What's New in This Edition

Java 1.1 Unleashed, Third Edition, is an entirely revised edition of the best-selling book, *Java Unleashed*. It includes full coverage of the enhancements in Java 1.1.

Three new parts have been added to this edition:

- **Part IV, "Programming the AWT,"** provides an in-depth look at the Abstract Windowing Toolkit and Java graphics fundamentals.

- **Part VIII, "Java Archives and JavaBeans,"** takes you inside the new Java archive facilities in Java 1.1, which allow you to package and deliver Java applets and components in a compressed form for better organization, loading efficiency, and security. This section also introduces you to JavaBeans, the exciting new software component technology in Java 1.1. Using JavaBeans, you can create reusable Java components that can be easily connected together in visual design tools to build applets and applications.

- **Part IX, "Java Databases,"** covers the new database enhancements in Java 1.1, also known as JDBC. With JDBC, you can build applets and applications that seamlessly interact with just about any database.

In addition to these entirely new parts, new individual chapters cover everything from the new Java 1.1 API packages to Java internationalization to remote Java objects. All other chapters have been completely revamped to accommodate and highlight the changes in Java 1.1. Some have even been condensed to facilitate the inclusion of more timely material.

If these additions and changes haven't gotten you excited, consider the updated reference material that has been packed between these covers. This book includes an updated Java language class summary and class hierarchy diagrams.

Basically, this book has been revised and expanded to address just about everything you want to know about Java 1.1.

Java™ 1.1
Third Edition

Michael Morrison, et al.

201 West 103rd Street
Indianapolis, IN 46290

UNLEASHED

Copyright © 1997 by Sams.net Publishing

THIRD EDITION

International Standard Book Number: 1-57521-298-6

Library of Congress Catalog Card Number: 97-65137

2000 99 98 97   4 3 2

Interpretation of the printing code: the rightmost double-digit number is the year of the book's printing; the rightmost single-digit is the number of the book's printing. For example, a printing code of 97-1 shows that the first printing of the book occurred in 1997.

Composed in Garamond and MCPdigital by Macmillan Computer Publishing

Printed in the United States of America

Trademarks

Publisher	*Richard K. Swadley*
Publishing Manager	*Mark Taber*
Acquisitions Manager	*Beverly M. Eppink*
Director of Editorial Services	*Cindy Morrow*
Director of Marketing	*Kelli S. Spencer*
Assistant Marketing Managers	*Kristina Perry*
	Rachel Wolfe

Acquisitions Editor
Beverly M. Eppink

Development Editor
Scott D. Meyers

Software Development Specialist
Bob Correll

Production Editor
Alice Martina Smith

Indexer
Cheryl Dietsch

Technical Reviewers
Brad Seifert
bci.assoc

Technical Edit Coordinator
Lorraine Schaffer

Resource Coordinator
Deborah Frisby

Editorial Assistants
Carol Ackerman
Andi Richter
Rhonda Tinch-Mize

Cover Designer
Tim Amrheim

Book Designer
Gary Adair

Copy Writer
David Reichwein

Production Team Supervisors
Brad Chinn
Charlotte Clapp

Production
Svetlana Dominguez
Brad Lenser
Chris Livengood
Mark Walchle

Overview

Contents

8   Introduction to Applet Programming   185

9   Overview of the Standard Packages   219

Part XIII Appendixes

A Java Language Summary   1297

B Class Hierarchy Diagrams   1307

C Java Class Library   1333

Dedication

To Mahsheed, who is the closest thing to perfect I've found.
—Michael Morrison

Acknowledgments

I would like to thank **Beverly Eppink** for being such a great editor and for taking all my personal crises in stride. A big thanks goes to **Alice Martina Smith**, for being so incredibly easy to work with…again! I'd also like to thank all the contributing authors, who are truly responsible for making this book as rich in content as it is.

I would like to thank my family and friends, especially my mom and dad, who simply are the best.

Thanks also goes out to the folks at **Cumberland Transit Skate Shop**, who are generous enough to help sponsor my skateboarding endeavors.

Finally, I'd like to thank the wooden bowl at **XXX Sports** (www.xxxsports.com), which taught me by way of a fractured wrist that I'm really not as invincible as I once thought.

—Michael Morrison

About the Authors

Lead Author:

Michael Morrison (mmorrison@thetribe.com, www.thetribe.com) is a writer and skateboarder living in Nashville, Tennessee. Michael is the author of *Presenting JavaBeans* and *Teach Yourself Internet Game Programming with Java in 21 Days*, he is also a contributing author to *Teach Yourself Java in 21 Days*, Professional Reference Edition, and *Late Night Visual J++*. When not working late into the night by the sounds of Miles Davis and Phish, Michael enjoys skateboarding on ramps of all shapes and sizes. Michael single-handedly (pun intended) wrote Chapters 2, 3, 4, 5, 9, 10, 12, 20, 30, 38, 39, 40, 41, 47, 53, and 57.

Contributing Authors:

Jerry Ablan (munster@mcs.net) is best described as a computer nut. He has been involved with computers since 1982, has programmed in many languages, and is a senior software engineer at the Chicago Board Options Exchange. He lives in a Chicago suburb with his wife, Kathryn, and when not playing WarCraft II with his friends, working, writing, or otherwise cavorting, Jerry and his brother, Dan, operate NetGeeks (http://www.netgeeks.com), an Internet consulting firm. He is the author of *Developing Intranet Applications with Java,* coauthor of the *Web Site Administrator's Survival Guide,* and a contributing author to *Special Edition: Using Java*; *Platinum Edition: Using CGI, HTML, and Java*; and *Intranets Unleashed.* Jerry wrote Chapter 49.

Michael Afergan (mikea@ai.mit.edu) began working with Java as early as the spring of 1995 through his research work at the MIT AI Labs. Since then, he has carefully studied its growth and developed practical applets for companies as an independent consultant. Michael is the author of *Java Quick Reference* and has taught Java overseas to both managers and programmers. Although only 19, Michael has been programming for 11 years and has even taught a class on computer science at MIT. Captain of his high-school wrestling team, he is currently attending Harvard University. Michael wrote Chapter 27.

Billy Barron (billy@metronet.com; http://www.utdallas.edu/~billy) is currently a new technology specialist for the University of Texas at Dallas and has an M.S. in computer science from the University of North Texas. He has written and edited so many books that he can't remember them all anymore. Some examples are *Netscape 3 Unleashed, Web Site Administrator's Survival Guide*, and *Tricks of the Internet Gurus.* Billy revised Chapter 11 and Appendixes A and C.

Chris Burdess, originally trained in cognitive science, started using Java to develop platform-independent neural network models of mammalian midbrain and cerebellar reflexes. He is currently working as an analyst and developer of intelligent systems and human-computer interaction methodologies on the Internet. For further biographical information and interests, you may consult his Web site at http://www.dog.net.uk. Chris revised Chapter 14.

Eric Burke is currently working on a Java development environment for a major Silicon Valley computer manufacturer. He received his master's degree in computer engineering from Purdue University in December 1994. In addition to programming in Java, Eric coaches youth football and is cofounder of a Web site devoted to mountain biking at http://www.mtbinfo.com. Eric wrote Chapter 15.

Eddie Burris is currently a research associate at the University of Missouri at Kansas City. He has an M.S. degree from Michigan State University and over 14 years of experience as a software engineer including appointments at IBM and Los Alamos National Research Lab. In addition to working with cutting-edge information technologies, Eddie enjoys listening to and restoring vintage radios from the 1930s. His home page on the World Wide Web is located at http://sol.cstp.umkc.edu/~burris/. Eddie wrote Chapter 17.

Bruce Campbell lives in Seattle, Washington, and works with Internet technologies related to 3D collaboration such as VRML. Having gained an appreciation for information flow and sharing in large corporations, he enjoys envisioning the future effects of computer networking on information-access efficiency. Admittedly utopian in his outlook, he enjoys discussing appropriate uses of new technologies for the betterment of society. Bruce revised Chapter 45.

Rogers Cadenhead (rcade@airmail.net, http://www.oruel.com/rcade) is a Web developer, computer programmer, and writer who created the multiuser games Czarlords and Super Video Poker. Thousands of readers see his work on the Fort Worth Star-Telegram question-and-answer column "Ask Ed Brice." Rogers has developed Java applets for Tele-Communications, Inc., and other clients, and is the author of *Teach Yourself Java 1.1 in 24 Hours* and the co-author of *Teach Yourself SunSoft's Java Workshop in 21 Days*. Rogers wrote Chapter 1.

David R. Chung (dchung@inav.net, http://soli.inav.net/~dchung) is a senior programmer in the Church Software Division of Parsons Technology in Hiawatha, Iowa. His current projects include Windows and the Internet, and he moonlights teaching C and C++ to engineers for a local community college. In his spare time, David enjoys bicycling, teaching adult Sunday school, rollerblading, skiing, windsurfing, preaching in a nursing home, tennis, two-player and six-player volleyball, playing the clarinet, and speaking French. He is the father of six children whose names all begin with *J* and has contributed to *Tricks of the Java Programming Gurus*. David wrote Chapters 7 and 22 and was the original author of Chapter 14.

Justin Couch (justin@vlc.com.au, http://www.vlc.com.au/~justin) works as a software engineer for ADI Ltd. He also runs The Virtual Light Company, a small VRML and Java Web publishing company located in Sydney, Australia. Coauthor of *Laura Lemay's Web Workshop: 3D Graphics and VRML 2,* Justin is an active member of both the VRML standards and

Java-VRML mailing lists. Currently, he is involved in research on using VRML to create seamless worlds on the Internet and can be found most days in the CyberGate community Point World under the name Mithrandir. When not pushing the limits, he relaxes by playing bassoon, clarinet, and going gliding. Justin was the original author of Chapter 45.

Rick Darnell (`darnell@montana.com`), a contributing author to *FrontPage Unleashed* and *Microsoft Internet Explorer 3 Unleashed,* is a midwest native currently living with his wife and two daughters in Missoula, Montana. He began his career in print at a small weekly newspaper after graduating from Kansas State University with a degree in broadcasting. While spending time as a freelance journalist and writer, Rick has seen the full gamut of personal computers—since starting out with a Radio Shack Model I in the late 1970s. When not in front of his computer, he serves as a volunteer firefighter and member of a regional hazardous materials response team. Rick wrote Chapters 8 and 46 and Appendix D.

Mike Fletcher (`lemur1@mindspring.com`) graduated from the Georgia Institute of Technology in 1994 and now works for BellSouth Wireless' AIN Services Group as a systems administrator. Mike was a contributing author to the first two editions of *Java Unleashed.* He once played tuba on stage with Jimmy Buffet, and his interests include reading science fiction and juggling. Mike wrote Chapters 13, 35, 36, 37, 54 and 55, and was the original author of Chapters 24 and 25.

Michael Girdley (`girdleyj@allwilk.com`, `http://www.lafayette.edu/~girdleyj/`) contributed to *Web Programming with Java* and is the chief consultant at Allwilk Consulting (`http://www.allwilk.com/`), an organization specializing in Web site creation and Java programming. He is currently pursuing a Bachelor of Science degree in computer science at Lafayette College in Easton, Pennsylvania, and will earn his fourth varsity letter in 1996-1997 as a member of the varsity swimming team. Originally from San Antonio, Texas, Michael hopes to find a job or go to graduate school after possibly graduating on time in May 1997. Michael was an original coauthor of Chapter 11.

K.C. Hopson is President of Geist Software and Services, Inc., an independent consulting firm in the Baltimore/ Washington D.C. metro area. He was a lead architect of the software used in Bell Atlantic's Stargazer interactive television system and has developed a variety of Intranet applications. K.C. has a bachelor's degree in applied mathematics from the University of California at Irvine, and a masters in computer science from the University of Maryland, Baltimore County. He writes regularly about Java and Internet tools and can be reached at `chopson@universe.digex.net`. You can also visit his home page at `http://www.universe.digex.net/~chopson`. K.C. wrote Chapter 23 and coauthored Chapter 51.

Steve Ingram (`singram@mnsinc.com`) is a computer consultant in the Washington D.C. metro area specializing in Internet communications and object-oriented design. Coauthor of *Developing Professional Java Applets* and contributor to *Tricks of the Java Gurus,* Steve holds an electrical engineering degree from Virginia Tech. He was the architect behind the language for Bell Atlantic's Stargazer interactive television project, where he first encountered Java. When he's not working, Steve likes to sail the Chesapeake Bay with his wife, Anne, and their two children. Steve wrote Chapters 26, 32, and 33, coauthored Chapter 51, and revised Chapters 24 and 25.

Corey Klaasmeyer (corey@webset.com) is a professional software engineer and active partner in WebSet Technologies, an Intranet software development firm. He teaches object-oriented programming in Java at Denver University. Corey wrote Chapter 18.

John J. Kottler (73157.335@compuserve.com, jkottler@aol.com, or jay_kottler@msn.com) has been programming for fourteen years and has spent the past six years developing applications for the Windows platform. He has programmed multimedia applications for more than two years and has spent this past year developing for the Web. His knowledge includes C/C++, Visual Basic, Lotus Notes, PowerBuilder, messaging-enabled applications, multimedia and digital video production, and Web page development. John contributed to *Presenting ActiveX, Web Publishing Unleashed, Netscape 2 Unleashed,* and *Programming Windows 95 Unleashed*; he codeveloped the shareware application virtual monitors. A graduate of Rutgers University with a degree in computer science, he enjoys rollerblading, cycling, and playing digital music in his spare time. John wrote Chapter 48.

Laura Lemay (lemay@lne.com, http://www.lne.com/lemay/)is the author of several best-selling books about the Internet and the World Wide Web, including *Teach Yourself Java in 21 Days* and *Teach Yourself Web Publishing with HTML*. After receiving her degree in technical writing from Carnegie-Mellon University in 1989, she wrote documentation at various Silicon Valley software companies before writing her first book in 1994. She also writes a monthly column on HTML and Web page design for *Web Techniques Magazine*. Laura has won awards of merit and excellence from the Society of Technical Communication for her work and has spoken to diverse audiences ranging from programmers to industry pundits to librarians to junior high school girls. She makes frequent appearances and lectures in the San Francisco Bay area. Laura is the original author of Appendixes A and C.

Richard Lesh (rich@micros.umsl.edu) is an instructor with the microcomputing program at the University of Missouri at St. Louis. He has developed a variety of applications for the Macintosh, PC, and various UNIX platforms. A number of software products he has developed are in national distribution, including PLANMaker, a business plan-building product, and a number of screen-saver modules published by Now Software in Now Fun! and by Berkeley Systems in After Dark. Richard was an original contributor to Chapter 11.

Tim Macinta (twm@mit.edu) is currently working towards a degree in computer science and electrical engineering at the Massachusetts Institute of Technology. He has been working with Java since the summer of 1995 when he joined Dimension X, one of the leaders in Java development. While at Dimension X, Tim developed the first commercial-quality Java chat applet along with several applets for commercial sites such as the Disney and Monopoly sites. More recently, he has been using Java to write several client/server applications (SMTP, POP, and IRC, to name a few) from the ground up. After graduating from MIT, Tim plans to start a company whose sole purpose will be to grab market share from Microsoft. Tim wrote Chapter 50.

Qusay H. Mahmoud is a graduate student in computer science at the University of New Brunswick at Saint John, Canada. This term, he is teaching a course on multimedia and the information highway. As part of his thesis, he developed a distributed computing system over the Web using Java, and he is in the process of writing up the thesis. His interests include computer networks, distributed objects, and cryptography and network security. You can reach him at `qusay@garfield.csd.unbsj.ca`. Qusay wrote Chapter 16.

Jim Mathis is a freelance Java and JavaScript consultant by night and a communications systems architect by day. He has been active in the Internet community from its very beginnings, wrote one of the first implementations of TCP/IP, and served on the Internet Activities Board. He received his B.S. from Stanford University in electrical engineering during that most interesting time when the Internet was being created. He is interested in object-oriented technology and the impact of CORBA on the Internet. You can contact Jim at `jmathis@ais.net`. Jim wrote Chapter 31.

Tim F. Park (`tpark@corp.webtv.net`) is a recent graduate of the Stanford Graduate School of Electrical Engineering. Now employed by a major computer company in Silicon Valley, he is currently working on a Java 3D graphics library for the Internet. Tim contributed to *Tricks of the Java Programming Gurus,* and his interests include distributed computing, computer graphics, and mountain biking. Tim wrote Chapter 28.

Charles L. Perkins (`virtual@rendezvous.com`) is the founder of Virtual Rendezvous (`http://rendezvous.com/java`), a company building a Java-based service that fosters socially focused, computer-mediated, real-time filtered interactions between people's personas in the virtual environments of the near future. In previous lives, he has evangelized NeXTSTEP, Smalltalk, and UNIX, and has degrees in both physics and computer science. Charles is the author of Appendix B.

Shelley Powers has her own company, YASD, and is a freelance writer. She also provides Web/Internet training and consulting. She contributed to two Java books by Sams Publishing and has coauthored several other books, including ones about JavaScript, PowerBuilder 5.0, and CGI/Perl. She is currently working on other books about Web authoring technology. She contributes articles to various online magazines and has a regular column on scripting with NetscapeWorld. Shelley originated in Portland, Oregon, but moved to Vermont in 1997. She can be reached at `shelleyp@yasd.com`; her site is at `http://www.yasd.com`. Shelley wrote Chapters 19, 42, 43, and 44.

George Reese (`borg@imaginary.com`) holds a degree in philosophy from Bates College in Lewiston, Maine. He currently works as a lead systems analyst for Carlson Marketing Group's Internet and intranet development team. In addition, he does consulting through Caribou Lake software, where he markets a Java persistence library. His Java writing has appeared in several Sams titles as well as in articles for the *Java Developer's Journal.* He was the creator of the first JDBC driver, the mSQL-JDBC driver for the MiniSQL database engine. George lives in Bloomington, Minnesota, with his two cats, Gypsy and Misty. George wrote Chapter 29.

Chris Seguin (seguin@uiuc.edu) completed a B.S. in mathematics at the University of Delaware in 1991. On June 25, 1994, he married his long-time sweetheart, Angela DiNunzio. Chris is currently working toward a Ph.D. at the University of Illinois in computer science. He is currently employed by NCSA and is working on a collaborative software project called Habanero (http://www.ncsa.uiuc.edu/SDG/Software/Habanero/). His research interests include creating artificial neural networks and developing collaboration tools. Chris wrote Chapter 21.

Jeff Shockley is the data processing manager at Total Response, Inc., an Indiana-based integrated marketing firm. Jeff has designed client/server systems and written multiple applications in languages such as C++, Visual Basic, Java, and SQLWindows. He is also experienced in Oracle and SQL Server databases, and has been a technical editor on topics such as Java programming, Visual Basic programming, Web databases, Web page design, and client/server technologies. Jeff lives in Indianapolis with his wife, Larryssa, and his three daughters, Lindi, Danielle, and Erin. You can reach him with e-mail at shockle@totalresponse.com or visit http:\\www.totalresponse.com to see what he does daily. Jeff revised Appendix C.

William R. Stanek (director@tvpress.com,http://tvp.com/) is a leading Internet technology expert and a working professional who directs an Internet start-up company called The Virtual Press. As a publisher and writer with over ten years experience on networks, William brings a solid voice of experience about the Internet and electronic publishing to his many projects. He has been involved in the commercial Internet community since 1991 and was first introduced to Internet e-mail in 1988 when he worked for the government. His years of practical experience are backed by a solid education: a master of science in information systems and a bachelor of science in computer science. He is the author of Sams.net's *Netscape ONE Developer's Guide, Web Publishing Unleashed*, and *Microsoft FrontPage Unleashed*. William wrote Chapter 56.

Glenn Vanderburg (glv@vanderburg.org, http://www.vanderburg.org/~glv/) is a software architect with BusinessWorks, Inc., where he is using Java to support multimedia educational systems. Glenn lives in Plano, Texas, with his wife, Deborah. He holds a B.S. degree in computer science from Texas A&M University. Glenn is the lead author of *Maximum Java 1.1* and is interested in using Java to build dynamically extensible, upgradable network applications. Glenn wrote Chapters 34 and 52.

Eric Williams (williams@sky.net, http://www.sky.net/~williams) is a team leader and software engineer for Sprint's Long Distance Division. Although he is currently focusing on C++ and Smalltalk development, Eric is active in the Java community, contributing to the comp.lang.java newsgroup and delivering presentations about Java to various user groups. Eric is also responsible for identifying a Java 1.0.1 security flaw related to sockets and DNS. Eric wrote Chapter 6.

Tell Us What You Think!

As a reader, you are the most important critic and commentator of our books. We value your opinion and want to know what we're doing right, what we could do better, what areas you'd like to see us publish in, and any other words of wisdom you're willing to pass our way. You can help us make strong books that meet your needs and give you the computer guidance you require.

Do you have access to CompuServe or the World Wide Web? Then check out our CompuServe forum by typing GO SAMS at any prompt. If you prefer the World Wide Web, check out our site at http://www.mcp.com.

> **NOTE**
>
> If you have a technical question about this book, call the technical support line at 317-581-3833.

As the publishing manager of the group that created this book, I welcome your comments. You can fax, e-mail, or write me directly to let me know what you did or didn't like about this book—as well as what we can do to make our books stronger. Here's the information:

FAX: 317-581-4669

E-mail: newtech_mgr@sams.mcp.com

Mail: Mark Taber
Sams.net Publishing
201 W. 103rd Street
Indianapolis, IN 46290

Introduction

Just over a year and a half after its inception, Java is still the dominant technology bringing interactive content to the World Wide Web. In a world where just about everyone has his or her own opinion about where the future of the Web is headed, this is no small feat. JavaSoft, the division of Sun Microsystems responsible for Java, has managed to stay ahead of the development curve and rapidly improve Java to accommodate the ever-changing environment known as the Web. Even so, Java is still a young technology and has plenty of room to evolve to meet the demands of Web developers. The release of Java 1.1 marks a significant step forward for Java.

The fact that Java is an evolving technology has played a critical role in its wide acceptance by Web developers; many developers who struggled with limitations in earlier releases of Java should feel reassured by the abundance of new features included in the latest 1.1 release. This confidence depends greatly on JavaSoft's willingness and desire to solicit input from experts in the field when expanding Java to solve new problems and provide new features. Since initially releasing Java, JavaSoft has been steadily improving Java to meet the needs of the demanding Web community. Even with Java 1.1 out the door, JavaSoft still has big plans for even more Java-related technologies.

Our goal in this edition of *Java 1.1 Unleashed* is to explore the Java technology from a variety of angles so that you can see the bigger picture of what Java has to offer as a Web technology. Our contention is that if you understand Java in its entirety, you will be much better suited to make decisions regarding its efficient use in your own Web development projects. Beyond that, we also thought it would be a lot of fun to chart some new territory and see for ourselves what Java could do. As you will see, Java 1.1 presents plenty of new territory to chart!

In this book, you learn about the following topics related to the Java 1.1 technology:

- Getting started with Java
- The Java language
- The standard Java programming packages
- The Java Advanced Windowing Toolkit (AWT)
- Networking with Java
- Java programming strategies
- Advanced Java programming
- Java archives
- JavaBeans software components
- Java databases

- Integrating Java with other technologies
- Applied Java
- Related Java technologies

The book also contains extensive reference material covering the following topics:

- Java language summary
- Java class hierarchy diagrams
- Java resources
- Java class library

Part I: Getting Started with Java

Every exploration has to start somewhere—you're ready to begin learning about the vast world of Java. You want to know why Java is an object-oriented language and what this really means in a practical sense. You'd also like to know exactly where to begin as far as setting up your own Java development environment.

Part II: The Java Language

The cornerstone of the Java technology is the Java programming language. You understand Java in general terms, but you want to know more about the Java language and what it can do for you. You are curious about Java classes and how they relate to all the object-oriented hype you've heard about Java. You also want to know what in the world *threads* and *exceptions* are, and why so many people seem so worried about them.

Part III: The Standard Java Programming Packages

The real power of Java is spelled out in the standard Java programming packages. You're ready to move past the Java language and see exactly what Java provides in the way of specific programming features such as mathematical functions, I/O, networking, and security. You're also curious about graphical user interfaces and what kinds are available in the standard Java packages.

Part IV: The Java Advanced Windowing Toolkit

Although Java is certainly strong in many ways that aren't immediately obvious, its user interface and graphics support make up the first impression for most users and developers alike. The AWT encompasses all the visual characteristics of the Java environment, providing support for things such as fancy user interfaces and advances and advanced image processing. If you're familiar with the AWT in a previous version of Java, you're in for a treat; Java 1.1 is chock full of neat new enhancements.

Part V: Networking with Java

Can you possibly imagine a programming language for the Web that doesn't provide extensive support for networking? Of course not! You want to know all about networking with Java and exactly what it can do for you. You've heard a lot about client/server networking and want to know how it is supported in Java. You're also interested in writing a multiuser applet in Java.

Part: VI Java Programming Strategies

You realize the importance of smart programming and want to know some Java programming strategies to improve your development efficiency. You understand the inherent nature of programming bugs and want to know how to debug Java code. You want to employ a documentation strategy so that your code can be better maintained. You are also interested in speeding up your code, because performance is a very critical issue in Java programming.

Part VII: Advanced Java Programming

You are ready to press on to some more advanced areas of Java programming. More specifically, you want to learn about *persistence* and *serialization*, which are techniques for storing and retrieving the state of Java objects. You are also interested in how Java integrates with native C code, as well as finding out more about the Java virtual machine, Java security, and Java's new reflection services.

Part VIII: Java Archives and JavaBeans

The idea of bundling all the files and resources required for an applet or application into one compressed, secure entity is nothing short of a breakthrough in terms of safely and efficiently distributing Java products. JAR files are something you simply must learn about so that you can improve the distribution of your own applets.

Have you ever wondered why building Java applications isn't as straightforward as building applications in other languages with visual development tools such as Visual Basic and Delphi? It's because earlier versions of Java didn't support a highly structured software component model for defining reusable components. JavaBeans, which is an integral part of Java 1.1, addresses this problem head-on. You won't believe how easy it is to build and use JavaBeans components.

Part IX: Java Databases

There has been lots of talk recently about how Java will support databases. Well, talk no more because Java 1.1 spells out exactly how Java supports databases with the JDBC API, which fully supports SQL (Structured Query Language) interaction with all major types of databases. Let the client/server Java madness begin!

Part X: Integrating Java with Other Technologies

Although Java is a pretty complete technology, there are still instances in which you may want to integrate Java with another technology such as VRML or ActiveX. You want to know some details surrounding the integration of Java with technologies such as VRML, ActiveX, JavaScript, and VBScript.

Part XI: Applied Java

A software development technology is only as useful as its range of application. Knowing this, you want to see some specific areas of application where Java can be used. More specifically, how can Java be applied to intranets, games, image processing, and internationalization?

Part XII: Related Java Technologies

You're interested in tying up some loose ends by learning about a variety of related Java technologies. More specifically, you want to find out more about just-in-time compilers, remote objects, Java server support, and what's in store for Java in the near future.

Even though Java has come a long way, the story of Java is still very much being written. We can certainly use Java's past as a means of forecasting its future, but ultimately, we must keep an open mind and be willing to adapt to changes in Java as they unfold. In the meantime, there's a lot to learn and a lot of fun to be had with Java in the present. Knowing that, I encourage you to set out on your own exploration of Java using this book as your guide. Have fun!

—Michael Morrison

IN THIS PART

Getting Started

I

PART

Introducing Java

by Rogers Cadenhead

IN THIS CHAPTER

CHAPTER 1

This represents the end result of nearly 15 years of trying to come up with a better programming language and environment for building simpler and more reliable software.

—Sun Microsystems cofounder Bill Joy

A year and a half ago, Java was just an island and one of the cooler synonyms for *coffee* (along with *joe* and *demitasse*). But anyone who has come within five feet of a Web page, computer magazine, or business newspaper since then has heard of Java, the programming language from Sun Microsystems.

If you haven't been initiated into the Secret Personhood of Java yet, you might be wondering what all the fuss is about. It's just a programming language, for cryin' out loud! It's not some kind of cross-dressing basketball player, Latino dance craze, or teeth whitener.

Figure 1.1 shows a Java program being used to test students on Egyptian history.

FIGURE 1.1.

A Java program to administer student testing (courtesy of David Benjamin and Auburn University).

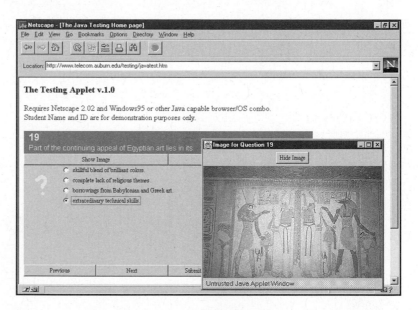

The test software itself isn't remarkable—numerous computer-based education programs are being used in schools today. What is noteworthy about the program are the following points:

- It runs on a World Wide Web page, making the test instantly accessible to the entire planet.
- The types of computer and operating system being used by the student don't matter—the student can use a Windows 95 PC clone, an Apple MacOS computer, or any other setup that has a Java interpreter.
- No special installation is required. The program loads itself when needed and unloads when it's done.

Java represents a fundamental shift in the way software can be designed and experienced. This, more than anything else, is why Sun's invention is the computer nerd's Macarena.

> **NOTE**
>
> The Macarena is a Latino dance craze that involves lots of repetitive motion, arm gyration, and an occasional pelvic swivel. If you're unfamiliar with the term, insert your own annoying aerobic trend into the previous paragraph and repeat as desired.

Shortly after Sun introduced Java in late 1995, company cofounder Bill Joy described the language as follows:

> *Java is just a small, simple, safe, object-oriented, interpreted or dynamically optimized, byte-coded, architecture-neutral, garbage-collected, multithreaded programming language with a strongly typed exception-handling mechanism for writing distributed, dynamically extensible programs.*

At this point, you probably are saying one of two things: "Duh!" or "Huh?"

If you're in the "huh?" camp, this chapter is for you. It discusses what Java is, where Java came from, and where Java is going. The "duh!" camp can benefit from this overview as well—and there's enough advanced material in *Java 1.1 Unleashed* for even the most grizzled Java veteran.

> **NOTE**
>
> Java's first official beta release was in November 1995, two months after Netscape became the first company to license the language from Sun. You may be questioning whether someone can become a "grizzled veteran" after little more than a year. However, many of us in the computer programming community have rather—shall we say—*unique* approaches to wellness and diet that contribute to premature grizzling.

The first thing to discuss, before getting into what Bill Joy meant in that Mother of All Sentences, is where Java came from.

How Java Was Developed

The story of Java is a tale of two situations—the worst of times followed by the best of times. It's a story about how a promising language didn't amount to a hill of coffee beans in this crazy world—until the crazy world got a little crazier and a new mass medium was born: the World Wide Web.

One for the Toasters

Five years ago, James Gosling was part of Green, an isolated research project at Sun that was studying how to put computers into everyday household items. The researchers wanted to make smart appliances such as thoughtful toasters, lucid lamps, and sagacious Salad Shooters—the Jetsons' vision of the future realized. The group also wanted these devices to communicate with each other.

To get a hands-on look at the issue, the Greens built a prototype device called Star7. This gadget was a handheld remote control operated by touching animated objects on the screen. A Star7 user could navigate by fingertip through a universe of rooms and objects. The universe featured Duke—immortalized later as Java's mascot (see Figure 1.2).

FIGURE 1.2.

Duke (courtesy of Sun Microsystems).

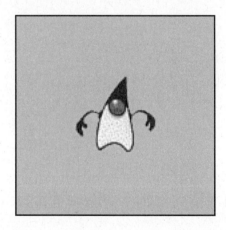

The most remarkable ability of the Star7 device was how it communicated with other Star7 devices. An on-screen object could be passed from one device to another. The prototype was a distributed operating system in which each device was a part of the whole—exactly the kind of thing that would be needed for the freezer to tell the vacuum to tell the humans that the ice machine is on strike until someone cleans it.

The original plan was for the Star7 operating system to be developed in C++. However, as Gosling said in a speech at the JavaOne conference in May 1996, "The tools kept breaking. It was at a fairly early breaking point when I was so disgusted that I went to my office and started typing." He wasn't writing hate mail to Bjarne Stroustrup, the primary developer of C++. Instead, Gosling holed up in his office and wrote a new language that was better for the purposes of the Green project than C++. He called the language Oak in honor of a tree that could be seen from his office window.

From the start, Gosling's language was created so that simple, bug-free, network-capable programs could be written with it. Like C++, Oak was object-oriented—a powerful way of developing computer programs that has many advantages over other methods but is difficult to master. Oak was designed to be easier to learn and use than other object-oriented languages.

Oak programs had to be platform independent because consumer appliance manufacturers need the ability to replace a higher-priced CPU with a cheaper one whenever possible to cut costs. Unlike computer owners, an appliance consumer isn't looking for a math coprocessor and 33MHz of added computational speed when buying a lawn edger. The consumer also is less likely to tolerate a bug in the edger's software or hardware, especially if said glitch causes unexpected limb loss.

The Green project had an impressive demonstration device, operating system, and programming language. Sun's higher-ups gave the go-ahead and the project was incorporated as FirstPerson in November 1992. The group focused its efforts on cable set-top boxes and the potentially billion-dollar interactive television (ITV) industry. Don't laugh—this was the early 1990s.

As the FirstPerson team was busy gunning to do Time-Warner's interactive TV trial in Spring 1993, an event took place that would become very important later to the FirstPerson people, long after they struck out in the ITV business. The first visual World Wide Web browser, Mosaic 1.0, was developed by Marc Andreesen, an undergraduate student working at the National Center for Supercomputing Applications.

Caught in the Web

For the next 12 months, the FirstPerson project tried to sell one of the ITV or consumer electronics companies on the use of Oak and the Green operating system. The future of Java can trace its roots back to the project's failure to attract a big client in its chosen field. After Time-Warner chose SGI over FirstPerson, and a deal with 3DO for the FirstPerson OS did not materialize, the project was cut in half and it started scrambling for a new *raison d'être*.

In mid-1994, the folks who stuck with Oak found their reason for being: the World Wide Web. When Oak was created, the Web was a little-known service bouncing around the high-energy physics community. However, Andreesen's graphical Web browser had sparked an international phenomenon, and the Web was rapidly becoming a mass medium. The Oak technology was well-suited for this medium, especially because of its ability to run on multiple platforms. More importantly, it introduced something that wasn't available anywhere else—programs that could be run on user's computers safely from a Web page.

Patrick Naughton and Jonathan Payne finished WebRunner, a Web browser that brought back the star of the Star7, Duke. Sun realized it had something promising on its hands, but soon found that Oak could not be trademarked because a product was already using the name.

> **NOTE**
>
> When Sun needed to rename Oak, no one used Gosling's "look out the office window" method of naming. This is perhaps fortunate. Ask yourself if Java would have been as successful under any of the following names:
>
> - Shrubbery
> - OfficeBuildingNextDoor
> - LightPole
> - WindowWasher
> - SecretaryLeavingForLunch
> - WeirdSecurityGuard
> - FatGuyMowing

After brainstorming sessions in January 1995 to supplant the *Oak* name, *Java* won for the language and *HotJava* replaced *WebRunner* as the browser's name. Java does not stand for Just Another Vague Acronym, or any other acronym or meaningful term. Like rock bands (Deep Blue Something, Smashing Pumpkins) and celebrity offspring (Moon Unit Zappa, Chastity Bono), Java was the name chosen because it sounded the coolest. It won out over DNA, Silk, Ruby, and WRL (WebRunner Language).

The project now had a cool name, a cool new purpose, and a HotJava browser to show it off. On March 23, 1995, it attracted a cool new admirer: that Andreesen kid. In a front-page story, the *San Jose Mercury News* reported that Sun was working on a project to make Web pages "as lively as a CD-ROM." The story included the following quote from Andreesen, who had become a vice president at Netscape (and had also become a self-contained Bill Gates starter kit): "What these guys are doing is undeniably, absolutely new," Andreesen told the *Mercury News*. "It's great stuff. There's so much stuff that people want to do over the network that they haven't had the software to do. These guys are really pushing the envelope."

The phenomenon was on. Netscape licensed the Java language for use in its browser a few months after the article ran, putting the language in front of millions of Netscape users. The first beta release of Java was made available for download in November 1995. Sun made a developer's kit and the source code for its product freely available to anyone who wanted it—and by that time, thousands of people and companies did.

Toasters are no smarter today than they were in 1991, so in that regard, Sun's research project has been a total failure. However, a new object-oriented, made-for-the-Internet programming language was created instead.

Now that you know about Java's ancestors, it's time to be introduced to the language.

What Java Is

The basics: Java is an object-oriented programming language developed by Sun Microsystems that plays to the strengths of the Internet.

Object-oriented programming (OOP) is an unusual but powerful way to develop software. In OOP, a computer program is considered to be a group of objects that interact with each other. Consider an embezzlement program implemented with Java: A Worker object skims some Money objects from the CompanyFunds object and puts them in its own BankAccount object. If another Worker object uses the DoubleCheckFunds object, a Police object will be called.

The feature that is best known about Java is that it can be used to create programs that execute from World Wide Web pages. These programs are called *applets*.

Java programs made a big splash on the Web because they offered interactivity in a medium that was largely one way. The Web distributes almost all information in a passive manner. Someone using a browser asks for a page, looks it over, asks for another, looks it over, and so on. Lather, rinse, repeat.

A Java applet running on a Web page provides a much richer experience—both in terms of information and user interaction. Information can change in response to user input or be updated dynamically as a Web page is viewed. Figure 1.3 shows an example of a Java applet that dynamically updates itself. The applet, offered by *JavaWorld* magazine (at the URL `http://www.javaworld.com`) in conjunction with Quote.Com, updates a stock portfolio dynamically with quotes updated in real time.

FIGURE 1.3.

A Java applet that updates a stock portfolio in real time (courtesy of JavaWorld *magazine).*

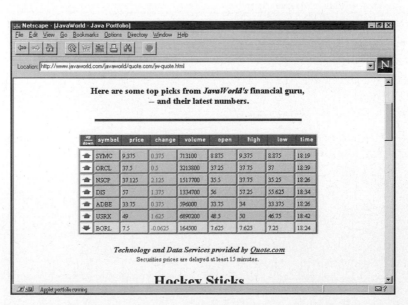

Although Web-based programs are a strength of the language, Java is a general-purpose language that can be used to develop all kinds of programs.

A Java program is created as a text file with the file extension `.java`. It is compiled into one or more files of bytecodes with the extension `.class`. *Bytecodes* are a set of instructions similar to the machine code instructions created when a computer program is compiled. The difference is that machine code must run on the computer system it was compiled for; bytecodes can run on any computer system equipped to handle Java programs.

The next section describes why Java is being used and takes a closer look at Bill Joy's adjective-stuffed description of the language.

Why Java Is Internationally Beloved

Although "internationally beloved" might be pushing it a bit, Java has quickly become a popular choice for computer programming—both on and off the Internet. A lot of the initial interest undoubtedly came from people who wanted to know whether Java lived up to the hype. In a short time, the language has become one of the biggest buzzwords of the Internet, spawning magazines, Web sites, training courses, conferences, and lots of books. And I'm not talking about small books either; I mean big, heavy books you can hurt yourself with. Try dropping *this* book on your toes and you'll see (feel) exactly what I mean!

Even if Java was as underpublicized as Tonya Harding's singing career, the programming language has some advantages over other languages such as C++ and Visual Basic. These can be found in Bill Joy's description of the language.

As a reminder, Joy sang its praises as follows:

> *Java is just a small, simple, safe, object-oriented, interpreted or dynamically optimized, byte-coded, architecture-neutral, garbage-collected, multithreaded programming language with a strongly typed exception-handling mechanism for writing distributed, dynamically extensible programs.*

These adjectives can be tackled by dividing them into more manageable groups.

Java Is Small and Simple

When James Gosling retreated to his office to write the language that became Java, it was modeled after C and C++. The object-oriented approach, and most of Java's syntax, is adapted from C++. Programmers who are familiar with that language (or with C) will have a much easier time learning Java because of the common features.

However, Java has been described as "C++ minus" because of elements of C++ that were omitted. Gosling wanted to avoid the problems that the Green project had encountered when using C++ as it developed the Star7 prototype. The most complex parts of C++ were excluded from Java, such as pointers and memory management. These elements are complicated to use, and are thus easy to use incorrectly. Finding a pointer error in a large program is an experience not unlike searching for the one-armed man who framed you for murder. Memory management occurs automatically in Java—programmers do not have to write their own garbage-collection routines to free up memory.

Another design decision to make Java simpler is its elementary data types and objects. The language enforces very strict rules regarding variables—in almost all cases, you have to use variables as the data type they were declared to be, or use explicit casts to manipulate them. This arrangement permits mistakes in variable use to be caught when the program is compiled, rather than letting them creep into a running program where they're harder to find. As a result, programs behave in a more predictable manner.

Experienced programmers may have trouble adjusting to some of the changes and reductions from C++. However, Java's architects were trying to make the language easier to write, debug, and learn.

Java Is Object Oriented

Object-oriented programming (OOP) is a powerful way of organizing and developing software. The short-form description of OOP is that it organizes a program as a set of components called *objects*. These objects exist independently of each other, and they have rules for communicating with other objects and for telling those objects to do things. Think back to how Star7 devices were developed as a group of independent devices with methods for communicating with each other. Object-oriented programming is highly compatible with what the Green project was created to do and, by extension, for Java as well.

Java inherits its object-oriented concepts from C++ and other languages such as Smalltalk. The fact that a programming language is object oriented may not seem like a benefit to some. Object-oriented programming can be an intimidating subject to tackle, even if you have some experience programming with other languages. However, object-oriented programs are more adaptable for use in other projects, easier to understand, and more bugproof.

The Java language includes a set of class libraries that provide basic variable types, system input and output capabilities, and other functions. It also includes classes to support networking, Internet protocols, and graphical user interface functions.

There's a lot of excitement in the programming community because Java provides a new opportunity to use object-oriented techniques on the job. Smalltalk, the language that pioneered object-oriented programming in the 1970s, is well-respected but has never been widely adopted as a software-development choice. As a result, getting the go-ahead to develop a project using Smalltalk can be an uphill struggle. C++ is object-oriented, but concerns about its use have already been described. Java is overcoming the hurdle in terms of usage, especially in regard to Internet programming and the development of distributed applications.

Tim Berners-Lee, the inventor of the World Wide Web, told the attendees at the JavaOne conference one big reason he's excited about the language: "We now have an excuse to really use object-oriented programming."

Java Is Safe

Another thing essential to Java's success is that it is safe. The original reason for Java to execute reliably was that people expect their waffle irons not to kill them or to exhibit any other unreliable behavior. This emphasis on security was well-suited for Java's adaptation to the World Wide Web.

A Java program that executes from a Web page is called an *applet*. All other Java programs are called *applications*. When an applet is encountered on a Web page (if the user's browser can handle Java), the browser downloads the applet along with the text and images on the page. The applet then runs on the user's computer. This act should raise a red flag—danger! danger!—because a lot of harmful things can occur when programs are executed: viruses, Trojan horses, the Microsoft Network, and so on.

Java provides security on several different levels. First, the language was designed to make it extremely difficult to execute damaging code. The elimination of pointers is a big step in this regard. Pointers are a powerful feature, as the programmers of C-like languages can attest, but pointers can be used to forge access to parts of a program where access is not allowed, and to access areas in memory that are supposed to be unalterable. By eliminating all pointers except for a limited form of references to objects, Java is a much more secure language.

Another level of security is the bytecode verifier. As described earlier, Java programs are compiled into a set of instructions called bytecodes. Before a Java program is run, a verifier checks each bytecode to make sure that nothing suspicious is going on.

In addition to these measures, Java has several safeguards that apply to applets. To prevent a program from committing random acts of violence against a user's disk drives, an applet cannot, by default, open, read, or write files on the user's system. Also, because Java applets can open new windows, these windows have a Java logo and text that identifies them. This arrangement prevents one of these pop-up windows from pretending to be something such as a user name and password dialog box.

The latest release of Java (version 1.1) offers a more advanced approach to security that allows applets to be digitally signed for verification purposes. In other words, you can create an applet and put your stamp of approval on it, which users are supposed to be able to trust. This new approach to security loosens the security constraints of earlier versions of Java, but it also pushes some responsibility onto the user. You can think of this type of security as similar to a fisheye peephole in your front door—without the peephole, you wouldn't even consider opening the door for visitors; but with the peephole, you can see enough to decide who you want to let in.

There is no system of security that is completely foolproof; several security bugs in the first year after Java's release were brought to Sun's attention by programmers such as David Hopwood. The following Web site describes some of these incidents and outlines the issues regarding safe Internet programming:

`http://www.cs.princeton.edu/sip/News.html`

Because of the multiple levels of security, and the continued efforts to improve these measures, Java is generally regarded as a secure way to execute code over the World Wide Web.

CAUTION

These safeguards are not an absolute guarantee against malicious programming. Several security experts found ways to circumvent Java applet security during the first year of the language's availability, and the details were sent to JavaSoft and browser developers. In the future, there will undoubtedly be new security holes found with Java, as there are with any system. If you are concerned about running Java applets on your computer, you should run only applets that have been approved by a Java directory such as Gamelan or another trusted source. Gamelan, which can be found at the URL `http://www.gamelan.com`, tests applets before offering them. You also should back up any essential data on your computer regularly—which is good practice in any case.

Java Is Platform Independent

Platform independence is another way of saying that Java is architecture neutral. If both terms leave you saying "huh?," they basically mean that Java programs don't care what system they're running on.

Most computer software is developed for a specific operating system. If Sid Software wanted its two-fisted 17th-century shootemup *Quaker* to run on Windows and Mac systems, it had to develop two versions of the software at a significant effort and expense. *Platform independence* is the capability of the same program to work on different operating systems; Java is completely platform independent.

Java's variable types have the same size across all Java development platforms—so an integer is always the same size, no matter which system a Java program was written and compiled on. Also, as shown by the use of applets on the Web, a Java `.class` file of bytecode instructions can execute on any platform without alteration.

Sun Microsystems has been aggressive in making Java available on different systems. As JavaSoft President Alan Baratz says, "Anything that feels, smells, walks, or talks like it has a processor—we'd like the Java platform to live on it." There are Java interpreters that can run programs for Microsoft Windows 95 and NT, Apple Macintosh 7.5, SPARC Solaris 2.3 or higher, and Intel x86 Solaris; other systems have Java versions under development.

Java's declaration of platform independence is often trumpeted by Java advocates as a major accomplishment because it opens up a much larger audience for programs than has been readily available in the past. Although no major commercial releases of Java-based software have been introduced as of this writing (other than JavaSoft products such as HotJava and the Java WorkShop programming environment), several have been announced. In the absence of major commercial Java-based applications, Java has still managed to rapidly expand its presence on the Web as Web developers realize the value of Java applets.

> **NOTE**
>
> One particularly interesting and long-awaited commercial Java release is Corel Office for Java, which is the first suite of office productivity applications written entirely in Java. As of this writing, a free beta version of Corel Office for Java is available for download at this URL:
>
> ```
> http://officeforjava.corel.com/
> ```

Java Is that Other Stuff, Too

One adjective that has been left out thus far is that Java is *multithreaded*. Threads represent a way for a computer program to do more than one task at the same time. Many operating systems are multitasking. Windows 95, for example, enables a person to write a book chapter with Word in one window while using Netscape Navigator to download every known picture of E! host Eleanor Mondale in the other. (Speaking hypothetically, of course.)

A multithreaded language extends this schizophrenic behavior to programs so that more than one set of instructions can be executed concurrently. Java provides the tools to write multithreaded programs and to make these programs reliable in execution.

Another thing that should be highlighted is Java's network-centric nature. Sun, the company that trademarked the phrase, "the network is the computer," has created a language that backs it up. Star7 was able to pass an object from one device to another using radio signals, and Java makes it possible to create applications that communicate across the Internet in the same way.

Its networkability may be the area in which Java truly separates itself from other languages that can be used for development. As language creator James Gosling has remarked, "The thing that distinguishes Java is its approach to distributed programming."

Most of Bill Joy's accolades should make more sense to you at this point, although it may take a complete reading of *Java 1.1 Unleashed* before you're ready to string together technical jargon like his with the proficiency of a *Dilbert* character.

Java Today

Now that you have an idea about what Java is and why you should use it, forsaking all others (or maybe not), you're ready to get started. To understand the status of Java development today, you should learn more about the Java Development Kit, the language Application Programming Interface (API), future APIs, and some examples of Java in action.

The Java Development Kit

The Java Development Kit (JDK) is a set of command-line tools that can be used to create Java programs. As of this writing, version 1.1 is the latest release of the JDK, and it can be down-loaded from the following Web address:

```
http://java.sun.com/products/JDK/index.html
```

Sun supports the following platforms: Microsoft Windows 95 and NT, Solaris 2.x for SPARC and x86 systems, and Apple MacOS. The JDK version 1.1 includes the following tools: a compiler, an interpreter to run compiled Java standalone applications, an applet viewer to run Java applets, an archiver to create compressed archives, and other utilities.

There are numerous alternatives to the JDK 1.1 that offer graphical user interfaces, tools to speed up debugging and program development, and other niceties. Some of these alternatives use the JDK transparently; others replace the JDK's tools entirely. Chapter 2, "Tools for Getting Started," introduces a few of these alternatives.

The Java API

The Java Application Programming Interface (API) is a set of classes used to develop Java programs. These classes are organized into groups called *packages*. There are packages for the following tasks:

- Numeric variable and string manipulation
- Image creation and manipulation
- File input and output
- Networking
- Windowing and graphical user interface design
- Applet programming
- Error handling
- Security
- Database access
- Distributed application communication
- JavaBeans components

The API includes enough functionality to create sophisticated applets and applications. The Java API must be supported by all operating systems and Web software equipped to execute Java programs, so you can count on the existence of Java API class files when developing programs.

The Java API is at version 1.1 at this time; Sun promises to make no changes in future versions that would require changes to source code. Although enhancements are planned for future releases of the API, there will be no removals or changes to class behavior. However, the natural tendency of software evolution dictates that some parts of the API will become obsolete, but they will still be supported.

Extended APIs

In addition to the core API that must be present with all Java implementations, Sun is developing extended APIs that further extend the features of the language. As if Java 1.1 doesn't provide a rich enough set of APIs!

All but one of the following new APIs are in various stages of development at Sun:

- Commerce API, for secure commercial transactions
- Media API, which adds multimedia classes for graphics, sound, video, 3D, VRML, and telephony
- Servlet API, which creates applet-like Java programs that can run on a Web server
- Management API, to integrate with network management systems, which will be offered as part of the Solstice WorkShop development tool
- Socratic API, which answers the questions that have befuddled mankind for centuries, including the chicken-or-egg dilemma, the doctrine of original sin, the noise caused by trees falling in uninhabited forests, and actress Susan Lucci's lack of success at the Daytime Emmy awards

If you guessed that the Socratic API was the false one, move forward two spaces—you're right. However, Microsoft could not take the risk that another company would be first to implement it—the Socratic API will begin development with ActiveX later this year.

JavaOS

In May 1996, JavaSoft announced plans to develop JavaOS, a compact operating system intended to run Java programs. The stated goal was to create the fastest and smallest platform possible that can handle Java. In addition to being a competitor to operating systems such as Microsoft Windows 95, JavaOS was targeted to put the language where it was originally intended to be: in appliances.

As of this writing, JavaOS is finished and has been ported to several different processor architectures. A complete network computer implementation of JavaOS—including the HotJava browser, class libraries, and over a megabyte of fonts—requires 4M of disk space (or ROM) and 4M of memory. JavaOS and HotJava together use less than 2.5M of RAM, leaving more than 1.5M to handle the storage of cached Web pages, images or client applications, and data.

No specific products using JavaOS have been announced as of yet, but I expect to see some interesting applications of JavaOS in the near future. Maybe a palmtop Web box or a programmable, networkable, electronic toothbrush.

Web Sites

One of the advantages of a Web-based phenomenon like Java is that it generates megabytes of information on the World Wide Web. Documentation, news, source code, and other material about Java is offered at thousands of sites. The following should get you started:

- `http://www.javasoft.com` is the official JavaSoft site. It offers online documentation, news on the latest developments, Java software to download or purchase, and links to other pertinent sites. The Java Development Kit is available from this site, as are trial versions of the Java WorkShop integrated development environment and HotJava Web browser.

- `http://www.gamelan.com` is the largest directory of Java applets and Java-related Web sites. This site also offers links to the winners of the Java Cup applet programming contest, and a chat applet that uses Java to offer America Online-style discussions.

- `http://www.jars.com` is the Java Applet Rating Service, a group that reviews Java applets. If you see an apple logo accompanying a Java program on the Web, it has been reviewed by JARS.

- `http://www.j-g.com/java/` is another directory of Java applets that is smaller than Gamelan's collection. However, a nice collection of Java programs have been assembled here.

- `http://www.mbmdesigns.com/macjava/` is Apple-flavored Java, a site devoted to Macintosh implementations of Java development software and Java programs.

- `http://sunsite.unc.edu/javafaq/javafaq.html` is a list of frequently asked questions about Java programming answered by participants in the Java-related Usenet newsgroups.

- `http://k2.scl.cwru.edu/~gaunt/java/java-faq.html` is another list of questions about Java called the "Unofficial Obscure Java FAQ," which was established for some answers to infrequently asked questions about the language.

- `http://www.javaworld.com/` is the home page of *JavaWorld* magazine, which puts a lot of articles, sample source code, and news stories online.

- `http://www.yahoo.com/Computers_and_Internet/Programming_Languages/Java/` is a section of the Yahoo! directory devoted to Java, with more than 300 links to Web sites.

Usenet Newsgroups

Numerous messages are posted on Usenet newsgroups each day by people who are interested in Java. Some are from developers with experience in the language who can comment on advanced aspects of the language. Many are from newcomers who need help in their efforts to learn Java. In any case, Usenet is a great place to get technical assistance. Some other Usenet messages are from America Online users who have become lost in their search for pictures of Pamela Anderson Lee, but that's another story entirely.

The following newsgroups currently are available on Usenet, which can be accessed with an Internet account, a subscription to online services such as CompuServe and America Online, and other means:

- `comp.lang.java.advocacy` is a newsgroup for debate and diatribes about Java and other languages that can be compared to it.

- `comp.lang.java.announce` is a moderated newsgroup with announcements related to Java—often used for company press releases, Web site launches, and similar information.

- `comp.lang.java.api` is a newsgroup for discussion of the Java Application Programming Interface, the full class library that comes with Java WorkShop, and other development environments for the language.

- `comp.lang.java.programmer` is a newsgroup for questions, answers, and other talk related to Java programming.

- `comp.lang.java.security` is a newsgroup where the security issues related to Java are discussed, with an emphasis on the security of executing Java applets over the World Wide Web.

- `comp.lang.java.setup` is a newsgroup for the discussion of installation problems regarding Java development tools and similar issues.

- `comp.lang.java.tech` is an advanced newsgroup where technical issues of the Java language are discussed.

- `comp.lang.java.misc` is a newsgroup for everything else related to Java. It generally is the most active of the newsgroups.

Java Tomorrow

During its first year and a half of public life, Java has enjoyed the same advantages bestowed on child prodigies. Most of the talk has been about its great potential; criticism has been overshadowed by excited anticipation about what it will do in the future.

As an example of this, consider the words of Marc Andreesen, himself a child prodigy of sorts, after creating Mosaic while he was an undergraduate. Andressen's endorsement was one of the reasons for Java's astonishing growth. He said the following at the JavaOne conference:

> *Java is a huge opportunity for all of us, all the developers in the industry, who are, all of a sudden, able to develop applications in days or weeks, instead of months or years; who have new ways of distributing those applications, making money from those applications without having to fight for retail shelf space.*

One of the applications that has been announced is the WordPerfect Office Suite. Corel has shown off a beta version of Office Suite—redesigned entirely using Java, which makes it available for a wide range of platforms. IBM is redesigning its OS/2 Warp operating system to make it optimized for Java programs. Microsoft has even talked about integrating Java with the Windows platform.

The technology venture capital firm, Kleiner, Perkins, Caufield, and Byers (KPCB), has offered $100 million to support companies doing work with Java.

The next year is going to be a little tougher on the tyke. If Java is to remain the object-oriented language of people's affections, it has to start fulfilling some of its promises. Granted, the release of Java 1.1 has certainly quieted some of the skeptics, but until some major commercial software becomes available in Java form, there will continue to be questions surrounding Java's practical usefulness.

Growing up isn't always an easy process for those who have achieved outlandish success early in life. Ask any former child star who has traded in a Screen Actors Guild card for a life of crime or a career in talk shows.

By picking up a book of this kind and learning about Java, you're one of the people who is expected to do something remarkable with it. The developers of Java, the nation's press, and those of us who make our living writing Java books by the ton are depending on you. Not to mention the folks at KPCB who gave up $100 million of their allowances to fund Java-related programming.

It's one of the prices you pay for being in the right place at the right time.

CHAPTER 2

Tools for Getting Started

by Michael Morrison

IN THIS CHAPTER

When the Java programming language was introduced in 1995, the only development tool available was the Java Development Kit (JDK) from Sun. This set of command-line tools makes it possible to write, compile, and debug Java programs (among other things). However, the JDK is a far cry from integrated development environments such as Visual Basic and Borland C++. An *integrated development environment* (IDE) is software that combines several development tools into a single, cohesive package. The assortment usually includes a source code editor, compiler, debugger, and other utilities. These tools work together through the development process; most packages are highly visual and rely on windows, drag-and-drop, and other graphical elements. The goal is to make software design faster, more efficient, and easier to debug.

Many IDEs make use of *rapid application development* (RAD) methods. RAD is a broad strategy to use tools such as an interface designer and prototyping to speed up the design process. For most of the Java programming environments that have been released, the RAD tools in evidence are graphical user interface builders. Some of these have a direct connection from the interface design tool to the source code so that you can design a component such as a button and go directly to the event-handling code to make something happen when the button is clicked.

This chapter focuses on both the standard JDK 1.1 development tools and on some of the more popular third-party Java IDEs. The goal is to get you up to speed with the types of tools available so that you can begin assembling your own Java toolkit.

The following development environments are described in this chapter:

- The Java Development Kit 1.1
- Symantec Café
- SunSoft Java WorkShop
- Microsoft Visual J++
- Asymetrix SuperCede
- Roaster Technologies' Roaster
- SourceCraft NetCraft
- Pro-C WinGEN for Java
- Rogue Wave JFactory
- Metrowerks Code Warrior

The Java Development Kit 1.1

Before you get started learning about the Java Development Kit, it's important to make sure that you have the latest version. As of this writing, the latest version of the JDK is release 1.1. JavaSoft is expected to release a version 1.1.1 with minor bug fixes in the very near future; you can check Sun's Java Web site at http://www.javasoft.com/ to see what the latest version is.

This Web site provides all the latest news and information regarding Java, including the latest release of the JDK. Keep in mind that Java is still a new technology in a state of rapid change; be sure to keep an eye on this Java Web site for the latest information.

The Java Development Kit contains a variety of tools and Java development information. Following is a list of the main components of the JDK:

- Runtime interpreter
- Compiler
- Applet viewer
- Debugger
- Class file disassembler
- Header and stub file generator
- Documentation generator
- Archiver
- Digital signer
- Remote Method Invocation tools
- Sample demos and source code
- API source code

The runtime interpreter is the core runtime module for the Java system. The compiler, applet viewer, debugger, class file disassembler, header and stub file generator, and documentation generator are the primary tools used by Java developers. The demos are interesting examples of Java applets, which all come with complete source code. And finally, if you are interested in looking under the hood of Java, the complete source code for the Java API (Application Programming Interface) classes is provided.

The Runtime Interpreter

The Java runtime interpreter (`java`) is used to run standalone Java executable programs in compiled, bytecode format. The runtime interpreter acts as a command-line tool for running Java programs that are either nongraphical or that manage their own window frame (applications); graphical programs requiring the display support of a Web browser (applets) are executed entirely within a browser. The syntax for using the runtime interpreter follows:

```
java Options ClassName Arguments
```

The `ClassName` argument specifies the name of the class you want to execute. If the class resides in a package, you must fully qualify the name. You learn about classes and packages in Chapter 5, "Classes, Packages, and Interfaces." For example, if you want to run a class called `Roids` that is located in a package called `ActionGames`, you execute it in the interpreter like this:

```
java ActionGames.Roids
```

When the Java interpreter executes a class, what it is really doing is executing the `main()` method of the class. The interpreter exits when the `main()` method and any threads created by it are finished executing. Don't worry if you aren't yet familiar with the `main()` method or Java threads—they aren't critical to understanding the runtime interpreter at this point. You'll learn about them soon enough in the coming chapters. The `main()` method accepts a list of arguments that can be used to control the program. The *Arguments* argument to the interpreter specifies the arguments passed into the `main()` method. For example, if you have a Java class called `TextFilter` that performs some kind of filtering on a text file, you would likely pass the name of the file as an argument, like this:

```
java TextFilter SomeFile.txt
```

The *Options* argument specifies options related to how the runtime interpreter executes the Java program. Please refer to the JDK documentation for more information about the options supported in the runtime interpreter.

The Compiler

The Java compiler (`javac`) is used to compile Java source code files into executable Java bytecode classes. In Java, source code files have the extension `.java`. The Java compiler takes files with this extension and generates executable class files with the `.class` extension. The compiler creates one class file for each class defined in a source file. This means that it is possible for a single Java source code file to compile into multiple executable class files. When this happens, it means that the source file contains multiple class definitions.

> **NOTE**
>
> Even though Java source files and classes are typically given the extensions `.java` and `.class`, it is important to note that some operating systems aren't capable of fully representing these extensions because of their length. For example, Windows 3.1 is limited to three-character extensions, so Java source files and classes must use the extensions `.jav` and `.cla`.

The Java compiler is a command-line utility that works in a manner similar to the Java runtime interpreter. The syntax for the Java compiler follows:

```
javac Options Filename
```

The *Filename* argument specifies the name of the source code file you want to compile. The *Options* argument specifies options related to how the compiler creates the executable Java classes. Please refer to the JDK documentation for more information about the options supported by the compiler.

The Applet Viewer

The applet viewer is a tool that serves as a minimal test bed for final release Java applets. You can use the applet viewer to test your programs instead of using a full-blown Web browser. You invoke the applet viewer from a command line like this:

```
appletviewer Options URL
```

The `URL` argument specifies a document URL containing an HTML page with an embedded Java applet. The `Options` argument specifies how to run the Java applet. There is only one option supported by the applet viewer: `-debug`. The `-debug` option starts the applet viewer in the Java debugger, which enables you to debug the applet. To see the applet viewer in action, check out Figure 2.1.

FIGURE 2.1.

The `MoleculeViewer`
applet running in the
Java applet viewer.

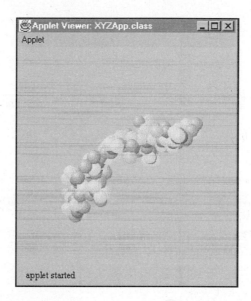

Figure 2.1 shows the `MoleculeViewer` demo applet (which comes with the JDK) running in the applet viewer. This program was launched in the applet viewer by changing to the directory containing the `MoleculeViewer` HTML file and executing the following statement at the command prompt:

```
appletviewer example1.html
```

`example1.html` is the HTML file containing the embedded Java applet. As you can see, there's nothing complicated about running Java applets using the applet viewer. The applet viewer is a useful tool for testing Java applets in a simple environment.

The Debugger

The Java debugger (jdb) is a command-line utility that enables you to debug Java applications. The Java debugger uses the Java Debugger API to provide debugging support within the Java runtime interpreter. The syntax for using the Java debugger follows:

```
jdb Options
```

The Options argument is used to specify different settings within a debugging session. For more information about the options supported in the debugger, see Chapter 28, "Java Debugging."

The Class File Disassembler

The Java class file disassembler (javap) is used to disassemble executable Java class files. Its default output consists of the public data and methods for a class. The class file disassembler is useful in cases where you don't have the source code for a class, but you want to know a little more about how it is implemented. The syntax for the disassembler follows:

```
javap Options ClassNames
```

The ClassNames argument specifies the names of one or more classes to be disassembled. The Options argument specifies how the classes are to be disassembled. Refer to the JDK documentation for more information about the options supported in the class file disassembler.

The Header and Stub File Generator

The Java header and stub file generator (javah) is used to generate C header and source files for implementing Java methods in C. The files generated can be used to access member variables of an object from C code. The header and stub file generator accomplishes this by generating a C structure whose layout matches that of the corresponding Java class. The syntax for using the header and stub file generator follows:

```
javah Options ClassName
```

The ClassName argument is the name of the class from which to generate C source files. The Options argument specifies how the source files are to be generated. Refer to the JDK documentation for more information about the options supported in the header and stub file generator.

The Documentation Generator

The Java documentation generator (javadoc) is a useful tool for generating API documentation directly from Java source code. The documentation generator parses through Java source files and generates HTML pages based on the declarations and comments. The syntax for using the documentation generator follows:

```
javadoc Options FileName
```

The `FileName` argument specifies either a package or a Java source code file. In the case of a package, the documentation generator creates documentation for all the classes contained in the package. The `Options` argument enables you to change the default behavior of `javadoc`.

Because the Java documentation generator is covered in detail in Chapter 29, "Documenting Your Code," you'll have to settle for this brief introduction for now. Or you could jump ahead to Chapter 29 to learn more now.

The Archiver

The Java archiver (`jar`) is a tool used to combine and compress multiple files (usually applets or applications) into a single archive file, which is also commonly referred to as a *JAR file*. Combining the components of an applet or application into a single archive allows them to be downloaded by a browser in a single HTTP transaction instead of requiring a new connection for each individual file. This approach, coupled with the data compression provided by the archiver, dramatically improves download times. Additionally, the archiver can be used with the digital signer (described in the following section) to sign applets and applications so that they can be authenticated at runtime. The syntax for using the archiver follows:

```
jar Options ManifestFileName OuputFileName InputFileNames
```

The `ManifestFileName` argument specifies a manifest file used to describe the contents of the archive being created. The `OutputFileName` argument specifies the name of the archive to be created. The `InputFileNames` argument specifies the files to be added to the archive. The `Options` argument enables you to change the default behavior of `jar`. You learn all about manifest files, code signing, and the ins and outs of the `jar` tool in Part VIII of this book, "Java Archives and JavaBeans."

The Digital Signer

The Java digital signer (`javakey`), also known as the Java security tool, is an interesting tool that generates digital signatures for archive files. *Signatures* are used to verify that a file came from a specified entity, or *signer*. To generate a signature for a particular file, the signer must first be associated with a public/private key pair and must also have one or more certificates authenticating the signer's public key. The digital signer is responsible for managing this database of entities, along with their keys and certificates. The syntax for using the digital signer follows:

```
javakey Options
```

The `Options` argument is used to control the operation of `javakey`. You learn all about digital code signing, public and private keys, and the specifics of how to use the `javakey` tool in Chapter 37, "Code Signing and JAR Security."

The Remote Method Invocation Tools

The JDK includes three different tools for working with and managing remote method invocation (RMI). These tools consist of an RMI stub compiler, a remote object registry tool, and a serial version tool. For more information about the RMI tools, please refer to Chapter 17, "The RMI Package."

Examples and Source Code

The JDK comes with a variety of interesting Java examples, all of which include complete source code. Following is a list of the Java example applets that come with the JDK:

- Animator
- ArcTest
- BarChart
- Blink
- BouncingHeads
- CardTest
- DitherTest
- DrawTest
- Fractal
- GraphicsTest
- GraphLayout
- ImageMap
- ImageTest
- JumpingBox
- MoleculeViewer
- NervousText
- ScrollingImages
- SimpleGraph
- SpreadSheet
- TicTacToe
- TumblingDuke
- UnderConstruction
- WireFrame

Rather than go through the tedium of describing each of these examples, I'll leave most of them for you to explore and try out on your own. However, it's worth checking out a few of them here and discuss how they impact the Web.

The first demo applet we're concerned about is the BarChart applet, shown in Figure 2.2.

FIGURE 2.2.

The BarChart *Java applet.*

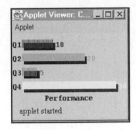

The BarChart applet is a good example of how Java can be used to show statistical information on the Web graphically. The data represented by the bar graph could be linked to a live data source, such as a group of stock quotes. Then you could actually generate a live, to-the-minute, dynamically changing stock portfolio.

The GraphicsTest applet is a good example of how to use Java graphics. Java includes an extensive set of graphics features, including support for drawing primitive shapes as well as more elaborate drawing routines. Figure 2.3 shows what the GraphicsTest applet looks like.

FIGURE 2.3.

The GraphicsTest *Java applet.*

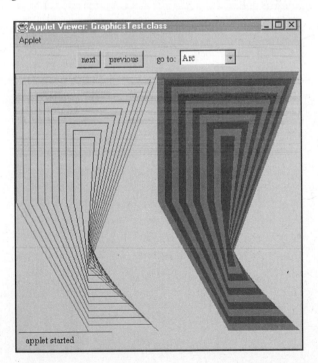

Keeping the focus on graphics, the `SimpleGraph` applet shows how Java can be used to plot a two-dimensional graph. There are plenty of scientific and educational applications for plotting. Using Java, data presented in a Web page can come to life with graphical plots. `SimpleGraph` is shown in Figure 2.4.

FIGURE 2.4.

The `SimpleGraph` *Java applet.*

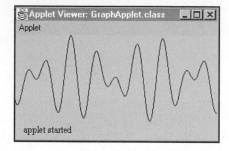

On the business front, there's nothing like a good spreadsheet. The `SpreadSheet` Java applet shows how to implement a simple spreadsheet in Java. I don't think I even need to say how many applications there are for interactive spreadsheets on the Web. Check out the `SpreadSheet` applet in Figure 2.5.

FIGURE 2.5.

The `SpreadSheet` *Java applet.*

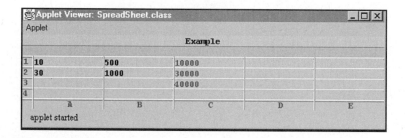

Once you've gotten a headache playing with the `SpreadSheet` applet, it's time to blow off a little steam with a game. The applet in Figure 2.6 demonstrates a simple Java version of TicTacToe. This demo opens a new window of opportunity for having fun on the Web. Games are an interesting application for Java, so keep your eyes peeled for new and interesting ways to have fun on the Web with Java games.

FIGURE 2.6.

The `TicTacToe` *Java applet.*

The last applet mentioned in this chapter is the `UnderConstruction` applet, which is a neat little applet that can be used to jazz up unfinished Web pages. This applet shows an animation of the Java mascot, Duke, with a jackhammer. Because the applet also has sound, it's a true multimedia experience! Although this applet is strictly for fun, it nevertheless provides a cool alternative to the usual "under construction" messages that are often used in unfinished Web pages. The `UnderConstruction` applet is shown in Figure 2.7.

FIGURE 2.7.

The `UnderConstruction` *Java applet.*

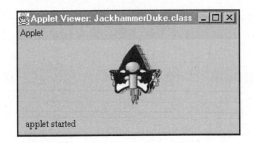

Although running these example applets is neat, the real thing to keep in mind is that they all come with complete source code. This means that you can rip them apart and figure out how they work, and then use similar techniques in your own Java programs. The most powerful way to learn is by example, and the sample applets that come with the JDK are great examples of robust Java applets.

API Source Code

The final component of the Java Development Kit is the source code for the Java API. That's right—the JDK comes with the complete source code for all the classes that make up the Java API. Sun isn't concerned with keeping the internals of Java top secret. They followed the lead of the UNIX world and decided to make Java as available and readily understood as possible. Besides, the real value of Java is not the specific code that makes it work, it's the idea behind it.

The API source code is automatically installed to your hard drive when you decompress the JDK, but it may remain in compressed form, depending on your particular platform. It is sometimes very useful to be able to look under the hood to see how something works. The API source code comes compressed in a file called `src.zip`, located in the `java` directory created on your hard drive during installation of the JDK. All the classes that make up the Java API are included in this file.

Selecting an IDE

Although the JDK is certainly sufficient for professional Java development, the advanced features of third-party IDEs (integrated development environments) can improve productivity significantly. Even so, IDEs aren't necessarily for everyone. When you evaluate an IDE for any language, you should ask yourself some questions about what you want to have on hand when you're ready to develop a program. Although this approach is true for any language and any environment, you should consider some specific issues related to Java's unique programming features (such as portability). Ask yourself the following questions:

■ How important is graphical interface design to your programs?

■ Do your programs have to be completely portable across platforms?

■ What is your comfort zone with IDE tools?

■ Do you want to program in other languages at the same time?

GUI Development Tools

The popularity of windowing systems is well established; users have begun to shy away from software that does not make use of these features. Although some of us grizzled veterans have an Amish-like love of the old ways—DOS utilities, the command prompt, batch processing, 1970s dance funk—most users today expect their software to have features such as mouse control, point-and-click, and resizable program windows. Because these requirements make graphical user interface design an important element of most Java programming, it is important to select an IDE that is strong in this area.

Most Java IDEs are distinguishing themselves from each other by their approach to interface design and the functionality possible from within the interface development tool. Also, software such as Rogue Wave JFactory is primarily an interface builder rather than an entire IDE.

Most Java interface builders work in largely the same way—like a painting program. You start with a blank form and a palette of user interface components. These components are usually Abstract Windowing Toolkit (AWT) objects, and the interface builder generates AWT code that can be modified by a programmer who is fluent in dealing with the toolkit. Some IDEs such as SunSoft Java WorkShop introduce a layer between the AWT and the programmer's source code. The goal of a layer such as this is to make it easier to deal with windowing and interface issues. The IDE handles things behind the scenes so that the programmer can concentrate on larger issues.

For some programmers, especially those who spent a lot of time learning the intricacies of the AWT, this may not be an attractive feature. Others may be more interested in the power offered by these interface builders or may be ready to leave the complexity of the AWT behind.

One of the nicest features of these interface builders is their capability to generate event-handling code at the same time they create a user interface component. Anyone who has used Visual Basic is familiar with this approach: You plunk down a text field where you want it on a dialog box, double-click the text field, and then begin entering the source code to control how it operates.

Portability of Code

One of the features to watch for when choosing an IDE is whether it produces code that is fully compatible with the standard Java class library. Several of the development environments such as Café and Java WorkShop come with their own versions of the JDK instead of using an existing implementation of the JDK.

This usually does not matter because one of the goals of any Java IDE is to take advantage of the language's portability across any platform. Many development environments such as SourceCraft NetCraft work entirely within the JDK to create software that does not enhance those features with proprietary extensions.

Others environments, such as Microsoft Visual J++, add features that require new classes. Visual J++ provides extensions to the Java language that are specific to the Windows operating system. For an applet or application designed with Visual J++ to be fully portable, it must not make use of these extensions. Because this IDE is relatively new, it remains to be seen whether the advantage of extended features makes up for the significant disadvantage of platform specificity. This issue is being hotly debated within the community of Java developers because many believe that the continued growth of the language depends on its ability to stay cohesive and fully cross platform.

An interesting side issue to the portability question is that most Java development environments are not cross platform themselves—even when the IDE is touted as being a Java program. All the major IDEs that have been introduced to date are offered for specific platforms—primarily because of the use of native code.

IDE Experience

One element of IDE use that sometimes gets lost in the shuffle is the skill level required to use them. If the idea of an IDE is to improve your programming, this can't happen if you can't figure out the IDE! An integrated development environment is a complex type of software. It often makes use of a multiple-document interface where you can have several windows open at once and a dizzying array of options.

For experienced programmers, this functionality is a great boon. You want to have as much power at your control as possible. However, a new programmer can easily get lost in some of the available IDEs—especially if the programmer is still learning the Java language. When you are busy clearing out space in your brain for a new programming language, you shouldn't have to find room for an IDE at the same time.

Several of the IDEs available for Java are more suited for the code warrior—the multilingual veteran who can throw around jargon like *OOP*, *MUMPS*, and *male-female connector* with the greatest of ease. However, a few of the development environments are more suited for the newcomer because their interface is more approachable and less complex.

The best example of this kind of interface is Java WorkShop from SunSoft, which uses the familiar Web browser interface. People coming to Java from a limited programming background—such as HTML developers looking to upgrade their skills—may find this kind of IDE more suited to their tastes.

There is a trade-off for this ease of use, of course. An environment like Java WorkShop may require more steps to get a task done—either because the functions are not immediately available or because the environment may not offer some of the functionality of a more complex IDE.

Multiple Language Development

Another factor regarding the use of an IDE for some programmers is its use with other languages. Several of these environments, including Metrowerks CodeWarrior and Microsoft Visual J++, are designed to handle more than one language or are fully equivalent to the company's other development tools.

If the IDE is a complex one (as these are), you learn how to use it and don't have to learn another when you shift gears and program in a nonJava language. Also, if you write native methods for use in your Java programs, you can use some multilanguage IDEs to write that code. The Visual J++ environment integrates completely with the Visual C++ environment, so native methods can be written alongside Java methods in an integrated manner.

The Bottom Line

The goal of an IDE is to make you a better programmer. As Java developer Chuck McManis wrote in his August 1996 *JavaWorld* column, "I rate the IDEs by my ability to get productive work done while using them."

As you go over the details of the software products discussed in the following sections, you get a clearer picture of how each environment can help you. Given the number of IDEs already available for Java, you should be able to match one with your skill level, programming tasks, and personal taste.

If not, as the Amish coder might tell you—there's always the JDK. You can match it with word processors, custom interface builders, and other single-feature design tools to create a personalized IDE.

CAUTION

If you are downloading tryout or beta copies of several IDEs—as I did in the course of preparing this material—be advised that these rival products may not coexist peacefully. Many Java development tools make use of environment variables such as CLASSPATH and JAVAHOME, and they are not happy if another software tool has claimed these variables for its own purposes. As an example, Café and Java WorkShop are the Prince Charles and Lady Diana of software—they should be kept apart for the benefit of everyone involved. If possible, deinstall one IDE before installing the next one on your system and make sure that your boot files are cleaned out as well. If you need more than one IDE active on your system, you can establish multiple configuration files that are executed when a particular environment is used.

NOTE

As of this writing, none of the IDEs mentioned here support Java 1.1 because Java 1.1 is so new. There will no doubt be a mad rush by tool vendors to support Java 1.1, so you can expect support for the new Java version by these IDEs in the very near future—if it's not available by the time you read this.

Symantec Café

Symantec Café, originally released in March 1996, is the first development environment that became widely available for Java programming after the JDK. Symantec calls it an *integrated development and debugging environment* (IDDE), but the added *D* doesn't make it different from most IDEs—the others usually include a debugger, too. Café is based on Symantec's C++ environment, but Café is a standalone product that does not require a C++ platform to run.

System Requirements

Symantec has released versions of Café for the Microsoft Windows 95, Windows NT 3.5x, and Macintosh systems.

For Microsoft users, an Intel 386 processor and 8M of memory are required, but a 486 or better and 16M of memory are recommended. A VGA monitor is needed, but Symantec recommends that an SVGA monitor be used if available. The software and all its sample files and Help files require 60M of disk space and a CD-ROM drive.

For Macintosh owners, a Power Macintosh, 68030, or 68040 Macintosh is required, and 16M of memory is recommended. The full installation of the software requires 30M of disk space.

Café incorporates the JDK into its release with a full implementation of the Java class libraries and source code samples. You do not have to have the JDK before installing Café. In fact, it is prudent to deinstall the JDK before implementing Café to avoid system conflicts between the two.

Overview

Café is a sophisticated IDE that offers an excellent source editor with color highlighting of syntax, an editor for class and hierarchy modification, a Studio tool for interface design, and numerous example applets. To aid in the design of a class hierarchy, Café has a class editor for navigating through classes and editing class methods, and a hierarchy editor for viewing and modifying Java class relationships. Changes in the source code that affect the class hierarchy can be seen as the program is being written, instead of requiring that it be compiled before changes are reflected in the hierarchy. You can also change the source code from within the class editor—clicking the function or method within a class brings up its source code in a window you can use to edit the code.

With AppExpress, the process of creating a skeleton Java program speeds up. This and several other *Express Agents*—Café's term for wizards—make it easier to begin projects and new programs.

In the source editor, Java syntax is highlighted, making it easier to spot typos and other errors immediately. The editor can be customized to behave like several popular programmers' editors such as Brief, Emacs, and Epsilon. The editor also uses the standard Windows cut, copy, and paste commands.

With Café Studio, designing a graphical user interface for your Java programs can be done in a visual, drag-and-drop manner. Studio enables programmers to develop the dialog boxes and other visual elements visually, and it creates event handlers for these components automatically. There's also a menu editor with an active window in which you can test the menu. These resources are saved in separate `.rc` files that can be edited later (just as source files are edited); the `.rc` format is compatible with other design tools that generate `.rc` files.

One interesting aspect of Café Studio is the ability it gives you to design a form and dictate exactly how it looks. With the JDK and its Abstract Windowing Toolkit, GUI designers have to allow their work to be changed depending on the platform the applet or application is running on. This approach is similar to the way HTML can be modified to fit the large number of platforms used on the World Wide Web. It's an approach well suited to cross-platform design. With Café Studio, programmers can choose to use one of these variable layout managers or to dictate the position and size of all interface elements.

When you're ready to compile a program, Café provides the option to use Sun's JDK compiler or the Café compiler, which operates more quickly than the current JDK version.

The Café debugger provides several different ways to temporarily halt the execution of code, including a quick-breakpoint feature for a one-time run that stops at a specific line. The debugger also enables a large amount of control over threads in multithreaded programs. During debugging, you can use a watch view to monitor the contents of variables.

The environment of Symantec Café is highly customizable—all toolbars and palettes can be resized and placed where you want them on-screen. Several windows can be open at the same time, making it possible to view the object hierarchy while entering source code and using the form editor, for example.

How to Get It

In addition to retail and mail-order outlets, you can purchase Café from Symantec's Web site. The home page for Symantec Café is at the following URL:

```
http://cafe.symantec.com/
```

The customer service number for the company is (800) 441-7234, and its e-mail address for Java-related comments and questions is javainfo@symantec.com.

SunSoft Java WorkShop

SunSoft Java WorkShop, the development tool offered by the language's home team, is an IDE written almost entirely in Java. Its development has been used to help improve the Java language. The mindset at Sun is that committing to such a large-scale undertaking in the company's own language gives it insight into the issues other developers are facing and reveals any kinks in Java that still have to be straightened out.

However, all that talk doesn't benefit the developer looking for a tool to write software. Java WorkShop is evaluated here on the basis of its applicability to this task.

System Requirements

Versions of Java WorkShop are available for the following systems: Microsoft Windows 95, Windows NT 3.5.1, SPARC Solaris (2.4 or later), and Intel x86 Solaris systems.

Microsoft Windows 95 and NT systems must be running a 90-megahertz Pentium or better with 16M of memory and 45M of hard disk space. Solaris systems must have 32M of memory, 45M of disk space, and an OSF/Motif 1.2.3-compliant windowing system. The recommended display resolution to use with Java WorkShop is 800×600 pixels.

Java WorkShop comes with its own modified version of the JDK, so it cannot be used in conjunction with an existing installation of the kit. Like Café, Java WorkShop requires that any existing JDK copies be deinstalled before you can install and run WorkShop correctly.

Overview

Java WorkShop, one of the most approachable IDEs for a novice programmer, uses a Web interface to offer the following features: a source editor, class browser, debugger, project management system, and Visual Java (a tool for the visual design of a graphical interface and an easier means to create windowing software).

The most striking difference between Java WorkShop and other IDEs is its interface. Java WorkShop looks more like a Web browser than a programming development environment. It *is* a Web browser, in fact—users of Sun's HotJava browser will recognize elements from that software in the design of WorkShop. In addition, you can view any Web page while working in Java WorkShop.

Java WorkShop's browser interface is easier to use for programmers who are unfamiliar with IDEs and similar software; the browser interface is frustrating to some of those who are comfortable with these tools.

WorkShop has a source browser for viewing a class hierarchy, public methods, and variables. The browser creates HTML pages in the same format as HTML documentation generated by the JDK's javadoc utility. The WorkShop source editor works in conjunction with WorkShop's debugger—compilation errors create links directly into the source editor for fixing. The WorkShop debugger provides breakpoints and other methods of debugging.

The Visual Java feature provides a way to graphically design an interface, much as Café Studio does. Visual Java enables programmers to develop dialog boxes and other visual elements and automatically creates event handlers for these components. There's also a menu editor. Resources are saved in separate .gui files that can be edited later, just as source files are edited.

The environment is not customizable in the way Café is, but the Web interface makes it easy to integrate other tools and programs into WorkShop. The program is a collection of Web pages with Java programs embedded in and around them. You can go to a different page from within Java WorkShop as easily as you can enter a URL in a Web browser. This approach makes it possible for a user to create original pages of Java development tools that can be linked to WorkShop pages. This arrangement may be unusual for someone accustomed to development environments written as cohesive, single-executable files that can't be changed (as most are). However, it suits the spirit of Java—independent programs linked together by HTML pages, which can be modified as individual elements without affecting the other parts of the whole.

How to Get It

Java WorkShop can be downloaded freely for evaluation. For more detail and the opportunity to download an evaluation copy, visit the following URL:

http://www.sun.com/sunsoft/Developer-products/java/index.html

The customer service number to use for the company is (800) 786-7638 (SUN-SOFT) in the United States, or (512) 434-1511 elsewhere. The company's e-mail address for comments and questions is sunsoft@selectnet.com.

Microsoft Visual J++

Microsoft Visual J++ is Microsoft's answer to a Java development environment. Designed to integrate with Microsoft's Visual Studio suite of development tools, Visual J++ features extensions to the Java class library that are specific to the Windows platform. Visual J++ sports the look and feel of the popular Visual C++ development environment, as well as most of its advanced features. Visual J++ provides the only real support of any IDE for fully integrating Java with ActiveX.

System Requirements

Visual J++ is currently available only for the Windows 95/NT platform. It requires a minimum of a 486 or higher processor with 8M of memory for Windows 95 (12M recommended), or 16M of memory for Windows NT Workstation (20M recommended). A typical installation requires 20M of hard disk space, while a minimum installation weighs in at 14M.

Overview

For Windows developers familiar with the Visual C++ IDE, it will be very easy to hit the ground running with Visual J++. Even for developers new to Microsoft's visual development environments, Visual J++ presents a reasonable learning curve. For Java programmers who really want a jumpstart, Visual J++ includes wizards that give step-by-step assistance for building applets. It also sports the fastest Java 1.02 source code compiler, at 10,000 lines of code per second. It isn't clear whether Microsoft will be able to maintain this record with its Java 1.1 compiler—we'll just have to wait and see.

The Visual J++ editor is very nice and fully supports color syntax highlighting. There is also a class viewer, which shows all the Java classes that have definitions as well as the members of those classes, including properties and methods. Visual J++ has a very powerful graphical Java debugger that supports the debugging of multiple applets simultaneously from within a browser. The debugger comes complete with bytecode disassembly, bytecode-level stepping and tracing, and the ability to assign values to variables while debugging.

All things considered, Visual J++ is one of the better Java IDEs available. There are some valid concerns over Microsoft's proprietary extensions for Java, but Microsoft knows it must adhere to the core Java API to lure developers. As long as the company continues to do that, it can bundle in as many proprietary extensions as it wants.

How to Get It

Visual J++ is currently not available for download. However, you can find out lots more information about it and even purchase a copy online at Microsoft's Visual J++ home page:

```
http://www.microsoft.com/visualj/
```

Asymetrix SuperCede

SuperCede, by Asymetrix, is a forms-based IDE geared toward being an easy-to-use environment for learning and using Java. SuperCede's tight integration between forms and source editors makes it easy to navigate between user interface objects and their associated event handlers. SuperCede also includes a very interesting compiler technology known as *flash compilation*, which allows developers to modify the source code of a running application and instantly see the impact of the change. The flash compiler in SuperCede also provides developers with the option of generating portable Java bytecode or native Intel machine code for higher performance.

System Requirements

SuperCede is currently available only for the Windows 95/NT platform. It requires a minimum of a 486/66 or higher processor with 32M of memory and 50M of hard disk space.

Overview

The SuperCede integrated development environment includes a project manager, browsers, a color syntax-highlighting source editor, a drag-and-drop form editor, and a graphical debugger, among other things. The browsers included with SuperCede include source, form, and class and content file browsers. The forms-centric development approach used by SuperCede streamlines application development.

The one thing that really sets SuperCede apart as a Java development environment is its flash compiler technology, which allows you to interactively modify running applications. Additionally, the flash compiler in SuperCede allows you to choose between generating standard Java bytecode executables or native x86 executables that perform significantly better but specifically target Intel processors.

How to Get It

You can get more information about SuperCede and even download an evaluation copy from Asymetrix's SuperCede home page:

```
http://www.asymetrix.com/products/supercede/
```

Roaster Technologies' Roaster

Roaster Technologies' Roaster was made available to developers in January 1996, making it the first Java IDE for the Macintosh. As of this writing, the current version is Developer release 2.3, which contains significant enhancements over Roaster's debut version. Roaster includes a visual interface builder, a compiler that can be targeted for Macintosh or Microsoft Windows systems, and an extended class library.

System Requirements

The minimum requirements for Roaster are a 68030 or greater processor, Macintosh System 7.1.2 or later (7.5 or later preferred), and 8M of RAM.

Overview

In many ways, Roaster is the Java IDE of choice for Macintosh developers, primarily because it was the first IDE for the Mac and has had more time to evolve. Roaster includes a fully integrated browser, class tree viewer, and editor. Roaster also fully supports AppleScript and includes an AppleScript class wizard that guides you through building AppleScript classes.

Roaster provides support for running and testing applets over a network, as well as Java classes for accessing databases using ODBC. Roaster is the only Java IDE that gives registered users a free subscription to *Java Report* magazine, a SIGS publication.

How to Get It

You can find out more about Roaster by dropping by Roaster Technologies' Roaster home page at this URL:

```
http://www.roaster.com/roaster/
```

SourceCraft NetCraft

SourceCraft, the developer of the ObjectCraft development environment, is making its NetCraft Java IDE available as freeware. For those unfamiliar with the term, *freeware* is software available for no cost as long as you comply with the developer's terms and conditions for use.

This fact makes NetCraft attractive if cost is a criteria—obviously!—but the IDE still must be well designed or you will pay in terms of lost time and efficiency.

System Requirements

Versions of NetCraft are available for Microsoft Windows 95 and Windows NT 3.5.1 systems running a 486 or better with 8M of memory. NetCraft comes bundled with the current version of the JDK; SourceCraft also makes NetCraft available for download without the JDK if you already have the JDK installed.

Overview

SourceCraft NetCraft is somewhat less ambitious in its approach than other IDEs because it has a smaller set of available features. However, it is a fully featured replacement for the JDK, and it creates Java programs compatible across all Java implementations. NetCraft has an editor, a class inspector, a user interface designer, and a compiler.

NetCraft is an IDE that can be used for any type of Java applet or application. In its approach to the software, SourceCraft focuses on Java's applicability in intranet environments.

The Package Inspector, part of NetCraft's system for organizing projects, includes a way to browse the methods used in a class. NetCraft also has a Class Inspector for looking at the following aspects of a class: its position in the hierarchy, its methods, and its variables. When you are looking at a method with this tool, you can view the source code of the method and how it is used in a program.

NetCraft, like Café and Java WorkShop, includes a way to visually develop a graphical user interface. The NetCraft UI Builder generates Java code that uses the Abstract Windowing Toolkit as its raw material, so the code does not rely on any new classes introduced with the development environment. When you create an interface component, NetCraft generates source code for that component, complete with a TODO comment line where the event-handling code for that component is placed. It's a simpler approach than some of the alternatives; a programmer comfortable with the AWT should be comfortable with it.

The source editor uses Windows cut-and-paste commands and is similar to other small word processors with which you are probably familiar. And the NetCraft UI builder is not much more difficult to use than a word processor. A nice feature of the builder is its ability to set the specific coordinates (height and width) of a component by entering numbers into text fields.

The environment is simpler to use and master than other IDEs. However, this may be a problem when you are developing sophisticated programs with numerous windows and interactions; some of the tools you need to manage this software are not available in NetCraft. Its strength for use with complex programs depends on where SourceCraft, the maker of other development tools, plans to go with this freeware product.

For basic tasks and applets, NetCraft appears to be a good substitute for JDK users seeking to migrate to a graphical interface. Because it is free, it is a fitting place for novices to start when choosing a Java IDE.

How to Get It

For more details, and the opportunity to download NetCraft at no cost, visit the home page for NetCraft at this URL:

```
http://www.sourcecraft.com:4800/about/netcraft/
```

The customer service number for the company is (617) 221-5665; the company's e-mail address for comments and questions is edc@sourcecraft.com.

Pro-C WinGEN for Java

WinGEN for Java, the development software from Pro-C, is an IDE designed with the nonprogrammer in mind. The focus is on automatically generating code so that HTML designers and other programming novices can develop Java applets and applications. The graphical interface of a program can be developed using drag-and-drop features; elements such as animation can be introduced without writing a single line of code. The IDE calls the Java Development Kit from within WinGEN to compile and run programs.

System Requirements

Versions of WinGEN are available for Microsoft Windows 95 and Windows NT 3.5.1 systems running a 486 or better with 8M of memory and 10M of hard disk space. Unpacking WinGEN Lite, the evaluation edition of the software, requires a program that can unpack ZIP files into long filenames. (For users of Windows systems, the Windows 95 operating system introduced filenames longer than eight characters and a three-character extension.) If you use a ZIP unpack program that does not support long filenames, files are not named correctly and the setup will fail. WinGEN includes the current version of the JDK, which must be installed *before* WinGEN is installed so that the IDE will function.

Overview

WinGEN augments the existing JDK rather than replacing it, enabling you to run the compiler and interpreter from within WinGEN rather than using the JDK's command-line tools.

As software that strives to put nonprogrammers to work developing Java applets and applications, WinGEN puts its emphasis on its point-and-click approach to the creation of graphical user interfaces. Many simple user events can be created through WinGEN without writing any Java code; graphics and animation features can also be created without programming.

The user interface is designed in a manner that should be familiar to programmers who have used other GUI design tools—especially Visual Basic developers. The version currently available is a bit difficult to use when it comes to aligning components (because of the lack of a snap-to grid feature). Otherwise, laying out things such as text fields and labels is easier than doing so in some other IDEs.

The IDE takes a resource-centric view of development. Instead of starting from the code and using it to create things such as menus and dialog boxes, you start with the menus and dialog boxes and use them to generate the required code. One feature missing from WinGEN is the ability to see the interface before any code has been generated. The Java program that uses the interface must be compiled and run before you can see how the interface will look.

The commercial version of WinGEN for Java includes some features not commonly available in other IDEs at this time, such as support for specific types of ASCII text databases and tables.

A system called CodeHooks handles advanced programming—for writing Java code to handle special circumstances that WinGEN can't handle. These *hooks*—blocks of code that accomplish specific tasks such as a special event handler—are kept separate from the code WinGEN automatically generates. This separation of code enables programmers to change the GUI and plug CodeHooks back in without reentering any code.

How to Get It

For more details about WinGEN, the opportunity to download WinGEN Lite at no cost, or to purchase the full version online, visit the home page for WinGEN:

```
http://www.pro-c.com/products/wfj/java.html
```

The phone number at Pro-C for inquiries related to the software is (813) 227-7762; the company's e-mail address for comments and questions regarding WinGEN is support@ pro-c.com.

Rogue Wave JFactory

Unlike most of the development tools being introduced for Java, JFactory is being offered as an interface builder rather than an IDE. However, because JFactory enables the placement of event-handling code from within the program and also provides a way to compile and test programs during development, it's close enough to a full IDE to be worthy of consideration. Although JFactory can be used in conjunction with any editor and Java compiler, a default editor is provided and JFactory is initially set up to use the JDK compiler.

System Requirements

Versions of JFactory are available for the following platforms:

- Microsoft Windows 95 and Windows NT systems running a 486 or better with 16M of memory, 25M of hard disk space, and the Java Developer's Kit version 1.0.2.
- SPARC Solaris 2.4 or 2.5 running UNIX with 25M of hard disk space, an applet browser, JDK version 1.0.2, and X11R5. You must have enough memory to run X11R5, the JDK compiler, and an applet browser.
- HP-UX 10.01 systems with 25M of hard disk space, an applet browser, the JDK version 1.0.2, and X11R5. The memory requirements are the same as for Solaris systems.
- IBM OS/2 Warp 3.0 systems with 25M of hard disk space, 4M of memory not used by OS/2, a two-button mouse or pointing device, and the JDK version 1.0.2 build os2-19960412.

Overview

JFactory is a sophisticated interface builder based on zApp Factory, a multiplatform C++ application framework from Rogue Wave. The software has a large number of features that facilitate rapid application design, and the product benefits from the experience Rogue Wave has accumulated with its other programming tools. The primary offering of JFactory is its visual, drag-and-drop editor for interface creation. This graphical user interface developer is head-and-shoulders above many of the other visual development tools currently available.

The JFactory software is not considered to be a full IDE because it does not provide its own compiler, debugger, or other tools. However, JFactory's visual editor is so easy to use, and so capable, that it may compensate for the loss of some integrated development offerings. This open environment, a trait of Rogue Wave's programming software, enables any compiler or debugger to be used from within JFactory.

At any stage in the development process, you can test the interface you have created. Another useful feature is that custom components can be integrated easily into the toolbar alongside standard components such as text labels, text fields, and radio buttons. One thing JFactory offers that sets it apart from most other IDEs is its ability to import `.rc` and `.dlg` files created with other programming environments.

A lot of the source code associated with interface components is generated automatically by JFactory. Custom code that must be added is protected from modification so that you can change the interface afterward without overwriting your changes to the source code.

JFactory has a robust system for creating the interface: You can use drag-and-drop and mouse movements to place components, and you can also place components with numeric input. The height, width, and x,y coordinates of a component can be set from a properties dialog box. This approach makes it much easier to cure the problem of wandering components that are difficult to align correctly.

How to Get It

For more details about JFactory and the opportunity to download a demo version or to purchase it online, visit Rogue Wave's home page for JFactory:

`http://www.roguewave.com/products/jfactory/jfactory.html`

The e-mail address for comments and questions regarding JFactory is support@roguewave.com.

Metrowerks CodeWarrior

Metrowerks CodeWarrior is the only Java IDE that supports three other programming languages (C, C++, and Pascal) in the same environment. In addition, CodeWarrior supports all these languages on both the Macintosh and Windows 95/NT platforms. CodeWarrior ships standard with support for all four languages, meaning that Java developers have the option of using other languages without purchasing any additional software.

System Requirements

The minimum requirements for the Macintosh version of CodeWarrior are a 68020 or greater processor (or a PowerPC 601 or greater), Macintosh System 7.1 or later, 8M of RAM (16M preferred), and 65M of hard disk space. The Windows version of CodeWarrior requires at least a 486 or higher processor, Windows 95 or NT, and 16M of RAM.

Overview

CodeWarrior has been well established in the Macintosh community for some time now as the standard Macintosh C/C++ development environment. For this reason, it isn't surprising that it has quickly gained popularity as a Java development environment—at least on the Mac. The CodeWarrior IDE includes a project manager, resource editor, text editor, graphical debugger, and class browsers—basically everything you expect in a professional development environment.

CodeWarrior's wide support for Macintosh C/C++ developers migrating to Java will no doubt give it a broad user base and establish it as a major player on the Java front. It still isn't clear how it will fare in the much more competitive Windows development tool market (where Microsoft, Symantec, and Borland have traditionally ruled). Only time will tell, but Metrowerks is certainly in the race with a solid product.

How to Get It

You can find out more about CodeWarrior if you drop by Metrowerks' products home page:

```
http://www.metrowerks.com/products/
```

Summary

The Java Development Kit provides a wealth of information, including the tools essential to Java programming. In this chapter, you learned about the different components of the JDK, including tools, applet demos, and the Java API source code. Although you learn more about some of these tools throughout the rest of the book, it's important to understand what role each tool plays in the development of Java programs. A strong knowledge of the information contained in the Java Development Kit is necessary to becoming a successful Java developer.

However, you shouldn't stop with the Java Development Kit. In this chapter, you also saw how third-party IDEs can make Java development much easier. Hopefully, you now have a good idea about the types of tools available so that you can begin putting together your own Java development toolkit.

Java Language Fundamentals

by Michael Morrison

CHAPTER 3

Java is an object-oriented language. This means that the language is based on the concept of an *object*. Although a knowledge of object-oriented programming is necessary to put Java to practical use, it isn't required to understand the fundamentals of the Java language. This chapter focuses on the language and leaves the object-oriented details of Java for Chapter 5, "Classes, Packages, and Interfaces."

If you already have some experience with another object-oriented language such as C++ or Smalltalk, much of Java will be familiar territory. In fact, you can almost consider Java a new, revamped C++. Because Java evolved from C++, many of the similarities and differences between Java and C++ will be highlighted throughout the next few chapters.

This chapter covers the essentials of the Java language, including a few sample programs to help you hit the ground running.

Hello, World!

 The best way to learn a programming language is to jump right in and see how a real program works. In keeping with a traditional introductory programming example, your first program is a Java version of the classic "Hello, World!" program. Listing 3.1 contains the source code for the HelloWorld class, which also is located on the CD-ROM that accompanies this book in the file HelloWorld.java.

Listing 3.1. The HelloWorld class.

```
class HelloWorld {
  public static void main(String args[]) {
    System.out.println("Hello, World!");
  }
}
```

After compiling the program with the Java compiler (javac), you are ready to run it in the Java interpreter. The Java compiler places the executable output in a file called HelloWorld.class. This naming convention might seem strange considering the fact that most programming languages use the .EXE file extension for executables. Not so in Java! Following the object-oriented nature of Java, all Java programs are stored as Java classes that are created and executed as objects in the Java runtime environment. To run the HelloWorld program, type **java HelloWorld** at the command prompt. As you may have guessed, the program responds by displaying Hello, World! on your screen. Congratulations! You just wrote and tested your first Java program!

Obviously, HelloWorld is a very minimal Java program. Even so, there's still a lot happening in those few lines of code. To fully understand what is happening, let's examine the program line by line. First, you must understand that Java relies heavily on classes. In fact, the first statement of `HelloWorld` reminds you that `HelloWorld` is a class, not just a program. Furthermore, by looking at the `class` statement in its entirety, you can see that the name of the class is defined as `HelloWorld`. This name is used by the Java compiler as the name of the executable output class. The Java compiler creates an executable class file for each class defined in a Java source file. If there is more than one class defined in a `.java` file, the Java compiler stores each class in a separate `.class` file.

The `HelloWorld` class contains one *method*, or member function. For now, you can think of this function as a normal procedural function that happens to be linked to the class. The details of methods are covered in Chapter 5, "Classes, Packages, and Interfaces." The single method in the `HelloWorld` class is called `main()` and should be familiar if you have used C or C++. The `main()` method is where execution begins when the class is executed in the Java interpreter. The `main()` method is defined as being `public static` with a `void` return type. `public` means that the method can be called from anywhere inside or outside the class. `static` means that the method is the same for all instances of the class. The `void` return type means that `main()` does not return a value.

The `main()` method is defined as taking a single parameter, `String args[]`. `args` is an array of `String` objects that represent command-line arguments passed to the class at execution. Because `HelloWorld` doesn't use any command-line arguments, you can ignore the `args` parameter. You learn a little more about strings later in this chapter.

The `main()` method is called when the `HelloWorld` class is executed. `main()` consists of a single statement that prints the message `Hello, World!` to the standard output stream, as follows:

```
System.out.println("Hello, World!");
```

This statement may look a little confusing at first because of the nested objects. To help make things clearer, examine the statement from right to left. First, notice that the statement ends in a semicolon, which is standard Java syntax borrowed from C/C++. Moving to the left, you see that the `"Hello, World!"` string is in parentheses, which means that it is a parameter to a function call. The method being called is actually the `println()` method of the `out` object. The `println()` method is similar to the `printf()` method in C, except that it automatically appends a newline character (`\n`) at the end of the string. The `out` object is a member variable of the `System` object that represents the standard output stream. Finally, the `System` object is a global object in the Java environment that encapsulates system functionality.

That pretty well covers the `HelloWorld` class—your first Java program. If you got a little lost in the explanation of the `HelloWorld` class, don't be too concerned. `HelloWorld` was presented with no previous explanation of the Java language and was only meant to get your feet wet with Java code. The rest of this chapter focuses on a more structured discussion of the fundamentals of the Java language.

3

JAVA LANGUAGE FUNDAMENTALS

Tokens

When you submit a Java program to the Java compiler, the compiler parses the text and extracts individual tokens. A *token* is the smallest element of a program that is meaningful to the compiler. (Actually, this definition is true for all compilers, not just the Java compiler.) These tokens define the structure of the Java language. All the tokens that comprise Java are known as the Java *token set*. Java tokens can be broken into five categories: identifiers, keywords, literals, operators, and separators. The Java compiler also recognizes and subsequently removes comments and whitespaces.

The Java compiler removes all comments and whitespaces while tokenizing the source file. The resulting tokens are then compiled into machine-independent Java bytecode capable of being run from within an interpreted Java environment. The bytecode conforms to the hypothetical Java virtual machine, which abstracts processor differences into a single virtual processor. For more information on the Java virtual machine, check out Chapter 33, "Java Under the Hood: Inside the Virtual Machine." Keep in mind that an interpreted Java environment can be either the Java command-line interpreter or a Java-capable browser.

Identifiers

Identifiers are tokens that represent names. These names can be assigned to variables, methods, and classes to uniquely identify them for the compiler and give them meaningful names for the programmer. `HelloWorld` is an identifier that assigns the name `HelloWorld` to the class residing in the `HelloWorld.java` source file developed earlier.

Although you can be creative in naming identifiers in Java, there are some limitations. All Java identifiers are case sensitive and must begin with a letter, an underscore (_), or a dollar sign ($). Letters include both uppercase and lowercase letters. Subsequent identifier characters can include the numbers `0` to `9`. The only other limitation to identifier names is that the Java keywords, which are listed in the next section, cannot be used. Table 3.1 contains a list of valid and invalid identifier names.

Table 3.1. Valid and invalid Java identifiers.

Valid	Invalid
HelloWorld	Hello World (uses a space)
Hi_Mom	Hi Mom! (uses a space and punctuation mark)
heyDude3	3heyDude (begins with a numeral)
tall	short (this is a Java keyword)
poundage	#age (does not begin with a letter)

In addition to the mentioned restrictions in naming Java identifiers, you should follow a few stylistic rules to make your Java programming easier and more consistent. It is standard Java practice to name multiple-word identifiers in lowercase except for the beginning letter of words in the middle of the name. For example, the variable toughGuy is in correct Java style; the variables toughguy, ToughGuy, and TOUGHGUY are all in violation of this style rule. The rule isn't etched in stone—it's just a good rule to follow because most other Java code you run into follows this style.

Another more critical naming issue regards the use of underscore and dollar-sign characters at the beginning of identifier names. Using either of these characters at the beginning of identifier names is a little risky because many C libraries use the same naming convention for libraries that can be imported into your Java code. To eliminate the potential problem of name-clashing in these instances, it's better to stay away from the underscore and dollar-sign characters at the beginning of your identifier names. A good use of the underscore character is to use it to separate words where you normally would use a space (Hi_Mom).

> **NOTE**
>
> With Java 1.1, the style conventions in naming identifiers has become significantly more important. JavaBeans, which is the new component technology in Java 1.1, depends in part on the standard identifier-naming conventions if it is to function properly. You learn more about JavaBeans and the naming conventions it relies on in Part VIII, "Java Archives and JavaBeans."

3

JAVA LANGUAGE
FUNDAMENTALS

Keywords

Keywords are predefined identifiers reserved by Java for a specific purpose and are used only in a limited, specified manner. Java has a richer set of keywords than C or C++, so if you are learning Java with a C/C++ background, be sure to pay attention to the Java keywords. The following keywords are reserved for Java:

abstract	double	int	super
boolean	else	interface	switch
break	extends	long	synchronized
byte	false	native	this
byvalue	final	new	threadsafe
case	finally	null	throw
catch	float	package	transient
char	for	private	true

```
class            goto            protected       try

const            if              public          void

continue         implements      return          while

default          import          short

do               instanceof      static
```

Literals

Program elements used in an invariant manner are called *literals,* or *constants.* Literals can be numbers, characters, or strings. Numeric literals include integers, floating-point numbers, and booleans. Booleans are considered numeric because of the C influence on Java. In C, the boolean values for `true` and `false` are represented by 1 and 0. Character literals always refer to a single Unicode character. Strings, which contain multiple characters, are still considered literals even though they are implemented in Java as objects.

> **NOTE**
>
> If you aren't familiar with the Unicode character set, you should know that it is a 16-bit character set that replaces the ASCII character set. Because it is a 16-bit character set, there are enough entries to represent many symbols and characters from other languages. Unicode is quickly becoming the standard for modern operating systems.

Integer Literals

Integer literals are the primary literals used in Java programming. They come in a few different formats: decimal, hexadecimal, and octal. These formats correspond to the base of the number system used by the literal. Decimal (base 10) literals appear as ordinary numbers with no special notation. Hexadecimal numbers (base 16) appear with a leading `0x` or `0X`, similar to the way they do in C/C++. Octal (base 8) numbers appear with a leading `0` in front of the digits. For example, an integer literal for the decimal number 12 is represented in Java as `12` in decimal, `0xC` in hexadecimal, and `014` in octal.

Integer literals default to being stored in the `int` type, which is a signed 32-bit value. If you are working with very large numbers, you can force an integer literal to be stored in the `long` type by appending an `l` or `L` to the end of the number, as in `79L`. The `long` type is a signed 64-bit value.

Floating-Point Literals

Floating-point literals represent decimal numbers with fractional parts, such as `3.142`. They can be expressed in either standard or scientific notation, meaning that the number `563.84` also can be expressed as `5.6384e2`.

Unlike integer literals, floating-point literals default to the `double` type, which is a 64-bit value. You have the option of using the smaller 32-bit `float` type if you know the full 64 bits are not required. You do this by appending an `f` or `F` to the end of the number, as in `5.6384e2f`. If you are a stickler for details, you also can explicitly state that you want a `double` type as the storage unit for your literal, as in `3.142d`. But because the default storage for floating-point numbers is `double` already, this addition isn't necessary.

Boolean Literals

Boolean literals are certainly welcome if you are coming from the world of C/C++. In C, there is no `boolean` type, and therefore no boolean literals. The boolean values `true` and `false` are represented by the integer values `1` and `0`. Java fixes this problem by providing a `boolean` type with two possible states: `true` and `false`. Not surprisingly, these states are represented in the Java language by the keywords `true` and `false`.

Boolean literals are used in Java programming about as often as integer literals because they are present in almost every type of control structure. Any time you have to represent a condition or state with two possible values, a `boolean` is what you want. You learn a little more about the `boolean` type later in this chapter. For now, just remember the two boolean literal values: `true` and `false`.

Character Literals and Special Characters

Character literals represent a single Unicode character and appear within a pair of single quotation marks. Similar to C/C++, *special characters* (control characters and characters that cannot be printed) are represented by a backslash (\) followed by the character code. A good example of a special character is \n, which forces the output to a new line when printed. Table 3.2 shows the special characters supported by Java.

Table 3.2. Special characters supported by Java.

Description	Representation
Backslash	\\
Continuation	\
Backspace	\b
Carriage return	\r
Form feed	\f
Horizontal tab	\t
Newline	\n
Single quote	\'

continues

Table 3.2. continued

Description	Representation
Double quote	\ "
Unicode character	\udddd
Octal character	\ddd

An example of a Unicode character literal is \u0048, which is a hexadecimal representation of the character *H*. This same character is represented in octal as \110.

> **NOTE**
>
> To find out more information about the Unicode character set, check out the Unicode home page at this URL:
>
> http://www.unicode.org

String Literals

String literals represent multiple characters and appear within a pair of double quotation marks. Unlike all the other literals discussed in this chapter, string literals are implemented in Java by the String class. This arrangement is very different from the C/C++ representation of strings as an array of characters.

When Java encounters a string literal, it creates an instance of the String class and sets its state to the characters appearing within the double quotation marks. From a usage perspective, the fact that Java implements strings as objects is relatively unimportant. However, it is worth mentioning at this point because it is a reminder that Java is very object oriented in nature—much more so than C++, which is widely considered the current object-oriented programming standard.

Operators

Operators, also known as *operands*, specify an evaluation or computation to be performed on a data object or objects. These operands can be literals, variables, or function return types. The operators supported by Java follow:

+	-	*	/	%	&	¦
^	~	&&	¦¦	!	<	>
<=	>=	<<	>>	>>>	=	?
++	- -	==	+=	-=	*=	/=
%=	&=	¦=	^=	!=	<<=	>>=
>>>=	.	[	]	(	)	

Just seeing these operators probably doesn't help you a lot in determining how to use them. Don't worry—you'll learn a lot more about operators and how they are used in the next chapter, "Expressions, Operators, and Control Structures."

Separators

Separators are used to inform the Java compiler of how things are grouped in the code. For example, items in a list are separated by commas much like lists of items in a sentence. Java separators go far beyond commas, however, as you discover in the next chapter. The separators supported by Java follow:

{   }   ;   ,   :

Comments and Whitespaces

Earlier in this chapter, you learned that comments and whitespaces are removed by the Java compiler during the tokenization of the source code. You may be wondering, "What qualifies as whitespace and how are comments supported?" First, *whitespace* consists of spaces, tabs, and linefeeds. All occurrences of spaces, tabs, and linefeeds are removed by the Java compiler, as are comments. Comments can be defined in three different ways, as shown in Table 3.3.

Table 3.3. Types of comments supported by Java.

Type	*Usage*
/* comment */	All characters between /* and */ are ignored.
// comment	All characters after the // up to the end of the line are ignored.
/** comment */	Same as /* */, except that the comment can be used with the javadoc tool to create automatic documentation.

The first type of comment (/* comment */) should be familiar if you have programmed in C. All characters inside the /* and */ comment delimiters are ignored by the compiler. The second type of comment (// comment) should also be familiar if you have used C++. All characters appearing after the // comment delimiter up to the end of the line are ignored by the compiler. These two comment types are borrowed from C and C++. The final comment type (/** comment */) works in the same fashion as the C-style comment type, with the additional benefit that it can be used with the Java documentation generator tool, javadoc, to create automatic documentation from the source code. The javadoc tool is covered in Chapter 29, "Documenting Your Code." Following are a few examples using the various types of comments:

```
/* This is a C style comment. */
// This is a C++ style comment.
/** This is a javadoc style comment. */
```

Data Types

One of the fundamental concepts of any programming language is data types. *Data types* define the storage methods available for representing information, along with how the information is interpreted. Data types are linked tightly to the storage of variables in memory because the data type of a variable determines how the compiler interprets the contents of the memory. You already have received a little taste of data types in the discussion of literal types.

To create a variable in memory, you must declare it by providing the type of the variable as well as an identifier that uniquely identifies the variable. The syntax of the Java declaration statement for variables follows:

```
Type Identifier [, Identifier];
```

The declaration statement tells the compiler to set aside memory for a variable of type `Type` with the name `Identifier`. The optional bracketed `Identifier` indicates that you can make multiple declarations of the same type by separating them with commas. Finally, as in all Java statements, the declaration statement ends with a semicolon.

Java data types can be divided into two categories: simple and composite. Simple data types are core types not derived from any other types. Integer, floating-point, boolean, and character types are all simple types. Composite types, on the other hand, are based on simple types and include strings, arrays, and both classes and interfaces in general. You learn about arrays later in this chapter. Classes and interfaces are covered in Chapter 5, "Classes, Packages, and Interfaces."

Integer Data Types

Integer data types are used to represent signed integer numbers. There are four integer types: `byte`, `short`, `int`, and `long`. Each of these types takes up a different amount of space in memory, as shown in Table 3.4.

Table 3.4. Java integer types.

Type	*Size*
byte	8 bits
short	16 bits
int	32 bits
long	64 bits

To declare variables using the integer types, use the declaration syntax mentioned previously with the desired type. Following are some examples of declaring integer variables:

```
int i;
short rocketFuel;
long angle, magnitude;
byte red, green, blue;
```

Floating-Point Data Types

Floating-point data types are used to represent numbers with fractional parts. There are two floating point types: `float` and `double`. The `float` type reserves storage for a 32-bit single-precision number; the `double` type reserves storage for a 64-bit double-precision number.

Declaring floating-point variables is very similar to declaring integer variables. Following are some examples of floating-point variable declarations:

```
float temperature;
double windSpeed, barometricPressure;
```

Boolean Data Type

The *boolean data type* (`boolean`) is used to store values with one of two states: `true` or `false`. You can think of the `boolean` type as a 1-bit integer value (because 1 bit can have only two possible values: 1 or 0). However, instead of using 1 and 0, you use the Java keywords `true` and `false`. `true` and `false` aren't just conveniences in Java; they are actually the only legal boolean values. This means that you can't interchangeably use booleans and integers as you can in C/C++. To declare a boolean value, just use the `boolean` type declaration:

```
boolean gameOver;
```

Character Data Type

The *character data type* (`char`) is used to store single Unicode characters. Because the Unicode character set is composed of 16-bit values, the `char` data type is stored as a 16-bit unsigned integer. You create variables of type `char` as follows:

```
char firstInitial, lastInitial;
```

Remember that the `char` type is useful only for storing single characters. If you come from a C/C++ background, you may be tempted to fashion a string by creating an array of `char`s. In Java, this isn't necessary because the `String` class takes care of handling strings. This doesn't mean that you should never create arrays of characters, it just means that you shouldn't use a character array when you really want a string. C and C++ do not distinguish between character arrays and strings, but Java does.

Casting Types

Inevitably, there will be times when you have to convert from one data type to another. The process of converting one data type to another is called *casting*. Casting is often necessary when a function returns a type different than the type you need to perform an operation. For example, the read() member function of the standard input stream (System.in) returns an int. You must cast the returned int type to a char type before storing it, as in the following:

```
char c = (char)System.in.read();
```

The cast is performed by placing the desired type in parentheses to the left of the value to be converted. The System.in.read() function call returns an int value, which then is cast to a char value because of the (char) cast. The resulting char value is then stored in the char variable c.

CAUTION

The storage size of the types you are attempting to cast is very important. Not all types can be safely cast to other types. To understand this, consider the outcome of casting a long to an int. A long is a 64-bit value and an int is a 32-bit value. When casting a long to an int, the compiler chops off the upper 32 bits of the long value so that it will fit into the 32-bit int. If the upper 32 bits of the long contain any useful information, that information is lost and the number changes as a result of the cast. Information loss can also occur when you cast between different fundamental types, such as between integer and floating-point numbers. For example, casting a double to a long results in the loss of the fractional information, even though both numbers are 64-bit values.

When casting, the destination type should always be equal to or larger in size than the source type. Furthermore, you should pay close attention to casting across fundamental types, such as from floating-point to integer types. Table 3.5 lists the casts that are guaranteed to result in no loss of information.

Table 3.5. Casts that result in no loss of information.

From Type	To Type
byte	short, char, int, long, float, double
short	int, long, float, double
char	int, long, float, double
int	long, float, double
long	float, double
float	double

Blocks and Scope

In Java, source code is divided into parts separated by opening and closing curly braces: { and }. Everything between curly braces is considered a *block* and exists more or less independently of everything outside the braces. Blocks aren't important just from a logical sense—they are required as part of the syntax of the Java language. If you don't use braces, the compiler has trouble determining where one section of code ends and the next section begins. And from a purely aesthetic viewpoint, it is very difficult for someone else reading your code to understand what is going on if you don't use the braces. For that matter, it isn't very easy for you to understand your own code without the braces!

Braces are used to group related statements together. You can think of everything between matching braces as being executed as one statement. In fact, from an outer block, that's exactly what an inner block appears like: a single statement. But what's a block? A *block* is simply a section of code. Blocks are organized in a hierarchical fashion, meaning that code can be divided into individual blocks *nested* under other blocks. One block can contain one or more nested subblocks.

It is standard Java programming style to identify different blocks with indentation. Every time you enter a new block, you should indent your source code by a number of spaces—preferably two. When you leave a block, you should move back, or *deindent*, two spaces. This is a fairly established convention in many programming languages. However, indentation is just a style issue and is not technically part of the language. The compiler produces identical output even if you don't indent anything. Indentation is used for the programmer, not the compiler; it simply makes the code easier to follow and understand. Following is an example of the proper indentation of blocks in Java:

```
for (int i = 0; i < 5; i++) {
  if (i < 3) {
    System.out.println(i);
  }
}
```

Following is the same code without any block indentations:

```
for (int i = 0; i < 5; i++) {
if (i < 3) {
System.out.println(i);
}
}
```

The first bit of code clearly shows the breakdown of program flow through the use of indentation; it is obvious that the `if` statement is nested within the `for` loop. The second bit of code, on the other hand, provides no visual clues about the relationship between the blocks of code. Don't worry if you don't know anything about `if` statements and `for` loops; you'll learn plenty about them in the next chapter, "Expressions, Operators, and Control Structures."

The concept of *scope* is tightly linked to blocks and is very important when you are working with variables in Java. Scope refers to how sections of a program (blocks) affect the lifetime of variables. Every variable declared in a program has an associated scope, meaning that the variable is used only in that particular part of the program.

Scope is determined by blocks. To better understand blocks, take a look again at the HelloWorld class in Listing 3.1, earlier in this chapter. The HelloWorld class is composed of two blocks. The outer block of the program is the block defining the HelloWorld class:

```
class HelloWorld {
...
}
```

Class blocks are very important in Java. Almost everything of interest is either a class itself or belongs to a class. For example, methods are defined inside the classes to which they belong. Both syntactically and logically, everything in Java takes place inside a class. Getting back to HelloWorld, the inner block defines the code within the main() method, as follows:

```
public static void main (String args[]) {
...
}
```

The inner block is considered to be nested within the outer block of the program. Any variables defined in the inner block are local to that block and are not visible to the outer block; the scope of the variables is defined as the inner block.

To get an even better idea of what's behind the usage of scope and blocks, take a look at the HowdyWorld class in Listing 3.2.

Listing 3.2. The HowdyWorld class.

```
class HowdyWorld {
  public static void main (String args[]) {
    int i;
    printMessage();
  }
  public static void printMessage () {
    int j;
    System.out.println("Howdy, World!");
  }
}
```

The HowdyWorld class contains two methods: main() and printMessage(). main() should be familiar to you from the HelloWorld class, except that in this case, it declares an integer variable i and calls the printMessage() method. printMessage() is a new method that declares an integer variable j and prints the message Howdy, World! to the standard output stream, much like the main() method does in HelloWorld.

You've probably figured out already that HowdyWorld results in basically the same output as HelloWorld because the call to printMessage() results in a single text message being displayed.

What you may not see right off is the scope of the integers defined in each method. The integer i defined in `main()` has a scope limited to the body of the `main()` method. The body of `main()` is defined by the curly braces around the method (the method block). Similarly, the integer j has a scope limited to the body of the `printMessage()` method. The importance of the scope of these two variables is that the variables aren't visible beyond their respective scopes; the `HowdyWorld` class block knows nothing about the two integers. Furthermore, `main()` doesn't know anything about j, and `printMessage()` knows nothing about i.

Scope becomes more important when you start nesting blocks of code within other blocks. The `GoodbyeWorld` class shown in Listing 3.3 is a good example of variables nested within different scopes.

Listing 3.3. The GoodbyeWorld class.

```
class GoodbyeWorld {
  public static void main (String args[]) {
    int i, j;
    System.out.println("Goodbye, World!");
    for (i = 0; i < 5; i++) {
      int k;
      System.out.println("Bye!");
    }
  }
}
```

The integers i and j have scopes within the `main()` method body. The integer k, however, has a scope limited to the for loop block. Because k's scope is limited to the for loop block, it cannot be seen outside that block. On the other hand, i and j still can be seen within the for loop block. What this means is that scoping has a top-down hierarchical effect—variables defined in outer scopes can still be seen and used within nested scopes; however, variables defined in nested scopes are limited to those scopes. Incidentally, don't worry if you aren't familiar with for loops—you learn all about them in the next chapter.

For more reasons than visibility, it is important to pay attention to the scope of variables when you declare them. Along with determining the visibility of variables, the scope also determines the lifetime of variables. This means that variables are actually destroyed when program execution leaves their scope. Look at the `GoodbyeWorld` example again: Storage for the integers i and j is allocated when program execution enters the `main()` method. When the for loop block is entered, storage for the integer k is allocated. When program execution leaves the for loop block, the memory for k is freed and the variable is destroyed. Similarly, when program execution leaves `main()`, all the variables in its scope (i and j) are freed and destroyed. The concepts of variable lifetime and scope become even more important when you start dealing with classes. You'll get a good dose of this in Chapter 5, "Classes, Packages, and Interfaces."

Arrays

An *array* is a construct that provides for the storage of a list of items of the same type. Array items can have either a simple or composite data type. Arrays also can be multidimensional. Java arrays are declared with square brackets: []. Following are a few examples of array declarations in Java:

```
int numbers[];
char[] letters;
long grid[][];
```

If you are familiar with arrays in another language, you may be puzzled by the absence of a number between the square brackets specifying the number of items in the array. Java doesn't allow you to specify the size of an empty array when declaring the array. You must always explicitly set the size of the array with the new operator or by assigning a list of items to the array at the time of creation. The new operator is covered in the next chapter, "Expressions, Operators, and Control Structures."

> **NOTE**
>
> It may seem like a hassle to have to explicitly set the size of an array with the new operator. The reason for doing this is because Java doesn't have pointers like C or C++ and therefore doesn't allow you to point anywhere in an array to create new items. Because the Java language handles memory management this way, the bounds-checking problems common with C and C++ have been avoided.

Another strange thing you may notice about Java arrays is the optional placement of the square brackets in the array declaration. You can place the square brackets either after the variable type or after the identifier.

Following are a couple examples of arrays that have been declared and set to a specific size by using the new operator and by assigning a list of items in the array declaration:

```
char alphabet[] = new char[26];
int primes = {7, 11, 13};
```

More complex structures for storing lists of items, such as stacks and hash tables, are also supported by Java. Unlike arrays, these structures are implemented in Java as classes. You'll get a crash course in some of these other storage mechanisms in Chapter 11, "The Utilities Package."

Strings

In Java, *strings* are handled by a special class called String. Even literal strings are managed internally by an instantiation of a String class. An *instantiation of a class* is simply an object that has been created based on the class description. This method of handling strings is very different from languages like C and C++, where strings are represented simply as an array of characters. Following are a few strings declared using the Java String class:

```
String message;
String name = "Mr. Blonde";
```

At this point, it's not that important to know the String class inside and out. You'll learn all the gory details of the String class in Chapter 10, "The Language Package."

Summary

This chapter took a look at the core components of the Java language. Hopefully, you now have more insight about why Java has become popular in such a relatively short time. With vast improvements over the weaknesses of the C and C++ languages—arguably the industry's language standards—Java is making huge waves and may conceivably replace C and C++ at some point in the near future. The language elements covered in this chapter are just the tip of the iceberg when it comes to the benefits of programming in Java.

Now that you are armed with the fundamentals of the Java language, you are no doubt ready to press onward and learn more about the Java language. The next chapter, "Expressions, Operators, and Control Structures," covers exactly what its title suggests. In it, you learn how to work with and manipulate much of the information you learned about in this chapter. In doing so, you will be able to start writing programs that do a little more than display cute messages on the screen.

PART

II

IN THIS PART

The Java Language

## CHAPTER 4

Expressions, Operators, and Control Structures

by Michael Morrison

IN THIS CHAPTER

In Chapter 3, "Java Language Fundamentals," you learned about some of the basic components of a Java program. This chapter focuses on how to use these components to do more useful things. Data types are interesting, but without expressions and operators, you can't do much with them. Even expressions and operators alone are somewhat limited in what they can do. Throw in control structures and you have the ability to do some interesting things.

This chapter covers all these issues and pulls together many of the missing pieces of the Java programming puzzle you've begun to assemble. You'll not only expand your knowledge of the Java language a great deal, you'll also learn what it takes to write some more interesting programs.

Expressions and Operators

Once you create variables, you typically want to do something with them. *Operators* enable you to perform an evaluation or computation on a data object or objects. Operators applied to variables and literals form expressions. An *expression* can be thought of as a programmatic equation. More formally, an expression is a sequence of one or more data objects (operands) and zero or more operators that produce a result. An example of an expression follows:

```
x = y / 3;
```

In this expression, x and y are variables, 3 is a literal, and = and / are operators. This expression states that the y variable is divided by 3 using the division operator (/), and the result is stored in x using the assignment operator (=). Notice that the expression was described from right to left. Although this approach of analyzing the expression from right to left is useful in terms of showing the assignment operation, most Java expressions are, in fact, evaluated from left to right. You get a better feel for this in the next section.

Operator Precedence

Even though Java expressions are typically evaluated from left to right, there still are many times when the result of an expression would be indeterminate without other rules. The following expression illustrates the problem:

```
x = 2 * 6 + 16 / 4
```

Strictly using the left-to-right evaluation of the expression, the multiplication operation 2 * 6 is carried out first, which leaves a result of 12. The addition operation 12 + 16 is then performed, which gives a result of 28. The division operation 28 / 4 is then performed, which gives a result of 7. Finally, the assignment operation x = 7 is handled, in which the number 7 is assigned to the variable x.

If you have some experience with operator precedence from another language, you might already be questioning the evaluation of this expression, and for good reason—it's wrong! The problem is that using a simple left-to-right evaluation of expressions can yield inconsistent results, depending on the order of the operators. The solution to this problem lies in *operator* *precedence*, which determines the order in which operators are evaluated. Every Java operator has an associated precedence. Following is a list of all the Java operators from highest to lowest precedence. In this list of operators, all the operators in a particular row have equal precedence. The precedence level of each row decreases from top to bottom. This means that the [ ] operator has a higher precedence than the * operator, but the same precedence as the () operator.

```
    .          [ ]        ()

++         --         !          ~

*          /          %

+          -

<<         >>         >>>

<          >          <=         >=

==         !=

&

^

&&

||

?:

=
```

Evaluation of expressions still moves from left to right, but only when dealing with operators that have the same precedence. Otherwise, operators with a higher precedence are evaluated before operators with a lower precedence. Knowing this, take another look at the sample equation:

```
x = 2 * 6 + 16 / 4
```

Before using the left-to-right evaluation of the expression, first look to see whether any of the operators have differing precedence. Indeed they do! The multiplication (*) and division (/) operators both have the highest precedence, followed by the addition operator (+), and then the assignment operator (=). Because the multiplication and division operators share the same precedence, evaluate them from left to right. Doing this, you first perform the multiplication operation 2 * 6 with the result of 12. You then perform the division operation 16 / 4, which results in 4. After performing these two operations, the expression looks like this:

```
x = 12 + 4;
```

Because the addition operator has a higher precedence than the assignment operator, you perform the addition operation 12 + 4 next, resulting in 16. Finally, the assignment operation x = 16 is processed, resulting in the number 16 being assigned to the variable x. As you can see, evaluating the expression using operator precedence yields a completely different result.

Just to get the point across, take a look at another expression that uses parentheses for grouping purposes:

```
x = 2 * (11 - 7);
```

Without the grouping parentheses, you would perform the multiplication operation first and then the subtraction operation. However, referring back to the precedence list, the () operator comes before all other operators. So the subtraction operation 11 - 7 is performed first, yielding 4 and the following expression:

```
x = 2 * 4;
```

The rest of the expression is easily resolved with a multiplication operation and an assignment operation to yield a result of 8 in the variable x.

Integer Operators

There are three types of operations that can be performed on integers: unary, binary, and relational. Unary operators act on only single integer numbers, and binary operators act on pairs of integer numbers. Both unary and binary integer operators typically return integer results. Relational operators, on the other hand, act on two integer numbers but return a boolean result rather than an integer.

Unary and binary integer operators typically return an int type. For all operations involving the types byte, short, and int, the result is always an int. The only exception to this rule is when one of the operands is a long, in which case the result of the operation is also of type long.

Unary Integer Operators

Unary integer operators act on a single integer. Table 4.1 lists the unary integer operators.

Table 4.1. The unary integer operators.

Description	Operator
Increment	++
Decrement	--
Negation	-
Bitwise complement	~

The increment and decrement operators (++ and --) increase and decrease integer variables by 1. Similar to their complements in C and C++, these operators can be used in either prefix or postfix form. A *prefix operator* takes effect before the evaluation of the expression it is in; a *postfix operator* takes effect after the expression has been evaluated. Prefix unary operators are placed immediately before the variable; postfix unary operators are placed immediately following the variable. Following are examples of each type of operator:

```
y = ++x;
z = x--;
```

In the first example, x is *prefix incremented*, which means that it is incremented before being assigned to y. In the second example, x is *postfix decremented*, which means that it is decremented after being assigned to z. In the latter case, z is assigned the value of x before x is decremented. Listing 4.1 contains the IncDec program, which uses both types of operators. Please note that the IncDec program is actually implemented in the Java class IncDec. This is a result of the object-oriented structure of Java, which requires programs to be implemented as classes. When you see a reference to a Java *program*, keep in mind that it is really referring to a Java *class*.

Listing 4.1. The IncDec class.

```
class IncDec {
  public static void main (String args[]) {
    int x = 8, y = 13;
    System.out.println("x = " + x);
    System.out.println("y = " + y);
    System.out.println("++x = " + ++x);
    System.out.println("y++ = " + y++);
    System.out.println("x = " + x);
    System.out.println("y = " + y);
  }
}
```

The IncDec program produces the following results:

```
x = 8
y = 13
++x = 9
y++ = 13
x = 9
y = 14
```

The negation unary integer operator (-) is used to change the sign of an integer value. This operator is as simple as it sounds, as indicated by the following example:

```
x = 8;
y = -x;
```

In this example, x is assigned the literal value 8 and then is negated and assigned to y. The resulting value of y is -8. To see this code in a real Java program, check out the Negation program in Listing 4.2.

Listing 4.2. The Negation class.

```
class Negation {
  public static void main (String args[]) {
    int x = 8;
    System.out.println("x = " + x);
    int y = -x;
    System.out.println("y = " + y);
  }
}
```

The last Java unary integer operator is the *bitwise complement operator* (~), which performs a bitwise negation of an integer value. *Bitwise negation* means that each bit in the number is toggled. In other words, all the binary 0s become 1s and all the binary 1s become 0s. Take a look at an example very similar to the one for the negation operator:

```
x = 8;
y = ~x;
```

In this example, x is assigned the literal value 8 again, but it is bitwise complemented before being assigned to y. What does this mean? Well, without getting into the details of how integers are stored in memory, it means that all the bits of the variable x are flipped, yielding a decimal result of -9. This result has to do with the fact that negative numbers are stored in memory using a method known as *two's complement* (see the following note). If you're having trouble believing any of this, try it yourself with the BitwiseComplement program shown in Listing 4.3.

NOTE

Integer numbers are stored in memory as a series of binary bits that can each have a value of 0 or 1. A number is considered negative if the highest-order bit in the number is set to 1. Because a bitwise complement flips all the bits in a number—including the high-order bit—the sign of a number is reversed.

Listing 4.3. The BitwiseComplement class.

```
class BitwiseComplement {
  public static void main (String args[]) {
    int x = 8;
    System.out.println("x = " + x);
    int y = ~x;
    System.out.println("y = " + y);
  }
}
```

Binary Integer Operators

Binary integer operators act on pairs of integers. Table 4.2 lists the binary integer operators.

Table 4.2. The binary integer operators.

Description	Operator
Addition	+
Subtraction	-
Multiplication	*
Division	/
Modulus	%
Bitwise AND	&
Bitwise OR	¦
Bitwise XOR	^
Left-shift	<<
Right-shift	>>
Zero-fill-right-shift	>>>

The addition, subtraction, multiplication, and division operators (+, -, *, and /) all do what you expect them to. An important thing to note is how the division operator works; because you are dealing with integer operands, the division operator returns an integer divisor. In cases where the division results in a remainder, the modulus operator (%) can be used to get the remainder value. Listing 4.4 contains the `Arithmetic` program, which shows how the basic binary integer arithmetic operators work.

Listing 4.4. The Arithmetic class.

```
class Arithmetic {
  public static void main (String args[]) {
    int x = 17, y = 5;
    System.out.println("x = " + x);
    System.out.println("y = " + y);
    System.out.println("x + y = " + (x + y));
    System.out.println("x - y = " + (x - y));
    System.out.println("x * y = " + (x * y));
    System.out.println("x / y = " + (x / y));
    System.out.println("x % y = " + (x % y));
  }
}
```

The results of running the Arithmetic program follow:

```
x = 17
y = 5
x + y = 22
x - y = 12
x * y = 85
x / y = 3
x % y = 2
```

These results shouldn't surprise you too much. Just notice that the division operation x / y, which boils down to 17 / 5, yields the result 3. Also notice that the modulus operation x % y, which is resolved down to 17 % 5, ends with a result of 2 (the remainder of the integer division).

Mathematically, a division by zero results in an infinite result. Because representing infinite numbers is a big problem for computers, division or modulus operations by zero result operations in an error. To be more specific, a runtime exception is thrown. You learn a lot more about exceptions in Chapter 7, "Exception Handling."

The bitwise AND, OR, and XOR operators (&, ¦, and ^) all act on the individual bits of an integer. These operators are sometimes useful when an integer is being used as a bit field. An example of this is when an integer is used to represent a group of binary flags. An int is capable of representing up to 32 different flags, because it is stored in 32 bits. Listing 4.5 contains the program Bitwise, which shows how to use the binary bitwise integer operators.

NOTE

Java actually includes a class that provides specific support for storing binary flags. The class is called BitSet, and you learn about it in Chapter 11, "The Utilities Package."

Listing 4.5. The Bitwise class.

```
class Bitwise {
  public static void main (String args[]) {
    int x = 5, y = 6;
    System.out.println("x = " + x);
    System.out.println("y = " + y);
    System.out.println("x & y = " + (x & y));
    System.out.println("x ¦ y = " + (x ¦ y));
    System.out.println("x ^ y = " + (x ^ y));
  }
}
```

The output of running `Bitwise` follows:

```
x = 5
y = 6
x & y = 4
x ¦ y = 7
x ^ y = 3
```

To understand this output, you must first understand the binary equivalents of each decimal number. In `Bitwise`, the variables x and y are set to 5 and 6, which correspond to the binary numbers 0101 and 0110. The bitwise AND operation compares each bit of each number to see whether they are the same. It then sets the resulting bit to 1 if both bits being compared are 1; it sets the resulting bit to 0 otherwise. The result of the bitwise AND operation on these two numbers is 0100 in binary, or decimal 4. The same logic is used for both of the other operators, except that the rules for comparing the bits are different. The bitwise OR operator sets the resulting bit to 1 if either of the bits being compared is 1. For these numbers, the result is 0111 binary, or 7 decimal. Finally, the bitwise XOR operator sets resulting bits to 1 if exactly one of the bits being compared is 1, and 0 otherwise. For these numbers, the result is 0011 binary, or 3 decimal.

The left-shift, right-shift, and zero-fill-right-shift operators (<<, >>, and >>>) shift the individual bits of an integer by a specified integer amount. Following are some examples of how these operators are used:

```
x << 3;
y >> 7;
z >>> 2;
```

In the first example, the individual bits of the integer variable x are shifted to the left three places. In the second example, the bits of y are shifted to the right seven places. Finally, the third example shows z being shifted to the right two places, with zeros shifted into the two leftmost places. To see the shift operators in a real program, check out `Shift` in Listing 4.6.

Listing 4.6. The `Shift` class.

```
class Shift {
  public static void main (String args[]) {
    int x = 7;
    System.out.println("x = " + x);
    System.out.println("x >> 2 = " + (x >> 2));
    System.out.println("x << 1 = " + (x << 1));
    System.out.println("x >>> 1 = " + (x >>> 1));
  }
}
```

The output of `Shift` follows:

```
x = 7
x >> 2 = 1
x << 1 = 14
x >>> 1 = 3
```

The number being shifted in this case is the decimal 7, which is represented in binary as 0111. The first right-shift operation shifts the bits two places to the right, resulting in the binary number 0001, or decimal 1. The next operation, a left-shift, shifts the bits one place to the left, resulting in the binary number 1110, or decimal 14. The last operation is a zero-fill-right-shift, which shifts the bits one place to the right, resulting in the binary number 0011, or decimal 3. Pretty simple, eh? And you probably thought it was difficult working with integers at the bit level!

Based on these examples, you may be wondering what the difference is between the right-shift (>>) and zero-fill-right-shift (>>>) operators. The right-shift operator appears to shift zeros into the leftmost bits, just like the zero-fill-right-shift operator, right? Well, when dealing with positive numbers, there is no difference between the two operators; they both shift zeros into the upper bits of a number. The difference arises when you start shifting negative numbers. Remember that negative numbers have the high-order bit set to 1. The right-shift operator preserves the high-order bit and effectively shifts the lower 31 bits to the right. This behavior yields results for negative numbers similar to those for positive numbers. That is, -8 shifted right by one results in -4. The zero-fill-right-shift operator, on the other hand, shifts zeros into *all* the upper bits, including the high-order bit. When this shifting is applied to negative numbers, the high-order bit becomes 0 and the number becomes positive.

Relational Integer Operators

The last group of integer operators is the relational operators, which all operate on integers but return a type boolean. Table 4.3 lists the relational integer operators.

Table 4.3. The relational integer operators.

Description	Operator
Less-than	<
Greater-than	>
Less-than-or-equal-to	<=
Greater-than-or-equal-to	>=
Equal-to	==
Not-equal-to	!=

These operators all perform comparisons between integers. Listing 4.7 contains the Relational program, which demonstrates the use of the relational operators with integers.

Listing 4.7. The Relational class.

```
class Relational {
  public static void main (String args[]) {
    int x = 7, y = 11, z = 11;
    System.out.println("x = " + x);
    System.out.println("y = " + y);
    System.out.println("z = " + z);
    System.out.println("x < y = " + (x < y));
    System.out.println("x > z = " + (x > z));
    System.out.println("y <= z = " + (y <= z));
    System.out.println("x >= y = " + (x >= y));
    System.out.println("y == z = " + (y == z));
    System.out.println("x != y = " + (x != z));
  }
}
```

The output of running `Relational` follows:

```
x = 7
y = 11
z = 11
x < y = true
x > z = false
y <= z = true
x >= y = false
y == z = true
x != y = true
```

As you can see, the `println()` method is smart enough to print boolean results correctly as `true` and `false`.

Floating-Point Operators

Similar to integer operators, there are three types of operations that can be performed on floating-point numbers: unary, binary, and relational. Unary operators act only on single floating-point numbers, and binary operators act on pairs of floating-point numbers. Both unary and binary floating-point operators return floating-point results. Relational operators, however, act on two floating-point numbers but return a boolean result.

Unary and binary floating-point operators return a `float` type if both operands are of type `float`. If one or both of the operands are of type `double`, however, the result of the operation is of type `double`.

Unary Floating-Point Operators

The unary floating point operators act on a single floating-point number. Table 4.4 lists the unary floating-point operators.

Table 4.4. The unary floating-point operators.

Description	Operator
Increment	++
Decrement	- -

As you can see, the only two unary floating-point operators are the increment and decrement operators. These two operators respectively add and subtract 1.0 from their floating-point operand.

Binary Floating-Point Operators

The binary floating-point operators act on a pair of floating-point numbers. Table 4.5 lists the binary floating-point operators.

Table 4.5. The binary floating-point operators.

Description	Operator
Addition	+
Subtraction	-
Multiplication	*
Division	/
Modulus	%

The binary floating-point operators consist of the four traditional binary operations (+, -, *, /), along with the modulus operator (%). You might be wondering how the modulus operator fits in here, considering that its use as an integer operator relied on an integer division. If you recall, the integer modulus operator returned the remainder of an integer division of the two operands. But a floating-point division never results in a remainder, so what does a floating-point modulus do? The floating-point modulus operator returns the floating-point equivalent of an integer division. What this means is that the division is carried out with both floating-point operands, but the resulting divisor is treated as an integer, resulting in a floating-point remainder. Listing 4.8 contains the FloatMath program, which shows how the floating-point modulus operator works along with the other binary floating-point operators.

Listing 4.8. The FloatMath class.

```
class FloatMath {
  public static void main (String args[]) {
    float x = 23.5F, y = 7.3F;
```

```
        System.out.println("x = " + x);
        System.out.println("y = " + y);
        System.out.println("x + y = " + (x + y));
        System.out.println("x - y = " + (x - y));
        System.out.println("x * y = " + (x * y));
        System.out.println("x / y = " + (x / y));
        System.out.println("x % y = " + (x % y));
    }
}
```

The output of FloatMath follows:

```
x = 23.5
y = 7.3
x + y = 30.8
x - y = 16.2
x * y = 171.55
x / y = 3.21918
x % y = 1.6
```

The first four operations no doubt performed as you expected, taking the two floating-point operands and yielding a floating-point result. The final modulus operation determined that 7.3 divides into 23.5 an integral amount of 3 times, leaving a remaining result of 1.6.

Relational Floating-Point Operators

The relational floating-point operators compare two floating-point operands, leaving a boolean result. The floating-point relational operators are the same as the integer relational operators listed in Table 4.3, earlier in this chapter, except that they work on floating-point numbers.

Boolean Operators

Boolean operators act on boolean types and return a boolean result. The boolean operators are listed in Table 4.6.

Table 4.6. The boolean operators.

Description	Operator
Evaluation AND	&
Evaluation OR	¦
Evaluation XOR	^
Logical AND	&&
Logical OR	¦¦

continues

Table 4.6. continued

Description	Operator
Negation	!
Equal-to	==
Not-equal-to	!=
Conditional	?:

The evaluation operators (&, ¦, and ^) evaluate both sides of an expression before determining the result. The logical operators (&& and ¦¦) avoid the right-side evaluation of the expression if it is not needed. To better understand the difference between these operators, take a look at the following two expressions:

```
boolean result = isValid & (Count > 10);
boolean result = isValid && (Count > 10);
```

The first expression uses the evaluation AND operator (&) to make an assignment. In this case, both sides of the expression are always evaluated, regardless of the values of the variables involved. In the second example, the logical AND operator (&&) is used. This time, the isValid boolean value is first checked. If it is false, the right side of the expression is ignored and the assignment is made. This operator is more efficient because a false value on the left side of the expression provides enough information to determine the false outcome.

Although the logical operators are more efficient than the evaluation operators, there still may be times when you want to use the evaluation operators to ensure that the entire expression is evaluated. The following code shows how the evaluation AND operator is necessary for the complete evaluation of an expression:

```
while ((++x < 10) & (++y < 15)) {
  System.out.println(x);
  System.out.println(y);
}
```

In this example, the second expression (++y < 15) is evaluated after the last pass through the loop because of the evaluation AND operator. If the logical AND operator had been used, the second expression would not have been evaluated and y would not have been incremented after the last time around.

The three boolean operators—negation, equal-to, and not-equal-to (!, ==, and !=)—perform exactly as you might expect. The negation operator toggles the value of a boolean from false to true or from true to false, depending on the original value. The equal-to operator simply determines whether two boolean values are equal (both true or both false). Similarly, the not-equal-to operator determines whether two boolean operands are unequal.

The conditional boolean operator (?:) is the most unique of the boolean operators and is worth a closer look. This operator also is known as the *ternary operator* because it takes three items: a condition and two expressions. The syntax for the conditional operator follows:

Condition ? Expression1 : Expression2

The `Condition`, which itself is a boolean, is first evaluated to determine whether it is `true` or `false`. If `Condition` evaluates to a `true` result, `Expression1` is evaluated. If `Condition` ends up being `false`, `Expression2` is evaluated. To get a better feel for the conditional operator, check out the `Conditional` program in Listing 4.9.

Listing 4.9. The Conditional class.

```
class Conditional {
  public static void main (String args[]) {
    int x = 0;
    boolean isEven = false;
    System.out.println("x = " + x);
    x = isEven ? 4 : 7;
    System.out.println("x = " + x);
  }
}
```

The results of the `Conditional` program follow:

```
x = 0
x = 7
```

The integer variable x is first assigned a value of `0`. The boolean variable `isEven` is assigned a value of `false`. Using the conditional operator, the value of `isEven` is checked. Because it is `false`, the second expression of the conditional is used, which results in the value `7` being assigned to x.

String Operator

Just as integers, floating-point numbers, and booleans can be, strings can be manipulated with operators. Actually, there is only one string operator: the concatenation operator (+). The concatenation operator for strings works very similarly to the addition operator for numbers—it adds strings together. The concatenation operator is demonstrated in the `Concatenation` program shown in Listing 4.10.

Listing 4.10. The Concatenation class.

```
class Concatenation {
  public static void main (String args[]) {
    String firstHalf = "What " + "did ";
    String secondHalf = "you " + "say?";
    System.out.println(firstHalf + secondHalf);
  }
}
```

The output of Concatenation follows:

What did you say?

In the Concatenation program, literal strings are concatenated to make assignments to the two string variables, firstHalf and secondHalf, at time of creation. The two string variables are then concatenated within the call to the println() method.

Assignment Operators

One final group of operators you haven't seen yet is the assignment operators. Assignment operators actually work with all the fundamental data types. Table 4.7 lists the assignment operators.

Table 4.7. The assignment operators.

Description	Operator
Simple	=
Addition	+=
Subtraction	-=
Multiplication	*=
Division	/=
Modulus	%=
AND	&=
OR	¦=
XOR	^=

With the exception of the simple assignment operator (=), the assignment operators function exactly like their nonassignment counterparts, except that the resulting value is stored in the operand on the left side of the expression. Take a look at the following examples:

```
x += 6;
x *= (y - 3);
```

In the first example, x and 6 are added and the result stored in x. In the second example, 3 is subtracted from y and the result is multiplied by x. The final result is then stored in x.

Control Structures

Although performing operations on data is very useful, it's time to move on to the issue of program flow control. The flow of your programs is dictated by two different types of constructs: branches and loops. *Branches* enable you to selectively execute one part of a program instead of another. *Loops*, on the other hand, provide a means to repeat certain parts of a program. Together, branches and loops provide you with a powerful means to control the logic and execution of your code.

Branches

Without branches or loops, Java code executes in a sequential fashion, as shown in Figure 4.1.

FIGURE 4.1.

A program executing sequentially.

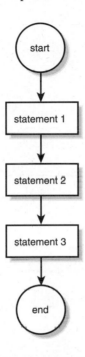

In Figure 4.1, each statement is executed sequentially. But what if you don't always want every single statement executed? Then you use a branch. Figure 4.2 shows how a conditional branch gives the flow of your code more options.

By adding a branch, you give the code two optional routes to take, based on the result of the conditional expression. The concept of branches might seem trivial, but it would be difficult if not impossible to write useful programs without them. Java supports two types of branches: if-else branches and switch branches.

FIGURE 4.2.

A program executing with a branch.

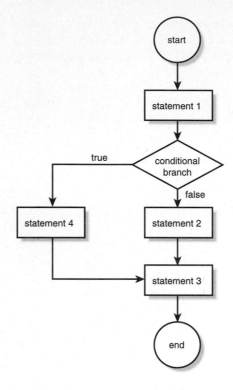

if-else Branches

The if-else branch is the most commonly used branch in Java programming. It is used to select conditionally one of two possible outcomes. The syntax for the if-else statement follows:

```
if (Condition)
  Statement1
else
  Statement2
```

If the boolean *Condition* evaluates to true, *Statement1* is executed. Likewise, if *Condition* evaluates to false, *Statement2* is executed. The following example shows how to use an if-else statement:

```
if (isTired)
  timeToEat = true;
else
  timeToEat = false;
```

If the boolean variable isTired is true, the first statement is executed and timeToEat is set to true. Otherwise, the second statement is executed and timeToEat is set to false. You may have noticed that the if-else branch works in a manner very similar to the conditional operator

(?:) described earlier in this chapter. In fact, you can think of the if-else branch as an expanded version of the conditional operator. One significant difference between the two is that you can include compound statements in an if-else branch, which you cannot do with the conditional operator.

> **NOTE**
>
> *Compound statements* are blocks of code surrounded by curly braces {} that appear as a single, or simple, statement to an outer block of code.

If you have only a single statement that you want to execute conditionally, you can leave off the else part of the branch, as shown in the following example:

```
if (isThirsty)
  pourADrink = true;
```

On the other hand, if you need more than two conditional outcomes, you can string together a series of if-else branches to get the desired effect. The following example shows multiple if-else branches used to switch between different outcomes:

```
if (x == 0)
  y = 5;
else if (x == 2)
  y = 25;
else if (x >= 3)
  y = 125;
```

In this example, three different comparisons are made, each with its own statement executed on a true conditional result. Notice, however, that subsequent if-else branches are in effect nested within the previous branch. This arrangement ensures that at most one statement is executed.

The last important topic to cover in regard to if-else branches is compound statements. As mentioned in the preceding note, a compound statement is a block of code surrounded by curly braces that appears to an outer block as a single statement. Following is an example of a compound statement used with an if branch:

```
if (performCalc) {
  x += y * 5;
  y -= 10;
  z = (x - 3) / y;
}
```

Sometimes, when nesting if-else branches, it is necessary to use curly braces to distinguish which statements go with which branch. The following example illustrates the problem:

```
if (x != 0)
  if (y < 10)
    z = 5;
else
  z = 7;
```

In this example, the style of indentation indicates that the `else` branch belongs to the first (outer) `if`. However, because there was no grouping specified, the Java compiler assumes that the `else` goes with the inner `if`. To get the desired results, you must modify the code as follows:

```java
if (x != 0) {
  if (y < 10)
    z = 5;
}
else
  z = 7;
```

The addition of the curly braces tells the compiler that the inner `if` is part of a compound statement; more importantly, it completely hides the `else` branch from the inner `if`. Based on what you learned from the discussion of blocks and scope in Chapter 3, "Java Language Fundamentals," you can see that code within the inner `if` has no way of accessing code outside its scope, including the `else` branch.

Listing 4.11 contains the source code for the `IfElseName` class, which uses a lot of what you've learned so far.

Listing 4.11. The `IfElseName` class.

```java
class IfElseName {
  public static void main (String args[]) {
    char firstInitial = (char)-1;
    System.out.println("Enter your first initial:");
    try {
      firstInitial = (char)System.in.read();
    }
    catch (Exception e) {
      System.out.println("Error: " + e.toString());
    }
    if (firstInitial == -1)
      System.out.println("Now what kind of name is that?");
    else if (firstInitial == 'j')
      System.out.println("Your name must be Jules!");
    else if (firstInitial == 'v')
      System.out.println("Your name must be Vincent!");
    else if (firstInitial == 'z')
      System.out.println("Your name must be Zed!");
    else
      System.out.println("I can't figure out your name!");
  }
}
```

When typing the letter **v** in response to the input message, `IfElseName` yields the following results:

```
Your name must be Vincent!
```

The first thing in IfElseName you probably are wondering about is the read() method. The read() method simply reads a character from the standard input stream (System.in), which is typically the keyboard. Notice that a cast is used because read() returns an int type. Once the input character has been successfully retrieved, a succession of if-else branches is used to determine the proper output. If there are no matches, the final else branch is executed, which notifies users that their names could not be determined. Notice that the value of read() is checked to see whether it is equal to -1. The read() method returns -1 if it has reached the end of the input stream.

> **NOTE**
>
> You may have noticed that the call to the read() method in IfElseName is enclosed within a try-catch clause. The try-catch clause is part of Java's support for exception handling and is used in this case to trap errors encountered while reading input from the user. You'll learn more about exceptions and the try-catch clause in Chapter 7, "Exception Handling."

switch Branches

Similar to the if-else branch, the switch branch is specifically designed to conditionally switch among multiple outcomes. The syntax for the switch statement follows:

```
switch (Expression) {
  case Constant1:
    StatementList1
  case Constant2:
    StatementList2
  default:
    DefaultStatementList
}
```

The switch branch evaluates and compares *Expression* to all the case constants and branches the program's execution to the matching case statement list. If no case constants match *Expression*, the program branches to the *DefaultStatementList*, if one has been supplied (the *DefaultStatementList* is optional). You might be wondering what a statement list is. A *statement list* is simply a series, or list, of statements. Unlike the if-else branch, which directs program flow to a simple or compound statement, the switch branch directs the flow to a list of statements.

When the program execution moves into a case statement list, it continues from there in a sequential manner. To better understand this, take a look at Listing 4.12, which contains a switch version of the name program developed earlier with if-else branches.

Listing 4.12. The SwitchName1 class.

```
class SwitchName1 {
  public static void main (String args[]) {
    char firstInitial = (char)-1;
    System.out.println("Enter your first initial:");
    try {
      firstInitial = (char)System.in.read();
    }
    catch (Exception e) {
      System.out.println("Error: " + e.toString());
    }
    switch(firstInitial) {
      case (char)-1:
        System.out.println("Now what kind of name is that?");
      case 'j':
        System.out.println("Your name must be Jules!");
      case 'v':
        System.out.println("Your name must be Vincent!");
      case 'z':
        System.out.println("Your name must be Zed!");
      default:
        System.out.println("I can't figure out your name!");
    }
  }
}
```

When typing the letter **v** in response to the input message, SwitchName1 produces the following results:

```
Your name must be Vincent!
Your name must be Zed!
I can't figure out your name!
```

Hey, what's going on here? That output definitely does not look right. The problem lies in the way the switch branch controls program flow. The switch branch matched the v entered with the correct case statement, as shown in the first string printed. However, the program continued executing all the case statements from that point onward, which is *not* what you wanted. The solution to the problem lies in the break statement. The break statement forces a program to break out of the block of code it is currently executing. Check out the new version of the program in Listing 4.13, which has break statements added where appropriate.

Listing 4.13. The SwitchName2 class.

```
class SwitchName2 {
  public static void main (String args[]) {
    char firstInitial = (char)-1;
    System.out.println("Enter your first initial:");
    try {
      firstInitial = (char)System.in.read();
    }
    catch (Exception e) {
      System.out.println("Error: " + e.toString());
    }
```

```
    switch(firstInitial) {
      case (char)-1:
        System.out.println("Now what kind of name is that?");
        break;
      case 'j':
        System.out.println("Your name must be Jules!");
        break;
      case 'v':
        System.out.println("Your name must be Vincent!");
        break;
      case 'z':
        System.out.println("Your name must be Zed!");
        break;
      default:
        System.out.println("I can't figure out your name!");
    }
  }
}
```

When you run SwitchName2 and enter **v**, you get the following output:

```
Your name must be Vincent!
```

That's a lot better! You can see that placing break statements after each case statement kept the program from falling through to the next case statements. Although you will use break statements in this manner the majority of the time, there may still be some situations where you will want a case statement to fall through to the next one.

Loops

When it comes to program flow, branches really tell only half of the story; loops tell the other half. Put simply, *loops* enable you to execute code repeatedly. There are three types of loops in Java: for loops, while loops, and do-while loops.

Just as branches alter the sequential flow of programs, so do loops. Figure 4.3 shows how a loop alters the sequential flow of a Java program.

for Loops

The for loop provides a means to repeat a section of code a designated number of times. The for loop is structured so that a section of code is repeated until some limit has been reached. The syntax for the for statement follows:

```
for (InitializationExpression; LoopCondition; StepExpression)
  Statement
```

The for loop repeats the *Statement* lines the number of times that is determined by the *InitializationExpression*, the *LoopCondition*, and the *StepExpression*. The *InitializationExpression* is used to initialize a loop control variable. The *LoopCondition* compares the loop control variable to some limit value. Finally, the *StepExpression* specifies how the loop control variable should be modified before the next iteration of the loop. The following example shows how a for loop can be used to print the numbers from 1 to 10:

```
for (int i = 1; i < 11; i++)
  System.out.println(i);
```

FIGURE 4.3.

A program executing with a loop.

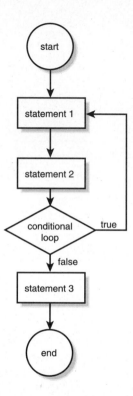

First, i is declared as an integer. The fact that i is declared within the body of the for loop might look strange to you at this point. Don't despair—this is completely legal. i is initialized to 1 in the *InitializationExpression* part of the for loop. Next, the conditional expression i < 11 is evaluated to see whether the loop should continue. At this point, i is still equal to 1, so *LoopCondition* evaluates to true and the *Statement* is executed (the value of i is printed to standard output). i is then incremented in the *StepExpression* part of the for loop, and the process repeats with the evaluation of *LoopCondition* again. This continues until *LoopCondition* evaluates to false, which is when x equals 11 (ten iterations later).

Listing 4.14 shows the ForCount program, which shows how to use a for loop to count a user-entered amount of numbers.

Listing 4.14. The ForCount class.

```
class ForCount {
  public static void main (String args[]) {
    char input = (char)-1;
    int  numToCount;
    System.out.println("Enter a number to count to between 0 and 10:");
    try {
      input = (char)System.in.read();
    }
    catch (Exception e) {
      System.out.println("Error: " + e.toString());
    }
    numToCount = Character.digit(input, 10);
    if ((numToCount > 0) && (numToCount < 10)) {
      for (int i = 1; i <= numToCount; i++)
        System.out.println(i);
    }
    else
      System.out.println("That number was not between 0 and 10!");
  }
}
```

When the ForCount program is run and the number 4 is entered, the following output results:

```
1
2
3
4
```

ForCount first prompts the user to enter a number between 0 and 10. A character is read from the keyboard using the read() method and the result is stored in the input character variable. The static digit method of the Character class then is used to convert the character to its base 10 integer representation. This value is stored in the numToCount integer variable. numToCount is then checked to make sure that it is in the range 0 to 10. If so, a for loop is executed that counts from 1 to numToCount, printing each number along the way. If numToCount is outside the valid range, an error message is printed.

Before you move on, there is one small problem with ForCount that you may not have noticed. Run it and try typing in a number greater than 9. What happened to the error message? The problem is that ForCount grabs only the first character it sees from the input. So if you type 10, ForCount just gets the 1 and thinks everything is fine. You don't have to worry about fixing this problem right now because it will be resolved when you learn more about input and output in Chapter 12, "The I/O Package."

while Loops

Like the for loop, the while loop has a loop condition that controls the execution of the loop statement. Unlike the for loop, however, the while loop has no initialization or step expressions. The syntax for the while statement follows:

```
while (LoopCondition)
  Statement
```

If the boolean *LoopCondition* evaluates to true, the *Statement* is executed and the process starts over. It is important to understand that the while loop has no step expression as the for loop does. This means that the *LoopCondition* must somehow be affected by code in the *Statement* or the loop will infinitely repeat, which is a bad thing. This is bad because an infinite loop causes a program to never exit, which hogs processor time and can ultimately hang the system.

Another important thing to notice about the while loop is that its *LoopCondition* occurs before the body of the loop *Statement*. This means that if the *LoopCondition* initially evaluates to false, the *Statement* is never executed. Although this may seem trivial, it is in fact the only thing that differentiates the while loop from the do-while loop, which is discussed in the next section.

To better understand how the while loop works, take a look at Listing 4.15, which shows how a counting program works using a while loop.

Listing 4.15. The WhileCount class.

```
class WhileCount {
  public static void main (String args[]) {
    char input = (char)-1;
    int  numToCount;
    System.out.println("Enter a number to count to between 0 and 10:");
    try {
      input = (char)System.in.read();
    }
    catch (Exception e) {
      System.out.println("Error: " + e.toString());
    }
    numToCount = Character.digit(input, 10);
    if ((numToCount > 0) && (numToCount < 10)) {
      int i = 1;
      while (i <= numToCount) {
        System.out.println(i);
        i++;
      }
    }
    else
      System.out.println("That number was not between 0 and 10!");
  }
}
```

Arguably, WhileCount doesn't demonstrate the best usage of a while loop. Loops that involve counting should almost always be implemented with for loops. However, seeing how a while loop can be made to imitate a for loop can give you insight into the structural differences between the two types of loops.

Because while loops don't have any type of initialization expression, you first have to declare and initialize the variable i to 1. Next, the loop condition for the while loop is established as i <= numToCount. Inside the compound while statement, you can see a call to the println() method, which outputs the value of i. Finally, i is incremented and program execution resumes back at the while loop condition.

do-while Loops

The do-while loop is very similar to the while loop, as you can see in the following syntax:

```
do
  Statement
while (LoopCondition);
```

The major difference between the do-while loop and the while loop is that, in a do-while loop, the *LoopCondition* is evaluated *after* the *Statement* is executed. This difference is important because there may be times when you want the *Statement* code to be executed at least once, regardless of the *LoopCondition*.

The *Statement* is executed initially, and from then on it is executed as long as the *LoopCondition* evaluates to true. As with the while loop, you must be careful with the do-while loop to avoid creating an infinite loop. An infinite loop occurs when the *LoopCondition* remains true indefinitely. The following example shows a very obvious infinite do-while loop:

```
do
  System.out.println("I'm stuck!");
while (true);
```

Because the *LoopCondition* is always true, the message I'm Stuck! is printed forever, or at least until you press Ctrl+C and break out of the program.

break and continue Statements

You've already seen how the break statement works with the switch branch. The break statement is also useful when dealing with loops. You can use the break statement to jump out of a loop and effectively bypass the loop condition. Listing 4.16 shows how the break statement can help you out of the infinite loop problem shown earlier.

Listing 4.16. The BreakLoop class.

```
class BreakLoop {
  public static void main (String args[]) {
    int i = 0;
    do {
      System.out.println("I'm stuck!");
      i++;
      if (i > 100)
        break;
    }
    while (true);
  }
}
```

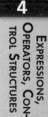

In BreakLoop, a seemingly infinite do-while loop is created by setting the loop condition to true. However, the break statement is used to exit the loop when i is incremented past 100.

Another useful statement that works similarly to the break statement is the continue statement. Unlike break, the continue statement is useful only when working with loops; it has no real application to the switch branch. The continue statement works like the break statement in that it jumps out of the current iteration of a loop. The difference with continue is that program execution is restored to the test condition of the loop. Remember that break jumps completely out of a loop. Use break when you want to jump out and terminate a loop; use continue when you want to jump immediately to the next iteration of the loop. The following example shows the difference between the break and continue statements:

```java
int i = 0;
while (i++ < 100) {
  System.out.println("Looping with i.");
  break;
  System.out.println("Please don't print me!");
}
int j = 0;
while (j++ < 100) {
  System.out.println("Looping with j!");
  continue;
  System.out.println("Please don't print me!");
}
```

In this example, the first loop breaks out because of the break statement after printing the looping message once. Note that the second message is never printed because the break statement occurs before we get to it. Contrast this with the second loop, which prints the looping message 100 times. The reason for this is that the continue statement allows the loop to continue its iterations. In this case, the continue statement serves only to skip over the second message, which still isn't printed.

Summary

This chapter covered a lot of territory. You started off by learning about expressions and then moved right into operators, learning how they work and how they affect each data type. You won't regret the time spent working with operators in this chapter—they are at the core of almost every mathematical or logical Java expression.

From operators, you moved on to control structures, learning about the various types of branches and loops. Branches and loops provide the means to alter the flow of Java programs and are just as important as operators in Java programming.

With the concepts presented in this chapter firmly set in your mind, you are ready to dig a little deeper into Java. Next stop: object-oriented programming with classes, packages, and interfaces!

Classes, Packages, and Interfaces

by Michael Morrison

IN THIS CHAPTER

So far, you've managed to avoid the issue of object-oriented programming and how it relates to Java. Actually, Chapter 3, "Java Language Fundamentals," touched on some object-oriented programming issues, but it purposely avoided a thorough discussion. This chapter aims to remedy that hole in your education. It begins with a basic discussion of object-oriented programming in general. With this background in place, you can then move into the rest of the chapter, which covers the specific elements of the Java language that provide support for object-oriented programming—namely, classes, packages, and interfaces.

You can think of this chapter as the chapter that finishes helping you to your feet in regard to learning the Java language. Classes are the final core component of the Java language you must learn before becoming a proficient Java programmer. Once you have a solid understanding of classes and how they work in Java, you'll be ready to write some serious Java programs. So, what are you waiting for? Read on!

Object-Oriented Programming Primer

You may have been wondering what the big deal is with objects and object-oriented technology. Is it something you should be concerned with, and if so, why? If you sift through the hype surrounding the whole object-oriented issue, you'll find a very powerful technology that provides a lot of benefits to software design. The problem is that object-oriented concepts can be difficult to grasp. And you can't embrace the benefits of object-oriented design if you don't completely understand what they are. Because of this, a complete understanding of the theory behind object-oriented programming is usually developed over time through practice.

A lot of the confusion among developers in regard to object-oriented technology has led to confusion among computer users in general. How many products have you seen that claim they are object-oriented? Considering the fact that object orientation is a software design issue, what can this statement possibly mean to a software consumer? In many ways, "object-oriented" has become to the software industry what "new and improved" is to the household cleanser industry. The truth is that the real world is already object oriented, which is no surprise to anyone. The significance of object-oriented technology is that it enables programmers to design software in much the same way that they perceive the real world.

Now that you've come to terms with some of the misconceptions surrounding the object-oriented issue, try to put them aside and think of what the term object-oriented might mean to software design. This primer lays the groundwork for understanding how object-oriented design makes writing programs faster, easier, and more reliable. And it all begins with the object. Even though this chapter ultimately focuses on Java, this object-oriented primer section really applies to all object-oriented languages.

Objects

Objects are software bundles of data and the procedures that act on that data. The *procedures* are also known as *methods*. The merger of data and methods provides a means of more accurately representing real-world objects in software. Without objects, modeling a real-world problem in software requires a significant logical leap. Objects, on the other hand, enable programmers to solve real-world problems in the software domain much easier and more logically.

As evident by its name, objects are at the heart of object-oriented technology. To understand how software objects are beneficial, think about the common characteristics of all real-world objects. Lions, cars, and calculators all share two common characteristics: state and behavior. For example, the state of a lion includes color, weight, and whether the lion is tired or hungry. Lions also have certain behaviors, such as roaring, sleeping, and hunting. The state of a car includes the current speed, the type of transmission, whether it is two-wheel or four-wheel drive, whether the lights are on, and the current gear, among other things. The behaviors for a car include turning, braking, and accelerating.

As with real-world objects, software objects also have these two common characteristics (state and behavior). To relate this back to programming terms, the state of an object is determined by its data; the behavior of an object is defined by its methods. By making this connection between real-world objects and software objects, you begin to see how objects help bridge the gap between the real world and the world of software inside your computer.

Because software objects are modeled after real-world objects, you can more easily represent real-world objects in object-oriented programs. You can use the lion object to represent a real lion in an interactive software zoo. Similarly, car objects would be very useful in a racing game. However, you don't always have to think of software objects as modeling physical real-world objects; software objects can be just as useful for modeling abstract concepts. For example, a thread is an object used in multithreaded software systems that represents a stream of program execution. You'll learn a lot more about threads and how they are used in Java in the next chapter, "Threads and Multithreading."

Figure 5.1 shows a visualization of a software object, including the primary components and how they relate. The software object in Figure 5.1 clearly shows the two primary components of an object: data and methods. The figure also shows some type of communication, or access, between the data and the methods. Additionally, it shows how messages are sent through the methods, which result in responses from the object. You learn more about messages and responses later in this chapter.

The data and methods within an object express everything that the object represents (state), along with what it can do (behavior). A software object modeling a real-world car would have variables (data) that indicate the car's current state: It's traveling at 75 mph, it's in 4th gear, and the lights are on. The software car object would also have methods that allow it to brake, accelerate, steer, change gears, and turn the lights on and off. Figure 5.2 shows what a software car object might look like.

FIGURE 5.1.

A software object.

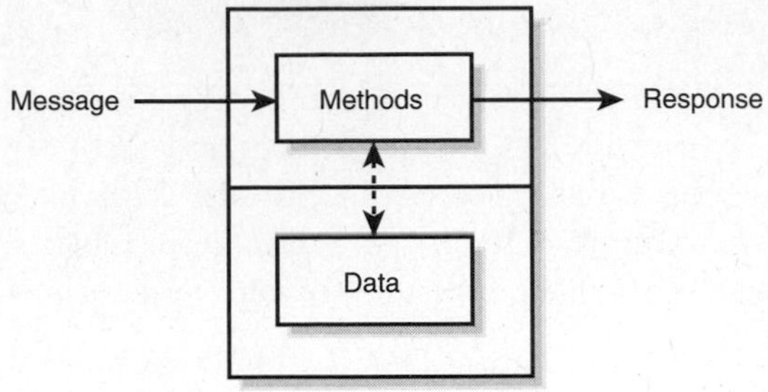

FIGURE 5.2.

A software car object.

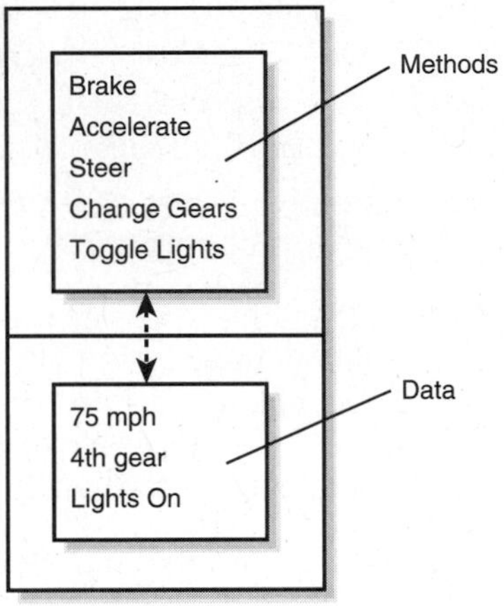

In both Figures 5.1 and 5.2, notice the line separating the methods from the data within the object. This line is a little misleading because methods have full access to the data within an object. The line is there to illustrate the difference between the visibility of the methods and the data to the outside world. In this sense, an object's *visibility* refers to the parts of the object to which another object has access. Because object data defaults to being invisible, or inaccessible to other objects, all interaction between objects must be handled through methods. This hiding of data within an object is called *encapsulation*.

Encapsulation

Encapsulation is the process of packaging an object's data together with its methods. A powerful benefit of encapsulation is the hiding of implementation details from other objects. This means that the internal portion of an object has more limited visibility than the external portion. This arrangement results in the safeguarding of the internal portion against unwanted external access.

The external portion of an object is often referred to as the object's *interface* because it acts as the object's interface to the rest of the program. Because other objects must communicate with the object only through its interface, the internal portion of the object is protected from outside tampering. And because an outside program has no access to the internal implementation of an object, the internal implementation can change at any time without affecting other parts of the program.

Encapsulation provides two primary benefits to programmers:

- **Implementation hiding.** This refers to the protection of the internal implementation of an object. An object is composed of a public interface and a private section that can be a combination of internal data and methods. The internal data and methods are the sections of the object hidden. The primary benefit is that these sections can change without affecting other parts of the program.

- **Modularity.** This means that an object can be maintained independently of other objects. Because the source code for the internal sections of an object is maintained separately from the interface, you are free to make modifications with confidence that your object won't cause problems to other areas. This makes it easier to distribute objects throughout a system.

Messages

An object acting alone is rarely useful; most objects require other objects to do much of anything. For example, the car object is pretty useless by itself with no other interaction. Add a driver object, however, and things get more interesting! Knowing this, it's pretty clear that objects need some type of communication mechanism to interact with each other.

Software objects interact and communicate with each other through *messages*. When the driver object wants the car object to accelerate, it sends the car object a message. If you want to think of messages more literally, think of two people as objects. If one person wants the other person to come closer, they send the other person a message. More accurately, they may say to the other person "Come here, please." This is a message in a very literal sense. Software messages are a little different in form, but not in theory—they tell an object what to do.

Many times, the receiving object needs—along with a message—more information so that it knows exactly what to do. When the driver tells the car to accelerate, the car must know by how much. This information is passed along with the message as *message parameters*.

From this discussion, you can see that messages consist of three things:

1. The object to receive the message (car)
2. The name of the action to perform (accelerate)
3. Any parameters the method requires (15 mph)

These three components are sufficient information to fully describe a message for an object. Any interaction with an object is handled by passing a message. This means that objects anywhere in a system can communicate with other objects solely through messages.

So that you don't get confused, understand that "message passing" is another way of saying "method calling." When an object sends another object a message, it is really just calling a method of that object. The message parameters are actually the parameters to a method. In object-oriented programming, messages and methods are synonymous.

Because everything an object can do is expressed through its methods (interface), message passing supports all possible interactions between objects. In fact, interfaces allow objects to send and receive messages to each other even if they reside in different locations on a network. Objects in this scenario are referred to as *distributed objects*. Java is specifically designed to support distributed objects.

> **NOTE**
>
> Actually, complete support for distributed objects is a very complex issue and isn't entirely handled by the standard Java class structure. However, new extensions to Java do provide thorough support for distributed objects. You find out about these new extensions in Chapter 54, "Remote Objects and the Java IDL System."

Classes

Throughout this discussion of object-oriented programming, you've dealt only with the concept of an object that already exists in a system. You may be wondering how objects get into a system in the first place. This question brings you to the most fundamental structure in object-oriented programming: the class. A *class* is a template or prototype that defines a type of object. A class is to an object what a blueprint is to a house. Many houses can be built from a single blueprint; the blueprint outlines the makeup of the houses. Classes work exactly the same way, except that they outline the makeup of objects.

In the real world, there are often many objects of the same kind. Using the house analogy, there are many different houses around the world, but all houses share common characteristics. In object-oriented terms, you would say that your house is a specific instance of the class of objects known as houses. All houses have states and behaviors in common that define them as houses. When builders start building a new neighborhood of houses, they typically build them all from a set of blueprints. It wouldn't be as efficient to create a new blueprint for every single house, especially when there are so many similarities shared between each one. The same thing is true in object-oriented software development; why rewrite tons of code when you can reuse code that solves similar problems?

In object-oriented programming, as in construction, it's also common to have many objects of the same kind that share similar characteristics. And like the blueprints for similar houses, you can create blueprints for objects that share certain characteristics. What it boils down to is that classes are software blueprints for objects.

As an example, the car class discussed earlier would contain several variables representing the state of the car, along with implementations for the methods that enable the driver to control the car. The state variables of the car remain hidden underneath the interface. Each instance, or instantiated object, of the car class gets a fresh set of state variables. This brings you to another important point: When an instance of an object is created from a class, the variables declared by that class are allocated in memory. The variables are then modified through the object's methods. Instances of the same class share method implementations but have their own object data.

Where objects provide the benefits of modularity and information hiding, classes provide the benefit of reusability. Just as the builder reuses the blueprint for a house, the software developer reuses the class for an object. Software programmers can use a class over and over again to create many objects. Each of these objects gets its own data but shares a single method implementation.

Inheritance

What happens if you want an object that is very similar to one you already have, but that has a few extra characteristics? You just inherit a new class based on the class of the similar object. *Inheritance* is the process of creating a new class with the characteristics of an existing class, along with additional characteristics unique to the new class. Inheritance provides a powerful and natural mechanism for organizing and structuring programs.

So far, the discussion of classes has been limited to the data and methods that make up a class. Based on this understanding, all classes are built from scratch by defining all the data and all the associated methods. Inheritance provides a means to create classes based on other classes. When a class is based on another class, it inherits all the properties of that class, including the data and methods for the class. The class doing the inheriting is referred to as the *subclass* (or the *child class*), and the class providing the information to inherit is referred to as the *superclass* (or the *parent class*).

Using the car example, child classes could be inherited from the car class for gas-powered cars and cars powered by electricity. Both new car classes share common "car" characteristics, but they also add a few characteristics of their own. The gas car would add, among other things, a fuel tank and a gas cap; the electric car would add a battery and a plug for recharging. Each subclass inherits state information (in the form of variable declarations) from the superclass. Figure 5.3 shows the car parent class with the gas and electric car child classes.

Inheriting the state and behaviors of a superclass alone wouldn't do all that much for a subclass. The real power of inheritance is the ability to inherit properties and methods and add new ones; subclasses can add variables and methods to the ones they inherited from the superclass. Remember that the electric car *added* a battery and a recharging plug. Additionally, subclasses have the ability to override inherited methods and provide different implementations for them. For example, the gas car would probably be able to go much faster than the electric car. The accelerate method for the gas car could reflect this difference.

FIGURE 5.3.
Inherited car objects.

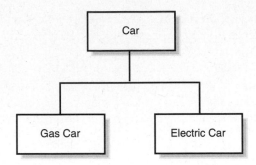

Class inheritance is designed to allow as much flexibility as possible. A group of interrelated classes is called an *inheritance tree*, or *class hierarchy*. An inheritance tree looks much like a family tree: it shows the relationships between classes. Unlike a family tree, the classes in an inheritance tree get more specific as you move down the tree. You can create inheritance trees as deep as necessary to carry out your design, although it is important to not go so deep that it becomes cumbersome to see the relationship between classes. The car classes in Figure 5.3 are a good example of an inheritance tree.

By understanding the concept of inheritance, you understand how subclasses can allow specialized data and methods in addition to the common ones provided by the superclass. This enables programmers to reuse the code in the superclass many times, thus saving extra coding effort and eliminating potential bugs.

One final point to make in regard to inheritance: It is possible and sometimes useful to create superclasses that act purely as templates for more usable subclasses. In this situation, the superclass serves as nothing more than an abstraction for the common class functionality shared by the subclasses. For this reason, these types of superclasses are referred to as *abstract classes*. An abstract class cannot be instantiated, meaning that no objects can be created from an abstract class. The reason an abstract class can't be instantiated is that parts of it have been specifically left unimplemented. More specifically, these parts are made up of methods that have yet to be implemented—abstract methods.

Using the car example once more, the accelerate method really can't be defined until the car's acceleration capabilities are known. Of course, how a car accelerates is determined by the type of engine it has. Because the engine type is unknown in the car superclass, the accelerate method could be defined but left unimplemented, which would make both the accelerate method and the car superclass abstract. Then the gas and electric car child classes would implement the accelerate method to reflect the acceleration capabilities of their respective engines or motors.

The Java Class Hierarchy

No doubt, you're probably about primered out by now and are ready to get on with how classes work in Java. Well, wait no longer! In Java, all classes are subclassed from a superclass called Object. Figure 5.4 shows what the Java class hierarchy looks like in regard to the Object superclass.

FIGURE 5.4.

Classes derived from the Object *superclass.*

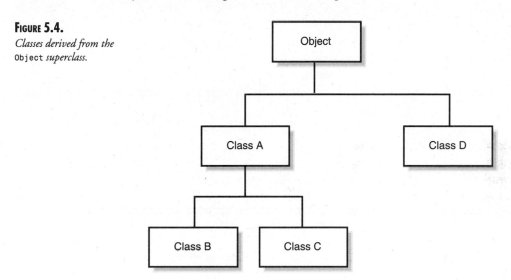

As you can see, all the classes fan out from the Object base class. In Java, Object serves as the superclass for all derived classes, including the classes that make up the Java API.

Declaring Classes

The syntax for declaring classes in Java follows:

```
class Identifier {
  ClassBody
}
```

Identifier specifies the name of the new class, which is by default derived from Object. The curly braces surround the body of the class, *ClassBody*. As an example, take a look at the class declaration for an Alien class, which could be used in a space game:

```
class Alien {
  Color color;
  int   energy;
  int   aggression;
}
```

The state of the Alien object is defined by three data members, which represent the color, energy, and aggression of the alien. It's important to notice that the Alien class is inherently derived from `Object`. So far, the `Alien` class isn't all that useful; it needs some methods. The most basic syntax for declaring methods for a class follows:

```
ReturnType Identifier(Parameters) {
  MethodBody
}
```

ReturnType specifies the data type that the method returns, *Identifier* specifies the name of the method, and *Parameters* specifies the parameters to the method, if there are any. As with class bodies, the body of a method, *MethodBody*, is enclosed by curly braces. Remember that in object-oriented design terms, a method is synonymous with a message, with the return type being the object's response to the message. Following is a method declaration for the `morph()` method, which would be useful in the `Alien` class because some aliens like to change shape:

```
void morph(int aggression) {
  if (aggression < 10) {
    // morph into a smaller size
  }
  else if (aggression < 20) {
    // morph into a medium size
  }
  else {
    // morph into a giant size
  }
}
```

The `morph()` method is passed an integer as the only parameter, `aggression`. This value is then used to determine the size to which the alien is morphing. As you can see, the alien morphs to smaller or larger sizes based on its aggression.

If you make the `morph()` method a member of the `Alien` class, it is readily apparent that the `aggression` parameter isn't necessary. This is because `aggression` is already a member variable of `Alien`, to which all class methods have access. The `Alien` class, with the addition of the `morph()` method, looks like this:

```
class Alien {
  Color color;
  int    energy;
  int    aggression;

  void morph() {
    if (aggression < 10) {
      // morph into a smaller size
    }
    else if (aggression < 20) {
      // morph into a medium size
    }
    else {
      // morph into a giant size
    }
  }
}
```

Deriving Classes

So far, the discussion of class declaration has been limited to creating new classes inherently derived from Object. Deriving all your classes from Object isn't a very good idea because you would have to redefine the data and methods for each class. The way you derive classes from classes other than Object is by using the extends keyword. The syntax for deriving a class using the extends keyword follows:

```
class Identifier extends SuperClass {
  ClassBody
}
```

Identifier refers to the name of the newly derived class, *SuperClass* refers to the name of the class you are deriving from, and *ClassBody* is the new class body.

Let's use the Alien class introduced in the preceding section as the basis for a derivation example. What if you had an Enemy class that defined general information useful for all enemies? You would no doubt want to go back and derive the Alien class from the new Enemy class to take advantage of the standard enemy functionality provided by the Enemy class. Following is the Enemy-derived Alien class using the extends keyword:

```
class Alien extends Enemy {
  Color color;
  int   energy;
  int   aggression;

  void morph() {
    if (aggression < 10) {
      // morph into a smaller size
    }
    else if (aggression < 20) {
      // morph into a medium size
    }
    else {
      // morph into a giant size
    }
  }
}
```

This declaration assumes that the Enemy class declaration is readily available in the same package as Alien. In reality, you will likely derive from classes in a lot of different places. To derive a class from an external superclass, you must first import the superclass using the import statement.

> **NOTE**
>
> You'll get to packages a little later in this chapter. For now, just think of a *package* as a group of related classes.

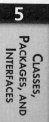

5

CLASSES, PACKAGES, AND INTERFACES

If you had to import the Enemy class, you would do so like this:

```
import Enemy;
```

Overriding Methods

There are times when it is useful to *override* methods in derived classes. For example, if the Enemy class had a move() method, you would want the movement to vary based on the type of enemy. Some types of enemies may fly around in specified patterns, while other enemies may crawl in a random fashion. To allow the Alien class to exhibit its own movement, you would override the move() method with a version specific to alien movement. The Enemy class would then look something like this:

```
class Enemy {
...
  void move() {
    // move the enemy
  }
}
```

Likewise, the Alien class with the overridden move() method would look something like this:

```
class Alien {
  Color color;
  int    energy;
  int    aggression;

  void move() {
    // move the alien
  }

  void morph() {
    if (aggression < 10) {
      // morph into a smaller size
    }
    else if (aggression < 20) {
      // morph into a medium size
    }
    else {
      // morph into a giant size
    }
  }
}
```

When you create an instance of the Alien class and call the move() method, the new move() method in Alien is executed rather than the original overridden move() method in Enemy. Method overriding is a simple yet powerful usage of object-oriented design.

Overloading Methods

Another powerful object-oriented technique is method overloading. *Method overloading* enables you to specify different types of information (parameters) to send to a method. To overload a method, you declare another version with the same name but different parameters.

For example, the move() method for the Alien class could have two different versions: one for general movement and one for moving to a specific location. The general version is the one you've already defined: it moves the alien based on its current state. The declaration for this version follows:

```
void move() {
  // move the alien
}
```

To enable the alien to move to a specific location, you overload the move() method with a version that takes x and y parameters, which specify the location to move to. The overloaded version of move() follows:

```
void move(int x, int y) {
  // move the alien to position x,y
}
```

Notice that the only difference between the two methods is the parameter lists; the first move() method takes no parameters; the second move() method takes two integers.

You may be wondering how the compiler knows which method is being called in a program, when they both have the same name. The compiler keeps up with the parameters for each method along with the name. When a call to a method is encountered in a program, the compiler checks the name and the parameters to determine which overloaded method is being called. In this case, calls to the move() methods are easily distinguishable by the absence or presence of the int parameters.

Access Modifiers

Access to variables and methods in Java classes is accomplished through access modifiers. *Access modifiers* define varying levels of access between class members and the outside world (other objects). Access modifiers are declared immediately before the type of a member variable or the return type of a method. There are four access modifiers: the default access modifier, public, protected, and private.

Access modifiers affect not only the visibility of class members, but also of classes themselves. However, class visibility is tightly linked with packages, which are covered later in this chapter.

The Default Access Modifier

The default access modifier specifies that only classes in the same package can have access to a class's variables and methods. Class members with default access have a visibility limited to other classes within the same package. There is no actual keyword for declaring the default access modifier; it is applied by default in the absence of an access modifier. For example, the Alien class members all had default access because no access modifiers were specified. Examples of a default access member variable and method follow:

```
long length;
void getLength() {
  return length;
}
```

Notice that neither the member variable nor the method supply an access modifier, so they take on the default access modifier implicitly.

The `public` Access Modifier

The `public` access modifier specifies that class variables and methods are accessible to anyone, both inside and outside the class. This means that `public` class members have global visibility and can be accessed by any other objects. Some examples of `public` member variables follow:

```
public int count;
public boolean isActive;
```

The `protected` Access Modifier

The `protected` access modifier specifies that class members are accessible only to methods in that class and subclasses of that class. This means that `protected` class members have visibility limited to subclasses. Examples of a `protected` variable and a `protected` method follow:

```
protected char middleInitial;
protected char getMiddleInitial() {
  return middleInitial;
}
```

The `private` Access Modifier

The `private` access modifier is the most restrictive; it specifies that class members are accessible only by the class in which they are defined. This means that no other class has access to `private` class members, even subclasses. Some examples of `private` member variables follow:

```
private String firstName;
private double howBigIsIt;
```

The `static` Modifier

There are times when you need a common variable or method for all objects of a particular class. The `static` modifier specifies that a variable or method is the same for all objects of a particular class.

Typically, new variables are allocated for each instance of a class. When a variable is declared as being `static`, it is allocated only once regardless of how many objects are instantiated. The result is that all instantiated objects share the same instance of the `static` variable. Similarly, a `static` method is one whose implementation is exactly the same for all objects of a particular class. This means that `static` methods have access only to `static` variables.

Following are some examples of a `static` member variable and a `static` method:

```
static int refCount;
static int getRefCount() {
  return refCount;
}
```

A beneficial side effect of `static` members is that they can be accessed without having to create an instance of a class. Remember the `System.out.println()` method used in the last chapter? Do you recall ever instantiating a `System` object? Of course not. `out` is a `static` member variable of the `System` class, which means that you can access it without having to actually instantiate a `System` object.

The `final` Modifier

Another useful modifier in regard to controlling class member usage is the `final` modifier. The `final` modifier specifies that a variable has a constant value or that a method cannot be overridden in a subclass. To think of the `final` modifier literally, it means that a class member is the final version allowed for the class.

Following are some examples of `final` member variables:

```
final public int numDollars = 25;
final boolean amIBroke = false;
```

If you are coming from the world of C++, `final` variables may sound familiar. In fact, `final` variables in Java are very similar to `const` variables in C++; they must always be initialized at declaration and their value can't change any time afterward.

The `synchronized` Modifier

The `synchronized` modifier is used to specify that a method is *thread safe*. This means that only one path of execution is allowed into a `synchronized` method at a time. In a multithreaded environment like Java, it is possible to have many different paths of execution running through the same code. The `synchronized` modifier changes this rule by allowing only a single thread access to a method at once, forcing the other threads to wait their turn. If the concepts of threads and paths of execution are totally new to you, don't worry; they are covered in detail in the next chapter, "Threads and Multithreading."

The `native` Modifier

The `native` modifier is used to identify methods that have native implementations. The `native` modifier informs the Java compiler that a method's implementation is in an external C file. It is for this reason that `native` method declarations look different from other Java methods; they have no body. Following is an example of a `native` method declaration:

```
native int calcTotal();
```

Notice that the method declaration simply ends in a semicolon; there are no curly braces containing Java code. This is because `native` methods are implemented in C code, which resides in external C source files. To learn more about `native` methods, check out Chapter 32, "Integrating Native Code with the Native Method Interface."

Abstract Classes and Methods

In the object-oriented primer earlier in this chapter, you learned about abstract classes and methods. To recap, an *abstract class* is a class that is partially implemented and whose purpose is solely a design convenience. Abstract classes are made up of one or more *abstract methods*, which are methods that are declared but left bodiless (unimplemented).

The `Enemy` class discussed earlier is an ideal candidate to become an abstract class. You would never want to actually create an `Enemy` object because it is too general. However, the `Enemy` class serves a very logical purpose as a superclass for more specific enemy classes, like the `Alien` class. To turn the `Enemy` class into an abstract class, you use the `abstract` keyword, like this:

```
abstract class Enemy {
  abstract void move();
  abstract void move(int x, int y);
}
```

Notice the usage of the `abstract` keyword *before* the class declaration for `Enemy`. This tells the compiler that the `Enemy` class is abstract. Also notice that both `move()` methods are declared as being abstract. Because it isn't clear how to move a generic enemy, the `move()` methods in `Enemy` have been left unimplemented (abstract).

There are a few limitations to using `abstract` of which you should be aware. First, you can't make constructors abstract. (You'll learn about constructors in the next section covering object creation.) Second, you can't make static methods abstract. This limitation stems from the fact that static methods are declared for all classes, so there is no way to provide a derived implementation for an abstract static method. Finally, you aren't allowed to make private methods abstract. At first, this limitation may seem a little picky, but think about what it means. When you derive a class from a superclass with abstract methods, you must override and implement all the abstract methods or you won't be able to instantiate your new class, and it will remain abstract itself. Now consider that derived classes can't see private members of their superclass, methods included. This results in you not being able to override and implement private abstract methods from the superclass, which means that you can't implement (nonabstract) classes from it. If you were limited to deriving only new abstract classes, you couldn't accomplish much!

Casting

Although casting between different data types was discussed in Chapter 3, "Java Language Fundamentals," the introduction of classes puts a few new twists on casting. Casting between classes can be broken into three different situations:

■ Casting from a subclass to a superclass

■ Casting from a superclass to a subclass

■ Casting between siblings

In the case of casting from a subclass to a superclass, you can cast either implicitly or explicitly. *Implicit casting* simply means that you do nothing; *explicit casting* means that you have to provide the class type in parentheses, just as you do when casting fundamental data types. Casting from subclass to superclass is completely reliable because subclasses contain information tying them to their superclasses. When casting from a superclass to a subclass, you are required to cast explicitly. This cast isn't completely reliable because the compiler has no way of knowing whether the class being cast to is a subclass of the superclass in question. Finally, the cast from sibling to sibling isn't allowed in Java. If all this casting sounds a little confusing, check out the following example:

```
Double d1 = new Double(5.238);
Number n = d1;
Double d2 = (Double)n;
Long l = d1;   // this won't work!
```

In this example, data type wrapper objects are created and assigned to each other. If you aren't familiar with the data type wrapper classes, don't worry, you'll learn about them in Chapter 10, "The Language Package." For now, all you need to know is that the Double and Long sibling classes are both derived from the Number class. In the example, after the Double object d1 is created, it is assigned to a Number object. This is an example of implicitly casting from a subclass to a superclass, which is completely legal. Another Double object, d2, is then assigned the value of the Number object. This time, an explicit cast is required because you are casting from a superclass to a subclass, which isn't guaranteed to be reliable. Finally, a Long object is assigned the value of a Double object. This is a cast between siblings and is not allowed in Java; it results in a compiler error.

Object Creation

Although most of the design work in object-oriented programming is creating classes, you don't really benefit from that work until you create instances (objects) of those classes. To use a class in a program, you must first create an instance of it.

The Constructor

Before getting into the details of how to create an object, there is an important method you need to know about: the *constructor*. When you create an object, you typically want to initialize its member variables. The constructor is a special method you can implement in all your classes; it allows you to initialize variables and perform any other operations when an object is created from the class. The constructor is always given the same name as the class.

Listing 5.1 contains the complete source code for the `Alien` class, which contains two constructors.

Listing 5.1. The Alien class.

```
class Alien extends Enemy {
  protected Color color;
  protected int   energy;
  protected int   aggression;

  public Alien() {
    color = Color.green;
    energy = 100;
    aggression = 15;
  }

  public Alien(Color c, int e, int a) {
    color = c;
    energy = e;
    aggression = a;
  }

  public void move() {
    // move the alien
  }

  public void move(int x, int y) {
    // move the alien to the position x,y
  }

  public void morph() {
    if (aggression < 10) {
      // morph into a smaller size
    }
    else if (aggression < 20) {
      // morph into a medium size
    }
    else {
      // morph into a giant size
    }
  }
}
```

The `Alien` class uses method overloading to provide two different constructors. The first constructor takes no parameters and initializes the member variables to default values. The second constructor takes the color, energy, and aggression of the alien and initializes the member variables with them. As well as containing the new constructors, this version of `Alien` uses access modifiers to explicitly assign access levels to each member variable and method. This is a good habit to get into.

 This version of the `Alien` class is located in the source file `Enemy1.java` on the CD-ROM that accompanies this book. The `Enemy1.java` source code file also includes the Enemy class. Keep in mind that these classes are just example classes with little functionality. However, they are good examples of Java class design and can be compiled into Java classes.

The new Operator

To create an instance of a class, you declare an object variable and use the new operator. When dealing with objects, a declaration merely states what type of object a variable is to represent. The object isn't actually created until the new operator is used. Following are two examples that use the new operator to create instances of the Alien class:

```
Alien anAlien = new Alien();
Alien anotherAlien;
anotherAlien = new Alien(Color.red, 56, 24);
```

In the first example, the variable anAlien is declared and the object is created by using the new operator with an assignment directly in the declaration. In the second example, the variable anotherAlien is declared first; the object is created and assigned in a separate statement.

> **NOTE**
>
> If you have some C++ experience, you no doubt recognize the new operator. Even though the new operator in Java works in a somewhat similar fashion to its C++ counterpart, keep in mind that you must *always* use the new operator to create objects in Java. This is in contrast to the C++ version of new, which is used only when you are working with object pointers. Because Java doesn't support pointers, the new operator must always be used to create new objects.

Object Destruction

When an object falls out of scope, it is removed from memory, or deleted. Similar to the constructor that is called when an object is created, Java provides the ability to define a destructor that is called when an object is deleted. Unlike the constructor, which takes on the name of the class, the destructor is called finalize(). The finalize() method provides a place to perform chores related to the cleanup of the object, and is defined as follows:

```
void finalize() {
  // cleanup
}
```

It is worth noting that the finalize() method is not guaranteed to be called by Java as soon as an object falls out of scope. The reason for this is that Java deletes objects as part of its system garbage collection, which occurs at inconsistent intervals. Because an object isn't actually deleted until Java performs a garbage collection, the finalize() method for the object isn't called until then either. Knowing this, it's safe to say that you shouldn't rely on the finalize() method for anything that is time critical. In general, you will rarely need to place code in the `finalize()` method simply because the Java runtime system does a pretty good job of cleaning up after objects on its own.

Packages

Java provides a powerful means of grouping related classes and interfaces together in a single unit: packages. (You learn about interfaces a little later in this chapter.) Put simply, *packages* are groups of related classes and interfaces. Packages provide a convenient mechanism for managing a large group of classes and interfaces while avoiding potential naming conflicts. The Java API itself is implemented as a group of packages.

As an example, the `Alien` and `Enemy` classes developed earlier in this chapter would fit nicely into an `Enemy` package—along with any other enemy objects. By placing classes into a package, you also allow them to benefit from the default access modifier, which provides classes in the same package with access to each other's class information.

Declaring Packages

The syntax for the `package` statement follows:

```
package Identifier;
```

This statement must be placed at the beginning of a compilation unit (a single source file), before any class declarations. Every class located in a compilation unit with a `package` statement is considered part of that package. You can still spread classes out among separate compilation units; just be sure to include a package statement in each.

Packages can be nested within other packages. When this is done, the Java interpreter expects the directory structure containing the executable classes to match the package hierarchy.

Importing Packages

When it comes time to use classes outside of the package you are working in, you must use the `import` statement. The `import` statement enables you to import classes from other packages into a compilation unit. You can import individual classes or entire packages of classes at the same time if you want. The syntax for the `import` statement follows:

```
import Identifier;
```

Identifier is the name of the class or package of classes you are importing. Going back to the `Alien` class as an example, the `color` member variable is an instance of the `Color` object, which is part of the Java AWT (Abstract Windowing Toolkit) class library. For the compiler to understand this member variable type, you must import the `Color` class. You can do this with either of the following statements:

```
import java.awt.Color;
import java.awt.*;
```

The first statement imports the specific class `Color`, which is located in the `java.awt` package. The second statement imports all the classes in the `java.awt` package. Note that the following statement doesn't work:

```
import java.*;
```

This statement doesn't work because you can't import nested packages with the * specification. This wildcard works only when importing all the classes in a particular package, which is still very useful.

There is one other way to import objects from other packages: *explicit package referencing*. By explicitly referencing the package name each time you use an object, you can avoid using an `import` statement. Using this technique, the declaration of the `color` member variable in `Alien` would look like this:

```
java.awt.Color color;
```

Explicitly referencing the package name for an external class is generally not required; it usually serves only to clutter up the class name and can make the code harder to read. The exception to this rule is when two packages have classes with the same name. In this case, you are required to explicitly use the package name with the class names.

Class Visibility

Earlier in this chapter, you learned about access modifiers, which affect the visibility of classes and class members. Because class member visibility is determined relative to classes, you're probably wondering what *visibility* means for a class. Class visibility is determined relative to packages.

For example, a `public` class is visible to classes in other packages. Actually, `public` is the only explicit access modifier allowed for classes. Without the `public` access modifier, classes default to being visible to other classes in a package but not visible to classes outside of the package.

Inner Classes

Most Java classes are defined at the package level, meaning that each class is a member of a particular package. If you don't explicitly specify a package association for a class, the default package is assumed. Classes defined at the package level are known as *top-level classes*. Before Java 1.1, top-level classes were the only types of classes supported. However, Java 1.1 has ushered in a more open-minded approach to class definition. Java 1.1 supports *inner classes*, which are classes that can be defined in any scope. This means that a class can be defined as a member of another class, within a block of statements, or anonymously within an expression.

Although they may seem to be a minor enhancement to the Java language, inner classes actually represent a significant modification. When you consider that inner classes are the *only* modification to the Java language itself in Java 1.1, you'll start to get the picture. The rest of the enhancements introduced with Java 1.1 came in the form of new APIs. Why bother changing the language itself for something as seemingly abstract as inner classes? The answer to this question is not exactly simple. Rather than get into a discussion beyond the scope of this chapter, let me sum up the need for inner classes by saying that the new Java 1.1 AWT event model specifically needed a mechanism like the one provided by inner classes to function properly.

Rules governing the scope of an inner class closely match those governing variables. An inner class's name is not visible outside its scope, except in a fully qualified name (which helps in structuring classes within a package). The code for an inner class can use simple names from enclosing scopes—including class and member variables of enclosing classes—as well as local variables of enclosing blocks. In addition, you can define a top-level class as a static member of another top-level class. Unlike an inner class, a top-level class cannot directly use the instance variables of any other class. The ability to nest classes in this way allows any top-level class to provide a package-style organization for a logically related group of secondary top-level classes.

Following is a simple example of an inner class:

```
public class Outer {
  int x, y;

  public int calcArea() {
    return x * y;
  }
  class Inner {
    int z;
    public int calcVolume() {
      return calcArea() * z;
    }
  }
}
```

In this example, an inner class named Inner is declared within a class called Outer. As you can see, the inner class declaration looks just like a normal (outer) class declaration. Admittedly, this example isn't too useful, but it nevertheless gives you an idea of how inner classes are structured.

NOTE

The support for inner classes in Java 1.1 was provided entirely by the Java compiler and did not require any changes to the Java virtual machine (VM). This is a major part of the reason why the Java architects were willing to modify the Java language to support inner classes because they knew it wouldn't impact the VM.

Interfaces

The last stop on this object-oriented whirlwind tour of Java is a discussion of interfaces. An *interface* is a prototype for a class and is useful from a logical design perspective. This description of an interface may sound vaguely familiar…. Remember abstract classes?

Earlier in this chapter, you learned that an abstract class is a class that has been left partially unimplemented because it uses abstract methods, which are themselves unimplemented. Interfaces are abstract classes that are left completely unimplemented. *Completely unimplemented* in this case means that *no* methods in the class have been implemented. Additionally, interface member data is limited to static final variables, which means that they are constant.

The benefits of using interfaces are much the same as the benefits of using abstract classes. Interfaces provide a means to define the protocols for a class without worrying about the implementation details. This seemingly simple benefit can make large projects much easier to manage; once interfaces have been designed, the class development can take place without worrying about communication among classes.

Another important use of interfaces is the capacity for a class to implement multiple interfaces. This is a twist on the concept of multiple inheritance, which is supported in C++ but not in Java. *Multiple inheritance* enables you to derive a class from multiple parent classes. Although powerful, multiple inheritance is a complex and often tricky feature of C++ that the Java designers decided they could do without. Their workaround was to allow Java classes to implement multiple interfaces.

The major difference between inheriting multiple interfaces and true multiple inheritance is that the interface approach enables you to inherit only method *descriptions*, not *implementations*. If a class implements multiple interfaces, that class must provide all the functionality for the methods defined in the interfaces. Although this approach is certainly more limiting than multiple inheritance, it is still a very useful feature. It is this feature of interfaces that separates them from abstract classes.

Declaring Interfaces

The syntax for creating interfaces follows:

```
interface Identifier {
  InterfaceBody
}
```

`Identifier` is the name of the interface and `InterfaceBody` refers to the abstract methods and static final variables that make up the interface. Because it is assumed that all the methods in an interface are abstract, it isn't necessary to use the `abstract` keyword.

Implementing Interfaces

Because an interface is a prototype, or template, for a class, you must implement an interface to arrive at a usable class. Implementing an interface is similar to deriving from a class, except that you are required to implement any methods defined in the interface. To implement an interface, you use the implements keyword. The syntax for implementing a class from an interface follows:

```
class Identifier implements Interface {
  ClassBody
}
```

Identifier refers to the name of the new class, *Interface* is the name of the interface you are implementing, and *ClassBody* is the new class body. Listing 5.2 contains the source code for Enemy2.java, which includes an interface version of Enemy along with an Alien class that implements the interface.

Listing 5.2. The Enemy interface and Alien class.

```
package Enemy;

import java.awt.Color;

interface Enemy {
  abstract public void move();
  abstract public void move(int x, int y);
}

class Alien implements Enemy {
  protected Color color;
  protected int   energy;
  protected int   aggression;

  public Alien() {
    color = Color.green;
    energy = 100;
    aggression = 15;
  }

  public Alien(Color c, int e, int a) {
    color = c;
    energy = e;
    aggression = a;
  }

  public void move() {
    // move the alien
  }

  public void move(int x, int y) {
    // move the alien to the position x,y
  }
```

```
   public void morph() {
      if (aggression < 10) {
         // morph into a smaller size
      }
      else if (aggression < 20) {
         // morph into a medium size
      }
      else {
         // morph into a giant size
      }
   }
}
```

Summary

This chapter covered the basics of object-oriented programming as well as the specific Java constructs that enable you to carry out object-oriented concepts: classes, packages, and interfaces. You learned the benefits of using classes—and how to implement objects from them. The communication mechanism between objects, messages (methods), were covered. You also learned how inheritance provides a powerful means of reusing code and creating modular designs. You then learned how packages enable you to logically group similar classes together, making large sets of classes easier to manage. Finally, you saw how interfaces provide a template for deriving new classes in a structured manner.

You are now ready to move on to more-advanced features of the Java language, such as threads and multithreading. The next chapter covers exactly these topics.

Threads and Multithreading

by Eric Williams

IN THIS CHAPTER

CHAPTER 6

Multithreading

One of the characteristics that makes Java a powerful programming language is its support for multithreaded programming as an integrated part of the language. This provision is unique because most modern programming languages either do not offer multithreading or provide multithreading as a nonintegrated package. Java, however, offers a single, integrated view of multithreading.

Multithreaded programming is an essential aspect of programming in Java. To master the Java programming language, you should first become familiar with the concepts of multithreaded programming. Then you should learn how multithreaded and concurrent programming are done *in Java.*

This chapter presents a complete introduction and reference to Java threads, including these topics:

- How to write and start your own threads
- A comprehensive reference to the `Thread` and `ThreadGroup` classes
- How to make your classes thread safe
- An introduction to Java monitors
- How to coordinate the actions of multiple threads

> **NOTE**
>
> Multithreading and concurrent programming are unfamiliar concepts for most new Java programmers. If you are familiar with only single-threaded languages like Visual Basic, Delphi, Pascal, Cobol, and so on, you may be worried that threads are too hard to learn. Although learning to use Java threads is not trivial, the model is simple and easy to understand. Threads are a normal everyday aspect of developing Java applications and applets.

What Is a Thread?

In the early days of computing, computers were *single tasking*—that is, they ran a single job at a time. The big, lumbering machine would start one job, run that job to completion, then start the next job, and so on. When engineers became overly frustrated with these batch-oriented systems, they rewrote the programs that ran the machines and thus was born the modern multitasking operating system.

Multitasking refers to a computer's capability to perform multiple jobs concurrently. For the most part, modern operating systems like Windows 95 or Solaris can run two or more programs at the same time. While you are using Netscape to download a big file, you can be running Solitaire in a different window; both programs are running at the same time.

Multithreading is an extension of the multitasking paradigm. But rather than multiple programs, multithreading involves multiple threads of control within a single program. Not only is the operating system running multiple programs, each program can run multiple threads of control—think of threads as subprograms—within the program. For example, using a Web browser, you can print one Web page, download another, and fill out a form in a third—all at the same time.

A *thread* is a single sequence of execution within a program. Until now, you have probably used Java to write single-threaded applications, something like this:

```
class MainIsRunInAThread {
    public static void main(String[] args) {
        // main() is run in a single thread
        System.out.println(Thread.currentThread());
        for (int i=0; i<1000; i++) {
            System.out.println("i == " + i);
        }
    }
}
```

This example is simplistic, but it demonstrates the use of a single Java thread. When a Java application begins, the virtual machine (VM) runs the main() method inside a Java thread. (You have already used Java threads and didn't even know it!) Within this single thread, this simple application's main() method counts from 0 to 999, printing out each value as it is counted.

Programming within a single sequence of control can limit your ability to produce usable Java software. (Imagine using an operating system that could execute only one program at a time, or a Web browser that could load only a single page at a time.) When you write a program, you often want the program to do multiple things at the same time. For example, you may want the program to retrieve an image over the network at the same time it is requesting an updated stock report and also running several animations—and you want all this to occur concurrently. This is the kind of situation in which Java threads become useful.

Java threads allow you to write programs that do many things at once. Each thread represents an independently executing sequence of control. One thread can write a file out to disk while a different thread responds to user keystroke events.

Before jumping into the details about Java threads, let's take a peek at what a multithreaded application looks like. Listing 6.1 modifies the preceding single-threaded application to take advantage of threads. Instead of counting from 0 to 999 in one thread, this application uses five different threads to count from 0 to 999—each thread counts 200 numbers: 0 to 199, 200 to 399, and so on. Don't worry if you don't understand the details of this example yet; it is presented only to introduce you to threads.

Listing 6.1. A simple multithreaded application.

```java
class CountThreadTest extends Thread {
    int from, to;
    public CountThreadTest(int from, int to) {
        this.from = from;
        this.to = to;
    }
    // the run() method is like main() for a thread
    public void run() {
        for (int i=from; i<to; i++) {
            System.out.println("i == " + i);
        }
    }
    public static void main(String[] args) {
        // spawn 5 threads, each of which counts 200 numbers
        for (int i=0; i<5; i++) {
            CountThreadTest t = new CountThreadTest(i*200, (i+1)*200);
            // starting a thread will launch a separate sequence
            // of control and execute the run() method of the thread
            t.start();
        }
    }
}
```

When this application starts, the VM invokes the main() method in its own thread. main() then starts five separate threads to perform the counting operations. Figure 6.1 shows the threads in the CountThreadTest application.

FIGURE 6.1.

Parallel Java threads.

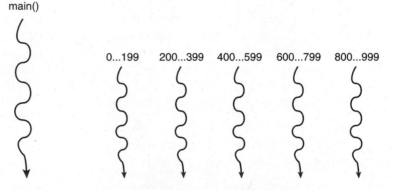

NOTE

Even though multiple threads may appear to perform tasks *at the same time*, technically speaking, this may not be true. Even today, most computers are equipped with a single processor—such computers can perform at most one task at a time. On single-processor systems, the operating system continuously switches between different tasks and threads, allowing each active task or thread to use the CPU for a small amount of time. This subject is discussed in detail in "Thread Scheduling," later in this chapter.

Java Threads

Support for multiple threads of execution is not a Java invention. Threads have been around for a long time and have been implemented in many programming languages. However, programmers have had to struggle with a lack of thread standards. Different platforms have different thread packages, each with a different API. Operating systems do not have uniform support for threads; some support threads in the OS kernel, and some do not. Only recently has a standard emerged for threads—POSIX threads (IEEE standard 1003.1c-1995). However, the POSIX threads standard defines only a C programming interface (not a Java interface) and is not yet widely implemented.

One of the greatest benefits of Java is that it presents the Java programmer with a unified multithreading API—one that is supported by all Java virtual machines on all platforms. When you use Java threads, you do not have to worry about which threading packages are available on the underlying platform or whether the operating system supports kernel threads. The virtual machine isolates you from the platform-specific threading details. The Java threading API is identical on all Java implementations.

Creating New Threads

The first thing you need to know about threads is how to create and run a thread. This process involves two steps: writing the code that is executed in the thread and writing the code that starts the thread.

As discussed earlier, you are already familiar with how to write single-threaded programs. When you write a main() function, that method is executed in a single thread. The Java virtual machine provides a multithreaded environment, but it starts user applications by calling main() in a single thread.

An application's `main()` method provides the central logic for the main thread of the application. Writing the code for a thread is similar to writing `main()`. You must provide a method that implements the main logic of the thread. This method is always named `run()` and has the following signature:

```
public void run();
```

Notice that the `run()` method is not a static method as `main()` is. The `main()` method is static because an application starts with only one `main()` method. But an application may have many threads, so the main logic for a thread is associated with an object—the `Thread` object.

You can provide an implementation for the `run()` method in two ways. Java supports the `run()` method in subclasses of the `Thread` class. Java also supports `run()` through the `Runnable` interface. Both methods for providing a `run()` method implementation are described in the following sections.

Subclassing the Thread Class

This section discusses how to create a new thread by subclassing `java.lang.Thread`.

Let's start with a plausible situation in which a thread might be useful. Suppose that you are building an application; in one part of this application, a file must be copied from one directory to a different directory. But when you run the application, you find that if the file is large, the application stalls during the time that the file is being copied. You determine that the cause of the stall is this: When the application is copying the file, it is unable to respond to user-interface events.

To improve this situation, you decide that the file-copy operation should be performed concurrently, in a separate thread. To move this logic to a thread, you provide a subclass of the `Thread` class that contains this logic, implemented in the `run()` method. The `FileCopyThread` class shown in Listing 6.2 contains this logic.

Listing 6.2. The file-copy logic in `FileCopyThread`.

```
// subclass from Thread to provide your own kind of Thread
class FileCopyThread extends Thread {
    private File from;
    private File to;
    public FileCopyThread(File from, File to) {
        this.from = from;
        this.to = to;
    }
    // implement the main logic of the thread in the run()
    // method [run() is equivalent to an application's main()]
    public void run() {
        FileInputStream in = null;
        FileOutputStream out = null;
        byte[] buffer = new byte[512];
        int size = 0;
```

```
        try {
            // open the input and output streams
            in = new FileInputStream(from);
            out = new FileOutputStream(to);
            // copy 512 bytes at a time until EOF
            while ((size = in.read(buffer)) != -1) {
                out.write(buffer, 0, size);
            }
        } catch(IOException ex) {
            ex.printStackTrace();
        } finally {
            // close the input and output streams
            try {
                if (in != null) { in.close(); }
                if (out != null) { out.close(); }
            } catch (IOException ex) {
            }
        }
    }
}
```

Let's analyze the `FileCopyThread` class. Note that the `FileCopyThread` subclasses from `Thread`. By subclassing from `Thread`, `FileCopyThread` inherits all the state and behavior of a `Thread`— the property of "being a thread."

The `FileCopyThread` class implements the main logic of the thread in the `run()` method. (Remember that the `run()` method is the initial method for a Java thread, just as the `main()` method is the initial method for a Java application.) Within `run()`, the input file is copied to the output file in 512-byte chunks. When a `FileCopyThread` instance is created and started, the entire `run()` method is executed in one separate sequence of control (you'll see how this is done soon).

Now that you are familiar with how to write a `Thread` subclass, you have to learn how to use that class as a separate control sequence within a program. To use a thread, you must *start* the concurrent execution of the thread by calling the `Thread` object's `start()` method. The following code demonstrates how to launch a file-copy operation as a separate thread:

```
File from = getCopyFrom();
File to = getCopyTo();
// create an instance of the thread class
Thread t = new FileCopyThread(from, to);
// call start() to activate the thread asynchronously
t.start();
```

Invoking the `start()` method of a `FileCopyThread` object begins the concurrent execution of that thread. When the thread starts running, its `run()` method is called. In this case, the file copy begins its execution concurrently with the original thread. When the file copy is finished, the `run()` method returns (and the concurrent execution of the thread ends). This process is shown in Figure 6.2.

FIGURE 6.2.
Concurrent file copy.

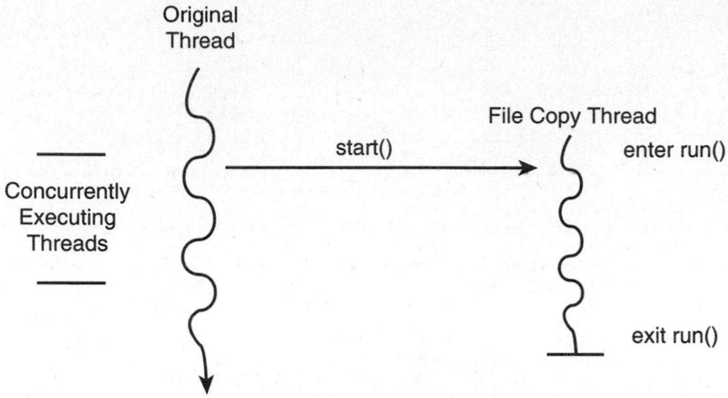

Implementing the Runnable Interface

There are situations in which it is not convenient to create a Thread subclass. For example, you may want to add a run() method to a preexisting class that does not inherit from Thread. The Java Runnable interface makes this possible.

The Java threading API supports the notion of a thread-like entity that is an interface: java.lang.Runnable. Runnable is a simple interface, with only one method:

```
public interface Runnable {
    public void run();
}
```

This interface should look familiar. In the previous section, we covered the Thread class, which also supported the run() method. To subclass Thread, we redefined the Thread run() method. To use the Runnable interface, you must write a run() method and add the text implements Runnable to the class. Reimplementing the FileCopyThread (of the previous example) as a Runnable interface requires few changes:

```
// implementing Runnable is a different way to use threads
class FileCopyRunnable implements Runnable {
    // the rest of the class remains mostly the same
    ...
}
```

To use a Runnable interface as a separate control sequence requires the cooperation of a Thread object. Although the Runnable object contains the main logic, Thread is the only class that encapsulates the mechanism of launching and controlling a thread. To support Runnable, a separate Runnable parameter was added to several of the Thread class constructors. A thread that has been initialized with a Runnable object will call that object's run() method when the thread begins executing.

Here is an example of how to start a thread using FileCopyRunnable:

```
File from = new File("file.1");
File to = new File("file.2");
```

```
// create an instance of the Runnable
Runnable r = new FileCopyRunnable(from, to);
// create an instance of Thread, passing it the Runnable
Thread t = new Thread(r);
// start the thread
t.start();
```

Thread States

Although you have learned a few things about threads, we have not yet discussed one aspect that is critical to your understanding of how threads work in Java—thread states. A Java thread, represented by a Thread object, traverses a fixed set of states during its lifetime (see Figure 6.3).

FIGURE 6.3.

Thread states.

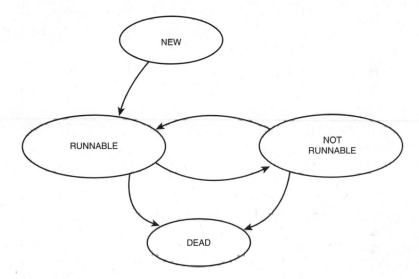

When a Thread object is first created, it is in the NEW state. At this point, the thread is not executing. When you invoke the Thread's start() method, the thread changes to the RUNNABLE state.

When a Java thread is RUNNABLE, it is *eligible* for execution. However, a thread that is RUNNABLE is not necessarily *running*. RUNNABLE implies that the thread is alive and that it can be allocated CPU time by the system when the CPU is available—but the CPU may not always be available. On single-processor systems, Java threads must share the single CPU; additionally, the Java virtual machine task (or process) must also share the CPU with other tasks running on the system. How a thread is allocated CPU time is covered in greater depth in "Scheduling and Priority," later in the chapter.

When certain events happen to a RUNNABLE thread, the thread may enter the NOT RUNNABLE state. When a thread is NOT RUNNABLE, it is still alive, but it is not eligible for execution. The thread is not allocated time on the CPU. Some of the events that may cause a thread to become NOT RUNNABLE include the following:

- The thread is waiting for an I/O operation to complete
- The thread has been put to sleep for a certain period of time (using the `sleep()` method)
- The `wait()` method has been called (as discussed in "Synchronization," later in this chapter)
- The thread has been suspended (using the `suspend()` method)

A NOT RUNNABLE thread becomes RUNNABLE again when the condition that caused the thread to become NOT RUNNABLE ends (I/O has completed, the thread has ended its `sleep()` period, and so on). During the lifetime of a thread, the thread may frequently move between the RUNNABLE and NOT RUNNABLE states.

When a thread terminates, it is said to be DEAD. Threads can become DEAD in a variety of ways. Usually, a thread dies when its `run()` method returns. A thread may also die when its `stop()` or `destroy()` method is called. A thread that is DEAD is permanently DEAD—there is no way to resurrect a DEAD thread.

> **NOTE**
>
> When a thread dies, all the resources consumed by the thread—including the `Thread` object itself—become eligible for reclamation by the garbage collector (if, of course, they are not referenced elsewhere). Programmers are responsible for cleaning up system resources (closing open files, disposing of graphics contexts, and so on) *while* a thread is terminating, but no cleanup is required *after* a thread dies.

The Thread API

The following sections present a detailed analysis of the Java `Thread` API.

Constructors

The `Thread` class has seven different constructors:

```
public Thread();
public Thread(Runnable target);
public Thread(Runnable target, String name);
public Thread(String name);
public Thread(ThreadGroup group, Runnable target);
public Thread(ThreadGroup group, Runnable target, String name);
public Thread(ThreadGroup group, String name);
```

These constructors represent most of the combinations of three different parameters: thread *name*, thread *group*, and a `Runnable` *target* object. To understand the constructors, you must understand the three parameters:

- name is the (string) name to be assigned to the thread. If you fail to specify a name, the system generates a unique name of the form Thread-N, where N is a unique integer.

- target is the Runnable instance whose run() method is executed as the main method of the thread.

- group is the ThreadGroup to which this thread will be added. (The ThreadGroup class is discussed in detail later in this chapter.)

Constructing a new thread does not begin the execution of that thread. To launch the Thread object, you must invoke its start() method.

When creating a thread, the priority and daemon status of the new thread are set to the same values as the thread from which the new thread was created.

> **CAUTION**
>
> Although it is possible to allocate a thread using new Thread(), it is not useful to do so. When constructing a thread directly (without subclassing), the Thread object requires a target Runnable object because the Thread class itself does not contain your application's logic.

Naming

```
public final String getName();
public final void setName(String name);
```

Every Java thread has a name. The name can be set during construction or with the setName() method. If you fail to specify a name during construction, the system generates a unique name of the form Thread-N, where N is a unique integer; the name can be changed later using setName().

The name of a thread can be retrieved using the getName() method.

Thread names are important because they provide the programmer with a useful way to identify particular threads during debugging. You should name a thread in such a way that you (or others) will find the name helpful in identifying the purpose or function of the thread during debugging.

Starting and Stopping

To start and stop threads once you have created them, you need the following methods:

```
public void start();
public final void stop();
public final void stop(Throwable obj);
public void destroy();
```

To begin a new thread, create a new `Thread` object and call its `start()` method. An exception is thrown if `start()` is called more than once on the same thread.

As discussed in "Thread States," earlier in this chapter, there are two main ways a thread can terminate: The thread can return from its `run()` method, ending gracefully. Or the thread can be terminated by the `stop()` or `destroy()` method.

When invoked on a thread, the `stop()` method causes that thread to terminate by throwing an exception *to* the thread (a `ThreadDeath` exception). Calling `stop()` on a thread has the same behavior as executing `throw new ThreadDeath()` within the thread, except that `stop()` can also be called from other threads (whereas the `throw` statement affects only the current thread).

To understand why `stop()` is implemented this way, consider what it means to stop a running thread. Active threads are part of a running program, and each runnable thread is in the middle of *doing* something. It is likely that each thread is consuming system resources: file descriptors, graphics contexts, monitors (to be discussed later), and so on. If stopping a thread caused all activity on the thread to cease immediately, these resources might not be cleaned up properly. The thread would not have a chance to close its open files or release the monitors it has locked. If a thread were stopped at the wrong moment, it would be unable to free these resources; this leads to potential problems for the virtual machine (running out of open file descriptors, for example).

To provide for clean thread shutdown, the thread to be stopped is given an opportunity to clean up its resources. A `ThreadDeath` exception is thrown to the thread, which percolates up the thread's stack and through the exception handlers that are currently on the stack (including `finally` blocks). Monitors are also released by this stack-unwinding process.

Listing 6.3 shows how calling `stop()` on a running thread generates a `ThreadDeath` exception.

Listing 6.3. Generating a ThreadDeath exception with `stop()`.

```
class DyingThread extends Thread {
    // main(), this class is an application
    public static void main(String[] args) {
        Thread t = new DyingThread();           // create the thread
        t.start();                              // start the thread
        // wait for a while
        try { Thread.sleep(100); } catch (InterruptedException e) { }
        t.stop();                               // now stop the thread
    }
    // run(), this class is also a Thread
    public void run() {
        int n = 0;
        PrintStream ps = null;
        try {
            ps = new PrintStream(new FileOutputStream("big.txt"));
            while (true) {                      // forever
                ps.println("n == " + n++);
                try { Thread.sleep(5); } catch (InterruptedException e) { }
            }
```

```
        } catch (ThreadDeath td) {              // watch for the stop()
            System.out.println("Cleaning up.");
            ps.close();                          // close the open file
            // it is very important to rethrow the ThreadDeath
            throw td;
        } catch (IOException e) {
        }
    }
}
```

The DyingThread class has two parts. The main() method spawns a new DyingThread, waits for a period of time, and then sends a stop() to the thread. The DyingThread run() method, which is executed in the spawned thread, opens a file and periodically writes output to that file. When the thread receives the stop(), it catches the ThreadDeath exception and closes the open file. It then rethrows the ThreadDeath exception.

When you run the code shown in Listing 6.3, you see the following output:

```
Cleaning up.
```

> **NOTE**
>
> Java provides a convenient mechanism for programmers to write "cleanup" code—code that is executed when errors occur or when a program or thread terminates. (Cleanup involves closing open files, disposing of graphics contexts, hiding windows, and so on.) Exception handler catch and finally blocks are good locations for cleanup code.
>
> Programmers use a variety of styles to write cleanup code. Some programmers place cleanup code in catch(ThreadDeath td) exception handlers (as was done in Listing 6.3). Others prefer to use catch(Throwable t) exception handlers. Both these methods are good, but writing cleanup code in a finally block is the best solution for most situations. A finally block is executed unconditionally, whether the exception handler exited because of a thrown exception or not. If an exception was thrown, it is automatically rethrown after the finally block has completed.

Although the ThreadDeath solution allows the application a high degree of flexibility, there are problems. By catching the ThreadDeath exception, a thread can actually prevent stop() from having the desired effect. The code to do this is trivial:

```
// prevent stop() from working
catch (ThreadDeath td) {
    System.err.println("Just try to stop me. I'm invincible.");
    // oh no, I've failed to rethrow td
}
```

Calling stop() is not sufficient to guarantee that a thread will end. This is a serious problem for Java-enabled Web browsers; there is no guarantee that an applet will terminate when stop() is invoked on a thread belonging to the applet.

The destroy() method is stronger than the stop() method. The destroy() method is designed to terminate the thread without resorting to the ThreadDeath mechanism. The destroy() method stops the thread immediately, without cleanup; any resources held by the thread are not released.

CAUTION

The destroy() method is not implemented in the Java Development Kit, in all versions up to and including 1.1. Calling this method results in a NoSuchMethodError exception. Although there has been no comment about when this method will be implemented, it is likely that it will not become available until JavaSoft can implement it in a way that cleans up the dying thread's environment (locked monitors, pending I/O, and so on).

Scheduling and Priority

Thread *scheduling* is defined as the mechanism used to determine how RUNNABLE threads are allocated CPU time (that is, when they actually get to execute for a period of time on the computer's CPU). In general, scheduling is a complex subject that uses terms such as *preemptive, round-robin scheduling, priority-based scheduling, time-sliced*, and so on.

A thread-scheduling mechanism is either *preemptive* or *nonpreemptive*. With preemptive scheduling, the thread scheduler preempts (pauses) a running thread to allow different threads to execute. A nonpreemptive scheduler never interrupts a running thread; instead, the nonpreemptive scheduler relies on the running thread to *yield* control of the CPU so that other threads can execute. Under nonpreemptive scheduling, other threads may *starve* (never get CPU time) if the running thread fails to yield.

Among thread schedulers classified as preemptive, there is a further classification. A preemptive scheduler can be either *time-sliced* or *nontime-sliced*. With time-sliced scheduling, the scheduler allocates a period of time for which each thread can use the CPU; when that amount of time has elapsed, the scheduler preempts the thread and switches to a different thread. A nontime-sliced scheduler does not use elapsed time to determine when to preempt a thread; it uses other criteria such as priority or I/O status.

Different operating systems and thread packages implement a variety of scheduling policies. But Java is intended to be platform independent. The correctness of a Java program should not depend on what platform the program is running on, so the designers of Java decided to isolate the programmer from most platform dependencies by providing a single guarantee about thread scheduling: *The highest priority* RUNNABLE *thread is always selected for execution above lower priority threads.* (When multiple threads have equally high priorities, only one of those threads is guaranteed to be executing.)

Java threads are guaranteed to be preemptive, but not time sliced. If a higher priority thread (higher than the current thread) becomes RUNNABLE, the scheduler preempts the current thread. However, if an equal or lower priority thread becomes RUNNABLE, there is no guarantee that the new thread will ever be allocated CPU time until it becomes the highest priority RUNNABLE thread.

> **NOTE**
>
> The current implementation of the Java VM uses different thread packages on different platforms; thus, the behavior of the Java thread scheduler varies slightly from platform to platform. It is best to check with your Java VM supplier to determine whether the VM uses native threads and whether the platform's native threads are time sliced (some native threading packages, most notably Solaris threads, are not time sliced).

Even though Java threads are not guaranteed to be time sliced, this should not be a problem for the majority of Java applications and applets. Java threads release control of the CPU when they become NOT RUNNABLE. If a thread is waiting for I/O, is sleeping, or is waiting to enter a monitor, the thread scheduler will select a different thread for execution. Generally, only threads that perform intensive numerical analysis (without I/O) will be a problem. A thread would have to be coded like the following example to prevent other threads from running (and such a thread would starve other threads only on some platforms—on Windows NT, for example, other threads would still be allowed to run):

```
int i = 0;
while (true) {
    i++;
}
```

There are a variety of techniques you can implement to prevent one thread from consuming too much CPU time:

- Don't write code such as `while (true) { }`. It is acceptable to have infinite loops—as long as what takes place inside the loop involves I/O, `sleep()`, or interthread coordination (using the `wait()` and `notify()` methods, discussed later in this chapter).
- Occasionally call `Thread.yield()` when performing operations that are CPU intensive. The `yield()` method allows the scheduler to spend time executing other threads.
- Lower the priority of CPU-intensive threads. Threads with a lower priority run only when the higher priority threads have nothing to do. For example, the Java garbage collector thread is a low priority thread. Garbage collection takes place when there are no higher priority threads that need the CPU; this way, garbage collection does not needlessly stall the system.

By using these techniques, your applications and applets will be well behaved on any Java platform.

Setting Thread Priority

```
public final static int MAX_PRIORITY = 10;
public final static int MIN_PRIORITY = 1;
public final static int NORM_PRIORITY = 5;
public final int getPriority();
public final void setPriority(int newPriority);
```

Every thread has a priority. When a thread is created, it inherits the priority of the thread that created it. The priority can be adjusted subsequently using the setPriority() method. The priority of a thread can be obtained using getPriority().

There are three symbolic constants defined in the Thread class that represent the range of priority values: MIN_PRIORITY, NORM_PRIORITY, and MAX_PRIORITY. The priority values range from 1 to 10, in increasing priority. An exception is thrown if you attempt to set priority values outside this range.

Waking Up a Thread

```
public void interrupt();
public static boolean interrupted();
public boolean isInterrupted();
```

To send a wake-up message to a thread, call interrupt() on its Thread object. Calling interrupt() causes an InterruptedException to be thrown in the thread and sets a flag that can be checked by the running thread using the interrupted() or isInterrupted() method. Calling Thread.interrupted() checks the interrupt status of the current thread and resets the interrupt status to false (in versions before 1.1, the interrupt status is not reset). Calling isInterrupted() on a Thread object (which can be other than the current thread) checks the interrupt status of that thread but does not change the status.

The interrupt() method is useful in waking a thread from a blocking operation such as I/O, wait(), or an attempt to enter a synchronized method.

CAUTION

The interrupt() method is not fully implemented in the JDK 1.0.x. Calling interrupt() on a thread sets the interrupted flag but does not throw an InterruptedException or end a blocking operation in the target thread; threads must check interrupted() to determine whether the thread has been interrupted.

The interrupt() method is fully implemented in the Java virtual machine, version 1.1.

Suspending and Resuming Thread Execution

```
public final void suspend();
public final void resume();
```

Sometimes, it is necessary to pause a running thread. You can do so using the suspend() method. Calling the suspend() method ensures that a thread will not be run. The resume() method reverses the suspend() operation.

A call to suspend() puts the thread in the NOT RUNNABLE state. However, calling resume() does not guarantee that the target thread will become RUNNABLE; other events may have caused the thread to be NOT RUNNABLE (or DEAD).

Putting a Thread to Sleep

```
public static void sleep(long millisecond);
public static void sleep(long millisecond, int nanosecond);
```

To pause the current thread for a specified period of time, call one of the varieties of the sleep() method. For example, Thread.sleep(500) pauses the current thread for half a second, during which time the thread is in the NOT RUNNABLE state. When the specified time expires, the current thread again becomes RUNNABLE.

> **CAUTION**
>
> In the JDK versions 1.0.x and 1.1, the sleep(int *millisecond*, int *nanosecond*) method uses the *nanosecond* parameter to round the *millisecond* parameter to the nearest millisecond. Sleeping is not yet supported in nanosecond granularity.

Making a Thread Yield

```
public static void yield();
```

The yield() method is used to give a hint to the thread scheduler that now would be a good time to run other threads. If many threads are RUNNABLE and waiting to execute, the yield() method is guaranteed to switch to a different RUNNABLE thread only if the other thread has at least as high a priority as the current thread.

Waiting for a Thread to End

```
public final void join();
public final void join(long millisecond);
public final void join(long millisecond, int nanosecond);
```

Programs sometimes have to wait for a specific thread to terminate; this is referred to as *joining* the thread. To wait for a thread to terminate, invoke one of the join() methods on its Thread object. For example:

```
Thread t = new OperationINeedDoneThread();
t.start();
....            // do some other stuff
t.join();       // wait for the thread to complete
```

The two join() methods with time parameters are used to specify a timeout for the join() operation. If the thread does not terminate within the specified amount of time, join() returns anyway. To determine whether a timeout has happened, or whether the thread has ended, use the Thread method isAlive().

join() with no parameters waits forever for the thread to terminate.

> **CAUTION**
>
> In the JDK versions 1.0.x and 1.1, the join(int *millisecond*, int *nanosecond*) method uses the *nanosecond* parameter to round the *millisecond* parameter to the nearest millisecond. Joining is not yet supported in nanosecond granularity.

Understanding Daemon Threads

```
public final boolean isDaemon();
public final void setDaemon(boolean on);
```

Some threads are intended to be "background" threads, providing service to other threads. These threads are referred to as *daemon threads*. When only daemon threads remain alive, the Java virtual machine process exits.

The Java virtual machine has at least one daemon thread, known as the garbage collection thread. The garbage collection thread is a low priority thread, executing only when there is nothing else for the system to do.

The setDaemon() method sets the daemon status of this thread. The isDaemon() method returns true if this thread is a daemon thread; it returns false otherwise.

Miscellaneous Thread Methods

The countStackFrames() method returns the number of active stack frames (method activations) currently on this thread's stack. The thread must be suspended when this method is invoked. Following is this method's signature:

```
public int countStackFrames();
```

The getThreadGroup() method returns the ThreadGroup class to which this thread belongs. A thread is always a member of a single ThreadGroup class. Following is this method's signature:

```
public final ThreadGroup getThreadGroup();
```

The isAlive() method returns true if start() has been called on this thread and if this thread has not yet died. In other words, isAlive() returns true if this thread is RUNNABLE or NOT RUNNABLE and false if this thread is NEW or DEAD. Following is this method's signature:

```
public final boolean isAlive();
```

The `currentThread()` method returns the `Thread` object for the current sequence of execution. Following is this method's signature:

```
public static Thread currentThread();
```

The `activeCount()` method returns the number of threads in the currently executing thread's `ThreadGroup` class. Following is this method's signature:

```
public static int activeCount();
```

The `enumerate()` method returns (through the `tarray` parameter) a list of all threads in the current thread's `ThreadGroup` class. Following is this method's signature:

```
public static int enumerate(Thread tarray[]);
```

The `dumpStack()` method is used for debugging. It prints a method-by-method list of the stack trace for the current thread to the `System.err` output stream. Following is this method's signature:

```
public static void dumpStack();
```

The `toString()` method returns a debugging string that describes this thread. Following is this method's prototype:

```
public String toString();
```

The `ThreadGroup` API

Each Java thread belongs to exactly one `ThreadGroup` instance. The `ThreadGroup` class is used to assist with the organization and management of similar groups of threads. For example, thread groups can be used by Web browsers to group all threads belonging to a single applet. Single commands can be used to manage the entire group of threads belonging to the applet.

`ThreadGroup` objects form a tree-like structure; groups can contain both threads and other groups. The top thread group is named `system`; it contains several system-level threads (such as the garbage collector thread). The `system` group also contains the `main` `ThreadGroup` object; the `main` group contains a `main` `Thread`—the thread in which `main()` is run. Figure 6.4 is a graphical representation of the `ThreadGroup` tree.

Constructors

The `ThreadGroup` class has two constructors. Both constructors require that you specify a name for the new thread group. One of the constructors takes a reference to the parent group of the new `ThreadGroup`; the constructor that does not take the *parent* parameter uses the group of the currently executing thread as the parent of the new group.

```
public ThreadGroup(String name);
public ThreadGroup(ThreadGroup parent, String name);
```

Initially, the new `ThreadGroup` object contains no threads or other thread groups.

FIGURE 6.4.

The ThreadGroup *tree.*

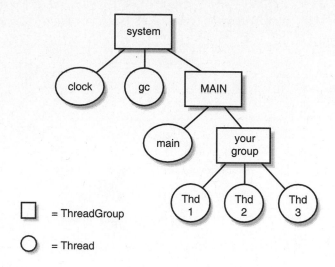

Thread Helper Methods

The ThreadGroup class contains a few methods that operate on the threads within the group. These methods are "helper" in nature; they invoke the same-named Thread method on all threads within the group (recursively, to thread groups within this group).

```
public final void suspend();
public final void resume();
public final void stop();
public final void destroy();
```

The helper methods include suspend(), resume(), stop(), and destroy(). Here is an example of how to stop an entire group of threads with a single method call:

```
ThreadGroup group = new ThreadGroup("client threads");
while (some_condition) {
    Thread t = new Thread(group);
    t.start();
    ...
}
...
if (kill_em_all) {    // stop all of the threads
    group.stop();
}
```

The other thread group helper methods can be called in a similar manner.

Priority

ThreadGroup trees can assist in the management of thread priority. After calling setMaxPriority() on a ThreadGroup object, no thread within the group's tree can use setPriority() to set a priority higher than the specified maximum value. (Priorities of threads already in the group are not affected.)

```
public final int getMaxPriority();
public final void setMaxPriority(int pri);
```

The `getMaxPriority()` method returns the maximum priority value of this `ThreadGroup` tree.

ThreadGroup Tree Navigation

Each thread group can contain both threads and thread groups. The `activeCount()` and `activeCountGroup()` methods return the number of contained threads and groups, respectively. Following are the method signatures:

```
public int activeCount();
public int activeGroupCount();
```

The `activeCount()` method returns the number of threads that are members of this `ThreadGroup` tree (recursively).

The `activeCountGroup()` method returns the number of `ThreadGroups` that are members of this `ThreadGroup` tree (recursively).

The following `enumerate()` methods can be used to retrieve the list of threads or groups in this `ThreadGroup` object:

```
public int enumerate(Thread list[]);
public int enumerate(Thread list[], boolean recurse);
public int enumerate(ThreadGroup list[]);
public int enumerate(ThreadGroup list[], boolean recurse);
```

The `recurse` parameter, if `true`, causes the retrieval of all the threads or groups within this `ThreadGroup` tree (recursively). If *recurse* is `false`, only the threads or groups in this immediate `ThreadGroup` object are retrieved. The `enumerate()` methods lacking the `recurse` parameter perform in the same way as the `enumerate()` methods with `recurse` set to `true`.

The `parentOf()` method returns `true` if this thread group is the parent of the specified group; it returns `false` otherwise. Following is this method's syntax:

```
public final boolean parentOf(ThreadGroup g);
```

The `getParent()` method returns the parent of this thread group, or `null` if this `ThreadGroup` is the top-level `ThreadGroup`. Following is this method's syntax:

```
public final ThreadGroup getParent();
```

The `list()` method prints debugging information about this `ThreadGroup`'s tree (threads and groups) to `System.out`. Following is this method's syntax:

```
public void list();
```

Miscellaneous `ThreadGroup` Methods

The `getName()` method returns the name of this thread group. Following is this method's syntax:

```
public final String getName();
```

Some thread groups, like some threads, can be referred to as *daemons*. When a `ThreadGroup` object is a daemon group (`setDaemon(true)` has been called), the group is destroyed once all its threads and groups have been removed.

```
public final boolean isDaemon();
public final void setDaemon(boolean daemon);
```

The `isDaemon()` method returns `true` if this thread group is a daemon; it returns `false` otherwise.

The `toString()` method returns debugging information about this thread group. Following is this method's syntax:

```
public String toString();
```

When a thread exits because it failed to catch an exception, the `uncaughtException()` method of the thread's group is invoked with the `Thread` object and the exception (`Throwable`) as parameters:

```
public void uncaughtException(Thread t, Throwable e);
```

The default behavior of `uncaughtException()` is to pass the thread and exception to the parent of this thread group. The `system` thread group, if reached, calls the `Throwable` exception's `printStackTrace()` method, dumping the stack trace of the exception to `System.err`.

Security Features

Threads and thread groups are considered critical system resources that must be protected by Java's security features. The precise implementation of the security policy depends on the environment. When running a Java application, there is no security unless you install a `SecurityManager` using `System.setSecurityManager()`. Applets, however, use the `SecurityManager` installed by the browser environment. When you run an applet under Netscape Navigator 3.0, for example, the applet is allowed to modify only the threads and thread groups created by the current applet; attempts to modify other threads or groups result in a `SecurityException`.

The `Thread` class has security (as implemented by the current `SecurityManager` object) implemented for the following methods:

- `Thread(ThreadGroup group)`
- `Thread(ThreadGroup group, Runnable target, String name)`
- `Thread(ThreadGroup group, String name)`
- `stop()`

- ■ suspend() and resume()
- ■ setPriority()
- ■ setName()
- ■ setDaemon()

The ThreadGroup class has security (as implemented by the current SecurityManager object) implemented for the following methods:

- ■ ThreadGroup(ThreadGroup *parent*, String *name*)
- ■ setDaemon()
- ■ setMaxPriority()
- ■ stop()
- ■ suspend() and resume()
- ■ destroy()

Concurrency

One of the most powerful features of the Java programming language is that it can run multiple threads of control. Performing multiple tasks at the same time seems natural from the user's perspective—for example, simultaneously downloading a file from the Internet, performing a spreadsheet recalculation, and printing a document. From a programmer's point of view, however, managing concurrency is not as natural as it seems. Concurrency requires the programmer to take special precautions to ensure that Java objects are accessed in a thread-safe manner.

There is nothing *obvious* about threads that makes threaded programs unsafe; nevertheless, threaded programs can be subject to hazardous situations unless you take appropriate measures to make them safe.

The following example demonstrates how a threaded program can be *unsafe*:

```java
public class Counter {
    private int count = 0;
    public int incr() {
        int n = count;
        count = n + 1;
        return n;
    }
}
```

As Java classes go, the Counter class is simple, having only one attribute and one method. As its name implies, the Counter class is used to count things, such as the number of times a button is pressed or the number of times the user visits a particular Web site. The incr() method is the heart of the class, returning and incrementing the current value of the counter. However, the incr() method has a problem; it is a source of unpredictable behavior in a multithreaded environment.

Consider a situation in which a Java program has two runnable threads, both of which are about to execute this line of code (affecting the same `Counter` object):

```
int cnt = counter.incr();
```

The programmer cannot predict or control the order in which these two threads are run. The Java thread scheduler has full authority over thread scheduling. There are no guarantees about which thread will receive CPU time, when the threads will execute, or how long each thread will be allowed to execute. Either thread may be interrupted by the scheduler at any time (remember that Java's thread scheduler is preemptive). On a multiprocessor machine, both threads may execute concurrently on separate processors.

Table 6.1 describes one possible sequence of execution of the two threads. In this scenario, the first thread is allowed to run until it completes its call to `counter.incr()`; then the second thread does the same. There are no surprises in this scenario. The first thread increments the `Counter` value to 1, and the second thread increments the value to 2.

Table 6.1. Counter scenario I.

Thread 1	*Thread 2*	*Count*
`cnt = counter.incr();`	——	0
`n = count;      // 0`	——	0
`count = n + 1; // 1`	——	1
`return n;      // 0`	——	1
——	`cnt = counter.incr();`	1
——	`n = count;      // 1`	1
——	`count = n + 1;  // 2`	2
——	`return n;      // 1`	2

Table 6.2 describes a somewhat different sequence of execution. In this scenario, the first thread is interrupted by a *context switch* (a switch to a different thread) during execution of the `incr()` method. The first thread remains temporarily suspended, and the second thread is allowed to proceed. The second thread executes its call to the `incr()` method, incrementing the `Counter` value to 1. When the first thread resumes, a problem becomes evident. The `Counter`'s value is not updated to the value 2, as you would expect, but is instead set again to the value 1.

Table 6.2. Counter scenario II.

Thread 1	*Thread 2*	*Count*
`cnt = counter.incr();`	——	0
`n = count;      // 0`	——	0

Thread 1	*Thread 2*	*Count*
——	`cnt = counter.incr();`	0
——	`n = count;      // 0`	0
——	`count = n + 1;  // 1`	1
——	`return n;       // 0`	1
`count = n + 1; // 1`	——	1
`return n;      // 0`	——	1

By examining Thread 1 in Table 6.2, you can see a problematic sequence of operations. After entering the `incr()` method, the value of the `count` attribute (`0`) is stored in a local variable, `n`. The thread is then suspended for a period of time while a different thread executes. (It is important to note that the `count` attribute is modified by the second thread during this time.) When Thread 1 resumes, it stores the value `n + 1` (`1`) back in the `count` attribute. Unfortunately, this is no longer a correct value for the counter because the counter was already incremented to `1` by Thread 2.

The problem outlined by Table 6.2 is called a *race condition*—the outcome of the program is affected by the order in which the program's threads are allocated CPU time. It is usually considered inappropriate to allow race conditions to affect a program's result. Consider a medical device that monitors a patient's blood pressure. If this device were affected by race conditions in its software, it might report an incorrect reading to the physician. The physician would base medical treatment decisions on incorrect information—a bad situation for the patient, doctor, insurance company, and software vendor!

All multithreaded programs, even Java programs, can suffer from race conditions. Fortunately, Java provides the programmer with the necessary tools to manage concurrency—monitors.

Monitors

Many texts on computer science and operating systems deal with the issue of concurrent programming. Concurrency has been the subject of much research over the years, and many concurrency-control solutions have been proposed and implemented. These solutions include the following:

- Critical sections
- Semaphores
- Mutexes
- Database record locking
- Monitors

Java implements a variant of the monitor approach to concurrency.

The concept of a *monitor* was introduced by C. A. R. Hoare in a 1974 paper published in the *Communications of the ACM*. Hoare described a special-purpose object, called a monitor, which applies the principle of mutual exclusion to groups of procedures (*mutual exclusion* is a fancy way of saying "one thread at a time"). In Hoare's model, each group of procedures requiring mutual exclusion is placed under the control of a single monitor. At run time, the monitor allows only one thread at a time to execute a procedure controlled by the monitor. If another thread tries to invoke a procedure controlled by the monitor, that thread is suspended until the first thread completes its call.

Java monitors remain true to Hoare's original concept, with a few minor variations (which are not discussed here). Monitors in Java enforce mutually exclusive access to methods; more specifically, Java monitors enforce mutually exclusive access to synchronized methods. (The synchronized keyword is an optional method modifier. If the synchronized keyword appears before the return type and signature of the method, the method is referred to as a "synchronized method.")

Every Java object has an associated monitor. synchronized methods that are invoked on an object use that object's monitor to limit concurrent access to that object. When a synchronized method is invoked on an object, the object's monitor is consulted to determine whether any other thread is currently executing a synchronized method on the object. If no other thread is executing a synchronized method on that object, the current thread is allowed to *enter* the monitor. (Entering a monitor is also referred to as *locking* the monitor, or *acquiring ownership of* the monitor.) If a different thread has already entered the monitor, the current thread must wait until the other thread *leaves* the monitor.

Metaphorically, a Java monitor acts as an object's gatekeeper. When a synchronized method is called, the gatekeeper allows the calling thread to pass and then closes the gate. While the thread is still in the synchronized method, subsequent synchronized method calls to that object from other threads are blocked. Those threads line up outside the gate, waiting for the first thread to leave. When the first thread exits the synchronized method, the gatekeeper opens the gate, allowing a single waiting thread to proceed with its synchronized method call. The process repeats.

In plain English, a Java monitor enforces a one-at-a-time approach to concurrency. This is also known as *serialization* (not to be confused with "object serialization," which is the Java library for reading and writing objects on a stream).

NOTE

Programmers already familiar with multithreaded programming in a different programming language often confuse monitors with *critical sections*. Java monitors are not like traditional critical sections. Declaring a method synchronized does not imply that only one thread at a time can execute that method, as is the case with a critical section. Monitors imply that only one thread can invoke that method (or any synchronized method) on a particular object at any given time. Java monitors are associated with objects, not with blocks of code. Two threads can concurrently execute the same synchronized method, provided that the method is invoked on different objects (that is, a.method() and b.method(), where a != b).

To demonstrate how monitors operate, let's rewrite the Counter example from the preceding section to take advantage of monitors, using the synchronized keyword:

```java
public class Counter2 {
    private int count = 0;
    public synchronized int incr() {
        int n = count;
        count = n + 1;
        return n;
    }
}
```

Note that the incr() method has not been modified except for the addition of the synchronized keyword.

What would happen if this new Counter2 class were used in the scenario presented in Table 6.2 (the race condition)? The outcome of the same sequence of context switches is listed in Table 6.3.

Table 6.3. Counter scenario II, revised.

Thread 1	*Thread 2*	*Count*
cnt = counter.incr();	——	0
(acquires the monitor)	——	0
n = count; // 0	——	0
——	cnt = counter.incr();	0
——	(can't acquire monitor)	0
count = n + 1; // 1	(blocked)	1
return n; // 0	(blocked)	1
(releases the monitor)	(blocked)	1
——	(acquires the monitor)	1
——	n = count; // 1	1
——	count = n + 1; // 2	2
——	return n; // 1	2
——	(releases the monitor)	2

In Table 6.3, the sequence of operations begins the same as the scenario in Table 6.2. Thread 1 starts executing the incr() method of the Counter2 object but is interrupted by a context switch. In this example, however, when Thread 2 attempts to execute the incr() method on the same Counter2 object, the thread can't acquire the monitor and is blocked; the monitor is already owned by Thread 1. Thread 2 is suspended until the monitor becomes available. When Thread 1 releases the monitor, Thread 2 can then acquire the monitor and continue running.

The synchronized keyword is Java's solution to the concurrency control problem. As you saw in the Counter example, the potential race condition was eliminated by adding the synchronized modifier to the incr() method. All accesses to the incr() method of a counter were serialized by the addition of the synchronized keyword. Generally speaking, any method that modifies an object's attributes should be synchronized with the synchronized keyword.

> **NOTE**
>
> You may be wondering when you will see an actual monitor object. Anecdotal information has been presented about monitors, but you probably want to see some official documentation about what a monitor is and how you access it. Unfortunately, that is not possible. Java monitors have no official standing in the language specification, and their implementation is not directly visible to the programmer. Monitors are not Java objects—they have no attributes or methods. Monitors are a concept beneath Java's implementation of multithreading and concurrency. It is possible to access Java monitors at the native code level in the 1.x release of the Java virtual machine from Sun—the 1.1 Java Native Interface specification defines two methods that operate on monitors: MonitorEnter() and MonitorExit().

Non-synchronized Methods

Java monitors are used only in conjunction with synchronized methods. Methods that are not declared synchronized do not attempt to acquire ownership of an object's monitor before executing—they ignore monitors entirely. At any given moment, at most one thread can execute a synchronized method on an object, but an arbitrary number of threads can execute non-synchronized methods. This can lead to some surprising situations if you are not careful in deciding which methods should be synchronized. Consider the Account class in Listing 6.4.

Listing 6.4. The Account class.

```
class Account {
  private int balance;
  public Account(int balance) {
    this.balance = balance;
  }
  public synchronized void transfer(int amount, Account destination) {
    synchronized (destination) {
```

```
      this.withdraw(amount);
      Thread.yield();        // force a context switch
      destination.deposit(amount);
    }
  }
  public synchronized void withdraw(int amount) {
    if (amount > balance) {
      throw new RuntimeException("No overdraft protection!");
    }
    balance -= amount;
  }
  public synchronized void deposit(int amount) {
    balance += amount;
  }
  public int getBalance() {
    return balance;
  }
}
```

The attribute-modifying methods of the Account class are declared synchronized, but the getBalance() method is not synchronized. It appears that this class has no problem with race conditions—but it does!

To understand the race condition to which the Account class is subject, consider how a bank deals with accounts. To a bank, the correctness of its accounts is of the utmost importance—a bank that makes accounting errors or reports incorrect information would not have happy customers. To avoid reporting incorrect information, a bank would likely disable "inquiries" on an account while a transaction involving the account is in progress. This prevents the customer from viewing the result of a partially complete transaction. In Listing 6.4, the Account class's getBalance() method is not synchronized, and this can lead to problems.

Consider two Account objects and two different threads performing actions on these accounts. One thread is performing a balance transfer from one account to the other. The second thread is performing a balance inquiry. This code demonstrates the suggested activity:

```
public class XferTest implements Runnable {
  public static void main(String[] args) {
    XferTest xfer = new XferTest();
    xfer.a = new Account(100);
    xfer.b = new Account(100);
    xfer.amount = 50;
    Thread t = new Thread(xfer);
    t.start();
    Thread.yield();        // force a context switch
    System.out.println("Inquiry: Account a has : $" + xfer.a.getBalance());
    System.out.println("Inquiry: Account b has : $" + xfer.b.getBalance());
  }
  public Account a = null;
  public Account b = null;
  public int amount = 0;
```

```
    public void run() {
      System.out.println("Before xfer: a has : $" + a.getBalance());
      System.out.println("Before xfer: b has : $" + b.getBalance());
      a.transfer(amount, b);
      System.out.println("After xfer: a has : $" + a.getBalance());
      System.out.println("After xfer: b has : $" + b.getBalance());
    }
}
```

In this example, two Accounts are created, each with a $100 balance. A transfer is then initiated to move $50 from one account to the other. The transfer is not an operation that should affect the total balance of the two accounts; that is, the sum of the balance of the two accounts should remain constant at $200. If the balance inquiry is performed at just the right time, however, it is possible that the total amount of funds in these accounts could be incorrectly reported. If this program is run using the JDK version 1.0 for Solaris, the following output is printed:

```
Before xfer: a has : $100
Before xfer: b has : $100
Inquiry: Account a has : $50
Inquiry: Account b has : $100
After xfer: a has : $50
After xfer: b has : $150
```

The inquiry reports that the first account contains $50 and the second account contains $100. That's not $200! What happened to the other $50? Nothing has "happened" to the money—except that it is in the process of being transferred to the second account when the balance inquiry scans the accounts. Because the getBalance() method is not synchronized, a customer would have no problem executing an inquiry on accounts involved in the balance transfer. The lack of synchronization can leave some customer wondering why the accounts are $50 short.

If the getBalance() method is declared synchronized, the application has a different result. The modified code follows:

```
public synchronized int getBalance() {
return balance;
}
```

The balance inquiry is blocked until the balance transfer is complete. Here is the modified program's output:

```
Before xfer: a has : $100
Before xfer: b has : $100
Inquiry: Account a has : $50
Inquiry: Account b has : $150
After xfer: a has : $50
After xfer: b has : $150
```

Advanced Monitor Concepts

Monitors sound pretty simple. Add the synchronized modifier to your methods, and that's all there is to it. Well, not quite. Monitors themselves may be simple, but taken together with the rest of the programming environment, there are a few issues you should understand before you use synchronized methods. The following sections present a few tips and techniques you should master to become expert in concurrent Java programming.

static synchronized Methods

Methods that are declared synchronized attempt to acquire ownership of the target object's monitor. But what about static methods (methods that do not have an associated object)?

The language specification is fairly clear, if brief, about static synchronized methods. When a static synchronized method is called, the monitor acquired is said to be a *per-class* monitor—that is, there is one monitor for each class that regulates access to all static methods of that class. Only one static synchronized method in a class can be active at a given moment.

The synchronized Statement

It is not possible to use synchronized methods on some types of objects. For example, it is not possible to add *any* methods to Java array objects (much less synchronized methods). To get around this restriction, Java has a second way of interacting with an object's monitor. The synchronized *statement* is defined to have the following syntax:

```
synchronized ( Expression ) Statement
```

Executing a synchronized statement has the same effect as calling a synchronized method—ownership of an object's monitor is acquired before a block of code can be executed. With the synchronized statement, the object whose monitor is up for grabs is the object resulting from Expression (which must be an object type, not an elemental type like int, double, and so on).

One of the most important uses of the synchronized statement involves controlling access to array objects. The following example demonstrates how to use the synchronized statement to provide thread-safe access to an array:

```
void safe_lshift(byte[] array, int count) {
    synchronized(array) {
        System.arraycopy(array, count, array, 0, array.size - count);
    }
}
```

Before modifying the array in this example, the virtual machine assigns ownership of array's monitor to the currently executing thread. Other threads trying to acquire array's monitor are forced to wait until the array-copy operation is complete. Of course, accesses to the array that are not guarded by a synchronized statement are not blocked; so be careful!

The synchronized statement is also useful when modifying an object's public variables directly. Here's an example:

```
void call_method(SomeClass obj) {
    synchronized(obj) {
        obj.variable = 5;
    }
}
```

PUBLIC OR NOT?

There is debate within the Java community about the potential danger of declaring attributes to be public. When concurrency is considered, it becomes apparent that public attributes can lead to thread-unsafe code. Here's why: public attributes can be accessed by any thread without the benefit of protection by a synchronized method. When you declare an attribute public, you relinquish control over updates to that attribute; any programmer using your code has a license to access (and update) public attributes directly.

In general, it is not a good idea to declare non-final attributes to be public. Not only can doing so introduce thread-safety problems, it can make your code difficult to modify and support in later revisions.

Note, however, that Java programmers frequently define immutable symbolic constants as public final class attributes (such as Event.ACTION_EVENT). Attributes declared this way do not have thread-safety issues. (Race conditions involve only objects whose values can be modified.)

When Not to Be synchronized

By now, you should be able to write thread-safe code using the synchronized keyword. When should you really use the synchronized keyword? Are there situations in which you should *not* use synchronized? Are there drawbacks to using synchronized?

The most common reason developers don't use synchronized is that they write single-threaded, single-purpose code. For example, CPU-bound tasks do not benefit much from multithreading. A compiler does not perform much better if it is threaded. The Java compiler from Sun does not contain many synchronized methods. For the most part, it assumes that it is executing in its own thread of control, without having to share its resources with other threads.

Another common reason for avoiding synchronized methods is that they do not perform as well as non-synchronized methods. In simple tests in the JDK version 1.0.1 from Sun, synchronized methods have been shown to be three to four times slower than their non-synchronized counterparts. Although this doesn't mean your entire application will be three or four times slower, it is a performance issue nonetheless. Some programs demand that every ounce of performance be squeezed out of the runtime system. In this situation, it may be appropriate to avoid the performance overhead associated with synchronized methods.

Java 1.1 Inner Classes

With the release of Java 1.1, Java now supports *inner classes* (refer to Chapter 5, "Classes, Packages, and Interfaces," for an introduction to inner classes). Inner classes are classes declared within another class. An instance of an inner class has a special relationship to an instance of the outer class—referred to as the *enclosing instance*. Inner-class instances are permitted to access all the fields of the enclosing instance, including `private` fields. Additionally, an inner-class instance can modify the variables of its enclosing instance.

Inner classes introduce potential problems for programs that use threads. Consider the following example of an inner class and an enclosing class:

```
public class Enclosing {
  private int privateVar = 1;
  public synchronized void update() {
    privateVar = privateVar + 1;
  }
  public class Inner {
    public synchronized void update() {
      privateVar = privateVar + 1;
    }
  }
}
```

The `Enclosing` class has three fields: a `private` variable, a synchronized method, and the `Inner` class. This example demonstrates that the `private` variables of an enclosing instance can be updated from methods of the enclosing instance *and* the inner instance—both `Enclosing` and `Inner` have an `update()` method that modifies `privateVar`.

Calling a synchronized method from the enclosing instance is a safe way to update the enclosing instance:

```
Enclosing enclosingInstance = getEnclosingInstance();
enclosingInstance.update();       // SAFE
```

However, it is not particularly safe to call a synchronized method from an inner instance to update the enclosing instance:

```
Enclosing enclosingInstance = getEnclosingInstance();
Enclosing.Inner innerInstance = enclosingInstance.new Inner();
innerInstance.update();           // UNSAFE
```

This second code example is unsafe because the use of inner classes involves more than one object—and thus, more than one monitor. When the code `innerInstance.update()` is called, the only monitor acquired is that of the `innerInstance`. The monitor of the `enclosingInstance` is never acquired, even though its `privateVar` is updated. To make the code thread safe, the `Inner` class's `update()` method should acquire the monitor of its enclosing instance, like this:

```
class Inner {
  public synchronized void update() {
    synchronized (Enclosing.this) {      // must also lock the enclosing instance
      privateVar = privateVar + 1;
    }
  }
}
```

In general, inner classes that access variables from an enclosing instance should use the `synchronized` statement to lock the enclosing instance while its variables are being accessed. The generalized form for this type of lock follows:

```
synchronized (name-of-enclosing-class . this) {
  // your code here
}
```

Deadlocks

Sometimes referred to as a *deadly embrace*, a *deadlock* is one of the worst situations that can happen in a multithreaded environment. Java programs are not immune to deadlocks, and programmers must take care to avoid them.

A deadlock is a situation that causes two or more threads to *hang*, that is, to be unable to proceed. In the simplest case, two threads are each trying to acquire a monitor that is already owned by the other thread. Each thread goes to sleep, waiting for the desired monitor to become available—but the monitors never become available. (The first thread waits for the monitor owned by the second thread, and the second thread waits for the monitor owned by the first thread. Because each thread is waiting for the other, it never releases its monitor to the other thread.)

The sample application in Listing 6.5 should give you an understanding of how a deadlock happens.

Listing 6.5. A deadlock.

```
public class Deadlock implements Runnable {
  public static void main(String[] args) {
        Deadlock d1 = new Deadlock();
        Deadlock d2 = new Deadlock();
        Thread t1 = new Thread(d1);
        Thread t2 = new Thread(d2);
        d1.grabIt = d2;
        d2.grabIt = d1;
        t1.start();
        t2.start();
        try { t1.join(); t2.join(); } catch(InterruptedException e) { }
        System.exit(0);
  }
  Deadlock grabIt;
  public synchronized void run() {
        try { Thread.sleep(2000); } catch(InterruptedException e) { }
        grabIt.sync_method();
  }
  public synchronized void sync_method() {
        try { Thread.sleep(2000); } catch(InterruptedException e) { }
        System.out.println("in sync_method");
  }
}
```

In this class, main() launches two threads, each of which invokes the synchronized run() method on a Deadlock object. When the first thread wakes up, it attempts to call the sync_method() of the other Deadlock object. Obviously, the second Deadlock's monitor is owned by the second thread, so the first thread begins waiting for the monitor. When the second thread wakes up, it tries to call the sync_method() of the first Deadlock object. Because that Deadlock's monitor is already owned by the first thread, the second thread begins waiting. Because the threads are waiting for each other, neither will ever wake up.

NOTE

If you run the deadlock application shown in Listing 6.5, you will notice that it never exits. That is understandable; after all, that is what a deadlock is. How can you tell what is really going on inside the virtual machine? There is a trick you can use with the Solaris/UNIX JDK to display the status of all threads and monitors: Press Ctrl+\ in the terminal window in which the Java application is running. This action sends the virtual machine a signal to dump the state of the VM. Here is a partial listing of the monitor table dumped several seconds after launching the deadlock application:

```
Deadlock@EE300840/EE334C20 (key=0xee300840):      monitor owner: "Thread-5"
    Waiting to enter:
        "Thread-4"
Deadlock@EE300838/EE334C18 (key=0xee300838):      monitor owner: "Thread-4"
    Waiting to enter:
        "Thread-5"
```

Numerous algorithms are available for preventing and detecting deadlock situations, but those algorithms are beyond the scope of this chapter (many database and operating system texts cover deadlock-detection algorithms in detail). Unfortunately, the Java virtual machine itself does not perform any deadlock detection or notification. There is nothing that prevents the virtual machine from doing so, however, so this behavior may be added to future versions of the virtual machine.

Using volatile

It is worth mentioning that the volatile keyword is supported as a variable modifier in Java. The language specification states that the volatile qualifier instructs the compiler to generate loads and stores on each access to an attribute, rather than caching the value in a register. The intent of the volatile keyword is to provide thread-safe access to an attribute, but volatile falls short of this goal.

In the 1.x JDK virtual machine, the volatile keyword is ignored. It is unclear whether volatile has been abandoned in favor of monitors and synchronized methods or whether the keyword was included solely for a C and C++ look and feel. Regardless, volatile is useless—use synchronized methods rather than the volatile keyword.

Synchronization

After learning how synchronized methods are used to make Java programs thread safe, you may wonder what the big deal is about monitors. They are just object locks, right? Not true! Monitors are more than locks; monitors are also used to coordinate multiple threads by using the wait() and notify() methods available in every Java object.

The Need for Thread Coordination

In a Java program, threads are often interdependent—one thread can depend on another thread to complete an operation or to service a request. For example, a spreadsheet program can run an extensive recalculation as a separate thread. If a user-interface (UI) thread attempts to update the spreadsheet's display, the UI thread should coordinate with the recalculation thread, starting the screen update only when the recalculation thread has successfully completed.

There are many other situations in which it is useful to coordinate two or more threads. The following list identifies only some of the possibilities:

- **Shared buffers are often used to communicate data between threads.** In this scenario, one thread writes to a shared buffer (the writer) and one thread reads from the buffer (the reader). When the reader thread attempts to read from the buffer, it should coordinate with the writer thread, retrieving data from the shared buffer only after the writer thread has put it there. If the buffer is empty, the reader thread should wait for the data. The writer thread notifies the reader thread when it has completed filling the buffer so that the reader can continue.

- **Many threads may have to perform an identical action, such as loading an image file across the network.** These threads can reduce the overall system load if only one thread performs the work while the other threads wait for the work to be completed. (The waiting threads must wait without consuming CPU time by temporarily transitioning into the NOT RUNNABLE thread state; this is possible, and is discussed later in this chapter.) This is precisely the model used in the java.awt.MediaTracker class.

It is no accident that the previous examples repeatedly use the words *wait* and *notify*. These words express the two concepts central to thread coordination: A thread *waits* for some condition or event to occur, and you *notify* a waiting thread that a condition or event has occurred. The words *wait* and *notify* are also used in Java as the names of the methods you call to coordinate threads: wait() and notify(), in class Object.

As noted in "Monitors," earlier in this chapter, every Java object has an associated monitor. That fact turns out to be useful at this point because monitors are also used to implement Java's thread-coordination primitives. Although monitors are not directly visible to the programmer, an API is provided in class Object that enables you to interact with an object's monitor. This API consists of two methods: wait() and notify().

Conditions, `wait()`, and `notify()`

Threads are usually coordinated using a concept known as a condition, or a condition variable. A *condition* is a logical statement that must hold true in order for a thread to proceed; if the condition does not hold true, the thread must wait for the condition to become true before continuing. In Java, this pattern is usually expressed as follows:

```
while ( ! the_condition_I_am_waiting_for ) {
    wait();
}
```

First, check to see whether the desired condition is already true. If it is true, there is no need to wait. If the condition is not yet true, call the `wait()` method. When `wait()` ends, recheck the condition to make sure that it is now true.

Invoking `wait()` on an object pauses the current thread and adds the thread to the *condition variable wait queue* of the object's monitor. This queue contains a list of all the threads that are currently blocked inside `wait()` on that object. The thread is not removed from the wait queue until `notify()` is invoked on that object from a different thread. A call to `notify()` wakes a single waiting thread, notifying the thread that a condition of the object has changed.

There are two additional varieties of the `wait()` method. The first version takes a single parameter—a timeout value in milliseconds. The second version has two parameters—a more precise timeout value, specified in milliseconds *and* nanoseconds. These methods are used when you do not want to wait indefinitely for an event. If you want to abandon the wait after a fixed period of time (referred to as *timing out*), you should use either of the following methods:

- `wait(long milliseconds);`
- `wait(long milliseconds, int nanoseconds);`

Unfortunately, these methods do not provide a way to determine how the `wait()` was ended—whether a `notify()` occurred or whether the method timed out. This is not a big problem, however, because you can recheck the wait condition and the system time to determine which event has occurred.

> **CAUTION**
>
> In the JDK versions 1.0.x and 1.1, the `wait(int millisecond, int nanosecond)` method uses the *nanosecond* parameter to round the *millisecond* parameter to the nearest millisecond. Waiting is not yet supported in nanosecond granularity.

The `wait()` and `notify()` methods must be invoked from within a `synchronized` method or from within a `synchronized` statement. This requirement is discussed in further detail in "Monitor Ownership," later in this chapter.

A Thread Coordination Example

A classic example of thread coordination used in many computer science texts is the *bounded buffer* problem. This problem involves using a fixed-size memory buffer to communicate between two processes or threads. To solve this problem, you must coordinate the reader and writer threads so that the following are true:

- When the writer thread attempts to write to a full buffer, the writer is suspended until some items are removed from the buffer.

- When the reader thread removes items from the full buffer, the writer thread is notified of the buffer's changed condition and may continue writing.

- When the reader thread attempts to read from an empty buffer, the reader is suspended until some items are added to the buffer.

- When the writer adds items to the empty buffer, the reader thread is notified of the buffer's changed condition and may continue reading.

The following class listings demonstrate a Java implementation of the bounded buffer problem. There are three main classes in this example: the `Producer`, the `Consumer`, and the `Buffer`. Let's start with the `Producer`:

```
public class Producer implements Runnable {
  private Buffer buffer;
  public Producer(Buffer b) {
      buffer = b;
  }
  public void run() {
     for (int i=0; i<250; i++) {
          buffer.put((char)('A' + (i%26)));   // write to the buffer
      }
  }
}
```

The `Producer` class implements the `Runnable` interface (which should give you a hint that it will be used in a `Thread`). When the `Producer`'s `run()` method is invoked, 250 characters are written in rapid succession to a buffer.

The `Consumer` class is as simple as the `Producer`:

```
public class Consumer implements Runnable {
  private Buffer buffer;
  public Consumer(Buffer b) {
      buffer = b;
  }
  public void run() {
      for (int i=0; i<250; i++) {
        System.out.println(buffer.get());   // read from the buffer
      }
  }
}
```

The Consumer is also a Runnable interface. Its run() method greedily reads 250 characters from a buffer.

The Buffer class has been mentioned already, including two of its methods: put(char) and get(). Listing 6.6 shows the Buffer class in its entirety.

Listing 6.6. The Buffer class.

```java
public class Buffer {
  private char[] buf;   // buffer storage
  private int last;     // last occupied position
  public Buffer(int sz) {
      buf = new char[sz];
      last = 0;
  }
  public boolean isFull()  { return (last == buf.length); }
  public boolean isEmpty() { return (last == 0);          }
  public synchronized void put(char c) {
      while(isFull()) {                       // wait for room to put stuff
        try { wait(); } catch(InterruptedException e) { }
      }
      buf[last++] = c;
      notify();
  }
  public synchronized char get() {
      while(isEmpty()) {                      // wait for stuff to read
        try { wait(); } catch(InterruptedException e) { }
      }
      char c =  buf[0];
      System.arraycopy(buf, 1, buf, 0, —last);
      notify();
      return c;
  }
}
```

NOTE

When you first begin using wait() and notify(), you may notice a contradiction. The wait() and notify() methods must be called from synchronized methods, so if wait() is called inside a synchronized method, how can a different thread enter a synchronized method in order to call notify()? Doesn't the waiting thread own the object's monitor, preventing other threads from entering the synchronized method?

The answer to this paradox is that wait() temporarily releases ownership of the object's monitor; before wait() can return, however, it must reacquire ownership of the monitor. By releasing the monitor, the wait() method allows other threads to acquire the monitor (which gives them the ability to call notify()).

The `Buffer` class is just that—a storage buffer. You can use `put()` to put items into the buffer (in this case, characters), and you can use `get()` to get items out of the buffer.

Note the use of `wait()` and `notify()` in these methods. In the `put()` method, a `wait()` is performed while the buffer is full; no more items can be added to the buffer while it is full. At the end of the `get()` method, the call to `notify()` ensures that any thread waiting in the `put()` method will be activated and allowed to continue adding an item to the buffer. Similarly, a `wait()` is performed in the `get()` method if the buffer is empty; no items can be removed from an empty buffer. The `put()` method calls `notify()` to ensure that any thread waiting in `get()` will be wakened.

> **NOTE**
>
> Java provides two classes similar to the `Buffer` class presented in this example. These classes, `java.io.PipedOutputStream` and `java.io.PipedInputStream`, are useful in communicating streams of data between threads. If you unpack the `src.zip` file shipped with the JDK, you can examine these classes to see how they handle interthread coordination.

Advanced Thread Coordination

The `wait()` and `notify()` methods simplify the task of coordinating multiple threads in a concurrent Java program. However, to make full use of these methods, you should understand a few additional details. The following sections present more material about thread coordination in Java.

Monitor Ownership

The `wait()` and `notify()` methods have one major restriction you must observe: You can call these methods only when the current thread owns the monitor of the object. Most frequently, `wait()` and `notify()` are invoked from within a `synchronized` method, as in the following example:

```
public synchronized void method() {
    ...
    while (!condition) {
      wait();
    }
    ...
}
```

In this case, the `synchronized` modifier guarantees that the thread invoking the `wait()` call already owns the monitor when it calls `wait()`.

If you attempt to call `wait()` or `notify()` without first acquiring ownership of the object's monitor (for example, from a non-synchronized method), the virtual machine throws an

IllegalMonitorStateException. The following example demonstrates what happens when you call wait() without first acquiring ownership of the monitor:

```
public class NonOwnerTest {
  public static void main(String[] args) {
        NonOwnerTest not = new NonOwnerTest();
        not.method();
  }
  public void method() {
        try { wait(); } catch(InterruptedException e) { }   // a bad thing to do!
  }
}
```

If you run this Java application, the following text is printed to the terminal:

```
java.lang.IllegalMonitorStateException: current thread not owner
        at java.lang.Object.wait(Object.java)
        at NonOwnerTest.method(NonOwnerTest.java:10)
        at NonOwnerTest.main(NonOwnerTest.java:5)
```

When you invoke the wait() method on an object, you must own the object's monitor if you are to avoid this exception.

MONITORS AND THE synchronized STATEMENT

All Java objects can participate in thread synchronization by using the wait() and notify() methods. However, the "monitor ownership" requirement introduces a quirk for some object types, such as arrays. (Strangely enough, Java array types inherit from the java.lang.Object class, where the wait() and notify() methods are defined.) The wait() and notify() methods can be called on Java array objects, but monitor ownership must be established using the synchronized statement rather than a synchronized method. The following code demonstrates monitor usage as applied to a Java array:

```
// wait for an event on this array
Object[] array = getArray();
synchronized (array) {
  array.wait();
}
...
// notify waiting threads
Object[] array = getArray();
synchronized (array) {
  array.notify();
}
```

Multiple Waiters

It is possible for multiple threads to be waiting on the same object. This can happen when multiple threads wait for the same event. For example, recall the Buffer class described earlier; the buffer was operated on by a single Producer and a single Consumer. What would happen if there were multiple Producers? If the buffer filled, different Producers might attempt to use put() to place items into the buffer; they would all block inside the put() method, waiting for a Consumer to come along and free up space in the buffer.

When you call notify(), there may be zero, one, or more threads blocked in a wait() on the monitor. If there are no threads waiting, the call to notify() is a *no-op*—it does not affect any other threads. If there is a single thread in wait(), that thread is notified and begins waiting for the monitor to be released by the thread that called notify(). If two or more threads are in a wait(), the virtual machine picks a single waiting thread and notifies that thread. (The method used to "pick" a waiting thread varies from platform to platform—your programs should not rely on the VM to select a specific thread from the pool of waiting threads.)

Using notifyAll()

In some situations, you may want to notify *every* thread currently waiting on an object. The Object API provides a method to do this: notifyAll(). The notify() method wakes only a single waiting thread, but the notifyAll() method wakes every thread currently waiting on the object.

When would you want to use notifyAll()? Consider the java.awt.MediaTracker class. This class is used to track the status of images being loaded over the network. Multiple threads may wait on the same MediaTracker object, waiting for all the images to be loaded. When the MediaTracker detects that all images have been loaded, notifyAll() is called to inform every waiting thread that the images have been loaded. notifyAll() is used because the MediaTracker does not know how many threads are waiting; if notify() were used, some of the waiting threads may not receive notification that the transfer was completed. These threads would continue waiting, probably hanging the entire applet.

Listing 6.6, earlier in this chapter, can also benefit from the use of notifyAll(). In that code, the Buffer class used the notify() method to send a notification to a single thread waiting on an empty or a full buffer. However, there was no guarantee that only a single thread was waiting; multiple threads may have been waiting for the same condition. Listing 6.7 shows a modified version of the Buffer class (named Buffer2) that uses notifyAll().

Listing 6.7. The Buffer2 class, using notifyAll().

```
public class Buffer2 {
  private char[] buf;                    // storage
  private int last = 0;                  // last occupied position
  private int writers_waiting = 0;  // # of threads waiting in put()
  private int readers_waiting = 0;  // # of threads waiting in get()
  public Buffer2(int sz) {
        buf = new char[sz];
}
  public boolean isFull()  { return (last == buf.length); }
  public boolean isEmpty() { return (last == 0);          }
```

```
public synchronized void put(char c) {
      while(isFull()) {
         try     { writers_waiting++;  wait(); }
         catch   (InterruptedException e) { }
         finally { writers_waiting--; }
      }
      buf[last++] = c;
      if (readers_waiting > 0) {
         notifyAll();
      }
}
public synchronized char get() {
      while(isEmpty()) {
         try     { readers_waiting++;  wait(); }
         catch   (InterruptedException e) { }
         finally { readers_waiting--; }
      }
      char c =  buf[0];
      System.arraycopy(buf, 1, buf, 0, --last);
      if (writers_waiting > 0) {
         notifyAll();
      }
      return c;
   }
}
```

The get() and put() methods have been made more intelligent. They now check to see whether any notification is necessary and then use notifyAll() to broadcast an event to all waiting threads.

Summary

This chapter was a whirlwind tour of multithreaded programming in Java. Among other things, the chapter covered the following:

- Creating your own thread classes by subclassing Thread or implementing Runnable
- Using the ThreadGroup class to manage groups of threads
- Understanding thread states and thread scheduling
- Making your classes thread-safe by using the synchronized keyword to protect objects from concurrent modification
- Understanding how monitors affect concurrent programming in Java
- Coordinating the actions of multiple threads by calling the wait() and notify() methods

Java threads are not difficult to use. After reading this chapter, you should begin to see how threads can be used to improve your everyday Java programming.

Exception Handling

by David R. Chung

IN THIS CHAPTER

CHAPTER 7

Errors are a normal part of programming. Some of these errors are flaws in a program's basic design or implementation—these are called *bugs*. Other types of errors are not really bugs; rather, they are the result of situations like low memory or invalid filenames.

The way you handle the second type of error determines whether they become bugs. Unfortunately, if your goal is to produce robust applications, you probably find yourself spending more time handling errors than actually writing the core of your application.

Java's exception-handling mechanism lets you handle errors without forcing you to spend most of your energy worrying about them.

What Is an Exception?

As the name implies, an *exception* is an exceptional condition. An exception is something out of the ordinary. Most often, exceptions are used as a way to report error conditions. Exceptions can be used as a means of indicating other situations as well. This chapter concentrates primarily on exceptions as an error-handling mechanism.

Exceptions provide notification of errors and a way to handle them. This control structure allows you to specify exactly where to handle specific types of errors.

NOTE

Other languages like C++ and Ada provide exception handling. Java's exception handling is similar to the one used by C++.

Tennyson Understood the Problem

In his poem, *Charge of the Light Brigade*, Andrew Lord Tennyson describes an actual battle. In this battle, a cavalry brigade is ordered to attack a gun emplacement. It turns out that the valley they attack is a trap. There are big guns on three sides, and the brave soldiers on horseback with their sabers are massacred. The poem describes an actual battle from the Crimean War.

The battle as Tennyson describes it highlights a classic problem. Someone (probably far from the front) had given the order to attack. The men who led the charge became aware very quickly that an error had been made. Unfortunately, they did not have the authority to do anything about it. In Tennyson's immortal words, "Theirs not to reason why, theirs but to do and die: into the valley of Death rode the 600."

Using exceptions in Java allows you to determine exactly who handles an error. In fact, low-level functions can detect errors while higher-level functions decide what to do about them. Exceptions provide a way to communicate information about errors up through the chain of methods until one of them can handle it.

If Exceptions Are the Answer, What Is the Question?

Most procedural languages like C and Pascal do not use exception handling. In these languages, a variety of techniques are used to determine whether an error has occurred. The most common means of error checking is the function's return value.

Consider the problem of calculating the retail cost of an item and displaying it. For this example, the retail cost is twice the wholesale cost:

```
int retailCost( int wholesale ) {
    if ( wholesale <= 0 ) {
        return 0 ;
    }
    return (wholesale * 2 ) ;
}
```

The `retailCost()` method takes the wholesale price of an item and doubles it. If the wholesale price is negative or zero, the function returns zero to indicate that an error has occurred. This method can be used in an application as follows:

```
int wholesalePrice = 30 ;
int retailPrice    = 0 ;
retailPrice = retailCost( wholesalePrice ) ;
System.out.println( "Wholesale price = " + wholesalePrice ) ;
System.out.println( "Retail price = "     + retailPrice ) ;
```

In this example, the `retailCost()` method calculates the correct retail cost and prints it. The problem is that the code segment never checks whether the `wholesalePrice` variable is negative. Even though the method checks the value of `wholesalePrice` and reports an error, there is nothing that forces the calling method to deal with the error. If this method is called with a negative `wholesalePrice` value, the function blindly prints invalid data. Therefore, no matter how diligent you are in ensuring that your methods return error values, the callers of your methods are free to ignore them.

You can prevent bad values from being printed by putting the whole operation in a method. The `showRetail()` method takes the wholesale price, doubles it, and prints it. If the wholesale price is negative or zero, the method does not print anything and returns the `boolean` value `false`:

```
boolean showRetail( int wholesale ) {
    if ( wholesale <= 0 ) {
        return false ;
    }
    int retailPrice ;
    retailPrice = wholesalePrice * 2 ;
    System.out.println( "Wholesale price = " + wholesale ) ;
    System.out.println( "Retail price = "     + retailPrice ) ;
    return true ;
}
```

Using this new and improved method guarantees that *bad* values are never printed. However, once again, the caller does not have to check to see whether the method returned true.

The fact that the caller can choose to ignore return values is not the only problem with using return values to report errors. What happens if your method returns a boolean and both true and false are valid return values? How does this method report an error?

Consider a method to determine whether a student passes a test. The pass() method takes the number of correct answers and the number of questions. The method calculates the percentage; if it is greater than 70 percent, the student passes. Consider the passingGrade() method:

```
boolean passingGrade( int correct, int total ) {
    boolean returnCode = false ;
    if ( (float)correct / (float)total > 0.70 ) {
        returnCode = true ;
    }
return returnCode ;
}
```

In this example, everything works fine as long as the method arguments are well behaved. What happens if the number correct is greater than the total? Or worse, if the total is zero (because this causes a division by zero in the method.) By relying on return values in this case, there is *no way* to report an error in this function.

Exceptions prevent you from making your return values do double duty. Exceptions allow you to use return values to return only useful information from your methods. Exceptions also *force* the caller to deal with errors—because exceptions cannot be ignored.

Some Terminology

Exception handling can be viewed as a nonlocal control structure. When a method *throws* an exception, its caller must determine whether it can *catch* the exception. If the calling method can catch the exception, it takes over and execution continues in the caller. If the calling method cannot catch the exception, the exception is passed on to *its* caller. This process continues until either the exception is caught or the top (or bottom, depending on how you look at it) of the call stack is reached and the application terminates because the exception has not been caught.

Java exceptions are class objects subclassed from java.lang.Throwable. Because exceptions are class objects, they can contain both data and methods. In fact, the base class Throwable implements a method that returns a String describing the error that caused the exception. This is useful for debugging and if you want to give users a meaningful error message.

Don't Throw Up Your Hands— throw an Exception

The passingGrade() method presented in the preceding section was unable to report an error condition because all its possible return values were valid. Adding exception handling to the method makes it possible to uncouple the reporting of results from the reporting of errors.

The first step is to modify the passingGrade() method definition to include the throws clause. The throws clause lists the types of exceptions that can be thrown by the method. In the following revised code, the method throws only an exception of type Exception:

```
static boolean passingGrade( int correct, int total ) throws Exception {
    boolean returnCode = false ;
```

The rest of the method remains largely unchanged. This time, the method checks to see whether its arguments make sense. Because this method determines passing grades, it would be unreasonable to have more correct responses than total responses. Therefore, if there are more correct responses than total responses, the method throws an exception.

The method instantiates an object of type Exception. The Exception constructor takes a String parameter. The string contains a message that can be retrieved when the exception is caught. The throw statement terminates the method and gives its caller the opportunity to catch it:

```
    if( correct > total ) {
        throw new Exception( "Invalid values" ) ;
    }
    if ( (float)correct / (float)total > 0.70 ) {
        returnCode = true ;
    }
    return returnCode ;
}
```

throw, try, and catch Blocks

To respond to an exception, the call to the method that produces it must be placed within a try block. A try block is a block of code beginning with the try keyword followed by a left and right curly brace. Every try block is associated with one or more catch blocks. Here is a try block:

```
try
    {
    // method calls go here
    }
```

7

EXCEPTION HANDLING

If a method is to catch exceptions thrown by the methods it calls, the calls must be placed within a try block. If an exception is thrown, it is handled in a catch block. Different catch blocks handle different types of exceptions. This is a try block and a catch block set up to handle exceptions of type Exception:

```
try
    {
    // method calls go here
    }
catch( Exception e )
    {
    // handle exceptons here
    }
```

When any method in the try block throws any type of exception, execution of the try block ceases. Program control passes immediately to the associated catch block. If the catch block can handle the given exception type, it takes over. If it cannot handle the exception, the exception is passed to the method's caller. In an application, this process goes on until a catch block catches the exception or the exception reaches the main() method uncaught and causes the application to terminate.

An Exceptional Example

Because *all* Java methods are class members, the passingGrade() method is incorporated in the gradeTest application class. Because main() calls passingGrade(), main() must be able to catch any exceptions passingGrade() might throw. To do this, main() places the call to passingGrade() in a try block. Because the throws clause lists type Exception, the catch block catches the Exception class. Listing 7.1 shows the entire gradeTest application.

Listing 7.1. The gradeTest application.

```
import java.io.* ;
import java.lang.Exception ;
public class gradeTest {
    public static void main( String[] args ) {
        try
            {
            // the second call to passingGrade throws
            // an exception so the third call never
            // gets executed
            System.out.println( passingGrade( 60,  80 ) ) ;
            System.out.println( passingGrade( 75,   0 ) ) ;
            System.out.println( passingGrade( 90, 100 ) ) ;
            }
        catch( Exception e )
            {
            System.out.println( "Caught exception -" +
                            e.getMessage() ) ;
            }
    }
```

```
    static boolean passingGrade( int correct, int total )
                                  throws Exception {
        boolean returnCode = false ;
        if( correct > total ) {
            throw new Exception( "Invalid values" ) ;
        }
        if ( (float)correct / (float)total > 0.70 ) {
            returnCode = true ;
        }
        return returnCode ;
    }
}
```

The second call to passingGrade() fails in this case because the method checks to see whether the number of correct responses is less than the total responses. When passingGrade() throws an exception, control passes to the main() method. In this example, the catch block in main() catches the exception and prints Caught exception - Invalid values.

Multiple catch Blocks

In some cases, a method may have to catch different types of exceptions. Java supports multiple catch blocks. Each catch block must specify a different type of exception:

```
try
    {
    // method calls go here
    }
catch( SomeExceptionClass e )
    {
    // handle SomeExceptionClass exceptions here
    }
catch( SomeOtherExceptionClass e )
    {
    // handle SomeOtherExceptionClass exceptions here
}
```

When an exception is thrown in the try block, it is caught by the first catch block of the appropriate type. Only one catch block in a given set will be executed. Notice that the catch block looks a lot like a method declaration. The exception caught in a catch block is a local reference to the actual exception object. You can use this exception object to help determine what caused the exception to be thrown in the first place.

Does Every Method Have to Catch Every Exception?

What happens if a method calls another method that throws an exception but chooses not to catch it? In the example in Listing 7.2, main() calls foo(), which in turn calls bar(). bar() lists Exception in its throws clause; because foo() is not going to catch the exception, it must also have Exception in its throws clause. The application in Listing 7.2 shows a method, foo(), that ignores exceptions thrown by the called method.

7

EXCEPTION
HANDLING

Listing 7.2. A method that ignores exceptions thrown by the method it calls.

```java
import java.io.* ;
import java.lang.Exception ;
public class MultiThrow {
    public static void main( String[] args ) {
        try
            {
            foo() ;
            }
        catch( Exception e )
            {
            System.out.println( "Caught exception " +
                                  e.getMessage() ) ;
            }
    }
    static void foo() throws Exception {
        bar() ;
    }
    static void bar() throws Exception {
        throw new Exception( "Who cares" ) ;
    }
}
```

In the example in Listing 7.3, main() calls foo() which calls bar(). Because bar() throws an exception and doesn't catch it, foo() has the opportunity to catch it. The foo() method has no catch block, so it cannot catch the exception. In this case, the exception propagates up the call stack to foo()'s caller, main().

Listing 7.3. A method that catches and rethrows an exception.

```java
import java.io.* ;
import java.lang.Exception ;
public class MultiThrow {
    public static void main( String[] args ) {
        try
            {
            foo() ;
            }
        catch( Exception e )
            {
            System.out.println( "Caught exception " +
                                  e.getMessage() ) ;
            }
    }
    static void foo() throws Exception {
        try
            {
            bar() ;
            }
        catch( Exception e )
            {
            System.out.println( "Re throw exception - " +
                                  e.getMessage() ) ;
```

```
            throw e ;
        }    }
    static void bar() throws Exception {
        throw new Exception( "Who cares" ) ;
    }
}
```

The foo() method calls bar(). The bar() method throws an exception and foo() catches it. In this example, foo() simply *rethrows* the exception, which is ultimately caught in the application's main() method. In a *real* application, foo() could do some processing and then rethrow the exception. This arrangement allows both foo() and main() to handle the exception.

The finally Clause

Java introduces a new concept in exception handling: the finally clause. The finally clause sets apart a block of code that is always executed. Here's an example of a finally clause:

```
import java.io.* ;
import java.lang.Exception ;
public class MultiThrow {
    public static void main( String[] args ) {
        try
            {
            alpha() ;
            }
        catch( Exception e }
            {
            System.out.println( "Caught exception " ) ;
            }
        finally()
            {
            System.out.println( "Finally. " ) ;
            }
    }
}
```

In normal execution (that is, when no exceptions are thrown), the finally block is executed immediately after the try block. When an exception is thrown, the finally block is executed before control passes to the caller.

If alpha() throws an exception, it is caught in the catch block and *then* the finally block is executed. If alpha() does not throw an exception, the finally block is executed after the try block. If any code in a try block is executed, the finally block is executed as well.

The Throwable Class

All exceptions in Java are subclassed from the class Throwable. If you want to create your own exception classes, you must subclass Throwable. Most Java programs do not have to subclass their own exception classes.

Following is the `public` portion of the class definition of `Throwable`:

```
public class Throwable {
    public Throwable() ;
    public Throwable(String message) ;
    public String getMessage()
    public String toString() ;
    public void printStackTrace() ;
    public void printStackTrace(
                        java.io.PrintStream s) ;
    private native void printStackTrace0(
                        java.io.PrintStream s);
    public native Throwable fillInStackTrace();
}
```

The constructor takes a string that describes the exception. Later, when an exception is thrown, you can call the `getMessage()` method to get the error string that was reported.

Types of Exceptions

The methods of the Java API and the language itself also throw exceptions. These exceptions can be divided into two classes: `Exception` and `Error`.

Both the `Exception` and `Error` classes are derived from `Throwable`. `Exception` and its subclasses are used to indicate conditions that may be recoverable. `Error` and its subclasses indicate conditions that are generally not recoverable and that should cause your applet to terminate.

The various packages included in the Java Development Kit throw different kinds of `Exception` and `Error` exceptions, as described in the following sections.

java.awt Exceptions

The AWT classes have members that throw one error and two exceptions:

- `AWTException` (exception in AWT)
- `IllegalComponentStateException` (a component is not in the proper state for a requested operation)
- `AWTError` (error in AWT)

java.awt.datatransfer Exception

Classes of the AWT data transfer package may throw this exception:

- `UnsupportedFlavorException` (data in improper format)

> **NOTE**
>
> In the JDK 1.1 data transfer model, Java uses the word *Flavor* in place of the more common term *Format*.

java.beans Exceptions

The classes of the java.beans package throw the following exceptions:

- IntrospectionException (unable to resolve object during introspection)
- PropertyVetoException (illegal property change)

java.io Exceptions

The classes in the java.io package throw a variety of exceptions, as shown in Table 7.1 and Figure 7.1. Any classes that work with I/O are good candidates to throw recoverable exceptions. For example, activities such as opening files or writing to files are likely to fail from time to time. The classes of the java.io package do not throw errors at all.

Table 7.1. The java.io exceptions.

Exception	Cause
CharConversionException	Root class for character conversion exceptions
IOException	Root class for I/O exceptions
EOFException	End of file
FileNotFoundException	Unable to locate file
InterruptedIOException	I/O operation was interrupted; contains a member bytesTransferred that indicates how many bytes were transferred before the operation was interrupted
InvalidClassException	Class is not valid for serialization
InvalidObjectException	Class explicitly forbids serialization
NotActiveException	Serialization not active
NotSerializableException	Class may not be serialized
ObjectStreamException	Root class for object stream exceptions

continues

Table 7.1. continued

Exception	Cause
OptionalDataException	Contains data members to indicate end of file or optional data to read
StreamCorruptedException	Stream fails internal consistency test
SyncFailedException	Synchronization failed
UTFDataFormatException	Malformed UTF-8 string
UnsupportedEncodingException	Character-encoding mechanism not supported
WriteAbortException	Exception in stream

Figure 7.1.

The java.io *exception hierarchy.*

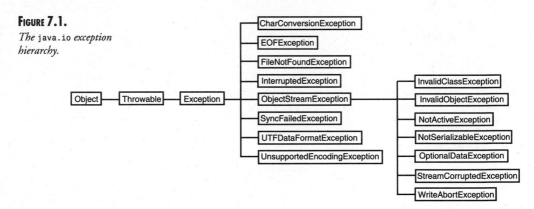

java.lang Exceptions

The java.lang package contains much of the core Java language. The exceptions subclassed from RuntimeException do not have to be declared in a method's throws clause. These exceptions are considered *normal* because nearly any method can throw them. Table 7.2 and Figure 7.2 show the recoverable exceptions from the java.lang package. Table 7.3 and Figure 7.3 show the nonrecoverable errors in the java.lang package.

Table 7.2. The java.lang exceptions.

Exception	Cause
ArithmeticException	Arithmetic error condition (for example, divide by zero)
ArrayIndexOutOfBoundsException	Array index less than zero or greater than actual size of array
ArrayStoreException	Object type mismatch between array and object to be stored in array

Exception	Cause
ClassCastException	Cast of object to inappropriate type
ClassNotFoundException	Unable to load requested class
CloneNotSupportedException	Object does not implement cloneable interface
Exception	Root class of exception hierarchy
IllegalAccessException	Class is not accessible
IllegalArgumentException	Method received illegal argument
IllegalMonitorStateException	Improper monitor state (thread synchronization)
IllegalStateException	Method invoked at improper time
IllegalThreadStateException	Thread is in improper state for requested operation
IndexOutOfBoundsException	Index is out of bounds
InstantiationException	Attempt to create instance of abstract class
InterruptedException	Thread interrupted
NegativeArraySizeException	Array size less than zero
NoSuchFieldException	Attempt to access invalid field
NoSuchMethodException	Unable to resolve method
NullPointerException	Attempt to access null object member
NumberFormatException	Unable to convert string to number
RuntimeException	Base class for many java.lang exceptions
SecurityException	Security settings do not allow operation
StringIndexOutOfBoundsException	Index is negative or greater than size of string

Table 7.3. The java.lang errors.

Error	Cause
AbstractMethodError	Attempt to call abstract method
ClassCircularityError	This error is no longer used
ClassFormatError	Invalid binary class format
Error	Root class of error hierarchy
ExceptionInInitializerError	Unexpected exception in initializer
IllegalAccessError	Attempt to access inaccessible object

continues

Table 7.3. continued

Error	Cause
IncompatibleClassChangeError	Improper use of class
InstantiationError	Attempt to instantiate abstract class
InternalError	Error in interpreter
LinkageError	Error in class dependencies
NoClassDefFoundError	Unable to find class definition
NoSuchFieldError	Unable to find requested field
NoSuchMethodError	Unable to find requested method
OutOfMemoryError	Out of memory
StackOverflowError	Stack overflow
ThreadDeath	Indicates that thread will terminate; can be caught to perform clean up (if caught, must be rethrown)
UnknownError	Unknown virtual machine error
UnsatisfiedLinkError	Unresolved links in loaded class
VerifyError	Unable to verify bytecode
VirtualMachineError	Root class for virtual machine errors

FIGURE 7.2.

The java.lang *exception hierarchy.*

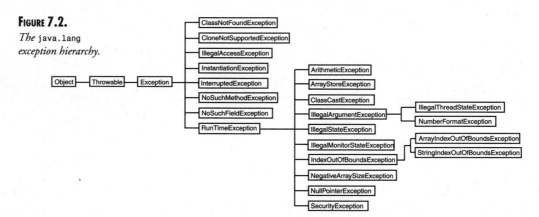

java.lang.reflect Exception

The classes of java.lang.reflect throw the following exception:

■ InvocationTargetException (invoked method has thrown an exception)

Figure 7.3.

The java.lang *error hierarchy.*

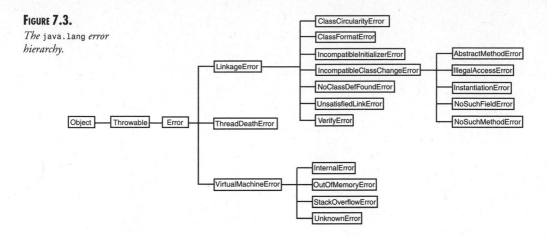

java.net Exceptions

The java.net package handles network communications. Its classes most often throw exceptions to indicate connect failures and the like. Table 7.4 and Figure 7.4 show the recoverable exceptions from the java.net package. The classes of the java.net package do not throw errors at all.

Table 7.4. The java.net exceptions.

Exception	Cause
BindException	Unable to bind socket—port in use
ConnectException	Remote socket refused connection—no listening socket
MalformedURLException	Unable to interpret URL
NoRouteToHostException	Unable to reach host—firewall in the way
ProtocolException	Socket class protocol error
SocketException	Socket class exception
UnknownHostException	Unable to resolve host name
UnknownServiceException	Connection does not support service

Figure 7.4.

The java.net *exception hierarchy.*

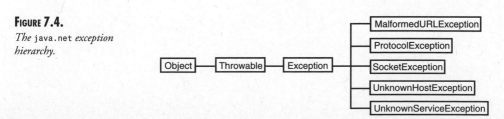

java.rmi Error

The Java Remote Method Invocation classes allow Java objects to exist on remote machines. These classes throw the following error:

- ■ ServerError (remote server indicates error)

java.rmi Exceptions

Java objects whose methods are invoked remotely through RMI may throw exceptions. Table 7.5 and Figure 7.5 show the exceptions thrown from the java.rmi package.

Table 7.5. The java.rmi exceptions.

Exception	Cause
AccessException	Operation not allowed
AlreadyBoundException	Name is already bound
ConnectException	Host refused connection
ConnectIOException	I/O exception during connection
MarshalException	Error during marshaling
NoSuchObjectException	Object no longer exists
NotBoundException	Name is not bound
RMISecurityException	RMISecurityManager throws exception
RemoteException	Invalid remote method
ServerException	Remote server throws exception
ServerRuntimeException	Remote server throws runtime exception
StubNotFoundException	Remote object not exported
UnexpectedException	Unknown error
UnknownHostException	Exception not in method signature
UnmarshalException	Error in unmarshaling; possible stream corruption

java.rmi.server Exceptions

RMI servers throw exceptions. Table 7.6 shows these java.rmi.server exceptions.

FIGURE 7.5.

The java.rmi *exception hierarchy.*

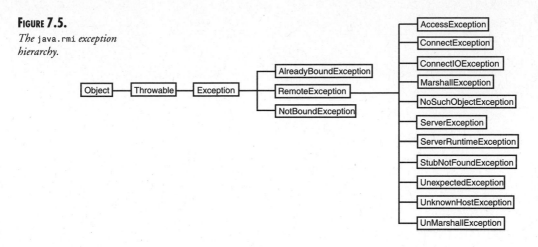

Table 7.6. The java.rmi.server exceptions.

Exception	Cause
ExportException	Port in use
ServerCloneException	Unable to clone
ServerNotActiveException	Server not executing remote method
SkeletonMismatchException	Stub and skeleton do not match
SkeletonNotFoundException	Skeleton not found or invalid
SocketSecurityException	Attempt to use invalid port

java.security Exceptions

The Java security API allows users to implement security features in Java. The API includes support for digital signatures, data encryption, key management, and access control. Table 7.7 and Figure 7.6 show the exceptions thrown from the java.security package.

Table 7.7. The java.security exceptions.

Exception	Cause
DigestException	Generic digest error
InvalidKeyException	Key invalid
InvalidParameterException	Actual method parameter invalid
KeyException	Generic key error

continues

7

EXCEPTION
HANDLING

Table 7.7. continued

Exception	*Cause*
KeyManagementException	Key management system error
NoSuchAlgorithmException	Algorithm does not exist
NoSuchProviderException	Security provider is not available
ProviderException	Security provider exception
SignatureException	Generic signature error

FIGURE 7.6.

The java.security *exception hierarchy.*

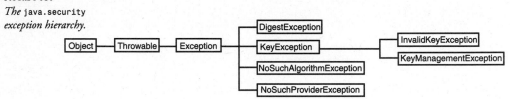

java.security.acl Exceptions

The Java security access control list API allows Java developers to control access to specific users. The classes of java.security.acl throw the following exceptions:

- ACLNotFoundException (unable to find access control list)
- LastOwnerException (attempt to delete last owner of ACL)
- NotOwnerException (only the owner may modify)

java.sql Exceptions

The Java SQL API throws the following exceptions:

- DataTruncation (unexpected data truncation)
- SQLException (SQL error—contains detailed SQL information)
- SQLWarning (SQL warning)

java.text Exception

The Java text API throws the following exception:

- FormatException (format or parsing error)

java.util Exceptions

The classes of the java.util package throw the following exceptions:

- EmptyStackException (no objects on stack)
- MissingResourceException (resource missing)
- NoSuchElementException (no more objects in collection)
- TooManyListenersException (thrown by unicast event listeners)

> **NOTE**
>
> *Unicast* is Java terminology for a singleton server object. *Singletons* are objects that can be instantiated only once.

java.utils.zip Exceptions

The Java utilities zip API throws the following exceptions:

- DataFormatException (format error)
- ZipException (Zip error)

Built-In Exceptions

In the example in Listing 7.4, you see how the *automatic* exceptions in Java work. This application creates a method and forces it to divide by zero. The method does not have to explicitly throw an exception because the division operator throws an exception when required.

Listing 7.4. An example of a built-in exception.

```
import java.io.* ;
import java.lang.Exception ;
public class DivideBy0 {
    public static void main( String[] args ) {
    int a = 2 ;
    int b = 3 ;
    int c = 5 ;
    int d = 0 ;
    int e = 1 ;
    int f = 3 ;
    try
        {
        System.out.println( a+"/"+b+" = "+div( a, b ) ) ;
        System.out.println( c+"/"+d+" = "+div( c, d ) ) ;
        System.out.println( e+"/"+f+" = "+div( e, f ) ) ;
        }
```

continues

Listing 7.4. continued

```
catch( Exception except )
    {
    System.out.println( "Caught exception " +
                            except.getMessage() ) ;
    }
}
static int div( int a, int b ) {
    return (a/b) ;
}
}
```

The output of this application is shown here:

```
2/3 = 0
Caught exception / by zero
```

The first call to div() works fine. The second call fails because of the divide-by-zero error. Even though the application did not specify it, an exception was thrown—and caught. So you can use arithmetic in your code without writing code that explicitly checks bounds.

Summary

The exception-handling mechanism in Java allows your methods to report errors in a manner that cannot be ignored. Every exception that is thrown must be caught, or the application terminates. Exceptions are actually class objects derived from the Throwable class. Therefore, exceptions combine data and methods; an exception object generally contains a string explaining what the error is.

Exception handling helps you combine error processing in one place. It uncouples the reporting of results and the reporting of errors. If you use exception handling, you can create much more powerful and robust code.

Introduction to Applet Programming

by Rick Darnell

CHAPTER 8

IN THIS CHAPTER

Although Java is a general-purpose programming language suitable for a large variety of tasks, the task most people use it for is applet programming. An *applet* is a Java program that can operate only within a compatible Web browser, such as Netscape Navigator or Microsoft Internet Explorer.

Your first experience with Java may have been one of the demonstration applets released in 1995 with the first Java Development Kit—spinning heads, an animated "Duke" cartoon doing cartwheels, and so on. Today, applets are used to accomplish far more than demonstrative goals. Current uses of applets include these:

- Tickertape-style news and sports headline updates
- Animated graphics
- Video games
- Student tests
- Imagemaps that respond to mouse movement
- Advanced text displays
- Database reports

For example, the Instant Ballpark applet from Instant Sports (`http://www.instantsports.com/ballpark.html`) takes real-time data from live baseball games and updates its graphical display to reflect what's happening in the game. Players run the bases, the ball goes to the place it was hit, and sound effects are used for strike calls, crowd noise, and other elements. The program, which was unique enough to qualify for a U.S. patent, is reminiscent of the old-time baseball tradition of presenting the play-by-play for road games by moving metal figures on the side of a building. In addition to the live coverage, Instant Ballpark can be used to review the play-by-play action of past games.

With HTML and some kind of gateway programming language such as Perl, a Web page can offer textual updates to a game in progress. In addition to the text, Instant Ballpark offers a visual presentation of a live game and can respond immediately to user input. This interactive nature of Java is used to provide information to Web users in a more compelling way, which is often the reason site providers offer applets.

With Microsoft's and Apple's encouragement of windowing software in the past five years, users now expect software to make use of graphical window features like buttons and scrollbars. In Java, windows and other graphical user interface functions are handled by the Abstract Windowing Toolkit (AWT).

The AWT is one of the most useful packages included with the Java API, but it is also one of the hardest to become familiar with. The AWT is a set of classes used to build graphical user interfaces for Java applications and applets. It enables programmers to easily create the following features for programs:

- Windows and dialog boxes
- Pull-down menus

- Buttons, labels, checkboxes, and other simple user interface components
- Text areas, scrollbars, and other more sophisticated user interface components
- Layout managers to control the placement of user interface components

The AWT also includes classes to handle graphics, fonts, and color, plus an Event class to enable programs to respond to mouse clicks, mouse movements, and keyboard input.

In the early days of Java, the Java Developer's Kit (JDK) and a text editor was the only choice available to programmers for developing applets and applications. Today, there are numerous ways to develop programs with Java, including SunSoft Java WorkShop, Symantec Café and Visual Café, and Rogue Wave JFactory. Java WorkShop, Café, and Visual Café include tools for drag-and-drop development of windows, dialog boxes, and other elements common to windowing systems. JFactory is an interface builder that can be used with different Java programming environments.

Providing Security

Java applets are programs that run on a Web user's machine. As you know, anything that can execute code is a potential security risk because of the damaging things that can occur. Viruses can damage a computer's file system and reproduce onto other disks, Trojan horses can masquerade as helpful programs while doing harmful things, and programs can be written to retrieve private information surreptitiously. Even Microsoft applications such as Word and Access have security risks because of Visual Basic for Applications—an executable programming language that can be used in conjunction with application documents.

Security is one of the primary concerns of Java's developers, and they have implemented safeguards at several levels. Some of these safeguards affect the language as a whole: removal of pointers, verification of bytecodes, and restricted remote and local file access. This means that some of Java's functionality is blocked for applets because of security concerns.

- Applets cannot read or write files on the Web user's disk. If information must be saved to disk as an applet is executing (as in the case of a video game saving the top 10 scores), the storage of information must be done on the disk from which the Web page is served.
- Applets cannot make a network connection to a computer other than the one from which the Web page is served, except to direct the browser to a new location.
- Popup windows opened by applets are identified clearly as Java windows. A Java cup icon and text such as Untrusted Applet Window appear in the window's border to prevent a window opened by Java from pretending to be something else, such as a Windows dialog box requesting a user's name and password.
- Applets cannot use dynamic or shared libraries from any other programming language. Although Java *applications* can use programs written in languages such as Visual C++, *applets* cannot make use of this feature because there's no way to adequately verify the security of the nonJava code.

■ Applets cannot run any programs on the Web user's system, including browser plug-ins, ActiveX controls, or other browser-related items.

These restrictions limit Java applets more than standalone Java applications. The loss is a tradeoff for the security that must be in place for the language to run remotely on users' computers. Refer to Chapter 34, "Java Security," for more information about security and Java.

Understanding the Basics of Applet Programming

Now that you understand what applets are, it's time to get out some power tools and see what it takes to put one together. We'll begin with a quick introduction to some basic elements of applet programming.

Each applet starts out with a class definition, like this:

```
public class LearnPigLatin extends java.applet.Applet {
    // to do
}
```

In this example, `LearnPigLatin` is the name of the applet's class. An applet must be declared as a `public` class. All applets extend the `java.applet.Applet` class, also referred to simply as the `Applet` class. Another way to write the class definition is to use `import` to load the `Applet` class and simplify the declaration:

```
import java.applet.Applet
public class LearnPigLatin extends Applet {
    // to do
}
```

NOTE

`Applet` extends the `java.awt.Panel` class, which is a Java container. This evolution enables an applet to hold a physical place on the Web page within the browser's window. For more information, see "Containers: A Place for Your Components," later in this chapter.

The superclasses of `Applet` give all applets a framework on which you can build user interface elements and mouse events. These superclasses also provide a structure for the applet that must be used when the program is developed.

Applet Methods

The structure of an applet takes its form from four events that take place during the life of an applet. When each stage is reached, a method is automatically called. There are default versions of each of the methods if you choose not to override them:

- **init():** This is the initialization method used to set the stage for the applet's activity; the method usually includes things such as loading graphics, initializing variables, and creating objects.

- **start():** Starting the applet's execution is next on the agenda. This method is where the meat and potatoes of the applet are found. The start() method is the body of the applet; this method is also used to restart the applet after it has stopped.

- **stop():** Stopping an applet interrupts its execution but leaves its resources intact so that it can start again. You should always stop an applet before you destroy it; you can also use the stop() method to stop applet execution when a pause in the flow is needed.

- **destroy():** When an applet is destroyed, all its resources—memory, processor time, swap disk space—are cleared and returned to the system. This method is the last thing that happens when the user leaves the page containing the applet.

APPLETS AND APPLICATIONS

This chapter focuses on applets, but it's important to make clear the distinction between the two types of Java programs. *Applets* are programs offered on Web pages that require the use of a Web browser to execute. *Applications* are everything else: general-purpose programs run by executing the Java interpreter with the name of the Java program as an argument. For example, to run the Java program ReadNews.class, enter the following at a command-line prompt:

```
java ReadNews
```

Applications do not have many of the restrictions that are in place for applets, although features such as bytecode verification are still implemented.

Many programmers are initially confused by the lack of a main() method to start applet operation. Understand that the browser provides all the necessary support and responsibility for running the applet. In other words, the browser is the main() method, and the applet is a subroutine running within its context.

For more information on techniques for working with Java programs, see Part VI of this book, "Programming Strategies."

Other important methods—although not directly required for program execution—are paint() and repaint(). These methods apply only to the display in the applet window and occur automatically at certain times, such as when the applet window is redisplayed after being covered or when the applet window is resized. An applet can call repaint() directly to update the window whenever necessary.

Of all the methods, repaint() is the only one that requires a parameter. This parameter is an instance of the Graphics class, as in the following method definition:

```
public void paint(Graphics g) {
    g.drawString("One moment, please", 5, 50);
}
```

The `Graphics` object used as the parameter represents the applet window. The `g.drawString()` line uses this `Graphics` object to indicate where a string should be drawn. Every time the `repaint()` method is called, the applet window is updated with the string `One moment, please` drawn at the x, y position `5, 50`.

Each of these applet methods—`init()`, `destroy()`, `start()`, `stop()`, and `paint()`—is inherited by an applet. However, each of the applet methods is empty by default. If something specific is supposed to happen in an applet, some or all of these methods must be overridden. Although you do not have to override any of these methods, as a general rule, you always provide your own `start()` method.

Viewing Applets

Applets are displayed as a part of a Web page by using the HTML tag `<APPLET>`. To run an applet, you need a Web browser or some other software that serves the function of a browser, such as the applet viewer program that ships with the Java Development Kit from JavaSoft.

The browser acts as the operating system for the applet—you cannot run an applet as a standalone program in the same way you can run an executable file. The two leading browsers—Netscape Navigator (version 2.02 and later) and Microsoft Internet Explorer (version 3.0 and later)—both support Java applets. A third choice—Sun's HotJava—also handles applets but is not widely used.

These programs load applets from a Web page and run them remotely on the Web user's computer. This arrangement raises security issues that must be handled by the Java language itself and by Java-enabled browsers.

The <APPLET> Tag

Running Java applets on a Web page requires the use of two special HTML tags: `<APPLET>` and `<PARAM>`. These tags are included on a Web page along with all other HTML code. In this respect, inserting a Java applet on your Web page is no different than inserting a picture, as the following lines demonstrate:

```
<APPLET CODE="NowShowing.class" CODEBASE="progdir" WIDTH=376 HEIGHT=104>
<PARAM NAME="speed" value="100">
<PARAM NAME="blink" value="5">
<PARAM NAME="text" value="FREE THE BOUND PERIODICALS!">
<PARAM NAME="fontsize" value="21">
<PARAM NAME="pattern" value="random">
<H5>This applet requires the use of a Java-enabled browser!</H5>
</APPLET>
```

When included on a Web page, this HTML code causes the following to take place on a Java-enabled browser:

1. An applet called `NowShowing.class` is loaded from a directory called `progdir`. The `CODE` attribute specifies the applet's filename, and the optional `CODEBASE` attribute refers to a directory where the applet is found.

   If the `CODEBASE` attribute is used without a leading slash (`/`), it indicates the path from the Web page's directory to the directory containing the applet's class file. For example, `CODEBASE="usr"` indicates that the applet is in a directory called usr that is a subdirectory of the Web page's directory. `CODEBASE` can also specify a complete path on the Web site separate from the page's current location.

2. The applet is set to a width of 376 pixels and a height of 104 pixels using the `WIDTH` and `HEIGHT` attributes. These attributes work the same with `<APPLET>` as they do with `<IMG>`.

   The `ALIGN` attribute used with images also can be used with `<APPLET>`. The `ALIGN` attribute determines how the applet is positioned in relation to the other parts of the Web page; it can have the value `TOP`, `MIDDLE`, or `BOTTOM`.

3. A parameter named `speed` is sent to the applet with a value of `100`. Four other parameters are sent to the applet: `blink`, `text`, `fontsize`, and `pattern`. Parameters are optional; you can include as many as you want. The `NAME` attribute indicates the name a parameter should be given; the `VALUE` attribute indicates the value to associate with the parameter.

WHY PASS NUMBERS AS STRINGS?

All parameters passed from an HTML page to an applet are passed as strings, no matter what the parameter is or how it's formatted on the page. Any conversion to other types (such as `integer`, `boolean`, or `date`) must happen within the applet itself.

For example, `<PARAM NAME="speed" value=100>` and `<PARAM NAME="speed" value="100">` both pass the string `"100"` to the applet. This restriction eliminates a lot of guesswork between the browser and the applet because neither has to guess what kind of value is being sent. Everything is converted to a string, and the programmer can take care of casting the value to a new type after it enters the applet.

---

4. The line `<H5>This applet requires a Java-enabled browser!</H5>` is ignored unless the page is loaded by a nonJava browser. An incompatible browser won't recognize the two `<APPLET>` tags and ignores each line until it reaches the line with the `<H5>` heading tag. Because the browser knows what to do with this tag, it displays the appropriate text.

> **TIP**
>
> You can insert any standard HTML code before the closing </APPLET> tag. Many page designers include an image or similar item that occupies the same amount of space as the applet. This arrangement helps maintain consistent page layout regardless of the browser being used.

If the applet makes use of class files that are not part of the standard Java API, these class files must be located in the same directory as the applet's class file.

Putting the Applet on the Web

It's easy to make your applet available on the Web after it's created and placed on an HTML page using the <APPLET></APPLET> tags. Put all .class files required by the applet on your Web site, making sure that you put the files in the directory specified by the CODEBASE attribute (if this attribute has been used). If the CODEBASE attribute has not been used, put the .class files in the same directory as the Web page that includes the applet.

That's all it takes. Unlike CGI programming (which requires special access to the computer providing the Web pages), Java applets can be added by anyone who can put pages on a Web site.

More about Using Parameters

As you saw earlier, parameters are sent to an applet using the <PARAM> tag and its attributes of NAME and VALUE. For example, <PARAM NAME="blink" VALUE="100"> sends a parameter named blink with a value of 100 to the applet.

> **TIP**
>
> Unlike everything else relating to Java, the parameter name is *not* case sensitive. You can send a rose, a Rose, or a ROSE to the applet, and they'll all smell the same.

Parameters are passed to the applet after it's loaded; all parameters are sent as strings whether or not they are encased in quotation marks. All parameters are converted to other data types within the applet. For an applet to use a parameter, the applet must retrieve the parameter using the getParameter() method, which is usually used within the init() portion of applet execution.

For example, use the following line in a Java applet to store the blink parameter in a variable called blinkValue:

```
String blinkValue = getParameter("blink");
```

If you want to retrieve the value and convert it to an integer, use the following code:

```
int blinkValue = -1;
try { blinkValue = Integer.parseInt(getParameter("blink")); }
catch (NumberFormatException e) { }
```

This example uses the parseInt() method of the java.lang.Integer class to convert a String to an int. The try and catch block is used to trap errors if the String cannot be converted to a number.

An Example: The ColorCycle Applet

In subsequent chapters, you delve into the specific details of programming, including user interface design and event handling. For now, it is worthwhile to take a look at a working example of an applet to get a clearer picture of how applets are constructed.

 ColorCycle is a simple applet with one button labeled Next Color. When you click this button with the mouse, the background color of the applet changes. The program demonstrates basic applet structure and a simple bit of event handling. The source code for this applet is shown in Listing 8.1 and can be found on the CD-ROM that accompanies this book.

Listing 8.1. The source code for ColorCycle.java.

```
1: import java.awt.*;
2:
3: public class ColorCycle extends java.applet.Applet {
4:     float hue = (float).5;
5:     float saturation = (float)1;
6:     float brightness = (float)0;
7:     Button b;
8:
9:     public void init() {
10:        b = new Button("Next Color");
11:        add(b);
12:    }
13:
14:    public void start() {
15:        setBackground(Color.black);
16:        repaint();
17:    }
18:
19:    public boolean action(Event evt, Object o) {
20:        if (brightness < 1)
21:            brightness += .25;
22:        else
23:            brightness = 0;
24:        Color c = new Color(Color.HSBtoRGB(hue, saturation, brightness));
25:        setBackground(c);
26:        repaint();
27:        return true;
28:    }
29: }
```

Don't worry if some aspects of this program are unfamiliar to you at this point. Several aspects of this applet are discussed later in this chapter, including the creation of user interface components such as buttons and the action() method.

The following things are taking place in the applet:

- **Line 1:** The applet imports several classes by using the wildcard character with java.awt.*. The awt stands for Abstract Windowing Toolkit and is a set of classes that handle most visual and interactive aspects of Java programming—graphics, fonts, and keyboard and mouse input.

- **Lines 4 through 6:** Three instance variables are created to store the HSB values of the color being displayed. HSB (Hue, Saturation, and Brightness) is a method of describing a color as three numeric values from 0 to 1.

- **Line 7:** A Button object is created.

- **Lines 9 through 12:** The applet's init() method is called automatically when the applet is first run; this method provides instantiation for Button object b with the label Next Color.

- **Lines 14 through 17:** The start() method sets the background color of the applet to black using a constant of the Color class (Color.black). In addition, the repaint() method is called to redraw the applet window because something—the background color—has changed and we want to display that change.

- **Line 19:** The action() method is called whenever a user interface component generates an action event. In this applet, an event occurs when the button is clicked. For more information on event handling, see Chapter 7, "Exception Handling," and Chapter 22, "Creating User Interface Components."

- **Lines 20 through 23:** The value of brightness is changed to cycle the background color through several shades from black to light blue.

- **Lines 24 through 26:** A Color object is created to store the value of the background color, which is created based on the values of the variables hue, saturation, and brightness. The new background color is reflected with another call to repaint().

- **Line 27:** The boolean value true is returned at the end of the action() method, indicating that the action event generated by clicking the button was handled.

Notice that there are no stop() or destroy() methods defined in this applet because we have no need to override either one of these method's activities. When the user moves to a different Web page or otherwise dumps this applet page from the viewer, the applet will stop and its resources will be recovered.

Designing the HTML Page for ColorCycle

Once the ColorCycle applet has been written and compiled using your development software, you can put it on a Web page using the HTML tags <APPLET>, </APPLET>, and <PARAM>, described earlier in this chapter.

Listing 8.2 shows the full text of an HTML page that loads the `ColorCycle.class` applet. (This code can also be found on the CD-ROM that accompanies this book.) Because the `CODEBASE` attribute is not used with the `<APPLET>` tag, the `.class` file must be placed in the same directory as the Web page containing the applet.

Listing 8.2. The source code for `ColorCycle.html`.

```
1: <html>
2: <body>
3: <applet code=ColorCycle.class height=250 width=250>
4: </applet>
5: </body>
6: </html>
```

Although the applet loses something in the translation from color to black and white, Figure 8.1 shows how the `ColorCycle` applet looks when viewed with the applet viewer provided with the Java Development Kit from Sun.

FIGURE 8.1.

The ColorCycle *applet consists of a square frame whose background color changes when the* Next Color *button is clicked.*

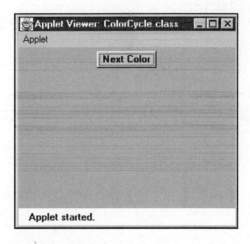

Making ColorCycle an Application

To underscore the difference between applets and applications, let's now turn the `ColorCycle` applet into an application that can run independently of a browser (see Listing 8.3 and the code on the CD-ROM). Remember that the application must provide the basic framework normally supplied for the applet by the browser, and must also invoke each of the applet methods in turn.

Listing 8.3. The source code for the `ColorCycleApplication.java` application.

```
1:  import java.applet.Applet;
2:  import java.awt.*;
3:
4:  public class ColorCycleApplication extends Applet {
5:      float hue = (float).5;
6:      float saturation = (float)1;
7:      float brightness = (float)0;
8:      Panel p;
9:      Button b;
10:
11:     public static void main(String args[]) {
12:      ColorCycleFrame app = new ColorCycleFrame("ColorCycle Application Window");
13:          app.resize(200,200);
14:          app.show();
15:          app.applet.start();
16:     }
17:
18:     public void init() {
19:          b = new Button("Next Color");
20:          add(b);
21:     }
22:
23:     public void start() {
24:          setBackground(Color.black);
25:          repaint();
26:     }
27:
28:     public boolean action(Event event, Object obj) {
29:          if (brightness < 1)
30:              brightness += .25;
31:          else
32:              brightness = 0;
33:          Color c = new Color(Color.HSBtoRGB(hue, saturation, brightness));
34:          setBackground(c);
35:          repaint();
36:          return true;
37:     }
38: }
39:
40: class ColorCycleFrame extends Frame {
41:     ColorCycleApplication applet;
42:
33:     public ColorCycleFrame(String frameName) {
44:          super(frameName);
45:          applet = new ColorCycleApplication();
46:          add("Center",applet);
47:          applet.init();
48:     }
49:
50:     public boolean handleEvent(Event event) {
51:          if(event.id == Event.WINDOW_DESTROY) {
52:              applet.stop();
53:              applet.destroy();
54:              System.exit(0); }
55:          return false;
56:     }
57: }
```

An extra class and method are added to the ColorCycle applet so that the necessary overhead normally provided by the browser is now supplied by the application itself. This allows the same piece of code to run as an applet or an application (see Figure 8.2).

FIGURE 8.2.

The ColorCycle *applet transformed into a standalone application.*

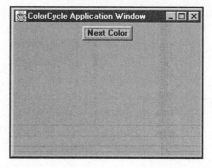

In Listing 8.3, the application begins by importing the classes needed to support both types of operation (lines 1 and 2). The imported classes include the Applet class for the applet and the awt.Frame class for the application.

TIP

Because the Frame class is a part of the AWT, it's easier to import it along with the rest of the AWT classes by using the import java.awt.* statement. You should use this approach (instead of a long list of import statements for each individual item needed) when more than two or three subclasses are used within a program. This results in cleaner code and fewer opportunities for typing mistakes when the code is compiled.

The next step is ensuring that the code can run on a browser: in line 4, the ColorCycleApplication class extends the Applet class. Then the main() method required by an application is placed as the first method within the class. This method creates and displays a frame to hold the program (line 11), which in turn starts the body of the program. If the program is run as an applet, main() is never used and the browser begins with the init() method. If the class runs as an application, the main() method is executed first, which creates a frame to hold the applet functions using the ColorCycleFrame class. After the frame is created, the applet is centered within it.

Remember that a browser normally supplies all the overhead required by an applet; the browser also is responsible for calling each of the four required methods in turn—init(), start(), stop(), and destroy(). However, when the program runs as an application, we must replace this overhead because the browser is not available. These details are handled primarily by the ColorCycleApplication.main() method and the ColorCycleFrame class. Let's look closer at the ColorCycleFrame class.

When an applet runs on a browser, the browser provides a frame for it to reside in. Because the application is not a browser, it doesn't know about this requirement, so the `ColorCycleFrame` class provides the first bit of necessary overhead. Next, the program has to provide an instance of the application class to use as an applet (line 41). Lines 33 through 46 actually create the physical frame and add an instance of `ColorCycleApplication` within it. The first method of the applet, `init()`, is called to prepare the applet for operation.

After the frame and applet are instantiated, control is passed back to the `main()` method. Lines 13 and 14 set the initial size of the window and force its display on the screen. The main method of the applet, `start()`, is then called. At this point, the program performs its tricks and functions until the user closes the window.

Any action concerning the frame triggers an event. An event can be moving the mouse into or out of the frame, resizing the frame, or minimizing or maximizing the frame. Each event is handled using `ColorCycleFrame.handleEvent()` on line 50. Line 51 looks at the event to see whether the user has closed the window. If the window has been closed, the last two applet methods, `stop()` and `destroy()`, are called to close program operation and shut down the Java system.

> **NOTE**
>
> You may have noticed that the `stop()` and `destroy()` methods are called but not explicitly defined in the `ColorCycleApplication` class. This is because the `Applet` class includes default definitions for these two methods. If one of these methods is not included as part of a user-defined class, the Java system automatically invokes the default `Applet` version.

By adding the frame class and an extra bit of code to virtually any applet, you enable the applet to run on machines that don't have a compatible browser but that do have a Java virtual machine.

Working with the Java AWT

Now that you understand the basic framework in which you develop an applet, it's time to take a closer look at the Abstract Windowing Toolkit (AWT). The AWT is used to build the graphical user interface with standard windowing elements. Each window element is represented by its own component. There are components for buttons you can click, components for text fields you can type into, and components for scrollbars you can control. There also are components for some things you cannot directly manipulate, such as labels.

For more information about the other capabilities and classes within the AWT, see Part IV of this book, "Programming the AWT."

Containers: A Place for Your Components

To use AWT components in a program, you must contain them. After all, buttons floating freely in the computer don't do anyone any good. A Java *container* is a blank slate that holds the interface components. All containers in Java are subclasses of the Container class.

There are two basic types of containers:

- **The Window class:** This class creates popup windows separate from the main program. There are two subclasses of Window: Frame (windows that have a border and a menu bar) and Dialog (a special window used in applications to select a file).

- **The Panel class:** A container that represents a section of an existing window. The Applet class is a container that is a subclass of the Panel class. You can place components directly on an applet panel or use additional Panel objects to subdivide the applet into smaller sections.

A Panel container is not visible when it is added to an applet. Its purpose is to provide a way to organize components as they're laid out in a window.

 Listing 8.4 is the source code for an applet that has a new Panel added to its surface. The applet is also located on the CD-ROM that accompanies this book. This code does not produce any output other than a blank window. However, it is useful as a template for the components you will learn to add throughout this chapter.

Listing 8.4. The source code for `ContainerAndPanel.java`.

```
1: import java.applet.Applet;
2: import java.awt.*;
3: public class ContainerAndPanel extends Applet {
4:     Panel p = new Panel();
5:
6:     public void init() {
7:         add(p);
8:     }
9: }
```

The statement that puts the instance of panel p in the applet window is add(p) (line 7). The add() method is used whenever a component of any kind is added to a container.

By default, components are added to a container in left-to-right, top-to-bottom order. If a component does not fit on a line, it is placed at the leftmost edge of the next line. In addition, there are several *layout managers* that offer greater control of component placement. Organizing components using layout managers is covered later in this chapter and also in Chapter 14, "The Windowing (AWT) Package."

Now it's time to look at the various components you can add to your applet. Detailed information about the various AWT components can be found in Chapter 22, "Creating User Interface Components," and Chapter 23, "Working with Dialog Boxes."

Labels

The Label component is a string displayed in the container that cannot be modified by the user. Figure 8.3 shows an example of an applet with a label next to a text field.

FIGURE 8.3.

A Label *component to the left of a text field.*

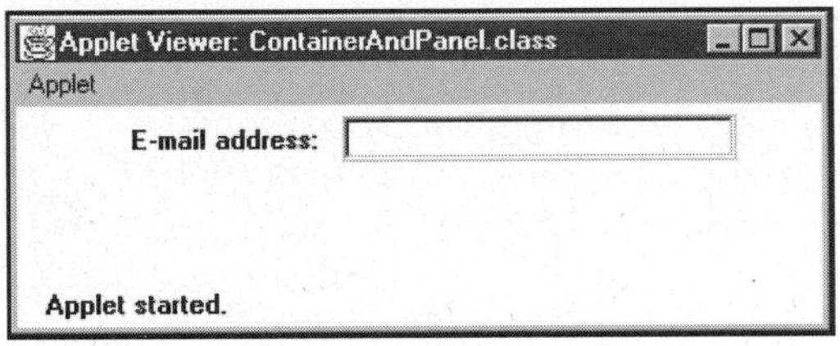

The following code is used to create a Label component and add it to an applet window:

```
Label l = new Label("E-mail address: ");
add(l);
```

The parameter in the constructor Label("E-mail address: ") identifies the text to be displayed.

Text Fields

The TextField component is an input box in which a user can type a single line of text. The number of characters visible in the text field is configurable. Figure 8.4 shows an example of an applet with a text field.

FIGURE 8.4.

A TextField *component.*

Adding a TextField component to a window is the same as adding a button or any other component:

```
TextField t = new TextField(12);
add(t);
```

The parameter 12 in the constructor `TextField(12)` sets up the text field so that the field is limited to displaying approximately 12 characters. The user can type more characters than that, but only some of the characters will be displayed.

> **NOTE**
>
> The actual number of characters displayed depends on which characters are typed. A text field can display more *is* than *ms* because the former characters are narrower than the latter.

If a string is specified as a parameter, such as `TextField t = TextField("your name")`, the text field is created with that string as the default text in the input area of the field.

You can specify default text and a width at the same time by using a statement such as this:

```
TextField country = new TextField("United States", 20)
```

> **TIP**
>
> There is no default length for the text field. If you don't supply a length parameter, the result is a one-character-wide text field.

Text Areas

The `TextArea` component is an extended input box that makes it possible for the user to enter more than one line of text. The number of lines and the number of characters per line visible in the text area are configurable. Figure 8.5 shows an example of an applet with a text area.

FIGURE 8.5.

A `TextArea` component.

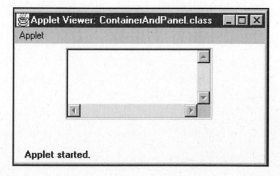

The following code is used to create a `TextArea` component and add it to an applet window:

```
TextArea t = new TextArea(5,20);
add(t);
```

The parameters 5 and 20 specify the text area's number of lines and the number of characters per line, respectively. If the text extends beyond the borders of the text area, a scrollbar appears to enable the user to scroll to the different sections of the text area.

If a string is specified as a parameter to the constructor, as in the statement TextArea t = TextArea("It was a dark and stormy night.", 7, 25); the text area is created with the string as the default text in the input area of the field. To cause parts of this text to start at the beginning of the next line, use a newline character (\n) in the text of the parameter. For example, to put the text "stormy night" at the beginning of a new line, use the following statement:

```
TextArea t = TextArea("It was a dark and \nstormy night", 7, 25);
```

Buttons

The Button component is a rectangular button that can be clicked with a mouse. The ColorCycle applet, earlier in this chapter, used a Button component to change the background color. Creating a Button component and adding it to an applet window requires two lines:

```
Button b = new Button("Cancel");
add(b);
```

Because the add(b) method does not refer to a specific container object, it defaults to adding the button to the applet surface. You can also create a new Panel and add a new Button component to that panel:

```
Panel p = new Panel();
Button b = new Button("Cancel");
p.add(b);
```

Checkboxes

The Checkbox component is a toggle box that can be either selected or deselected. When selected, the checkbox displays a checkmark. This element usually has a line of text next to it explaining what the box signifies. Figure 8.6 shows an example of an applet with a checkbox.

FIGURE 8.6.

A Checkbox *component.*

The following code is used to create a Checkbox component and add it to an applet window:

```
Checkbox c = new Checkbox("Never Mind");
add(c);
```

The parameter in the constructor Checkbox("Never Mind") identifies the text to be displayed. If you omit this parameter, a checkbox is displayed without any text next to it.

A checkbox is often used with a group of related checkboxes so that only one of the boxes can be selected at one time. In HTML, such groups of checkboxes are known as *radio buttons*. To create a group of checkboxes, you use the CheckboxGroup class. The setCheckboxGroup() method associates a checkbox with a particular group. The setCurrent() method of CheckboxGroup is used to make one of the boxes the selected box. Listing 8.5 shows the use of Checkbox and CheckboxGroup; the code is also located on the CD-ROM that accompanies this book.

Listing 8.5. An applet that creates a group of checkboxes similar to an HTML radio button group.

```
1:   import java.applet.Applet;
2:   import java.awt.*;
3:
4:   public class ContainerAndPanel extends Applet {
5:       CheckboxGroup cbg = new CheckboxGroup();
6:
7:       public void init() {
8:           Checkbox c1 = new Checkbox("I hug trees.");
9:           c1.setCheckboxGroup(cbg);
10:          c1.setState(false);
11:          add(c1);
12:
13:          Checkbox c2 = new Checkbox("I cut trees.",cbg,false);
14:          add(c2);
15:
16:          Checkbox c3 = new Checkbox("I've never seen a tree",cbg,true);
17:          add(c3);
18:      }
19: }
```

When adding a checkbox to a group, note the difference between lines 8 through 10 and line 13. Line 8 creates the checkbox with its label; line 9 adds it to the group; line 10 sets its initial state to false. Line 13 combines these three operations into a single statement by merging the three parameters into the Checkbox method instantiation. Figure 8.7 shows the checkbox group that results from Listing 8.5.

TIP

By default, all checkboxes are set to false (deselected) when they are instantiated. There is no need to use setState() for a new checkbox unless you want to ensure its state or set it to true.

FIGURE 8.7.

A group of Checkbox *components.*

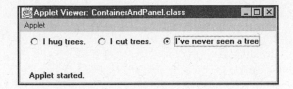

Choice List

The Choice component is a popup list of strings from which a single string can be selected, similar to a group of checkboxes. A choice list provides a group of options and enables selection of one at a time. Figure 8.8 shows an example of an applet with a choice list.

FIGURE 8.8.

A Choice *component.*

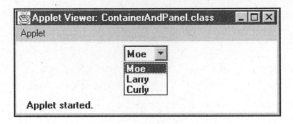

The addItem() method of the Choice class is used to build the choice list. To create a list, you instantiate the list, add individual items to it, and then add the loaded list to an applet window:

```
Choice c = new Choice();
c.addItem("Moe");
c.addItem("Larry");
c.addItem("Curly");
add(c);
```

Scrolling Lists

The List component is a scrolling list of strings from which one or more strings can be selected. Figure 8.9 shows an example of an applet with a scrolling list.

FIGURE 8.9.

A List *component.*

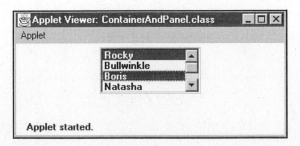

The addItem() method of the List class is used to build the scrolling list. The following code is used to create a scrolling list, add items to it, and then add the list to an applet window:

```
List l = new List(4,true);
l.addItem("Rocky");
l.addItem("Bullwinkle");
l.addItem("Boris");
l.addItem("Natasha");
l.addItem("Dudley Do-Right");
l.addItem("Nell");
add(l);
```

The List() constructor can be used with no parameters or with two parameters. The List l = new List(4, true) statement uses two parameters; the first parameter indicates the number of list items to display in the list window and the second parameter determines how many list items can be selected. If the second parameter is true, multiple items can be selected. Otherwise, only one choice is allowed at a time, similar to the choice list.

Scrollbars

The Scrollbar component is an up-down or left-right slider that can be used to set a numeric value. You use this component by clicking the mouse on an arrow or by grabbing the box on the slider. Figure 8.10 shows an example of an applet with a scrollbar.

FIGURE 8.10.

A Scrollbar *component.*

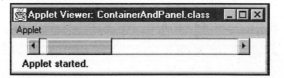

The first parameter of the Scrollbar constructor determines whether it is a vertical or horizontal scrollbar. If you want the bar to be vertical, use the constant Scrollbar.VERTICAL. Otherwise, use the constant Scrollbar.HORIZONTAL. Four other parameters follow the alignment parameter; these parameters determine the slider's initial setting, the size of the scrollable area, the minimum value, and the maximum value.

Consider the following statement:

```
Scrollbar sb = new Scrollbar(Scrollbar.HORIZONTAL, 50, 500, 0, 1000);
add(sb);
```

This code creates a horizontal Scrollbar component with the slider initially set to 50. When the user moves the slider, the scrollable area can return a value from 0 (the minimum value on the left) to 1000 (the maximum value on the right). The value changes in increments of 2 because the overall size of the scrollbar is limited to 500 elements (half the maximum value).

Canvases

The Canvas component is a section of a window used primarily as a place to draw graphics or display images. In that respect, a canvas is more similar to a container than a component—however, a Canvas component cannot be used as a place to put components. The following code creates a Canvas component, resizes it to 50×50 pixels, sets the background of the canvas to the color black, and adds the canvas to an applet window:

```
Canvas c = new Canvas();
c.resize(50,50);
c.setBackground(Color.black);
add(c);
```

Figure 8.11 shows the code as it appears to the user: a black area on a white applet background.

FIGURE 8.11.

A Canvas *component.*

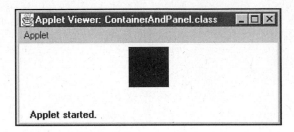

Organizing the Interface

Up to this point, all the components have been added to a container in a manner similar to the way HTML elements are arranged on a Web page. Things are loosely organized from left to right and from top to bottom; the look of the container is highly dependent on the size of its display area.

This approach is an easy way to implement Java's multiplatform capability. Because the language must work on any system that has a Java implementation, the windowing environment must be flexible. This also means that the same Java applet *looks* dramatically different when shown on a Windows 95 system, a Macintosh system, and a SPARC workstation, although it *works* exactly the same.

However, Java's developers understood the need for organizing the components in a user interface. Therefore, they extended Java's capability to customize your applet's interface to work on each of the platforms and to look close enough in appearance on different platforms to ensure cross-platform usability.

The tools added for this purpose are called *layout managers*. In the preceding sections, when you added components to a container—the main applet window—you were using the default layout manager: a class called FlowLayout. There are four other layout managers you can use as you organize your interface: BorderLayout, GridLayout, GridBagLayout, and CardLayout.

The FlowLayout Class

The FlowLayout class is the default layout manager for all panels, including the Applet class. It's the simplest to use. Components placed under the rules of FlowLayout are arranged in order from left to right. When a component is too big to be added to the current row, a new line of components is begun below the first line.

Each row of components can be aligned to the left, right, or centered. The only parameter used with the add() method is the name of the object to add.

The following setLayout() statement sets up a container to use the FlowLayout manager:

```
setLayout( new FlowLayout() );
```

The BorderLayout Class

The BorderLayout class is the default layout manager for all Window, Dialog, and Frame classes. In a border layout, components are added to the edges of the container; the center area is allotted all the space that's left over. The add() method takes an additional parameter—a string that can be North, South, East, West, or Center. This parameter specifies the location in the border layout for the component. For example, the following statements create five buttons and add them to a container laid out with the BorderLayout manager, as shown in Figure 8.12:

```
Button b1 = new Button("Climb");
Button b2 = new Button("Dive");
Button b3 = new Button("Left");
Button b4 = new Button("Right");
Button b5 = new Button("Fire!");
setLayout( new BorderLayout() );
add("North", b1);
add("South", b2);
add("West", b3);
add("East", b4);
add("Center", b5);
```

Note the use of the setLayout() method to select a layout manager for the container. Its single parameter is an instance of the desired layout. Remember to capitalize the directional parameter to the add() method. Like many other case-sensitive aspects of the Java language, the BorderLayout manager requires the directions to be capitalized consistently as North, South, East, West, and Center.

The GridLayout Class

The GridLayout class puts each component into a place on a grid that is equal in size to all the other places. The grid is given specific dimensions when created; components are added to the grid in order, starting with the upper-left corner. This is similar to the way components are added with the FlowLayout manager, but with GridLayout, components are given equal amounts of space in the container.

FIGURE 8.12.

Components arranged by the BorderLayout *manager.*

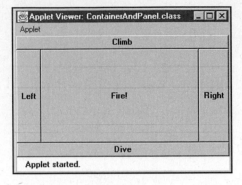

Components added to the container with the GridLayout manager are arranged in order from left to right. When there are no more grids remaining on a row, the next component to be added is placed in the leftmost grid on the next line. New rows are added as needed—if you create a three-by-three grid and add a tenth item, a fourth row is added. The only parameter used with the add() method is the name of the object to add.

The following setLayout() statements set up a container to use the GridLayout manager with three rows and two columns and then add a series of buttons:

```
setLayout( new GridLayout(3, 2));
Button b1 = new Button("Lefty");
Button b2 = new Button("Righty");
Button b3 = new Button("Loosey");
Button b4 = new Button("Tighty");
Button b5 = new Button("White on Right");
Button b6 = new Button("Red on Ribs");
add(b1);
add(b2);
add(b3);
add(b4);
add(b5);
add(b6);
```

Figure 8.13 shows an example of an applet with all the components arranged according to the rules of the GridLayout manager.

The GridBagLayout Class

The GridBagLayout class is similar to the GridLayout class except that GridBagLayout provides much more control over how the grid is organized and how components are presented. Cells in the grid are not required to take up the same amount of space, and components can be aligned in different ways in each grid cell.

A special GridBagConstraints object is used to determine how a component is placed in a cell and how much space the cell will occupy. Unlike the FlowLayout and GridLayout managers, the GridBagLayout manager permits you to add components to the grid in any order.

FIGURE 8.13.

Components arranged by the GridLayout *manager.*

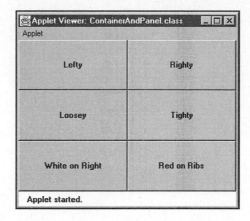

The first step you take to use the GridBagLayout manager is to set up the layout and the GridBagConstraints object, as shown here:

```
GridBagLayout gl = new GridBagLayout();
setLayout ( gl );
GridBagConstraints gb = new GridBagConstraints();
```

Before you can add a component to the container, you use instance variables of the GridBagConstraints object to determine the component's location and alignment within its grid cell.

The following GridBagConstraints variables can be set:

- **gridx and gridy:** These variables specify the cell in the grid where the component should be placed. gridx represents the rows, and gridy represents the columns. The (1,1) position is the upper-left corner.

- **gridheight and gridwidth:** These variables specify the number of cells a component should occupy. gridheight determines the number of rows, and gridwidth determines the number of columns.

- **fill:** This variable specifies the directions in which a component should expand if it has room to grow inside its cell. This can happen because of larger components in other cells. The constants GridBagConstraints.HORIZONTAL, GridBagConstraints.VERTICAL, GridBagConstraints.BOTH, and GridBagConstraints.NONE can be used with this variable. This example sets the fill variable to expand in both the horizontal and the vertical directions:

  gb.fill = GridBagConstraints.BOTH;

- **anchor:** This variable specifies the way a component should be aligned in its cell. The following GridBagConstraints constants are used: NORTH, NORTHEAST, EAST, SOUTHEAST, SOUTH, SOUTHWEST, WEST, NORTHWEST, and CENTER.

8

INTRODUCTION TO APPLET PROGRAMMING

Listing 8.6 shows an example of placing a component on a page using the GridBagLayout class. The code can also be found on the CD-ROM that accompanies this book.

Listing 8.6. Placing a component with the GridBagLayout manager.

```
// declare variables
GridBagLayout gl = new GridBagLayout();
GridBagConstraints gb = new GridBagConstraints();
// choose a layout manager
setLayout ( gl );
// create components
Label l1 = new Label("Full e-mail address:");
Label l2 = new Label("Captain Kirk");
Label l3 = new Label("Crate of oranges");
// set up the constraints and add component
gb.gridx = 1;
gb.gridy = 1;
gb.gridwidth = 2;
gl.setConstraints(l1, gb);
add(l1);
// set up the constraints and add component
gb.gridx = 5;
gb.gridy = 3;
gb.gridwidth = 2;
gl.setConstraints(l2, gb);
add(l2);
// set up the constraints and add component
gb.gridx = 3;
gb.gridy = 5;
gb.gridwidth = 2;
gl.setConstraints(l3, gb);
add(l3);
```

In this example, the first component is placed in row 1, column 1 of the grid and takes up two cells in width. The second component is placed in row 5, column 3; the third component is placed in row 3, column 5. Figure 8.14 shows an example of an applet with all components arranged according to the rules of the GridBagLayout manager and its GridBagConstraints.

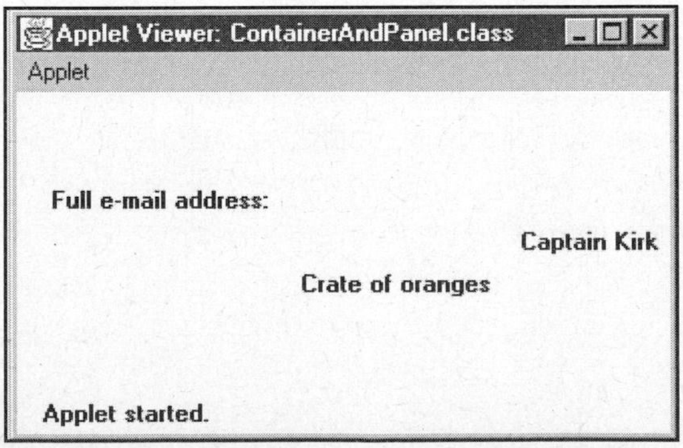

FIGURE 8.14.

Components arranged by the GridBagLayout *manager.*

```
Applet Viewer: ContainerAndPanel.class   _ □ ✕
Applet



    Full e-mail address:
                                        Captain Kirk
                      Crate of oranges




Applet started.
```

The CardLayout Class

The CardLayout class is a special type of layout organizer. Instead of displaying several panels concurrently, it creates a stack of panels that can then be displayed one at a time, much like the stack of cards in the ubiquitous Solitaire game. The CardLayout class has its own group of methods that are used to control which panel is displayed.

 Listing 8.7 uses a series of panels with different-colored canvases to illustrate the CardLayout class. Clicking on the applet area causes the layout manager to load the next panel. If the last panel is already loaded, the CardLayout manager automatically returns to the first panel. This code is also located on the CD-ROM that accompanies this book.

Listing 8.7. Using the CardLayout class to display three panels with different colors.

```java
import java.applet.Applet;
import java.awt.*;

public class cardStack extends Applet {
    private Panel    canvasCards = new Panel(),
        p1 = new Panel(), p2 = new Panel(), p3 = new Panel();
    private CardLayout cardDeck = new CardLayout();

    public void init() {
        canvasCards.setLayout( cardDeck );

        p1.setLayout (new BorderLayout());
        p2.setLayout (new BorderLayout());
        p3.setLayout (new BorderLayout());

        Canvas c1 = new Canvas(), c2 = new Canvas(), c3 = new Canvas();
        c1.setBackground(Color.black);
        c2.setBackground(Color.red);
        c3.setBackground(Color.green);

        p1.add("Center", c1);
        p2.add("Center", c2);
        p3.add("Center", c3);

        canvasCards.add("p1", p1);
        canvasCards.add("p2", p2);
        canvasCards.add("p3", p3);

        setLayout(new BorderLayout());
        add("Center", canvasCards);
    }

    public boolean mouseDown(Event event, int x, int y) {
        cardDeck.next(canvasCards);
        return true;
    }
}
```

Combining Layouts with Nested Panels

Although the Abstract Windowing Toolkit offers several different kinds of layout managers, frequently, one specific manager does not fit the user interface you are trying to create.

The solution to this problem is to nest one type of container inside another so that the nested container can have one type of layout manager and the larger container can use another. You can nest containers as many times as necessary because containers can contain other containers; each container can use its own layout manager.

The following code creates a container that uses the BorderLayout manager and then adds a panel of choice boxes to that container. Because no layout manager is specified for the boxes, they default to the FlowLayout manager.

```
setLayout( new BorderLayout() );
Button b1 = new Button("Purchase");
add("North", b1);
Button b2 = new Button("Exit");
add("West", b2);
Button b3 = new Button("Help");
add("East", b3);
Button b4 = new Button("Browse Catalog");
add("South", b4);
Panel p = new Panel();
// add check boxes to panel
Checkbox c1 = new Checkbox("Brazil: $9.95");
p.add(c1);
Checkbox c2 = new Checkbox("Time Bandits: $12.95");
p.add(c2);
Checkbox c3 = new Checkbox("12 Monkeys: $39.95");
p.add(c3);
// add panel to main container
add("Center",p);
```

Figure 8.15 shows an applet that uses this code. By using nested panels and different types of layout managers, you can create many different types of user interface windows.

FIGURE 8.15.

A container organized by the BorderLayout *manager with a nested panel in the center organized by the* FlowLayout *manager.*

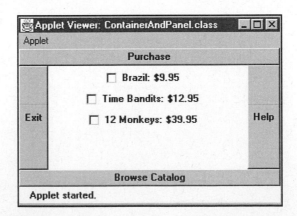

Event Handling

At this point, you have the tools necessary to build an impressive graphical user interface for a Java applet. You can use text fields to enter characters, click buttons, move scrollbars from side to side, and so on.

However, the interface has no way to respond to any of this user input. In a windowing environment such as the one provided by the Abstract Windowing Toolkit, user input—whether from the mouse, keyboard, or other means—generates an event.

An *event* is a way for a program to communicate that something has taken place. Events generate automatic calls to methods in the same way that a paint() method can be called automatically when an applet window has to be redrawn, or that an init() method is called automatically when an applet is first run.

Events can involve a user interface element—such as a button that has been clicked. Events can also be something unrelated to the interface—such as an error condition that causes the program to stop execution.

In Java, the class java.awt.Event handles all events related to the user interface.

For the purposes of controlling the user interface components you can create for use with applets, there are two kinds of events to consider: action events and scrollbar events.

Action Events

An *action event* is generated by most user interface components to signify that something has happened. This means different things depending on the component:

- For buttons, an event means that the button has been clicked.
- For checkboxes, an event means that the box has been selected or deselected.
- For lists or choice lists, an event means that one of the list items has been selected.
- For text fields, an event means that the Enter key has been pressed to indicate that user input is completed.

The action() method is part of the Event class and follows this syntax:

```
public boolean action(Event e, Object o) {
    // method code here
}
```

All user interface components that must generate an action event use the action() method. Two parameters to the method determine which component generated the event and gather some other information about what occurred. These two parameters are an instance of an Event and an Object class.

The Event class has several instance variables that provide information about the event that has taken place. The one you use most with action() events is the target variable, which indicates which component generated the event.

 The code in Listing 8.8 creates three buttons on an applet window and sets a TextField in response to the button that was pressed, as shown in Figure 8.16. The code can also be found on the CD-ROM that accompanies this book.

Listing 8.8. The full source code of Buttons.java.

```
1: import java.awt.*;
2:
3: public class Buttons extends java.applet.Applet {
4:     Button b1 = new Button("Swing Away");
5:     Button b2 = new Button("Bunt");
6:     Button b3 = new Button("Renegotiate Contract");
7:     TextField t = new TextField(50);
8:
9:     public void init() {
10:         add(b1);
11:         add(b2);
12:         add(b3);
13:         add(t);
14:     }
15:
16:     public boolean action(Event e, Object o) {
17:         if (e.target instanceof Button) {
18:             String s = (String)o;
19:             if ( s.equals("Swing Away") )
20:                 t.setText("A long fly to center ... caught.");
21:             else if ( s.equals("Bunt") )
22:                 t.setText("You reach on a throwing error!");
23:             else
24:                 t.setText("You're now America's newest multimillionaire!");
25:             return true;
26:         }
27:         return false;
27:     }
28: }
```

FIGURE 8.16.

The Buttons *applet.*

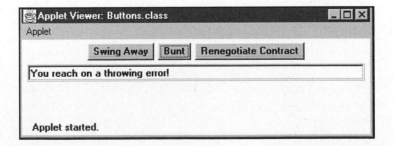

Scrollbar Events

The action() method is generated by every component described in this chapter except for
Scrollbar. The Scrollbar component uses the handleEvent() method. Unlike the action()
method, handleEvent() takes only one parameter: an instance of the Event class:

```
public boolean handleEvent(Event e) {
    // method code here
}
```

 Using the target variable of the Event class, you can determine which component
generated the event and respond to it. Listing 8.9 sets a value in a text field based on
user input to a scrollbar. You can find the code on the CD-ROM that accompanies
this book.

Listing 8.9. The full source code of Scroller.java.

```
 1: import java.awt.*;
 2:
 3: public class Scroller extends java.applet.Applet {
 4:     Scrollbar s = new Scrollbar(Scrollbar.HORIZONTAL,
 5:                   50,100,0,100);
 6:     Label l = new Label("Choose Your Own Tax Rate: ");
 7:     TextField t = new TextField("50%", 3);
 8:
 9:     public void init() {
10:         add(s);
11:         add(l);
12:         add(t);
13:     }
14:
15:     public boolean handleEvent(Event e) {
16:         if (e.target instanceof Scrollbar) {
17:             int taxrate = ((Scrollbar)e.target).getValue();
18:             t.setText(taxrate + "%");
19:             return true;
20:         }
21:     return false;
22:     }
23: }
```

When you use a Web browser or the JDK applet viewer utility to view the completed applet,
it should resemble Figure 8.17.

FIGURE 8.17.

The Scroller applet.

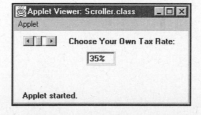

Summary

As you will find when programming your own applets, the Java API has built-in functionality that handles a lot of the work for you. The user interface provides many components such as buttons, text fields, and choice boxes—and subclassing makes it possible to extend these components without requiring a lot of new code.

Tasks that can be arduous in some languages—such as animation and event handling—are relatively easy with Java. One of Java's original design goals was simplicity. Some folks argue that object-oriented programming is never simple. However, applet programming is a good area for novice Java programmers to begin because it can be easy to develop useful Web programs without a lot of coding.

This introduction to applet programming and the Abstract Windowing Toolkit demonstrated a lot of Java's functionality as it's built into the class libraries. For many applets, creating the user interface represents the bulk of the work because a lot of the code required to control the interface has already been written.

Each of the user interface components has methods you can use to retrieve or change their values, enable or disable their operation, and perform other tasks. The full reference to these methods is available in Appendix C, "Java Class Library."

III

PART

IN THIS PART

The Standard Packages

Overview of the Standard Packages

by Michael Morrison

IN THIS CHAPTER

CHAPTER 9

Code reuse is one of the most significant benefits of using object-oriented design practices. Creating reusable, inheritable classes can save amazing amounts of time and energy—which in turn greatly boosts productivity. Java itself takes code reuse to heart in its implementation of a wide variety of standard objects available to Java programmers. The standard Java objects are known collectively as the Java *standard packages*.

The Java standard packages contain groups of related classes. Along with classes, the standard Java packages also include interfaces, exception definitions, and error definitions. Java is composed of ten standard packages: the language package, the utilities package, the I/O package, the networking package, the windowing package, the text package, the security package, the RMI package, the reflection package, and the SQL package. In this chapter, you learn what each package is and what classes and interfaces comprise each.

The Language Package

The Java language package, also known as java.lang, provides classes that make up the core of the Java language. The language package contains classes at the lowest level of the Java standard packages. For example, the Object class, from which all classes are derived, is located in the language package.

It's impossible to write a Java program without dealing with at least a few of the elements of the language package. You'll learn much more about the inner workings of the language package in the next chapter. The most important classes contained in the language package follow:

- The Object class
- Data type wrapper classes
- The Math class
- String classes
- System and Runtime classes
- Thread classes
- Class classes
- Exception-handling classes
- The Process class

NOTE

The Java reflection package, java.lang.reflect, is technically a subpackage of the java.lang package. However, because of its significance to the overall architecture of Java, it is treated in this book as its own package. You learn about it later in this chapter and in Chapter 18, "The Reflection Package."

The Object Class

The Object class is the superclass for all classes in Java. Because all classes are derived from Object, the methods defined in Object are shared by all classes. This results in a core set of methods that all Java classes are guaranteed to support. Object includes methods for making copies of an object, testing objects for equality, and converting the value of an object to a string.

Data Type Wrapper Classes

Java's fundamental data types (int, char, float, and so on) are not implemented as classes. It is frequently useful, however, to know more information about a fundamental type than just its value. By implementing *class wrappers* for the fundamental types, you can maintain additional information—you can also define methods that act on the types. The data type wrapper classes serve as class versions of the fundamental data types and are named similarly to the types they wrap. For example, the type wrapper for int is the Integer class. Following are the Java data type wrapper classes:

- Boolean
- Character
- Double
- Float
- Integer
- Long

Type wrappers are also useful because many of Java's utility classes require *classes* as parameters instead of simple types. It is worth pointing out that type wrappers and simple types are *not* interchangeable. However, you can get a simple type from a wrapper through a simple method call, which you learn about in the next chapter.

The Math Class

The Math class groups mathematical functions and constants. It is interesting to note that all the variables and methods in Math are static and that the Math class itself is final. This means that you can't derive new classes from Math. Additionally, you can't instantiate the Math class. It's best to think of the Math class as just a conglomeration of methods and constants for performing mathematical computations.

The Math class includes the E and PI constants, methods for determining the absolute value of a number, methods for calculating trigonometric functions, and minimum and maximum methods, among others.

String Classes

For various reasons (mostly security related), Java implements text strings as classes rather than forcing the programmer to use character arrays. The two Java classes that represent strings are String and StringBuffer. The String class is useful for working with constant strings that can't change in value or length. The StringBuffer class is used to work with strings of varying value and length.

The System and Runtime Classes

The System and Runtime classes provide a means for your programs to access system and runtime environment resources. Like the Math class, the System class is final and is composed entirely of static variables and methods. The System class basically provides a system-independent programming interface to system resources. Examples of system resources include the standard input and output streams, System.in and System.out, which typically model the keyboard and monitor.

The Runtime class provides direct access to the runtime environment. An example of a runtime routine is the freeMemory() method, which returns the amount of free system memory available.

Thread Classes

Java is a multithreaded environment and provides various classes for managing and working with threads. Following are the classes and interfaces used in conjunction with multithreaded programs:

- Thread: Used to create a thread of execution in a program.
- ThreadDeath: Used to clean up after a thread has finished execution.
- ThreadGroup: Useful for organizing a group of threads.
- Runnable: Provides an alternative means of creating a thread without subclassing the Thread class.

Threads and multithreading are covered in detail in Chapter 6, "Threads and Multithreading."

Class Classes

Java provides two classes for working with classes: Class and ClassLoader. The Class class provides runtime information for a class, such as the name, type, and parent superclass. Class is useful for querying a class for runtime information, such as the class name. The ClassLoader class provides a means to load classes into the runtime environment. ClassLoader is useful for loading classes from a file or for loading distributed classes across a network connection.

Exception-Handling Classes

Runtime error handling is a very important facility in any programming environment. Java provides the following classes for dealing with runtime errors:

- `Throwable`: Provides low-level error-handling capabilities such as an execution stack list.

- `Exception`: Derived from `Throwable` to provide the base level of functionality for all the exception classes defined in the Java system. Used to handle normal errors.

- `Error`: Derived from `Throwable` (as is the `Exception` class) but is used to handle abnormal errors that aren't expected to occur. Very few Java programs use the `Error` class; most use the `Exception` class to handle runtime errors.

Error handling with exceptions is covered in detail in Chapter 7, "Exception Handling."

The Process Class

Java supports system processes with a single class, `Process`. The `Process` class represents generic system processes that are created when you use the `Runtime` class to execute system commands.

The Utilities Package

The Java utilities package, also known as `java.util`, provides various classes that perform different utility functions. The utilities package includes a class for working with dates, a set of data structure classes, a class for generating random numbers, and a string tokenizer class, among others. You'll learn much more about the classes that make up the utilities package in Chapter 11, "The Utilities Package." The most important classes contained in the utilities package follow:

- The `Date` class
- Data structure classes
- The `Random` class
- The `StringTokenizer` class
- The `Properties` class
- Observer classes

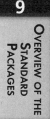

The Date Class

The `Date` class represents a calendar date and time in a system-independent fashion. The `Date` class provides methods for retrieving the current date and time as well as computing days of the week and month.

Data Structure Classes

The Java data structure classes and interfaces implement popular data structures for storing data. The data structure classes and interfaces are as follows:

- ■ BitSet: Represents a set of bits, also known as a *bitfield*.
- ■ Dictionary: An abstract class that provides a lookup mechanism for mapping keys to values.
- ■ Hashtable: Derived from Dictionary to provide additional support for working with keys and values.
- ■ Properties: Derived from Hashtable to provide the additional functionality of being readable and writable to and from streams.
- ■ Vector: Implements an array that can dynamically grow.
- ■ Stack: Derived from Vector to implement a classic stack of last-in-first-out (LIFO) objects.
- ■ Enumeration: This interface specifies a set of methods for counting (iterating) through a set of values.

The Random Class

Many programs, especially programs that model the real world, require some degree of randomness. Java provides randomness with the Random class. The Random class implements a random-number generator by providing a stream of pseudo-random numbers. A slot-machine program is a good example of one that can make use of the Random class.

The StringTokenizer Class

The StringTokenizer class provides a means of converting text strings into individual tokens. By specifying a set of delimiters, you can parse text strings into tokens using the StringTokenizer class. String tokenization is useful in a wide variety of programs, from compilers to text-based adventure games.

The Observer Classes

The model-view paradigm is becoming increasingly popular in object-oriented programming. This model divides a program into data and views on the data. Java supports this model with the Observable class and the Observer interface. The Observable class is subclassed to define the observable data in a program. This data is then connected to one or more observer classes. The observer classes are implementations of the Observer interface. When an Observable object changes state, it notifies all its observers of the change.

The I/O Package

The Java I/O package, also known as `java.io`, provides classes with support for reading and writing data to and from different input and output devices—including files. The I/O package includes classes for inputting streams of data, outputting streams of data, working with files, and tokenizing streams of data. You'll learn a lot more about the classes that make up the I/O package in Chapter 12, "The I/O Package." The most important classes contained in the I/O package follow:

- Input stream classes
- Output stream classes
- File classes
- The `StreamTokenizer` class

Input Stream Classes

Java uses input streams to handle reading data from an input source. An *input source* can be a file, a string, memory, or anything else that contains data. The input stream classes follow:

- `InputStream`
- `BufferedInputStream`
- `ByteArrayInputStream`
- `DataInputStream`
- `FileInputStream`
- `FilterInputStream`
- `LineNumberInputStream`
- `PipedInputStream`
- `PushbackInputStream`
- `SequenceInputStream`
- `StringBufferInputStream`

The `InputStream` class is an abstract class that serves as the base class for all input streams. The `InputStream` class defines an interface for reading streamed bytes of data, finding the number of bytes available for reading, and moving the stream position pointer, among other things. All the other input streams provide support for reading data from different types of input devices.

Output Stream Classes

Output streams are the counterpart to input streams; they handle writing data to an output source. Similar to input sources, *output sources* include files, strings, memory, and anything else that can contain data. The output stream classes defined in java.io follow:

- OutputStream
- BufferedOutputStream
- ByteArrayOutputStream
- DataOutputStream
- FileOutputStream
- FilterOutputStream
- PipedOutputStream
- PrintStream

The OutputStream class is an abstract class that serves as the base class for all output streams. OutputStream defines an interface for writing streamed bytes of data to an output source. All the other output streams provide support for writing data to different output devices. Data written by an output stream is formatted to be read by an input stream.

File Classes

Files are the most widely used method of data storage in computer systems. Java supports files with two different classes: File and RandomAccessFile. The File class provides an abstraction for files that takes into account system-dependent features. The File class keeps up with information about a file, including the location where it is stored and how it can be accessed. The File class has no methods for reading and writing data to and from a file; it is useful only for querying and modifying the attributes of a file. In actuality, you can think of the File class data as representing a filename, and the class methods as representing operating system commands that act on filenames.

The RandomAccessFile class provides a variety of methods for reading and writing data to and from a file. RandomAccessFile contains many different methods for reading and writing different types of information, namely the data type wrappers.

The StreamTokenizer Class

The StreamTokenizer class provides the functionality for converting an input stream of data into a stream of tokens. StreamTokenizer provides a set of methods for defining the lexical syntax of tokens. Stream tokenization can be useful in parsing streams of textual data.

The Networking Package

The Java networking package, also known as `java.net`, contains classes that allow you to perform a wide range of network communications. The networking package includes specific support for URLs, TCP sockets, IP addresses, and UDP sockets. The Java networking classes make it easy and straightforward to implement client/server Internet solutions in Java. You learn much more about the classes that make up the networking package in Chapter 13, "The Networking Package." The classes included in the networking package follow:

- The `InetAddress` class
- URL classes
- Socket classes
- The `ContentHandler` class

The InetAddress Class

The `InetAddress` class models an Internet IP address and provides methods for getting information about the address. For example, `InetAddress` contains methods for retrieving either the text name or the raw IP representation of the host represented by the address. `InetAddress` also contains static methods that allow you to find out about hosts without actually creating an `InetAddress` object.

URL Classes

The URL classes are used to represent and interact with Uniform Resource Locators (URLs), which are references to information on the Web. Following are the URL classes included in the networking package:

- `URL`: Represents a Uniform Resource Locator. `URL` objects are constant, meaning that their values cannot change once they have been created. In this way, `URL` objects more closely represent physical URLs, which are also constant.
- `URLConnection`: An abstract class that defines the overhead necessary to facilitate a connection through a URL. This class must be subclassed to provide functionality for a specific type of URL connection.
- `URLStreamHandler`: An abstract class that defines the mechanism required to open streams based on URLs.
- `URLEncoder`: Allows you to convert a string of text information into a format suitable for communication through a URL.

Socket Classes

The socket classes are perhaps the most important classes contained in the networking package. They provide the entire framework for performing network communication through a couple of different approaches. The classes that comprise Java's socket support follow:

- SocketImpl: An abstract class that defines a base level of functionality required by all sockets. This functionality includes both member variables and a substantial collection of methods. Specific socket implementations are derived from SocketImpl.

- Socket: Provides client-side streamed socket support. *Streamed sockets* are sockets that communicate in real time over a live connection with a high degree of reliability.

- ServerSocket: Used to implement the server side of streamed socket support.

- DatagramSocket: Contains everything necessary to perform datagram socket communication. A *datagram socket* is a socket that sends out packets of information with little regard for reliability or timing. Unlike streamed sockets, datagram sockets don't rely on a live connection, meaning that they send and receive data whenever it is convenient. Data being transferred with a datagram socket must be encapsulated by a DatagramPacket object.

- DatagramPacket: Includes information critical to a packet of information being transferred with a datagram socket.

The ContentHandler Class

The ContentHandler class serves as a framework for handling different Internet data types. For example, you can write a content handler to process and display a proprietary file format. To do this, you derive a class from ContentHandler and write code to build an object from a stream of data representing the object type.

The Windowing (AWT) Package

The Java windowing package, also known as java.awt, consists of classes that provide a wide range of graphics and user interface features. This package includes classes representing graphical interface elements such as windows, dialog boxes, menus, buttons, checkboxes, scrollbars, and text fields, as well as general graphics elements such as fonts. You learn much more about the classes in the windowing package in Chapter 14, "The Windowing (AWT) Package." The most important classes included in the windowing package follow:

- Graphical classes
- Layout manager classes
- Font classes
- Dimension classes
- The MediaTracker class

> **NOTE**
>
> The windowing package is also often referred to as the Abstract Windowing Toolkit (AWT), which is where the name `java.awt` comes from.

Graphical Classes

The graphical classes are all based on serving a particular graphical user input or display need. For this reason, the graphical classes are often indispensable in applet programming. The graphical classes include support for everything from checkboxes and menus to canvases and color representations.

> **NOTE**
>
> Although I mention the graphical classes here only in terms of Java applets, these classes are equally useful in graphical standalone Java applications. Just keep in mind that standalone applications must create their own frame window to house any graphical elements; an applet can simply use the applet window that has been allotted to it on the containing Web page.

One of the most important GUI classes is the `Graphics` class, which serves as an all-purpose graphical output class capable of performing all kinds of different drawing functions. The `Graphics` class is ultimately responsible for all graphical output generated by a Java applet.

The `Component` class is another fundamental graphical class and serves as the parent for many of the other graphical classes. It is used this way primarily because `Component` provides all the overhead necessary for a basic graphical element.

Layout Manager Classes

The layout manager classes provide a framework for controlling the physical layout of GUI elements. For example, if you want a row of buttons arranged in a certain way across the top of an applet window, you use a layout manager to accomplish this. Following are the layout manager classes implemented in the windowing package:

- `BorderLayout`: Arranges graphical elements (also called *components*) along a window border, with one element in each position (north, south, east, west, and center).
- `CardLayout`: Arranges components on top of each other like a stack of cards; you can flip through the "cards" to display different components.
- `FlowLayout`: Arranges components from left to right across a window until no more fit; then the components are wrapped around to the next line.

- ■ GridLayout: Arranges equally sized components in a grid with a specific number of rows and columns.
- ■ GridBagLayout: Similar to the GridLayout class except that the components in GridBagLayout don't have to be the same size; this layout provides the programmer with a great deal of flexibility.

All the layout classes are derived from the LayoutManager interface, which defines the core functionality required of a graphical layout manager.

Font Classes

The font classes consist of the Font class and the FontMetrics class. The Font class represents graphical font objects with attributes such as name, size, and style. Furthermore, Font objects can also be made **bold** or *italic*. The FontMetrics class provides a means to find information about the size of a font. For example, you can use a FontMetrics object to ascertain the height of a font, or something more specific such as a font's line spacing (leading).

Dimension Classes

The dimension classes provide a convenient way to represent different graphical dimensions in Java. The following dimension classes are defined in the windowing package:

- ■ Dimension: Represents the basic rectangular dimensions of a graphical element. The class includes two public member variables for storing the width and height of a rectangular object.
- ■ Rectangle: Similar to Dimension, except that Rectangle also includes the x and y coordinates of the upper-left corner of a graphical element. In other words, the Rectangle class keeps up with the dimension of a graphical element as well as its position.
- ■ Point: Similar to the Rectangle class, except that Point keeps up only with an x,y position.
- ■ Polygon: Represents a polygon, which is basically a series of connected points.

The MediaTracker Class

The MediaTracker class provides a means to track when media resources have finished transmitting across a network connection. Currently, the MediaTracker class supports only the tracking of images, but a future release of Java will no doubt add support for sounds and other media types as they gain popularity. The MediaTracker class serves a very useful purpose for applets because it allows them to know when a particular image is ready to be displayed. For some applets, this knowledge is critical.

The Text Package

The Java text package, also known as `java.text`, is a key part of Java's support for internationalization. The text package contains classes and interfaces for handling text specific to a particular locale. In other words, the text package provides the underlying mechanism that enables text to be mapped to a specific language and region. The classes and interfaces defined in the text package rely on Unicode 2.0 character encoding and can be used to adapt text, numbers, dates, currency, and user-defined objects to the conventions of any country. You learn a great deal more about the classes and interfaces in the text package in Chapter 15, "The Text Package." Some of the more important classes included in the text package follow:

- Formatting classes
- The `Collator` class
- The `TextBoundary` class

Formatting Classes

The text package provides a variety of classes for formatting data according to different cultural conventions. These formatting classes can also parse formatted strings back into their original form. The `Format` class is an abstract base class that encapsulates locale-sensitive formatting and parsing. Three main subclasses are derived from `Format`: `NumberFormat`, `DateFormat`, and `MessageFormat`. These derived classes are used to format numbers, dates, and messages, respectively. More specific formatting classes are derived from these classes.

The Collator Class

The `Collator` class provides support for the locale-sensitive comparison of strings. Using the `Collator` class, you can compare two strings and factor in any special naming and formatting conventions specific to a particular locale. Java's internationalization facilities require this capability for text sorting and locale-sensitive searching.

The TextBoundary Class

The `TextBoundary` class determines different boundaries in text such as word, line, and sentence boundaries. These capabilities are critical if Java is to manage different languages; these features enable the programmer to allow intelligent text selection and line wrapping.

The Security Package

The Java security package, also known as `java.security`, contains the functionality for incorporating cryptographic security into Java-based applications. The cryptography framework in the security package includes support for DSA cryptography and is designed so that new algorithms can be added later without difficulty. For example, although DSA is the only

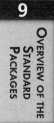

9

OVERVIEW OF THE STANDARD PACKAGES

built-in digital signature algorithm in Java version 1.1, the API can easily accommodate other algorithms such as RSA without requiring significant code changes. You learn more about the classes and interfaces in the security package in Chapter 16, "The Security Package." Some of the more important classes included in the security package follow:

- Digital signature classes
- The MessageDigest class
- Key management classes

Digital Signature Classes

The digital signature classes in the security package provide support for generating public/private key pairs as well as for signing and verifying arbitrary digital data. Digital signatures are used for authentication and integrity assurance of digital data. The Signature class is used to provide the functionality of a digital signature algorithm such as DSA. The Identity class represents *identities*: real-world objects such as people, companies, or organizations whose identities can be authenticated using their public keys. The Signer class represents an identity that can also digitally sign data.

The MessageDigest Class

The MessageDigest class provides the functionality of a message digest algorithm, such as MD5 or SHA. *Message digests* are secure, one-way hash functions that take arbitrary-sized data and output a fixed-length hash value. Message digests are useful for producing "digital fingerprints" of data, which are frequently used in digital signatures and other applications that need unique and unforgeable identifiers for digital data.

Key Management Classes

The key management classes included in the security package are used to manage the public and private keys used in the digital signature process. The Key interface is the top-level interface for all keys; it defines the functionality shared by all key objects. The KeyPair class is a simple container for a key pair (that is, a public key and a private key). Finally, the KeyPairGenerator class is used to generate pairs of public and private keys.

The RMI Package

The Java RMI (Remote Method Invocation) package, also known as java.rmi, enables developers to create distributed Java-to-Java applications that rely on remote method invocation. When you use RMI, you can invoke methods of remote Java objects from other Java virtual machines—even on different hosts. The RMI support provided in the RMI package uses object serialization to process parameters being passed between methods. You learn more about the RMI package in Chapter 17, "The RMI Package."

The Reflection Package

The Java reflection package, also known as `java.lang.reflect`, enables Java code to examine and find detailed information regarding the structure of classes at runtime. More specifically, the reflection services can be used to discover information about the fields, methods, and constructors of classes. The reflection package accommodates applications that require access to either the public members of a target object or the members declared by a given class. You learn more about the reflection package in Chapter 18, "The Reflection Package."

> **NOTE**
>
> JavaBeans relies heavily on the reflection API to give application builder tools the capability of assessing the exported properties of JavaBeans components.

The SQL Package

The Java SQL package, also known as `java.sql`, contains the overhead required for developers to write database applications capable of performing SQL queries. The SQL package is also sometimes referred to as JDBC (Java Database Connectivity). SQL is the industry standard querying language for accessing and manipulating databases. The SQL package makes it possible for a Java application to interact with virtually any relational database using SQL. The only requirement is that the database have a SQL driver. The capability of accessing multiple databases in a consistent fashion with Java is a huge breakthrough for Java developers. For example, the SQL package makes it possible to publish a Web page containing an applet that uses information obtained from a remote database. Intranet database applications will also benefit a great deal from the SQL package. You learn more about the SQL package in Chapter 19, "The SQL Package." Some of the more important classes and interfaces included in the SQL package follow:

- The `DriverManager` class
- The `Connection` interface
- The `Statement` and `ResultSet` interfaces

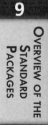

9

OVERVIEW OF THE
STANDARD
PACKAGES

The DriverManager Class

The `DriverManager` class provides the overhead to manage a set of JDBC drivers, which is necessary to establish a connection with a particular database. When the `DriverManager` class is initialized, it tries to load the drivers identified in the system settings. It then attempts to select and use one of these drivers when the user tries to establish a database connection.

The Connection Interface

The Connection interface defines the functionality required of a database connection. When a successful database connection is established through the DriverManager class, a Connection-derived object is returned to the user. This object is then used as the context through which SQL statements are constructed and executed and through which subsequent results are returned.

The Statement and ResultSet Interfaces

The Statement interface defines the functionality required of a SQL statement to be executed on a database. SQL statements are always issued through a particular connection context. The results of an executed SQL statement are returned in a ResultSet-derived object. In accordance with standard relational database result handling, the ResultSet interface provides access to a tabular set of result data. The ResultSet interface is used to access this data on a row-by-row basis.

Summary

This chapter provided a thumbnail sketch of the contents of the ten standard Java packages: the language package, the utilities package, the I/O package, the networking package, the windowing package, the text package, the security package, the RMI package, the reflection package, and the SQL package. Although you didn't learn a lot of gritty details, or how to use any of these classes in a real program, you should now have a general sense of what these packages can do. The standard Java packages provide a rich set of classes for overcoming a wide variety of programming obstacles.

This chapter has given you an idea of which standard classes you can use in your own Java programs, and which classes you will have to implement yourself.

Having seen the types of features these packages provide, you're probably eager to start learning how to use the classes included in each package. The next ten chapters focus on the standard Java packages.

The Language
Package

by Michael Morrison

IN THIS CHAPTER

CHAPTER 10

The Java language package is the heart of the Java language. In this chapter, you learn more about some of the classes that make up the language package (java.lang). You'll find that many of the classes in the language package are indispensable when you are writing Java programs.

The language package contains many classes, each with a variety of member variables, member constants, and methods. You don't learn about every class and every method in this chapter (that would simply be too much material to cover in a single chapter). Rather, you focus on the most important classes in the language package—the classes that are the most useful as you begin developing your own Java classes. Please note that although the multithreading and error-handling classes are part of the language package, they aren't covered in this chapter; Chapter 6, "Threads and Multithreading," and Chapter 7, "Exception Handling," are devoted to these classes.

The Object Class

The Object class is probably the most important of all Java classes, simply because it is the superclass of all Java classes. It is important to have a solid understanding of the Object class because all the classes you develop inherit the variables and methods of Object. The Object class implements the following important methods:

- `Object clone()`
- `boolean equals(Object obj)`
- `int hashCode()`
- `final Class getClass()`
- `String toString()`

The clone() Method

`Object clone()`

The Object `clone()` method creates a clone of the object on which it is called. `clone()` creates and allocates memory for the new object being copied to. `clone()` actually creates a new object and then copies the contents of the calling object to the new object. An example of using the `clone()` method follows:

```
Circle circle1 = new Circle(1.0, 3.5, 4.2);
Circle circle2 = circle1.clone();
```

In this example, the circle1 object is created, but the circle2 object is only declared. circle2 is not created by using the new operator; it is created when circle1 calls the `clone()` method to create a clone of itself.

The equals() Method

```
boolean equals(Object obj)
```

The equals() method compares two objects for equality. equals() is applicable only when both objects have been stored in a hash table.

The hashCode() Method

```
int hashCode()
```

The hashCode() method returns the hashcode value for an object. *Hashcodes* are integers that uniquely represent objects in the Java system.

The getClass() Method

```
final Class getClass()
```

The getClass() method returns the runtime class information for an object in the form of a Class object. The Class object keeps up with runtime class information such as the name of a class and the parent superclass.

The toString() Method

```
String toString()
```

The toString() method returns a string representing the value of an object. Because the value of an object varies depending on the class type, it is assumed that each class will override the toString() method to display information specific to that class. The information returned by toString() can be very valuable for determining the internal state of an object when you are debugging your code.

Data Type Wrapper Classes

The data type wrapper classes provide object versions of the fundamental Java data types. Type wrapping is important because many Java classes and methods operate on classes rather than on fundamental types. Furthermore, by creating object versions of the simple data types, it is possible to add useful member functions for each data type. Following are the type wrapper classes supported by Java:

- Boolean
- Byte

- Short
- Character
- Integer
- Long
- Float
- Double
- Void

Although each wrapper implements methods specific to each data type, a handful of methods are applicable to all the wrappers except the Void class. This is because the Void class serves merely as a placeholder for the primitive void type. The common methods implemented in the other wrapper classes follow:

- ClassType(*type*)
- type *type*Value()
- int hashCode()
- String toString()
- boolean equals(Object *obj*)
- static boolean valueOf(String *s*)

> **NOTE**
>
> Actually, the valueOf() method isn't implemented in the Character class, but it is implemented in all the other wrapper classes.

The ClassType() Method

ClassType(*type*)

The ClassType() method is actually the constructor for each class. The wrapper constructors take as their only parameter the type of data they are wrapping. This arrangement enables you to create a type wrapper from a fundamental type. For example, you can use the constructor for the Character class like this:

```
Character c1 = new Character('x');
```

The *type*Value() Method

```
type typeValue()
```

The *type*Value() method is used to get the fundamental type back from a wrapper. *type*Value() returns a value of the same type as the fundamental type it wraps. Following is an example of how a fundamental type can be extracted from a wrapper object:

```
char c2 = c1.charValue();
```

> **NOTE**
>
> Remember that fundamental types are not represented in Java by classes or objects. Data type wrapper classes provide a way of representing a fundamental type as an object, which is often useful. Wrapper classes are different from other Java classes in that their only purpose is to allow fundamental types to be represented as objects. You can easily distinguish wrapper classes from primitive types because the first letter of wrapper class names is always capitalized.

The hashCode() Method

```
int hashCode()
```

The hashCode() method returns the hashcode for a type wrapper object. This hashCode() method is simply an overridden version of the hashCode() method contained in the Object class.

The toString() Method

```
String toString()
```

The toString() method is used to get a string representation of the internal state of an object. toString() is typically overridden in each class so that it reflects unique state implementations. Following is an example of how you can output the state of a wrapper variable using toString():

```
System.out.println(c1.toString());
```

The equals() Method

```
boolean equals(Object obj)
```

The equals() method is used to test for equality between two wrapper objects. This is the same equals() method that is implemented in Object and inherited by all other objects in Java.

The valueOf() Method

```
static boolean valueOf(String s)
```

The valueOf() method is implemented in all the type wrappers except Character. valueOf(), which is static, is used to convert a string to a value of a particular wrapper type. valueOf() parses the String parameter s and returns its value.

Now that you have an idea of what functionality all the wrapper classes share, it's time to take a look at some of the specifics of each class.

The Boolean Class

The Boolean class wraps the boolean fundamental data type. Boolean implements only one method in addition to the common wrapper methods already mentioned: getBoolean().

The getBoolean() Method

```
static boolean getBoolean(String name)
```

The getBoolean() method returns a type boolean that represents the boolean property value of the String parameter *name*. The *name* parameter refers to a property name that represents a boolean property value. Because getBoolean() is static, it is typically meant to be used without actually instantiating a Boolean object.

> **NOTE**
>
> Java *properties* are system variables that define the characteristics of the Java runtime environment. For example, there is a property called os.name that specifies the name of the operating system in which the Java runtime is executing. In my case, os.name is set to "Windows 95".

Member Constants

The Boolean class also includes three final static (constant) data members: TRUE, FALSE, and TYPE. TRUE and FALSE represent the two possible states that the Boolean class can represent. It is important to note the difference between true and false and Boolean.TRUE and Boolean.FALSE. The first pair applies to boolean fundamental types; the second pair applies to Boolean classes; they cannot be interchanged. The TYPE member constant specifies the runtime Class object representing the boolean value.

The Byte and Short Classes

The Byte class wraps the fundamental byte type and provides a variety of methods for working with byte numbers. Some of the more important methods implemented by Byte follow:

- static int parseByte(String *s*, int *radix*)
- static int parseByte(String *s*)
- long shortValue()
- long longValue()
- long intValue()
- float floatValue()
- double doubleValue()

The parseByte() Methods

```
static byte parseByte(String s, int radix)
static byte parseByte(String s)
```

The parseByte() methods parse strings for a byte value and return the value as a byte. The version of parseByte() with the *radix* parameter enables you to specify the base of the byte; the other version of parseByte() assumes a base of 10.

The shortValue(), longValue(), intValue(), floatValue(), and doubleValue() Methods

```
short shortValue()
long longValue()
int intValue()
float floatValue()
double doubleValue()
```

The shortValue(), longValue(), intValue(), floatValue(), and doubleValue() methods return the value of a byte converted to the appropriate type. For example, the following code shows how to convert a byte to a double:

```
Byte b = new Byte(43);
Double d = b.doubleValue();
```

In this example, the value of the Byte variable b is converted to a double value and stored in the Double variable d.

Member Constants

The Byte class also includes three final static (constant) data members: MIN_VALUE, MAX_VALUE, and TYPE. MIN_VALUE and MAX_VALUE specify the smallest and largest numbers that can be represented by a Byte object. TYPE specifies the runtime Class object representing the byte value.

10

THE LANGUAGE PACKAGE

The Short class is similar to the Byte class except that it wraps the fundamental type short. Short implements methods similar to those of the Byte class, with the exception that they act on short-type numbers rather than on byte-type numbers.

The Character Class

The Character class wraps the char fundamental type and provides some useful methods for manipulating characters. Some of the more important methods implemented by Character follow:

- static boolean isLowerCase(char *ch*)

- static boolean isUpperCase(char *ch*)

- static boolean isDigit(char *ch*)

- static boolean isSpace(char *ch*)

- static char toLowerCase(char *ch*)

- static char toUpperCase(char *ch*)

- static int digit(char *ch*, int *radix*)

- static char forDigit(int *digit*, int *radix*)

All these methods are static, which means that they can be used without instantiating a Character object.

The isLowerCase() and isUpperCase() Methods

```
static boolean isLowerCase(char ch)
static boolean isUpperCase(char ch)
```

The isLowerCase() and isUpperCase() methods return whether or not a character is an uppercase or lowercase character. An example of using the isLowerCase() method follows:

```
Character c = new Character('g');
boolean isLower = Character.isLowerCase(c);
```

In this case, the boolean variable isLower is set to true because 'g' is a lowercase character.

The isDigit() Method

```
static boolean isDigit(char ch)
```

The isDigit() method simply returns whether or not a character is a digit (0 to 9). Following is an example of how to use the isDigit() method:

```
boolean isDigit = Character.isDigit('7');
```

Here, the boolean variable isDigit is set to true because '7' is in fact a numeric digit.

The `isSpace()` Method

```
static boolean isSpace(char ch)
```

The `isSpace()` method returns whether or not a character is whitespace. (*Whitespace* is defined as any combination of the space, tab, newline, carriage return, or linefeed characters.) Following is an example of how to use `isSpace()`:

```
boolean isSpace = Character.isSpace('\t');
```

In this example, the `isSpace` boolean variable is set to `true` because the tab (`'\t'`) character is considered whitespace.

The `toLowerCase()` and `toUpperCase()` Methods

```
static char toLowerCase(char ch)
static char toUpperCase(char ch)
```

The `toLowerCase()` and `toUpperCase()` methods convert a character to a lowercase or uppercase character. If a character is already lowercase and `toLowerCase()` is called, the character is not changed. Similarly, `toUpperCase()` does nothing to uppercase characters. Following are a few examples of how to use these methods:

```
char c1 = Character.toUpperCase('g');
char c2 = Character.toLowerCase('M');
```

In the first example, c1 is converted from `'g'` to `'G'` with the call to the `toUpperCase()` method. In the second example, c2 is converted from `'M'` to `'m'` with the call to `toLowerCase()`.

The `digit()` Method

```
static int digit(char ch, int radix)
```

The `digit()` method returns the numeric (integer) value of a character digit in base 10. The *radix* parameter specifies the base of the character digit for conversion. If the character is not a valid digit, `-1` is returned. Following are a few examples of using the `digit()` method:

```
char c1 = '4';
char c2 = 'c';
int four = Character.digit(c1, 10);
int twelve = Character.digit(c2, 16);
```

In the first example, the character `'4'` is converted to the integer number 4 using the `digit()` method. In the second example, the hexadecimal number represented by the character `'c'` is returned as the base 10 integer number 12.

The forDigit() Method

```
static char forDigit(int digit, int radix)
```

The forDigit() method performs the reverse of the digit() method: It returns the character representation of an integer digit. Once again, *radix* specifies the base of the integer number. Following is an example of how to use forDigit():

```
int i = 9;
char c = Character.forDigit(i, 10);
```

In this example, the integer number 9 is converted to the character '9' by the forDigit() method.

Member Constants

The Character class provides three final static data members for specifying the radix limits for conversions: MIN_RADIX, MAX_RADIX, and TYPE. The *radix* for a number is its base, such as binary, octal, or hexadecimal. These common radixes have values of 2, 8, and 16, respectively. MIN_RADIX specifies the minimum radix (base 2) for performing numeric-to-character conversions and vice-versa. Likewise, MAX_RADIX specifies the maximum radix (base 36) for conversions. TYPE specifies the runtime Class object representing the character value.

> **NOTE**
>
> The Character class also includes a variety of member constants representing different types of commonly used characters. Please refer to the Java 1.1 API documentation for more information on these member constants.

The Integer and Long Classes

The Integer and Long classes wrap the fundamental integer types int and long and provide a variety of methods for working with integer numbers. The methods implemented by Integer follow:

- ◼ `static int parseInt(String s, int radix)`
- ◼ `static int parseInt(String s)`
- ◼ `short shortValue()`
- ◼ `long longValue()`
- ◼ `float floatValue()`
- ◼ `double doubleValue()`
- ◼ `byte byteValue()`
- ◼ `static Integer getInteger(String name)`
- ◼ `static Integer getInteger(String name, int val)`
- ◼ `static Integer getInteger(String name, Integer val)`

The parseInt() Methods

```
static int parseInt(String s, int radix)
static int parseInt(String s)
```

The parseInt() methods parse strings for an integer value and return the value as an int. The version of parseInt() with the *radix* parameter enables you to specify the base of the integer; the other version of parseInt() assumes a base of 10.

The shortValue(), longValue(), floatValue(), doubleValue(), and byteValue() Methods

```
short shortValue()
long longValue()
float floatValue()
double doubleValue()
byte byteValue()
```

The shortValue(), longValue(), floatValue(), doubleValue(), and byteValue() methods return the value of an integer converted to the appropriate type. For example, the following code shows how to convert an integer to a double:

```
Integer i = new Integer(17);
float f = i.floatValue();
```

In this example, the value of the Integer variable i is converted to a float value and is stored in the float variable f. The result is that the Integer value 17 is converted to the float value 17.0.

The getInteger() Methods

```
static Integer getInteger(String name)
static Integer getInteger(String name, int val)
static Integer getInteger(String name, Integer val)
```

The getInteger() methods return an integer property value specified by the String property name parameter *name*. Notice that all three of the getInteger() methods are static, which means that you don't have to instantiate an Integer object to use these methods. The differences among these three methods is what happens when the integer property isn't found. The first version returns 0 if the property isn't found, the second version returns the int parameter val, and the last version returns the Integer object value val.

Member Constants

The Integer class also includes three final static (constant) data members: MIN_VALUE, MAX_VALUE, and TYPE. MIN_VALUE and MAX_VALUE specify the smallest and largest numbers that can be represented by an Integer object. TYPE specifies the runtime Class object representing the integer value.

The Long class is similar to the Integer class except that it wraps the fundamental type long. The Long class implements methods similar to those of the Integer class, with the exception that they act on long-type numbers rather than on int-type numbers.

The `Float` and `Double` Classes

The Float and Double classes wrap the fundamental floating-point types float and double. These two classes provide a group of methods for working with floating-point numbers. The methods implemented by the Float class follow:

- ▪ `boolean isNaN()`
- ▪ `static boolean isNaN(float v)`
- ▪ `boolean isInfinite()`
- ▪ `static boolean isInfinite(float v)`
- ▪ `short shortValue()`
- ▪ `long longValue()`
- ▪ `int intValue()`
- ▪ `double doubleValue()`
- ▪ `byte byteValue()`
- ▪ `static int floatToIntBits(float value)`
- ▪ `static float intBitsToFloat(int bits)`

The `isNaN()` Methods

```
boolean isNaN()
static boolean isNaN(float v)
```

The isNaN() method returns whether or not the Float value is the special not-a-number (NaN) value. The first version of isNaN() operates on the value of the calling Float object. The second version is static and takes the float to test as its parameter, v.

The `isInfinite()` Methods

```
boolean isInfinite()
static boolean isInfinite(float v)
```

The isInfinite() method returns whether or not the Float value is infinite, which is represented by the special NEGATIVE_INFINITY and POSITIVE_INFINITY final static member constants. Like the isNaN() method, isInfinite() comes in two versions: a class value version and a static version that takes a float as an argument.

The shortValue(), longValue(), intValue(), doubleValue(), and byteValue() Methods

```
short shortValue()
long longValue()
int intValue()
double doubleValue()
byte byteValue()
```

The shortValue(), longValue(), intValue(), doubleValue(), and byteValue() methods return the values of a floating-point number converted to the appropriate type. For example, the following code shows how to convert a Float object to a long type:

```
Float f = new Float(5.237);
long l = f.longValue();
```

In this example, the value of the Float variable f is converted to a long and stored in the long variable l. This action results in the floating-point value 5.237 being converted to the long value 5.

The floatToIntBits() and intBitsToFloat() Methods

```
static int floatToIntBits(float value)
static float intBitsToFloat(int bits)
```

The last two methods implemented by the Float class are floatToIntBits() and intBitsToFloat(). The floatToIntBits() and intBitsToFloat() methods convert floating-point values to their integer bit representations and back.

Member Constants

The Float class also has a group of final static (constant) data members: MIN_VALUE, MAX_VALUE, NEGATIVE_INFINITY, POSITIVE_INFINITY, NaN, and TYPE. MIN_VALUE and MAX_VALUE specify the smallest and largest numbers that can be represented by a Float object. NEGATIVE_INFINITY and POSITIVE_INFINITY represent negative and positive infinity, while NaN represents the special not-a-number condition. TYPE specifies the runtime Class object representing the floating-point value.

The Double class is very similar to the Float class. The only difference is that Double wraps the fundamental type double instead of float. Double implements methods similar to those of the Float class, with the exception that the methods act on double-type numbers rather than on float-type numbers.

The Void Class

The Void class is a placeholder class wrapping the primitive void Java data type. The Void class has no constructors or methods and only one member constant: TYPE. The TYPE member constant specifies the runtime Class object representing the void type.

The Math Class

The Math class contains many invaluable mathematical functions along with a few useful constants. The Math class isn't intended to be instantiated; it is basically just a holding class for mathematical functions. Additionally, the Math class is declared as `final`—you can't derive from it. The most useful methods implemented by the Math class follow:

- `static double sin(double a)`
- `static double cos(double a)`
- `static double tan(double a)`
- `static double asin(double a)`
- `static double acos(double a)`
- `static double atan(double a)`
- `static double exp(double a)`
- `static double log(double a)`
- `static double sqrt(double a)`
- `static double pow(double a, double b)`
- `static double ceil(double a)`
- `static double floor(double a)`
- `static int round(float a)`
- `static long round(double a)`
- `static double rint(double a)`
- `static double atan2(double a, double b)`
- `static synchronized double random()`
- `static int abs(int a)`
- `static long abs(long a)`
- `static float abs(float a)`
- `static double abs(double a)`
- `static int min(int a, int b)`
- `static long min(long a, long b)`
- `static float min(float a, float b)`
- `static double min(double a, double b)`
- `static int max(int a, int b)`
- `static long max(long a, long b)`
- `static float max(float a, float b)`
- `static double max(double a, double b)`

> **NOTE**
>
> Be sure that you don't confuse the `Math` class with the `java.math` package. The `Math` class is included in the `java.lang` package and provides a wide range of mathematical functions; the `java.math` package is a package unto itself that provides two support classes (`BigDecimal` and `BigInteger`) for working with large numbers.

Trigonometric Methods

```
static double sin(double a)
static double cos(double a)
static double tan(double a)
static double asin(double a)
static double acos(double a)
static double atan(double a)
```

The trigonometric methods `sin()`, `cos()`, `tan()`, `asin()`, `acos()`, and `atan()` perform the standard trigonometric functions on `double` values. All the angles used in the trigonometric functions are specified in radians. Following is an example of calculating the sine of an angle:

```
double dSine = Math.sin(Math.PI / 2);
```

Notice in the example that the `PI` constant member of the `Math` class was used in the call to the `sin()` method. You learn about the `PI` member constant of `Math` at the end of this section.

The `exp()`, `log()`, `sqrt()`, and `pow()` Methods

```
static double exp(double a)
static double log(double a)
static double sqrt(double a)
static double pow(double a, double b)
```

The `exp()` method returns the exponential number E raised to the power of the `double` parameter `a`. Similarly, the `log()` method returns the natural logarithm (base E) of the number passed in the parameter `a`. The `sqrt()` method returns the square root of the parameter number `a`. The `pow()` method returns the result of raising a number to a power. `pow()` returns `a` raised to the power of `b`. Following are some examples of using these `Math` methods:

```
double d1 = 12.3;
double d2 = Math.exp(d1);
double d3 = Math.log(d1);
double d4 = Math.sqrt(d1);
double d5 = Math.pow(d1, 3.0);
```

The ceil(), floor(), round(), and rint() Methods

```
static double ceil(double a)
static double floor(double a)
static int round(float a)
static long round(double a)
static double rint(double a)
```

The ceil() and floor() methods return the "ceiling" and "floor" for the passed parameter *a*. The *ceiling* is the smallest whole number greater than or equal to *a*; the *floor* is the largest whole number less than or equal to *a*. The round() methods round float and double numbers to the nearest integer value, which is returned as type int or long. Both round() methods work by adding 0.5 to the number and then returning the largest integer that is less than or equal to the number. The rint() method returns an integer value, similar to round(), that remains a type double. Following are some examples of using these methods:

```
double d1 = 37.125;
double d2 = Math.ceil(d1);
double d3 = Math.floor(d1);
int i = Math.round((float)d1);
long l = Math.round(d1);
double d4 = Math.rint(d1);
```

Notice in the first example that uses round() that the double value d1 must be explicitly cast to a float. This is necessary because this version of round() takes a float and returns an int.

The atan2() Method

```
static double atan2(double a, double b)
```

The atan2() method converts rectangular coordinates to polar coordinates. The double parameters *a* and *b* represent the rectangular x and y coordinates to be converted to polar coordinates, which are returned together as a single double value.

The random() Method

```
static synchronized double random()
```

The random() method generates a pseudo-random number between 0.0 and 1.0. random() is useful for generating random floating-point numbers. To generate random numbers of different types, you should use the Random class, which is located in the utilities package, java.util. The utilities package, including the Random class, is covered in the next chapter.

The abs() Methods

```
static int abs(int a)
static long abs(long a)
static float abs(float a)
static double abs(double a)
```

The abs() methods return the absolute values of numbers of varying types. There are versions of abs() for the following types: int, long, float, and double. Following is an example of using the abs() method to find the absolute value of an integer number:

```
int i = -5, j;
j = Math.abs(i);
```

The min() and max() Methods

```
static int min(int a, int b)
static long min(long a, long b)
static float min(float a, float b)
static double min(double a, double b)
static int max(int a, int b)
static long max(long a, long b)
static float max(float a, float b)
static double max(double a, double b)
```

The min() and max() methods return the minimum and maximum numbers given a pair of numbers to compare. Like the abs() methods, the min() and max() methods come in different versions for handling the types int, long, float, and double. Following are some examples of using the min() and max() methods:

```
double d1 = 14.2, d2 = 18.5;
double d3 = Math.min(d1, d2);
double d4 = Math.max(d1, 11.2);
```

Beyond the rich set of methods provided by the Math class, there are also a couple of important member constants: E and PI. The E member represents the exponential number (2.7182...) used in exponential calculations. The PI member represents the value of π (3.1415...).

The String Classes

Text strings in Java are represented with classes rather than with character arrays (as they are in C and C++). The two classes that model strings in Java are String and StringBuffer. The reason for having two string classes is that the String class represents constant (immutable) strings and the StringBuffer class represents variable (mutable) strings.

The String Class

The String class is used to represent constant strings. The String class has less overhead than StringBuffer, which means that you should use it if you know that a string is constant. The constructors for the String class follow:

■ String()

■ String(String *value*)

■ String(char *value*[])

■ String(char *value*[], int *offset*, int *count*)

■ String(byte *ascii*[], int *offset*, int *count*, String *enc*)

■ String(byte *ascii*[], String *enc*)

■ String(StringBuffer *buffer*)

It should be readily apparent from the number of constructors for String that there are many ways to create String objects. The first constructor simply creates a new string that is empty. All the other constructors create strings that are initialized in different ways from various types of text data. Following are examples of using some of the String() constructors to create String objects:

```
String s1 = new String();
String s2 = new String("Hello");
char cArray[] = {'H', 'o', 'w', 'd', 'y'};
String s3 = new String(cArray);
String s4 = new String(cArray, 1, 3);
```

In the first example, an empty String object (s1) is created. In the second example, a String object (s2) is created from a literal String value, "Hello". The third example shows a String object (s3) being created from an array of characters. The fourth example shows a String object (s4) being created from a subarray of characters. The subarray is specified by passing 1 as the offset parameter and 3 as the count parameter. This means that the subarray of characters is to consist of the three consecutive characters starting one character into the array. The resulting subarray in this case consists of the characters 'o', 'w', and 'd'.

Once you have some String objects created, you are ready to work with them using some of the powerful methods implemented in the String class. Some of the most useful methods provided by the String class follow:

■ int length()

■ char charAt(int *index*)

■ boolean startsWith(String *prefix*)

■ boolean startsWith(String *prefix*, int *toffset*)

■ boolean endsWith(String *suffix*)

■ int indexOf(int *ch*)

■ int indexOf(int *ch*, int *fromIndex*)

■ int indexOf(String *str*)

■ int indexOf(String *str*, int *fromIndex*)

■ int lastIndexOf(int *ch*)

■ int lastIndexOf(int *ch*, int *fromIndex*)

■ int lastIndexOf(String *str*)

■ int lastIndexOf(String *str*, int *fromIndex*)

■ String substring(int *beginIndex*)

■ String substring(int *beginIndex*, int *endIndex*)

■ boolean equals(Object *anObject*)

■ boolean equalsIgnoreCase(String *anotherString*)

■ int compareTo(String *anotherString*)

■ String concat(String *str*)

■ String replace(char *oldChar*, char *newChar*)

■ String trim()

■ String toLowerCase()

■ String toUpperCase()

■ static String valueOf(Object *obj*)

■ static String valueOf(char *data*[])

■ static String valueOf(char *data*[], int *offset*, int *count*)

■ static String valueOf(boolean *b*)

■ static String valueOf(char *c*)

■ static String valueOf(int *i*)

■ static String valueOf(long *l*)

■ static String valueOf(float *f*)

■ static String valueOf(double *d*)

The length(), charAt(), startsWith(), and endsWith() Methods

```
int length()
char charAt(int index)
boolean startsWith(String prefix)
boolean startsWith(String prefix, int toffset)
boolean endsWith(String suffix)
```

The length() method simply returns the length of a string, which is the number of Unicode characters in the string. The charAt() method returns the character at a specific index of a string specified by the int parameter *index*. The startsWith() and endsWith() methods determine whether or not a string starts or ends with a prefix or suffix string, as specified by the *prefix* and *suffix* parameters. The second version of startsWith() enables you to specify an offset to begin looking for the string *prefix*. Following are some examples of using these methods:

```
String s1 = new String("This is a test string!");
int len = s1.length();
char c = s1.charAt(8);
boolean b1 = s1.startsWith("This");
boolean b2 = s1.startsWith("test", 10);
boolean b3 = s1.endsWith("string.");
```

In this series of examples, a String object is first created with the value "This is a test string!". The length of the string is calculated using the length() method and stored in the integer variable len. The length returned is 22, which specifies how many characters are contained in the string. The character at offset 8 into the string is then obtained using the charAt() method. As is true with C and C++, Java offsets start at 0, not 1. If you count eight characters into the string, you can see that `charAt()` returns the `'a'` character. The next two examples use the `startsWith()` method to determine whether specific strings are located in the `String` object. The first `startsWith()` example looks for the string `"This"` at the beginning of the `String` object. This example returns `true` because the string is in fact located at the beginning of the `String` object. The second `startsWith()` example looks for the string `"test"` beginning at offset `10` into the `String` object. This call also returns `true` because the string `"test"` is located 10 characters into the `String` object. The last example uses the `endsWith()` method to check for the occurrence of the string `"string."` at the end of the `String` object. This call returns `false` because the `String` object actually ends with `"string!"`.

The `indexOf()` and `lastIndexOf()` Methods

```
int indexOf(int ch)
int indexOf(int ch, int fromIndex)
int indexOf(String str)
int indexOf(String str, int fromIndex)
int lastIndexOf(int ch)
int lastIndexOf(int ch, int fromIndex)
int lastIndexOf(String str)
int lastIndexOf(String str, int fromIndex)
```

The `indexOf()` method returns the location of the first occurrence of a character or string within a `String` object. The first two versions of `indexOf()` determine the index of a single character within a string; the second two versions determine the index of a string of characters within a string. Each pair of `indexOf()` methods contains a version for finding a character or string based on the beginning of the `String` object, as well a version that enables you to specify an offset into the string to begin searching for the first occurrence. If the character or string is not found, `indexOf()` returns `-1`.

The `lastIndexOf()` methods work very much like `indexOf()`, with the exception that `lastIndexOf()` searches backwards through the string. Following are some examples of using these methods:

```
String s1 = new String("Saskatchewan");
int i1 = s1.indexOf('t');
int i2 = s1.indexOf("chew");
int i3 = s1.lastIndexOf('a');
```

In this series of examples, a `String` object is created with the value `"Saskatchewan"`. The `indexOf()` method is then called on this string with the character value `'t'`. This call to `indexOf()` returns `5` because the first occurrence of `'t'` is five characters into the string. The second call to `indexOf()` specifies the string literal `"chew"`. This call returns `6` because the substring `"chew"` is located six characters into the `String` object. Finally, the `lastIndexOf()` method is called with a character parameter of `'a'`. The call to `lastIndexOf()` returns `10`, indicating the position of the third `'a'` in the string. (Remember that `lastIndexOf()` searches *backwards* through the string to find the first occurrence of a character.)

The substring() Methods

```
String substring(int beginIndex)
String substring(int beginIndex, int endIndex)
```

The substring() methods return a substring of the calling String object. The first version of substring() returns the substring beginning at the index specified by *beginIndex*, through the end of the calling String object. The second version of substring() returns a substring beginning at the index specified by *beginIndex* and ending at the index specified by *endIndex*. Following is an example using some of the substring() methods:

```
String s1 = new String("sasquatch");
String s2 = s1.substring(3);
String s3 = s1.substring(2, 7);
```

In this example, a String object is created with the value "sasquatch". A substring of this string is then retrieved using the substring() method and passing 3 as the *beginIndex* parameter. This results in the substring "quatch", which begins at the string index of 3 and continues through the rest of the string. The second version of substring() is then used with starting and ending indices of 2 and 7, yielding the substring "squat".

The equals(), equalsIgnoreCase(), and compareTo() Methods

```
boolean equals(Object anObject)
boolean equalsIgnoreCase(String anotherString)
int compareTo(String anotherString)
```

There are two methods for determining equality between String objects: equals() and equalsIgnoreCase(). The equals() method returns a boolean value based on the equality of two strings. equalsIgnoreCase() performs a similar function except that it compares the strings with case insensitivity. Similarly, the compareTo() method compares two strings and returns an integer value that specifies whether the calling String object is less than, greater than, or equal to the *anotherString* parameter. The integer value returned by compareTo() specifies the numeric difference between the two strings. It is a positive value if the *calling* String object is greater; it is negative if the *passed* String object is greater. If the two strings are equal, the return value is 0.

Wait a minute—if strings are just text, how can you get a numeric difference between two strings or establish which one is greater than or less than the other? When strings are compared using the compareTo() method, each character is compared to the character at the same position in the other string until they don't match. When two characters are found that don't match, compareTo() converts them to integers and finds the difference. This difference is what is returned by compareTo(). Check out the following example to get a better idea of how this works:

```
String s1 = new String("abcfj");
String s2 = new String("abcdz");
System.out.println(s1.compareTo(s2));
```

10

THE LANGUAGE PACKAGE

Each pair of characters is compared until two are encountered that don't match. In this example, the `'f'` and `'d'` characters are the first two that don't match. Because the `compareTo()` method is called on the s1 `String` object, the integer value of `'d'` (100) is subtracted from the integer value of `'f'` (102) to determine the difference between the strings. Notice that all characters following the two nonmatching characters are ignored in the comparison.

The concat() Method

```
String concat(String str)
```

The `concat()` method is used to concatenate two `String` objects. The string specified in the str parameter is concatenated on to the end of the calling `String` object. Following are a few examples of string concatenation:

```
String s1 = new String("I saw sasquatch ");
String s2 = new String(s1 + "in Saskatchewan.");
String s3 = s1.concat("in Saskatchewan.");
```

In these concatenation examples, a `String` object is first created with the value `"I saw sasquatch"`. The first concatenation example shows how two strings can be concatenated using the addition operator (+). The second example shows how two strings can be concatenated using the `concat()` method. In both examples, the resulting string is the sentence `"I saw sasquatch in Saskatchewan."`.

The replace() Method

```
String replace(char oldChar, char newChar)
```

The `replace()` method is used to replace characters in a string. All occurrences of *oldChar* are replaced with *newChar*. Using the strings from the previous concatenation examples, you can replace all the s characters with m characters like this:

```
String s4 = s3.replace('s', 'm');
```

This results in the string `"I maw mamquatch in Samkatchewan."`. Notice that the uppercase S character wasn't replaced.

The trim(), toLowerCase(), and toUpperCase() Methods

```
String trim()
String toLowerCase()
String toUpperCase()
```

The `trim()` method trims leading and trailing whitespace from a `String` object. The `toLowerCase()` and `toUpperCase()` methods are used to convert all the characters in a `String` object to lowercase and uppercase characters. Following are some examples of these methods using the strings from the previous two examples:

```
String s5 = new String("\t  Yeti\n");
String s6 = s5.trim();
```

```
String s7 = s3.toLowerCase();
String s8 = s4.toUpperCase();
```

In this example, the `trim()` method is used to strip off the leading and trailing whitespace, resulting in the string `"Yeti"`. The call to `toLowerCase()` results in the string `"i saw sasquatch in saskatchewan."`. The only characters modified were the `I` and `S` characters, which were the only uppercase characters in the string. The call to `toUpperCase()` results in the string `"I MAW MAMQUATCH IN SAMKATCHEWAN."`. All the lowercase characters were converted to uppercase, as you might have guessed!

The `valueOf()` Methods

```
static String valueOf(Object obj)
static String valueOf(char data[])
static String valueOf(char data[], int offset, int count)
static String valueOf(boolean b)
static String valueOf(char c)
static String valueOf(int i)
static String valueOf(long l)
static String valueOf(float f)
static String valueOf(double d)
```

Finally, the `valueOf()` methods all return `String` objects that represent the particular type taken as a parameter. For example, the `valueOf()` method that takes an `int` returns the string `"123"` when passed the integer number `123`.

The `StringBuffer` Class

The `StringBuffer` class is used to represent variable, or nonconstant, strings. The `StringBuffer` class is useful when you know that a string will change in value or in length. The constructors for the `StringBuffer` class follow:

- `StringBuffer()`

- `StringBuffer(int length)`

- `StringBuffer(String str)`

The first constructor simply creates a new string buffer that is empty. The second constructor creates a string buffer that is *length* characters long, initialized with spaces. The third constructor creates a string buffer from a `String` object. This last constructor is useful when you have to modify a constant `String` object. Following are examples of using the `StringBuffer` constructors to create `StringBuffer` objects:

```
String s1 = new String("This is a string!");
String sb1 = new StringBuffer();
String sb2 = new StringBuffer(25);
String sb3 = new StringBuffer(s1);
```

Some of the most useful methods implemented by `StringBuffer` follow:

- `int length()`

- `int capacity()`

■ `synchronized void setLength(int `*`newLength`*`)`

■ `synchronized char charAt(int `*`index`*`)`

■ `synchronized void setCharAt(int `*`index`*`, char `*`ch`*`)`

■ `synchronized StringBuffer append(Object `*`obj`*`)`

■ `synchronized StringBuffer append(String `*`str`*`)`

■ `synchronized StringBuffer append(char `*`c`*`)`

■ `synchronized StringBuffer append(char `*`str`*`[])`

■ `synchronized StringBuffer append(char `*`str`*`[], int `*`offset`*`, int `*`len`*`)`

■ `StringBuffer append(boolean `*`b`*`)`

■ `StringBuffer append(int `*`I`*`)`

■ `StringBuffer append(long `*`l`*`)`

■ `StringBuffer append(float `*`f`*`)`

■ `StringBuffer append(double `*`d`*`)`

■ `synchronized StringBuffer insert(int `*`offset`*`, Object `*`obj`*`)`

■ `synchronized StringBuffer insert(int `*`offset`*`, String `*`str`*`)`

■ `synchronized StringBuffer insert(int `*`offset`*`, char `*`c`*`)`

■ `synchronized StringBuffer insert(int `*`offset`*`, char `*`str`*`[])`

■ `StringBuffer insert(int `*`offset`*`, boolean `*`b`*`)`

■ `StringBuffer insert(int `*`offset`*`, int `*`I`*`)`

■ `StringBuffer insert(int `*`offset`*`, long `*`l`*`)`

■ `StringBuffer insert(int `*`offset`*`, float `*`f`*`)`

■ `StringBuffer insert(int `*`offset`*`, double `*`d`*`)`

■ `String toString()`

The `length()`, `capacity()`, and `setLength()` Methods

```
int length()
int capacity()
synchronized void setLength(int newLength)
```

The `length()` method is used to get the length of, or number of characters in, the string buffer. The `capacity()` method is similar to `length()` except that it returns how many characters a string buffer has allocated in memory, which is sometimes greater than the length. Characters are allocated for a string buffer as they are needed. Frequently, more memory is allocated for a string buffer than is actually being used. In these cases, the `capacity()` method returns the amount of memory allocated for the string buffer. You can explicitly change the length of a string buffer using the `setLength()` method. An example of using `setLength()` is to truncate a string by specifying a shorter length. The following example shows the effects of using these methods:

```
StringBuffer s1 = new StringBuffer(14);
System.out.println("capacity = " + s1.capacity());
System.out.println("length = " + s1.length());
s1.append("Bigfoot");
System.out.println(s1);
System.out.println("capacity = " + s1.capacity());
System.out.println("length = " + s1.length());
s1.setLength(3);
System.out.println(s1);
System.out.println("capacity = " + s1.capacity());
System.out.println("length = " + s1.length());
```

The resulting output of this example follows:

```
capacity = 14
length = 0
Bigfoot
capacity = 14
length = 7
Big
capacity = 14
length = 3
```

In this example, the newly created string buffer shows a capacity of 14 (based on the value passed in the constructor) and a length of 0. After appending the string "Bigfoot" to the buffer, the capacity remains the same but the length grows to 7, which is the length of the string. Calling setLength() with a parameter of 3 truncates the length down to 3, but leaves the capacity unaffected at 14.

The charAt() and setCharAt() Methods

```
synchronized char charAt(int index)
synchronized void setCharAt(int index, char ch)
```

The charAt() method returns the character at the location in the string buffer specified by the *index* parameter. You can change characters at specific locations in a string buffer using the setCharAt() method. The setCharAt() method replaces the character at *index* with the *ch* character parameter. The following example shows the use of these two methods:

```
StringBuffer s1 = new StringBuffer("I saw a Yeti in Yellowstone.");
char c1 = s1.charAt(9);
System.out.println(c1);
s1.setCharAt(4, 'r');
System.out.println(s1);
```

In this example, the call to charAt() results in the character e, which is located nine characters into the string. The call to setCharAt() results in the following output, based on the w in saw being replaced by r:

```
I sar a Yeti in Yellowstone.
```

10

THE LANGUAGE
PACKAGE

The append() and insert() Methods

```
synchronized StringBuffer append(Object obj)
synchronized StringBuffer append(String str)
synchronized StringBuffer append(char c)
synchronized StringBuffer append(char str[])
synchronized StringBuffer append(char str[], int offset, int len)
StringBuffer append(boolean b)
StringBuffer append(int I)
StringBuffer append(long l)
StringBuffer append(float f)
StringBuffer append(double d)
synchronized StringBuffer insert(int offset, Object obj)
synchronized StringBuffer insert(int offset, String str)
synchronized StringBuffer insert(int offset, char c)
synchronized StringBuffer insert(int offset, char str[])
StringBuffer insert(int offset, boolean b)
StringBuffer insert(int offset, int I)
StringBuffer insert(int offset, long l)
StringBuffer insert(int offset, float f)
StringBuffer insert(int offset, double d)
```

The StringBuffer class implements a variety of overloaded append() and insert() methods. The append() methods allow you to append various types of data on to the end of a String object. Each append() method returns the String object on which it was called. The insert() methods enable you to insert various data types at a specific offset in a string buffer. insert() works in a manner similar to append(), with the exception of where the data is placed. Following are some examples of using append() and insert():

```
StringBuffer sb1 = new StringBuffer("2 + 2 = ");
StringBuffer sb2 = new StringBuffer("The tires make contact ");
sb1.append(2 + 2);
sb2.append("with the road.");
sb2.insert(10, "are the things on the car that ");
```

In this set of examples, two string buffers are created using the constructor for StringBuffer that takes a string literal. The first StringBuffer object initially contains the string "2 + 2 = ". The append() method is used to append the result of the integer calculation 2 + 2. In this case, the integer result 4 is converted by the append() method to the string "4" before it is appended to the end of the StringBuffer object. The value of the resulting StringBuffer object is "2 + 2 = 4". The second string buffer object begins life with the value "The tires make contact ". The string "with the road." is then appended to the end of the string buffer using the append() method. Then the insert() method is used to insert the string "are the things on the car that ". Notice that this string is inserted at index 10 within the StringBuffer object. The string that results after these two methods are called follows:

```
The tires are the things on the car that make contact with the road.
```

The toString() Method

```
String toString()
```

The last method of interest in StringBuffer is the toString() method. toString() returns the String object representation of the calling StringBuffer object. toString() is useful when you have a StringBuffer object but need a String object.

The System and Runtime Classes

The System and Runtime classes provide access to the system and runtime environment resources. The System class is defined as final and is composed entirely of static variables and methods, which means that you never actually instantiate an object of it. The Runtime class provides direct access to the runtime environment and is useful for executing system commands and determining things like the amount of available memory.

The System Class

The System class contains the following useful methods:

- static long currentTimeMillis()
- static void arraycopy(Object *src*, int *src_position*, Object *dst*, int *dst_position*, int *length*)
- static Properties getProperties()
- static String getProperty(String *key*)
- static String getProperty(String *key*, String *def*)
- static void setProperties(Properties *props*)
- static void gc()
- static void loadLibrary(String *libname*)

The currentTimeMillis() Method

```
static long currentTimeMillis()
```

The currentTimeMillis() method returns the current system time in milliseconds. The time is specified in GMT (Greenwich Mean Time) and reflects the number of milliseconds that have elapsed since midnight on January 1, 1970. This is a standard frame of reference for computer time representation.

The arraycopy() Method

```
static void arraycopy(Object src, int src_position, Object dst,
    int dst_position, int length)
```

The arraycopy() method copies data from one array to another. arraycopy() copies *length* elements from the *src* array beginning at position *src_position* to the *dst* array starting at *dst_position*.

The `getProperties()`, `getProperty()`, and `setProperties()` Methods

```
static Properties getProperties()
static String getProperty(String key)
static String getProperty(String key, String def)
static void setProperties(Properties props)
```

The getProperties() method gets the current system properties and returns them using a Properties object. There are also two getProperty() methods in the System class that allow you to get individual system properties. The first version of getProperty() returns the system property matching the *key* parameter passed into the method. The second version of getProperty() does the same as the first except that it returns the default *def* parameter if the property isn't found. The setProperties() method takes a Properties object and sets the system properties with it.

The `gc()` Method

```
static void gc()
```

The gc() method stands for *garbage collection* and does exactly that. gc() forces the Java runtime system to perform a memory garbage collection. You can call gc() if you think the system is running low on memory because a garbage collection event usually frees up memory.

The `loadLibrary()` Method

```
static void loadLibrary(String libname)
```

The Java system supports executable code in dynamic link libraries. A *dynamic link library* is a library of Java classes that can be accessed at run time. The loadLibrary() method is used to load a dynamic link library. The name of the library to load is specified in the *libname* parameter.

Member Variables

The System class contains three member variables that are very useful for interacting with the system: in, out, and err. The in member is an InputStream object that acts as the standard input stream. The out and err members are PrintStream objects that act as the standard output and error streams.

The Runtime Class

The Runtime class is another very powerful class for accessing Java system-related resources. Following are a few of the more useful methods in the Runtime class:

- `static Runtime getRuntime()`
- `long freeMemory()`
- `long totalMemory()`

■ void gc()

■ synchronized void loadLibrary(String *libname*)

The getRuntime(), freeMemory(), and totalMemory() Methods

```
static Runtime getRuntime()
long freeMemory()
long totalMemory()
```

The static method getRuntime() returns a Runtime object representing the runtime system environment. The freeMemory() method returns the amount of free system memory in bytes. Because freeMemory() returns only an estimate of the available memory, it is not completely accurate. If you want to know the total amount of memory accessible by the Java system, you can use the totalMemory() method. The totalMemory() method returns the number of bytes of *total* memory; the freeMemory() method returns the number of bytes of *available* memory. Listing 10.1 contains the source code for the Memory program, which displays the available free memory and total memory.

Listing 10.1. The Memory class.

```
class Memory {
  public static void main (String args[]) {
    Runtime runtime = Runtime.getRuntime();
    long freeMem = runtime.freeMemory() / 1024;
    long totalMem = runtime.totalMemory() / 1024;
    System.out.println("Free memory : " + freeMem + "KB");
    System.out.println("Total memory : " + totalMem + "KB");
  }
}
```

An example of the output of running the Memory program follows:

```
Free Memory : 3068KB
Total Memory : 3071KB
```

The Memory class uses the getRuntime(), freeMemory(), and totalMemory() methods of the Runtime class. Note that you can convert the amount of memory returned by each method from bytes to kilobytes by dividing by 1024.

The gc() and loadLibrary() Methods

```
void gc()
synchronized void loadLibrary(String libname)
```

The other two methods of importance in the Runtime class (gc() and loadLibrary()) work exactly the same as the versions that belong to the System class.

The Class Classes

Java provides two classes in the language package for dealing with classes: Class and ClassLoader. The Class class allows you access to the runtime information for a class. The ClassLoader class provides support for dynamically loading classes at run time.

The Class Class

Some of the more useful methods implemented by the Class class follow:

- ▪ static Class forName(String *className*)
- ▪ String getName()
- ▪ Class getSuperclass()
- ▪ ClassLoader getClassLoader()
- ▪ boolean isInterface()
- ▪ String toString()

The forName() Method

```
static Class forName(String className)
```

The forName() method is a static method used to get the runtime class descriptor object for a class. The String parameter *className* specifies the name of the class about which you want information. forName() returns a Class object containing runtime information for the specified class. Notice that forName() is static and is the method you typically use to get an instance of the Class class for determining class information. Following is an example of how to use the forName() method to get information about the StringBuffer class:

```
Class info = Class.forName("java.lang.StringBuffer");
```

The getName() Method

```
String getName()
```

The getName() method retrieves the string name of the class represented by a Class object. Following is an example of using the getName() method:

```
String s = info.getName();
```

The getSuperclass(), getClassLoader(), and isInterface() Methods

```
Class getSuperclass()
ClassLoader getClassLoader()
boolean isInterface()
```

The getSuperclass() method returns a Class object containing information about the superclass of an object. The getClassLoader() method returns the ClassLoader object for a class or null if no class loader exists. The isInterface() method returns a boolean indicating whether or not a class is an interface.

The toString() Method

```
String toString()
```

Finally, the toString() method returns the name of a class or interface. toString() automatically prepends the string "class" or "interface" to the name based on whether the Class object represents a class or an interface.

The ClassLoader Class

The ClassLoader class provides the framework that enables you to dynamically load classes into the runtime environment. Following are the methods implemented by ClassLoader:

- abstract Class loadClass(String *name*, boolean *resolve*)
- final Class defineClass(byte *data*[], int *offset*, int *length*)
- final void resolveClass(Class *c*)
- final Class findSystemClass(String *name*)

The loadClass() and defineClass() Methods

```
abstract Class loadClass(String name, boolean resolve)
final Class defineClass(byte data[], int offset, int length)
```

The loadClass() method is an abstract method that must be defined in a subclass of ClassLoader. loadClass() resolves a class name passed in the String parameter *name* into a Class runtime object. loadClass() returns the resulting Class on success or null if not successful. The defineClass() method converts an array of byte data into a Class object. The class is defined by the *data* parameter beginning at *offset* and continuing for *length* bytes.

The resolveClass() Method

```
final void resolveClass(Class c)
```

A class defined with defineClass() must be resolved before it can be used. You can resolve a class by using the resolveClass() method, which takes a Class object as its only parameter.

10

THE LANGUAGE
PACKAGE

The `findSystemClass()` Method

`final Class findSystemClass(String name)`

Finally, the `findSystemClass()` method is used to find and load a system class. A *system class* is a class that uses the built-in (primordial) class loader, defined as `null`.

Summary

In this chapter, you learned a great deal about the classes and interfaces that make up the Java language package. The language package lays out the core classes, interfaces, and errors of the Java class libraries. Although some of the classes implemented in the language package are fairly low level, a solid understanding of these classes is necessary to move on to other areas of the Java class libraries.

This chapter explained how fundamental data types can become objects using the data type wrappers. You then learned about the many mathematical functions contained in the `Math` class. And don't forget about the string classes, which provide a powerful set of routines for working with strings of text. You finished up with a tour of how to access the system and runtime resources of Java, along with the lower-level runtime and dynamic class support.

The following chapter provides the next stop on this guided tour of the Java class libraries: the Java utilities package.

The Utilities Package

by Michael Girdley and Richard Lesh
revised by Billy Barron

IN THIS CHAPTER

This chapter describes the classes in the java.util package in the Java class library. These classes implement many of those features or functions usually left for the programmer or someone else to implement. In programming experiences, I regularly find myself saying, "It would be so much easier if there were a built-in object that would do *some common but complicated task.*" The java.util package is a well-designed and effective attempt to satisfy many of these specialized needs.

In many languages, you find yourself implementing a stack or a hash table class and all the corresponding methods. Java has a built-in stack type that enables you to quickly and efficiently include your own stack data structures in your Java programs. This frees you to deal with more important design and implementation issues. These classes are also useful in a variety of other ways and are the fundamental building blocks of the more complicated data structures used in other Java packages and in your own applications.

This chapter covers the following topics:

- Each of the features of the utilities package
- The implementation of most of the different classes in the utilities package

> **NOTE**
>
> Unless otherwise noted, all the interfaces and classes discussed in this chapter extend the java.lang.Object class.

Table 11.1 shows the classes that are part of the utilities package and that are discussed in this chapter.

Table 11.1. Important classes in the utilities package.

Class	*Description*
BitSet	Implements a collection of binary values
Calendar	Used to implement a calendar
Date	Used for date and time data storage and use
Dictionary	Used to store a collection of key and value pairs
GregorianCalendar	Used to implement a Gregorian calendar
Hashtable	Used to store a hash table
Locale	Used to implement a location
Observable	Used to store observable data
Properties	Used for storage of a properties list that can be saved

Class	Description
Random	Used to generate a pseudo-random number
SimpleTimeZone	Used to implement a simplified time zone
Stack	Used to store and implement a stack
StringTokenizer	Used to tokenize a string
TimeZone	Used to store information about a time zone
Vector	Used to store a vector data type

NOTE

You may not be familiar with some of these data types. The Dictionary class is used to implement a dictionary in your program. A Hashtable is a storage data type whose speed in searching is much greater than that of other data structures because it stores data items based on a key derived from some given formula. A Stack, of course, functions as if you were stacking data items on the floor, one on top of the other, in a single stack. As a consequence, the only two manipulations you can make to the stack are to remove the top item or to place another item on top. The Vector class implements an interesting data structure that has the capability to begin with a limited capacity and then change in size to accommodate the data items you insert into it. The Vector class can be described as a "growable array."

Linked Lists, Queues, Search Trees, and Other Dynamic Data Structures

One would expect that the Vector class would eliminate the necessity for creating your own data structures. But there may be times when you may want to conserve space to the maximum or access your data in a specialized way. In these cases, there is a technique to implement such data structures in Java.

As you know, Java has no pointers. Because dynamically linked lists and queues are implemented using pointers, is it then impossible to create these two data structures in Java? Not quite. Just as with many other tasks in Java, you need to do a little "funky stepping" to get it right because the implementation of lists, queues, and other dynamic data structures is not intuitive.

To define your own dynamic data structures, you will want to make use of the fact that references to objects in Java are already dynamic. This is demonstrated and necessitated by the practices Java uses, such as interfaces and abstract implementations.

If you are accustomed to implementing dynamically linked lists or queues in C++, the format you use in Java to create your own version of these structures should seem very familiar to you. For example, the following code creates a `Node` class for the list that contains a string:

```
class Node {
    String Name;
    Node Prev;
    Node Next;
}
```

Of course, this code creates a *doubly linked list*, which has links backward and forward to other nodes containing strings. You could just as easily convert this type to link objects in just about any way to exhibit just about any behavior you want: queues, stacks (remember, there is already a `Stack` object in the class library), doubly linked lists, circular lists, binary search trees, and the list goes on.

To implement such a list, you create a `DoubleList` class that contains one such `Node` object and links strung out from there. You can use the keyword `null` to represent an empty object. Here is an example of the `DoubleList` declaration:

```
class DoubleList {
    // Declare the listhead to be of the Node type we created earlier.
    // Also, set it to be an empty object.
    Node ListHead = null;
    .
    .
    .
}
```

You then create methods to act on the list, such as `InsertNode()` or `ClearMyListJerk()`—whatever you want.

You may also want to create a constructor method for the `Node` class that accepts parameters to set the previous and next nodes at construction time; or you may want to create a method such as `SetNext()` or `SetNextToNull()`. Either choice would work just fine.

> **NOTE**
>
> Out of all this you get a surprise bonus: No worry about freeing space allocated to create nodes because the Java garbage collection processes take care of all that for you. Just create objects when you need them and let Java take care of it.

Using the Utilities Package

The utilities package has three interfaces, but you typically use only two: `Enumeration` and `Observer`. The other interface is `EventListener`; it is most commonly used internally by the AWT for handling events. Programmers only rarely implement the `EventListener` interface.

An *interface* is a set of methods that must be written for any class that claims to implement the interface. This arrangement provides a way to consistently use all classes that implement the interface. Following is a summary of the Enumeration and Observer interfaces:

- Enumeration. Interface for classes that can enumerate a vector
- Observer. Interface for classes that can observe observable objects

The Enumeration interface is used for classes that can retrieve data from a list, element by element. For example, there is an Enumeration class in the utilities package that implements the Enumeration interface for use with the Vector class. This frees you from hard-core traversal of the different classes of data structures.

The Observer interface is useful in designing classes that can watch for changes that occur in other classes.

CAUTION

Some of the examples in this chapter are not applets—they are applications. Many of these data structures are best exhibited by just plain text input and output. Removing the baggage that would have come along with applets allows the examples to be simplified so that the topic being demonstrated is clearer.

When you apply any code segments from this chapter in your own applets, remember that some of the examples are not true applets; you must deal with the differences inherent between applets and applications.

The Enumeration Interface

The Enumeration interface specifies a set of methods used to *enumerate*—that is, iterate through—a list. An object that implements this interface can be used to iterate through a list only once because the Enumeration object is consumed through its use.

For example, an Enumeration object can be used to print all the elements of a Vector object, v, as follows:

```
for (Enumeration e=v.elements();e.hasMoreElements();)
    System.out.print(e.nextElement()+" ");
```

The Enumeration interface specifies only two methods: hasMoreElements() and nextElement(). The hasMoreElements() method must return true if there are elements remaining in the enumeration. The nextElement() method must return an object representing the next element within the object being enumerated. The details of how the Enumeration interface is implemented and how the data is represented internally are left up to the implementation of the specific class.

The `Observer` Interface

The `Observer` interface, if implemented by a class, allows an object of the class to observe other objects of the class `Observable`. The `Observer` interface is notified whenever the `Observable` object that it is watching changes.

The interface only specifies one method, `update(Observable, Object)`. This method is called by the observed object to notify the `Observer` of changes. A reference to the observed object is passed along with any additional object that the observed object wants to pass to the `Observer`. The first argument enables the `Observer` to operate on the observed object; the second argument is used to pass information from the observed to the `Observer`.

Classes

The utilities package supplies many different classes that provide a wide variety of functionality. Although these classes don't generally have much in common, they all provide support for the most common data structures used by programmers. The techniques described in the next sections enable you to create your own specialized classes to supplement those missing from the package.

The classes supplied in the `java.util` package, however limited they are, do provide a great advantage over other languages. The main advantage is that these classes simplify some things and eliminate a lot of the garbage you were stuck with in the past, in terms of freeing memory and doing mundane programming tasks.

However, there are a number of limitations. For example, you have to "dance a little bit" to implement some of the more complicated data structures. And if you want speed, there are much faster languages to choose from. Java provides a combination of power and simplicity while sacrificing speed. However, don't worry that your programs will be slugs. Although Java is not nearly as efficient as C++ and C, it still beats Visual Basic in terms of size and speed.

The `BitSet` Class

The `BitSet` class implements a data type that represents a collection of bits. The collection grows dynamically as more bits are required. The class is useful for representing a set of `true` and `false` values. Specific bits are identified using nonnegative integers. The first bit is bit `0`.

The `BitSet` class is most useful for storing a group of related `true`/`false` values, such as user responses to Yes and No questions. For example, if the applet has a number of radio buttons, you can slap those values into an instance of the `BitSet` class.

The class is also useful in terms of bitmapping your own graphics. You can create bitsets that represent a pixel at a time (of course, it would be much easier to use the `Graphics` class for this purpose instead).

Individual bits in the set are turned on or off with the set() and clear() methods. Individual bits are queried with the get() method. These methods all take the specific bit number as their only argument. The basic boolean operations AND, OR, and XOR can be performed on two bitsets using the and(), or(), and xor() methods. Because these methods modify one of the bitsets, you generally use the clone() method to create a duplicate of one bitset, and then use the AND, OR, or XOR operation on the clone with the second bitset. The result of the operation then ends up in the cloned bitset. The BitSet1 program in Listing 11.1 shows the basic BitSet operations.

Listing 11.1. BitSet1.java: a sample BitSet program.

```java
import java.io.DataInputStream;
import java.io.BufferedReader;
import java.io.InputStreamReader;
import java.util.BitSet;
class BitSet1 {
    public static void main(String args[])
        throws java.io.IOException
    {
        BufferedReader dis=new BufferedReader(new InputStreamReader(System.in));
        String bitstring;
        BitSet set1,set2,set3;
        set1=new BitSet();
        set2=new BitSet();
        // Get the first bit sequence and store it
        System.out.println("Bit sequence #1:");
        bitstring=dis.readLine();
        for (short i=0;i<bitstring.length();i++){
            if (bitstring.charAt(i)=='1')
                set1.set(i);
            else
                set1.clear(i);
        }
        // Get the second bit sequence and store it
        System.out.println("Bit sequence #2:");
        bitstring=dis.readLine();
        for (short i=0;i<bitstring.length();i++){
            if (bitstring.charAt(i)=='1')
                set2.set(i);
            else
                set2.clear(i);
        }
        System.out.println("BitSet #1: "+set1);
        System.out.println("BitSet #2: "+set2);
        // Test the AND operation
        set3=(BitSet)set1.clone();
        set3.and(set2);
        System.out.println("set1 AND set2: "+set3);
        // Test the OR operation
        set3=(BitSet)set1.clone();
        set3.or(set2);
        System.out.println("set1 OR set2: "+set3);
```

continues

Listing 11.1. continued

```
        // Test the XOR operation
        set3=(BitSet)set1.clone();
        set3.xor(set2);
        System.out.println("set1 XOR set2: "+set3);
    }
}
```

The output from this program looks like this:

```
Bit sequence #1:
1010
Bit sequence #2:
1100
BitSet #1: {0, 2}
BitSet #2: {0, 1}
set1 AND set2: {0}
set1 OR set2: {0, 1, 2}
set1 XOR set2: {1, 2}
```

Table 11.2 summarizes all the methods available in the BitSet class.

Table 11.2. Methods in the BitSet interface.

Method	Description
Constructors	
BitSet()	Constructs an empty BitSet
BitSet(int)	Constructs an empty BitSet of a given size
Methods	
and(BitSet)	Logically ANDs the object's bitset with another BitSet object
clear(int)	Clears a specific bit
clone()	Creates a clone of the BitSet object
equals(Object)	Compares this object against another BitSet object
get(int)	Returns the value of a specific bit
hashCode()	Returns the hash code
or(BitSet)	Logically ORs the object's bitset with another BitSet object
set(int)	Sets a specific bit
size()	Returns the size of the set
toString()	Converts bit values to a string representation
xor(BitSet)	Logically XORs the object's bitset with another BitSet object

In addition to extending the `java.lang.Object` class, `BitSet` implements the `java.lang.Cloneable` interface. This, of course, allows instances of the object to be cloned to create another instance of the class.

The Calendar Class

The `Calendar` class is an abstract class used to convert dates. You can use this class to convert a `Date` object to fields, such as YEAR, MONTH, HOUR, and so on. You can also use these fields to update a `Date` object.

In the API definition, only one subclass of `Calendar` exists: `GregorianCalendar`. Because most people and virtually all businesses in the world use the Gregorian calendar, you will find all the details about calendars in that section, later in this chapter.

Table 11.3 summarizes the methods available in the `Calendar` class.

Table 11.3. Methods in the Calendar class.

Method	*Description*
Constructors	
`Calendar()`	Creates a calendar with the default `TimeZone` and `Locale`
`Calendar(TimeZone,Locale)`	Creates a calendar with the given `TimeZone` and `Locale`
Static Methods	
`getDefault()`	Returns a calendar with the default `TimeZone` and `Locale`
`getDefault(TimeZone)`	Returns a calendar with the default `Locale` and given `TimeZone`
`getDefault(Locale)`	Returns a calendar with the given `Locale` and default `TimeZone`
`getDefault(TimeZone,Locale)`	Returns a calendar with the given `TimeZone` and `Locale`
`getAvailableLocales()`	Returns an array of all available locales
Methods	
`getTime()`	Returns the date and time
`setTime(Date)`	Sets the date and time
`get(byte)`	Returns the specified field
`set(byte,int)`	Sets the specified field to the specified value

continues

Table 11.3. continued

Method	*Description*
	Methods
set(int,int,int)	Sets the year, month, and date
set(int,int,int,int,int)	Sets the year, month, date, hour, and minute
set(int,int,int,int,int,int)	Sets the year, month, date, hour, minute, and second
clear()	Clears all fields
clear(byte)	Clears the specified field
isSet(int)	Returns true if the specified field is set
equals(Object)	Returns true if two objects are the same
before(Object)	Returns true if this object is before the given object
after(Object)	Returns true if this object is after the given object
add(byte,int)	Adds the given value to the field
roll(byte,boolean)	Increments or decrements (depending on the boolean value) the specified field by one unit
setTimeZone(TimeZone)	Sets the time zone this object is in
setValidationMode(boolean)	If the boolean value is set to true, invalid dates are allowed
getValidationMode()	Returns whether or not invalid dates are allowed
setFirstDayOfWeek(byte)	Sets the first day of the week
getFirstDayOfWeek()	Returns the first day of the week
setMinimumDaysInFirstWeek(byte)	Sets how many days are required to define the first week of the month
getMinimumDaysInFirstWeek()	Returns how many days are required to define the first week of the month
getMinimum(byte)	Returns the minimum possible value for the given field
getMaximum(byte)	Returns the maximum possible value for the given field
getGreatestMinimum(byte)	Returns the greatest possible minimum value for the field
getLeastMaximum(byte)	Returns the least possible maximum value for the given field
Clone()	Makes a copy of this object

NOTE

The use of the terms *greatest minimum* and *least maximum* may have confused you in Table 11.3. An example of *least maximum* is the question "what is the least maximum day in any month?" The answer is 28—from February, where the maximum day is 28 (in most years). For the Gregorian calendar (which most of us use), getGreatestMinimum() always returns the same value as getMinimum().

The Date Class

Before Java 1.1, the Date class was an extremely important class for handling dates and times. However, it was weak in some areas such as internationalization and dealing with the differences in daylight saving time in different locations.

With Java 1.1, the Date class has been relegated to just storing the exact time. Most of the old Date class methods have been deprecated and should no longer be used. All the methods for converting time between binary and human-readable form are now handled by the Calendar, GregorianCalendar, TimeZone, SimpleTimeZone, and Locale classes. An example of how these classes can work together is found in Listing 11.3, in "The GregorianCalendar Class," later in this chapter.

The default constructor is used when the current date and time are required. The other constructor takes a millisecond representation of time and creates a Date object based on it.

When a date is converted to a string by an automatic coercion, the toString() method is used. The resulting string returned by the toString() function follows UNIX time and date standards.

Dates can be compared to each other by using their UTC values (the UTC value is the number of seconds since January 1, 1970) or by using the methods after(), before(), and equals().

CAUTION

Don't try to launch space shuttles or coordinate nuclear attacks based on your operating system's local time as reflected by Java. Although the API is intended to reflect UTC (Coordinated Universal Time), it doesn't do so exactly. This inexact behavior is inherited from the time system of the underlying OS. The vast majority of all modern operating systems assume that one day equals 3600 seconds/hour multiplied by 24 hours, and as such, they reflect time to the accuracy that UTC does.

continues

continued

Under the UTC, about once a year, there is an extra second, called a "leap second," added to account for the wobble of the earth. Most computer clocks are not accurate enough to reflect this distinction.

Between UTC and standard OS time (UT/GMT), there is this subtle difference; one is based on an atomic clock and the other is based on astronomical observations, which, for all practical purposes, is an invisibly fine hair to split.

For more information, Sun suggests you visit the U.S. Naval Observatory site, particularly the Directorate of Time at `http://tycho.usno.navy.mil` and its definitions of different systems of time at `http://tycho.usno.navy.mil/systime.html`.

Table 11.4 summarizes all the nondeprecated methods available in the Date class. You can find the deprecated methods by looking at the API reference included with the JDK or found on JavaSoft's Web site (`http://www.javasoft.com/`).

Table 11.4. Useable methods available in the Date interface.

Method	*Description*
Constructors	
`Date()`	Constructs a date using today's date and time
`Date(long)`	Constructs a date using a single UTC value
Methods	
`after(Date)`	Returns `true` if the date is later than the specified date
`before(Date)`	Returns `true` if the date is earlier than the specified date
`equals(Object)`	Returns `true` if the date and the specified date are equal
`getTime()`	Returns the time as a single UTC value
`hashCode()`	Computes a hash code for the date
`setTime(long)`	Sets the time using a single UTC value
`toString()`	Converts a date to text using UNIX `ctime()` conventions

You will also find the `before()` and `after()` functions useful. They enable you to send in another instance of the Date class and compare that date to the value in the calling instance.

The sample applet in Listing 11.2 demonstrates the use of the Date class.

Listing 11.2. Using the Date class.

```java
import java.awt.*;
import java.util.*;
import java.awt.event.ActionEvent;
import java.awt.event.ActionListener;

public class MichaelSimpleClock extends java.applet.Applet {
    Button DateButton = new Button(
        "                    Click me!                    ");
    public void init()  {
        ButtonListener bl = new ButtonListener(DateButton);
        add(DateButton);
     DateButton.addActionListener(bl);
    }
}

class ButtonListener implements ActionListener {
    Date TheDate = new Date();
    Button theButton;

    public ButtonListener(Button aButton) {
     theButton = aButton;
    }

    public void actionPerformed (ActionEvent e) {
            theButton.setLabel(TheDate.toString());
    }
}
```

Figure 11.1 shows the MichaelSimpleClock applet. Note that the clock in the applet is wrong: it is not actually 8:00 A.M. There is no way I would write that early in the morning!

FIGURE 11.1.
The
MichaelSimpleClock
applet.

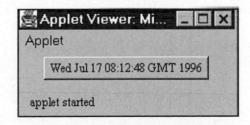

What about a real-time clock that updates as the clock changes? To accomplish this small feat, you must include in the applet a loop that has each iteration reconstructing the internal Date instance. Then you regularly repaint that value inside the applet's paint() method. You also have to include threading to keep your system from locking up during the applet's execution. Threading is covered in Chapter 6, "Threads and Multithreading," so a real-time clock was not included in this chapter.

The GregorianCalendar Class

Before 1582, the western world used the Julian calendar system, which was adopted by Julius Caesar. The problem with the Julian calendar was that it had too many leap years (3 too many every 400 years). Pope Gregory XIII fixed that problem. In addition, the Julian year started on March 25; the Gregorian calendar year starts on January 1. At the time of the switch, the last day of the Julian calendar was October 4, 1582, and the first day of the Gregorian calendar was October 15, 1582. The dates in between never occurred. However, this was not true for England and America, which kept the Julian calendar until 1752. When England and America switched, the last Julian day was September 2, 1752, and the first Gregorian date was September 14, 1752. If you are working on historical dates, I strongly recommend that you do some additional reading on this subject!

The GregorianCalendar class handles conversions between actual dates and data fields such as month for the Gregorian calendar. The Gregorian calendar is the most widely used calendar system in the world. However, in fact, this class also handles the Julian calendar system.

Table 11.5 summarizes the methods available in the GregorianCalendar class.

Table 11.5. Methods in the GregorianCalendar class.

Method	Description
Constructors	
GregorianCalendar()	Creates a Gregorian calendar using the current time with the default TimeZone and Locale
GregorianCalendar(TimeZone)	Creates a Gregorian calendar using the current time with the default Locale and the given TimeZone
GregorianCalendar(TimeZone,Locale)	Creates a Gregorian calendar with the current time and the given TimeZone and Locale
GregorianCalendar(int,int,int)	Creates a Gregorian calendar at the given year, month, and date with the default TimeZone and Locale
GregorianCalendar(int,int,int,int,int)	Creates a Gregorian calendar at the given year, month, date, hour, and minute with the default TimeZone and Locale

Method	Description
Constructors	
`GregorianCalendar(int,int,int,int,int,int)`	Creates a Gregorian calendar at the given year, month, date, hour, minute, and second with the default `TimeZone` and `Locale`
`GregorianCalendar(Locale)`	Creates a Gregorian calendar at the current time with the default `TimeZone` and the given `Locale`
Methods	
`setGregorianChange(Date)`	Sets the date that the Julian calendar changed to the Gregorian calendar
`getGregorianChange()`	Returns the date that the Julian calendar changed to the Gregorian calendar
`isLeapYear()`	Returns `true` if the year of this object is a leap year
`equals(Objects)`	Returns `true` if the two objects are equal
`before(Object)`	Returns `true` if this object is before the date of the object given
`after(Object)`	Returns `true` if the object is after the date of the object given
`add(byte,amount)`	Adds the `amount` given to the field specified by `byte`
`roll(byte,boolean)`	Increments or decrements (depending on the `boolean` value) the specified field by one unit
`getMinimum(byte)`	Returns the minimum value for the specified field
`getMaximum(byte)`	Returns the maximum value for the specified field
`getGreatestMinimum(byte)`	Returns the greatest minimum value for the specified field
`getLeastMaximum(byte)`	Returns the least maximum value for the specified field
`clone()`	Makes a copy of this object

Listing 11.3 shows the use of the GregorianCalendar class as well as many other classes in the utilities package.

Listing 11.3. A program to calculate the day of week.

```
import java.util.*;
public class cal {
    public static void main(String args[]) {
        int msecsInHour = 60*60*1000;
        SimpleTimeZone cst = new SimpleTimeZone(-6*msecsInHour,"CST");
        cst.setStartRule(Calendar.APRIL, 1, Calendar.SUNDAY, 2*msecsInHour);
        cst.setEndRule(Calendar.OCTOBER, -1, Calendar.SUNDAY, 2*msecsInHour);
        Calendar calendar = new GregorianCalendar(cst);

        System.out.println("Day of Week: " + calendar.get(Calendar.DAY_OF_WEEK));
    }
}
```

The Locale Class

The Locale class is used to define a locale. A *locale* is a combination of a geographic location, a language, and a variant. The *variant* is usually a browser-specific code. The Locale class is key in using internationalization in your Java code. The Locale class enables you to write your program independent of country and language. Specific behaviors for each country and language can easily be added later when they are needed.

The ISO (International Standards Organization) language codes are documented in standard ISO-639 (http://www.ics.uci.edu/pub/ietf/http/related/iso639.txt). The ISO country codes are documented in standard ISO-3166 (http://www.chemie.fu-berlin.de/diverse/doc/ISO_3166.html). An example of a country code is "US" (for the United States). An example of a language code is "EN" (for English). Some example of variants are WIN (for Windows), MAC (for Macintosh), and POSIX (for UNIX).

Table 11.6 lists the methods available in the Locale class.

Table 11.6. Methods available with the Locale class.

Method	Description
	Constructor
Locale(String, String)	Creates a locale based on a given language and country
Locale(String, String, String)	Creates a locale based on a given language, country, and variant

Method	Description
	Static Methods
getDefault()	Returns the default `Locale`
setDefault(Locale)	Sets the default `Locale`
	Methods
getLanguage()	Returns the language in use
getCountry()	Returns the country in use
getISO3Language()	Returns the three-character ISO code for the language
getISO3Country()	Returns the three-character ISO code for the country
getVariant()	Returns the variant in use
toString()	Returns the object as a `String`
getDisplayLanguage()	Returns the language to display to the user
getDisplayLanguage(Locale)	Returns the language to display to the user based on the given `Locale`
getDisplayCountry()	Returns the country to display to the user
getDisplayCountry(Locale)	Returns the country to display to the user for the given `Locale`
getDisplayVariant()	Returns the variant to display to the user
getDisplayVariant(Locale)	Returns the variant to display to the user for the given `Locale`
getDisplayName()	Returns the language, country, and variant to display to the user
getDisplayName(Locale)	Returns the language, country, and variant to display to the user for the given `Locale`
clone()	Makes a copy of this locale
hashCode()	Returns the hash code for this locale
equals(Object)	Returns `true` if two locales are equal

The Random Class

For the programming of games and many other program types, it is important to be able to generate random numbers. Java includes the capability to generate random numbers efficiently and effectively.

The Random class implements a pseudo-random number data type that generates a stream of seemingly random numbers. To create a sequence of different pseudo-random values each time the application is run, create the Random object as follows:

```
Random r=new Random();
```

This statement seeds the random generator with the current time. On the other hand, consider the following statement:

```
Random r=new Random(326);    // Pick any value
```

This statement seeds the random generator with the same value each time, resulting in the same sequence of pseudo-random numbers each time the application runs. The generator can be reseeded at any time using the setSeed() method.

TIP

Want to get really random numbers? Well, you can't. But a common practice to simulate actual random numbers in computer programs is to seed the random number generator with some variant of the current time or date. If, for example, you want to seed a random number generator with the sum of the current seconds, minutes, and hours, you could use this code, which should suffice for most tasks:

```
int OurSeed = ADate.getSeconds() + ADate.getHours() + ADate.getMinutes();
Random = new Random(OurSeed);
```

Pseudo-random numbers can be generated using one of these functions: nextInt(), nextLong(), nextFloat(), nextDouble(), or nextGaussian(). The first four functions return integers, longs, floats, and doubles. For more information about the Gaussian distribution, refer to the following sidebar. The Random1 program in Listing 11.4 prints five pseudo-random uniformly distributed values using these functions.

Listing 11.4. Random1.java: A sample Random program.

```
import java.lang.Math;
import java.util.Date;
import java.util.Random;
class Random1 {
    public static void main(String args[])
        throws java.io.IOException
    {
        int count=6;
        Random randGen=new Random();
        System.out.println("Uniform Random Integers");
        for (int i=0;i<count;i++)
        System.out.print(randGen.nextInt()+" ");
        System.out.println("\n");
        System.out.println("Uniform Random Floats");
```

```
      for (int i=0;i<count;i++)
      System.out.print(randGen.nextFloat()+" ");
      System.out.println("\n");
      System.out.println("Gaussian Random Floats");
      for (int i=0;i<count;i++)
          System.out.print(randGen.nextGaussian()+" ");
      System.out.println("\n");
      System.out.println("Uniform Random Integers [1,6]");
      for (int i=0;i<count;i++)
          System.out.print((Math.abs(randGen.nextInt())%6+1)+" ");
      System.out.println("\n");
      }
}
```

The output from the preceding program looks like this:

```
Uniform Random Integers
1704667569 -1431446235 1024613888 438489989 710330974 -1689521238
Uniform Random Floats
0.689189 0.0579988 0.0933537 0.748228 0.400992 0.222109
Gaussian Random Floats
-0.201843 -0.0111578 1.63927 0.205938 -0.365471 0.626304
Uniform Random Integers [1,6]
4 6 1 6 3 2
```

If you want to generate uniformly distributed random integers within a specific range, the output from nextInt(), nextLong(), or nextDouble() can be scaled to match the required range. However, a simpler approach is to take the remainder of the result of nextInt() divided by the number of different values plus the first value of the range. For example, if the values 10 to 20 are needed, you can use the formula nextInt()%21+10. Unfortunately, although this method is much simpler than scaling the output of nextInt(), it is guaranteed to work only on truly random values. Because the pseudo-random generator may have various undesired correlations, the modulus operator may not provide acceptable results—you might get all odd numbers, for example. In other words, don't plan on simulating the detonation of your new H-bomb in Java because you may find yourself a couple miles too close.

GAUSSIAN AND NORMAL DISTRIBUTIONS

Uniformly distributed random numbers are generated using a modified linear congruential method with a 48-bit seed. Uniformly distributed random numbers within a given range all appear with the same frequency. The Random class can also generate random numbers in a Gaussian or normal distribution. The Gaussian frequency distribution curve is also referred to as a *bell curve*. For information on the Gaussian frequency distribution curve, see *The Art of Computer Programming*, Volume 2, by Donald Knuth.

Table 11.7 summarizes the complete interface of the Random class.

Table 11.7. The methods available in the Random interface.

Method	Description
	Constructors
Random()	Creates a new random number generator
Random(long)	Creates a new random number generator using a seed
	Methods
nextDouble()	Returns a pseudo-random, uniformly distributed double
nextFloat()	Returns a pseudo-random, uniformly distributed float
nextGaussian()	Returns a pseudo-random, Gaussian distributed double
nextInt()	Returns a pseudo-random, uniformly distributed integer
nextLong()	Returns a pseudo-random, uniformly distributed long
setSeed(long)	Sets the seed of the pseudo-random number generator

The applet shown in Listing 11.5 demonstrates a bit of what you can do with the Random class.

Listing 11.5. Using the Random class.

```java
import java.awt.*;
import java.util.*;
import java.awt.event.ActionListener;
import java.awt.event.ActionEvent;

public class TheWanderer extends java.applet.Applet {
        int xpos = 100;
        int ypos = 100;
    // Our current date.
    Calendar C = new GregorianCalendar();
        // The movement button
        Button theButton = new Button("Click Me");
        // Our random number generator.
        Random R;
        public void init() {
                SimpleListener simple = new SimpleListener(this);
                add(theButton);
                theButton.addActionListener(simple);
                setBackground(Color.white);
        // Our random number generator seeded with the current seconds.
        int seed = C.get(Calendar.SECOND);
                R = new Random(seed);
        }
    public void paint(Graphics g) {
                g.setColor(Color.black);
                g.fillOval(xpos,ypos, 50, 50);
        }
```

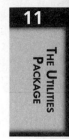

```
    public void move() {
                    // Move our thing.
                    xpos = xpos + (Math.abs(R.nextInt())%10-7);
                    ypos = ypos + (Math.abs(R.nextInt())%10-7);
        // repaint the sucker.
                    repaint();
    }
}

class SimpleListener implements ActionListener {
      private TheWanderer theClass;

      public SimpleListener(TheWanderer aClass) {
            theClass = aClass;
      }
      public void actionPerformed (ActionEvent e) {
            theClass.move();
      }
   }
```

Figure 11.2 shows `TheWanderer` applet during its execution.

FIGURE 11.2.

`TheWanderer` *applet.*

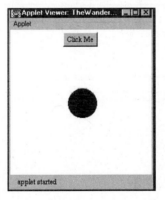

The `SimpleTimeZone` Class

The `SimpleTimeZone` class is a simple `TimeZone` that can be used with the `GregorianCalendar` class. The `SimpleTimeZone` class assumes that time-zone rules have not changed historically. Additionally, it assumes that the rules are of a simple nature. Even with these limitations, this class can handle the needs of the majority of programmers. Listing 11.3, earlier in this chapter, provides an example of how to use this class. Table 11.8 summarizes the methods available with the `SimpleTimeZone` class.

Table 11.8. Methods available with the `SimpleTimeZone` class.

Method	Description
Constructor	
`SimpleTimeZone(int,String)`	Creates a `TimeZone` with the given offset and time-zone name
`SimpleTimeZone(int,String,int,int,` `int,int,int,int,int,int)`	Creates a `TimeZone` with the given offset, time-zone name, and time to start and end daylight saving time
Methods	
`setStartYear(int)`	Sets the first year that daylight saving time started
`setStartRule(int,int,int,int)`	Sets the rule for the beginning of daylight saving time based on the month, week, day of week, and time of day
`setEndRule(int,int,int,int)`	Sets the rule for the end of daylight saving time based on the month, week, day of week, and time of day
`getOffset(int,int,int,int,int,int)`	Returns the Greenwich mean time (GMT) offset for a given time
`getRawOffset()`	Returns the GMT offset for the current time
`setRawOffset(int)`	Sets the base GMT offset
`useDaylightTime()`	Returns `true` if this `TimeZone` uses daylight saving time
`inDaylightTime(Date)`	Returns `true` if the given date is in daylight saving time
`clone()`	Makes a copy of this object
`hashCode()`	Returns the hash code for this object
`equals(Object)`	Returns `true` if this object is equal to the one given

The `StringTokenizer` Class

This section describes the function of the `StringTokenizer` class, which also could have been appropriately grouped with the other classes in Chapter 12, "The I/O Package," because it is so vital to the input and output functions demonstrated in that chapter. The `StringTokenizer` class enables you to parse a string into a number of smaller strings called *tokens*. This class works specifically for what is called "delimited text," which means that each individual substring of the string is separated by a delimiter. The delimiter can be anything ranging from an * to YabaDaba. You simply specify what you want the class to look for when tokenizing the string.

This class is included in this chapter because it has uses that prove helpful in everything from a spreadsheet applet to an arcade game applet.

The delimiter set can be specified when the StringTokenizer object is created, or it can be specified on a per-token basis. The default delimiter set is the set of *whitespace* characters. With this delimiter set, the class would find all the separate words in a string and tokenize them. For example, the StringTokenizer1 code in Listing 11.6 prints out each word of the string on a separate line.

Listing 11.6. StringTokenizer1.java: A sample StringTokenizer program.

```java
import java.io.DataInputStream;
import java.io.BufferedReader;
import java.io.InputStreamReader;
import java.util.StringTokenizer;
class StringTokenizer1 {
    public static void main(String args[])
        throws java.io.IOException
    {
        BufferedReader dis=new BufferedReader(new InputStreamReader(System.in));
        System.out.println("Enter a sentence: ");
        String s=dis.readLine();
        StringTokenizer st=new StringTokenizer(s);
        while (st.hasMoreTokens())
            System.out.println(st.nextToken());
    }
}
```

Here is the output from this listing:

```
Enter a sentence:
Four score and seven
Four
score
and
seven
```

Pure excitement. The method countTokens() returns the number of tokens remaining in the string using the current delimiter set—that is, the number of times nextToken() can be called before generating an exception. This is an efficient method because it does not actually construct the substrings that nextToken() must generate.

In addition to extending the java.lang.Object class, the StringTokenizer class implements the java.util.Enumeration interface.

Table 11.9 summarizes the methods of the StringTokenizer class.

Table 11.9. The methods available in the `StringTokenizer` interface.

Method	Description
Constructors	
`StringTokenizer (String)`	Constructs a `StringTokenizer` given a string using whitespace as delimiters
`StringTokenizer (String, String)`	Constructs a `StringTokenizer` given a string and a delimiter set
`StringTokenizer (String, String, boolean)`	Constructs a `StringTokenizer` given a string and a delimiter set; the final parameter is a boolean value which, if `true`, says that the delimiters must be returned as tokens (if this parameter is `false`, the tokens are not returned)
Methods	
`countTokens()`	Returns the number of tokens remaining in the string
`hasMoreTokens()`	Returns `true` if more tokens exist
`nextToken()`	Returns the next token of the string
`nextToken(String)`	Returns the next token, given a new delimiter set
`hasMoreElements()`	Returns `true` if more elements exist in the enumeration
`nextElement()`	Returns the next element of the enumeration using the current delimiter set

The `TimeZone` Class

The `TimeZone` class is a generic class that represents any kind of time zone. This class contains the offset from Greenwich mean time (GMT) and can deal with daylight saving time. Table 11.10 lists the methods available with the `TimeZone` class.

Table 11.10. Methods available with the `TimeZone` class.

Method	Description
Constructor	
`TimeZone()`	Creates a `TimeZone`
Static Methods	
`getTimeZone(String)`	Returns the `TimeZone` object given the name of the time zone
`getAvailableIDs()`	Returns an array of all `TimeZone` names

Method	Description
Static Methods	
getAvailableIDs(int)	Returns an array of all TimeZone names that apply to a particular offset
getDefault()	Returns the default TimeZone for this machine
setDefault(TimeZone)	Sets the default TimeZone for this machine
Methods	
getOffset(int,int,int,int,int,int)	Returns the GMT offset for the local TimeZone at the time given
getRawOffset()	Returns the GMT offset for the local TimeZone at the current time
getID()	Returns the name of the TimeZone
setID(String)	Sets the name of the TimeZone
useDaylightTime()	Returns true if this TimeZone uses daylight saving time
inDaylightTime(Date)	Returns true if the date given is in daylight saving time for this TimeZone
clone()	Makes a copy of this object

The Vector Class

As stated earlier in this chapter, Java doesn't include dynamically linked lists, queues, or other data structures of that type. Instead, the designers of Java envisioned the Vector class, which handles the occasions when you need to dynamically store objects. Of course, there are positive and negative consequences of this decision by the designers at Sun. On the positive side, the Vector class contributes to the simplicity of the language. The major negative point is that, at face value, the Vector class severely limits programmers from using more sophisticated programs.

In any case, the Vector class implements a dynamically allocated list of objects. It attempts to optimize storage by increasing the storage capacity of the list when needed by increments larger than just one object. Typically, with this mechanism, there is some excess capacity in the list. When this capacity is exhausted, the list is reallocated to add another block of objects at the end of the list. Setting the capacity of the Vector object to the needed size before inserting a large number of objects reduces the need for incremental reallocation. Because of this mechanism, it is important to remember that the *capacity* (the available elements in the Vector object) and the *size* (the number of elements currently stored in the Vector object) usually are not the same.

Suppose that a Vector with capacityIncrement equal to 3 has been created. As objects are added to the Vector, new space is allocated in chunks of three objects. After five elements have been added, there is still room for one more element without the need for any additional memory allocation.

After the sixth element has been added, there is no more excess capacity. When the seventh element is added, a new allocation is made to add three additional elements, giving a total capacity of nine. After the seventh element is added, there are two remaining unused elements.

The initial storage capacity and the capacity increment can both be specified in the constructor. Even though the capacity is automatically increased as needed, the ensureCapacity() method can be used to increase the capacity to a specific minimum number of elements; the trimToSize() method can be used to reduce the capacity to the minimum number of elements needed to store the current amount. New elements can be added to the Vector using the addElement() and insertElementAt() methods. The elements passed to be stored in the Vector must be derived from type Object. Elements can be changed using the setElementAt() method. Removal of elements is accomplished with the removeElement(), removeElementAt(), and removeAllElements() methods. Elements can be accessed directly using the elementAt(), firstElement(), and lastElement() methods; elements can be located using the indexOf() and lastIndexOf() methods. Information about the size and the capacity of the Vector are returned by the size() and capacity() methods. The setSize() method can be used to directly change the size of the Vector.

For example, the Vector1 code in Listing 11.7 creates a Vector of integers by adding new elements to the end. Then, using a variety of techniques, it prints the Vector.

Listing 11.7. Vector1.java: A sample Vector program.

```java
import java.lang.Integer;
import java.util.Enumeration;
import java.util.Vector;
class Vector1 {
    public static void main(String args[]){
        Vector v=new Vector(10,10);
        for (int i=0;i<20;i++)
            v.addElement(new Integer(i));
        System.out.println("Vector in original order using an Enumeration");
        for (Enumeration e=v.elements();e.hasMoreElements();)
            System.out.print(e.nextElement()+" ");
        System.out.println();
        System.out.println("Vector in original order using elementAt");
        for (int i=0;i<v.size();i++)
            System.out.print(v.elementAt(i)+" ");
        System.out.println();
        // Print out the original vector
        System.out.println("\nVector in reverse order using elementAt");
        for (int i=v.size()-1;i>=0;i++)
            System.out.print(v.elementAt(i)+" ");
        System.out.println();
```

```
        // Print out the original vector
        System.out.println("\nVector as a String");
        System.out.println(v.toString());
    }
}
```

The output from this program looks like this:

```
Vector in original order using an Enumeration
0 1 2 3 4 5 6 7 8 9 10 11 12 13 14 15 16 17 18 19
Vector in original order using elementAt
0 1 2 3 4 5 6 7 8 9 10 11 12 13 14 15 16 17 18 19
Vector in reverse order using elementAt
19 18 17 16 15 14 13 12 11 10 9 8 7 6 5 4 3 2 1 0
Vector as a String
[0, 1, 2, 3, 4, 5, 6, 7, 8, 9, 10, 11, 12, 13, 14, 15, 16, 17, 18, 19]
```

NOTE

The expression new Integer() was used to create integer objects to store because the fundamental types, such as int, are not objects in Java. This technique is used many times throughout this chapter.

Notice the use of the Enumeration object as one way to access the elements of a Vector. Look at the following lines:

```
for (Enumeration e=v.elements();e.hasMoreElements();)
    System.out.print(e.nextElement()+" ");
```

You can see that an Enumeration object, which represents all the elements in the Vector, is created and returned by the Vector method elements(). With this Enumeration object, the loop can check to see whether there are more elements to process using the Enumeration method hasMoreElements(); the loop can get the next element in the Vector using the Enumeration method nextElement().

The Vector2 program in Listing 11.8 shows some of the vector-accessing techniques. It first generates a vector of random integers; then it allows the user to search for a specific value. The locations of the first and last occurrences of the value are printed by the program using the indexOf() and lastIndexOf() methods.

Listing 11.8. Vector2.java: Another sample Vector program.

```
import java.io.DataInputStream;
import java.io.InputStreamReader;
import java.io.BufferedReader;
import java.lang.Integer;
```

continues

Listing 11.8. continued

```java
import java.lang.Math;
import java.util.Enumeration;
import java.util.Random;
import java.util.Vector;
class Vector2 {
    public static void main(String args[])
        throws java.io.IOException
    {
        int numElements;
        BufferedReader dis=new BufferedReader(new InputStreamReader(System.in));
        Vector v=new Vector(10,10);
        Random randGen=new Random();
        System.out.println("How many random elements? ");
        numElements=Integer.valueOf(dis.readLine()).intValue();
        for (int i=0;i<numElements;i++)
            v.addElement(new Integer(Math.abs(
                randGen.nextInt())%numElements));
        System.out.println(v.toString());
        Integer searchValue;
        System.out.println("Find which value? ");
        searchValue=Integer.valueOf(dis.readLine());
        System.out.println("First occurrence is element "+
            v.indexOf(searchValue));
        System.out.println("Last occurrence is element "+
            v.lastIndexOf(searchValue));
    }
}
```

The output from this program looks like this:

```
How many random elements?
10
[0, 2, 8, 4, 9, 7, 8, 6, 3, 2]
Find which value?
8
First occurrence is element 2
Last occurrence is element 6
```

In addition to extending the `java.lang.Object` class, the `Vector` class implements the `java.lang.Cloneable` interface. Table 11.11 summarizes the methods of the `Vector` class.

Table 11.11. The variables and methods available in the Vector interface.

Variable	Description
capacityIncrement	Size of the incremental allocations, in elements
elementCount	Number of elements in Vector
elementData	Buffer in which the elements are stored

Method	*Description*
	Constructors
Vector()	Constructs an empty vector
Vector(int)	Constructs an empty vector with the specified storage capacity
Vector(int, int)	Constructs an empty vector with the specified storage capacity and capacity increment
	Methods
addElement(Object)	Adds the specified object at the end of the Vector
capacity()	Returns the capacity of the Vector
clone()	Creates a clone of the Vector
contains(Object)	Returns true if the specified object is in the Vector
copyInto(Object[])	Copies the elements of this vector into an array
elementAt(int)	Returns the element at the specified index
elements()	Returns an Enumeration of the elements
ensureCapacity(int)	Ensures that the Vector has the specified capacity
firstElement()	Returns the first element of the Vector
indexOf(Object)	Returns the index of the first occurrence of the specified object within the Vector
indexOf(Object, int)	Returns the index of the specified object within the Vector, starting the search at the index specified and proceeding toward the end of the Vector
insertElementAt(Object, int)	Inserts an object at the index specified
isEmpty()	Returns true if the Vector is empty
lastElement()	Returns the last element of the Vector
lastIndexOf(Object)	Returns the index of the last occurrence of the specified object within the Vector
lastIndexOf(Object, int)	Returns the index of the specified object within the Vector, starting the search at the index specified and proceeding toward the beginning of the Vector
removeAllElements()	Removes all elements of the Vector
removeElement(Object)	Removes the specified object from the Vector
removeElementAt(int)	Removes the element with the specified index

continues

Table 11.11. continued

Method	Description
	Methods
setElementAt(Object, int)	Stores the object at the specified index in the Vector
setSize(int)	Sets the size of the Vector
size()	Returns the number of elements in the Vector
toString()	Converts the Vector to a string
trimToSize()	Trims the Vector's capacity down to the specified size

The Stack Class

The stack data structure is key to many programming efforts, ranging from building compilers to solving mazes. The Stack class in the Java library implements a *Last In, First Out* (LIFO) stack of objects. Even though they are based on (that is, they extend) the Vector class, Stack objects are typically not accessed in a direct fashion. Instead, values are pushed onto and popped off the top of the stack. The net effect is that the values most recently pushed are the first to pop.

The Stack1 code in Listing 11.9 pushes strings onto the stack and then retrieves them. The strings end up printed in the reverse order from which they were stored.

Listing 11.9. Stack1.java: A sample Stack program.

```java
import java.io.DataInputStream;
import java.io.BufferedReader;
import java.io.InputStreamReader;
import java.util.Stack;
import java.util.StringTokenizer;
class Stack1 {
    public static void main(String args[])
        throws java.io.IOException
    {
        BufferedReader dis=new BufferedReader(new InputStreamReader(System.in));
        System.out.println("Enter a sentence: ");
        String s=dis.readLine();
        StringTokenizer st=new StringTokenizer(s);
        Stack stack=new Stack();
        while (st.hasMoreTokens())
            stack.push(st.nextToken());
        while (!stack.empty())
            System.out.print((String)stack.pop()+" ");
        System.out.println();
    }
}
```

The output from this program looks like this:

```
Enter a sentence:
The quick brown fox jumps over the lazy dog
dog lazy the over jumps fox brown quick The
```

Even though Stack objects normally are not accessed in a direct fashion, it is possible to search the Stack for a specific value using the search() method. search() accepts an object to find and returns the distance from the top of the Stack where the object was found. It returns -1 if the object is not found.

The method peek() returns the top object on the Stack without actually removing it from the Stack. The peek() method throws an EmptyStackException if the stack has no items.

Table 11.12 summarizes the complete interface of the Stack class.

Table 11.12. The methods available in the Stack interface.

Method	*Description*
Constructor	
Stack()	Constructs an empty Stack
Methods	
empty()	Returns true if the Stack is empty
peek()	Returns the top object on the Stack without removing the element
pop()	Pops an element off the Stack
push(Object)	Pushes an element onto the Stack
search(Object)	Finds an object on the Stack

The Dictionary Class

The Dictionary class is an abstract class used as a base for the Hashtable class. It implements a data structure that allows a collection of key and value pairs to be stored. Any type of object can be used for the keys or the values. Typically, the keys are used to find a particular corresponding value.

Because the Dictionary class is an abstract class that cannot be used directly, the code examples presented in this section cannot actually be run. They are presented only to explain the purpose and use of the methods declared by this class. The following code would, hypothetically, be used to create a Dictionary with these values:

```
Dictionary products = new Dictionary();
products.put(new Integer(342), "Widget");
```

```
products.put(new Integer(124), "Gadget");
products.put(new Integer(754), "FooBar");
```

The put() method is used to insert a key and value pair into the Dictionary. Both arguments must be derived from the class Object. The key is the first argument and the value is the second argument.

A value can be retrieved using the get() method and a specific key to be found. get() returns the null value if the specified key is not found. Here's an example:

```
String name = products.get(new Integer(124));
if (name != null) {
    System.out.println("Product name for code 124 is " + name);
}
```

Although an individual object can be retrieved with the get() method, it is sometimes necessary to access all the keys or all the values. Two methods, keys() and elements(), return Enumerations that can be used to access the keys and the values.

Table 11.13 summarizes the complete interface of the Dictionary class.

Table 11.13. The methods available in the Dictionary interface.

Method	Description
Constructor	
Dictionary()	Constructs an empty Dictionary
Methods	
elements()	Returns an Enumeration of the values
get(Object)	Returns the object associated with the specified key
isEmpty()	Returns true if the Dictionary has no elements
keys()	Returns an Enumeration of the keys
put(Object, Object)	Stores the specified key and value pair in the Dictionary
remove(Object)	Removes an element from the Dictionary based on its key
size()	Returns the number of elements stored

The Hashtable Class

The hash table data structure is very useful when searching for and manipulating data. You should use the Hashtable class if you will be storing a large amount of data in memory and then searching it. The time needed to complete a search of a hash table is decidedly less than what it takes to search a Vector. Of course, for small amounts of data, it doesn't make much difference whether you use a hash table or a linear data structure, because the overhead time is much greater than any search time would be. See the following sidebar for more information about search times in the different classes.

Hash table organization is based on *keys*, which are computed based on the data being stored. For example, if you want to insert a number of words into a hash table, you can base your key on the first letter of the word. When you come back later to search for a word, you can then compute the key for the item being sought. By using this key, search time is drastically reduced because the items are stored based on the value of their respective key.

The `Hashtable` class implements a hash table storage mechanism for storing key and value pairs. Hash tables are designed to quickly locate and retrieve stored information by using a key. Keys and values can be of any object type, but the key object's class must implement the `hashCode()` and `equals()` methods.

SEARCH TIMES

Big "O" notation is used to measure the "worst case scenario" time requirements in terms of searching while using different data structures. Linear searching, such as that used in the `Vector` class, is $O(n)$; hash table searching is $O(\log n)$. This means that for a large number of objects, you can save a lot of search time when you use a hash table because the *log* of a number is always less than the number itself. If you will be doing a large amount of searching through data, a hash table is likely to be much more efficient.

The sample `Hashtable1` in Listing 11.10 creates a `Hashtable` object and stores 10 key and value pairs using the `put()` method. It then uses the `get()` method to return the value corresponding to a key entered by the user.

Listing 11.10. Hashtable1.java: A sample Hashtable program.

```java
import java.io.DataInputStream;
import java.lang.Integer;
import java.lang.Math;
import java.util.Random;
import java.util.Hashtable;
class Hashtable1 {
    public static void main(String args[])
        throws java.io.IOException
    {
        DataInputStream dis=new DataInputStream(System.in);
        int numElements=10;
        String keys[]={"Red","Green","Blue","Cyan","Magenta",
            "Yellow","Black","Orange","Purple","White"};
        Hashtable ht;
        Random randGen=new Random();
        ht=new Hashtable(numElements*2);
        for (int i=0;i<numElements;i++)
            ht.put(keys[i],new Integer(Math.abs(
                randGen.nextInt())%numElements));
        System.out.println(ht.toString());
        String keyValue;
```

continues

Listing 11.10. continued

```
        System.out.println("Which key to find? ");
        keyValue=dis.readLine();
        Integer value=(Integer)ht.get(keyValue);
        if (value!=null) System.out.println(keyValue+" = "+value);
    }
}
```

The output from this program looks like this:

```
{Cyan=4, White=0, Magenta=4, Red=5, Black=3,
Green=8, Purple=3, Orange=4, Yellow=2, _Blue=6}
Which key to find?
Red
Red = 5
```

In addition to the get() method, the contains() and containsKey() methods can be used to search for a particular value or key. Both return true or false depending on whether the search was successful. The contains() method must perform an exhaustive search of the table and is not as efficient as the containsKey() method, which can take advantage of the hash table's storage mechanism to find the key quickly.

Because hash tables must allocate storage for more data than actually is stored, a measurement called the *load factor* indicates the number of used storage spaces as a fraction of the total available storage spaces. The load factor is expressed as a value between 0 and 100 percent. Typically, the load factor should not be higher than about 50 percent for efficient retrieval of data from a hash table. When specifying the load factor in a program, use a fractional value in the range 0.0 to 1.0 to represent load factors in the range 0 to 100 percent.

Hash tables can be constructed in three different ways: by specifying the desired initial capacity and load factor; by specifying only the initial capacity; or by specifying neither the initial capacity nor the load factor. If the load factor is not specified, the Hashtable is rehashed into a larger table when it is full—otherwise, it is rehashed when it exceeds the load factor. The constructors throw an IllegalArgumentException if the initial capacity is less than or equal to zero, or if the load factor is less than or equal to zero.

The clone() method can be used to create a copy (a clone) of the Hashtable. However, it creates a *shallow copy* of the Hashtable, which means that the keys and values themselves are not clones. This local method overrides the inherited clone() method.

CAUTION

The clone() method is a relatively expensive operation to perform in terms of memory usage and execution time. Because the new Hashtable still refers directly to the objects (keys and values) stored in the old table, use caution to avoid making changes that will disrupt the original Hashtable.

The Hashtable class extends the java.util.Dictionary class and implements the java.lang.Cloneable interface. Table 11.14 summarizes the methods of the Hashtable class.

Table 11.14. The methods available in the Hashtable interface.

Method	Description
Constructors	
Hashtable()	Constructs an empty Hashtable
Hashtable(int)	Constructs an empty Hashtable with the specified capacity
Hashtable(int, float)	Constructs an empty Hashtable with the given capacity and load factor
Methods	
clear()	Deletes all elements from the Hashtable
clone()	Creates a clone of the Hashtable
contains(Object)	Returns true if the specified object is an element of the Hashtable
containsKey(Object)	Returns true if the Hashtable contains the specified key
elements()	Returns an Enumeration of the Hashtable's values
get(Object)	Returns the object associated with the specified key
isEmpty()	Returns true if the Hashtable has no elements
keys()	Returns an Enumeration of the keys
put(Object, Object)	Stores the specified key and value pair in the Hashtable
rehash()	Rehashes the contents of the table into a bigger table
remove(Object)	Removes an element from the Hashtable based on its key
size()	Returns the number of elements stored
toString()	Converts the contents to a very long string

The Properties Class

The Properties class is what enables end-users to customize their Java program. For example, you can easily store values such as foreground colors, background colors, font defaults, and so on and then have those values available to be reloaded. This arrangement is most useful for Java applications, but you can also implement it for applets. If you have an applet that is regularly used by multiple users, you can keep a properties file on your server for each different user; the properties file is accessed each time that user loads the applet.

The Properties class is a Hashtable, which can be repeatedly stored and restored from a stream. It is used to implement persistent properties. The Properties class also allows for an unlimited level of nesting, by searching a default property list if the required property is not found. The fact that this class is an extension of the Hashtable class means that all methods available in the Hashtable class are also available in the Properties class.

The sample program Properties1 in Listing 11.11 creates two properties lists. One is the default property list and the other is the user-defined property list. When the user property list is created, the default Properties object is passed. When the user property list is searched, if the key value is not found, the default Properties list is searched.

Listing 11.11. Properties1.java: A sample Properties program.

```
import java.io.DataInputStream;
import java.lang.Integer;
import java.util.Properties;
class Properties1 {
    public static void main(String args[])
        throws java.io.IOException
    {
        int numElements=4;
        String defaultNames[]={"Red","Green","Blue","Purple"};
        int defaultValues[]={1,2,3,4};
        String userNames[]={"Red","Yellow","Orange","Blue"};
        int userValues[]={100,200,300,400};
        DataInputStream dis=new DataInputStream(System.in);
        Properties defaultProps=new Properties();
        Properties userProps=new Properties(defaultProps);
        for (int i=0;i<numElements;i++){
            defaultProps.put(defaultNames[i],
                Integer.toString(defaultValues[i]));
            userProps.put(userNames[i],
                Integer.toString(userValues[i]));
        }
        System.out.println("Default Properties");
        defaultProps.list(System.out);
        System.out.println("\nUser Defined Properties");
        userProps.list(System.out);
        String keyValue;
        System.out.println("\nWhich property to find? ");
        keyValue=dis.readLine();
        System.out.println("Property '"+keyValue+"' is '"+
            userProps.getProperty(keyValue)+"'");
    }
}
```

Notice that the getProperties() method is used instead of the inherited get() method. The get() method searches only the current Properties object. The getProperties() method must be used to search the default Properties list. An alternative form of the getProperties() method has a second argument: a Properties list that is to be searched instead of the default specified when the Properties object was created.

The propertyNames() method can be used to return an Enumeration, which can be used to index all the property names. This Enumeration includes the property names from the default Properties list. Likewise, the list() method, which prints the Properties list to the standard output, lists all the properties of the current Properties object and those in the default Properties object.

Properties objects can be written to and read from a stream using the save() and load() methods. In addition to the output or input stream, the save() method has an additional string argument that is written at the beginning of the stream as a header comment.

Table 11.15 summarizes the methods of the Properties class.

Table 11.15. The variables and methods available in the Properties interface.

Variable	Description
defaults	Default Properties list to search

Method	Description
Constructors	
Properties()	Constructs an empty property list
Properties(Properties)	Constructs an empty property list with the specified default
Methods	
getProperty(String)	Returns a property given the key
getProperty(String, String)	Returns a property given the specified key and default
list(PrintStream)	Lists the properties to a stream for debugging
load(InputStream)	Reads the properties from an InputStream
propertyNames()	Returns an Enumeration all the keys
save(OutputStream, String)	Writes the properties to an OutputStream

The Observable Class

The Observable class acts as a base class for objects you want to have observed by other objects that implement the Observer interface. An Observable object can notify its Observers whenever the Observable object is modified using the notifyObservers() method. This method accomplishes the notification by invoking the update() method of all its Observers, optionally passing a data object that is passed to notifyObservers(). Observable objects can have any number of Observers.

Table 11.16 summarizes the complete interface of the Observable class.

Table 11.16. The methods available in the Observable interface.

Method	Description
	Constructor
Observable()	Constructs an instance of the Observable class.
	Methods
addObserver(Observer)	Adds an Observer to the observer list
clearChanged()	Clears an observable change
countObservers()	Returns the number of Observers
deleteObserver(Observer)	Deletes an Observer from the observer list
deleteObservers()	Deletes all Observers from the observer list
hasChanged()	Returns true if an observable change has occurred
notifyObservers()	Notifies all Observers when an observable change has occurred
notifyObservers(Object)	Notifies all Observers of a specific observable change
setChanged()	Sets a flag to indicate that an observable change has occurred

Summary

This chapter described the classes that make up the Java utilities package. This package provides complete implementations of the basic data structures and some of the most useful data types (other than the fundamental numeric types) needed by programmers. Many of the data types and data structures you will develop using Java will be based on the classes found in the utilities package. For smaller applets, many of these classes are not necessary. However, as your applets increase in complexity, you will find these classes to be very useful. In any case, this chapter has been a good starting point for understanding the utility of these important Java classes and for understanding how to use them effectively.

The I/O Package

by Michael Morrison

IN THIS CHAPTER

It would be impossible for a program to do anything useful without performing some kind of input or output of data. Most programs require input from the user; in return, they output information to the screen, printer, and often to files. The Java I/O package provides an extensive set of classes that handle input and output to and from many different devices. In this chapter, you learn about the primary classes contained in the I/O package, along with some examples that show off the capabilities of these classes.

The I/O package, also known as `java.io`, contains many classes, each with a variety of member variables and methods. This chapter does not take an exhaustive look at every class and method contained in the I/O package. Instead, you can view this chapter as a tutorial on how to perform basic input and output using the more popular I/O classes. Armed with the information from this chapter, you will be ready to begin using the Java I/O classes in your own programs. And should you choose to explore the more complex I/O classes supported by Java, you will be prepared for the challenge.

Input Stream and Reader Classes

The Java input model is based on the concept of an input stream. An *input stream* can be thought of much like a physical (and certainly more literal) stream of water flowing from a water plant into the pipes of a water system. The obvious difference is that an input stream deals with binary computer data rather than physical water. The comparison is relevant, however, because the data going into an input stream flows like the water being pumped into a pipe. Data pumped into an input stream can be directed in many different ways, much as water is directed through the complex system of pipes that make up a water system. The data in an input stream is transmitted one byte at a time, which is roughly analogous to individual drops of water flowing into a pipe.

More practically speaking, Java uses input streams as the means of reading data from an *input source*, such as the keyboard. The basic input stream classes supported by Java follow:

- `InputStream`
- `BufferedInputStream`
- `DataInputStream`
- `FileInputStream`
- `StringBufferInputStream`

Java version 1.1 introduces support for *character input streams*, which are virtually identical to the input streams just listed except that they operate on characters rather than on bytes. The character input stream classes are called *readers* instead of input streams. Corresponding reader classes implement methods similar to the input stream classes just listed except for the `DataInputStream` class. The purpose of providing character-based versions of the input stream classes is to help facilitate the internationalization of character information. To find out more about the support for internationalization in Java, check out Chapter 52, "Java Internationalization." Following are the basic reader classes provided by Java:

■ Reader

■ BufferedReader

■ FileReader

■ StringReader

Throughout this chapter, you use both input streams and reader classes. Because their supported methods are very similar, it's pretty easy to use one once you've learned about the other.

The InputStream Class

The InputStream class is an abstract class that serves as the base class for all other input stream classes. InputStream defines a basic interface for reading streamed bytes of information. The methods defined by the InputStream class will become very familiar to you because they serve a similar purpose in every InputStream-derived class. This design approach enables you to learn the protocol for managing input streams once and then apply it to different devices using an InputStream-derived class.

The typical scenario when using an input stream is to create an InputStream-derived object and then tell it you want to input information by calling an appropriate method. If no input information is currently available, the InputStream uses a technique known as *blocking* to wait until input data becomes available. An example of when blocking takes place is the case of using an input stream to read information from the keyboard. Until the user types information and presses Return or Enter, there is no input available to the InputStream object. The InputStream object then waits (blocks) until the user presses Return or Enter, at which time the input data becomes available and the InputStream object can process it as input.

The InputStream class defines the following methods:

■ abstract int read()

■ int read(byte *b*[])

■ int read(byte *b*[], int *off*, int *len*)

■ long skip(long *n*)

■ int available()

■ synchronized void mark(int *readlimit*)

■ synchronized void reset()

■ boolean markSupported()

■ void close()

InputStream defines three different read() methods for reading input data in various ways. The first read() method takes no parameters and simply reads a byte of data from the input stream and returns it as an integer. This version of read() returns -1 if the end of the input stream is reached. Because this version of read() returns a byte of input as an int, you must cast it to a char if you are reading characters. The second version of read() takes an array of bytes as its only parameter, enabling you to read multiple bytes of data at once. The data that is read is stored in this array. You have to make sure that the byte array passed into read() is large enough to hold the information being read or an IOException is thrown. This version of read() returns the actual number of bytes read, or -1 if the end of the stream is reached. The last version of read() takes a byte array, an integer offset, and an integer length as parameters. This version of read() is very similar to the second version except that it enables you to specify where in the byte array you want to place the information that is read. The *off* parameter specifies the offset into the byte array to start placing read data, and the *len* parameter specifies the maximum number of bytes to read.

The skip() method is used to skip over bytes of data in the input stream. skip() takes a long value *n* as its only parameter, which specifies how many bytes of input to skip. It returns the actual number of bytes skipped or -1 if the end of the input stream is reached.

The available() method is used to determine the number of bytes of input data that can be read without blocking. available() takes no parameters and returns the number of available bytes. This method is useful if you want to ensure that there is input data available (and therefore avoid the blocking mechanism).

The mark() method marks the current position in the stream. You can later return to this position using the reset() method. The mark() and reset() methods are useful in situations in which you want to read ahead in the stream but not lose your original position. An example of this situation is verifying a file type, such as an image file. You would probably read the file header first and mark the position at the end of the header. You would then read some of the data to make sure that it follows the format expected for that file type. If the data doesn't look right, you can reset the read pointer and try a different technique.

Notice that the mark() method takes an integer parameter, *readlimit*. *readlimit* specifies how many bytes can be read before the mark becomes invalidated. In effect, *readlimit* determines how far you can read ahead and still be able to reset the marked position. The markSupported() method returns a boolean value representing whether or not an input stream supports the mark/reset functionality.

Finally, the close() method closes an input stream and releases any resources associated with the stream. It is not necessary to explicitly call close() because input streams are automatically closed when the InputStream object is destroyed. Although it is not necessary, calling close() immediately after you are finished using a stream is a good programming practice. The reason is that close() causes the stream buffer to be flushed, which helps avoid file corruption.

The System.in Object

The keyboard is the standard device for retrieving user input. The System class contained in the language package contains a member variable that represents the keyboard, or standard input stream. This member variable is called in and is an instance of the InputStream class. This variable is useful for reading user input from the keyboard. Listing 12.1 contains the ReadKeys1 program, which shows how the System.in object can be connected with an InputStreamReader object to read user input from the keyboard. This program can be found in the file ReadKeys1.java on the CD-ROM that accompanies this book.

> **NOTE**
>
> I mentioned the keyboard as being the standard input stream. This isn't entirely true because the standard input stream can receive input from any number of sources. Although the keyboard certainly is the most common method of feeding input to the standard input stream, it is not the only method. An example of the standard input stream being driven by a different input source is the redirection of an input file into a stream.

Listing 12.1. The ReadKeys1 class.

```java
import java.io.*;
class ReadKeys1 {
  publio statio void main (String args[]) {
    StringBuffer s = new StringBuffer();
    char c;
    try {
      Reader in = new InputStreamReader(System.in);
      while ((c = (char)in.read()) != '\n') {
        s.append(c);
      }
    }
    catch (Exception e) {
      System.out.println("Error: " + e.toString());
    }
    System.out.println(s);
  }
}
```

The ReadKeys1 class first creates a StringBuffer object called s. It then creates a reader object connected to the standard input stream and enters a while loop that repeatedly calls the read() method until a newline character (\n) is detected (that is, the user presses Return). Notice that the input data returned by read() is cast to a char type before being stored in the character variable c. Each time a character is read, it is appended to the string buffer using the append() method of StringBuffer. It is important to see how any errors caused by the read() method are handled by the try/catch exception-handling blocks. The catch block simply prints an error message to the standard output stream based on the error that occurred. Finally, when a newline character is read from the input stream, the println() method of the standard output stream is called to output the string to the screen. You learn more about the standard output stream a little later in this chapter.

Listing 12.2 contains ReadKeys2, which is similar to ReadKeys1 except that it uses the second version of the read() method. This read() method takes an array of characters as a parameter to store the input that is read. ReadKeys2 can be found in the file ReadKeys2.java on the CD-ROM that accompanies this book.

Listing 12.2. The ReadKeys2 class.

```java
import java.io.*;
class ReadKeys2 {
  public static void main (String args[]) {
    char buf[] = new char[80];
    try {
      Reader in = new InputStreamReader(System.in);
      in.read(buf, 0, 80);
    }
    catch (Exception e) {
      System.out.println("Error: " + e.toString());
    }
    String s = new String(buf);
    System.out.println(s);
  }
}
```

In ReadKeys2, an array of characters 80 characters long is created. A reader object is created and connected to the standard input stream, and a single read() method call is performed that reads everything the user has typed. The input is blocked until the user presses Return, at which time the input becomes available and the read() method fills the character array with the new data. A String object is then created to hold the constant string previously read. Notice that the constructor used to create the String object takes an array of characters (buf) as the first parameter. Finally, println() is again used to output the string.

 The ReadKeys3 program in Listing 12.3 shows how to use the last version of the read() method. This version of read() again takes an array of characters, as well as an offset and length for determining how to store the input data in the character array. ReadKeys3 can be found in the file ReadKeys3.java on the CD-ROM that accompanies this book.

Listing 12.3. The ReadKeys3 class.

```java
import java.io.*;
class ReadKeys3 {
  public static void main (String args[]) {
    char buf[] = new char[10];
    try {
      Reader in = new InputStreamReader(System.in);
      in.read(buf, 0, 10);
    }
    catch (Exception e) {
      System.out.println("Error: " + e.toString());
    }
```

```
        String s = new String(buf);
        System.out.println(s);
    }
}
```

ReadKeys3 is very similar to ReadKeys2, with one major difference: The third version of the read() method is used to limit the maximum number of characters read into the array. The size of the character array is also shortened to 10 characters to show what this version of read() does when more data is available than the array can hold. Remember that this version of read() can also be used to read data into a specific offset of the array. In this case, the offset is specified as 0 so that the only difference is the maximum number of characters that can be read (10). This useful technique guarantees that you don't overrun the array.

The BufferedInputStream Class

As its name implies, the BufferedInputStream class provides a buffered stream of input. This means that more data is read into the buffered stream than you might have requested so that subsequent reads come straight out of the buffer rather than from the input device. This arrangement can result in much faster read access because reading from a buffer is really just reading from memory. BufferedInputStream implements all the same methods defined by InputStream. As a matter of fact, it doesn't implement any new methods of its own. However, the BufferedInputStream class does have two different constructors, which follow:

- BufferedInputStream(InputStream *in*)
- BufferedInputStream(InputStream *in*, int *size*)

Notice that both constructors take an InputStream object as the first parameter. The only difference between the two is the size of the internal buffer. In the first constructor, a default buffer size is used; in the second constructor, you specify the buffer size with the *size* integer parameter. To support buffered input, the BufferedInputStream class also defines a handful of member variables, which follow:

- byte *buf*[]
- int *count*
- int *pos*
- int *markpos*
- int *marklimit*

The *buf* byte array member is the buffer in which input data is actually stored. The *count* member variable keeps up with how many bytes are stored in the buffer. The *pos* member variable keeps up with the current read position in the buffer. The *markpos* member variable specifies the current mark position in the buffer as set using the mark() method. *markpos* is equal to -1 if no mark has been set. Finally, the *marklimit* member variable specifies the maximum number of bytes that can be read before the mark position is no longer valid. *marklimit* is set by the *readlimit* parameter passed into the mark() method. Because all these member variables are specified as protected, you will probably never actually use any of them. However, seeing these variables should give you some insight into how the BufferedInputStream class implements the methods defined by InputStream.

 The BufferedReader class is very similar to the BufferedInputStream class except that it deals with characters instead of bytes. Listing 12.4 contains the ReadKeys4 program, which uses a BufferedReader object instead of an InputStreamReader object to read input from the keyboard. ReadKeys4 can be found in the file ReadKeys4.java on the CD-ROM that accompanies this book.

Listing 12.4. The ReadKeys4 class.

```
import java.io.*;
class ReadKeys4 {
  public static void main (String args[]) {
    Reader in = new BufferedReader(new InputStreamReader(System.in));
    char buf[] = new char[10];
    try {
      in.read(buf, 0, 10);
    }
    catch (Exception e) {
      System.out.println("Error: " + e.toString());
    }
    String s = new String(buf);
    System.out.println(s);
  }
}
```

The BufferedReader object is created by passing the System.in input stream into an InputStreamReader object. This approach is necessary because the BufferedReader() constructor requires a Reader-derived object. From there on, the program is essentially the same as ReadKeys3, except that the read() method is called on the BufferedReader object rather than on an InputStreamReader object.

The DataInputStream Class

The DataInputStream class is useful for reading primitive Java data types from an input stream in a portable fashion. There is only one constructor for DataInputStream, which simply takes an InputStream object as its only parameter. This constructor is defined as follows:

```
DataInputStream(InputStream in)
```

`DataInputStream` implements the following useful methods beyond those defined by `InputStream`:

- `final int skipBytes(int n)`
- `final void readFully(byte b[])`
- `final void readFully(byte b[], int off, int len)`
- `final boolean readBoolean()`
- `final byte readByte()`
- `final int readUnsignedByte()`
- `final short readShort()`
- `final int readUnsignedShort()`
- `final char readChar()`
- `final int readInt()`
- `final long readLong()`
- `final float readFloat()`
- `final double readDouble()`

The `skipBytes()` method works in a manner very similar to `skip()`; the exception is that `skipBytes()` blocks until all bytes are skipped. The number of bytes to skip is determined by the integer parameter *n*. There are two `readFully()` methods implemented by `DataInputStream`. These methods are similar to the `read()` methods except that they block until *all* data has been read. The normal `read()` methods block only until *some* data is available, not all. The `readFully()` methods are to the `read()` methods what `skipBytes()` is to `skip()`.

The rest of the methods implemented by `DataInputStream` are variations of the `read()` method for different fundamental data types. The type read by each method is easily identifiable by the name of the method.

The `FileInputStream` Class

The `FileInputStream` class is useful for performing simple file input. For more advanced file input operations, you will more than likely want to use the `RandomAccessFile` class, discussed a little later in this chapter. The `FileInputStream` class can be instantiated using one of the following three constructors:

- `FileInputStream(String name)`
- `FileInputStream(File file)`
- `FileInputStream(FileDescriptor fdObj)`

The first constructor takes a `String` object parameter called *name*, which specifies the name of the file to use for input. The second constructor takes a `File` object parameter that specifies the file to use for input. You learn more about the `File` object near the end of this chapter. The third constructor for `FileInputStream` takes a `FileDescriptor` object as its only parameter.

The `FileInputStream` class functions exactly like the `InputStream` class except that it is geared toward working with files. Similarly, the `FileReader` class functions like the `FileInputStream` class except that it operates on characters instead of bytes. Listing 12.5 contains the `ReadFile` program, which uses the `FileReader` class to read data from a text file. `ReadFile` can be found in the file `ReadFile.java` on the CD-ROM that accompanies this book.

Listing 12.5. The ReadFile class.

```
import java.io.*;
class ReadFile {
  public static void main (String args[]) {
    char buf[] = new char[64];
    try {
      Reader in = new FileReader("Grocery.txt");
      in.read(buf, 0, 64);
    }
    catch (Exception e) {
      System.out.println("Error: " + e.toString());
    }
    String s = new String(buf);
    System.out.println(s);
  }
}
```

In `ReadFile`, a `FileReader` object is first created by passing a string with the name of the file (`"Grocery.txt"`) as the input file. The `read()` method is then called to read from the input file into a character array. The character array is then used to create a `String` object, which is in turn used for output. Pretty simple!

The `StringBufferInputStream` Class

Aside from having a very long name, the `StringBufferInputStream` class is a pretty neat class. `StringBufferInputStream` enables you to use a string as a buffered source of input. `StringBufferInputStream` implements all the same methods defined by `InputStream`, and no more. The `StringBufferInputStream` class has a single constructor, which follows:

`StringBufferInputStream(String s)`

The constructor takes a `String` object, from which it constructs the string buffer input stream. Although `StringBufferInputStream` doesn't define any additional methods, it does provide a few of its own member variables, which follow:

■ String *buffer*
■ int *count*
■ int *pos*

The *buffer* string member is the buffer in which the string data is actually stored. The *count* member variable specifies the number of characters to use in the buffer. Finally, the *pos* member variable keeps up with the current position in the buffer. As is true with the BufferedInputStream class, you will probably never see these member variables, but they are important in understanding how the StringBufferInputStream class is implemented.

 The StringReader class is a character version of the StringBufferInputStream class. Listing 12.6 shows the ReadString program, which uses a StringReader object to read data from a string of text data. ReadString can be found in the file ReadString.java on the CD-ROM that accompanies this book.

Listing 12.6. The ReadString class.

```
import java.io.*;
class ReadString {
  public static void main (String args[]) {
    // Get a string of input from the user
    char buf1[] = new char[64];
    try {
      Reader in = new InputStreamReader(System.in);
      in.read(buf1, 0, 64);
    }
    catch (Exception e) {
      System.out.println("Error: " + e.toString());
    }
    String s1 = new String(buf1);
    // Read the string and output it
    Reader in = new StringReader(s1);
    char buf2[] = new char[64];
    try {
      in.read(buf2, 0, 64);
    }
    catch (Exception e) {
      System.out.println("Error: " + e.toString());
    }
    String s2 = new String(buf2);
    System.out.println(s2);
  }
}
```

The ReadString program enables the user to type text, which is read and stored in a string. This string is then used to create a StringReader object that is read into another string for output. Obviously, this program goes to a lot of trouble to do very little; it's meant only as a demonstration of how to use the StringReader class. It's up to you to find an interesting application to which you can apply this class.

The first half of the ReadString program should look pretty familiar; it's essentially the guts of the ReadKeys3 program (discussed earlier in this chapter), which reads data entered by the keyboard into a string. The second half of the program is where you actually get busy with the

`StringReader` object. A `StringReader` object is created using the `String` object (s1) containing the text entered from the keyboard. The contents of the `StringReader` object are then read into a character array using the `read()` method. The character array is in turn used to construct another `String` object (s2), which is output to the screen.

Output Stream and Writer Classes

In Java, output streams are the logical counterparts to input streams; they handle writing data to output sources. Using the water analogy from the discussion of input streams earlier in this chapter, an *output stream* is equivalent to the water spout on your bathtub. Just as water travels from a water plant through the pipes and out the spout into your bathtub, so must data flow from an input device through the operating system and out an output device. A leaky water spout is an even better way to visualize the transfer of data out of an output stream; each drop of water falling out of the spout represents a byte of data. Each byte of data flows to the output device just like the drops of water falling one after the other out of the bathtub spout.

Getting back to Java, you use output streams to output data to various output devices, such as the screen. The primary output stream classes used in Java programming follow:

- `OutputStream`
- `PrintStream`
- `BufferedOutputStream`
- `DataOutputStream`
- `FileOutputStream`

The Java output streams provide a variety of ways to output data. The `OutputStream` class defines the core behavior required of an output stream. The `PrintStream` class is geared toward outputting text data, such as the data sent to the standard output stream. The `BufferedOutputStream` class is an extension to the `OutputStream` class that provides support for buffered output. The `DataOutputStream` class is useful for outputting primitive data types such as `int` or `float`. Finally, the `FileOutputStream` class provides the support necessary to output data to files.

Java also supports character output streams, which are virtually identical to the output streams just listed except that they operate on characters rather than bytes. The character output stream classes are called *writers* instead of output streams. A corresponding writer class implements methods similar to the output stream classes just listed except for the `DataOutputStream` class. The purpose of providing character-based versions of the output stream classes is to help facilitate the internationalization of character information. To find out more about the support for internationalization in Java, check out Chapter 52, "Java Internationalization." Following are the basic writer classes provided by Java:

- `Writer`
- `PrintWriter`

■ BufferedWriter

■ FileWriter

Throughout this chapter, you use both output streams and writer classes. Because their supported methods are very similar, it's pretty easy to use both types after you learn about one of them.

The OutputStream Class

The OutputStream class is the output counterpart to InputStream; it serves as an abstract base class for all the other output stream classes. OutputStream defines the basic protocol for writing streamed data to an output device. As you did with the methods for InputStream, you will become accustomed to the methods defined by OutputStream because they act very much the same in every OutputStream-derived class. The benefit of this common interface is that you can essentially learn a method once and then be able to apply it to different classes without starting the learning process over again.

You typically create an OutputStream-derived object and call an appropriate method to tell it you want to output information. The OutputStream class uses a technique similar to the one used by InputStream: It blocks until data has been written to an output device. While blocking (waiting for the current output to be processed), the OutputStream class does not allow any further data to be output.

The OutputStream class implements the following methods:

■ abstract void write(int *b*)

■ void write(byte *b*[])

■ void write(byte *b*[], int *off*, int *len*)

■ void flush()

■ void close()

OutputStream defines three different write() methods for writing data in a few different ways. The first write() method writes a single byte to the output stream, as specified by the integer parameter *b*. The second version of write() takes an array of bytes as a parameter and writes them to the output stream. The last version of write() takes a byte array, an integer offset, and a length as parameters. This version of write() is very much like the second version except that it uses the other parameters to determine where in the byte array to begin outputting data, along with how much data to output. The *off* parameter specifies an offset into the byte array from which you want to begin outputting data, and the *len* parameter specifies how many bytes are to be output.

The flush() method is used to flush the output stream. Calling flush() forces the OutputStream object to output any pending data.

12

THE I/O PACKAGE

Finally, the `close()` method closes an output stream and releases any resources associated with the stream. As with `InputStream` objects, it isn't usually necessary to call `close()` on an `OutputStream` object because streams are automatically closed when they are destroyed.

The PrintStream Class

The `PrintStream` class is derived from `OutputStream` and is designed primarily for printing output data as text. `PrintStream` has two constructors:

- `PrintStream(OutputStream out)`
- `PrintStream(OutputStream out, boolean autoflush)`

Both `PrintStream` constructors take an `OutputStream` object as their first parameter. The only difference between the two methods is how the newline character is handled. In the first constructor, the stream is flushed based on an internal decision by the object. In the second constructor, you can specify that the stream be flushed every time it encounters a newline character. You specify this through the boolean *autoflush* parameter.

The `PrintStream` class also implements a rich set of methods, which follow:

- `boolean checkError()`
- `void print(Object obj)`
- `synchronized void print(String s)`
- `synchronized void print(char s[])`
- `void print(char c)`
- `void print(int i)`
- `void print(long l)`
- `void print(float f)`
- `void print(double d)`
- `void print(boolean b)`
- `void println()`
- `synchronized void println(Object obj)`
- `synchronized void println(String s)`
- `synchronized void println(char s[])`
- `synchronized void println(char c)`
- `synchronized void println(int I)`
- `synchronized void println(long l)`
- `synchronized void println(float f)`
- `synchronized void println(double d)`
- `synchronized void println(boolean b)`

The checkError() method flushes the stream and returns whether or not an error has occurred. The return value of checkError() is based on whether an error has ever occurred on the stream, meaning that once an error occurs, checkError() always returns true for that stream.

PrintStream provides a variety of print() methods to handle all your printing needs. The version of print() that takes an Object parameter simply outputs the results of calling the toString() method on the object. Each of the other print() methods takes a different type parameter that specifies which data type is to be printed.

The println() methods implemented by PrintStream are very similar to the print() methods. The only difference is that the println() methods print a newline character following the data that is printed. The println() method that takes no parameters simply prints a newline character by itself.

The System.out Object

The monitor is the primary output device on modern computer systems. The System class has a member variable that represents the standard output stream, which is typically the monitor. The member variable is called out and is an instance of the PrintStream class. The out member variable is very useful for outputting text to the screen. But you already know this because you've seen the out member variable in most of the sample programs developed thus far.

The BufferedOutputStream Class

The BufferedOutputStream class is very similar to the OutputStream class except that it provides a *buffered* stream of output. This class enables you to write to a stream without causing a bunch of writes to an output device. The BufferedOutputStream class maintains a buffer that is written to when you write to the stream. When the buffer gets full or is explicitly flushed, it is written to the output device. This output approach is much more efficient because most of the data transfer takes place in memory. And when it does come time to output the data to a device, it all happens at once.

The BufferedOutputStream class implements the same methods defined in OutputStream, meaning that there are no additional methods except for constructors. The two constructors for BufferedOutputStream follow:

- BufferedOutputStream(OutputStream *out*)
- BufferedOutputStream(OutputStream *out*, int *size*)

Both constructors for BufferedOutputStream take an OutputStream object as their first parameter. The only difference between the two is the size of the internal buffer used to store the output data. In the first constructor, a default buffer size of 512 bytes is used; in the second constructor, you specify the buffer size with the *size* integer parameter. The buffer itself within the BufferedOutputStream class is managed by two member variables, which follow:

- byte *buf*[]
- int *count*

The *buf* byte array member variable is the actual data buffer in which output data is stored. The *count* member keeps up with how many bytes are in the buffer. These two member variables are sufficient to represent the state of the output stream buffer.

 The `BufferedWriter` class is a character-based version of the `BufferedOutputStream` class. Listing 12.7 shows the `WriteStuff` program, which uses a `BufferedWriter` object to output a character array of text data. `WriteStuff` can be found in the file `WriteStuff.java` on the CD-ROM that accompanies this book.

Listing 12.7. The WriteStuff class.

```
import java.io.*;
class WriteStuff {
  public static void main (String args[]) {
    // Copy the string into a byte array
    String s = new String("Dance, spider!\n");
    char[] buf = new char[64];
    s.getChars(0, s.length(), buf, 0);
    // Output the byte array (buffered)
    Writer out = new BufferedWriter(new OutputStreamWriter(System.out));
    try {
      out.write(buf, 0, 64);
      out.flush();
    }
    catch (Exception e) {
      System.out.println("Error: " + e.toString());
    }
  }
}
```

The `WriteStuff` program fills a character array with text data from a string and outputs the array to the screen using a buffered output stream. `WriteStuff` begins by creating a `String` object containing text, and a character array. The `getChars()` method of `String` is used to copy the characters of data in the string to the character array. The `getChars()` method copies each character in the string to the array. Once the character array is ready, a `BufferedWriter` object is created by passing `System.out` into the constructor for an `OutputStreamWriter` object, which in turn is passed to the constructor for the `BufferedWriter` object. The character array is then written to the output buffer using the `write()` method. Because the stream is buffered, it is necessary to call the `flush()` method to actually output the data.

The DataOutputStream Class

The `DataOutputStream` class is useful for writing primitive Java data types to an output stream in a portable way. `DataOutputStream` has only one constructor, which simply takes an `OutputStream` object as its only parameter. This constructor is defined as follows:

```
DataOutputStream(OutputStream out)
```

The DataOutputStream class implements the following useful methods beyond those inherited from OutputStream:

- ▪ `final int size()`
- ▪ `final void writeBoolean(boolean v)`
- ▪ `final void writeByte(int v)`
- ▪ `final void writeShort(int v)`
- ▪ `final void writeChar(int v)`
- ▪ `final void writeInt(int v)`
- ▪ `final void writeLong(long v)`
- ▪ `final void writeFloat(float v)`
- ▪ `final void writeDouble(double v)`
- ▪ `final void writeBytes(String s)`
- ▪ `final void writeChars(String s)`

The size() method is used to determine how many bytes have been written to the stream thus far. The integer value returned by size() specifies the number of bytes written.

The rest of the methods implemented in DataOutputStream are all variations of the write() method. Each version of write*Type*() takes a different data type that is in turn written as output.

The FileOutputStream Class

The FileOutputStream class provides a means to perform simple file output. For more advanced file output, check out the RandomAccessFile class, discussed a little later in this chapter. A FileOutputStream object can be created using one of the following constructors:

- ▪ `FileOutputStream(String name)`
- ▪ `FileOutputStream(File file)`
- ▪ `FileOutputStream(FileDescriptor fdObj)`

The first constructor takes a String parameter, which specifies the name of the file to use for output. The second constructor takes a File object parameter, which specifies the output file. You learn about the File object later in this chapter. The third constructor takes a FileDescriptor object as its only parameter.

The FileWriter class functions exactly like the FileOutputStream class except that it is specifically designed to work with characters instead of with bytes. Listing 12.8 contains the WriteFile program, which uses the FileWriter class to write user input to a text file. WriteFile can be found in the file WriteFile.java on the CD-ROM that accompanies this book.

Listing 12.8. The WriteFile class.

```java
import java.io.*;
class WriteFile {
  public static void main (String args[]) {
    // Read the user input
    char buf[] = new char[64];
    try {
      Reader in = new InputStreamReader(System.in);
      in.read(buf, 0, 64);
    }
    catch (Exception e) {
      System.out.println("Error: " + e.toString());
    }
    // Output the data to a file
    try {
      Writer out = new FileWriter("Output.txt");
      out.write(buf, 0, 64);
      out.flush();
    }
    catch (Exception e) {
      System.out.println("Error: " + e.toString());
    }
  }
}
```

In WriteFile, user input is read from the standard input stream into a character array using the read() method of InputStreamReader. A FileWriter object is then created with the filename Output.txt, which is passed in as the only parameter to the constructor. The write() method is then used to output the character array to the stream.

You can see that working with writers is just as easy as working with readers.

File Classes

If the FileInputStream and FileOutputStream classes don't quite meet your file-handling expectations, don't despair! Java provides two more classes for working with files that are sure to meet your needs. These two classes are File and RandomAccessFile. The File class models an operating system directory entry, providing you with access to information about a file including file attributes and the full path where the file is located, among other things. The RandomAccessFile class, on the other hand, provides a variety of methods for reading and writing data to and from a file.

The File Class

The File class can be instantiated using one of three constructors, which follow:

- File(String *path*)
- File(String *path*, String *name*)
- File(File *dir*, String *name*)

The first constructor takes a single `String` parameter that specifies the full path name of the file. The second constructor takes two `String` parameters: *path* and *name*. The *path* parameter specifies the directory path where the file is located; the *name* parameter specifies the name of the file. The third constructor is similar to the second except that it takes another `File` object as the first parameter instead of a string. The `File` object in this case is used to specify the directory path of the file.

The most important methods implemented by the `File` class follow:

- `String getName()`
- `String getPath()`
- `String getAbsolutePath()`
- `String getParent()`
- `boolean exists()`
- `boolean canWrite()`
- `boolean canRead()`
- `boolean isFile()`
- `boolean isDirectory()`
- `boolean isAbsolute()`
- `long lastModified()`
- `long length()`
- `boolean mkdir()`
- `boolean mkdirs()`
- `boolean renameTo(File dest)`
- `boolean delete()`
- `String[] list()`
- `String[] list(FilenameFilter filter)`

The `getName()` method gets the name of a file and returns it as a string. The `getPath()` method returns the path of a file—which may be relative—as a string. The `getAbsolutePath()` method returns the absolute path of a file. The `getParent()` method returns the parent directory of a file or `null` if a parent directory is not found.

The `exists()` method returns a boolean value that specifies whether or not a file actually exists. The `canWrite()` and `canRead()` methods return boolean values that specify whether a file can be written to or read from. The `isFile()` and `isDirectory()` methods return boolean values that specify whether a file is valid and whether the directory information is valid. The `isAbsolute()` method returns a boolean value that specifies whether a filename is absolute.

The `lastModified()` method returns a `long` value that specifies the time at which a file was last modified. The `long` value returned is useful only in determining differences between modification times; it has no meaning as an absolute time and is not suitable for output. The `length()` method returns the length of a file in bytes.

The `mkdir()` method creates a directory based on the current path information. `mkdir()` returns a boolean value indicating the success of creating the directory. The `mkdirs()` method is similar to `mkdir()`, except that it can be used to create an entire directory structure. The `renameTo()` method renames a file to the name specified by the `File` object passed as the *dest* parameter. The `delete()` method deletes a file. Both `renameTo()` and `delete()` return a boolean value indicating the success or failure of the operation.

Finally, the `list()` methods of the `File` object obtain listings of the directory contents. Both `list()` methods return a list of filenames in a `String` array. The only difference between the two methods is that the second version takes a `FilenameFilter` object that enables you to filter out certain files from the list.

 Listing 12.9 shows the source code for the `FileInfo` program, which uses a `File` object to determine information about a file in the current directory. The `FileInfo` program is located in the `FileInfo.java` source file on the CD-ROM that accompanies this book.

Listing 12.9. The `FileInfo` class.

```java
import java.io.*;
class FileInfo {
  public static void main (String args[]) {
    System.out.println("Enter file name: ");
    char c;
    StringBuffer buf = new StringBuffer();
    try {
      Reader in = new InputStreamReader(System.in);
      while ((c = (char)in.read()) != '\n')
        buf.append(c);
    }
    catch (Exception e) {
      System.out.println("Error: " + e.toString());
    }
    File file = new File(buf.toString());
    if (file.exists()) {
      System.out.println("File Name  : " + file.getName());
      System.out.println("     Path  : " + file.getPath());
      System.out.println("Abs. Path  : " + file.getAbsolutePath());
      System.out.println("Writable   : " + file.canWrite());
      System.out.println("Readable   : " + file.canRead());
      System.out.println("Length     : " + (file.length() / 1024) + "KB");
    }
    else
      System.out.println("Sorry, file not found.");
  }
}
```

The `FileInfo` program uses the `File` object to get information about a file in the current directory. The user is first prompted to type a filename; the resulting input is stored in a `String` object. The `String` object is then used as the parameter to the `File` object's constructor. A call to the `exists()` method determines whether the file actually exists. If so, information about the file is obtained through the various `File()` methods and the results are output to the screen.

Following are the results of running `FileInfo` and specifying `FileInfo.java` as the file for which you want to get information:

```
File Name  : FileInfo.java
     Path  : FileInfo.java
Abs. Path  : C:\Books\Jul11PRE\Source\Chap12\FileInfo.java
Writable   : true
Readable   : true
Length     : 0KB
```

The RandomAccessFile Class

The `RandomAccessFile` class provides a multitude of methods for reading and writing to and from files. Although you can certainly use `FileInputStream` and `FileOutputStream` for file I/O, `RandomAccessFile` provides many more features and options. Following are the constructors for `RandomAccessFile`:

- `RandomAccessFile(String name, String mode)`
- `RandomAccessFile(File file, String mode)`

The first constructor takes a `String` parameter specifying the name of the file to access, along with a `String` parameter specifying the type of mode (read or write). The mode type can be either `"r"` for read mode or `"rw"` for read/write mode. The second constructor takes a `File` object as the first parameter, which specifies the file to access. The second parameter is a mode string, which works exactly the same as it does in the first constructor.

The `RandomAccessFile` class implements a variety of powerful file I/O methods. Following are some of the most useful ones:

- `int skipBytes(int n)`
- `long getFilePointer()`
- `void seek(long pos)`
- `int read()`
- `int read(byte b[])`
- `int read(byte b[], int off, int len)`
- `final boolean readBoolean()`
- `final byte readByte()`
- `final int readUnsignedByte()`
- `final short readShort()`

- final int readUnsignedShort()
- final char readChar()
- final int readInt()
- final long readLong()
- final float readFloat()
- final double readDouble()
- final String readLine()
- final void readFully(byte *b*[])
- final void readFully(byte *b*[], int *off*, int *len*)
- void write(byte *b*[])
- void write(byte *b*[], int *off*, int *len*)
- final void writeBoolean(boolean *v*)
- final void writeByte(int *v*)
- final void writeShort(int *v*)
- final void writeChar(int *v*)
- final void writeInt(int *v*)
- final void writeLong(long *v*)
- void writeFloat(float *v*)
- void writeDouble(double *v*)
- void writeBytes(String *s*)
- void writeChars(String *s*)
- long length()
- void close()

From looking at this method list, you no doubt are thinking that many of these methods look familiar. And they should look familiar—most of the methods implemented by RandomAccessFile are also implemented by either FileInputStream or FileOutputStream. The fact that RandomAccessFile combines them into a single class is a convenience in and of itself. But you already know how to use these methods because they work just as they do in the FileInputStream and FileOutputStream classes. What you are interested in are the new methods implemented by RandomAccessFile.

The first new method you may have noticed is the getFilePointer() method. getFilePointer() returns the current position of the file pointer as a long value. The *file pointer* indicates the location in the file where data will next be read from or written to. In read mode, the file pointer is analogous to the needle on a phonograph or the laser in a CD player. The seek() method is the other new method that should catch your attention. seek() sets the file pointer to the absolute position specified by the long parameter *pos*. Calling seek() to move the file pointer is analogous to moving the phonograph needle with your hand. In both cases, the read point of the data or music is being moved. A similar situation occurs when you are writing data.

> **NOTE**
>
> It's worth noting that Java's file pointers are not pointers in the traditional sense (that is, a pointer meaning a direct reference to a memory location). As you may know, Java doesn't support memory pointers. File pointers are more conceptual in nature: They "point" to a specific location in a file.

 Listing 12.10 shows the source code for `FilePrint`, a program that uses the `RandomAccessFile` class to print a file to the screen. The source code for the `FilePrint` program can be found in the file `FilePrint.java` on the CD-ROM that accompanies this book.

Listing 12.10. The FilePrint class.

```java
import java.io.*;
class FilePrint {
  public static void main (String args[]) {
    System.out.println("Enter file name: ");
    char c;
    StringBuffer buf = new StringBuffer();
    try {
      Reader in = new InputStreamReader(System.in);
      while ((c = (char)in.read()) != '\n')
        buf.append(c);
      System.out.println(buf.toString());
      RandomAccessFile file = new RandomAccessFile(buf.toString(), "rw");
      while (file.getFilePointer() < file.length())
        System.out.println(file.readLine());
    }
    catch (Exception e) {
      System.out.println("Error: " + e.toString());
    }
  }
}
```

The `FilePrint` program begins very much like the `FileInfo` program in Listing 12.9 in that it prompts the user to type a filename and stores the result in a string. It then uses that string to create a `RandomAccessFile` object in read/write mode, which is specified by passing `"rw"` as the second parameter to the constructor. A `while` loop is then used to repeatedly call the `readLine()` method until the entire file has been read. The call to `readLine()` is performed within a call to `println()` so that each line of the file is output to the screen.

Summary

Whew! This chapter covered a lot of ground! Hopefully, you've managed to make it this far relatively unscathed. On the up side, you've learned just about all there is to know about fundamental Java I/O and the most important classes in the I/O package. That's not to say that there isn't still a wealth of information inside the I/O package that you haven't seen. The point is that the Java class libraries are very extensive, which means that some of the classes are useful only in very special circumstances. The goal of this chapter was to highlight the more mainstream classes and methods within the I/O package.

One of the neatest uses of I/O streams is in sending and receiving data across a network. You're in luck because the next chapter takes a look at the Java networking package, java.net. You learn all about the built-in networking support provided by the networking package and how it can be used to build network Java programs.

## CHAPTER 13

The Networking Package

by Mike Fletcher

IN THIS CHAPTER

This chapter serves as an introduction to the package containing Java's networking facilities. It covers the classes, interfaces, and exceptions that make up the `java.net` package.

Unless otherwise noted, classes, exceptions, and interfaces are members of the `java.net` package. The full package name is given for members of other classes (for example, `java.io.IOException`). Method names are shown followed by parentheses `()` (for example, `close()`).

Classes

The classes in the networking package fall into three general categories:

- **Web interface classes.** The `URL` and `URLConnection` classes provide a quick and easy way to access content using Uniform Resource Locators. This content may be located on the local machine or anywhere on the WWW. The `URLEncoder` class provides a way to convert text for use as arguments for CGI scripts.

- **Raw network interface classes.** `Socket`, `ServerSocket`, `DatagramSocket`, and `InetAddress` are the classes that provide access to plain, bare-bones networking facilities. They are the building blocks for implementing new protocols, talking to preexisting servers, and the like. Chapter 26, "Java Socket Programming," covers using these classes in detail.

- **Extension classes.** The `ContentHandler` and `URLStreamHandler` abstract classes are used to extend the capabilities of the `URL` class. Chapter 25, "Developing Content and Protocol Handlers," explains how to write handlers for new protocols and content types.

Keep in mind that some of the `java.net` classes (such as `URLConnection` and `ContentHandler`) are abstract classes and cannot be directly instantiated. Subclasses provide the actual implementations for the different protocols and contents.

Table 13.1 lists all the classes in the package along with brief descriptions of the functionality each provides.

Table 13.1. Classes of the `java.net` package.

Class	Purpose
`URL`	Represents a Uniform Resource Locator
`URLConnection`	Retrieves content addressed by `URL` objects
`Socket`	Provides a TCP (connected, ordered stream) socket
`ServerSocket`	Provides a server (listening) TCP socket
`DatagramSocket`	Provides a UDP (connectionless datagram) socket

Class	Purpose
DatagramPacket	Represents a datagram to be sent using a DatagramSocket object
InetAddress	Represents a host name and its corresponding IP number or numbers
URLEncoder	Encodes text in the x-www-form-urlencoded format
URLStreamHandler	Subclasses implement communications streams for different URL protocols
ContentHandler	Subclasses know how to turn MIME objects into corresponding Java objects
SocketImpl	Subclasses provide access to TCP/IP facilities

The URL Class

The URL class represents a Web Uniform Resource Locator. Along with the URLConnection class, the URL class provides access to resources located on the World Wide Web using the HTTP protocol. The URL class also allows resources to be accessed from the local machine or from the FTP protocol with file: URLs.

Constructors. The constructors for the URL class allow the creation of absolute and relative URLs. One constructor takes a whole String as a URL; other constructors allow the protocol, host, and file to be specified in separate String objects. The class also provides for relative URLs with a constructor that takes another URL object for the context and a String as the relative part of the URL.

Constructor	Description
URL(String *url*)	Takes the entire URL as a String.
URL(String *protocol*, String *host*, int *port*, String *file*)	Takes each component of the URL as a separate argument.
URL(String *protocol*, String *host*, String *file*)	As above, but uses the default port number for the protocol.
URL(URL *context*, String *file*)	Replaces the file part of the URL with the second argument.

Methods. The methods for the URL class retrieve individual components of the represented URL (such as the protocol and the host name). The class also provides comparison methods for determining whether two URL objects reference the same content.

Probably the most important method is getContent(). This method returns an object representing the content of the URL. Another method, openConnection(), returns a URLConnection object that provides a connection to the remote content. The connection object can then be used to retrieve the content, as it can be with the getContent() method.

The URLConnection Class

The URLConnection class does the actual work of retrieving the content specified by URL objects. This class is an abstract class; as such, it cannot be directly instantiated. Instead, subclasses of the class provide the implementation to handle different protocols. The subclasses know how to use the appropriate subclasses of the URLStreamHandler class to connect and retrieve the content.

Constructor. The only constructor provided for the URLConnection class takes a URL object and returns a URLConnection object for that URL. However, because URLConnection is an abstract class, it cannot be directly instantiated. Instead of using a constructor, you will probably use the URL class openConnection() method. The Java runtime system creates an instance of the proper connection subclass to handle the URL.

Methods. The getContent() method acts just like the URL class method of the same name. The URLConnection class also provides methods to get information such as the content type of the resource or HTTP header information sent with the resource. Examples of these methods are getContentType(), which returns what the HTTP content-type header contained, and the verbosely named guessContentTypeFromStream(), which tries to determine the content type by observing the incoming data stream.

Methods also are provided to obtain a java.io.InputStream object that reads data from the connection. For URLs that provide for output, there is a corresponding getOutputStream() method. The remaining URLConnection methods deal with retrieving or setting class variables.

Variables. Several protected members describe aspects of the connection, such as the URL connected to and whether the connection supports input or output. A variable also notes whether or not the connection uses a cached copy of the object.

The Socket Class

A Socket object is the Java representation of a TCP connection. When a Socket is created, a connection is opened to the specified destination. Stream objects can be obtained to send and receive data to the other end.

Constructors. The constructors for the Socket class take two arguments: the name (or IP address) of the host to connect to, and the port number on that host to connect to. The host name can be given as either a String or as an InetAddress object. In either case, the port number is specified as an integer.

Constructor	Description
Socket(String *host*, int *port*, boolean *stream*)	Takes the host name and port to contact, and whether to use a stream (true) or datagram connection.
Socket(String *host*, int *port*)	As above, but defaults to a stream connection.
Socket(InetAddress *host*, int *port*, boolean *stream*)	Uses an InetAddress object rather than a String to specify the host name.
Socket(InetAddress *host*, int *port*)	As above, but defaults to a stream connection.

Methods. The two most important methods in the Socket class are getInputStream() and getOutputStream(), which return stream objects that can be used to communicate through the socket. A close() method is provided to tell the underlying operating system to terminate the connection. Methods also are provided to retrieve information about the connection such as the local and remote port numbers and an InetAddress representing the remote host.

New in Java 1.1 are three methods that control how the TCP connection represented by a Socket object behaves. These new methods are listed here with a short description of what each does. A more detailed explanation of the options that can be set for a connection is given later in this chapter, in the discussion of the SocketOptions interface.

Constructor	Description
setSoLinger(boolean *on*, int *val*)	Sets whether the close() method blocks for *val* seconds until all pending data is sent and acknowledged by the receiver. If *val* is zero, the connection is closed immediately.
setTcpNoDelay(boolean *on*)	Controls whether data is buffered until an acknowledgment is received for any data already sent.
setSoTimeout(int *timeout*)	Sets a timeout (in milliseconds) for read() calls on the socket. A *timeout* value of zero indicates an infinite timeout (wait until data is ready).

Three corresponding methods read the options set by the three methods just described: The `getSoLinger()` and `getSoTimeout()` methods both return an `int` representing the corresponding delay. A `-1` for `getSoLinger()` and a `0` for `getSoTimeout()` indicate that the option is disabled. The `getTcpNoDelay()` method returns a boolean value indicating whether the option is enabled.

The ServerSocket Class

The `ServerSocket` class represents a listening TCP connection. Once an incoming connection is requested, the `ServerSocket` object returns a `Socket` object representing the connection. In normal use, another thread is spawned to handle the connection. The `ServerSocket` object is then free to listen for the next connection request.

Constructors. Both constructors for this class take as an argument the local port number to listen to for connection requests. One constructor also takes the maximum time to wait for a connection as a second argument.

Constructor	Description
`ServerSocket( int port, int count )`	Takes the port number to listen to for connections and the amount of time to listen.
`ServerSocket( int port )`	As above, but the socket waits until a connection is received.

Methods. The most important method in the `ServerSocket` class is `accept()`. This method blocks the calling thread until a connection is received. A `Socket` object is returned representing this new connection. The `close()` method tells the operating system to stop listening for requests on the socket. Also provided are methods to retrieve the host name on which the socket is listening (in `InetAddress` form) and the port number being listened to.

The DatagramSocket Class

The `DatagramSocket` class represents a connectionless datagram socket. This class works with the `DatagramPacket` class to provide for communication using the UDP (User Datagram Protocol).

Constructors. Because UDP is a connectionless protocol, you do not have to specify a host name when creating a `DatagramSocket`—only the port number on the local host. A second constructor takes no arguments. When this second constructor is used, the port number is assigned arbitrarily by the operating system.

Constructor	Description
DatagramSocket(int *port*)	Creates a socket on the specified port number.
DatagramSocket()	Creates a socket on an available port.

Methods. The two most important methods for the DatagramSocket class are send() and receive(). Each takes as an argument an appropriately constructed DatagramPacket (described in the following section). In the case of the send() method, the data contained in the packet is sent to the specified host and port. The receive() method blocks execution until a packet is received by the underlying socket, at which time the data is copied into the packet provided.

A close() method is also provided, which asks for the underlying socket to be shut down, as is a getLocalPort() method, which returns the local port number associated with the socket. This last method is particularly useful when you let the system pick the port number for you.

The DatagramPacket Class

DatagramPacket objects represent one packet of data that is sent using the UDP protocol (using a DatagramSocket).

Constructors. The DatagramPacket class provides two constructors: one for outgoing packets and one for incoming packets. The incoming version takes as arguments a byte array to hold the received data and an int specifying the size of the array. The outgoing version also takes the remote host name (as an InetAddress object) and the port number on that host to send the packet to.

Constructor	Description
DatagramPacket(byte[] *buffer*, int *length*)	Creates a packet to receive the specified number of bytes into the given buffer.
DatagramPacket(byte[] *buffer*, int *length*, InetAddress *addr*, int *port*)	Creates a packet to send the specified number of bytes from the given buffer to the host and port given.

Methods. Four methods in the DatagramPacket class allow the data, datagram length, and addressing (InetAdress and port number) information for the packet to be extracted. The methods are named, respectively, getData(), getLength(), getAddress(), and getPort().

The MulticastSocket Class

The MulticastSocket class extends the DatagramSocket class to provide a way of sending and receiving multicast UDP packets. A multicast packet is sent to all members of a multicast group on the Internet (network routing and firewalls willing). Each group is specified by an IP address between 224.0.0.1 and 239.255.255.255 (inclusive) as well as a port number.

In addition to the methods provided by the DatagramSocket class, the MulticastSocket class provides methods to set and get the limit of the number of network hops the packet will travel, methods to join and leave a particular multicast group, and methods to specify which network interface is used to send multicast messages.

The InetAddress Class

The InetAddress class represents a host name and its IP numbers. The class itself also provides the functionality to obtain the IP number for a given host name—similar to the C gethostbyname() function on UNIX and UNIX-like platforms.

Constructors. There are no explicit constructors for InetAddress objects. Instead, you use the static class method getByName(), which returns a reference to an InetAddress. Because some hosts may be known by more than one IP address, there also is a method getAllByName(), which returns an array of InetAddress objects.

Methods. In addition to the static methods just listed, the getHostName() method returns a String representation of the host name that the InetAddress represents; the getAddress() method returns an array of the raw bytes of the address. The equals() method compares address objects. The class also supports a toString() method, which prints out the host name and IP address textually.

The URLEncoder Class

The URLEncoder class provides a method to encode arbitrary text in the x-www-form-urlencoded format. The primary use for this format is when you are encoding arguments in URLs for CGI scripts. Nonprinting or punctuation characters are converted to a two-digit hexadecimal number preceded by a percent (%) character. Space characters are converted to plus (+) characters.

Constructors. There is no constructor for the URLEncoder class. All the functionality is provided by means of a static method.

Methods. The URLEncoder class provides one static class method, encode(), which takes a String representing the text to encode and returns the translated text as a String.

The URLStreamHandler Class

The subclasses of the URLStreamHandler class provide the implementation of objects that know how to open communications streams for different URL protocol types. More information on how to write handlers for new protocols can be found in Chapter 25, "Developing Content and Protocol Handlers."

Constructors. The constructor for the URLStreamHandler class cannot be called because URLStreamHandler is an abstract class.

Methods. Each subclass provides its own implementation of the openConnection() method, which opens an input stream to the URL specified as an argument. The method should return an appropriate subclass of the URLConnection class.

The ContentHandler Class

Subclasses of the ContentHandler abstract class are responsible for turning a raw data stream for a MIME type into a Java object of the appropriate type.

Constructors. Because ContentHandler is an abstract class, ContentHandler objects cannot be instantiated. An object implementing the ContentHandlerFactory interface decides what the appropriate subclass is for a given MIME content type.

Methods. The important method for ContentHandler objects is the getContent() method, which does the actual work of turning into a Java object the data read using URLConnection. This method takes as its argument a reference to a URLConnection that provides an InputStream at the beginning of the representation of an object.

The SocketImpl Class

The SocketImpl abstract class provides a mapping from the raw networking classes to the native TCP/IP networking facilities of the host. This means that the Java application does not have to concern itself with the operating system specifics of creating network connections. At run time, the Java interpreter loads the proper native code for the implementation, which is accessed by means of a SocketImpl object. Each Socket or ServerSocket then uses the SocketImpl object to access the network.

This scheme also allows for flexibility in different network environments. An application does not have to bother with details such as being behind a firewall because the interpreter takes care of loading the proper socket implementation (such as one that knows how to use the SOCKS proxy TCP/IP service).

13

THE NETWORKING PACKAGE

TIP

SOCKS provides TCP and UDP access through a firewall. A SOCKS daemon runs on the firewall (or the inside machine of a DMZ setup). Clients on the inside network call up the SOCKS daemon and ask it to make a connection to an outside host. The daemon connects to the outside host directly or through another SOCKS daemon. SOCKS is pretty cool because the client application doesn't even know it's there if things are set up properly.

For more information about SOCKS, take a look at this URL:

```
http://www.socks.nec.com/socks5.html
```

Unless you are porting Java to a new platform or adding support for something such as connecting through a firewall, you probably will never see or use `SocketImpl`.

Constructors. The `SocketImpl` abstract class has one constructor that takes no arguments.

Methods. The methods provided by the `SocketImpl` class look very familiar to anyone who has done socket programming under a UNIX variant. All the methods are protected and may be used only by subclasses of `SocketImpl` that provide specific socket implementations.

The `create()` method creates a socket with the underlying operating system. It takes one boolean argument that specifies whether the created socket should be a stream (TCP) or datagram (UDP) socket. Two calls, `connect()` and `bind()`, cause the socket to be associated with a particular address and port.

For server sockets, there is the `listen()` method, which tells the operating system how many connections may be pending on the socket. The `accept()` method waits for an incoming connection request. It takes another `SocketImpl` object as a parameter, which represents the new connection once it has been established.

To allow reading and writing from the socket, the class provides the `getInputStream()` and `getOutputStream()` methods, which return a reference to the corresponding stream. Once communication on a socket is finished, the `close()` method can be used to ask the operating system to close the connection. The remaining methods allow read access to the member variables as well as a `toString()` method for printing a textual representation of the object.

Variables. Each `SocketImpl` object has four protected members:

Member	Description
fd	A `java.io.FileDescriptor` object used to access the underlying operating system network facilities.
address	An `InetAddress` object representing the host at the remote end of the connection.
port	The remote port number, stored as an `int`.
localport	The local port number, stored as an `int`.

Exceptions

Java's exception system allows for flexible error handling. The `java.net` package defines five exceptions, which are described in the following sections. All these exceptions provide the same functionality as any `java.lang.Exception` object. Because each exception is a subclass of `java.io.IOException`, the exceptions can be handled with code such as this:

```
try {
    // Code that might cause an exception goes here
}
catch( java.net.IOException e ) {
    System.err.println( "Error on socket operation:\n" + e );
    return;
}
```

This code can be placed inside a `for` loop—for example, when trying to create a `Socket` to connect to a heavily loaded host.

The `UnknownHostException` Exception

The `UnknownHostException` exception is thrown when a host name cannot be resolved into a machine address. The most probable causes for this condition are listed here:

- The host name is misspelled.
- The host does not actually exist.
- There is a problem with the network and the host, or the host that is providing name-to-IP number mapping is unreachable.

TIP

If you are sure that you are using the right host name and are still getting this exception, you may have to fix the name-to-IP number mapping. How to go about this depends on the platform you are using. If you are using DNS, you must contact the administrator for the domain. If you are using Sun's NIS, you must have the system administrator change the entry on the NIS server. Finally, you may have to change the local machine's host file, usually named `hosts` or `HOSTS` (`/etc/hosts` on UNIX variants, `\WINDOWS\HOSTS` on Windows 95). In any case, using the IP number itself to connect to the host should work.

The `UnknownServiceException` Exception

The `URLConnection` class uses the `UnknownServiceException` exception to signal that a given connection does not support a requested facility such as input or output. If you write your own protocol or content handlers and do not override the default methods for getting input or output stream objects, the inherited method throws this exception. An application to which a user can give an arbitrary URL should watch for this exception. (Users being the malicious creatures they are!)

The `SocketException` Exception

The `SocketException` exception is the superclass for the exceptions thrown when there is a problem using a socket. An exception is thrown if a bad value is passed for a socket option (see "The `SocketOptions` Interface," later in this chapter).

The `SocketException` exception is also thrown if you try to use the `setSocketImplFactory()` method of the `Socket` or `ServerSocket` classes when the `SocketImplFactory` already has been set. Usually, the Java interpreter sets this to a reasonable value for you, but if you are writing your own socket factory (for example, to provide sockets through a firewall), this exception may be thrown.

The `BindException` Exception

A `BindException` exception is thrown to indicate an error binding a socket to a local address and port number. One possible cause for this exception is that the local port you are asking for is already in use (that is, another process already has that particular port open). Some operating systems may wait for a period of time after a socket has been closed before allowing it to be reopened.

Another cause for this exception is that the user cannot bind to that particular port. On most UNIX systems, ports numbered less than 1024 cannot be used by accounts other than the root or superuser account. This is a security measure; most well-known services reside on ports in this range. Normal users cannot start their own servers in place of the system version. While you are developing a service, you may want to run the server on a port with a higher number. Once the service has been developed and debugged, you can move it to a normal port.

The `ProtocolException` Exception

The `ProtocolException` exception is raised by the underlying network support library. It is thrown by a native method of the `PlainSocketImpl` class when the underlying socket facilities return a protocol error.

The `MalformedURLException` Exception

The URL class throws the `MalformedURLException` exception if it is given a syntactically invalid URL. One cause can be that the URL specifies a protocol that the URL class does not support. Another cause is that the URL cannot be parsed. A URL for the `http` or `file` protocols should have the following general form:

```
protocol://hostname[:port]/[/path/_/path]/object
```

In this syntax, the following components are used:

Component	Description
protocol	The protocol to use to connect to the resource (http or file).
hostname[:port]	The host name to contact, optionally followed by a colon (:) and the port number to connect to (for example, kremvax. gov.su:8000). The host name also may be given as an IP address.
[/path/.../path]	The (optional) path to the object, separated by / characters.
object	The name of the actual object itself.

This syntax for a URL depends on the protocol. The complete URL specification can be found in RFC 1738 (see Chapter 24, "Introduction to Network Programming," for details on retrieving RFC documents, or check out the World Wide Web Consortium's site at http://www.w3.org/ for the latest version).

The ConnectException and NoRouteToHostException Exceptions

These two exceptions are thrown if an error occurs while you are trying to connect to a remote host. A ConnectException exception indicates that a connection could not be made, usually because there is a problem with the destination host or because nothing is listening on the other end. A NoRouteToHostException exception indicates that the remote host cannot be reached. This condition can be caused by network problems or if a firewall machine is blocking the connection.

Other Exceptions

In addition to the exceptions in the java.net package, several methods throw exceptions from the java.io package. The most common of these is java.io.IOException—which is thrown when there is a problem reading a Web resource by the URL class or if there is a problem creating a Socket object.

Interfaces

The java.net package defines five interfaces. These interfaces are used primarily behind the scenes by the other networking classes rather than by user classes. Unless you are porting Java to a new platform or are extending it to use a new socket protocol, you probably will have no need to implement these interfaces in a class. They are included here for completeness and for those people who like to take off the cover and poke around in the innards to find out how things work.

The `SocketImplFactory` Interface

The `SocketImplFactory` interface defines a method that returns a `SocketImpl` instance appropriate to the underlying operating system. The socket classes use an object implementing this interface to create the `SocketImpl` objects they need to use the network.

The `SocketOptions` Interface

The `SocketOptions` interface provides methods that allow options to be set or read on socket connections provided by the underlying implementation classes (such as `SocketImpl`). Unless you are writing a subclass of one of the socket implementation classes, you should not use these methods directly; instead, use the access methods provided by the socket class.

The `URLStreamHandlerFactory` Interface

Classes that implement the `URLStreamHandlerFactory` interface provide a mapping from protocols such as HTTP or FTP into the corresponding `URLStreamHandler` subclasses. The `URL` class uses this factory object to obtain a protocol handler.

The `ContentHandlerFactory` Interface

The `URLStreamHandler` class uses the `ContentHandlerFactory` interface to obtain `ContentHandler` objects for different content types. The interface specifies one method, `createContentHandler()`, which takes the MIME type for which a handler is desired as a `String`.

The `FileNameMap` Interface

The `FileNameMap` interface provides one method, `getContentTypeFor()`, which provides a way to map between a filename and a `string` containing the MIME type. This interface is used by the `URLConnection` class to provide the `guessContentTypeFromName()` method.

Summary

This chapter provided a quick introduction to the networking facilities that the `java.net` package provides. For more specific information about `java.net` classes, consult the online class documentation that accompanies the JDK. You can also refer to Part V of this book, "Networking with Java"; the four chapters in that part of the book go into more detail about how to use Java's network capabilities and also provide examples of their use.

The Windowing (AWT) Package

by David R. Chung
revised by Christopher Burdess

IN THIS CHAPTER

CHAPTER 14

The Abstract Windowing Toolkit (AWT) package in the JDK is a library of Java classes you can use to create graphical user interfaces (GUIs). These interfaces allow users to interact with the Java application or applet in the same way they are accustomed to interacting with other applications on their native platforms.

Because Java is a multiplatform language, the AWT is not intended to implement all the features of any *specific* GUI operating system, merely the features common to *all* operating systems. Programming with the AWT is therefore a highly portable user interface solution.

The AWT classes can essentially be divided into the following three categories:

- Components
- Layouts
- Utility classes

This chapter examines each of these categories and provides examples of how to incorporate AWT classes into your Java applications and applets. Additionally, this chapter presents a discussion of peer components and their advantages and limitations.

Components

Otherwise known as user interface control elements, controls, or widgets, *components* is the name given to a wide variety of interface elements that can be displayed to the user. Components can also be programmed to respond to interaction by the user with the mouse or keyboard. This *event handling* is an important part of GUI programming and is discussed later in this chapter in the "Events" section.

Most AWT components are derived from the Component class. The notable exception is the MenuComponent class and its subclasses; these are discussed later in this section.

The Component class is an abstract class that defines elements common to all components: font, color, painting, reshaping, and event handling.

> **NOTE**
>
> *Abstract classes are classes that declare one or more methods as* abstract. *Abstract methods must be overridden by a subclass; abstract classes cannot be instantiated.*

The Component class tree is shown in Figure 14.1. All classes belong to the java.awt package except the Applet class, which is in the java.applet package.

NOTE

A class in one package can be derived from a superclass in another package. Thus, the `Applet` class, in the `java.applet` package, is derived from the `Panel` class in the `java.awt` package. A package is not an indication of class hierarchy, merely a convenient way to bundle certain kinds of functionality. The aspect of primary functional importance of `Applet` objects is that they can be embedded in Web documents and be interpreted by a Web browser according to certain security rules, not that they form part of a graphical user interface to a Java program.

FIGURE 14.1.

The Component *class tree.*

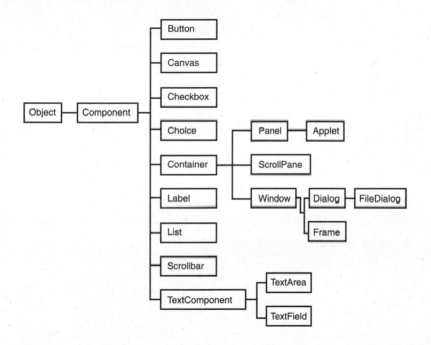

Components can be further subdivided into four main functional groups:

- Simple widgets
- Text components
- Containers
- The `Canvas` class

This chapter also discusses menus. Although menus are not derived from the `Component` class and do not share some of the properties of components (such as position, width, color, and so forth), menus do have other properties similar to components—notably fonts and event handling. In any case, I will continue to refer to menu elements as components because they are evidently visible elements of the user interface. See the "Menus" section, later in this chapter, for further details.

Simple Widgets

Simple widgets are components for which the user interaction required is minimal or nonexistent and which are not containers for any other kind of component. Simple widgets include the `Button`, `Checkbox`, `Choice`, `Label`, `List`, and `Scrollbar` classes. Correlations of these components exist on most GUI operating systems. The `SimpleWidgetApplet` applet in Figure 14.2 shows the AWT's simple widgets on the Microsoft Windows NT 4.0 platform. The code for the `SimpleWidgetApplet` applet is shown in Listing 14.1 and is provided on the CD-ROM that accompanies this book.

FIGURE 14.2.

The
SimpleWidgetApplet
applet shows the AWT's
simple widgets.

Listing 14.1. The `SimpleWidgetApplet` applet.

```java
import java.awt.*;

public class SimpleWidgetApplet extends java.applet.Applet {

    Button button = new Button("Click me!");
    Checkbox checkbox = new Checkbox("Tick me!");
    Choice choice = new Choice();
    Label label = new Label("This just displays some text.");
    List list = new List();
    Scrollbar scrollbar = new Scrollbar();

    public void init() {
        choice.add("Item 1");
        choice.add("Item 2");
        choice.add("Item 3");

        list.add("Item 1");
        list.add("Item 2");
        list.add("Item 3");

        add(button);
        add(checkbox);
        add(choice);
```

```
        add(label);
        add(list);
        add(scrollbar);
    }
}
```

First of all, we create the widgets. Some of them have handy constructors that can be used to set their initial values; for example, the Button class can be passed a String in its constructor to initialize the button's label. Other components do not have useful constructors, usually because the number of values that must be passed is not known (as is the case with the Choice and List components). In this case, you use the default constructor and set its properties later. With the Choice widget in SimpleWidgetApplet, we use its add(String) method to set the strings we want to appear in the choice list. Note that when you add items to a list (and later to menus) in this way, no sorting takes place—the strings appear in the order you add them.

Then we are ready to add these components to the applet using the applet's add(Component) method. Sometimes, you can cut out a step by creating a component and adding it at the same time:

```
add(new Button("Hello!"));
```

This approach is sometimes useful for labels. However, you usually want to keep a reference to the object you have created, as we do in SimpleWidgetApplet. Keeping a reference to the object allows you to easily refer to the objects you have created in other methods in the class—especially event-handling methods—so that you can examine and set their properties.

The functionality provided by the simple widgets is as follows:

- The Label component, as we have discovered, is used just to display text for the user—the user can't do anything with a label.
- The Button component is used to trigger an associated action.
- The Checkbox component is used to represent the state of a boolean variable (true or false, on or off). Checkboxes can be associated with a particular CheckboxGroup object, either by constructing them with it or by using the setCheckboxGroup(CheckboxGroup) method. When a checkbox is part of a group, only one of the checkboxes can be selected at a time; if one is selected, the others are all deselected.
- The Choice component is used to select one of a number of string options. Only the selected option is shown—other options are displayed in a popup window when the Choice component is clicked.

- The List component can be used in the same way as the Choice component: to select one of a number of string options. Additionally, a List component can contain multiple selections; you can specify this either in the constructor or using the setMultipleMode(*boolean*) method. For a multiple-selection List component, the user can select several options at a time.

- The Scrollbar component is used to represent a bounded numeric value. Normally, this value is itself used to represent the amount of a component that is visible in a container. See the discussion about the ScrollPane class in the "Containers" section, later in this chapter, for details.

Text Components

You can add to your Java applications and applets two AWT components into which the user can enter text with the keyboard. These text components are TextField and TextArea; they are both subclasses of TextComponent (refer back to Figure 14.1).

 The TextComponent class is an abstract base class that encapsulates much that is common to the two components. The TextField class is a simple one-line text editing component; the TextArea class supports multiple lines and vertical scrolling. Both components can be used to display and let the user specify string values. An example is shown in Figure 14.3. The code for the TextComponentApplet applet is given in Listing 14.2 and on the CD-ROM that accompanies this book.

Figure 14.3.

The
TextComponentApplet
applet.

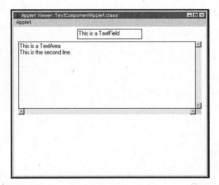

Listing 14.2. The TextComponentApplet applet.

```java
import java.awt.*;

public class TextComponentApplet extends java.applet.Applet {
    TextField textfield = new TextField("This is a TextField");
    TextArea textarea = new TextArea("This is a TextArea\nThis is the second
    line.");
```

```
    public void init() {
        add(textfield);
        add(textarea);
    }
}
```

TIP

As you can see from this example, text components have handy constructors you can use to specify the strings to be displayed initially. You can also set other properties of text components: Both TextField and TextArea allow you to specify the number of (character) columns in the component; the TextArea component also allows you to set the number of rows (lines) in the component.

Containers

A *container* is a component that can hold other components. All containers in the AWT are derived from the Container abstract class (refer back to Figure 14.1). The main containers are Panel, ScrollPane, and Window.

Panels are normally used to group components into specific areas of the display. Because every component can be given a separate layout, panels are useful if you want to position components according to a different layout than what was used by its parent container (usually either some form of Window or an Applet). An Applet is a kind of panel with additional properties relating to browser implementations; the Applet class in the java.applet package is the only AWT-derived class that is not in the java.awt package or one of its subpackages.

Scroll panes are a form of panel. You can add a child component to the ScrollPane container that may have dimensions greater than the ScrollPane container itself. When this is the case, the scroll pane provides horizontal and/or vertical scrollbars that allow the user to display different areas of the child component.

The Window class encapsulates a top-level window. By itself, the Window class represents a window with no title bar or border. Subclasses of the Window class provide titles, icon images, and window user control functions such as close commands and minimize/maximize capabilities. These subclasses are Frame and Dialog.

TIP

You can use the Window class as a base superclass for popup windows and components, such as ToolTips.

The `Frame` class provides all the functionality of an application window in the native operating system—with the notable exception that you cannot access the operating system's handle or PID for the window (or other windows in the environment). Frames are the basis for the majority of Java GUI applications. Because frames also implement the `MenuContainer` interface, they can possess a menu bar (see "Menus," later in this chapter).

The `Dialog` class represents a window that normally appears for a short time to display or request transient information. If some information is needed for a step in a computation (for example, `This file has been edited. Do you want to save it?`) but is not required after that step, you should use a dialog box. In the same way, if your application must notify the user that some step has been carried out and requires feedback from the user indicating that the user has understood the notification, you should use a dialog box. A `Dialog` object can be declared *modal* either by constructing it as such or by calling `setModal(true)`. A *modal dialog box* is one that does not allow user interaction with its parent frame until the dialog box has been dismissed.

The `FileDialog` class represents a special kind of dialog box that prompts the user for a path or filename. Because paths and filenames are specified differently under different operating systems, this class is used to remove the associated difficulty of catering for all possible specifications.

Note that all windows are initially invisible when they are created. To make a window you have created visible, you must invoke its `show()` method. Normally, you do this after you have added all the components to it (unless, of course, you are developing dynamic components).

For an example of how frames and dialog boxes work, look at the `DialogFrame` application detailed in "Events," later in this chapter.

Menus

Menu components, as mentioned earlier in this chapter, are not derived from the `Component` class. Menu components all derive from the abstract `MenuComponent` class. Figure 14.4 shows the `MenuComponent` hierarchy.

FIGURE 14.4.

The `MenuComponent` *class tree.*

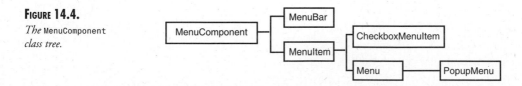

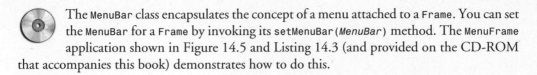

The MenuBar class encapsulates the concept of a menu attached to a Frame. You can set the MenuBar for a Frame by invoking its setMenuBar(*MenuBar*) method. The MenuFrame application shown in Figure 14.5 and Listing 14.3 (and provided on the CD-ROM that accompanies this book) demonstrates how to do this.

FIGURE 14.5.

The MenuFrame *application.*

Listing 14.3. The MenuFrame application.

```java
import java.awt.*;

public class MenuFrame extends Frame {
    MenuItem fileNew = new MenuItem("New");
    MenuItem fileOpen = new MenuItem("Open...");
    MenuItem fileSave = new MenuItem("Save");
    MenuItem fileExit = new MenuItem("Exit");
    MenuItem editUndo = new MenuItem("Undo");
    MenuItem editCut = new MenuItem("Cut");
    MenuItem editCopy = new MenuItem("Copy");
    MenuItem editPaste = new MenuItem("Paste");
    MenuItem helpContents = new MenuItem("Contents");
    MenuItem helpAbout = new MenuItem("About MenuFrame...");

    public MenuFrame() {
        super("Menu example");

        MenuBar menubar = new MenuBar();
        Menu fileMenu = new Menu("File");
        Menu editMenu = new Menu("Edit");
        Menu helpMenu = new Menu("Help");

        fileMenu.add(fileNew);
        fileMenu.add(fileOpen);
        fileSave.setEnabled(false);
        fileMenu.add(fileSave);
        fileMenu.addSeparator();
        fileMenu.add(fileExit);

        editUndo.setEnabled(false);
        editMenu.add(editUndo);
        editMenu.addSeparator();
        editCut.setEnabled(false);
```

14

THE WINDOWING
(AWT) PACKAGE

continues

Listing 14.3. continued

```
            editMenu.add(editCut);
            editCopy.setEnabled(false);
            editMenu.add(editCopy);
            editPaste.setEnabled(false);
            editMenu.add(editPaste);

            helpMenu.add(helpContents);
            helpMenu.addSeparator();
            helpMenu.add(helpAbout);

            menubar.add(fileMenu);
            menubar.add(editMenu);
            menubar.add(helpMenu);
            menubar.setHelpMenu(helpMenu);

            setMenuBar(menubar);
            setSize(new Dimension(400, 300));
            show();
    }

    public static void main(String[] args) {
        MenuFrame me = new MenuFrame();
    }
}
```

As well as specifying the label to appear on menu items, the `MenuItem` class also allows you to construct the menu with a hotkey that can activate the specific `MenuItem`.

As you may have noticed, the code in Listing 14.3 disables menu items that are not applicable. In this small example, it is redundant to do so because there will never be a time when the `MenuFrame` object has any content that must be saved or edited. The menu items were disabled only for purposes of explanation. Furthermore, nothing actually happens when the menu items are selected because we have not yet added any event-handling functionality to the application. To see an example of an application that responds to user interaction, see the "Events" section, later in this chapter.

Popup Menus

Popup menus, used to provide contextual functions for the underlying object of a referential component, have become very common on platforms such as Windows 95, NT 4.0, and CDE. The base class for creating popup menus is `PopupMenu`, derived from `MenuComponent`. You can compose a popup menu with this class and display it relative to the referential component by means of its `show(Component, int, int)` method. The other two variables in the `show()` method are the x and y coordinates (in pixels) relative to the specified component. You must add the popup menu to a valid component first, which may or may not be the component from which you specify its position.

One of the issues relating to popup menus is the event used to trigger the menu; this event differs from platform to platform. For example, in Motif, the menu pops up on a mouse-down event; in Windows, the menu appears on a mouse-up event. The MouseEvent class has a special isPopupTrigger() function to deal with this problem.

The Canvas Class and Graphics Contexts

The Canvas class is a generic component class that can be used to implement graphics methods. By itself, the Canvas class appears similar to a Panel class but it is not a container and you cannot add other components to it. Essentially, the Canvas class is just an instantiable Component class. Canvases are subclassed extensively to display images, draw graphs, and create custom components such as progress bars, tabbed folders, and custom buttons. This is achieved by overriding the paint(Graphics) method. With the provided Graphics context, you can invoke graphics methods to draw points, lines, text, and images into the canvas.

The Graphics object provides an encapsulation of the state information required for the various rendering methods Java uses, such as the current color, font, and rendering translation origin. Coordinates passed to Graphics methods are considered relative to this origin; rendering methods invoked on the Graphics object only modify pixels within the bounds of its clipping rectangle. Some of the more useful methods provided by this object include drawImage(), which is used to render an Image into the graphics context; drawLine(), which is used to draw lines; drawOval(), which is used to draw ellipses and circles; drawString(), which is used to draw text; fillRect(), which is used to draw filled rectangles; getFontMetrics(), which retrieves a FontMetrics object containing information about the current font, which can then be used to calculate where to draw text; and setColor() and setFont(), which are used to select colors and fonts for drawing. For more information about fonts, colors, and images, refer to "Utility Classes," later in this chapter.

The ImageButton class demonstrates how to subclass the Canvas class to draw a button that can display an image *and* text. Figure 14.6 shows an ImageButton object added to a Frame object on the Windows NT 4.0 platform. Listing 14.4 shows the code to accomplish this feat (the code is also provided on the CD-ROM that accompanies this book).

FIGURE 14.6.

The ImageButton *component displayed in a frame.*

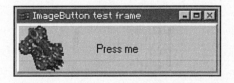

14

THE WINDOWING (AWT) PACKAGE

Listing 14.4. The ImageButton class.

```java
import java.awt.*;

public class ImageButton extends Canvas {

    private String label;
    private Image image;

    public ImageButton() {
        this(null, null);
    }

    public ImageButton(String label) {
        this(label, null);
    }

    public ImageButton(Image image) {
        this(null, image);
    }

    public ImageButton(String label, Image image) {
        this.label = label;
        this.image = image;
    }

    public String getLabel() {
        return label;
    }

    public Image getImage() {
        return image;
    }

    public void setLabel(String label) {
        if(!label.equals(this.label)) {
            this.label = label;
            repaint();
        }
    }

    public void setImage(Image image) {
        if(!image.equals(this.image)) {
            this.image = image;
            repaint();
        }
    }

    public void paint(Graphics g) {
        Color b = getBackground();
        Font f = g.getFont();
        Rectangle r = g.getClipBounds();

        super.paint(g);

        // Draw the image.
        // Scale it so it fits in the clip rectangle and center it vertically.
```

```
    if(image != null && r.width>4 && r.height>4) {
        Dimension d = new Dimension(image.getWidth(this),
                        image.getHeight(this));
        float scale = 1;
        float fdwidth = (new Integer(d.width)).floatValue();
        float frwidth = (new Integer(r.width)).floatValue();
        float fdheight = (new Integer(d.height)).floatValue();
        float frheight = (new Integer(r.height)).floatValue();
        if((fdwidth*scale) > (frwidth*scale))
            scale = scale * (frwidth/fdwidth);
        if((fdheight*scale) > (frheight*scale))
            scale = scale * (frheight/fdheight);
        int ndwidth = (new Float(fdwidth * scale)).intValue() - 4;
        int ndheight = (new Float(fdheight * scale)).intValue() - 4;
        int yOffset = (r.height - ndheight) / 2;
        g.drawImage(image, 2, yOffset, ndwidth, ndheight, this);
    }

    // Draw the label.
    // Center it in the clip rectangle.
    if(label!=null) {
        FontMetrics fm = g.getFontMetrics();
        g.drawString(label, (r.width - fm.stringWidth(label)) / 2,
                    (r.height/2) + (fm.getAscent()/2));
    }

    // Draw the button bevel.
    // We need to draw the lines twice to make them thicker.
    g.setColor(b.brighter());
    g.drawLine(0, r.height-1, 0, 0);
    g.drawLine(1, r.height-2, 1, 1);
    g.drawLine(0, 0, r.width-1, 0);
    g.drawLine(1, 1, r.width-2, 1);
    g.setColor(b.darker());
    g.drawLine(r.width-1, 0, r.width-1, r.height-1);
    g.drawLine(r.width-2, 1, r.width-2, r.height-2);
    g.drawLine(r.width-1, r.height-1, 0, r.height-1);
    g.drawLine(r.width-2, r.height-2, 1, r.height-2);
    }
}
```

You may have noticed that in the paint() routine, the variables height and width refer to the height and width of the ImageButton. These numbers are 1 greater than the index of the last pixel in the clip rectangle; the pixels are numbered 0 to width-1 and 0 to height-1, in the same way that the length of an array is 1 greater than the index of the last element of the array.

The ImageButton class is far from encapsulating a real button that can be clicked to trigger events. To make it a clickable button, you must define a boolean instance variable (for example, down) that is flagged when the button receives a mouse-down event and unflagged when it receives a mouse-up event. The paint() routine can then examine the down variable and draw the button appropriately. For example, you may want to switch the g.setColor() calls in the bevel-drawing routine to reverse the bevel; you may also want to offset the image and text to the right and down by some factor to give the user some feedback that the button has been clicked. In Windows, button backgrounds are dithered when they are clicked; you may want to implement this feature.

To bring some life to the `ImageButton` object, it must handle events. Event handling is discussed next.

Events

Event handling is one of the largest concerns for GUI developers. The other is layout management, which is dealt with in "Layout Management," later in this chapter. Fortunately, the AWT makes event handling relatively easy to learn and implement. Before the JDK 1.1 API, an inheritance event model was used, which was found to have considerable overhead and was cumbersome to deploy. In the current version of the JDK, the AWT uses a delegation event model, which is much more robust and flexible and allows for a greater degree of compile-time checking.

When the user initiates some event, such as clicking the mouse or typing at the keyboard, the event is generated and made available to your Java application or applet. The following sections describe how to catch these events and process them.

Listeners and Adapters

An event is propagated from a source object (component) to a "listener" object. The source object is the GUI object the user clicked on, typed text into, or otherwise interacted with. Listeners are objects that register themselves as interested in certain kinds of events on that source. Listeners can be other GUI objects or separate objects responsible for delegated events; in the latter case, you can write event-handling code that separates the GUI elements from their functionality. In the AWT, events that are passed are typically derived from the `AWTEvent` class.

The AWT provides for two conceptually different kinds of events: low-level and semantic. *Low-level events* are concerned with the specific user input or window system-level event occurrences. *Semantic events* are concerned not with the specifics of what interaction occurred, but with its meaning. For example, when you press the Enter key after typing something into a text field, you want to perform some action (such as validating the contents of the text field). In the same way, when you click a button or double-click an item in a list, you want to perform an action. However, if you click a scrollbar (or drag its marker), you want to adjust the value of something. You can see that the low-level event (the click with the mouse) does not perform the same role for different components; this is why you need semantic events.

Low-level events and semantic events are both subclassed from the `AWTEvent` class, which is subclassed from `java.util.EventObject`. `AWTEvent` is in the `java.awt` package. All other events discussed here are in the `java.awt.event` package. Figure 14.7 shows the class tree for low-level events.

FIGURE 14.7.

The class tree for low-level events.

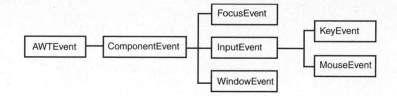

There is, in fact, one more event, the (very) low-level `PaintEvent`, which is normally used only internally; it is not designed to be used with the listener model. Figure 14.8 shows the corresponding class tree for the semantic events.

FIGURE 14.8.

The class tree for semantic events.

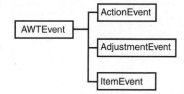

The `ActionEvent` encapsulates our notion of "doing something" or "performing an action." The other two events are more specific: The `AdjustmentEvent` is representative of a numeric variable being adjusted; the `ItemEvent` indicates that the state of an item has changed.

According to this model, all your class has to do is to implement a certain listener interface and get itself registered with the source object. However, listeners for low-level events are designed to listen to multiple event types (the `WindowListener`, for example, listens to window activation, closed, closing, deactivation, deiconification, iconification, and opened events); if your class implements such an interface, you must supply the methods that handle these events.

TIP

To make things simpler, the AWT event model includes *adapter* classes for low-level event listeners. These classes, located in the `java.awt.event` package, provide default implementations of all the methods so that you can choose which methods to override in your code. Because the body of the adapter method is empty, using adapters is equivalent to using the listener interfaces directly except that you don't have to specify every method in the listener interface.

Figure 14.9 shows the low-level event listener and adapter hierarchy; Figure 14.10 shows the semantic event listener interfaces. All listeners inherit the `java.util.EventListener` interface and are contained in the `java.awt.event` package.

FIGURE 14.9.
Low-level event listeners and adapters.

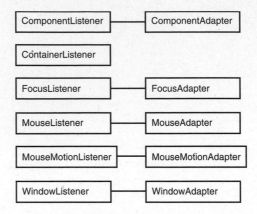

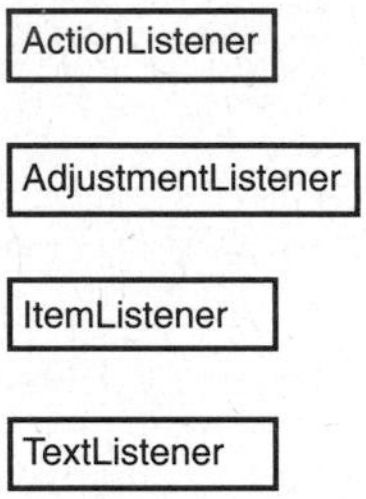

FIGURE 14.10.
Semantic event listeners.

ActionListener

AdjustmentListener

ItemListener

TextListener

The Event Queue

The AWT provides a system event queue, which is represented by the `java.awt.EventQueue` class. The `EventQueue` class provides a static method to return the current system event queue: `getEventQueue()`. You can use the event queue to get sneak previews of events destined for objects in the system, and, most importantly, you can push new events onto the queue.

There are security issues involved here: Although applications can make free use of the event queue, allowing untrusted applets to freely manipulate events can have serious implications. Thus, the `getEventQueue()` method is protected by a `SecurityManager` check that does not allow untrusted applets direct access to the queue. Instead, appropriate `Applet` methods for peeking at the queue exist. These methods are restricted so that applets can only access events contained on components within their own containment hierarchy.

Event Handling

The `DialogFrame` application in Listing 14.5 (and included on the CD-ROM that accompanies this book) demonstrates the use of the various event objects and methods, as well as how the `Frame` and `Dialog` classes work.

Listing 14.5. The DialogFrame application.

```java
import java.awt.*;
import java.awt.event.*;

public class DialogFrame extends Frame implements ActionListener, WindowListener {

    Dialog dialog;
    Button openDialogButton;
    Button closeDialogButton;
    Button closeFrameButton;

    public DialogFrame() {
        super("Dialog and Frame example");
        setLayout(new FlowLayout());
        addWindowListener(this);

        openDialogButton = new Button("Open dialog");
        openDialogButton.addActionListener(this);

        closeFrameButton = new Button("Close me");
        closeFrameButton.addActionListener(this);

        add(openDialogButton);
        add(closeFrameButton);

        pack();
        show();
    }

    public void showDialog() {
        dialog = new Dialog(this, "This is the dialog", true);
        dialog.setLayout(new FlowLayout());
        dialog.addWindowListener(this);

        closeDialogButton = new Button("Close dialog");
        closeDialogButton.addActionListener(this);

        dialog.add(closeDialogButton);

        dialog.pack();
        dialog.show();
    }

    public void actionPerformed(ActionEvent e) {
        String buttonCommand = e.getActionCommand();
        if(buttonCommand.equals("Open dialog"))
            showDialog();
        else if(buttonCommand.equals("Close dialog"))
            dialog.dispose();
        else if(buttonCommand.equals("Close me"))
            processEvent(new WindowEvent(this, WindowEvent.WINDOW_CLOSING));
    }
```

14

THE WINDOWING (AWT) PACKAGE

continues

Listing 14.5. continued

```java
        public void windowClosing(WindowEvent e) {
            Window originator = e.getWindow();
            if(originator.equals(this)) {
                this.dispose();
                System.exit(0);
            } else if(originator.equals(dialog))
                dialog.dispose();
        }

        public void windowActivated(WindowEvent e) { }
        public void windowDeactivated(WindowEvent e) { }
        public void windowDeiconified(WindowEvent e) { }
        public void windowClosed(WindowEvent e) { }
        public void windowIconified(WindowEvent e) { }
        public void windowOpened(WindowEvent e) { }

        public static void main(String[] args) {
            DialogFrame me = new DialogFrame();
        }
}
```

First, we ensure that the DialogFrame class can receive events from the sources it is interested in. And it is interested in the clicking of buttons (which are semantic events) and window events (so that it can intercept low-level window closing events—otherwise, the user cannot terminate the application by closing the window). Thus, DialogFrame implements the ActionListener and WindowListener interfaces and provides methods to handle the events it receives as a result.

When DialogFrame is constructed, it first calls the superconstructor in the Frame class with a string argument that sets the specified string to be the window title. The next line sets the layout (as described in "Layout Management," later in this chapter). The next method, addWindowListener(*WindowListener*), registers the DialogFrame with itself for the purposes of receiving window events. Then the code creates the buttons that go on the frame and registers itself as an ActionListener for action events on those buttons. Because windows are always created invisible, the code then calls show() to display the frame.

The showDialog() function constructs a modal dialog box and registers DialogFrame as a window listener for it. The method also creates a button on the dialog box and registers DialogFrame as an action listener for the button.

Now we implement the event-handling methods for DialogFrame. First, we implement the actionPerformed(*ActionEvent*) method for the button clicks. We work out which button has been clicked and perform the relevant action for it. In this example, we use the ActionEvent's getActionCommand() method to return the button label. Alternatively, we could have used ActionEvent's getSource() method to return the actual source object and then compared it with the button references we have (openDialogButton and so on). The openDialogButton click calls showDialog() to show the dialog box; the closeDialogButton click calls dispose() on the dialog box, which hides it and removes any excess system resources used to manage the window. The `closeFrameButton` click, however, does not close the frame directly; it posts a new window-closing event to the frame. This event is picked up by `DialogFrame` in its role as window listener and is processed as if it is a request to close the window (which, effectively, it is). Why would we bother to go through this tortuous arrangement of posting events to ourselves in this way, when disposing of the window and calling `System.exit()` is easy and straight-forward? In this case, that *is* all the processing to be done by the window listener's closing routine, but when you develop more complex applications, you will find that you must frequently do more processing before the application can exit successfully. If you start off duplicating code in different methods, and you have to change the code in some way at a later date, you must always consider all the other code snippets that are supposed to be providing the same functionality. Many experienced programmers write special methods such as `closeAndExit()`, which is called by any routine that wants to close down the application, thereby ensuring that there is only one way that the system can exit.

> **TIP**
>
> Because `DialogFrame` is an application and not an applet, instead of calling `processEvent()`, we could easily have requested a handle to the system event queue and posted the window-closing event there:
>
> ```
> EventQueue.getEventQueue().postEvent(new WindowEvent(this,
>     WindowEvent.WINDOW_CLOSING));
> ```
>
> However, because `processEvent()` causes the event to be handled immediately, this method is usually more useful.

Next, we must override the relevant methods in `WindowListener` to handle window events. We compare the source window with our references to `DialogFrame` and its child dialog box and then dispose of the windows accordingly. We must also provide empty implementations of the other `WindowListener` methods because we are not using a separate adapter object.

Note that because this is an application and not an applet, we must provide a `main()` method with the following form:

```
public static void main(String[])
```

In this form, the `String` array parameter references any command-line parameters passed to the application. As soon as we have compiled this class, we can run it with a Java interpreter from the command line, like this:

```
java DialogFrame
```

The Focus and Keyboard Events

The *focus* is a term used to describe which component is to receive keyboard events. Because numerous components, each potentially capable of handling keyboard events, may be visible in the same window, the focus is used to determine the destination of the keyboard events. For example, if you want to receive keyboard events on a Frame or Canvas object, the component must first request the focus using the requestFocus() method.

The AWT provides for mouseless focus traversal, which is implemented by pressing the Tab key (to move forwards) or Shift+Tab (to move backwards). Some components (those based on peers in the underlying platform) have this ability innately. For example, if you develop new components derived from Canvas that are destined to receive keyboard events, you should override the isTabbable() method to return true and catch the mouse-down event on the component to call requestFocus(). Most user-interface component designers also implement additional drawing routines when the component has the focus; a button, for example, may have a dotted line around the inside of the bevel.

Clipboard Functions

Most GUI users expect to be able to transfer data such as text and images between applications using the clipboard functions cut, copy, and paste. The API for transferable objects is based around the java.awt.datatransfer.Transferable interface. Objects that implement this interface must provide a list of "flavors" or formats in which it can provide the actual data. The java.awt.datatransfer package provides one convenient class for the most common data type: the StringSelection class implements the Transferable interface.

The Clipboard class encapsulates a clipboard in Java. You are free to create as many of these objects as you like for private purposes. One clipboard object, however, called System, is used to interface with the system clipboard and hence nonJava applications. You can retrieve the System clipboard with a call to getSystemClipboard() on a valid Toolkit object. To write data to a Clipboard object, you must implement the ClipboardOwner interface. Transfer occurs with two methods: To write data to a clipboard, you use the Clipboard method setContents(*Transferable, ClipboardOwner*); to read from the clipboard, use the getContents(*Object*) method. The *ClipboardOwner* and *Object* parameters refer to the calling object; the *Transferable* objects involved are the clipboard data. When you read from the clipboard, you must also request a list of available flavors from the *Transferable* object and read the data in the desired flavor with the *Transferable* object's getTransferData() method.

Layout Management

So far in this chapter, the examples have just been adding components to containers without any indication of how those components are to be arranged in the display. The AWT provides a group of classes known as *layout managers*, or *layouts*, that handle this kind of placement. All layouts implement the LayoutManager interface. Once you set a layout for a container using the setLayout(*LayoutManager*) method, and then add a component to the container, you also add the component to the container's layout. The layouts provided with the AWT library are discussed in the following sections.

The FlowLayout Manager

The FlowLayout manager sets out the components in rows. This layout is most useful for implementing button toolbars and the like. The FlowLayout manager fits as many components as it can on one row before populating the row below. The order of the components in the row is determined by the order in which they are added to the container. FlowLayout is the default layout for the Panel class, so applets also use this layout manager if none is specified.

You can specify the spacing between components in a FlowLayout by using the setHgap() and setVgap() methods or by constructing it with these values (the default is 5 pixels for both horizontal and vertical gaps). The FlowLayout manager respects a component's Insets, so these are added to the total gap between components if they are specified.

> **TIP**
>
> You can also specify the alignment of the flow (which side it aligns the components against) either in the constructor or with the setAlignment() method.

The ToolbarApplet shown in Figure 14.11 and Listing 14.6 (and included on the CD-ROM that accompanies this book) displays a set of buttons positioned with a FlowLayout manager with RIGHT alignment.

FIGURE 14.11.

The ToolbarApplet *applet.*

Listing 14.6. The ToolbarApplet applet.

```java
import java.awt.*;

public class ToolbarApplet extends java.applet.Applet {

    public void init() {
        setLayout(new FlowLayout(FlowLayout.RIGHT));
        add(new Button("Button 1"));
        add(new Button("Button 2"));
```

continues

Listing 14.6. continued

```
        add(new Button("Button 3"));
        add(new Button("Button 4"));
        add(new Button("Button 5"));
    }
}
```

The BorderLayout Manager

The BorderLayout manager is a simple layout that places controls so that they fill their container. When you add a component to a container that has a BorderLayout layout, you can also specify one of five constraints in the form of a string: "North", "East", "South", "West", and "Center". The first four constraints specify which edge of the container the component will be attached to (north, east, south, or west). The "Center" constraint places the component in the center of the container. If you do not specify a constraint, the default constraint is "Center". A maximum of five components can be displayed in the container, although you can create more complex arrangements by embedding containers within one another. The BorderLayout manager is the default layout for the Window class, so frames and dialog boxes use the BorderLayout manager if none is specified.

> **TIP**
>
> You can specify horizontal and vertical gaps with the BorderLayout manager in the same way you can with the FlowLayout manager.

Figure 14.12 shows how components are laid out with the BorderLayout manager; Listing 14.7 shows the code used to accomplish this. This code is also included on the CD-ROM that accompanies this book.

FIGURE 14.12.
The
BorderButtonApplet
applet.

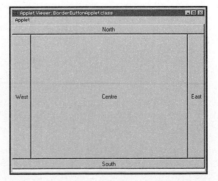

Listing 14.7. The BorderButtonApplet applet.

```java
import java.awt.*;

public class BorderButtonApplet extends java.applet.Applet {

    public void init() {
        setLayout(new BorderLayout());
        add(new Button("North"), "North");
        add(new Button("East"), "East");
        add(new Button("South"), "South");
        add(new Button("West"), "West");
        add(new Button("Centre"));
    }
}
```

The CardLayout Manager

The CardLayout manager is an interesting layout in that it does not attempt to resize components to display them all in the container. Instead, it displays them one at a time in a Rolodex fashion. Listing 14.8 shows the ThreePagesApplet applet (the applet is also located on the CD-ROM that accompanies this book); Figure 14.13 shows this CardLayout container displaying its third control, a panel with some buttons and text.

FIGURE 14.13.
The ThreePagesApplet
applet.

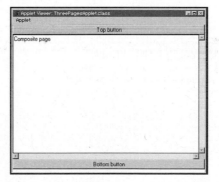

Listing 14.8. The ThreePagesApplet applet.

```java
import java.awt.*;
import java.awt.event.*;

public class ThreePagesApplet extends java.applet.Applet implements MouseListener {

    Button page1Button;
    Label page2Label;
    TextArea page3Text;
    Button page3Top;
```

14

THE WINDOWING
(AWT) PACKAGE

continues

Listing 14.8. continued

```
    Button page3Bottom;
    CardLayout layout;

    public void init() {
        setLayout(layout = new CardLayout());

        add(page1Button = new Button("Button page"), "page1Button");
        page1Button.addMouseListener(this);

        add(page2Label = new Label("Label page"), "page2Label");
        page2Label.addMouseListener(this);

        Panel panel = new Panel();
        panel.setLayout(new BorderLayout());

        panel.add(page3Text = new TextArea("Composite page"));
        page3Text.addMouseListener(this);

        panel.add(page3Top = new Button("Top button"), "North");
        page3Top.addMouseListener(this);

        panel.add(page3Bottom = new Button("Bottom button"), "South");
        page3Bottom.addMouseListener(this);

        add(panel, "panel");
    }

    public void mouseClicked(MouseEvent e) {
        layout.next(this);
    }

    public void mouseEntered(MouseEvent e) { }
    public void mouseExited(MouseEvent e) { }
    public void mousePressed(MouseEvent e) { }
    public void mouseReleased(MouseEvent e) { }

}
```

When the user clicks any of the components in the applet, the ThreePagesApplet shows the next component in its layout. This is done by calling the next() method on the layout. The position methods for the CardLayout are listed here:

- ◼ first(*Container*)
- ◼ next(*Container*)
- ◼ previous(*Container*)
- ◼ last(*Container*)

These methods move to the first, next, previous, and last components in the layout, respectively.

TIP

All these methods require a container to be specified, because you can use the same layout manager object for more than one container at a time. Normally (unless you have a good reason not to), you create a separate layout manager for each container. Doing so allows you to modularize your code more easily. If, however, you want to minimize the total number of objects in a large application, sharing a layout manager between containers may be one of your solutions.

When components are added to the container, you specify a string that the `CardLayout` manager uses to identify the control. Instead of calling position methods such as `next()` and `first()`, you can also jump to the component with the specified label by calling the `show(`*`Container`*`, `*`String`*`)` method on the layout. For example, if you want to jump to the second page in the `ThreePagesApplet`, you can use this call:

```
layout.show(this, "page2Label");
```

The `GridLayout` Manager

The `GridLayout` manager is used to lay out components in a grid of evenly spaced cells. The default constructor creates a grid with one column per component, but you can use other constructors to specify the exact number of rows and columns you need as well as the spacing between the cells. As you can see in Figure 14.14, the `GridLayout` manager populates its cells from left to right and top to bottom. Listing 14.9 shows the code used to create this applet. This applet is also located on the CD-ROM that accompanies this book.

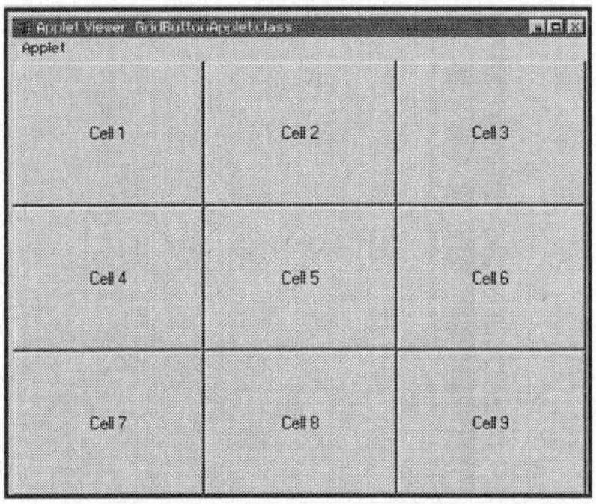
Applet Viewer: GridButtonApplet.class
Applet
Cell 1
Cell 2
Cell 3
Cell 4
Cell 5
Cell 6
Cell 7
Cell 8
Cell 9

FIGURE 14.14.
The `GridButtonApplet` *applet.*

Listing 14.9. The GridButtonApplet applet.

```
import java.awt.*;

public class GridButtonApplet extends java.applet.Applet {

    public void init() {
        setLayout(new GridLayout(3, 3));
        add(new Button("Cell 1"));
        add(new Button("Cell 2"));
        add(new Button("Cell 3"));
        add(new Button("Cell 4"));
        add(new Button("Cell 5"));
        add(new Button("Cell 6"));
        add(new Button("Cell 7"));
        add(new Button("Cell 8"));
        add(new Button("Cell 9"));
    }
}
```

The GridBagLayout Manager

The GridBagLayout manager is the most complex and highly flexible layout manager in the AWT. Once you get used to it, you will use it all the time to develop form-like interfaces. However, it is difficult to learn and has many options.

The basis of the GridBagLayout manager is a grid. Unlike the GridLayout manager, components in the GridBagLayout manager are not constrained to a single, regular cell. Each cell has a horizontal and vertical *weight*, which is used to determine the proportion of the space it takes up as a double-precision floating-point value between 0 (none of the available space) and 1 (all the available space). Also, each component can take up more than one cell. A number of other factors control the placement and sizing of components in a GridBagLayout manager; any or all of these factors are specified to the layout by means of a GridBagConstraints object, which is added to the layout at the same time as the component, and which specifies the factors for that component. The GridBagConstraints class contains the following data members:

- ■ **gridx, gridy:** These variables specify the cell coordinates for the northwest corner of the component. You can use the default value GridBagConstraints.RELATIVE to specify a horizontal or vertical offset of 1 from the cell of the most recently added component.

- ■ **gridwidth, gridheight:** These variables specify the number of horizontal and vertical cells the component is to take up. You can use GridBagConstraints.REMAINDER to take up all the remaining cells in a row or column.

- ■ **fill:** If the component is smaller than its cell(s), this variable determines whether (and if so, how) to resize the component to fit into the available area. Valid arguments are GridBagConstraints.NONE (don't resize), GridBagConstraints.HORIZONTAL (make use of all the width), GridBagConstraints.VERTICAL (make use of all the height), and GridBagConstraints.BOTH (make use of all the space).

- **anchor:** If the component is smaller than its cell(s), this variable determines what corner or edge of the cell area to attach the component to. Valid arguments are GridBagConstraints.CENTER (the default), GridBagConstraints.NORTH, GridBagConstraints.EAST, GridBagConstraints.SOUTH, GridBagConstraints.WEST, GridBagConstraints.NORTHWEST, GridBagConstraints.NORTHEAST, GridBagConstraints.SOUTHEAST, and GridBagConstraints.SOUTHWEST.

- **weightx, weighty:** These variables are used to determine the weight of a cell, or to what extent excess space is added to the row or column. If you do not specify the weight of at least one row and column, the components are laid out in the center because specifying a weight of 0 (the default) adds any extra space at the edges.

- **Insets:** The Insets object specifies the distance in pixels between the edges of the component and the edges of its cell(s).

- **ipadx, ipady:** These variables control the horizontal and vertical padding between the component's edge and that of its cell(s).

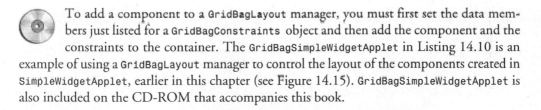

CAUTION

Although the variables ipadx and ipady are still supported in GridBagConstraints and by the layout manager, they are essentially superseded by the Insets variable and their use is no longer recommended.

To add a component to a GridBagLayout manager, you must first set the data members just listed for a GridBagConstraints object and then add the component and the constraints to the container. The GridBagSimpleWidgetApplet in Listing 14.10 is an example of using a GridBagLayout manager to control the layout of the components created in SimpleWidgetApplet, earlier in this chapter (see Figure 14.15). GridBagSimpleWidgetApplet is also included on the CD-ROM that accompanies this book.

14

FIGURE 14.15.

The GridBag-
SimpleWidgetApplet
applet.

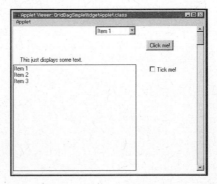

Listing 14.10. The `GridBagSimpleWidgetApplet` applet.

```java
import java.awt.*;

public class GridBagSimpleWidgetApplet extends java.applet.Applet {

    public void init() {

        GridBagConstraints gbc;
        setLayout(new GridBagLayout());

        Button button = new Button("Click me!");
        Checkbox checkbox = new Checkbox("Tick me!");
        Choice choice = new Choice();
        Label label = new Label("This just displays some text.");
        List list = new List();
        Scrollbar scrollbar = new Scrollbar();

        choice.add("Item 1");
        choice.add("Item 2");
        choice.add("Item 3");

        list.add("Item 1");
        list.add("Item 2");
        list.add("Item 3");

        gbc = new GridBagConstraints();
        gbc.gridx = gbc.gridy = 0;
        gbc.anchor = GridBagConstraints.SOUTH;
        gbc.weightx = gbc.weighty = 1.0;
        add(label, gbc);

        gbc = new GridBagConstraints();
        gbc.gridx = 0;
        gbc.fill = GridBagConstraints.BOTH;
        gbc.gridwidth = 2;
        gbc.gridheight = 3;
        gbc.weightx = 1.0;
        gbc.weighty = 3.0;
        add(list, gbc);

        gbc = new GridBagConstraints();
        gbc.gridy = 0;
        gbc.fill = GridBagConstraints.HORIZONTAL;
        gbc.anchor = GridBagConstraints.NORTH;
        gbc.weightx = gbc.weighty = 1.0;
        add(choice, gbc);

        gbc = new GridBagConstraints();
        gbc.gridy = 0;
        gbc.weightx = gbc.weighty = 1.0;
        add(button, gbc);

        gbc = new GridBagConstraints();
        gbc.gridy = 2;
        gbc.anchor = GridBagConstraints.NORTHEAST;
```

```
            gbc.weightx = gbc.weighty = 1.0;
            add(checkbox, gbc);

            gbc = new GridBagConstraints();
            gbc.gridy = 0;
            gbc.gridheight = GridBagConstraints.REMAINDER;
            gbc.fill = GridBagConstraints.VERTICAL;
            gbc.anchor = GridBagConstraints.EAST;
            gbc.weightx = gbc.weighty = 1.0;
            add(scrollbar, gbc);

        }
}
```

Custom Layouts

If you still can't get the required layout behavior for your container, you can write your own layout manager. You must implement either the LayoutManager or LayoutManager2 interface and supply the relevant methods. LayoutManager2 is an interface that provides a minimal extension to LayoutManager for the purpose of assigning components to the layout based on a constraints object, such as a GridBagConstraints object for the GridBagLayout manager, or the "North" string object for the BorderLayout manager.

Utility Classes

Utility classes represent useful structures and resources, many of which are fundamental to graphics programming and can act as properties of widgets. The utility classes are grouped as follows:

- **Vectors:** Dimension, Insets, Point, Polygon, Rectangle, Shape
- **Colors:** Color, SystemColor
- **Resources:** Cursor, Font, FontMetrics, Graphics, Image, PrintGraphics, PrintJob, Toolkit
- **Resource-manipulation utilities:** MediaTracker

Because the vector classes are primarily intended to store and retrieve position information, all their relevant fields are public. An Insets object is attached to a component to give an idea of the spacing between that component and the ones around it; Insets objects are handled by the layout manager.

The color classes effectively encapsulate color to a depth of 16,777,216 colors, which is as many as most current operating systems support. The SystemColor class can be used to retrieve information about the current desktop colors, including text and window foreground and background colors.

Cursor objects encapsulate the shape of the mouse pointer. They can be one of a number of predefined types, including the default cursor (usually an arrow), a text cursor for positioning the caret, a wait cursor to show that some uninterruptable task is in progress, a hand cursor to select relevant items (such as hypertext links), a crosshair cursor for graphics positioning, and various resizing cursors. You cannot define your own cursor shapes; the cursor shapes are determined from the shapes of the platform's cursors.

Fonts and font metrics provide a way to describe fonts in Java. Every implementation of Java is guaranteed to have at least six fonts: Courier, Dialog, DialogInput, Helvetica, Times Roman, and ZapfDingbats. The actual font used by the platform depends on the specific platform. For example, Windows uses the MS Sans Serif font for the Dialog font.

The Toolkit class encapsulates a windowing toolkit on the underlying platform. The Toolkit class is used to create peers (see "Peers," later in this chapter), return lists of fonts and current print jobs, and provide a way to request information such as screen resolution and size.

Loading Images

The Image class represents an image. There are two standard ways you can load an image into Java, depending on whether you are developing an applet or an application. For an applet, you can use the getImage(*URL*) method on the applet itself. For an application, you can use Toolkit.getDefaultToolkit().getImage(*URL*) independently. Images in GIF and JPEG format are currently supported by the AWT. When you call getImage(), it returns immediately with a valid image reference but loads the image in a separate thread. The MediaTracker class can be used to keep track of the process of loading images; for example, if you want to wait until an image is completely loaded before showing a frame, you can use the MediaTracker class as follows:

```
Frame f = new Frame("MediaTracker test");
MediaTracker mt = new MediaTracker(f);
Image img = Toolkit.getDefaultToolkit().getImage(new URL("http://myserver.com/
    myimage.gif"));
mt.addImage(img, 0);
mt.waitForAll();
f.show();
```

Printing

The PrintJob class and PrintGraphics interface are used to provide the printing API. Printing in Java is very simple. First, you initiate a print job by calling getPrintJob(*Frame*, *String*, *Properties*) on a valid Toolkit object. The Properties object allows you to assign default values for the print job, which is specific to the platform (and sometimes to the printer). The getPrintJob() method displays a print dialog box to the user, so the returned PrintJob object will be complete with all the properties specified by the user. Next, you can call getGraphics() on the PrintJob. This method provides a Graphics object that implements the PrintGraphics interface, which you can pass to the paint() or print() method, or simply use graphics methods on. When you finish with the graphics context, you can flush it to the printer by calling dispose(). Each graphics context represents a page, so you can print multiple pages by making multiple calls to getGraphics(). You can determine page attributes and resolution with the getPageDimensions() and getPageResolution() methods on the PrintJob. Note that the initiation of a print job is an operation bound by security considerations: Untrusted applets are not allowed to print potentially subversive material on the printer of their choice.

Peers

The simple widgets (and the Panel and Canvas classes) in the AWT class library use a peer mechanism to provide the visual aspects of the component. A *peer* is an object created by the native windowing platform that the Java virtual machine manages. Peers have the same "look and feel" as other, nonJava components on the same platform. For example, a Choice list instantiated on a Motif desktop creates a raised component with a small 3D hyphen that pops up a 3D menu centered on the item currently selected, but on a Windows 95 desktop, the same Choice list creates a recessed component (like a text field) with a button showing a down arrow that pops up a flat menu below the button.

The advantage of using a peer mechanism is that users of a particular windowing platform can always be provided with GUI components that resemble those they are used to, and it allows simple data transfer to and from the system clipboard, because the objects that are created are managed by the platform and not by the Java virtual machine.

There are a number of disadvantages with peers, however. First, the area covered by the bounding box of peer-based components will always be filled with the background color of that component. If you want a background image to your application, for example, the image will always be covered by any peer-based components you add to the application. Second, the windowing platform requires additional overhead in the form of system resources to manage the peers that are created, and calls from the Java virtual machine to the operating system to synchronize operations on components with their peer correlates can add to overall processing time.

There is an alternative to using peers, however. Instead of subclassing components from Canvas and Panel, you can instead derive them directly from Component and Container, writing paint() methods in the same way but without the overhead of maintaining a peer. For example, you can derive the ImageButton class (described in the preceding section on the Canvas class) from Component instead of from Canvas. This approach means that any painting that occurred on the ImageButton's container would show through the button, unless you first chose to fill the clip rectangle with the button's background color.

One other advantage to writing your own peerless components is that you have a great deal of control over the specifics of how the components look. You can also correct failings in the platform-specific implementations of peer classes that you otherwise have no control over in

Java. For example, a peer-based List widget on a Windows 95 platform always has a black border. If the user wants a black background, he or she will not be able to see the border of their List widget. You can correct this possible problem in your peerless component by examining the system colors (described in "Utility Classes," earlier in this chapter) and drawing the border in an appropriate color.

> **NOTE**
>
> Sun intends to distribute a larger set of peerless simple widget components (also called *lightweight* components) in the next version of the AWT. The next version of the AWT should also have, as standards, more complex rendering abilities and drag-and-drop functionality.

Summary

The Java AWT contains a collection of components and ways to lay them out that you can use as-is or extend to provide a complete and consistent multiplatform graphical user interface. Presenting information to the user and being able to respond to a wide variety of ways that users manipulate the application is a complex and challenging task; this task is made considerably easier by the encapsulation of function and display features in AWT objects. By using the AWT, you can create small applets as well as fully featured applications that run on a variety of hardware and software platforms.

The Text Package

by Eric Burke

IN THIS CHAPTER

CHAPTER

15

This chapter describes the classes in the java.text package, new to the Java Development Kit 1.1. The text package contains a number of classes that allow the programmer to create internationalized and localized programs that do not contain location-dependent code. In my experience, localization is one of the most overlooked aspects of released software. This problem is compounded by the global characteristics of the World Wide Web. Any Web application—based on Java or not—has to be understood by many users who speak many different languages.

When used properly, the classes contained in java.text allow the developer to cleanly and correctly implement a localized program to be used the world over. Table 15.1 shows the classes and interfaces that are part of the java.text package.

Table 15.1. Classes and interfaces available in the text package.

Class	*Description*
BreakIterator	Finds boundary locations in text
CharacterIterator	Interface for bidirectional text iteration
ChoiceFormat	Attaches a format to a range of numbers
CollationElementIterator	Walks through each character of an international string
CollationKey	Compares strings that are part of a Collator class
Collator	Abstract class that provides Unicode text-comparison services
DateFormat	Abstract base class for date and time formatting
DateFormatSymbols	Encapsulates date and time formatting functionality for changes across languages and countries
DecimalFormat	Formats decimal numbers
DecimalFormatSymbols	Represents symbols such as decimal separators and grouping separators required by DecimalFormat when formatting numbers
FieldPosition	Aligns columns of formatted text
Format	Abstract base class for all formats
MessageFormat	Formats localizable concatenated messages
NumberFormat	Abstract base class for all number formats
ParsePosition	Records the parsing position for formatted strings
SimpleDateFormat	Formats and parses dates in a localized way
StringCharacterIterator	Implements the CharacterIterator interface for strings
RuleBasedCollator	Simple Collator implementation
SimpleDateFormat	Concrete class for parsing and formatting dates

Class	Description
BreakIterator	Iterates through word and line boundaries in a stringParseException; thrown when an error occurs while parsing or formatting

Formats

Formats provide a way for the programmer to easily handle the formatting of text, numbers, dates, times, and so on, in a localized way. For example, in the United States, the number 4.00 written as a monetary amount is $4.00, but in Germany, it is DM4,00. By using classes derived from java.text.Format, you are spared the details of how a particular locale writes its numbers or strings for any representation such as money, time, and so on. Instead, you can concentrate on writing the application at hand. The JDK 1.1 provides classes you can use to format numbers, dates and times, and text messages. Formats rely heavily on the use of java.util.Locale, so let's take a look at that before continuing. Table 15.2 lists the important methods supported by the Format class.

Table 15.2. Methods in the Format class.

Method	Description
format()	Formats the given object
parseObject()	Parses the given string using the current format

The NumberFormat Class

The java.text.NumberFormat class is the abstract base class for all classes that support number formatting and parsing. Code that uses a NumberFormat-derived class can be written to be completely independent of the current locale with respect to number conventions (that is, decimal sign, percent sign, separator for thousands, and so on).

The NumberFormat class provides a few static methods that return an appropriate number, currency, or percent format for a specific locale:

```
NumberFormat defFormat = NumberFormat.getInstance();
NumberFormat defCurrFmt = NumberFormat.getCurrencyInstance();
NumberFormat defPctFmt = NumberFormat.getPercentInstance();
NumberFormat frFormat = NumberFormat.getInstance( Locale.FRENCH );
NumberFormat usCurrFmt = NumberFormat.getCurrencyInstance( Locale.US );
getPercentInstanceNumberFormat usPctFmt = NumberFormat.getPercentInstance(
   Locale.US );
```

The first three methods in this list return the NumberFormat objects for the default Locale for numbers, currencies, and percents, respectively.

The second three methods also return NumberFormat objects for numbers, currencies, and percents; however, these methods also accept a Locale object (in these examples, Locale.FRENCH and Locale.US) as a parameter and use that as the Locale whose NumberFormat should be returned.

Once you retrieve a NumberFormat object, you can use it to generate a properly formatted number. The following line creates the string for 4.00 monetary units in the default locale:

```
String moneyString = NumberFormat.getCurrencyInstance().format( 4.00 );
```

You can also use the NumberFormat class to parse a string that you know is a representation of a number in the current locale. For example, the following statement parses the string "$4.00" and finds the value 4.00 to store in the variable myFour:

```
Number myFour = NumberFormat.getCurrencyInstance(Locale.US).parse( "$4.00" );
```

Finally, you can use the NumberFormat class in conjunction with the FieldPosition class to provide a simple way of aligning numbers on different fields, such as the decimal sign, the percent sign, and so on. Table 15.3 lists the important methods in the NumberFormat class.

Table 15.3. Methods in the NumberFormat class.

Method	Description
format()	Formats the given object into a string; overrides the Format class
parseObject()	Parses a string and creates an Object object
parse()	Parses a string and returns a Number object
isParseIntegerOnly()	Returns true if this parser stops when it hits a decimal point
setParseIntegerOnly()	Specifies whether the parser should read past the decimal point
getInstance()	Gets the default NumberFormat object for a locale
getNumberInstance()	Gets a general-purpose formatter for a locale
getCurrencyInstance()	Gets a currency formatter for a locale
getPercentInstance()	Gets a percent formatter for a locale
getAvailableLocales()	Returns all locales supported by the NumberFormat class
isGroupingUsed()	Returns true if grouping is used; *example*: The number 12345 would be 12,345 with grouping turned on

Method	Description
setGroupingUsed()	Specifies whether grouping should be used
get/setMaximumIntegerDigits()	Gets or sets the maximum number of integer digits to be used
get/setMinimumIntegerDigits()	Gets or sets the minimum number of integer digits to be used
get/setMaximumFractionDigits()	Gets or sets the maximum number of fraction digits to be used
get/setMinimumFractionDigits()	Gets or sets the minimum number of fraction digits to be used

 Listing 15.1 shows how to use the NumberFormat class. You can find this code on the CD-ROM that accompanies this book.

Listing 15.1. NumberFormatExample.java: A sample NumberFormat program.

```java
import java.text.*;
import java.util.*;

public class NumberFormatExample {

    public static void main( String args[] ) {

        try {
            double averages[] = { 0.456, 0.78, 0.3, 1.0, .25, .345 };
            String spaces = "                    ";

            System.out.println( "Available Locales for NumberFormat" );
            Locale availLocs[] = NumberFormat.getAvailableLocales();

            for( int i=0; i<availLocs.length; i++ ) {
                System.out.println( "\t" + availLocs[i].getDisplayName() );
                DecimalFormat fmt = (DecimalFormat) NumberFormat.getInstance(
                    availLocs[i] );
                String pattern = fmt.toPattern();
                int len = pattern.length();
                String newPattern = pattern.substring(0,len-4) + ".000";
                fmt = new DecimalFormat( newPattern, new
                    DecimalFormatSymbols(availLocs[i]) );
                FieldPosition status = new FieldPosition(
                    NumberFormat.FRACTION_FIELD );

                for( int j=0; j<averages.length; j++ ) {
                    StringBuffer sb = new StringBuffer();
                    fmt.format( averages[j], sb, status );
                    System.out.println( spaces.substring(0, 20-
                            status.getEndIndex()) + sb.toString() );
                }
```

continues

Listing 15.1. continued

```
                System.out.println("");
        }

    } catch (Exception e) {
        e.printStackTrace();
    }
  }
}
```

The output from this program looks like this:

```
Available Locales for NumberFormat
    Belorussian (Belarus)
                0,456
                0,780
                0,300
                1,000
                0,250
                0,345

    Bulgarian (Bulgaria)
                0,456
                0,780
                0,300
                1,000
                0,250
                0,345
                etc.
```

As you can see, the same code block produces different output strings depending on the locale.

The DateFormat Class

The java.text.DateFormat class is an abstract base class for all classes that parse and format dates and times in a localized manner. Like the NumberFormat class, the DateFormat class also provides a number of static functions that retrieve default formats for dates and times:

```
DateFormat fmt = DateFormat.getDateInstance();
DateFormat fmt = DateFormat.getDateInstance( DateFormat.SHORT );
DateFormat fmt = DateFormat.getDateInstance( DateFormat.LONG, Locale.FRENCH );
DateFormat fmt = DateFormat.getDateTimeInstance();
DateFormat fmt = DateFormat.getDateInstance( DateFormat.LONG, DateFormat.SHORT );
DateFormat fmt = DateFormat.getDateInstance( DateFormat.LONG, DateFormat.SHORT,
    Locale.US );
DateFormat fmt = DateFormat.getTimeInstance();
DateFormat fmt = DateFormat.getTimeInstance( DateFormat.SHORT );
DateFormat fmt = DateFormat.getTimeInstance( DateFormat.LONG, Locale.FRENCH );
```

The getDateFormat() method returns the default date format for the default locale. The second version of this method, getDateFormat(DateFormat.SHORT), returns the default date format for the given style for the default locale. The style attribute can be SHORT, MEDIUM, LONG,

FULL, or DEFAULT. The third form of this method, getDateFormat(DateFormat.LONG, Locale.FRENCH), returns the default date format for the given style in the given locale. The getDateTimeFormat() method returns the default date and time format for the default locale. The getDateFormat(DateFormat.LONG, DateFormat.SHORT) method returns the default date and time format for the given date and time formatting styles for the default locale. The next version of this method, getDateFormat(DateFormat.LONG, DateFormat.SHORT, Locale.US), returns the default date and time format for the given date and time formatting styles for the given locale. The getTimeFormat() method returns the default time format for the default locale. The second version of this method, getTimeFormat(DateFormat.SHORT), returns the default time format with the given style for the default locale. The style attribute for the time methods can have the same value as the style attribute for the date methods: SHORT, LONG, FULL, or DEFAULT. The third version of this method, getTimeFormat(DateFormat.LONG, Locale.FRENCH), returns the default time format with the given style in the given locale.

Here are some examples of the DateFormat attributes:

Attribute	Example
SHORT	4/2/97 (completely numeric)
MEDIUM	Apr 2, 1997
LONG	April 2, 1997
FULL	Wednesday, April 2, 1997 AD

The object returned by these functions is usually of type java.text.SimpleDateFormat, which provides a concrete implementation of the abstract DateFormat class. Once you have retrieved a DateFormat object, you can use it to properly format a date or parse a string to find a date.

These field constants are also available in the DateFormat class: AM_PM_FIELD, DATE_FIELD, and DAY_OF_WEEK_FIELD, among others. These field constants are used with the FieldPosition class to help properly align strings formatted with a DateFormat object. For example, if the formatted date is Friday, April 4, 1997, and the FieldPosition class is using the DAY_OF_WEEK_FIELD for alignment, the DateFormat object determines that the day of the week begins in string[0] and ends in string[5]; the FieldPosition object sets its getBeginIndex() and getEndIndex() methods to 0 and 5, respectively.

Table 15.4 lists the important methods in the DateFormat class.

Table 15.4. Methods in the DateFormat class.

Method	Description
format()	Formats the given object into a string; overrides class Format
parseObject()	Parses a string and creates an Object object

continues

Table 15.4. continued

Method	Description
parse()	Parses a string and returns a Number object
getTimeInstance()	Gets a time formatter for a locale
getDateInstance()	Gets a date formatter for a locale
getDateTimeInstance()	Gets a date and time formatter for a locale
getInstance()	Gets the default DateFormat for a locale
getAvailableLocales()	Gets all the locales supported by DateFormat
get/setCalendar()	Gets or sets the Calendar to be used by the DateFormat object
get/setNumberFormat()	Gets or sets the NumberFormat to be used by the DateFormat object
get/setTimeZone()	Gets or sets the TimeZone object for the calendar of this DateFormat object
is/setLenient()	Gets or sets whether this object uses lenient parsing; if lenient parsing is used, the parser will use heuristics to interpret the input; if lenient parsing is off, the parser will use strict parsing rules

 Listing 15.2 shows some examples of the use of the DateFormat class. You can find this code on the accompanying CD-ROM.

Listing 15.2. DateFormatExample.java: A sample DateFormat program.

```
import java.text.*;
import java.util.*;

public class DateFormatExample {

    public static void main( String args[] ) {

        try {
            System.out.println( "Available Locales for DateFormat" );
            Locale availLocs[] = DateFormat.getAvailableLocales();
            for( int i=0; i<availLocs.length; i++ ) {
                System.out.println( "\t" + availLocs[i].getDisplayName() );
            }

            SimpleDateFormat fmt =
                new SimpleDateFormat( "'It is now' H:mm 'on' EEEE',' MMMM d','
                                        yyyy" );
            FieldPosition status = new FieldPosition( DateFormat.DAY_OF_WEEK_FIELD );
```

```
                // format today's date
                Date today = new Date();
                StringBuffer sbToday = new StringBuffer();
                fmt.format( today, sbToday, status );
                int todayOffset = status.getEndIndex();

                // format tomorrow's date
                Date tomorrow = new Date( today.getTime() + 86400000 );
                StringBuffer sbTmw = new StringBuffer();
                fmt.format( tomorrow, sbTmw, status );
                int tmwOffset = status.getEndIndex();

                // format tomorrow+1
                Date tp1 = new Date( tomorrow.getTime() + 86400000 );
                StringBuffer sbTp1 = new StringBuffer();
                fmt.format( tp1, sbTp1, status );
                int tp1Offset = status.getEndIndex();

                // align all dates in column 40 of the screen using the DAY_OF_WEEK
                String spaces = "                     ";
                System.out.println("Dates");
                System.out.print( spaces.substring(0, 40-todayOffset) );
                System.out.println( sbToday.toString() );
                System.out.print( spaces.substring(0, 40-tmwOffset) );
                System.out.println( sbTmw.toString() );
                System.out.print( spaces.substring(0, 40-tp1Offset) );
                System.out.println( sbTp1.toString() );

                // parse a date from a string (reverse-formatting)
                String dateStr = "It is now 16:26 on Tuesday, February 4, 1997";
                Date date = fmt.parse( dateStr );
                System.out.println("Parsing");
                System.out.println( "\t" + date.toString() );

        } catch (Exception e) {
            e.printStackTrace();
        }
    }
}
```

The output of this program looks something like the following. The actual output from your system may vary depending on which `locales` are installed.

```
Available Locales for DateFormat
    Arabic (Egypt)
    Belorussian (Belarus)
    Bulgarian (Bulgaria)
    Catalan (Spain)
    Czech (Czech Republic)
    Danish (Denmark)
    German (Germany)
    <more locales here>
Dates
            It is now 14:37 on Monday, April 7, 1997
           It is now 14:37 on Tuesday, April 8, 1997
         It is now 14:37 on Wednesday, April 9, 1997
Parsing
    Tue Feb 04 16:26:00 PST 1997
```

As you can see, the dates are aligned on the day of the week, and the string we made up is parsed into a `java.util.Date` object, just as we expected!

The `ChoiceFormat` Class

The `java.text.ChoiceFormat` class is a formatter that allows you to attach a pattern to a range of numbers (of type `double`). Its most common use is in conjunction with the `MessageFormat` class to handle cases with plurals (for example, "zero objects," "one object," and "many objects"), although it is certainly not limited to such use.

A `ChoiceFormat` object is specified with a list of ascending numbers (`double`s) that determine the limits to be used. A number X falls into a given interval between `list[j]` and `list[j+1]` if and only if `list[j] <= X < list[j+1]`. If X < `list[0]`, then `list[0]` is used. Similarly, if X > `list[N-1]` (where there are N items in the list), `list[N-1]` is used.

For example, if the list is {`1.0`, `2.0`, `3.0`}, then the following are true:

> 0.5 maps to `list[0]` because 0.5 is less than 1.0 (`list[0]`)
>
> 1.5 also maps to `list[0]` because 1.0 <= 1.5 < 2.0
>
> 2.5 maps to `list[1]` because 2.0 <= 2.5 < 3.0
>
> 3.5 maps to `list[2]` because 3.0 <= 3.5

Along with the list of numbers that determine the limits is a list of objects. The list of objects has the same number of items as the list of limits and contains the items to be used as the formats for the corresponding limits. Although it sounds confusing, it is really very simple. Table 15.5 lists the important methods in the `ChoiceFormat` class.

Table 15.5. Methods in the `ChoiceFormat` class.

Method	*Description*
`applyPattern()`	Sets the pattern for a `ChoiceFormat` object
`toPattern()`	Gets the pattern for a `ChoiceFormat` object
`setChoices()`	Sets the limits for a `ChoiceFormat` object
`getLimits()`	Gets the limits for a `ChoiceFormat` object
`getFormats()`	Gets the formats for a `ChoiceFormat` object
`format()`	Formats an object into a string
`parse()`	Parses a string and creates a `Number` object
`nextDouble()`	Finds the next double greater than or equal to a given value
`previousDouble()`	Finds the next double less than or equal to a given value

Listing 15.3 shows a simple example. You can also find this example on the CD-ROM that accompanies this book.

Listing 15.3. SimpleChoiceFormatExample.java: A sample ChoiceFormat program.

```java
import java.text.*;
import java.util.*;

public class SimpleChoiceFormatExample {

    public static void main( String args[] ) {

        try {
            double[] limits = { 1, 4, 7, 10 };
            String[] seasons = { "Winter", "Spring", "Summer", "Autumn" };
            ChoiceFormat fmt = new ChoiceFormat( limits, seasons );

            for (int i = 1; i <= 12; ++i) {
                System.out.println( "Month number " + i + " falls in " +
                                    fmt.format(i) );
            }

        } catch (Exception e) {
            e.printStackTrace();
        }
    }
}
```

This program prints the following output:

```
Month number 1 falls in Winter
Month number 2 falls in Winter
Month number 3 falls in Winter
Month number 4 falls in Spring
Month number 5 falls in Spring
Month number 6 falls in Spring
Month number 7 falls in Summer
Month number 8 falls in Summer
Month number 9 falls in Summer
Month number 10 falls in Autumn
Month number 11 falls in Autumn
Month number 12 falls in Autumn
```

By letting the formatter do the work, you save the effort of doing many comparisons to determine the season in which a particular month falls. The next section makes it clearer why the ChoiceFormat class is useful.

The MessageFormat Class

The java.text.MessageFormat class provides a simple way to get concatenated messages in a language-neutral (localized) way. A MessageFormat object has a specified pattern and, optionally, a list of Format objects associated with it. A MessageFormat object's specification is of the following form:

15

THE TEXT PACKAGE

```
MessageFormat fmt = new MessageFormat( "The incoming fax from {0} has a total of
                                        {1} pages.");
```

The *string* passed in is called the *pattern*. The pattern is used by the `MessageFormat` object when formatting and is subject to the following set of rules:

1. The syntax `{N}` (`0 <= N <= 9`) indicates that the `Nth` argument in the list of arguments passed to `format()` should be formatted using format `N` (which is specified by calling `setFormat()`). An example pattern for this rule is `"The person's name is {0}"`.

2. The optional syntax `{N, <elementType>}` indicates that the `Nth` argument should be formatted with the `Nth` format, subject to the constraints set by `<elementType>`. The valid element types are `time`, `date`, `number`, and `choice`. If an element type is provided, the formatter assumes that the argument is of the type indicated and throws an exception if it is not. If no element type is provided (as in rule 1 just listed), it is assumed to be a string. A sample pattern is `"It is now {0,time} on {1,date}, and I am {3,number} years old."` The formatter assumes that argument `0` represents a time, argument `1` represents a date, and argument `3` represents a number.

3. The *elementType* can have a style. Valid styles for dates and times are `SHORT`, `MEDIUM`, `LONG`, and `FULL`. Valid styles for numbers are `currency`, `percent`, and `integer`.

Table 15.6 lists the important methods found in the `MessageFormat` class.

Table 15.6. Methods in the `MessageFormat` class.

Method	Description
`get/setLocale()`	Gets or sets the locale for the `MessageFormat` object
`applyPattern()`	Sets the pattern for the object
`toPattern()`	Gets the pattern for the object
`setFormats()`	Sets all the formats to be used by the object
`setFormat()`	Sets an individual format to be used by the object
`getFormats()`	Gets all the formats for the object
`format()`	Formats an object and returns a string
`parse()`	Parses a string and returns an array of objects
`parseObject()`	Parses a string and returns the next object

 Listing 15.4 shows a simple example of how to use `MessageFormat` objects. You can find the code on the CD-ROM that accompanies this book.

Listing 15.4. `MessageFormatExample.java`: **A sample** `MessageFormat` **program.**

```java
import java.text.*;
import java.util.*;

public class MessageFormatExample {

    public static void main( String args[] ) {
        try {
            MessageFormat fmt = new MessageFormat( "The fax from {1} has {0}
                                                    pages." );
            Object fmtArgs[] = { new Long(5), "Joe Schmo" };
            System.out.println( fmt.toPattern() + "; " + fmt.format(fmtArgs) );

        } catch (Exception e) {
            e.printStackTrace();
        }
    }
}
```

The output of this short code snippet is as follows:

```
The fax from {1} has {0} pages.; The fax from Joe Schmo has 5 pages.
```

 Because we did not specify any formats for the particular arguments, the `MessageFormat` object simply substituted `fmtArgs[0]` for `{0}` and `fmtArgs[1]` for `{1}`. Listing 15.5 uses a `ChoiceFormat` object in conjunction with a `MessageFormat` object to create a formatted string. You can find this file on the CD-ROM that accompanies this book.

Listing 15.5. `MessageFormatExample2.java`: **A more complex** `MessageFormat` **program.**

```java
import java.text.*;
public class MessageFormatExample2 {
    public static void main( String args[] ) {
        try {
            // the limits to use for ChoiceFormat
            double[] limits = { 0, 1, 2};

            // strings for 0, 1, and >1 pages
            String[] pages = { "no pages", "one page", "{1,number} pages" };

            // a ChoiceFormat object based on the given limits
            ChoiceFormat chFmt = new ChoiceFormat( limits, pages );

            // senders of faxes
            String[] senders = { "Joe", "Fred", "Mary" };

            // formats to use for the arguments in the MessageFormat
            Format[] testFormats = { null, chFmt };
```

continues

Listing 15.5. continued

```
        MessageFormat messFmt =
                new MessageFormat( "The fax from {0} has {1}." );

        messFmt.setFormat( 1, chFmt );

        for (int i = 0; i < 3; ++i) {

            // an array of Objects to pass to the MessageFormat
            Object[] testArgs = { senders[i], new Long(i) };

            // format the arguments and print out the resulting string
            System.out.println( messFmt.toPattern() + " -> " +
            messFmt.format(testArgs) );
        }

    } catch (Exception e) {
        e.printStackTrace();
    }
  }
}
```

The output of this code is as follows:

```
The fax from {0} has {1,choice,0.0#no pages¦1.0#one page¦2.0#{1,number} pages}. ->
The fax from Joe has no pages.
The fax from {0} has {1,choice,0.0#no pages¦1.0#one page¦2.0#{1,number} pages}. ->
The fax from Fred has one page.
The fax from {0} has {1,choice,0.0#no pages¦1.0#one page¦2.0#{1,number} pages}. ->
The fax from Mary has 2 pages.
```

Collators

The `java.text.Collator` class is an abstract class that provides a common interface for the language-sensitive comparison of strings, text searches, and alphabetical sorting. The `Collator` class hides from the developer the nuances of any individual locale so that you can use the same code in any local setting. Table 15.7 lists the important methods used in the `Collator` class.

Table 15.7. Methods in the `Collator` class.

Method	*Description*
`getInstance()`	Gets a `Collator` for a locale
`compare()`	Compares two strings according to the rules for a `Collator`
`getCollationKey()`	Transforms a string into a set of bits that can be compared (bitwise) to other `CollationKeys` from the same `Collator`

Method	Description
get/setStrength()	Gets or sets the strength of the Collator; legal values are PRIMARY, SECONDARY, and TERTIARY
get/setDecomposition()	Gets or sets the decomposition mode for the Collator; legal values are NO_DECOMPOSITION, CANONICAL_DECOMPOSITION, and FULL_DECOMPOSITION
getAvailableLocales()	Gets a list of locales supported by the Collator class

Basic Collation

Languages throughout the world differ with respect to both the characters they use and the way they treat those characters when comparing and sorting them. There are four areas that apply to correct string comparison and sorting: ordering characters, grouping characters, expanding characters, and ignoring characters. The following sections explain these areas in more detail.

NOTE

Java uses the Unicode representation of strings instead of using multibyte representation.

Ordering

There are three types of orderings: primary, secondary, and tertiary. When you compare two strings, you first do so by comparing characters at the same positions in each string. The first difference in this *primary ordering* determines the order of the strings, regardless of the remaining characters. For example, "deed" is less than "definition". The first primary difference is in the third character, where "e" is less than "f". In languages such as English and German, the primary ordering is in base letters. For example, "a" is different than "b" but is not different from "A". Remember that Java uses the Unicode representation of characters, which is actually a superset of the ASCII character set. Punctuation such as spaces and quotation marks precede numbers, which precede letters in the ordering.

If the primary ordering shows that the strings are identical, the comparison then moves to secondary ordering. In English, the secondary ordering is in the case of the characters. Thus, "apple" is less than "Apple". In this example, the primary ordering of the characters is the same, but the first characters have a secondary difference. In languages such as Czech and French, the secondary ordering is in accents.

Finally, if all secondary orderings are also identical, the comparison moves to tertiary ordering. For example, in Czech, the *secondary* ordering is based on accent marks ("e" is less than "è") and the *tertiary* ordering is based on case.

Groups of Characters

Some languages stipulate that a certain sequence of characters should be treated as a single character. For example, in Spanish, "c" is less than "ch" which is less than "d", because "ch" is treated as a base character in itself and is placed in the ordering between the characters "c" and "d".

Note that the language normally determines when a set of characters should be treated as a single character (as in the Spanish "ch" example), but the programmer can also insert his or her own grouped characters, as we will see later in this chapter with the RuleBasedCollator example.

Expanding Characters

Some languages stipulate that a single character be treated as a sequence of characters. For example, in German, "s" is less than "ß" which is less than "t". In this case, the character "ß" is treated as though it is the characters "ss" for ordering purposes.

Ignorable Characters

Most languages have certain characters that can be ignored when you compare and sort strings. That is, some characters are not significant unless there are no differences in the remainder of the string. In English, one such character is the dash (-). For example, "foobar" is less than "foo-bar" which is less than "foobars".

For any given collation operation, you can specify a strength (PRIMARY, SECONDARY, or TERTIARY). The *strength* of a collation is the highest level at which comparisons are made; differences in levels beyond the specified strength are ignored. For example, if you set the strength of a collation to SECONDARY, any characters that have tertiary differences are reported as being equal. The strength of a collator can be set using Collator.setStrength().

Comparing Strings Using the CollationKey Class

It is simple to compare two strings using the Collator.compare() method. However, the comparison algorithm used by Collator.compare() is very complex. If you are sorting long lists of strings, the operation may be very slow because compare() repetitively compares the same strings. As an alternative, you can use the java.text.CollationKey class, which is a key representing a given string in a collation. You can generate CollationKey objects for all your strings and cache them for use in all comparisons instead of using the strings themselves. Because they are bit-ordered, CollationKey objects allow you to do bitwise comparisons; in addition, once the keys are generated, comparisons are faster than direct comparisons of the two strings.

Table 15.8 lists the important methods in the CollationKey class.

Table 15.8. Methods in the CollationKey class.

Method	Description
compareTo()	Compares the CollationKey to another CollationKey object from the same Collator
getSourceString()	Returns a reference to the actual string which maps to the CollationKey under the given Collator
toByteArray()	Converts the CollationKey to a sequence of bits; used for bitwise comparison of keys

---

TIP

Here is a good rule of thumb when deciding whether to use direct comparison or comparisons using CollationKeys: If you compare the strings more than once, use CollationKeys; if you compare the strings only once, use the direct comparison. Also note that you cannot compare CollationKey objects from different Collator objects.

Decomposition Modes

Decomposing characters is another way of saying *preparing characters for sorting*. Decomposing characters involves the four attributes discussed earlier: ordering, grouping, expanding, and ignoring characters. Decomposing characters is the process of actually applying a language's rules to a given set of characters.

When you are dealing with Unicode characters, there are three decomposition modes to consider:

- **No decomposition.** Accented characters are not sorted correctly. You should use this mode only if you can guarantee that the source text has absolutely no accented characters. ***This mode is not recommended.***

- **Canonical decomposition.** Characters that are *canonical variants* under Unicode 2.0 (such as accents) are decomposed when collated. This is the default mode, and must be used if accents and other canonical variants are to be correctly collated. Canonical variants are letters such as "e" and "è", which differ only in that one has an accent mark.

- **Full decomposition.** Both canonical variants and compatibility variants are decomposed. A *compatibility variant* is a character that has a special format to be sorted with its normalized form, such as half-width and full-width ASCII and Katakana characters.

15

THE TEXT PACKAGE

> **NOTE**
>
> Although NO_DECOMPOSITION is the fastest decomposition mode, it is not correct if accented characters appear. For correctness, it is recommended that you use either CANONICAL_DECOMPOSITION or FULL DECOMPOSITION. To set the decomposition mode for a collator, use the setDecomposition() method.

The RuleBasedCollator Class

The `java.text.RuleBasedCollator` class is a concrete class that provides a very simple `Collator` implementation using tables (hence the name). This class uses a set of collation rules to determine the result of comparisons. The rules can take on three different forms:

- `<modifier>`
- `<relation> <text argument>`
- `<reset> <text argument>`

The definitions for each component of these rules are as follows:

Component	Description
modifier	There is only one modifier, "@", which indicates that all secondary differences are ordered in reverse.
relation	There are four relations. The first three—"<", ";", and ","— mean "greater than" for primary, secondary, and tertiary differences, respectively. The fourth relation is "=", which means "equal."
reset	There is only one reset, "&", which specifies that the next rule follows the position in which the *reset* argument would be sorted. The *reset* argument follows the "&", as in "a < b & a < c". In this case, "a" is the *reset* argument and "c" is placed in the list after "a", yielding "a < c < b".
text argument	Any sequence of characters, excluding "special" characters (those characters contained in whitespace or used as modifiers, relations, and resets). To use a special character within a string, place it in single quotation marks (for example, '&').

Here are some simple examples of rules:

Example	Comment
a < b < c	
a < c & a < b	Equivalent to a < b < c
a < b & b < c	Equivalent to a < b < c
- < a < b < c	' - ' can be ignored because it preceded the first relation

Here are some rules that create errors (and thus throw FormatException exceptions):

Example	Comment
a < b & c < d	c has not been put into the rules and thus cannot be used as a reset argument
w < x y < z	There is no relation between x and y
w <, x	There is no text argument between the relations < and ,

> **NOTE**
>
> The RuleBasedCollator class has a few restrictions for efficiency:
>
> - It uses the secondary ordering rules for the French language for the entire object
> - Any unmentioned Unicode characters come at the end of the collation order
> - Private-use characters (that is, Unicode characters 0xe800 through 0xf8ff) are all treated as identical
>
> These restrictions should be important only to advanced users of the RuleBasedCollator class; they are mentioned here for completeness.

Table 15.9 lists the important methods in the RuleBasedCollator class.

Table 15.9. Methods in the RuleBasedCollator class.

Method	Description
getRules()	Returns a string representation of the rules for the object
getCollationElementIterator()	Gets a CollationElementIterator object for a given string under the RuleBasedCollator
compare()	Compares two strings based on the rules in the RuleBasedCollator
getCollationKey()	Gets a CollationKey for a given string under the rules for the RuleBasedCollator

To explain the use of the `RuleBasedCollator` class, we need a useful example. Many companies assign a "grade level" to their employees; this grade level consists of a letter followed by a number. Our fictional company uses this ordering system: A1, A2, B1, A3, B2, and B3. Additionally, for the A grades, a lowercase *a* represents someone who is in training to become that given grade, but is not quite there. Thus, we define a tertiary difference between a lowercase *a* and an uppercase *A* grade. Listing 15.6 augments the basic United States `RuleBasedCollator` rules with our rules and sorts a list of grade levels using these rules (the code is also located on the CD-ROM that accompanies this book). Note that each of the grade levels is considered by the `Collator` class to be a single group character, not a string of multiple characters.

Listing 15.6. RuleBasedCollatorExample.java: A sample RuleBasedCollator program.

```java
import java.text.*;
import java.util.*;

public class RuleBasedCollatorExample {

    public static void main( String args[] ) {

        try {
            // make a collation with rules from the US
                RuleBasedCollator collUS = (RuleBasedCollator)
                Collator.getInstance(Locale.US);

            // provide the ordering for levels
            // no need to do the C's because they will have a primary difference

            String newRules = "< B1 < a1, A1 < a2, A2 < a3, A3 < B2 < B3";
            String sampleInput[] = { "B1", "a1", "A3", "A1", "B3", "B2", "a2",
                                     "A2", "B1" };

            RuleBasedCollator newColl = new RuleBasedCollator( newRules );
            newColl.setStrength( Collator.TERTIARY );

            CollationKey keys[] = new CollationKey[sampleInput.length];

            // print the original list
            for( int i=0; i<sampleInput.length; i++ ) {
                System.out.print( sampleInput[i] + " " );
                keys[i] = newColl.getCollationKey( sampleInput[i] );
            }
            System.out.println("");

        // sort the list
            for( int i=0; i<sampleInput.length-1; i++ ) {
                for (int j=i+1; j<sampleInput.length; j++ ) {

                    if( keys[i].compareTo(keys[j]) > 0 ) {
                        CollationKey tmpkey = keys[i];
                        keys[i] = keys[j];
                        keys[j] = tmpkey;
```

```
                String tmp = sampleInput[i];
                sampleInput[i] = sampleInput[j];
                sampleInput[j] = tmp;
            }
        }
    }

    // print the sorted list
    for( int i=0; i<sampleInput.length; i++ ) {
        System.out.print( sampleInput[i] + " " );
    }
    System.out.println("");
} catch (Exception e) {
    e.printStackTrace();
}
    }
}
```

The output of the program is as follows:

```
B1 a1 A3 A1 B3 B2 a2 A2 B1
B1 B1 a1 A1 a2 A2 A3 B2 B3
```

Iterators

There are two classes of iterators in the java.text package: the CollationElementIterator, which is used to iterate through each character of an international string; and StringCharacterIterator, which implements the CharacterIterator interface and is used for bidirectional iteration over a given string.

The CollationElementIterator Class

The java.text.CollationElementIterator class allows you to go through each character of an international string and return the ordering priority of the positioned character. The "key" of a character is an integer that comprises the primary, secondary, and tertiary orders for the character. The primary order is of type short (16 bits); the secondary and tertiary orders are of type byte (8 bits). This integer is formed internally to the iterator based on other characters in the string.

NOTE

Java strictly defines the size and sign of the types short and byte. To ensure that the key value for a given character is correct, the function primaryOrder() returns an int (not a short) because we need a true, unsigned, 16-bit number. Similarly, the functions secondaryOrder() and tertiaryOrder() return values of type short (and not byte).

Table 15.10 lists the important methods in the `CollationElementIterator` class.

Table 15.10. Methods in the `CollationElementIterator` class.

Method	Description
`reset()`	Resets the iterator's marker to the beginning of the string
`next()`	Gets the next character from the iterator
`primaryOrder()`	Gets the primary order of the given character
`secondaryOrder()`	Gets the secondary order of the given character
`tertiaryOrder()`	Gets the tertiary order of the given character

 Listing 15.7 provides an example using the `CollationElementIterator` class. It is similar to Listing 15.6 in that it uses the same `RuleBasedCollator` object. As usual, you can find this code on the CD-ROM that accompanies this book.

Listing 15.7. `CollationElementIteratorExample.java`: A sample `CollationElementIterator` program.

```java
import java.text.*;
import java.util.*;

public class CollationElementIteratorExample {

    public static void main( String args[] ) {
        try {
            // make a collation with rules from the US
            RuleBasedCollator collUS = (RuleBasedCollator)
              Collator.getInstance(Locale.US);

            // provide the ordering for levels
            String newRules = "< B1 < a1, A1 < a2, A2 < a3, A3 < B2 < B3";

            // sample list
            String sampleInput[] = { "B1a1A3A1B3B2a2A2B1" };
            RuleBasedCollator newColl = new RuleBasedCollator( collUS.getRules() +
              newRules );

            // sort the list
            for( int i=0; i<sampleInput.length; i++ ) {
                CollationElementIterator iter =
                newColl.getCollationElementIterator( sampleInput[i] );
                int next;
                int count = 0;
                while( (next = iter.next()) != CollationElementIterator.NULLORDER ) {
                    int pri = CollationElementIterator.primaryOrder( next );
                    int sec = CollationElementIterator.secondaryOrder( next );
                    int ter = CollationElementIterator.tertiaryOrder( next );
```

```
                    System.out.println( "orderings for character " + count +
                                        " of string " + i + " are " +
                                        pri + "," + sec + "," + ter );
                    count++;
                }
                System.out.println("");
            }
        } catch (Exception e) {
            e.printStackTrace();
        }
    }
}
```

The output of this program is as follows:

```
orderings for character 0 of string 0 are 96,0,0
orderings for character 1 of string 0 are 97,0,0
orderings for character 2 of string 0 are 99,0,1
orderings for character 3 of string 0 are 97,0,1
orderings for character 4 of string 0 are 101,0,0
orderings for character 5 of string 0 are 100,0,0
orderings for character 6 of string 0 are 98,0,0
orderings for character 7 of string 0 are 98,0,1
orderings for character 8 of string 0 are 96,0,0
```

Notice that characters 6 and 7 have the same primary value (the value 98); this is because a2 and A2 are the same as far as primary comparisons go. However, there is a case difference between a2 and A2 as our rules are written; thus, there is a tertiary difference (the third value; character 6 has value 0 and character 7 has value 1).

The StringCharacterIterator Class

The StringCharacterIterator class implements the CharacterIterator interface for strings. The CharacterIterator interface specifies a protocol for the bidirectional iteration over text, on a range of character positions bounded by startIndex and endIndex-1.

Table 15.11 shows four methods from this class which allow you to manipulate and query the indices of this iterator.

Table 15.11. Methods from the StringCharacterIterator class.

Method	Description
startIndex()	Retrieves the starting index for the given iterator
endIndex()	Retrieves the ending index
getIndex()	Retrieves the index of the character currently being used by the iterator
setIndex()	Changes the current index

Three methods allow you to retrieve the actual characters from the text stored in the iterator:

Method	Description
current()	Returns the character at the current index
previous()	Decrements the index by 1 and returns the character at the new index
next()	Increments the index by 1 and returns the character at the new index

With these seven methods, you can easily find a combination that enables you to iterate through any given string in any manner you choose. In Listing 15.9, we start at position 7 of a given string and iterate through the string in two directions: from position 7 to the end (forward) and from position 7 to the beginning (backward). Finally, we use the java.text.BreakIterator class to break up the string at each word. You can find this code on the CD-ROM that accompanies this book.

Listing 15.9. StringCharacterIteratorExample.java: A sample StringCharacterIterator program.

```java
import java.text.*;
import java.util.*;

public class StringCharacterIteratorExample {

    public static void main( String args[] ) {
        try {
            String source = "This is my string!  Hey there.";
            StringCharacterIterator iter =
                new StringCharacterIterator( source );

            int pos = 7;
            System.out.println( "Starting from position " + pos );
            System.out.print( "\t" );
            for (char c = iter.setIndex(pos);
                    c != CharacterIterator.DONE && iter.getIndex() <=
                        iter.getEndIndex();
                    c = iter.next()) {
                System.out.print( c );
            }
            System.out.print( "\n" );
            System.out.print( "\t" );
            for (char c = iter.setIndex(pos);
                    c != CharacterIterator.DONE && iter.getIndex() >=
                        iter.getBeginIndex();
                    c = iter.previous()) {
                System.out.print( c );
            }
            System.out.print( "\n" );

            BreakIterator bd = BreakIterator.getWordInstance();
            bd.setText( iter );
```

```
            int start = bd.first();
            for ( int end = bd.next();
                    end != BreakIterator.DONE;
                    start = end, end = bd.next() ) {
                System.out.println( source.substring(start, end) );
            }
        } catch (Exception e) {
            e.printStackTrace();
        }
    }
}
```

The output of this program is as follows:

```
Starting from position 7
        my string!  Hey there.
        si sihT
This
is
my
string
!
Hey
there.
```

Summary

Writing inherently international code is not easy; many large software houses spend a lot of money in their efforts to make localization simpler. What the JDK 1.1 provides in the java.text package is a huge first step toward helping all Java developers create clean, international code. Clean, international code, in turn, will help make Java the global language we all want it to be. As the Web grows, we can no longer assume anything about the demographics of those who use what we publish.

This chapter has given you some insight not only into how to use the package, but also into what it means to make a program international and localizable. As a developer, you must shift your thought processes when you write international code; as you do that, the ideas behind the java.text package will become clearer and you will fully understand how to use all the classes described in this chapter. *Good luck! Viel Glück! Bonne chance! Chuk li ho wan! Kou-unn wo Negattemasu! Bueno suerte!*

The Security Package

by Qusay H. Mahmoud

IN THIS CHAPTER

CHAPTER

16

The introduction of worldwide computer networks has led to issues related to communication channels protection. Communication channels are accessible to eavesdroppers, and the only way to enforce protection for those communication channels is to apply cryptography. Cryptography is used to protect information to which illegal access is possible. *Cryptography* is defined as "the science of secret writing."

An Introduction to Cryptography

The Java Security API is based on cryptography. A quick review of some of the concepts of cryptography will help you better understand how the security package works.

In cryptography, the main operation is encryption. *Encryption* is a special computation that converts messages into representations that are meaningless to all parties except the intended receiver. Because there are many encryption algorithms, you have a choice to make—and your choice depends on the sensitivity of the data you want to encrypt. There are two types of encryption: conventional encryption and public-key encryption.

Conventional Encryption

Conventional encryption is also known as *symmetric encryption*, or *single-key encryption*, or *private-key encryption*. Conventional encryption was the only type available before the development of public-key encryption.

In conventional encryption, the process of encryption consists of an algorithm and a key. The *key* is shared between the sender of the message and the intended receiver. The original message, referred to as *plain text*, is converted into scrambled text known as *cipher text*. The output of the algorithm used depends on the key; different keys return different output. Once the message has been encrypted, it can be transmitted. After it is received, it can be converted back to plain text by using a decryption algorithm with the same key used to encrypt the message. Note that the key must be kept secret.

An example of conventional encryption is DES (Data Encryption Standard).

Public-Key Encryption

Public-key encryption is also known as *asymmetric encryption*. One of the main reasons that led to the development of this type of encryption was the problem of distributing the keys (key management) in conventional encryption. In public-key encryption, there are two keys (rather than the one key used in conventional encryption): One is public (can be seen by anyone), and one is private (must be kept secret and only its owner should know it).

An example of public-key encryption is RSA (Rivest-Shamir-Adleman).

Digital Signatures

In the real world, it is easy to differentiate between originals and copies. In the digital world, the task of differentiating between originals and copies is almost impossible because all information is represented as bits. Therefore, in the digital world, we need a mechanism by which one party can send a "signed" message to another party so that:

- The receiver can verify the claimed identity of the sender.
- The sender cannot duplicate the message at a later time.

A digital signature therefore establishes sender authenticity. It is analogous to an ordinary written signature in that:

- It must be able to verify the author, data, and time of the signature.
- It must be verifiable by third parties to resolve disputes.

For digital signatures to be of practical use, they must have the following properties:

- They must be easy to produce.
- They must be easy to recognize and verify.
- It must be computationally infeasible to forge a digital signature, either by constructing a new message for an existing digital signature or by constructing a fraudulent digital signature for a given message.

Public-key cryptosystems provide a simple scheme for implementing digital signatures. However, note that conventional cryptosystems, such as DES, do not in themselves provide sender authenticity because the sender and receiver share the same key.

An example of digital signature is DSA (Digital Signature Algorithm), which is supported by the security API in JDK 1.1.

Certification

One of the limitations of public-key encryption is its inability to verify that a public key belongs to the individual you believe it does. It is possible that a hostile individual can send you a message signed with a secret key, claiming to be from another party. The attacker then advertises a public key; you retrieve that key and decrypt the signature. Believing that you have verified the author, you now trust information written by that hostile source. Thus, there is a need for a certificate and a certification authority.

A *certificate* is a block of data that identifies a user and is signed by a third party, the certification authority. The most common certificate format is the X.509. The X.509 certificate contains standard information about the user name, organization, e-mail address, and so on, along with the user's public key.

Certification Authorities (CA) have four primary functions: to issue new certificates and key pairs to users, to store a copy of each user's private key, to answer queries for users' certificates, and to keep an updated list of revoked and invalid certificates.

Java Security Mechanisms in JDK 1.0

Until now, applets have been one of the most exciting uses of the Java platform. However, the use of applets adds security vulnerabilities to your programming tasks. The automatic distribution and execution of applets makes it likely that software can be obtained from untrusted third parties; because this software is downloaded to the user's machine and run locally, the untrusted software can potentially steal or damage information and files stored on the user's machine.

The beta release of JDK 1.0 introduced the `SecurityManager` class. The `SecurityManager` class defines and implements a security policy by centralizing all access-control decisions. Web browsers such as HotJava, Netscape, and Microsoft IE use the `SecurityManager` class to define and implement their own browser security policies when dealing with applets. When executing untrusted code from an applet, the browser installs its own security manager.

Java protects its users from the dangers of untrusted code by placing strict limitations on applets:

- Applets cannot read from or write to the local disk.
- Applets cannot make network connections to computers other than the one from which they were downloaded.

How Can Cryptography Help?

Encryption can expand the capabilities of applets. If an applet is digitally signed with a public key, you can identify the person who has created the applet. With the Java Security API, you can establish trust relationships. In a *trust relationship*, applets do not have the restrictions just listed and can do the following:

- Read from and write to files residing on your computer
- Make network connections to computers throughout the Internet

Overview of the Java Security API

The `java.security` package lets developers incorporate low-level and high-level security functionality into their Java applications (both applets and standalone applications). The Java Security API provides APIs for digital signatures, message digests, key management, and access control lists. A *message digest* is a condensed form of the original message, produced using a hash function that maps a variable-length message into a fixed-length value called a hash code.

Key management refers to the technique used for the distribution of public keys and the use of public-key encryption for the distribution of private keys. An *access control list* lists users and their permitted access rights to objects.

The JDK 1.1 includes the `javakey` utility for managing keys and certificates and for digitally signing files. The JDK also includes facilities for signing and verifying Java ARchive (JAR) files.

The Java Security API introduces the notion of a Security Package Provider (SPP). A *provider* is a package or a set of packages that provides a particular implementation of a subset of the Java Security API. The Java Security API itself provides mostly interfaces and abstract classes. To put security to work, you need implementations for the interfaces and abstract classes; this is where SPPs come in to play. SPPs are explicitly installed and configured according to the developer's preferences.

The JDK 1.1 comes with a default security provider known as the Sun Security Provider, or SUN. The `sun.security.provider` package provides implementations for the following:

- The digital signature standard
- The message digests MD5 and SHA (Secure Hash Algorithm)

In addition, the SUN provider provides implementations of a simple key system and a trust management mechanism. Note that the `sun.security.provider` classes should not be accessed directly. If the requested security provider is SUN, those classes are instantiated and used by the Java Security API.

The Java Security API Core Classes

The following sections describe the core classes of the Java Security API.

The Signature Class

The `Signature` class is a subclass of `Object`. The `Signature` class provides the functionality of the Digital Signature Algorithm (DSA). Once a `Signature` object has been created, it can be used for two purposes:

- To sign data
- To verify that an alleged signature is in fact the authentic signature of the data associated with it

A `Signature` object can be in one of three states: UNINITIALIZED, SIGN, or VERIFY. Thus, a `Signature` object can do only one type of operation at a given time.

When you first create a `Signature` object, it is in the UNINITIALIZED state. Two initialization methods are defined in the `Signature` class: `initSign()` and `initVerify()`. These methods change the state of the `Signature` object to SIGN and VERIFY, respectively.

Once a `Signature` object has been created and initialized, it can be used to sign data or verify a signature.

Creating a `Signature` Object

Some developers may be interested in implementing other digital signature algorithms (that is, the developer may want to request a particular signature algorithm). If a developer wants to implement a particular signature algorithm, he or she has to provide a Security Provider Package (SPP). Thus, it is possible to call a particular signature algorithm from a particular package.

To create a `Signature` object, the programmer has the choice of specifying an algorithm or both an algorithm and a provider using one of the following methods:

```
public static Signature getInstance(String algorithm) throws
    NoSuchAlgorithmException
public static Signature getInstance(String algorithm, String provider) throws
    NoSuchAlgorithmException, NoSuchProviderException
```

A call to the first method generates a `Signature` object that implements the specified algorithm as the argument to `getInstance()`. If no such algorithm exists, the exception, `NoSuchAlgorithmException`, is thrown.

A call to the second method generates a `Signature` object that implements the specified algorithm supplied by the specified provider. If no such algorithm is implemented by the specified provider, the exception, `NoSuchAlgorithmException`, is thrown. If the specified provider does not exist, the exception, `NoSuchProviderException`, is thrown.

Once a `Signature` object has been created, it must be initialized. As mentioned earlier, a `Signature` object can be in one of three states: `UNITIALIZED` (when the object is created), `SIGN`, and `VERIFY`. The state to which you initialize a `Signature` object depends on whether the object is going to be used for signing data or verifying a signature.

If the `Signature` object is going to be used for signing data, that object must be initialized with the private key of the entity whose signature is going to be generated. You can initialize the `Signature` object to the `SIGN` state by calling this method:

```
public final void initSign(PrivateKey priv) throws InvalidKeyException
```

If the key provided is invalid, the exception, `InvalidKeyException`, is thrown. Once this method is called, the state of the `Signature` object becomes `SIGN`.

If the `Signature` object is going to be used for verifying a signature, it must be initialized with the public key of the entity whose signature is going to be verified. In this case, you initialize the `Signature` object to the `VERIFY` state by calling this method:

```
public final void initVerify(PublicKey pub) throws InvalidKeyException
```

Again, if the key provided is invalid, the exception, `InvalidKeyException`, is thrown.

Signing Data

If a `Signature` object is in the `SIGN` state (that is, it has been initialized for signing with the `initSign()` method), the data to be signed can be supplied to the object by making one or more calls to one of the following `update()` methods:

- `public final void update(byte b) throws SignatureException`
  Updates the data to be signed by byte.

- `public final void update(byte data[]) throws SignatureException`
  Updates the data to be signed using the specified array of bytes.

- `public final void update(byte data[], int off, int len) throws SignatureException`
  Updates the data to be signed or verified using the specified array of bytes, starting at the specified offset.

A `SignatureException` is thrown by any of these methods if the `Signature` object is not initialized properly.

To generate the signature, you simply call the `sign()` method:

`public final byte[] sign() throws SignatureException`

Verifying a Signature

If a `Signature` object is in the `VERIFY` state (that is, it has been initialized with the `initVerify()` method), the data to be verified can be supplied to the object by making one or more calls to the three `update()` methods just described.

Once the updating process is complete, the signature can be verified simply by calling the `verify()` method:

`public final boolean verify(byte signature[]) throws SignatureException`

Listing 16.1 is an example of how to sign a file by using the private key of a signer defined and generated by the `javakey` tool. The example uses some of the other classes' methods, explained later in this chapter.

Listing 16.1. Signing a file with a private key defined and generated by the `javakey` tool.

```
// package java.security
import java.io.*;
import java.util.*;
import java.security.*;

public class SigFile {
public static void main(String argv[]) {
        IdentityScope ss = IdentityScope.getSystemScope();
        Signer sig = (Signer) ss.getIdentity("alice");
```

continues

Listing 16.1. continued

```java
        PrivateKey priv = sig.getPrivateKey();
        PublicKey pub = sig.getPublicKey();
        try {
          Signature signature;
          signature = Signature.getInstance("DSA");
          signature.initSign(priv);
          File file = new File("test.data");
          FileInputStream fis = new FileInputStream(file);
          while (fis.available() != 0) {
            signature.update((byte)fis.read());
          }
          byte[] realSignature = signature.sign();
          System.out.println(realSignature);
          signature.initVerify(pub);
          File f = new File("test.data");
          FileInputStream fx = new FileInputStream(f);
          while (fx.available() != 0) {
            signature.update((byte)fx.read());
          }
          if (signature.verify(realSignature)) {
            System.out.println("Signature checks out");
          } else {
            System.out.println("Signature does not check out");
          }
        }
        catch(Exception e) {
          System.err.println(e);
        }
    }
}
```

To run the program in Listing 16.1, you must first create a file called `test.data`. Put anything you like in that file. Note that a signer with the user name `alice` must exist in the database managed by `javakey`. When you run the program, you should see something like this:

```
% java SigFile
[B@1dc62277
Signature checks out
```

The first line of the output of the program is the signature used for signing the file; the second line tells us that `alice`'s signature has been verified.

The `java.security.Key` Interface

The `Key` interface is the base interface for all keys. The `Key` interface defines the characteristics shared by all `Key` objects. These characteristics are listed here:

■ **An algorithm:** This is the algorithm for that particular key. It is an encryption algorithm such as RSA or DSA. The name of the algorithm of a key can be obtained using this method:

```java
public abstract String getAlgorithm()
```

This method returns the name of the algorithm for that key. A `null` value is returned if the algorithm for this key is unknown.

■ **An encoded form**: This is an external encoded form for the key used when a representation of the key is required outside the Java virtual machine. The key is encoded according to a standard format: X.509. The encoded key can be obtained by calling this method:

```
public abstract byte[] getEncoded()
```

A `null` value is returned if the key does not support encoding.

■ **A format**: This is the name of the format of the encoded key, which can be obtained by a call to this method:

```
public abstract String getFormat()
```

A `null` value is returned if the key does not support encoding.

In addition to the `Key` interface, you should be aware of two other key interfaces that are part of the Security API. The `PrivateKey` interface provides neither methods nor constants. It groups all private-key interfaces. Specialized private-key interfaces such as `DSAPrivateKey` extend this interface.

The `PublicKey` interface provides neither methods nor constants. It groups all public-key interfaces. Specialized public-key interfaces such as `DSAPublicKey` extend this interface.

> **NOTE**
>
> Interfaces are useful for designing reusable object-oriented software libraries and frameworks. The `PublicKey` and `PrivateKey` interfaces are methodless and are used mainly for type safety and type identification purposes.

The KeyPair Class

The `KeyPair` class extends the `Object` class. This class is a holder for a *key pair*—a public key and a private key. This class has two methods: `public PublicKey getPublic()` returns the public key, and `public PrivateKey getPrivate()` returns the private key.

The KeyPairGenerator Class

The `KeyPairGenerator` class is used to generate a pair of keys: a public key and a private key. You can generate keys using `KeyPairGenerator` in two ways: by using *algorithm-independent* or *algorithm-specific* methods. The only difference between the two approaches is the initialization of the object. You must initialize a `KeyPairGenerator` before you can use it to generate keys. Note that algorithm-independent initialization is sufficient for most cases; however, if you want more control over the parameter of the algorithm, you can use a particular algorithm initialization approach.

To generate a pair of keys, follow these steps:

1. Create a `KeyPairGenerator` object for generating keys. This line of Java code creates an instance object of `KeyPairGenerator` to generate keys for the DSA algorithm:

```
KeyPairGenerator keys = KeyPairGenerator.getInstance("DSA");
```

2. Initialize the `KeyPairGenerator`. Before you initialize the `KeyPairGenerator`, you must decide whether you want to generate keys using an algorithm-independent or algorithm-specific approach. For demonstration purposes, let's do it both ways:

Algorithm-independent initialization:

Initialization can be done using `KeyPairGenerator`'s method, `initialize()`:

```
public abstract void initialize(int strength, SecureRandom random)
```

The *strength* argument refers to the strength of the key; the *random* argument refers to the source of randomness—which can be obtained from the `SecureRandom` class, described later in this chapter. If you want to generate your keys with a modulus length of 1024 and an automatically seeded random number, you can use the following code:

```
keys.initialize(1024, new SecureRandom());
```

Algorithm-specific initialization:

As you can see in the preceding line of code, we have accepted the default parameters supplied by the SUN provider. However, if you want to have control over those parameters, you may use algorithm-specific initialization. In this approach, you must set the DSA-specific parameters: p, q, and g. q is a 160-bit prime number. p is a prime number with a length between 512 and 1,024 bits such that q divides (p-1); g is a number of the form $h^{((p-1)/q)}$ mod p where h is an integer between 1 and (p-1).

If you don't want to accept the default values for these parameters, set them yourself. You can do this with the following code:

```
DSAParams params = new DSAParams(p, q, g);
DSAKeyPairGenerator dsaKeys = (DSAKeyPairGenerator)keys;
dsaKeys.initialize(params, new SecureRandom());
```

In this example, we cast the `KeyPairGenerator` object created with `KeyPairGenerator.getInstance()` to a specific algorithm—DSA in this case, because that is what we want to use. The DSA algorithm implements the `DSAKeyPairGenerator`.

3. Generate the key pair using this code:

```
KeyPair pair = keys.generateKeyPair();
```

This statement generates a pair of keys: a public key and a private key. If you want to extract the public key from the pair, use the `getPublic()` method of `KeyPair`:

```
pair.getPublic();
```

To extract the private key, use the `getPrivate()` method of `KeyPair`:

```
pair.getPrivate();
```

Listing 16.2 shows the complete program for using an algorithm-independent initialization.

Listing 16.2. Key pairs generation using an algorithm-independent initialization.

```
import java.security.*;

class Ks {
    public static void main(String argv[]) {
        KeyPairGenerator keys = null;
        try {
          keys = KeyPairGenerator.getInstance("DSA");
        } catch(NoSuchAlgorithmException e) {
          System.err.println(e);
        }
        keys.initialize(1024, new SecureRandom());
        KeyPair pair = keys.generateKeyPair();

        System.out.println(pair.getPublic().toString());  // public key
        System.out.println(pair.getPrivate().toString()); // private key
    }
}
```

If you compile the code in Listing 16.2 and run it, you generate a pair of keys using algorithm-independent initialization. You should see something similar to the following. In this output, the y value refers to the public key, and the x value refers to the private key.

```
% java Ks        # the % is my csh prompt under unix
Sun DSA Public Key
parameters:
p:  fd7f53811d75122952df4a9c2eece4e7f611b7523cef4400c31e3f80b6512669455d402251fb593d8d58fabfc5f
5ba30f6cb9b556cd7813b801d346ff26660b76b9950a5a49f9fe8047b1022c24fbba9d7feb7c61bf83b57e7c6a8a61
50f04fb83f6d3c51ec3023554135a169132f675f3ae2b61d72aeff22203199dd14801c7


q: 9760508f15230bccb292b982a2eb840bf0581cf5
g:  f7e1a085d69b3ddecbbcab5c36b857b97994afbbfa3aea82f9574c0b3d0782675159578ebad4594fe67107108180b4
49167123e84c281613b7cf09328cc8a6e13c167a8b547c8d28e0a3ae1e2bb3a675916ea37f0bfa213562f1fb627a01243
bcca4f1bea8519089a883dfe15ae59f06928b665e807b552564014c3bfecf492a

y:  47006b52c5c2b766f6e6864758f4a79fd4f069317de66a13093f42ac32176217f23d174899dc02ffca009c21f78f77c
4c258bdfa8069fd493148b78da6d5860216793a1b51faa9a7800867bcba912ca762847d30a57f87e4676dff91bbeb0d35c
a2591d4c4293b910435fc552a346fc2bfef921f6b398d1a9531a486fbc28ff0

Sun DSA Private Key
parameters:
p:  fd7f53811d75122952df4a9c2eece4e7f611b7523cef4400c31e3f80b6512669455d402251fb593d8d58fabfc5f5ba30f
6cb9b556cd7813b801d346ff26660b76b9950a5a49f9fe8047b1022c24fbba9d7feb7c61bf83b57e7c6a8a6150f04fb83f6d
3c51ec3023554135a169132f675f3ae2b61d72aeff22203199dd14801c7
```

q: 9760508f15230bccb292b982a2eb840bf0581cf5
g: f7e1a085d69b3ddecbbcab5c36b857b97994afbbfa3aea82f9574c0b3d0782675159578ebad4594fe67107108180b4
49167123e84c281613b7cf09328cc8a6e13c167a8b547c8d28e0a3ae1e2bb3a675916ea37f0bfa213562f1fb627a01243bcca4f1b
ea8519089a883dfe15ae59f06928b665e807b552564014c3bfecf492a
x: 3669898a02adf49267ac1f07fd49952132c133b4

The SecureRandom Class

This SecureRandom class extends Random and provides a platform-independent, cryptographically strong random-number generator. You can create an instance of SecureRandom in two ways: by using the default (automatically generated) seed or by providing the seed yourself. Not surprisingly, then, there are two constructors of SecureRandom:

```
SecureRandom()
SecureRandom(byte[] seed)
```

The SecureRandom class provides five methods for using and reseeding a SecureRandom object:

- `public synchronized void setSeed(byte seed[])`
  This method reseeds the SecureRandom object, where the given *seed* supplements (rather than replaces) the existing seed. Repeated calls never reduce randomness.

- `public void setSeed(long seed)`
  This method reseeds a SecureRandom object using the eight bytes in the given long argument. As with the preceding method, the given *seed* supplements the existing one.

- `public synchronized void nextBytes(byte bytes[])`
  This method generates a user-specified number of random bytes. The array given as argument is filled with random bytes.

- `protected final int next(int numBits)`
  This method generates an integer containing the user-specified number of random bits.

- `public static byte[] getSeed(int numBytes)`
  This method returns the given number of seed bytes,.

You have already seen how to use methods from this class in the example in Listing 16.2.

The Identity Class

The Identity class is one of the key-management classes and is the basic key-management entity. This class represents real-world objects such as people, organizations, and so on whose identities can be authenticated using their public keys.

An `Identity` object has a name and a public key. An `Identity` object may also have a scope, as described in the following section. An `Identity` object also has a set of certificates that certify its public key. The `Identity` class can be inherited so that you can add your e-mail address, an image of your face, and so on.

The `Identity` class has a handful of methods. However, the most important ones are those that return the object's name, public key, and scope:

```
public final String getName()
public final IdentityScope getScope()
public PublicKey getPublicKey()
```

Note that the methods `getName()` and `getScope()` are `final`, thus the name and scope of the `Identity` object are immutable.

The IdentityScope Class

The `IdentityScope` class is a subclass of the `Identity` class. This class merely serves as an abstraction for repositories of `Identity` objects. These repositories can be used, for example, to assign permission and verify classes being loaded. They can also be used by signing tools to retrieve private keys and generate digital signatures.

An `IdentityScope` object is an `Identity` object itself. Thus, an `IdentityScope` object has a name, a public key, and a scope. Note that no two objects in the same scope can have the same public key.

Some of the important methods in the `IdentityScope` class are listed here:

- `public abstract void addIdentity(Identity identity) throws KeyManagementException`
  This method adds an *identity* to this `IdentityScope`. An exception is thrown if the identity is not valid, if there is a name conflict, or if another identity has the same public key.

- `public abstract Identity getIdentity(String name)`
  `public abstract Identity getIdentity(PublicKey key)`
  With these two methods, you can retrieve an identity, given either its name or its public key.

- `public abstract void removeIdentity(Identity identity) throws KeyManagementException`
  This method removes an *identity* from this `IdentityScope`. An exception is thrown if the *identity* is missing.

- `public abstract Enumeration identities()`
  With this method, you can get an enumeration of all identities in this identity scope.

Listings 16.3 through 16.5 show some examples of how to retrieve identities.

Listing 16.3. Retrieving an identity, given its name.

```
import java.security.*;

// retrieve an identity given its name
class ID {
    public static void main(String argv[]) {
        IdentityScope id = IdentityScope.getSystemScope();
        // please see javakey tool below to see how we created the identity "alice".
        Identity d  = id.getIdentity("alice");
        System.out.println(d.toString());
    }
}
```

Compiling and running this program gives an output similar to the following. Note that if an identity with the user name alice has not been created, the program returns an error.

```
% java ID
[Signer]alice[identitydb.obj][trusted]
```

Listing 16.4. Retrieving an identity, given its public key.

```
import java.security.*;

// retrieve an identity given its public key
class ID2 {
    public static void main(String argv[]) {
        IdentityScope id = IdentityScope.getSystemScope();
        Signer sig = (Signer) id.getIdentity("alice");
         // please see the signer class below
        PublicKey pk = sig.getPublicKey();
        Identity d = id.getIdentity(pk);
        System.out.println(d.toString());
    }
}
```

Compiling and running this code gives the following output:

```
% java ID2
[Signer]alice[identitydb.obj][trusted]
```

Listing 16.5. Retrieving all identities in the system scope.

```
import java.util.*;
import java.security.*;

// retrieve all the identities in the system scope
class Ids {
    public static void main(String argv[]) {
        IdentityScope id = IdentityScope.getSystemScope();
        Enumeration e = id.identities();
        while (e.hasMoreElements()) {
```

```
            System.out.println(e.nextElement());
        }
    }
}
```

Compiling and running this program gives the following output. Note that your output will differ depending on how many identities have you created.

```
% java Ids
[Signer]duke[identitydb.obj][trusted]
jane[identitydb.obj][not trusted]
[Signer]alice[identitydb.obj][trusted]
```

The Signer Class

The `Signer` class extends the `Identity` class. The `Signer` class can be used to represent an entity that can sign data. Such an entity must have a public and a private key.

There are two main methods in the `Signer` class:

■ `public PrivateKey getPrivateKey()`
    This method returns the signer's private key.

■ `public final void setKeyPair(KeyPair pair) throws InvalidParameterException, KeyException`
    This method is used to set the key pair for the signer. An exception is thrown if the key pair is not properly initialized.

An example of how to use this class was shown in Listing 16.4, which retrieved an identity given its public key.

The Provider Class

The `Provider` class represents a Security Package Provider (SPP, but *provider* for short). A provider is a package or a set of packages that implements some or all parts of Java security, including algorithms (such as DSA, RSA, MD5, and so on) and key-generation and key-management facilities.

Each provider has a name and a version number. JDK 1.1 comes with a default provider with the name SUN. The main methods in the `Provider` class are listed here:

■ `public String getName()`
    This method returns the name of the provider.

■ `public double getVersion()`
    This method returns the version number of the provider.

■ public String getInfo()
  This method returns information about the provider such as a description of the provider and its services.

Listing 16.6 shows an example of the usage of this class.

Listing 16.6. Using the SUN provider and the Provider class methods.

```java
import java.security.*;

class Supp {
    public static void main(String argv[]) {
        Provider p = Security.getProvider("SUN");  // please see the Security class
                                                    // below
        System.out.println(p.getName());            // name of the security package
                                                    // provider (SPP)
        System.out.println(p.getVersion());         // the version number
        System.out.println(p.getInfo());            // information about the SPP
    }
}
```

Compile and run this code to see the following output:

```
% java Supp
SUN
1.0
SUN Security Provider v1.0, DSA signing and key generation, SHA-1 and MD5 message
digests.
```

The Security Class

The Security class is a subclass of Object. The Security class has two main purposes:

■ To manage security properties
■ To manage Security Package Providers (SPPs)

The Security class provides only static methods and is never instantiated. Thus, the methods in this class can be called only from a trusted program. Here, a *trusted program* refers to either a local application or a trusted applet.

One of the main purposes of the Security class is to manage providers. Thus, this class provides methods to do just that:

■ public static int addProvider(Provider *provider*)
  This method adds a *provider* to the next position available. The method returns either the position in which the provider was added or -1 if the provider was not added for some reason (for example, it is already installed).

■ public static void removeProvider(String *name*)
  This method removes the provider with the specified *name*. Nothing is returned if the provider is not installed.

■ `public static Provider[] getProviders()`

This method returns an array of all providers currently installed.

The small program in Listing 16.7 shows how to get a list of currently installed providers.

Listing 16.7. Getting a list of currently installed providers.

```
import java.security.*;

class Supps {
    public static void main(String argv[]) {
        Provider p[] = Security.getProviders();
        for (int i=0; i<p.length; i++) {
            System.out.println(p[i].toString());
        }
    }
}
```

Compiling and running this program gives the following output:

```
% java Supps
SUN version 1.0
```

The MessageDigest Class

The `MessageDigest` class is an engine that provides a cryptographically secure message digest such as SHA-1 (Secure Hashing Algorithm) or MD5. Message *digests*, or *digital fingerprints*, are used to produce unique identifiers of data. A digest has the following properties:

■ It should be computationally infeasible to find another input string that generates the same digest.

■ The digest does not reveal anything about the input string that was used to generate it.

There are three steps to follow in computing a message digest:

1. Create a `MessageDigest` object by calling this method:

   `public static MessageDigest getInstance(String algorithm)`

   If you want to specify a particular provider, call this method:

   `public static MessageDigest getInstance(String algorithm, String provider)`

2. Update the `MessageDigest` object by making one or more calls to one of the `update()` methods:

   ```
   public void update(byte input)
   public void update(byte[] input)
   public void update(byte[] input, int offset, int len)
   ```

3. Compute the digest (hash) by calling one of the `digest()` methods:

   ```
   public byte[] digest()
   public byte[] digest(byte[] input)
   ```

Listing 16.8 is an example that shows how to compute a digest.

Listing 16.8. Computing a digest.

```java
import java.util.*;
import java.security.*;

// message digest
class Med {
    public static void main(String argv[]) {
        MessageDigest md = null;
        try {
            md = MessageDigest.getInstance("SHA");
        } catch(NoSuchAlgorithmException nsa) {
            System.err.println("Error: "+nsa);
        }
        String alg = md.getAlgorithm();   // what algorithm are we using?
                                          // obviously, SHA

        System.out.println(alg);

        byte b[] = new byte[100];
        for (int i=0; i<100; i++) {
            b[i] = (byte) i;
        }
        md.update(b);
        byte[] hash = md.digest();
        System.out.println(hash.toString());


    }
}
```

Compile and run this program to see the following output. The first line of output is the algorithm used (SHA), and the second line is the hash code generated.

```
% java Med
SHA
[B@1dc607a2
```

The javakey Tool

The javakey tool manages a database of entities, their key pairs (public key and private key), and certificates. The tool is also used to generate and verify signatures for Java ARchive (JAR) files.

The javakey tool always generates signatures using the Digital Signature Algorithm (DSA). In its current implementation, there is one database per user.

The javakey tool manages two kinds of entities: identities and signers. *Identities* are real-world objects, such as people and organizations that have a public key associated with them; *signers* have private keys in addition to public keys associated with them. Note that you can sign files only with private keys—you cannot use public keys to sign files. Also note that before signing files, you must generate a public and private key pair. Using `javakey`, you can either import existing keys or generate new ones for entities and signers.

Entities (identities and signers) have a *user name* in the database managed by `javakey`. The user name is local to the database, so it does not have to be the same user name as your login ID on a UNIX machine, for example. User names can be specified when you add entities to the database. The `javakey` tool has many options you can specify on the command line, as shown in the following examples:

- Create a trusted signer called `alice`:

```
% javakey -cs alice true
Created identity [Signer]alice[identitydb.obj][trusted]
```

- Create a trusted entity called `bob`:

```
% javakey -c bob true
Created identity bob[identitydb.obj][trusted]
```

- Generate a key pair for `alice` using `512` as the key size and writing a copy of the public key to the file `/tmp/pk`:

```
% javakey -gk alice DSA 512 /tmp/pk
Generated DSA keys for [Signer]alice[identitydb.obj][trusted] (strength:512).
Saved public key to /tmp/pk.
```

- Get detailed information about the signer `alice`:

```
% javakey -li alice
Identity: alice
[Signer]alice[identitydb.obj][trusted]
public and private keys initialized
certificates:
No further information available.
```

Certificates

A *certificate* is a digitally signed statement from one signer that says the public key of some other entity (the identity of a signer) has a particular value. If you trust the entity that signed the certificate, then you trust that the association between the specified public key and another entity is authentic.

Generating a Certificate

You must first generate a directive file before generating a certificate. In the directive file, you must supply the following information:

- Information about the signer of the certificate
- Information about the entity whose public key is being authenticated
- Information about the certificate itself
- The name of a file in which to save a copy of the certificate (this is optional)

Listing 16.9 shows an example of a directive file. Note that lines starting with a pound sign (#) are comments. Note that the serial number must be unique to distinguish this certificate from other certificates signed by the issuer.

Also note that in the example in Listing 16.9, the `signature.algorithm` field is missing. This means that we are using the DSA algorithm. If you want to use another algorithm, you must use the `signature.algorithm` field to specify the algorithm you want to use.

Listing 16.9. A sample directive file.

```
# Filename: directivefile
# Information about the signer
issuer.name=alice
issuer.real.name=Alice Johnson
issuer.org.unit=Management
issuer.org=Sekurity Inc
issuer.country=SomeCountry

# Information about the entity whose public key is being authenticated
subject.name=alice
subject.real.name=Alice Johnson
subject.org.unit=Management
subject.org=Sekurity Inc
subject.country=SomeCountry

# Information about the certificate
state.date=1 March 1997
end.date=1 March 1997
serial.number=1002

# Name of a file in which to save a copy of the certificate
out.file=certif
```

To generate a certificate, issue the following command:

```
% javakey -gc directivefile
Generated certificate from directive file directivefile.
```

To display information about the certificate, issue this command:

```
% javakey -dc certif
[
X.509v1 certificate,
Subject is CN=Alice Johnson, OU=Management, O=Sekurity Inc, C=SomeCountry
Key:  Sun DSA Public Key
parameters:
p: fca682ce8e12caba26efccf7110e526db078b05edecbcd1eb4a208f3ae1617ae01f35b91a47e6df63413c5e12ed
0899bcd132acd50d99151bdc43ee737592e17
```

q: 962eddcc369cba8ebb260ee6b6a126d9346e38c5
g:678471b27a9cf44ee91a49c5147db1a9aaf244f05a434d6486931d2d14271b9e35030b71fd73da179069
b32e2935630e1c2062354d0da20a6c416e50be794ca4
y:2bfe2d23d60ce90554965bbb065b910c9fa874fa3b771a21850fd28222706c93409119b42f7d555ff86
c267dae7241a93e97c8a202dbe9f885e642e29bcad441
Validity <Fri Feb 28 16:00:00 PST 1997> until <Fri Feb 28 16:00:00 PST
1997>
Issuer is CN=Alice Johnson, OU=Management, O=Sekurity Inc, C=SomeCountry
Issuer signature used [SHA1withDSA]
Serial number =   03ea
]

Table 16.1 lists the options you can use with the javakey tool.

> **NOTE**
>
> The hyphen before each option is not necessary; however, you are encouraged to use it.
> Note that only one of the following options can be specified for each javakey command.

Table 16.1. The javakey tool options.

Option	Description
-c *identity* {true ¦ false}	Creates a new identity in the database with the user name *identity*. The optional true or false specifies whether or not an identity is to be considered trusted. The default is false.
-cs *signer* {true ¦ false}	Creates a new signer in the database with the user name *signer*. The optional true or false specifies whether or not an identity is to be considered trusted. The default is false.
-t *identityOrSigner* {true ¦ false}	This option sets or resets the trust level for the specified identity or signer.
-l	Lists all the user names in the database.
-ld	Lists the user names in the database with detailed information about them.
-li *identityOrSigner*	Gives detailed information about the specified identity or signer.
-r *identityOrSigner*	Deletes the specified identity or signer from the database.

continues

Table 16.1. continued

Option	Description
-ik *identity keyfile*	Imports the public key in the file *keyfile* and associates it with the specified *identity*.
-ikp *signer pubfile privfile*	Imports the public key in the file *pubfile*, and the private key in the file *privfile*, and associates them with the *signer*.
-ic *identityOrSigner certificateFile*	Imports the public key certificate in the file *certificateFile* and associates it with the specified identity or signer. If a public key is associated with the identity or signer in the database, javakey makes sure that the public key is the same as the one in the file *certificateFile*.
-ii *identityOrSigner*	Sets information for the specified identity or signer. When using this option, you can type as many lines of information as you want; when you are finished, type a period on a line by itself to exit.
-gk *signer algorithm keysize* {*pubfile*} {*privfile*}	Generates a key pair for the specified *signer* using the specified *algorithm* with the *keysize* (strength). The key size has to be between 512 and 1024 bits. Optionally, you can specify a public key file and/or a private key file. If those options are specified, the generated keys are also written in those files. When you use this option to generate keys, you must type some random characters and end with a period on a line by itself. These random characters are used to generate the random number to be used by DSA.

Option	Description
-g *signer algorithm keysize* {*pubfile*} {*privfile*}	This option is a shortcut for the -gk option to generate a key pair for the specified *signer*.
-gc *directivefile*	Generates a certificate according to the information provided in the file *directivefile*.
-dc *certfile*	Shows the certificate stored in the file *certfile*.
-gs *directivefile* *jarfile*	Signs the *jarfile* according to information supplied in the *directivefile*.

Summary

After reading this chapter, you should be familiar with the Java Security API. This chapter introduced you to the important classes from the Java Security API that you can incorporate into your Java-based applications.

Although some of the examples given in this chapter are not full-fledged applications, they do demonstrate how to use the Java Security API. You can find more information about Java security issues in Chapter 34, "Java Security."

The RMI Package

by Eddie Burris

CHAPTER 17

The Java programming language is designed to be a programming language for the Internet. Any language with such aspirations must include native support for communication between programs on different machines. To be more precise, the language must include native support for communication between process address spaces or, when both programs are written in Java, between virtual machines.

The first version of the Java programming language provided support for interprocess communication in the java.net package. The main feature of this package is support for interprocess communication through sockets. The implementation of sockets in java.net was a welcome relief to many programmers struggling with add-on network APIs (Application Programming Interfaces). Although using the Java implementation of sockets is easier than using other implementations, programmers are still required to do a fair amount of work at the application level just to send simple data types between applications.

This chapter discusses RMI (Remote Method Invocation), a new alternative for interprocess communication between Java virtual machines. The chapter is organized around the capabilities RMI provides. Each new concept and capability is explained and examples are given to demonstrate exactly how the capabilities are used in practice.

What Is RMI?

RMI is a term used to describe both the act of invoking a method defined in a different address space and the changes made to the Java language to support remote method calls. The changes made to the Java language to support RMI include new tools, APIs, and runtime support. RMI is part of the core Java programming language that all licensees are required to support.

As its name implies, RMI enables remote method invocations. RMI enables the method of an object in one virtual machine to call the method of an object in another virtual machine with the same syntax and ease as a local method invocation. RMI supports not only the transfer of control between virtual machines but also the passing of objects either by reference or by copy.

RMI supports interprocess communication at a higher level of abstraction. This capability alone makes RMI an attractive alternative to sockets for interprocess communication. However, RMI provides much more than support for passing data types between processes. RMI also provides support for new capabilities such as these:

- Dynamic class loading
- Callbacks to applets
- Distributed object model

Don't worry if you don't completely understand the significance of these capabilities. They are explained in detail throughout this chapter.

Where Does RMI Fit?

We already mentioned one alternative for interprocess communication—sockets. If you are writing a distributed application that requires some form of interprocess communication, there are at least two other options you may want to consider: RPC (Remote Procedure Call) and CORBA (Common Object Request Broker Architecture). The following sections compare RMI to these alternatives to help you decide which is best for your specific situation.

Sockets

Sockets provide a low-level, general-purpose solution to interprocess communication. Because sockets have near planet-wide support, you should have no trouble using sockets for communication in a heterogeneous environment. Sockets support both TCP and UDP transport protocols and are the most efficient method for moving data between process address spaces. However, sockets are not the most efficient solution in terms of programmer time. Sockets require the programmer to invent application-level protocols. For example, to send a sound file, you must decide on a protocol for transferring the binary data. One such method may be to first send the type of file followed by the number of bytes in the file; the program on the receiving end can read just that number of bytes and interpret them as the type of file that was sent.

With RMI, sending a complex data type such as a sound file to a remote process is as easy as passing the data type to an internal method. Because there is some overhead for each RMI method call, sending data using RMI is not as fast as sending the data through a socket. The upside of using RMI is that RMI programs are much easier to write and maintain without the extra code to support an application-level protocol.

Remote Procedure Call

The abstraction provided by RPC (Remote Procedure Call) is similar to the abstraction provided by RMI. RPC makes calling an external procedure that resides in a different address space as simple as calling a local procedure. Arguments and return values are packaged and sent between the local and external procedures to keep the semantics of a remote procedure call the same as those of a local call.

RPC was designed for a heterogeneous environment. In a heterogeneous environment, fewer assumptions can be made about the machine at the other end of the network. For example, because integer byte ordering can be different between machines (big-endian versus little-endian), parameters in RPC must be packaged in an architecture-neutral format before they can be passed to a remote procedure.

Because RMI supports calls only between Java virtual machines, certain assumptions can be made about the communicating processes. These assumptions reduce the overhead associated with a method invocation and make RMI a more efficient method than RPC for external calls.

With RPC, the programmer is limited to passing parameters between external routines. RMI supports passing objects. Remote objects passed between virtual machines support polymorphism and casting between the implementation types supported by the remote object.

Dynamic class loading is another, more powerful capability provided by RMI that is not provided by RPC. With RPC, you are limited to passing only the argument types expected by the destination process. More specifically, you can pass only the data types known to or compiled into the client. When you invoke a remote method with RMI, class definitions can be downloaded from the server at run time. This capability enables the client to execute code and make calls to methods created long after the client has been compiled. (The mechanism used is the same mechanism that supports the downloading of applets to Web browsers.)

CORBA

CORBA (Common Object Request Broker Architecture) defines a specification for a standard heterogeneous object-oriented distributed computing environment. Part of the specification describes an industry standard IDL (Interface Definition Language) that all CORBA implementations must support. A CORBA implementation maps the capabilities defined by the IDL to the capabilities of the specific language environment. The object model of CORBA doesn't provide all the services of any one native language; instead, it defines a subset of services that is reasonable for all languages to implement.

RMI doesn't have an IDL or separate object model for distributed computing. The object model of RMI is the object model of Java. Consequently, RMI supports a feature-rich distributed computing object model. One such feature supported by RMI not supported by CORBA is garbage collection. Programmers writing to the CORBA specification must keep track of objects that are created so that they can be specifically removed when the objects are no longer needed. RMI objects are automatically garbage collected when there are no more references to them.

Another capability exposed by the Java object model but not available in CORBA is the ability to pass an object as its actual type rather than as its declared type. With CORBA, when an object reference is passed from a server to a client, the object must be of a type the client recognizes. If the actual object is a more derived type, the object is converted to the declared type before being sent to the client. With the RMI object model, an object can be passed around and referenced as any of the types implemented by the remote object. The instanceof operator can be used to determine the actual type of the object. If the object is actually of a more derived type, it can be cast back to the more derived type. Any class definitions required for the cast are downloaded automatically by the runtime system. This capability allows you to manipulate objects at a more abstract level.

One capability in the CORBA specification not supported by RMI is automatic object activation. Before you can invoke a method on a remote object with RMI, the object must be active (that is, instantiated) and exported.

Communication Comparison Wrap-Up

When you compare RMI, sockets, RPC, and CORBA, the one you decide is "better" depends on your specific requirements. If you are programming a very performance-sensitive application, sockets may be your only alternative. If you are working in a heterogeneous environment and have to communicate between applications written in different object-oriented programming languages, CORBA may be the best solution.

RMI is the clear winner for Java-to-Java interprocess communication. If you like the features of RMI but have to communicate with nonJava programs, you may want to consider adding a Java front-end to the nonJava destinations. With this Java front-end, or wrapper, in place, you can communicate across the network with RMI and with your nonJava applications by using native function calls.

A Simple Example

One of the best ways to learn about a new programming feature is to see an example. Listings 17.1 through 17.3 show all the code necessary to create a simple but complete client/server application that uses RMI to communicate. The client retrieves a Date object created on the server. The client makes two separate calls to the server to retrieve two Date objects. The difference between the two Date objects is computed to estimate the amount of time a remote method invocation takes.

 The source code for all the examples used in this chapter is available on the companion CD-ROM. You can find the source code for this simple example in the calendar directory.

> **NOTE**
>
> With some distributed applications, it is not always clear which is the client and which is the server. This is especially true with RMI systems because RMI supports a peer-to-peer communication model. For the rest of this chapter, the term *client* is used to refer to the process invoking a method on a remote object. The term *server* is used to refer to the process that created the remote object.

Listing 17.1. iCalendar.java: The interface declaration for a remote object.

```
import java.rmi.*;
public interface iCalendar extends Remote {
  java.util.Date getDate () throws RemoteException;
}
```

17

THE RMI
PACKAGE

Listing 17.2. `CalendarImpl.java`: The remote object and server definition.

```java
import java.util.Date;
import java.rmi.*;
import java.rmi.registry.*;
import java.rmi.server.*;
public class CalendarImpl
        extends UnicastRemoteObject
        implements iCalendar {
  public CalendarImpl() throws RemoteException {}
  public Date getDate () throws RemoteException {
    return new Date();
  }
  public static void main(String args[]) {
    CalendarImpl cal;
    try {
      LocateRegistry.createRegistry(1099);
      cal = new CalendarImpl();
      Naming.bind("rmi:///CalendarImpl", cal);
      System.out.println("Ready for RMI's");
    } catch (Exception e) {
      e.printStackTrace();
    }
  }
}
```

Listing 17.3. `CalendarUser.java`: The client definition.

```java
import java.util.Date;
import java.rmi.*;
public class CalendarUser {
  public CalendarUser() {}
  public static void main(String args[]) {
    long      t1=0,t2=0;
    Date      date;
    iCalendar  remoteCal;
    try {
      remoteCal = (iCalendar)
                  Naming.lookup("rmi://ctr.cstp.umkc.edu/CalendarImpl");
      t1 = remoteCal.getDate().getTime();
      t2 = remoteCal.getDate().getTime();
    } catch (Exception e) {
      e.printStackTrace();
    }
    System.out.println("This RMI call took " + (t2-t1) +
                        " milliseconds");
  }
}
```

Figure 17.1 shows the order in which the components should be created and on which machine they should be placed. As with most client/server applications, both the client and server portions can run on the same machine. This example shows the client and server portions running on different machines to make clear on which machine each component belongs and on which machine each activity takes place. For example, notice that the `rmic` command is used on the server to create the stub file `CalendarImpl_Stub.class` and the skeleton file `CalendarImpl_Skel.class`. Also notice that the stub file is copied to the client before run time. The `rmic` command and the purpose of the stub and skeleton files are explained in a moment.

FIGURE 17.1.

Compilation steps for the Calendar example.

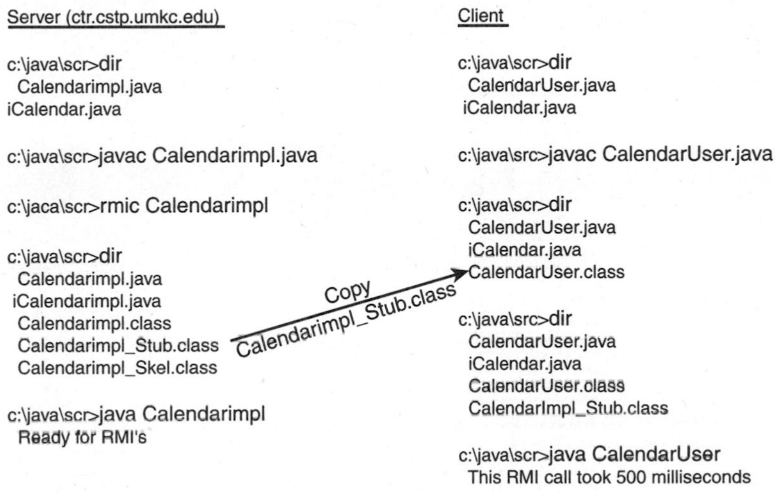

Before looking at the details of this example, here is a high-level description of the application: the `CalendarImpl` class creates and exports a remote object. The `CalendarUser` class looks up the remote object in a registry and calls the `getDate()` method defined for the remote object. `CalendarImpl` defines the implementation for the remote object. A `Date` object is created on the server and a copy is sent back to the client. The `getDate()` method is called twice in succession; the values of the calls are subtracted (with the difference being the amount of time between the calls) to estimate the amount of time a remote method invocation takes.

Listing 17.1 shows the source code for `iCalendar.java`, the remote interface declaration for the remote object. A *remote interface* declares the remote methods for a remote object. A *remote object* is an object with remote methods that can be called from another Java virtual machine.

Listing 17.2 shows the source code for `CalendarImpl.java`, the server portion of the system. The first thing to notice about this code is the new import libraries. The API support for RMI is contained in the four packages `java.rmi`, `java.rmi.server`, `java.rmi.registry`, and `java.rmi.dgc`.

`CalendarImpl.java` is defined as extending `UnicastRemoteObject` and implementing the remote interface `iCalendar`. `UnicastRemoteObject` is covered more thoroughly later in this chapter. For now, it's enough to know that by extending `UnicastRemoteObject`, `ClientImpl` becomes "exported" and is ready to be used outside the virtual machine in which it was created.

CalendarImpl.java defines getDate(), the implementation for the remote method declared in the iCalendar interface. The main() method creates a registry on port 1099 (the default port for registry services), creates an instance of the remote object CalendarImpl, and binds that instance to the name CalendarImpl in the registry just created. Placing an object in a registry makes it available to clients on other virtual machines. Once an object is placed in a registry, any client that has access to the machine with the registry can get a reference to the remote object by specifying the machine name, port number (if it is different than the default port number), and the name given to the object when it was exported to the registry.

> **TIP**
>
> A remote object can be bound to any name in the registry. To prevent name collisions, it's a good idea to use the full package qualified name of an object you export to the registry.

CalendarUser.java (in Listing 17.3) defines the client side of our client/server application. Notice that CalendarUser.java is compiled with the remote interface iCalendar.java (see Figure 17.1). On the client side, the type of a remote object reference must be one of the remote interface types implemented by the remote object. In this simple example, the remote interface class is copied to the client at compile time. In another example later in this chapter, you see how you can use dynamic class loading to transparently copy the remote interface classes at run time.

The first executable statement in CalendarUser.java is a call to the static method Naming.lookup(String url). This method retrieves a reference to a remote object specified with URL-like syntax. In this case, the remote object resides on the machine ctr.cstp.umkc.edu and was bound to the name CalendarImpl. Because no port number is specified, the default port number of 1099 is used. The next two statements in the application are remote method invocations. The objects returned are copies of the Date object created on the remote system. The final statement prints the difference in time between the two Date objects returned from the server.

So far, this example has concentrated almost exclusively on the client and server programmer interfaces that support remote method invocations. We haven't said much about *how* RMI works. To effectively use RMI, you have to look below the surface and learn something about how it is implemented.

One of the advantages of using RMI is the abstraction it provides from the details of interprocess communication. Part of this abstraction is provided by special classes called stubs and skeletons. A *stub* is a client-side proxy that implements the remote methods of a remote object. A *skeleton* is a server-side proxy that accepts a method invocation from a client and dispatches the invocation to the target method on the server. Figure 17.2 shows the relationship between these special classes and the client and server portions of an RMI application. When a client invokes a remote method, there is the illusion of directly invoking the method on the remote object. In reality, the remote method invocation starts as a local method invocation on a stub. The stub packages any parameters and sends the request to the skeleton for the remote object. The skeleton unpacks the parameters that were sent and dispatches the invocation to the target method. The stub and skeleton are also responsible for marshaling any return values.

TIP

A *stub* is best described as a client-side proxy, but the stub for a remote object must also be available to the server process. The stub for a remote object is instantiated when the remote object is exported. When a client makes a request for a reference to the remote object, it is the stub for the remote object that is sent to the client.

Figure 17.2.

Communication layers.

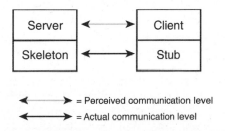

NOTE

Looking at abstraction in network programming is a lot like peeling an onion. Each time you peel away a layer of abstraction, you find another layer of abstraction. Certainly, stubs and skeletons don't communicate *directly*. Beneath the stubs and skeletons is the remote reference layer. The remote reference layer implements the semantics of the server and the specific invocation. Beneath the remote reference layer is the transport layer. The transport layer is responsible for setting up and managing the connection. Currently, only one type of remote reference layer and transport layer is supported.

You must be aware of stubs and skeletons because, when you create a remote object, you also have to create the stub and skeleton for that remote object. Stubs and skeletons are created by the `rmic` compiler. Figure 17.1 shows the stub and skeleton being created for this simple example. Also notice that the stub is copied to the client machine. Later in this chapter, you see how you can use dynamic loading to automatically deliver stubs to clients at run time.

This simple example introduces many of the concepts that are explained in more detail in the following sections.

17

THE RMI PACKAGE

Remote Objects and the Remote Interface

A *remote object* was defined as an object with methods that can be called from another Java virtual machine; a *remote interface* was defined as an interface that declares the remote methods for a remote object. This section gives a more precise definition of both these terms and how they work together to define the semantics of a remote object.

A *remote interface* is a Java interface that extends (directly or indirectly) the interface `java.rmi.Remote`. `java.rmi.Remote` declares no methods:

```
public interface Remote {}
```

The `java.rmi.Remote` interface is used exclusively to identify remote objects. Remote objects must directly or indirectly implement this interface.

A remote object can implement any number of remote interfaces and can extend other remote implementation classes. Java's cast and `instanceof` operators can be used to cast between and test for any of the remote interface types supported by the implementation of the remote object.

Remote objects outside the virtual machine on which they were created must be declared as their remote interface type rather than as their implementation type. The client's interface to a remote object is through the stub generated for the remote object. The stub implements only those methods declared in a remote interface. Only the methods declared in a remote interface can be invoked from another Java virtual machine.

A method defined in a remote interface must have `java.rmi.RemoteException` declared in its `throws` clause. A remote method invocation across a network is fraught with perils. This exception, which extends `java.io.IOException`, provides a mechanism to gracefully handle unlikely but possible failure scenarios.

The remote objects in all the examples we have looked at so far extend `java.rmi.server.UnicastRemoteObject`. However, remote objects aren't required to extend this class. As stated earlier, a remote object is a class that implements a remote *interface*. You should, however, be aware of the semantics inherited by extending `UnicastRemoteObject`.

`UnicastRemoteObject` is currently the only type of server object supported by RMI. `UnicastRemoteObject` provides support for point-to-point active object references. The most important features inherited from `UnicastRemoteObject` are these:

- Automatic export
- `java.lang.Object` behavior

Before a remote object can be passed as a parameter or returned as a result, it must be exported. A remote object that extends UnicastRemoteObject is exported in the constructor of the UnicastRemoteObject class. Remote objects that don't extend UnicastRemoteObject must be exported explicitly with the static method java.rmi.server.UnicastRemoteObject .exportObject().

The other feature inherited by extending UnicastRemoteObject is *correct* java.lang.Object behavior. Remote objects that extend UnicastRemoteObject inherit more appropriate behavior for the equals(), hashCode(), and toString() methods.

To understand why the default java.lang.Object behavior for equals(), hashCode(), and toString() doesn't work for remote objects, consider the following scenario. A server creates and exports a remote object that doesn't extend any other objects and doesn't redefine the equals() method inherited from java.lang.Object. The server receives back from a client a reference to the remote object it exported. The server now has two references to the same remote object: one to the implementation class and one to the stub for the remote object. Because both references are to the same object, you would expect them to compare equally, but they don't. The equals() method for the implementation class is inherited from java.lang.Object and knows nothing about remote objects. UnicastRemoteObject redefines equals(), hashCode(), and toString() to work correctly for remote objects.

The Remote Object Registry

When a client/server system using RMI first starts, there must be some way for a client to get its first reference to a remote object. Once a client has a remote object reference, other remote references can be passed to the client in the form of parameters or return values. A *remote object registry* is the mechanism a client can use to get its first remote object reference.

A remote object registry provides a simple name service that binds a character string name to a remote object reference. A remote object registry has both a client and a server interface. A server can bind, unbind, or rebind a name to a remote reference; a client can look up the remote reference for a certain name. A remote object registry, like other TCP/IP-based tools, listens for requests on a certain port. You can have multiple registries running on the same machine as long as they are listening on different ports. The default port number for the registry is 1099.

> **NOTE**
>
> The remote object registry is not completely open. To bind, unbind, or rebind an object in the registry, you must be running on the same computer as the registry. The simple registry mechanisms provided with the JDK are not intended to be fully featured object request brokers. Instead, they are intended to provide a simple bootstrap mechanism for clients that don't require a lot of security.

There are two ways to start a registry. A simple tool (`rmiregistry`) is provided with the JDK that will start a registry on the specified port. (This tool is described in more detail in "RMI Tools," later in this chapter.) You can also start a registry from within your Java application. The static method `java.rmi.registry.LocateRegistry.createRegistry(port)` will create a registry on the specified port number. A registry created within one Java application can be used by other servers on the same machine to export remote references.

There are two classes for working with remote object registries:

- `java.rmi.Naming`
- `java.rmi.registry.LocateRegistry`

The `java.rmi.Naming` class provides a group of static methods for binding and looking up objects using familiar URL-like syntax. Each method takes a `String` URL in this form:

`rmi://machine:port/name`

For example, the following URL identifies the object named `StudentDB` in the registry listening on port `1098` running on the machine named `ctr.cstp.umkc.edu`:

`rmi://ctr.cstp.umkc.edu:1098/StudentDB`

The `java.rmi.registry.LocateRegistry` class provides a group of static methods for retrieving the registry on a particular host and for creating a registry on the local host. Note that an application is allowed to create only one registry. Although other registries can be running on the host, each process is allowed to create only one registry.

Dynamic Class Loading

The Internet is becoming one of the most efficient software distribution channels ever to be used. On the very day programs are released and made available on the Internet, hundreds of users download and use them immediately. The dynamic class loading capabilities of RMI take software distribution over the Internet one step further by providing support for automatically downloading applications and application components at run time.

To fully understand the dynamic class loading capabilities in RMI, you should know what a class loader is and how it is used during the execution of a Java program.

A Java application or applet is defined by one or more classes. A class can be a system class or one written by the developer of the application or applet. At run time, the classes are loaded into the system for execution. As part of the runtime behavior of a Java virtual machine, *class loaders* are used to load the classes that make up an application. The class loaders give the Java programming language a measure of security and flexibility.

You may already be familiar with two existing types of class loaders: the `AppletClassLoader` and the default class loader.

The `AppletClassLoader` is used to download an applet class and all the classes used directly by the applet. The `AppletClassLoader` follows a well-defined search path as it searches for a class. The local class file is searched first. If the class loader doesn't find a match, it looks for the class at the code base for the applet.

The *default class loader* is used when a Java application is started from the command line with the `java` interpreter. The default class loader looks for classes in the locations designated by the environment variable `CLASSPATH`.

The RMI runtime system introduces a new type of class loader called the `RMIClassLoader`. The `RMIClassLoader` supports two types of dynamic class loading. First, the `RMIClassLoader` can be used to download stubs, skeletons, and the extended classes of parameters and return values. These are the classes that a client may require to make a remote method invocation but that aren't specifically used within the client application.

Second, the `RMIClassLoader` can be used to download arbitrary classes and all the classes used within the class. With this capability, a small bootstrap client application can be delivered to the end user. During execution, this bootstrap client connects to the server and downloads all the classes that make up the application.

The `RMIClassLoader`—like the `AppletClassLoader` and the default class loader—follows a certain search order when looking for classes at run time. The `RMIClassLoader` looks for classes in the following order:

1. The local `CLASSPATH` environment variable.
2. The URL encoded with a local or remote object being passed as a parameter or return value. When local and remote objects are passed as parameters or return values, the URL of the object's class loader is encoded with the object. If the class of the object was originally loaded by the default class loader, the value of the property `java.rmi.server.codebase`, if defined, is associated with the object. If the class was originally loaded by any other class loader, the URL of that class loader is used instead.
3. For stubs and skeletons of objects created in the local machine, the URL specified by the `java.rmi.server.codebase` property is used.

When the locations of class files are specified by a URL, the URL points to a directory on the Internet using standard Internet Web protocols like HTTP and FTP. For example, the following URL points to a directory on a Web server that contains the class files for some objects:

```
http://ctr.cstp.umkc.edu/java/classes/
```

Let's look at how this capability can be used in practice. In the simple example presented earlier in this chapter, the stub of the remote object had to be copied to the client by hand before the client could be started. Now we'll show two ways to copy the stub for the remote object to the client at run time using the `RMIClassLoader`.

The first method relies on the URL's being coded into the stub for the remote object being retrieved from the server. To encode the URL into the stream for the remote object, you must add the following four lines as the first executable statements in the code for the server `CalendarImpl.java`:

```
System.setSecurityManager(new RMISecurityManager());
System.getProperties().put(
        "java.rmi.server.codebase",
        "http://ctr.cstp.umkc.edu/java/classes/");
```

The stub for the remote object (`CalendarImpl_Stub.class`) must be placed in the directory on the server defined by the URL `http://ctr.cstp.umkc.edu/java/classes/`.

Before the `RMIClassLoader` can load a class from a remote source, a security manager must be in place. (The security manager for the RMI class loader is discussed in more detail later in this chapter.) Because the client will now be loading the stub for the remote object over the network, you must add the following line as the first executable statement in the client `CalendarUser.java`:

```
System.setSecurityManager(new RMISecurityManager());
```

 Both the classes `CalendarUser` and `iCalendar` must be copied to—or created on—the client. This time, when `CalendarUser` starts, the `RMIClassLoader` loads the stub from the URL specified in the byte stream for the remote object reference passed to the client. The complete source code for this example is included on the companion CD-ROM in the directory `dynload1`.

The second method for copying the stub for the remote object to the client relies on the property `java.rmi.server.codebase` being set on the client machine at the time a reference to the remote object is requested. This method requires no changes to the server application `CalendarImpl` in Listing 17.2. Instead, you must add the following lines as the first executable statements in the client application `CalendarUser.java`:

```
System.setSecurityManager(new RMISecurityManager());
System.getProperties().put(
        "java.rmi.server.codebase",
        "http://ctr.cstp.umkc.edu/java/classes/");
```

 Notice that these are the same lines we added to the server to set the value of the URL in the stream for the stub of the remote object. When the lines are added to the client application instead of to the server, the `RMIClassLoader` doesn't find a valid URL in the object stream (the second place it looks, as listed earlier in this section). The next place the `RMIClassLoader` looks for the URL is the local `java.rmi.server.codebase` property. Here it finds a valid URL; if the stub has been copied to the directory pointed to by the URL, the remote object stub is downloaded from the server. The complete source code for this example is included on the companion CD-ROM in the directory `dynload2`.

The other type of dynamic class loading supported by the `RMIClassLoader` is the downloading of a complete class and all the classes used within it. The application shown in Listings 17.4 and 17.5 demonstrates this capability.

Listing 17.4. NetworkApp.java: A class to be loaded remotely.

```
import java.lang.Runnable;
import java.awt.*;
public class NetworkApp implements Runnable {
  Frame f;
  public NetworkApp(Frame f) {
    this.f = f;
  };
  public void run() {
    Label l = new Label("Latest version of your application.",
                        Label.CENTER);
    f.add("Center",l);
    f.pack();
    f.repaint();
  }
}
```

Listing 17.5. BootstrapClient.java: A class to bootstrap NetworkApp.

```
import java.lang.Runnable;
import java.rmi.server.RMIClassLoader;
import java.rmi.RMISecurityManager;
import java.net.URL;
import java.awt.*;
import java.lang.reflect.Constructor;
import java.awt.event.*;

public class BootstrapClient {
  public static void main(String args[]) {
    System.setSecurityManager(new RMISecurityManager());
    Frame of = new CloseableFrame("NetworkApp");
    cf.show();

    try {
      URL url = new
          URL("http://ctr.cstp.umkc.edu/java/NetworkApp/");
      Class cl = RMIClassLoader.loadClass(url,"NetworkApp");
      Class argTypes[] = {Class.forName("java.awt.Frame")};
      Object argArray[] = {cf};
      Constructor cntr = cl.getConstructor(argTypes);
      Runnable client = (Runnable)cntr.newInstance(argArray);
      client.run();
    } catch (Exception e) {
      e.printStackTrace();
    }
  }
}

class CloseableFrame extends Frame
      implements WindowListener {
  public CloseableFrame(String s) {
```

continues

Listing 17.5. continued

```
    super(s);
    addWindowListener(this);
}

public void windowClosing(WindowEvent e){this.dispose();}
public void windowOpened(WindowEvent e){}
public void windowIconified(WindowEvent e){}
public void windowDeiconified(WindowEvent e){}
public void windowClosed(WindowEvent e){}
public void windowActivated(WindowEvent e){}
public void windowDeactivated(WindowEvent e){}
}
```

The file NetworkApp.java (shown in Listing 17.4) should be compiled and the resulting class file moved to the directory pointed to by the URL http://ctr.cstp.umkc.edu/java/NetworkApp/.

 The bootstrap application, BootstrapClient.java, should be moved to the client machine and compiled. When started, BootstrapClient downloads the class file NetworkApp from the HTTP server on ctr.cstp.umkc.edu and creates an instance of the class for local execution. The complete source code for this example is included on the companion CD-ROM in the directory netapp.

RMI to and from Applets

RMI also works with applets. An applet can look up a reference to a remote object and invoke remote methods defined for the remote object. Applets can retrieve a reference to a remote object only from the server from which the applet came. This restriction exists for the same reason that an applet can open a socket only on the server from which the applet came. If an applet could set up a communication path between any two hosts, it could create a security risk by opening a communication path to a machine with more restrictive access and tunneling information from outside the network to this otherwise secure machine. For the same reason, applets also are not allowed to listen on a port.

> **NOTE**
>
> The restriction that you can connect only to the server from which the applet came is enforced by the security manager of the applet viewer or browser. Some applet viewers can be configured to relax some or all of the network restrictions.

These restrictions make programming some systems difficult. For example, a common requirement for applets that make up a groupware application is the ability to be notified by the server when some condition changes. Because applets can't listen on a socket, the applet programmer must open a connection back to the server, keep the connection open, and wait to be notified of any updates. One of the design goals of RMI is to allow callbacks to an applet.

A *callback* is a convention used by an object to request notification of a future event. An object that wants to receive notification from a server object of some future event can leave with the server a reference to a method that should be called when the information arrives.

RMI supports callbacks to applets. Rather than opening a connection back to the server, an applet can create a remote object, export it, and send a reference back to the server. The server can make a remote method call on the reference to send a message to the applet.

Compiling and Running the Weather Forecast Application

Listings 17.6 through 17.11 show a complete example that uses callbacks to communicate with applets. The example demonstrates a client/server application for delivering weather forecasts. The forecasts originate on the server and are broadcast to remote applets. Client applets interested in knowing the most up-to-date weather forecast register a callback with the server. When the server detects a change in the forecast, it sends the new forecast to all the clients that have registered a callback with the server. (So that we can focus on the RMI concepts in this sample application, the "forecast" is limited to the current temperature.)

Listing 17.6 shows the interface for the remote object exported by the server. Through this interface, client applets can request the current forecast or register a callback with the server to receive future forecasts.

To register a callback with the server, the client applet creates and exports a remote object and then passes a reference to the server. Listing 17.7 shows the interface for the remote object exported by the client applet. The interface declares one remote method. The server uses this interface to pass a new forecast back to client applets.

Listing 17.8 shows the source code for the server. The server implements the remote methods for getting a new forecast and for registering a callback to receive a new forecast. The server implements the Runnable interface and keeps a separate thread running as long as there are clients waiting for a new forecast. To simulate a fluctuating forecast, the server generates a random number between +3 and –3. If the random number generated is not zero, the number is added to the current temperature to get the new forecast. Client references are kept in a hash table. A *client reference* is a reference to the remote object exported by the client. A new forecast is sent back to the client by invoking a remote method on the remote object.

Listing 17.9 shows the source code for the client applet. The client applet implements a remote interface and is therefore a remote object. The applet exports itself, gets a reference to the remote object exported by the server, and registers a callback with the server.

Because this chapter is about RMI and not about good programming practices, we show how to compile and run the application from a single directory under a Web server. In practice, you will probably want to keep your source code outside your Web server directory tree.

The complete source code for this example is included on the companion CD-ROM in the directory forecast. Copy the contents of this directory (the files shown in Listings 17.6 through 17.11) to a location under your Web server. Run the make.bat file to compile the application and start the server. You can now connect to the server through the applet in this directory. For example, if you copy the files to the directory /java/forecast/ off the Web server root on the machine ctr.cstp.umkc.edu, give the following command to start the applet viewer on the forecast applet:

```
appletviewer http://ctr.cstp.umkc.edu/java/forecast/forecast.html
```

Listing 17.6. iForecast.java: The interface to the weather forecast server.

```
import java.rmi.*;
public interface iForecast extends java.rmi.Remote {
  int  currentTemperature()
      throws RemoteException;
  void requestUpdates(iUpdatedForecast client)
      throws RemoteException;
}
```

Listing 17.7. iUpdateForecast.java: The interface for the callback.

```
import java.rmi.*;
public interface iUpdatedForecast extends java.rmi.Remote {
  void newForecast (int newTemperature) throws RemoteException;
}
```

Listing 17.8. WeatherForecastServer.java: The server and remote object implementation.

```
import java.rmi.*;
import java.rmi.server.*;
import java.rmi.registry.LocateRegistry;
import java.util.*;

public class WeatherForecastServer extends UnicastRemoteObject
      implements iForecast, Runnable {

  private Hashtable clientTable = new Hashtable();
  private Random rand = new Random();
  private Thread notifier = null;
  private int fahrenheit = 0;

  public WeatherForecastServer() throws RemoteException {
    fahrenheit = 78;
  }

  public int  currentTemperature() throws RemoteException {
    return fahrenheit;
  }
```

```
      public synchronized void requestUpdates (iUpdatedForecast client)
            throws RemoteException {
        iUpdatedForecast prevEntry = (iUpdatedForecast)clientTable.get(client);
        if (prevEntry == null) {
          clientTable.put(client,client);
        }
        if (notifier == null) {
          notifier = new Thread(this);
          notifier.start();
        }
      }

      public void removeClient(iUpdatedForecast client) {
        clientTable.remove(client);
        if (clientTable.isEmpty()) {
          Thread thread = notifier;
          notifier = null;
          thread.stop();
        }
      }

      public void run() {
        int newFahrenheit = 0;
        while (true) {
          try {Thread.currentThread().sleep(2000);}
          catch (InterruptedException e) { }
          // Generate a random number between -3 and +3.
          newFahrenheit = fahrenheit + (rand.nextInt() % 4);

          if (newFahrenheit != fahrenheit) {
            fahrenheit = newFahrenheit;
            Enumeration enum = clientTable.keys();
            while (enum.hasMoreElements()) {
              iUpdatedForecast client = (iUpdatedForecast)enum.nextElement();
              try {
                System.out.println("sending update ");
                client.newForecast(fahrenheit);
              } catch (RemoteException e) {
                System.out.println("client passed away");
                removeClient(client);
              }
            } // while client table has more elements
          } // if temperature has changed
        } // while(true)
      } // void run()

      public static void main(String args[]) {
        try {
          System.out.println("main: creating registry");
          LocateRegistry.createRegistry(1099);
          iForecast server = new WeatherForecastServer();
          Naming.rebind("///WeatherForecastServer", server);
          System.out.println("Ready for RMI's.");
        } catch (Exception e) {
          e.printStackTrace();
        }
      } // static void main()
}
```

Listing 17.9. WeatherForecastApplet.java: The applet with the callback.

```java
import java.applet.Applet;
import java.awt.*;
import java.net.URL;
import java.rmi.*;
import java.rmi.server.*;

public class WeatherForecastApplet extends Applet
        implements iUpdatedForecast {
  int currentTemp = 0;

  public void init() {
    try {
      UnicastRemoteObject.exportObject(this);
      URL base = getDocumentBase();
      String serverName = "//" + base.getHost() +
                          "/WeatherForecastServer";
      iForecast server = (iForecast) Naming.lookup(serverName);
      currentTemp = server.currentTemperature();
      server.requestUpdates(this);
    } catch (Exception e) {
      e.printStackTrace();
      return;
    }
    setLayout(null);
  }

  public  void newForecast (int newTemperature) {
    currentTemp = newTemperature;
    repaint();
  }

  public void paint(Graphics g) {
    g.drawString("Temp: " + currentTemp,25,25);
  }
}
```

Listing 17.10. make.bat: The batch file that builds the application.

```
javac WeatherForecastApplet.java WeatherForecastServer.java
rmic WeatherForecastServer WeatherForecastApplet
java WeatherForecastServer
```

Listing 17.11. forecast.html: The HTML file that downloads the applet.

```html
<HTML>
<title>Weather Monitor</title>
<center> <h1>Weather Monitor</h1> </center>
<p>
```

```
<applet
  code="WeatherForecastApplet"
  width=100
  height=50>
</applet>
</HTML>
```

Distributed Object-Oriented Programming

The RMI examples shown so far have focused on using RMI to pass control and simple data types between virtual machines. This section explains how RMI can be used to enable object-oriented solutions in a distributed environment.

Just as C++ can be used as a better C, RMI can be used as an alternative to sockets for moving data between virtual machines. The most significant benefit of using C++ as a programming language is that it enables a new class of object-oriented solutions. Similarly, the benefits of RMI are only fully realized when it is also used to enable object-oriented solutions for distributed computing problems.

An object-oriented solution in a distributed environment is characterized by passing objects—and not just simple data types—between virtual machines. Objects encapsulate both methods and data. The objects can be of the base type or of a more derived type that overrides the methods in the base type.

The example in Listings 17.12 through 17.15 shows an object-oriented solution to the problem of providing personal information to organizations and acquaintances. There are many situations in which you are required to provide personal information about yourself. Ideally, you would have a "smart card" that contains all your personal information that you can pass to the requester. The card has to be "smart" because the type and amount of information you want to divulge is most likely determined by the status and intentions of the requester. In the example shown here, an object with a well-known interface is used as a smart card.

Listing 17.12 shows the source code for the base class of our smart card. Clients are expected to extend the base class and specialize the methods with their own preferences. Notice that the base class implements `java.io.Serializable`. The arguments and return values of remote methods must implement the `Serializable` interface. This interface has no methods defined for it; it is only there to remind the compiler that special information must be saved with the class. This information is used by the runtime system to package and ship the contents of the class across the network. You don't have to write any special routines for marshaling the contents of the class; implementing the `Serializable` interface is all that is required to pass a new class you have defined as a parameter or return value.

Listing 17.13 shows the source code for the interface to the remote object exported by the server. The server exports a remote object with only one remote method. The method is used by clients to pass a smart card to the server.

Listing 17.14 shows the source code for the server. The server has many of the elements discussed in earlier examples. The server is itself a remote object. It creates and exports an instance of itself, and the server sets the codebase property to the location where the client can find the stub for the remote object it exports. The one new element is in the implementation for the remote method. The server expects from the client an object rather than a primitive data type. The server invokes a method on the object to retrieve a primitive data type. Also notice that the server passes some data to the method on the object. In this example, the server passes a primitive data type. In a more realistic example, the server would probably pass another object with a well-known interface.

Listing 17.15 shows the source code for the client. The client creates MyID, an extended class of the smart card base class. This extended class is passed to the server in a remote method invocation. When the extended class arrives at the server, the server searches its CLASSPATH path for the class definition for MyID. Of course, the server won't find the class locally. The second place the server looks is at the location specified in the marshaling stream for the object. Because the client has specified the codebase property, the server will find a URL in the marshaling stream. The client should have copied the class file for MyID to the location defined by the URL specified for the codebase property.

 The complete source code for this example is included on the companion CD-ROM in the directory ID.

Listing 17.12. SmartCard.java: The base class for a smart ID.

```java
public class SmartCard implements java.io.Serializable {
  public String name(boolean commercial) {
    return "(Name withheld)";
  }
}
```

Listing 17.13. iRegister.java: The interface for the registration server.

```java
import java.rmi.*;
public interface iRegister extends Remote {
  void register(SmartCard id) throws RemoteException;
}
```

Listing 17.14. RegistrationServer.java: The registration server.

```java
import java.rmi.*;
import java.rmi.registry.*;
import java.rmi.server.*;
```

```
public class RegistrationServer
        extends UnicastRemoteObject
        implements iRegister {

  public RegistrationServer() throws RemoteException {}

  public void register (SmartCard id) throws RemoteException {
    boolean commercial = false;
    System.out.println("Name: " + id.name(commercial));
  }

  public static void main(String args[]) {
    RegistrationServer rs;

    System.setSecurityManager(new RMISecurityManager());

    System.getProperties().put(
          "java.rmi.server.codebase",
          "http://ctr.cstp.umkc.edu/java/classes/");
    try {
      LocateRegistry.createRegistry(1099);
      rs = new RegistrationServer();
      Naming.bind("rmi:///RegistrationServer", rs);
      System.out.println("Ready for RMI's");
    } catch (Exception e) {
      e.printStackTrace();
    }
  }
}
```

Listing 17.15. RegistrationClient.java: The registration client.

```
import java.rmi.*;

public class RegistrationClient {

  public RegistrationClient() {}

  public static void main(String args[]) {
    iRegister  regServer;

    System.setSecurityManager(new RMISecurityManager());
    System.getProperties().put(
          "java.rmi.server.codebase",
          "http://ehscott.cstp.umkc.edu/java/classes/");
    try {
      regServer = (iRegister)
                  Naming.lookup("rmi://ctr.cstp.umkc.edu/RegistrationServer");
      MyID id = new MyID();
      regServer.register(id);
    } catch (Exception e) {
      e.printStackTrace();
    }
  }
}
```

continues

Listing 17.15. continued

```
class MyID extends SmartCard {

  public String name(boolean commercial) {
    if (commercial)
      return super.name(commercial);
    else
      return "Eddie Burris";
  }
}
```

Security

As a programming language, Java gets high marks for security. From the beginning, Java has supported *applets*—the local execution of classes from remote, unknown, and possibly untrusted sources.

Many of the security capabilities already provided in the language have been adapted for RMI applications. This section identifies the potential security risks inherent in an RMI application, describes Java's built-in capabilities for guarding against these risks, and discusses some options for making RMI applications more secure.

Most security issues in a distributed system fall into one of the following categories:

- ■ **Runtime integrity.** Dynamic class loading allows class files to be downloaded from remote sources. Safeguards are required to ensure that when the methods of these classes are invoked, they don't violate the integrity of the system.

- ■ **Encryption.** During a remote method invocation, data in the form of parameters and return values may be sent across the network. Encryption is wanted when the data is sensitive; it is not wanted when transfer efficiency is more important.

- ■ **Authentication.** For some applications, it may be desirable to allow only authorized users to access a remote object.

Runtime integrity is provided by the RMIClassLoader and RMISecurityManager. The RMIClassLoader is responsible for loading stubs, skeletons, and the extended classes of parameters and return values. For example, if B extends A, and an object of type B is passed to a remote method defined to accept an object of type A, the extended class of A (that is, B) is loaded by the RMIClassLoader. The RMIClassLoader also does bytecode verification on classes loaded from remote sources. *Bytecode verification* is the process of scanning the bytecodes to make sure that they represent a valid Java class. An invalid class can violate the integrity of the VM in many ways. For example, an invalid class could craft a pointer and write to a different stack frame, possibly changing the behavior of another method. An authentic Java compiler does not let you create an invalid Java class, but because the Java runtime environment can't be sure that a "trusted" compiler was used, bytecode verification is done inside the Java VM.

As mentioned earlier, the RMIClassLoader looks for a class file first in the locations defined by the CLASSPATH environment variable, then it looks at the URL encoded with the object being passed, and then it looks at the URL defined by the java.rmi.server.codebase property. If you don't want a specific class to be loaded over the network, you can put it in one of the directories specified on the CLASSPATH environment variable. If you want to be sure of the location from which classes are loaded, set java.rmi.server.useCodebaseOnly to true. If the class isn't found on the CLASSPATH or at the URL specified by the java.rmi.server.codebase property, you get an exception.

Certain system services (such as starting a process or writing to a file) are considered privileged. Before the system performs one of these privileged services, it checks to see whether a security manager is defined. If one is defined, the system queries the security manager to determine whether the requested operation is currently allowed. Before you can load a class from a remote source, you must set a security manager. You can define your own security manager or use the restrictive RMISecurityManager() with this call:

```
System.setSecurityManager(new java.rmi.RMISecurityManager());
```

The default behavior of RMISecurityManager() is to not allow most privileged services if any of the methods on the execution stack belong to a class loaded from a remote source.

RMI doesn't support encryption directly, but it does have built-in support that allows you to add encryption.

RMI uses the socket abstraction for communication. The RMI transport layer requests a client or server socket; subsequent communication is performed through the abstract methods of these objects. RMI supports encryption using a socket factory design pattern.

If you want to communicate over an encrypted channel, you must do the following:

- Define client and server sockets that implement the encryption algorithm you want.
- Create and set a socket factory that returns the client and server sockets you have defined.

The one drawback to this solution is that *all* RMI communication is then done using the sockets you define—including communication with the RMI registry and all clients. It is expected that the next release of the language will contain support for a more flexible method of communicating over a secure channel.

17

THE RMI
PACKAGE

For more information about creating a socket factory, see the documentation for the `RMISocketFactory` class in the `java.rmi.server` package. This class contains the methods for setting a socket factory.

There is really no special support built into RMI to enable authentication. If you want to authenticate clients, you have to build that support on top of RMI.

RMI Tools

There are two RMI-related command-line utilities: `rmic` and `rmiregistry`.

The `rmic` command is used to generate the stub and skeleton for a remote object. It has one required parameter: the package-qualified name of the remote object. Here is an example that shows how to call `rmic`:

```
rmic database.EmployeeImpl
```

A *stub* is a class file used as a proxy on the client side. A *skeleton* is a class file used as a proxy on the server side. The stub is responsible for packaging the arguments of a remote method invocation and passing control to the server. The skeleton on the server side unpacks any arguments and dispatches the invocation to the implementation of the remote object.

Both the stub and skeleton class files for a remote object must be available to the virtual machine that is exporting the remote object. The clients of a remote object need access to only the stub class file. You can copy the stub file to the client or make it available from a URL.

When you create a remote object in one virtual machine, there must be a way for a client in another VM to get a reference to the remote object. The remote object registry is the mechanism for making references to remote objects available to clients. The `rmiregistry` command creates a remote object registry on a specific port. Here is an example of the use of this command:

```
rmiregistry 1088
```

The port number is optional. If you omit it, a remote object registry is created on the default port, `1099`. You can also create a remote object registry from within an application with a call to `java.rmi.registry.LocateRegistry.createRegistry(int port)`. Other processes on the same machine can export remote objects to a registry created with `createRegistry(port)`, but if the process that started the registry terminates, the registry is no longer available.

Summary

RMI expands the scope of the runtime Java object model from a single virtual machine to a collection of networked virtual machines. Remote objects can be created and published through a remote object registry. Clients can retrieve a reference to a remote object and invoke methods on the remote object with the same syntax and ease as they can make a local method invocation. Local and remote objects can be passed between virtual machines. Local objects are passed by copy; remote objects are passed by reference.

Two of the more interesting capabilities enabled by RMI are dynamic class loading and callbacks to applets. Dynamic class loading allows class files to be loaded across the network. Stubs, skeletons, and the extended classes of parameters and return values are loaded transparently. Support is also provided for loading specific classes. You can control how much freedom these downloaded classes have by specifying a security manager.

The freedom to export a remote object from an applet allows applets to register a callback with a server running on the machine from which the applet came. This capability makes writing distributed systems using applets much easier.

CHAPTER 18

The Reflection Package

by Corey Klaasmeyer

IN THIS CHAPTER

The reflection package (`java.lang.reflect`) allows you to peer into the Java virtual machine and gather information about classes and objects. JavaBeans application builder tools make use of these classes as do compilers and debuggers that need access to class-level information. Object serialization classes must also inspect objects to pack and unpack objects. This chapter describes the major classes of the reflection package and their uses.

Java 1.1 added new methods to the `Class` class to support reflection. Although the `Class` class should really be a member of the `java.lang.reflect` package, it remains a member of `java.lang` for backwards compatibility. For this reason, a portion of the `Class` methods are covered in Chapter 10, "The Language Package," as part of the `java.lang` package; the rest of the methods of `Class` are covered in this chapter. This chapter focuses on methods relevant to the `java.lang.reflect` subpackage. The `Exception` classes defined in this package are covered in Chapter 7, "Exception Handling."

The Class Class

The `Class` class plays a central role in the reflection package by providing runtime access to classes and interfaces through `Class` objects. Instances of these `Class` objects are created by calling the static method `forName()` of class `Class`. These `Class` objects are representations, or *reflections*, of their respective classes and interfaces. Methods of the `Class` class return instances of `Field`, `Method`, `Constructor`, `Array`, and `Modifier` classes, which you can then use to access and modify members of the reflected classes and interfaces.

> **NOTE**
>
> The `Class`, `Field`, `Method`, `Constructor`, and `Array` classes all have private constructors. Only the Java virtual machine can create new instances of these classes.

The following methods play important roles in the `java.lang.reflect` classes:

- `boolean isInstance(Object obj)`
- `boolean isInterface()`
- `boolean isArray()`
- `boolean isPrimitive()`
- `int getModifiers()`
- `Field[] getFields()`
- `Field getField(String name)`
- `Method[] getMethods()`

■ Method getMethod(String *name*, Class[] *parameterTypes*)

■ Constructor[] getConstructors()

■ Constructor getConstructor(Class[] *parameterTypes*)

■ Class[] getDeclaredClasses()

■ Field[] getDeclaredFields()

■ Method[] getDeclaredMethods()

The isInstance() Method

```
boolean isInstance(Object obj)
```

The isInstance() method works like the instanceof operator. If the Object argument is not null and can be cast to the type of the Class object without throwing an exception, the method returns true.

```
Object o = new Object();
Class instance = Class.forName("java.lang.StringBuffer");
System.out.println( instance.isInstance( o ) );
```

This code segment prints false because a reference of type Object cannot be cast to a StringBuffer type.

The isInterface() Method

```
boolean isInterface()
```

The isInterface() method returns true if the Class object represents an interface type. The isInterface() method can be used in the following way:

```
Class instance = Class.forName("java.lang.image.ImageObserver");
System.out.println( instance.isInterface() );
```

This code prints true because ImageObserver is an interface.

The isArray() Method

```
boolean isArray()
```

The isArray() method returns true if the Class object represents an array type; it returns false if not. This method can be used as follows:

```
Class instance = Class.forName("java.awt.image.ImageObserver");
System.out.println( instance.isArray() );
```

This example outputs false because the ImageObserver class is not an array type.

18

THE REFLECTION PACKAGE

The isPrimitive() Method

```
boolean isPrimitive()
```

The isPrimitive() method returns true if the Class object represents a primitive type; it returns false if not. The following is an example of its use:

```
System.out.println( Integer.TYPE.isPrimitive() );
```

This example prints true because the final static class variable Integer.TYPE is an object representing the primitive type int. This TYPE class variable is a member of all the type wrapper classes, including the new class Void. In fact, Void contains nothing but the TYPE class variable.

The getModifiers() Method

```
int getModifiers()
```

Although you may guess that the getModifiers() method returns an array of modifiers, it actually returns an int. The static method toString() of the Modifier class can then be used to return the set of modifiers represented by this int value. The following example illustrates this process:

```
Class instance = Class.forName("java.lang.StringBuffer");
int modifiers = instance.getModifiers();
System.out.println(Modifier.toString(modifiers));
```

This code segment prints all the modifiers found in the definition of the StringBuffer class:

```
public final synchronized
```

The getFields() Method

```
Field[] getFields()
```

The getFields() method returns an array of Field objects representing all the member fields of the reflected interface or class. All the public fields of the superclass or superinterface are included in this array. Each of the Field objects in the array represents a single class (static) variable or instance variable. If no public fields are found in the reflected class, an array of length zero is returned. The following example uses the getFields() method to gather information about the Event class; the method returns an array of 74 public instance and class variables:

```
Class instance = Class.forName( "java.awt.Event" );
Field[] result = null;
result = instance.getFields();
for( int i = 0 ; i < Array.getLength( result ) ; i++ ) {
System.out.println( result[i].toString() ); }
```

See the discussion of the toString() method, in the section "The Field Class," later in this chapter for information about what the output from this code snippet looks like.

The getField() Method

```
Field getField(String name)
```

The getField() method returns a single Field object with a name matching the String argument. To find the field with the specified name, the getField() method searches all the public instance fields or static fields of the reflected class or object and all the public fields of the superclass or superinterface. If no fields matching that name are found, a NoSuchFieldException exception is thrown. The following example shows how to find the id variable in the Event object:

```
Class instance = Class.forName( "java.awt.Event" );
Field result = instance.getField( "id" );
System.out.println( result.toString() );
```

In this example, the getField() method searches for the instance variable "id" within the reflected Event class. It finds the field and prints the following information about the field:

```
public int java.awt.Event.id
```

The getMethods() Method

```
Method[] getMethods()
```

The getMethods() method can be used in the same way as the getFields() method just described. Instead of returning Field objects, however, the getMethods() method returns all the public methods of the reflected interface or class and the public methods of any superclasses or superinterfaces. If no public methods are found, the method returns an array of length zero. Here is an example showing how this method is called on a Class object representing the String class:

```
Class instance = Class.forName( "java.lang.String" );
Method[] result = instance.getMethods();
for( int i = 0 ; i < result.length ; i++ ) {
System.out.println( result[i].toString() ); }
```

This example prints out all the public methods in the String class as well as all the public methods of the Object class. The toString() method of the Method class describes more fully how the output from this example is formatted.

The getMethod() Method

```
Method getMethod(String name, Class[] parameterTypes)
```

The getMethod() method returns a Method object representing a method with the same name as the String argument. An array of Class objects is sent as the second argument to the method to distinguish between overridden and overloaded methods with the same names. Because a method signature is defined by number of parameters, types of parameters, as well as order of parameters, the order of the Class objects in the Class[] array parameter is important. If no method by that signature is found, the method throws a `NoSuchMethodException` exception. The `getMethod()` method can be used as in the following example:

```
Class instance = Class.forName("java.lang.String");
Class[] array = new Class[2];
array[0] = Class.forName("java.lang.String");
array[1] = Integer.TYPE;
System.out.println(instance.getMethod("indexOf",array).toString());
```

The fourth line in this code segment is interesting because it uses the new `static final` class variable `TYPE`, which is a member of the `Integer` class. The variable contains a reference to an object of class `Class`, which in this case represents the `int` type. The new primitive `Class` objects are discussed in the example code of the `isPrimitive()` method, presented earlier in this chapter.

The getConstructors() Method

```
Constructor[] getConstructors()
```

The `getConstructors()` method returns an array containing `Constructor` objects. If the reflected class represents an interface or a primitive type or there are no public constructors, an array of length zero is returned. The following example enumerates all the constructors of the `String` class:

```
Class instance = Class.forName( "java.lang.String" );
Constructor[] result = instance.getConstructors();
for( int i = 0 ; i < result.length ; i++ ) {
System.out.println( result[i].toString() ); }
```

This example prints the 11 constructors defined in the `String` class. See the description of the `toString()` method in "The `Constructor` Class," later in this chapter, for details about the formatting of this output.

The getConstructor() Method

```
Constructor getConstructor(Class[] parameterTypes)
```

The `getConstructor()` method returns a single `Constructor` object that represents the constructor member of the reflected class with a matching signature. The name of the constructor is not specified because this name is always the same as the name of the constructor's class. Only the number, types, and order of the parameters determine which constructor is returned. If a zero-length array of `Class` objects is sent as a parameter, the default constructor is returned. If no constructor is found within the reflected class, a `NoSuchMethodException` exception is returned. Interfaces and classes with no `public` constructors also throw this exception. The following example uses this method to find a specific constructor in the `String` class:

```
Class instance = Class.forName("java.lang.String");
Class[] array = new Class[1];
array[0] = Class.forName("java.lang.String");
System.out.println(instance.getConstructor(array).toString());
```

This program outputs the following line:

```
public java.langString(java.lang.String)
```

The getDeclaredClasses() Method

```
Class[] getDeclaredClasses()
```

The `getDeclaredClasses()` method can be used to find the public, private, or protected member classes declared within the reflected class or interface. Inherited member classes are not returned by this method. If the `Class` object represents a primitive type, or the class declares no classes or interfaces as members, this method returns an array of length zero. The following code is an example of the usage of the `getDeclaredClasses()` method:

```
Class instance = Class.forName( "java.net.URLConnection" );
Class[] result = instance.getDeclaredClasses();
```

The getDeclaredFields() Method

```
Field[] getDeclaredFields()
```

Like the `getDeclaredClasses()` method, the `getDeclaredFields()` method returns all the private, protected, or public fields declared by the reflected class or interface (excluding inherited methods). If the `Class` object represents a primitive type or the class declares no fields, this method returns an array of length zero. The following example lists all the declared fields of the `URLConnection` class:

```
Class instance = Class.forName( "java.net.URLConnection" );
Field[] result = instance.getDeclaredFields();
for( int i = 0 ; i < result.length ; i++ ) {
System.out.println( result[i].toString() ); }
```

The getDeclaredMethods() Method

```
Method[] getDeclaredMethods()
```

The `getDeclaredMethods()` method returns all the private, protected, or public methods of the reflected class or interface (excluding inherited methods). If the `Class` object represents a primitive type or the class declares no fields, this method returns an array of length zero. The following example lists all the declared methods within the `URLConnection` class:

```
Class instance = Class.forName( "java.net.URLConnection" );
Field[] result = instance.getDeclaredFields();
for( int i = 0 ; i < result.length ; i++ ) {
System.out.println( result[i].toString() ); }
```

The Member Interface

The Member interface defines a number of methods implemented by the Field, Method, and Constructor classes. Because all these classes are members of classes or interfaces, it is logical that they share some functionality. A detailed explanation of the functionality of these methods is included in this section rather than in each of the classes that implement these member interfaces. Examples of the use of these methods and brief descriptions of their functionality are included in each of the classes that implement the Member interface. Following is a list of the methods defined by the Member interface:

- ■ Class getDeclaringClass()
- ■ String getName()
- ■ int getModifiers()

The getDeclaringClass() Method

```
Class getDeclaringClass()
```

The getDeclaringClass() method returns a Class object that represents the class or interface that declared this member. This method is typically used after the getFields(), getMethods(), or getConstructors() method has returned an array of one of the Field, Method, or Constructor classes. Because these methods return member types from superclasses or superinterfaces, getDeclaringClass() is required to determine the class to which a member field, method, or constructor belongs.

The getName() Method

```
String getName()
```

The getName() method returns a String indicating the name of this member or constructor.

The getModifiers() Method

```
int getModifiers()
```

The getModifiers() method returns the modifiers for the reflected member or constructor. The int returned is an encoded representation of some combination of modifiers in a standard order. The Java virtual machine stores modifiers internally in the same format (that is, as encoded ints). The static toString() method of the Modifier class can be used to translate an encoded int into a string of modifiers.

The Field class

The Field class provides access to the fields of a class or object. The term *field* refers to both instance and class variables. The Field object is typically used to get a field or set a field. This list shows the member methods of the Field class:

- Class getDeclaringClass()
- String getName()
- int getModifiers()
- Class getType()
- boolean equals(Object *obj*)
- String toString()
- Object get(Object *obj*)
- boolean getBoolean(Object *obj*)
- byte getByte(Object *obj*)
- char getChar(Object *obj*)
- short getShort(Object *obj*)
- int getInt(Object *obj*)
- long getLong(Object *obj*)
- float getFloat(Object *obj*)
- double getDouble(Object *obj*)
- int hashCode()
- void set(Object *obj*, Object *value*)
- void setBoolean(Object *obj*, boolean *z*)
- void setByte(Object *obj*, byte *b*)
- void setChar(Object *obj*, char *c*)
- void setShort(Object *obj*, short *s*)
- void setInt(Object *obj*, int *i*)
- void setLong(Object *obj*, long *l*)
- void setFloat(Object *obj*, float *f*)
- void setDouble(Object *obj*, double *d*)

The getDeclaringClass() Method

```
Class getDeclaringClass()
```

The getDeclaringClass() method returns an instance of Class to which the instance or class variable represented by the Field object belongs. If an array of Field objects is received in response to a call to the getFields() method of the Class class, the getDeclaringClass() method can be used to find the declaring class for a particular Field object. For example, if you want to find the Class of the third element of an array of Field objects defined within the Panel class and its superclasses, you can use the getDeclaringClass() method in this way:

```
Class instance = Class.forName( "java.awt.Panel" );
Field[] result = instance.getFields();
System.out.println( result[2].getDeclaringClass().toString() );
```

The output from this example is as follows:

```
interface java.awt.image.ImageObserver
```

The method did not return a Class object representing the Panel class as you may have expected. Instead, it returned an interface-type class called ImageObserver from the image subpackage of java.awt because the getFields() method also returns public fields from the superclass of the reflected class.

The getName() Method

```
String getName()
```

The getName() method returns the name of the instance or class variable represented by this Field object. This example demonstrates the use of getName():

```
System.out.println( result[2].getName() );
```

If we add this line to the example from the description of getDeclaringClass() in the preceding section, the output includes a second line: PROPERTIES. PROPERTIES is the name of the public instance variable contained in the third element of the array of Field objects.

The getModifiers() Method

```
int getModifiers()
```

The getModifiers() method returns an int value that represents the set of modifiers found in the definition of the field represented by the Field object. This example demonstrates the use of the getModifiers() method:

```
Class instance = Class.forName("java.awt.Event");
Field field = instance.getField("id");
System.out.println(Modifier.toString(field.getModifiers()));
```

Because the instance variable of class java.awt.Event is public, this example results in the following output:

```
public
```

The getType() Method

```
Class getType()
```

The getType() method returns the type of field represented by the Field object as a Class object. The following example demonstrates the use of this method on a Field object:

```
Class instance = Class.forName("java.awt.Event");
Field field = instance.getField("id");
System.out.println( field.getType().toString() );
```

In this example, the Field object represents the instance variable "id" of class java.awt.Event. Because its type is int, this code outputs the string "int".

The hashCode() Method

```
int hashCode()
```

The hashCode() method returns an integer representation of the class created by taking the exclusive-OR of the hashcode of the declaring class and the name of the field represented by this Field object. The following example returns the hashcode for the id field in the Event class:

```
Class class = Class.forName("java.awt.Event");
Field field = class.getField("id");
System.out.println( field.hashCode() );
```

The equals() Method

```
boolean equals(Object obj)
```

The equals() method compares two Field objects for equality. The two objects are equal and the method returns true if they both have the same declaring class and the same name. The following example shows a case in which two Field objects are defined within the class Event. Because they both exist in the same class, they cannot be equal.

```
Class instance = Class.forName( "java.awt.Event" );
Field[] result = instance.getFields();
System.out.println( result[2].equals( result[3]  ) );
```

This code outputs false because these two modifiers do not have the same name.

The toString() Method

```
String toString()
```

The toString() method overrides the Object class toString() method. The string returned from this method includes all the modifiers that describe the field represented by the Field object. The modifiers are followed by the return type, package name, and class. The name of the instance variable or class variable is then appended to the end of the class. In this example, the toString() method is called on the second element of the array of Field objects from the Event class:

```
Class instance = Class.forName( "java.awt.Event" );
Field[] result = instance.getFields();
System.out.println( result[2].toString()  );
```

The following output is printed:

```
public final static int java.awt.image.ImageObserver.PROPERTIES
```

In general, this method first outputs the modifier public, protected, or private, then outputs static, final, transient, or volatile, and finally outputs the type. The modifiers are followed by the fully qualified class name, a period (.), and the name of the field represented by the Field object.

The get(), getBoolean(), getByte(), getChar(), getShort(), getInt(), getLong(), getFloat(), and getDouble() Methods

```
Object get(Object obj)
boolean getBoolean(Object obj)
byte getByte(Object obj)
char getChar(Object obj)
short getShort(Object obj)
int getInt(Object obj)
long getLong(Object obj)
float getFloat(Object obj)
double getDouble(Object obj)
```

You can use the get() method to get the value of the instance or class variable represented by a Field object. The Object argument of this method specifies the object from which the value should be taken. The first method always returns a reference to an Object. If the field value contains a primitive type, that type is turned into a reference using an appropriate type wrapper class. The remaining get methods return specific primitive types without wrapping the primitive type. For this reason, they operate more efficiently than the get() method when returning a primitive type.

Java access rules still control access to instance variables. Private variables remain private to an object. If an attempt to access a nonaccessible instance or class variable is made, the get() method throws an IllegalAccessException exception.

In the following example, a value is retrieved from an object of class `Button`:

```
Class instance = Class.forName( "java.awt.Button" );
Field result = instance.getField("label");
Button button = new Button("This is a label.");
System.out.println( result.get( button ) );
```

This example prints the following output:

```
This is a label
```

Because the `label` field of the `Button` class is `protected`, the preceding code has to be declared as part of the `java.awt` package to avoid throwing an `IllegalAccessException`. If the field is `public` rather than `protected`, this is not a concern.

The set(), setBoolean(), setByte(), setChar(), setShort(), setInt(), setLong(), setFloat(), and setDouble() Methods

```
Object set(Object obj, Object value)
void setBoolean(Object obj, boolean z)
void setByte(Object obj, byte b)
void setChar(Object obj, char c)
void setShort(Object obj, short s)
void setInt(Object obj, int i)
void setLong(Object obj, long l)
void setFloat(Object obj, float f)
void setDouble(Object obj, double d)
```

The `set()` method can be used to set the value of an instance variable or class variable represented by the `Field` object. A value is set within the object specified by the `Object` argument. The `set()` method takes a reference to an object as its second parameter; the remaining methods take one of the primitive types as their second parameter. As is true with the get methods, the set methods that return a specific primitive type operate more efficiently than the `set()` method itself because they do not take the extra step of unwrapping the value to be set when dealing with primitive types. The following example shows how the `label` field of the `Button` class can be set within an instance of that class:

```
Class instance = Class.forName( "java.awt.Button" );
Field result = instance.getDeclaredField("label");
Button button = new Button("This is a label.");
result.set(button,"This is a set label");
System.out.println( result.get( button ) );
```

In this example, a `Field` object representing the field `label` is returned using the `getDeclaredField()` method. The `getField()` method would not work in this case because the instance variable is protected. In addition, to gain access to the `label` field, this code segment must declare itself as part of the `java.awt` package. After the `Field` object is created, a new instance of `Button` is created. The `set()` method sets the `label` field of this object to a new value by passing a reference to the `Button` object as the first parameter and the new value as the second parameter. In a call to the `set()` method, if the second value happens to be an object of some primitive type, the object is automatically unwrapped. The new value in the `label` field is then printed by accessing the `Field` object with the `get()` method. The example prints the following line:

```
This is a set label
```

The Method Class

The `Method` class provides access to a method of a class or interface. The method represented by the `Method` object can be an `abstract`, `static`, or `instance` method. As with the `Field` and `Class` classes, instances of the `Method` class can be created only by the Java virtual machine; these instances are always `final`. The `Method` object can be used to get information about the reflected method; the `Method` object can also be used to invoke that method on an instance of the declaring class. All the methods of the `Method` class are listed here:

- `Class getDeclaringClass()`
- `String getName()`
- `int getModifiers()`
- `Class getReturnType()`
- `Class[] getParameterTypes()`
- `Class[] getExceptionTypes()`
- `boolean equals(Object obj)`
- `int hashCode()`
- `String toString()`
- `Object invoke(Object obj, Object[] args)`

The getDeclaringClass() Method

```
Class getDeclaringClass()
```

The `getDeclaringClass()` method returns a `Class` object that represents the class in which the reflected method is declared. This method can be used as in this example:

```
Class instance = Class.forName("java.lang.String");
Class[] array = new Class[2];
array[0] = Class.forName("java.lang.String");
array[1] = Integer.TYPE;
Method method = instance.getMethod("indexOf",array);
System.out.println(method.getDeclaringClass().getName());
```

In this example, `getDeclaringClass()` returns a `Class` object representing the declaring class for the `indexOf(String, int)` method of the `String` class. The name of the class is printed as output:

```
java.lang.String
```

NOTE

The first four lines of code in the preceding example are used in the descriptions of the rest of the methods of the Method class.

The getName() Method

```
String getName()
```

The getName() method returns the name of the reflected method as a string. The getName() method can be used as follows:

```
System.out.println( method.getName() );
```

If the variable method reflects the indexOf(String, int) method of the String class (refer back to the getDeclaringClass() example), this code segment prints the name of the method:

```
indexOf
```

The getModifiers() Method

```
int getModifiers()
```

The getModifiers() method returns an int representing the set of modifiers that belongs to the reflected method. This method can be used in the following way:

```
System.out.println(Modifier.toString(method.getModifiers()));
```

If the variable method reflects the indexOf(String, int) method of the String class (refer back to the getDeclaringClass() example), this code segment prints the modifiers of this method:

```
public
```

The getReturnType() Method

```
Class getReturnType()
```

The getReturnType() method returns a Class object representing the return type for the reflected method. The following example demonstrates how this method can be used:

```
System.out.println(method.getReturnType().toString());
```

If the variable method reflects the indexOf(String, int) method of the String class (refer back to the getDeclaringClass() example), this code segment prints the return type of this method:

```
int
```

18

THE REFLECTION
PACKAGE

The getParameterTypes() Method

```
Class[] getParameterTypes()
```

The getParameterTypes() method returns an array of Class objects that represent the order and types of the parameters in the reflected method. The method is used as follows:

```
Class[] params = method.getParameterTypes();
for(int c=0;c<params.length;c++)
{System.out.println(params[c].toString());}
```

If the variable method reflects the indexOf(String, int) method of the String class (refer back to the getDeclaringClass() example), this code segment prints the parameter types of this method in the correct order:

```
class java.lang.String
int
```

The getExceptionTypes() Method

```
Class[] getExceptionTypes()
```

The getExceptionTypes() method returns an array of Class objects that represent the exceptions thrown by the reflected method. This method can be used as follows:

```
Class[] params = method.getExceptionTypes();
for(int c=0;c<params.length;c++)
{System.out.println(params[c].toString());}
```

If the variable method reflects the indexOf(String, int) method of the String class (refer back to the getDeclaringClass() example), this code segment prints nothing because the reflected method throws no exceptions and an array of length zero is returned from the getParameterTypes() method.

The equals() Method

```
boolean equals(Object obj)
```

The equals() method tests two Method objects for equality. Two Method objects are equal if they have the same declaring class, name, and formal parameter types.

The hashCode() Method

```
int hashCode()
```

The hashCode() method returns a hashcode for the reflected method. The *hashcode* is an exclusive-OR of the hashcodes of the reflected method's declaring class and the reflected method's name. The following example demonstrates how this method can be used:

```
System.out.println( method.hashCode() );
```

If the variable `method` reflects the `indexOf(String, int)` method of the `String` class (refer back to the `getDeclaringClass()` example), this code segment prints the following:

```
74190650
```

The `toString()` Method

```
String toString()
```

The `toString()` method returns a string representation of the reflected field with modifiers, return type, package name, method name, and parameters.

In general, this method first outputs the modifier `public`, `protected`, or `private`, then outputs `static`, `final`, `transient`, or `volatile`, and finally outputs the return type. The modifiers are followed by a fully qualified class name, a period (.), and the name of the method represented by this `Method` object. A set of parentheses at the end encloses a list of fully qualified type names representing the methods parameter list. Finally, the word `throws` is tacked on to the end with a comma-separated list of all the exceptions thrown by this method. The following example shows how the `toString()` method can be used:

```
System.out.println( method.toString() );
```

If the variable `method` reflects the `indexOf(String, int)` method of the `String` class (refer back to the `getDeclaringClass()` example), this code segment prints this line:

```
public int java.lang.String.indexOf(java.lang.String, int)
```

The `invoke()` Method

```
Object invoke(Object obj, Object[] args)
```

The `invoke()` method is used to call a method on an object. The object name is passed as the first parameter to the method. The second parameter is an array with the arguments to be sent to the method. The following example shows how this method is used:

```
String string = new String("The day's soma ration");
Object[] arguments = { "soma", new Integer(0) };
System.out.println(method.invoke(string,arguments));
```

If the variable `method` reflects the `indexOf(String, int)` method of the `String` class (refer back to the `getDeclaringClass()` example), this code segment prints `10` because the word `soma` is found at position 10 in the string `The day's soma ration`.

The Constructor Class

The `Constructor` class provides access to a constructor of a class. Instances of the `Constructor` class can be created only by the Java virtual machine; these instances are always `final`. The

Constructor object can be used to get information about the reflected constructor or to create new instances of the declaring class. All the methods of the Constructor class are listed here:

- ▪ Class getDeclaringClass()
- ▪ String getName()
- ▪ int getModifiers()
- ▪ Class[] getParameterTypes()
- ▪ Class[] getExceptionTypes()
- ▪ boolean equals(Object *obj*)
- ▪ int hashCode()
- ▪ String toString()
- ▪ Object newInstance(Object *initargs*[])

The getDeclaringClass() Method

```
Class getDeclaringClass()
```

The getDeclaringClass() method returns a Class object representing the class in which the reflected constructor is declared. This method can be used as follows:

```
Class instance = Class.forName("java.lang.String");
Constructor[] constructors = instance.getConstructors();
System.out.println(constructors[0].getDeclaringClass().getName());
```

In this example, the getDeclaringClass() method is called on the first Constructor object in the array. The getName() method of the Class object name returns java.lang.String.

> **NOTE**
>
> The first two lines of code in this example are used in the descriptions of the rest of the methods of the Constructor class.

The getName() Method

```
String getName()
```

The getName() method returns the name of the constructor reflected by the Constructor object. This is the same name as the declaring class. The getName() method in the following example returns the string java.lang.String:

```
Class instance = Class.forName("java.lang.String");
Constructor[] constructors = instance.getConstructors();
System.out.println(constructors[0].getName());
```

The getModifiers() Method

```
int getModifiers()
```

The getModifiers() method returns an int that represents the modifiers for the constructor reflected by this Constructor object. The following example prints public as the modifier for the first constructor from the java.lang.String class:

```
Class instance = Class.forName("java.lang.String");
Constructor[] constructors = instance.getConstructors();
System.out.println(Modifier.toString(constructors[0].getModifiers()));
```

The getParameterTypes() Method

```
Class[] getParameterTypes()
```

The getParameterTypes() method returns an ordered list of all the parameters of a constructor in an array of Class objects. The following example shows how the getParameterTypes() method is used:

```
Class instance = Class.forName("java.lang.String");
Constructor[] constructors = instance.getConstructors();
Class[] parameters = constructors[1].getParameterTypes();
System.out.println(parameters[0].getName());
```

The only parameter in the second constructor in the String class is a String parameter type. This method prints the following output:

```
java.lang.String
```

The getExceptionTypes() Method

```
Class[] getExceptionTypes()
```

The getExceptionTypes() method returns an array of Class objects that represent the exceptions thrown by the reflected constructor. This method is used as follows:

```
System.out.println(constructor.getExceptionTypes());
```

The equals() Method

```
boolean equals(Object obj)
```

The equals() method returns true if the Constructor objects are equal; that is, if they have the same declaring class and the same parameter types, order, and number. The method is used as follows:

```
System.out.println(constructor1.equals(constructor2));
```

This example outputs true if constructor1 and constructor2 meet the conditions for equality. If not, the method outputs false.

The hashCode() Method

```
int hashCode()
```

The `hashCode()` method overrides the `hashCode()` method defined in class `Object` and returns a hashcode. The returned hashcode is the same as the hashcode of the declaring class. This method is used as shown here:

```
System.out.println(constructor1.hashCode());
```

This example prints the hashcode representing the `constructor1` `Constructor` object.

The toString() Method

```
String toString()
```

The `toString()` method returns a string representation of the constructor reflected by this `Constructor` object. An example of the use and format of the output string is shown here:

```
Class instance = Class.forName("java.lang.String");
Constructor[] constructors = instance.getConstructors();
System.out.println(constructors[0].toString());
```

This example sends the following output:

```
public java.lang.String()
```

In general, this method first outputs the modifier `public`, `protected`, or `private`, and then outputs `static`, `final`, `transient`, or `volatile`. The modifiers are followed by a fully qualified class name, a period (.), and the name of the method represented by this `Method` object. A set of parentheses at the end encloses a list of fully qualified type names representing the method's parameter list. Finally, the word `throws` is tacked on to the end with a comma-separated list of all the exceptions thrown by this method.

The newInstance() Method

```
public Object newInstance(Object initargs[]))
```

The `newInstance()` method can be used to create a new instance of the `Constructor` object's declaring class. The method cannot instantiate instances of abstract classes or create a new instance with a constructor that has been declared `private`. The new object is returned if the number of the arguments match.

```
Class instance = Class.forName("java.lang.String");
Constructor[] constructors = instance.getConstructors();
Object[] arguments = { "We made a new object!" };
String newObject = (String)constructors[1].newInstance(arguments);
System.out.println( newObject );
```

In the preceding example, all the constructors that belong to class `String` are stored in the array `constructors`. The second array element (at index 1) contains the `String` constructor that takes a string argument. To instantiate the new object, the arguments must be specified in an array of type Object[]. The first element of this array is set to the string that is used to construct the new String class. Finally, the new instance is created by calling the newInstance() method of the appropriate constructor object; the result is stored in the identifier newObject. This is a convoluted way to send the following output:

```
We made a new object!
```

The Array Class

The Array class provides access to array objects and classes. The following methods can be used to instantiate new array objects and to access or modify elements within arrays:

- Object newInstance(Class *componentType*, int *length*)
- int getLength(Object *array*)
- int get(Object *array*, int *index*)
- boolean getBoolean(Object *array*, int *index*)
- byte getByte(Object *array*, int *index*)
- char getChar(Object *array*, int *index*)
- short getShort(Object *array*, int *index*)
- int getInt(Object *array*, int *index*)
- long getLong(Object *array*, int *index*)
- float getFloat(Object *array*, int *index*)
- double getDouble(Object *array*, int *index*)
- void set(Object *array*, int *index*, Object *value*)
- void setBoolean(Object *array*, int *index*, boolean *z*)
- void setByte(Object *array*, int *index*, byte *b*)
- void setChar(Object *array*, int *index*, char *c*)
- void setShort(Object *array*, int *index*, short *s*)
- void setInt(Object *array*, int *index*, int *i*)
- void setLong(Object *array*, int *index*, long *l*)
- void setFloat(Object *array*, int *index*, float *f*)
- void setDouble(Object *array*, int *index*, double *d*)

18

THE REFLECTION
PACKAGE

The `newInstance()` Methods

```
Object newInstance(Class componentType, int length)
Object newInstance(Class componentType, int[] dimensions)
```

The `newInstance()` methods return arrays with the specified component type and dimensions. The first version of the method returns a single dimensional array whose length is specified by the second argument. The second version of the method returns a multidimensional array whose dimensions are specified by the second array argument.

Both methods return an array just as if it had been created in the standard way:

```
new int[dimensions]
new int[dimensions][dimensions]
```

In the following example, a new four-element array of type `String[]` is created using the `Array` class's `newInstance()` method. The elements of the array are then initialized and concatenated in a print statement:

```
String[] strings =
        (String[])Array.newInstance(Class.forName("java.lang.String"),4);
strings[0] = "I ";
strings[1] = "am ";
strings[2] = "human ";
strings[3] = "not an array! ";
System.out.println( strings[0] + strings[1] + strings[2] + strings[3] );
```

The output from this example is shown here:

```
I am human not an array!
```

Notice that the returned type had to be cast as type `String[]` because the method returns an array of type `Object`. If the array has to be multidimensional, you can send an array of `int`s as the second argument to the `newInstance()` method.

The `getLength()` Method

```
int getLength(Object array)
```

The `getLength()` method returns the length of the array argument. If `getLength()` is called on the `strings` object created in the example in the preceding section, the method would return 4 as the length of the array. The following example shows this usage:

```
strings.getLength()
```

The get(), getBoolean(), getByte(), getChar(), getShort(), getInt(), getLong(), getFloat(), and getDouble() Methods

```
Object get(Object array, int index)
boolean getBoolean(Object array, int index)
byte getByte(Object array, int index)
char getChar(Object array, int index)
short getShort(Object array, int index)
int getInt(Object array, int index)
long getLong(Object array, int index)
float getFloat(Object array, int index)
double getDouble(Object array, int index)
```

The get methods return a value of the array object argument at the index specified by the int argument. If the type returned is a primitive type, it is wrapped in its corresponding type wrapper class. Because the methods that get a primitive type do not have to wrap the returned primitive type in a type wrapper, they operate more efficiently.

The following example gets the String value from the second element of the strings array created in the example for the newInstance() method, earlier in this section:

```
System.out.println( (String)Array.get(strings,1) );
```

The string "am" is printed as the output for this example.

The set(), setBoolean(), setByte(), setChar(), setShort(), setInt(), setLong(), setFloat(), and setDouble() Methods

```
void set(Object array, int index, Object value)
void setBoolean(Object array, int index, boolean z)
void setByte(Object array, int index, byte b)
void setChar(Object array, int index, char c)
void setShort(Object array, int index, short s)
void setInt(Object array, int index, int i)
void setLong(Object array, int index, long l)
void setFloat(Object array, int index, float f)
void setDouble(Object array, int index, double d)
```

These methods set a value of the array object argument at the index specified by the int argument. If the value to set is a primitive type, the value sent in must be wrapped in the appropriate type wrapper class. Because the methods that set a primitive type do not have to unwrap the value to be set, they operate more efficiently than the more general set() method.

The following example resets the second element of the strings object created in the example for the newInstance() method, earlier in this section:

```
Array.set(strings,1,"am not ");
Array.set(strings,3,"but an array! ");
System.out.println( strings[0] + strings[1] + strings[2] + strings[3] );
```

The Modifier Class

The Modifier class provides a number of static methods that take an integer as their argument. This integer represents an encoded set of variable or method modifiers. The integer is returned from one of the getModifier() methods described earlier in this chapter. The Java virtual machine stores modifiers internally as encoded integers.

The Modifier class methods return a boolean or String. Typically, the modifier is being tested to determine whether it contains a specific modifier, or it is being decoded and returned as a string representation. The following list includes all the member methods of the Modifier class:

- boolean isPublic(int *mod*)
- boolean isPrivate(int *mod*)
- boolean isProtected(int *mod*)
- boolean isStatic(int *mod*)
- boolean isFinal(int *mod*)
- boolean isSynchronized(int *mod*)
- boolean isVolatile(int *mod*)
- boolean isTransient(int *mod*)
- boolean isNative(int *mod*)
- boolean isInterface(int *mod*)
- boolean isAbstract(int *mod*)
- String toString(int *mod*)

These methods test the integer for a modifier of a particular type. For example, the isPublic() method tests the integer argument and returns true if the integer represents a set of modifiers that contains the public modifier.

The toString() method returns a string of the set of modifiers contained by the integer. This method can be used as follows:

```
Modifier.toString( method.getModifiers() );
```

In this example, method is an instance of the Method class, and the getModifiers() method returns an int representing the modifiers declared for the reflected method. The method toString() decodes the int representation; it first outputs a string with the modifier public, protected, or private, and then outputs static, final, transient, or volatile. For example, if the method object in the preceding example is declared as private, final, and static, the following string is output:

```
private static final
```

Summary

This chapter described the reflection package new to the Java Development Kit version 1.1. If you are using object serialization or are developing JavaBeans components, you will use this package indirectly. If you happen to be developing debuggers or other applications that require runtime information about, and access to, classes and objects, you may use this package directly.

The `Field`, `Method`, `Constructor`, and `Array` classes provide the core functionality for inspection and modification of classes and objects. These classes can be created only by the Java virtual machine. The `Modifier` class contains a number of utility methods that allow you to decode the integer representation of a set of modifiers belonging to a field, method, or class.

The SQL Package

by Shelley Powers

IN THIS CHAPTER

CHAPTER 19

When the Java Developer's Kit (JDK) was first released in January 1996, it did not include any classes for relational database access. For many of us who had hoped Java would enable database access on the Web, this omission was a disappointment. However, in February 1996, JavaSoft announced the JDBC (Java Database Connectivity) API, which was eventually released as a set of classes and interfaces under the package name `java.sql` in the JDK version 1.1. This chapter provides an overview of the JDBC package.

> **NOTE**
>
> The remainder of this chapter refers to the `java.sql` package as the JDBC.

This chapter provides an overview of the JDBC classes and interfaces. For a more detailed look at the JDBC—including several complete examples—refer to these chapters: Chapter 42, "Databases and Java," Chapter 43, "Getting Started with JDBC," and Chapter 44 "Building Database Applets with JDBC."

The JDBC Architecture

The JDBC is implemented in two specific layers: the *driver layer* and the *business layer*. The driver layer consists of specific implementations of interfaces (provided by the developer of the driver) that work with a specific relational database. The business layer is the JDBC `DriverManager` and the classes provided by the JDBC driver to connect with a particular business database. Based on this DBMS (Database Management System) abstraction, if the underlying database changes, and there is a JDBC-compliant driver for the new database, the developer can switch the applet to the new database with very little change to existing code. This abstraction also enables the developer to connect to and access data from multiple heterogeneous databases at the same time using the same methods and techniques.

In addition to providing a database abstraction layer, the JDBC also hides lower level implementation details from the developer. Instead of having to create and manage sockets and input and output streams, the developer can issue one call to create a connection, one call to issue a query, and one or more simple calls to manipulate the results.

The real key to the JDBC is the `DriverManager`, a class that queries the type of driver being used and pulls in the driver-specific classes. Once this is done, the job of the `DriverManager` class is pretty much done; the driver itself has control of all activity at that point, including connecting to the database, issuing a transaction, and processing a result. The `DriverManager` and JDBC drivers are covered in more detail later in this chapter.

The JDBC Members

The JDBC consists of the following interfaces:

- `CallableStatement`
- `Connection`
- `DatabaseMetaData`
- `Driver`
- `PreparedStatement`
- `ResultSet`
- `ResultSetMetaData`
- `Statement`

As mentioned in Chapter 5, "Classes, Packages, and Interfaces," *interfaces* are abstract classes with no implementation methods.

The SQL package also provides several classes:

- `Date`
- `DriverManager`
- `DriverPropertyInfo`
- `Time`
- `TimeStamp`
- `Types`

The most important of these classes is `DriverManager`.

The JDBC Drivers

The JDBC drivers are implementations of JDBC that are specific to a database or middleware layer. JavaSoft has categorized drivers into four categories:

- **The JDBC-ODBC bridge.** This type of driver uses the ODBC driver specific to the database. It also requires that the ODBC driver be available on the client machine running the Java application, and that the JDBC-ODBC binary code be installed where the system can access it. This approach is best reserved for intranet, local, or client/server-based data access.

- **Native-API driver.** This type of driver uses Java to make calls to a database-access API on the client, which, in turn, provides connectivity to the database. The driver is only partially implemented in Java and depends on the API binary code being available on the client.

■ **JDBC-Net driver.** This type of driver uses the network protocols that come with the JDK to connect to a server. The server, in turn, translates the request into DBMS-specific transactions. This approach does not require any client-side binary code and implies that a middleware layer exists to process specific transactions.

■ **Native protocol—All Java drivers.** This type of driver uses the DBMS network protocol to connect to the database. As with drivers from the JDBC-Net driver category, the drivers in the Native protocol—All Java drivers category also use Java exclusively.

Drivers that require binary code such as ODBC drivers or native APIs are not effective for Internet use and should be used exclusively in corporate intranets, Java applications that connect to a local database, or in a client/server environment. Pure Java JDBC drivers such as the last two in the preceding list are very effective for use in internets.

Driver developers provide implementations of the JDBC interfaces specifically for the DBMS or middleware layer. As an example, a Java application developer can connect to an mSQL database using the following code:

```
Class.forName("imaginary.sql.iMsqlDriver");
String url = "jdbc:msql://yasd.com:1112/yasd";
Connection con = DriverManager.getConnection(url);
Statement stmt = con.createStatement();
```

This code loads the Imaginary mSQL driver written by Darryl Reese. If the driver is not located on the client machine, it is downloaded from the Web server. A connection string is then created that contains the type of database (mSQL), the host and port of the database, and the name of the database. This string can also contain any required user name and password to connect to the database. The connection made by this code is to an mSQL database located on a UNIX box and accessed remotely.

> **TIP**
>
> The mSQL JDBC driver can be found on the CD-ROM that comes with this book. An evaluation copy of mSQL can be downloaded from the Hughes Technologies home site at http://www.hughes.com.au/.

After the connection string is created, it is used with the DriverManager class to create the database connection. This connection is then used to make a JDBC SQL object.

The beauty of the JDBC becomes apparent when you compare the preceding code using a pure Java-based JDBC driver with the following code using the JDBC-ODBC bridge to connect to an ODBC database:

```
Class.forName("sun.jdbc.odbc.JdbcOdbcDriver");
String url = "jdbc:odbc:zoo";
Connection con = DriverManager.getConnection(url);
Statement stmt = con.createStatement();
```

Aside from differences in the use of the forName() method and how the connection string is formed, there are virtually no differences between this code and the preceding code. However, this second bit of code generates a connection to a local Access database using an ODBC driver and the JDBC-ODBC bridge.

Without using some form of trusted applet (described in Chapter 8, "Introduction to Applet Programming"), the second piece of code cannot be used by an applet downloaded from a Web server. This code uses the JDBC-ODBC driver, which uses native method calls to access the ODBC driver. Calls to native methods normally violate the security standards currently implemented by most browsers. Additionally, the second approach requires that the JDBC-ODBC driver binary code be installed on the client, and that the ODBC driver for the database be installed and configured for use with the database.

The first code sample, however, uses a driver created purely in Java and that has no requirements of the client.

In spite of these differences, the code itself is very similar and the driver and connectivity issues are transparent to the developer.

The JDBC Classes

The JDBC classes are discussed in the following sections. The most important class is the DriverManager class, which controls the loading of the driver classes.

The DriverManager Class

The DriverManager class controls the loading of driver-specific classes. The classes can be loaded using a system variable to specify the drivers to be loaded; they can also be loaded dynamically at run time.

To load classes for a driver at run time, you typically use the following command:

```
Class.forName("sun.jdbc.odbc.JdbcOdbcDriver");
```

This code snippet uses the standard forName() method to force the loading of the classes specified in the string passed to the method. If the classes cannot be located locally using the CLASSPATH system variable, they are downloaded from the Web server using the same class loader that downloaded the applet.

Another method to load driver classes at run time is to create a new instance of the object. This technique also looks for the driver classes locally and then looks to the Web server if the classes are not found:

```
new imaginary.sql.iMsqlDriver();
```

19

THE SQL
PACKAGE

More than one driver can be loaded at a time; the `DriverManager` class methods are responsible for determining which driver's classes to use to establish the database connection. The string passed to the `Connection()` method makes this determination. Each driver requires that the string used in the `getConnection()` method follows a pattern specific to that particular driver:

```
// JDBC-ODBC driver
String url = "jdbc:odbc:zoo";
Connection con = DriverManager.getConnection(url);
// mSQL-JDBC driver
String url = "jdbc:msql://yasd.com:1112/test";
Connection con = DriverManager.getConnection(url);
```

The applet or application developer uses some of the methods provided by the `DriverManager` class, and the driver developer uses other methods. The call to `getConnection()` is an example of a method called from the Java application. An example of a method called from the driver is `registerDriver()`, which registers a newly loaded driver class using the `DriverManager` class methods. The following code would most likely be called from the constructor of the driver class:

```
java.sql.DriverManager.registerDriver(this);
```

Other methods provided by the `DriverManager` class are listed here:

- `public static void deregisterDriver(Driver driver) throws SQLException`
  This method removes *driver* from the list of those drivers currently available to the `DriverManager`.

- `public static synchronized Connection getConnection(String url) throws SQLException`
  This method creates a connection to the database specified in the *url* passed to the method. This method also forces the `DriverManager` to look for a driver that works with the URL specification.

- `public static synchronized Connection getConnection(String url, Properties info) throws SQLException`
  This method creates a connection to the database specified in the *url* passed to the method. This function also accepts properties in a tag-value format such as `"user=username"`.

■ public static synchronized Connection getConnection(String *url*, String *user*, String *password*) throws SQLException
This method creates a connection to the database specified in the *url* passed to the method. The connection also passes as additional parameters *user* (the username) and *password*.

■ public static Driver getDriver(String *url*) throws SQLException
This method attempts to load a driver to match the *url* passed as a parameter.

■ public static Enumeration getDrivers()
This method returns an enumeration of all loaded JDBC drivers. The names of the drivers can be accessed and printed using the methods provided with the Enumeration class.

■ public static int getLoginTimeout()
This method returns the time a driver can wait to connect to the database.

■ public static PrintStream getLogStream()
This method gets the logging/tracing of the PrintStream. You can use the PrintStream object to print information about the driver.

■ public static void println(String *message*)
This method prints a string to the current logging stream. The *logging stream* is an output stream (to a file or standard output) used for logging messages or errors.

■ public static synchronized void registerDriver(Driver *driver*) throws SQLException
This method registers a newly created and loaded driver. It is called by the driver class itself.

■ public static void setLoginTimeout(int *seconds*)
This method sets the timeout all drivers can wait to establish a connection to a database.

■ public static void setLogStream(PrintStream *out*)
This method sets the logging/tracing of the PrintStream. The PrintStream handles all output of logging and tracing calls using the println() method.

19

THE SQL PACKAGE

TIP

In the preceding list of methods, the synchronized modifier means that the method is thread safe. A *thread-safe method* is one that forces threads to enter the method one thread at a time; the method blocks entry to other threads until the first thread is through.

The Date Type Classes

There are three date classes in the JDBC: Date, Time, and TimeStamp. Each of these classes is basically a wrapper around the associated java.util.Date class. Creating a wrapper extends the base object methods to work with SQL.

The java.util.Date object provides both date and time. SQL, however, requires a separate date value, a separate time value, and a timestamp value that includes date, time, and a fractional second value in nanoseconds.

The JDBC date classes provide methods that get and set values in the associated class objects, and that convert those values to different data types and formats.

The Date Class

The Date class can be created using a single long value that represents the number of milliseconds since January 1, 1997; it can also be created by providing three integers that represent the year, month, and date:

```
java.sql.Date somedate;
somedate = new java.sql.Date(9,0,20);
```

The preceding statements create a Date object that is equivalent to "January 20, 1909". Once the object has been created, you can access the Date class's methods to modify, access, and convert the date.

Modify the date value using one of the set override methods by using a statement like this:

```
somedate.setHours(20);
```

The other set methods are listed a little later in this section. You can also convert a SQL date to a formatted string. The following statement produces a string that is equivalent to the date value and that is formatted in the pattern "YYYY-MM-DD":

```
String somestring = somedate.toString();
```

To create a SQL date value from a string, use the following statement:

```
somedate = somedate.valueOf("1998-01-01");
```

The valueOf() method converts the string date to a SQL-specific date, converting it into a format that is understandable by the target DBMS.

> **TIP**
>
> When creating a Date object, note that the value for the year is equal to the year minus 1900. For example, if you want the value "1978", enter "78". A required value of "2009" is entered as "109".

Using the `valueOf()` and `toString()` methods, the developer can convert easily between Java and SQL dates. The `Date` methods and their arguments follow:

- ◼ `public int getHours()`
  This method returns hours. The get methods return a value based on the unit specified (in this example, the get method returns the hours), and how the `Date` object was created (for example, using local time).

- ◼ `public int getMinutes()`
  This method returns the minutes value of the defined `Date` object.

- ◼ `public int getSeconds()`
  This method returns the seconds value of the defined `Date` object.

- ◼ `public void setHours(int i)`
  This method sets the hour value of the defined `Date` object.

- ◼ `public void setMinutes(int i)`
  This method sets the minutes value of the defined `Date` object.

- ◼ `public void setSeconds(int i)`
  This method sets the seconds value of the defined `Date` object.

- ◼ `public void setTime(long date)`
  This method sets the value of the `Date` object using the number of milliseconds since January 1, 1971.

- ◼ `public static Date valueOf(String s)`
  This method returns the date value given a string containing a date, such as `"01/01/99"`.

- ◼ `public String toString()`
  This method returns a formatted date string from the given `Date` object.

The Time Class

The `Time` class extends the `java.util.Date` object to identify SQL time. As does the JDBC `Date` class, the `Time` class also provides for conversions between time values in Java and those applicable to a DBMS.

There are two constructors for the `Time` class:

- ◼ `public Time(int hour, int minute, int second)`

- ◼ `public Time(long time)`

Once a time object has been instantiated, the following methods can be used with it:

- ◼ `public int getDate()`
  This method returns the day of the month of the `Time` object.

- ◼ `public int getDay()`
  This method returns the current day of the week of the `Time` object; the range is from `0` to `6`, with Sunday being `0`.

- `public int getMonth()`
  This method returns the current month of the `Time` object; the range is from 0 to 11, with January being 0.

- `public int getYear()`
  This method returns the current year of the defined `Time` object.

- `public int setDate(int i)`
  This method sets the month of the date for the `Time` object.

- `public void setDay(int i)`
  This method sets the day of the week for the defined `Time` object.

- `public void setMonth(int i)`
  This method sets the month, with a value in the range from 0 to 11, with January being 0.

- `public void setYear(int i)`
  This method sets the year for the `Time` object.

- `public static Time valueOf(String s)`
  This method returns the value of the specified string in time format (`"hh:mm:ss"`).

- `public String toString()`
  This method returns a formatted time string in JDBC escape syntax (for use directly with the databases) for the defined `Time` object.

The `TimeStamp` Class

When you work with relational databases, you are aware of the `timestamp` data type. Database developers and administrators use timestamps in most (if not all) of their tables—to mark when a table row has been inserted, when values in a row have been changed, or both.

The `TimeStamp` class extends the `java.util.Date` class to include the concept of date, time, and a fractional second value.

The `TimeStamp` object can be created with a long `timestamp` value or by providing separate values for each component of the `timestamp`:

```
Timestamp newdate = new Timestamp(97,0,1,12,12,20,10);
```

This statement creates a new `TimeStamp` object and sets its value to `"January 1, 1997 12:12:20.00000001"`. As you can with the JDBC `Date` class, you can use the `TimeStamp` class to set database field values and convert the `timestamp` values returning from a database into a string you can display:

```
Timestamp origtimestamp = new Timestamp(97,0,1,12,12,20,10);
Timestamp newtimestamp = origtimestamp.valueOf("1998-03-01 10:10:10.00000001");
String stimestamp = newtimestamp.toString();
g.drawString(stimestamp, 20,20);
```

This code creates a new `TimeStamp` object, which is then used to create another `TimeStamp` object using the `valueOf()` method and a string representing a new value. This value is then converted back to a string using `toString()`. The new string is displayed using `Graphics.drawString()`. This timestamp value would display as follows:

```
1998-03-01 10:10:10.00000001
```

The `TimeStamp` class has the following methods:

- `public boolean after(TimeStamp ts)`
  This method returns `true` if the timestamp of the defined `TimeStamp` object is later than the timestamp argument.

- `public boolean before(TimeStamp ts)`
  This method returns `true` if the timestamp of the defined `TimeStamp` object is earlier than the timestamp argument.

- `public boolean equals(TimeStamp ts)`
  This method returns `true` if the timestamp and the timestamp argument are equal.

- `public int getNanos()`
  This method returns the timestamp nanoseconds value of the `TimeStamp` object.

- `public void setNanos(int i)`
  This method sets the timestamp nanoseconds value of the defined `TimeStamp` object.

- `public String toString()`
  This method returns a formatted string derived from the `TimeStamp` object.

Of course, you do not use the JDBC `Date`, `Time`, and `TimeStamp` classes to convert values back and forth between strings and dates. However, the classes are very useful for displaying date values pulled from a database and for inserting date values retrieved from a Java input field. These techniques are demonstrated in the chapters in Part IX of this book, "Java Databases."

The `DriverPropertyInfo` Class

The `DriverPropertyInfo` class helps advanced developers provide information to a driver for a connection. Java application developers are not required to use this class; it is included here to complete the coverage of the SQL package classes rather than as a suggestion that you use it.

If you do not have the database connection information during development, but it can be provided by the user at runtime, the `DriverPropertyInfo` class provides the way to prompt the user for name-value pairs that represent connection-specific properties. The `DriverPropertyInfo` class is used with the `Driver` interface's `getPropertyInfo()` method to determine which values have been specified and which are still needed to establish the connection.

No methods are associated with this class. Its constructor requires two strings: the property name and the property value. Here is an example:

```
DriverPropertyInfo somevalue = new DriverPropertyInfo("password", "somepassword");
```

19

THE SQL
PACKAGE

The Types Class

The last of the JDBC classes is `Types`, which defines constants that identify SQL types. These constants are then used to map between the SQL data type and its associated Java data type.

The types are defined as follows:

```
public final static int BIGINT
```

Each of the types is defined with the following modifiers: `public` (accessible by all classes), `final` (the value is constant), and `static` (the value is the same for all objects). The types currently defined are listed here:

SQL Type	Description of Java Data Type
BIGINT	Mapped to a Java `long`
BINARY	Mapped to a byte array
BIT	Mapped to a Java `boolean`
CHAR	Mapped to a Java `String`
DATE	Mapped to the JDBC `Date` class
DECIMAL	Mapped to the class `java.math.BigDecimal`
DOUBLE	Mapped to a `double`
FLOAT	Mapped to a `double`
INTEGER	Mapped to an `int`
LONGVARBINARY	Mapped to a byte array
LONGVARCHAR	Mapped to a Java `String`
NULL	No mapping provided
NUMERIC	Mapped to the `java.math.BigDecimal` class
OTHER	Mapped using `getObject()` and `setObject()`
REAL	Mapped to a `float`
SMALLINT	Mapped to a `short`
TIME	Mapped to the `java.sql.Time` class
TIMESTAMP	Mapped to the `java.sql.TimeStamp` class
TINYINT	Mapped to a byte
VARBINARY	Mapped to a byte array
VARCHAR	Mapped to a Java `String`

NOTE

As this book went to press, the JDK 1.1 was changing, resulting in a modification to the JDBC. The `java.lang.Bignum` class was being replaced with the `java.math.BigDecimal` and `java.math.BigInteger` classes.

The JDBC Interfaces

The JDBC *interfaces* are abstract classes implemented by developers who are building JDBC drivers. Interfaces have no implementations themselves; they are used to derive the driver classes. Once the derived classes are implemented, the applet or application developer can use these classes to connect to a database, issue a transaction, and process a result set without being concerned about the underlying database.

The Driver Interface

The `Driver` interface provides the methods to establish a connection to a specific DBMS or DBMS middleware layer. `Driver` is usually a small class; it contains only what is necessary to register the driver using the `DriverManager` class methods to test whether the driver can process the connection URL, to get driver properties if the connection information is being processed dynamically, and to connect to the database.

Here are the methods provided with the `Driver` interface and implemented by the driver:

- `public abstract boolean accceptsURL(String url) throws SQLException`
This method tests whether the driver can understand the protocol specified in the connection *url*.

- `public abstract Connection connect(String url, Properties info) throws SQLException`
This method establishes a connection to the DBMS and returns a `Connection` object. The `DriverManager` class methods call this method for each driver loaded. If the driver cannot process the connection, it returns a `null` value.

- `public abstract int getMajorVersion()`
This method returns the driver's major version number.

- `public abstract int getMinorVersion()`
This method returns the driver's minor version number.

19

THE SQL
PACKAGE

■ `public abstract DriverPropertyInfo[] getPropertyInfo (String url,`
  `Properties info) throws SQLException`
This method enables a user interface to query for which properties already exist for a connection and then to query for additional properties the connection may need.

■ `public abstract boolean jdbcCompliant()`
This method is coded to return `true` if the driver developer determines that the driver is JDBC compliant; else it returns `false`.

NOTE

JDBC-compliant drivers are drivers that implement the full set of JDBC functionality and are developed for a DBMS that is SQL 92-entry level compliant. The mSQL-JDBC driver (mentioned earlier in this chapter and provided on the CD-ROM that accompanies this book) is *not* JDBC compliant because the mSQL database is not SQL 92-entry compliant.

The Connection Interface

The `Connection` interface is used by driver developers to create a DBMS-specific implementation of the `Connection` class that is, in turn, used by the applet or application developer to establish a database connection. Statements are created using the `createStatement()` and `PrepareStatement()` methods; result sets are created using specific methods provided with the `Statement`, `PreparedStatement`, and `CallableStatement` classes.

Each of the methods defined for the `Connection` interface has an associated implementation in the driver. An example of how this happens is shown here:

```
public class iSomeDriverConnection implements java.sql.Connection
{
  ...
  public Statement createStatement() throws SQLException {
    // code to implement createStatement for driver
    ...
  }
}
```

The driver implements the `java.sql.Connection` and provides implementations for each of the classes, as shown here with the `createStatement()` implementation.

The applet or application developer uses the driver-specific `Connection` class to create statements and process result sets:

```
new imaginary.sql.iMsqlDriver();
java.sql.Connection con = java.sql.DriverManager.getConnection(
                          "jdbc:msql://yasd.com:1112/test");
java.sql.Statement stmt = con.createStatement();
String stringSelect = "Select retail_item.item_nbr from retail_item";
java.sql.ResultSet rs = stmt.executeQuery(stringSelect);
```

NOTE

If the import java.sql.* statement is issued at the beginning of the applet or application, the java.sql statement modifiers are not necessary for each object.

The Connection interface methods listed here are those defined for the interface. The driver must redefine the methods as nonabstract classes with the same parameters and return types.

- public abstract void clearWarnings() throws SQLException
  This method results in the getWarnings() method returning null until a new warning is generated for the current Connection object.

- public abstract void close() throws SQLException
  This method closes a database connection and releases JDBC resources without waiting for traditional garbage collection (when the program goes out of the Connection object's scope).

- public abstract void commit() throws SQLException
  This method commits changes to the database and releases database locks. commit() applies only if auto commit has been turned off. Auto commit is a flag that can be set with the setAutoCommit() method. *Auto commit* means that every transaction is automatically committed if it is successful.

- public abstract Statement createStatement() throws SQLException
  This method creates and returns a Statement object.

- public abstract boolean getAutoCommit() throws SQLException
  This method gets the status of the auto commit.

- public abstract String getCatalog() throws SQLException
  This method returns the current catalog name. *Catalogs* are the names of the meta database (or database about the database) and contain information about the database objects themselves.

- public abstract DatabaseMetaData getMetaData() throws SQLException
  This method returns a DatabaseMetaData object with information about the database (such as stored procedures, SQL grammar, and so on).

- public abstract int getTransactionIsolation() throws SQLException
  This method gets the current transaction isolation mode. The transaction modes are listed in Table 19.1.

- public abstract SQLWarning getWarnings() throws SQLException
  This method returns the SQLWarning object associated with the first warning reported with the Connection. Additional warnings are chained onto the object.

- public abstract boolean isClose() throws SQLException
  This method tests to see whether the connection is still open.

■ `public abstract boolean isReadOnly() throws SQLException`
This method tests to see whether the database is read-only.

■ `public abstract String nativeSQL(String sql) throws SQLException`
This method returns the native form of the SQL. *Native form* means that the SQL is converted by the database driver before being sent to the database.

■ `public abstract CallableStatement prepareCall(String sql) throws SQLException`
This method processes the JDBC procedure `call` statement and returns a `CallableStatement` object.

■ `public abstract PreparedStatement prepareStatement(String sql) throws SQLException`
This method processes a string that contains one or more ? placeholders and returns a `PreparedStatement` object.

■ `public abstract void rollback() throws SQLException`
This method rolls back all database changes that have occurred since the previous rollback or commit statement. Any database locks being maintained are released. This method is applicable only if auto commit is turned off.

■ `public abstract void setAutoCommit(boolean autocommit) throws SQLException`
This method turns on or off the auto commit feature if the database allows.

■ `public abstract void setCatalog(String catalog) throws SQLException`
This method sets a subspace of the database `catalog` if this feature is supported in the database.

■ `public abstract void setReadOnly(boolean readonly) throws SQLException`
This method sets the read-only mode for succeeding transactions to enable some database optimizations.

■ `public abstract void setTransactionIsolation(int level) throws SQLException`
This method attempts to change the transaction level using one of the transaction modes listed in Table 19.1.

Several variables are defined for the `Connection` class that you can use to set the transaction level for the database (if this is allowed by the DBMS). Table 19.1 lists these transaction modes.

Table 19.1. Transaction modes.

Variable Name	Description
TRANSACTION_NONE	Transactions are not supported
TRANSACTION_READ_COMMITTED	Prevents dirty reads but allows nonrepeatable and phantom reads
TRANSACTION_READ_UNCOMMITTED	Allows dirty, nonrepeatable, and phantom reads

Variable Name	Description
TRANSACTION_REPEATABLE_READ	Prevents dirty and nonrepeatable reads but allows phantom reads
TRANSACTION_SERIALIZABLE	Prevents dirty, nonrepeatable, and phantom reads

Chapter 42, "Databases and Java," details what these transaction levels mean.

The Statement Classes

The JDBC provides three different statement classes: PreparedStatement, CallableStatement, and Statement. The Statement class is the simplest; it is used primarily for static SQL statements that do not result in multiple result sets or update counts. The PreparedStatement class is used to compile a SQL statement and invoke the compiled statement multiple times; PreparedStatement is an extension of the Statement class. The CallableStatement class is used to invoke a stored procedure call that may return multiple result sets or update counts; CallableStatement is an extension of the PreparedStatement class.

The Statement Class

The Statement class is used for SQL statements that are executed only once and that do not have to pass parameters with the statement. Some of the SQL statement types this class can process are those that perform one-time queries that process a static SQL statement:

```
Connection con = DriverManager.getConnection(someurl);
Statement stmt = con.createStatement();
String stmt = "Select * from retail_item where retail_item_nbr =  " +
               somejavavariable;
ResultSet rs = stmt.executeQuery(stmt);
```

The statement being executed does not process any input variables and passes a hard-coded SQL statement to the executeQuery() method. The statement may or may not contain references to Java variables. A ResultSet class is returned from the executeQuery() method call.

A statement may return multiple result sets when the statement executes a stored procedure that performs several statements (a statement may also return multiple result sets for some other reason). When the SQL statement is unknown, the results are unknown. When this is the case, the developer must use the execute statement and then process the result sets by using the getResultSet(), getUpdateCount(), and getMoreResults() methods. An example of this situation is presented in Chapter 43, "Getting Started with JDBC."

The SQL statement can be an update statement such as this:

```
Connection con = DriverManager.getConnection(someurl);
Statement stmt = con.createStatement();
int i = stmt.executeUpdate("Insert into company_codes(company_cd, company_desc)
                    values('" + value1 + "','" + value2 + "')");
```

19

THE SQL PACKAGE

This statement inserts a row into the table company_codes. This type of statement can also be used to update or delete from a database table.

The methods defined for the Statement interface are listed here:

- public abstract void cancel() throws SQLException
  In a multithreaded application, this method can be used to cancel the execution of a statement occurring in another thread.

- public abstract void clearWarnings() throws SQLException
  This method results in the getWarnings() method returning null until a new warning is generated for the defined Statement object.

- public abstract void close() throws SQLException
  This method releases the resources being maintained for the statement instead of waiting for them to be released with the standard garbage collection (when the Statement object falls out of scope).

- public abstract boolean execute(String *sql*) throws SQLException
  This method is used when processing a SQL statement that may have multiple result sets, multiple update counts, or both.

- public abstract ResultSet executeQuery(String *sql*) throws SQLException
  This method executes a SQL statement that returns only one result set. Additionally, the SQL statement is static (that is, it is not dynamically created at run time).

- public abstract int executeUpdate(String *sql*) throws SQLException
  This method executes a SQL INSERT, UPDATE, or DELETE statement and returns a count of the rows impacted by the statement.

- public abstract int getMaxFieldSize() throws SQLException
  The value returned by this method is the maximum size of the data returned by any of the columns.

- public abstract int getMaxRows() throws SQLException
  The value returned by this method is the maximum number of rows that can be returned in a result set.

- public abstract boolean getMoreResults() throws SQLException
  This method tests to see whether the statement's next result contains a result set. It also closes the open result set.

- public abstract int getQueryTimeout() throws SQLException
  The value returned by this method is the number of seconds allowed for the statement to execute.

- public abstract ResultSet getResultSet() throws SQLException
  This method returns the result set for the execute statement if the current result is a result set; the method returns -1 otherwise.

- `public abstract int getUpdateCount() throws SQLException`
  This method returns the current results as a count; it returns -1 if there are no results or the current result is a result set.

- `public abstract SQLWarning getWarnings() throws SQLException`
  This method returns the `SQLWarning` object with the first warning reported with the `Statement`. Additional warnings for the `Statement` object are appended to the `SQLWarning` object.

- `public abstract void setCursorName(String name) throws SQLException`
  This method defines the cursor name used by each execute method call that follows.

- `public abstract void setEscapeProcessing(boolean enable) throws SQLException`
  If escapes are processes, the driver will do the escape substitution before sending SQL. This method enables or disables escape processing.

- `public abstract void setMaxFieldSize(int max) throws SQL Exception`
  This method sets the maximum field size for any column that can be returned. You can set only certain data types such as VARCHAR, LONGVARCHAR, BINARY, VARBINARY, and CHAR fields.

- `public abstract void setMaxRows(int max) throws SQLException`
  This method sets the maximum number of rows that can be returned in a result set. Excess rows are discarded.

- `public abstract void setQueryTimeout(int seconds) throws SQLException`
  This method sets how long a driver will wait for a query to execute.

The PreparedStatement Class

The `PreparedStatement` class allows the developer to create a SQL statement that is compiled and stored in the database. The statement can then be efficiently invoked several times, passing in parameters for each execution.

Here is an example of the use of a `PreparedStatement`:

```
ResultSet rs;
Connection con = DriverManager.getConnection(someurl);
PreparedStatement prepstmt = con.prepareStatement("Select var1,
    var2 from sometable where varx = ?");
for (int i = 1; i < 10; i++) {
   rs = prepstmt.executeQuery(prepstmt);
   // process rs
}
```

The `PreparedStatement` class contains the same methods used in the `Statement` class and are not repeated here. However, this class has some additional methods. The set methods listed here set a parameter to the named Java value. This parameter is then converted to the appropriate database type based on the SQL-to-Java type mapping listed earlier in this chapter.

19

THE SQL PACKAGE

■ public abstract void clearParameters() throws SQLException
This method clears all parameters currently in effect for the statement.

■ public abstract void setAsciiStream(int *parameterindex*, InputStream *x*,
int *length*) throws SQLException
This method inputs a parameter of LONGVARCHAR that can be very large. This method is more efficient and makes use of java.io.InputStream.

■ public abstract void setBignum (int *parameterindex*, Bignum *x*) throws SQLException
This method sets a parameter to a type of java.lang.Bignum. Note that this class is currently being replaced with the java.math.BigDecimal and java.math.BigInteger classes.

■ public abstract void setBinaryStream(int *parameterindex*, InputStream *x*,
int *length*) throws SQLException
This method inputs a parameter of type LONGVARBINARY that can be quite large. This method is more efficient than using a LONGVARCHAR data type directly in a statement going to the database and makes use of java.io.InputStream class.

■ public abstract void setBoolean(int *parameterindex*, boolean *b*) throws SQLException
This method sets a parameter to a boolean value.

■ public abstract void setByte(int *parameterindex*, byte *x*) throws SQLException
This method sets a parameters to a Java byte value.

■ public abstract void setBytes(int *parameterindex*, byte *x*[]) throws SQLException
This method sets a parameter to a Java array of bytes. Values convert to VARBINARY or LONGVARBINARY before reaching the database.

■ public abstract void setDate(int *parameterindex*, Date *x*) throws SQLException
This method sets a parameter to a Java Date value.

■ public abstract void setDouble (int *parameterindex*, double *x*) throws SQLException
This method sets a parameter to a Java double value.

■ public abstract void setFloat(int *parameterindex*, float *f*) throws SQLException
This method sets a parameter to a Java float value.

■ public abstract void setInt (int *parameterindex*, int *I*)
This method sets a parameter to a Java int value.

■ public abstract void setLong(int *parameterindex*, long *l*)
This method sets a parameter to a Java long value.

■ public abstract void setNull(int *parameterindex*, int *SqlType*) throws SQLException
This method sets a parameter to SQL NULL. The second argument is type *SqlType* as defined in java.sql.Types.

■ public abstract void setObject(int *parameterindex*, Object *x*) throws SQLException
This method sets the parameter to an Object, which is a generic Java object that can be used to dynamically pass in any class or Java object as a parameter.

- public abstract void setObject (int *parameterindex*, Object *x*,
  int *targetsqltype*) throws SQLException
  This method sets the parameter to an Object and provides the SQL type defined by
  `java.sql.Types`.

- public abstract void setShort(int *parameterindex*, short *s*) throws SQLException
  This method sets a parameter to a Java short value.

- public abstract void setString(int *parameterindex*, String *s*) throws SQLException
  This method sets a parameter to a Java string value.

- public abstract void setTime(int *parameterindex*, Time *t*) throws SQLException
  This method sets a parameter to a Java Time value.

- public abstract void setTimestamp(int *parameterindex*, TimeStamp *tstmp*)
  throws SQLException
  This method sets a parameter to a Java TimeStamp value.

- public abstract void setUnicodeStream(int parameterindex, InputStream x, int
  length) throws SQLException
  This method inputs a parameter of Unicode to LONGVARCHAR that can be very large.
  This method is more efficient than supplying a LONGVARCHAR data type directly, and
  makes use of `java.io.InputStream` class.

The CallableStatement Class

The CallableStatement class is an extension of the PreparedStatement class with the added
capability of processing stored procedure results. The methods defined for this class allow the
developer to pull different database types from a result set using a series of functions that convert the SQL type to the appropriate Java type:

- public abstract boolean getBoolean(int *parameterindex*) throws SQLException
  This method gets the value of the column indicated by the index and returns it as a
  Java boolean value.

- public abstract byte getByte(int *parameterindex*) throws SQLException
  This method gets the value of the column indicated by the index and returns it as a
  Java byte value.

- public abstract byte[] getBytes(int *parameterindex*) throws SQLException
  This method gets the value of the column indicated by the index and returns it as a
  Java byte array value.

- public abstract Date getDate(int *parameterindex*) throws SQLException
  This method gets the value of the column indicated by the index and returns it as a
  Java Date value.

- public abstract double getDouble(int *parameterindex*) throws SQLException
  This method gets the value of the column indicated by the index and returns it as a
  Java double value.

■ public abstract float getFloat(int *parameterindex*) throws SQLException
This method gets the value of the column indicated by the index and returns it as a
Java float value.

■ public abstract int getInt(int *parameterindex*) throws SQLException
This method gets the value of the column indicated by the index and returns it as a
Java int value.

■ public abstract long getLong(int *parameterindex*) throws SQLException
This method gets the value of the column indicated by the index and returns it as a
Java long value.

■ public abstract Object getObject(int *parameterindex*) throws SQLException
This method gets the value of the column indicated by the index and returns it as a
Java generic Object. This method can be used to dynamically access an object as any
Java class.

■ public abstract short getShort(int *parameterindex*) throws SQLException
This method gets the value of the column indicated by the index and returns it as a
Java short value.

■ public abstract String getString(int *parameterindex*) throws SQLException
This method gets the value of the column indicated by the index and returns it as a
Java string value.

■ public abstract Time getTime(int *parameterindex*) throws SQLException
This method gets the value of the column indicated by the index and returns it as a
Java Time value.

■ public abstract Timestamp getTimestamp(int *parameterindex*) throws SQLException
This method gets the value of the column indicated by the index and returns it as a
Java TimeStamp value.

■ public abstract void registerOutParameter(int *parameterindex*, int *SqlType*)
throws SQLException
This method must be called for each parameter to register the java.sql.Type of the
parameter.

■ public abstract void registerOutParameter(int *parameterindex*, int *SqlType*,
int *scale*) throws SQLException
This method registers Numeric or Decimal java.sql.Type parameters.

■ public abstract boolean wasNull() throws SQLException
This method is used to report whether the last parameter was SQL NULL. This method
is used in combination with the appropriate get OUT parameter method.

The ResultSet Class

After a connection is opened and a statement is created and executed, you will most likely want
to process the return values from a query; the ResultSet class is the object to use.

The following code creates a connection, issues a statement, executes a simple query, and then processes the results:

```
Connection con = DriverManager.getConnection(someurl);
Statement stmt = con.createStatement();
String stmt = "Select item_desc, item_cat from retail_item where retail_item_nbr =
               " + somejavavariable;
ResultSet rs = stmt.executeQuery(stmt);
String stringResult = "";
while (rs.next()) {
   tmpString = "Item Description is " + rs.getObject(1) + "\n";
   stringResult+=tmpString;
   tmpString = "Item Category is " + rs.getObject(2) + "\n";
   stringResult+=tmpString;
}
resultsTextArea.setText(stringResult);
```

As you can see, the `ResultSet` class provides methods that allow you to access the individual fields for each row returned from a query. A `ResultSet` object also maintains a cursor pointing to the row currently being accessed. The get methods defined for this type of object return the Java data type specified in the method, applying the appropriate SQL-data-type to Java-data-type conversion approach.

- ■ `publio abstract void clearWarnings() throws SQLException`
  This method results in the `getWarnings()` method returning `null` until a new warning is generated for the result set.

- ■ `public abstract void close() throws SQLException`
  This method releases the resources being maintained for the result set rather than waiting for them to be released with the standard garbage collection (when the result set object falls out of scope).

- ■ `public abstract int findColumn(String colname) throws SQLException`
  This method returns the column index of the specified column name beginning with column number 1.

- ■ `public abstract InputStream getAsciiStream(String colname) throws SQLException`
  This method returns ASCII characters as a stream. All the data for the column must be read before proceeding to another column.

- ■ `public abstract InputStream getBinaryStream(int columnindex) throws SQLException`
  This method returns a stream that can then be read in chunks. The index provides the location of the column in which the binary stream is located.

- ■ `public abstract InputStream getBinaryStream(String colname) throws SQLException`
  This method returns a stream that can then be read in chunks. The name of the column is passed to the method.

- ■ `public abstract boolean getBoolean(int columnindex) throws SQLException`
  This method gets the value of the column indicated by the index and returns it as a Java `boolean` value, given the column index.

19

THE SQL PACKAGE

■ public abstract boolean getBoolean(string *colname*) throws SQLException
This method gets the value of the column indicated by the index and returns it as a Java boolean, given the column name.

■ public abstract byte getByte (int *columnindex*) throws SQLException
This method gets the value of the column indicated by the index and returns it as a Java byte value, given the column index.

■ public abstract byte getByte (String *colname*) throws SQLException
This method gets the value of the column indicated by the index and returns it as a Java byte value, given the column name.

■ public abstract byte[] getBytes (int *columnindex*) throws SQLException
This method gets the value of the column indicated by the index and returns it as a Java byte array, given the column index.

■ public abstract byte[] getBytes (String *colname*) throws SQLException
This method gets the value of the column indicated by the index and returns it as a Java byte array, given the column name.

■ public abstract String getCursorName()throws SQLException
This method returns the name of the cursor being used by the result set.

■ public abstract Date getDate(int *columnindex*) throws SQLException
This method gets the value of the column indicated by the index and returns it as a Java Date value, given the column index.

■ public abstract Date getDate(String *colname*) throws SQLException
This method gets the value of the column indicated by the index and returns it as a Java Date value, given the column name.

■ public abstract double getDouble(int *columnindex*) throws SQLException
This method gets the value of the column indicated by the index and returns it as a Java double value, given the column index.

■ public abstract double getDouble(String *colname*) throws SQLException
This method gets the value of the column indicated by the index and returns it as a Java double value, given the column name.

■ public abstract float getFloat(int *columnindex*) throws SQLException
This method gets the value of the column indicated by the index and returns it as a Java float value, given the column index.

■ public abstract float getFloat(String *colname*) throws SQLException
This method gets the value of the column indicated by the index and returns it as a Java float value, given the column name.

■ public abstract int getInt(int *columnindex*) throws SQLException
This method gets the value of the column indicated by the index and returns it as a Java int value, given the column index.

- `public abstract int getInt(String `*`colname`*`) throws SQLException`
  This method gets the value of the column indicated by the index and returns it as a Java `int` value, given the column name.

- `public abstract long getLong(int `*`columnindex`*`) throws SQLException`
  This method gets the value of the column indicated by the index and returns it as a Java `long` value, given the column index.

- `public abstract long getLong(String `*`colname`*`) throws SQLException`
  This method gets the value of the column indicated by the index and returns it as a Java `long` value, given the column name.

- `public abstract Object getObject(int `*`columnindex`*`) throws SQLException`
  This method returns a `java.lang.Object` type and can also be used to handle abstract SQL data types, given a column index.

- `public abstract Object getObject(String `*`colname`*`) throws SQLException`
  This method returns a `java.lang.Object` type and can also be used to handle abstract SQL data types, given a column name.

- `public abstract short getShort(int `*`columnindex`*`) throws SQLException`
  This method gets the value of the column indicated by the index and returns it as a Java `short` value, given a column index.

- `public abstract short getShort(String `*`colname`*`) throws SQLException`
  This method gets the value of the column indicated by the index and returns it as a Java `short` value, given a column name.

- `public abstract String getString(int `*`columnindex`*`) throws SQLException`
  This method gets the value of the column indicated by the index and returns it as a Java string value, given a column index.

- `public abstract String getString(String `*`colname`*`) throws SQLException`
  This method gets the value of the column indicated by the index and returns it as a Java string value, given a column name.

- `public abstract Time getTime(int `*`columnindex`*`) throws SQLException`
  This method gets the value of the column indicated by the index and returns it as a Java `Time` value, given a column index.

- `public abstract Time getTime(String `*`colname`*`) throws SQLException`
  This method gets the value of the column indicated by the index and returns it as a Java `Time` value, given a column name.

- `public abstract TimeStamp getTimestamp(int `*`columnindex`*`) throws SQLException`
  This method gets the value of the column indicated by the index and returns it as a Java `TimeStamp` value, given a column index.

- `public abstract TimeStamp getTimestamp(String `*`colname`*`) throws SQLException`
  This method gets the value of the column indicated by the index and returns it as a Java `TimeStamp` value, given a column name.

- `public abstract InputStream getUnicodeStream(int columnindex) throws SQLException`
  This method returns a stream of Unicode characters that can then be read in chunks, given a column index.

- `public abstract long getLong(String colname) throws SQLException`
  This method returns a stream of Unicode characters that can then be read in chunks, given a column name.

- `public abstract SQLWarning getWarnings() throws SQLException`
  This method returns the `SQLWarning` object with the first warning reported with the result set object. Additional warnings are then chained to this `SQLWarning` object.

- `public abstract boolean next() throws SQLException`
  Calls to `next()` move the position of the current row of the result set; returns `false` when no more rows can be read. This method also implicitly closes the input stream from the previous row.

- `public abstract boolean wasNull() throws SQLException`
  This method is used to report whether the column contains a SQL `NULL`. This method is used in combination with the appropriate get method.

The ResultSetMetaData and DatabaseMetaData Classes

The remaining JDBC interfaces are the `ResultSetMetaData` and `DatabaseMetaData` classes. The `ResultSetMetaData` class provides information about properties of the columns in a result set. The `DatabaseMetaData` class provides information about the database itself. Because neither of these classes is commonly used when developing Java applets or applications, the individual methods and variables for each of the interfaces are not listed here; they are listed instead in Chapter 42, "Databases and Java."

Summary

The JDBC is a powerful mechanism that allows Java applets to provide database access over an internet or intranet. The JDBC is also valuable when you are using Java to create local or client/server applications that have to access one or more databases.

This chapter provided an overview of the JDBC classes and interfaces as well as a description of the multiple-layer approach to using JDBC. Brief examples of some of the more commonly used JDBC classes were given, and descriptions of most of the JDBC methods were provided.

For more detailed information and complete code examples, refer to the chapters in Part IX of this book, "Java Databases": Chapter 42, "Databases and Java," provides a detailed description of the way Java accesses databases, gives sample code for database utility tools, and discusses some non-JDBC database techniques currently being used with Java. Chapter 43, "Getting Started with JDBC," provides several examples that use JDBC to create Java applications, including a more thorough look at the different statement types. Chapter 44, "Building Database Applets with JDBC," provides code for several applets that use the JDBC to both query and update a database.

19

THE SQL PACKAGE

Programming the AWT

Java Graphics Fundamentals

by Michael Morrison

IN THIS CHAPTER

Few Java applets, and few Java applications for that matter, would be interesting without at least some graphics. Knowing this, it's important for you to understand the fundamentals of Java graphics so that you can make the most of graphics in your applets. This chapter focuses on some of the basic Java graphics techniques that will be important as you start building your own applets. Although some of the graphics techniques you learn about in this chapter may seem fairly simple, keep in mind that they form the basis for more advanced graphics.

The chapter begins by explaining the Java graphics coordinate system and the class used as the basis for most of the Java graphics operations. The chapter then moves on to text and how it is drawn using the standard Java graphics features. You finish up the chapter by learning how images are used in the context of a Java applet. By the end of the chapter, you will have a solid understanding of graphics and how they are handled in Java applets and applications.

The Graphics Coordinate System

All graphical computing systems use some sort of coordinate system to specify the nature of points in the system. Coordinate systems typically spell out the origin (0,0) of a graphical system, as well as the axes and directions of increasing value for each of the axes. The traditional mathematical coordinate system familiar to most of us is shown in Figure 20.1.

FIGURE 20.1.
The traditional coordinate system.

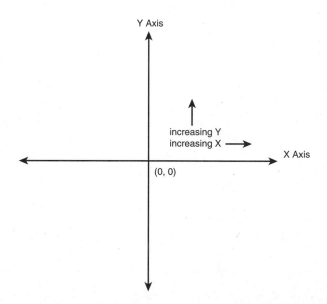

The graphics system in Java uses a coordinate system of its own to specify how and where drawing operations take place. Because all drawing in Java takes place within the confines of an applet or application window, the Java coordinate system is realized by the window. The coordinate system in Java has an origin located in the upper-left corner of the window; positive x values increase to the right and positive y values increase down. All values in the Java coordinate system are positive integers. Figure 20.2 shows how this coordinate system looks.

FIGURE 20.2.
The Java graphics coordinate system.

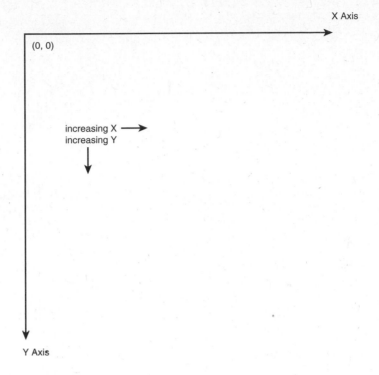

The Basics of Color

A topic that impacts almost every area of Java graphics is color. Therefore, it's important to understand the underlying nature of color and how it is modeled in Java and in computer systems in general. Most computer systems take a similar approach to representing color. The main function of color in a computer system is to accurately reflect the physical nature of color within the confines of a graphical system. This physical nature isn't hard to figure out; anyone who has experienced the joy of Play-Doh can tell you that colors react in different ways when they are combined with each other. Like Play-Doh, a computer's color system must be able to mix colors with accurate, predictable results.

Color computer monitors provide possibly the most useful insight into how software systems implement color. A color monitor has three electron guns: red, green, and blue. The output from these three guns converge on each pixel of the screen, exciting phosphors to produce the appropriate color (see Figure 20.3). The combined intensities of the guns determine the resulting pixel color. This convergence of different colors from the monitor guns is very similar to the convergence of different colored Play-Doh.

20

JAVA GRAPHICS FUNDAMENTALS

> **NOTE**
>
> Technically speaking, the result of combining colors on a monitor is different than that of combining similarly colored Play-Doh. Color combinations on a monitor are *additive*, meaning that mixed colors are emitted by the monitor; Play-Doh color combinations are *subtractive*, meaning that mixed colors are absorbed. The additive or subtractive nature of a color combination depends on the physical properties of the particular medium involved.

FIGURE 20.3.

Electron guns in a color monitor converge to create a unique color.

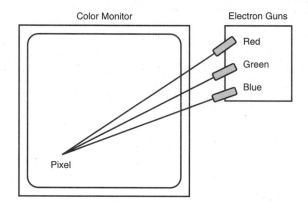

The Java color system is very similar to the physical system used by color monitors; it forms unique colors by using varying intensities of the colors red, green, and blue. Therefore, Java colors are represented by the combinations of the numeric intensities of the primary colors (red, green, and blue). This color system is known as RGB (Red Green Blue) and is standard across most graphical computer systems.

> **NOTE**
>
> Although RGB is the most popular computer color system in use, there are others. Another popular color system is HSB, which stands for Hue Saturation Brightness. In this system, colors are defined by varying degrees of hue, saturation, and brightness. The HSB color system is also supported by Java.

Table 20.1 shows the numeric values for the red, green, and blue components of some basic colors. Notice that the intensities of each color component range from 0 to 255 in value.

Table 20.1. RGB component values for some basic colors.

Color	Red	Green	Blue
White	255	255	255
Black	0	0	0
Light Gray	192	192	192
Dark Gray	128	128	128
Red	255	0	0
Green	0	255	0
Blue	0	0	255
Yellow	255	255	0
Purple	255	0	255

Java provides a class, `Color`, for modeling colors. The `Color` class represents an RGB color and provides methods for extracting and manipulating the primary color components. The `Color` class also includes constant members representing many popular colors. You typically use the `Color` class to specify the color when you are using many of Java's graphical functions, which you learn about next.

The Graphics Class

Most of Java's graphics functions are accessible through a single class, `Graphics`, found in the Java AWT (Abstract Windowing Toolkit) package. The `Graphics` class models a graphics context. A *graphics context* is an abstract representation of a graphical surface that you can draw on. A graphics context is basically a way for you to draw in a generic manner, without worrying about where the drawing is physically taking place.

Graphics contexts are necessary so that the same graphics routines can be used regardless of whether you are drawing to the screen, to memory, or to a printer. The `Graphics` class provides you with a graphics context to which you perform all graphics functions. As you learn about the functionality provided by the `Graphics` class, keep in mind that its output is largely independent of the ultimate destination, thanks to graphics contexts.

Graphical output code in a Java applet or application is usually implemented in the `paint()` method. A `Graphics` object is passed into the `paint()` method, which is then used to perform graphical output to the applet or application window (output surface). Because the `Graphics` object is provided by `paint()`, you never explicitly create a `Graphics` object. Actually, you couldn't explicitly create a `Graphics` object even if you wanted to because it is an abstract class.

Even though graphics operations often take place within the context of a window, the output of the Graphics object is really tied to a component. A *component* is a generic graphical window and forms the basis for all other graphical elements in the Java system. Java components are modeled at the highest level by the Component class, which is defined in the AWT package.

An applet or application window is just a specific type of component. Thinking of graphics in terms of the Component class rather than a window shows you that graphics can be output to any object derived from the Component class. As a matter of fact, every Component object contains a corresponding Graphics object that is used to render graphics on its surface.

Java graphics contexts (Graphics objects) have a few attributes that determine how different graphical operations are carried out. The most important of these attributes is the color attribute, which determines the color used in graphics operations such as drawing lines. You set this attribute using the setColor() method defined in the Graphics class. setColor() takes a Color object as its only parameter. Similar to setColor() is setBackground(), which is a method in the Component class that determines the color of the component's background. Graphics objects also have a font attribute that determines the size and appearance of text. This attribute is set using the setFont() method, which takes a Font object as its only parameter. You learn more about drawing text and using the Font object in the section "Drawing Text," later in this chapter.

Most of the graphics operations provided by the Graphics class fall into one of the following categories:

- Drawing graphics primitives
- Drawing text
- Drawing images

Drawing Graphics Primitives

Graphics primitives consist of lines, rectangles, circles, polygons, ovals, and arcs. You can create pretty impressive graphics by mixing these primitives together; the Graphics class provides methods for drawing these primitives. There are also methods that act on primitives that form closed regions. *Closed regions* are graphical elements with a clearly distinguishable inside and outside. For example, circles and rectangles are closed regions, but lines and points are not. You can also use the methods defined in the Graphics class to erase the area defined by a primitive or fill it with a particular color.

Lines

Lines are the simplest of the graphics primitives and are therefore the easiest to draw. The drawLine() method handles drawing lines, and is defined as follows:

```
void drawLine(int x1, int y1, int x2, int y2)
```

The first two parameters, *x1* and *y1*, specify the starting point for the line; the *x2* and *y2* parameters specify the ending point. To draw a line in an applet, call `drawLine()` in the applet's `paint()` method, as in this example:

```
public void paint(Graphics g) {
  g.drawLine(5, 10, 15, 55);
}
```

The results of this code are shown in Figure 20.4.

FIGURE 20.4.

A line drawn with the `drawLine()` *method.*

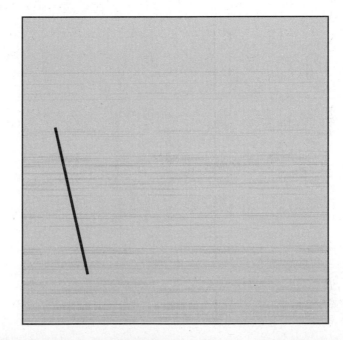

> **NOTE**
>
> Most graphical programming environments provide a way to draw lines (and other graphics primitives) in various widths. Java doesn't currently provide a facility to vary the width of lines, which is a pretty big limitation.

Rectangles

Rectangles are also very easy to draw in Java. The `drawRect()` method enables you to draw rectangles by specifying the upper-left corner and the width and height of the rectangle. The `drawRect()` method is defined in `Graphics` as follows:

```
void drawRect(int x, int y, int width, int height)
```

The *x* and *y* parameters specify the location of the upper-left corner of the rectangle; the *width* and *height* parameters specify their namesakes, in pixels. To draw a rectangle using drawRect(), just call it from the paint() method like this:

```
public void paint(Graphics g) {
  g.drawRect(5, 10, 15, 55);
}
```

The results of this code are shown in Figure 20.5.

FIGURE 20.5.

A rectangle drawn with the drawRect() *method.*

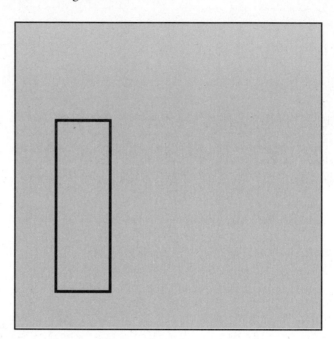

There is also a drawRoundRect() method that allows you to draw rectangles with rounded corners:

```
void drawRoundRect(int x, int y, int width, int height, int arcWidth,
  int arcHeight)
```

The drawRoundRect() method requires two more parameters than drawRect(): *arcWidth* and *arcHeight*. These parameters specify the width and height of the arc forming the rounded corners of the rectangle. Following is an example that uses drawRoundRect() to draw a rectangle with rounded corners:

```
public void paint(Graphics g) {
  g.drawRoundRect(5, 10, 15, 55, 6, 12);
}
```

The results of this code are shown in Figure 20.6.

FIGURE 20.6.
A rounded rectangle drawn with the drawRoundRect() *method.*

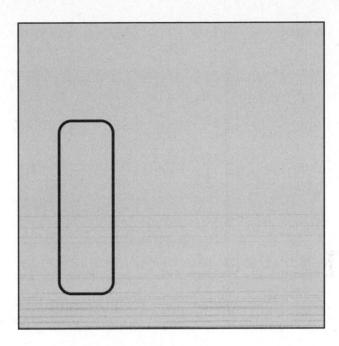

In addition to these two basic rectangle-drawing methods, there is also a method for drawing 3D rectangles with shadow effects along the edges: draw3DRect(). However, because Java has the limitation of only supporting a line width of one pixel, the 3D effect is pretty subtle.

The Graphics class also provides versions of each of these rectangle-drawing methods that fill the interior of a rectangle with the current color in addition to drawing the rectangle itself. These methods are fillRect(), fillRoundRect(), and fill3DRect(). The support for drawing both filled and unfilled rectangles is common throughout the Graphics class when dealing with closed regions.

> **NOTE**
>
> To draw a perfect square using any of the rectangle-drawing methods, simply use an equivalent width and height.

Polygons

Polygons are shapes consisting of a group of interconnected points; each point in a polygon is connected in a series by lines. To draw a polygon, you provide a list of points in the order in which they are to be connected to form the polygon shape. Polygons are not closed regions by default; to make a polygon a closed region, you must provide the same point as the starting and ending point for the polygon.

20
JAVA GRAPHICS
FUNDAMENTALS

Java provides two approaches to drawing polygons: a method and a class. The most straight-forward approach is using the `drawPolygon()` method, which is defined as follows:

```
void drawPolygon(int xPoints[], int yPoints[], int nPoints)
```

The first two parameters, *xPoints* and *yPoints*, are arrays containing the x and y components of each coordinate in the polygon. For example, *xPoints*[0] and *yPoints*[0] form the starting point for the polygon. The last parameter to `drawPolygon()`, *nPoints*, is the number of points in the polygon; this value is typically equal to the length of the *xPoints* and *yPoints* arrays.

The following example uses the `drawPolygon()` method to draw a closed polygon:

```java
public void paint(Graphics g) {
  int xPts[] = {5, 25, 50, 30, 15, 5};
  int yPts[] = {10, 35, 20, 65, 40, 10};

  g.drawPolygon(xPts, yPts, xPts.length);
}
```

The results of this code are shown in Figure 20.7.

FIGURE 20.7.

A closed polygon drawn with the `drawPolygon()` *method.*

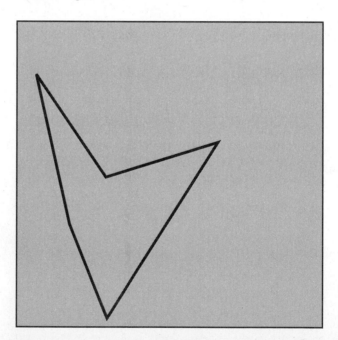

> **NOTE**
>
> The polygon in Figure 20.7 is closed because the same point (5, 10) is defined both at the beginning and end of the polygon coordinate list. Without duplicating this point at the end of the list, the last point would not have been connected back to the first point and the polygon would have remained an open region.

The other approach to drawing polygons involves using the Polygon class to construct a Polygon object. Once you have a Polygon object, you can simply pass it to drawPolygon() instead of passing the x and y point arrays. You construct a Polygon object using one of the Polygon class constructors, which are defined as follows:

```
Polygon()
Polygon(int xpoints[], int ypoints[], int npoints)
```

The first constructor simply creates a default polygon with an empty coordinate list; the second constructor is initialized with a coordinate list much like the one taken by the drawPolygon() method just described. Regardless of how you create a Polygon object, you can add points to the polygon by using the addPoint() method, which is defined as follows:

```
void addPoint(int x, int y)
```

The following example uses a Polygon object to draw a closed, filled polygon:

```
public void paint(Graphics g) {
  int      xPts[] = {5, 25, 50, 30, 15, 5};
  int      yPts[] = {10, 35, 20, 65, 40, 10};
  Polygon  poly = new Polygon(xPts, yPts, xPts.length);

  g.fillPolygon(poly);
}
```

The results of this code are shown in Figure 20.8.

FIGURE 20.8.

A closed polygon drawn with a Polygon *object and the* fillPolygon() *method.*

In the previous section, I mentioned that many of the methods for drawing graphics primitives in Java support both unfilled and filled versions. Figure 20.8 is an example of using the filled version for polygons, `fillPolygon()`.

You may not see why there is ever a need to use a `Polygon` object, considering the fact that I used the same technique for representing the set of points that make up the polygon for both the `drawPolygon()` method and the `Polygon` object. The truth is that `Polygon` objects are very useful whenever you know you have to draw a particular polygon again. Consider the asteroids floating around in a space game; you can easily model the asteroids as polygons and use a `Polygon` object to represent each. When it comes time to draw the asteroids, all the messy co-ordinates are already stored within each `Polygon` object, so you only have to pass the object to the `drawPolygon()` or `fillPolygon()` method.

Ovals

Another useful graphics primitive supported by Java is the *oval*, which is a rounded, closed region. You specify an oval using a coordinate for the top-left corner of the oval, along with the width and height of the oval. This is basically the same approach used when drawing rectangles with square corners; the difference, of course, is that ovals are round regions, not rectangular regions. The primary method for drawing ovals is `drawOval()`, which is defined as follows:

```
void drawOval(int x, int y, int width, int height)
```

The *x* and *y* parameters specify the location of the upper-left corner of the oval; the *width* and *height* parameters specify their namesakes. You draw an oval using the `drawOval()` method, like this:

```
public void paint(Graphics g) {
  g.drawOval(5, 10, 15, 55);
}
```

The results of this code are shown in Figure 20.9.

Like the drawing methods you learned about for other graphics primitives, the `Graphics` class also provides a method to draw filled ovals: `fillOval()`.

> **NOTE**
>
> To draw a perfect circle using the `drawOval()` or `fillOval()` methods, simply use equivalent width and height values.

FIGURE 20.9.

An oval drawn with the drawOval() *method.*

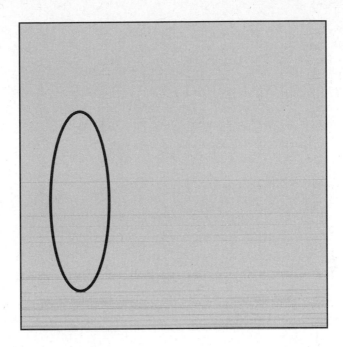

Arcs

Unlike the graphics primitives you've learned about so far, arcs are a little more complex to handle. An *arc* is basically a section of an oval; just picture erasing part of an oval and what you have left is an arc. Because an arc is really just part of an oval, you draw an arc in relation to the complete oval it is a part of. In other words, to specify an arc, you must specify a complete oval along with what section of the oval the arc comprises. If you still don't quite follow, maybe taking a look at the Java method for drawing arcs will help clear things up:

```
void drawArc(int x, int y, int width, int height, int startAngle, int arcAngle)
```

As you can see, the first four parameters of the drawArc() method are the same ones used in the drawOval() method. In fact, these parameters define the oval of which the arc is a part. The remaining two parameters define the arc as a section of this oval. To understand how these parameters define an arc, refer to Figure 20.10, which shows an arc as a section of an oval.

As you can see in Figure 20.10, an arc can be defined within an oval by specifying the starting and ending angles for the arc. Alternatively, you can specify just the starting angle and a number of degrees to sweep in a particular direction. In the case of Java, an arc is defined in the latter manner: with a starting angle and a sweep angle, or arc angle. The sweep direction in Java is counterclockwise, meaning that positive arc angles are counterclockwise and negative arc angles are clockwise. The arc shown in Figure 20.10 has a starting angle of 95 degrees and an arc angle of 115 degrees. The resulting ending angle is the sum of these two angles, which is 210 degrees.

FIGURE 20.10.

An arc defined as a section of an oval.

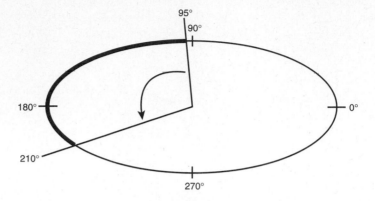

Following is an example of drawing a similar arc using the drawArc() method:

```
public void paint(Graphics g) {
  g.drawArc(5, 10, 150, 75, 95, 115);
}
```

The results of this code are shown in Figure 20.11.

FIGURE 20.11.

An arc drawn with the drawArc() method.

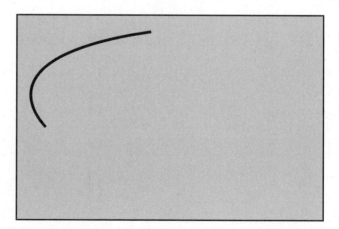

Like most of the graphics primitives in Java, there is a method for drawing filled arcs: fillArc(). The fillArc() method is very useful because you can use it to draw pie-shaped pieces of a circle or oval. For example, if you are writing an applet that has to draw a pie graph for a set of data, you can use the fillArc() method to draw each piece of the pie.

Drawing Text

Because Java applets (and graphical Java applications) are entirely graphical in nature, you must use the Graphics object even when you want to draw text. Fortunately, drawing text is very easy and yields very nice results. You typically create a font for the text and select it as the font to be used by the graphics context before actually drawing any text. As you learned earlier, the setFont() method selects a font into the current graphics context. This method is defined as follows:

```
void setFont(Font font)
```

The Font object models a textual font and includes the name, point size, and style of the font. The Font object supports three different font styles, which are implemented as the following constant members: BOLD, ITALIC, and PLAIN. These styles are really just constant numbers and can be added together to yield a combined effect. The constructor for the Font object is defined as follows:

```
Font(String name, int style, int size)
```

As you can see, the constructor takes as its parameters the name, style, and point size of the font. If you are wondering exactly how font names work, you simply provide the string name of the font you want to use. The names of the most common fonts supported by Java are TimesRoman, Courier, and Helvetica. To create a bold, italic, Helvetica, 22-point font, you use the following code:

```
Font f = new Font("Helvetica", Font.BOLD + Font.ITALIC, 22);
```

> **CAUTION**
>
> Some systems may support other fonts in addition to the three common fonts mentioned here (TimesRoman, Courier, and Helvetica). Even though you are free to use other fonts, keep in mind that these three common fonts are the only ones guaranteed to be supported across all systems. In other words, it's much safer to stick with these three fonts if you want your programs to be truly cross platform.

After you create a font, you often want to create a FontMetric object to find out the details of the font's size. The FontMetric class models very specific placement information about a font, such as the ascent, descent, leading (pronounced *ledding*), and total height of the font. Figure 20.12 shows what these font metric attributes represent.

You can use the font metrics to precisely control the location of the text you are drawing. After you have the metrics under control, you just have to select the original Font object into the Graphics object using the setFont() method, as in the following example:

```
g.setFont(f);
```

Now you're ready to draw some text using the font you've created, sized up, and selected. The drawString() method, defined in the Graphics class, is exactly what you need. drawString() is defined as follows:

```
void drawString(String str, int x, int y)
```

FIGURE 20.12.

The different font metric attributes.

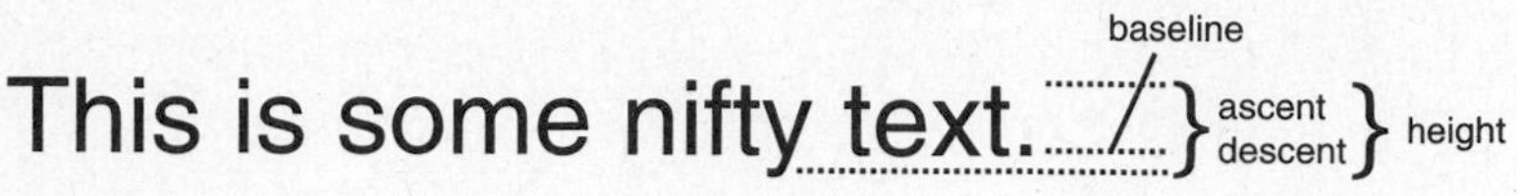

This is some nifty text.

baseline
} ascent
descent } height

The drawString() method takes a String object as its first parameter, which determines the text to be drawn. The last two parameters specify the location at which the string is drawn; *x* specifies the left edge of the text and *y* specifies the baseline of the text. The baseline of the text is the bottom of the text, not including the descent. Refer to Figure 20.12 if you are having trouble visualizing these pieces.

The DrawText sample applet in Listing 20.1 demonstrates how to draw a string centered in the applet window. Figure 20.13 shows the DrawText applet in action.

Listing 20.1. The DrawText sample applet.

```
// DrawText Class
// DrawText.java

// Imports
import java.applet.*;
import java.awt.*;

public class DrawText extends Applet {
  public void paint(Graphics g) {
    Font        font = new Font("Helvetica", Font.BOLD +
      Font.ITALIC, 22);
    FontMetrics fm = g.getFontMetrics(font);
    String      str = new
      String("The highest result of education is tolerance.");

    g.setFont(font);
    g.drawString(str, (getSize().width - fm.stringWidth(str)) / 2,
      ((getSize().height - fm.getHeight()) / 2) + fm.getAscent());
  }
}
```

The DrawText applet uses the font-related methods you just learned about to draw a string centered in the applet window. You may be wondering about the calls to the size() method when the location to draw the string is being calculated. The size() method is a member of Component and returns a Dimension object that specifies the width and height of the applet window.

That sums up the basics of drawing text using the Graphics object. Now it's time to move on to one of the most important aspect of Java graphics: images.

FIGURE 20.13.

The DrawText *sample applet.*

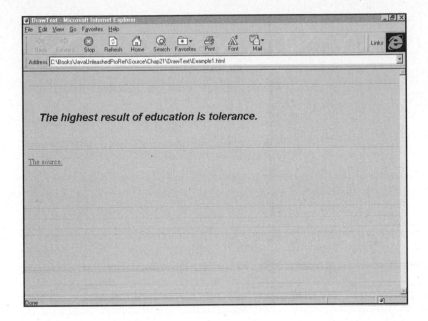

Drawing Images

Images are rectangular graphical objects composed of colored pixels. Each pixel in an image describes the color at that particular location of the image. Pixels can have unique colors that are usually described using the RGB color system. Java provides support for working with 32-bit images, which means that each pixel in an image is described using 32 bits. The red, green, and blue components of a pixel's color are stored in these 32 bits, along with an alpha component. The *alpha component* of a pixel refers to the transparency or opaqueness of the pixel.

Before getting into the details of how to draw an image, you must first learn how to load images. The getImage() method, defined in the Applet class, is used to load an image from a URL. getImage() comes in two versions, which are defined as follows:

```
Image getImage(URL url)
Image getImage(URL url, String name)
```

These two versions essentially perform the same function; the only difference is that the first version expects a fully qualified URL, including the name of the image, and the second version enables you to specify a separate URL and image name.

You probably noticed that both versions of getImage() return an object of type Image. The Image class represents a graphical image, such as a GIF or JPEG file image, and provides a few methods for determining the width and height of the image. Image also includes a method for retrieving a graphics context for the image, which enables you to draw directly onto an image.

The Graphics class provides a handful of methods for drawing images, which follow:

```
boolean drawImage(Image img, int x, int y, ImageObserver observer)
boolean drawImage(Image img, int x, int y, int width, int height,
  ImageObserver observer)
boolean drawImage(Image img, int x, int y, Color bgcolor, ImageObserver observer)
boolean drawImage(Image img, int x, int y, int width, int height, Color bgcolor,
  ImageObserver observer)
boolean drawImage(Image img, int dx1, int dy1, int dx2, int dy2, int sx1,
  int sy1, int sx2, int sy2, ImageObserver observer)
boolean drawImage(Image img, int dx1, int dy1, int dx2, int dy2, int sx1,
  int sy1, int sx2, int sy2, Color bgcolor, ImageObserver observer)
```

All these methods are variations on the same theme: They all draw an image at a certain location as defined by the parameters *x* and *y*. The last parameter in each method is an object of type ImageObserver, which is used internally by drawImage() to get information about the image.

The first version of drawImage() draws the image at the specified *x* and *y* location—*x* and *y* represent the upper-left corner of the image. The second version draws the image inside the rectangle formed by *x*, *y*, *width*, and *height*. If this rectangle is different than the image rectangle, the image is scaled to fit the defined rectangle. The third version of drawImage() draws the image with transparent areas filled in with the background color specified in the *bgcolor* parameter. The fourth version of drawImage() combines the capabilities of the first three, enabling you to draw an image within a given rectangle and with a background color.

The last two versions of drawImage() are new to Java 1.1 and provide support for clipping and flipping images. Before these versions of drawImage() were available, you had to clip an image using a cropping filter or the clipping mechanism provided in the Graphics class. The clipping mechanism in the Graphics class is limited because it can be set only to a more restrictive value—which means that it isn't very versatile. Furthermore, Java 1.0 really provided no direct means of flipping images. The last two drawImage() methods support both clipping and flipping by allowing you to specify the source and destination rectangles for the draw. Flipping is accomplished by swapping the x and y extents of the destination rectangle, which results in a reverse draw. The last of the drawImage() methods allows you to specify a background color to be drawn in transparent areas of the image.

The process of drawing an image involves calling the getImage() method to load the image, followed by a call to drawImage(), which actually draws the image on a graphics context. The DrawImage sample applet (presented in Listing 20.2) shows how easy it is to draw and flip an image (see Figure 20.14). This applet also shows how easy it is to immortalize your friends by plastering their images on the Web; Figure 20.14 displays a picture of my good friend, Keith Nash, and his twin brother Ned. Actually, "both" people shown in the applet are Keith—the applet inverts the original image horizontally to draw it a second time.

Listing 20.2. The DrawImage sample applet.

```
// DrawImage Class
// DrawImage.java

// Imports
import java.applet.*;
import java.awt.*;

public class DrawImage extends Applet {
  public void paint(Graphics g) {
    Image img = getImage(getCodeBase(), "Dude.gif");

    g.drawImage(img, 0, 0, this);
    g.drawImage(img, img.getWidth(this) * 2, 0, img.getWidth(this),
      img.getHeight(this), 0, 0, img.getWidth(this), img.getHeight(this),
      this);
  }
}
```

Figure 20.14.

The DrawImage *sample applet.*

The DrawImage sample applet loads an image in the paint() method using getImage(). The getCodeBase() method is used to specify the applet directory in which applet resources are usually located, while the image name itself is simply given as a string. The image is then drawn in the applet window using the basic drawImage() method. The more versatile drawImage() method is then used to draw the same image flipped horizontally next to the first image. The flipping is carried out simply by swapping the horizontal values on the destination rectangle, resulting in a reverse draw horizontally. It's as simple as that!

Summary

This chapter bombarded you with a lot of information about the graphics support in Java. Most of it was centered around the Graphics object, which is fortunately pretty straightforward to use. You began by learning about color and what it means in the context of Java. You moved

20

**Java Graphics
Fundamentals**

on to drawing a variety of different graphics primitives. You then learned how text is drawn in Java through the use of fonts and font metrics. Finally, you concluded the chapter by taking a look at images and how they are drawn.

This chapter showed you that Java not only provides a rich set of graphics features, but that it also has a very clean interface through which you can explore the use of graphics in your own applets. If the graphics features you learned about in this chapter seem a little tame, you may be ready to jump into the next chapter, which covers animation programming.

Basic Animation Programming

by Christopher A. Seguin

IN THIS CHAPTER

CHAPTER 21

History, as the cliché claims, repeats itself. Consider this: Between 4,000 and 6,000 years ago, the Sumerians began communicating using pictograms. In 1827, Joseph Niepce produced the first photographs on a metal plate. Eighty-eight years later, the motion picture camera was created and in 1937, the first full-length animation feature was released. Since then, animation has transformed from a novelty to an art form. We regularly see animation in commercials, television, and movies.

The history of the Web is similar. At first, Web pages could contain only text and links to other pages. In the early 1990s, a browser called Mosaic was released that added the ability to incorporate pictures and sound. Mosaic started a flurry of interest in the Internet. But after a while, even the carefully designed Web pages with elaborate background images and colored text began to grow stale. Java, a recent extension to the World Wide Web, allows programs to be added to Web pages.

Animations have been available on the Web since the early versions of Mosaic, where Mosaic would download the MPEG file and launch a separate viewer. With the release of Netscape version 1.1, CGI files could use a push-and-pull method of creating animations. The browser would receive instructions to reread the information or read the next URL address after a set delay. The client could keep the connection open and push new information onto the browser every so often. However, this type of animation was available only on Netscape. And it was slow. One of the popular uses of Java is to create animations. Because the Java animations are on the page, they serve to call attention to the Web page, rather than away from the page the way a separate viewer does. Java is also faster than the Netscape method and works on any browser that supports Java.

This chapter covers the following topics:

- The `Animator` class
- Design of simple animation systems
- Double buffering
- Advanced animation techniques

The design of simple animation systems is explained with animated text and images. This chapter covers double buffering, which is the easiest way to eliminate animation flicker. The advanced animation techniques include in-betweens, backgrounds, z-order, and collision detection.

The Animator Class

Before we dive into the programming of animation applets, let's start with the hands-down easiest way to create an animation: use someone else's applet. Herb Jellinek and Jim Hagen at Sun Microsystems have created an `Animator` class, an applet that creates an animation. This class is provided as a demonstration program with the Java Development Kit.

To use the `Animator` applet, do the following:

1. After installing Sun's Java Development Kit, copy the following three files to your classes directory: `Animator.class`, `ParseException.class`, and `ImageNotFoundException.class`. These files can be found in the examples provided with the JDK provided by Sun and are located on the CD-ROM that accompanies this book. They should be in a directory called `java/demo/Animator`.

2. Create the image and sound files for your animations.

3. Put the applet tag on your Web page. Table 21.1 shows the parameters that the `Animator` applet reads from your HTML file.

4. View your animation on your favorite Java-enabled browser.

Table 21.1. Animator applet parameters.

Tag	Description	Default
IMAGESOURCE	The directory that contains the image files	The same directory that contains the HTML file
STARTUP	The image to be displayed while the program loads the other images	None
BACKGROUNDCOLOR	A 24-bit number that specifies the color of the background	A filled, light-gray rectangle that covers the entire applet
BACKGROUND	The image to be displayed in the background	A filled, light-gray rectangle that covers the entire applet
STARTIMAGE	The number of the first image	1
ENDIMAGE	The number of the last image	1
NAMEPATTERN	Specifies the name of the image files	`T%N.gif` (`%N` means number, so `T%N.gif` uses images called `T1.gif`, `T2.gif`, `T3.gif,...`")
IMAGES	A list of indexes of the images to be displayed, in the order in which they are to be displayed	None
HREF	The page to visit on a mouse click	None
PAUSE	The number of milliseconds for the pause between frames	3900

continues

Table 21.1. continued

Tag	Description	Default
PAUSES	The number of milliseconds for the pause between each frame	The value of PAUSE
REPEAT	A boolean value: Does the animation cycle through the images? (yes or true/no or false)	true
POSITIONS	The coordinates of where each image will be displayed in the applet	(0,0)
SOUNDSOURCE	The directory that contains the sound files	The value of IMAGESOURCE
SOUNDTRACK	The background music	None
SOUNDS	The sounds to be displayed for each image in the animation	None

Most of the tags are straightforward in their use, but some tags need additional explanation. We'll begin with the images and then describe how to use the tags that accept multiple inputs.

The default name of images used by the Animator class must start with the letter T followed by a number. For example, if you have three GIF files that form the changing part of the animation, you can name them T1.gif, T2.gif, and T3.gif. However, you can change this default by using the NAMEPATTERN parameter. For example, if your images are called myImage1.jpg, myImage2.jpg, and myImage3.jpg, you would use the following parameter:

```
<PARAM NAME=NAMEPATTERN VALUE="myImage%N.jpg">
```

The background image and startup image have no constraints on their names.

There are two ways to specify the order of the images. First, you can specify the first and last image with the STARTIMAGE and ENDIMAGE tags. If the value of the STARTIMAGE tag is greater than the value of the ENDIMAGE tag, the images are displayed starting at STARTIMAGE and decrementing to ENDIMAGE. Second, you can specify the order of the images with the IMAGES tag. This tag takes multiple inputs, so let's consider how to give multiple inputs to the Animator applet.

Several tags take multiple inputs. The Animator class has implemented these tags using a ¦ as a separator between values. For example, the IMAGES tag requires the list of numbers of the images to be displayed. If you want to display the images T1.gif, T3.gif, and T2.gif in that order, you would write this:

```
<PARAM NAME=IMAGES VALUE=1¦3¦2>
```

The SOUNDS tag works the same way except that values can be left blank. A blank value in the SOUNDS tag means that no sound is played for that image. The PAUSES tag also takes multiple inputs, but if an input is left out, it defaults to the standard pause between images. For example, the following statements display the first image for 1000ms (1000 milliseconds), the second image for 250ms, and the third image for 4ms:

```
<PARAM NAME=PAUSE VALUE=250>
<PARAM NAME=PAUSES VALUE=1000¦¦4>
```

The POSITION tag is a set of coordinates. As with the IMAGES and SOUNDS tags, the coordinates are separated by a ¦ character. The x and y values of the coordinate are separated by an @ character. If a coordinate is left blank, the image remains in the same location as the previous image. For example, if you want to draw the first and second images at (30, 25), and the third image at (100, 100), you would write this code:

```
<PARAM NAME=POSITION VALUE=30@25¦¦100@100>
```

The Animator class enables you to create an animation quickly and easily. If, however, you have more than one moving object or you want to draw your objects as the animation runs, you have to write your own animation applet. The next section begins with the design of an animator and gives four examples.

Simple Animation

Let's dive right into programming simple animations in Java. Although these animations may not be perfectly smooth in their presentation, they do explain the basic design of an animation. We will also look at what makes a good animation. Let's begin by creating an abstract animated object interface, and then create several examples of the animation in action.

The AnimationObject Interface

When writing a program in an object-oriented language, the first step is to decompose the problem into things that interact. The things, called *objects*, that are similar are grouped into classes. The class holds all the information about an object. Sometimes, classes are very similar, and you can have a class to represent the similarities of the class. Such a class is called a *base class*. If the base class doesn't actually store information, but provides a list of methods that all the members of the class have, the class is called an *abstract class*.

Java is an objected-oriented language, so in creating a design for a program, first find similarities in the components of the program. When designing an animation, begin by looking for similarities. Each image or text message that moves is an object. But if you consider these objects, you find that they are very similar. Each object has to be able to paint itself in the applet window. In addition to painting the object, something about the objects is changing (or it wouldn't be an animation). So the object must know when to change.

Let's create a class with the following two methods:

- paint()—directs the object to paint itself
- clockTick()—tells the object to change

Java provides two ways to create an abstract class. First, if there is some basic method that is used for any object of the class, you can create an abstract class. The methods that are the same can be filled in. If there is no similarity in the actual methods, you can create an interface. The advantage of using an interface is that a class can inherit from multiple interfaces, but it can inherit only from a single class.

Because a moving text object and an image have nothing in common other than the names of their paint() and clockTick() methods, I have created the following interface:

```
public interface AnimationObject {
    public void paint (Graphics G, Applet parent);
    public void clockTick ();
}
```

This skeleton enables you to simplify the design of the applet object. For example, the paint() routine just erases the screen and sends each animation object a paint() method:

```
public void paint (Graphics g) {
    update (g);
    }
public void update (Graphics g) {
    //  Erase the screen
    g.setColor (Color.lightGray);
    g.fillRect (0, 0, nWidth, nHeight);
    g.setColor (Color.black);

    //  Paint each object
    for (int ndx = 0; ndx < AnimatedObjects.length; ndx++)
        AnimatedObjects[ndx].paint (g, this);
    }
```

For now, assume that the update() method and the paint() method are essentially the same, although a description of the difference is given later in this chapter in the section on double buffering. The update() method is straightforward, but it may cause your animation to flicker. Code to fix the flicker is given in the section on double buffering.

The run() method is only three steps. First, the applet tells each object that one time unit has passed, and then the applet repaints itself. Finally, the program pauses. Here's what the run() method looks like:

```
public void run() {
        int ndx = 0;

        //  Set the priority of the thread
        Thread.currentThread().setPriority(Thread.MIN_PRIORITY);
```

```
//  Do the animation
while (size().width > 0 &&
       size().height > 0 &&
       kicker != null) {

    for (ndx = 0; ndx < AnimatedObjects.length; ndx++)
        AnimatedObjects[ndx].clockTick ();

    repaint();

    try { Thread.sleep(nSpeed); }
        catch (InterruptedException e) {}
    }
}
```

The hard part is initially creating the applet, and that depends on how difficult it is to create each of the animation objects. Let's start with moving text.

Moving Text

NOTE

The code in this section is in Example 21.1 in file exmp21_1.java on the CD-ROM that accompanies this book.

Everyone has seen animated text, such as weather warnings that slide across the bottom of the TV screen during storms. Let's start with an animation object that moves a text message around the applet drawing area and consider why this is effective.

Java provides the drawString (String s, int x, int y) routine in the java.awt.Graphics class that draws a string at a specific location. To animate text, the applet repeatedly draws the string at a different location.

If we want to scroll text across the applet, what do we have to store? First, we need a text message. For this example, assume that the message slides only to the left. (It's easy to extend this code so that the message can also slide right, up, or down.) In addition to the message, we need some internal variables to store the x and y locations of where the message should be printed next.

The next question is, "How do you compute when the message is no longer visible?" We have to know about the length of the message and the width of the applet to determine when the message disappears from view and where it should reappear. We won't be able to determine the length of the message until we have the java.awt.Graphics object, so we'll postpone this computation until the first time we paint() the text message.

Let's begin by creating an object that stores each of these values:

```
class TextScrolling implements AnimationObject {

    // Internal Variables
    String pcMessage;

    int nXPos;
    int nYPos;
    int nAppletWidth;
    int nMessageWidth;
```

Now we need to initialize these variables in the constructor method. The constructor needs the text message and the applet width. The other values are computed in the paint() method. Here's the constructor:

```
public TextScrolling (String pcMsg, int nWide) {
    pcMessage = pcMsg;

    nAppletWidth = nWide;
    nMessageWidth = -1;

    nXPos = nWide;
    nYPos = -1;
    }
```

Use the drawString() method to draw the text message. The paint() routine is more complex, however, because we have to compute nYPos and nMessageWidth. The constructor assigned both of these variables the value -1 to flag them as unknown values. Now that a Graphics object is available, their values can be computed:

```
public void paint (Graphics g, Applet parent) {
    if (nYPos < 0) {
        // Determine the y position
        nYPos = (g.getFontMetrics ()).getHeight ();

        // Determine the size of the message
        char pcChars [];
        pcChars = new char [pcMessage.length()];
        pcMessage.getChars (0, pcMessage.length(),
                            pcChars, 0);
        nMessageWidth = (g.getFontMetrics ()).charsWidth
                            (pcChars, 0, pcMessage.length());
        }

    // Draw the object here
    g.drawString (pcMessage, nXPos, nYPos);
    }
```

TIP

Drawing in an applet is easy because the applet draws only the graphics that fall inside its boundaries. This process is called *clipping*—limiting the drawing area to a specific rectangle. All graphics output that falls outside the rectangle is not displayed. You can further limit the region where the graphics are drawn using java.awt.Graphics.clipRect().

Now, whenever the clock ticks, the message shifts to the left. You can do this by adjusting the nXPos variable. We reset the nXPos whenever the message is no longer visible:

```
public void clockTick () {
        //  Do nothing until the message width is known
        if (nMessageWidth < 0)
            return;

        //  Move Right
        nXPos -= 10;
        if (nXPos < -nMessageWidth)
            nXPos = nAppletWidth - 10;
        }

//  END of TextScrolling Object
}
```

At this point, I could point out the lack of computation in the paint() and clockTick() methods and say how it is important to avoid extensive computations during an animation. But either you already know that, or you would discover it very quickly with the first complex animation you write.

How can you avoid complex computations? You have two options:

- Perform the computations offline
- Do each computation once and save the results

In this animation object, the value of the variables nMessageWidth and nYPos were computed once in the paint() routine. Before then, the information wasn't available.

Let's consider some more examples. First, we'll write two programs to display a series of images in an applet and to move a single image around an applet. These programs demonstrate the first possibility. For the second possibility, we draw and copy a stick person.

Images

In the past ten years, computer animations of many different objects have been created using the physical equations that model movement. Interactions between rigid bodies are easy to animate, but more advanced techniques have created realistic animations of rubber bands and elastic cubes that deform as they interact. The computations required for these are extensive and are not suitable for the online nature of applets.

The first animation object uses the flip-book principle of animation. For this approach, you generate all the pictures in advance and allow Java to display the images in sequence to create the illusion of motion. This second approach is useful for rigid body motion and interactions, where you take a single image and move it around the applet drawing area.

But first, let's review some information about images.

The `MediaTracker` Class

Images take a while to load into the computer's memory, and they look very strange if you display them before they are completely ready. Have you ever seen the top of a head bouncing around a Web page? Very unnerving :-) To avoid this gruesome possibility, the creators of Java have provided a `MediaTracker` class. A `MediaTracker` object enables you to determine whether an image is correctly loaded.

> **NOTE**
>
> Although the `MediaTracker` class will eventually be able to determine whether an audio object has loaded correctly, it currently supports only images.

The `MediaTracker` object provides three types of methods:

- Those that register or check in images
- Those that start loading images
- Those that determine whether the images are successfully loaded

The methods that register images are named `AddImage()`; there are two versions of this method:

- `AddImage (Image img, int groupNumber)` begins tracking an image and includes the image in the specified group
- `AddImage (Image img, int groupNumber, int width, int height)` begins tracking a scaled image

You can organize images with the group number. Doing so enables you to check logical groups of images at once.

The methods that start loading the images are listed here:

- `checkAll (true)` starts loading all the images and returns immediately
- `checkID (int groupNumber, true)` starts loading all the images in the group specified by *groupNumber* and returns immediately
- `waitForAll()` starts loading all images and returns when all images are loaded
- `waitForID(int groupNumber)` starts loading all images in the group specified by *groupNumber* and returns when all images in the group are loaded

> **NOTE**
>
> In `checkAll()` and `checkID()`, the last input is `true`. It is not a variable but the `boolean` constant.

Because the routines that start with check return immediately, you can continue with other processing and occasionally monitor the progress with checkID(groupNumber) and checkAll().

> **TIP**
>
> Be careful not to monitor an image that has already been loaded. You should only track the loading of an image once. If you ask the media tracker to wait for an image that has already been loaded, it might never return.

The final two methods that determine whether the images loaded successfully are shown here:

- ■ isErrorAny() returns true if any errors were encountered loading any image
- ■ isErrorID(int *groupNumber*) returns true if any errors were encountered loading the images in the specified group

Now we are ready to start working with the image object animators. Let's begin with a *changing* image animation. Then we'll discuss a special type of changing image where all the individual frames are *tiled* in one large image and a different frame is shown at each time step. Finally, we'll create a *moving* image animation.

Changing Images

The flip-book method of animation in Java is the most popular on Web sites. Flip books contain pictures but no words. The first picture is slightly different from the second, and the second picture is slightly different from the third. When you thumb through a flip book as shown in Figure 21.1, the pictures appear to move. In this section, we create an applet that takes a series of images and repeatedly displays them in the applet window to create the illusion of motion.

> **NOTE**
>
>
> The code in this section is in Example 21.2 in file exmp21_2.java on the CD-ROM that accompanies this book.

This program has to store two values: the images to be displayed and the MediaTracker to determine whether the images are ready. Internally, we will also keep track of the number of the image to be displayed next:

```
class ChangingImage extends AnimationObject {

    //  Internal Variables
    Image ImageList [];
    int nCurrent;
    MediaTracker ImageTracker;
```

FIGURE 21.1.

Thumbing through a flip book creates the illusion of motion.

The constructor initializes the variables with the constructor's inputs and starts the animation sequence with the first image:

```
public ChangingImage (Image il[], MediaTracker md,
            Applet parent) {
      ImageList = il;
      nCurrent = 0;
      ImageTracker = md;
      }
```

As mentioned earlier, it is important to check that the image is available before it is drawn:

```
public void paint (Graphics g, Applet Parent) {
      //  Draw the object here
      if (ImageTracker.checkID(1)) {
          g.drawImage (ImageList [nCurrent], 100, 100, Parent);
          }
      else
          System.out.println
              ("Not Ready Yet " + (nCurrent+1));
      }
```

Remember that this object is only one part of a possibly large animation; you may have to sacrifice the first few pictures to keep all the parts of the animation together. Therefore, the object doesn't check the ImageTracker to see whether the images are ready in the clockTick method:

```
public void clockTick () {
      nCurrent++;
      if (nCurrent >= ImageList.length)
          nCurrent = 0;
      }

//  END of ChangingImage Object
}
```

With this approach, most of the work is done ahead of time, either as you draw all the images or by a computer program that generates and saves the images. In Java, this method is how you animate objects with elastic properties or realistic lighting because of the amount of computation involved.

Tiling Image Frames

> **NOTE**
>
> The code in this section is in Example 21.3 in file exmp21_3.java on the CD-ROM that accompanies this book.

One problem with loading multiple images is that you have to make a separate connection for each image file you want to download. This operation takes extra time because of the overhead involved in making a connection back to the server. One way to get around this delay is to place all the images side by side in a single image file. Figure 21.2 shows an example of laying the images side by side.

FIGURE 21.2.

Frames are stored side by side in a single image.

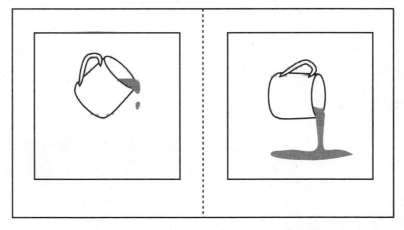

Frame 1   Frame 2

With this arrangement, you have to read only one large image from the server—hence, you make only one connection. But how do you draw the image since you don't want to write all the images onto the screen at the same time? The solution is to use java.awt.Graphics.clipRect(). First, block out the area we want to draw in. This should have the x and y coordinates of where you want the image to be, and the size of the frame. Let's call the location of the image nX and nY; call the width and height of the frame nFrameWidth and nFrameHeight:

```
public void paint (Graphics g, Applet Parent) {
    //  Draw the object here
    g.clipRect (nXPos, nYPos, nFrameWidth, nFrameHeight);
    g.drawImage (Picture, nXImagePos, nYPos, Parent);
    }
```

The tricky part was recognizing this use of the clipRect() method. The only thing left is to explain the nXImagePos variable. All we have to do is shift what part of the image is in the visible part. The shifting is done in the variable nXImagePos. Let's say that we have nImageWidth that stores the width of the entire image (with all the frames); when we do a clock tick, we just decrease the nXImagePos until it becomes less than the nImageWidth parameter, at which point we reset it to zero:

```
public void clockTick () {
    nXImagePos -= nFrameWidth;
    if (nXImagePos <= nImageWidth)
        nXImagePos = 0;
    }
```

Because that is so easy, why isn't it done all the time? Well, you will run into problems with this approach if you use multiple changing images in your animations. clipRect() computes the intersection of the current clipping rectangle (which initially is the entire area of the applet) and the rectangle that was just given as the input to clipRect. So there is no way to make the clipping region bigger! This AnimationObject must be the only one of its type, and it must be the last object to be painted. If only there was a way to break up the framed image once you've loaded it into the applet....

We don't have the mechanism yet to do this operation, but I promise to show you how before the end of the chapter.

Moving Images

NOTE

The code in this section is in Example 21.4 in file exmp21_4.java on the CD-ROM that accompanies this book.

For rigid bodies, there is an easier way to create a 2D animation: You can take an image of the object and move it around the applet drawing area. An example of a *rigid body* is a rock or a table (they don't deform or change while they move). A cube of gelatin, on the other hand, wiggles as it moves and deforms when it runs into another object.

The MovingImage class is very similar to the ChangingImage class described in the preceding section. The variables are a picture and the x and y locations where it will be drawn. In this object, the nCurrent variable keeps track of the location in the object's path, rather than the image:

```
class MovingImage extends AnimationObject {
    //  Internal Variables
    Image Picture;
    MediaTracker ImageTracker;
    int nCurrent;

    int pnXPath [];
    int pnYPath [];
```

The constructor for MovingImage is nearly identical to the constructor for ChangingImage except that it has two extra variables to save:

```
public MovingImage (Image img, MediaTracker md,
               int pnXs [], int pnYs [],
               Applet parent) {
    Picture = img;
    nCurrent = 0;

    ImageTracker = md;

    pnXPath = pnXs;
    pnYPath = pnYs;
    }
```

Instead of changing images, we simply draw the image at the next location in the path:

```
public void paint (Graphics g, Applet Parent) {
    //  Draw the object here
    if (ImageTracker.checkID(1))
        g.drawImage (Picture,
                    pnXPath[nCurrent], pnYPath[nCurrent],
                    Parent);
    }
```

The clockTick() program is nearly identical to the method written for the ChangingImage object.

The Copy Area

NOTE

The code in this section is in Example 21.5 in file exmp21_5.java on the CD-ROM that accompanies this book.

Remember that we are trying to minimize the amount of computation performed during an animation. If we don't have an image we can use, we have to draw the image using graphic primitives. Suppose that we want to slide a stick figure across the applet. Here is a small method that draws a stick person at a specified location:

```
public void drawStickFigure (Graphics g, int nX, int nY) {
        g.drawOval (nX +  10, nY +  20, 20, 40);
        g.drawLine (nX +  20, nY +  60, nX +  20, nY + 100);
        g.drawLine (nX +  10, nY +  70, nX +  30, nY +  70);
```

```
        g.drawLine (nX +  10, nY + 150, nX +  20, nY + 100);
        g.drawLine (nX +  20, nY + 100, nX +  30, nY + 150);
        }
```

The original stick figure is drawn in `black` on a `lightGray` background. To continue the animation, we can erase it by redrawing the figure in `lightGray` over the `black` figure, and then drawing a new figure in `black` a little to the right. For such an uncomplicated drawing, this method is effective. For the purpose of this illustration, however, let's animate the stick figure using the `copyArea()` method:

```
public void paint (Graphics g, Applet Parent) {
        if (bFirstTime) {
            bFirstTime = false;
            drawStickFigure (g, nX, nY);
            }
        else {
            g.copyArea (nX, nY, 35, 155, 5, 0);
            }
        }
```

The first time the `paint()` method is called, the figure is drawn using the `drawStickFigure()` routine. After the first time, the `paint()` routine recopies the stick figure a few pixels to the right. To erase the old copy of the figure, some blank space is copied with the stick figure. The result: the figure slides across the applet.

There are two problems with this animation so far. The first problem is that sometimes part of the stick figure is left behind. When you make a `repaint()` method call to draw the next frame in the animation, you sometimes get repainted and you sometimes do not. Whether or not the `repaint()` call is processed depends on how much additional computation is being done at the time. If multiple repaint requests have been made since the drawing thread has last been allowed to execute, it combines all of these repaints into a single call. To solve this problem, you just have to remember where the stick figure was last drawn in the applet window, and copy the figure with extra blank space from there. You can do this easily in the `paint()` routine:

```
public void paint (Graphics g, Applet Parent) {
    static int nLastX;
    if (bFirstTime) {
        bFirstTime = false;
        drawStickFigure (g, nX, nY);
        nLastX = nX;
        }
    else {
        int nSkipped = nX - nLastX;
        g.copyArea (nX - (nSkipped - 5), nY, 30 + nSkipped, 155, nSkipped, 0);
        nLastX = nX;
        }
    }
```

The second problem is that our previous animations repeatedly cycle across the screen. Once our little figure is out of the viewing area, it is gone for good. If only there was a way to draw an image in Java and save it. Then we could use the animation techniques in the previous section to move the image around the applet drawing area repeatedly.

Fortunately, such a facility is available in Java. In addition to enabling us to create an image offline so that it can be used repeatedly, this facility generates a cleaner flicker-free animation.

Double-Buffered Animation

Double buffering is a common trick to eliminate animation flicker. Instead of drawing directly onto the applet's drawing area where a person can see it, a second drawing area is created in the computer's main memory. The next frame of the animation is drawn on the drawing area in main memory. When the frame is complete, it is copied onto the screen where a person can see it. It sounds complicated, but it is really quite simple.

To double buffer your animation, you have to do the following:

■ Create an off-screen image and get the associated graphics object

■ Draw on the off-screen graphics object

■ Copy the off-screen image onto the applet's graphic object

> **NOTE**
>
> An example that shows the flickering effect and the improvement created by using double buffering is in Example 21.6 in file `exmp21_6.java` on the CD-ROM that accompanies this book.

The first step requires that you create an image in which you will do all the work. To create the off-screen image, you must know the height and width of the drawing area. Once that is determined, you can get the graphics object from the image with the `getGraphics()` method:

```
offScreenImage = createImage(width, height);
offScreenGraphic = offScreenImage.getGraphics();
```

The graphics object extracted from the image is now used for all drawing. This part of the program is the same as the `paint()` program explained in "Simple Animation," earlier in this chapter—except that, instead of using g, you use `offScreenGraphic`:

```
//  Erase the screen
offScreenGraphic.setColor (Color.lightGray);
offScreenGraphic.fillRect (0, 0, width, height);
offScreenGraphic.setColor (Color.black);

//  Paint each object
for (int ndx = 0; ndx < AnimatedObjects.length; ndx++)
    AnimatedObjects[ndx].paint (offScreenGraphic, this);
```

Finally, you copy the off-screen image into the applet's graphics object:

```
g.drawImage(offScreenImage, 0, 0, this);
```

You have succeeded in improving the clarity of your animation. You may wonder why this change improves the animation. After all, the number of pixels that are drawn has increased! There are three reasons for this improvement:

- Most machines have an efficient way to copy a block of bits onto the screen, and an image is just a block of bits.

- No extra computations interrupt the drawing of the picture. These extra computations come from drawing lines, determining the boundaries of a filled area, and looking up fonts.

- Video memory cannot be cached in the CPU, while an off-screen image can be anywhere in memory.

- All the image appears at once, so even though more work is done between frames, a human perceives that all the work is done instantaneously.

Now we have reduced the flicker by creating an off-screen image. In the first section, the theme was to reduce the computation the applet performed. Using the off-screen image increases the computations but improves the visual effect. Now we will eliminate the extra computations in the program by using the off-screen image.

The update() and paint() Methods

> **NOTE**
>
> To see when the paint() and update() methods are called, the ChangingImage example has been modified to print a message to the output describing which method was called. This method is in Example 21.7 in exmp21_7.java on the CD-ROM that accompanies this book.

Earlier, I said that the paint() and update() methods were essentially the same. In fact, most of the sample code that Sun Microsystems provides does basically what I did in the "Simple Animation" section: the update() method calls the paint() method. So what is the difference?

The paint() method is called when the applet begins execution and when the applet is exposed. An applet is said to be *exposed* when more area or a different area can be viewed by the user. For example, when an applet is partially covered by a window, it must be redrawn after the covering window is removed. The removal of the covering window exposes the applet (changes the screen to enable the user to see more of a viewing area of a window). See Figure 21.3 for an example.

FIGURE 21.3.
Moving another window exposes the applet.

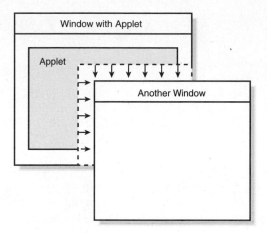

The update() method is called whenever a repaint() method is called. For example, in the run() method of the applet, a repaint() method is called on every iteration through the loop.

So what does that mean? If the paint() method calls the update() method, the applet does extra work by recomputing what the image should be. Yet less than a second ago, update() created a perfectly good picture—and it is still available for paint() to use. It is better if the paint() method copies the image created by update() onto the screen again.

Here is a more efficient pairing of paint() and update():

```
public void paint (Graphics g) {
    if (offScreenImage != null)
        g.drawImage(offScreenImage, 0, 0, this);
    }

public void update (Graphics g) {
    if (offScreenImage != null) {
        //  Erase the screen
        offScreenGraphic.setColor (Color.lightGray);
        offScreenGraphic.fillRect (0, 0, nWidth, nHeight);
        offScreenGraphic.setColor (Color.black);

        //  Paint each object
        for (int ndx = 0; ndx < AnimatedObjects.length; ndx++)
            AnimatedObjects[ndx].paint (offScreenGraphic,
                                            this);

        g.drawImage(offScreenImage, 0, 0, this);
        }
    }
```

> **TIP**
>
> One problem with this approach is that the paint() method is called as the applet begins running. At this time in the execution of the applet, there is no image to display because update() has not yet been called. The effect: The first screen the user sees is a filled white rectangle that covers the entire applet. You can remedy this situation by printing a text message in the off-screen image when it is created.

Because it takes only three lines of code to overload the paint() and the update() methods, we've been doing this from the very beginning. However, you don't have to overload the update() method. You could just put all your drawing commands in the paint() method, and your code would work just fine. The default method for update() erases the screen with the background color and calls the paint() method. And our earlier code has already showed us what happens if you do this—it creates lots of flicker. If you want a cleaner-looking animation, you should always overload the update() method.

Breaking Tiled Images

Earlier in this chapter, I said that the problem with using tiled images to store the frames of an animation is that you can use only one of them. But now that we have the mechanism to create an off-screen image, we can break the tiled image into multiple off-screen images after the image with the frames is loaded.

The easy way to do this is to create a new object similar to the ChangingImage object. Most of the code is identical to the ChangingImage object except that once the MediaTracker reports that the image is completely loaded, the object should break the image into its separate frames. We can do this in the prepare() method. First, we create an array of the images called ImageList. Then we create an off-screen image for each. Now we just act as if we are doing double buffering—we get the graphic and draw each frame using the graphic:

```
private void prepare () {
    ImageList = new Image [nFrameCount];
    Graphic tempGraphic;
    for (int ndx = 0; ndx < nFrameCount; ndx++) {
        ImageList [ndx] = createImage(nFrameWidth, nFrameHeight);
        tempGraphic = pimgFrames [ndx].getGraphics();
        tempGraphic.drawImage (imgAllFrames, -1 * ndx * nFrameWidth, 0, this);
        }
}
```

The double-buffered approach is one of the most widely used algorithms to improve animation. Part of the reason that this algorithm is widely used is that it is so simple. The next section discusses other algorithms that help improve your animation or simplify your life.

Advanced Tricks of the Trade

The following sections present four tactics for better animations. First, you learn about *in-betweens*, which reduce the amount of time you spend creating the animation. Second, *backgrounds* provide an alternative method to erase the screen and spice up the animation. Third, we consider the *order* in which images are drawn in the applet to produce the illusion of depth. Finally, we discuss *collisions*.

In-Betweens

When the first movie-length animation was finished, it required over two million hand-drawn pictures. Because there were only four expert artists, it would have been impossible for these people to create the entire film. Instead, the master artists drew the main, or key, frames (the frames specified by the creator of the animation). Other artists drew the in-between frames (frames created to move objects between their key positions).

This approach is used today to create animations, except that now the computer creates the in-between frames. Generally, a computer needs more key frames than does a human artist because computers don't have common-sense knowledge about how something should move. For example, a falling rock increases speed as it falls (which is obvious), but a computer does not know this obvious fact. You can compensate for the computer's lack of common sense by specifying how the objects move between key positions. Four common trajectories are shown in Figure 21.4.

FIGURE 21.4.

These graphs show four different trajectories for moving objects.

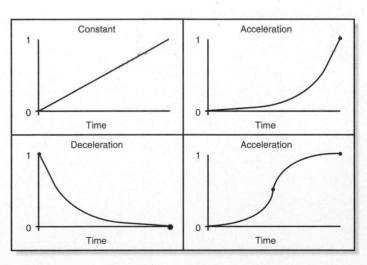

To see how in-betweens work, consider Figure 21.5, which shows a ball moving upwards using the first acceleration trajectory from Figure 21.4. At first, the ball object moves slowly, but then the distance between successive positions of the ball increases. The successive positions of the balls are numbered, with 1 being the starting image and 10 being the final image.

Figure 21.5.

The motion of an image corresponds to the location on the trajectory graph.

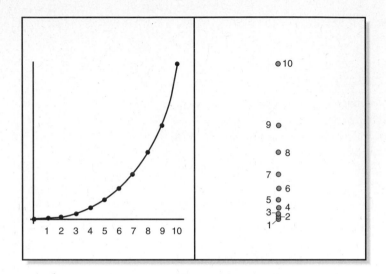

You can create these object paths with the following code:

```
class InBetweenGenerator extends Object {

    public int[] InBetweens (int pnValues[], String sTypes[],
                          int pnWidths [])
        {
        int pnResult [];
        int ndx;
        int nArraySize = 1;

        //  Create the array of the correct size
        for (ndx = 0; ndx < pnWidths.length; ndx++) {
            nArraySize += 1 + pnWidths [ndx];
            }

        pnResult = new int [nArraySize];

        //  Fill in the array
        int nItem = 0;
        for (ndx = 0; ndx < pnWidths.length; ndx++) {
            pnResult [nItem] = pnValues [ndx];
            fillIn (pnResult, nItem + 1,
                    pnWidths[ndx], sTypes [ndx],
                    pnValues[ndx], pnValues[ndx+1]);
            nItem += (pnWidths[ndx] + 1);
            }
```

```
        pnResult [nItem] = pnValues [pnWidths.length];

        return pnResult;
        }
```

First, we call the method InBetweens(), which creates an array and fills it in. Each segment of the array can contain a different type of motion. For each type of motion, we will fill in a separate portion of the array using the method fillIn():

```
void fillIn (int pnArray [], int nStart, int nHowMany,
             String sType, int nLow, int nHigh)
    {
    double dIncr = 1.0 / ((double) (nHowMany + 2));
    double dTemp = dIncr;

    for (int ndx = 0; ndx < nHowMany; ndx++) {
        pnArray [ndx + nStart] = (int) (nLow +
            (nHigh - nLow) * interpolate (sType, dTemp));
        dTemp += dIncr;
        }
    }
```

How these values are filled in depends on the type of interpolation occurring between each point. We can compute the actual value with the following method:

```
double interpolate (String sType, double dValue)
    {
    if (sType.equalsIgnoreCase ("c")) {
        return dValue;
        }
    else if (sType.equalsIgnoreCase ("a")) {
        return dValue * dValue;
        }
    else if (sType.equalsIgnoreCase ("d")) {
        return (dValue * (2.0 - dValue));
        }
    else { //  Both
        if (dValue < 0.5) {
            double dTemp = 2.0 * dValue;
            return 0.5 * dTemp * dTemp;
            }
        else {
            double dTemp = 2.0 * dValue - 1.0;
            double dTemp2 = 0.5 * dTemp * (2.0 - dTemp);
            return 0.5 + dTemp2;
            }
        }
    }
//  End of InBetweenGenerator
}
```

In-betweens reduce the amount of information an animation artist must enter to create the desired animation. The next section presents a few hints for using a background image. Basically, a *background image* is a combination image that contains all the unchanging pictures. Using a background can reduce the computations involved in the animation.

> **NOTE**
>
> One thing in-betweens allow you to do is to specify the velocity or acceleration of the object.

Background

Another trick animators use is to draw the background on one sheet of paper and then draw the characters and moving objects on a piece of plastic. Because the background remains the same, it is drawn once. By overlaying the different plastic pictures, you can create the illusion of movement in a world. The same trick can be used with a computer. You first create a background image and save it. Then, instead of erasing the image with the `fillRect()`, you use `drawImage()` to initialize the off-screen image and draw the moving parts on top of the background.

The borders of your moving images should be transparent—just as though the characters were drawn on plastic. The GIF89a graphics image format allows you to designate one of the colors in a GIF image as transparent. When Java recognizes one of the pixels in the image as being the transparent color, it does not draw anything, so the background shows through. You can either create your images with a software program that allows you to specify the transparent color, or you can use a separate program to read the graphics file and set the transparent color. One program that allows you to specify the transparent color is called `giftrans`, available at anonymous ftp sites such as this one:

`http://www-genome.wi.mit.edu/WWW/tools/graphics/giftrans/`

This site contains a DOS executable file and the C source code. Many more sites have this program, and you can find at least 20 more by searching Lycos or Yahoo! with the keyword `giftrans`.

> **NOTE**
>
> You can load either JPG or GIF images for animations in Java, but there is no facility to specify transparent regions in images stored in the JPG format.

Z-Order

You will notice in your animations that some objects appear to be in front of others because of the way they are painted. For example, the last object painted appears to be the closest object to the viewer. Such an arrangement is called a *2-$\frac{1}{2}$- dimensional picture.*

We can specify the order in which the objects are drawn by associating a number with each AnimationObject. This number reflects how far forward in the viewer's field of vision the object is. This number is called the *z coordinate*, or the *z-order number*. Because the x axis is generally from left to right on the screen, and the y axis is up and down, the z axis comes out of the screen at you.

The z-order number can be stored in a base class from which the other animated objects are subclassed. Let's call this new object a DepthObject. Although we could store an integer in this class of objects, we might tempt users of the DepthObject to manipulate the number directly. Instead, we'll use good data-hiding techniques and require the implementation of a method that returns the z-order number:

```
public interface DepthObject implements AnimationObject {
    public int queryZOrder ();
  }
```

The next step is to create an object to store all the animated objects and keep them in order. This object should be able to add a new animated object at any time, as well as paint each object and inform them all of the passage of time:

```
public class ThreeSpaceAnimation {
    Vector vecAnimations;

    public int addElement (DepthObject doNew) {
        int nStart = 0;
        int nEnd = vecAnimations.size ();
        int nOrder = doNew.queryZOrder ();

        try {
            while (nStart + 1 <= nEnd) {
                int nCurrent = (nStart + nEnd) / 2;
                int nCurrentDepth = ((DepthObject) vecAnimations.elementAt
                                        (nCurrent)).queryZOrder ();
                if (nCurrentDepth < nOrder)
                    nStart = nCurrent;
                else if (nCurrentDepth == nOrder) {
                    nStart = nCurrent;
                    nEnd = nCurrent;
                    }
                else
                    nEnd = nCurrent;
                }

            if (((DepthObject) vecAnimations.elementAt (nStart)).queryZOrder () >
                    nOrder) {
                // Insert before
                vecAnimations.insertElementAt (doNew, nStart);
                }
            else if (((DepthObject) vecAnimations.elementAt (nEnd)).queryZOrder ()
                        < nOrder) {
                // Insert after
                vecAnimations.insertElementAt (doNew, nEnd+1);
                }
```

```
              else {
                  //  Insert between
                  vecAnimations.insertElementAt (doNew, nEnd);
                  }
              } catch (ClassCastException cce) {}
          }

      public void clockTick () {
          allAnimationObjects = vecAnimations.elements ();
          while (allAnimationObjects.hasMoreElements ()) {
              try {
                  AnimationObject aniObj = (AnimationObject)
                                          allAnimationObjects.nextElement ();
                  aniObj.clockTick ();
                  } catch (ClassCastException cce) {}
              }
          }
      public void paint (Graphics g, Applet parent) {
          allAnimationObjects = vecAnimations.elements ();
          while (allAnimationObjects.hasMoreElements ()) {
              try {
                  AnimationObject aniObj = (AnimationObject)
                                          allAnimationObjects.nextElement ();
                  aniObj.paint (g, parent);
                  } catch (ClassCastException cce) {}
              }
          }
```

Before we finish with this class, note that the way DepthObject was created allows the object to change its depth at any time. To make changing the depth more efficient, we will ask the object to send a message to the ThreeSpaceAnimation to inform it of the change. The method to inform the object is called informDepthChange and it takes the object that is changing as input:

```
public void informDepthChange (DepthObject obj) {
    vecAnimations.removeElement (obj);
    addElement (obj);
    }
```

Collision Detection

One final item to cover is how you can tell if two objects have collided. In many animations where the path of each object is predetermined, this question is not important. But sometimes, you may want to create an animated object controlled by the user (in a video game, for example). In such situations, it becomes important to determine when two objects collide.

The easiest way to detect collisions is to simply consider whether the two images overlap. This calculation is easy because we can extract the size of the images from the images themselves. But it is not very accurate, especially if there are transparent pixels along the edge. For an example of this approach, see Figure 21.6.

FIGURE 21.6.

*An example of collision
detection using a
rectangle covering the
entire image.*

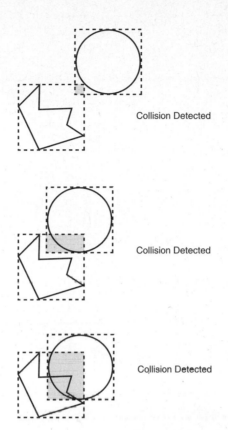

Collision Detected

Collision Detected

Collision Detected

The hard way to detect a collision is to check each pixel in each image and see whether two non-transparent pixels are at the same location. Figure 21.7 shows this option. This is a very costly operation because you have to check each pixel; this approach is really not suited to an interpreted language like Java.

As a compromise, a third method is suggested. You can associate with each image a smaller rectangle that lies inside the image. This smaller rectangle more closely matches where the nontransparent pixels are (see Figure 21.8). There are two reasons that this algorithm is better. First, comparing two rectangles to determine whether they intersect is much quicker than comparing all the colored pixels of each image to determine if they overlap. Second, a large portion of the image near the edge may be transparent. Generally, you don't want to make this transparent region an invisible force field that transforms near misses into collisions.

If you choose the correct rectangle for each image, the rectangle will cover most of the colored pixels and not too many of the transparent pixels. Choosing the best rectangle is the hard part, and I can't help you there, but we can plan to make collision detection a part of the animation design by creating an interface. This interface, called Collidable, returns the bounding rectangle. You determine whether an object can collide by casting it to an instance of this interface. If it can be cast, then you check its rectangle with the object that it collides with.

FIGURE 21.7.
Exact collision detection is possible if you compare nontransparent pixels.

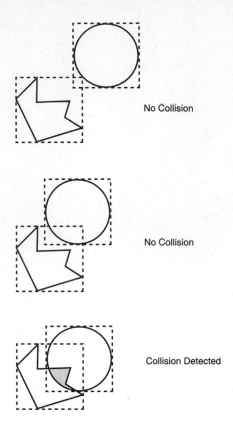

No Collision

No Collision

Collision Detected

```
public interface Collidable {
    public Rectangle queryHitArea ();
    }
```

With this interface, we can check to see whether two animated objects collide with the following code:

```
if ((animatedObject1.queryHitArea()).intersects (animatedObject2.queryHitArea())) {
    // The two objects have collided
    }
else {
    //  The two objects missed each other
    }
```

This algorithm makes use of the Rectangle object provided in java.awt.

FIGURE 21.8.
Using a smaller rectangle for detecting collisions is faster and has fewer errors than using the image's entire area.

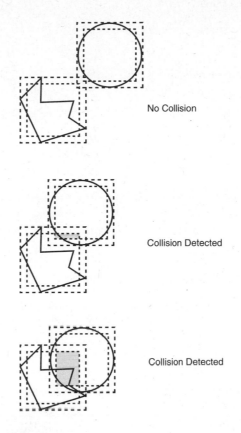

No Collision

Collision Detected

Collision Detected

Example Object Animator

Now let's take some of the ideas discussed in this chapter and make a multiple-object animator. In this section, we'll see some of the highlights of this chapter. First, we want the code to be able to read from the HTML file the number and motion of the animation objects. Second, we'll review how some of the advanced animation techniques are used in this example.

NOTE

The full source code for this example is provided on the CD-ROM that accompanies this book. The code for this example is in exmp21_8.java.

To enable the program to read the motion specifications from the applet tag, we have to do the following:

- Store the images and animation objects in a vector
- Generalize the `ChangingImage` and `MovingImage` to a single object
- Add routines to the `init()` method to load the required information

The first step is to store the images and the animation objects in a vector. The applet then dynamically stores however many objects or images there will be in the animation. For more information about how to use a vector, see Chapter 11, "The Utilities Package."

The effect of an `AnimatedImage` object is a moving changing picture. It requires an array of images and two arrays for the path the object travels. However, the `AnimatedImage` object sometimes is used as a `ChangingImage` object, and it would be easier on the user if numbers could be passed for the path variables. The constructor has been overloaded for this purpose. The other change is the use of a vector to store the images, which allows us to store an arbitrary number of images.

The `init()` method is standard, but the applet generates the tags it needs as it runs. It does this by concatenating strings with numbers:

```
String at = getParameter ("IL" + 3);
```

This arrangement enables us to load an arbitrary number of animation objects. For the tags and what they mean, consult Table 21.2.

Table 21.2. Tags for `exmp21_8.java` (located on the CD-ROM).

Tag	Description
IL?	Image letter, what should prefix the image filenames
IC?	The number of images
IO?	Image offset, which image you should start with
KF?	The number of key frames
X?_?	The x coordinates of the key frame
Y?_?	The y coordinates of the key frame
XT?_?	The type of motion between x values
YT?_?	The type of motion between y values
W?_?	The number of points between values

The first ? in the tag refers to the number of the animated object. The second ? in the tag is the number of the frame. For example, X3_7 refers to the x value of the third animated object in the seventh key frame.

Now consider some of the advanced techniques and how they were used in this example. This program provides the functionality to create in-betweens and to use a background image. To keep the animation from flickering, this code also uses the double-buffered approach to painting the image.

The paths of the moving objects are specified in the HTML file, but they are filled in as suggested by the user with the InBetweenGenerator object. This object requires three values: the key locations, how many frames to produce between each set of key locations, and the type of motion between each key location. It then generates an array of integers that represent the path that object traverses. To extend the InBetweenGenerator object to create another type of motion between endpoints, rewrite the interpolation() method to include your new motion. All the equations in this method take a number between 0 and 1, and return a number between 0 and 1. However, if you want the object to overshoot the source or the destination, you can create equations that produce values outside this range.

Notice that a background image is an image that doesn't move and doesn't change. To create a background for the animation, just make the background image the first animated object.

FOR MORE INFORMATION

Here are some Web sites you can browse for more information about animations. The best collection of Java applets is Gamelan, and it has a page on animations. Its URL is as follows:

`http://www.gamelan.com/Gamelan.animation.html`

The following sites have many links to animations. Viewing some of these sites can give you ideas for your animations:

- `http://www.xm.com/cafe/AnimatePLUS/slideshow.html`
  Description of the slideshow applet

- `http://www.auburn.edu/~harshec/WWW/Cinema.html`
  An example of the slideshow in action

- `http://www-itg.lbl.gov/vbart/`
  BART schedule animation

- `http://www.intrinsa.com/personal/steve/ClickBoard/ClickBoard.html`
  Interactive animation

continues

continued

- http://www.sealevelsoftware.com/sealevel/javademo.htm
  Animation of falling raindrops
- http://www.dimensionx.com/dnx/StreamingAnimation/index.html
  Smooth-loading animation
- http://www.geom.umn.edu/~daeron/apps/flag.html
  United States flag blowing in the wind

More information about animation can be found at this URL:
http://java.sun.com/people/avh/javaworld/animation/

Summary

In this chapter, we created the AnimationObject interface that simplifies design. This animation class was then used to create moving text, to create a flip-book-style animation, to animate an image that contains frames, and to create a moving-image animation. Double buffering was used to eliminate flicker, and we discussed the difference between the paint() and update() methods. The final algorithms discussed were the use of in-betweens, background images, z-order numbers, and collision detection.

What really launched Java into the spotlight for many people was its capability to perform animations on the World Wide Web. With the release of Netscape 2.0, Java is not the only way to create animations on Web pages. Increasingly, there are specialized programs that help you create animations that can be visible on Web pages. One of these is Shockwave for Director, which enables you to create animations in Director; Shockwave also allows the animations to be viewed. VRML is a language that specifies three-dimensional animations by specifying the locations, objects, and a viewing path. However, VRML currently requires special graphics hardware to view. It seems, then, that Java is still the least expensive way to create an animation.

Creating User Interface Components

by David R. Chung

IN THIS CHAPTER

CHAPTER

22

The Java Abstract Window Toolkit (AWT) consists of classes that encapsulate basic GUI controls. Because Java is a multiplatform solution, the AWT provides a lowest common denominator interface. Any interface you develop should appear about the same on any platform. Often, the AWT is called *Another Window Toolkit* or (affectionately) *Awful Window Toolkit*. Chapter 14, "The Windowing (AWT) Package," provides an overview of the AWT.

Now don't be misled—the AWT provides many useful controls and your applications or applets may not require anything more. Sometimes, however, an application needs something extra. This chapter examines two methods for creating custom user interface components: extending controls and combining controls.

Extending Controls

In this chapter, you learn how to extend the TextField class to create a password control. The new class is a TextField that allows users to enter a password. Instead of displaying the password, however, the control displays asterisks as the user types.

The mechanism you use to extend the control is called subclassing. *Subclassing* is just a fancy object-oriented term for changing the way a class works. The actual process creates a new class from the old one and adds new features along the way.

The passField Class

You create the passField class by subclassing the TextField class. The new control allows the user to type passwords. You provide an implementation of the processKeyEvent() method for the class. When the user enters a character, processKeyEvent() responds and *consumes* the event. You keep track of the key the user presses and place an asterisk in the control (to keep the password hidden).

Notice that this control does not actually verify that the password is valid. Instead, the control keeps track of user input and hides the actual characters. Later in the chapter, you see how to combine this control with other methods to create a useful password control.

Member Data

The passField class has to keep track of the characters entered by the user. To do so, it requires a data member of type String:

```
import java.awt.*;
import java.awt.event.*;

class passField extends java.awt.TextField {
    String pass ;
```

The class constructor has to know how many characters the control can contain. To convey that information, the class constructor takes an integer parameter, chars. Because passField is derived from `TextField`, the first line in the constructor must be a call to the superclass constructor.

> **NOTE**
>
> To understand how classes are derived from (or extend) other classes, you must be familiar with some object-oriented terminology. In this example, `passField` is derived from `TextField`. `TextField` is referred to as the *superclass*, *parent class*, or *base class*; `passField` is referred to as the *subclass*, *child class*, or *derived class*.

The call to `super(int)` actually calls the superclass constructor, `TextField(int)`. The `enableEvents()` method indicates that this class processes keyboard events. The next line in the constructor simply creates the `String`:

```
public passField( int chars ) {
    super( chars ) ;
    enableEvents( AWTEvent.KEY_EVENT_MASK ) ;
    pass = new String() ;
}
```

The reason for subclassing this control is to hide user input. To do this, the control must handle user input in the derived class. Events are then *consumed* so that the `TextField` base class does not respond to those events. To handle user input, this control overrides the class's `processKeyEvent()` method, which is called every time the user presses a key.

The overridden `processKeyEvent()` method must do the following:

- Add an asterisk to the control.
- Store the actual key value entered.
- Position the cursor at the end of the string.

Because this class does not actually display the user-entered values, the call to `getText()` returns a `String` full of asterisks. Next, the method adds an asterisk to the `String` and puts it back in the control. The `select()` method is used to position the cursor at the end of the line; because the two parameters are the same, nothing is actually selected:

```
protected void processKeyEvent( KeyEvent e ) {
    switch ( e.getID() ) {
        case KeyEvent.KEY_PRESSED :
            String text = getText() ;
            setText( text + "*" ) ;
            select( text.length() + 1, text.length() + 1 ) ;
```

The next item of business is to store the keystroke in a `String`. Because the `key` parameter is an `int`, you must cast it to a `char` and then use the `String.valueOf()` method to convert it to a `String`. This new `String` is then concatenated to the existing `String`. The `processKeyEvent()` method has fully handled the keyboard event. The call to `consume()` prevents any other method from responding to the event.

```
        pass = pass + String.valueOf( (char)key ) ;
        e.consume() ;
}
```

The `getString()` method is provided to allow `containers` that use this control to get the user-entered value:

```
public String getString() {
    return pass ;
}
}
```

To test the `passField` class, let's embed it in a simple applet, as shown here:

```
import java.awt.*;
public class testPassField extends java.applet.Applet {
    public void init() {
        add( new passField( 40 ) ) ;
    }
}
```

Figure 22.1 shows the `testPassField` applet.

FIGURE 22.1.

The `testPassField`
applet.

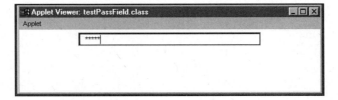

If you run the applet and type some letters, you will see that there are some strange behaviors. When you press Backspace, instead of erasing an asterisk as you might expect, the control adds another one! The reason is that when the `processKeyEvent()` method gets a keystroke—any keystroke—it simply adds it to the string and displays another asterisk.

To fix this behavior, you must somehow handle certain keystrokes differently. If you call `consume()` only for the keystrokes you want to handle, the superclass's `processKeyEvent()` method handles the other keystrokes. Replace the call to `consume()` with this code:

```
        if ( arg > 20 ) {
            e.consume();
        }
```

Although this is only a partial solution, it is a beginning. If the keystroke has an ASCII value less than `20` (that is, if it is a nonprinting character), it is not consumed and the superclass's `processKeyEvent()` method handles it. If your `processKeyEvent()` method consumes the event, the event is not passed on. In this example, this small modification causes the control to accept Backspaces. To really make this method useful, however, you must also change the value of the `String` to reflect any deletions.

Combining Controls

If you have ever served on a committee, you know how hard it is for a group of people to work together to reach a common goal. Without leadership, everyone seems to go their own way. Without well-coordinated communication, duplication of effort can occur. Likewise, if you try to put together a Java applet by combining several AWT controls, it may seem that you have a big committee—lots of activity but no leadership and no communication.

However, if you combine your controls into *composite controls*, they will then act like all the rest of the AWT controls. You can use the new composite controls anywhere you use regular AWT controls. To demonstrate composite controls, the following sections explain how to create a scrolling picture-window control. This control takes an image and makes it scrollable. All the interaction between the AWT components that make up the control is handled internally. To use the control, all you have to do is create one and add it to your applet's layout.

Using Panels to Combine User Interface (UI) Elements

The base class for all composite controls is `Panel`. The `Panel` class allows you to embed other AWT components in it. Because this class is derived from `Container`, it can contain UI components. The `Panel` class also contains functions for managing embedded components.

Some functions in the `Panel` class can retrieve references to the embedded components. These functions allow the class to iteratively call methods in the embedded components. Other functions handle layout issues.

PANELS ARE COMPONENTS, TOO

The primary advantage of using `Panel` as your composite component base class is that it is a component itself. Consequently, you can use your composite components like any other AWT components. You can take these new components and combine them to form composite components from other composite components, and so on.

The new components can be added to layouts; they can generate existing events or create new ones. They are full-fledged UI components and can be used anywhere AWT components are used.

The composite controls will be more versatile if you implement them with the appropriate layout manager. Because you want the controls to be self-contained, they should be able to lay themselves out properly no matter what size they are.

A Scrolling Picture-Window Example

In this example, you create a scrolling picture window. You derive a class from Panel called ScrollingPictureWindow. The class contains three member objects: an ImageCanvas object (derived from Canvas) to hold the picture and two scrollbars.

To respond to the scrollbars, the ScrollingPictureWindow class implements AdjustmentListener. Therefore, the class is the listener object for its own scrollbars.

This composite control provides a self-contained way to display a picture. A user simply has to pass an Image object to the control and the control does the rest. The control handles scrolling and updating the image. Figure 22.2 shows the scrolling picture-window applet.

FIGURE 22.2.

The testPictureWindow *applet.*

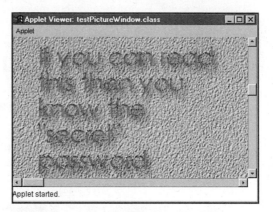

The testPictureWindow applet uses a ScrollingPictureWindow object. The applet creates the ScrollingPictureWindow in *exactly* the same way you would use an AWT control. The source code for the testPictureWindow class is given in Listing 22.1. This class and the ScrollingPictureWindow class in Listing 22.2, found later in this chapter, make up the testPictureWindow applet. Both classes can be found on the CD-ROM that accompanies this book.

Listing 22.1. The source code for the testPictureWindow class.

```
import java.applet.*;
import java.awt.*;
import java.awt.event.*;

public class testPictureWindow extends Applet {

    ScrollingPictureWindow pictureWindow ;

public void init() {
    Image img = getImage( getCodeBase(), "picture.gif" ) ;
    pictureWindow = new ScrollingPictureWindow( img ) ;
```

```
        setLayout( new BorderLayout() );
        add( "Center", pictureWindow ) ;
        pictureWindow.setEnabled( true ) ;
        }
};
```

The ImageCanvas Class

The ImageCanvas class is derived from Canvas. Canvas is provided in the AWT as a generic class for painting and drawing. You use this class to display your image. The class contains one instance variable:

```
Image canvasImg ;
```

The ImageCanvas constructor takes an Image object as a parameter. Because object parameters are passed by reference, img becomes a local reference to the Image object in the class:

```
public ImageCanvas( Image img ) {
    canvasImg = img ;
}
```

The only other method provided in the ImageCanvas class is paint(). The paint() method actually draws the image. Before doing any painting, however, the control has to determine whether its parent is enabled. This check allows the entire control to be turned off.

Because the picture scrolls, the class has to know where to draw it. The location of the image depends on the position of the scrollbars. In your scheme, the ScrollingPictureWindow object handles communication between the member objects. You have to query the ScrollingPictureWindow object to determine where to draw the image:

```
    public void paint(Graphics g) {
        if ( getParent().isEnabled() ) {
            g.drawImage( canvasImg,
                -1 * ((ScrollingPictureWindow)getParent()).imgX,
                -1 * ((ScrollingPictureWindow)getParent()).imgY,
                this ) ;
        }
    }
```

To get the information, use the getParent() method. The getParent() method is a member of the Component class. This method returns a reference to the Container object that holds the Component.

When you call getParent(), you get a reference to the ScrollingPictureWindow object. Because this reference is the Container type, you have to cast it to a ScrollingPictureWindow reference. Now you can access the public instance variables in the ScrollingPictureWindow object.

The imgX and imgY members contain the x and y coordinates of the point (in terms of the Image) that will be displayed in the upper-left corner of the window. If you want the point (10,5) to be displayed in the upper-left corner, pass -10 and -5 to drawImage().

Instance Variables

The ScrollingPictureWindow class contains several instance variables. These variables include the embedded controls and state variables. The embedded controls are stored as follows:

```
public ImageCanvas imageCanvas ;
Scrollbar    vertBar ;
Scrollbar    horzBar ;
Image        image ;
```

The last instance variable in this list is a reference to an Image object, which is passed in by the owner of your class object.

The remaining instance variables all contain information about the state of the control. The first two contain the size (in pixels) of the entire image:

```
int imgWidth ;
int imgHeight ;
```

The next two instance variables contain the current position of the image. These variables also reflect the current position of the scrollbars. Because the scrollbars and the image are tied together, both classes use these variables. The scrollbars set their values, and the ImageCanvas uses these values to place the image:

```
int imgX ;
int imgY ;
```

The last variable is used by the scrollbars. This value specifies the amount the scrollbar moves when you request a page up or page down:

```
int block ;
```

Class Construction

The class constructor performs all the initialization for your class. The constructor must do the following:

- Initialize the state variables
- Determine the size of the image
- Instantiate the member controls
- Set up the GridBagLayout layout manager
- Set the constraints for each control
- Add the class as the listener

Initialize State Variables

Begin construction by setting the local Image reference to the Image argument:

```
    public ScrollingPictureWindow ( Image img ) {
        image = img ;
```

The next step in the construction process is simple. You have to initialize `imgX` and `imgY` to zero. What this really does is set the initial position of the image and the scrollbars. These two instance variables contain the x and y offsets at which to display the image:

```
imgX = 0 ;
imgY = 0 ;
```

The `ImageCanvas` class needs these variables to determine how to place the image. The `ImageCanvas paint()` method accesses these instance variables directly and uses them in its call to `drawImage()`.

Determine the Image Size

Your composite control has to know how large the image is. Once you have this information, you know it will remain constant. Unfortunately, determining the image size is not as straightforward as you may think.

Your class has been designed to take an `Image` object as a parameter, giving the users of the class a great deal of flexibility to load the image any way they want. The image you receive may be one of many in an array. It may be in use by other objects in the applet. It may also have been just recently loaded by the calling applet. It is this last case that causes problems.

In your class constructor, it is possible that the reference you receive is to an image that is not yet fully loaded. To get the image size, you make a call to `Image.getHeight()`. If the image is not fully loaded, however, `getHeight()` returns -1. To get the size of the image, you must loop until `getHeight()` returns a value other than -1. Both `while` loops that follow have `null` bodies:

```
while ((imgHeight = image.getHeight(this)) == -1 ) {
    // loop until image loaded
}

while ((imgWidth  = image.getWidth(this)) == -1 ) {
    // loop until image loaded
}
```

Instantiate Member Controls

Next you must create the embedded member objects. The `ImageCanvas()` takes the `Image` as a parameter. The scrollbar constructors each take a constant that determines whether the scrollbar is vertical or horizontal:

```
imageCanvas = new ImageCanvas( image ) ;

vertBar = new Scrollbar( Scrollbar.VERTICAL ) ;
horzBar = new Scrollbar( Scrollbar.HORIZONTAL ) ;
```

Set Up `GridBagLayout`

You use the `GridBagLayout` layout manager to lay out the embedded control. `GridBagLayout` is the most versatile layout manager in the AWT; it provides precisely the control you need to arrange the components.

First you create a GridBagLayout object. Then you call setLayout() to make it the current layout manager:

```
GridBagLayout gridbag = new GridBagLayout();
setLayout( gridbag ) ;
```

Set Up Constraints for Each Control

The GridBagLayout class uses the GridBagConstraints class to specify how the controls are laid out. First you create a GridBagConstraints object. Then you use the GridBagConstraints object to determine how to lay out the individual components:

```
GridBagConstraints c = new GridBagConstraints();
```

You add the ImageCanvas object to your panel first. Because the ScrollingPictureWindow control is supposed to act like the native AWT controls, it must be resizeable. Because you have to specify that the control can grow in both x and y directions, set the fill member to BOTH:

```
c.fill        = GridBagConstraints.BOTH ;
```

Because you want the image to fill all the available space with no padding, set the weight parameters to 1.0:

```
c.weightx     = 1.0;
c.weighty     = 1.0;
```

Finish laying out the image by calling setConstraints() to associate the ImageCanvas object with the GridBagConstraints object. Then add the image to the layout:

```
gridbag.setConstraints(imageCanvas, c);
add( imageCanvas ) ;
```

Then you lay out the scrollbars. Start with the vertical scrollbar. The vertical scrollbar should shrink or grow vertically when the control is resized, so set the fill member to VERTICAL:

```
c.fill        = GridBagConstraints.VERTICAL ;
```

Look at your layout in terms of rows. You see that the first row contains two controls: the ImageCanvas and the vertical scrollbar. You indicate that the scrollbar is the last control in the row by setting the gridwidth member to REMAINDER.

```
c.gridwidth   = GridBagConstraints.REMAINDER ;
```

Complete the vertical scrollbar layout by associating it with the constraint object and then add it to the layout:

```
gridbag.setConstraints(vertBar, c);
add( vertBar ) ;
```

Finally, lay out the horizontal scrollbar. Because this scrollbar should be horizontally resizeable, set its fill member to HORIZONTAL:

```
c.fill        = GridBagConstraints.HORIZONTAL ;
```

The reason for using a `GridBagLayout` layout manager is to prevent the horizontal scrollbar from filling the entire width of the control. You want to guarantee that the horizontal scrollbar remains the same width as the `ImageCanvas` object. Fortunately, the `GridBagConstraint` class provides a way to tie the width of one object to the width of another.

You use the `gridwidth` member of the `GridBagConstraint` class to specify the width of the scrollbar in terms of grid *cells*. Set this member to 1 so that the horizontal scrollbar takes up the same width as the `ImageCanvas` object (they are both one cell wide). It is the `ImageCanvas` object that sets the cell size.

```
c.gridwidth  = 1 ;
```

Then add the horizontal scrollbar. First associate it with the constraints object and then add it to the layout:

```
gridbag.setConstraints(horzBar, c);
add( horzBar ) ;
```

Finally, declare `ScrollingPictureWindow` to be the `AdjustmentListener` object for both scrollbars:

```
        vertBar.addAdjustmentListener( this ) ;
        horzBar.addAdjustmentListener( this ) ;
```

Depending on where your control is used, it may be resizeable. You handle resizing by overriding the `Component.setBounds()` method. This method is called every time a control is resized. The first thing your function does is to call the superclass's `setBounds()` method. The superclass method does the real work of sizing. Because you are using a `GridBagLayout`, the `LayoutManager` resizes the individual components:

```
public synchronized void setBounds( int x,
                                    int y,
                                    int width,
                                    int height) {
        super.setBounds( x, y, width, height ) ;
```

You let the superclass do the resizing, so now you must update the image and scrollbars. First, determine whether the width of the control is greater than the image width plus the width of the vertical scrollbar. If the control width is greater, disable the horizontal scrollbar:

```
        if ( width > imgWidth + vertBar.getBounds().width ) {
            horzBar.setEnabled( false ) ;
```

If the control width is not greater than the horizontal scrollbar, enable the horizontal scrollbar:

```
        } else {
            horzBar.setEnabled( true ) ;
```

Next, determine how to reposition the horizontal scrollbar. Start by getting the size of the entire control and the width of the vertical scrollbar:

```
            Rectangle bndRect = getBounds() ;
            int barWidth = vertBar.getPreferredSize().width ;
```

> **NOTE**
>
> When working with scrollbars, you have to set several values:
> - The thumb position
> - The maximum and minimum values
> - The size of the viewable page
> - The page increment

Now you can calculate the maximum value for the scrollbar. You always set the minimum value of the scrollbar to zero. The maximum value is the image width minus the width of the ImageCanvas. You set the page size and page increment to one-tenth of the maximum size:

```
int max = imgWidth - (bndRect.width - barWidth);
block = max/10 ;
```

Before setting the new values, you must determine how to translate the old position to the new scale. Start by getting the old maximum value. If the old value is zero, you make the position zero:

```
int oldMax = horzBar.getMaximum() ;
if ( oldMax == 0) {
    imgX = 0 ;
```

If the old maximum value is not zero, you calculate the new position. First, express the old position as a fraction of the old maximum. Then multiply the fraction by the new maximum. The resulting value gives you the new position:

```
} else {
    imgX = (int)(((float)imgX/(float)oldMax) *
                  (float)max) ;
}
```

The last thing you have to do is set the scrollbar parameters:

```
horzBar.setValues( imgX, block, 0, max ) ;
horzBar.setBlockIncrement( block ) ;
}
```

Use the same algorithm to set the vertical scrollbar.

Add the Class as the Listener

The scrolling picture-window control is especially concerned with scrollbar events. All other types of events are passed on and handled outside your program.

You start by implementing the `AdjustmentListener` interface and overriding the `adjustmentValueChanged()` method. Because the `ScrollingPictureWindow` class is designated as the listener for both scrollbars, it gets all the scrollbar events. When the user adjusts the scrollbars, you reset the `imgX` and `imgY` variables and call `repaint()`:

```
public void adjustmentValueChanged(AdjustmentEvent e) {
        imgY = vertBar.getValue() ;
        imgX = horzBar.getValue() ;
        imageCanvas.repaint();
    }
```

Putting It Together

You now have a composite control that can become a drop-in replacement for other AWT controls. It handles its own events and responds to external resizing. You use this class by combining it with the `testPictureWindow` applet class from Listing 22.1, earlier in this chapter. The `ScrollingPictureWindow` class appears in Listing 22.2 and can also be found on the accompanying CD-ROM.

Listing 22.2. The ScrollingPictureWindow class.

```
class ScrollingPictureWindow
                    extends Panel
                    implements AdjustmentListener{

    ImageCanvas  imageCanvas ;
    Scrollbar    vertBar ;
    Scrollbar    horzBar ;
    Image        image ;

    int imgWidth ;
    int imgHeight ;
    int imgX ;
    int imgY ;
    int block ;

    public ScrollingPictureWindow ( Image img ) {
        image = img ;
        imgX = 0 ;
        imgY = 0 ;

        while ((imgHeight = image.getHeight(this)) == -1 ) {
        // loop until image loaded
        }

        while ((imgWidth  = image.getWidth(this)) == -1 ) {
        // loop until image loaded
        }

        imageCanvas = new ImageCanvas( image ) ;
        vertBar = new Scrollbar( Scrollbar.VERTICAL ) ;
        horzBar = new Scrollbar( Scrollbar.HORIZONTAL ) ;
        GridBagLayout gridbag = new GridBagLayout();
        setLayout( gridbag ) ;
```

continues

Listing 22.2. continued

```
        {
        GridBagConstraints c = new GridBagConstraints();
        c.fill      = GridBagConstraints.BOTH ;
        c.weightx   = 1.0;
        c.weighty   = 1.0;
        gridbag.setConstraints(imageCanvas, c);
        add( imageCanvas ) ;
        }

        {
        GridBagConstraints c = new GridBagConstraints();
        c.fill      = GridBagConstraints.VERTICAL ;
        c.gridwidth = GridBagConstraints.REMAINDER ;
        gridbag.setConstraints(vertBar, c);
        add( vertBar ) ;
        }

        {
        GridBagConstraints c = new GridBagConstraints();
        c.fill      = GridBagConstraints.HORIZONTAL ;
        c.gridwidth = 1 ;
        gridbag.setConstraints(horzBar, c);
        add( horzBar ) ;
        }

        vertBar.addAdjustmentListener( this ) ;
        horzBar.addAdjustmentListener( this ) ;
    }

    public synchronized void setBounds( int x,
                                         int y,
                                         int width,
                                         int height) {

        super.setBounds( x, y, width, height ) ;
        if ( width > imgWidth + vertBar.getBounds().width ) {
            horzBar.setEnabled( false ) ;
        } else {
            horzBar.setEnabled( true ) ;
            Rectangle bndRect = getBounds() ;
            int barWidth = vertBar.getPreferredSize().width ;
            int max = imgWidth - (bndRect.width - barWidth);
            block = max/10 ;
            int oldMax = horzBar.getMaximum() ;
            if ( oldMax == 0) {
                imgX = 0 ;
            } else {
            imgX = (int)(((float)imgX/(float)oldMax) *
                                         (float)max) ;
            }
            horzBar.setValues( imgX, block, 0, max ) ;
            horzBar.setBlockIncrement( block ) ;
        }
```

```
        if (height > imgHeight + horzBar.getBounds().height) {
            vertBar.setEnabled( false ) ;
        } else {
            vertBar.setEnabled( true ) ;
            Rectangle bndRect = getBounds() ;
            int barHeight = horzBar.getPreferredSize().height ;
            int max = imgHeight - (bndRect.height - barHeight) ;
            block = max/10 ;
            int oldMax = vertBar.getMaximum() ;
            if ( oldMax == 0) {
                imgY = 0 ;
            } else {
            imgY = (int)(((float)imgY/(float)oldMax) *
                                          (float)max) ;
            }
            vertBar.setValues( imgY, block, 0, max ) ;
            vertBar.setBlockIncrement( block ) ;
        }
    }

    public void adjustmentValueChanged(AdjustmentEvent e) {
        imgY = vertBar.getValue() ;
        imgX = horzBar.getValue() ;
        imageCanvas.repaint();
    }
};

class ImageCanvas extends Canvas {
    Image canvasImg ;
    public ImageCanvas( Image img ) {
        canvasImg = img ;
    }

    public void paint(Graphics g) {
        if ( getParent().isEnabled() ) {
            g.drawImage( canvasImg,
                -1 * ((ScrollingPictureWindow)getParent()).imgX,
                -1 * ((ScrollingPictureWindow)getParent()).imgY,
                this ) ;
        }
    }
};
```

A Password-Protected Picture Control

The versatility of composite or extended controls becomes apparent when they are combined into a single applet. The applet presented in this section is a password-protected picture control. This control combines a passField control with a ScrollingPictureWindow control. Figures 22.3 and 22.4 show the testPassWindow applet.

FIGURE 22.3.

The testPassWindow
*applet before entering
the password.*

FIGURE 22.4.

The testPassWindow
*applet after entering the
password.*

This applet combines passField, ScrollingPictureWindow and Button objects. Because the passField and ScrollingPictureWindow classes are self-contained, they are used here just like the AWT Button control. Because Java applets are reusable components themselves, the applet is like a new control itself. In fact, in Java, you create applets to embed in your Web pages in the same way you create controls to embed in your applets.

The testPassWindow applet begins by creating passField, Button, and ScrollingPictureWindow objects:

```
import java.applet.*;
import java.awt.*;
import java.awt.event.*;
```

```
public class testPassWindow
                    extends Applet
                    implements ActionListener {
    passField               passwordField ;
    Button                  verifyButton ;
    ScrollingPictureWindow pictureWindow ;
```

The `init()` method creates the member objects and places them in the control using the `GridBagLayout` layout manager (see Chapter 14, "The Windowing (AWT) Package," for details on the `GridBagLayout` layout manager and the associated `GridBagConstraints` classes). Notice that the `passField` and `ScrollingPictureWindow` controls are used as if they were *native* AWT controls. Finally, `init()` registers `testPassWindow` as the listener for the `Verify` button:

```
public void init() {
    GridBagLayout gridbag = new GridBagLayout();
    setLayout( gridbag ) ;
    {
    GridBagConstraints c = new GridBagConstraints();
    passwordField = new passField( 30 ) ;
    c.fill       = GridBagConstraints.BOTH ;
    c.gridx      = 1 ;
    c.gridy      = 1 ;
    c.weightx    = 1.0;
    gridbag.setConstraints(passwordField, c);
    add( passwordField ) ;
    }

    {
    GridBagConstraints c = new GridBagConstraints();
    verifyButton = new Button( "Verify" ) ;
    c.gridx      = 2 ;
    c.gridy      = 1 ;
    c.gridwidth  = GridBagConstraints.REMAINDER ;
    gridbag.setConstraints(verifyButton, c);
    add( verifyButton ) ;
    }

    {
    GridBagConstraints c = new GridBagConstraints();
    Image img = getImage( getCodeBase(), "picture.gif" ) ;
    pictureWindow = new ScrollingPictureWindow( img ) ;
    c.fill       = GridBagConstraints.BOTH ;
    c.gridx      = 1 ;
    c.gridy      = 2 ;
    c.gridwidth  = 2 ;
    c.weightx    = 1.0 ;
    c.weighty    = 1.0 ;
    gridbag.setConstraints(pictureWindow, c);
    add( pictureWindow ) ;
    }

    pictureWindow.setEnabled( false ) ;
    verifyButton.addActionListener( this ) ;
}
```

To tie all these controls together, the `testPassWindow` class implements the `ActionListener` interface. This combination of the password control and the picture-window control is a good candidate for encapsulation in a `Panel` so that it would become one big composite control.

The `testPassWindow` class implements `actionPerformed()` from the `ActionListener` interface. This function simply checks whether the password entered by the user is valid and then enables and paints the image:

```
public void actionPerformed(ActionEvent e) {
    if ( passwordField.getString().equals( "secret" ) ) {
        pictureWindow.setEnabled( true ) ;
        pictureWindow.imageCanvas.invalidate() ;
        pictureWindow.imageCanvas.repaint() ;
        verifyButton.setEnabled( false ) ;
        passwordField.setEnabled( false ) ;
    }
}
```

Summary

Sometimes, your applets or applications require UI functionality beyond what is provided by the AWT. You can use subclassing and composite controls to extend the AWT and create new classes from the basic AWT classes.

When you extend the AWT, you can create self-contained controls that respond to their own events. Your enhanced controls can often be used as drop-in replacements for the associated AWT control.

The `passField` class developed in this chapter is an example of a subclassed control. This class takes the basic functionality of an AWT `TextField` and enhances it. The result is a control that can be plugged in anywhere you might use a `TextField`.

The `ScrollingPictureWindow` class created in this chapter is a good example of a composite control. This class combines the techniques of subclassing and encapsulation. It is a subclass of `Panel` and serves to encapsulate the `Canvas` control and two scrollbars.

When you design an applet or application in Java, you have at your disposal the basic AWT controls. Now you can create enhanced controls by combining and subclassing them. These new controls will become part of your personal Java toolbox and you can use them in all your future Java programming projects.

Working with Dialog Boxes

by K.C. Hopson

IN THIS CHAPTER

CHAPTER 23

This chapter focuses on the Dialog class, which is the basis for writing dialog boxes in Java. The class is explained with several dialog box examples that provide tips about how to use some of the more obscure features of Abstract Windowing Toolkit (AWT). The FileDialog class is discussed at the end of this chapter.

To get a proper understanding of the Dialog class, however, it is important to review how the Window and Frame classes work. This chapter begins with a quick review of these two classes.

Windows and Frames

The Window class is used in AWT to create popup windows that appear outside the constraints of the normal browser area allocated to an applet. Because the Window class is derived from the Container class, it can contain other components. Unlike applet components tied directly to a browser page, Window classes are not restricted to a prespecified area of the screen. Window objects can be resized as their immediate requirements dictate. AWT can perform this adjustment automatically using the Window class's pack() method; this method works with the Window layout manager (by default, BorderLayout) to arrive at the optimal presentation of the window, given its contained components and screen resolution. Typically, pack() is called before a window is displayed. Windows are not made visible until the show() method is called. Windows are removed from the screen and their resources are freed when the dispose() method is invoked.

The Frame class extends the Window class by adding a title bar, a border for resizing, and support for menus. For most GUI platforms, the frame's title bar is tied to system control boxes, such as minimize, maximize, and destroy. Consequently, the Frame class has all the elements necessary to make an applet look like a "real" application, complete with menus and system controls.

Listing 23.1 presents a simple Frame applet that changes its title based on the button selected. The applet class, FrameTestApplet, does little more than launch the main frame, FrameTitles. The main listener class, FrameTitleListener, simply takes action commands and sets the frame title to the command name. The constructor for the frame itself, FrameTitles(), begins by calling the frame super constructor. The sole parameter for the constructor is the caption displayed on the title bar. The layout for the frame is then set. The default is BorderLayout, but because we want a 3×2 grid matrix in this case, we use GridLayout. Then the buttons are added to the frame, with names representing the new title of the frame. Each button is hooked to the same instance of FrameTitleListener; when the button is clicked, the listener is called, and the frame's title is changed. After all the components have been added, another listener, FrameListener, is hooked to the frame; this listener simply shuts down the frame when the user tries to close it. Finally, the pack() method is invoked so that the button placement can be optimized. Because this optimized placement results in a small frame (six buttons placed closely around the label text doesn't take much space), the resize() method is called to make the frame a larger size. Finally, the frame is displayed with the show() method.

Listing 23.1. Code for the Frame applet that changes the frame title.

```java
import java.awt.*;
import java.awt.event.*;
import java.lang.*;
import java.applet.*;
// This applet simply starts up the frame use to
// show different frame titles...
public class FrameTestApplet extends Applet  {
   public void init() {
      // Create the frame with a title...
      new FrameTitles("Frame Titles");
   }
}
// Listen for changes to the frame title
class FrameTitleListener implements ActionListener {
   Frame fr;  // Frame to use...
   // Constructor...
   public FrameTitleListener(Frame fr) {
       this.fr = fr;
   }
   // Handle the action to be performed...
   public void actionPerformed(ActionEvent e) {
       // Get the action that occurred...
       String selection = e.getActionCommand();
       fr.setTitle(selection);
   }
}
// Handle close events...
class FrameListener implements WindowListener {
   Frame fr;  // Frame to use...
   // Constructor...
   public FrameListener(Frame fr) {
       this.fr = fr;
   }
   // This closes the window...
   public void windowClosing(WindowEvent e) {
       fr.dispose();
   }
   public void windowOpened(WindowEvent e) {
   }
   public void windowClosed(WindowEvent e) {
   }
   public void windowIconified(WindowEvent e) {
   }
   public void windowDeiconified(WindowEvent e) {
   }
}
// The frame for letting the user pick different
// titles to display...
class FrameTitles extends Frame {
   // Create the frame with a title...
   public FrameTitles(String title) {
       // Call the superclass constructor...
       super(title);
       // Create a grid layout to place the buttons...
       setLayout(new GridLayout(3,2));
       // Create the listener...
```

continues

Listing 23.1. continued

```
        // Add the buttons for choosing the titles...
        FrameTitleListener listener = new FrameTitleListener(this);
        Button b = new Button("Frame Title #1");
        b.addActionListener(listener);
        add(b);
        b = new Button("Frame Title #2");
        b.addActionListener(listener);
        add(b);
        b = new Button("Frame Title #3");
        b.addActionListener(listener);
        add(b);
        b = new Button("Frame Title #4");
        b.addActionListener(listener);
        add(b);
        b = new Button("Frame Title #5");
        b.addActionListener(listener);
        add(b);
        b = new Button("Frame Title #6");
        b.addActionListener(listener);
        add(b);
        // Have a listener for shutting down the frame...
        addWindowListener(new FrameListener(this));
        // Pack and display...
        pack();
        resize(300,200); // Make it a reasonable size...
        show();
    }
}
```

Introduction to the Dialog Class

Like the Frame class, the Dialog class is a subclass of Window. Dialog boxes differ from frames in a couple of subtle ways, however. The most important of these differences is that dialog boxes can be *modal*. When a modal dialog box is displayed, input to other windows in the applet is blocked until the dialog box is disposed. This feature points to the general purpose of dialog boxes, which is to give the user a warning or a decision to be made before the program can continue. Although support for nonmodal, or *modeless*, dialog boxes is supported, most dialog boxes are modal.

There are three constructors for the Dialog class. All three take a Frame object as an initial parameter, indicating the owner of the constructor. Two of the constructors take an additional String parameter for the title, and one constructor takes a third boolean parameter to indicate whether or not it is a modal dialog box. Many of your dialog boxes will be modal, meaning that they take all input from the user until the dialog box is destroyed.

Listing 23.2 shows the code of a variation of the applet in Listing 23.1; in this second version, a dialog box is used to change the frame's title. A frame class, called FrameMenuTest, and its corresponding listener, FrameMenuListener, work with a menu that has two options: show the dialog box or quit using the `dispose()` method. The dialog box is called `ChangeTitleDialog`. Notice that, like the frame example, this dialog box example has two event listener classes.

The main thing to note about the code in this listing is how the dialog box is instantiated in the `FrameMenuListener` class (the first parameter is `FrameMenuTest`):

```
ChangeTitleDialog dlg;
dlg = new ChangeCursorDialog(fr,true,"Change the cursor");
```

When it is time to display the dialog box, you can declare it as follows:

```
dlg.show(); // Make the dialog visible...
```

Notice how similar the dialog box in Listing 23.2 is to the frame in Listing 23.1.

Listing 23.2. Code for the `Dialog` class that changes the frame title.

```
import java.awt.*;
import java.lang.*;
import java.applet.*;
import java.awt.event.*;
// This applet simply starts up the frame
// which provides a menu for setting the frame title...
public class DialogTestApplet extends Applet  {
    public void init() {
        // Create the frame with a title...
        new FrameMenuTest("Menu Based Test");
    }
}
// Listen for changes to the frame title
class FrameMenuListener implements ActionListener {
    // The dialog to change the title...
    ChangeTitleDialog dlg;
    Frame fr;  // Frame to use...
    // Constructor...
    public FrameMenuListener(Frame fr) {
        this.fr = fr;
        // Instantiate the dialog...
        dlg = new ChangeTitleDialog(fr,true,"Change the title");
    }
    // Handle the action to be performed...
    public void actionPerformed(ActionEvent e) {
        // Get the action that occurred...
        String selection = e.getActionCommand();
        if (selection.equals("Quit"))
            fr.dispose();
        // Otherwise call the Dialog...
        if (selection.equals("Change Title Dialog"))
            dlg.show(); // Make the dialog visible...
    }
}
// The frame that creates a dialog that
// changes the frame's title
class FrameMenuTest extends Frame {
    // Create the frame with a title...
    public FrameMenuTest(String title) {
```

continues

23

WORKING WITH
DIALOG BOXES

Listing 23.2. continued

```java
        // Call the superclass constructor...
        super(title);
        // Add the menus...
        // First create the menu bar
        MenuBar mbar = new MenuBar();
        setMenuBar(mbar); // Attach to the frame...
        // Add the File submenu...
        Menu m = new Menu("File");
        mbar.add(m);  // Add to menu bar
        // Create action listener for the menu items...
        FrameMenuListener listener = new FrameMenuListener(this);
        // Add Dialog to the submenu...
        MenuItem item = new MenuItem("Change Title Dialog");
        item.addActionListener(listener);
        m.add(item);
        // Add a separator
        m.addSeparator();
        // Add Quit to the submenu...
        item = new MenuItem("Quit");
        item.addActionListener(listener);
        m.add(item);
        // Pack and display...
        pack();
        resize(300,200); // Make it a reasonable size...
        show();
    }
}
// Listen for changes to the frame title
class DialogTitleListener implements ActionListener {
    Frame fr;  // Frame to use...
    // Constructor...
    public DialogTitleListener(Frame fr) {
        this.fr = fr;
    }
    // Handle the action to be performed...
    public void actionPerformed(ActionEvent e) {
        // Get the action that occurred...
        String selection = e.getActionCommand();
        fr.setTitle(selection);
    }
}
// Handle close events...
class DialogListener implements WindowListener {
    Dialog dlg;  // Dialog to use...
    // Constructor...
    public DialogListener(Dialog dlg) {
        this.dlg = dlg;
    }
    // This closes the window...
    public void windowClosing(WindowEvent e) {
        dlg.dispose();
    }
    public void windowOpened(WindowEvent e) {
    }
    public void windowClosed(WindowEvent e) {
    }
    public void windowIconified(WindowEvent e) {
    }
```

```
        public void windowDeiconified(WindowEvent e) {
        }
}
// Dialog that presents a grid of buttons
// for changing the Frame title.
class ChangeTitleDialog extends Dialog {
    Frame fr;
    // Create the dialog and store the title string...
    public ChangeTitleDialog(Frame parent,boolean modal,String title) {
        // Create dialog with title
        super(parent,title,modal);
        fr = parent;
        // Create a grid layout to place the buttons...
        setLayout(new GridLayout(3,2));
        // Add the buttons for choosing the titles...
        DialogTitleListener listener = new DialogTitleListener(fr);
        Button b = new Button("Frame Title #1");
        b.addActionListener(listener);
        add(b);
        b = new Button("Frame Title #2");
        b.addActionListener(listener);
        add(b);
        b = new Button("Frame Title #3");
        b.addActionListener(listener);
        add(b);
        b = new Button("Frame Title #4");
        b.addActionListener(listener);
        add(b);
        b = new Button("Frame Title #5");
        b.addActionListener(listener);
        add(b);
        b = new Button("Frame Title #6");
        b.addActionListener(listener);
        add(b);
        // Have a listener for shutting down the dialog...
        addWindowListener(new DialogListener(this));
        // Pack and size for display...
        pack();
        resize(300,200);
    }
}
```

The Color Dialog Box Example

In this section, a color dialog box is created to further explain how to use the Dialog class. The example lets the you associate a color with the foreground and background states of the text. Figure 23.1 shows how the dialog box appears in a browser.

How the Color Dialog Box Is Used

When the color dialog box appears, a list control at the top left of the dialog box shows which elements of the text can be modified. These colors are normal foreground, normal background, highlighted foreground, and highlighted background. When you select an item from the list, the radio button for the corresponding color is highlighted. A text display underneath the list shows what the text would look like with the given colors. The text display shows either the normal state (with both foreground and background colors) or the background state. If you select a new color with the radio buttons, the Canvas object is updated to show what the new foreground and background combination would look like. When you select the Update button, the text is updated with the color settings for the current list item.

FIGURE 23.1.

The color dialog box.

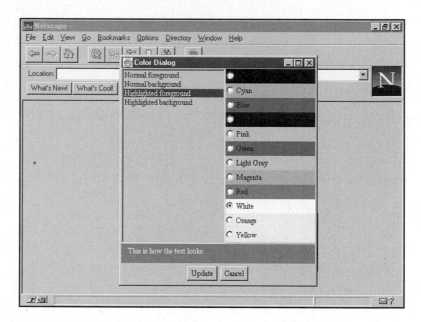

The Construction of the Color Dialog Box

Four classes are used to construct the color dialog box. The ChooseColorDialog class is a subclass of the Dialog class and controls the main display of the dialog box. The colorDisplay class is a Canvas class derivative that draws text with colors corresponding to the selected foreground and background display. The ColoredCheckbox class draws a checkbox associated with a certain Color object; the background of the box is drawn with that color. The ColoredCheckboxGroup class groups ColoredCheckbox items together so that they can function as part of a radio-button group. In addition to these main classes, there are three listener classes attached to the dialog box.

The discussion of the color dialog box begins with its underlying components. Listing 23.3 shows the code for the ColoredCheckbox class. Its most interesting feature is that it associates itself with a given Color object. It paints its background according to the Color object and, by using the setIfColorMatches() method, turns its checkbox on if the color sent to it matches its internal color. The checkbox in this case is a radio button because the class is associated with a CheckboxGroup object. Checkbox objects have radio buttons only if they are associated with a

CheckboxGroup object; only one radio button in a checkbox group can be selected at a time. If no checkbox group is specified for a checkbox object, there are no restrictions on which checkboxes can be selected.

Listing 23.3. The ColoredCheckbox class.

```
// Class for creating a checkbox associated
// with a given color...
class ColoredCheckbox extends Checkbox {
   Color color;  // The color of this checkbox...
   // Constructor creates checkbox with specified color...
   public ColoredCheckbox(Color color, String label,
         CheckboxGroup grp, boolean set) {
         // Call the default constructor...
         super(label,grp,set);
         this.color = color;
         setBackground(color);
   }
   // Sets itself to true if it matches the color
   public void setIfColorMatches(Color match) {
      if (color == match)
         setState(true);
      else
         setState(false);
   }
   // Return the color matching this box...
   public Color getColor() {
      return color;
   }
}
```

The ColoredCheckboxGroup class is used to contain ColoredCheckbox objects. Its constructor creates a preselected number of colored checkboxes associated with a Panel object. Here are the first few lines of the ColoredCheckboxGroup class declaration:

```
class ColoredCheckboxGroup extends CheckboxGroup {
   // Array to hold checkboxes...
   ColoredCheckbox c[] = new ColoredCheckbox[12];
   // Constructor. Create the checkboxes with
   // no default color chosen...
   public ColoredCheckboxGroup(Panel p,ItemListener listener) {
      // Call the default constructor...
      super();
      // Create the checkboxes and store in panel and reference array...
      c[0] = new ColoredCheckbox(Color.black,"Black",this,false);
      c[0].addItemListener(listener);
      p.add(c[0]);
      c[1] = new ColoredCheckbox(Color.cyan,"Cyan",this,false);
      c[1].addItemListener(listener);
      p.add(c[1]);
```

Strangely enough, ColoredCheckboxGroup is not a Container object. Consequently, the checkboxes must be associated with a Panel object to meet the needs at hand. Note the use of the Color constants in the construction of the ColoredCheckbox objects. The reference array (variable c) is used in the other method of the class, setMatchingColor(), which is used to set the radio button of the ColoredCheckbox object that matches a certain color:

```
public void setMatchingColor(Color match) {
    for (int i = 0; i < c.length; ++i)
        c[i].setIfColorMatches(match);
}
```

Because ColoredCheckbox objects are self-identifying by color, this technique prevents a long and cumbersome walk through hard-coded color names to determine which radio button should be turned on.

You may also have noticed that an ItemListener class is attached to each checkbox. This listener is called every time a checkbox is selected. As discussed in the following section, "Using the Dialog Box," the listener is used to set the colors for the dialog box whenever a color checkbox is selected.

The colorDisplay class is a Canvas derivative that draws text (specified in the displayText string variable) with a specified foreground and background color. Listing 23.4 highlights some of the more interesting features of the colorDisplay class.

Listing 23.4. Portions of the colorDisplay class.

```
// The layout will call this to get the minimum size
// of the object.  In this case, you want it to be at
// least big enough to fit the display text...
    public Dimension minimumSize() {
        // Get the metrics of the current font...
        FontMetrics fm = getFontMetrics(getFont());
        return new Dimension(fm.stringWidth(displayText),
            2 * fm.getHeight());
    }
    // Paint the colors and text...
    public synchronized void paint(Graphics g) {
        if ((foreground == null) || (background == null))
            return;
        // Set background...
        Dimension dm = size();
        g.setColor(background);
        g.fillRect(0,0,dm.width,dm.height);
        // Draw the string
        g.setColor(foreground);
        // Set dimensions. Move just from left...
        FontMetrics fm = getFontMetrics(getFont());
        int x = fm.charWidth('W');
        // And center in height...
        int y = fm.getHeight();
        g.drawString(displayText,x,y);
    }
```

The paint() method draws the canvas if a background and foreground color have been selected. The method starts by getting the size of its drawing area from the size() method (a standard part of subclasses of `Component`). The `paint()` method then fills in the background color using the `setColor()` and `fillRect()` methods of the `Graphics` class. The method then sets the color of the text to be displayed (the foreground). By getting the current `FontMetrics`, the canvas can figure out a good location for the text string; the `getHeight()` method returns the total height of the font. The `drawString()` method then draws the text at the specified location.

The `minimumSize()` method is used with layouts, which are discussed in Chapter 22, "Creating User Interface Components." When the AWT constructs the display of a group of components, it works with the layouts to decide the position and size of a component. Sometimes, you may want a component to have some input into what its size will be. Two methods of the `Component` class can be invoked to do this. The `preferredSize()` method returns the dimensions of the preferred size of the component. The `minimumSize()` method returns the smallest size in which the component should be made. For the `colorDisplay()` class, the `minimumSize()` method returns the information that the component should be wide enough to display the text string and twice as high as its current font. The method does this by getting the `FontMetrics` of the current font and calling the `stringWidth()` and `getHeight()` methods respectively.

Finally, the dialog box is ready to be constructed. Listing 23.5 shows the complete code for the color dialog box. The `createComponents()` method adds the components to the dialog box by using the complex `GridBagLayout` class. The main thing to be done here is to set up the list control to take up most of one half of the dialog box and to place the color checkboxes on the other half (refer back to Figure 23.1). The key reason for doing this is to set the `GridBagConstraints` `weighty` and `gridheight` variables to the appropriate values. By setting the former to `1.0`, you tell the layout that the associated components should be given preeminence in terms of the layout's height. When `weighty` is set to `0.0`, the height of the corresponding components is given lower priority.

The `preferredSize()` method in Listing 23.5 returns the desired dimensions of the dialog box. The dialog box should be 3 times as wide as the longest string in the list component, and 24 times as high as the current font. With these settings, everything should fit comfortably in the dialog box.

Listing 23.5. The construction of the `ChooseColorDialog` class.

```
// Dialog box for choosing display colors...
class ChooseColorDialog extends Dialog {
    ColoredCheckboxGroup colorGrp;  // To hold radio buttons of colors...
    List choiceList;  // List of color choices...
    colorDisplay d; // This is the text display...
    // Defines for listbox values...
    static final int NORMAL_FORE = 0;
    static final int NORMAL_BACK = 1;
    static final int HILITE_FORE = 2;
    static final int HILITE_BACK = 3;
    Color normalForeColor;
```

continues

Listing 23.5. continued

```
    Color normalBackColor;
    Color highlightedForeColor;
    Color highlightedBackColor;
    // Construct dialog to allow color to be chosen...
    public ChooseColorDialog(Frame parent,boolean modal) {
        // Create dialog with title
        super(parent,"Color Dialog",modal);
        // Initialize the colors...
        normalForeColor = Color.black;
        normalBackColor = Color.white;
        highlightedForeColor = Color.black;
        highlightedBackColor = Color.white;
        // Create the dialog components...
        createComponents();
        pack();  // Compact...
        // Resize to fit everything...
        resize(preferredSize());
    }
    // The layout will call this to get the preferred size
    // of the dialog.  Make it big enough for the listbox text,
    // the checkboxes, canvas, and buttons...
    public Dimension preferredSize() {
        // Get the metrics of the current font...
        FontMetrics fm = getFontMetrics(getFont());
        int width = 3 * fm.stringWidth("Highlighted foreground");
        int height = 24 * fm.getHeight();
        return new Dimension(width,height);
    }
    // Create the main display panel...
    void createComponents() {
     // Use gridbag constraints...
     GridBagLayout g = new GridBagLayout();
     setLayout(g);
     GridBagConstraints gbc = new GridBagConstraints();
     // Set the constraints for the top objects...
     gbc.fill = GridBagConstraints.BOTH;
     gbc.weightx = 1.0;
     gbc.weighty = 1.0;
     gbc.gridheight = 10;
     // Add the listbox of choices...
     choiceList = new List();
     choiceList.addItem("Normal foreground");
     choiceList.addItem("Normal background");
     choiceList.addItem("Highlighted foreground");
     choiceList.addItem("Highlighted background");
     g.setConstraints(choiceList,gbc);
     add(choiceList);
     // Add the listeners...
     ColorListboxListener listListener = new ColorListboxListener(this);
     choiceList.addItemListener(listListener);
     // Create the checkbox panel
     Panel checkboxPanel = new Panel();
     checkboxPanel.setLayout(new GridLayout(12,1));
     // Create the checkbox group and add radio buttons...
     colorGrp = new ColoredCheckboxGroup(checkboxPanel,new
             ColorCheckboxListener(this));
     colorGrp.setMatchingColor(Color.magenta);
```

```
    // Create add checkbox panel to right...
    gbc.gridwidth = GridBagConstraints.REMAINDER;
    g.setConstraints(checkboxPanel,gbc);
    add(checkboxPanel);
    // Display the color chosen...
    d = new colorDisplay("This is how the text looks.");
    // Add to grid bag...
    gbc.weighty = 0.0;
    gbc.weightx = 1.0;
    gbc.gridwidth = GridBagConstraints.REMAINDER;
    gbc.gridheight = 1;
    g.setConstraints(d,gbc);
    add(d);
    // Two buttons: "Update" and "Cancel"
    Panel p = new Panel();
    ChooseActionListener listener = new ChooseActionListener(this);
    Button b = new Button("Update");
    b.addActionListener(listener);
    p.add(b);
    b = new Button("Cancel");
    b.addActionListener(listener);
    p.add(b);
    // Add to grid bag...
    gbc.gridwidth = GridBagConstraints.REMAINDER;
    g.setConstraints(p,gbc);
    add(p);
}
// Set up defaults upon showing...
public synchronized void show() {
    super.show(); // Call the default show method...
    // Set the listbox default...
    choiceList.select(0);
}
// Update the global color fields with current settings...
public void update()
{
    // Set canvas colors based on state...
    int index = choiceList.getSelectedIndex();
    switch (index) {
      case NORMAL_FORE:
          normalForeColor = d.getForeColor();
          break;
      case NORMAL_BACK:
          normalBackColor = d.getBackColor();
          break;
      case HILITE_FORE:
          highlightedForeColor = d.getForeColor();
          break;
      case HILITE_BACK:
          highlightedBackColor = d.getBackColor();
          break;
      default:
          break;
    }
}
// Set up caption colors and color choice highlight
// according to current listbox value...
public void selectedChoiceListItem() {
```

continues

23

WORKING WITH
DIALOG BOXES

Listing 23.5. continued

```
    Color fore,back;  // Display canvas colors
    // Set canvas colors based on state...
    int index = choiceList.getSelectedIndex();
    if ((index == NORMAL_FORE) || (index == NORMAL_BACK)) {
        fore = normalForeColor;
        back = normalBackColor;
    }
    // Otherwise it's the background...
    else {
        fore = highlightedForeColor;
        back = highlightedBackColor;
    }
    // Update the canvas...
    d.setForeColor(fore);
    d.setBackColor(back);
    d.repaint();
    // Update the color radio buttons...
    Color radioColor;
    // Even numbers are fore, odd are back...
    if ((index % 2) == 0)
        radioColor = fore;
    else
        radioColor = back;
    colorGrp.setMatchingColor(radioColor);
}

// Update display canvas when radio color changes...
public void selectedRadioItem() {
    // Get choice from Color box...
    ColoredCheckbox box = (ColoredCheckbox)colorGrp.getCurrent();
    Color color = box.getColor();
    // If normal set canvas colors...
    Color fore,back;
    int index = choiceList.getSelectedIndex();
    // Set background or foreground color based on
    // current listbox selection...
    if ((index == NORMAL_FORE) || (index == HILITE_FORE))
        d.setForeColor(color);
    else
        d.setBackColor(color);
    // Repaint the canvas...
    d.repaint();
}
}
```

Using the Dialog Box

Three listener classes are used to control the actions of the color dialog box. They are tied to the dialog box in the createComponents() method of the ChooseColorDialog class. The first class, ColorListboxListener, is called whenever an item in the list is selected. The ColorListboxListener class is based on the ItemListener interface, which invokes the itemStateChanged() method when an item is selected from the list. The ColorCheckboxListener class is similar to the ItemListener interface except that it is called when checkboxes (in this case, radio buttons) are selected. The ColorCheckboxListener class notifies the dialog box that a new color has been displayed. Finally, the ChooseActionListener class is used to indicate which of the two buttons has been selected: The Update button permanently sets a color, and the Cancel button causes the dialog box to be destroyed.

Listing 23.6. The listener classes of the color dialog box.

```
// Listeners for the Color Dialog
// This one is for the listbox...
class ColorListboxListener implements ItemListener {
    ChooseColorDialog dlg; // The color dialog...
    // Constructor...
    public ColorListboxListener(ChooseColorDialog dlg) {
        this.dlg = dlg;
    }
    // Handle the action to be performed...
    public void itemStateChanged(ItemEvent e) {
        dlg.selectedChoiceListItem();
    }
}
// This one is for the checkboxes......
class ColorCheckboxListener implements ItemListener {
    ChooseColorDialog dlg; // The color dialog...
    // Constructor...
    public ColorCheckboxListener(ChooseColorDialog dlg) {
        this.dlg = dlg;
    }
    // Handle the action to be performed...
    public void itemStateChanged(ItemEvent e) {
        dlg.selectedRadioItem();
    }
}
class ChooseActionListener implements ActionListener {
    // Actions on the dialog...
    ChooseColorDialog dlg; // The color dialog...
    // Constructor...
    public ChooseActionListener(ChooseColorDialog dlg) {
        this.dlg = dlg;
    }
    // Handle the action to be performed...
    public void actionPerformed(ActionEvent e) {
        // Get the action that occurred...
        String selection = e.getActionCommand();
        if (selection.equals("Update"))
            dlg.update();
        // Otherwise destroy the Dialog...
        if (selection.equals("Cancel"))
            dlg.dispose();
    }
}
```

Calling the Dialog Box

The Frame object is responsible for displaying the color dialog box. It can declare a variable of the color dialog class as follows:

```
ChooseColorDialog colorDialog;  // Color Dialog...
```

In its constructor, the frame instantiates the color dialog box with the following call:

```
colorDialog = new ChooseColorDialog(this, true);
```

This code fragment states that the frame is the parent of the dialog box and its appearance is modal. Recall that a modal dialog box does not allow input to other windows while it is being displayed.

A dialog box does not automatically appear when it is constructed; you display the dialog box with a specific call to the show() method.

The Font Dialog Box Example

The discussion of the font dialog box example is not as lengthy as the preceding discussion of the color dialog box. In many ways, the two examples are similar, so a detailed explanation of the font dialog box isn't required.

Figure 23.2 shows the font dialog box. It is based on the ChooseFontDialog class, which displays its components in a two-column style similar to that of the color dialog box. The current font family, style, and size is shown in a Canvas display object of the fontDisplay class, which is very similar to the colorDisplay class.

FIGURE 23.2.

The font dialog box.

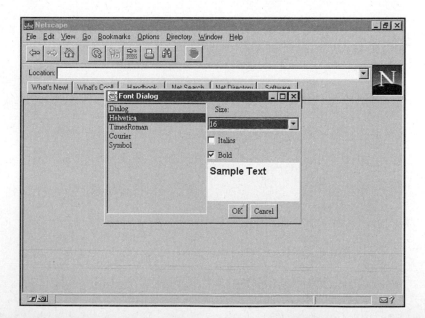

The list component on the left side of the dialog box shows the fonts available on the current platform. It uses the AWT `Toolkit` class to get this information. Here is the code that creates the control and adds the font families:

```
// Add the listbox of choices...
    // Get the selection from the toolkit...
    choiceList = new List();
    String fontList[] = Toolkit.getDefaultToolkit().getFontList();
    for (int i = 0; i < fontList.length; ++i)
        choiceList.addItem(fontList[i]);
```

A choice box is added to the dialog box to enumerate font sizes that can be used. Two checkboxes are used to set the bold and italicized styles. If none of these options are selected, the font's style is set to plain.

Every time one of these controls changes, the font display is updated to show the change. This change happens in the `paintSample()` method, as shown in Listing 23.7.

Listing 23.7. The full source code for the font dialog box.

```
// Listeners for the Font Dialog
// This one is for all the repaint routines...
class FontItemListener implements ItemListener {
    ChooseFontDialog dlg; // The color dialog...
    // Constructor...
    public FontItemListener(ChooseFontDialog dlg) {
        this.dlg = dlg;
    }
    // Handle the action to be performed...
    public void itemStateChanged(ItemEvent e) {
        dlg.paintSample();
    }
}
class ChooseActionListener implements ActionListener {
    // Actions on the dialog...
    ChooseFontDialog dlg; // The color dialog...
    // Constructor...
    public ChooseActionListener(ChooseFontDialog dlg) {
        this.dlg = dlg;
    }
    // Just shut down...
    public void actionPerformed(ActionEvent e) {
        dlg.dispose();
    }
}
// Dialog box for choosing display colors...
class ChooseFontDialog extends Dialog {
    List choiceList;  // List of color choices...
    fontDisplay d; // This is the text display...
    Choice choiceSize;  // Size of font...
    Checkbox checkItalics;
    Checkbox checkBold;
    Frame fr;
    Font currentFont;  // Current font in sample...
    Font defaultFont; // Store font dialog was created with...
```

23

WORKING WITH
DIALOG BOXES

continues

Listing 23.7. continued

```
// Construct dialog to allow color to be chosen...
public ChooseFontDialog(Frame parent,boolean modal) {
    // Create dialog with title
    super(parent,"Font Dialog",modal);
    fr = parent;
    defaultFont = getFont();
    // Create the dialog components...
    createComponents();
}
// Get the default font and set up display...
private void setDefaultFont() {
    // Get the latest font...
    currentFont = getFont();
    // Get default list...
    String s = currentFont.getName();
    int index = findListString(choiceList,s);
    if (index >= 0)
        choiceList.select(index);
    else
        choiceList.select(0);
    // Get default size
    int sizeFont = currentFont.getSize();
    index = findChoiceString(choiceSize,
        String.valueOf(sizeFont));
    if (index >= 0)
        choiceSize.select(index);
    else
        choiceSize.select(0);
    // Set the style displays...
    int styleFont = currentFont.getStyle();
    if ((styleFont & Font.BOLD) != 0)
        checkBold.setState(true);
    else
        checkBold.setState(false);
    if ((styleFont & Font.ITALIC) != 0)
        checkItalics.setState(true);
    else
        checkItalics.setState(false);
    // Set the canvas style...
    d.setFont(currentFont);
}
// The layout will call this to get the preferred size
// of the dialog.  Make it big enough for the listbox text,
// the checkboxes, canvas, and buttons...
public Dimension preferredSize() {
    // Get the metrics of the current font...
    FontMetrics fm = getFontMetrics(getFont());
    int width = 3 * fm.stringWidth("Highlighted foreground");
    int height = 14 * fm.getHeight();
    return new Dimension(width + 40,height + 40);
}
// Create the main display panel...
private void createComponents() {
    // Use gridbag constraints...
    GridBagLayout g = new GridBagLayout();
    setLayout(g);
    GridBagConstraints gbc = new GridBagConstraints();
```

```
// Set the constraints for the top objects...
gbc.fill = GridBagConstraints.BOTH;
gbc.weightx = 1.0;
gbc.weighty = 1.0;
gbc.gridheight = 10;
// Add the listbox of choices...
// Get the selection from the toolkit...
choiceList = new List();
String fontList[] = Toolkit.getDefaultToolkit().getFontList();
for (int i = 0; i < fontList.length; ++i) {
    choiceList.addItem(fontList[i]);
} // end if
g.setConstraints(choiceList,gbc);
add(choiceList);
// Set the default values...
gbc.weighty = 0.0;
gbc.weightx = 1.0;
gbc.gridheight = 1;
gbc.gridwidth = GridBagConstraints.REMAINDER;
// Create a label for display...
Label l = new Label("Size:");
// Add to grid bag...
g.setConstraints(l,gbc);
add(l);
// Create the choice box...
choiceSize = new Choice();
choiceSize.addItem("8");
choiceSize.addItem("10");
choiceSize.addItem("12");
choiceSize.addItem("14");
choiceSize.addItem("16");
choiceSize.addItem("20");
// Add to grid bag...
g.setConstraints(choiceSize,gbc);
add(choiceSize);
// Add Italics...
checkItalics = new Checkbox("Italics");
g.setConstraints(checkItalics,gbc);
add(checkItalics);
// Add Bold...
checkBold = new Checkbox("Bold");
g.setConstraints(checkBold,gbc);
add(checkBold);
// Set listeners...
FontItemListener itemListener = new FontItemListener(this);
choiceList.addItemListener(itemListener);
choiceSize.addItemListener(itemListener);
checkItalics.addItemListener(itemListener);
checkBold.addItemListener(itemListener);
// Display the color chosen...
d = new fontDisplay("Sample Text");
// Add to grid bag...
g.setConstraints(d,gbc);
add(d);
// Two buttons: "OK" and "Cancel"
Panel p = new Panel();
ChooseActionListener actionListener = new ChooseActionListener(this);
Button b = new Button("OK");
```

continues

23

WORKING WITH
DIALOG BOXES

Listing 23.7. continued

```
    b.addActionListener(actionListener);
    p.add(b);
    b = new Button("Cancel");
    b.addActionListener(actionListener);
    p.add(b);
    // Add to grid bag...
    gbc.gridwidth = GridBagConstraints.REMAINDER;
    g.setConstraints(p,gbc);
    add(p);
  }
  // Set up defaults upon showing...
  public void show() {
    setFont(defaultFont);
    // Set up defaults...
    setDefaultFont();
    pack();  // Compact...
    // Resize to fit everything...
    resize(preferredSize());
    // Set the font dialog started off with...
    super.show(); // Call the default constructor...
}
  // Set the display canvas to show itself with
  // the currently selected font
  public synchronized void paintSample() {
    // Get the family to display
    String fontName = choiceList.getSelectedItem();
    // Get its point size
    String fontSize = choiceSize.getSelectedItem();
    // Set its style
    int fontStyle = Font.PLAIN;
    if (checkItalics.getState())
        fontStyle += Font.ITALIC;
    if (checkBold.getState())
        fontStyle += Font.BOLD;
    // Create a font with the proper attributes...
    currentFont = new Font(fontName,fontStyle,
        Integer.parseInt(fontSize));
    // Set the new font on the canvas...
    d.setFont(currentFont);
    // Repaint it so the new font is displayed..
    d.repaint();
  }
  // Return index of string in list...
  // -1 means not found
  public int findListString(List l,String s) {
    for (int i = 0; i < l.countItems(); ++i) {
      if (s.equals(l.getItem(i)) )
          return i;
    }
    return -1;
  }
  // Return index of string in choice...
  // -1 means not found
  public int findChoiceString(Choice c,String s) {
```

```
            for (int i = 0; i < c.countItems(); ++i) {
                if (s.equals(c.getItem(i)) )
                    return i;
            }
            return -1;
        }
}
// A small class that illustrates the
// current highlight and background
class fontDisplay extends Canvas {
    String displayText;
    // Construct the display by storing the
    // text to be displayed...
    public fontDisplay(String displayText) {
        super();
        this.displayText = displayText;
    }
    // The layout will call this to get the minimum size
    // of the object.  In this case we want it to be at
    // least big enough to fit the display text...
    public Dimension minimumSize() {
        // Get the metrics of the current font...
        FontMetrics fm = getFontMetrics(getFont());
        return new Dimension(fm.stringWidth(displayText),
            4 * fm.getHeight());
    }
    // Paint the colors and text...
    public synchronized void paint(Graphics g) {
        // Set background...
        Dimension dm = size();
        g.setColor(Color.white);
        g.fillRect(0,0,dm.width,dm.height);
        // Draw the string
        g.setColor(Color.black);
        // Set dimensions. Move just from left...
        FontMetrics fm = getFontMetrics(getFont());
        int x = fm.charWidth('I');
        // And center in height...
        int y = fm.getHeight();
        g.drawString(displayText,x,y);
    }
}
```

The FileDialog Class

The FileDialog class is a subclass of Dialog and is used to provide a platform-independent approach to letting the user select the files to be loaded or saved. Instances of the FileDialog class usually mirror the underlying GUI conventions. For example, a FontDialog object for loading a file in the Windows 95 environment follows the Windows 95 Open dialog box conventions.

The FileDialog object can be constructed in the mode to load a file or in the mode to save a file. These dialog boxes look similar but perform slightly differently. For example, the Save version of the dialog box notifies the user that a file exists if a filename is given for a preexisting file. Here's the code you need to construct dialog boxes for both the load and save cases:

```
FileDialog openFileDialog;  // File Open Dialog...
FileDialog saveFileDialog;  // File Save Dialog...
openFileDialog = new FileDialog(this,"Open File",
            FileDialog.LOAD);
saveFileDialog = new FileDialog(this,"Save File",
            FileDialog.SAVE);
```

The integer flag in the last parameter of the constructors indicates the mode in which the dialog box should function.

When the dialog box is displayed with the show() method, it acts in a modal fashion so that input to the frame is blocked while the dialog box is displayed. After a choice has been made, the chosen file and directory can be retrieved with the getFile() and getDirectory() methods. The getFile() method returns a null value if the user cancels out of the dialog box.

It is interesting to note that the FileDialog objects constructed here do not appear when the applet is run in Netscape Navigator. For security reasons, Netscape does not allow any file-based methods to be invoked from an applet. In the latest incarnation of Microsoft Internet Explorer, you actually get a security exception if you even attempt to reference the FileDialog class! Consequently, the FileDialog class is really useful only for standalone applications.

Summary

As the examples in this chapter have shown, most of the work in creating a dialog box is setting up the component controls. The techniques for doing this are very similar to those for creating controls in an applet, with the difference that you may have to call the pack() or preferredSize() method to give your dialog box the exact appearance you want.

The other big issue with dialog boxes is related to security. Some browsers, such as Netscape Navigator, consider dialog boxes to be a possible security threat. For this reason, a warning or an "untrusted window" message may appear in the browser's status bar. In the worst case, the dialog box may not even appear or may be flagged with a security exception (as is the case with the FileDialog class in the Microsoft Internet Explorer). For these reasons, you must use great caution when placing dialog boxes in applets. When all is said and done, dialog boxes may be best suited for standalone Java applications.

V

PART

Networking with Java

Introduction to Network Programming

by Mike Fletcher
revised by Stephen Ingram

IN THIS CHAPTER

One of the best features of Java is its networking support. Java has classes that range from low-level TCP/IP connections to ones that provide instant access to resources on the World Wide Web. Even if you have never done any network programming before, Java makes it easy.

The following chapters introduce you to the networking classes and how to use them. A guide to what is covered by each chapter follows:

- **Chapter 24, "Introduction to Network Programming"**
  The chapter you are reading contains an introduction to TCP/IP networking, a list of the concepts you should be familiar with before reading the rest of the networking chapters, an overview of the networking facilities provided by Java, and an introduction to client/server fundamentals.
- **Chapter 25, "Developing Content and Protocol Handlers"**
  This chapter explains what protocol and content handlers are and how they can be applied; it also provides an introduction to writing your own handlers.
- **Chapter 26, "Java Socket Programming"**
  This chapter shows you how to use Java's low-level TCP/IP socket facilities.
- **Chapter 27, "Multiuser Network Programming"**
  This chapter presents techniques for creating applets that allow multiple users to interact with each other.

Prerequisites

Although networking with Java is fairly simple, there are a few concepts and classes from other packages you should be familiar with before reading this part of the book. If you are interested only in writing an applet that interacts with an HTTP daemon, you probably can concentrate just on the URL class for now. For the other network classes, you need at least a passing familiarity with the World Wide Web, java.io classes, threads, and TCP/IP networking.

World Wide Web Concepts

If you are using Java, you probably already have a familiarity with the Web. You need some knowledge of how Uniform Resource Locators (URLs) work to use the URL and URLConnection classes.

java.io Classes

Once you have a network connection established using one of the low-level classes, you will use java.io.InputStream and java.io.OutputStream objects or appropriate subclasses of these objects to communicate with the other endpoint. You should also know that many of the java.net classes throw a java.io.IOException when they encounter a problem.

Threads

Although not strictly needed for networking, threads make using the network classes easier. Why tie up your user interface waiting for a response from a server when a separate communications thread can wait instead of your main interface thread? Server applications also can service several clients simultaneously by spawning off a new thread to handle each incoming connection.

TCP/IP Networking

Before using the networking facilities of Java, you should be familiar with the terminology and concepts of the TCP/IP networking model. The next part of this chapter gets you up to speed.

Internet Networking: A Quick Overview

TCP/IP (Transmission Control Protocol/Internet Protocol) is the set of networking protocols used by Internet hosts to communicate with other Internet hosts. If you have ever had any experience with networks or network programming in general, you should be able to skim this section and check back when you find a term you are not familiar with. A list of references is given at the end of this section if you want more detailed information. The Glossary at the end of this book is another excellent reference.

TCP/IP and Networking Terms

Like any other technical field, computer networking has its own jargon. These definitions should clear up what the terms mean:

- **host.** An individual machine on a network. Each host on a TCP/IP network has at least one unique address (*see* IP number).

- **hostname.** A symbolic name that can be mapped into an IP number. Several methods exist for performing this mapping, such as DNS (Domain Name Service) and Sun's NIS (Network Information Services).

- **IETF.** The Internet Engineering Task Force, a group responsible for maintaining Internet standards and defining new ones.

- **internet.** A network of networks. When capitalized as the *Internet*, the term refers to the globally interconnected network of networks.

- **intranet.** A term used to describe a network that uses TCP/IP protocols and that either is not connected to the Internet or is connected through a firewall.

- **IP number.** A unique address for each host on the Internet (unique in the sense that a given number can be used by only one particular machine, but a particular machine may be known by multiple IP numbers). Currently, this is a 32-bit number that consists of a network part and a host part. The network part identifies the network on which the host resides; the host part is the specific host on that network. Sometimes, the IP number is referred to as the *IP address* of a host.

- **packet.** A single message sent over a network. Sometimes a packet is referred to as a *datagram,* but the former term usually refers to data at the network layer; the latter term refers to a higher-layer message.

- **protocol.** A set of data formats and messages used to transmit information. Different network entities must speak the same protocol if they are to understand each other.

- **protocol stack.** Networking services can be thought of as different layers that use lower-level services to provide services to higher-level services. The set of layers that provides network functionality is known as a *protocol stack.*

- **RFC.** Request For Comments—documents in which proposed Internet standards are released. Each RFC is issued a sequential number, which is how they are usually referenced. Examples are RFC 791, which specifies the Internet Protocol (the IP of TCP/IP), and RFC 821, which specifies the protocol used for transferring e-mail between Internet hosts (SMTP).

- **router.** A host that knows how to forward packets to different networks. A router can be a specialized piece of network hardware or can be something as simple as a machine with two network interfaces (each on a different physical network).

- **socket.** A communications *endpoint* (that is, one end of a conversation). In the TCP/IP context, a socket usually is identified by a unique pair consisting of the source IP address and port number, and the destination IP address and port number.

The Internet Protocols

TCP/IP is a set of communications protocols for communicating between different types of machines and networks (hence the name *internet*). The name TCP/IP comes from two of the protocols: the Transmission Control Protocol and the Internet Protocol. Other protocols in the TCP/IP suite are the User Datagram Protocol (UDP), the Internet Control Message Protocol (ICMP), and the Internet Group Multicast Protocol (IGMP).

These protocols define a standard format for exchanging information between machines (known as *hosts*) regardless of the physical connections between them. TCP/IP implementations exist for almost every type of hardware and operating system imaginable. Software exists to transmit IP datagrams over network hardware ranging from modems to fiber-optic cable.

TCP/IP Network Architecture

There are four layers in the TCP/IP network model. Each of the protocols in the TCP/IP suite provides for communication between entities in one of these layers (see Figure 24.1). These lower-level layers are used by higher-level layers to transfer data from host to host. The layers are as follows, with examples of which protocols live at each layer:

- Physical (Ethernet, Token Ring, PPP)
- Network (IP)
- Transport (TCP, UDP)
- Application (Telnet, HTTP, FTP, Gopher)

FIGURE 24.1.

The TCP/IP protocol stack.

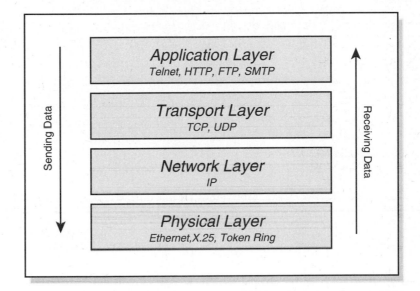

Each layer in the stack takes data from the one above it and adds the information needed to get the data to its destination, using the services of the layer below. One way to think of this layering is to compare it to the layers of an onion. Each protocol layer adds a layer to the packet going down the protocol stack (see Figure 24.2). When the packet is received, each layer peels off its addressing to determine where next to send the packet.

FIGURE 24.2.

Addressing information is added and removed at each layer.

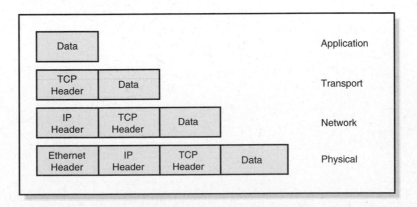

Suppose that your Web browser wants to retrieve something from a Web server running on a host on the same physical network. The browser sends an HTTP request using the TCP layer. The TCP layer asks the IP layer to send the data to the proper host. The IP layer then uses the physical layer to send the data to the appropriate host.

At the receiving end, each layer strips off the addressing information that the sender added and determines what to do with the data. Continuing the example, the physical layer passes the received IP packet to the IP layer. The IP layer determines that the packet is a TCP packet and passes it to the TCP layer. The TCP layer passes the packet to the HTTP daemon process. The HTTP daemon then processes the request and sends the data requested back through the same process to the other host.

When the hosts are not on the same physical network, the IP layer handles the routing of the packet through the correct series of hosts (known as *routers*) until the packet reaches its destination. One of the nice features of the IP protocol is that individual hosts do not have to know how to reach every host on the Internet. The host simply passes to a default router any packets for networks it does not know how to reach.

For example, a university may have only one machine with a physical connection to the Internet. All the campus routers know to forward all packets destined for the Internet to this host. Similarly, any host on the Internet has to send packets only to this one router to reach any host at the university. The router forwards the packets to the appropriate local routers (see Figure 24.3).

FIGURE 24.3.
An example of IP routing.

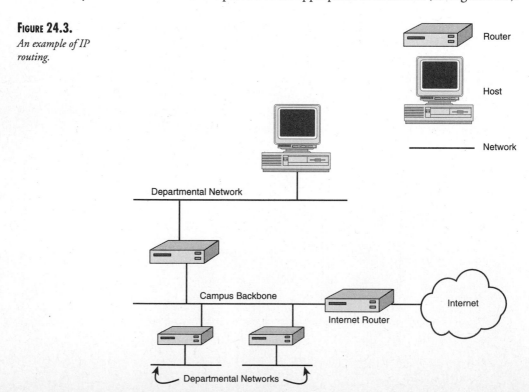

NOTE

A publicly available program for UNIX platforms, called `traceroute`, is useful if you want to find out what routers are actually responsible for sending a packet from one host to another and how long each hop takes. The source for `traceroute` can be found by consulting an Archie server for an FTP site near you or from `ftp://ee.lbl.gov`.

The Future: IP Version 6

Back when the TCP/IP protocols were being developed in the early 1970s, 32-bit IP numbers seemed more than capable of addressing all the hosts on an internet. Although there currently is not a lack of IP numbers, the explosive growth of the Internet in recent years is rapidly consuming the remaining unassigned addresses. To address this lack of IP numbers, a new version of the IP protocols is being developed by the IETF.

This new version, known as either IPv6 or IPng (IP Next Generation), will provide a much larger address space of 128 bits. This address space will allow for approximately 3.4×10^{38} different IP addresses. Where IP addresses used to be expressed as four decimal numbers (with values 0 to 255) separated by periods (.)—as in `192.242.139.42`—IPv6 addresses are expressed as eight groups of four hexadecimal digits separated by colons, like this:

`5A02:1364:DD03:0432:0031:12CA:0001:BEEF`

IPv6 will be backward compatible with current IP implementations to allow older clients to operate with newer ones. Provisions are contained in the protocol for tunneling IPv6 traffic over an IPv4 network (and vice versa). Other benefits of the new version are as follows:

- Improved support for *multicasting* (sending packets to several destinations at one time)
- Simplified packet header formats
- Support for authentication and encryption of packet contents at the network layer
- Support for designating a connection as a special flow that should be given special treatment (such as real-time audio data that requires quick delivery)

Several new protocols are being added to the TCP/IP suite. The RTP (Real-Time Protocol) and RTCP (Real-Time Control Protocol) protocols provide support for applications such as video and audio conferencing. Some protocols are being done away with, and the functionality they provide is being merged into other existing protocols. For example, IGMP (Internet Group Membership Protocol), which provided support for membership in multicast groups, has been done away with; multicast membership is now handled with ICMP messages.

These enhancements to TCP/IP should allow the Internet to continue the phenomenal growth it has experienced over the past few years.

24

INTRODUCTION
TO NETWORK
PROGRAMMING

Where to Find More Information

This chapter is not meant to completely cover the subject of TCP/IP. If your curiosity has been piqued, the following online documents and books may be of interest to you.

RFCs

The definitive source of information on the IP protocol family is the Request For Comments documents defining the standards themselves. An index of all the RFC documents is available through the Web at `http://ds.internic.net/ds/rfc-index.html`. This page has pointers to all currently available RFCs (organized in groups of 100) as well as a searchable index.

Table 24.1 gives the numbers of some relevant RFCs and what they cover. Keep in mind that a given RFC may have been made obsolete by a subsequent RFC. The InterNIC site's index will note in the description any documents that were made obsolete by a subsequent RFC.

Table 24.1. RFC documents of interest.

RFC Number	Topic
791	The Internet Protocol (IPv4)
793	The Transmission Control Protocol (TCP)
768	The User Datagram Protocol 2(UDP)
894	Transmission of IP Datagrams over Ethernet Networks
1171	The PPP Protocol
1883	IP version 6
1602	The Internet Standards Process: How an RFC Becomes a Standard
1880	Current Internet Standards

Books on TCP/IP

A good introduction to TCP/IP is the book *TCP/IP Network Administration*, by Craig Hunt (O'Reilly and Associates, ISBN 0-937175-82-X). Although it was written as a guide for systems administrators of UNIX machines, the book contains an excellent introduction to all aspects of TCP/IP, such as routing and the Domain Name Service (DNS).

Another book worth checking out is *The Design and Implementation of the 4.3BSD UNIX Operating System*, by Samuel J. Leffler, et al. (Addison-Wesley, ISBN 0-201-06196-1). In addition to covering how a UNIX operating system works, it contains a chapter on the TCP/IP implementation.

If you are a beginner, another way to get started get started with TCP/IP is by reading *Teach Yourself TCP/IP in 14 Days*, by Timothy Parker (Sams Publishing, ISBN 0-672-30549-6).

IPng and the TCP/IP Protocols, by Stephan A. Thomas (John Wiley & Sons, ISBN 0-471-13088-5) offers an overview of version 6 of the Internet protocols.

Network Class Overview

The following sections give a short overview of the capabilities and limitations of the different network classes provided in the java.net package. If you have never done any network programming, these sections should help you decide the type of connection class on which you need to base your application. The overview can help you pick the Java classes that best fit your networking application. An overview of Java security, as it relates to network programming, is also provided.

Which Class Is Right for Me?

The answer to this question depends on what you are trying to do and what type of application you are writing. Each network protocol has its own advantages and disadvantages. If you are writing a client for someone else's protocol, the decision probably has been made for you. If you are writing your own protocol from scratch, the following should help you decide which transport method (and hence, which Java classes) best fit your application.

The URL Class

The URL class is an example of what can be accomplished using the other, lower-level network objects. The URL class is best suited for applications or applets that have to access content on the World Wide Web. If all you use Java for is to write Web browser applets, the URL and URLConnection classes, in all likelihood, will handle your network communications needs.

The URL class enables you to retrieve a resource from the Web by specifying the Uniform Resource Locator for it. The content of the URL is fetched and turned into a corresponding Java object (such as a String containing the text of an HTML document). If you are fetching arbitrary information, the URLConnection object provides methods that try to deduce the type of the content either from the filename in the URL or from the content stream itself.

The Socket Class

The Socket class provides a reliable, ordered stream connection (that is, a TCP/IP socket connection). The host and port number of the destination are specified when the Socket is created.

The connection is reliable because the transport layer (the TCP protocol layer) acknowledges the receipt of sent data. If one end of the connection does not receive an acknowledgment within a reasonable period of time, the other end re-sends the unacknowledged data (a technique known as *Positive Acknowledgment with Retransmission,* often abbreviated as PAR). Once you have written data into a Socket object, you can assume that the data will get to the other side (unless you receive an IOException, of course).

The term *ordered stream* means that the data arrives at the opposite end in the exact same order it is written. However, because the data is a stream, write boundaries are not preserved. What this means is that if you write 200 characters, the other side *can* read all 200 characters at once. But it might get the first 10 characters one time and the next 190 the next time data is received from the socket. In any case, the receiver cannot tell where each group of data was written.

The reliable stream connection provided by `Socket` objects is well suited for interactive applications. Examples of protocols that use TCP as their transport mechanism are Telnet and FTP. The HTTP protocol used to transfer data for the Web also uses TCP to communicate between hosts.

The ServerSocket Class

The `ServerSocket` class represents the thing with which `Socket`-type connections communicate. Server sockets listen on a given port for connection requests when their `accept()` method is called. The `ServerSocket` offers the same connection-oriented, ordered stream protocol (TCP) that the `Socket` object does. In fact, once a connection has been established, the `accept()` method returns a `Socket` object to talk with the remote end.

The DatagramSocket Class

The `DatagramSocket` class provides an unreliable, connectionless, datagram connection (that is, a UDP/IP socket connection).

Unlike the reliable connection provided by a `Socket`, there is no guarantee that what you send over a UDP connection actually gets to the receiver. The TCP connection provided by the `Socket` class takes care of retransmitting any packets that get lost. Packets sent through UDP simply are sent out and forgotten, which means that if you need to know that the receiver got the data, you will have to send back some sort of acknowledgment. This arrangement does not mean that your data will never get to the other end of a UDP connection. If a network error happens (your cat jiggles the Ethernet plug out of the wall, for example), the UDP layer does not try to send it again or even know that the packet did not get to the recipient.

Connectionless means that the socket does not have a fixed receiver. You can use the same `DatagramSocket` to send packets to different hosts and ports; however, you can use a `Socket` connection to connect only to a given host and port. Once a `Socket` is connected to a destination, that destination cannot be changed. The fact that UDP sockets are not bound to a specific destination also means that the same socket can listen for packets as well as originate them. There is no UDP `DatagramServerSocket` equivalent to the TCP `ServerSocket`.

Datagram refers to the fact that the information is sent as discrete packets rather than as a continuous ordered stream. The individual packet boundaries are preserved. It may help to think of this process as dropping fixed-size postcards in a mailbox. If you send four packets, the order in which they arrive at the destination is not guaranteed to be the same as they were sent. The receiver may get them in the same order they were sent or the packets may arrive in reverse order. In any case, each packet is received whole.

Given the above constraints, why would anyone want to use a DatagramSocket? There are several advantages to using UDP:

- **You have to communicate with several different hosts.** Because a DatagramSocket is not bound to a particular host, you can use the same object to communicate with different hosts by specifying the InetAddress when you create each DatagramPacket.

- **You are not worried about reliable delivery.** If the application you are writing does not have to know that the data it sends was received at the other end, using a UDP socket eliminates the overhead of acknowledging each packet as TCP does. Another example is when the protocol you are implementing has its own method of handling reliable delivery and retransmission.

- **The amount of data being sent does not merit the overhead of setting up a connection and the reliable delivery mechanism.** An application that is sending only 100 bytes for each transaction every 10 minutes is an example of this kind of situation.

The NFS (Network File System) protocol version 2, originally developed by Sun with implementations available for most operating systems, is an example of an application that uses UDP for its transport mechanism. Another example of an application in which a DatagramSocket may be appropriate is a multiplayer game. The central server must communicate with all the players involved and does not necessarily have to know that a position update got to the player.

> **NOTE**
>
> An actual game that uses UDP for communication is Netrek, a space combat simulation loosely based on the *Star Trek* series. Information on Netrek can be found using the Yahoo! subject catalog at this URL:
>
> http://www.yahoo.com/Recreation/Games/Internet_Games/Netrek/
>
> There is also a Usenet newsgroup for this game:
>
> news:rec.games.netrek

Decisions, Decisions

Now that you know what the classes are capable of, you can choose the one that best fits your application. Table 24.2 sums up the type of connection each of the base networking classes creates. The *Direction* column indicates where a connection originates; *Outgoing* indicates that your application is opening a connection out to another host; *Incoming* indicates that some other application is initiating a connection to yours.

24

INTRODUCTION TO NETWORK PROGRAMMING

Table 24.2. Summary of low-level connection objects.

Class	Connection Type	Direction
Socket	Connected, ordered byte stream (TCP)	Outgoing
ServerSocket	Connected, ordered byte stream (TCP)	Incoming
DatagramSocket	Connectionless datagram (UDP)	Incoming or Outgoing

You should look at the problem you are trying to solve, any constraints you have, and the transport mechanism that best fits your situation. If you are having problems choosing a transport protocol, take a look at some of the RFCs that define Internet standards for applications (such as HTTP or SMTP). One of them might be similar to what you are trying to accomplish. As an alternative, you can be indecisive and provide both TCP and UDP versions of your service, duplicating the processing logic and customizing the network logic. Trying both transport protocols with a pared-down version of your application can give you an indication of which protocol better serves your purposes. Once you've looked at these factors, you should be able to decide what class to use.

The Client/Server Model

A common application for networking classes is the implementation of the client/server model. The client/server model is based on the idea that one computer specializing in information presentation displays the data stored and processed on a remote machine.

Today, the Internet provides home computers with the same networking power institutions outside the home have traditionally used. Many of the Internet applications you have come to know are client/server applications: the Web, e-mail, FTP, Telnet, and so on. Specifically, your home PC serves as the *client* side of the architecture. It displays information located on *servers* around the world.

Basic Client/Server Architecture

The Web implements a simple form of client/server architecture for multiple client machines. Your computer, the client, uses a Web browser to display HTML documents stored somewhere on the Internet on a Web server.

There are four software components to the Web system:

■ A browser such as Netscape Navigator that displays HTML documents on a client machine

■ A server program running on the server that hands HTML documents to client browsers

- The HTML documents stored on the server machine
- The communications protocol that handles the communication of data between the client and server

The diagram in Figure 24.4 shows how this architecture fits together.

FIGURE 24.4.
The client/server architecture of the Web.

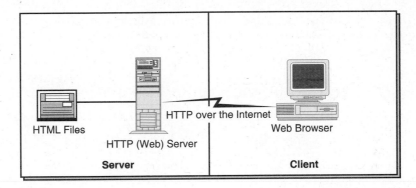

Dividing the Work

The client/server architecture provides us with a logical breakdown of application processing. In an ideal environment, the server side of the application handles all common processing, and the client side handles user-specific processing. With the Web, the server stores the HTML documents shown to all the clients. Each client, on the other hand, has different display needs. Suppose that a user at a dumb terminal is limited to using the character-mode Lynx client. A Windows user, on the other hand, may have a GUI browser that uses the power of the graphical interface to display the document with full multimedia effects. The presentation of the HTML documents delivered by the server is thus left up to the client.

Client/Server Communication

The two most common protocols for client/server communication are TCP/IP (Transmission Control Protocol/Internet Protocol) and UDP/IP (User Datagram Protocol/Internet Protocol). The choice of Java socket classes is dictated by the protocol you select for transmission because Socket objects are optimized for the underlying transmission protocol.

- **Using TCP/IP.** Because of the way Java socket classes are engineered, client and server operations are nearly identical. The major differences are that the server communicates with multiple clients but the client communicates with only a single server—and that the server has to create a listening port for initial connections. The symmetry between TCP clients and servers allows clean implementations that can be maintained with relative ease.

■ **Using UDP/IP.** You may wonder at first why you would use an unreliable communications protocol such as UDP. After all, if you are sending data, can't you assume that you want it to get to its destination? Not necessarily. Sometimes, an application sends information but the arrival of individual packets is unimportant. For example, a server repeatedly broadcasting sports scores 24 hours a day does not really care whether a given score arrives at its destination. It does care, however, about the overhead any error correction might introduce. Such an application is a perfect situation for UDP/IP.

UDP/IP sockets require a lot more base manipulation than do TCP/IP sockets because you have to specify a destination address for every single packet you send. The payoff is enhanced performance for communication that does not depend on any one socket actually arriving at its destination.

Two-Tier versus Three-Tier Design

Now that you understand how to make computers talk to one another on the Internet with Java, it helps to understand how to design a client/server application that you want to build. As discussed earlier in this chapter, the client/server architecture assigns processing responsibility where it logically belongs. A simple system can be broken into two layers: a server (where data and common processing occurs) and a client (where user-specific processing occurs). This kind of architecture is more commonly known as a *two-tier architecture*. A simple time server is one example of a two-tier architecture.

Business applications—and, increasingly, Internet applications—are generally much more complex than simple two-tier applications. These more complex applications can involve relational databases and advanced server-side processing. Because client machines are becoming increasingly powerful, client/server development has enabled applications to move processing off the server and onto the client to facilitate the use of cheaper servers. This trend has led to a problem known as the problem of the fat client.

A *fat client* is a client in a client/server system that has absorbed an inordinate amount of the system's processing needs. Although a fat-client architecture is as capable as any other client/server configuration, it is harder to scale as your application grows over time. Using a common client/server tool such as PowerBuilder, your client application has direct knowledge of exactly how your data is stored and what it looks like in the data store (usually a database). If you ever change where that data is stored or how it is stored, you have to do significant rework of your client application.

The solution to the problem of the fat client is a three-tier client/server architecture that creates another layer of processing across the network. In Figure 24.5, you can see how the three-tier design divides application work into the following three tasks:

■ User interface

■ Data processing or business rules

■ Data storage

FIGURE 24.5.
The three-tier client/server architecture.

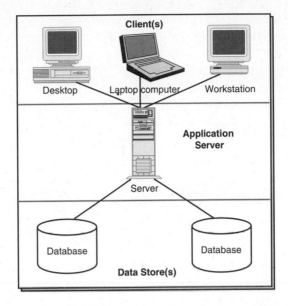

One of the primary advantages of three-tier architecture is that, as your data storage needs grow, you can change the way data is stored without affecting your clients. The middle layer of the system, commonly referred to as the *application server,* can thus concentrate on centralizing business rule processing. (Business rule processing is the processing of data going to and from the clients in a way that is common to all clients.)

Distributed Objects

New technologies are on the horizon to help deliver you from the tedium of socket programming in a client/server environment. The most exciting of these technologies is distributed objects. A *distributed* application is a single application that has individual objects located on many machines. In an ideal world, these objects communicate with one another through simple method calls. Unfortunately, the ideal world is not here yet.

With the release of Java 1.1, Sun has provided a new API designed to allow you to distribute your Java applications. This new API, called Remote Method Invocation (RMI), enables a program on one machine to communicate with a program on another machine using simple Java method calls. Instead of writing a complex socket interface and an application-specific communication protocol, your application acts as though all the separate pieces were part of a single program on one machine. You call methods in any object, no matter where they exist, just as you call any other Java method.

A discussion of RMI is beyond the scope of this chapter (refer to Chapter 17, "The RMI Package," for more information). As a seamless method-based communications API, RMI provides an attractive alternative to writing socket code. Unfortunately, RMI works only when all the pieces of your application are Java pieces. In a hybrid system, sockets are still the best method of enabling communication among networked machines.

Java Security and the Network Classes

One of the purposes of Java is to enable executable content from an arbitrary network source to be retrieved and run securely. To accomplish this goal, the Java runtime system enforces certain limitations on what the classes obtained through the network can do. You should be aware of these constraints because they affect the design of applets and how the applets must be loaded. You must take into consideration the security constraints imposed by your target environment as well as your development environment when you design your application or applet.

For example, Netscape Navigator 2.0 allows code loaded from a local disk more privileges than code loaded over a network connection. A class loaded from an HTTP daemon may create only outgoing connections back to the host from which it was loaded. If the class is loaded from the local host (that is, if it is located somewhere in the class search path on the machine running Navigator), the class can connect to an arbitrary host. Contrast this with the applet viewer provided with Sun's Java Development Kit. The applet viewer can be configured to act in a way similar to Navigator or to enforce no restrictions on network connectivity.

If you require full access to all Java's capabilities, there is always the option of writing a standalone application. A standalone application (that is, one that does not run in the context of a Web browser) has no restrictions on what it can do. Sun's HotJava Web browser is an example of a standalone application.

> **NOTE**
>
> For a more detailed discussion of Java security and how it is designed into the language and runtime system, take a look at Chapter 34, "Java Security."
>
> In addition, Sun has several white-paper documents and a collection of frequently asked questions available at `http://www.javasoft.com/sfaq/`.

These security checks are implemented by a subclass of `java.lang.SecurityManager`. Depending on the security model, the object allows or denies certain actions. You can check beforehand whether a capability your applet needs is present by calling the `SecurityManager` yourself. The `java.lang.System` object provides a `getSecurityManager()` method that returns a reference to the `SecurityManager` active for the current context. If your applet has to open a `ServerSocket`, for example, you can call the `checkListen()` method yourself and print an error message (or pop up a dialog box) alerting the users and referring them to installation instructions.

Summary

This chapter is a roadmap to the next three chapters. It has described the concepts you must be familiar with before you dive into network programming in Java. You should be comfortable with how TCP/IP networking operates in general (or at least know where to look for more information). You also should have an idea of which Java class provides which functionality and how the Java classes fit into client/server architectures.

Developing Content and Protocol Handlers

by Mike Fletcher
revised by Stephen Ingram

IN THIS CHAPTER

CHAPTER

25

Java's URL class gives applets and applications easy access to the World Wide Web using the HTTP protocol. This is fine and dandy if you can get the information you need into a format that a Web server or CGI script can access. However, wouldn't it be nice if your code could talk directly to the server application without going through an intermediary CGI script or some sort of proxy? Wouldn't you like your Java-based Web browser to be able to display your wonderful new image format? This is where protocol and content handlers come in.

What Are Protocol and Content Handlers?

Handlers are classes that extend the capabilities of the standard URL class. The URL class actually hides a complex web of classes that facilitate extensible support for any number of protocols and content types.

The entire *protocol scheme* is implemented by a tandem of classes: URLStreamHandler and URLConnection. When you create a URL object, the protocol name is parsed out of the string and used to create a URLStreamHandler descendant. By itself, URLStreamHandler is rather unimpressive. What it provides is a layer of abstraction that isolates a protocol's implementation from the search and load architecture of the URL class. Although URLStreamHandler acts much like an interface, because it is a class and not an interface, it can be represented by a physical class file and is thus eligible for dynamic loading. URLStreamHandler provides openConnection()— the bridge method to jump from a standard URL to the implementation. What is returned is the class that performs the actual protocol processing: a descendant of URLConnection. If you examine the URL class methods getContent() and openStream(), you find a two-method sequence that first creates and then calls a URLConnection:

```
return handler.openConnection().getContent();      // URL code for getContent()
return handler.openConnection().getInputStream(); // URL code for openStream()
```

In this way, the URLConnection class performs all the protocol-specific work for the URL class. Implementing a protocol handler actually involves implementing both URLStreamHandler and URLConnection descendants. The only class that is aware of the existence of your descendant URLConnection class is your specific URLStreamHandler object.

Content handlers work in a way similar to protocol handlers, but because content handlers interpret streams of input into a single Java object (String or Image and so on), all the processing can be isolated to a single descendant of the ContentHandler class. There is no need for the extra layer of abstraction that protocol handlers implement. Protocol handlers allow two-stage interaction—before and after connection. Content handlers have only a single direct access method (getContent()) and so can implement all their processing directly in the handler.

The URL object cannot parse the content type from the input string. Instead, it has to wait until a protocol handler executes and extracts the content type from the resulting stream. How are content types encoded in the data stream? They are represented as MIME types.

MIME Types

MIME (Multipurpose Internet Mail Extensions) is the Internet standard for specifying the type of content a resource contains. As you may have guessed from the name, MIME was originally proposed for the context of enclosing nontextual components in Internet e-mail. MIME allows different platforms (PCs, Macintoshes, UNIX workstations, and others) to exchange multimedia content in a common format.

The MIME standard, described in RFC 1521, defines an extra set of headers similar to those on Internet e-mail. The headers describe attributes such as the method of encoding the content and the MIME content type. MIME types are written as *type/subtype*, where *type* is a general category such as text or image and *subtype* is a more specific description of the format such as html or jpeg. For example, when a Web browser contacts an HTTP daemon to retrieve an HTML file, the daemon's response looks something like this:

```
Content-type: text/html
<HEAD><TITLE>Document moved</TITLE></HEAD>
<BODY><H1>Document moved</H1>
```

The Web browser parses the Content-type: header and sees that the data is text/html—an HTML document. If it was a GIF image file, the header would have been Content-type: image/gif.

IANA (Internet Assigned Numbers Authority), the group that maintains the lists of assigned protocol numbers and the like, is responsible for registering new content types. A current copy of the official MIME types is available from ftp://ftp.isi.edu/in-notes/iana/assignments/media-types/. This site also has specifications or pointers to specifications for each type.

Getting Java to Load New Handlers

The exact procedure for loading a protocol or content handler depends on the Java implementation. The following instructions are based on Sun's Java Development Kit and should work for any implementation derived from Sun's. If you have problems, check the documentation for your particular version of Java.

In the JDK implementation, the URL class and helpers look for classes in the sun.net.www package. Protocol handlers should be in a package called sun.net.www.protocol.*ProtocolName*, where *ProtocolName* is the name of the protocol (such as ftp or http). The handler class itself should be named `Handler`. For example, the full name of the HTTP protocol handler class, provided by Sun with the JDK, is `sun.net.www.protocol.http.Handler`. To load your new protocol handler, you must construct a directory structure corresponding to the package names and add the directory to your CLASSPATH environment variable. Assume that you have a handler for a protocol—let's call it the `foo` protocol—and that your Java library directory is `.../java/lib/` (`...\java\lib\` on Windows machines). You must take the following steps to load the `foo` protocol:

1. Create the directories `.../java/lib/sun`, `.../java/lib/sun/net`, and so on. The last directory should be named like this:

   `.../java/lib/sun/net/www/protocol/foo`

2. Place your `Handler.java` file in the last directory. Name it like this:

   `.../java/lib/sun/net/www/protocol/foo/Handler.java`

3. Compile the `Handler.java` file.

 If you place the `netClass.zip` file containing the network classes (located on the CD-ROM that accompanies this book) in your CLASSPATH, the sample handlers should load correctly.

Creating a Protocol Handler

Let's start extending Java with a handler for the `finger` protocol. The `finger` protocol is defined in RFC 762. The server listens on TCP port 79; it expects either the user name for which you want information followed by ASCII carriage return and linefeed characters, or (if you want information for all users currently logged in) just the carriage return and linefeed characters. The information is returned as ASCII text in a system-dependent format (although most UNIX variants give similar information). We will use an existing class (`fingerClient`) to handle contacting the `finger` server and concentrate on developing the protocol handler.

Design

The first decision we must make is how to structure URLs for our protocol. We'll imitate the HTTP URL and specify that `finger` URLs should be of the following format:

`finger://host/user`

In this syntax, *host* is the host to contact, and *user* is an optional user to ask for information about. If the user name is omitted, we will return information about all users.

Because Sun already provides a `fingerClient` class (`sun.net.www.protocol.finger.fingerClient`), we will rely on it to do the actual implementation of the `finger` protocol. We have to write the subclasses to `URLStreamHandler` and `URLConnection`. Our stream handler will use the client object to format the returned information using HTML. The handler will write the content into a

StringBuffer object, which will be used to create a StringBufferInputStream. The fingerConnection—a subclass of URLConnection—will take this stream and implement the getInputStream() and getContent() methods.

In our implementation, the protocol stream handler object does all the work of retrieving the remote content; the connection object simply retrieves the data from the stream provided. Usually, the connection object handler would retrieve the content. The openConnection() method would open a connection to the remote location, and the getInputStream() method would return a stream to read the contents. In our case, the protocol is very simple (compared to something as complex as FTP or HTTP), and we can handle everything in the URLStreamHandler descendant.

The fingerConnection Source

The source for the fingerConnection class should go in the same file as the Handler class. The constructor copies the InputStream passed and calls the URLConnection constructor. It also sets the URLConnection member to indicate that the connection cannot take input. Listing 25.1 contains the source for this class.

Listing 25.1. The fingerConnection class.

```
class fingerConnection extends URLConnection {
  InputStream in;
  fingerConnection( URL u, InputStream in ) {
    super( u );
    this.in = in;
    this.setDoInput( false );
  }
  public void connect( ) {
    return;
  }
  public InputStream getInputStream( ) throws IOException {
    return in;
  }
  public Object getContent( ) throws IOException {
    String retval;
    int nbytes;
    byte buf[] = new byte[ 1024 ];
    try {
      while( (nbytes = in.read( buf, 0, 1024 )) != -1 ) {
        retval += new String( buf, 0, 0, nbytes );
      }
    } catch( Exception e ) {
      System.err.println(
        "fingerConnection::getContent: Exception\n" + e );
      e.printStackTrace( System.err );
    }
    return retval;
  }
}
```

> **NOTE**
>
> URLConnections normally go through a two-stage existence. First they are created, then they are connected. Separating the two stages allows a user to interact with the created object to specify input options such as request methods, cache usage, and the like. Once connected, these options can no longer be altered. The fingerConnection class was connected at creation time because of the work performed by the stream handler. Other URLConnection descendants may not operate the same way and so may allow user interaction between the times they are created and connected.

Handler Source

Let's rough out the skeleton of the Handler.java file. We need the package statement so that our classes are compiled into the package where the runtime handler will look for them. We also import the fingerClient object here. The outline of the class is shown in Listing 25.2.

Listing 25.2. The protocol handler skeleton.

```
package sun.net.www.protocol.finger;
import java.io.*;
import java.net.*;
import sun.net.www.protocol.finger.fingerClient;
// fingerConnection source goes here
public class Handler extends URLStreamHandler {
   // openConnection() method
}
```

> **NOTE**
>
> Because the fingerConnection class appears with default visibility within the handler file, the URLStreamHandler descendant is the only class that has any knowledge of or access to the implementation. All access outside of the handler occurs through virtual methods of URLConnection—fingerConnection's parent class. This is not a requirement; the fingerConnection class could just as easily have existed as an external public class. Often, external existence is necessary to allow specific user input alterations that are not part of the URLConnection base class.

The openConnection() Method

Now let's develop the method responsible for returning an appropriate URLConnection object to retrieve a given URL. The method starts out by allocating a StringBuffer to hold our return data. We also will parse out the host name and user name from the URL argument. If the host was omitted, we default to localhost. The code for openConnection() is given in Listings 25.3 through 25.6.

Listing 25.3. The openConnection() method: Parsing the URL.

```
public synchronized URLConnection openConnection( URL u ) {
  StringBuffer sb = new StringBuffer( );
  String host = u.getHost( );
  String user = u.getFile( ).substring( 1, u.getFile( ).length() );
  if( host.equals( "" ) ) {
    host = "localhost";
  }
```

Notice how the connection class relies on the URL class for parsing. Other than its function as a gateway to the handlers, parsing is the main feature of the URL class.

Next, the method writes an HTML header into the buffer (see Listing 25.4). This enables a Java-based Web browser to display the finger information in a nice-looking format.

Listing 25.4. The openConnection() method: Writing the HTML header.

```
sb.append( "<HTML><head>\n");
sb.append( "<title>Fingering " );
sb.append( (user.equals("") ? "everyone" : user) );
sb.append( "@" + host );
sb.append( "</title></head>\n" );
sb.append( "<body>\n" );
sb.append( "<pre>\n" );
```

Now we'll use Sun's fingerClient class to get the information into a String and then append it to our buffer. If there is an error while getting the finger information, we will put the error message from the exception into the buffer instead (see Listing 25.5).

Listing 25.5. The openConnection() method: Retrieving the finger information.

```
try {
  String info = null;
  info = (new fingerClient( host, user )).getInfo( );
  sb.append( info );
} catch( Exception e ) {
  sb.append( "Error fingering: " + e );
}
```

Finally, we'll close all the open HTML tags and create a fingerConnection object that will be returned to the caller (see Listing 25.6).

Listing 25.6. The openConnection() method: Finishing the HTML and returning a `fingerConnection` object.

```
sb.append( "\n</pre></body>\n</html>\n" );
return new fingerConnection( u,
    (new StringBufferInputStream( sb.toString( ) ) ) );
}
```

Using the Handler

Once all the code is compiled and in the right locations, load the `urlFetcher` applet provided on the CD-ROM that accompanies this book and enter a `finger` URL. If everything loads right, you should see something like Figure 25.1. If you get an error with a message such as `BAD URL "finger://...": unknown protocol`, check that you have your `CLASSPATH` set correctly.

FIGURE 25.1.

The `urlFetcher` *applet displaying a* `finger` *URL.*

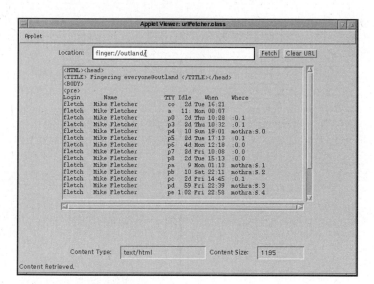

Creating a Content Handler

The content handler example presented in this section is for MIME-type text and tab-separated values. If you have ever used a spreadsheet or database program, this type will be familiar. Many applications can import and export data in an ASCII text file, where each column of data in a row is separated by a tab character (\t). The first line is interpreted as the names of the fields, and the remaining lines are the actual data.

Design

Our first design decision is to figure out what type of Java object or objects to use to map the tab-separated values. Because this is textual content, some sort of `String` object would seem to be the best solution. The spreadsheet characteristics of rows and columns of data can be represented by arrays. Putting these two facts together gives us a data type of `String[][]`, or an array of arrays of `String` objects. The first array is an array of `String[]` objects, each representing one row of data. Each of these arrays consists of a `String` for each cell of the data.

Because we also require some way of breaking the input stream into separate fields, we'll make a subclass of `java.io.StreamTokenizer` to handle this task. The `StreamTokenizer` class provides methods for breaking an `InputStream` into individual tokens.

Content Handler Skeleton

Content handlers are implemented by subclassing the `java.net.ContentHandler` class. These subclasses are responsible for implementing a `getContent()` method. We'll start with the skeleton of the class and then import the networking and I/O packages as well as the `java.util.Vector` class. We will also define the skeleton for our `tabStreamTokenizer` class. Listing 25.7 shows the skeleton for this content handler.

Listing 25.7. Content handler skeleton.

```
/*
 *  Handler for text/tab-separated-values MIME type.
 */
// This needs to go in this package for JDK-derived
// Java implementations
package sun.net.www.content.text;
import java.net.*;
import java.io.*;
class tabStreamTokenizer extends StreamTokenizer {
  public static final int TT_TAB = ''\t'
  // Constructor
}
import java.util.Vector;
public
  class tab_separated_values extends ContentHandler {
  // getContent method
}
```

The `tabStreamTokenizer` Class

Let's first define the class that breaks the input into separate fields. Most of the functionality we require is provided by the `StreamTokenizer` class, so we only have to define a constructor

25

CONTENT AND PROTOCOL HANDLERS

that specifies the character classes needed to get the behavior we want. For the purposes of this content handler, there are three types of tokens: TT_TAB tokens, which represent fields; TT_EOL tokens, which signal the end of a line (that is, the end of a row of data); and TT_EOF tokens, which signal the end of the input file. Because this class is relatively simple, it is presented in its entirety in Listing 25.8.

Listing 25.8. The tabStreamTokenizer class.

```
class tabStreamTokenizer extends StreamTokenizer {
  public static final int TT_TAB = '\t';
  tabStreamTokenizer( InputStream in ) {
    super(new BufferedReader(new InputStreamReader(in)) );
    // Undo parseNumbers() and whitespaceChars(0, ' ')
    ordinaryChars( '0', '9' );
    ordinaryChar( '.' );
    ordinaryChar( '-' );
    ordinaryChars( 0, ' ' );
    // Everything but TT_EOL and TT_TAB is a word
    wordChars( 0, ('\t'-1) );
    wordChars( ('\t'+1), 255 );
    // Make sure TT_TAB and TT_EOL are returned verbatim.
    whitespaceChars( TT_TAB, TT_TAB );
    ordinaryChar( TT_EOL );
  }
}
```

The getContent() Method

Subclasses of ContentHandler must provide an implementation of getContent() that returns a reference to an Object. The method takes as its parameter a URLConnection object from which the class can obtain an InputStream to read the resource's data.

The getContent() Skeleton

First, let's define the overall structure and method variables. We need a flag (which we'll call done) to signal when we've read all the field names from the first line of text. The number of fields (columns) in each row of data will be determined by the number of fields in the first line of text and will be kept in an int variable called numFields. We also will declare another integer, index, for use while inserting the rows of data into a String[].

We need some method of holding an arbitrary number of objects because we cannot determine the number of data rows in advance. To do this, we'll use the java.util.Vector object, which we'll call lines, to keep each String[] array. Finally, we will declare an instance of our tabStreamTokenizer, using the getInputStream() method from the URLConnection passed as an argument to the constructor. Listing 25.9 shows the skeleton code for the getContent() method.

Listing 25.9. The getContent() skeleton.

```
public Object getContent( URLConnection con )
  throws IOException
{
  boolean done = false;
  int numFields = 0;
  int index = 0;
  Vector lines = new Vector();
  tabStreamTokenizer in =
    new tabStreamTokenizer( con.getInputStream( ) );
  // Read in the first line of data (Listings 25.10 & 25.11)
  // Read in the rest of the file (Listing 25.12)
  // Stuff all data into a String[][] (Listing 25.13)
}
```

Reading the First Line

The first line of the file tells us the number of fields and the names of the fields in each row for the rest of the file. Because we don't know beforehand how many fields there are, we'll keep each field in Vector firstLine. Each TT_WORD token that the tokenizer returns is the name of one field. We know we are done once it returns a TT_EOL token and can set the done flag to true. We use a switch statement on the ttype member of our tabStreamTokenizer to decide what action to take (see Listing 25.10).

Listing 25.10. Reading the first line of data.

```
Vector firstLine = new Vector( );
while( !done && in.nextToken( ) != in.TT_EOF  ) {
  switch( in.ttype ) {
  case in.TT_WORD:
    firstLine.addElement( new String( in.sval ) );
    numFields++;
    break;
  case in.TT_EOL:
    done = true;
    break;
  }
}
```

Now that we have the first line in memory, we have to build an array of String objects from those stored in the Vector. To accomplish this, we'll first allocate the array to the size just determined. Then we will use the copyInto() method to transfer the strings into the array just allocated. Finally, we'll insert the array into lines (see Listing 25.11).

Listing 25.11. Copying field names into an array.

```
// Copy first line into array
  String curLine[] = new String[ numFields ];
  firstLine.copyInto( curLine );
  lines.addElement( curLine );
```

Read the Rest of the File

Before reading the remaining data, we have to allocate a new array to hold the next row. Then we loop until we encounter the end of the file, signified by TT_EOF. Each time we retrieve a TT_WORD, we insert the String into curLine and increment index.

The end of the line lets us know when a row of data is done, at which time we copy the current line into Vector. Then we allocate a new String[] to hold the next line and set index back to zero (to insert the next item starting at the first element of the array). The code to implement this is given in Listing 25.12.

Listing 25.12. Reading the rest of the data.

```
curLine = new String[ numFields ];
while( in.nextToken( ) != in.TT_EOF ) {
  switch( in.ttype ) {
  case in.TT_WORD:
    curLine[ index++ ] = new String( in.sval );
    break;
  case in.TT_EOL:
    lines.addElement( curLine );
    curLine = new String[ numFields ];
    index = 0;
    break;
  }
}
```

Stuff All Data into `String[][]`

At this point in the code, all the data has been read in. All that remains is to copy the data from lines into an array of arrays of String, as shown in Listing 25.13.

Listing 25.13. Returning tab-separated value (TSV) data as `String[][]`.

```
String retval[][] = new String[ lines.size() ][];
lines.copyInto( retval );
return retval;
```

Using the Content Handler

To show how the content handler works, we'll modify the `urlFetcher` applet (used earlier in this chapter to demonstrate the `finger` protocol handler). We'll change it to use the `getContent()` method to retrieve the contents of a resource rather than reading the data from the stream returned by `getInputStream()`. We'll show the changes to the `doFetch()` method of the `urlFetcher` applet necessary to determine what type of `Object` was returned and to display it correctly. The first change is to call the `getContent()` method and get an `Object` back rather than getting an `InputStream`. Listing 25.14 shows this change.

Listing 25.14. Modified `urlFetcher.doFetch()` code: Calling `getContent()` to get an `Object`.

```
try {
  boolean displayed = false;
  URLConnection con = target.openConnection();
  Object obj = con.getContent( );
```

Next we must perform tests using the `instanceof` operator. We handle `String` objects and arrays of `String` objects by placing the text into the `TextArea`. Arrays are printed item by item. If the object is a subclass of `InputStream`, we read the data from the stream and display it. `Image` content is just noted as being an `Image`. For any other content type, we simply throw our hands up and remark that we cannot display the content (because the `urlFetcher` applet is not a full-fledged Web browser). The code to do this is shown in Listing 25.15.

Listing 25.15. Modified `urlFetcher.doFetch()` code: Determining the type of the `Object` and displaying it.

```
if( obj instanceof String ) {
  contentArea.setText( (String) obj );
  displayed = true;
}
if( obj instanceof String[] ) {
  String array[] = (String []) obj;
  StringBuffer buf = new StringBuffer( );
  for( int i = 0; i < array.length; i++ )
    buf.append( "item " + i + ": " + array[i] + "\n" );
  contentArea.setText( buf.toString( ) );
  displayed = true;
}
if( obj instanceof String[][] ) {
  String array[][] = (String [][]) obj;
  StringBuffer buf = new StringBuffer( );
  for( int i = 0; i < array.length; i++ ) {
    buf.append( "Row " + i + ":\n\t" );
    for( int j = 0; j < array[i].length; j++ )
      buf.append( "item " + j + ": "
                    + array[i][j] + "\t" );
    buf.append( "\n" );
  }
```

25

CONTENT AND PROTOCOL HANDLERS

continues

Listing 25.15. continued

```
        contentArea.setText( buf.toString() );
        displayed = true;
    }
    if( obj instanceof Image ) {
      contentArea.setText( "Image" );
      diplayed = true;
    }
    if( obj instanceof InputStream ) {
      int c;
      StringBuffer buf = new StringBuffer( );
      while( (c = ((InputStream) obj).read( )) != -1 )
        buf.append( (char) c );
      contentArea.setText( buf.toString( ) );
      displayed = true;
    }
    if( !displayed ) {
      contentArea.setText( "Don't know how to display "
        obj.getClass().getName( ) );
    }
    // Same code to display content type and length
} catch( IOException e ) {
    showStatus( "Error fetching \"" + target + "\": " + e );
    return;
}
```

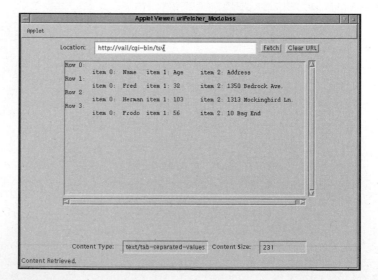

The complete modified applet source is on the CD-ROM that accompanies this book as `urlFetcher_Mod.java`. Figure 25.2 shows what the applet will look like when displaying text/tab-separated values. The file displayed in the figure is included on the CD-ROM as `example.tsv`.

FIGURE 25.2.

The `urlFetcher_Mod` *applet.*

Most HTTP daemons should return the correct content type for files ending in `.tsv`. Many Web browsers have a menu option that shows you information such as the content type about a URL (for example, the View | Document Info option in Netscape Navigator does this). You can use this feature to see what MIME type the sample data is being returned as. If the data does not show up as text/tab-separated values, try one of the following suggestions:

■ Ask your Webmaster to look at the MIME configuration file for your HTTP daemon. The Webmaster will either be able to tell you the proper file suffix or modify the daemon to return the proper type.

 ■ If you can install CGI scripts on your Web server, you may want to look at a sample script on the CD-ROM that accompanies this book (named `tsv.sh`); it has the content handler example that returns data in the proper format.

Summary

After reading this chapter, you should have an understanding of how Java can be extended fairly easily to deal with new application protocols and data formats. You now know the classes from which you have to derive your handlers (`URLConnection` and `URLStreamHandler` for protocol handlers; `ContentHandler` for content handlers) and how to get Java to load the new handler classes.

25

CONTENT AND
PROTOCOL
HANDLERS

Java Socket Programming

by Stephen Ingram

IN THIS CHAPTER

CHAPTER 26

For full Java client/server applet connectivity, an applet server is required. This chapter initiates the development of a Java HTTP server. Before beginning the development of the server, however, you need some background knowledge of socket programming. This chapter begins with a socket overview followed by an exploration of Java's socket classes. The remainder of the chapter focuses on the construction of a Java HTTP Web server.

After reading this chapter, you should be able to do the following:

- Understand the socket abstraction
- Know the different modes of socket operation
- Have a working knowledge of the HTTP protocol
- Be able to apply the Java socket classes
- Understand applet socket use and limitations
- Comprehend the HTTP Java server

An Introduction to Sockets

Computers on the Internet are connected by the TCP/IP protocol. In the 1980s, the Advanced Research Projects Agency (ARPA) of the U.S. government funded the University of California at Berkeley to provide a UNIX implementation of the TCP/IP protocol suite. What was developed was termed the *socket interface* (although you may hear it called the *Berkeley-socket interface* or just *Berkeley sockets*). Today, the socket interface is the most widely used method for accessing a TCP/IP network.

A *socket* is nothing more than a convenient abstraction. It represents a connection point into a TCP/IP network, much like the electrical sockets in your home provide a connection point for your appliances. When two computers want to converse, each uses a socket. One computer is termed the *server*—it opens a socket and listens for connections. The other computer is termed the *client*—it calls the server socket to start the connection. To establish a connection, all that's needed is a server's destination address and port number.

Each computer in a TCP/IP network has a unique address. *Ports* represent individual connections within that address. This is analogous to corporate mail—each person within a company shares the same address, but a letter is routed within the company by the person's name. Each port within a computer shares the same address, but data is routed within each computer by the port number. When a socket is created, it must be associated with a specific port—this process is known as *binding to a port*.

Socket Transmission Modes

Sockets have two major modes of operation: connection-oriented and connectionless modes. *Connection-oriented sockets* operate like a telephone: they must establish a connection and then hang up. Everything that flows between these two events arrives in the same order it was sent. *Connectionless sockets* operate like the mail: delivery is not guaranteed, and multiple pieces of mail may arrive in an order different from that in which they were sent.

The mode you use is determined by an application's needs. If reliability is important, connection-oriented operation is better. File servers must have all their data arrive correctly and in sequence. If some data is lost, the server's usefulness is invalidated. Some applications—time servers, for example—send discrete chunks of data at regular intervals. If data were to get lost, the server would not want the network to retry because by the time the re-sent data arrived, it would be too old to have any accuracy. When you need reliability, be aware that it does come with a price. Ensuring data sequence and correctness requires extra processing and memory usage; this extra overhead can slow down the response times of a server.

Connectionless operation uses the User Datagram Protocol (UDP). A *datagram* is a self-contained unit that has all the information needed to attempt its delivery. Think of it as an envelope—it has a destination and return address on the outside and contains the data to be sent on the inside. A socket in this mode does not have to connect to a destination socket; it simply sends the datagram. The UDP protocol promises only to make a best-effort delivery attempt. Connectionless operation is fast and efficient, but not guaranteed.

Connection-oriented operation uses the Transport Control Protocol (TCP). A socket in this mode must connect to the destination before sending data. Once connected, the sockets are accessed using a *streams interface*: open-read-write-close. Everything sent by one socket is received by the other end of the connection in exactly the same order it was sent. Connection-oriented operation is less efficient than connectionless operation, but it's guaranteed.

Sun Microsystems has always been a proponent of internetworking, so it isn't surprising to find rich support for sockets in the Java class hierarchy. In fact, the Java classes have significantly reduced the skill needed to create a sockets program. Each transmission mode is implemented in a separate set of Java classes. This chapter discusses the connection-oriented classes first.

Java Connection-Oriented Classes

The connection-oriented classes within Java have both a client and a server representative. The client half tends to be the simplest to set up, so we cover it first.

Listing 26.1 shows a simple client application. It requests an HTML document from a server and displays the response to the console.

Listing 26.1. A simple socket client.

```java
import java.io.*;
import java.net.*;

/**
 * An application that opens a connection to a Web server and reads
 * a single Web page from the connection.
 */
public class SimpleWebClient {
    public static void main(String args[])
    {
        try
        {
            // Open a client socket connection
            Socket clientSocket1 = new Socket("www.javasoft.com", 80);
            System.out.println("Client1: " + clientSocket1);

            // Get a Web page
            getPage(clientSocket1);
        }
        catch (UnknownHostException uhe)
        {
            System.out.println("UnknownHostException: " + uhe);
        }
        catch (IOException ioe)
        {
            System.err.println("IOException: " + ioe);
        }
    }

    /**
     * Request a Web page using the passed client socket.
     * Display the reply and close the client socket.
     */
    public static void getPage(Socket clientSocket)
    {
        try
        {
            // Acquire the input and output streams
            DataOutputStream outbound = new DataOutputStream(
                clientSocket.getOutputStream() );
            BufferedReader inbound = new BufferedReader(
                new InputStreamReader(clientSocket.getInputStream()) );
            // Write the HTTP request to the server
            outbound.writeBytes("GET / HTTP/1.0\r\n\r\n");

            // Read the response
            String responseLine;
            while ((responseLine = inbound.readLine()) != null)
            {
                // Display each line to the console
                System.out.println(responseLine);
            }

            // Clean up
            outbound.close();
```

```
        inbound.close();
        clientSocket.close();
    }
    catch (IOException ioe)
    {
        System.out.println("IOException: " + ioe);
    }
  }
}
```

NOTE

The examples in this chapter are coded as applications to avoid security restrictions. Run the code from the command line as `java ClassName`.

Recall that a client socket issues a connect call to a listening server socket. Client sockets are created and connected by using a constructor from the `Socket` class. The following line creates a client socket and connects it to a host:

```
Socket clientSocket = new Socket("merlin", 80);
```

The first parameter is the name of the host you want to connect to; the second parameter is the port number. A host name specifies only the destination computer. The port number is required to complete the transaction and allow an individual application to receive the call. In this case, port number 80 was specified (the well-known port number for the HTTP protocol). Other well-known port numbers are shown in Table 26.1. Port numbers were not originally mandated by any governing body, but were assigned by convention—this is why they are said to be "well known." Currently, port numbers are assigned by the Internet Assigned Numbers Authority (IANA), although port numbers less than 1024 are still referred to as "well known."

Table 26.1. Well-known port numbers.

Service	Port
echo	7
daytime	13
ftp	21
telnet	23
smtp	25
finger	79
http	80
pop3	110

Because the Socket class is connection oriented, it provides a streams interface for reads and writes. Classes from the java.io package should be used to access a connected socket:

```
DataOutputStream outbound = new DataOutputStream( clientSocket.getOutputStream() );
BufferedReader inbound = new BufferedReader(new
InputStreamReader(clientSocket.getInputStream()) );
```

Once the streams are created, normal stream operations can be performed. The following code snippet requests a Web page and echoes the response to the screen:

```
outbound.writeBytes("GET / HTTP/1.0\r\n\r\n);
String responseLine;
while ( (responseLine = inbound.readLine()) != null)
{
    System.out.println(responseLine);
}
```

When the program is done using the socket, the connection must be closed, like this:

```
outbound.close();
inbound.close();
clientSocket.close();
```

Notice that the socket streams are closed first. All socket streams should be closed before the socket is closed. This application is relatively simple, but all client programs follow the same basic script:

1. Create the client socket connection.
2. Acquire read and write streams to the socket.
3. Use the streams according to the server's protocol.
4. Close the streams.
5. Close the socket.

Client Socket Options

JDK 1.1 has added capabilities that allow a subset of Berkeley-style socket options. Options give you tighter control over the socket's behavior. For client sockets, there are three socket options under user control:

- SO_LINGER
- SO_TIMEOUT
- TCP_NODELAY

Each option entails significant complexity and should be exercised only when you have a thorough understanding of their operation.

The SO_LINGER Socket Option

The SO_LINGER option is referenced by these complimentary socket methods:

- public int getSoLinger()
- public void setSoLinger(boolean *on*, int *val*)

When sockets are told to close, they undertake an orderly shutdown. This shutdown is an end-to-end cooperative process: First a TCP finish (<FIN>) command is sent. The other side responds with a TCP acknowledgment (<ACK><FIN>). Finally, the closing socket sends <ACK>. Each connected socket maintains a record of the average time required by round-trip transmissions. If no acknowledgment is received before the average round-trip timeout, a TCP abort (<RST>) is sent and the connection is closed unilaterally. This timeout is controllable with the SO_LINGER option. Additionally, setting a SO_LINGER time of zero causes an abortive close. *Abortive closes* cause any queued data to be discarded and a TCP <RST> command to be transmitted.

> **CAUTION**
>
> It is normally best to leave the SO_LINGER option disabled. This is the default setting and should be changed only with great caution. Most TCP protocol stacks choose a close timeout based on a historical analysis of the connection. It is presumptive to assume that you can choose this value more accurately.

The SO_TIMEOUT Socket Option

The SO_TIMEOUT option is much more useful than SO_LINGER. Where SO_LINGER exists for expert-level users, SO_TIMEOUT has practical applications for the average Java programmer. Normally, reading from a connected socket blocks the calling thread until data is received or the socket is closed. Setting SO_TIMEOUT allows this behavior to change. There are two complimentary methods for SO_TIMEOUT:

- public synchronized int getSoTimeout()
- public synchronized void setSoTimeout(int *timeout*)

This option represents the timeout in milliseconds. Any read operation returns an InterruptedIOException if no data is received before the timeout expires. The default is -1 (not set).

The TCP_NODELAY Socket Option

The final socket option allows selective application of the Nagle algorithm. John Nagle had a congestion problem in his large internetwork at Ford Aerospace. In response, he formulated a simple algorithm: no TCP packets can be sent until either all previous packets are acknowledged or a maximum segment size (MSS) is reached. Such a simple algorithm had dramatic results, but also caused data to be accumulated in buffers rather than being immediately transmitted.

The default setting for the `TCP_NODELAY` option is disabled; in reality, there is little reason to change this setting. Only applications that require immediate application-level acknowledgment to sent packets would experience any noticeable effects of a change to this setting. The classic example is a UNIX X-server client. This application sends mouse movements and expects immediate responses in order to position the cursor. The Nagle algorithm would queue mouse movements, thus skewing the cursor's placement. For this application, `TCP_NODELAY` should be enabled.

There are two complimentary methods for manipulating `TCP_NODELAY`:

- `public boolean getTcpNoDelay()`
- `public void setTcpNoDelay(boolean on)`

TCP Interfaces

JDK 1.1 also added support for multihomed computers. A *multihomed computer* has more than one TCP interface (typically found on machines that have both local Ethernet and Internet access). In response to the need to use a specific interface, the socket class has an additional pair of constructors that allow users to choose a local network interface address:

- `public Socket(String host, int port, InetAddress localAddr, int localPort)`
- `public Socket(InetAddress address, int port, InetAddress localAddr, int localPort)`

Using a server socket is only slightly more complicated than using a client socket, as explained in the following section.

Server Sockets

Listing 26.2 is a partial listing of a simple server application. The complete server example can be found on the CD-ROM that accompanies this book in the file `SimpleWebServer.java`.

Listing 26.2. A simple server application.

```
/**
 * An application that listens for connections and serves a simple
 * HTML document.
 */
class SimpleWebServer {
    public static void main(String args[])
```

```java
    {
        ServerSocket serverSocket = null;
        Socket clientSocket = null;
        int connects = 0;
        try
        {
            // Create the server socket
            serverSocket = new ServerSocket(80, 5);

            while (connects < 5)
            {
                // Wait for a connection
                clientSocket = serverSocket.accept();

                //Service the connection
                ServiceClient(clientSocket);
                connects++;
            }
            serverSocket.close();
        }
        catch (IOException ioe)
        {
            System.out.println("Error in SimpleWebServer: " + ioe);
        }
    }

    public static void ServiceClient(Socket client)
        throws IOException
    {

        BufferedReader inbound = null;
        OutputStream outbound = null;
        try
        {
            // Acquire the input stream
            inbound = new BufferedReader(
                new InputStreamReader(client.getInputStream()) );


            // Format the output (response header and tiny HTML document)
            StringBuffer buffer = PrepareOutput();

            String inputLine;
            while ((inputLine = inbound.readLine()) != null)
            {
                // If end of HTTP request, send the response
                if ( inputLine.equals("") )
                {
                    outbound = client.getOutputStream();
                    outbound.write(buffer.toString().getBytes());
                    break;

                }
            }
        }
        finally
        {
```

continues

Listing 26.2. continued

```
                // Clean up
                System.out.println("Cleaning up connection: " + client);
                outbound.close();
                inbound.close();
                client.close();
            }
        }
    ...
    }
```

Servers do not actively create connections. Instead, they passively listen for a client connect request and then provide their services. Servers are created with a constructor from the `ServerSocket` class. The following line creates a server socket and binds it to port `80`:

```
ServerSocket serverSocket = new ServerSocket(80, 5);
```

The first parameter is the port number on which the server should listen. The second parameter is an optional listen stack depth. A server can receive connection requests from many clients at the same time, but each call is processed one at a time. The *listen stack* is a queue of unanswered connection requests. The preceding code instructs the socket driver to maintain the last five connection requests. If the constructor omits the listen stack depth, a default value of `50` is used.

Once the socket is created and listening for connections, incoming connections are created and placed on the listen stack. The `accept()` method is called to lift individual connections off the stack:

```
Socket clientSocket = serverSocket.accept();
```

This method returns a connected client socket used to converse with the caller. No conversations are ever conducted over the server socket itself. Instead, the server socket spawns a new socket in the `accept()` method. The server socket is still open and queuing new connection requests.

As you do with the client socket, the next step is to create input and output streams:

```
BufferedReader inbound = new BufferedReader(new
InputStreamReader(client.getInputStream()) );
OutputStream outbound = client.getOutputStream();
```

Normal I/O operations can now be performed by using the newly created streams. This server waits for the client to send a blank line before sending its response. When the conversation is finished, the server closes the streams and the client socket. At this point, the server tries to accept more calls. What happens when there are no calls waiting in the queue? The method waits for one to arrive. This behavior is known as *blocking*. The `accept()` method blocks the server thread from performing any other tasks until a new call arrives. When five connections have been serviced, the server exits by closing its server socket. Any queued calls are canceled.

NOTE

The SimpleWebServer application produces no output. To exercise it, you can either use a browser or the SimpleWebClient application from Listing 26.1. Both cases require the current machine's name. You can substitute localhost if you are unsure of your machine's name. Browsers should be pointed to http://localhost/.

All servers follow the same basic script:

1. Create the server socket and begin listening.
2. Call the accept() method to get new connections.
3. Create input and output streams for the returned socket.
4. Conduct the conversation based on the agreed protocol.
5. Close the client streams and socket.
6. Go back to step 2 or continue to step 7.
7. Close the server socket.

Figure 26.1 summarizes the steps needed for client/server connection-oriented applications.

FIGURE 26.1.
Client and server connection-oriented applications.

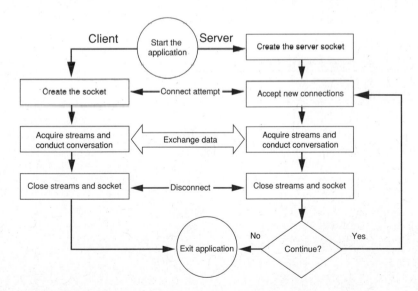

Iterative and Concurrent Servers

The client/server application just presented is known as an *iterative server* because the code accepts a client connection and completely processes it before it accepts another connection. More complex servers are *concurrent servers*: Instead of accepting connections and immediately processing them, a concurrent server spawns a new thread to process each new request, so it seems as though the server is processing many requests simultaneously. All commercial Web servers are concurrent servers.

Java Datagram Classes

Unlike the client and server portions of connection-oriented classes, the datagram versions of the client and server behave in nearly identical manners—the only difference occurs in implementation. For the datagram model, the same class is used for both client and server halves. The following lines create client and server datagram sockets:

```
DatagramSocket serverSocket = new DatagramSocket( 4545 );
DatagramSocket clientSocket = new DatagramSocket();
```

The server specifies its port using the lone constructor parameter 4545. Because the client calls the server, the client can use any available port. The omitted constructor parameter in the second call instructs the operating system to assign the next available port number. The client could have requested a specific port, but the call would fail if some other socket had already bound itself to that port. It's better not to specify a port unless the intent is to be a server.

Because streams can't be acquired for communication, how do you talk to a DatagramSocket object? The answer lies in the DatagramPacket class.

Receiving Datagrams

The DatagramPacket class is used to receive and send data over DatagramSocket classes. The packet class contains connection information as well as the data. As was explained earlier, datagrams are self-contained transmission units. The DatagramPacket class encapsulates these units. The following lines receive data from a datagram socket:

```
DatagramPacket packet = new DatagramPacket(new byte[512], 512);
clientSocket.receive(packet);
```

The constructor for the packet must know where to place the received data. A 512-byte buffer is created and passed to the constructor as the first parameter. The second constructor parameter is the size of the buffer. Like the accept() method in the ServerSocket class, the receive() method blocks until data is available.

Sending Datagrams

Sending datagrams is really very simple; all that's needed is a complete address. Addresses are created and tracked using the InetAddress class. This class has no public constructors, but it does contain several static methods that can be used to create an instance of the class. The following list shows the public methods that create InetAddress class instances:

Public InetAddress *Creation Methods*

```
InetAddress getByName(String host);

InetAddress[] getAllByName(String host);

InetAddress getLocalHost();
```

Getting the local host is useful for informational purposes, but only the first two methods are actually used to send packets. Both getByName() and getAllByName() require the name of the destination host. The first method merely returns the first match it finds. The second method is needed because a computer can have more than one address. When this occurs, the computer is said to be *multihomed*: The computer has one name, but multiple ways to reach it.

All the creation methods are marked as static. They must be called as follows:

```
InetAddress addr1 = InetAddress.getByName("localhost");
InetAddress addr2[] = InetAddress.getAllByName("localhost");
InetAddress addr3 = InetAddress.getLocalHost();
```

Any of these calls can throw an UnknownHostException. If a computer is not connected to a Domain Name Server (DNS), or if the host is really not found, an exception is thrown. If a computer does not have an active TCP/IP configuration, then getLocalHost() is likely to fail with this exception as well.

Once an address is determined, datagrams can be sent. The following lines transmit a string to a destination socket:

```
String toSend = "This is the data to send!";

byte sendbuf[] = toSend.getBytes();
DatagramPacket sendPacket = new DatagramPacket( sendbuf, sendbuf.length, addr,
                                                port);
clientSocket.send( sendPacket );
```

First, the string must be converted to a byte array. The getBytes() method takes care of the conversion. Then a new DatagramPacket instance must be created. Notice the two extra parameters at the end of the constructor. Because this will be a send packet, the address and port of the destination must also be placed into the packet. An applet may know the address of its server, but how does a server know the address of its client? Remember that a datagram is like an envelope—it has a return address. When any packet is received, the return address can be extracted from the packet by using getAddress() and getPort(). This is how a server would respond to a client packet:

```
DatagramPacket sendPacket = new DatagramPacket( sendbuf, sendbuf.length,
    recvPacket.getAddress(), recvPacket.getPort() );
serverSocket.send( sendPacket );
```

Datagram Servers

Unlike connection-oriented operation, datagram servers are actually less complicated than the datagram client. The basic script for a datagram server is as follows:

1. Create the datagram socket on a specific port.
2. Call receive() to wait for incoming packets.
3. Respond to received packets according to the agreed protocol.
4. Go back to step 2 or continue to step 5.
5. Close the datagram socket.

Listing 26.3 shows a simple datagram echo server. This server echoes back any packets it receives.

Listing 26.3. A simple datagram echo server.

```java
import java.io.*;
import java.net.*;

public class SimpleDatagramServer
{
    public static void main(String[] args)
    {
        DatagramSocket socket = null;
        DatagramPacket recvPacket, sendPacket;
        try
        {
            socket = new DatagramSocket(4545);
            while (socket != null)
            {
                recvPacket= new DatagramPacket(new byte[512], 512);
                socket.receive(recvPacket);
                sendPacket = new DatagramPacket(
                    recvPacket.getData(), recvPacket.getLength(),
                    recvPacket.getAddress(), recvPacket.getPort() );
                socket.send( sendPacket );
            }
        }
        catch (SocketException se)
        {
            System.out.println("Error in SimpleDatagramServer: " + se);
        }
        catch (IOException ioe)
        {
            System.out.println("Error in SimpleDatagramServer: " + ioe);
        }
    }
}
```

Datagram Clients

The corresponding datagram client uses the same process as the datagram server with one exception: the client must initiate the conversation. The basic recipe for datagram clients is as follows:

1. Create the datagram socket on any available port.
2. Create the address to send to.
3. Send the data according to the server's protocol.
4. Wait for incoming data.
5. Go back to step 3 (send more data), go back to step 4 (wait for incoming data) or go to step 6 (exit).
6. Close the datagram socket.

Figure 26.2 summarizes the steps needed for client/server datagram applications. The symmetry between client and server is evident in this figure; compare Figure 26.2 with Figure 26.1.

FIGURE 26.2.

Client and server datagram applications.

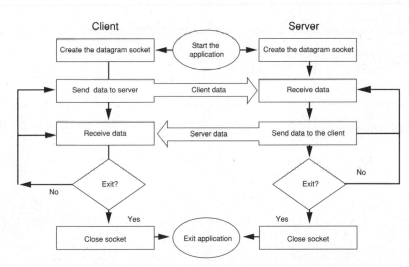

Listing 26.4 shows a simple datagram client. It reads user input strings and sends them to the echo server presented in Listing 26.3. The echo server sends the data right back, and the client prints the response to the console.

Listing 26.4. A simple datagram client.

```java
import java.io.*;
import java.net.*;

public class SimpleDatagramClient
{
    private DatagramSocket socket = null;
    private DatagramPacket recvPacket, sendPacket;
    private int hostPort;

    public static void main(String[] args)
    {
        DatagramSocket socket = null;
        DatagramPacket recvPacket, sendPacket;
        try
        {
            socket = new DatagramSocket();
            InetAddress hostAddress = InetAddress.getByName("localhost");

            BufferedReader userData = new BufferedReader(
                new InputStreamReader(System.in) );
            while (socket != null)
            {
                String userString = userData.readLine();
                if (userString == null || userString.equals(""))
                    return;

                byte sendbuf[] = userString.getBytes();
                sendPacket = new DatagramPacket(
                    sendbuf, sendbuf.length, hostAddress, 4545 );
                socket.send( sendPacket );
                recvPacket= new DatagramPacket(new byte[512], 512);
                socket.receive(recvPacket);
                System.out.write(recvPacket.getData(), 0,
                    recvPacket.getLength());
                System.out.print("\n");
            }
        } catch (SocketException se)
        {
            System.out.println("Error in SimpleDatagramClient: " + se);
        } catch (IOException ioe)
        {
            System.out.println("Error in SimpleDatagramClient: " + ioe);
        }
    }
}
```

Multicast Sockets

In JDK 1.1, Sun chose to move the Multicast class into the java.net package. Multicast descends from Datagram and so shares many similarities. A *multicast address* is a class D address in the range 224.0.0.1 to 239.255.255.255, inclusive. The most noticeable difference between Datagram and Multicast is Multicast's capability to transmit to all listening hosts simultaneously. In fact, when you send on a multicast socket, you also receive everything you send. The downside to multicast sockets is the lack of support for multicast routing. Normally, multicasting operates only over a local network. Most routers still will not forward multicast packets to the Internet at large.

Multicasting is based on the Internet Group Management Protocol (IGMP). To begin receiving multicast transmissions, a host must join a multicast group using an IGMP packet. The `Multicast` class provides two methods for manipulating group membership:

- `public void joinGroup(InetAddress mcastaddr)`
- `public void leaveGroup(InetAddress mcastaddr)`

Two additional methods control the time to live (TTL):

- `public byte getTTL()`
- `public void setTTL(byte ttl)`

Each network router examines a packet's `ttl` parameter and decrements it before forwarding the packet. If the `ttl` parameter goes to zero, the packet is not forwarded. In the event that a network's router supports multicasting, the `ttl` parameter becomes critical. To avoid flooding the Internet with your multicast packets, it is best to leave the `ttl` parameter set to 1.

> **NOTE**
>
> Chapter 24, "Introduction to Network Programming," mentions the UNIX utility `traceroute`. This program reveals the address and names of the routes traversed to arrive at a specific destination. This utility works by manipulating the `ttl` parameter and relying on the intermediate routers to send back an error when `ttl` goes to zero. By continuously incrementing `ttl` and resending the same packet, `traceroute` can log the resulting errors, thus revealing the exact route to a destination.

Listing 26.5 contains the source for a multicast test class. When executed, the test class sends and receives its own string.

Listing 26.5. A multicast test class.

```
class MultiTest
{
    public static void main(String[] args)
    {
        try
        {
            //byte[] msg = {'H', 'e', 'l', 'l', 'o'};
            InetAddress group = InetAddress.getByName("227.1.2.3");
            MulticastSocket s = new MulticastSocket(4567);
            s.joinGroup(group);
            String usermsg = "Hello";
```

continues

Listing 26.5. continued

```
            byte msg[] = usermsg.getBytes();
            DatagramPacket hi = new DatagramPacket(msg, msg.length,
                group, 4567);
            s.send(hi);
            byte[] buf = new byte[1000];
            DatagramPacket recv = new DatagramPacket(buf, buf.length);
            s.receive(recv);
            System.out.write(buf, 0, recv.getLength());
            s.leaveGroup(group);
        }
        catch (Exception se)
        {
            System.out.println("Exception: " + se);
        }
    }
}
```

So far, all the examples in this chapter have been Java standalone applications. Running these examples within the framework of an applet presents an extra complication: security.

APPLET SECURITY AND SOCKETS

When writing applications, you don't have to be concerned with security exceptions. This fact changes when the code under development is executed from an applet. Browsers use very stringent security measures where sockets are concerned. An applet can open a socket only back to the host name from which it was loaded. If any other connection is attempted, a SecurityException is thrown.

Because datagram sockets don't open connections, how is security ensured for these sockets? When an inbound packet is received, the host name is checked. If the packet did not originate from the server, a SecurityException is immediately thrown. Obviously, sending comes under the same scrutiny. If a datagram socket tries to send to any destination except the server, a SecurityException is thrown. These restrictions apply only to the address, not the port number. Any port number on the host may be used.

Multicast sockets are completely illegal within an applet. Only applications can create and use multicast sockets.

An HTTP Server Application

Client applets need an HTTP Web server so that they can open sockets under the prevailing security restrictions. If an applet is loaded into a browser from a hard drive, any socket actions are permissible. This presents a significant hurdle to Java client applet development and testing. A simple solution is to write an HTTP server application. Once written, additional server threads can be added to provide all types of back-end connectivity. The server example can also demonstrate how to subclass `Socket` and `ServerSocket`. JDK 1.1 has removed the `final` keyword restriction from the socket classes; thus, it now allows subclassing. In addition, slight modifications were added to `ServerSocket` to allow the newly allowed descendant classes access to the underlying implementation.

HTTP Primer

Before diving into this project, you need some background information about the HTTP protocol. The Hypertext Transfer Protocol (HTTP) has been in use on the World Wide Web since 1990. All applet-bearing Web pages are sent over the Net with HTTP. Our server will support a subset of HTTP version 1.0 in that it will handle only file requests. As long as browser page requests can be fulfilled, the server will have accomplished its goal.

HTTP uses a stream-oriented (TCP) socket connection. Typically, port 80 is used, but other port numbers can be substituted. All of the protocol is sent in plain-text format. An example of a conversation was demonstrated in Listings 26.1 and 26.2. The server listens on port 80 for a client request, which takes this format:

```
GET FILE HTTP/1.0
```

The first word is referred to as the "method" of the request. Table 26.2 lists all the request methods for HTTP version 1.0.

Table 26.2. HTTP version 1.0 request methods.

Method	Use
GET	Retrieve a file
HEAD	Retrieve only file information
POST	Send data to the server
PUT	Send data to the server
DELETE	Delete a resource
LINK	Link two resources
UNLINK	Unlink two resources

The second parameter of a request is a file path. Each of the following URLs is followed by the request that will be formulated and sent:

```
HTTP://www.qnet.com/
GET / HTTP/1.0

HTTP://www.qnet.com/index.html
GET /index.html HTTP/1.0

HTTP://www.qnet.com/classes/applet.html
GET /classes/applet.html HTTP/1.0
```

The request does not end until a blank line containing only a carriage return (\r) and a linefeed (\n) is received. After the method line, a number of optional lines can be sent. Netscape Navigator 2.0 produces the following request:

```
GET / HTTP/1.0
Connection: Keep-Alive
User-Agent: Mozilla/2.0 (Win95; I)
Host: merlin
Accept: image/gif, image/x-xbitmap, image/jpeg, image/pjpeg, */*
```

Responses use a header similar to the request:

```
HTTP/1.0 200 OK
Content-type: text/html
Content-Length: 128
```

Like the request, the response header is not complete until a blank line is sent containing only a carriage return and a linefeed. The first line contains a version identification string followed by a status code indicating the results of the request. Table 26.3 lists all the defined status codes. Our server sends only two of these: 200 and 404. The text that follows the status code is optional; it may be omitted. If it is present, it may not match the definitions given in the table.

Table 26.3. HTTP response status codes.

Status Code	Optional Text Description
200	OK
201	Created
202	Accepted
204	No Content
300	Multiple Choices
301	Moved Permanently
302	Moved Temporarily
304	Not Modified
400	Bad Request
401	Unauthorized
403	Forbidden
404	Not Found
500	Internal Server Error
501	Not Implemented
502	Bad Gateway
503	Service Unavailable

Immediately after the response header, the requested file is sent. When the file is completely transmitted, the socket connection is closed. Each request-response pair consumes a new socket connection.

That's enough information for you to construct a basic Web server. Full information on the HTTP protocol can be retrieved from this URL:

```
HTTP://www.w3.org/
```

A Basic Web Server

This basic Web server example follows the construction of the `SimpleWebServer` presented in Listing 26.2. Many improvements will be made to method and response handling. Perhaps the largest improvement is the addition of specialized socket classes. Because `ServerSocket` and `Socket` are no longer `final` classes, you are free to create more specialized descendant classes. This project creates `HttpServerSocket` and `HttpSocket` classes. Before developing the specialized classes, the `HttpServer` shell class is presented.

HttpServer Application Class

The outer class for the server is actually quite simple. All the complex protocol work is relegated to the specialized HTTP sockets. Listing 26.6 shows the socket access routines of the `HttpServer` class.

Listing 26.6. HttpServer class socket access routines.

```
/**
 * The only method to begin server operation.
 * The server port is hard coded to 80 by HTTP_PORT.
 * Any additional server threads should be started from
 * this routine.
 */
public void start()
{
    HttpServerSocket serverSocket = null;
    HttpSocket clientSocket = null;

    try
    {
        // Create the server socket
        serverSocket = new HttpServerSocket(HTTP_PORT, 5);
    }
    catch (IOException e)
    {
        System.out.println(
            "Couldn't open listen socket " + HTTP_PORT + " " + e);
        System.exit(10);
    }
```

continues

Listing 26.6. continued

```java
        try
        {
            do
            {
                /* the main loop for processing incoming requests */
                clientSocket = (HttpSocket)serverSocket.accept();
                System.out.println("Connect from: " + clientSocket );
                ServiceClientRequest(clientSocket);
                clientSocket.close();
            } while (clientSocket != null);
        }
        catch (IOException e)
        {
            System.out.println(
                "Accept failure on port " + HTTP_PORT + " " + e);
            System.exit(10);
        }
    }

    /**
     * Read the client request and formulate a response.
     */
    private void ServiceClientRequest(HttpSocket client)
    {
        if ( client.method.equals("GET") || client.method.equals("HEAD") )
            ServicegetRequest(client);
        else
        {
            System.out.println("Unimplemented method: " + client.method);
            client.sendNegativeResponse();
        }
    }
    /**
     * Get the file stream and pass it to the HttpSocket.
     * Handles GET and HEAD request methods.
     * @param client = the HttpSocket to respond to
     */
    private void ServicegetRequest(HttpSocket client)
    {
        String mimeType = "application/octet-stream";

        try
        {
            if (client.file.indexOf("..") != -1)
                throw new ProtocolException("Relative paths not supported");
            String fileToGet = "htdocs" + client.file;
            FileInputStream inFile = new FileInputStream(fileToGet);
            if (fileToGet.endsWith(".html")) mimeType = "text/html";
            client.sendFile(inFile, inFile.available(), mimeType);
            inFile.close();
        }
        catch (FileNotFoundException fnf)
        {
            client.sendNegativeResponse();
        }
```

```
        catch (ProtocolException pe)
        {
            System.out.println("ProtocolException: " + pe);
            client.sendNegativeResponse();
        }
        catch (IOException ioe)
        {
            System.out.println("IOException: Unknown file length: " + ioe);
            client.sendNegativeResponse();
        }
    }
```

Implementing subclassed socket servers actually involves creating two cooperating classes. ServerSocket performs only listening chores; the real protocol work is done by the connected Socket class. HttpServerSocket subclasses ServerSocket and creates a connected HttpSocket object to parse the incoming HTTP request. Because the accept() method of ServerSocket returns only a plain Socket, you must perform an explicit cast to store the actual object type:

```
clientSocket = (HttpSocket)serverSocket.accept();
```

Listing 26.7 shows the HttpServerSocket class. The key element is the overridden accept() method. To allow subclasses to perform connection services, ServerSocket provides the implAccept() method. This method takes an existing Socket object and connects it to the next call. This is how the HttpServerSocket connects an HttpSocket to incoming requests. After connecting a socket, the server simply calls the HttpSocket getRequest() method to parse the protocol. Once it has been processed, the connected socket is simply returned to the caller.

Listing 26.7. The HttpServerSocket implementation.

```
/**
 * A class that provides HTTP protocol services.
 */
public class HttpServerSocket extends ServerSocket
{
    HttpServerSocket(int port, int depth) throws IOException
    {
        super(port, depth);
    }

    public Socket accept () throws IOException
    {
        HttpSocket s = new HttpSocket();
        implAccept(s);
        s.getRequest();
        return s;
    }
}
```

The HttpSocket performs all the protocol-specific work. Listing 26.8 shows the methods used to parse and store the inbound HTTP request. First, an input stream is acquired. The specifics of the HTTP header are then parsed and stored as class member variables. These are public variables so that consuming classes can make decisions based on the HTTP header.

Listing 26.8. The HttpSocket class.

```java
public class HttpSocket extends Socket
{
    protected BufferedReader inbound = null;

    public String version = null;
    public String method = null;
    public String file = null;
    public NameValue headerpairs[];
    public String extraHdr = null;

    HttpSocket()
    {
        super();
        headerpairs = new NameValue[0];
    }

    /**
     * Read an HTTP request and parse it into class attributes.
     * @exception ProtocolException If not a valid HTTP header
     * @exception IOException
     */
    public void getRequest()
        throws IOException, ProtocolException
    {
        try
        {
            // Acquire an input stream for the socket
            inbound = new BufferedReader(
                new InputStreamReader(getInputStream()) );

            // Read the header into a String
            String reqhdr = readHeader(inbound);

            // Parse the string into parts
            parseReqHdr(reqhdr);
        }
        catch (ProtocolException pe)
        {
            if ( inbound != null )
                inbound.close();
            throw pe;
        }
        catch (IOException ioe)
        {
            if ( inbound != null )
                inbound.close();
            throw ioe;
        }
    }
```

```java
/**
 * Assemble an HTTP request header String
 * from the passed BufferedReader.
 * @param is the input stream to use
 * @return a continuous String representing the header
 * @exception ProtocolException If a pre HTTP/1.0 request
 * @exception IOException
 */
private String readHeader(BufferedReader is)
    throws IOException, ProtocolException
{
    String command;
    String line;

    // Get the first request line
    if ( (command = is.readLine()) == null )
        command = "";
    command += "\n";

    // Check for HTTP/1.0 signature
    if (command.indexOf("HTTP/") != -1)
    {
        // Retrieve any additional lines
        while ((line = is.readLine()) != null  && !line.equals(""))
            command += line + "\n";
    }
    else
    {
        throw new ProtocolException("Pre HTTP/1.0 request");
    }
    return command;
}


/**
 * Parsed the passed request String and populate an HTTPrequest.
 * @param reqhdr the HTTP request as a continous String
 * @return a populated HTTPrequest instance
 * @exception ProtocolException If name,value pairs have no ':'
 * @exception IOException
 */
private void parseReqHdr(String reqhdr)
    throws IOException, ProtocolException
{
    // Break the request into lines
    StringTokenizer lines = new StringTokenizer(reqhdr, "\r\n");
    String currentLine = lines.nextToken();

    // Process the initial request line
    // into method, file, version Strings
    StringTokenizer members = new StringTokenizer(currentLine, " \t");
    method = members.nextToken();
    file = members.nextToken();
    if (file.equals("/")) file += "index.html";
    version = members.nextToken();
```

continues

Listing 26.8. continued

```java
            // Process additional lines into name/value pairs
            while ( lines.hasMoreTokens() )
            {
                String line = lines.nextToken();

                // Search for separating character
                int slice = line.indexOf(':');

                // Error if no separating character
                if ( slice == -1 )
                {
                    throw new ProtocolException(
                        "Invalid HTTP header: " + line);
                }
                else
                {
                    // Separate at the slice character into name, value
                    String name = line.substring(0,slice).trim();
                    String value = line.substring(slice + 1).trim();
                    addNameValue(name, value);
                }
            }
        }

    /**
     * Add a name/value pair to the internal array
     */
    private void addNameValue(String name, String value)
    {
        try
        {
            NameValue temp[] = new NameValue[ headerpairs.length + 1 ];
            System.arraycopy(headerpairs, 0, temp, 0, headerpairs.length);
            temp[ headerpairs.length ] = new NameValue(name, value);
            headerpairs = temp;
        }
        catch (NullPointerException npe)
        {
            System.out.println("NullPointerException while adding name-value: " +
                npe);
        }
    }
}
```

The method readHeader() interrogates the inbound socket stream searching for the blank line.
If the request is not of HTTP/1.0 format, this method throws an exception. Otherwise, the
resulting string is passed to parseReqHdr() for processing.

These routines reject any improperly formatted requests, including requests made in the older
HTTP/0.9 format. Parsing makes heavy use of the StringTokenizer class found in the java.util
package described in Chapter 11, "The Utilities Package."

Normally, it is preferable to close the inbound stream as soon as the request has been completely read. If this is done, subsequent output attempts will fail with an IOException. This is why the inbound parameter is stored as a class attribute rather than allocated within the getRequest() method. When the output has been completely sent, both the output and the input streams are closed.

> **CAUTION**
>
> Do not be tempted to close an inbound stream after all input has been read. Prematurely closing the input stream causes subsequent output attempts to fail with an IOException. Close both streams only after all socket operations are finished.

Once a request has been processed, methods for sending responses must be provided. Because only the GET and HEAD requests are honored, HttpSocket only provides methods for sending files or negative responses. Listing 26.9 shows the two response routines. Once a valid file is found, the sendFile() function can be called. The file is read and sent in 1K blocks. This design keeps memory usage down while seeking to balance the number of disk accesses attempted. Negative responses are sent only for errors that occur after the request has been built. As a consequence, improperly formatted requests generate no response.

Listing 26.9. HttpSocket response methods.

```
/**
 * Send a negative (404 NOT FOUND) response
 */
public void sendNegativeResponse()
{
    OutputStream outbound = null;

    try
    {
        // Acquire the output stream
        outbound = getOutputStream();

        // Write the negative response header
        String hdr = "HTTP/1.0 404 NOT_FOUND\r\n\r\n";
        outbound.write(hdr.getBytes());

        // Cleanup
        outbound.close();
        inbound.close();
    }
    catch (IOException ioe)
    {
        System.out.println("IOException while sending -rsp: " + ioe);
    }
}
```

continues

Listing 26.9. continued

```java
/**
 * Send the passed file
 * @param inFile the opened input file stream to send
 * @param fileSize the size of the stream (used to report Content-Length)
 * @param MimeType String used to report Content-Type
 */
public void sendFile(FileInputStream inFile, int fileSize, String MimeType)
{
    OutputStream outbound = null;

    try
    {
        // aquire the output stream
        outbound = getOutputStream();

        // Send the response header
        String hdr = "HTTP/1.0 200 OK\r\n";
        hdr += "Content-type: " + MimeType + "\r\n";
        hdr += "Content-Length: " + fileSize + "\r\n";
        if (extraHdr != null) hdr += extraHdr;
        hdr += "\r\n";

        outbound.write(hdr.getBytes());

        // If not a HEAD request, send the file body.
        // HEAD requests only solicit a header response.
        if (!method.equals("HEAD"))
        {
            byte dataBody[] = new byte[1024];
            int cnt;
            while ((cnt = inFile.read(dataBody)) != -1)
            {
                outbound.write(dataBody, 0, cnt);
            }
        }
    }
    catch (IOException ioe)
    {
        System.out.println("IOException while sending file: " + ioe);
    }
    try
    {
        // Cleanup
        outbound.close();
        inbound.close();
    }
    catch (IOException ioe)
    {
        System.out.println("IOException closing streams in sendFile: " + ioe);
    }
}
```

The `SimpleWebServer` project is now finished; compile all the source code and start the server. If you maintained the directory structure used on the CD-ROM that accompanies this book, you should be able to start the server and connect to it. The default HTML document is in `htdocs/index.html`.

Summary

In this chapter, you learned about the socket abstraction as well as the Java implementation of sockets. Remember that socket use requires at least two applications: a client and a server. The server waits for a client application to call and request attention. Multiple clients can make use of the same server—either at the same time (concurrent server) or one at a time (iterative server). Server behavior was demonstrated with the development of an iterative Java HTTP server. You should now have a working knowledge of HTTP and an appreciation of the limitations imposed by the socket security model. Namely, an applet can only open a socket back to the same server that loaded the applet.

Sockets provide a rich communications medium that allows your Java applications to exploit a wired world.

Multiuser Network Programming

by Michael Afergan

IN THIS CHAPTER

Without doubt, Java is one of the more spectacular products to hit the computer market in recent years. Inasmuch as its initial support came from academia, most initial Java applets have been limited to decorative roles. However, now that Java's popularity has increased, Java has recently been used for more practical purposes. Applets have been used to provide live-time, ticker-like feeds and to create interactive environments for such purposes as retrieving financial information. In essence, by employing the power of Java, users can now do much of what they think they should be able to do on the Internet—but have not been able to do before.

One of the more exciting powers of Java is that it gives programmers the ability to create multiuser environments in which many users can interact and share information. In a simple multiuser environment such as the one in Figure 27.1, several users are connected to each other through a server running on a mutually accessible host. As a result, all actions by one user can instantaneously be displayed on the screens of other users across the world—without any requirement that the users know each other beforehand.

FIGURE 27.1.
A multiuser environment.

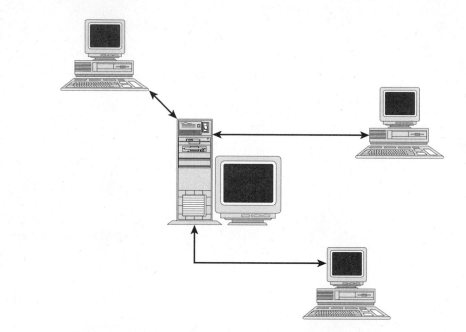

This ability to link computers in live time enables Java programmers to accomplish feats never before possible in a Web page. A business can now set up a system so that people who desire information can talk with a customer service representative directly on the Web page rather than sending e-mail to a service department. Moreover, because of the graphical nature of the Web and Java, the customer service representative can demonstrate information in a visual manner (for example, by pointing out items on a diagram). Additionally, an enterprising company can allow people from around the world to participate in a real-time live auction. In general, by facilitating multiple-user environments that enable such sharing of information, Java has the power to revolutionize the Web.

WHY JAVA?

The concept of servers, sockets, and communication is nothing new, nor is the idea of linking many users together in a live-time environment. In fact, the Web, without Java, can be considered a multiuser environment inasmuch as multiple users can access the same information in the form of a simple HTML page. Furthermore, methods exist by which a user can directly affect what another user sees on a given page (such as the hit counters found at the bottom of many HTML pages).

What, then, does Java offer that is so revolutionary? It offers the capacity to perform actions while the user is viewing the same HTML page. The architecture of the Web enables users to view Web pages from around the world. However, once this page is displayed on your screen, it cannot change. In the example of the hit counters—although more users may access the given page—you are never informed of this fact unless you reload that page. Java, however, brings life into Web pages by means of applets, enabling the pages to perform actions such as communicating with a server. Java enables programmers to create applets as potent and effective as the applications on your own computer. It is this capacity that enables us to create multiuser environments.

This chapter discusses the elements required to create a multiuser environment in Java. Although no entirely new topics in Java are presented, this chapter shows you how to bring several powerful aspects of Java together and highlights some of the more interesting applications of Java. Through explanation of the processes as well as sample code, this chapter enables you, the Java programmer, to code and establish your own multiuser environment. This chapter deals with subjects including the handling of the connections to the server, the graphical interface, and various animation and threading techniques necessary to make your applet Webworthy. Although each of these topics is explained with code, keep in mind that the essence of a multiuser environment is *what* you do, not *how* you do it. Furthermore, the code for each multiuser application depends heavily on the environment itself, and therefore is significantly different in each. Consequently, although the code offered here can supply you with a suitable framework, it may be advisable to envision your own multiuser application. As each topic is presented, imagine how you would deal with each of the issues involved. Remember that in programming—and Java in particular—the limits of the language are the limits of your imagination. Be creative and have fun!

SOCKETS AND NETSCAPE

With any new technology come new concerns and problems. Java is definitely not an exception to this rule. The chief concern of many has been the fact that Java applets can connect to servers from around the world and transmit information from the host that its

continues

27

MULTIUSER
NETWORK
PROGRAMMING

continued

owner might not want to make public. Although there are several solutions to this problem, Netscape has chosen to place stringent restrictions on Java socket connections for now.

Currently, Java sockets can connect only to servers running on the host that served the applet. For example, an applet residing in `http://www.xyz.com/page.html` can connect back only to a server running on `www.xyz.com`. Therefore, when developing a multiuser environment as discussed in this chapter, make sure that the server to which the applet connects is running on the same host as the HTML page in which the applet resides. (See Chapter 34, "Java Security," for more details about applet security.)

Our Mission—Should We Choose to Accept It

In this chapter, we develop a multiuser environment for a museum that is opening an exhibition of Haphazard Art. The museum believes that the most beautiful art is created by human-controlled whims and has hired you to create an environment through which users from around the world can "weave" a quilt. The user should be able to access the Web page, select a color and a blank tile, and "paint" the tile. Not only should this tile change colors on the screen of the user, but it also should instantaneously become painted on the screens of all the users around the world who are working on that quilt. (The museum will then save these designs and display them at its upcoming exhibit.)

Although this is a rather simplistic example of the power of multiuser environments, it is an excellent model for the explanation of the concepts involved.

The Requirements of the Server

Although it is not of our direct concern, the server in this environment plays an extremely large role. Because the server can be written in virtually any language, we won't spend much time dealing with it here. However, it is necessary that we discuss the essentials for the server in a multiuser environment.

As you can see from Figure 27.1, the server acts as the intermediate agent between the various users. Thus, the server must be able to do the following:

- Accept multiple connections from clients on a given port
- Receive information from the clients
- Send information to the clients

As the application becomes more involved, it is necessary to add additional functionality to the server. Even in the simple example of the museum quilt, the server must keep track of the color of all the tiles. Furthermore, if a new client begins work on an in-progress quilt, it's necessary for the server to inform the client of the current status of the quilt.

Nevertheless, these subjects are extremely context-dependent and deal more with computer science than with Java. Therefore, we now move on to more exciting matters, such as the socket communication required to provide the interaction.

Integrating a Communication Class in Your Applet

For an effective implementation, it's necessary to create a class that handles all the interaction with the server. This class manages such responsibilities as connecting and disconnecting from the server as well as the actual sending and receiving of data. By encapsulating this functionality in a separate class, we can deal with our problem in a more effective and logical manner.

A more important reason for encapsulating this functionality in a separate class, however, is the fact that, in a multiuser environment, the applet must do two things at the exact same time: listen for user interactions (such as a mouse click) and listen for new information from the server. The best way to do this is to create a separate class to handle the server interaction and make that class a thread. (See Chapter 6, "Threads and Multithreading," for details on creating threads.) This threaded class runs continually for the lifetime of the applet, updating the quilt when required to do so. With this problem out of our hands, we can allow the applet class to respond to user interactions without worrying about the socket connection.

How to Connect to a Server

Assuming that we have a suitable server running, the actual communication is not a very complicated process. In essence, the applet needs only to connect to the server and read and write information to the appropriate streams. Conveniently, Sun has wrapped most of these methods and variables in the `java.net.Socket` class.

Here is the beginning of our `Client` class that handles the actual communication:

```
import java.net.Socket;
import java.io.*;

public class Client extends Thread
{

   private Socket soc;
   public void connect ()
   {
     String       host = "www.museum.com";
     int          port = 2600;

     soc = new Socket(host, port);
   }
}
```

Note that it is necessary for you to know both the name of the host on which the server is running as well as the port on which the server can accept connections.

In theory, the `connect()` method in the preceding class is sufficient to connect to a server on a known port. However, any experienced programmer knows that what works in theory does not always work in practice. Consequently, it is good practice to place all communication statements in a `try-catch` block. (Those unfamiliar with the `throw` and `try-catch` constructs can refer to Chapter 7, "Exception Handling.") In fact, forgetting to place all statements that deal with the server in a `try-catch` block will produce a compile-time error with the Java compiler.

Consequently, the preceding method should actually look like this:

```
import java.net.Socket;
import java.io.*;

public class Client extends Thread
{
   private Socket soc;
   public boolean connect ()
   {
   String          host = "www.museum.com";
   int             port = 2600;

   try {
        soc = new Socket(host, port);
      }
   catch (Exception e)
       return(false);
   return(true);
}
```

Note that the method now returns a `boolean` variable that corresponds to whether or not it was successful in connecting.

How to Communicate with the Server

Inasmuch as different situations require different constructs, Java supplies several options for the syntax of communication with a server. Although all such approaches can work, some are more useful and flexible than others. Consequently, what follows is a rather generic method of communicating with a server. Keep in mind that there are some nice wrapper methods in the `java.io.InputStream` subclasses that you may want to use to simplify the processing of the parsing involved with the communication.

Sending Information

Once we have established our connection, the output is then passed through the `java.net.Socket.outputStream`, which is a `java.io.outputStream`. Because `OutputStream` is a protected variable, however, we cannot reference it as simply as you may imagine. To access this stream, we must employ the `java.net.Socket.getOutputStream()` method. A simple method to send data resembles the following:

```
public boolean SendInfo(int choice) {
   OutputStream out;
   try {
        out = soc.getOutputStream();
        out.write(choice);
        out.flush();
      }
   catch (Exception e)
      return(false);
   return(true);
}
```

Although the preceding code is sufficient to send information across a socket stream, communication is not that simple in a true multiuser environment. Because we will have multiple clients in addition to the server, it is necessary to define a common protocol that all parties can speak. Although this may be as simple as a specific order to a series of integers, it is nevertheless vital to the success of the environment.

PROTOCOLS

Although we will adopt a rather simple protocol for this applet, there are a few issues you should keep in mind when developing more complex protocols:

- Preface each command with a title, such as a letter or short word. For example, B123 could be the command to buy property lot 123, and S123 could be the command to sell lot 123.

- Make all titles of the same format. Doing so makes parsing the input stream much easier. For example, B and S are good titles. B and Sell would cause some headaches.

- Terminate each command with a common character. Doing so signifies the end of information and also gives you a starting point in case some of the information becomes garbled. For the sake of simplicity, the newline character (\n) is usually best.

In the case of our quilt-making applet for the museum, each update packet consists of three things: the x coordinate of the recently painted tile, the y coordinate of the recently painted tile, and the color to be applied (which can also be represented by an integer). Additionally, we will use the newline character (\n) as our terminating character. All this can be accomplished with the following method:

```
public boolean SendInfo(int x, int y, int hue) {
   OutputStream out;

   try {
        out = soc.getOutputStream();
        out.write(x);
        out.write(y);
        out.write(hue);
        out.write('\n');
```

```
/*  Now flush the output stream to make sure that everything is sent. */
        out.flush();
      }
   catch (Exception e)
      return(false);
   return(true);
}
```

Reading Information

Another factor that complicates the reading of information from the socket is that we have absolutely no idea when new information will travel across the stream. When we send data, we are in complete control of the stream and thus can employ a rather simple method as we did earlier. When reading from the socket, however, we do not know when new information will arrive. Thus we need to employ a method that runs constantly in a loop. As discussed previously, the best way to do this is to place our code in the `run()` method of a threaded class.

A REFRESHER ON THREADS

Before we proceed in our development of this threaded subclass, it is important to review a key concept. As presented in Chapter 6, "Threads and Multithreading," a class that extends the definition of the `java.lang.Thread` class can continually execute code while other portions of the applet are running. Nevertheless, this is not true of all the methods of the threaded class.

Only the `run()` method has the power attributed to threads (namely the capacity to run independently of other operations). This method is automatically declared in every thread, but has no functionality unless you override the original declaration in your code. Although other methods can exist within the threaded subclass, remember that only the code contained in the `run()` method can execute concurrently with the rest of the processes in the application. Furthermore, remember that the `run()` method of class `foo` is begun by invoking `foo.start()` from the master class.

Also note that because we are overriding a method first declared in the `java.lang.Runnable` interface, we are forced to employ the original declaration: `public void run()`. Your code won't compile if you choose to use another declaration, such as `public boolean run()`. (We deal with ways of returning data in the section on sharing information, later in this chapter.)

What results from all this planning is the method shown in Listing 27.1. In reading it, pay attention to how we are able to stop the method from reading from the socket once the user is done; how the method deals with garbled input; and how the method returns information to the main applet. (You will be quizzed later!)

Listing 27.1. Our method to read information from the socket.

```
public void run() {
   int spot = 0;
   int stroke[];
   stroke = new int[10];                          // an array for storing the commands
   DataInputStream in;

   in = new DataInputStream(soc.getInputStream());

   while (running) {
      do {                                        // reads the information
         try {
                stroke[spot] = in.readByte();
         }
         catch (Exception e)
                stroke[spot] = '\n';  // restarts read on error
      } while (  (stroke[spot] != '\n') && (++spot < 9) );
                                    // reads until the newline flag or limit of
      spot = 0;                     // array
                                    // resets the counter
      quilt.sew(stroke[0],stroke[1],stroke[2]);
   }
}
```

Okay. Time is up. Here are the answers.

First of all, remember that we are designing this class to serve within a larger applet. It would be rather difficult for the Client class to decide when the "painting session" is over because it has no idea what is going on inside the applet. Thus, the applet, not the Client class, must have control of when the class will be looking for information. The best way to retain control of the run() method is to create a boolean field (running) inside the Client class itself. This variable can be set to true on connection to the server and can be set to false when the applet decides to close the connection. Thus, once the user has decided to close the connection, the run() method exits the while loop and runs through to its completion.

Second, remember that while we plan on receiving three integers followed by a newline character, in real life, things do not always work as we plan them. Inasmuch as we do not know exactly what the error will be, there is no ideal way of handling garbled information. The run() method in Listing 27.1 uses the newline character as its guide, and continues to read until it reaches one. If, however, there are nine characters before a newline character, it exits the do loop regardless and calls the sew() method. This means that the sew() method in our main applet must be well constructed to handle such errors.

Third, and most important, is the means by which the class returns data to the applet. As discussed earlier, this Client class will be a subclass of our main applet. Consequently, we will be able to call all public methods of the applet class. (In this example, the applet is referenced by the variable `quilt`.) Although we will discuss this process in more detail later, keep in mind that the last line of code simply passes the appropriate values to a method in the applet that will in turn process them:

```
quilt.sew(stroke[0],stroke[1],stroke[2]);
```

A NOTE FOR ADVANCED READERS

You will notice that in our example, all the information coming across the stream is read in the form of integers. Obviously, in the real world, other data types such as characters—or even mixed data types such as three numbers and a letter—could be passed. Although accommodating these data types would require slight alterations to the preceding code, doing so would not be a dramatic hack.

Although you could deal with such a situation by having separate `read()` statements for each data type, remember the ASCII relationship between characters and numbers. Because the ASCII value of a number is 48 more than that number (for example, the ASCII value for '1' is 1 + 48), you can choose to read all the data in as integers and then translate certain values to their character equivalents—or vice versa, depending on how you sent the information to the server.

Finally, keep in mind that `serverInput` is a basic `java.lang.Inputstream` that can be manipulated in several ways using the powers of the `java.lang` and `java.io` classes and methods. (See Chapter 10, "The Language Package," and Chapter 12, "The I/O Package," for more details on `java.lang` and `java.io`, respectively.)

How to Disconnect from the Server

So far, we have been able to connect to the server and communicate with it. From the point of view of the user, we have begun the application and have successfully painted our quilt. There is only one essential functionality we haven't included in our `Client` class thus far: the capacity to disconnect from the server.

Although the capacity to disconnect from the server may appear trivial, it is in fact very essential to a successful multiuser environment. A server can be constructed to accept numerous clients, but because of hardware constraints, there is an inherent limit to the number of clients a server can have connected at the same time. Consequently, if the socket connections remain open even when the clients leave, the server eventually becomes saturated with lingering sockets. In general, it's good practice to close sockets; doing so benefits all aspects of the environment, ranging from the Internet-access software the user is running to the person managing the server.

Without further ado, here is an appropriate `disconnect()` method for our `Client` class:

```
public boolean disconnect () {
    running = false;
    try {
            soc.close()
        }
    catch (Exception e)
        return(false);
    return(true);
}
```

Although the code itself is nothing extraordinary, note the use of the `boolean` variable `running` (also used in the `run()` method). Remember that the function of the `running` variable is to serve as a flag that allows the client to listen to the socket stream. Inasmuch as we do not want the client to listen to the socket stream after the user has decided to disconnect, we set the variable to `false` in this method. Also note that the `running = false` statement comes *before* the `soc.close()` statement. This arrangement is made because regardless of the success of the `disconnect` statement, we no longer want to listen to the stream.

The Graphical Interface

Now that we have developed the framework of our `Client` subclass, let's switch gears to develop the applet class that will act as the heart of our application. Although it is not extremely intricate, the applet must be able to respond to user input and present the user with a friendly and attractive display. Fortunately, as a Web-based programming language, Java is very well suited for this. Each applet you create inherits various methods that enable it to respond to virtually anything the user can do. Furthermore, the `java.awt` package provides us with some excellent classes for creating good-looking interactive features such as buttons and text areas.

Responding to Input

The most important aspect of a graphical interface is its capacity to monitor the user's responses to the system. As you saw in Chapter 14, "The Windowing (AWT) Package," Java supplies us with an excellent system for doing this in the form of the `java.awt.Event` class. Additionally, the `java.awt.Component` class, of which `java.applet.Applet` is a subclass, provides many methods that we can use to catch and process events. These methods seize control of the applet under appropriate conditions and enable the applet to react to specific user events.

For our museum quilt applet, the user must be able to change the current color, select a tile, and quit the application. If we decide that the user will select the tile through a mouse click and will change colors and quit with the keyboard, we require two interactive methods from the `java.awt.Component` class: `keyDown(Event, int)` and `mouseDown(Event, int, int)`.

In this setup, the keyboard has two purposes: to enable the user to change colors and to enable him or her to quit. If we choose to present the user with a pallet of numbered colors (`0` to `9`, for example) from which he or she can select, our `keyDown()` method can be as simple as this:

```
public boolean keyDown(Event evt, int key) {
   if ( (key >= '0') && (key <= '9') ) {          // if a valid key
         current_color = key - 48;                // converts ASCII key to
         return(true);                            // numeric equivalent
   }
   else if ( key = 'Q') {
         leave();                                 // a method that will handle
         return(true);                            // cleanup
   }
   return(false);
}
```

In this method, `current_color` is a field that keeps track of the currently selected color.

If we declare `museum` to be an instance of the `Client` socket class (which we have almost completed), the `mouseDown()` method can be accomplished with the following code:

```
public boolean mouseDown(Event evt, int x, int y) {
   int x_cord, y_cord;

   if ( (x >= xoff) && (x =< xoff + xsize) && (y >= yoff) && (y =< yoff + ysize) {
                                 // checks to see if the click was within the
                                 // grid
        x_cord = (x - xoff)/scale;   // determines the x and y coordinates
        y_cord = (y- yoff)/scale;    //  of the click
        museum.sendInfo(x_cord, y_cord, current_color);  // makes use of the
                                                         // sendInfo method to send
                                                         // the data
        return(true);                            // the click was valid
     }
   return(false);                    // the click was outside the bounds of the
                                     // grid
}
```

Note that in the previous method, it is necessary to have already declared the x and y offsets, the size of each tile (scale), and the size of the grid itself as global fields of the class.

Displaying Information

Chapter 20, "Java Graphics Fundamentals," gave an overview of how to create a background and fill it in with whatever you want. In a dynamic graphical interface, however, various properties will change and thus must be tracked in some manner. Our quilt application may consist of nothing more than a single colored background on which tiles of different colors are drawn. Consequently, the only information we are concerned with is the colors (if any) that have been assigned to the individual tiles.

A simple way of doing this is to create an array of `java.awt.Color` (`hues[ ]`) and assign each color to be used a given value (`hues[1]` = `Color.blue`, for example). Thus, we can store the design in simple array of integers, such as `tiles[ ][ ]`, with each integer element representing a color. If we do so, our `paint()` method can be accomplished by the following code:

```
public void paint(Graphics g) {
   for (int i = 0; i < size; i++) {
      for(int j = 0; j < size; j++) {
         g.setColor(hues[ (tiles[i][j]) ]);
         g.fillRect( (i*scale+xoff) , (j*scale+yoff), scale,scale);
      }
   }
}
```

Note that in the preceding example, g.fillRect((i*scale+xoff) , (j*scale+yoff), scale,scale) paints squares with length and width equal to a final field, scale. These squares are located on the grid with respect to the initial x and y offsets.

How to Thread the Client Class

So far, we have been successful in creating the interface that the user will find on our Web page, as well as some of the methods necessary to facilitate the user's interaction with the applet. We have also assembled a Client subclass that will serve as our means of communication. Our next step is to integrate the Client class within the applet class to produce a cohesive application.

Nevertheless, it is important to keep in mind that we are not using this subclass merely as a means of keeping the information separate. The main reason for creating a separate class is that, by making it a thread as well, we can perform two tasks *at the exact same time*.

> **NOTE**
>
> Although it may seem as if we can perform two tasks at the exact same time, this is not entirely true on a standard single-processor computer. What Java does (and other time-sharing applications such as Windows as well) is to allocate "time-slices" to each thread, allowing each thread to run for a brief moment before switching control to another thread. Because this process is automatically done by the Java virtual machine, and because the time for which a given thread is not running is so small, we can think of the two threads as running at the same time.

Although we almost forget about its existence, we must retain some control over the Client class. We do not want it to check for new commands before the socket connection has been opened or after it has been closed. Additionally, we want to be able to control socket events such as opening and closing in a manner that isolates them from the main applet, but also impacts the status of the run() method. Conveniently for us, we developed the Client class in such a manner: We kept the connect() and disconnect() methods separate entities, both of which have control over the run() method (by means of the boolean variable running).

Consequently, within the applet class, the code necessary to control communications is quite simple:

```
public class Project extends Applet {
   public Client museum;
         .
         .
         .
   public void init() {
      museum = new Client();
            .
            .
      museum.connect();
      museum.start();
   }
            .
            .
   public void leave() {
      museum.disconnect();
   }
}
```

First of all, note that this is the first time we have dealt with the applet itself. So far, its only important property is that it is named `Project`.

Also note the use of the constructor `Client()`. Like any other class, the `Client` class requires not only a declaration, but also a `new` statement to actually create and allocate memory for the class. We deal with this constructor again in the next section.

Finally, note that we established the connection by means of the `museum.connect()` statement located in the `init()` method. Most likely (and in the case of the museum applet), you will want to establish the socket stream as soon as the applet starts up. The most logical place for the `museum.connect()` statement is in the `init()` method. Nevertheless, you can place this code anywhere you like in your applet. (You can, for example, have a Connect to Server button somewhere in your applet.)

CAUTION

Although giving the user the ability to initiate connection may be a good idea, be careful that you do not allow the same user to connect to the server more than once without first disconnecting. Neglecting to screen for multiple connections for the same user can lead to all sorts of headaches and improper results.

How to Share Information

We have created the framework of both the Project (applet) and Client classes and have begun the process of intertwining them by creating an instance of the Client class in the Project class. However, there is more to the interaction between the two classes than what we have seen thus far.

Remember that the purpose of the Client subclass is to provide information to the applet. Nevertheless, we are required to employ the run() method of the threaded Client class, which does not allow us to return information through a simple return() statement. Also, in most cases (as well as in the museum application), we must return several pieces of information (the x and y coordinates of the tile being painted as well as its color).

With a little construction, we can easily solve this problem. First, we must enable the Client class to refer to the Project class; this involves a few alterations to the Client class. The changes will allow the Client class to accept the Project applet class in its constructor method and make use of it during its lifetime:

```
public class Client extends Thread
{
    private Project quilt;

    public Client (Project proj) {
        quilt = proj;
    }
...
}
```

> **NOTE**
>
> In this setup, the parent class is required to pass itself as an argument to the constructor method. Therefore, when we add the code to do so to our program, the syntax resembles the following:
>
> ```
> museum = new Client(this);
> ```

What exactly does the preceding code accomplish? First, it establishes a constructor method for the Client class. (Remember that, as in C++, constructor methods must have the same name as the class itself.) Although this constructor may serve other purposes, its most important function is to accept a reference to a Project class as one of its arguments.

Further, the code creates a public variable, quilt, of type Project. By doing so, each method of the Client class can now reference all public methods and variables in the Project class. For example, if we had the following definitions in the Project class, the Client subclass could reference quilt.tiles_remaining and quilt.sew():

```
public int tiles_remaining;

public void sew(int x, int y, int hue) {
...
}
```

The Translating Method

Okay, time for an assessment of where we stand. The museum applet is now able to do the following:

- Connect to the server
- Monitor the user's actions
- Display the current design
- Receive and send information
- Create a client "within" the main applet
- Enable the client to reference the main applet

At this point, whenever the user clicks a square, the "request to paint" is immediately sent to the server by the sendInfo() method. But we have not yet developed a true method of translating a command after it comes back across the server stream.

We have, however, laid the foundation for such a process. By enabling the Client subclass to refer to all public variables and methods of the Project applet class, we have given ourselves access to all the necessary information. In fact, we have many options for updating the data in the applet once it has been parsed from the server stream. Nevertheless, some approaches are much better than others.

The most secure and flexible approach is to create a "translating" method in the applet class, such as the sew() method in the Project class—the sew() method has been mentioned several times in this chapter. This method serves as the bridge between the client and applet classes. Why is this approach the best? Why can't we create some public variables in the Project class that can be changed by the Client class? There are several reasons.

Why Use a Translating Method?

The first reason we use a translating method is that doing so makes life a great deal easier for the programmer. By employing a translating method, we can maintain the encapsulation enjoyed thus far in our application. The sew() method is contained entirely within the Project class and thus has all the necessary resources (such as private variables that would be hidden from the Client subclass). Furthermore, when we actually code the application, we can focus on each class independently. When we code the Client class, we can effectively forget how the sew() method works; when we code the Project class, we can trust that the appropriate information will be sent to it.

The second reason for having the Client class rely on a foreign method is flexibility. If we decided to revamp this application and changed the manner in which we store the data, we would have no need to drastically change the Client class. In fact, in the worst case, the only changes necessary would be to increase the amount of data being read from the stream and the number of parameters passed to the sew() method.

The third reason for employing a translating method is that by linking the two classes with a method rather than direct access, we can prevent the corruption and intermingling of data that can occur when two processes attempt to access the same data at the same time. For example, if we made tiles[ ][ ] (the array that contains the design in the applet class) to be public, we could change the colors with a statement such as this one:

```
quilt.tiles[(stroke[0])][(stroke[1])] = stroke[2];
```

However, what would happen if, at the exact moment that the paint() method was accessing tiles[1][2], the Client class was changing its value? What if more data had to be stored (the color, the design, the author's name, and so on)? Would the paint() method get the old data, the new data, a mixture, or none? As you can see, this could be a catastrophic problem. However, if we use a separate translating method in our applet class, this problem can easily be solved through use of the synchronized modifier. If our applet grew to the point that this problem presented itself, we could make the paint() method synchronized and place any necessary statements in a synchronized block. As a result, these portions of our code would never be able to run at the exact same time, thereby solving our problem.

How to Create a Translating Method

Now that we have seen why the sew() method is necessary, let us discuss its actual code. As mentioned earlier, each command in the museum application consists of three integers: the x coordinate, the y coordinate, and the new color. Also remember from the discussion of the Client class that the sew() method must be able to handle corrupted data. Consequently, the sew() method could look something like this:

```
public void sew(int x, int y, int hue) {
   if ( (x>=0) && (x <= size) && ( y >= 0) &&
      (y <= size) && (hue >= 0) && (hue <= _9) ) { // 9 colors
         tiles[x][y] = hue;
         repaint();
   }
}
```

The first statement is self-explanatory, but the second statement deserves some comment (if not a complete explanation). The first statement performs the actual task of changing the color on the tile—even though the user does not see anything unless the repaint() method is called. Thus, by setting the array and calling repaint(), the sew() method updates the quilt in the mind of the computer as well as on the screen itself.

In a moment, we will also harness the sew() method to perform another vital function for us.

Now that we have developed the entire functionality of the `Client` subclass, let's tie it together once and for all and put it aside. First look the final product over, as shown in Listing 27.2.

Listing 27.2. The final version of the `Client` class.

```java
import java.net.Socket;
import java.io.*;

public class Client extends Thread
{
   private Socket soc;
   private Boolean running;
   private Project quilt;

   public Client (Project proj) {
     quilt = proj;
   }
   public void connect () {
     String          host;
     int             port = 2600;

     host = "www.museum.com";
     try {
          soc = new  Socket(host, port);
        }
     catch (Exception e)
          return(false);
   }

   public boolean SendInfo(int x, int y, int hue) {
     OutputStream out;

     try {
          out = soc.getOutputStream();
          out.write(x);
          out.write(y);
          out.write(hue);
          out.write('\n');
          out.flush();
        }
     catch (Exception e)
          return(false);
     return(true);
   }

   public void run() {
     int spot;
     int stroke[];
     stroke = new int[10];                    // an array for storing the commands
     spot = 0;
     DataInputStream in;

     in = new DataInputStream(soc.getInputStream());
```

```
    while (running) {
        do {                                   // reads the information
            stroke[spot] = in.readByte();
        } while (  (stroke[spot] != '\n') && (++spot < 9) );
                                               // until the newline flag or limit of
                                               // array
    spot = 0;              // resets counter
    quilt.sew(stroke[0],stroke[1],stroke[2]);
    }

    public boolean disconnect () {
      running = false;
      try {
          soc.close()
          }
      catch (Exception e)
            return(false);
      return(true);
    }
}
```

Although none of the methods used in Listing 27.2 are new, there is a very important piece of the class that has been completely installed for the first time—the boolean field running. As a field, it is accessible to all methods within the Client subclass. Nevertheless, by making it private, we have ensured that, if it is changed, its change will be associated with an appropriate change in the status of the socket connection—a connection or disconnection, for example.

Although the Client class may require application-dependent changes, the version shown in Listing 27.2 is sufficient to satisfy most requirements. However, as of yet, we have dealt very little with the applet itself. This is primarily because each multiuser applet is inherently very different. Nevertheless, there are a few topics that should be discussed if you want to develop a quality multiuser applet.

Advanced Topics of Applet Development

What we have developed thus far in the chapter is entirely sufficient to satisfy the demands of the museum. Nevertheless, there are several other topics regarding efficiency, architecture, and appearance that we have not dealt with yet. The next few sections discuss these issues as well as those regarding the development of an effective server on the other end.

Animation and Dynamic Changes to the Screen

Although a programmer may appreciate the intricacies of a multiuser environment, users are attracted to those applications that look nice and help them to do interesting things. Although a multiuser environment is certainly one of the latter variety, we must still keep in mind the first criteria: making the applet look nice and run smoothly.

Although this chapter's purpose is not to deal with such issues as the graphical layout of applets, the communication structures developed in this chapter do have a direct impact on the "smoothness" of the changes that will occur on the user's screen. In the case of the museum applet developed earlier in this chapter, every time a user clicks on a tile, his or her request to paint must be sent to the server and then returned to the client. Once this information is finally returned to the client, the applet must then repaint each and every tile. Although this process occurs in a matter of seconds, for users who have to wait three seconds to see their changes reflected, as well as users who can actually observe each tile being repainted, this process may be a few seconds too slow.

A SHOT OF JAVA JARGON

As we have learned, the method that actually handles the creation of graphics in a Java applet is `paint()`. Although various actions such as drawing lines, changing the background color, and displaying messages may be performed in this method, this functionality is nevertheless commonly referred to as the "painting" of the applet.

This slow graphical process can produce a very choppy effect, commonly referred to as "flickering," and can nevertheless be easily remedied. Although this requires a few changes to our applet, the main idea behind it is noticing that *we do not have to repaint those items that have not changed*. Even though this may seem a rather elementary observation, when developing an applet, it may seem a great deal easier to simply repaint the entire screen. (In fact, if you take a look at some of the Java applets on the Web, you will notice that many applets exhibit the problem of flickering.)

In the case of our museum applet, you will see that we have to paint only the tile that has been changed. Because we know the coordinates and size of each tile, this should not be much of a problem at all. It would seem as if all we have to do is modify the `paint()` method to paint only one tile; when the `sew()` method calls `repaint()`, only the most recently changed tile must change.

There are two problems with such a simplistic approach. First of all, the `paint()` method is called not only by explicit calls to `repaint()`, it is also called whenever the applet "appears" (such as when it first starts up or after the browser has been hidden behind another application). If we change the `paint()` method to paint only one tile, we may be left with only one tile on the screen, rather than the full quilt.

Another problem is that we cannot pass information to the `paint()` method because (as with the `run()` method for threads) we are overriding an already created method.

Don't worry. These problems can be handled easily. Peruse the additions to our code in Listing 27.3 and see whether you can determine how the two problems were solved.

Listing 27.3. Revised code to provide smoother animation.

```java
public class Project extends Applet {
  private boolean FullPaint;
  private java.awt.Point Changed;

  public void init() {
      ...
    FullPaint = true;
    Changed = new Point();
  }

  public void paint(Graphics g) {
    if (FullPaint) {
        for (int i = 0; i < size; i++)
            for(int j = 0; j < size; j++) {
                g.setColor(hues[ (tiles[i][j]) ]);
                g.fillRect( (i*scale+xoff) , (j*scale+yoff), scale,scale);
            }
    }
    else
      g.fillRect( (Changed.x*scale+xoff) , (Changed.y*scale+yoff), scale,scale);
    FullPaint = true;
  }

  public void sew(int x, int y, int hue) {
    if ( (x>=0) && (x <= size) && ( y >= 0) &&
       (y <= size) && (hue >= 0) && (hue _<= 9) ) { // 9 colors
        tiles[x][y] = hue;
        Changed.x = x;
        Changed.y = y;
        FullPaint = false;
        repaint();
    }
  }
}
```

Okay, let's see how the problems were solved.

Most notably, we added two new variables, one for each problem. The first variable is a boolean named FullPaint. As you can probably guess, its function is to tell the paint() method whether it should repaint all the tiles or just the newest one. Note that the key to this variable is that we want it to be true as much as possible so that we prevent the "one tile quilts" scenario discussed earlier. In this setup, the FullPaint variable is set to false only one line before the call to repaint() and is reset to true at the end of the paint() method.

CAUTION

Remember to reset the FullPaint to true at the end of your paint() statement! If you don't, you'll defeat the purpose of the variable—and ruin the appearance of your applet.

How did we deal with the second problem of being unable to inform the `paint()` method which tile has changed? Notice the use of the `private` variable `Point Changed`. Because the field is accessible by all methods, by setting the x and y values of this variable in the `sew()` method, we can indirectly pass this information along to the `paint()` method.

A LOOK INSIDE THE EVOLUTION OF THE LANGUAGE

The code in Listing 27.3 employed `Changed`, a variable of type `Point`, which can be found in the `java.awt` package. This is a useful class, but it has not always been part of Java. When the alpha releases came out, authors (especially those who were making graphical interfaces) were forced to develop their own `Point`-type classes. Even though this was not much of a problem, Sun chose to respond to this need by including the `Point` class in the beta and later API libraries.

Ensuring that the Sockets Close Properly

Although we have developed a sufficient `disconnect()` method, remember that things do not always work as well as they should. In fact, the `disconnect()` method in the socket class has had some problems in Java—further complicated by the fact that we are running our applet through a browser. As discussed earlier, not closing sockets can become a serious problem in a multiuser environment. It is good practice to develop into your protocol a "close" command. Although it should resemble the other commands in your protocol, the close command need not be anything elaborate. In the museum example, if `123` were the command to paint tile `(1,2)` in color `3`, sending `-123` could be the defined close command because it would be an aberration from the rest of the commands—something easily distinguishable.

Are You Still There?

Another related issue is that some users may not tell the applet that they are leaving—so the `disconnect()` method does not have a chance to execute. For example, the user may go to another HTML page or his or her computer might be struck with a sudden power outage. To handle either case, it is advisable to have some method by which the server can ensure that all its clients are still active.

A simple way of doing this is to develop another command into your protocol, the semantics of which are irrelevant. Regardless of the syntax, the server should send out some kind of "are you there?" command periodically. In terms of the applet itself, you should develop the translating method in such a manner that when such a command is received, it responds with an appropriate answer.

Consequently, if this functionality is built into the applet, the server will know that any client that does not respond within a reasonable amount of time (20 seconds, for example) is no longer active and can be closed.

Requests versus Commands

This chapter has repeatedly referred to the information passed from each client to the server as a *request* that describes what the user would like as opposed to a *command* that defines a particular action to be taken. Furthermore, note that in the system developed in this chapter, although a user may click a square, his or her screen is not updated until the request has been echoed back from the server. These two facts may seem a bit abnormal: It may seem more natural to have the applet update itself and then inform the server of what was done. As you will soon see, these two procedures are very necessary for the exact same reason.

In the example of the museum applet, users can paint only blank (unpainted) tiles. Imagine for a moment what would happen if user A decided to paint tile (1,2) black, and a moment later user B decided to paint tile (1,2) yellow. User A's command is received first and user B's command is received second. (It is impossible for the server to receive two commands at the same time on the same socket. Subsequent commands are normally placed in a queue.) If the applets were designed to paint themselves *before* the commands were echoed, user A and user B would have different images of the same quilt at the same time. Disaster!

Consequently, in a multiuser environment in which the status is really important (or even in a game application), it is essential that you develop your environment in such a manner that the status of whatever is being displayed on the screen (such as the position of the players) is updated *only* by what is returned from the server. That means that the server should be developed so that any invalid requests (such as a request to paint an already painted tile) are simply "sucked up" by the server and are not echoed to any clients. If two users attempt to paint the same tile, only the request of the first user should be honored, and the second request should simply be swallowed up by the server. Even better, you could enable your server to send user-specific error messages that cause some form of error message on the user's screen.

Limiting and Keeping Track of Users

In several situations—such as error messages—the server wants to speak with just one user. Additionally, your situation may require that only five users be in the environment at a given moment. These are real-world problems, but ones that are easily solved.

At the heart of these solutions is the idea of having more than one server for your multiuser environment. Such a configuration may involve one central server that has the power to spawn other servers (on other ports), or a central server that acts as a "gatekeeper," accepting clients only if there are openings (see Figure 27.2).

Either case requires the development of a richer protocol, but also provides you with opportunities for greater power over your environment. For example, you can establish several two-player games managed by a central server. By designing the applet to connect on a given port (1626, for example) and to request entrance to a game, the server on that port can act as a manager by beginning a new game on another port (1627, for example) and informing the applet of the new port number. The applet can then disconnect from port 1626, connect to port 1627, and wait for the central server to send another user to the same port. Once the central server has sent two players to port 1627, it starts a new server on the next available port (1628, for example) and can continue in this manner indefinitely (see Figure 27.3).

FIGURE 27.2.
*An example of a
gatekeeper system.*

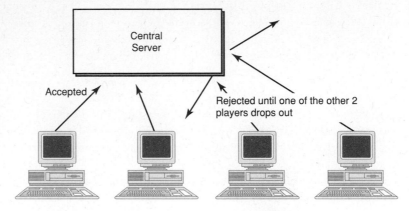

FIGURE 27.3.
*An example of a central
server/children server
system.*

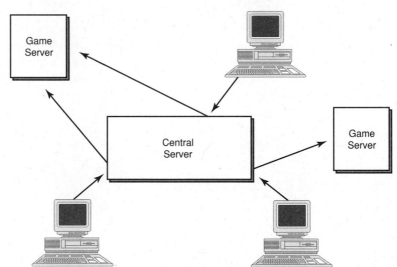

In the cases of the central server/children server system and the gatekeeper system, the server can assign each client an identification number at connection time. This arrangement not only allows the server to keep track of who is sending the information, it also enables the server to send user-specific messages (for example, Player One: You can't do that). Both of these tasks can be facilitated by appending a simple identification letter or number to each command in the protocol. (B112 could mean, for example, that player 1 just bought plot 12.)

Summary

Even though this chapter did not deal with many topics, keep in mind that the power of Java is its abstract capability to facilitate a multiuser environment, not its specific lexical constructs. Here are a few issues relating to the Java language that you should keep in mind when developing a multiuser environment:

- Develop a user-friendly graphical interface. By using the `java.awt.Event` class, you can respond to the user's interactions in an effective manner.

- Create a client class that extends the `java.lang.Thread` class. Although you can create as many methods as you want within this class, the best approach is to harness the `run()` method's capacity to run concurrently to develop an effective means of reading data from the stream. Also, remember to use some form of flag that provides you with a way of controlling the lifetime of the `run()` method.

- Develop the framework by which the applet and client classes will be able to communicate. This is best done by making an instance of the client class a field in the applet class. By making the appropriate methods of the client class `public`, your applet class can perform such tasks as connecting, disconnecting, and sending data.

- Create a "translating" method in your applet class. Doing so enables the client class to send the parsed data to the applet class to elicit the proper response.

VI
PART

Programming Strategies

Java Debugging

by Tim Park

IN THIS CHAPTER

Bugs are an unfortunate fact of life in software design. As most development environments have done, Sun has included a debugger with the Java Development Kit (JDK) to help you fix your Java applets and applications. JDB (short for Java DeBugger) isn't a fancy visual debugging environment like the debuggers you may be familiar with from other professional development systems, but it does make the task of finding and exterminating bugs in your Java programs much easier.

Most of this chapter shows you how to use JDB to debug your programs. The last section uses Symantec Café to show you how to debug your Java programs using Café's very popular visual environment.

Debugging with JDB

In the first part of the chapter, we use a simple Java applet to explain how to use JDB to help you debug your programs. As you can see from the output of the JDB `help` command in Listing 28.1, the range of commands available in JDB is extensive.

Listing 28.1. Output from the JDB `help` command.

```
> help
** command list **
threads [threadgroup]     — list threads
thread <thread id>        — set default thread
suspend [thread id(s)]    — suspend threads (default: all)
resume [thread id(s)]     — resume threads (default: all)
where [thread id] ¦ all   — dump a thread's stack
threadgroups              — list threadgroups
threadgroup <name>        — set current threadgroup

print <id> [id(s)]        — print object or field
dump <id> [id(s)]         — print all object information

locals                    — print all local variables in current stack frame

classes                   — list currently known classes
methods <class id>        — list a class's methods

stop in <class id>.<method> — set a breakpoint in a method
stop at <class id>:<line> — set a breakpoint at a line
up [n frames]             — move up a thread's stack
down [n frames]           — move down a thread's stack
clear <class id>:<line>   — clear a breakpoint
step                      — execute current line
cont                      — continue execution from breakpoint

catch <class id>          — break for the specified exception
ignore <class id>         — ignore when the specified exception

list [line number]        — print source code
use [source file path]    — display or change the source path
```

```
memory                          — report memory usage
gc                              — free unused objects (gc means garbage collection)

load classname                  — load Java class to be debugged
run <class> [args]              — start execution of a loaded Java class
!!                              — repeat last command
help (or ?)                     — list commands
exit (or quit)                  — exit debugger
>
```

Using JDB to Debug Your Program

From our experience, the easiest way to learn JDB is by using it. Without further ado, then, let's use JDB to debug the simple class that follows. We chose a simple class for the benefit of people skipping ahead to learn how to use the basic features of the debugger. But don't worry if you've read all the previous chapters of this book—we'll still cover all the advanced features of JDB!

AddNumbers is a simple class that implements both the user interface and the algorithm to add two numbers together. Well, at least this is what it's supposed to do. In reality, the class has a simple bug that will be located using JDB (see Listing 28.2).

 On the CD-ROM that accompanies this book, you will find two Java classes: StartApplet, which is the requisite subclass of the Applet class that instantiates the AddNumbers class, and StartApplet.html, which is used by the applet viewer to load the applet. Use the bundled installation program to install the files for this chapter onto your hard drive.

Listing 28.2. The AddNumbers.java file—complete with bug.

```java
import java.awt.*;
import java.awt.event.*;

public class AddNumbers extends Frame implements ActionListener {
  int LeftNumber = 5;
  int RightNumber = 2;
  TextArea taResult;

  public AddNumbers() {
    setTitle("JDB Sample Java Program");
    setLayout(new BorderLayout());
    Panel p = new Panel();
    Button b = new Button("5");
    b.addActionListener(this);
    p.add(b);
    b = new Button("1");
    b.addActionListener(this);
    p.add(b);
    add("West", p);
```

continues

28

JAVA DEBUGGING

Listing 28.2. continued

```
      Panel g = new Panel();
      b = new Button("2");
      b.addActionListener(this);
      g.add(b);
      b = new Button("3");
      b.addActionListener(this);
      g.add(b);
      add("East", g);
      taResult = new TextArea(2,1);
      taResult.setEditable(false);
      add("South", taResult);
      pack();
      setSize(300,200);
      show();
    }

    public void ComputeSum () {
      int Total = LeftNumber - RightNumber;
      String ConvLeft  = String.valueOf(LeftNumber);
      String ConvRight = String.valueOf(RightNumber);
      String ConvTotal = String.valueOf(Total);
      taResult.setText(ConvLeft + " + " + ConvRight + " = " +  ConvTotal);
    }

    public void paint(Graphics g) {
      ComputeSum();
    }

    public void actionPerformed(ActionEvent e) {
      // Was the "5" button pressed?
      if (e.getActionCommand().equals("5")) {
        LeftNumber = 5;
        ComputeSum();
      }

      // Was the "1" button pressed?
      if (e.getActionCommand().equals("1")) {
        LeftNumber = 1;
        ComputeSum();
      }

      // Was the "2" button pressed?
      if (e.getActionCommand().equals("2")) {
        RightNumber = 2;
        ComputeSum();
      }

      // Was the "3" button pressed?
      if (e.getActionCommand().equals("3")) {
        RightNumber = 3;
        ComputeSum();
      }
    }
}
```

Compiling for JDB

Before starting the debugging session, you must first compile the Java applet to include extra information needed only for debugging. This information is required so that the debugger can display information about your applet or application in a human-comprehensible form instead of a confusing wash of hexadecimal numbers. (Don't laugh—the first debuggers required you to do this translation, so count your lucky stars!)

To compile your program with debugging information enabled, change to the \java\classes\AddNumbers directory and issue the following commands:

```
C:\java\classes\AddNumbers> javac_g -g AddNumbers.java
C:\java\classes\AddNumbers> javac_g -g StartApplet.java
```

The javac_g compiler is functionally identical to the javac compiler used in previous chapters, except that it doesn't perform any optimizations to your applet or application. Optimizations rearrange the statements in your applet or application to make them faster. This rearrangement makes it more difficult to conceptualize program flow when you are debugging, so using javac_g in conjunction with JDB is useful for keeping your program in the order in which you wrote it.

The -g command-line option tells the compiler to include line number and object names in the output file. This option allows the debugger to reference objects and line numbers in a program by source code names instead of using the Java interpreter's internal representations.

Setting Up a Debugging Session

The next step in debugging a Java application or applet is to start JDB. There are two ways to do this, depending on whether you are debugging an applet or an application. Because we are debugging an applet in our example, we will use the applet viewer program supplied in the Java Development Kit to load JDB indirectly. If we were trying to debug *an application* instead, we would use the following command to start JDB:

```
C:\java\classes\AddNumbers> jdb MyApplication
```

Because we are debugging an applet in our example and not an application, ***do not start JDB*** in the preceding manner. However, for future reference, after you invoke the debugger, using JDB on a Java application is identical to using it on an applet.

With that important distinction covered, start the applet viewer with the following command:

```
C:\java\classes\AddNumbers> appletviewer -debug StartApplet.html
```

The -debug flag specifies to the applet viewer that it should start up in JDB instead of by directly executing the AddNumbers class.

28

JAVA DEBUGGING

Once the applet viewer loads, it opens its applet window and displays something similar to the following in the command-line window:

```
C:\java\classes\AddNumbers> appletviewer -debug AddNumbers.html
Initializing jdb...
0x139f2f8:class(sun.applet.Appletviewer)
>_
```

The first thing you should notice about JDB is that it is command-line based. Although this makes the learning curve for JDB a little steeper, it doesn't prevent you from doing anything you may be familiar with in a visual debugging environment.

Before going further, examine the third line of the preceding output. This line indicates where the debugger stopped in its execution of the applet. In this case, it stopped during the execution of Sun's `applet.Appletviewer` class. This is logical, because `applet.Appletviewer` is the class that is transparently loaded and executed to load an applet. (See, you're learning things by using JDB already!) The hexadecimal number that prefixes this on the third line is the ID number assigned to the `sun.applet.Appletviewer` object by the Java interpreter. (Aren't you glad now that you can see the English version because you used the `-g` option for `javac`?) The > prompt on the fourth line indicates that there is currently no default thread that we are watching—more on this later.

To understand the bug in `AddNumbers`, we will start the applet running in the debugger as follows:

```
> run
run sun.applet.AppletViewer MA.html
running ...
main[1]
```

The debugger should open the applet's frame and start executing it. Because the debugger and the applet are in different threads of execution, you can interact with the debugger and the applet at the same time. The preceding `main[1]` prompt indicates that the debugger is monitoring the applet thread (the `main` thread); the `[1]` indicates that we are currently positioned at the topmost stack frame on the method call stack (we'll explain what this means later).

The `AddNumbers` applet contains two buttons on each side of the applet window with numbers as their labels (see Figure 28.1). The applet is supposed to use the number of the button pressed on the left and add it to the number of the button pressed on the right. Try this out: Press some of the buttons and check the applet's math.

Hmm—unless you learned math differently than we did, there seems to be something wrong with the computation of the applet. (Maybe we found another Pentium processor flaw?)

FIGURE 28.1.

The AddNumbers *applet with its numbered buttons.*

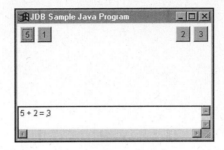

Basic Debugger Techniques

To find out what is going on, let's examine the ComputeSum() method of the AddNumbers class. We would like to stop directly in this method without having to move slowly and tediously through the rest of the code.

Setting and Clearing Breakpoints

Fortunately, JDB has a set of commands called *breakpoints* that let you stop at particular places in your code. We'll use breakpoints to stop program execution in the ComputeSum() method; but first, press the 5 and 3 buttons on the applet to make sure that you see the same things as we do when the program is stopped. After pressing 5 and 3, type the following in the debugger window:

```
main[1] stop in AddNumbers.ComputeSum
Breakpoint set in AddNumbers.ComputeSum
main[1]
```

As you probably can guess, the stop in command tells JDB to stop when the ComputeSum() method in the AddNumbers class is entered. This is convenient to do because the computation part of method we are interested in is very close to the start of the method. If the statement was farther down in the method, it would be tedious to manually move down to the statement of interest every time we hit the breakpoint at the beginning of the method. In this case, we would want to use the stop at command in JDB.

The stop at command works exactly like the stop in command in JDB, except that you specify the line number you want JDB to stop on instead of the method. For example, look at the handleEvent() method of AddNumbers class. If you want to stop at the if statement where the program checked for a push of the number 2 button, enter the following:

```
main[1] stop at AddNumbers:90
Breakpoint set in AddNumbers:90
main[1]
```

28

JAVA DEBUGGING

However, ***don't do this*** because we want to examine the ComputeSum() method and not the handleEvent() method. We can verify this and see all the breakpoints currently set by using the clear command as follows:

```
AWT-Callback-Win32[1] clear
Current breakpoints set:
      AddNumbers:37
AWT-Callback-Win32[1]
```

As expected, there is only one breakpoint set. Note that it is specified as AddNumbers:37 instead of as AddNumbers:ComputeSum. JDB converts the command stop in AddNumbers.ComputeSum to the command stop at AddNumbers:37 to make its internal bookkeeping easier.

Of course, the real use of the clear command is to clear breakpoints when they have outgrown their usefulness. ***Don't do this now***, but if you have to clear the breakpoint you just set, enter the following:

```
AWT-Callback-Win32[1] clear AddNumbers.ComputeSum
Breakpoint cleared at AddNumbers.ComputeSum
AWT-Callback-Win32[1]
```

Let's get back to debugging our applet. When we left our applet, it was still running and there was no prompt in the JDB window. Why hasn't JDB stopped at ComputeSum()? If you look at the applet code, you notice that the ComputeSum() method is called only when you press a button in the applet. Press the 2 button to provide this ComputeSum() method call:

```
main[1]
Breakpoint hit: AddNumbers.ComputeSum (AddNumbers: 37)
AWT-Callback-Win32[1]
```

As you can see, when you press the 2 button, the debugger stops at the ComputeSum() method as instructed. Note that we are now in a different thread (as shown by the change in prompts from main[1] to AWT-Callback-Win32[1]) because the AWT window manager thread calls the handleEvent() method in the AddNumbers class when a button is pressed in the applet.

Although we know we are stopped in the ComputeSum() method, let's get a better sense of our bearings and refresh our memory by looking at where this method is in the source code. Fortunately, the line-number information is stored in the class when you compile with the -g option; you can access this information by using the JDB list command as follows:

```
AWT-Callback-Win32[1] list
33           }
34    35          public void ComputeSum() {
36
37    =>          int Total = LeftNumber - RightNumber;
38
39            String ConvLeft  = String.valueOf(LeftNumber);
40            String ConvRight = String.valueOf(RightNumber);
41            String ConvTotal = String.valueOf(Total);
AWT-Callback-Win32[1]
```

As expected, this output shows that we are stopped in ComputeSum() on the first statement—and as luck would have it, right before the computation statement. The observant reader probably already can tell what is wrong, but just pretend that it's a much more complicated computation and that you can't, okay?

Examining Objects

First, let's check our operands for the computation to make sure that they are correct. JDB provides three commands to display the contents of objects: locals, print, and dump. The locals command displays the current values of all the objects defined in the local scope. The print and dump commands are very similar and are used to display the contents of any object in any scope, including objects defined in the interface for the class. The main difference is that dump displays more information about complex objects (objects with inheritance or multiple data members) than print does.

Because LeftNumber and RightNumber are class members, we'll have to use print to display them, as follows:

```
AWT-Callback-Win32[1] print LeftNumber
this.LeftNumber = 5
AWT-Callback-Win32[1] print RightNumber
this.RightNumber = 2
AWT-Callback-Win32[1]
```

The operands seem to be exactly as we entered them in the applet. Let's take a look at the local objects to get a feeling for where we are by using the locals command as follows:

```
AWT-Callback-Win32[1] locals
  this = AddNumbers[0,0,300x200,layout=java.awt.BorderLayout,
resizable,title=JDB Sample Java Program]
  Total is not in scope.
  ConvLeft is not in scope.
  ConvRight is not in scope.
  ConvTotal is not in scope.
AWT-Callback-Win32[1]
```

As expected, JDB is telling us that none of the local objects have been instantiated yet, so none of the objects are within the local scope yet. Let's move the execution of the method along one statement so that we can see what the value of the computation is. To do this, use the JDB step command as follows:

```
AWT-Callback-Win32[1] step
AWT-Callback-Win32[1]
Breakpoint hit: AddNumbers.ComputeSum (AddNumbers:39)
AWT-Callback-Win32[1]
```

JDB moves the execution along one statement and stops. Doing this also triggers another breakpoint, because we are still in AddNumbers.ComputeSum(). Look at the following output to determine how the computation turned out:

```
AWT-Callback-Win32[1] locals
this = AddNumbers[0,0,300x200,layout=java.awt.BorderLayout,
resizable,title=JDB Sample Java Program]
  Total = 3
  ConvLeft is not in scope.
  ConvRight is not in scope.
  ConvTotal is not in scope.
AWT-Callback-Win32[1]
```

We see that `Total` was instantiated, the addition carried out, and the result put in `Total`. But wait: 5 + 2 doesn't equal 3! Take a look at the following source code:

```
AWT-Callback-Win32[1] list
35           public void ComputeSum() {
36
37               int Total = LeftNumber - RightNumber;
38
39     =>        String ConvLeft   = String.valueOf(LeftNumber);
40               String ConvRight = String.valueOf(RightNumber);
41               String ConvTotal = String.valueOf(Total);
42
43               taResult.setText(ConvLeft + " + " + ConvRight + " = " +
AWT-Callback-Win32[1]
```

Oops—a minus sign was used instead of a plus sign! So much for finding another bug in the Pentium processor! But congratulations—you've found your first applet bug in JDB.

Additional JDB Functions

We've found our bug, but don't quit out of the applet viewer yet. We'll use it and the `AddNumbers` class to demonstrate a few more features of JDB that you might find useful in future debugging sessions.

Walking the Method Call Stack with JDB

In the previous section, we used the JDB `locals` command to look at the objects in the current scope. Using the JDB `up` command, you can also look at the local objects in previous stack frames (which consist of all the methods that either called `ComputeSum()` or called a method that called `ComputeSum()`, and so on). For example, look at the following output to see the state of the `handleEvent()` method right before it called the `ComputeSum()` method:

```
AWT-Callback-Win32[1] up
AWT-Callback-Win32[2] locals
this = AddNumbers[0,0,300x200,layout=java.awt.BorderLayout,
resizable,title=JDB Sample Java Program]
evt = java.awt.Event[id=1001,x=246,y=28,
target=java.awt.Button[5,5,20x24,label=2],arg=2]
AWT-Callback-Win32[2]
```

As you can see, the `handleEvent` stack frame has two objects in its local frame: the pointer to this `AddNumbers` instance and the `Event` object passed to `handleEvent()`.

It's possible to use the up command as many times as your method call stack is deep. To undo the up function and return to a higher method call in the stack, use the JDB down command as follows:

```
AWT-Callback-Win32[2] down
AWT-Callback-Win32[1] locals
this = AddNumbers[0,0,300x200,layout=java.awt.BorderLayout,
resizable,title=JDB Sample Java Program]
  Total = 3
  ConvLeft is not in scope.
  ConvRight is not in scope.
  ConvTotal is not in scope.
AWT-Callback-Win32[1]
```

As expected, we are now back in the ComputeSum() local stack frame.

Using JDB to Get More Information about Classes

JDB also has two commands for getting more information about classes: methods and classes. The methods command enables you to display all the methods in a class. For example, you can examine the AddNumbers class with the methods command:

```
AWT-Callback-Win32[1] methods
void <init>()
void ComputeSum()
void paint(Graphics)
boolean handleEvent(Event)
AWT-Callback-Win32[1]
```

The classes function lists all the classes currently loaded in memory. Here is partial output from the execution of classes on AddNumbers (the actual output listed more than 80 classes):

```
AWT-Callback-Win32[1] classes
...
...
0x13a5f70:interface(sun.awt.UpdateClient)
0x13a6160:interface(java.awt.peer.MenuPeer)
0x13a67a0:interface(java.awt.peer.ButtonPeer)
0x13a6880:class(java.lang.ClassNotFoundException)
0x13a6ea8:class(sun.tools.debug.Field)
0x13a7098:class(sun.tools.debug.BreakpointSet)
0x13a7428:class(sun.tools.debug.Stackframe)
0x13a7478:class(sun.tools.debug.LocalVariable)
AWT-Callback-Win32[1]
```

Monitoring Memory Usage and Controlling finalize()

For some large applets or applications, the amount of free memory may become a concern. JDB's memory command enables you to monitor the amount of used and free memory during your debugging session, as follows:

```
AWT-Callback-Win32[1] memory
Free: 2554472, total: 3145720
AWT-Callback-Win32[1]
```

28

JAVA DEBUGGING

JDB also lets you explicitly demand that the `finalize()` method be run on all freed objects through the `gc` (garbage collection) command. This is useful for proving that your applet or application correctly handles deleted objects—which can be difficult to prove normally with small applets and applications because the `finalize()` methods are normally called only when the applet or application has run out of free memory.

Controlling Threads of Execution

As you know from Chapter 6, "Threads and Multithreading," Java applets have multiple threads of execution. Using JDB and the `threads` command, you can view these threads as follows:

```
AWT-Callback-Win32[1] threads
Group sun.applet.AppletViewer.main:
 1.  (java.lang.Thread)0x13a3a00          AWT-Win32                  running
 2.  (java.lang.Thread)0x13a2a58          AWT-Callback-Win32    running
 3.  (sun.awt.ScreenUpdater)0x13a2d98    Screen Updater running Group group
applet-StartApplet.class:
 4.     (java.lang.Thread)0x13a28f0 class running AWT-Callback-Win32[1]
```

As you can see from this output, there are four threads of simultaneous applet execution. Two correspond to the AWT window management system (threads 1 and 2), one is for updating the screen (thread 3), and one is for the actual applet itself (thread 4).

JDB provides two commands for controlling the execution of threads: `suspend` and `resume`. Suspending a thread isn't very worthwhile in our simple example, but in multithreaded applications, it can be very worthwhile—you can suspend all but one thread and focus on that thread.

But let's try `suspend` and `resume` on our applet to get a feel for their use. To suspend the AWT-Win32 thread, you should note its ID from the `threads` list and then use this information as the argument to `suspend`, as follows:

```
AWT-Callback-Win32[1] threads
Group sun.applet.AppletViewer.main:
 1.  (java.lang.Thread)0x13a3a00               AWT-Win32                      running
...
AWT-Callback-Win32[1] suspend 1
AWT-Callback-Win32[1] threads
Group sun.applet.AppletViewer.main:
 1.  (java.lang.Thread)0x13a3a00        AWT-Win32                  suspended
 2.  (java.lang.Thread)0x13a2a58        AWT-Callback-Win32    running
 3.  (sun.awt.ScreenUpdater)0x13a2d98 Screen Updater running Group group
applet-StartApplet.class:
 4.     (java.lang.Thread)0x13a28f0 class running AWT-Callback-Win32[1]
```

As expected, the AWT-Win32 thread is now suspended. Threads are resumed in a completely analogous manner—with the `resume` command, as follows:

```
AWT-Callback-Win32[1] resume 1
AWT-Callback-Win32[1] threads
```

```
Group sun.applet.AppletViewer.main:
 1.  (java.lang.Thread)0x13a3a00         AWT-Win32                  running
 2.  (java.lang.Thread)0x13a2a58         AWT-Callback-Win32      running
 3.  (sun.awt.ScreenUpdater)0x13a2d98 Screen Updater running Group group
applet-StartApplet.class:
 4.      (java.lang.Thread)0x13a28f0 class running AWT-Callback-Win32[1]
```

Using use to Point the Way to Your Java Source Code

To execute the list command, JDB takes the line number and grabs the required lines of Java from the source file. To find that source file, JDB reads your CLASSPATH environment variable and searches all the paths contained in it. If that path doesn't contain your source file, JDB is unable to display the source for your program.

This wasn't a problem for this example because the search path contained the current directory, but if you set up your applet or application and the source is located in a directory outside the search path, you'll have to use the use command to add to your path. The use command without any arguments displays the current search path as follows:

```
AWT-Callback-Win32[1] use
\java\classes;.;C:\JAVA\BIN\..\classes;
AWT-Callback-Win32[1]
```

Appending a directory to the search path is unfortunately slightly tedious. You have to retype the *entire current path* and add the new path. To add the path \myclasses to the preceding path, do the following:

```
AWT-Callback-Win32[1] use \java\classes;.;C:\JAVA\BIN\..\classes;\myclasses
AWT-Callback-Win32[1]
```

Getting More Information about Your Objects with dump

Earlier in this chapter, you saw an example of how to display an object's value using the print command. In this section, we'll look at JDB's dump command, which is a more useful display command for objects that contain multiple data members. The AddNumbers class is a good example (note that this in this case refers to the instantiation of AddNumbers for our applet), as follows:

```
AWT-Callback-Win32[1] dump this
this = (AddNumbers)0x13a3000 {
    ComponentPeer peer = (sun.awt.win32.MFramePeer)0x13a31b0
    Container parent = null
    int x = 0
    int y = 0
    int width = 300
    int height = 200
    Color foreground = (java.awt.Color)0x13a2bb0
    Color background = (java.awt.Color)0x13a2b98
```

```
    Font font = (java.awt.Font)0x13a31d0
    boolean visible = true
    boolean enabled = true
    boolean valid = true
    int ncomponents = 3
AWT-Callback-Win32[1] _
```

Contrast this with the output from `print`:

```
AWT-Callback-Win32[1] print this
this = AddNumbers[0,0,300x200,layout=java.awt.BorderLayout,
resizable,title=JDB Sample Java Program]
AWT-Callback-Win32[1]
```

As you can see, the `dump` command displays the data members for the class but `print` displays only the key attributes for the class.

Handling Exceptions with `catch` and `ignore`

JDB has two functions for dealing with exceptions: `catch` and `ignore`. The `catch` function, similar to a breakpoint, enables you to trap exceptions and stop the debugger. The `catch` command is useful when debugging because it is much easier to diagnose an exception when you know the conditions under which it occurred. To catch an exception, simply type `class` and the name of the exception class. To trap any exception in the `Exception` base class, do the following:

```
AWT-Callback-Win32[1] catch Exception
AWT-Callback-Win32[1]
```

The `ignore` function does exactly the opposite of `catch`. It squelches the specified class of exceptions raised by an applet or application. The use of `ignore` is completely analogous to `catch`, as shown by the following example:

```
AWT-Callback-Win32[1] ignore ArrayOutOfBoundsException
AWT-Callback-Win32[1]
```

Continuing Program Execution with `cont`

You may be wondering how to restart execution once you reach a breakpoint and execution has stopped. Why, you use the `cont` command, of course!

```
AWT-Callback-Win32[1] cont
```

The program resumes execution and the JDB prompt does not return until another breakpoint or exception is reached.

Leaving JDB Using `exit`

Although it may be obvious to you already, there is one final command that comes in handy at least once in any debugging session. The `exit` command lets you out of the debugger and back to the operating system command prompt.

Debugging with Symantec Café

If you want to be a more efficient Java developer, it is hard to find anything as important as adopting an integrated development environment for your development platform. One of the best such visual environments is Symantec Café for Java. In addition to excellent debugging support, it also features project management, a visual GUI builder, and object-oriented browsing of your Java classes. Because of its solid debugger, Café is the IDE we'll use in the next sections to teach you about graphical debugging.

Loading the AddNumbers Project

The first thing we have to do to use Symantec Café's debugger is to load the project file for the `AddNumbers` applet. This project file contains all the information required to build `AddNumbers.java` and `StartApplet.java`. After launching the Symantec Café IDE, use the mouse to pull down the Project menu and select the Open option. The Open Project dialog box appears. In this dialog box, type the path or navigate to the directory containing the same `AddNumbers` applet you used in the first part of this chapter. From this directory, you should be able to see a file named `AddNumbers.prj`. Select this file and click OK to load the project.

Building the AddNumbers Project

The `AddNumbers.prj` project should have come precompiled on the CD-ROM that accompanies this book. In case you want to do it yourself, let's rebuild it in Café. Pull down the Project menu again and select Build. Café pops up a build status window and builds the files one by one.

Running the AddNumbers Project

Before we jump into debugging the `AddNumbers` project, let's run it first and make sure that it still adds numbers wrong. To run it, pull down the Project menu and select Execute Program (or press its accelerator key, Ctrl+F5).

Debugging the AddNumbers Project

After you play with the `AddNumbers` applet for a while and confirm that it is broken, stop it at the applet's execution: Open the Debug menu and select Start/Restart Debugging. This command should bring up five windows: a source code window displaying `StartApplet.java`, a Data/Object window, a Call window, a Thread window, and an Output window. A thorough coverage of all these windows would require more than a single chapter. For the purposes of this chapter, we'll explain what all the windows do, but focus on the source code window and the Data/Object window—these are the only windows you'll use for 90 percent of your debugging tasks anyway.

At this point, the debugger is stopped at the first program statement and is waiting for your command. Suppose that, from your last test run, you have guessed that the error lies somewhere within the ComputeSum() method in the AddNumbers class. Let's set a breakpoint here using Café and run until we get to this point in the program.

To set a breakpoint, you must first open the AddNumbers.java file. With the AddNumbers file in the editor, move down in the file until you reach the ComputeSum() method. Pull down the Window menu in Café and make sure that the Debug Toolbox option is selected. Next, move the cursor down to line 37, which is the computation of TotalSum. Finally, find the Debug toolbar on your icon bar, which looks like the bar in Figure 28.2.

Figure 28.2.

Café's Debug toolbar.

The breakpoint toggle button is the one with the red and green flags on it. Click this button to toggle the breakpoint on for the computation line. A little red diamond should appear next to that line (see Figure 28.3).

Figure 28.3.

Setting a breakpoint in Café.

```
c:\temp2\AddNumbers.java
 File  Edit  Goto  Macro  New!

   import java.awt.*;

   public class AddNumbers extends Frame {

      int LeftNumber = 5;
      int RightNumber = 2;

      TextArea taResult;

      public AddNumbers() {

         setTitle("JDB Sample Java Program");
         setLayout(new BorderLayout());

         Panel p = new Panel();
         p.add(new Button("5"));
         p.add(new Button("1"));
         add("West", p);

         Panel g = new Panel();
         g.add(new Button("2"));
         g.add(new Button("3"));
         add("East", g);

         taResult = new TextArea(2,1);
         taResult.setEditable(false);
         add("South", taResult);

         pack();
         resize(300,200);
         show();

      }

      public void ComputeSum () {

         int Total = LeftNumber - RightNumber;

         String ConvLeft  = String.valueOf(LeftNumber);
         String ConvRight = String.valueOf(RightNumber);
         String ConvTotal = String.valueOf(Total);

         taResult.setText(ConvLeft + " + " + ConvRight + " = " + ConvTotal)
```
Line 37 Col 11

With the breakpoint set, we're now ready to let the program execute freely until it reaches the breakpoint. To do this, pull down the Debug menu and select Go Until Breakpoint. This action starts the applet viewer; the AddNumbers applet runs until it reaches the ComputeSum() method as part of the redraw. Execution stops at the line on which we put the breakpoint—as we expect (see Figure 28.4). Notice, however, that Café doesn't execute the line we set as the target of the breakpoint.

FIGURE 28.4.

Café stopped at a breakpoint.

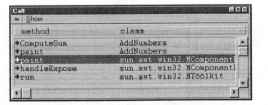

```
    taResult = new TextArea(2,1);
    taResult.setEditable(false);
    add("South", taResult);

    pack();
    resize(300,200);
    show();

}

public void ComputeSum () {

    int Total = LeftNumber - RightNumber;

    String ConvLeft  = String.valueOf(LeftNumber);
    String ConvRight = String.valueOf(RightNumber);
```

Café's Call window (shown in Figure 28.5) shows the stack of method calls that have been made to reach this point in program execution. We know that the ComputeSum() method was reached during the repaint of the window because it was called from the AddNumbers paint() method.

FIGURE 28.5.

Café's Call window.

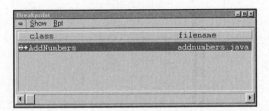

Café's Breakpoint window (shown in Figure 28.6) shows which breakpoint caused the stop in execution. In this example, there is only one breakpoint, so this information isn't very helpful—but for bigger debugging situations, the Breakpoint window is more useful as a central reference for all the breakpoints you have set in your program.

FIGURE 28.6.

Café's Breakpoint window.

The Thread window shows all the threads in operation for your program. Note that its output is exactly the same, if in a somewhat more readable format, as what we saw when we were using JDB.

But what we're really interested in is the Data/Object window (shown in Figure 28.7). This window contains the current values of all the data members for local objects. In looking at the values of `lLeftNumber` and `lRightNumber`, we can tell that the problem isn't caused by the operands to the computation because they are what we expect them to be.

FIGURE 28.7.

Café's Data/Object window before the `Total` *computation.*

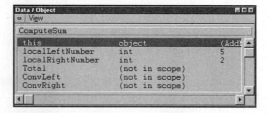

Let's move execution ahead one line so that we can see the result of the execution. To do this, press the F10 key or click the button in the Debug toolbar with the foot "stepping into" a yellow hole. The "stepping into" button differs from the "stepping over" button (the next button on the Debug bar) in that "stepping into" shows the execution of any and all function calls incurred on this line; "stepping over" shows only the output of the function.

Looking at the Data/Object window, we can now tell that something is wrong with the computation of `Total`: 5 + 2 certainly doesn't equal 3, as shown in the display of the Data/Object window in Figure 28.8. Hopefully, with this information, the bug is now obvious to you.

FIGURE 28.8.

Café's Data/Object window after the `Total` *computation.*

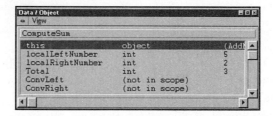

To complete the debug cycle, take Café out of debugging mode using the Stop Debugging option in the Debug menu. Then change the - operator in the `Total` computation to a + and rebuild using the Build option in the Project menu. Run the program again to prove that the problem has been fixed.

Summary

This chapter helped you learn how to debug by giving you hands-on experience with Sun's Java debugger, JDB, and Symantec's visual environment, Café. Debugging is a learned skill; don't be discouraged if it takes you a long time to debug your first applet or application. As you gain experience doing it, you'll start to recognize the effects of different classes of bugs and be able to solve each bug in shorter amounts of time. Patience is definitely a virtue in software debugging.

Documenting Your Code

by George Reese

IN THIS CHAPTER

If one single thing can define the difference between hackers and serious programmers, it is documentation. The trademark of a hacker is a quick-and-dirty solution developed without the use of any commonly understood process or anything other than the code itself to describe what was done. A programmer, on the other hand, develops an application based on documentation derived from a clearly defined development process. As a result, the quality of the applications built by programmers is worlds above the quality of applications built by hackers.

This chapter examines the role of documentation in object-oriented application development. It focuses on approaches to object-oriented development that help produce useful documentation and on the javadoc tool, which creates API documentation from comments in your source code.

The Role of Documentation

The complexity of software engineering can equal the complexity of fields like construction and manufacturing. In construction, you create buildings using a process that defines and documents what you are building before you build it. Specifically, an architect puts together a blueprint that others use to define how they will construct the building. Years down the road, if someone decides to expand the building, or simply update it to new fire standards, that old blueprint is brought out and used as the starting point for the changes.

Not all construction projects, however, have the same level of complexity. For example, building a doghouse is not quite the same as building a bridge. You do not really need to document the building of your doghouse; but if you are building a bridge, you better have it blueprinted and tested in computer simulations before constructing it. Why should software development be any different?

Over the life cycle of an application, documentation plays two important roles:

- Prescriptive
- Descriptive

Prescriptive Documentation

Prescriptive documentation outlines how your application *should* be built. How often have you finished a significant portion of an application that you failed to document only to realize that you forgot a piece? Because good documentation flows from a standard engineering process, you are less likely to find that you have missed a key element, and for each element, you will understand it thoroughly before you begin building it. The basic goal of prescriptive documentation is to provide you with a history of the issues you decided were important and how they fit into the application as a whole.

Descriptive Documentation

Descriptive documentation details how an application is actually built. In a well-structured project, your documentation evolves as the project evolves, continuing even after the application has been deployed. If you have ever had to modify someone else's existing code, you know that the tasks of application testing and maintenance are made much easier by well-written documentation. And *much easier* translates into *less time and money*.

The Software Engineering Process

Random documentation does not help you build an application. The documentation you create should tell you, and any potential reader, all the information known about the objects in your system and how they act together. Although scribbling notes into a notebook may be enough to capture this information for yourself, this approach does not help others understand what you are trying to do.

Good documentation comes from a sound software engineering process that challenges you to ask the right questions and record the answers in a standard format. It is often said that "it's the planning, not the plan"; to some degree, that cliché is true. A good software engineering process serves as a sort of preflight checklist that helps you be sure that you do not miss anything crucial before takeoff.

Let's start out by taking a brief look at object-oriented software engineering and how it relates to the documentation you produce. I first want to take a look at object-oriented software engineering; keep in mind, however, that many volumes have been written on the subject, so I cannot possibly cover all its nuances in this short chapter. Instead, I want to provide an introduction to the subject to help you understand its importance and whet your appetite for more.

Object-Oriented Design

Because Java is a purely object-oriented language, the process of designing applications using Java should follow well-established object-oriented software engineering methodologies. A *methodology* is simply a step-by-step process for performing a task; at each step along the way, you document what you did. An object-oriented methodology specifically looks at the system as an interplay of objects and thus seeks to understand the objects that make up that system and how they interact with each other.

Any software engineering process—object-oriented or otherwise—can be cleanly divided into six stages:

1. Analysis
2. Design
3. Development

4. Testing
5. Implementation
6. Maintenance

These steps proceed iteratively, meaning that once a subsystem comes out of testing, it probably goes back into development (or even, sometimes, back into design). This loop repeats as many times as necessary until all testing requirements are met.

Traditionally, 80 percent of software development is spent in the last stage: maintenance. In other words, the most effort on a system is spent fixing bugs and correcting things done poorly in the first five stages. Because getting something right the first time is always less costly than going back and redoing it, the goal of object-oriented software engineering is to shift time back to the first and second stages so that much less time is spent in the final stage.

Analysis

Before you begin any software development project, you first have to analyze the problem and understand what it is. The task of analysis is to prioritize system components by classifying them as either wants or needs. You must be able to accommodate the proper amount of time for the design and development of your system's needs. If you still have time on your planning chart after the *needs* have been accounted for, you then note which *wants* you will accommodate and which ones you will not. If you plan to implement a *want* in a future release, you should note that decision in your documentation so that designers can plan for that future expansion.

> **NOTE**
>
> This chapter offers a very distilled object-oriented software engineering process geared more towards the casual or small-project developer. There are actually several major object-oriented approaches in common use today. This chapter takes the major components of these well-known methodologies and describes their essence. Regardless of what sort of projects you are involved with, I highly recommend that you familiarize yourself with at least two of the major methodologies, such as OMT and the new Universal Methodology.
>
> Furthermore, if you are developing software professionally for a large audience, I strongly advise that you follow one of those methodologies for two reasons: First, a well-known methodology provides a common ground of understanding for a diverse set of people—from entry-level developers to senior architects and managers. Second, whenever you tell a potential customer that you follow object-oriented design practices, their first question, oddly enough, will be "Which methodology do you use?"

The documentation of your analysis can be fairly simple. It only has to show which pieces of your system will be considered *in scope*, that is, what will be built in the first release. For everything out of scope, you should note why it is out of scope and whether you plan to address it in a later release.

> **TIP**
>
> If you are building an application for a specific group of people, this is the best time to show them your analysis document and have them sign it. If, at a later date, they come back to you, asking why feature X was not included in the system, you can show them their approval of the document.

The following outline captures the essence of what an analysis document should look like:

  I. General-Use Cases

  II. Context Model

  III. Notes

To capture the proper wants and needs, you should sit down with potential users and document *general-use cases*, sometimes called *scenarios*. A general-use case is a simple statement describing a function of the system. For example, if I were building a program that predicted football games, I might have a use case like this:

The user requests a prediction for two teams.

Your use cases can help you identify high-level components that you can place into a diagram to graphically illustrate which pieces of the application are in scope and which are out of scope. This diagram is called a *context model*. Figure 29.1 shows a sample context model for the football game prediction program.

The content of a context model is simple. You design and build anything inside the box. Anything outside the box is out of scope. If there is a line connecting something inside the box with something outside the box, that means that your system is interfacing with an external system.

The last section of your analysis document should briefly describe any decisions you made about the scope of the application. Specifically, you want to record anything you cut from scope and why you cut it.

29

DOCUMENTING YOUR CODE

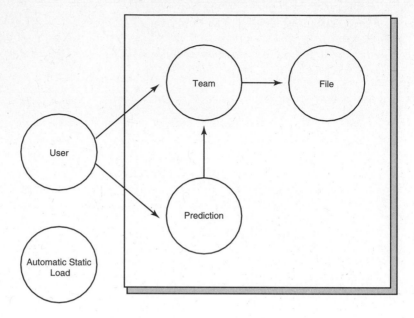

FIGURE 29.1.
The context model for a football game prediction program.

Design

By understanding the problem, you can go on to design a solution. During the design process, you break the application into objects and provide descriptions of how they interact to satisfy the general-use cases in the analysis document. The end product of your design should be a document that tells you exactly how to build your system without diving into coding details. The outline of a good design document should look something like this:

    I. Object Model

    II. Detailed-Use Cases

    III. Object Specifications

To put together the object model, you first have to identify all your objects. Identifying objects is a lot less complex than it sounds. A few people gather around a white board or a piece of paper and name things they think are objects straight off the top of their heads. At first, there are no wrong or right answers. Later, as you start applying the objects to use cases, you will see which objects best describe the system and eliminate from your design those that do not.

The following list of objects comes from a brainstorm session on the design for the football program:

- Team
- Statistic
- Game

- User
- Points-for
- Points-against
- File

Once you feel comfortable with the initial list of objects, the next step is to attempt to identify recurring patterns within those objects. The simplest form is that of inheritance, in which one object is simply an extension of another object. Clearly, the points-for and points-against objects are really extensions of a statistic. But is a statistic really a simple attribute of a team? Or is it a more complex object with independent behaviors? Because converting an object into a simple data type is easier than converting a simple data type into an object during the design process, you should keep anything as an object until you are certain it is not.

Completing the design involves iterating over the process of fitting objects into use cases, fleshing out those use cases, and then identifying opportunities for abstraction until you feel you have a clearly defined architecture for the development of your system. To reach this stage, you need documentation that identifies every single object you will build for the system, its attributes, and its behaviors.

The object model is a diagram that illustrates your understanding of the system as a whole. For a small system like the football game prediction program, the diagram can be simple as the one in Figure 29.2.

FIGURE 29.2.

The object model for the football game predictor.

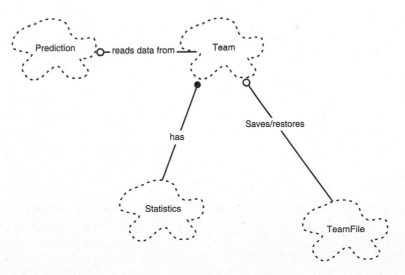

This diagram shows you exactly what you have to code. All that is left to figure out is how to code it. In object-oriented programming, an application consists of objects that are made up of methods and attributes. After putting together the object model, you next must detail each step of the general-use cases detailed in the analysis documentation. By going into deep detail on the use cases, you can visualize the things each object does and the data it requires to support that behavior. As you did with the general-use cases, you provide simple English sentences that describe what happens. The general-use case, "The user requests a prediction for two teams," can be divided into the following detailed scenario:

1. The user executes the program with the two teams as arguments.
2. The prediction object creates a team instance for each of the teams.
3. The prediction object requests relevant statistics from each team instance.
4. The prediction object calculates an outcome.
5. The prediction object displays the results to the user.

From this detailed-use case, you can see that the team object requires methods for retrieving statistics and the prediction object requires methods to instantiate team objects and predict games.

The final important section of a design document is a list of objects with their attributes and methods, called the *object specification*. Figure 29.3 shows the object specification for the Team object in the football predictor.

Into Development and Beyond

The final stages of the software engineering process form the traditional bulk of where work is done. During *development*, you write the code that becomes the system. As you complete each module or subsystem, you *test* it to make sure that it works. For the purposes of this chapter, testing is simply making sure that each subsystem does exactly what your design documents say it should do. In a very formal environment, however, the testing process is a very complex subject about which entire books have been written.

Once the application has been thoroughly tested and you know it does everything it is supposed to do, you release the code to the people who will actually use it. Using Java's ability to create zero-install applications, however, the time you spend in the *implementation* stage is greatly reduced. You make the classes available over the Internet or intranet and let people run the application. The rest of implementation stage is spent gathering feedback on how the application performs in the real world so that you can prepare and manage the maintenance stage.

After you first release a product, chances are you will want to enhance it and fix any bugs you didn't catch in testing. Perhaps you may even want to reengineer portions of it as your development experience grows. The final phase of software development, *maintenance*, is about doing just that. Of course, the creation of a new release is a full exercise in software development in itself. Maintenance thus brings you full circle back into the analysis stage of software development.

FIGURE 29.3.

The object specification for a Team *object.*

Team

Description

> The Team class represents a given football team. It is responsible for tracking its statistics and managing information received from recently completed games. In addition, it has a TeamFile object which it uses to save its statistics.

Attributes

Attribute Name	Data Type	Description
name	String	The name of the team.
wins	int	The number of wins to-date.
losses	int	The number of losses to-date.
points_for	int	The number of points scored by the team this season.
points_against	Int	The number of points scored by opponents against the team this season.
file	TeamFile	The TeamFile object managing the saving and restoring of team data.

Methods/Events

Method Name	Return Type	Parameters	Description
addGame	void	int points_scored, int points_allows	This method adds a new game to the Team's list of game stats.
getStat	int	String stat	Returns the number of wins, losses, points for, or points against depending on the stat requested.

29

Documenting Code

The documentation created in the analysis and design phases comprises the prescriptive documentation you need to build an application. During the iterative process of systems development, however, you will encounter issues that you simply missed in analysis and design. You therefore need a way to communicate to others exactly how your system was built.

Developers commonly write their descriptive documentation from memory after an application is built. They then fail to maintain the documentation along with the application. For someone trying to make a change to an application that has poorly maintained documentation, no documentation is almost as good as what he or she has to work with. Fortunately, Java provides the javadoc utility for documenting your code as you write it.

The javadoc Utility

The javadoc utility is a small Java program that comes with the JDK to help you create object documentation straight from your code. javadoc uses a combination of compiler information and comments made by you to build HTML documentation that describes everything about a Java object. As long as you maintain your comments with your code, your application documentation always reflects the current state of its objects when you use the javadoc utility.

If you have visited the JavaSoft API documentation pages at http://java.sun.com/products/JDK/CurrentRelease/api/, you have seen the kind of descriptive documentation produced by javadoc. To produce HTML pages that properly document your objects, you must include the following in each object source file:

- A description of the object
- A description of all public, protected, or private protected attributes
- A description of all public, protected, or private protected methods

Each description appears in Java code as a comment just before the element it is describing. To mark the comment as a javadoc comment, it must be in this format:

```
/** description */
```

Listing 29.1 shows what the Team class source code looks like.

Listing 29.1. The Team class source file, with javadoc comments.

```
/**
 * The Team class has statistics and receives updates from users.
 * It represents one football team and maintains the statistics for
 * that team.
 * @version 1.0
 * @author George Reese
 */
public class Team {
  private TeamFile file;
  private int wins, losses, points_for, points_against;
  /**
   * Constructs a new Team object based on a team name.
   * Specifically, it creates a TeamFile object to access
   * The file in which team data is stored.  It then uses
   * the file object to get all of the team's stats
   * from storage.
   * @exception FileException caused by a failure to read storage file
```

```
   * @param name the name of the team
   * @see TeamFile#getField
   */
  public Team(String name) {
    file = new TeamFile(name);
    wins = f.getField("wins");
    losses = f.getField("losses");
    points_for = f.getField("points_for");
    points_against = f.getField("points_against");
  }
  /**
   * Adds the statistics for a recently completed game.
   * In this release, we are ignoring ties.
   * @exception FileException thrown by a failed attempt to save the file
   * @param pf the points this team scored in the game
   * @param pa the points scored by the opponent
   * @see TeamFile#setField
   * @see TeamFile#save
   */
  public void addGame(int pf, int pa) {
    if( pf > pa ) wins++;
    else if( pa > pf ) losses++;
    points_for += pf;
    points_against += pa;
    file.setField("wins", wins);
    file.setField("losses", losses);
    file.setField("points_for", points_for);
    file.setField("points_against");
    file.save();
  }
  /**
   * Allows the Prediction class to get team statistics
   * for this team.
   * @exception NoSuchStatException thrown if a bad stat is requested
   * @param stat the desired stat
   * @return the value for the requested stat
   */
  protected int getStat(String stat) {
    if( stat.equals("wins") ) {
      return wins;
    }
    else if( stat.equals("losses") ) {
      return losses;
    }
    else if( stat.equals("points_for") ) {
      return points_for;
    }
    else if( stat.equals("points_against") ) {
      return points_against;
    }
    throw new NoSuchStatException(stat);
  }
}
```

Ideally, you should be commenting your code to this degree anyway. Why not have those comments help you get your documentation done?

You may have noticed some fields in the comments beginning with an @ symbol. The javadoc utility enables you to pass certain information using these @ keywords. In the Team class example, I used @version, @author, @exception, @param, @return, and @see to tell javadoc about the class version, class author, method exceptions, method parameters, method return values, and other references.

Table 29.1 lists all the keywords you can use in your javadoc comments, along with their meanings.

Table 29.1. Keywords used by javadoc.

Keyword	Description
@author	Used in class comments. Identifies who wrote the class. You can have multiple @author tags for a class.
@exception	Used in method comments. Identifies the full class name for any exceptions thrown by the method. You can have multiple @exception tags for a method.
@param	Used in method comments. Identifies a method parameter. You should specify as many of these as the method has parameters.
@return	Used in method comments. Describes what the method will return.
@see	Used in any comment type. Allows you to reference other classes, attributes, and methods with a hypertext link.
@version	Used in class comments. Identifies the version number for this class.

Among the advantages of this style of documentation is that you can embed HTML tags inside any comments that will appear in your final HTML documentation. You can even go so far as to embed applets inside your applet documentation! More importantly, this kind of documentation enables you to create links to related documentation that is beyond the ability of the @see keyword to handle. The only limitation is that you cannot embed an <HR> or <H1> through <H6> HTML tag inside a comment. Although doing so does not generate an error, it may produce unexpected results in your output documentation.

Once your source files are complete—both in terms of code and commenting—you are ready to build the documentation for the application. To do this, simply execute the javadoc command with the class file as an argument. The javadoc command creates five output HTML files with documentation for your class. The generated files are listed here:

Filename	Description
YourClassName.html	Detailed documentation for your class.
Package-YourPackageName.html	For each package, one of these files is created listing all the classes in that package.

Filename	Description
AllNames.html	A list of attributes and methods for all classes (in this case, just one class) in alphabetical order.
packages.html	A list of all packages in your application.
tree.html	A list of all classes shown as an inheritance tree.

Of course, you probably want to document more than one class at a time, and you probably do not want that documentation stuck in the same directory as your source code. The javadoc command accepts a host of options so that you can customize your documentation to your needs. Before you worry about those options, however, you should understand what Java does count on. It expects a directory tree that ships with the JDK, containing stock graphics as well as the Java API documentation (javadoc produces documentation that contains appropriate links to Java API documentation).

Managing links to existing documentation is one place in which javadoc gets a little messy. Unfortunately, javadoc likes to pile all your documentation into one huge directory. Additionally, javadoc is not smart enough to determine any class dependencies on its own. If you are generating documentation for classes with dependencies, you must tell javadoc so that it regenerates any old documentation. Finally, the HTML files created by javadoc expect an images subdirectory under the directory in which they are located. You can generally take care of this problem by creating a link to the images directory that came with the JDK.

On the command line, javadoc can take one of two forms:

- javadoc [*options*] *file*
- javadoc [*options*] *package*

You can customize javadoc output with the options listed in Table 29.2.

Table 29.2. Options for use with javadoc.

Option	Comment
-author	If there are @author tags in the comments, list them in the documentation.
-authors	Same as the -author option.
-classpath *path list*	Manually sets the classpath for finding source code. Remember that your CLASSPATH environment variable is generally set to where your .class files are located, so you almost always have to specify this option.
-d *directory*	The directory in which the generated documentation should be placed.

continues

Table 29.2. continued

Option	Comment
-depend *package list*	A list of dependencies for the package being documented.
-version	As with the @author tag, you must specify that version information should be included in the documentation.
-verbose	Print information about the progress of javadoc as it is generating documentation.

Summary

Although generating documentation may not be the most enjoyable part of software development, it is a necessity. Successful applications built in a timely fashion with small maintenance requirements invariably are well-documented applications flowing from a proven engineering methodology. The analysis and design stages of development provide you with prescriptive documentation that tells you exactly what has to be built before you build it. In the development stage, you can use the javadoc utility to create up-to-date descriptive documentation that helps people maintain and modify your code down the road—even if you are the one doing the maintenance and modification.

Optimizing Java Code

by Michael Morrison

IN THIS CHAPTER

Even with all Java's power and wonder, few people can argue the primary drawback to Java as a development platform: execution speed. It's certainly true that the execution speed of Java programs has improved dramatically with the advent of just-in-time (JIT) compilers, but there is still room for improvement. Rather than wait around for faster JIT compilers or enhanced Java virtual machines, you can empower yourself by taking control of your Java code and the speed at which it executes.

This chapter looks at Java code optimization and how you can improve the performance of your Java programs. In this chapter, you learn various optimization techniques that can help you become a more efficient Java programmer. To really understand how these optimization techniques help, you have to go under the hood of Java a little. However, I think you'll find that Java code optimization isn't all that difficult. So roll up your sleeves and prepare to get a little dirty.

What Is Code Optimization?

Code optimization is the process of modifying working code to a more optimal state based on a particular goal. The fact that optimization takes place on *working code* is an important point; always perform optimizations on code after you get the code working. Also make sure that you retest the code after validating your optimizations. The type of optimization performed depends on the desired goal; code optimization can be divided into three distinct types, which are based on the needs of the developer:

- Maintainability
- Size
- Speed

Based on this list, you probably realize now that code optimization isn't just about improving performance; speed optimization is simply one type of optimization. Nevertheless, it is usually the most important type of optimization to consider when dealing with Java code.

Maintainability Optimization

Maintainability optimization is performed to help make code more manageable in the future. This type of optimization is usually geared toward the structure and organization of code rather than modifications to the algorithms used in the code. In general, maintainability optimization involves a programmer's studying the code at large and making changes to help other programmers understand and modify the code in the future.

Fortunately, the rigid structure of the Java language goes a long way toward keeping things optimized for maintainability. In fact, if you adhere to basic object-oriented design principles, you really don't need to do anything else to keep your code optimized for maintainability.

Size Optimization

Another popular optimization is size optimization, which involves making changes to code that result in a smaller executable class file. The cornerstone of size optimization is code reuse, which comes in the form of inheritance for Java classes. Fortunately, good object-oriented design strategies naturally favor size optimization, so you rarely have to go out of your way to perform this type of optimization. For example, it's simply good design practice to put code that is reused more than once into a method. In this way, most size optimizations naturally take place during the initial code development.

Although it's not typically a huge issue, size optimization can't be completely ignored in Java programming. This is because the size of your compiled Java classes directly impacts the amount of time it takes your program to load and initially execute—especially over an Internet connection. If you leverage as much of the standard Java API code as possible and reuse code by deriving from other classes, you're probably doing enough for the cause of reducing class size.

Speed Optimization

Speed optimization is without a doubt the most important type of optimization when it comes to Java programming. Speed optimization includes all the techniques and tricks used to speed up the execution of code. Considering the performance problems inherent in Java, speed optimization takes on an even more important role in Java than it does in other languages such as C and C++. Because the Java compiler has the last word on how code is generated, most speed optimizations are performed with the compiler in mind.

The rest of this chapter focuses on issues of speed optimization and how to get the best performance out of your Java code. At times, you will sacrifice the other types of optimization for the sake of speed. In most cases, this sacrifice is entirely acceptable—even expected—because the organization of the code and size of the executable classes won't matter much if your programs are too slow to be useable.

Optimizing with the JDK Compiler

All optimizations begin and end with the Java compiler. If you don't understand the compiler, you're largely guessing at which optimizations will have a positive effect on your code. So let's take a look at the JDK compiler and see what role it plays in turning out speedy Java bytecodes. Bytecodes comprise the intermediate processor-independent code generated by the Java compiler. Bytecode executables (classes) are interpreted by the Java runtime system.

> **NOTE**
>
> Third-party Java compilers are being released that outclass the JDK compiler in regard to speed optimization. Nevertheless, the JDK compiler is the standard Java compiler and is currently the most reliable.

The JDK compiler (javac) includes a switch for generating optimized Java bytecode executables: -O. In the JDK version 1.1, this switch results in only two optimizations taking place: inline methods and exclusion of line numbers. The first of these optimizations is the only one that affects the speed of the executable bytecode; final, static, and private methods are inlined by the compiler, resulting in less method call overhead. *Method inlining* is the process of replacing each call to a method with the actual method code. Inlining can often increase the size of the resulting class file, but it can help improve performance.

The second optimization performed by the JDK compiler results in the exclusion of line number information from the executable class file. This is a size optimization and does nothing in terms of helping speed up the code. However, it does have the side benefit of making the executable class files a little smaller, which improves the download time of Java applets.

The truth is that the JDK compiler does little for you in regard to optimization. This means that you have to plan on doing a lot of optimization by hand. Although this may sound like a lot of responsibility, keep in mind that any insight you have into the efficiency of your code will ultimately pay off regardless of how good the compiler is. In other words, knowing how to optimize code by hand is an extremely valuable skill.

Understanding the Costs of Common Operations

Now that you understand what the JDK compiler does (or doesn't do) for you in regard to optimization, it's time to focus on the Java runtime system. By examining the runtime system, you can get an idea of how fast certain types of code run and make smarter decisions about the way you write Java code. What do I mean by *examining the runtime system*? Well, I mean running different types of code and timing each type to see how the speeds match up. This operation gives you a very realistic look at how code differs in terms of execution speed, and consequently gives you a place to start making appropriate code optimizations.

The speed of an operation is often referred to as the *cost* of the operation. Code optimization can almost be likened to accounting, in which you try to keep from blowing a performance budget with your code costs. Jonathan Hardwick developed a neat benchmark applet, called the Java Microbenchmark applet, for determining how long common Java operations take to execute. Tables 30.1 through 30.3 contain the results of running the Microbenchmark applet on my system with the JDK 1.1 applet viewer. These tables contain approximate times in microseconds for common Java operations. Incidentally, the system used to perform the cost analysis was a Pentium 100 running Windows 95. You can try the Microbenchmark applet yourself by visiting its Web site at www.cs.cmu.edu/~jch/java/microbench.html.

Table 30.1. The costs of Java variable accesses (speeds measured in microseconds).

Description	Operation	Cost
Method variable assignment	`i = 1;`	0.14
Instance variable assignment	`this.i = 1;`	0.19
Array element assignment	`a[0] = 1;`	0.29

Table 30.2. The costs of increment with Java data types.

Description	Operation	Cost
Byte variable increment	`byte b++;`	0.28
Short variable increment	`short s++;`	0.28
Int variable increment	`int i++;`	0.11
Long variable increment	`long l++;`	0.30
Float variable increment	`float f++;`	0.34
Double variable increment	`double d++;`	0.53

Table 30.3. The costs of miscellaneous Java operations.

Description	Operation	Cost
Object creation	`new Object();`	6.6
Method invocation	`null_func();`	0.79
Synchronized method	`sync_func();`	5.8
Math function	`Math.abs(x);`	3.2
Equivalent math code	`(x < 0) ? -x : x;`	0.17

30

OPTIMIZING JAVA CODE

These tables point out lots of interesting information regarding the performance of Java code. From Table 30.1, it's apparent that method variables are a little more efficient to use than instance variables. Furthermore, you can see that array element assignment is slower than method variable assignment because Java performs bounds checking operations whenever an array element is accessed. Keep in mind that this table isn't meant as an argument to get rid of all your class member data. Rather, think of it as providing insight into making decisions where the design could go either way.

Table 30.2 shows timing data related to the use of the standard Java data types. As you may have expected, the two 32-bit data types (int and float) showed the best performance because the tests were performed on a 32-bit system.

Even though the floating-point types show comparable performance to the integer types, don't be misled about using integer math over floating-point math. This timing table reflects only an increment operation, which is much different than more complex operations performed in the context of a practical Java program. Integer math is much more efficient than floating-point math. So use the table as a measure of the relative speeds among integer types, and then try to use integer math throughout your code.

Table 30.3 focuses on a few miscellaneous operations that are worth thinking about. First off, it shows the high cost of creating an object. This should serve as an incentive to eliminate the creation of temporary objects within a loop where the creation occurs over and over. Rather, you can place the temporary object above the loop and reinitialize its members as needed inside the loop.

Table 30.3 also shows the dramatic performance costs of using a normal method versus a synchronized method. Even though synchronization is very important in multithreaded programming, Table 30.3 should be some encouragement to minimize the usage of synchronized methods in situations where you're in a performance squeeze.

Finally, Table 30.3 shows you how using the standard Java math methods can sometimes be a burden. Even something as simple as taking the absolute value of a number imposes much greater performance costs when you call the Math.abs() method, as opposed to inlining the equivalent code yourself.

> **NOTE**
>
> It's worth noting that the performance of Java code in Java 1.1 has improved considerably over that of Java version 1.02. Various changes were made within the Java runtime system to improve the overall performance of Java code. For example, the Java 1.1 runtime system automatically discards unused classes, which enables it to operate more efficiently and with less memory.

Isolating Sluggish Code

The biggest mistake you can make in regard to optimizing your Java code is trying to optimize *all* the code. Being smart about what code you attack is crucial in not spending years trying to improve the performance of your code. More important, it's a well-established fact that a relatively small portion of code is usually responsible for the bulk of the performance drain. It's your job to isolate this code and then focus your optimization efforts accordingly.

Fortunately, isolating problem code isn't all that difficult if you use the proper tools. The most useful tool in finding bottlenecks in your code is a profiler. A profiler's job is to report the amount of time spent in each section of code as a program is executing. The Java runtime interpreter has an undocumented built-in profiler that is easy to use and works pretty well. To use the runtime interpreter profiler, simply specify the -prof option when using the interpreter, like this:

```
java -prof Classname
```

`Classname` is the name of the class you want to profile. Of course, this technique doesn't work too well for applets, because they must be run within the context of the applet viewer tool or a Web browser. Fortunately, you can use the profiler with applets by altering the arguments to the interpreter a little, like this:

```
java -prof sun.applet.AppletViewer Filename
```

In this case, `Filename` is the name of the HTML file containing a link to your applet. When you finish running the applet, the interpreter writes a file named java.prof to the current directory. This file contains profile information for the applet you just ran. The information consists of a list of methods sorted according to how many times each method is called over the course of the program. The methods are listed in order of decreasing method calls, meaning that the first method in the list is called more than any other method.

You can easily use this information as a guide to determine the code on which to focus your optimization efforts. The methods appearing at the top of the java.prof file should receive more of your attention because they are being called much more than methods farther down in the list. Making small performance gains in a method called 20,000 times has a much greater impact than speeding up a method that is called only a couple hundred times. The cool thing is that you can try different optimizations and then run the profiler again to see whether the relative times have changed. This is a very practical (if somewhat time-consuming) way to make great strides in speeding up your code.

Implementing Optimization Strategies

Now that you've isolated the code that is making your program crawl, it's time to look into exactly what optimizations you can perform to speed things up. You won't always be able to optimize every piece of problem code; the goal is to make big dents in the areas that can be optimized.

Rethink Algorithms

Many C/C++ programmers have traditionally resorted to assembler language when the issue of performance is raised. As a Java programmer, you don't have this option. This is actually a good thing because it forces you to take a closer look at your design approach instead of relying on heavier processor dependence to solve your problems. What the assembly heads don't realize is that much more significant gains can be made by entirely rethinking an algorithm than by porting it to assembly. And trust me, the amount of time spent hand-coding tedious assembly can easily result in a leaner, more efficient algorithm.

This same ideology applies to Java programming. Before you run off writing native methods and expanding loops to get every little ounce of performance (which you learn about in the next section), take a step back and see whether the algorithm itself has any weaknesses. To put this all into perspective, imagine if programmers had always resorted to optimizing the traditional bubble sort algorithm and had never thought twice about the algorithm itself. The quick sort algorithm, which is orders of magnitude faster than the bubble sort without any optimization, would never have come about.

Use Native Methods

I hate to recommend them, but the truth is that *native methods* (methods written in C or C++ that can be called from Java code) are typically much faster than Java methods. The reason I'm reluctant to promote their use is that they blow the platform-independence benefit of using Java, therefore tying your program to a particular platform. Additionally, you can't use native methods in applets, because native code imposes all kinds of security problems. If platform independence isn't high on your list and you aren't developing an applet, however, by all means look into rewriting problem methods in C. You learn how to connect Java to C code in Chapter 32, "Integrating Native Code with the Native Method Interface."

Use Inline Methods

Inline methods, whose bodies appear in place of each method call, are a fairly effective way of improving performance. Because the Java compiler already inlines `final`, `static`, and `private` methods when you have the optimization switch turned on, your best bet is to try to make as many methods as possible `final`, `static`, or `private`. If this isn't possible and you still want the benefits of inlined code, you can always inline methods by hand: Just paste the body of the method at each place where it is called. This is one of those cases in which you are sacrificing both maintainability and size for speed. (The things we do for speed!)

Replace Slow Java API Classes and Methods

There may be times when you are using a standard Java API class for a few of its features, but the extra baggage imposed by the generic design of the class is slowing you down. In situations like this, you may be better off writing your own class that performs the exact functionality you need and no more. This streamlined approach can pay off big, even though it comes at the cost of rewriting code that already works.

Another similar situation occurs when you are using a Java API class and you isolate a particular method in it that is dragging down performance. In this situation, instead of rewriting the entire class, just derive from it and override the troublesome method. This is a good middle-of-the-road solution because you leverage code reuse against performance in a reasonable manner.

Use Look-Up Tables

An established trick up the sleeve of every programmer who has wrestled with floating-point performance problems is the look-up table. *Look-up tables* are tables of constant integer values that are used in place of time-consuming calculations. For example, a very popular type of look-up table is one containing values for trigonometric functions, such as sine. The use of trigonometric functions is sometimes unavoidable in certain types of programs. If you haven't noticed, Java's trigonometric functions are all floating-point in nature, which is a bad thing in terms of performance. The solution is to write an integer version of the desired function using a look-up table of values. This relatively simple change is sometimes a necessity considering the performance hit you take by using floating-point math.

Eliminate Unnecessary Evaluations

Moving along into more detailed optimizations, you can often find unnecessary evaluations in your code that serve only to eat up extra processor time. Following is an example of some code that unnecessarily performs an evaluation that acts effectively as a constant:

```java
for (int i = 0; i < size(); i++)
  a = (b + c) / i;
```

The addition of b + c, although itself a pretty efficient piece of code, is being calculated each time through the loop. It is better off being calculated before the loop, like this:

```java
int tmp = b + c;
for (int i = 0; i < size(); i++)
  a = tmp / i;
```

This simple change can have fairly dramatic effects, depending on how many times the loop is iterated. Speaking of the loop, there's another optimization you might have missed. Notice that size() is a method call, which should bring to mind the costs involved in calling a method (you learned about this performance drag earlier in the chapter). You may not realize it, but size() is called every time through the loop as part of the conditional loop expression. The same technique used to eliminate the unnecessary addition operation can be used to fix this problem. Check out the resulting code:

```java
int s = size;
int tmp = b + c;
for (int i = 0; i < s; i++)
  a = tmp / i;
```

30

OPTIMIZING JAVA CODE

Eliminate Common Subexpressions

Sometimes, you may be reusing a costly subexpression without even realizing it. In the heat of programming, it's easy to reuse common subexpressions instead of storing them in a temporary variable, like this:

```
b = Math.abs(a) * c;
d = e / (Math.abs(a) + b);
```

The multiple calls to `Math.abs()` are costly compared to calling it once and using a temporary variable, like this:

```
int tmp = Math.abs(a);
b = tmp * c;
d = e / (tmp + b);
```

Expand Loops

One optimization that is popular among C/C++ programmers is loop expansion, or loop unrolling, which is the process of expanding a loop to get rid of the overhead involved in maintaining the loop. You may be wondering exactly what overhead I'm talking about. Well, even a simple counting loop has the overhead of performing a comparison and an increment each time through. This may not seem like much, but when you consider that some code is called thousands of times in a program, it's easy to see how small changes can sometimes yield big results.

Loop expansion basically involves replacing a loop with the brute-force equivalent. To better understand this process, consider the following piece of code:

```
for (int i = 0; i < 1000; i++)
  a[i] = 25;
```

That probably looks like some pretty efficient code and, in fact, it is. But if you want to go the extra distance and perform a loop expansion on it, here's one approach:

```
int i = 0;
for (int j = 0; j < 100; j++) {
  a[i++] = 25;
  a[i++] = 25;
  a[i++] = 25;
  a[i++] = 25;
  a[i++] = 25;
  a[i++] = 25;
  a[i++] = 25;
  a[i++] = 25;
  a[i++] = 25;
  a[i++] = 25;
}
```

In this code, you've reduced the loop overhead by an order of magnitude, but you've introduced some new overhead by having to increment the new index variable inside the loop. Overall, this code does outperform the original code, but don't expect any miracles. Loop expansion can be effective at times, but I don't recommend placing it too high on your list of optimization tricks.

Avoid the String Concatenation Operator

Although it may look innocent, the string concatenation operator (+) is actually quite costly in terms of performance. It is costly because it results in a call to `String.append()`, which copies the two strings being concatenated into a string buffer using `System.arrayCopy()` and returns the result with a call to `StringBuffer.toString()`. This sluggish overhead can be eliminated by working with a single string buffer to begin with.

Summary

This chapter covered a somewhat murky area of Java programming: code optimization. You began by learning about the fundamental types of optimization, including the most popular type of Java optimization: speed optimization. You then learned about the optimizations (or lack thereof) provided by the JDK compiler. From there, you got a little dose of realism by looking into the timing costs of common Java operations. You finished the chapter by taking an in-depth look at some practical code optimizations you can apply to your own Java programs.

This chapter rounds out Part VI of this book, "Programming Strategies." Armed with these strategies, you're no doubt ready to press on into Part VII, "Advanced Java." In Part VII, you learn about all kinds of advanced Java programming issues including persistence, security, and reflection, among other things.

30

OPTIMIZING JAVA CODE

IN THIS PART

VII

PART

Advanced Java

Persistence and Java Serialization

by Jim Mathis

IN THIS CHAPTER

CHAPTER 31

Your Java programs create and process various pieces of data or information. Some information is temporary, such as the visual elements of the AWT display; other pieces of information have meaning well beyond the execution lifetime of your program. In a traditional system, such permanent information is stored in files or databases; various conventions such as file types and extensions are used to identify the format of the data or the programs that can process the data. This model perpetuates the structured programming view of the separation of code and data.

In object-oriented languages such as Java, data and code are tightly bound together so that one does not exist without the other. To support permanent information in an object-oriented manner, you require a scheme to preserve the qualities of an object-oriented language when the object instances are temporarily written to a file and later restored. *Persistence* in an object-oriented programming language deals with the capability of objects to exist beyond the lifetime of the program that created them.

In this chapter, you learn about object persistence in general; more specifically, you learn how to make objects persistent using the new facilities provided in Java Development Kit version 1.1—the `Serialization` and `Externalization` interface classes. You indirectly use serialization in the Remote Method Invocation package, covered in Chapters 17, "The RMI Package," and 54, "Remote Objects and the Java IDL System," and in JavaBeans components, covered in Chapters 38 through 41.

Introducing Object Persistence

Persistence describes something that exists beyond its expected lifetime or that lasts after program completion (for example, a network drive-letter assignment). As applied to an object-oriented programming language, persistence describes objects that exist beyond the scope, in terms of time or location, of the original program that created the objects. You can store a persistent object in a file for later use or transmit a persistent object to another machine.

To provide persistence, you need the following:

- A way of converting the in-memory layout of objects into a serial, byte-stream form suitable for storage or for Internet transmission.
- A way of creating an object from the serial form that preserves the object-oriented properties of the programming language and produces an object identical to the original.
- A mechanism to trigger saving or restoring this object state, either automatically or on command.

Extending an Object's Lifetime

Java objects have a *lifetime*. An object begins its life when it is created by the new operator (for example, new String("hi")). After it is created, the object exists until it is destroyed by the Java virtual machine's garbage collector. (An object can be garbage collected only when the Java program no longer holds a reference to the object.)

To understand your need for persistent objects, consider an AddressBook class that contains names and addresses. You enter information into an address book so that it is available when you need it at a later date. If you use an AddressBook class to represent a real address book, you find that it does not support the "save it now, use it later" paradigm. All instances of the AddressBook class are destroyed when the Java program ends. To be useful, your AddressBook objects must exist for an extended period of time; they must be *persistent*.

Persistence is usually implemented by preserving the state (attributes) of an object between executions of the program. To preserve the state, the object is converted to a sequence of bytes (that is, it is serialized) and put on some kind of long-term storage media (usually a disk). When the object is needed again, it is restored from the long-term media; the restoration process creates a new Java object identical to the original. Although the restored object is not "the same object," its state and behavior are identical.

Persistence is different from the load() and save() behavior of the Properties class. In the Properties class, the data is limited to being a string, and only the contents of the strings are stored. Any subclass of Properties can load data stored by any other, possibly incompatible, subclass of Properties; no object attributes are stored. With persistence, all object attributes (such as the class name, field names, and access modifiers) are associated with the stored data so that accidentally restoring the data to the wrong type of object is prevented. Generally, objects are restored as exactly the same class they were before they were saved; however, interoperability between different versions of the same class can be supported.

What Does JDK 1.1 Support?

Java supports object persistence by providing standard mechanisms for the encoding and decoding of objects from their in-memory form to a byte-stream format. No longer is object persistence a task each programmer must independently implement for himself or herself. JDK 1.1 adds the following persistence-related classes for you to use:

Class	*Description*
ObjectOutputStream	Use this output stream to convert objects from the in-memory form to serial form. This stream implements the ObjectOutput interface.
ObjectInputStream	Use this input stream to restore objects from the serial form. This stream implements the ObjectInput interface.

continues

Class	Description
Serializable	Implement this interface to indicate that the class can be converted to a serial form and to define methods that can be overridden to control the encoding of the class.
Externalizable	Implement this subclass of Serializable to define methods that provide complete control over the encoding process of the object.
ObjectInputValidation	Use this callback interface to validate the decoding of an object.

The JDK 1.1 provides facilities for the versioning of class implementations while preserving the strong type-checking and type-safe casting provided by Java. It is inevitable that the implementation of a particular class will evolve over time; you may have to add methods or fields, or implement additional interfaces, to support new versions of the JDK or to add functionality to your classes. It is unacceptable to lose stored objects whenever you make any change to the class definition. Java provides a form of interoperation between different versions of the same class as long as you follow some simple rules in creating the new version of an existing class. Versioning is covered in more detail in "Supporting Class Versioning," later in this chapter.

In the next section, you learn how to use these classes to make objects persistent.

Using Java Object Serialization

The JDK 1.1 uses a manually controlled object persistence scheme; the storage and retrieval of persistent Java objects is completely under your control. To make an object persistent, you create an ObjectOutputStream and serialize the object by calling writeObject(). You specify where the output of the ObjectOutputStream, and hence the object, are sent. Wrap the ObjectOutputStream around a FileOutputStream, and you write the state of the object to a file as shown in the following code:

```
FileOutputStream fout = new FileOutputStream(filename);
ObjectOutputStream out = new ObjectOutputStream(fout);
out.writeObject(obj);
```

Wrap the ObjectOutputStream around an OutputStream retrieved from a socket (using getOutputStream()), and you transfer the state of the object (but not the code) across the Internet to another machine as shown here:

```
Socket s = new Socket(remotehost, remoteport);
ObjectOutputStream out = new ObjectOutputStream(s.getOutputStream());
out.writeObject(obj);
```

Wrap the ObjectOutputStream around a ByteArrayOutputStream, and you can access the encoded form of the object for storage in a database or for other processing using the following code:

Persistence and Java Serialization

CHAPTER 31

747

31

**PERSISTENCE
AND JAVA
SERIALIZATION**

```
ByteArrayOutputStream bout = new ByteArrayOutputStream();
ObjectOutputStream out = new ObjectOutputStream(bout);
out.writeObject(obj);
Byte barray[] = bout.toByteArray();
```

Conversely, to restore an object, you create an `ObjectInputStream` and call `readObject()`. You wrap `ObjectInputStream` around various types of input streams in a way similar to what you did with the `ObjectOutputStream` and the various types of output streams. The next object in the stream is reconstituted and returned from the `readObject()` call. Because the returned type of `readObject()` is `Object`, you usually want to cast the returned object to another type. Java's type-safe casting ensures that you do not cast the object to an incorrect type. You can also use `instanceof` or methods in the object reflection package to determine the type of received objects.

The next section provides a more detailed description of the serialization API.

The Serialization API

Table 31.1 describes the constructor and commonly used methods for the `ObjectOutputStream` class; Table 31.2 describes the constructor and commonly used methods for the `ObjectInputStream` class. Because these streams also implement the `DataOutput` or `DataInput` interface (as appropriate), methods are provided for writing Java data types to the stream in a standard, machine-independent format. Note that a few of the methods can be called only while the stream is actively encoding or decoding an object; these methods are covered in more detail in "Making Your Objects Persistent," later in this chapter.

Table 31.1. Commonly used `ObjectOutputStream` constructor and methods.

Constructor/Method	Description
`ObjectOutputStream(OutputStream)`	Creates an `ObjectOutputStream` that writes the serialized object to the indicated `OutputStream`.
`writeObject(Object)`	Serializes and writes the object to the `OutputStream`.
`close()`	Closes the stream.
`flush()`	Flushes the stream, forcing a write of any buffered data to the underlying `OutputStream`.
`reset()`	Resets the encoding state of the `ObjectOutputStream`, effectively discarding any objects already written to the stream, although the data has already been written.
`writeInt(int)`	Writes a 32-bit `int` to the stream.
`writeUTF(String)`	Writes a `String` to the stream in UTF format.

continues

Table 31.1. continued

Constructor/Method	Description
defaultWriteObject()	Writes the nonstatic and nontransient fields of the current class to this stream using the default encoding format. You can call this method only from the writeObject() method of the class being encoded.

Table 31.2. Commonly used ObjectInputStream constructor and methods.

Constructor/Method	Description
ObjectInputStream(InputStream)	Creates an ObjectInputStream that reads from the specified InputStream.
readObject()	Reads an object from the input stream; is the opposite of writeObject().
close()	Closes the input stream.
available()	Returns the number of bytes that can be read without blocking.
readInt()	Reads a 32-bit int from the stream.
readUTF()	Reads a UTF-formatted String from the stream.
defaultReadObject()	Reads the nonstatic and nontransient fields of the current class from the stream, ensuring the standard encoding format. You can call this method only from the readObject() method of the class being decoded.
registerValidation (ObjectInputValidation, int)	Registers a handler to validate the restored object. You can call this method only while a class is being decoded, as described in "Validating the Restored Object," later in this chapter. The int specifies a relative callback priority; typically, you just specify a priority of zero.

The Serializable interface defines no methods but is an indication that the class is compatible with serialization and may have private readObject() and writeObject() methods to control serialization.

Only the data in the objects and the declarations of the classes are encoded in the byte stream; the Java virtual machine bytecodes that implement the methods of the classes are not stored

Persistence and Java Serialization
CHAPTER 31

749

31

PERSISTENCE
AND JAVA
SERIALIZATION

when an object is serialized. When an object is retrieved from the stream, the class declaration is read and the normal class-loading mechanisms (for example, searching through the CLASSPATH) are used to load the code. If a matching class is not found, readObject() throws ClassNotFoundException. The JDK support for persistence does not deal with the issues of code distribution (which must be addressed if you are going to build Java agents that can migrate from machine to machine).

Object References

One complication of serializing an object is the correct handling of other referenced objects. When you store an object or send it across the Internet, the object must include a copy of all the objects it references, all the objects those objects reference, and so on. The object has to include all these other objects because all these objects are part of the total state of the one object you explicitly serialized. Serializing an object that has many object references produces a larger-than-expected serialization output. Saving an apparently simple object, such as a button, may entail many kilobytes of data.

Listing 31.1 is a very simple program that creates a frame with a button. You can find the chapter31.ex1 program on the CD-ROM that accompanies this book. The classes in this program, like many classes in JDK 1.1, are already designed to be persistent. After creating the frame, you serialize the button first without an event listener (lines 25 through 29) and then with a frame as the registered action event listener (lines 31 through 36). Just the button, without an action listener, requires approximately 1,064 bytes to serialize; add the application frame as an action listener (which is a common practice in the new JDK 1.1 event model), and the size more than doubles to approximately 2,609 bytes. Because of object references, serializing the button results in serializing the complete application.

> **NOTE**
>
> The writeObject() method does not explicitly synchronize on the object being serialized. If you have multiple threads using the same object, and one thread can possibly be serializing an object while another thread is manipulating fields of the same object, you must take steps to be thread safe: You can either add explicit synchronization code or make a clone of the object before serialization.

Listing 31.1. chapter31.ex1: Serializing a button.

```
01    import java.awt.*;
02    import java.awt.event.*;
03    import java.io.*;
04
05
```

continues

Listing 31.1. continued

```
06    public class Ex1 extends Frame
07      implements ActionListener{
08      Button button;
09
10      public Ex1() {
11        super("Button Serialization Test");
12        setSize(300,200);
13        button = new Button("Push");
14        add(button);
15        setVisible(true);
16      }
17
18      public void actionPerformed(ActionEvent event) {
19      // perform indicated action
20      }
21
22      public static void main(String args[]) {
23        Ex1 test = new Ex1();
24        try {
25          ByteArrayOutputStream bout = new ByteArrayOutputStream();
26          ObjectOutputStream out = new ObjectOutputStream(bout);
27          out.writeObject(test.button);
28          System.out.println("Serializing just the button takes " +
29            bout.size() + " bytes");
30          // add action listener to button
31          test.button.addActionListener(test);
32          bout = new ByteArrayOutputStream();
33          out = new ObjectOutputStream(bout);
34          out.writeObject(test.button);
35          System.out.println("Serializing this button takes " +
36            bout.size() + " bytes");
37          out.writeObject(test);
38          System.out.println("Serializing the button and frame takes " +
39            bout.size() + " bytes");
40          System.exit(0);
41        }
42        catch (Exception e) {
43          e.printStackTrace(System.out);
44        }
45      }
46    }
```

You may have several objects that reference a single object, or you may have objects that reference each other. When these objects are serialized, you want only one copy of each unique object written. For example, in Listing 31.1, the button has a reference to the frame (its action listener), and the frame has a reference to the button. You do not want two copies of the button object in the serialized output. Or worse, you do not want an infinite loop that serializes the button which, in turn, serializes the frame which, in turn, serializes the button, and so on. This problem is solved by saving the contents of the object once and using object references inside an ObjectOutputStream. If you are interested, the section "Looking Inside Object Serialization," later in this chapter, covers the implementation details on how object references are handled.

Persistence and Java Serialization

CHAPTER 31

751

31

PERSISTENCE
AND JAVA
SERIALIZATION

Here's an example of how object references are encoded: In lines 37 through 39 of Listing 31.1, you can write the frame object to the same stream (without resetting the ObjectOutputStream state), and the resulting size increases by only 5 bytes. These 5 bytes are simply a reference to the frame object that is already encoded in the stream.

Making Your Objects Persistent

Although you can indirectly use object serialization by simply referencing JDK package objects (most are already serializable), or subclassing JDK package classes (a subclass of a serializable class is assumed to be serializable), you eventually have to deal directly with serialization issues when you create new classes. In the following sections, you learn how to make your classes persistent.

The Serializable and Externalizable Interfaces

A class implements Serializable or Externalizable to indicate whether or not the instances of the class can be serialized for persistence storage or for transmission over the Internet. A class that is not meaningful when removed from its execution environment and later restored does not implement either interface. Attempts to serialize this class, either directly or indirectly because of a reference from another object being serialized, throw NotSerializableException.

Suitability Tests

You test whether or not a class is suitable for persistence by considering what happens to the object if it is serialized and later restored. Generally, objects that are tied to system resources (such as process identifiers, file descriptors, network sockets, and so on) are not candidates for serialization. For example, if you serialize an open FileInputStream object, can you continue reading from the stream when the object is serialized and restored at a later time? Probably not, because the open file descriptor used by the underlying operating system is gone, and the file may even no longer exist. The FileInputStream object state includes information outside the defined instance variables and is not normally available for serialization. In this example, such external information includes the file system descriptors and the file contents.

You can attempt to save the external state of the FileInputStream by serializing the complete path name of the file, the date of last file modification, and the logical byte offset for the next read. You would throw an exception if the file was not found or had a different modification date when the FileInputStream object was restored. Such nonstandard serialization is covered in "Custom Serialization," later in this chapter. When you implement custom encoding, consider whether the semantic meaning of the class is preserved or whether you are attempting to serialize the wrong class.

In this example, instead of making the FileInputStream class persistent, we define a new class, FileIdentifier, that holds the filename, modification date, and other identifying information; this new class also has a method that creates a FileInputStream. This approach clearly indicates that the reference to the file is persistent and not the input stream. Similarly, in JDK 1.1, the URL class is persistent but the URLConnection class is not.

Another clue to potential serialization problems is native methods. Such methods often interact with external software whose state is not automatically captured by serialization.

The Externalizable Interface

The Serializable and Externalizable interfaces differ in the amount of control they give you in the serialization process and the extent of customizations you can make. The Externalizable class is a subclass of Serializable for situations in which the class requires complete control over the encoding process; only the class identification of the object being serialized is automatically written to the output stream. By implementing Externalizable, your class can control whether or not the state of superclasses is stored in the stream and exactly which fields are stored. For an Externalizable class, you must implement the following public methods:

Method	*Description*
void readExternal(ObjectInput)	The object implements the readExternal() method to restore its contents by calling the methods of DataInput for primitive types and readObject() for objects, strings, and arrays.
void writeExternal(ObjectOutput)	The object implements the writeExternal() method to save its contents by calling the methods of DataOutput for its primitive values or calling the writeObject() method of ObjectOutput for objects, strings, and arrays.

The writeExternal() method obviously must encode the data of the object in a form and sequence supported by readExternal(). Unlike Serializable, the Externalizable interface does not handle code versioning automatically; you must provide your own versioning approach.

Because the state of superclasses can be indirectly manipulated by the publicly accessible readExternal() and writeExternal() methods, you must use Externalizable with extreme care so that you do not create a security problem. In most cases, you use the Serializable interface because its built-in, default object-encoding rules are suitable for most purposes, and it provides control over which fields are serialized. The remaining examples in this chapter use the Serializable interface.

Implementing Serializable: The Default Case

For many classes, you simply add implements Serializable to the class definition to use the default Java runtime serialization format to serialize the objects. Listing 31.2 (provided as chapter31.ex2 on the CD-ROM that accompanies this book) shows a simple AddressBook class that is used as the basis for the examples in the following sections. For brevity, only the essential fields and methods are defined and the javadoc comments are removed from the listing; a practical address book class would have to do much more than this limited version.

In this example, you have an AddressBook class that holds AddressEntry objects in a hash table and uses a ServerSocket (unused in this example, but perhaps it can handle network-client lookups). An AddressEntry contains a name and address string; the AddressBook lookup() method returns an AddressEntry based on a search key.

Listing 31.2. The serializable AddressBook class.

```
01    import java.io.*;
02    import java.net.*;
03    import java.util.*;
04
05
06    class AddressEntry implements Serializable {
07      String name;
08      String address;
09
10      /** create an AddressEntry from the supplied strings */
11      public AddressEntry(String name, String address) {
12        if ((name == null) || (address == null))
13          throw new IllegalArgumentException();
14        this.name = name;
15        this.address = address;
16      }
17
18      public boolean equals(AddressEntry e) {
19        return (name.equalsIgnoreCase(e.name)) &&
20                (address.equalsIgnoreCase(e.address));
21      }
22    }
23
24    class AddressBook implements Serializable {
25      Hashtable table;
26      transient ServerSocket socket;
27
28      public AddressBook() {
29        table = new Hashtable();
30        try {
31          socket = new ServerSocket(2020);
32        }
33        catch (IOException e) {
34          socket = null;
35        }
36      }
37
38      public AddressEntry lookup(String key) {
39        return (AddressEntry) table.get(key);
40      }
41
42      public AddressEntry add(String key, AddressEntry entry) {
43        return (AddressEntry) table.put(key, entry);
```

continues

Listing 31.2. continued

```
44      }
45
46    public int size() {
47      return table.size();
48    }
49
50    public boolean equals(AddressBook b) {
51      if ((b == null) || (size() != b.size()))
52        return false;
53      Enumeration keys = table.keys();
54      while (keys.hasMoreElements()) {
55        String key = (String)keys.nextElement();
56        AddressEntry mine = lookup(key);
57        AddressEntry other = b.lookup(key);
58        if (!mine.equals(other))
59          return false;
60      }
61      return true;
62    }
63  }
64
65  public class Ex2 {
66    public static void main(String args[]) {
67      String fname = "addrbook2.out";
68      AddressEntry dave = new AddressEntry("Dave", "Main Street");
69      AddressEntry tom = new AddressEntry("Tom", "1st Street");
70      AddressEntry bill = new AddressEntry("Bill", "Downtown");
71
72      AddressBook addr = new AddressBook();
73     addr.add("Dave", dave);
74     addr.add("Tom", tom);
75     addr.add("Bill", bill);
76     addr.add("SysAdmin", bill);
77
78      try {
79        FileOutputStream fout = new FileOutputStream(fname);
80        ObjectOutputStream out = new ObjectOutputStream(fout);
81        out.writeObject(addr);
82        out.close();
83
84        FileInputStream fin = new FileInputStream(fname);
85        ObjectInputStream in = new ObjectInputStream(fin);
86        AddressBook copy = (AddressBook) in.readObject();
87        if (copy.lookup("Bill") != copy.lookup("SysAdmin"))
88          System.out.println("Multiple keys to object not restored");
89        if (addr.equals(copy))
90          System.out.println("Objects are equal");
91        else
92          System.out.println("Objects are different");
93      }
94      catch (Exception e) {
95        e.printStackTrace(System.out);
96      }
97    }
98  }
```

Compared to a nonpersistent JDK 1.0.2 implementation, you make only three changes to enable the AddressBook to be persistent. First, in line 24, you declare the AddressBook class to be serializable using the following declaration:

```
24    class AddressBook implements Serializable {
```

This declaration results in the storing of every field in the object. This is exactly the behavior you want for the hash table because it holds the address-book information and is defined in the JDK as being serializable. However, because the ServerSocket is not serializable, your second change is to declare the ServerSocket as *transient* in line 26:

```
26      transient ServerSocket socket;
```

The transient modifier instructs the serialization routines to not serialize this field. Fields declared as static are also not serialized. When you serialize the hash table, each key and entry is serialized and these classes must implement Serializable or Externalizable. Your third change is in line 6, where you declare the AddressEntry to be serializable as follows:

```
06    class AddressEntry implements Serializable {
```

Because the strings stored in an AddressEntry object are themselves serializable, no further changes are necessary.

In the main() method, you perform a simple test of persistence by creating a small address book, storing it, restoring a copy, and verifying that the saved and restored object are equal. Here, *equals* means that the two objects have the same search keys that retrieve AddressEntry objects that contain equal name and address strings.

To check that object references are handled correctly, you define two search keys ("Bill" and "SysAdmin") that refer to the same AddressEntry object. Because the definition of equals does not detect this subtle difference, you add the following explicit test:

```
87        if (copy.lookup("Bill") != copy.lookup("SysAdmin"))
88          System.out.println("Multiple keys to object not restored");
```

Running this example, you see that both tests pass; the saved and restored objects are identical. In the next section, you implement custom encoding and explore the division of effort between the object being serialized and the ObjectOutputStream.

Setting Up Custom Serialization

In most cases, the use of the transient modifier is sufficient to control the encoding of your class. However, there are times when you want even more control to better deal with versioning issues or to produce a more compact representation. In these situations, you add both a private writeObject() and a private readObject() method to your class definition, defined exactly as follows:

■ private void readObject(ObjectInputStream) throws IOException, ClassNotFoundException

■ private void writeObject(ObjectOutputStream) throws IOException

Because the `ObjectOutputStream` implements the `DataOutput` methods, and `ObjectInputStream` implements the `DataInput` methods, you use methods such as `writeInt()` to store the contents of fields. This arrangement writes the data in a platform-independent manner.

 Listing 31.3 (provided as `chapter31.ex3` on the CD-ROM that accompanies this book) shows the `readObject()` and `writeObject()` methods you use for custom encoding of the `AddressBook` class. These methods serialize only the search key and `AddressEntry` from the address book rather than serializing the complete `AddressBook`, including the hash table. By serializing just the data from the hash table *table* rather than the hash table *object*, you can easily switch to a different internal data storage technique (such as binary trees) in later versions of the class. This representation is slightly smaller (105 bytes) because the class definition for the hash table is not included in the serialized output.

NOTE

 Because the program examples have similar code, the source code listings in this chapter have been condensed to highlight only the changed classes or methods. The full source code for each example is included on the CD-ROM that accompanies this book.

Listing 31.3. Customizing the serialization format.

```
01    /* the same AddressEntry class is used as defined in Listing 31.2 */
02
03    class AddressBook implements Serializable {
04      // do not automatically serialize the hashtable
05      transient Hashtable table;
06
07      /* this class has the same constructor, lookup(), add(),
08         size() and equals() methods as Listing 31.2 */
09
10      /** override writeObject to provide a custom serial format
11       * for an AddressBook    */
12      private void writeObject(ObjectOutputStream out)
13          throws IOException {
14        out.writeInt(table.size());
15        Enumeration enum = (Enumeration) table.keys();
16        while (enum.hasMoreElements()) {
17          String key = (String)enum.nextElement();
18          AddressEntry entry = (AddressEntry)table.get(key);
19          out.writeObject(key);
20          out.writeObject(entry);
21        }
22      }
24
25      /** override readObject to restore an AddressBook using
26       * customized format. At this point, our instance has been
27       * created but instance variables not initialized.   */
```

Persistence and Java Serialization

CHAPTER 31

757

31

PERSISTENCE
AND JAVA
SERIALIZATION

```
28      private void readObject(ObjectInputStream in)
29          throws IOException, ClassNotFoundException {
30        table = new Hashtable();
31        for (int count = in.readInt(); count > 0; count--) {
32          String key = (String)in.readObject();
33          AddressEntry entry = (AddressEntry)in.readObject();
34          if ((entry.name == null) || (entry.address == null))
35            throw new InvalidObjectException
36              ("name and address fields must be non-null");
37          table.put(key, entry);
38        }
39      }
40    }
```

In this example, you check for non-null AddressEntry fields in the readObject() method. In the next section, you add object validation to this example to ensure that the restored address book passes the same restrictions as those you impose in the constructor.

Validating the Restored Object

If your program logic requires certain conditions to operate correctly (such as a given field being non-null), you commonly place such checks in the constructor so that an invalid object cannot be created. But because restoring a Serializable object does not invoke the constructor, such checks must be performed in another method. The readObject() method uses a registration and callback scheme to an object that implements the ObjectInputValidation interface.

A class that implements ObjectInputValidation must define the validateObject() method. This method is called to validate the object just before ObjectInputStream.readObject() returns. This timing ensures that all object references are correct.

 Listing 31.4 (provided as chapter31.ex4 on the CD-ROM) shows the addition of input object validation to the AddressBook example. In this case, you require that the name and address fields of the AddressEntry be non-null and then you check for that requirement in the constructor. However, a different version of AddressEntry—either older or newer—may not include such a check and can potentially produce persistent objects with null name and address fields.

Listing 31.4. Validating deserialized objects.

```
01    /* the same AddressEntry class is used as defined in Listing 31.2 */
02
03    class AddressBook implements Serializable {
04      // do not automatically serialize the hashtable
05      transient Hashtable table;
06
07      /* this class has the same constructor, lookup(), add(),
08          size() and equals() methods as Listing 31.2 */
```

continues

Listing 31.4. continued

```
09
10     /** must override writeObject() if you also override readObject().
11      * Just do the normal serialization processing. */
12     private void writeObject(ObjectOutputStream out)
13         throws IOException {
14       out.defaultWriteObject();
15     }
16
17     /** override readObject for the sole purpose of registering a
18      * validation callback. This method is called after the complete
19      * object graph has been reconstructed. Otherwise, do the
20      * normal deserialization processing.    */
21     private void readObject(ObjectInputStream in)
22         throws IOException, ClassNotFoundException {
23       // register validation callback and read in object
24       in.registerValidation(this, 0);
25       in.defaultReadObject();
26     }
27
28     /** validateObject is called after the root object has been
29      * reconstructed to validate the entire contents of the
30      * AddressBook, rather than register individual callbacks
31      * for each AddressEntry instance.    */
32     public void validateObject() throws InvalidObjectException {
33       // ensure every entry has a both name and address
34       Enumeration enum = (Enumeration) table.elements();
35       while (enum.hasMoreElements()) {
36         AddressEntry entry = (AddressEntry)enum.nextElement();
37         if ((entry.name == null) || (entry.address == null))
38           throw new InvalidObjectException
39             ("name and address fields must be non-null");
40       }
41       System.out.println("validation passed");
42     }
43   }
```

You can call `registerValidation()` only while an object is being deserialized; the method throws `NotActiveException` if called at other times. To get this timing, you override `readObject()` for the sole purpose of registering the callback and then call `defaultReadObject()` to use the standard serialization format. Right before the `AddressBook` object is returned, the validation methods are called. Registering a single validation method for the `AddressBook` is much more efficient than registering a callback for each `AddressEntry`.

NOTE

So that your `writeObject()` and `readObject()` methods can be called, you must define *both* methods, even if, as in the case of registering a validation object, you need only one.

Persistence and Java Serialization

CHAPTER 31

759

31

PERSISTENCE
AND JAVA
SERIALIZATION

In the next section, you learn how to define your classes to support interoperation of objects between different versions of your class, such as between a version that has validation and one that does not, or a version that adds new fields.

Supporting Class Versioning

When you store an object in an `ObjectOutputStream`, the `serialVersionUID` of the class is written to the stream to ensure that the correct class is found when the object is restored. The `serialVersionUID` is a hash computed over various attributes of the class, including the class name, implemented interface names, field names, and method names. When the object is restored, the class is loaded by name and then verified to be identical by comparing the `serialVersionUID` of the class from the stream with the `serialVersionUID` computed for the class just loaded. If you add fields, interfaces, or methods to a class definition, the `serialVersionUID` changes and the new class is assumed to be incompatible with the old. This strict class compatibility matching poses a problem; a user's most important investment is his or her data, which becomes unreadable when even the most trivial changes are made to the class definition.

To provide for interoperation between different versions of the same class, you must explicitly declare the `serialVersionUID` of the class you are compatible with and follow some simple rules in creating the new version:

- Do not delete a field or change it to be `transient` or `static`
- Do not change a field's built-in type (for example, do not change a `short` to an `int`)
- Do not change a class from `Serializable` to `Externalizable` or vice versa

You can add fields, add methods, change access modifiers, and implement new interfaces. However, in all cases, you must deal with the consequences of class change, such as missing fields when restoring an object saved by an earlier version of the class.

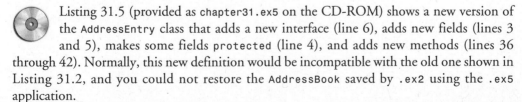 Listing 31.5 (provided as `chapter31.ex5` on the CD-ROM) shows a new version of the `AddressEntry` class that adds a new interface (line 6), adds new fields (lines 3 and 5), makes some fields `protected` (line 4), and adds new methods (lines 36 through 42). Normally, this new definition would be incompatible with the old one shown in Listing 31.2, and you could not restore the `AddressBook` saved by `.ex2` using the `.ex5` application.

To make this new class compatible with the `AddressEntry` class shown in Listing 31.2, you compute the `serialVersionUID` of the old class and indicate that your new class is compatible by including the following statement:

```
09      static final long serialVersionUID = -2357486172207358492L;
```

You obtain this `serialVersionUID` using the `serialver` tool included in JDK 1.1.

Because the earlier version of AddressEntry did not have a phone field, you add logic (lines 22 through 24) to deal with the missing field. In this case, you do not check the phone field for earlier versions when deciding whether two AddressEntry objects are equal. Fields that are missing from the ObjectInputStream are set to a type-specific default value. The main() method of this example (included in the CD-ROM source) tests version interoperability by restoring objects from the output of the program in Listing 31.5.

Listing 31.5. Interoperating with an older program version.

```
01   class AddressEntry implements Serializable, Cloneable {
02     String name;
03     protected int version;
04     protected String address;
05     protected String phone;
06
07     // indicate we are compatible with earlier name/address only
08     // version of AddressEntry defined in Listing 31.2
09     static final long serialVersionUID = -2357486172207358492L;
10
11     /** create an AddressEntry from the supplied strings */
12     public AddressEntry(String name, String address, String phone) {
13       if ((name == null) || (address == null))
14         throw new IllegalArgumentException();
15       this.name = name;
16       this.address = address;
17       this.phone = phone;
18       this.version = 1;
19     }
20
21     public boolean equals(AddressEntry e) {
22       if (version != e.version)
23         return (name.equalsIgnoreCase(e.name)) &&
24                 (address.equalsIgnoreCase(e.address));
25
26       if (phone == null)
27         return (name.equalsIgnoreCase(e.name)) &&
28                 (address.equalsIgnoreCase(e.address)) &&
29                 (e.phone == null);
30       else
31         return (name.equalsIgnoreCase(e.name)) &&
32                 (address.equalsIgnoreCase(e.address)) &&
33                 (phone.equalsIgnoreCase(e.phone));
34     }
35
36     public String getAddress() {
37       return address;
38     }
39
40     public String getPhone() {
41       return phone;
42     }
43   }
```

This completes the explanation of the commonly used functions of JDK 1.1 object serialization. In the next section, you take a look inside the implementation of serialization.

Looking Inside Object Serialization

In the next few sections, you briefly look inside the implementation of serialization in JDK 1.1 to understand the mechanism and get hints about how to reduce the size of the serialized output. You can skip these sections if you are not concerned about performance.

Comparison of Encoding Sizes

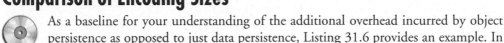 As a baseline for your understanding of the additional overhead incurred by object persistence as opposed to just data persistence, Listing 31.6 provides an example. In Listing 31.6 (provided as `chapter31.ex6` on the CD-ROM that accompanies this book), you implement a manual encoding of the `AddressBook` objects by writing fields using the `DataOutputStream` format. In hand-coding the `save()` and `restore()` methods, you save the contents of the entire address book by enumerating the keys of the hash table and saving each `AddressEntry` as two UTF-encoded strings. Although the data representation used by `DataOutputStream` can be further compacted, this is the format used by object serialization. For example, an `int` always takes four bytes—even if its value can be represented in a single byte. JDK serialization uses a fixed-size encoding technique instead of a variable-size one; the resulting output is slightly larger but encodes and decodes slightly faster. Running this example produced a serialized output of 95 bytes.

> **NOTE**
>
> UTF (Unicode Transfer Format) is a compressed way of exchanging or storing a Unicode string. The UTF form consists of a 16-bit length and the lower byte of each Unicode character in a given plane (that is, with the same high byte). Planes are changed using escape sequences. For the English (or Latin-1) character set, UTF encoding is essentially an ASCII string with a two-byte length.

Listing 31.6. The AddressBook example using `save()` and `restore()`.

```
01   class AddressEntry {
02     String name;
03     String address;
04
05     /** create an AddressEntry from the information in the file  */
06     public AddressEntry(DataInputStream in) throws IOException {
07       name = in.readUTF();
```

continues

Listing 31.6. continued

```
08        address = in.readUTF();
09    }
10
11    /** writes the contents of the entry to the output stream   */
12    void save(DataOutputStream out) throws IOException {
13      out.writeUTF(name);
14      out.writeUTF(address);
15    }
16  }
17
18  class AddressBook {
19    Hashtable table;
20
21    /* same constructor, lookup(), add(), and size() methods
22       as defined in Listing 31.2 */
23
24    public void save(String fname) throws IOException {
25      FileOutputStream fout = new FileOutputStream(fname);
26      DataOutputStream out = new DataOutputStream(fout);
27
28      Enumeration enum = (Enumeration) table.keys();
29      while (enum.hasMoreElements()) {
30        String key = (String)enum.nextElement();
31        AddressEntry entry = (AddressEntry)table.get(key);
32        out.writeUTF(key);
33        entry.save(out);
34      }
35      out.close();
36    }
37
38    void restore(String fname) throws IOException {
39      FileInputStream fin = new FileInputStream(fname);
40      DataInputStream in = new DataInputStream(fin);
41
42      while (fin.available() > 0) {
43        String key = in.readUTF();
44        AddressEntry entry = new AddressEntry(in);
45        table.put(key, entry);
46      }
47    }
48  }
```

Listing 31.2, earlier in this chapter, implemented the `Serializable` interface and used the standard encoding format. When you ran that example, you produced a serialized output of 333 bytes—which is 238 bytes larger than the same information content produced by the code in Listing 31.6. These extra bytes are used to convey type information. Encoded in the output stream is a complete description of the nonstatic, nontransient variables of all the classes serialized. This description includes the variable name and type. Listing the variables ensures that values are correctly restored even when new fields are added to a later version of the class. This is an important mechanism that supports version interoperability (as previously described). Listing 31.3 provided nonstandard serialization that did not include the hash table; running that example produced a serialized output of 228 bytes—133 bytes larger than the program in Listing 31.6 but 105 bytes smaller than the program in Listing 31.2. These extra 105 bytes were used to encode the hash table's class description and internal fields.

One subtle difference between the hand-coding approach and the Serializable approach is the object that controls the encoding. In Listing 31.6, you call the save() method of the AddressBook class and pass the stream as a parameter; in this case, the AddressBook and AddressEntry classes completely control the encoding. In Listing 31.2, you call the writeObject() method of the ObjectOutputStream and pass the AddressBook as a parameter; in that case, the stream controls the encoding. If you have to change the object encoding format rather than simply changing which fields are serialized, it is much easier to change the writeObject() method of the ObjectOutputStream than change the save() method of every persistent class.

Object Encoding Format

Variables that are primitive data types (such as int, long, and boolean) and some fundamental classes (such as String and Throwable) are identified by a one-byte flag. For example, this field declaration is encoded as an I followed by the UTF encoding of the field name string size:

int size;

Table 31.3 lists the flag bytes commonly used in encoding.

Table 31.3. Common encoding flag-byte values.

Code	Description	Code	Description
'B'	byte variable	0x70	Null (TC_NULL)
'C'	char variable	0x71	reference (TC_REFERENCE)
'D'	double variable	0x72	class descriptor (TC_CLASSDESC)
'F'	float variable	0x73	Object (TC_OBJECT)
'I'	int variable	0x74	String (TC_STRING)
'J'	long variable	0x75	array (TC_ARRAY)
'S'	short variable	0x76	class (TC_CLASS)
'Z'	boolean variable	0x77	block data start (TC_BLOCKDATA)
		0x78	block data end (TC_ENDBLOCKDATA)

Encoding Object References

The chapter31.ex6 example program in Listing 31.6 also shows one of the most common problems with hand-coded serialization routines: proper handling of object references. In this example, two names reference the single AddressEntry for Bill. The test code checks that a single AddressEntry is created. As coded, the test fails because two copies of Bill's AddressEntry will be created.

Rather than serializing an object's value (as is done in the chapter31.ex6 program), the JDK serialization methods serialize an object reference and enough information to recreate the instance. Each time writeObject() serializes a field that contains an object reference, the reference is first looked up in a hash table maintained for each ObjectOutputStream. If this instance has already been serialized to the stream, an entry is found in the table and a TC_REFERENCE flag and reference number is written to the stream. If no entry is found, a reference number is assigned to the object, an entry is made in the hash table, and writeObject() starts outputting the fields of this object. The result is that each unique object is serialized only once to a given ObjectOutputStream.

This completes a brief description of the internal mechanisms. In the next section, you learn about new research that aims to make object persistence even easier to use.

Introducing Persistent Stores

The persistence mechanisms specified for JDK 1.1 require you to explicitly manage the saving and restoring of objects. But just as databases can hide the details of storing, organizing, and retrieving data, a *persistent store* can automate the handling of persistent objects. An example of such a system is the University of Glasgow's PJava project. The following sections provide a very brief introduction to the interesting topic of persistent object stores. More information about persistent Java research projects in general, and about PJava in particular, can be found at ht.//www.dcs.gla.ac.uk/pjava.

Persistent Stores and Relational Databases

By far the most common type of client/server database system is the relational database (some examples are Oracle, Informix, Sybase, and DB2). Relational databases are organized in tabular data structures: tables, columns, and rows. Data from different tables can be joined to create new ways of looking at the data.

Relational databases, with their tabular data structures, do not mesh well with object-oriented programming languages for the following reasons:

- Relational data structures do not provide for class encapsulation. Java programmers are encouraged to model their domain by using classes, providing an API, and hiding all data within the class. Relational structures expose all data and do not allow encapsulation by an API.

- Because a Java class is a data type, it may be difficult or impossible to model efficiently in a relational structure. Examples include multidimensional arrays, dictionaries, and object references.

Persistence and Java Serialization

CHAPTER 31

765

31

PERSISTENCE
AND JAVA
SERIALIZATION

■ It is difficult to represent class inheritance in a relational database. Although it is possible, deep class inheritance trees can result in n-way joins on the database server, causing poor performance.

Tools that attempt to solve the object and relational mismatch are available. These tools map relational data structures into object-oriented classes using relatively simple rules (for example, they map tables to classes, columns to attributes, and foreign key attributes to object relationships). Although some of these products have been successful, they often suffer from performance issues—particularly when complex navigation is performed through the mapped data structures. Additionally, these products limit the type expressiveness of the language because not all the data types expressible in the object-oriented language can be easily expressed in a relational database.

Persistent stores are different from relational databases. Persistent stores do the following:

■ Eliminate the use of relational data structures; instead, they store whole objects directly in the database (such as a flat-file database)

■ Enable the programmer to write classes in a normal, object-oriented fashion to represent data that will be made persistent

■ Enable the programmer to take advantage of more data types than is possible when using a relational database

■ Provide a simpler interface than a relational database interface

Creating and Using Persistent Store Objects

Different persistent storage interfaces have different methods for creating persistent objects (or for making existing objects persistent). Some interfaces require the programmer to specify whether an object is to be persistent at the time the object is created. Other persistent stores implement a concept referred to as *persistent roots*. Persistent root objects are explicitly identified as objects that are persistent; any object referred to by the persistent root is also considered persistent. All objects that can be reached from the persistent root are also considered to be persistent and are saved in the persistent store. This concept is called *persistence via reachability*.

Retrieving objects from a persistent store is significantly different from retrieving data through SQL. When using SQL, the programmer must explicitly request data (using SELECT statements). With persistent stores, programmers seldom make explicit queries for objects. Persistent stores usually provide a mechanism to request only "top-level" objects, either through direct query or through a request for a particular persistent root.

Persistent storage interfaces almost universally employ a process known as *swizzling* (or *object faulting*) to retrieve objects from the database. Objects are retrieved on the fly, as they are needed. After obtaining a reference to a top-level object, programmers normally use that object to access related objects. When attempting to access an object that has not yet been retrieved from the database, the object is *swizzled* in. The attempt to access the object is trapped by the database interface, which then retrieves the object's storage block from the database, restores the object, and then allows the object access to continue.

Finally, persistent stores usually have a mechanism to identify objects uniquely: the object ID. Every object in a persistent store is assigned its own unique object ID, which can be used to differentiate objects of the same class whose values are equal.

The PJava Project

The stated goal of the PJava project is to provide orthogonal persistence in Java; that is, to create a persistent storage mechanism that can store objects of any type. Any object, without respect to type, can be made persistent. Many persistent stores and object databases do not support orthogonal persistence because it is extremely hard to implement in most programming languages.

Although the PJava project makes no changes to the Java language, the project's approach centers around a specially modified Java virtual machine that can interact with the persistent store to save and retrieve objects on an as-needed basis. Because of the special virtual machine modifications, PJava remains a research activity with no current plan for being commercially introduced.

Summary

A standard mechanism for object persistence was a significant omission from JDK 1.0 that has been partially corrected in JDK 1.1. As you have seen, use of the serialization facilities is easy and straightforward in most cases. In this chapter, you learned how to provide custom serialization and version interoperability.

However, some burden still falls on the programmer to manage the saving and restoring of objects. Ongoing research on projects such as PJava shows how even that burden can eventually be reduced by using persistent object stores.

Integrating Native Code with the Native Method Interface

by Stephen Ingram

IN THIS CHAPTER

CHAPTER

32

This chapter covers techniques for integrating nonJava code into your Java applications. The initial release of the JDK provided a mechanism for calling methods from C language libraries, but it was largely undocumented and extremely complicated. With the advent of Java 1.1, however, Sun decided to formalize and simplify the entire process. The result of all this work is embodied in the *Java Native Method Interface* (JNI). This chapter teaches you the five core techniques of the JNI:

- Working with Java arrays
- Working with Java strings
- Reading and writing Java `Object` fields
- Calling Java `Object` methods
- Throwing exceptions

These techniques are used to integrate both new and existing code libraries into your Java applications. In addition, this chapter introduces you to a powerful new feature that allows a standalone program to dynamically load and use Java classes. The *Java Invocation API* provides these capabilities. You'll learn how to use the API to add Java access to existing applications.

The Native Method Interface

Historically, native method programming required an intimate knowledge of the internal structures and representations of the virtual machine. Because Java was envisioned as a platform-independent system, Sun did not specify the internal design of a compliant Java virtual machine. Only external capabilities such as the class file format and bytecodes were rigidly dictated. This allowed vendors considerable latitude in the actual implementation of the Java runtime system.

The popularity of Java has caused a number of vendors to market their own Java virtual machine implementations. In fact, Sun's VM is a reference implementation, not a standard. Obviously, the internal structures of each vendor's implementation differ, so a standard methodology for accessing internal features was required. The earlier reliance on internal structures does not allow a native library to run on all implementations; native libraries for the Windows platform should operate correctly with any vendor's Windows VM. With this goal in mind, Sun's designers invented the Java Native Method Interface.

Overall Architecture

Figure 32.1 contrasts the general layout of the Java 1.0 and Java 1.1 runtime systems. The left side of the figure shows the old-style access; the right side shows the new-style access. Notice how Java 1.1 uses the interface layer to isolate the VM internals from the native library.

FIGURE 32.1.
Java 1.0 and Java 1.1 runtime architectures.

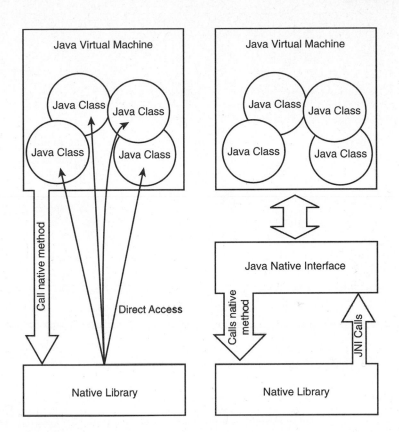

The Java Native Method Interface (JNI) is passed into all native libraries as a C pointer. It is actually a pointer to a pointer. The interface is structured much like a C++ virtual function table. This is the biggest change to old-style native method programming. Previously, the Java VM called your native method and passed only object pointers. The VM functions were accessed directly through shared library calls. This meant that the Java VM shared library had to be linked into the native library. With the JNI, all that has changed. Now, the Java VM calls your native method and passes an additional item: the JNI pointer. This extra parameter eliminates your having to link with the shared library. Every function you may need is now embedded in the JNI pointer.

The interface consists of a series of function calls that native methods use to access and exchange data with the Java runtime system. Before exploring the specifics of the interface, you should be fully introduced to native methods within Java classes.

Native Methods from the Java Side

Native methods within a Java class are very simple. Any Java method can be transformed into a native method—simply delete the method body, add a semicolon at the end, and add as a prefix the `native` keyword. Consider the following Java method:

```
public int myMethod(byte[] data)
{
    ...
}
```

This method becomes a native method that looks like this:

```
public native int myMethod(byte[] data);
```

Where is the method body implemented? In a Java-called native library that is loaded into Java at run time. The class of this example method has to cause the library to be loaded. The best way to accomplish the load is to add a `static` initializer to the class:

```
static
{
    System.loadLibrary("myMethodLibrary");
}
```

Static code blocks are executed once by the system when the class is first introduced. Any operations can be specified, but library loading is the most common use of the block. If the static block fails, the class is not loaded. This ensures that no native methods are executed without their underlying libraries. What happens if the class doesn't load the native library? An `UnsatisfiedLinkError` exception is generated when the first native method is called.

The Java VM appends the correct library extension to the name you provide. In the case of Microsoft Windows, Java adds `.dll`; for UNIX, it adds `.so`.

That's all there is to Java-side native methods. All the complexity is hidden within the native library. A native method appears to Java just like all other real Java methods. In fact, all the Java modifiers (`public`, `private`, and so forth) apply to native methods as well.

 Rather than encapsulating a complex native library, this chapter develops a straightforward library that attempts to exercise the major features of the Java Native Method Interface. Listing 32.1 contains the sample class that is developed in the remainder of this chapter. You can also find this file on the CD-ROM that accompanies this book.

Listing 32.1. Demonstration.java: The sample library.

```
public class Demonstration
{
    public String[] strs;
    public int[] vals;

    public native String[] createStrs(int siz);
    public native int[] createVals(int siz);
    public native void sortStrs();
    public native void reverseArray(int[] val);
    public native void genException();

    public void outputVals(String mess)
    {
        System.out.println(mess);
```

```java
        for (int x = 0; x < vals.length; x++)
        {
            System.out.println("vals[" + x + "] = " + vals[x]);
        }
    }

    public void outputStrs(String mess)
    {
        System.out.println(mess);
        for (int x = 0; x < strs.length; x++)
        {
            System.out.println("strs[" + x + "] = " + strs[x]);
        }
    }

    // a static method that provides a convenient entry point
    // for external processes (that are using the Invocation API)
    public static void start()
    {
        // Create the Demonstration class
        Demonstration demo = new Demonstration();

        demo.vals = demo.createVals(3);
        demo.outputVals("After Creation");
        demo.reverseArray(demo.vals);
        demo.outputVals("After reversing");

        demo.strs = demo.createStrs(3);
        demo.outputStrs("After creation");
        demo.sortStrs();
        demo.outputStrs("After sorting");
        demo.genException();
    }

    public static void main(String args[])
    {
        start();
    }

    static
    {
        System.loadLibrary("Demonstration");
    }
}
```

There are five native methods in this Demonstration class. The first two are used to create and fill arrays. The created arrays are stored within the class. The next two native methods alter the array data—either by sorting or by simple member reversal. To facilitate monitoring, two class methods print the contents of the arrays. The final native method generates an exception. The native methods within this class allow each of the five core techniques of the JNI to be demonstrated.

After compiling the class, the first step is to run javah on the class.

Using the javah Tool

javah is the tool you use to generate C header files for Java classes. Here's how you use it:

```
javah [options] class
```

Table 32.1 briefly lists the options available for use with javah. Java 1.1 adds a new option to accommodate the new native interface. You must use the -jni option to create the newer native interface header. Although old-style native methods are still supported by the javah tool, there are no guarantees for future compatibility. By default, javah creates a C header (.h) file in the current directory for each class listed on the command line. Class names are specified without the trailing .class. Therefore, to generate the header for SomeName.class, use the following command:

```
javah -jni SomeName
```

Table 32.1. The options for the javah tool.

Option	Description
-jni	Creates a JNI header file
-verbose	Causes progress strings to be displayed
-version	Displays the version of javah
-o *outputfile*	Overrides default file creation; uses only this filename
-d *directory*	Overrides placement of output in current directory
-td *tempdirectory*	Overrides default temporary directory use
-stubs	Creates a C code module instead of a header module
-classpath *path*	Overrides the default class path

> **NOTE**
>
> If the class you want is within a package, you must specify the package name along with the class name: javah java.net.Socket. In addition, javah prefixes the package name to the output filename: java_net_Socket.h.

To run javah on the compiled Demonstration class, use this command:

```
javah -jni Demonstration
```

 The result of this command is the C header file Demonstration.h (see Listing 32.2; the header file can also be found on the CD-ROM that accompanies this book). With this last action, you made the jump to the native library side of the fence.

Listing 32.2. The Demonstration.h file.

```c
/* DO NOT EDIT THIS FILE - it is machine generated */
#include <jni.h>
/* Header for class Demonstration */

#ifndef _Included_Demonstration
#define _Included_Demonstration
#ifdef _cplusplus
extern "C" {
#endif
/*
 * Class:     Demonstration
 * Method:    createStrs
 * Signature: (I)[Ljava/lang/String;
 */
JNIEXPORT jobjectArray JNICALL Java_Demonstration_createStrs
  (JNIEnv *, jobject, jint);

/*
 * Class:     Demonstration
 * Method:    createVals
 * Signature: (I)[I
 */
JNIEXPORT jintArray JNICALL Java_Demonstration_createVals
  (JNIEnv *, jobject, jint);

/*
 * Class:     Demonstration
 * Method:    sortStrs
 * Signature: ()V
 */
JNIEXPORT void JNICALL Java_Demonstration_sortStrs
  (JNIEnv *, jobject);

/*
 * Class:     Demonstration
 * Method:    reverseArray
 * Signature: ([I)V
 */
JNIEXPORT void JNICALL Java_Demonstration_reverseArray
  (JNIEnv *, jobject, jintArray);

/*
 * Class:     Demonstration
 * Method:    genException
 * Signature: ()V
 */
JNIEXPORT void JNICALL Java_Demonstration_genException
  (JNIEnv *, jobject);

#ifdef _cplusplus
}
#endif
#endif
```

Native Methods from the Library Side

The Demonstration.h header file created by javah provides you with the function prototypes for your native methods and also tells you what to name your functions so that Java can find them at run time. Normally, the function name is created by prefixing Java_ to the class and method names. If you have an overloaded method, the derived name also includes the argument list. Adding another createStrs() function with different arguments to the Demonstration class causes the derived name to look like this:

```
JNIEXPORT jobjectArray JNICALL Java_Demonstration_createStrs_I
  (JNIEnv *, jobject, jint);
```

This naming convention is used to allow Java to identify the correct implementation of createStrs() depending on the argument list of the caller.

JNI Data Types

To maintain consistency across multiple vendors, the JNI uses nine specific data types, contained in the JNI header file. Table 32.2 shows all these data types and their Java equivalents.

Table 32.2. JNI representation of Java basic types.

Java Type	JNI Representation
boolean	jboolean
byte	jbyte
char	jchar
short	jshort
int	jint
long	jlong
float	jfloat
double	jdouble
void	void

In addition to these basic types, Java objects are addressed and stored as pointers:

```
struct _jobject;

typedef struct _jobject *jobject;
typedef jobject jclass;
typedef jobject jthrowable;
typedef jobject jstring;
typedef jobject jarray;
typedef jarray jbooleanArray;
typedef jarray jbyteArray;
```

```
typedef jarray jcharArray;
typedef jarray jshortArray;
typedef jarray jintArray;
typedef jarray jlongArray;
typedef jarray jfloatArray;
typedef jarray jdoubleArray;
typedef jarray jobjectArray;
```

You may be wondering what the difference is between jobject and jclass. A class pointer (jclass) is a description or template for a class. It is used to construct a new object (jobject) of that class.

The second argument of a native method is of type jobject. This is a pointer to the Java object under which this method is acting. For you C++ programmers, jobject is equivalent to the this pointer. If the native method had been a static function, the second argument would have been of type jclass.

All native methods have as their first argument the Java Native Method Interface pointer, which is described in the next section.

Java Native Method Interface Pointer

With version 1.1—for the first time—the JDK now works with C++ directly! JNIEnv is a pointer to an interface structure which is defined differently depending on whether you are using standard C or C++. Both definitions are contained in the Java include file, jni.h. The JNIEnv structure provides all the interaction with Java; you will make constant use of its members. For standard C files, JNIEnv is defined as follows:

```
typedef const struct JNINativeInterface *JNIEnv;
struct JNINativeInterface {
    void *reserved0;
    void *reserved1;
    void *reserved2;

    void *reserved3;
    jint (JNICALL *GetVersion)(JNIEnv *env);
    jclass (JNICALL *DefineClass)
      (JNIEnv *env, const char *name, jobject loader, const jbyte *buf,
       jsize len);
    jclass (JNICALL *FindClass)
      (JNIEnv *env, const char *name);
    ...
};
```

In C++, JNIEnv is defined as a C++ structure with inline functions:

```
typedef JNIEnv_ JNIEnv;
struct JNIEnv_ {
    const struct JNINativeInterface *functions;
    void *reserved0;
    void *reserved1[6];
    jint GetVersion() {
        return functions->GetVersion(this);
    }
```

32

INTEGRATING
NATIVE CODE

```
    jclass DefineClass(const char *name, jobject loader, const jbyte *buf,
             jsize len) {
        return functions->DefineClass(this, name, loader, buf, len);
    }
    jclass FindClass(const char *name) {
        return functions->FindClass(this, name);
    }
        ...
};
```

> **NOTE**
>
> You may be wondering about the three reserved pointers at the top of the JNIEnv interface. These are present to allow the interface to conform to Microsoft's COM object model. Once COM cross-platform support is implemented, the JNI can become a COM interface to the Java VM!

The main advantage of this dual definition is in the calling convention used to invoke the interface functions. For standard C, you must use the pointer and call through the interface, like this:

```
(*env)->FindClass(env, "java/lang/String");
```

In C++, the same invocation can be accomplished in a much cleaner fashion:

```
env->FindClass("java/lang/String");
```

The extra calling complexity is hidden by the inline function. Ultimately, the C++ inline function resolves to exactly the same reference as its standard C cousin. The underlying functionality of the interface is not compromised in any way by the more streamlined C++ style.

Native Interface Functions

The functions available in the JNIEnv interface are too numerous to list in this chapter. I would rather convey the underlying concepts of the interface so that you can then understand any of the individual functions. The purpose of the JNI is to isolate the details of the Java VM from the native code. By providing a middle layer, the JNI allows native methods to run on any vendor's Java VM. It will always help your understanding if you keep the JNI's middle-layer interface nature in mind.

Perhaps the best place to start is with the representation of Java objects.

Object References

Scalar quantities, such as integers and characters, are copied between the Java VM and the native library. In contrast, Java objects are passed by reference. The native method is literally working with the same object as the Java VM. Allowing the Java garbage collector to function seamlessly with native methods is paramount. The interface solves this problem by dividing all object references into two distinct types: global and local.

A *local reference* has duration only for the life of the native method call and is freed when the native method returns. All arguments passed to, and returned from, a native method are local references. *Global references* must be explicitly freed. Any local reference can be turned into a global reference by using the interface function NewGlobalRef(). Both types of references are legal wherever a reference is needed. The only difference is in their scope of existence.

To facilitate efficient garbage collection, the interface contains a function that allows a native method to notify the VM that it no longer needs a particular local reference. Usually, this functionality is used only with a native method that is performing a particularly long computation. Rather than tie up the object for the entire length of the method, the native code can notify the VM that it no longer needs a local reference and the VM is free to garbage collect it before the method returns. Interface functions DeleteGlobalRef() and DeleteLocalRef() accomplish the removal notifications.

The JNI's ID System

I like to think of the JNI as having a distinct ID system for managing its parts. Whenever you want to interact with an object, you need an object reference (jobject). Similarly, whenever you want to interact with a specific field or method within a class, you need a field ID (jfieldID) or method ID (jmethodID). Identifying a specific class is accomplished with a class ID (jclass).

Together, these four types allow the native code to uniquely identify any individual feature of the Java hierarchy.

Java Arrays

The first major point to remember when dealing with Java arrays is that arrays are themselves Java objects. Arrays do have their own identifier (jobjectArray), but that is only to aid in readability. A jobjectArray reference can be passed and used by any routine expecting a jobject reference.

All Java arrays have a length parameter. The JNI provides the function GetArrayLength() to access any array's size:

```
jsize GetArrayLength(JNIEnv *env, jarray array);
```

To address the individual members of array objects, the JNI contains two major groups of functions. The group you use depends on the type of data held by the array. The first group allows access to arrays of Java objects or references. The second group allows access to arrays of scalar quantities.

In the case of arrays of objects, each array index can be set or retrieved by an interface function:

```
jobject GetObjectArrayElement(JNIEnv *env, jarray array, jsize index);
void SetObjectArrayElement(JNIEnv *env, jarray array, jsize index, jobject value);
```

Accessing each index with a function is very inefficient when dealing with a scalar quantity such as integers. Performing matrix calculations is horribly slow. To solve this problem, the JNI provides a set of functions that allow a scalar array to be accessed in the native address space.

Each scalar type has functions for manipulating arrays of that type. The following statement gives the calling format:

```
NativeType GetArrayElements(JNIEnv *env, jarray array, jboolean *isCopy);
```

There is no actual function called `GetArrayElements()`. Instead, there are variants for each scalar type. Table 32.3 lists all the flavors of `GetArrayElements()`.

The third argument (`isCopy`), is a boolean set by the VM depending on whether the array was originally stored as a C array. If the data of the Java array is stored contiguously, a pointer to that data is returned and `isCopy` is set to `false`. If, however, the internal storage is not contiguous, the VM makes a copy of the actual data and sets `isCopy` to `true`. The significance of this flag is that if the flag is `false`, you know you are manipulating the actual array data. Any changes you make are permanent changes. If, on the other hand, you are working with a copy, your changes can be released without saving.

Table 32.3. `GetArrayElements()` function types.

Function	Native Return Type	Java Array Type
GetBooleanArrayElements()	jboolean *	boolean[]
GetByteArrayElements()	jbyte *	byte[]
GetCharArrayElements()	jchar *	char[]
GetShortArrayElements()	jshort *	short[]
GetIntArrayElements()	jint *	int[]
GetLongArrayElements()	jlong *	long[]
GetFloatArrayElements()	jfloat *	float[]
GetDoubleArrayElements()	jdouble *	double[]

Releasing the local copy back to the Java object is accomplished with the various versions of `ReleaseArrayElements()`. This is its calling format:

```
void ReleaseArrayElements(JNIEnv *env, jarray array, NativeType elems, jint mode);
```

Again, the actual function name is specific to each scalar type. Table 32.4 lists the types of release functions. The fourth argument (`mode`) to `ReleaseArrayElements()` controls the release mode. It has three possible values:

0	Copy back the data and release the local storage
JNI_COMMIT	Copy back the data but do not release the storage
JNI_ABORT	Release the storage without copying back the data

Obviously, if the local data is not a copy, the mode parameter has no effect.

Table 32.4. ReleaseArrayElements() function types.

Function	Native Return Type	Java Array Type
ReleaseBooleanArrayElements()	jboolean *	boolean[]
ReleaseByteArrayElements()	jbyte *	byte[]
ReleaseCharArrayElements()	jchar *	char[]
ReleaseShortArrayElements()	jshort *	short[]
ReleaseIntArrayElements()	jint *	int[]
ReleaseLongArrayElements()	jlong *	long[]
ReleaseFloatArrayElements()	jfloat *	float[]
ReleaseDoubleArrayElements()	jdouble *	double[]

32

INTEGRATING
NATIVE CODE

NOTE

If you want to work with scalar array data in an unobtrusive manner, the JNI provides a second set of functions that allow the scalar array members to be copied into local storage allocated and managed by the native method. GetArrayRegion() and SetArrayRegion() operate on a subset of an array and use a locally allocated buffer.

Native methods can also create a new Java array. The NewArray() functions perform the work:

```
jarray NewObjectArray(JNIEnv *env, jsize length, jclass elementClass,
                    jobject initialElement);
jarray NewScalarArray(JNIEnv *env, jsize length);
```

Enough theory. It's time to apply what you have learned. You should now have enough knowledge to implement the createVals() and reverseArray() native methods from the Demonstration class. Listing 32.3 shows the completed methods; the code is also located on the CD-ROM that accompanies this book. In this example, the methods manipulate an integer array, so the scalar array functions are used.

Listing 32.3. The native methods createVals() and reverseArray().

```
/*
 * Class:      Demonstration
 * Method:     createVals
 * Signature: (I)[I
 */
JNIEXPORT jintArray JNICALL Java_Demonstration_createVals
  (JNIEnv *env, jobject DemoObj, jint len)
{
    jintArray RetArray;
    int x;
    jint *localArray;

    RetArray = env->NewIntArray(len);
    localArray = env->GetIntArrayElements(RetArray, NULL);
    for ( x = 0; x < len; x++)
        localArray[x] = len - x - 1;
    env->ReleaseIntArrayElements(RetArray, localArray, 0);
    return RetArray;
}



/*
 * Class:      Demonstration
 * Method:     reverseArray
 * Signature: ([I)V
 */
JNIEXPORT void JNICALL Java_Demonstration_reverseArray
  (JNIEnv *env, jobject DemoObj, jintArray vals)
{
        jint x, temp;
        jsize len;
        jboolean isCopy;
        jint *localArray;

        len = env->GetArrayLength(vals);
        localArray = env->GetIntArrayElements(vals, &isCopy);
        for (x = 0; x < len/2; x++)
        {
            temp = localArray[x];
            localArray[x] = localArray[len - x - 1];
            localArray[len - x - 1] = temp;
        }
        env->ReleaseIntArrayElements(vals, localArray, 0);
}
```

createVals() uses NewArray() to allocate the integer array. Because NewArray() creates a proper Java object, local access to the data must be acquired using GetIntArrayElements(). After the array has been initialized, the local elements are released back to the Java VM.

Reversing the array is similar to creating it. First, the array's length is determined. After the length is known, the array's contents can be acquired and manipulated as a standard C array.

Notice that the isCopy parameter is not required. createVals() passes null instead of a pointer because it doesn't care whether the data is a copy. reverseArray() passes a valid pointer, although it never uses the information. Either technique is valid.

Java Strings

Unlike C, Java treats strings as first-class objects. In C, a string is nothing more than a zero-terminated array of characters. This dichotomy is addressed by several string functions within the JNI.

String length is determined in a manner similar to the way array length is determined:

```
jsize GetStringLength(JNIEnv *env, jstring string);
```

Because Java supports strings in Unicode format, access to string data can be acquired in two distinct ways. Most C string routines can't work with Unicode, so the JNI provides translation functions that are more natural for C to use. Table 32.5 lists the string functions with brief comments. It is important to remember that strings in Java are immutable. This means that, unlike an array, you cannot change the data within a String object.

String data in Java is stored in UTF-8 format. This format represents all characters up to 0x7F (hexadecimal) in a single byte. Characters above 0x7F use an encoding mechanism that may take up to three bytes of storage. Standard ASCII data looks like C strings, but be aware of Unicode representation in international situations. Characters from 0x80 to 0x7FF consume two bytes, while characters from 0x800 to 0xFFFF use three bytes.

Table 32.5. String interface functions.

Function	Description
NewString()	Creates a String object from a jchar array (Unicode)
GetStringLength()	Returns the number of jchars in a string (Unicode)
GetStringChars()	Gets a jchar array of string characters (Unicode)
ReleaseStringChars()	Releases an acquired jchar array (Unicode)
GetStringUTFLength()	Returns the number of bytes in a string (UTF-8)
NewStringUTF()	Creates a String object from a byte array (UTF-8)
GetStringUTFChars()	Gets a byte array of string characters (UTF-8)
ReleaseStringUTFChar()	Releases an acquired byte array (UTF-8)

Listing 32.4 shows the code for creating an array of strings in the Demonstration class. The code is also located on the CD-ROM that accompanies this book.

Listing 32.4. The string array creation routine.

```
/*
 * Class:      Demonstration
 * Method:     createStrs
 * Signature: (I)[Ljava/lang/String;
 */
JNIEXPORT jobjectArray JNICALL Java_Demonstration_createStrs
  (JNIEnv *env, jobject DemoObj, jint len)
{
    jobjectArray RetArray;
    jobject StringObj;
    jclass StringClass;
    int x;
    char str[80];

    StringClass = env->FindClass("java/lang/String");
    RetArray = env->NewObjectArray(len, StringClass, NULL);
    for (x = 0; x < len; x++)
    {
        sprintf(str, "This is string #%04d", len - x - 1);
        StringObj = env->NewStringUTF(str);
        env->SetObjectArrayElement(RetArray, x, StringObj);
    }
    return RetArray;
}
```

This routine is considerably more complex than the integer array creation routine. To create arrays of objects, the class type of the array data must be known. The first step of the routine is to acquire a jclass reference to the String class. Once the array is constructed, each individual String object must be created and inserted into the array. Once each object is created, SetObjectArrayElement() is used to place the string into the array.

The string sort method is supposed to access the string array directly from the Demonstration object. To accomplish this, however, you must first learn how to access Java fields, as described in the following section.

Reading and Writing Java Object Fields

The variables within a Java object are referred to as *fields*. Before you can access an object field, you must first have a field ID. GetFieldID() takes a field name and signature and returns the variable's ID. The trick to the whole procedure is determining the field signature. Table 32.6 lays out the characters and their signature meanings.

Table 32.6. Signature symbols.

Type	Signature Character
array	[
byte	B

Type	Signature Character
char	C
class	L
end of class	;
float	F
double	D
function	(
end of function	)
int	I
long	J
short	S
void	V
boolean	Z

Using the information in Table 32.6, construct the field signatures of these two `public` variables within the `Demonstration` class:

```
public String[] strs;
public int[] vals;
```

The first variable is an array of strings, so its signature is `[Ljava/lang/String;`. The second variable is an array of integers, so its signature is `[I`.

> **NOTE**
>
> Signatures can be very confusing. The viewer tool described in Chapter 33, "Java Under the Hood: Inside the Virtual Machine," is very useful for displaying field and method signatures. Additionally, the JDK's `javap` tool can be used with the `-s` option to reveal signatures for a given class.

`GetFieldID()` requires one additional piece of information. It has to know the class that contains the desired field. If you know only the class name, use `FindClass()` to obtain the rest of this data. Most of the time, you already have an object reference to the class that contains the field. In this case, use `GetObjectClass()` to acquire the `jclass` reference of an existing object. Using the class, name, and signature yields the field ID:

```
demoClass = env->GetObjectClass(DemoObj);
strsArrayID = env->GetFieldID(demoClass, "strs", "[Ljava/lang/String;");
```

The field ID is valid for any instance of the class. If you have two instances of `Demonstration` objects, the same field ID can be used to reference the `strs` array in both objects.

Once the field ID is known, use the various types of `GetField()` functions to access the contents of the variable. Table 32.7 lists the various flavors of the `GetField()` function.

Table 32.7. The varieties of the `GetField()` function.

Function	Return Type	Field Type
GetObjectField()	jobject	Object
GetBooleanField()	jboolean	boolean
GetByteField()	jbyte	byte
GetCharField()	jchar	char
GetShortField()	jshort	short
GetIntField()	jint	int
GetLongField()	jlong	long
GetFloatField()	jfloat	float
GetDoubleField()	jdouble	double

Accessing the `strs` field in the `Demonstration` class is simple—once the field ID is known:

```
strsArray = env->GetObjectField(DemoObj, strsArrayID);
```

As you do when you read the field contents, when you set the field contents, you also use the field ID:

```
env->SetObjectField(DemoObj, strsArrayID, newArrayObj);
```

Table 32.8 lists the `SetField()` functions.

Table 32.8. The varieties of the `SetField()` function.

Function	Return Type	Field Type
SetObjectField()	jobject	Object
SetBooleanField()	jboolean	boolean
SetByteField()	jbyte	byte
SetCharField()	jchar	char
SetShortField()	jshort	short
SetIntField()	jint	int
SetLongField()	jlong	long
SetFloatField()	jfloat	float
SetDoubleField()	jdouble	double

Calling Java Object Methods

Like field operations, method operations use the concept of the central prominence of the method ID. As you do with fields, you acquire the method ID by using a class, name, and signature. In fact, the signature symbols in Table 32.6 are used to construct both field and method signatures.

There is a whole stable of functions for invoking Java methods. First you must recognize whether the target method is static. If it is not static, you must decide whether you are calling a virtual function or a specific function. Normal Java calls are always virtual. If a class overrides a function, you always call that new version when you have an object of that class or one of its descendants. If, however, you want to call a specific version of the function, you must issue a nonvirtual method invocation. This situation can arise when you want to execute the base class version of a virtual function but you have a descendant class object reference.

Once you decide which type of method invocation to use, you still must choose how you want to pass method arguments. There are three ways to pass arguments:

- Add them to the end of the method invocation
- Pass a `va_arg` structure
- Pass a `jvalue` array of arguments

The approach you use is based on personal preference. I favor the first method because it makes for the cleanest code. The generic calling formats are as follows:

- `CallMethod(jobject obj, jmethodID methodID, ...);`
- `CallMethodV(jobject obj, jmethodID methodID, va_list args);`
- `CallMethodA(jobject obj, jmethodID methodID, jvalue *args);`

Each return type has its own representative function. Table 32.9 lists the functions for invoking a virtual method.

Table 32.9. Virtual method invocations based on return type.

Function	Method Return Type
CallVoidMethod()	jvoid
CallObjectMethod()	jobject
CallBooleanMethod()	jboolean
CallByteMethod()	jbyte
CallCharMethod()	jchar
CallShortMethod()	jshort
CallIntMethod()	jint

continues

Table 32.9. continued

Function	Method Return Type
CallLongMethod()	jlong
CallFloatMethod()	jfloat
CallDoubleMethod()	jdouble

At this point, you are probably feeling a bit overwhelmed. That is understandable. Maybe an example would clear things up? Let's return to the sortStrs problem.

For simplicity, I chose an insertion sort. The sort compares two String objects. If you pull out your API reference, you will notice that the String class has a compareTo(String) function that seems tailor made for our purpose. The next step is to determine the method's signature. The method prototype is shown here:

```
public int compareTo(String anotherString);
```

 By using Table 32.6, we determine that the method signature is (Ljava/lang/String;)I. Listing 32.5 shows the code to implement the sortStrs() native method; the code is also located on the accompanying CD-ROM.

Listing 32.5. The sortStrs() method from Demonstration.cpp.

```cpp
/*
 * Class:     Demonstration
 * Method:    sortStrs
 * Signature: ()V
 */
JNIEXPORT void JNICALL Java_Demonstration_sortStrs
  (JNIEnv *env, jobject DemoObj)
{
    jobjectArray valsArray;
    jclass demoClass;
    jfieldID valsArrayID;
    jclass StringClass;
    jmethodID compID;

    demoClass = env->GetObjectClass(DemoObj);
    valsArrayID = env->GetFieldID(demoClass, "strs", "[Ljava/lang/String;");
    if ( valsArrayID == NULL ) return;

    valsArray = (jobjectArray)env->GetObjectField(DemoObj, valsArrayID);
    if ( valsArray == NULL ) return;

    StringClass = env->FindClass("java/lang/String");
    if (StringClass == NULL) return;

    compID = env->GetMethodID(StringClass, "compareTo", "(Ljava/lang/String;)I");
    if (compID == NULL) return;

    insertSort(env, valsArray, compID);
}
```

```
void insertSort(JNIEnv *env, jobjectArray valsArray, jmethodID compID)
{
    int i, j, len;
    jobject tmp, cobj, pobj;

    len = env->GetArrayLength(valsArray);

    for ( i = 1; i < len; i++ )
    {
        cobj = env->GetObjectArrayElement(valsArray, i);
        pobj = env->GetObjectArrayElement(valsArray, i - 1);
        if (env->CallIntMethod(cobj, compID, pobj) < 0)
        {
            for ( j = i - 1; j >= 0; j— )
            {
                tmp = env->GetObjectArrayElement(valsArray, j);
                env->SetObjectArrayElement(valsArray, j + 1, tmp);
                if ( j == 0 ) break;
                tmp = env->GetObjectArrayElement(valsArray, j - 1);
                if ( env->CallIntMethod(tmp, compID, cobj) < 0 ) break;
            }
            env->SetObjectArrayElement(valsArray, j, cobj);
        }
    }
}
```

Most of the work is done in the `insertSort()` function. Essentially, the routine parses the entire array, pulling each `String` object out and using `compareTo()` calls to insert the strings into the proper location. Although it would be much more efficient to create a local copy of the array, I wanted to exercise as many array calls as possible.

Throwing Exceptions

Java's rich support for exceptions also extends into the native method realm. A number of interface functions allow native code to issue, clear, retrieve, and describe exceptions. Table 32.10 lists all the exception functions for the JNI.

Table 32.10. The JNI exception functions.

Function	Description
Throw()	Throws an exception object
ThrowNew()	Creates a new exception object and throws it
ExceptionOccurred()	Determines whether an exception is pending and retrieves it
ExceptionDescribe()	Prints a description as a debugging convenience
ExceptionClear()	Clears a pending exception
FatalError()	Raises a fatal error (stops execution)

For the final native method in the `Demonstration` class, we have to generate an exception. Listing 32.6 displays the method used to do so (the code is located on the accompanying CD-ROM).

Listing 32.6. Generating an exception in native code.

```
/*
 * Class:      Demonstration
 * Method:     genException
 * Signature: ()V
 */
JNIEXPORT void JNICALL Java_Demonstration_genException
  (JNIEnv *env, jobject DemoObj)
{
    jclass exceptClass;

    exceptClass = env->FindClass("java/lang/Exception");
    env->ThrowNew(exceptClass, "genException()");
}
```

To generate an exception, you have to know only the class name of the exception you want to throw.

Putting It All Together

The final step is to actually create the native library. I used Microsoft Visual C++ 4.0 in a Windows 95/NT environment for this chapter. The JNI is generic enough to allow all the code in this chapter to be used on a different platform (such as many UNIX variants). That is one of the big advantages to the JNI's middle-layer status: All platforms are capable of hosting the interface.

To create the library, I used the following command-line statement:

```
cl Demonstration.cpp -FeDemonstration.dll -MD -LD
```

Invoking this command creates the library `Demonstration.dll`. You can test out the class by running the `Demonstration` class as an application:

```
java Demonstration
```

Before showing you the class output, I want to go one step further and execute the class from a compiled executable! For that, you have to learn to use the Invocation API.

The Invocation API

The JNI contains a facility for loading a Java VM into any existing native application. This facility presents exciting possibilities to application developers. Many developers agonize over how to add scripting or extensibility to their applications. By using the Invocation API, you can now use Java as your scripting language! All you have to supply is a few Java classes that expose their application's internals through native methods. Of course, you must also have some way to call the Java classes of your customers. This latter need is resolved with the Invocation API.

There are three functions for dealing with the VM:

- `jint JNI_CreateJavaVM(JavaVM **p_vm,JNIEnv **p_env, void *vm_args);`
  Loads the Java VM shared library and passes the initialization arguments.

- `jint DestroyJavaVM(JavaVM *vm);`
  Unloads the Java VM shared library.

- `void JNI_GetDefaultJavaVMInitArgs(void *vm_args);`
  Retreives the default initialization arguments passed into `CreateJavaVM()`.

 Listing 32.7 shows the code for a small executable program that uses these three functions to run the `Demonstration` class. The code is also located on the accompanying CD-ROM.

Listing 32.7. Dynamically loading the Java VM in `Invoke.cpp`.

```cpp
#include <jni.h>              /* where everything is defined */
#include <stdio.h>

JavaVM *jvm;                  /* denotes a Java VM */
JNIEnv *env;                  /* pointer to native method interface */
JDK1_1InitArgs vm_args;       /* VM initialization arguments */

void main(int argc, char **argv)
{
        jobject exceptObj;

        printf("Creating the Java VM\n");

        /* The default arguments are usually good enough. */
        JNI_GetDefaultJavaVMInitArgs(&vm_args);

        /* load and initialize a Java VM, return a native method interface
        * pointer in env */
        JNI_CreateJavaVM(&jvm, &env, &vm_args);

        /* invoke the Demonstration.main method using the JNI */
        jclass cls = env->FindClass("Demonstration");
        jmethodID mid = env->GetStaticMethodID(cls, "start", "()V");

        printf("Calling Demonstration.start()\n");
        env->CallStaticVoidMethod(cls, mid);
        if (env->ExceptionOccurred() != NULL) env->ExceptionDescribe();

        /* We are done. */
        printf("Destroying Java VM\n");
        jvm->DestroyJavaVM();
}
```

Unlike the JNI interface, the functions of the Invocation API are called directly by a native application. As a consequence, the Java VM library (`javai.lib`) must be linked with the application. Because the actual functions of the Java VM are contained in a shared library, platforms that do not support dynamic linking are not eligible for the Invocation API.

Notice that because `start()` is a static method, it can be executed without creating an instance of the `Demonstration` class. I used the following Visual C++ 4.0 command to create the `invoke` executable:

```
cl invoke.cpp javai.lib
```

Running `invoke.exe` produces the following output:

```
Creating the Java VM
Calling Demonstration.start()
After Creation
vals[0] = 2
vals[1] = 1
vals[2] = 0
After reversing
vals[0] = 0
vals[1] = 1
vals[2] = 2
After creation
strs[0] = This is string #0002
strs[1] = This is string #0001
strs[2] = This is string #0000
After sorting
strs[0] = This is string #0000
strs[1] = This is string #0001
strs[2] = This is string #0002
Exception in thread "main" java.lang.Exception: genException()
        at Demonstration.start(Demonstration.java:45)
Destroying Java VM
```

Because the generated exception is not handled by the Java code, it is caught by the native method. The debugging utility function `ExceptionDescribe` is used to display the error. If the exception check is omitted from the native code, the exception is not handled by any function. Normally, an unhandled exception is caught by the Java VM before it exits. In this case, the VM is being dynamically accessed, so no checks are made.

Summary

Programming to the Java Native Method Interface is a complicated issue. Take some time to absorb this chapter. The JNI provides a rich set of functions; only a subset of these have been presented in this chapter. All the additional functions operate on the same ID system. Remember to acquire the necessary `jobject`, `jclass`, `jfieldID`, or `jmethodID` before executing an interface function. This extra step is what enables the JNI to present a standard interface on all platforms and VM implementations. Remember that any operation that can be performed in a Java class can also be performed by a native method. The JNI has standardized and simplified native method programming.

Do not ignore the Invocation API. It enables you to include Java in your compiled applications. Once you link the API into your programs, the rich infrastructure of Java can be leveraged for scripting, information exchange, or remote access. Your programs will be limited only by the imagination of your users! The Invocation API is also useful for creating a single executable for running your Java applications. The coupling is much tighter than using simple batch files or shell scripts to launch your classes. The biggest advantage to executable access is that you can present custom icons and control initial arguments. Additionally, your users can always appreciate the ease of single-command access. I expect the Invocation API to play a large role in forthcoming Java-enabled business applications.

Java Under the Hood: Inside the Virtual Machine

by Stephen Ingram

IN THIS CHAPTER

CHAPTER 33

This chapter takes an in-depth look at the internals of the Java virtual machine (VM). Although an understanding of Java's internals is not required to be an effective Java programmer, comprehension of this chapter provides the basis for making the transition to expert-level Java coding. In any event, the VM internals shed light on the mindset of Java's original designers. Exploration at this level is a fascinating journey because of the elegance behind the Java architecture.

Looking at a virtual machine from the outside in is probably the best way to understand its workings. Incremental learning results when you move from the known to the unknown, so this chapter starts with the item you are most familiar with: the class file.

The Class File

The class file is similar to standard language object modules. When a C language file is compiled, the output is an object module. Multiple object modules are linked together to form an executable program. In Java, the class file replaces the object module and the Java virtual machine replaces the executable program.

You'll find all the information needed to execute a class contained within the class file; you'll also find extra information that aids debugging and source file tracking. Remember that Java has no "header" include files, so the class file format also has to fully convey class layout and members. Parsing a class file yields a wealth of class information, not just its runtime architecture.

Layout

The overall layout of the class file uses an outer structure and a series of substructures that contain an ever-increasing amount of detail. The outer layer is described by the following `ClassFile` structure:

```
ClassFile
{
    u4 magic;
    u2 minor_version;
    u2 major_version;
    u2 constant_pool_count;
    cp_info constant_pool[constant_pool_count - 1];
    u2 access_flags;
    u2 this_class;
    u2 super_class;
    u2 interfaces_count;
    u2 interfaces[interfaces_count];
    u2 fields_count;
    field_info fields[fields_count];
    u2 methods_count;
    method_info methods[methods_count];
    u2 attributes_count;
    attribute_info attributes[attribute_count];
}
```

In addition to the generic class information (`this_class`, `super_class`, `version`, and so on), there are three major substructures: `cp_info`, `field_info`, and `method_info`. The `attribute_info` structure is considered a minor substructure because attributes recur throughout the class file at various levels. Fields and methods contain their own set of attributes and some individual attributes also contain their own private attribute arrays.

The symbols u2 and u4 represent unsigned 2-byte and unsigned 4-byte quantities.

The Class Viewer

Simply regurgitating class file structures does not provide the best basis for actual learning. To better convey the overall class file structure, I wrote an interactive Java application that presents a class file in a tree format. Figure 33.1 shows the tool in action. With this tool, you can view any class and save it in ASCII format. Navigation is performed with the keyboard: The arrow keys provide movement and the spacebar expands and contracts the nodes.

 The Viewer.class tool and source code are provided on the CD-ROM that accompanies this book. Because it's an application, run the tool from the command line with this statement: `java Viewer`

FIGURE 33.1.

The class Viewer *application in action.*

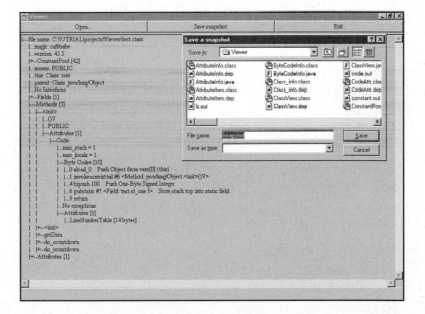

Now that you have a tool, you need a simple class to explore. Here's one, just waiting for you:

```java
public class test
{
    public static int st_one;

    public test()
    {
        st_one = 100;
    }

    public test(int v)
    {
        st_one = v;
    }

    public native boolean getData(int data[] );

    public int do_countdown()
    {
        int x = st_one;

        System.out.println("Performing countdown:");
        while ( x-- != 0 )
            System.out.println(x);
        return st_one;
    }

    public int do_countdown(int x)
    {
        int save = x;

        System.out.println("Performing countdown:");
        while ( x-- != 0 )
            System.out.println(x);
        return save;
    }
}
```

This class doesn't actually do very much, but it does provide a basis for class file exploration. Once compiled, the outer layer of the resulting class file is as follows:

```
----file name: test.class
      |....magic: cafebabe
      |....version: 45.3
      |+---ConstantPool [42]
      |....access: PUBLIC
      |....this: Class: test
      |....parent: Class: java/lang/Object
      |....No Interfaces
      |+---Fields [1]
      |+---Methods [5]
      |+---Attributes [1]
```

The `magic` number of a class is `0xcafebabe`. If a class file does not contain this number, the Java virtual machine will refuse to load the class. This number must appear in a class file or the file is assumed to be invalid. The current major version is 45; the current minor version is 3. Future Java compilers will increment these numbers when the underlying class file format changes. Version numbers allow future Java machines to recognize and disallow execution of older class files.

Access Flags

Access flags are used throughout the class file to convey the access characteristics of various items. The flag itself is a collection of 11 individual bits. Table 33.1 lays out the masks.

Table 33.1. Access flag bit values.

Flag Value	Indication
ACC_PUBLIC = 0x0001	Global visibility
ACC_PRIVATE = 0x0002	Local class visibility
ACC_PROTECTED = 0x0004	Subclass visibility
ACC_STATIC = 0x0008	One occurrence in system (not per class)
ACC_FINAL = 0x0010	No changes allowed
ACC_SYNCHRONIZED = 0x0020	Access with a monitor
ACC_VOLATILE = 0x0040	No local caching
ACC_TRANSIENT = 0x0080	Not a persistent value
ACC_NATIVE = 0x0100	Native method implementation
ACC_INTERFACE = 0x0200	Class is an interface
ACC_ABSTRACT = 0x0400	Class or method is abstract

Access flags are present for a class and its fields and methods. Only a subset of values appears in any given item. Some bits apply only to fields (for example, VOLATILE and TRANSIENT); others apply only to methods (for example, SYNCHRONIZED and NATIVE).

Attributes

Attributes, like access flags, appear throughout a class file. They have the following form:

```
GenericAttribute_info
{
    u2 attribute_name;
    u4 attribute_length;
    u1 info[attribute_length];
}
```

A generic structure exists to enable loaders to skip over attributes they don't understand. The actual attribute has a unique structure that can be read if the loader understands the format. As an example, the following structure specifies the format of a source file attribute:

```
SourceFile_attribute
{
    u2 attribute_name;
    u4 attribute_length;
    u2 sourcefile_index;
}
```

The name of an attribute is an index into the constant pool. You learn about the constant pool in the next section. If a loader does not understand the source file attribute structure, it can skip the data by reading the number of bytes specified in the *length* parameter. For the source file attribute, the length is 2.

Constant Pool

The *constant pool* forms the basis for all numbers and strings within a class file. Nowhere else do you find strings or numbers. Any time you need to reference a string or number, you substitute an index into the constant pool. Consequently, the constant pool is the dominant feature of a class. The pool is even used directly within the virtual machine itself.

There are 12 different types of constants:

- `CONSTANT_Utf8 = 1`
- `CONSTANT_Unicode = 2`
- `CONSTANT_Integer = 3`
- `CONSTANT_Float = 4`
- `CONSTANT_Long = 5`
- `CONSTANT_Double = 6`
- `CONSTANT_Class = 7`
- `CONSTANT_String = 8`
- `CONSTANT_Fieldref = 9`
- `CONSTANT_Methodref = 10`
- `CONSTANT_InterfaceMethodref = 11`
- `CONSTANT_NameAndType = 12`

Each constant structure leads off with a tag identifying the structure type. Following the type is data specific to each individual structure. The layout of each constant structure is shown in Listing 33.1.

Listing 33.1. The layout of all 12 constant structures.

```
CONSTANT_Utf8_info
{
    u1 tag;
    u2 length;
    u1 bytes[length];
}

CONSTANT_Unicode_info
{
    u1 tag;
    u2 length;
    u2 words[length];
}

CONSTANT_Integer_info
{
    u1 tag;
    u4 bytes;
}

CONSTANT_Float_info
{
    u1 tag;
    u4 bytes;
}

CONSTANT_Long_info
{
    u1 tag;
    u4 high_bytes;
    u4 low_bytes;
}

CONSTANT_Double_info
{
    u1 tag;
    u4 high_bytes;
    u4 low_bytes;
}

CONSTANT_Class_info
{
    u1 tag;
    u2 name_index;
}

CONSTANT_String_info
{
    u1 tag;
    u2 string_index;
}
```

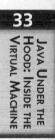

continues

Listing 33.1. continued

```
CONSTANT_Fieldref_info
{
    u1 tag;
    u2 class_index;
    u2 name_and_type_index;
}

CONSTANT_Methodref_info
{
    u1 tag;
    u2 class_index;
    u2 name_and_type_index;
}

CONSTANT_InterfaceMethodref_info
{
    u1 tag;
    u2 class_index;
    u2 name_and_type_index;
}

CONSTANT_NameAndType_info
{
    u1 tag;
    u2 name_index;
    u2 signature_index;
}
```

The CONSTANT_Utf8 structure contains standard ASCII text strings. These are not null-terminated because they use an explicit *length* parameter. Notice that most of the constants reference other constants for information. Methods, for example, specify a class and type by providing indexes to other constant pool members. Constant pool cross-references eliminate repetition of data.

The constant pool for the sample test class appears as follows:

```
¦---file name: test.class
   ¦...magic: cafebabe
   ¦...version: 45.3
   ¦---ConstantPool [42]
   ¦   ¦...String #28 -> Performing countdown:
   ¦   ¦...Class: java/lang/System
   ¦   ¦...Class: java/lang/Object
   ¦   ¦...Class: java/io/PrintStream
   ¦   ¦...Class: test
   ¦   ¦...Method: java/lang/Object.<init>()V
   ¦   ¦...Field: test.st_one I
   ¦   ¦...Field: java/lang/System.out Ljava/io/PrintStream;
   ¦   ¦...Method: java/io/PrintStream.println(I)V
   ¦   ¦...Method: java/io/PrintStream.println(Ljava/lang/String;)V
   ¦   ¦...NameAndType: st_one I
   ¦   ¦...NameAndType: println (I)V
   ¦   ¦...NameAndType: out Ljava/io/PrintStream;
   ¦   ¦...NameAndType: println (Ljava/lang/String;)V
```

```
          |...NameAndType: <init> ()V
          |...Utf8 [7] println
          |...Utf8 [4] (I)V
          |...Utf8 [3] ()I
          |...Utf8 [13] ConstantValue
          |...Utf8 [4] (I)I
          |...Utf8 [19] java/io/PrintStream
          |...Utf8 [10] Exceptions
          |...Utf8 [15] LineNumberTable
          |...Utf8 [1] I
          |...Utf8 [10] SourceFile
          |...Utf8 [14] LocalVariables
          |...Utf8 [4] Code
          |...Utf8 [21] Performing countdown:
          |...Utf8 [3] out
          |...Utf8 [21] (Ljava/lang/String;)V
          |...Utf8 [16] java/lang/Object
          |...Utf8 [6] <init>
          |...Utf8 [21] Ljava/io/PrintStream;
          |...Utf8 [16] java/lang/System
          |...Utf8 [12] do_countdown
          |...Utf8 [5] ([I)Z
          |...Utf8 [6] st_one
          |...Utf8 [7] getData
          |...Utf8 [9] test.java
          |...Utf8 [3] ()V
          |...Utf8 [4] test
   |...access: PUBLIC
   |...this: Class: test
   |...parent: Class: java/lang/Object
   |...No Interfaces
   |+--Fields [1]
   |+--Methods [5]
   |+--Attributes [1]
```

NOTE

The Viewer tool substitutes pool indexes with actual pool data whenever possible.

Fields

Field structures contain the individual data members of a class. Any class item that is not a method is placed into the fields section of the class file. The `field` structure looks like this:

```
field_info
{
    u2 access_flags;
    u2 name_index;
    u2 signature_index;
    u2 attribute_count;
    attribute_info attributes[attribute_count];
}
```

The sample test class contains one field:

```
¦---file name: test.class
    ¦...magic: cafebabe
    ¦...version: 45.3
    ¦+--ConstantPool [42]
    ¦...access: PUBLIC
    ¦...this: Class: test
    ¦...parent: Class: java/lang/Object
    ¦...No Interfaces
    ¦---Fields [1]
    ¦    ¦---st_one
    ¦           ¦...I
    ¦           ¦...PUBLIC STATIC
    ¦           ¦...No attributes
    ¦+--Methods [5]
    ¦+--Attributes [1]
```

Methods

The method section of the class file contains all the executable content of a class. In addition to the method name and signature, the structure contains a set of attributes. One of these attributes has the actual bytecodes that the virtual machine will execute. The method structure is shown here:

```
method_info
{
    u2 access_flags;
    u2 name_index;
    u2 signature_index;
    u2 attributes_count;
    attribute_info attributes[attribute_count];
}
```

The sample test class contains the following method section:

```
¦---file name: test.class
    ¦...magic: cafebabe
    ¦...version: 45.3
    ¦+--ConstantPool [42]
    ¦...access: PUBLIC
    ¦...this: Class: test
    ¦...parent: Class: java/lang/Object
    ¦...No Interfaces
    ¦+--Fields [1]
    ¦---Methods [5]
    ¦    ¦---<init>
    ¦    ¦      ¦...()V
    ¦    ¦      ¦...PUBLIC
    ¦    ¦      ¦---Attributes [1]
    ¦    ¦           ¦---Code
    ¦    ¦                  ¦...max_stack = 1
    ¦    ¦                  ¦...max_locals = 1
    ¦    ¦                  ¦+--Byte Codes [10]
    ¦    ¦                  ¦...No exceptions
    ¦    ¦                  ¦+--Attributes [1]
```

```
            |  |---<init>
            |  |   |...(I)V
            |  |   |...PUBLIC
            |  |   |---Attributes [1]
            |  |        |---Code
            |  |             |...max_stack = 1
            |  |             |...max_locals = 2
            |  |             |+--Byte Codes [9]
            |  |             |...No exceptions
            |  |             |+--Attributes [1]
            |  |---getData
            |  |   |...([I)Z
            |  |   |...PUBLIC NATIVE
            |  |   |...No attributes
            |  |---do_countdown
            |  |   |...()I
            |  |   |...PUBLIC
            |  |   |---Attributes [1]
            |  |        |---Code
            |  |             |...max_stack = 2
            |  |             |...max_locals = 2
            |  |             |+--Byte Codes [33]
            |  |             |...No exceptions
            |  |             |+--Attributes [1]
            |  |---do_countdown
            |  |   |...(I)I
            |  |   |...PUBLIC
            |  |   |---Attributes [1]
            |  |        |---Code
            |  |             |...max_stack = 2
            |  |             |...max_locals = 3
            |  |             |+--Byte Codes [29]
            |  |             |...No exceptions
            |  |             |+--Attributes [1]
            |+--Attributes [1]
```

Each method has a name and signature. Signatures are used by Java to determine calling arguments and return types. The format of a signature is as follows:

`"(args*)return_type"`

Arguments can be any combination of the characters listed in Table 33.2. Class name arguments are written as follows:

`Lclass_name;`

The semicolon (;) signals the end of the class name, just as the right parenthesis signals the end of an argument list. Arrays are followed by the array type:

```
[B for an array of bytes
[Ljava/langString; for an array of objects (in this case, Strings)
```

Table 33.2. Method signature symbols.

Type	Signature Character
byte	B
char	C
class	L
end of class	;
float	F
double	D
function	(
end of function	)
int	I
long	J
short	S
void	V
boolean	Z

All the methods except getData() have a code attribute. This method is marked as NATIVE, so the Java virtual machine expects the code to be in a native library. Each non-native method contains a code attribute that has the following format:

```
Code_attribute
{
    u2 attribute_name;
    u4 attribute_length;
    u2 max_stack;
    u2 max_locals;
    u4 code_length;
    u1 code[code_length];
    u2 exception_table_length;
    ExceptionItem exceptions[exception_table_length];
    u2 attributes_count;
    attribute_info attributes[attribute_count];
}
```

Code attributes contain a private list of other attributes. Typically, these are debugging lists, such as line-number information.

Exception Handling

The pc register points to the next bytecode to execute. Whenever an exception is thrown, the method's exception table is searched for a handler. Each exception table entry has this format:

```
ExceptionItem
{
    u2 start_pc;
    u2 end_pc;
    u2 handler_pc;
    u2 catch_type;
}
```

If the `pc` register is within the proper range and the thrown exception is the proper type, the entry's handler code block is executed. If no handler is found, the exception propagates up to the calling method. The procedure repeats itself until either a valid handler is found or the program exits.

Now that you've hit the code attribute, it's time to jump into the virtual machine.

The Virtual Machine

The Java virtual machine interprets Java bytecodes that are contained in code attributes. The virtual machine is stack based. Most computer architectures perform their operations on a mixture of memory locations and registers. The Java virtual machine performs its operations exclusively on a stack. This was done primarily to support portability. No assumptions could be made about the size or number of registers in a given CPU. Intel microprocessors are especially limited in their register composition.

Registers

The virtual machine does contain some registers, but these are used for tracking the current state of the machine:

- The `pc` register points to the next bytecode to execute
- The `vars` register points to the local variables for a method
- The `optop` register points to the operand stack
- The `frame` register points to the execution environment

All these registers are 32 bits wide and point into separate storage blocks. The blocks, however, can be allocated all at once because the code attribute specifies the size of the operand stack, the number of local variables, and the length of the bytecodes.

Operand Stack

Most Java bytecodes work on the operand stack. For example, to add two integers together, each integer is pushed onto the operand stack. The addition operator removes the top two integers, adds them, and places the result in their place back on the stack:

```
..., 4, 5 -> ..., 9
```

> **NOTE**
>
> Operand stack notation is used throughout the remainder of this chapter. The stack reads from left to right, with the stack top on the extreme right. Ellipses indicate indeterminate data buried on the stack. The arrow indicates an operation; the data to the right of the arrow represents the stack after the operation is performed.

Each stack location is 32 bits wide. Longs and doubles are 64 bits wide, so they take up two stack locations.

Local Variables

Each code attribute specifies the size of the local variables. A local variable is 32 bits wide, so long and double primitives take up two variable slots. Unlike C, all method arguments appear as local variables. The operand stack is reserved exclusively for operations.

Before detailing the bytecodes, I think a more holistic view of the virtual machine's operations would be instructive.

The Virtual Machine in Action

Consider the following method from the sample `test` class:

```
public int do_countdown(int x)
    {
        int save = x;

        System.out.println("Performing countdown:");
        while ( x-- != 0 )
            System.out.println(x);
        return save;
    }
```

The class file specifies that this method has a maximum operand stack of two and a local variable block of three. Figure 33.2 shows the initial state of these two blocks.

Notice how the method's input argument is placed into the local variable block. Java contains an extensive set of bytecodes dedicated to moving data between the local variable block and the operand stack. All data must be moved to the stack before it can be used. This is an important distinction between Java machine code and register-based machine architectures. Register machines reference memory directly from the contents of a register. Java must first move the contents of a variable to its operand stack before it can reference the location.

FIGURE 33.2.

The initial state of the operand stack and local variable blocks.

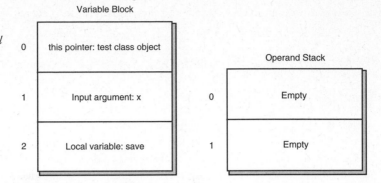

The do_countdown(int x) method contains 29 bytecodes. These two instructions store the input argument x into the local variable save:

```
0 iload_1    Move argument x onto the operand stack
1 istore_2   Store top of stack (x) into variable save
```

The next three bytecodes first load a target object (System.out) and a String onto the operand stack. At this point, println(String) is invoked. Notice that before the invocation, both elements of the operand stack are occupied. After the invocation, the operand stack is completely empty because invokevirtual removes all the stack elements it uses:

```
2 getstatic #8 <Field: java/lang/System.out Ljava/io/PrintStream;>
5 ldc1 #1 <String #28 -> Performing countdown:>
7 invokevirtual #10 <Method: java/io/PrintStream.println(Ljava/lang/String;)V>
```

This instruction transfers control to the test portion of the method's while loop. Most modern compilers code a loop with the loop test at the bottom:

```
10 goto 20
```

The loop body calls println(int):

```
13 getstatic #8 <Field: java/lang/System.out Ljava/io/PrintStream;>
16 iload_1    Move argument x onto the operand stack
17 invokevirtual #9 <Method: java/io/PrintStream.println(I)V>
```

Okay, this next bit is a little tricky. First, the current value of x is placed onto the stack. Next, 1 is subtracted from variable x. Finally, the value on the stack is checked for zero. Notice that the value on the stack is x before it was decremented. If the stack value is not zero, the body of the loop will be executed:

```
20 iload_1      Move argument x onto the operand stack
21 iinc 1 -1    Decrement argument x by one
24 ifne 13      Branch if stack top (x before decrement) not zero
```

The final two bytecodes move the value of the save variable onto the stack and then return this value to the calling method:

```
27 iload_2    Move variable save onto the operand stack
28 ireturn    Move integer on stack onto calling method's operand stack
```

The Verifier

When a class is loaded, it is passed through a bytecode verifier before it is executed. The verifier checks the internal consistency of the class and the validity of the code. Java uses a late binding scheme that puts the code at risk. In traditional languages, the object linker binds all the method calls and variable accesses to specific addresses. In Java, the virtual machine doesn't perform this service until the last possible moment. As a result, it is possible for a called class to have changed since the original class was compiled. Method names or their arguments may have been altered, or the access levels may have been changed. One of the verifier's jobs is to make sure that all external object references are correct and allowed.

No assumptions can be made about the origin of bytecodes. A hostile compiler could be used to create executable bytecodes that conform to the class file format, but specify illegal codes.

The verifier uses a conservative four-pass verification algorithm to check bytecodes.

Pass 1

The first pass through the verifier reads in the class file and ensures that it is valid. The magic number must be present and all the class data must be present with no truncation or extra data after the end of the class. Any recognized attributes must have the correct length and the constant pool must not have any unrecognized entries.

Pass 2

The second pass through the verifier involves validating class features other than the bytecodes. All methods and fields must have a valid name and signature, and every class must have a super class. Signatures are not actually checked, but they must appear valid. The next pass is more specific.

Pass 3

The third pass is the most complex because the bytecodes are validated. The bytecodes are analyzed to make sure that they have the correct type and number of arguments. In addition, a data-flow analysis is performed to determine each path through the method. Each path must arrive at a given point with the same stack size and types. Each path must call methods with the proper arguments, and fields must be modified with values of the appropriate type. Class accesses are not checked in this pass. Only the return type of external functions is verified.

Forcing all paths to arrive with the same stack and registers can lead the verifier to fail some otherwise legitimate bytecodes. This is a small price to pay for this high level of security.

Pass 4

The fourth pass loads externally referenced classes and checks that the method name and signatures match. This pass also validates that the current class has access rights to the external class. After complete validation, each instruction is replaced with a _quick alternative. These _quick bytecodes indicate that the class has been verified and need not be checked again.

Bytecodes

The bytecodes can be divided into 11 major categories:

- Pushing constants onto the stack
- Moving local variable contents to and from the stack
- Managing arrays
- Generic stack instructions (dup, swap, pop, and nop)
- Arithmetic and logical instructions
- Conversion instructions
- Control transfer and function return
- Manipulating object fields
- Method invocation
- Miscellaneous operations
- Monitors

Each bytecode has a unique tag and is followed by a fixed number of additional arguments. Notice that there is no way to work directly with class fields or local variables. They must be moved to the operand stack before any operations can be performed on the contents.

Generally, there are multiple formats for each individual operation. The addition operation provides a good example. There are actually four forms of addition: iadd, ladd, fadd, and dadd. Each type assumes the top two stack items are of the correct format: integers, longs, floats, or doubles.

Pushing Constants onto the Stack

Java uses the following instructions for moving object data and local variables to the operand stack.

Push One-Byte Signed Integer:

```
bipush=16 byte1      Stack: ... -> ..., byte1
```

Push Two-Byte Signed Integer:

```
sipush=17 byte1 byte2    Stack: ... -> ..., word1
```

Push Item from the Constant Pool (8-bit index):

```
ldc1=18 indexbyte1    Stack: ... -> ..., item
```

Push Item from the Constant Pool (16-bit index):

```
ldc2=19 indexbyte1 indexbyte2    Stack: ... -> ..., item
```

Push Long or Double from the Constant Pool (16-bit index):

```
ldc2w=20 indexbyte1 indexbyte2    Stack: ... -> ..., word1, word2
```

Push Null Object:

```
aconst_null=1    Stack: ... -> ..., null
```

Push Integer Constant -1:

```
iconst_m1=2   Stack: ... -> ..., -1
```

Push Integer Constants:

```
iconst_0=3   Stack: ... -> ..., 0
iconst_1=4   Stack: ... -> ..., 1
iconst_2=5   Stack: ... -> ..., 2
iconst_3=6   Stack: ... -> ..., 3
iconst_4=7   Stack: ... -> ..., 4
iconst_5=8   Stack: ... -> ..., 5
```

Push Long Constants:

```
lconst_0=9   Stack: ... -> ..., 0, 0
lconst_1=10  Stack: ... -> ..., 0, 1
```

Push Float Constants:

```
fconst_0=11  Stack: ... -> ..., 0
fconst_1=12  Stack: ... -> ..., 1
fconst_2=13  Stack: ... -> ..., 2
```

Push Double Constants:

```
dconst_0=14  Stack: ... -> ..., 0, 0
dconst_1=15  Stack: ... -> ..., 0, 1
```

Accessing Local Variables

The most commonly referenced local variables are at the first four offsets from the vars register. Because of this, Java provides single-byte instructions to access these variables for both reading and writing. A two-byte instruction is needed to reference variables greater than four deep. The variable at location zero is the class pointer itself (the this pointer).

Load Integer from Local Variable:

```
iload=21 vindex  Stack: ... -> ..., contents of varaible at vars[vindex]
iload_o=26       Stack: ... -> ..., contents of variable at vars[0]
iload_1=27       Stack: ... -> ..., contents of variable at vars[1]
iload_2=28       Stack: ... -> ..., contents of variable at vars[2]
iload_3=29       Stack: ... -> ..., contents of variable at vars[3]
```

Load Long Integer from Local Variable:

```
lload=22 vindex  Stack: .. -> ..., word1, word2  from vars[vindex] & vars[vindex+1]
lload_0=30       Stack: .. -> ..., word1, word2  from vars[0] & vars[1]
lload_1=31       Stack: .. -> ..., word1, word2  from vars[1] & vars[2]
lload_2=32       Stack: .. -> ..., word1, word2  from vars[2] & vars[3]
lload_3=33       Stack: .. -> ..., word1, word2  from vars[3] & vars[4]
```

Load Float from Local Variable:

```
fload=23 vindex  Stack: ... -> ..., contents from vars[vindex]
fload_0=34       Stack: ... -> ..., contents from vars[0]
fload_1=35       Stack: ... -> ..., contents from vars[1]
fload_2=36       Stack: ... -> ..., contents from vars[2]
fload_3=37       Stack: ... -> ..., contents from vars[3]
```

Load Double from Local Variable:

```
dload=24 vindex  Stack: ... -> ..., word1, word2  from vars[vindex] &
vars[vindex+1]
dload_0=38       Stack: ... -> ..., word1, word2  from vars[0] & vars[1]
dload_1=39       Stack: ... -> ..., word1, word2  from vars[1] & vars[2]
dload_2=40       Stack: ... -> ..., word1, word2  from vars[2] & vars[3]
dload_3=41       Stack: ... -> ..., word1, word2  from vars[3] & vars[4]
```

Load Object from Local Variable:

```
aload=25 vindex  Stack: ... -> ..., object  from vars[vindex]
aload_0=42       Stack: ... -> ..., object  from vars[0]
aload_1=43       Stack: ... -> ..., object  from vars[1]
aload_2=44       Stack: ... -> ..., object  from vars[2]
aload_3=45       Stack: ... -> ..., object  from vars[3]
```

Store Integer into Local Variable:

```
istore=54 vindex Stack: ..., INT -> ... into vars[vindex]
istore_0=59      Stack: ..., INT -> ... into vars[0]
istore_1=60      Stack: ..., INT -> ... into vars[1]
istore_2=61      Stack: ..., INT -> ... into vars[2]
istore_3=62      Stack: ..., INT -> ... into vars[3]
```

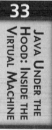

Store Long Integer into Local Variable:

```
lstore=55 vindex Stack: ..., word1, word2 -> ... into vars[vindex] &
vars[vindex+1]
lstore_0=63      Stack: ..., word1, word2 -> ... into vars[0] & vars[1]
lstore_1=64      Stack: ..., word1, word2 -> ... into vars[1] & vars[2]
lstore_2=65      Stack: ..., word1, word2 -> ... into vars[2] & vars[3]
lstore_3=66      Stack: ..., word1, word2 -> ... into vars[3] & vars[4]
```

Store Float into Local Variable:

```
fstore=56 vindex Stack: ..., FLOAT -> ... into vars[vindex]
fstore_0=67      Stack: ..., FLOAT -> ... into vars[0]
fstore_1=68      Stack: ..., FLOAT -> ... into vars[1]
fstore_2=69      Stack: ..., FLOAT -> ... into vars[2]
fstore_3=70      Stack: ..., FLOAT -> ... into vars[3]
```

Store Double into Local Variable:

```
dstore=57 vindex Stack: ..., word1, word2 -> ... into vars[vindex] &
vars[vindex+1]
dstore_0=71      Stack: ..., word1, word2 -> ... into vars[0] & vars[1]
dstore_1=72      Stack: ..., word1, word2 -> ... into vars[1] & vars[2]
dstore_2=73      Stack: ..., word1, word2 -> ... into vars[2] & vars[3]
dstore_3=74      Stack: ..., word1, word2 -> ... into vars[3] & vars[4]
```

Store Object into Local Variable:

```
astore=58 vindex Stack: ..., OBJ -> ... into vars[vindex]
astore_0=75      Stack: ..., OBJ -> ... into vars[0]
astore_1=76      Stack: ..., OBJ -> ... into vars[1]
astore_2=77      Stack: ..., OBJ -> ... into vars[2]
astore_3=78      Stack: ..., OBJ -> ... into vars[3]
```

Increment Local Variable (incrementing applies only to integers):

```
iinc=132 vindex constant   Stack: ... -> ...  vars[vindex] += constant
```

Managing Arrays

Arrays are treated as objects, but they don't use a method table pointer. Because of this uniqueness, arrays have special bytecodes to create and access them.

Allocate a New Array:

```
newarray=188 type Stack: ..., size -> ..., OBJ
```

Allocate a New Array of Objects:

```
anewarray=189 classindex1 classindex2 Stack: ..., size -> ..., OBJ
```

Allocate a New Multidimensional Array:

```
multianewarray=197 indexbyte1 indexbyte1 indexbyte2  Stack: ..., size1, size2,
     etc. -> ..., OBJ
```

Get the Array Length:

```
arraylength=190 Stack: ..., OBJ -> ..., length
```

Load Primitives from the Array:

```
iaload=46 Stack: ..., OBJ, index -> ..., INT
laload=47 Stack: ..., OBJ, index -> ..., LONG1, LONG2
faload=48 Stack: ..., OBJ, index -> ..., FLOAT
daload=49 Stack: ..., OBJ, index -> ..., DOUBLE1, DOUBLE2
aaload=50 Stack: ..., OBJ, index -> ..., OBJ
baload=51 Stack: ..., OBJ, index -> ..., BYTE
caload=52 Stack: ..., OBJ, index -> ..., CHAR
saload=53 Stack: ..., OBJ, index -> ..., SHORT
```

Store Primitives into the Array:

```
iastore=79 Stack: ..., OBJ, index, INT -> ...
lastore=80 Stack: ..., OBJ, index, LONG1, LONG2 -> ...
fastore=81 Stack: ..., OBJ, index, FLOAT -> ...
dastore=82 Stack: ..., OBJ, index, DOUBLE1, DOUBLE2 -> ...
aastore=83 Stack: ..., OBJ, index, OBJ -> ...
bastore=84 Stack: ..., OBJ, index, BYTE -> ...
castore=85 Stack: ..., OBJ, index, CHAR -> ...
sastore=86 Stack: ..., OBJ, index, SHORT -> ...
```

Generic Stack Instructions

Following are the basic operations that alter the stack.

Do Nothing:

```
nop=0    Stack: ... -> ...
```

Pop Stack Values:

```
pop=87  Stack: ..., VAL -> ...
pop2=88  Stack: ..., VAL1, VAL2 -> ...
```

Duplicate Stack Values and Possibly Insert below Stack Top:

```
dup=89     Stack: ..., V -> ..., V, V
dup2=92    Stack: ..., V1, V2 -> ..., V1, V2, V1, V2
dup_x1=90  Stack: ..., V1, V2 -> ..., V2, V1, V2
dup2_x1=93 Stack: ..., V1, V2, V3 -> ..., V2, V3, V1, V2, V3
dup_x2=91  Stack: ..., V1, V2, V3 -> ..., V3, V1, V2, V3
dup2_x2=94 Stack: ..., V1, V2, V3, V4 -> ..., V3, V4, V1, V2, V3, V4
```

Swap Two Stack Items:

```
swap=95    Stack: ..., V1, V2 -> ..., V2, V1
```

Arithmetic and Logical Instructions

All the arithmetic operations operate on four possible types: integer, long, float, or double. Logical instructions operate only on integer and long types.

Addition:

```
iadd=96 Stack: ..., INT1, INT2 -> ..., INT1+INT2
ladd=97 Stack: ..., L1_1, L1_2, L2_1, L2_2 -> ..., L1+L2 (high), L1+L2 (low)
fadd=98 Stack: ..., FLOAT1, FLOAT2 -> ..., FLOAT1+FLOAT2
dadd=99 Stack: ..., D1_1, D1_2, D2_1, D2_2 -> ..., D1+D2 (high), D1+D2 (low)
```

Subtraction:

```
isub=100 Stack: ..., INT1, INT2 -> ..., INT1-INT2
lsub=101 Stack: ..., L1_1, L1_2, L2_1, L2_2 -> ..., L1-L2 (high), L1-L2 (low)
fsub=102 Stack: ..., FLOAT1, FLOAT2 -> ..., FLOAT1-FLOAT2
dsub=103 Stack: ..., D1_1, D1_2, D2_1, D2_2 -> ..., D1-D2 (high), D1-D2 (low)
```

Multiplication:

```
imul=104 Stack: ..., INT1, INT2 -> ..., INT1*INT2
lmul=105 Stack: ..., L1_1, L1_2, L2_1, L2_2 -> ..., L1*L2 (high), L1*L2 (low)
fmul=106 Stack: ..., FLOAT1, FLOAT2 -> ..., FLOAT1*FLOAT2
dmul=107 Stack: ..., D1_1, D1_2, D2_1, D2_2 -> ..., D1*D2 (high), D1*D2 (low)
```

Division:

```
idiv=108 Stack: ..., INT1, INT2 -> ..., INT1/INT2
ldiv=109 Stack: ..., L1_1, L1_2, L2_1, L2_2 -> ..., L1/L2 (high), L1/L2 (low)
fdiv=110 Stack: ..., FLOAT1, FLOAT2 -> ..., FLOAT1/FLOAT2
ddiv=111 Stack: ..., D1_1, D1_2, D2_1, D2_2 -> ..., D1/D2 (high), D1/D2 (low)
```

Remainder:

```
irem=112 Stack: ..., INT1, INT2 -> ..., INT1%INT2
lrem=113 Stack: ..., L1_1, L1_2, L2_1, L2_2 -> ..., L1%L2 (high), L1%L2 (low)
frem=114 Stack: ..., FLOAT1, FLOAT2 -> ..., FLOAT1%FLOAT2
drem=115 Stack: ..., D1_1, D1_2, D2_1, D2_2 -> ..., D1%D2 (high), D1%D2 (low)
```

Negation:

```
ineg=116 Stack: ..., INT -> ..., -INT
lneg=117 Stack: ..., LONG1, LONG2 -> ..., -LONG1, -LONG2
fneg=118 Stack: ..., FLOAT -> ..., -FLOAT
dneg=119 Stack: ..., DOUBLE1, DOUBLE2 -> ..., -DOUBLE1, -DOUBLE2
```

Integer Logical Instructions:

>>> denotes an unsigned right shift

```
ishl=120 Stack: ..., INT1, INT2 -> INT1<<(INT2 & 0x1f)
ishr=122 Stack: ..., INT1, INT2 -> INT1>>(INT2 & 0x1f)
iushr=124 Stack: ..., INT1, INT2 -> INT1>>>(INT2 & 0x1f)
```

Long Integer Logical Instructions:

>>> denotes an unsigned right shift

```
lshl=121  Stack: ..., L1, L2, INT -> L1<<(INT & 0x3f), L2<<(INT & 0x3f)
lshr=123  Stack: ..., L1, L2, INT -> INT1>>(INT & 0x3f), L2>>(INT & 0x03)
lushr=125 Stack: ..., L1, L2, INT -> INT1>>>(INT & 0x3f), L2>>>(INT & 0x3f)
```

Integer Boolean Operations:

```
iand=126  Stack: ..., INT1, INT2 -> ..., INT1&INT2
ior=128   Stack: ..., INT1, INT2 -> ..., INT1|INT2
ixor=130  Stack: ..., INT1, INT2 -> ..., INT1^INT2
```

Long Integer Boolean Operations:

```
land=127  Stack: ..., L1_1, L1_2, L2_1, L2_2 -> ..., L1_1&L2_1, L1_2&L2_2
lor=129   Stack: ..., L1_1, L1_2, L2_1, L2_2 -> ..., L1_1|L2_1, L1_2|L2_2
lxor=131  Stack: ..., L1_1, L1_2, L2_1, L2_2 -> ..., L1_1^L2_1. L1_2^L2_2
```

Conversion Instructions

Because most of the previous bytecodes expect the stack to contain a homogenous set of operands, Java uses conversion functions. In code, you can add a float and an integer, but Java will first convert the integer to a float type before performing the addition.

Integer Conversions:

```
i2l=133      Stack: .., INT -> ..., LONG1, LONG2
i2f=134      Stack: .., INT -> ..., FLOAT
i2d=135      Stack: .., INT -> ..., DOUBLE1, DOUBLE2
int2byte=145 Stack: .., INT -> ..., BYTE
int2char=146 Stack: .., INT -> ..., CHAR
int2short=147 Stack: .., INT -> ..., SHORT
```

Long Integer Conversions:

```
l2i=136      Stack: .., LONG1, LONG2 -> ..., INT
l2f=137      Stack: .., LONG1, LONG2 -> ..., FLOAT
l2d=138      Stack: .., LONG1, LONG2 -> ..., DOUBLE1, DOUBLE2
```

Float Conversions:

```
f2i=139      Stack: .., FLOAT -> ..., INT
f2l=140      Stack: .., FLOAT -> ..., LONG1, LONG2
f2d=141      Stack: .., FLOAT -> ..., DOUBLE1, DOUBLE2
```

Double Conversions:

```
d2i=142      Stack: .., DOUBLE1, DOUBLE2 -> ..., INT
d2l=143      Stack: .., DOUBLE1, DOUBLE2 -> ..., LONG1, LONG2
d2f=144      Stack: .., DOUBLE1, DOUBLE2 -> ..., FLOAT
```

Control Transfer and Function Return

All branch indexes are signed 16-bit offsets from the current pc register.

Comparisons with Zero:

```
ifeq=153 branch1 branch2    Stack: ..., INT -> ...
ifne=154 branch1 branch2    Stack: ..., INT -> ...
iflt=155 branch1 branch2    Stack: ..., INT -> ...
ifge=156 branch1 branch2    Stack: ..., INT -> ...
ifgt=157 branch1 branch2    Stack: ..., INT -> ...
ifle=158 branch1 branch2    Stack: ..., INT -> ...
```

Comparisons with Null:

```
ifnull=198 branch1 branch2    Stack: ..., OBJ -> ...
ifnonnull=199 branch1 branch2 Stack: ..., OBJ -> ...
```

Compare Two Integers:

```
if_icmpeq=159 branch1 branch2  Stack: ..., INT1, INT2 -> ...
if_icmpne=160 branch1 branch2  Stack: ..., INT1, INT2 -> ...
if_icmplt=161 branch1 branch2  Stack: ..., INT1, INT2 -> ...
if_icmpge=162 branch1 branch2  Stack: ..., INT1, INT2 -> ...
if_icmpgt=163 branch1 branch2  Stack: ..., INT1, INT2 -> ...
if_icmple=164 branch1 branch2  Stack: ..., INT1, INT2 -> ...
```

Compare Two Long Integers:

```
lcmp=148  Stack: ..., L1_1, L1_2, L2_1, L2_2 -> ..., INT (One of [-1, 0, 1])
```

Compare Two Floats:

```
l->-1 on NaN, g->1 on NaN.
fcmpl=149  Stack: ..., FLOAT1, FLOAT2 -> ..., INT (One of [-1, 0, 1])
fcmpg=150  Stack: ..., FLOAT1, FLOAT2 -> ..., INT (One of [-1, 0, 1])
```

Compare Two Doubles:

```
l->-1 on NaN, g->1 on NaN.
dcmpl=151  Stack: ..., D1_1, D1_2, D2_1, D2_2 -> ..., INT (One of [-1, 0, 1])
dcmpg=152  Stack: ..., D1_1, D1_2, D2_1, D2_2 -> ..., INT (One of [-1, 0, 1])
```

Compare Two Objects:

```
if_acmpeq=165 branch1 branch2  Stack: ..., OBJ1, OBJ2 -> ...
if_acmpne=166 branch1 branch2  Stack: ..., OBJ1, OBJ2 -> ...
```

Unconditional Branching (16-bit and 32-bit branching):

```
goto=167 branch1 branch2                    Stack: ... -> ...
goto_w=200 branch1 branch2 branch3 branch4  Stack: ... -> ...
```

Jump Subroutine (16-bit and 32-bit jumps):

```
jsr=168 branch1 branch2                    Stack: ... -> ..., returnAddress
jsr_w=201 branch1 branch2 branch3 branch4  Stack: ... -> ..., returnAddress
```

Return from Subroutine:

The return address is retrieved from a local variable, not the stack.

```
ret=169 vindex    Stack: ... -> ...   (returnAddress <- vars[vindex])
ret_w=209 vindex1 vindex2  Stack: ... -> ...   (returnAddress <- vars[vindex])
```

Return Primitives:

The current stack frame is destroyed. The top primitive is pushed onto the caller's operand stack.

```
ireturn=172  Stack: ..., INT -> [destroyed]
lreturn=173  Stack: ..., LONG1, LONG2 -> [destroyed]
freturn=174  Stack: ..., FLOAT -> [destroyed]
```

```
dreturn=175  Stack: ..., DOUBLE1, DOUBLE2 -> [destroyed]
areturn=176  Stack: ..., OBJ -> [destroyed]
return=177   Stack: ... -> [destroyed]
```

Calling the Breakpoint Handler:

```
breakpoint=202 Stack: ..., -> ...
```

Manipulating Object Fields

A 16-bit index into the constant pool is used to retrieve the class and field name. These names are used to determine the field offset and width. The object reference on the stack is used as the source or target. Values are 32 or 64 bits, depending on the field information in the constant pool.

```
Getstatic=178  index1 index2   Stack: ..., -> ..., VAL
Putstatic=179  index1 index2   Stack: ..., VAL -> ...
Getfield=180   index1 index2   Stack: ..., OBJ -> ..., VAL
Putfield=181   index1 index2   Stack: ..., OBJ, VAL -> ...
```

Method Invocation

There are four types of method invocation:

- invokevirtual=182—This is the normal method dispatch in Java. Use the index bytes to create a 16-bit index into the constant table of the current class. Extract the method name and signature. Search the method table of the stack object to determine the method address. Use the method signature to remove the method arguments from the operand stack and transfer them to the new method's local variables.

- invokenonvirtual=183—Used when a method is called with the super keyword. Use the index bytes to create a 16-bit index into the constant pool of the current class. Extract the method name and signature. Search the named class's method table to determine the method address. Extract the object and arguments and place them in the new method's local variables.

- invokestatic=184—Used to call static methods. Create a 16-bit index into the current class's constant pool. Extract the method and search the named class's method table for the address. Transfer the arguments as before. There is no object to pass.

- invokeinterface=185—Invoke an interface function. Again, a 16-bit index is created to find the method name and signature. This time, however, the number of arguments is determined from the bytecodes, not the signature.

```
virtual index1 index2            Stack: ..., OBJ, [arg1, [arg2, ...]] -> ...
nonvirtual index1 index2         Stack: ..., OBJ, [arg1, [arg2, ...]] -> ...
static index1 index2             Stack: ..., [arg1, [arg2, ...]] -> ...
interface index1 index2 nargs resv Stack: ..., OBJ, [arg1, [arg2, ...]] -> ...
```

Miscellaneous Operations

The following instructions don't fall under any other heading; they deal with generic object operations, such as creation and casting.

Throw Exception:

```
athrow=191  Stack: ..., OBJ -> [undefined]
```

Create a New Object:

```
new=187 index1 index2  Stack: ... -> ..., OBJ
```

Check a Cast Operation:

```
checkcast=192 index1 index2  Stack: ..., OBJ -> ..., OBJ
```

Instanceof:

```
instanceof=193 index1 index2  Stack: ..., OBJ -> ... INT (1 or 0)
```

Monitors

Monitor instructions are used for synchronization.

Enter a Monitored Region of Code:

```
monitorenter=194  Stack: ..., OBJ -> ...
```

Exit a Monitored Region of Code:

```
monitorexit=195  Stack: ..., OBJ -> ...
```

Summary

This chapter revealed the internal structure of the Java virtual machine through use of the Viewer tool. You learned to interpret signatures and read Java machine code. The elegance of the Java class file was also presented.

Keep this information in mind when you are working with Java. An appreciation for the internal structure will help you become an expert Java programmer. I hope this introduction has heightened your curiosity; feel free to use the Viewer program to explore some of your own Java classes.

Java Security

by Glenn Vanderburg

IN THIS CHAPTER

Java's popularity and high profile are the product of several different characteristics, but none are more important than Java's claim to be a "secure" language. Java isn't the first language to have built-in security features, but it is *one* of the first; the others have been research projects or special-purpose languages. Certainly none can come close to Java's general-purpose, mainstream appeal.

This chapter presents a brief survey of Java security. First, you'll learn why security is important, and what kinds of threats Java protects against. You'll also learn the details of how Java security works, and how applications make use of the security features to implement their own security policies. Next, discussion turns to the new facilities in Java 1.1 for managing digitally signed classes and access control lists. Finally, the chapter discusses the quality of Java's security facilities: how strong they are, what weaknesses remain, and how Java security compares with other systems.

Why Is Security Important?

Since the introduction of Java in late 1995, it's been amusing to watch the varying reactions to Java's security claims. Java's creators recognize that security is important, and believe that they have devised a good solution. There are many who agree with them, but there are also many who don't, and the dissenters range all over the spectrum. Some decry the whole idea of indiscriminately bringing untrusted, possibly rogue programs onto your machine from the Internet, claiming that no language security model can be solid enough to hold up against clever crackers. Others wonder what all the fuss is about, and ask whether security is needed at all—wouldn't it be better if applets could actually read and write your files and do useful work for you? Many developers take a middle view; they understand the need for security in general, but they're frustrated when their own Java programs aren't allowed to do benign, helpful things.

All these groups have some good points, but they miss other important points about Java security and Internet security in general.

Is Java Security a Mirage?

If your computer and the data stored in it are important to you, it's easy to understand why you may not want to run Java applets at all. Java's creators claim that it's secure, but what if they're wrong? You would be opening the door for some malevolent programmer to enter your computer and steal, destroy, or alter important data.

But the same is true of software that you manually load from the Internet and install on your machine. Even if you never do that, you also risk your data when you purchase a shrink-wrapped program from a store and install it from disks or CD. Those programs could destroy or alter your data immediately, or steal it the next time you are connected to the Internet. Although this may sound unlikely to you, it has happened. Several companies have accidentally shipped viruses to their customers along with products. Early beta versions of the Microsoft Network software performed some data collection that many users considered to be an invasion of privacy.

Java may actually improve the overall security of our computers because it guards against accidents almost as much as it guards against deliberate damage. Most of us have had the experience of installing a buggy new program that caused problems on our computers so severe that we had to reinstall the operating system. In many cases, such experiences result in the loss of important data. Although Java may not completely eliminate such problems, Java applets won't be able to inflict such damage, even accidentally.

In fact, the only perfectly secure computer is one that is unplugged. To do useful things, you have to take some risks, and the essence of security is to have acceptable levels of risk and inconvenience. This is true of all security, not just computer security. That's not to say that good security has to be a lot of trouble, but perfect security is always more trouble than it's worth.

Is Java Security Really Necessary?

On the other extreme, if what's on your computer isn't vitally important to you, or if you're simply not convinced anyone would want to steal or destroy it, you may see Java's security restrictions as a nuisance. It would be great if applets, fetched on demand from Web pages (and free of charge), could actually be *useful* applications that you could use to accomplish your work.

That certainly would be great, even if the applets weren't free. Unfortunately, there are a couple things about this scenario that should make you uneasy. Traditional software requires your conscious intervention before it can do anything on your computer: you have to acquire and install it first, and then actually run it. An applet, on the other hand, can be invoked without forethought when you browse to a Web page that contains it. Furthermore, you may never know the applet is there—it may not take up any visible space on the Web page. So an applet can run on your system without any initiative on your part, and it may not leave a trace behind. With an applet, you have no choice, and the applet has no accountability.

You may wonder why anyone would want to attack your system. The unfortunate fact is that many crackers choose their targets randomly. They aren't searching for any particular data, or seeking to harm any particular individual. Instead, they are vandals, or they just want to practice their skills or find some random computer they can use to hide their tracks while they attack their true target. They search for vulnerable systems and zero in on them. Historically, most cracking incidents have focused on UNIX systems, but with the increasing prevalence of Windows and Macintosh systems on the Internet, things are bound to change.

Programs automatically fetched to your system and run locally really are different from those you install deliberately, and their security needs are different. Think of workers who come to your home: it's fine to let selected people in when you're there and expecting them, but you wouldn't leave all your doors open all the time just in case someone came by to do some work on your house.

Why Is Java Security So Strict?

Many users and applet developers understand the need for security, but wish Java security weren't so strict and inflexible. They say that users should be able to disable or weaken Java's security if they want to. To a large degree, they're right, and you can expect Java applications to have more flexibility in the future.

Java security isn't all or nothing. Applets run in the context of hosting applications—the programs that load the applets and initialize the security barriers around them. Examples include HotJava and Netscape Navigator. The hosting applications can grant or deny access to applets based on a wide variety of criteria: the name of an applet, where it came from, the type of resource it's trying to access, even the particular resource. Applications can choose to let applets read some files, but not others, for example.

If that's the case, then why is Java security in early hosting applications so inflexibly strict? There are two reasons.

The first is that such configurable, flexible security is difficult to get right. It is usually easy to build a high, impenetrable wall with no holes at all, but a wall with selective holes is much harder to develop. Flexible, selective schemes involve a lot of extra complexity, and with complexity comes the potential for mistakes. In addition, there are subtle, difficult questions surrounding flexible security schemes. For example, employees may have very different ideas about acceptable security than their employer does—how much control should be given to the users and how much to the site security administrator? Faced with numerous tough questions like that, the people behind Java decided to be careful at first. They started with an extremely conservative security model, which will become less rigid as time goes on. This is probably a good strategy because a big security scare early in Java's lifetime would have really dampened enthusiasm for the language.

The other problem is that, until recently, there hasn't been a good criterion for deciding which applets should be trusted and which should not. The best solution is probably to trust applets based on who wrote them, but that's difficult to verify. JavaSoft has developed a model based on digital signatures, and the support for that model is one of the new features of Java 1.1. As I write this, hosting applications are being prepared that use these features to provide more flexible security policies. Some of those applications (including Netscape Navigator 4.0) should be available by the time you read this.

Later in this chapter, you read more about the details of the security model and how the application security manager can make fine-grained decisions about access to system resources.

What Are the Dangers?

To really understand the Java security model—why it's important, how it works, and how to work with it—you should have a good idea about the kinds of security attacks that are possible and which system resources can be used to mount such attacks. Java takes care to protect these resources from untrusted code. If you are using a Java application that allows you to configure applet security, or if you are writing a Java application that loads classes from the Net, it helps to understand just what doors you might be opening when you give an applet access to a particular resource.

The Kinds of Attacks

There are several different kinds of security attacks that can be mounted on a computer system. Some of them are surprising to people who are new to computer security issues, but they are very real and can be devastating under the right circumstances. Table 34.1 lists some common types of attacks.

Table 34.1. Some common types of attacks against computers.

Type of Attack	*Description*
Theft of information	Nearly every computer contains some information that the owner or primary user of the machine would like to keep private.
Destruction of information	In addition to data that is private, *most* of the data on typical computers has some value, and losing it would be costly.
Theft of resources	Computers contain more than just data. They have valuable, finite resources that cost money: disk space and a CPU are the best examples. A Java applet on a Web page could quietly begin doing some extensive computation in the background, periodically sending intermediate results back to a central server, thus stealing some of your CPU cycles to perform part of someone else's large project. This would slow down your machine, wasting another valuable resource: your time.
Denial of service	Similar to theft of resources, denial-of-service attacks involve using as much as possible of a finite resource, not because the attacker really needs the resource, but simply to prevent someone *else* from being able to use it. Some computers (like mail servers) are extremely important to the day-to-day operations of businesses, and attackers can cause a lot of damage simply by keeping those machines so busy with worthless tasks that they can't do their real jobs.

continues

34

Java Security

Table 34.1. continued

Type of Attack	Description
Masquerade	By pretending to be from another source, a malicious program can persuade a user to reveal valuable information voluntarily.
Deception	If a malicious program were successful in interposing itself between the application and some important data source, the attacker could alter data—or substitute completely different data—before giving it to the application or the user. The user would take the data and act on it, assuming it to be valid.

In addition to these common attacks, Java applets can try another kind of attack. Because applets are fetched to your machine and run locally, they can try to assume your identity and do things while pretending to be you. For example, machines behind corporate firewalls often trust each other more than they trust machines on the wider Internet, so once an applet has started running on your machine behind the firewall, it may try to access other machines, exploiting that trust. (That's the reason current Java applets can make network connections only to the machine from which they were fetched.) Another example is mail forging: once on your machine, an applet may attempt to send threatening or offensive mail that appears to be from you. Of course, Internet mail can be forged from other machines besides your own, but doing it from your own machine makes it a little more convincing.

How Does Java Security Work?

Now that you understand why security features are important and what kinds of threats exist, it's time to learn how Java's security features work and how they protect against those threats.

The Java security model is composed of three layers, each dependent on those beneath it. The following sections cover each of the layers, describing how the security systems work from bottom to top.

The Three Layers of Security

The first line of defense against untrusted programs in a Java application is a part of the basic design of the language: Java is a *safe* language. When programming language theorists use the word *safety*, they aren't talking about protection against malicious programs. Rather, they mean protection against *incorrect* programs. Java achieves this in several ways:

- Array references are checked at run time to ensure that they are within the bounds of the array. This check prevents incorrect programs from running off the end of an array into storage that doesn't belong to the program or that contains values of the wrong type.

- Casts are carefully controlled so that they can't be used to violate the language's rules, and implicit type conversions are kept to a minimum.

- Memory management is automatic. This arrangement prevents "memory leaks" (when unused storage is never reclaimed) and "dangling pointers" (when valid storage is freed prematurely).

- The language does not allow programmers to manipulate pointers directly (although they are used extensively behind the scenes). This feature prevents many invalid uses of pointers, some of which could be used to circumvent the preceding restrictions.

All these qualities make Java a "safe" language. Put another way, they ensure that code written in Java actually does what it appears to do, or it fails. The surprising things that can happen in C (such as continuing to read data past the end of an array as though it were valid) cannot happen. In a safe language, the behavior of a particular program with a particular input should be entirely predictable—no surprises.

The second layer of Java security involves careful verification of Java class files—including the virtual machine bytecodes that represent the compiled versions of methods—as they are loaded into the virtual machine. This verification ensures that a garbled .class file won't cause an error within the Java interpreter itself, and it also ensures that the basic language safety is not violated. The rules about proper language behavior that were written into the language specification are good, but it's also important to make sure that those rules aren't broken. Checking everything in the compiler isn't good enough because it's possible for someone to write a completely new compiler that omits those checks. For that reason, the Java library carefully checks and verifies the bytecodes of every class loaded into the virtual machine to make sure that those bytecodes obey the rules. Some of the rules, such as bounds checking on references to array elements, are actually implemented in the virtual machine, so no real checks are necessary. Other rules, however, must be checked carefully. One particularly important rule that is verified rigorously is that objects must be true to their type—an object that is created as a particular type must never be able to masquerade as an object of some incompatible type. Otherwise, there would be a serious loophole through which explicit security checks could be bypassed.

This verification process doesn't mean that Java code can't be compiled to native machine code. As long as the validation is performed on the bytecodes first, a native compiled version of a class is still secure. "Just in time" (JIT) compilers run within the Java virtual machine, compiling bytecodes to native code as classes are loaded, just after the bytecode-verification stage. This compilation step doesn't usually take much time, and the resulting code runs much faster.

34

JAVA SECURITY

The third and final layer of the Java security model is the implementation of the Java class library. Classes in the library provide Java applications with their only means of access to sensitive system resources, such as files and network connections. Those classes are written so that they always perform security checks before granting access.

This third layer is the portion of the security system that an application can control—not by changing the library implementation, but by supplying the objects that actually make the decisions about whether to grant each request for access. Those objects—the security manager and the class loaders—are the core of an application's security *policy*, and you'll read more about them (including how to implement them) a little later in this chapter.

Protected System Resources

The first two layers of the Java security model are primarily concerned with protecting the security model itself. It's the third layer, the library implementation, in which explicit measures are taken to protect against the kinds of attacks listed in Table 34.1. To help thwart those attacks, Java checks each and every attempt to access particular system resources that could be used in an attack. Those resources fall into six categories, as listed in Table 34.2.

Table 34.2. Resources checked by Java security.

Resource	Description
Local file access	The ability to read or write files and directories. These capabilities can be used to steal or destroy information, as well as to deny service by destroying important system files or writing a huge file that fills the remaining space on your disk. Applets can also use local file access to deceive you by writing an official-looking file somewhere that you will find later and believe to be trustworthy.
System access	The ability to execute programs on the local machine, plus access to system properties and other system resources such as the clipboard, keyboard and mouse input events, and printer queues. These capabilities can be used for theft or destruction of information or denial of services in much the same way that direct file access can.
Network access	The ability to create network connections, both actively (by connecting to some machine) and passively (by listening and accepting incoming connections). Applets that actively create connections may be trying to usurp the user's identity, exploiting the trust that other machines place in him or her. Applets that try to listen for incoming connections may be taking over the job of a system service (such as a Web server).

Resource	Description
Thread manipulation	The ability to start, stop, suspend, resume, or destroy threads and thread groups, as well as other sorts of thread manipulation such as adjusting priorities, setting names, and changing the daemon status. Without restrictions on such capabilities, applets can destroy work by shutting down or disabling other components of the applications within which they run, or can do so to other applets. Rogue applets can also mount denial-of-service attacks by raising their own priority while lowering the priorities of other threads (including the system threads that may be able to control the errant applets).
Library manipulation	The ability to create factory objects that find and load extension classes from the network or other sources. An untrustworthy factory object can garble user data, transparently substitute incoming data from a completely different source, or even steal outgoing data—without the user of the application realizing what's happening. See "Further Reading," later in this chapter, for pointers to more information about factory objects.
Window creation	The ability to create new top-level windows. New top-level windows may appear to be under the control of a local, trusted application rather than an applet, and they can prompt unwary users for important information such as passwords. The Java security system permits applications to forbid applets from creating new windows, and it also permits tagging applet-owned windows with a special warning for users.

The third layer of the security model isn't just concerned with protecting system resources; it also provides protection for some Java runtime resources, to protect the integrity of the security model itself. You'll learn more about that kind of protection in "Protection for Security Facilities," later in this chapter.

Example: Reading a File

Let's look at an example to see how the security model works in practice. This example concentrates on what happens in the third layer, for two reasons: The lower two layers sometimes deal with some rather esoteric issues of type theory, and they are not within the programmer's control. The top layer, on the other hand, is relatively straightforward and can be controlled by Java application programmers.

Suppose that the Snark applet has been loaded onto your system and wants to read one of your files—say, diary.doc. To open the file for reading, Snark must use one of the core Java classes—in particular, FileInputStream or RandomAccessFile in the java.io package. Because those core classes are a part of the security model, before they allow reading from that particular file, they ask the system security manager whether it's okay. Those two classes make the request in their constructors; FileInputStream uses code like this:

```
// Gain access to the system security manager.
SecurityManager security = System.getSecurityManager();
if (security != null) {
    // See if reading is allowed.  If not, the security manager will
    // throw a SecurityException.  The variable "name" is a String
    // containing the file name.
    security.checkRead(name);
}
// If there is no security manager, anything goes!
```

The security manager is found using one of the static methods in the System class. If there is no security manager, everything is allowed; if there is a security manager, it is queried to see whether this access is permitted. If everything is fine, the SecurityManager.checkRead() method returns; otherwise, it throws a SecurityException. Because this code appears in a constructor, and because the exception isn't caught, the constructor never completes, and the FileInputStream object can't be created.

How does the security manager decide whether the request should be allowed or not? The SecurityManager class, an abstract class from which all application security managers are derived, contains several native methods that can be used to inspect the current state of the Java virtual machine. In particular, the execution stack—the methods in the process of executing when the security manager is queried—can be examined in detail. The security manager can thus determine which classes are involved in the current request, and it can decide whether all those classes can be trusted with the resource being requested.

In the Snark example, the security manager examines the execution stack and sees several classes, including Snark. That means something to us, but it probably doesn't mean a lot to the security manager. In particular, the security manager has probably never heard of a class called Snark, and presumably it doesn't even know that Snark is an applet. Yet that's the really important piece of information: if one of the classes currently on the execution stack is part of an applet or some other untrusted, dynamically loaded program, granting the request could be dangerous.

At this point, the security manager gets some help. For each class on the execution stack, it can determine which class loader is responsible for that class. *Class loaders* are special objects that load Java bytecode files into the virtual machine. One of their responsibilities is to keep track of where each class came from and other information that can be relevant to the application security policy. When the security manager consults Snark's class loader, the security manager learns (among other things) that Snark was loaded from the network. At last, the security manager knows enough to decide that Snark's request should be rejected.

An Applet's View of Java Security

Before we plunge ahead into the deeper details of how security managers and class loaders work, let's step to the other side of the security model for a moment and see what it looks like to untrusted classes. We've seen what happens backstage—but what does it look like if you don't have a backstage pass?

Applets and other untrusted (or partially trusted) classes, such as "servlets" in Java-based Web servers, or protocol handlers and content type handlers in HotJava, run within the confines of the application security policy. (In fact, depending on the security policy itself, it's possible that *all* classes except for the security manager and class loaders run under some security restrictions.) Such "unprivileged" classes are the kind that most Java programmers will be writing, so it's important to understand what the Java security facilities look like from the point of view of ordinary code.

Security violations are signaled when the security manager throws a `SecurityException`. It is certainly possible to catch that `SecurityException` and ignore it, or try a different strategy, so an attempt to access a secured resource doesn't have to mean the end of your applet. By trying different things and catching the exception, applets can build a picture of what they are and are not allowed to do. It's even possible to call the security manager's access-checking methods directly, so that you can find out whether a certain resource is accessible before actually attempting to access it.

> **NOTE**
>
> Such probing may seem sneaky, but there are plenty of legitimate uses for it. If you are writing a word processing applet, for example, it is a good idea to make the applet probe first to determine whether it is allowed to write a file to the local disk—before allowing the user to spend three hours typing an important document. As a user, wouldn't you much rather know from the beginning that saves are not allowed?

How to Build a Security Policy

This section delves a little deeper into the implementation of security managers and class loaders—deep enough to help you implement such classes yourself, should you have to. If you are building Java applets or other dynamic extensions, class libraries, or even standalone Java applications that don't need dynamic network extensibility, you may want to skip this section and proceed to "How Good Is Java Security?" later in this chapter. But if you are building a Java-based application that has to host applets or other untrusted classes, this section is important for you because those are the kinds of applications that need a security policy.

34

JAVA SECURITY

Unfortunately, the JDK doesn't come with a working security policy mechanism that's ready for an application to use. The `SecurityManager` class that comes with the JDK is an abstract class, so no instances can be created. It wouldn't be useful anyway, because every access-checking method throws a `SecurityException` immediately, in every case—whether any untrusted classes are active or not! Clearly, no program could accomplish anything useful with that security manager on watch.

Therefore, if your application plans to host untrusted classes, you need a new `SecurityManager` and one or more `ClassLoader` implementations. You'll probably have to build them yourself, because nobody is yet offering reusable security policy implementations that Java programmers can use "out of the box." I expect such third-party security support to be available at some point, but until that happens, the next sections explain how to do it yourself.

Building a Class Loader

Unlike most other portions of an application, class loaders must work both sides of the security fence. They must take care to consult the security manager before allowing certain operations, and they must cooperate with the security manager to help it learn about classes and make decisions about access requests. They must also avoid breaking any of the assumptions about classes on which the security manager relies.

When defining a class, the class loader must identify the package in which the class belongs and call `SecurityManager.checkPackageDefinition()` before actually loading the class into that package. Membership in a package gives a class special access to other classes in the package and can provide a way to circumvent security restrictions.

When the class loader defines a class, it must also *resolve* the class. Resolving a class involves locating and loading (if necessary) other classes that the new class requires. This is done by calling a native method called `ClassLoader.resolveClass(Class)`. If other classes are needed during the resolution process, the Java runtime system calls the `loadClass(String, boolean)` method in the same `ClassLoader` that loaded the class currently being resolved. (If the `boolean` parameter is `true`, the newly loaded class must be resolved, also.)

The class loader must be careful not to load a class from an untrusted source that will mirror a trusted class. The `CLASSPATH` should be searched first for system classes. This is especially important during the resolution process.

Additionally, the class loader should check with the security manager about whether the class being resolved is even allowed to use the classes in the requested package. The security manager may want to prevent untrusted code from using entire packages.

Listing 34.1 gives an example of the steps you can take to load a class securely.

Listing 34.1. Loading a class securely.

```java
protected Class loadClass(String cname, boolean resolve) {

    // Check to see if I've already loaded this one from my source.
    Class class = (Class) myclasses.get(cname);

    if (class == null) {
        // If not, then I have to do security checks.

        // Is the requestor allowed to use classes in this package?
        SecurityManager security = System.getSecurityManager();
        if (security != null) {
            int pos = cname.lastIndexOf('.');
            if (pos >= 0) {
                security.checkPackageAccess(cname.substring(0, pos));
            }
        }

        try {
            // If there's a system class by this name, use it.
            return findSystemClass(cname);
        }
        catch (Throwable e) {
            // otherwise, go find it and load it.
            class = fetchClass(cname);
        }
    }

    if (class == null) throw new ClassNotFoundException();

    if (resolve) resolveClass(class);

    return class;
}
```

In the preceding listing, the real work of actually retrieving a class and defining it is done in the `fetchClass()` method. The primary security responsibility of that method is to call `SecurityManager.checkPackageDefinition(package)` before actually defining the class, as described earlier.

The way this resolution process works (with the `ClassLoader` that loaded the class being responsible for resolving class dependencies) is one reason why applications typically define one class loader for each different source of classes. When a class from one source has a dependency on some class named `MyApplet`, for example, it would probably be a mistake to resolve the dependency using a class with the same name from another source.

The other side of the class loader's responsibility for security is to maintain information about classes and provide that information to the security manager. The type of information that is important to the security manager depends on the application. Currently, most Java applications base security decisions on the network host from which a class was loaded, but other information may soon be used instead. With digital signature facilities available, it will be feasible to allow certain classes special privileges based on the organization or authority that signed those classes.

Building a Security Manager

Implementing a security manager can involve a lot of work, but if you have a coherent security policy, the process isn't particularly complicated. Most of the work involved stems from the fact that the SecurityManager class has a lot of methods you must override with new, more intelligent implementations that make reasonable access decisions instead of automatically disallowing everything.

Once the security manager has decided to allow an operation, all it has to do is return. Alternatively, if the security manager decides to prohibit an operation, it just has to throw a SecurityException. Communicating the decision is easy—the hard part is deciding.

The section, "Example: Reading a File," earlier in this chapter, contains a simple example of the workings of the Java security system. That example omitted a few details for the sake of simplicity, but now you need to know the whole story. The security manager can examine the execution stack to find out which classes have initiated an operation. If an object's method is being executed at the time the security manager is called, the class of that object is requesting the current operation (either directly or indirectly). The important thing about the objects on the stack, from the security manager's point of view, is not the objects themselves but their classes and those classes' origins. In Java, each object contains a pointer to its Class object, and each class can return its class loader through the getClassLoader() method. The implementation of SecurityManager uses those facts, along with native methods that can find the objects on the stack itself, to find out the classes and class loaders that have objects on the execution stack. Figure 34.1 shows the Java execution stack while the security manager is executing.

NOTE

Because the security manager doesn't really care about the objects themselves—just the classes and class loaders—the documentation for the SecurityManager class blurs the distinction a bit. It refers to "the classes on the execution stack" and "the class loaders on the execution stack." This chapter uses the same phrases. Strictly speaking, the classes in question aren't actually on the stack, but they have instances that are. Likewise, the class loaders aren't really on the stack, but they are responsible for classes that are. It's just a lot easier to talk about "a ClassLoader on the stack" than "an object on the stack that is an instance of a class that was loaded by a ClassLoader."

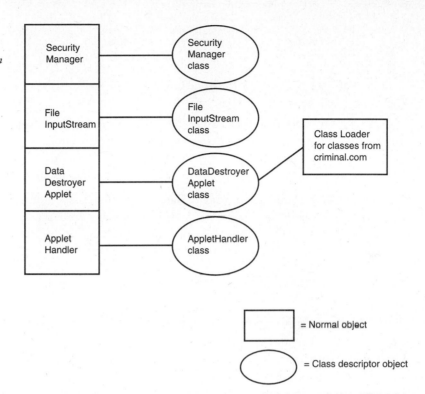

FIGURE 34.1.
The security manager and the Java execution stack.

The JDK applet viewer application and Netscape Navigator 3.0 have simple security models: If a class is not a system class (that is, if it wasn't loaded from CLASSPATH), it isn't trusted and isn't allowed to do very much. If your security model is that simple, your security manager will be simple, too. Calling SecurityManager.inClassLoader() tells you whether the operation is being requested by untrusted code. It returns true if there is any class loader at all on the stack. System classes loaded from CLASSPATH don't have a class loader, so if there's a class loader on the stack *anywhere*, there's an untrusted class in control.

If an operation is to be prohibited in general, but allowed if it comes from a particular trusted class, you can investigate further. SecurityManager.classLoaderDepth() tells you how deep on the stack the first class loader is. When classLoaderDepth() is used with SecurityManager.classDepth(String), it's possible to determine whether a particular trusted class is really in control. Imagine a distributed calendar-management system that makes use of applets. Such a system may include a trusted class, Invite, that records an invitation of some sort in your local calendar file. Applets can use the Invite class to issue invitations. Although you don't want an untrusted applet to write directly to your calendar file, you can trust Invite to write only invitations and not do any damage or reveal any private information. In such an application, the security manager's checkWrite() method might contain code like this:

```
if (classDepth("Invite") < classLoaderDepth()) {
    // The Invite class is in control, so we can allow the request.
    return;
}
else {
    throw new SecurityException("attempted to write file" + filename);
}
```

The inClass(String) method can also be helpful in this situation, if you're confident that the class you're interested in doesn't call any untrusted classes along the way. Be careful, however, because inClass() simply tells you that the specified class is on the stack *somewhere*. It says nothing about how deep the class is or what classes lie above it on the stack.

Now that digital signature technology is available for Java classes, it will be possible to verify the source of Java classes and loosen the security restrictions appropriately. If you are designing an application with such capability, you may need more information about the class loader responsible for the object requesting an operation. The currentClassLoader() method returns the ClassLoader object highest on the stack. You can query that object for application-specific information about the source of the class. (You learn more about authenticated, digitally signed classes later in this chapter.)

Finally, if all those other methods aren't enough to implement your security policy, SecurityManager provides the getClassContext() method. It returns an array of Class objects, in the order they appear on the stack from top to bottom. You can use any Class methods on these objects to learn various things: getName(), getSuperclass(), and getClassLoader(), among others.

Building your application's security manager takes work, and it can be complicated, but it doesn't have to be a nightmare. Just be sure to design a coherent security policy *first*.

Installing and Using Your Security Policy

We've talked about implementing class loaders and security managers, but there's one crucial question left: how are those new implementations installed so that they are called when classes have to be loaded from the network and when security decisions have to be made?

To answer that question, let's start with the security manager. One particular instance of SecurityManager serves as the security manager for an application. That instance is installed by using System.setSecurityManager(). Here's how to install a security manager in your application:

```
System.setSecurityManager(new mySecurityManager());
```

Likewise, the security manager can be accessed by using System.getSecurityManager(). Any Java method can query the security manager, but it's crucial that the methods that provide access to sensitive system resources query the security manager before they permit the access. Such checks are very simple, and all the Java library classes that consult the security manager use nearly identical code to do it. For example, here's the File.delete() method:

```
/**
 * Deletes the specified file. Returns true
 * if the file could be deleted.
 */
public boolean delete() {
    SecurityManager security = System.getSecurityManager();
    if (security != null) {
        security.checkDelete(path);
    }
    return delete0();
}
```

The `delete0()` method is what really does the work of deleting the file. (It's declared `private`, so other classes can't call it directly.) Before calling it, the `delete()` method checks with the security manager to see whether the operation is permitted. If everything is fine, the security manager's `checkDelete()` method simply returns, and the `delete0()` method is called. If the operation is not allowed, `checkDelete()` throws a `SecurityException`. Because `delete()` makes no attempt to catch the exception, it propagates up to the caller, and `delete0()` is never called.

In the `delete()` method, if there is no security manager defined, access is always granted. The same is true for all the methods that perform security checks. If no security manager is defined, everything is allowed. Thus, it's important that any application that is going to be loading untrusted classes create a security manager *before* the first untrusted class is loaded into the virtual machine.

What about the class loaders? How are they called to load classes from the network?

Classes are either loaded explicitly by the application or automatically by objects called *factory objects*. Some applications may have optional functionality that is loaded on demand. In that case, it may make sense for the application to have built-in knowledge of the classes required for those optional features. In other situations, the classes are supplied by third parties and should be loaded in response to some of the data being handled by the application. In such cases, it makes sense to have factory objects that search for a class that can handle the situation and load it. The core Java library can use factory objects to load protocol handlers and content type handlers in conjunction with the `URL` class. See "Further Reading," later in this chapter, for pointers to more information about factory objects.

In any case, a class loader is called explicitly by application code, whether it is a factory object or some other part of the application, so no "installation" of `ClassLoader` objects is usually necessary.

Protection for Security Facilities

Earlier in this chapter, you learned about the system resources that are protected by the Java security facilities. The security system must also take care to protect certain parts of the security model itself, so that applets cannot subvert the security system and slip in through the back door.

The first line of special protection for the security system is the mechanism for installing the security manager. Obviously, if an applet could install its own security manager, it could do anything it pleased. Therefore, installation of the security manager must be protected. But there's a "chicken and egg" problem here: when the security manager is first installed, there's no security manager to rule on whether it should be allowed!

The resolution of this problem is simple. If no security manager is installed, any class can install one. Once a security manager is active, however, it is *always* a security violation to attempt to replace it. This implies that applications must take care to establish their security policies before any untrusted code is brought into the virtual machine. Another implication is that during any individual execution, an application can have only one security manager. Thus, if it's desirable to adjust the security policy of an application while it is running, those adjustments must be handled dynamically by the security manager itself; they can't be accomplished by replacing the security manager.

The other defenses for the security system are more conventional in that they involve library routines that consult the security manager for access decisions. The protected aspects of the security system fall into two categories:

- **Interpreter manipulation:** The ability to stop the execution of the Java virtual machine or load new libraries of native methods into the virtual machine.
- **Class loading:** The ability to create new `ClassLoader` objects. Additionally, class loaders consult the security manager when loading classes to see whether a new class can be created within a particular package and whether the new class is allowed to access certain packages. For example, untrusted classes are not permitted to be in any of the core Java library packages.

Authentication and Trusted Applets

Java 1.1 includes important new features for building flexible security policies. *Authentication* is the process of verifying the identity or origin of someone or something. If you can verify that an applet originated with a particular person or company, you might be willing to trust it with additional privileges beyond those which you ordinarily grant to applets. The following sections discuss these facilities as well as some problems and limitations that currently apply.

Basics of Cryptographic Security

Before going into the details of cryptographic security as it relates to Java, you must know a few basics about cryptography in general. Because this chapter isn't about cryptography, I won't go into great depth—and I will certainly stay far away from the complex math involved. The `java.security` package hides all these details anyway, so the level of discussion presented here is sufficient for most developers.

Encryption and Authentication

Encryption is the process of transforming a message in such a way that it cannot be read without authorization. With the proper authorization (the message's *key*), the message can be decrypted and read in its original form. The theories and technologies of encryption and decryption processes are called *cryptography*.

Modern cryptography has its basis in some pretty heavy mathematics. Messages are treated as very large numbers, and an original, readable message (the *plain text*) is transformed into an encrypted message (the *cipher text*) and back again by means of a series of mathematical operations using appropriate keys. The keys are also large numbers. All this math means that cryptography is a somewhat specialized field, but it also means that computers are pretty good cryptographic tools. Because computers treat everything as numbers (at least at some level), cryptography and computers go together well.

The obvious use for encryption is to keep secrets. If you have a message that you need to save or send to a friend, but you don't want anyone else to be able to read it, you can encrypt it and give the key to only the people you want to trust with the secret message.

Less obvious, but just as important, is the possibility of using cryptography for *authentication*: that is, verifying someone's identity. After you know how to keep secrets, authentication comes naturally. For centuries, people have proved their identities to each other by means of shared secrets (secret handshakes, knocks, or phrases, for example). If you were to meet someone who claimed to be a childhood friend, but who had changed so much that you didn't recognize him or her, how would he or she go about convincing you? Probably by telling you details of memorable experiences that you two alone shared. The more personal, the better—the more likely that both of you would have kept the secret through the years. Cryptographic authentication works the same way: Alice and Bob share a key, which is their shared secret. To prove her identity, Alice encrypts an agreed-on message using that key and passes the encrypted message to Bob. When Bob decrypts it successfully, it is proof that the message originated from someone who shares the secret. If Bob has been careful to keep the secret and trusts Alice to do the same, he has his proof.

You may have noticed in the preceding two paragraphs that keeping secrets and proving identity both depend on keeping other secrets: the keys. If some enemy can steal a key, he or she can read the secret messages or pretend to be someone else. Thus, key security is very important. Worse still, for most uses of cryptography, keys must be traded between people who want to communicate securely; this *key exchange* represents a prime opportunity for the security of the keys to be compromised.

Public-Key Cryptography

Conventional cryptographic algorithms are *symmetric*: that is, the same key is used for both encryption and decryption. More recently, researchers have developed *asymmetric, public-key* cryptographic algorithms that use key pairs: If a message is encrypted with one key, it must be decrypted with the other key in the pair. The two keys are related mathematically, but in such a complex way that it's not feasible (that is, it's too costly or time consuming) to derive one key from the other, given sufficiently long keys.

Public-key cryptography simplifies key management immensely. You can treat one of the keys in the pair as your public key and distribute it widely, keeping the other as your secret key, known only to you. If Bob wants to create a message that only Alice can read, he can encrypt it using her public key. Because the public key can't be used to decrypt the message, others who also know Alice's public key can't read it, but Alice, using her secret key, can. Then, if Alice wants to prove her identity to Bob, she can encrypt an agreed-on message with her secret key. Bob (or anyone else) can decrypt it with her public key, thus demonstrating that it must have been encrypted with her secret key. Because only Alice knows her secret key, the message must really have come from her.

Public-key cryptography sounds unlikely and almost magical when you first encounter it, but it's not such an uncommon idea. Your own handwritten signature is somewhat like a key pair. Many of the people and organizations you deal with regularly probably recognize your signature (or have a copy on file for comparison), making the appearance of your signature a sort of public key. Actually placing your signature on a new piece of paper, however, is a skill that only you have: that's the secret key. Of course, signatures can be forged, but the point is that for all but one person, *creating* the signature is pretty difficult but having anyone *verify* it is easy. Public-key cryptography makes possible the creation of digital signatures that work in much the same way, except that forging a digital signature is much more difficult than forging a written signature.

If Alice wants to apply a digital signature to a document before sending it to Bob, a simple way for her to do so is to encrypt the document with her secret key. Because many people know her public key, the document isn't private—anyone with Alice's public key can decrypt it and read the contents (applying another layer of encryption with another key is possible; doing so produces a document that is both signed and private). When Bob successfully decrypts the message with Alice's public key, that action indicates that the message must have originally been encrypted with her secret key. What makes this effective as a signature is that, because only Alice knows her secret key, only she could have encrypted it in the first place.

Complications

Many other details enter into the practical use of cryptography, of course. For several reasons, practical digital signatures are not as simple as the preceding example. Even with public-key cryptography, key management and security are important (and tricky) issues. For example, once Bob has Alice's public key, how does he know for sure that it really is her key? If the key is actually a fake provided by an attacker, signed documents that appear to be from Alice would really be from the attacker, and the attacker would be able to read documents that Bob intended for Alice's eyes only. To reduce this risk, most systems provide a mechanism by which a third party can *certify* a key, attesting to the key's proper ownership.

Another complication is that public-key (asymmetric) cryptography is much more complicated (and thus much slower) than symmetric cryptography, so symmetric cryptography still has an important role to play. One serious problem is that, unlike most computer algorithms, most good cryptographic algorithms come with legal entanglements. Many are protected by patents, so they must be licensed from the patent holders. The United States government considers implementations of strong encryption algorithms to be in the same category as munitions, and it places heavy restrictions on their export (even though many of the best algorithms were invented outside the United States, and even though it's legal to export books containing cryptographic code). Some other governments prohibit the use of strong cryptography except for purposes of authentication, and a few governments ban it entirely. There are bills currently pending in the U.S. Congress to lift the export restrictions, but as I write this, those bills haven't yet become law, and the U.S. government's cryptography export policy is one of the factors currently delaying the release of some of the facilities planned for the java.security package.

Fortunately, the package hides most of the technical complications, and the Java license explains all the legal and political details. The rest of this chapter covers the basics of how you can use the java.security package with the rest of the Java library to make it possible for applets to do really useful work.

Signed Classes

The java.security package, along with the javakey tool, provide facilities for digitally signing classes (actually, for signing JAR bundles) so that the identity of the party responsible for the classes can be verified. It's the identity of the signer of the classes that is later used to make access decisions.

The javakey tool is somewhat difficult to use. It is a command-line tool that supports a wide variety of options that direct it to perform different tasks. It has two primary jobs: managing a database of entities (individuals or groups that may want to sign or be associated with some applets or Java classes), and applying digital signatures. In more detail, here are some of the things javakey can do:

- Create entities (what we typically think of as "identities")
- Generate public/private key pairs for entities
- Import key pairs generated by other programs
- Export key pairs from the entity database
- Certify keys (that is, generate key certificates)
- Import and export certificates
- List information about entities in the database
- Sign JAR bundles

When an application loads an applet from a signed JAR bundle, if the application has access to a certificate for the signer, the signature can be verified, thus providing fairly reliable

34

JAVA SECURITY

information about the origin of the applet. Signatures are represented by special signature files in the bundle, and verification is done using a suite of classes in the java.security package—the most important classes being Signature, MessageDigest, and Identity. Once the signatures have been verified, the identities of the signers can be recorded using the class loader's setSigners() method. When the time comes to make access decisions, the security manager can learn about the signers by using the Class.getSigners() method.

Unfortunately, the supported Java 1.1 classes don't provide all the facilities you need to build such an application yourself. In particular, the classes that understand the format of the signature files are a part of the sun.* packages, which are not supported (or documented, for that matter) for use outside of Sun Microsystems. As of this writing, the java.security package is useful for manipulating the identity database, and the javakey tool is useful for signing JAR bundles, but Java is still missing the features required to build applications that exploit digital signatures.

Access Control Lists

Assuming that you *could* verify the signer of a class, there would still remain the problem of making the access decision. How does the security manager know how much trust the user places in the provider of the class?

The other important new security feature in Java 1.1 is the access control list (ACL). ACLs are a useful way of representing information about permissions and privileges. Given an entity and a particular permission to be checked, the java.security.acl.Acl class can check whether the entity holds that permission by using the checkPermission() method.

ACLs have a structure that seems rather complex at first. An ACL consists of a set of ACL entries, each of which associates a set of permissions with a single *principal* (an individual entity or a group). An individual can be a member of multiple groups, and the effective permissions held by the individual are a composite of the directly associated individual permissions and those of all of the groups of which he or she is a member. (Individual permissions take precedence over group permissions.)

Another twist is that ACL entries come in both *positive* and *negative* varieties. A negative permission cancels an equivalent positive permission, so that permissions are not strictly additive. By using the relationship between negative and positive permissions, you can create special exceptions; for example, taking away a permission from someone who otherwise (by virtue of group membership) would hold the permission, or giving special privileges to individuals who are trusted more than others in a group.

ACLs are powerful, flexible, and simple to use. They are also general purpose and can be used for more than just trusted applets. Unfortunately, just as with the code-signing features, the Java 1.1 ACL implementation omits some important facilities. The classes in the java.security.acl package form a nice interface to ACLs that already exist, but they provide no way to create ACLs or to initialize them from a properties file or some other external resource.

How Good Is Java Security?

There remains one big topic to cover in this chapter: just how good is Java security? Does it really do all that it claims to do, and is it really the best thing out there, or does it have some serious weaknesses? Should we really be trusting our systems to Java applets?

Of course, the precise answer depends on who you ask. Network security is a complex topic, and we don't yet fully understand every detail of it. Nevertheless, some rough consensus is beginning to emerge about the strength of Java's security facilities. In the following sections, I attempt to answer the questions objectively, based on my own analysis as well as on the opinions of others, including some experts in the security community.

What the Java Security Model Does Not Address

Java security doesn't try to solve every security problem. There are some potential attacks that Java doesn't currently attempt to prevent (although work is in progress to extend the security facilities into these areas as well). These attacks involve the abuse of resources that aren't necessarily sensitive, such as CPU cycles, memory, and windows.

The current Java security model takes a yes-or-no approach to security: a class is either allowed access to a resource or it is not. There is no provision for allowing an untrusted class to use only a certain amount of some resource. Java does not enforce resource quotas. It doesn't even keep track of resource usage so that the application can enforce quotas.

Applets can exploit this fact to mount attacks of varying severity: denial-of-service attacks that render your machine unusable by allocating all your memory or some other finite resource; annoyances that make noises or pop up big, bouncing windows on your screen that flash and then disappear before you can destroy them; or resource theft attacks, where an applet stealthily lurks in the background, using your machine to perform part of some large calculation while you wonder why your computer seems a little slower than usual today.

Java's designers didn't simply forget about these issues. They decided not to deal with them at the time because they are extremely difficult to handle correctly. Especially when it comes to CPU time, it's difficult (and often impossible) to determine whether a class is doing useful work or simply wasting the resource. Researchers are currently investigating ways to prevent (or limit) these kinds of attacks, and future versions of Java will attempt to deal with them as well as possible.

Java Security Bugs

In addition to the kinds of attacks that were intentionally excluded from the scope of the Java security facilities, there have been a few accidental flaws. Several have been found by Drew Dean, Ed Felten, and Dan Wallach, a team of researchers at Princeton University. Others were found by David Hopwood, an Oxford researcher. Wallach and Hopwood have both consulted with Netscape, helping to strengthen Java security in Netscape products.

34

JAVA SECURITY

All these security holes permitted very serious attacks that could result in loss or theft of valuable data. It's comforting, however, to know that each of those holes was the result of a simple bug in the code that implemented part of the security architecture, rather than any fundamental flaw in the architecture itself. In each case, the bugs were fixed within a few days of discovery. In fact, the process in which researchers carefully examine Java for security weaknesses is one of the important reasons why Sun made the Java source code available for study. Java security is now much stronger because several security bugs have been found and eliminated.

That holes have been found in Java security is a reminder that we should be cautious, but there's no reason for panic. In truth, all network-oriented applications are candidates for serious security holes, and such problems are actually quite common in network applications. It's also common for security considerations to be almost an afterthought. Java actually seems to be stronger than many other programs because certain aspects of its security architecture have been central to Java's design from the beginning, and because all the Java hype has prompted some intense scrutiny.

Is the Architecture Sound?

What are the chances that someone will discover a really fundamental security flaw in Java—a serious flaw in the security architecture itself?

It's impossible to say for sure, of course, but we do know enough about security to be able to analyze the Java security model and make some guesses. It turns out that the Java security architecture is not perfect, and there are some things to watch out for. Dean, Felten, and Wallach, the Princeton researchers mentioned earlier, have expressed some concern about the complexity of Java's security architecture, but most who have studied the matter seem to believe that the outlook is good.

The biggest weakness in the Java security model is its complexity. Complexity begets mistakes. The problem is exacerbated by the fact that application authors currently must implement their own security manager and class loaders. Hopefully, a few flexible, configurable security policy implementations will be made available for reuse, so that they can be carefully tested and debugged once, and used many times. Such a development would greatly reduce the potential for new security holes.

Another weakness is that the security responsibility is split between the security manager and the class loaders. It would be better if the job were localized in one class.

Although we may wish things were simpler, as a whole, the Java security architecture appears to be strong enough, and we can expect it to grow stronger with time.

Java versus ActiveX

Microsoft has its own proposal for dynamically loaded code on the Internet: ActiveX. ActiveX is essentially a way to leverage the existing body of OLE controls that already exists for the

Windows environment. Questions have been raised about the security implications of the proposal, however. ActiveX certainly has considerable value in some situations, but there are good reasons to be worried about potential security problems.

ActiveX controls can be written in Java, and you can bet that Java-based controls will begin appearing in the near future. However, most of the large existing body of controls have been written in C or C++, and have been compiled into native Intel machine code. The ActiveX answer to securing these controls is based on a digital signature technology called Authenticode. Developers and software vendors sign their controls, and the ActiveX system verifies that signature against a registry of signature authorities, thereby verifying the origin of the control. Users can configure ActiveX to allow only controls from certain vendors to run on their system; for example, if you trust Microsoft and Corel, but nobody else, you can configure ActiveX to automatically fetch and run controls from those two companies, but to refuse all others.

That sounds okay, right? After all, it sounds a lot like the code-signing system for Java classes that is intended to help loosen the rigidly conservative Java security policy.

Actually, however, the two systems aren't all that similar. To understand why, you have to look at what a signature on a piece of software really means. A signature really only means "I signed this and it hasn't been changed since I did." The person or authority who applies the signature might actually mean more than that, but the Authenticode proposal doesn't require any guarantees. Even if guarantees were present, it's unlikely that they would be very strong, based on the weak (or nonexistent) warranties that are found on most software products today.

So a signature is not a guarantee of safety. If that's the case, what makes the Java code-signing technology better than Authenticode? The difference is that ActiveX security is all-or-nothing; Java security can be extremely fine grained and flexible. If you (or the ActiveX system) choose to allow a native-code ActiveX control to run on your system, that control has complete access to your system. It can read any file you can read, delete or change any file you can, make any network connection it chooses—even format your hard disk. Java, on the other hand, can grant access to classes selectively, even choosing which files a particular class is allowed to read. A word processing applet, invoked specifically to edit one particular document, can be allowed to write to that document and no other.

Authenticode is not really a security architecture; it's a trust management architecture. Furthermore, it's a very limited trust management architecture because it doesn't have any understanding of partial trust.

Some people say that ActiveX will probably be widely used on corporate intranets, with Java ruling the roost on the Internet at large. That's probably a good prediction—certainly ActiveX will be very useful on intranets because the security issues aren't quite as important there. However, even that thought makes me uneasy because security studies have shown that most security problems originate within an organization—and because of a prediction of my own: I believe that, over the next five to ten years, the walls between corporate intranets and the Internet will become more porous, often coming down altogether. Companies that rely heavily on intranet applications built with ActiveX will be at a disadvantage when that time comes.

FURTHER READING

Several Web pages, and at least one other book, provide more in-depth treatment of Java security topics. JavaSoft maintains a FAQ page on applet security issues (`http://java.sun.com/sfaq/`); the Princeton researchers who have found several serious Java security bugs maintain a similar page with an outsider's perspective (`http://www.cs.princeton.edu/sip/java-faq.html`).

For more information about the second layer of the security model (validation and verification of Java class files and bytecodes as they are loaded into the interpreter), read *The Java Virtual Machine Specification*, by Tim Lindholm and Frank Yellin. The book is a technical description of the architecture of the virtual machine and contains a precise description of the steps taken by the class verifier.

To see examples of applets that exploit some of the weaknesses in the current Java security facilities, take a look at Mark LaDue's Hostile Applets page (`http://www.math.gatech.edu/~mladue/HostileApplets.html`). (Don't worry, you can go at least that far without fear; Mark keeps the hostile applets off the main page.)

For more information about programming with the Java security system, read *Maximum Java* (published by Sams.net). It provides deeper coverage of several topics that readers of this chapter might find interesting, including these:

- What end users need to know about security
- Design considerations for security policies
- More details about the security facilities and security policy implementation
- Details of the `java.security` and `java.security.acl` packages
- The construction of factory objects and other ways to load classes from the network (with sample code)
- How to use a scripting language to provide security policy configurability
- A discussion about whether you should give both users and site administrators some say in security configuration
- How to integrate native method libraries (even dynamically loaded libraries) into the security model (with sample code)

Summary

Java's security model is possibly the least understood aspect of the Java system. Because it's unusual for a language environment to have security facilities, some people have been bothered by the danger; at the same time, because the security restrictions prevent some useful things as well as some harmful things, another group of people has wondered whether security is really necessary.

Java security is important because it makes exciting new things possible with very little risk. Early security holes caused by implementation bugs are being closed, and technology is being fielded that permits the strict security policy to be relaxed carefully and selectively. Resources that can be used to destroy or steal data are being protected, and researchers are examining ways to prevent applets from using other resources to cause annoyance or inconvenience.

Application developers can design their own security policies and supply parts of the third layer of the Java security model to implement those policies in their applications.

The Java security architecture is sound. Early weaknesses and bugs are not a surprise, and the process that has exposed those flaws has also helped remove them.

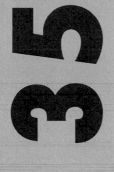

Java Reflection

by Mike Fletcher

IN THIS CHAPTER

This chapter covers the new Reflection API introduced in Java 1.1. The `java.lang.reflect` package contains classes that allow Java code to examine classes and interfaces dynamically. After a quick overview of the API (refer to Chapter 18, "The Reflection Package," for more detailed coverage of the package), this chapter presents a sample applet that uses the reflection classes to print out information about an arbitrary class.

An Overview of the Reflection Package

The Reflection API allows Java code to examine classes and objects at run time. The new reflection classes allow you to call another class's methods dynamically at run time. With the reflection classes, you can also examine an instance's fields and change the fields' contents. The reflection classes also enable you to create new class and array instances on the fly. All this new functionality is, of course, limited by the Java security model and the Java language access specifiers (for example, `private` and `protected`). The new Reflection API is intended to provide the functionality required by the JavaBeans package to access the `public` methods and fields of arbitrary classes at run time. The Reflection API also provides applications such as debuggers with access to the declared members of a class.

In addition to the new reflection classes, some additions have been made to the `java.lang` package. `Byte` and `Short` classes, analogous to the `Integer` class, have been added to serve as wrappers for the corresponding primitive types. New instances of the `Class` class, named `java.lang.Type.TYPE` (where *Type* is `Boolean`, `Character`, `Byte`, `Short`, `Integer`, `Long`, `Float`, `Double`, or `Void`), have been added to represent primitive field, parameter, and return value types.

The `java.lang.reflect` API

The Reflection API consists of the `java.lang.Class` class and the `java.lang.reflect` classes: `Field`, `Method`, `Constructor`, `Array`, and `Modifier`. The first three of these classes represent the corresponding members of classes and interfaces. The `Array` class provides methods for creating, accessing, and modifying arrays. The last class provides methods for decoding modifiers (such as `static` and `public`) returned for classes and their components. All these classes allow widening conversions when appropriate (for example, an `int` will be converted to a `long`), but throw an `IllegalArgumentException` if the value has to be narrowed (for example, the classes do not convert a `double` to a `float`).

The Class Class

The `Class` class, which remains in the `java.lang` package for backwards compatibility, provides running code with a representation of Java types. In Java 1.1, the `Class` class provides the same functionality as it did in Java 1.0, with the following additions:

■ Methods to determine whether an object represents an array or a primitive type.

■ Methods that return a representation of the modifiers for the class type.

■ Methods that return objects representing the fields, methods, and constructors, as well as the component type for arrays. Two versions are available for each type: One returns only the members declared specifically in the class, and the other returns all members of the class, including inherited members.

■ Methods that determine whether a class (or interface) is a superclass of a given class (or interface), as well as methods that determine whether an object is an instance of a type or implements an interface.

There are no `public` constructors for the `Class` class. The virtual machine constructs `Class` objects when classes are loaded. References to a `Class` object for a given class can be obtained with the `forName()` method.

The Member Interface

The `Member` interface defines shared functionality implemented by the `Field`, `Method`, and `Constructor` classes. It defines methods to get information such as the name, declaring class, and modifiers for type members. Two static constants, `PUBLIC` and `DECLARED`, are used by the security manager to determine whether code can access members.

The Field Class

`Field` instances give access to one field of a type. A `Field` object is created by the virtual machine when the `getField()`, `getFields()`, `getDeclaredField()`, or `getDeclaredFields()` method of `Class` is called. Both instance variables and class (`static`) variables can be represented by a `Field` object.

In addition to the methods declared by the `Member` interface, the `Field` class defines methods to retrieve and set the contents of a field. A generic `get()` method is provided that takes an `Object` reference as a parameter and returns an `Object` representing the value of the field. Specific methods are provided to return a value of the appropriate primitive type (or throw an `IllegalArgumentException` if the value represented by the `Field` object is not of that type). Similarly, a generic `set()` method and other type-specific methods are provided to set the contents of the field.

The Method Class

Just as the `Field` class represents the fields of a type, the `Method` class represents the methods of a class. References to `Method` objects can be obtained with the `getMethod()`, `getDeclaredMethod()`, `getMethods()`, and `getDeclaredMethods()` members of the `Class` class. The `Method` class implements the `Member` interface. The `Method` class provides methods to determine the return type, parameters, and exceptions thrown by the represented method. These are returned as references to `Class` objects for the first two methods, and arrays of `Class` objects for the last two methods.

35

JAVA REFLECTION

The invoke() method provides a way to call the method represented by the Method object. It takes as parameters the Object on which to call the method and an Object array representing the parameters. For class methods, the first parameter can be omitted. If you have problems with the arguments (for example, the first Object is not of the correct type, or one of the parameters is not the correct type), an IllegalArgumentException is thrown. If an exception is thrown by the method, it is caught and an InvocationTargetException is thrown with the original exception (which can be retrieved with the getTargetException() method).

The Constructor Class

The Constructor class represents a constructor for a class. A Constructor instance can be used to create a new instantiation of the declaring class. As with the Method and Field classes, instances can be created only by the virtual machine and are retrieved with the Class class's getConstructor() and related methods.

Methods are provided to return the parameter types and exceptions thrown by the constructor. A new instance can be obtained by calling the newInstance() method. As does the Method.invoke() method, the newInstance() method throws an IllegalArgumentException if there is a problem with the type of a parameter. An InvocationTargetException is thrown if the constructor throws an exception.

The Array Class

The Array class provides a way of dynamically creating new arrays at run time. Two methods, both with the name newInstance(), return a new array with a component type specified by the first parameter. One version takes a single int as the second parameter to specify the length of the array, the other takes an int[] for creating multidimensional arrays. A getLength() method takes an array reference as a parameter and returns the length of the array.

Methods similar to those of the Field class are provided by the Array class to get and set array components. The get() method as well as the type-specific versions of get() take an array reference and the index to retrieve as parameters. The set() method and its type-specific friends take an additional argument, which is the value to set the element.

The Modifier Class

The Modifier class is a convenience class that decodes the Java language modifiers returned by the other Reflection API classes. All the Modifier methods are static. Classes that implement the Member interface define a getModifiers() method, which returns an int. This integer can be passed to the methods of the Modifier class to determine which modifiers are present. Methods such as isPublic() are provided for all the Java modifiers: public, private, protected, static, final, synchronized, volatile, transient, native, interface, and abstract. A toString() method is also provided; it returns a space-separated list of the modifiers represented by the int parameter.

The `InvocationTargetException` Exception

The `InvocationTargetException` exception is used to represent an exception thrown by an underlying method or constructor called by the `Method.invoke()` or `Constructor.newInstance()` method. Either of these methods catches any exceptions thrown when the actual code is called. If an exception does occur, an `InvocationTargetException` is created with the exception that occurred, and this new exception is thrown. Two constructors are provided for this exception: One takes only an object extending `java.lang.Throwable`, and the other takes a `Throwable` and a message.

Security Concerns

Access to classes using the Reflection API is controlled by the security manager and by the standard Java language access controls. Before an instance representing a member (`Field`, `Method`, or `Constructor`) is returned, the `SecurityManager.checkMemberAccess()` method is called. If this check does not throw a `SecurityException`, access is granted, with the caveat of the standard checks for `private` and `protected` done by the virtual machine.

The access policy for applications is that code can access members for any class to which it can link within the standard language constraints. The JDK `AppletSeourity` class allows public members of public classes to access the public members of code loaded by the same loader; it also allows access to *public system classes* (classes that loaded from local disk somewhere in the `CLASSPATH`); the `AppletSecurity` class also allows access to nonpublic members of classes loaded by the same class loader. Code that has been signed by a trusted entity can access all members of system classes. In all cases, standard Java access controls are applied. For example, even though code can get a reference to a protected field, the code cannot get or set the value; it can only find out information about the member such as its declaring class and its name.

A Reflection Example

 To show how the Reflection API can be used, this part of the chapter develops a simple applet that displays information about a given class. The `classInfo` constructor takes two parameters: the `Class` to print the information to, and a `java.awt.TextArea` to display the information. A command-line version can easily be created by replacing the `TextArea` with a `PrintWriter` and converting the `appendText()` calls to `print()`. The final code for the finished `classInfo` example and a driver applet that shows how to use it is located on the accompanying CD-ROM.

Let's start with the overall skeleton for the class. Listing 35.1 shows the constructor and a convenience method called `smartTypePrint()`. The constructor copies its parameters into the corresponding instance variables. The `smartTypePrint()` method determines whether the `Class` parameter represents an array type and appends `[]` to the name if appropriate. The last three methods shown in Listing 35.1 are fleshed out in the next sections.

Listing 35.1. The `classInfo` skeleton.

```
import java.lang.reflect.*;
import java.io.*;
public class classInfo {
  protected Class myClass;
  protected java.awt.TextArea os;
  // Constructor
  public classInfo( Class c, java.awt.TextArea a ) {
    myClass = c;
    os = a;
  }
  public String smartTypePrint( Class c ) {
    if( c.isArray( ) ) {
      return new String( smartTypePrint( c.getComponentType() ) + "[]" );
    } else {
      return c.getName();
    }
  }
  public void generalInfo() { … }
  public void methodInfo() { … }
  public void fieldInfo() { … }
}
```

Class Name, Superclass, and Other Information

The `generalInfo()` method prints out information about the class in question. The general information it prints includes the class's name, whether it is a class or an interface, and any modifiers. Listing 35.2 shows the `generalInfo()` method.

Listing 35.2. The `generalInfo()` method.

```
public void generalInfo( ) {
    os.appendText( "Name: " + myClass.getName( ) + "\n" );
    os.appendText( "Class/Interface: "
            + (myClass.isInterface() ? "Interface" : "Class") );
    os.appendText( "\tSuperclass: " + myClass.getSuperclass().getName()
              + "\n" );
    os.appendText( "Primitive type: " + myClass.isPrimitive() + "\n" );
    os.appendText( "Interfaces: " );
    Class interfaces[] = myClass.getInterfaces();
    if( interfaces.length != 0 ) {
      for( int i = 0; i < interfaces.length; i++ ) {
        if( (i % 3) == 4) {
          os.appendText( "\n\t" );
        }
        os.appendText( interfaces[ i ].getName() + " " );
      }
      os.appendText( "\n" );
    } else {
      os.appendText( "None\n" );
    }
    os.appendText( "Class Modifiers: "
                + Modifier.toString( myClass.getModifiers() ) + "\n" );
}
```

Fields

The `fieldInfo()` method prints each of the fields declared by the class (see Listing 35.3). Inherited fields are ignored, although they can be obtained by using the `getFields()` method instead of `getDeclaredFields()`. The modifiers and type of the field are printed, followed by the name of the field. Although the `Field` class provides a `toString()` method that provides the same information, we'll do it ourselves here for the sheer fun of it.

Listing 35.3. The `fieldInfo()` method.

```java
public void fieldInfo( ) {
    Field fields[] = null;
    os.appendText( "Fields:\n" );
    try {
      fields = myClass.getDeclaredFields();
    } catch( SecurityException e ) {
      os.appendText( "Error getting fields: "
                       + e.getMessage() + "\n" );
      return;
    }
    if( fields != null ) {
      if( fields.length != 0 ) {
        for( int i = 0; i < fields.length; i++ ) {
          os.appendText( "\t" + Modifier.toString(
                                  fields[i].getModifiers() ) );
          os.appendText( " " + smartTypePrint( fields[i].getType() ) + " " );
          os.appendText( fields[ i ].getName() + "\n" );
        }
      } else {
        os.appendText( "\tNone\n" );
      }
    }
    os.appendText( "\n" );
}
```

Constructors

Next, the `constructorInfo()` method prints out any constructors for the class (see Listing 35.4). The modifiers for each constructor are printed, followed by any parameters the constructor takes. If the constructor throws any exceptions, these are printed next.

Listing 35.4. The `constructorInfo()` method.

```java
public void constructorInfo( ) {
    Constructor constructors[] = null;
    os.appendText( "Constructors:\n" );
    try {
      constructors = myClass.getDeclaredConstructors();
```

continues

Listing 35.4. continued

```
      } catch( SecurityException e ) {
        os.appendText( "Error getting constructors: " + e + "\n" );
        return;
      }
    if( constructors != null ) {
      Class a[] = null;
      if( constructors.length != 0 ) {
        for( int i = 0; i < constructors.length; i++ ) {
          os.appendText( " " + constructors[ i ].getName()
                        + "\n ----------\n" );
          os.appendText( "\tModifiers: " +
                        Modifier.toString( constructors[i].getModifiers() ) + "\n" );
          a = constructors[ i ].getParameterTypes();
          if( a.length != 0 ) {
            os.appendText( "\tParameters (" + a.length + "): " );
            for( int j = 0; j < a.length; j++ ) {
              if( (j % 8) == 7 ) {
                os.appendText( "\n\t\t" );
              }
              os.appendText( smartTypePrint( a[j] ) + " " );
            }
          } else {
            os.appendText( "\tParameters: none" );
          }
          os.appendText( "\n" );
          a = constructors[ i ].getExceptionTypes();
          if( a.length != 0 ) {
            os.appendText( "\tExceptions (" + a.length + "): " );
            for( int j = 0; j < a.length; j++ ) {
              if( (j % 8) == 7 ) {
                os.appendText( "\n\t\t" );
              }
              os.appendText( smartTypePrint( a[j] ) + " " );
            }
          } else {
            os.appendText( "\tExceptions: none" );
          }
          os.appendText( "\n\n" );
        }
      } else {
        os.appendText( "None\n" );
      }
    }
  }
}
```

Methods

The last method, methodInfo(), looks remarkably similar to the constructorInfo() method (see Listing 35.5). The methodInfo() method also makes use of the getReturnType() method to determine the return type of the method in question.

Listing 35.5. The `methodInfo()` method.

```
public void methodInfo( ) {
    Method methods[] = null;
    os.appendText( "Methods:\n" );
    try {
        methods = myClass.getDeclaredMethods();
    } catch( SecurityException e ) {
        os.appendText( "Error getting methods: " + e + "\n" );
        return;
    }
    if( methods != null ) {
        Class a[] = null;
        if( methods.length != 0 ) {
            for( int i = 0; i < methods.length; i++ ) {
                os.appendText( " " + methods[ i ].getName()
                        + "\n ---------\n" );
                os.appendText( "\tModifiers: " +
                        Modifier.toString( methods[i].getModifiers() ) + "\n" );
                os.appendText( "\tReturns: " +
                        smartTypePrint( methods[i].getReturnType() ) + "\n" );
                a = methods[ i ].getParameterTypes();
                if( a.length != 0 ) {
                    os.appendText( "\tParameters (" + a.length + "): " );
                    for( int j = 0; j < a.length; j++ ) {
                        if( (j % 8) == 7 ) {
                            os.appendText( "\n\t\t" );
                        }
                        os.appendText( smartTypePrint( a[j] ) + " " );
                    }
                } else {
                    os.appendText( "\tParameters: none" );
                }
                os.appendText( "\n" );
                a = methods[ i ].getExceptionTypes();
                if( a.length != 0 ) {
                    os.appendText( "\tExceptions (" + a.length + "): " );
                    for( int j = 0; j < a.length; j++ ) {
                        if( (j % 8) == 7 ) {
                            os.appendText( "\n\t\t" );
                        }
                        os.appendText( smartTypePrint( a[j] ) + " " );
                    }
                } else {
                    os.appendText( "\tExceptions: none" );
                }
                os.appendText( "\n\n" );
            }
        } else {
            os.appendText( "None\n" );
        }
    }
}
```

User Interface

The user interface for the applet is very simple, as shown in Listing 35.6. It consists of a TextField to allow the class name to be entered, a Button to click to print the information, and the TextArea in which to display the information.

When the button is clicked, the applet's action() method tries to get a Class reference for the class named in the field. If it retrieves a Class, it creates a classInfo object with the TextArea for output and calls each of the information methods. Figure 35.1 shows the classInfoApplet in action.

Listing 35.6. The classInfoApplet class.

```java
import java.applet.*;
import java.awt.*;
public class classInfoApplet
  extends Applet
{
  TextField className;              // For entering class name
  Button     goButton;             // Press button to do lookup
  TextArea  infoArea;              // Area to print output
  // init -- Create GUI.
  public void init( ) {
    setLayout( new BorderLayout( ) );

    Panel p = new Panel();
    p.setLayout( new FlowLayout( ) );
    className = new TextField( 40 );
    p.add( className );
    goButton = new Button( "Print Info" );
    p.add( goButton );
    add( "North", p );
    infoArea = new TextArea( 80, 80 );
    add( "Center", infoArea );
  }
  // action -- Dispatch events
  public boolean action( Event ev, Object arg ) {
    // If the target is our button
    if( ev.target == goButton ) {
      Class c = null;
      String name = className.getText(); // Get class name from field
      // Let user know what we're up to
      showStatus( "Trying class '" + name + "'" );
      // Try and get a Class object for that name
      try {
        c = java.lang.Class.forName( name );
      } catch( ClassNotFoundException e ) {
        // Gripe if class wasn't found
        showStatus( "Couldn't load class: " + e.getMessage() );
        return true;
      }
      if( c == null ) {
        // Paranoia check that we got a valid class object.
        showStatus( "Class is null??" );
      } else {
```

```
        infoArea.setText( "" );          // Clear out text area
        // Make a classInfo object with the Class and TextArea
        classInfo ci = new classInfo( c, infoArea );
        // Print information
        ci.generalInfo();
        ci.fieldInfo();
        ci.constructorInfo();
        ci.methodInfo();
        // Let user know we're done.
        showStatus( "Info for '" + name + "' done." );
      }
      return true;                        // Return that we handled event
    }
    // Let superclass handle event otherwise
    return super.action( ev, arg );
  }
}
```

FIGURE 35.1.

The classInfoApplet.

Summary

You should now have an understanding of what the Reflection API can do and how to use it. This new API provides useful functionality of interest to those who write utilities such as debuggers and object browsers, and to those who use the JavaBeans facilities.

35

JAVA REFLECTION

VIII

PART

Java Archives and JavaBeans

JAR Basics

by Mike Fletcher

IN THIS CHAPTER

Java Archive (JAR) files provide a way to bundle all the resources for an applet into a single file. This chapter introduces JAR files, explains how you can create them, describes the `java.util.zip` package, and provides a quick example of how to use JAR files with applets. More detailed information on JAR-related topics is given in Chapter 37, "Code Signing and JAR Security."

What Are JAR Files?

In versions of the JDK before version 1.1, if an applet was made up of several different class files or had resources such as GIFs or audio files, you had to download each resource individually. In addition to forcing the user of the applet to wait while the applet's pieces downloaded, this arrangement put an extra load on the HTTP server. To address this problem, Sun introduced JAR files. Based on the widely used ZIP file format developed by PKWare, a JAR file allows multiple resources (Java class files, graphics files, and others) to be bundled into a single, compressed archive file. In addition to making the server's job easier, applets and resources download quicker when they are compressed. A new package, `java.util.zip`, contains classes to manipulate JAR files (as well as normal ZIP files). You can simply store files in a JAR file, or you can compress them before storing to save space.

JAR files include a manifest file in the archive. This manifest (named `META-INF/MANIFEST.MF`) gives message digests of the component files in the archive. Additionally, digital signatures of component files can be included in the `META-INF` directory of the archive. Code signed by a trusted entity can be granted extra privileges (such as writing files). Code signing and related issues are covered in detail in Chapter 37.

Manipulating JAR Files with `jar`

Included with the JDK 1.1 is a tool to create and manipulate JAR files. This tool is called, logically enough, `jar`. The `jar` tool runs from the DOS command line or UNIX shell prompt (represented in the examples below by the `%` character). The following examples show how to use `jar` to create a JAR file, how to list the contents of an archive, and how to extract a file from an archive. In all cases, two extra options can be used with `jar` to change how it operates:

Option	Description
v	Tells `jar` to generate verbose output about the actions it is performing.
f	Specifies the filename to manipulate. If this option is not given, `jar` writes to standard output.

If you happen to forget how to use `jar`, you can run it with no arguments to generate a usage listing.

NOTE

Because JAR files are stored in the standard ZIP format, you do not have to use `jar` to create JAR files. You can use any application that can create ZIP files—as long as you generate your own manifest file and name it correctly (`META-INF/MANIFEST.MF`). You can find information about the manifest and signature file formats at this site:

`http://www.javasoft.com/products/JDK/1.1/docs/guide/jar/manifest.html`

Free ZIP and unZIP programs are available from the Info-ZIP group. Source code and binaries for many platforms are available from this site:

`http://www.cdrom.com/pub/infozip/Info-Zip.html`

Creating a JAR File

To create an archive, you use `jar` with the `c` flag. Suppose that we want to create a JAR file with three files: `sampleApplet.class`, a Java class file; `sampleGraphic.gif`, an image file; and `sampleSound.au`, an audio file. The following command places these three files into an archive named `sample.jar`. The options `cvf` specify that we want to create an archive, we want verbose output, and the archive filename should be `sample.jar`.

```
% jar cvf sample.jar sample.jar sampleApplet.class sampleGraphic.gif sampleSound.au
```

Here's what `jar` shows you as it's creating the archive:

```
adding: sampleApplet.class in=4480 out=2065 deflated 53.0%
adding: sampleGraphic.gif in=506 out=419 deflated 17.0%
adding: sampleSound.au in=5529 out=1088 deflated 80.0%
```

For each file, `jar` specifies the input size before compression and the output size after compression, as well as a ratio showing how well the file was compressed.

Listing the Contents of a JAR File

Next, let's list the contents of the archive file we just created. The `t` option tells `jar` that we want a table of contents for the JAR file; the `vf` options specify verbose mode and the filename for which we want information:

```
% jar tvf sample.jar
```

Here's the output from `jar`:

```
 402 Tue Feb 18 23:12:10 EST 1997 META-INF/MANIFEST.MF
4480 Mon Feb 17 02:03:46 EST 1997 sampleApplet.class
 506 Tue Feb 18 22:24:52 EST 1997 sampleGraphic.gif
5529 Mon Feb 17 00:16:02 EST 1997 sampleSound.au
```

Notice that there is an extra file named META-INF/MANIFEST.MF in the JAR archive file. This is a manifest of all the files contained in the archive and a message digest of the contents of each file (see Chapter 37, "Code Signing and JAR Security," for more information about message digests). The jar tool automatically generates a manifest file; alternatively, you can generate one yourself and pass the m flag to jar when you create the archive.

Extracting a File from a JAR File

Now let's extract sampleGraphic.gif from the sample.jar file. In the following command, the vf options are the same as they were in the preceding section (verbose mode and the filename from which you want to extract a file). The x option specifies that we want to extract files. If no extra arguments are given, jar extracts the entire contents of the archive. If arguments are given after the archive name, jar takes those as the names of the files to extract.

```
% jar xvf sample.jar sampleGraphic.gif
```

Here's the response from jar concerning the extraction request:

```
extracted: sampleGraphic.gif in=419 out=506 inflated 17.0%
```

An Overview of `java.util.zip`

The java.util.zip package contains several classes that facilitate the manipulation of compressed files.

The `ZipFile` Class

The ZipFile class provides a way to read the contents of a ZIP archive. There are two constructors: one that takes a String specifying the filename of the archive to open and one that takes a java.io.File object. The getName() method returns the path name of the ZIP file represented by the ZipFile object.

Two methods are provided to obtain ZipEntry objects representing the contents of the ZIP file. The getEntry() method takes a String and returns a ZipEntry for the corresponding file; it returns null if no such file exists in the archive. The entries() method returns a java.util.Enumeration of ZipEntry objects for all the entries in the ZIP file. The getInputStream() method is used to obtain an InputStream for the entry represented by the ZipEntry given as a parameter.

The `ZipEntry` Class

Each file in a ZIP archive can be represented by a ZipEntry object. ZipEntry objects can be obtained for an existing file from a ZipFile or ZipInputStream object; they can also be created when you make a new ZIP archive with a ZipOutputStream. The ZipEntry class provides methods to retrieve information about the entry (for example, the filename, the compressed and uncompressed size of the file, and the compression method used for the file). The isDirectory() method is provided to determine whether the entry in question is a normal file or a directory.

ZIP Stream Classes

In addition to the ZipFile class, the java.util.zip package has two stream classes that handle compressed data. The stream classes in java.util.zip extend either InflaterInputStream or DeflatorOutputStream as appropriate. These two filtered streams provide a generic interface for handling compressed data.

ZipInputStream reads data in the ZIP format from an InputStream. The getNextEntry() method returns a ZipEntry for the next component in the ZIP file and places the stream at the beginning of the data for that component. The closeEntry() method closes the current entry and advances the stream to return the next entry in the archive. Both methods throw a ZipException if a ZIP-related exception occurs.

The ZipOutputStream provides OutputStream functionality for writing compressed data. The putNextEntry() method takes a ZipEntry as a parameter. A new entry is created in the ZIP file and any data written to the stream goes to the current entry. Two methods are provided to control the compression used to store entries: setMethod() takes as a parameter either ZipOutputStream.DEFLATED (to specify that the next entries should be compressed) or ZipOutputStream.STORED (to specify that any subsequent entries should simply be stored with no compression). The setLevel() method takes an integer from 0 to 9, inclusive, with higher numbers indicating more compression (which takes longer to compress). The setComment() method allows the ZIP file comment to be set.

GNU Zip Stream Classes

In addition to classes for the ZIP compression format, the java.util.zip package provides two classes that support reading and writing files in the GNU Zip format. GNU Zip is a widely used compression format for UNIX. Unlike the ZIP format, the GNU Zip format handles only one file at a time, rather than multiple files and a directory structure. GNU Zip is most often used as a replacement for the UNIX compress utility, so there is no getNextEntry() method for the GZIPInputStream class. In addition, the GZIPOutputStream has no way to specify filenames for entries.

Using JAR Files

A new attribute has been added to the HTML <applet> tag: archives. This tag specifies one or more JAR files that should be downloaded with the applet (obviously, these JAR files contain components needed by the applet). You should still specify the code attribute, even if you give the archives attribute because code is used as the name of the applet class to load. Whenever the applet requests a class, image, or sound file, the archives specified are searched first. If the necessary resource is not contained in one of the JAR files downloaded, the applet contacts the server and searches for the resource as it did with the JDK version 1.0.2. You can specify multiple archive files by separating the filenames with + (a plus sign). A sample applet tag is shown in Listing 36.1.

Listing 36.1. A sample `<applet>` tag using JAR files.

```
<applet code="sampleApplet.class"
    archives="sample.jar + icons.jar + commonClasses.jar"
    width="550"
    height="300">
<param name="animal" value="lemur">
<param name="server" value="qa.nowhere.com">
</applet>
```

Summary

JAR files provide a way to simplify applet distribution. Along with the new code-signing facilities, JAR files should greatly increase the usefulness of applets by making them easier to distribute and allowing trusted code to step outside the narrow limits of the sandbox. Additionally, the `java.util.zip` package provides support for manipulating ZIP and GNU Zip archives in any Java program.

Code Signing and JAR Security

by Mike Fletcher

IN THIS CHAPTER

CHAPTER 37

Several additions and changes have been made to Java's security facilities in JDK 1.1. One of the most anticipated new features is the ability to digitally sign Java code—and to allow code signed by trusted entities to be granted access outside the normal applet sandbox. This chapter introduces the new `java.security` API, shows you how to use the `javakey` utility to create and manage digital keys, and shows you how to distribute signed code in JAR files.

Introduction to Digital Signatures

Before delving into the details of signed applets, you may find it useful to know how digital signatures work. Digital signatures provide a way to indicate that some piece of information was generated by some entity (for Java digital signatures, this "entity" is usually either a programmer or a company) and that the information has not been altered. Methods for generating signatures are designed so that it is mathematically impossible to create two different documents with the same signature in any reasonable period of time.

Public key cryptography differs from what is referred to as *conventional* or *secret key cryptography*. In public key cryptography, you have one key to encrypt a message and a different key to decrypt the message. For a well-designed algorithm, it is mathematically impossible to determine the secret key given the encrypting key. The encrypting key (usually referred to as the *public key*) can be given to anyone who wants to send an encrypted message to the holder of the corresponding secret key (usually referred to as the *private key*). Anyone can use the public key to encrypt, but only the secret key can decrypt the message and recover the original text.

Some public-key encryption algorithms can also be used to create digital signatures. Instead of the sender using the public key to encrypt a message to the private key holder, the private key holder encrypts the message using his or her private key. Anyone who has the public key can decrypt this message and verify that it did in fact come from the private key holder (because that person should be the only person with access to the private key). The signature algorithm used by the default JDK security package is known as DSA (Digital Signature Algorithm). DSA was created by the U.S. government's National Institute of Standards and Technology (the standard is FIPS 186, if you are interested) and the National Security Agency. The DSA has public keys that use anywhere from 512-bit to 1024-bit prime numbers and a 160-bit private key. Rather than using DSA to generate a signature of the entire document (a possibly time-consuming operation), a one-way hash of the document is generated using the MD5 algorithm; this hash is signed. MD5 generates a 128-bit string that is unique for a given input document. To verify the signature, the one-way hash of the received document is generated and checked against the signed 128-bit string from the sender. If the two match, the document has not been tampered with.

NOTE

For more information on digital signatures and public key cryptography, check out *Applied Cryptography*, Second Edition, by Bruce Shneier (published by John Wiley & Sons, ISBN 0-471-11709-9). This book is a very good introduction to cryptography in general, as well as an excellent reference for the details on specific algorithms. On the Web, the NIST's Computer Security Resource Clearing house (`http://csrc.ncsl.nist.gov/`) provides copies of the Federal Information Processing Standards for DSA and SHA. The `sci.crypt` newsgroup and its Frequently Asked Questions posting is another good starting place for cryptography resources.

The `java.security` API

The `java.security` package implements the new Java Security API. This API is intended to give developers access to security functionality in a standard, cross-platform way. In addition to the digital signatures, key management, and access control lists provided in the 1.1 release, future releases of `java.security` will provide support for exchanging digital keys and data encryption. For more information on the `java.security` package, see Chapter 16, "The Security Package."

The Signature Class

The `Signature` class represents a digital signature 94gorithm. The constructor takes as its parameter a `String` representing the name of the signature algorithm desired. Once a `Signature` reference has been obtained, it must be initialized with either the private key (for signing) or the public key (for verifying a signature). To generate a signature, call the `update()` method with the contents of the document to be signed. The `update()` method takes either a single `byte` argument or a `byte[]` array with an optional offset and length. After the contents of the document have been given to `Signature()`, the `sign()` method can be called to obtain a `byte[]` representing the signature. Verifying a signature is very similar to creating one: After calling the `initVerify()` method with the `PublicKey`, the contents of the document are passed to `update()`. Once the entire contents have been given, the `verify()` method is called with the `byte[]` representing what the signature should be. The `verify()` method returns a `boolean` specifying whether the signature was valid; the `Signature()` method is reset and ready to verify another signature by the same `PublicKey`.

The `KeyPairGenerator` and `KeyPair` Classes

These classes are used to generate a pair of public and private keys for use with other security packages. The `KeyPairGenerator` class's static method `getInstance()` returns a reference to an object, which in turn may be used to generate public and private keys for the algorithm specified. The `initialize()` method sets up the generator to provide a key of a specific *strength* (that is, a key of a certain length, such as 512 bits or 1,024 bits). The `generateKeyPair()` method returns a `KeyPair` object. The `KeyPair` class provides two methods, `getPrivateKey()` and `getPublicKey()`, which return the corresponding key references.

The `PrivateKey` and `PublicKey` Interfaces

These two interfaces represent key material for various algorithms. Each algorithm returns objects implementing these interfaces, which then behave as appropriate for the algorithm. For example, the DSA algorithm has the `DSAPrivateKey` and `DSAPublicKey` interfaces. In general (unless you are implementing an algorithm), you do not manipulate keys directly, only give them as parameters.

The `Identity`, `IdentityScope`, and `Certificate` Classes

The `Identity` class represents an entity that can be authenticated by a public key. The entity represented can be a person, a company, or even a particular computer. `Identity` objects have a name associated with them; this name should be unique within a given scope. An `IdentityScope` represents a scope for an `Identity`, giving the context in which the `Identity` object exists. Both `Identity` and `IdentityScope` objects can have one or more `Certificate` objects associated with them. A `Certificate` represents a guarantee by some entity that the `Identity` and its associated public key actually belong to the owner represented by the `Identity`.

For example, a programmer can be represented by an `Identity` object, which he or she uses to sign code he or she produces. The `IdentityScope` for this `Identity` object could be set to Acme Software, the company for which the programmer works. The programmer's `Identity` would have a `Certificate` signed by Acme Software. The `IdentityScope` for the company might have a `Certificate` signed by an entity providing certification of signatures (such as VeriSign or the U.S. Post Office). The `Certification` object can then be used to verify that the `Identity` is valid and belongs to the programmer.

Signing Code with `javakey`

The `javakey` utility included with the JDK provides facilities for managing identities and certificates, and for signing code. Along with the `jar` utility used to generate JAR files, `javakey` allows you to sign code and place the class files (and other resources used by an applet) into a single archive. Identities are stored in a database file named `identitydb.obj`, which is stored in a location specified in the java.security properties file in the JDK lib/security directory. When the applet is run in a properly configured browser, the signed code is granted privileges beyond those given to unsigned code. For example, a department can develop a signed applet for its intranet that stores its preferences in a local file on the user's computer. All the members of the department then set their browsers to allow code signed by the department to read and write files from their hard drives.

Creating an Identity and Key Pair

The first step in signing applets is to generate an identity and a public/private key pair for the identity. This is done with the following command:

```
% javakey -cs "MySigner" true
```

37

CODE SIGNING
AND JAR
SECURITY

> **NOTE**
>
> In this section, all the examples that show javakey commands use the % character to represent the command or shell prompt.

The -cs "MySigner" part of the preceding command tells javakey that we want to create an identity in our identitydb.obj database for a signer with the name MySigner. The true parameter indicates that we will trust code signed by this particular signer. If the last argument is omitted, signatures from this signer can be verified but the code signed is not granted extra privileges. Now that we have an identity in our database, we must have javakey generate a key pair for our identity.

The following command is used to have javakey create a key pair:

```
% javakey -gk "MySigner" DSA 512 MySigner.public MySigner.private
```

This command tells javakey to generate a key (-gk) for the signer named MySigner. The next two arguments specify that we want a key for the DSA algorithm that is 512 bits long. The last two arguments are optional; they specify that we want javakey to store a copy of the public and private keys in the files named MySigner.public and MySigner.private, respectively.

> **CAUTION**
>
> Be careful with your private keys. Anyone who can get a copy of a private key can generate signatures for the corresponding identity.

Generating an X.509 Certificate

Before you can sign code, `javakey` must generate a certificate for your identity. To do this, you have to create a text file containing the parameters for the certificate, such as the identity to create the certificate for and what period of time the certificate is valid for. For this example, the last line of the text file specifies that we want a copy of the certificate saved into the file named `MySigner.x509`. This certificate file can be distributed to people who want to verify signatures from our sample identity. You can embed comments in the directive file by preceding the comment with a # character. Listing 37.1 shows the contents of the directive file for our example.

Listing 37.1. The certificate directive file.

```
# This is a comment
issuer.name=MySigner

issuer.cert=1

subject.name=MySigner

subject.real.name=Example Signer
subject.org.unit=Bogus Organization
subject.org=Bogus Corporation
subject.country=US

start.date=15 Feb 1997
end.date=15 Feb 1998
serial.number=2000
out.file=MySigner.x509
```

Once we have the certificate directive in a file, we can use the `javakey -gc` options to generate the actual certificate. The following command assumes that the certificate directive in Listing 37.1 was placed in a file named `cdirective`:

```
% javakey -gc cdirective
```

Signing the JAR File

Now we are ready to sign a JAR file with our `MySigner` identity. Assume that a JAR file named `example.jar` has already been created, and that this JAR file contains an applet (see Chapter 36, "JAR Basics," for more information on creating JAR files). The next step is to create a signing directive file that tells `javakey` what identity to use to sign the file, what certificate to use, and what to name the signature file. The `signer` parameter in the directive file specifies which identity we want to use to create the signature. The `cert` directive specifies which certificate the identity is to use (for this example, we use 1 because our signer has only one certificate). The next parameter, `chain`, is not used in JDK 1.1 and should be set to zero. The final parameter gives the name of the signature file that will be generated and included in the JAR file. Listing 37.2 shows the complete signing directive file.

Listing 37.2. The signature directive file.

```
# This is a comment
signer=MySigner

cert=1

chain=0

signature.file=MySig
```

The last step is to have javakey sign the JAR file. The signed version of the JAR file has .sig appended to its name. Here is the command line to use to have javakey sign our example JAR file:

```
% javakey -gs sdirective example.jar
```

Distributing Signed Code

You now should have a JAR file named example.jar.sig which contains your applet resources and a signature by the MySigner identity. This JAR file can be manipulated with the jar utility in the same way as any other file. If you extract the contents of the JAR file, the META-INF directory contains the signature file just created. To grant trusted status to signed code, you must make available to users the X.509 certificate file created when the certificate was generated (this file is called MySigner.x509 in the preceding example). Once a user has a copy of the certificate file, he or she can use javakey to add the identity to his or her own database.

The first step in verifying a signature is similar to creating the identity—but instead of using the -cs flags, you use only the -c flag, as shown here:

```
% javakey -c MySigner true
```

After creating the identity, you must import the actual information about the identity from the certificate file. This is done using the javakey -ic options, which take the identity name and the filename containing the certificate as parameters:

```
% javakey -ic MySigner MySigner.x509
```

Now any code signed by the MySigner identity that is loaded over the network is given full access, just as if it had been loaded from a local disk.

Other javakey Operations

The javakey utility controls your database of identities and certificates. It can be used to list or remove identities as well as to create them. The -l option allows you to list a summary of all of the identities contained in identitydb.obj. You can use the -ld option to list detailed information for all entities in the database; use -li to limit the detailed display to a specific identity. Listing 37.3 shows what an identity listing looks like.

Listing 37.3. An identity listing.

```
% javakey -ld

Scope: sun.security.IdentityDatabase, source file: \fletch\identitydb.obj

MySigner[identitydb.obj][trusted]
        public key initialized
        certificates:
        certificate 1    for  : CN=Example Signer, OU=Bogus Organization,
                                O=Bogus Corporation, C=US
                        from : CN=Example Signer, OU=Bogus Organization,
                                O=Bogus Corporation, C=US

        No further information available.
```

If you want to remove an identity from the database, you can use the -r option with the name of the identity to delete:

```
% javakey -r MySigner
```

Summary

You should now have an idea how the new code-signing facilities in the JDK 1.1 extend the capabilities of applets. The new java.security API provides a framework for manipulating digital signatures in general, as well as for creating signed code. You now understand how to use javakey to create and manage identities and certificates for distributing and verifying signed code.

JavaBeans Basics

by Michael Morrison

IN THIS CHAPTER

When Sun released the Java programming language and runtime system, I don't think the company quite realized the impact Java would have on the software development community. The explosion of the Web and the need for a solid way to bring it interactivity created the perfect climate for an innovative technology like Java. So much so, in fact, that Sun decided to form a business unit solely devoted to Java—JavaSoft was born! The newly formed JavaSoft didn't waste any time planning a host of related technologies aimed at dealing with various issues facing software developers today. Some of these technologies were incorporated into Java 1.1; others were pushed off for inclusion in a future release. One of the technologies to make it into Java 1.1 is JavaBeans—JavaSoft's answer to the need for a comprehensive software component technology.

JavaBeans makes a concerted effort to address the multitude of challenges that must be overcome by a high-power software component technology. The fact that it is based on the Java environment is one reason JavaBeans has an excellent chance of becoming a hit with the software development community. Another significant advantage JavaBeans has as a component technology is that it was developed entirely from scratch, with no limitations imposed by a preexisting technology (except maybe from Java). In other words, JavaBeans is a completely new component technology specifically designed to deal with the problems software developers face today.

Software Components

The software development community has been exploring the idea of reusable software for a while. You may have heard *reusable software* referred to by its more popular name, *software components*. In case you've missed the hype, a *component* is a reusable piece of software that can be assembled easily to create applications with much greater development efficiency. Just in case you think this idea sounds groundbreaking, it is not. You only have to look back roughly a century to see this same idea applied to a very different type of application. I'm referring to the industrial revolution, in which the assembly-line approach to developing and assembling mechanical machinery was introduced. The idea as applied to software is to build small, reusable components once and then reuse them as much as possible, thereby streamlining the entire development process.

Although component software certainly has its merits, fully reusable software has yet to really establish itself, and for a variety of reasons. Not the least of which is that the software industry is still very young compared to the industries carved out in the industrial revolution. It only stands to reason that it should take time to iron out the kinks in the whole software-production process. If you're like me, you'll embrace the rapid changes taking place in the software world and relish the fact that you are a part of a revolution of sorts—an information revolution.

Perhaps the hardest thing component software has had to face is the wide range of disparate microprocessors and operating systems in use today. There have been a variety of reasonable attempts at component software, but they've always been limited to a specific operating system. Microsoft's VBX and OCX component architectures have had great success in the PC world, but they've done little to bridge the gap to the other types of operating systems. When you consider the amount of work required to get an inherently platform-dependent component technology running on a wide range of operating systems, it only makes sense that Microsoft has focused solely on the PC market.

> **NOTE**
>
> Actually, Microsoft's new ActiveX technology, which is a revamped version of its OCX technology, aims to provide an all-purpose component technology compatible across a wide range of platforms. However, considering the dependency of ActiveX on 32-bit Windows code, it has yet to be seen how Microsoft will solve the platform-dependency issue. Additionally, some developers are apprehensive about ActiveX's dependency on OCX, whose security measures pale in comparison to Java. You learn more about ActiveX and how it relates to Java in Chapter 47, "Integrating Java and ActiveX."

Before the explosion of the Internet, the platform-dependency issue wasn't that big a deal. PC developers didn't necessarily care too much that their products wouldn't run on a Solaris system. Some PC developers hedged their bets and ported their applications to the Macintosh platform—most with considerably lengthy and resource-intensive development efforts. The whole scenario changed with the operating system melting pot created by the Internet. The result was a renewed interest in developing software that everyone could use, regardless of which operating system they happened to be running. Java has been a major factor in making truly platform-independent software development a reality. However, until recently, Java has not provided an answer to the issue of component software.

If the platform dependency issue isn't enough, some existing component technologies also suffer because they must be developed using a particular programming language or within a particular development environment. Just as platform dependency cripples components at run time, limiting component development to a particular programming language or development environment equally cripples components at the development end. Software developers want to be able to decide for themselves which language is the most appropriate for a particular task. Likewise, developers want to be able to select the development environment that best fits their needs, instead of being forced to use one based on the constraints of a component technology.

Therefore, any realistic long-term component technology must deal with both the issue of platform dependency and the issue of language dependency. This brings you to JavaBeans: JavaSoft's JavaBeans technology is a component technology that answers both of these problems directly.

JavaBeans is implemented as an architecture-independent and platform-independent Application Programming Interface (API) for creating and using dynamic Java software components. JavaBeans picks up where other component technologies left off, using the portable Java platform as the basis for providing a complete component software solution readily applicable to the online world.

The Mission

Before getting into the details of JavaBeans, it's important to understand what JavaSoft wanted to accomplish by developing a component technology for Java. You might already be thinking about the many benefits provided by software components in general. However, let's focus instead on JavaSoft's specific plan to couple a component technology with Java. This plan can probably best be summarized by JavaSoft's own JavaBeans mission statement: "Write once, run anywhere, reuse everywhere."

This mission statement cuts through all the complexities surrounding component software and delivers a very simple, concise, and elegant set of requirements for the JavaBeans technology. To better understand exactly what the architects at JavaSoft have in mind, let's examine each part of this statement in more detail.

Write Once

By *write once*, the folks at JavaSoft aren't referring to kids writing home from summer camp. They are actually referring to the issue of software development and how programmers all too often have to rewrite code when they decide to make changes. JavaSoft is suggesting that a well-developed software component technology should fully encourage code to be written once and not require rewrites to add or improve functionality. Adhering to this premise, JavaBeans should provide a practical way to add and improve functionality in an existing code base without reworking the original code.

This goal of writing JavaBeans components once—in addition to making sense in terms of development resources—makes perfect sense in terms of version control. JavaBeans components encourage developers to make incremental changes to components instead of rewriting significant portions from scratch. The result is a steady progression of functionality, which in turn dictates a more consistent evolution of a component through subsequent versions.

Run Anywhere

The *run anywhere* statement doesn't refer to what you tell the cat after putting it outside. Instead, it refers to the capability of JavaBeans components to be executed (run) in any environment. What this statement really boils down to is the requirement for JavaBeans components to be cross platform. A software component technology simply must be cross platform to have a realistic chance of succeeding in the software climate of today and in the future. Fortunately for JavaBeans, cross-platform support comes easily because it is based on Java.

The *run anywhere* statement doesn't just refer to JavaBeans components executing on different platforms, however; it also refers to execution across distributed network environments. It is extremely important that distributed computing support be available in a component model. This part of the mission statement also addresses the need for JavaBeans to support distributed computing in some way.

Reuse Everywhere

Sorry, but I don't have a cute joke for this part of the JavaBeans mission statement, so I'll get straight to the point. The *reuse everywhere* part of the statement refers to the need for JavaBeans components to be reused in many different scenarios including (but not necessarily limited to) applications, other components, documents, Web sites, and application builder tools. This is perhaps the most critical part of the mission statement because it drives home the point that JavaBeans components should be capable of use in a wide range of situations. Furthermore, this requirement meets the primary goal of software components in general, which is code reuse.

Meeting Goals

Now that you know the fundamental ideas surrounding JavaSoft's drive to develop a component technology, it's time to move on to some of the specific goals the company pursued in making JavaBeans a reality. The primary design goals for JavaBeans are summarized by the following list of requirements for JavaBeans components:

- Compact and easy to create and use
- Fully portable
- Built on the inherent strengths of Java
- Flexible design-time component editor support
- Leverage for robust distributed computing mechanisms

JavaSoft felt it imperative that JavaBeans meet all these goals if it was to be taken seriously as a component technology. Fortunately, it accomplished these goals and succeeded in making JavaBeans a major contender for charting the future of software components. Now, take a closer look at how each of these goals was met.

Simple and Compact

The first requirement of JavaBeans—that it be very compact—is based on the fact that JavaBeans components often will be used in distributed environments in which entire components may be transferred across a low-bandwidth Internet connection. Clearly, components must be as compact as possible to facilitate a reasonable transfer time. The second part of this goal relates to the ease with which the components are built and used. Imagining components that are easy to use is not such a stretch, but creating a component architecture that makes building components easy is a different issue altogether. Existing attempts at component software often have been plagued by complex programming APIs that make it difficult for developers to create components without serious brain strain. JavaBeans components must be not only easy to use, but also easy to develop. This is a critical requirement for component developers because it means fewer ulcers and more time to embellish components with interesting features.

JavaBeans components are based largely on the class structure already in use with traditional Java applet programming. This approach is an enormous benefit to those people investing lots of time and energy in learning Java. This has the positive side effect of making JavaBeans components very compact, because Java applets already are very efficient in terms of size. Even though the goal is for JavaBeans components to be as compact as possible, this is in no way a limitation if you want to create complex and potentially bulkier components.

Portable

The second major goal of JavaSoft in creating JavaBeans was to make it fully portable. The JavaBeans API, coupled with the platform-independent Java system on which it is based, creates the platform-independent component solution alluded to earlier. As a result, developers don't have to worry about including platform-specific libraries with their Java applets. The end result will be reusable components that unify the world of computing under one happy, peaceful umbrella. Okay, maybe that's asking a little too much—I'll settle for just being able to develop a component and have it run unmodified on any Java-supported system.

Leveraging Java's Strengths

The existing Java architecture already offers a wide range of benefits easily applied to components. One of the more important, but rarely mentioned, features of Java is its built-in class-discovery mechanism, which enables objects to interact with each other dynamically at run time. This results in a system in which objects can be integrated with each other independently of their respective origins or development history. The class discovery mechanism is not just a neat feature of Java, it is a necessary requirement in any component architecture. Fortunately for JavaBeans, this functionality is already provided by Java at no additional cost, meaning that no extra overhead is required to support it. Other component architectures have had to implement complex mechanisms to achieve the same result.

Another example of JavaBeans inheriting existing Java functionality is *persistence* (the capability of an object to store and retrieve its internal state). Persistence is handled automatically in JavaBeans by way of the serialization mechanism already present in Java. Alternatively, developers can create their own customized persistence solutions whenever necessary.

Application Builder Support

Another design goal of JavaBeans relates to design-time issues and how developers build applications using JavaBeans components. The JavaBeans architecture includes support for specifying design-time properties and editing mechanisms to facilitate visual editing of JavaBeans components. The result is that developers can use visual application builder tools to assemble and modify JavaBeans components in a seamless fashion—much as existing visual development tools on the Windows platform work with components such as VBX or OCX controls. In this way, component developers specify the way in which the components are to be used and manipulated in a development environment. This feature alone will officially usher in the use of professional application builder tools and significantly boost the productivity of application developers.

Distributed Computing Support

Although it is not a core element of the JavaBeans architecture, support for distributed computing is a major issue with JavaBeans. Because distributed computing requires relatively complex solutions attributed to the complex nature of distributed systems, JavaBeans leverages the use of external distributed approaches based on need. In other words, JavaBeans enables developers to use distributed computing mechanisms whenever necessary, but it doesn't overburden itself with core support for distributed computing. Although this approach may seem that the folks at JavaSoft are just being lazy, this design approach enables JavaBeans components to be very compact. Remember that distributed computing solutions inevitably require a great deal of overhead.

JavaBeans component developers can select a distributed computing approach that best fits their needs. JavaSoft provides a distributed computing solution of its own in the Java Remote Method Invocation (RMI) technology, but JavaBeans developers are in no way handcuffed to this solution. (You learn more about RMI in Chapters 17, "The RMI Package," and 56, "Netscape's Internet Foundation Classes.") Other options include CORBA and Microsoft's DCOM, among others. The point is that distributed computing has been purposely left out of JavaBeans to keep things tight while still enabling developers who require distributed support a wide range of options.

The Relationship of JavaBeans to Java

Even though I've hopefully made a clear distinction between Java and JavaBeans, a common source of confusion about JavaBeans is the relationship it has with Java. To be fair, there certainly is some justification to this confusion. Hasn't Java been touted as an object-oriented technology capable of serving up reusable objects? Yes—and no. Java certainly enables you to build reusable objects, but there are few rules or standards governing how these objects interact with each other. JavaBeans builds on the existing design of Java by specifying a rich set of mechanisms that define interactions between objects, along with common actions most objects have to support (such as persistence and event handling).

Although the current Java component model works well, it is relatively limited in regard to delivering true reusability and interoperability. At the object level, there really is no straightforward mechanism for creating reusable Java objects that can interact with other objects dynamically in a consistent fashion. The closest thing you can do in Java is to create applets and try to enable them to communicate with each other on a Web page—not a very straightforward task. JavaBeans provides the framework by which this communication can take place with ease. Even more important is the fact that JavaBeans components can easily be tweaked with a standard set of well-defined properties. Basically, JavaBeans merges the power of full-blown Java applets with the compactness and reusability of Java AWT (Advanced Windowing Toolkit) components such as buttons.

However, JavaBeans components aren't limited to visual objects such as buttons. You can just as easily develop nonvisual JavaBeans components that perform background functions in concert with other components. In this way, JavaBeans merges the power of visual Java applets with nonvisual Java programs under a consistent component framework.

> **NOTE**
>
> A *nonvisual component* is any component that doesn't have visible output. When you think of components in terms of Java AWT objects such as buttons and menus, this might seem a little strange. However, keep in mind that a component is simply a tightly packaged program and has no specific requirement of being visual. A good example of a nonvisual component is a timer component, which fires timing events at specified intervals. Timer components are very popular in other component development environments such as Microsoft Visual Basic.

You can use a variety of JavaBeans components together in application builder tools without necessarily writing any code. The capability to use a variety of components together regardless of their origin is a major enhancement to the current Java model. You certainly can use other prebuilt objects in Java, but you must have an intimate knowledge of the object's interface at the code level. Additionally, you must integrate the object into your code programmatically. JavaBeans components expose their own interfaces visually, enabling you to edit their properties without programming. Furthermore, you can use a visual editor to simply "drop" a JavaBeans component directly into an application without writing any code. This is an entirely new level of flexibility and reuse not previously attainable in Java alone.

The Basic Structure of a Bean

So far, you've learned a fair amount about JavaBeans as a technology and what problems it tries to solve. However, you haven't really learned any details about JavaBeans components themselves. The time has come to get down to business and find out some specifics about what a JavaBeans component is made of. First, let me clarify some terminology that is sometimes used for JavaBeans: A JavaBeans component can also be referred to as a *bean* or a *JavaBean*. Therefore, from here·on, note that *bean*, *JavaBeans component*, and *JavaBean* all refer to the same thing. (Hey, variety keeps things interesting!) Also keep in mind that *JavaBeans* usually refers to the component technology itself, as opposed to multiple components.

Okay, so JavaBeans as a technology answers a lot of hopes and expectations as a component software solution, but what makes up a bean? A bean, like an object in any object-oriented environment, is comprised of two primary things: data and methods that act on the data. The data part of a bean completely describes the state of the bean; the methods provide a way for the bean's state to be modified and for actions to be taken accordingly. Figure 38.1 shows the two fundamental parts of a bean.

FIGURE 38.1.

The fundamental parts of a JavaBeans component.

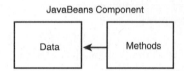

Just as a normal Java class can, a bean can have methods with different types of access. For example, `private` methods are accessible only within the internals of a bean, but `protected` methods are accessible both internally and in derived beans. The methods with the most accessibility are `public` methods, which are accessible internally, from derived beans, and from outside parties such as applications and other components. *Accessible* means that an application can call any of a component's public methods. Public methods have a unique importance to beans because they form the primary way a bean communicates with the outside world.

> **NOTE**
>
> A bean also communicates with the outside world through events, which are generated when the internal state of the bean changes. Events are handled and responded to by interested outside parties (event listeners) such as applications.

A bean's public methods are often grouped according to function. Functionally similar groups of public methods are also known as *interfaces*. A bean exposes its functionality to the outside world through these interfaces. Interfaces are important because they specify the protocol by which a particular bean is interacted with externally. A programmer only has to know a bean's interfaces to be able to successfully manipulate and interact with the bean. Figure 38.2 shows how interfaces expose a bean's functionality to the outside world.

FIGURE 38.2.

The relationship between interfaces and methods in a JavaBeans component.

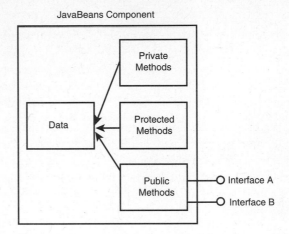

Although beans are expected to provide support for facilities such as persistence and application builder tool integration, all beans ultimately boil down to data and methods. These facilities are supported in the form of additional methods, data, and interfaces, which are themselves groups of methods. Therefore, no matter how complex a bean looks on the outside, just keep in mind that it is ultimately a combination of data and methods deep down. How simple!

Usage Scenarios

The last area to cover in your introductory tour of JavaBeans is how beans are used in practical scenarios. Because of their adherence to JavaSoft's goal of *reuse everywhere*, beans can be used in several ways. By going through a few bean-use scenarios, you'll get a better idea of how they fit into the software development process in general. Here are the two development-use scenarios for beans that are described in the following sections:

- Using an application builder tool to build an applet
- Hand-coding an applet

Using Beans with an Application Builder Tool

JavaBeans components can be used with a visual application builder tool to construct an application. Developers must purchase the builder tool along with whatever beans they want to use. Of course, you can also develop your own beans or download freeware beans developed by others. You learn how to develop your own beans in Chapter 40, "Creating Your Own Beans."

The next step is for the developer to lay out the application visually, using the builder tool and the beans. When the visual aspects of the application are finished and the appropriate beans are placed correctly, the developer moves on to customizing the beans. The developer edits the properties of the beans using visual property editors supplied by the beans themselves, which are invoked by the builder tool. At this point, the developer also connects the beans to each other and to the application by wiring events to appropriate handler routines. Again, this process is primarily performed in a visual fashion by virtue of the builder tool. I say "primarily" because it is usually necessary to write *some* code in the event-handling routines. When this step is completed, the developer tests everything and irons out the kinks. When he or she is happy with the outcome, the developer simply packages up the application along with the beans and distributes them together as one physical unit.

> **NOTE**
>
> Understand that I use the term *application* in a general sense throughout this discussion. In Java programming, an application is a standalone Java program, as opposed to an applet, which is a Java program that runs within the confines of a Web browser. In this discussion, the term *application* has a more general meaning and refers to both types of programs.

To summarize, the basic steps required to build an application with JavaBeans components using an application builder tool are as follows:

1. Visually lay out the application, using beans where appropriate.
2. Customize the beans using visual property editors.
3. Connect the beans using the builder tool's facilities, and write event-handler code.
4. Package the application with the beans and share it with the world.

As you can see, the entire development process described requires very little programming. Using beans in this way is very convenient because it alleviates many of the drudgeries of programming by putting a visual spin on the challenge of application development. Even though many of these conveniences are provided by the builder tool itself, they wouldn't be possible without the internal support provided by the beans. For example, the builder tool must be able to determine what features a bean provides, which is carried out by the introspection facilities of the JavaBeans component model. Also, the beans are responsible for providing a visual property editor to enable themselves to be edited and customized.

Using Beans in Handwritten Code

Using beans in code you write yourself isn't quite as rosy a scenario as connecting beans with a builder tool, but you can accomplish just as much. In this handwritten scenario, there is no fancy application builder tool and nothing is done visually. Instead, all the code for the application is written by hand, including the integration of the beans. This approach corresponds to a developer using the standard Java Development Kit provided by JavaSoft, which includes a command-line compiler and debugger. Although these tools aren't fancy, they *are* free. Even though the tools themselves are free, however, developers are still responsible for coming up with beans to use in building the application; developers are free to buy, borrow, or develop their own beans, just as in the first scenario.

The developer begins laying out the application by writing code to create and position the beans appropriately. With the beans created and positioned, the developer then moves on to customizing the beans by writing code that calls various methods that modify the properties of the beans. Calling these methods has the same effect as visually editing a bean with a property editor; you be the judge of which approach sounds easier for the developer.

When the beans are customized, the developer connects the beans to the application using event handlers. To accomplish this, the developer must write code to register each event listener with the appropriate component so that event notifications can be routed. The developer then must write code for the event handlers themselves. To be fair, the visual approach usually requires the event handlers to be written as well, but the event listener registration is typically handled automatically. When the beans are connected and everything is tested, the developer can package up the beans with the application and distribute the results.

To summarize, the basic steps required to build an application by hand with JavaBeans components are as follows:

1. Lay out the application by writing code to create and position the beans where appropriate.
2. Customize the beans by writing code that calls property-modifying methods on the beans.
3. Connect the beans by writing code that registers event listeners and handles bean events.
4. Package the application with the beans and distribute them.

This development scenario differs from the first scenario primarily in that everything is done by writing code. Although nothing is wrong with this approach, replacing handwritten code with more visual techniques generally results in a more rapid and intuitive development process. Even so, some developers are more comfortable getting dirty in the details of handwritten code, which is perfectly fine. The beauty of JavaBeans is that it fully enables and even encourages the existence of both scenarios. With JavaBeans, there's something for everyone!

Summary

This chapter introduced you to JavaBeans, JavaSoft's software component technology built on the rapid success and many benefits of Java. You began the chapter by learning about the fundamental criteria JavaBeans had to meet as specified in JavaSoft's concise mission statement: "Write once, run anywhere, reuse everywhere." This statement succinctly presents the ideal aspirations of any component model. The fact that JavaSoft chose this statement is testament to its desire to deliver a complete software component solution. This chapter examined each part of this statement and how it applies to JavaBeans.

You then moved on to the specific design goals for JavaBeans, which provide perhaps the best summary of the technology as a whole. Each of these design goals led directly to the development of a major part of the JavaBeans API, which you learn about in Chapter 39, "The JavaBeans API." By understanding the goals under which JavaBeans was developed, you are well on your way to understanding the technology as it exists in its final form.

In this chapter, you also learned how JavaBeans relates to Java, which is an interesting topic because of the way the JavaBeans technology is built on top of Java. From there, you moved on to the basic structure of a JavaBeans component, which was probably familiar to you from the structure of Java classes. You learned that JavaBeans components are internally composed of data and methods—which is to be expected because JavaBeans is fundamentally an object-oriented technology. You finished up the chapter by learning about a couple of development scenarios involving JavaBeans components, which gave you some insight into the options developers have in how they use JavaBeans.

38

JavaBeans Basics

The JavaBeans API

by Michael Morrison

IN THIS CHAPTER

With all the neat things JavaBeans accomplishes, you might imagine that there is some highly complex system pulling all kinds of magical tricks under the hood. The truth is, there is no magic behind JavaBeans and surprisingly little complexity considering how advanced it is as a software component technology. The lack of complexity in JavaBeans is because of the well-designed JavaBeans API, which is completely responsible for carrying out all the interesting ideas you learned about in the previous chapter.

In this chapter, you take a quick tour through the JavaBeans API to familiarize yourself with all emergency locations <grin>. Actually, the tour is meant to help you get the big picture of how the API is divided and what type of functionality each part of it addresses. Although there are a decent number of classes and interfaces defined in the API, you don't have to worry about them just yet. Being faced with a large amount of new information to process and digest is always somewhat overwhelming, so this chapter hits just the high points. This way, you'll have some perspective when you dig into more details in the next couple of chapters.

In this chapter, keep in mind that JavaBeans is ultimately a programming interface, which means that all its features are implemented in the `java.beans` package. The `java.beans` package is also referred to as the JavaBeans API and is provided as part of the standard Java 1.1 class library. The JavaBeans API itself is merely a suite of smaller APIs devoted to specific functions, or services. Following is a list of the main component services in the JavaBeans API that are necessary to facilitate all the features that make JavaBeans such an exciting technology:

- Property management
- Introspection
- Event handling
- Persistence
- Application builder support

By understanding these services and how they work, you'll have much more insight into exactly what type of technology JavaBeans is. This entire chapter is devoted to helping you understand the basics of these APIs and why they are necessary elements of the JavaBeans architecture.

Property Management

The property management facilities in the JavaBeans API are responsible for handling all interactions relating to bean properties. Properties reflect the internal state of a bean and constitute the data part of a bean's structure (remember that beans have two basic parts: a data part and a method part). More specifically, properties are discrete, named attributes of a bean that determine its appearance and behavior. Properties are important in any component technology because they isolate component state information into discrete pieces that can be easily modified.

To help you get a better idea of the importance of properties, consider some different scenarios that deal with properties. Following are some examples of how bean properties are accessed and used:

- As object fields in scripting environments such as JavaScript or VBScript
- Programmatically, using public accessor methods
- Visually, using property sheets in application builder tools
- Through the persistent storage and retrieval of a bean

As this list shows, properties come into play in a variety of ways when it comes to bean access and manipulation. Notice the flexibility properties provide: You can access them through scripting languages such as JavaScript, through full-blown programming languages such as Java, and through visual builder tools. This freedom to access and manipulate beans in a variety of ways is one of the critical design goals of the JavaBeans technology. And it is fulfilled by the property management facilities in the JavaBeans API. The next few sections discuss some of the major issues addressed by the JavaBeans API property management facilities.

Accessor Methods

The primary way properties are exposed in the JavaBeans API is through accessor methods. An *accessor method* is a public method defined in a bean that directly reads or writes the value of a particular property. Each property in a bean must have a corresponding pair of accessor methods: one for reading the property and one for writing. The accessor methods responsible for reading are known as *getter methods* because they get the value of a property. Likewise, accessor methods responsible for writing are known as *setter methods* because they set the value of a property.

Indexed Properties

So far, the discussion of properties has been limited to single-value properties, which are the most common properties used in JavaBeans. However, the JavaBeans API also supports *indexed properties*, which are properties that represent an array of values. Indexed properties work in a way very similar to arrays in traditional Java programming: You access a particular value using an integer index. Indexed properties are very useful in situations in which a bean must maintain a group of properties of the same type. For example, a container bean that keeps track of the physical layout of other beans might store references to them in an indexed property.

Bound and Constrained Properties

The JavaBeans API supports two mechanisms for working with properties at a more advanced level: bound and constrained properties. *Bound properties* are properties that provide notifications to an interested party based on changes in the property value. An interested party is an applet, application, or bean that wants to know about changes in the property. These properties are called bound properties because they are bound to some type of external behavior based on their own changes. Bound properties are defined at the component level, which means that a bean is responsible for specifying which components are bound. An example of a bound property is a visibility property; a bean's container might be interested in knowing the status of this property because the container has to graphically reorganize other beans based on a bean's visibility.

The other interesting property feature provided by the JavaBeans API is support for *constrained properties*, which are properties that enable an interested party to perform a validation on a new property value before accepting the modification. Constrained properties are useful in providing interested parties with control over how a bean is altered. An example of a constrained property is a date property for which the application containing the bean wants to limit the valid date property values to a certain range.

Introspection

The introspection facilities in the JavaBeans API define the mechanism by which components make their internal structure readily available to the outside world. These facilities consist of the functional overhead necessary to enable development tools to query a bean for its internal structure, including the interfaces, methods, and member variables that comprise the bean. Although the introspection services are primarily designed for use by application builder tools, they are grouped separately from the application builder services in the API because their role in making a bean's internal structure available externally is technically independent of builder tools. In other words, you may have other reasons for querying a bean about its internal structure beyond the obvious reasons used in builder tools.

The introspection services provided by the JavaBeans API are divided into two parts: low-level services and high-level services. These two types of services are distinguished by the level of access they provide to bean internals. The low-level API services are responsible for enabling wide access to the structural internals of a bean. These services are very important for application builder tools that heavily use bean internals to provide advanced development features. However, this level of access isn't appropriate for developers who are using beans to build applications because it exposes private parts of a bean that aren't meant to be used by developers at the application level. For these purposes, the high-level API services are more appropriate.

The high-level services use the low-level services behind the scenes to provide access to limited portions of a bean's internals (typically, the bean's public properties and methods). The difference between the two levels of services is that the high-level services don't enable access to internal aspects of a bean that aren't specifically designed for external use. The end result is two distinct services that offer bean introspection capabilities based on the level of access required by the interested party, be it an application builder tool or a user. The next few sections cover several of the major functions supported in the JavaBeans API introspection facilities.

Reflection and Design Patterns

The JavaBeans API has a very interesting technique for assessing the public properties, methods, and events for a bean. To determine information about a bean's public features, the bean's methods are analyzed using a set of low-level reflection services. These services gather information about a bean and determine its public properties, methods, and events by applying simple design patterns. You learned about the standard Java 1.1 reflection services in Chapter 18, "The Reflection Package." *Design patterns* are rules applied to a bean's method definitions that determine information about the bean. For example, when a pair of accessor methods are encountered in the analysis of a bean, the JavaBeans introspection facilities match them based on a design pattern and automatically determine the property they access.

The whole premise of design patterns is that method names and signatures conform to a standard convention. There are a variety of different design patterns for determining everything from simple properties to event sources. All these design patterns rely on some type of consistent naming convention for methods and their arguments. This approach to introspection is not only convenient from the perspective of JavaBeans, it also has the intended side effect of encouraging bean developers to use a consistent set of naming conventions.

Explicit Bean Information

Even though the design-pattern approach to introspection is very useful and encourages a consistent approach to naming, you may be wondering what happens if bean developers don't follow the convention. Fortunately, design patterns aren't the only option for introspection, meaning that obstinate developers are free to ignore the suggested naming conventions if they so choose. The developers who opt to cast convention to the wind must use another introspection facility in the JavaBeans API: They must explicitly list the public information about their beans. They must "spill the beans," to inject a painfully bad pun.

The explicit introspection facility in the JavaBeans API to which I'm referring involves creating a bean information class that specifies various pieces of information about a bean, including a property list, method list, and event list. This approach isn't automatic like the design-pattern approach, but it does provide a way to explicitly describe your bean to the world, which might be advantageous in some situations.

The Introspector

Just in case you're wondering how two different introspection approaches can possibly coexist to describe a single bean, you should know about another service that consolidates the whole introspection process. The introspection facilities provide an *introspector* used to obtain explicit bean information for a bean. The introspector is responsible for traversing the inheritance tree of a bean to determine the explicit bean information for all parent beans. If, at any point, explicit information is not defined, the introspector falls back on the reflection services and uses design patterns to automatically determine external bean information.

This two-tiered solution to assessing bean functionality is very nice because it first attempts to use information explicitly provided by a bean's developer and relies on automatic design patterns only if the explicit information isn't there. The other nice thing is that it supports a mixture of the two approaches, which means that methods for a bean can be explicitly defined in a provided bean information class, but the properties and events can be determined automatically using design patterns. This gives bean developers a lot of flexibility in deciding how they want their beans exposed.

Event Handling

The event-handling facilities in the JavaBeans API specify an event-driven architecture that defines interactions among beans and applications. If you're familiar with the Java AWT, you know that it provides a comprehensive event-handling model. This existing AWT event model forms the basis of the event-handling facilities in the JavaBeans API. These event-handling facilities are critical in that they determine how beans respond to changes in their state, as well as how these changes are propagated to applications and other beans.

The event-handling facilities hinge on the concepts of event sources and listeners. A bean capable of generating events is considered an event *source*; an application or bean capable of responding to an event is considered an event *listener*. Event sources and listeners are connected by an event registration mechanism that is part of the event-handling facilities. This registration mechanism basically boils down to an event listener being registered with an event source through a simple method call. When the source generates an event, a specified method is called on the event listener with an event state object being sent along as its argument. Event state objects are responsible for storing information associated with a particular event. In other words, event state objects carry with them any information related to the event being sent. The next few sections cover some of the major issues dealt with by the JavaBeans API event-handling facilities.

Unicast and Multicast Event Sources

Although most practical event sources support multiple listeners, the event-handling facilities provide for event sources that choose to limit their audience to a single listener. These sources are called *unicast event sources*; their more liberal counterparts are called *multicast event sources*. The primary functional difference between the two is that unicast event sources throw an exception if an attempt is made to register more than one listener.

Even though the JavaBeans API supports both unicast and multicast event sources, keep in mind that multicast event sources are much less limiting in terms of practical use. In other words, developers should avoid designing beans as unicast event sources whenever possible.

Event Adapters

Even though many bean events follow the standard source/listener model about which you just learned, the JavaBeans API provides a mechanism for dealing with more complex situations for which this model doesn't quite fit the bill. This mechanism is based on event *adapters,* which act as intermediaries between event sources and listeners. Event adapters sit between sources and listeners and provide a way of inserting specialized event-delivery behavior into the standard source/listener event model. Event adapters are important to the event-handling facilities because they open the door for the implementation of a highly specialized event-handling mechanism tailored to the unique challenges sometimes encountered in applications or application builder tools.

Persistence

The persistence facilities in the JavaBeans API specify the mechanism by which beans are stored and retrieved within the context of a container. The information stored through persistence consists of all the parts of a bean necessary to restore the bean to a similar internal state and appearance. This generally involves the storage of all public properties and, potentially, some internal properties, although the specifics are determined by each particular bean. Information not stored for a bean through persistence are references to external beans, including event registrations. These references are expected to be stored somehow by an application builder tool or through some programmatic means.

By default, beans are persistently stored and retrieved using the automatic serialization mechanism provided by Java, which is sufficient for most beans. However, bean developers are also free to create more elaborate persistence solutions based on the specific needs of their beans. Like the introspection facilities, the JavaBeans persistence facilities provide for both an explicit approach and an automatic approach to carrying out its functions.

Application Builder Support

The final area of the JavaBeans API deals with application builder support. The application builder support facilities provide the overhead necessary to edit and manipulate beans using visual application builder tools. Application builder tools rely heavily on these facilities to enable a developer to visually lay out and edit beans while constructing an application. These facilities fulfill a major design goal of the JavaBeans API: They enable beans to be used constructively with little or no programming effort.

One issue with which the JavaBeans architects wrestled is that application builder support for a specific bean is required only at design time. Consequently, it is somewhat wasteful to bundle this support code into a runtime bean. Because of this situation, the application builder facilities require that builder-specific overhead for a bean must be physically separate from the bean itself. This separation enables beans to be distributed by themselves for runtime use or in conjunction with the application builder support for design-time use. The next two sections cover some of the major issues dealt with by the JavaBeans API application builder support facilities.

Property Editors and Sheets

One of the ways in which the JavaBeans API supports the editing and manipulation of beans with application builder tools is through property sheets. A *property sheet* is a visual interface that provides editors for each public property defined for a bean. The individual editors used in a property sheet are called *property editors*. Each type of exported property in a bean must have a corresponding property editor if it is to be edited visually by a builder tool. Some standard property editors are provided by the JavaBeans API for built-in Java types, but user-defined properties require their own custom editors. The property editors for all the exported properties of a bean are presented together on a property sheet that enables users to edit the properties visually.

Customizers

The other way in which the JavaBeans API enables beans to be visually edited in an application builder tool is through *customizers*. Customizers are user interfaces that provide a specialized way of visually editing bean properties. Because customizers are implemented entirely by bean developers, there are no firm guidelines about how they present visual property information to the user. However, most customizers probably will be similar in function to "wizards," those popular user interfaces on the Windows platform that use multiple-step questionnaires to gather information from the user.

Summary

This chapter took you inside the JavaBeans technology by exploring the JavaBeans API. This API is ultimately responsible for delivering all the functionality of JavaBeans. You learned that the API has several major functional areas, each of which is devoted to a particular JavaBeans service. You covered the basics of each of these areas and looked at the kinds of problems they address and the different solutions they provide.

Although the discussions throughout this chapter were fairly general and avoided much technical detail, they still painted a pretty complete picture of the JavaBeans API—at least from a conceptual level. Armed with this knowledge, you're ready to press on and learn how to use the JavaBeans API in the next chapter, "Creating Your Own Beans." Roll up your sleeves and get ready for more thrills!

Creating Your Own Beans

by Michael Morrison

IN THIS CHAPTER

CHAPTER 40

In this chapter, you learn some practical aspects of JavaBeans programming that take you a step closer to being able to develop your own beans. Even though you don't actually create any beans in this chapter, you learn all about the tools and techniques necessary to do so. By the end of this chapter, you will have all the information you need to begin constructing and using your own beans.

This chapter recaps the major parts of a bean and what types of decisions you have to make in terms of these parts when you are developing a new bean. With these design concepts out of the way, you move on and learn how to install and configure the JavaBeans Development Kit (BDK). You then move on to possibly the most interesting topic of the chapter: the BeanBox. The BeanBox is a test container in which you can try out beans while you are developing them. You can use the BeanBox to easily test out all aspects of your beans, including visual property editing, event wiring, and bound property management. The chapter finishes with a look at Java Archive (JAR) files and how you use them to compress and group beans together for distribution.

Designing a Bean

Although beans typically are small development projects in terms of the amount of code involved, the fact that they are reusable makes their initial design critical. It's important for you to fully evaluate the functional requirements of a bean before you jump into writing code. Of course, this wisdom is good to apply to any programming situation, but it is especially important in JavaBeans because of the nature of bean components and how they are used. For example, the very fact that a bean must be backward compatible as it evolves is reason enough to make sure that the interfaces you define are extensible enough to provide room for future functionality.

The planning process you go through when you initially design a bean pays off in many ways when you start developing the bean as well as when you maintain the bean in the future. Too many programmers fall victim to the urge to get an object working in a hurry without thinking of the larger picture in which it will be used. Even though this narrow-minded approach can work in some limited environments with a certain degree of success, it must be strictly avoided when it comes to JavaBeans. Trying to hack together a bean in a hurry when the overall aim is to make beans widely reusable in a variety of different ways simply isn't smart.

Stepping down from my soap box, let me now soften the tone and add that the initial design phase for a typical bean isn't very involved. Beans usually are such small pieces of software that they just don't warrant a large or complex design. Furthermore, because beans are geared toward being simple and minimal at the very core, it only makes sense that bean developers should carry on with this tradition in the design of beans at a higher level. All I'm really suggesting is that you spend a little time pondering exactly what your bean is going to accomplish, how it will be practically used, and in what ways it might evolve in the future. Just so you get the idea, let me divide these ideas into three questions you can ask yourself while you are designing a bean:

1. What does the bean do?
2. How is the bean used?
3. How might the bean change in the future?

The first question is probably the easiest to answer because it is probably the question that drove you to design a bean in the first place. Even so, it's important to clearly identify what the bean is going to accomplish as a piece of reusable software. The second question is also fairly straightforward because you probably already have an application in mind that can use your bean. You may even be developing a bean as a specific part of an application, in which case you decided to make it a bean so that you would have the option of reusing it in other projects. Regardless of the motives that drove you to develop your bean, make sure that you have a good idea of how the bean is going to be used by an end user, whether that user is yourself or thousands of developers who are going to buy your bean for use in their own projects.

The third and final question is the one you probably haven't given much thought to because most people tend to think in terms of the present and the problems to be addressed immediately. However, a little insight on the front end of a bean development effort can make things infinitely easier for you later when, inevitably, you want to add a new feature or alter an old one. Try to assess any potential features or changes you see as being possible in the future, along with how they impact the bean in its current state. You might see that a small concession in an initial design can leave the door open for future enhancements. On the other hand, you may decide that your bean is fine for your purposes and that it will never have to evolve. That's a perfectly acceptable attitude to have—as long as you understand that it limits your options in the future. How far you want to go in assessing the future direction of a bean is ultimately up to you. All I can do is encourage you to at least entertain the thought of making a bean more open for future modification.

> **NOTE**
>
> Personally, I know I'm sometimes fickle enough to feel better with a design that is very extensible. I like the idea of knowing that decisions I make today are open for change in the future just in case I manage to figure out a better way of doing things. This attitude is actually useful far beyond the realm of programming and JavaBeans, but that's another book!

Now that I've grilled you about approaching bean development with at least some amount of planning, it's time to move on to some specifics. The design of a bean ultimately should culminate in a detailed description of the various parts of the bean. The following sections are devoted to the design issues surrounding the three primary parts of a bean:

■ Properties
■ Methods
■ Events

> **NOTE**
>
> Technically, events are implemented in beans through methods because methods are responsible for registering event listeners and responding to event notifications. So, it's a little misleading to mention events as if they are a part of a bean completely separate from methods. However, the conceptual role events play is very different than the role methods play, so it's worthwhile to consider events separately from a purely conceptual point of view. Just keep in mind that events rely on methods to function properly.

Laying Out the Properties

The heart of a bean is its internal state. Similar to normal Java classes, the internal state of a bean is reflected by the bean's member variables. *Properties* are public member variables that are accessible externally. Even though all member variables are important to a bean's functionality, properties take on a more critical importance because they enable you to query a bean for information or to modify a bean's state from outside the bean. Of course, you can never directly read or write properties externally; you must always do so through accessor methods.

Even if you aren't sure about all the data your bean needs to function properly, you should make a solid attempt to define all the bean's properties during the initial design. Trust me, this isn't asking too much. Properties are usually fairly easy to determine because they often directly relate to a piece of functionality. For example, it's pretty obvious that a button bean requires a property representing the label drawn on the button. In addition, you can define properties for the background and foreground colors of the button.

When you lay out the properties for your bean, be sure to decide whether the property is read-only, write-only, or read/write, because it will impact the accessor methods you have to implement later. Again, this should be a very simple and straightforward task because you've no doubt already thought about the characteristics of the bean that map to properties. At this point, you should also decide whether any of the properties are bound or constrained, because these decisions also impact methods you must implement later.

Although defining properties is an important step in the design of a bean, it is by no means something you can't go back and change later. It may happen that you later think of additional properties for the bean based on some new functionality you want to add. By all means, feel free to add or modify the properties of your bean while you are coding. I just want to encourage you to think about a core set of properties to begin with, because those properties will become the first member variables you define when you begin to code.

Defining Public Methods

After you've determined a set of suitable bean properties, you are ready decide on some methods that interact with them. At this point, you should focus on the public methods that are going to be accessible outside the bean. If you happen to already have an idea about nonpublic methods, go ahead and make note of them; just don't feel that you have to worry about them just yet. The primary goal here is to define the public interface that will be used to access your bean. This public interface is determined by the public methods implemented by the bean.

The first place to start when you are defining public methods is with accessor methods, which enable you to read and write the values of properties. Because you've already defined the properties for the bean, defining accessor methods is a simple task of listing getter and setter methods for each property based on its read/write capabilities. Keep in mind that these methods form the only direct link between a user and your bean's properties.

After you establish your bean's accessor methods, you have to check whether any of the bean's properties are bound or constrained. If so, you must add methods for registering and removing appropriate bound and constrained listeners. This process is very straightforward because these methods come in pairs and conform to a strict design pattern.

After the property-related methods are squared away, you have to assess any other public methods required by your bean. These methods are entirely bean dependent, so deciding what other public methods are required of your bean is totally up to you. Typically, public nonaccessor methods are used to perform some type of more involved function, as opposed to the simple getting and setting of properties performed by accessor methods. For example, you may have a bean that performs some complex calculation that impacts a variety of properties. Because you obviously want this functionality available externally, you place it in a public method.

Keep in mind that the constructors for your bean should also be defined at this stage. You can provide as many or as few constructors as you want; just remember that it's nice to give users a variety of constructors that use default values for some properties and require less explicit information.

Communicating with Events

The last major design area you have to assess is events. In terms of bean design, there are two different ways events come into play. The first has to do with the events a bean is capable of firing. The functionality of a bean determines the types of events it is capable of firing. Your bean can fire standard events defined in the Java API, or you can choose to define your own custom events and go from there. In the latter case, remember that you have to implement a class for each type of custom event you are going to use. Regardless of whether you decide on standard events, custom events, or a mixture of the two, the next step is to define the registration methods for listeners of each type. These methods are very similar to the methods defined for bound and constrained property listeners because they conform to similar design patterns.

The second way in which events come into play when you are designing beans relates to events a bean handles for itself. For example, a button bean has to catch and respond to mouse clicks, focus changes, and some key presses. These are the types of things you should decide how to handle up front so that you'll have fewer surprises when you start coding. The events processed by a bean basically result in overriding methods that handle different groups of events. Because most beans are derived from an AWT class such as `Canvas`, these event-processor methods are simply overridden in your bean class. Even so, go ahead and try to determine which ones you plan to override and why.

Now What?

After you have carefully designed the three major parts of your bean, you are ready to start actually building the bean. Although the initial design work isn't always the most thrilling part of bean development, it pays huge dividends when you begin coding. For example, you should be able to put together a pretty solid skeletal bean based on the properties and methods you planned for in the design phase. In other words, by merely defining properties and creating empty methods for the methods you listed in the design of the bean, you have a pretty good start on your bean class.

With a skeletal bean class in hand, you are ready to push on to the meat of JavaBeans development. Unfortunately, you'll have to wait until the next chapter to get into the gory details. However, the rest of this chapter covers some critical tool-related issues that are necessities for practical bean development.

Installing the BDK

Turning a bean design into reality wouldn't be possible without the JavaBeans Development Kit (BDK), which is freely available from JavaSoft. You can download the latest version of the BDK from JavaSoft's Web site at `http://www.javasoft.com`. The BDK comes complete with all the classes and documentation necessary to create and test your own beans. Please note that the BDK requires the Java Development Kit (JDK) version 1.1 or later, which provides all the core Java functionality used by JavaBeans.

> **NOTE**
>
> The BDK and JDK are both included on the CD-ROM that accompanies this book. Even so, you may want to check JavaSoft's Web site to ensure that you have the very latest version. Development kits like these tend to evolve rapidly, so new versions are released periodically.

The custom bean which you learn about in the next chapter was developed using a beta version of the BDK, which has a few caveats about how it must be installed. Because of these subtle installation details, I felt compelled to at least describe how I installed the JDK and BDK so that they work together seamlessly for bean development. Again, you can download both of these development kits for free directly from JavaSoft's Web site.

First, it's important that you install the JDK *before* you install the BDK because the JDK has all the core support required by the BDK. Although you are free to install the JDK however you choose, I recommend creating a `jdk` directory just below your root directory. Copy the JDK installation executable to this directory and execute it to install the JDK. The JDK expands into a `java` directory beneath the `jdk` directory you created.

After you install the JDK, you can install the BDK. Copy the BDK installation executable to the top-level `jdk` directory just as you did with the JDK executable, and then execute it to install the BDK. The BDK expands into a `beans` directory beneath the `jdk` directory.

> **NOTE**
>
> When you finish installing the JDK and BDK, be sure to delete the setup files used for the installation of each. These files are not cleaned up automatically and must be manually deleted.

After you install the JDK and BDK, you should have a directory structure like the one shown in Figure 40.1.

FIGURE 40.1.

The directory structure for the JDK and BDK installations.

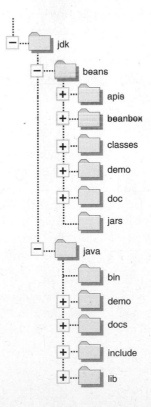

This directory structure is by no means a strict requirement for JavaBeans development, but it is consistent and has worked well for me. The consistency comes from the fact that the JDK and BDK are separate development kits for Java, which implies that they should reside at a similar level hierarchically. By creating a common jdk directory and installing different development kits below this directory, you have a very clear picture of how the development kits relate to each other.

Testing Beans with the BeanBox Test Container

As you learned in the previous chapter, one of the key benefits of JavaBeans is the capability for beans to be used in visual application builder tools. You've learned a great deal about the inner workings of JavaBeans that make this type of functionality possible, and now it's time to see it all in action and learn how to work with JavaBeans in a visual environment. The BDK ships with a test container called the BeanBox that enables you to lay out, edit, and interconnect beans visually. The BeanBox isn't intended to be a fully functional development tool for creating applications with beans; instead, it provides a simple example of how beans can be manipulated visually. Even so, the BeanBox is an indispensable tool for bean development because it provides a simple test bed for trying out beans.

The BeanBox is a standalone application executed using the JDK interpreter. Rather than running it directly using the interpreter, however, the BeanBox comes with a batch file, run.bat, which is in the BDK's beanbox directory and is responsible for setting the CLASSPATH environment variable before executing. You should use this batch file to run the BeanBox because it sets CLASSPATH to values specific to using the BeanBox. Following are the contents of the run.bat batch file used to execute the BeanBox:

```
set CLASSPATH=classes;unjar
java sun.beanbox.BeanBoxFrame
```

As you can see, the batch file first sets CLASSPATH to a few different paths; then it executes the BeanBox within the JDK interpreter. Don't worry too much about the CLASSPATH settings, because they are based on the internal workings of the BeanBox. To run the BeanBox, just execute the run batch file. When you run the batch file, the BeanBox executes and displays three different windows. Each of these windows performs a different function within the scope of the BeanBox. The first window is the ToolBox, which lists all the beans registered for use with the BeanBox. Figure 40.2 shows the BeanBox's ToolBox window.

As you can see, the ToolBox lists a variety of available beans. These beans are all demo beans provided with the BDK to demonstrate the development and use of beans. Notice that some of the beans have graphical icons associated with them. These beans use a bean information class to specify the icon to be displayed in visual development environments. Other beans are listed in the ToolBox by name only.

FIGURE 40.2.

The BeanBox's ToolBox window.

The second window associated with the BeanBox is the main container window, shown in Figure 40.3.

FIGURE 40.3.

The BeanBox's main container window.

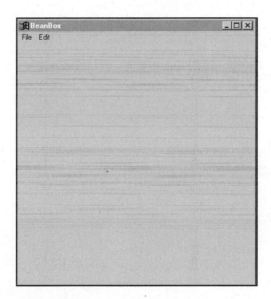

The main container window is the central BeanBox window because it is where you actually lay out beans. The main container window is very similar in function to form windows in other types of visual development environments such as Visual Basic. This window has two menu items: File and Edit. You use these menus to load and save BeanBox files and connect beans together.

The last window in the BeanBox is the PropertySheet window, which lists the properties associated with the currently selected bean. Figure 40.4 shows the PropertySheet window.

40

FIGURE 40.4.

*The BeanBox's
PropertySheet window.*

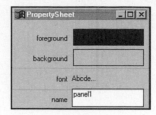

The PropertySheet window is responsible for providing the visual editing capabilities of the BeanBox because it displays a property editor for each property defined in a bean. When you first run the BeanBox, the PropertySheet window displays the properties for the BeanBox container itself. You can try to edit these properties by clicking one of them with the mouse. For example, try clicking the background property to change the background color for the container. Figure 40.5 shows the property editor dialog box displayed for changing the background color.

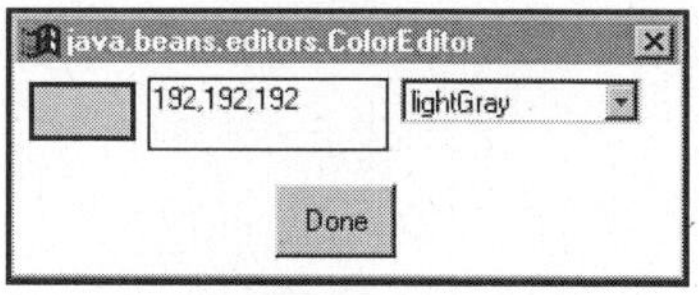

FIGURE 40.5.

*The property editor
dialog box for the
background color
property.*

This property editor dialog box enables you to easily change the background color for the container either by entering RGB (Red Green Blue) colors or by selecting a standard color from a drop-down list. Try selecting a different color and clicking Done to see how your choice affects the container.

> **NOTE**
>
> For beans that have an associated customizer, the Edit menu in the BeanBox includes a Customize command that runs the customizer on the bean.

Working with Beans in the BeanBox

Working with beans in the BeanBox is easy and demonstrates the real benefit of visual editing with beans. The first thing you do is select a bean from the ToolBox and add it to the main container window. You do this by clicking a bean's name or icon in the ToolBox window; this action turns the mouse pointer into a cross. Then click in the container window where you want to place the bean. A new bean appears in that location with a default size and set of properties.

Try laying out one of the demo beans that comes with the BDK. Click the OurButton bean in the ToolBox window, and then click somewhere in the container window to place the bean. After you do this, the container window should look similar to Figure 40.6.

FIGURE 40.6.

The main container window after adding the OurButton *bean to the BeanBox.*

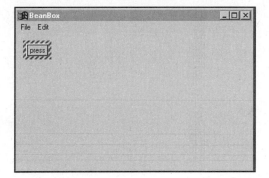

Notice that the new bean is drawn with a hashed boundary. This indicates that the bean is the currently selected bean, which means that the PropertySheet window reflects the properties for this bean. Beans are selected by default when you add them to the container window. To select a bean that isn't selected, just click outside the bean in the area where the hashed boundary is to appear. Some beans enable you to click anywhere on them to select them, but in the beta version of the BDK, this behavior is somewhat inconsistent. The version of the BeanBox in the final release of the BDK will no doubt be more robust.

In a moment, you'll use the OurButton bean you just laid out to control an animation bean, but first you have to change its label property. You do this using the PropertySheet window: Change the bean's label property to read Start Animation. Now add one more OurButton bean using the steps you just went through (click the bean in the ToolBox and position it in the container). Edit this button's label property and set the value to Stop Animation. After you've done this, the container window should look similar to Figure 40.7.

FIGURE 40.7.

The main container window after adding two OurButton *beans to the BeanBox.*

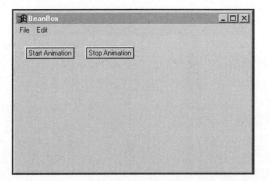

Now it's time to throw in a little excitement by adding a bean that displays an animation. Select the `Juggler` bean from the ToolBox and add it to the container just below the `OurButton` beans. After you've done this, the container window should look similar to Figure 40.8.

FIGURE 40.8.

The main container window after adding a `Juggler` *bean to the BeanBox.*

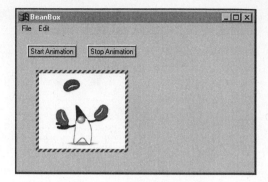

If your beans aren't lined up quite the way they are shown in the figure, feel free to move them around. You can do this by selecting one of the beans, clicking the hashed border and holding down the mouse button while you drag the mouse. With these actions, you can move the bean around in the container. You can also resize beans that support resizing by clicking one of the corners on the hashed border and dragging the mouse. There is no need to resize any of the beans in this example because they automatically size themselves to fit their content.

Wiring Beans Together with Events

A particularly useful function of the BeanBox is that you can wire beans together using events. For example, you can easily connect a bean's event to a public method defined in another bean, which effectively ties the two beans together functionally. The BeanBox enables you to do this visually, which makes the task very simple. As you might guess, the two buttons you've laid out thus far are perfectly situated to control the `Juggler` animation bean. Let's wire them up to see what happens.

Select the `Start` button and click the Edit menu in the BeanBox. You'll see an Events menu item that has a group of event types beneath it. Select the `action event` menu item and then the `actionPerformed` command beneath it. You'll see a line originating from the button that moves as you move the mouse around. Move the mouse over the `Juggler` bean and click to connect the button bean's action event to the `Juggler` bean. You'll be presented with a dialog box that shows the available target methods defined in the `Juggler` bean (see Figure 40.9).

Select the `start()` method from the dialog box to specify it as the receiver of the event action. When you do this, the `start()` method is called on the `Juggler` bean any time the `Start` button is clicked. Repeat this procedure to connect the `Stop` button to the `stop()` method of the `Juggler` bean. After you do this, you can test the buttons by clicking them to start and stop the animated `Juggler` bean. It's as simple as that!

FIGURE 40.9.

The EventTargetDialog dialog box for the Juggler *bean.*

> **NOTE**
>
> It's worth noting that the beta 3 version of the BeanBox available as of this writing is a little tricky to use at times. The selection of beans tends to be inconsistent at times, occasionally resulting in the addition of a new bean when you really wanted to select an existing bean. I think it's safe to assume that the final version of the BeanBox will be much more robust.

Saving Your Work

You can easily save the contents of the BeanBox using the Save command from the File menu. When you save the contents of the BeanBox, the persistence features of JavaBeans are used to store away the state of each bean. You then can reload the beans later using the Load command; the persistence features are used to reconstruct the beans just as you left them.

Packaging Beans with JAR Files

After you have developed and tested your bean, you have to consider packaging it so that others can use it. Things aren't so simple as they were in the good old days of Java 1.0 where you could just provide executable class files and everyone would be happy. The standard method of distributing beans involves packaging them into compressed archives called JAR (Java Archive) files. JAR files are similar to other types of compressed files such as ZIP or TAR files, except that they are specifically tailored to packaging up Java classes and resources. For more information about JAR files, refer to Chapters 36, "JAR Basics," and 37, "Code Signing and JAR Security."

> **NOTE**
>
> JAR files use a compression scheme based on the one used in ZIP files. Check out Chapter 11, "The Utilities Package," for more information about the `java.util.zip` package in Java 1.1.

JAR files basically enable you to group the classes and resources for beans into one compressed unit to organize them and conserve space. Bean resources can include anything from images and sounds to custom resources such as data files. Being able to group resources with the classes for a bean cleans up the delivery of beans considerably because it eliminates the chore of keeping up with a bunch of different support files. Additionally, having a single file for beans being delivered over an Internet connection results in only one HTTP transaction, which is much faster than transferring multiple individual files.

Just in case you are thinking you don't have to worry about bundling your bean in a JAR file, understand that most visual development tools *expect* beans to be included in JAR files. The BeanBox is an example of such a tool because it looks specifically for JAR files when it assembles the beans in its ToolBox. You may be wondering how a tool such as the BeanBox knows which beans are included in a JAR file—because JAR files are ultimately just a bunch of classes and associated resources. The answer to this question is found in the *manifest files*, which are text files that describe the beans contained in a JAR file (along with encryption information if so desired). The encryption information is used for code-signing purposes, which is a topic beyond the scope of this chapter. You learn about bean security and code signing in Chapter 37, "Code Signing and JAR Security." You learn more about manifest files in Chapter 36, "JAR Basics," and in the following chapter when you create your first bean.

> **NOTE**
>
> JAR files can store multiple beans. Just as with individual beans, the manifest file is responsible for formally listing all the beans contained in a JAR file.

The JDK version 1.1 ships with a tool called `jar` that enables you to create and modify JAR files. The `jar` tool works in a way similar to PKZip or `tar` in that you can combine and compress multiple files into a single archive. The `jar` utility also enables you to sign individual files in a JAR file for security purposes. The syntax for jar follows:

`jar Options Files`

The `Files` argument specifies the files to be used when working with a JAR file and varies according to the options. The `Options` argument specifies options related to how the `jar` utility manipulates a JAR file. Following is a list of the `jar` utility options:

Option	Description
c	Specifies that a new archive is to be created.
m	Specifies that the manifest file for the archive is to be created based on an external manifest file. The external manifest file is provided as the second file in the list of files following the options.

Option	Description
t	Used to list the contents of an archive.
x *File*	Extracts all the files in an archive; extracts just the named files if additional filenames are provided.
f	Specifies the name of the archive in question, where the name is provided as the first file in the file list. The f option is used in conjunction with all the other options.
v	Causes the jar utility to provide verbose output, which results in greater information about the actions being performed on a JAR file.

CAUTION

Unlike most command-line utilities, the jar utility doesn't require the use of a slash (/) or hyphen (-) when specifying options.

So that you can see how the jar utility works in a practical scenario, here is a jar command that compresses and adds all the Java classes in the current directory into a JAR file called BigStuff:

```
jar cf BigStuff.jar *.class
```

In this example, the c and f options are used to specify that a new archive is to be created with the name BigStuff.jar. The files to be added to the archive are specified by the wildcard *.class. As you can see, there's nothing complicated about JAR files. Granted, it gets a little messier when you start dealing with code signing, but you don't have to worry with any of that at this point.

Summary

This chapter tackled some practical issues concerning bean development. You first learned about initial design issues relating to beans, including the importance of carefully defining the different parts of a bean before you write any code. You then moved on to the installation of the JavaBeans Development Kit (BDK), which has a few caveats to consider if things are to work smoothly. From there, you dove straight into visual bean manipulation with the BeanBox test container. The BeanBox is perhaps the most significant tool provided by the BDK because it enables you to test the capabilities of your beans in a minimal environment. Finally, you ended the chapter with a look at JAR (Java Archive) files, which enable you to compress the classes and resources for a bean into a single file for distribution.

40

CREATING YOUR OWN BEANS

This chapter covered a variety of different topics to prepare you for developing your own beans from scratch. You now are ready to get into the specifics of building your own beans and testing them. Sure, concepts and theories are great, but at some point you want to see something real. The next chapter takes you through the design and development of a complete bean, a process that puts your newfound knowledge to the test and lets you have some fun along the way.

A Fancy Button Bean

by Michael Morrison

IN THIS CHAPTER

In this chapter, you learn to develop a bean that is somewhat similar in function to the standard AWT button provided in Java 1.1, but a little fancier. You develop this bean entirely from scratch—while observing the design suggestions covered in the previous chapter. The bean you create in this chapter serves as a great starting point for developing other beans because it tackles many of the common issues related to building practical beans. By the end of the chapter, you will have both the know-how and the source code necessary to start building beans of your own.

Along with developing the code for a custom bean in this chapter, you learn how to test the bean in the BeanBox test container, which is a vital part of the development process. You'll find that the BeanBox is a fun way to try out your beans as you develop them. You finish the chapter with a brainstorming session for some ways in which you can improve and extend the bean on your own.

Designing the Fancy Button Bean

As you learned in the previous chapter, the first step in building any bean is to come up with a preliminary design. This design should be carried out to some degree of detail before embarking on the actual coding of the bean. The bean you develop in this chapter is a *fancy button bean*, meaning that it functions similarly to the standard Java AWT button but adds some functionality to make it a little fancier. So that you can see how the design for the fancy button bean comes together, it doesn't derive from the AWT Button class but instead implements all its own button functionality from scratch.

A few things about the fancy button bean set it apart from the standard AWT button. Like the AWT button, the fancy button bean enables you to set the label for the button to any text you choose. However, it also enables you to set the font for the label, which can be one of a variety of typefaces in virtually any size. The fancy button bean knows how to automatically resize itself to accommodate the varying size of the label based on the font selection. Another neat feature of the fancy button bean is that you can change the background and foreground colors. The background color corresponds to the face of the button, and the foreground color determines the color of the label text.

The fancy button bean also supports a feature in which it can be used to represent an on/off state, much like a checkbox. In this mode—which we'll call *sticky mode*—instead of automatically raising after you click it, the button remains down. Another mouse click restores it to its normal position. This feature is useful in toolbars, where some buttons reflect a two-state option. A good example is the bold button in some popular word processor toolbars, which remains down when clicked to indicate that the bold option is turned on.

Now that you have an idea of what the fancy button does, let's move on to designing some specifics about it. Recall from the previous chapter that the design of a bean can be divided into three major parts: properties, methods, and events. The following sections focus on the fancy button bean and the design of these major functional parts.

Properties

The properties for the fancy button bean must somehow represent the information required to support the functionality you just learned about. Fortunately, you don't have to specifically define all these properties yourself because you are going to derive the bean from an existing AWT class, which provides a great deal of overhead and some very useful properties. The AWT class I'm referring to is Canvas, which represents a rectangular area onto which you can draw or trap input events from the user. The Canvas class provides the base functionality typically required of graphical beans, including background color, foreground color, name, and font properties. Actually, most of this functionality is provided by the Component class, which is the parent of Canvas.

Even though the Canvas and Component parent classes help out, you still must provide some properties of your own. You know that the fancy button bean will have a label, so you can start off with a string label property. You also know that the bean must support a sticky mode, which can easily be represented by a boolean property. Because the bean supports a sticky mode, you also need a property to keep track of whether the bean is up or down. Another boolean property serves this purpose just fine. These three properties are pretty well sufficient for modeling the high-level functionality required of the bean. In fact, combined with the properties provided by the Canvas class, these properties form the full set of properties for the fancy button bean. Keep in mind, however, that although these are the only three properties you must define yourself, there may be other member variables in the fancy button bean that aren't exposed as properties. You learn about these member variables when you start writing the actual code in the "Developing the Fancy Button Bean" section of this chapter.

Following are the properties required of the fancy button bean:

- Label
- Sticky mode (on/off)
- Button state (up/down)

Methods

Now that you've defined the properties, it's time to move on to determine the public methods required of the fancy button bean. The easiest place to start is with the accessor methods for the bean. You already know the properties for the bean, so determining the accessor methods is pretty easy. Both the label and sticky mode properties for the bean are readable and writeable, so you need a pair of accessor methods for each of them. The property representing the bean's up/down state is a little different because the state is determined by the user clicking the button. In other words, this property shouldn't be directly writeable like the other two properties; instead, it should always be set indirectly by interacting with the button visually. So, for this property, you need only one accessor method: a getter method.

Recall that the fancy button bean is supposed to resize itself based on the typeface and size of the font for the label text. This is necessary because selecting a larger font requires more physical space on the bean's surface to display the label text. Knowing that the bean must resize itself whenever the font property's value changes, what do you think this means in terms of accessor methods? If you're thinking you must override the setter method for the font property, you are exactly right. It turns out that the setter method for the font property is defined in the Component class, along with the font property itself. By overriding it in the fancy button bean, you can easily resize the bean after setting the new font value.

Beyond accessor methods, you have to consider the other public methods the bean must provide. The fancy button bean needs only two other public methods. The first of these, paint(), is overridden from the parent Canvas class to enable the bean to paint itself. The paint() method is pretty much required of all graphical beans because it provides a central location for placing all of a bean's drawing code. The other public method required of the bean isn't quite as obvious: It is the getPreferredSize() method, which calculates and returns the preferred size of the bean based on its current state. This method is necessary only because the fancy button bean has a preferred size based on the label text and font.

Following are the public methods required of the fancy button bean:

- Label property getter/setter methods
- Sticky mode property getter/setter methods
- Button state property getter method
- Overridden font property setter method
- Overridden paint() method
- Overridden getPreferredSize() method

Events

The last part of the fancy button bean you must focus on at this stage is events. Because the bean is a button, it has to fire an action event when the user clicks it. This is what enables the bean to be wired to other beans or applications in order to trigger them with a button click. Because the event fired in this case is an action event, part of supporting it is providing event listener registration methods. A pair of these methods is all you need to support the addition and removal of action event listeners.

The actual firing of the action event is another issue altogether. The bean is required to support some type of mechanism by which an action event is passed on to all the listeners registered. This mechanism must be handled by a single event-processing method that iterates through the listeners and dispatches the event to each one appropriately.

The final area of interest relating to events is how the bean processes events for itself. It's one thing to be able to broadcast events to others, but the fancy button bean must also manage events that occur within itself. For example, when the user clicks the bean, the bean must change its appearance to show the button pressing down. The events the bean must respond to are focus changes, mouse clicks, mouse drags, and key presses. The focus-change events must be processed because the button draws a focus rectangle on its surface whenever it has focus. The mouse click-and-drag events must be processed so that the bean can change its state appropriately and act like a button. Finally, the key-press events must be processed to provide a keyboard interface for the bean (so that it can simulate a mouse click for keys like the Enter key). These events are processed in individual event-processor methods that are overridden from the bean's parent class.

Following are the event-related methods required of the fancy button bean:

- Action event listener registration methods
- Action event-processing method for firing events
- Focus event-processing method
- Mouse click event-processing method
- Mouse drag event-processing method
- Key press event-processing method

Developing the Fancy Button Bean

Now that you have a pretty solid design, you're ready to jump into the code for the fancy button bean. You will probably be pleasantly surprised by how little difference there is between the code for beans and the code for normal Java classes. Beans are, in fact, normal Java classes with support for a few extra facilities such as introspection and serialization. In many cases, these extra facilities are handled automatically, so the bean code really does look just like a normal Java class.

 In the following sections, you learn about different parts of the code for the fancy button bean. Because the discussion tackles small parts of the code, you may not immediately see how everything fits into the overall bean class structure purely from a code perspective. If you are having trouble with this approach, check out the complete source code for the bean, which is included on the accompanying CD-ROM. The main code for the fancy button bean is in the `FancyButton` class, which appears on the CD-ROM in the file `FancyButton.java`.

Properties and Member Variables

The first place to start in developing the fancy button bean is laying out the properties. Following are the member variable properties for the bean based on the initial design:

```
private String    label;
private boolean   sticky;
private boolean   down;
```

As you can see, these member variables directly correspond to the properties mentioned in the initial design. Notice that they are all built-in Java types, which means that property editors are already provided by JavaBeans for each of them: You don't have to do any extra work to provide visual editing support for the fancy button bean's properties. Along with these properties, the bean also requires a few other member variables for internal use:

```
private transient ActionListener  actionListener = null;
private transient boolean          hasFocus;
```

The actionListener member is an ActionListener interface used to manage the list of action event listeners. This list is used by the action event-processing method to fire events to each listener. You learn more about the actionListener member later in the chapter when you get into the specifics of how the fancy button bean processes events. The hasFocus member is used to keep track of the focus state of the bean. The focus is important to keep up with because it affects the visual appearance of the bean.

You may be a little curious about why both of these member variables are declared as transient. *Transient* member variables are those that aren't saved and restored through bean persistence. The actionListener and hasFocus member variables represent information specific to a particular session, meaning that it isn't necessary to save them persistently as part of the bean's state. That sums up all the member variables for the bean. Let's move on to the constructors!

Constructors

The fancy button bean provides two constructors: a default constructor and a detailed constructor that takes all three properties as arguments. Following is the code for both of these constructors:

```
public FancyButton() {
  this("Push Me", false, false);
}
public FancyButton(String l, boolean s, boolean d) {
  // Allow the superclass constructor to do its thing
  super();
  // Set properties
  label = l;
  sticky = s;
  down = d;
  setFont(new Font("Dialog", Font.PLAIN, 12));
  setBackground(Color.lightGray);
  // Enable event processing
  enableEvents(AWTEvent.FOCUS_EVENT_MASK | AWTEvent.MOUSE_EVENT_MASK |
    AWTEvent.MOUSE_MOTION_EVENT_MASK | AWTEvent.KEY_EVENT_MASK);
}
```

The first constructor simply calls the second constructor with default property values. The second constructor is responsible for actually doing all the work. The second constructor begins by calling the superclass constructor and then moves on to set all the properties. Notice that the two inherited properties, `font` and `background color`, are set by calling their setter methods instead of directly setting the member variables. We do this because properties are always declared as `private`, which means that you are required to use a setter method to access them. In this case, it works out well because the fancy button bean provides its own setter method for the `font` property.

With the properties set, the constructor moves on to enabling a group of events for the bean to process by calling the `enableEvents()` method. If it didn't call this method, the bean would be incapable of directly trapping any events. The purpose of selectively enabling certain events is to optimize the event-handling procedure by looking for only the events in which you are specifically interested. In this case, the fancy button bean is interested in focus, mouse, mouse move, and key events.

Accessor Methods

Moving right along, the next piece of the bean puzzle is the accessor methods, which provide access to bean properties. Following is the code for the label property's accessor methods:

```
public String getLabel() {
  return label;
}
public void setLabel(String l) {
  label = l;
  sizeToFit();
}
```

The `getLabel()` getter method is pretty self-explanatory in that it simply returns the value of the `label` member variable. The `setLabel()` setter method is slightly more involved in that it calls the `sizeToFit()` method after setting the `label` member variable. The `sizeToFit()` method, which you learn about in detail in the "Support Methods" section, later in this chapter, is responsible for determining the optimal button size based on the label and font.

The accessor methods for the sticky property, `isSticky()` and `setSticky()`, are very minimal in that they simply get and set the value for the `sticky` member variable, with no additional functionality. Likewise, the getter method for the button state, `isDown()`, simply returns the value of the `down` member variable. Things get a little more interesting when you get to the overridden setter method for the font property, `setFont()`, which follows:

```
public void setFont(Font f) {
  super.setFont(f);
  sizeToFit();
}
```

The whole point of overriding this method is to make sure that the bean is resized when any change occurs in the value of the font property. Notice that the superclass's `setFont()` method is called to perform the actual setting of the property before the bean is resized with a call to `sizeToFit()`.

Public Methods

There are two important public methods in the bean to look at now: `paint()` and `getPreferredSize()`. The `paint()` method is used to paint the visual appearance of the bean; its source code follows:

```java
public synchronized void paint(Graphics g) {
  int width = getSize().width;
  int height = getSize().height;
  // Paint the background with 3D effects
  g.setColor(getBackground());
  g.fillRect(1, 1, width - 2, height - 2);
  g.draw3DRect(0, 0, width - 1, height - 1, !down);
  g.setColor(Color.darkGray);
  if (down) {
    g.drawLine(1, height - 3, 1, 1);
    g.drawLine(1, 1, width - 3, 1);
  }
  else {
    g.drawLine(2, height - 2, width - 2, height - 2);
    g.drawLine(width - 2, height - 2, width - 2, 1);
  }
  // Paint the foreground text
  g.setColor(getForeground());
  g.setFont(getFont());
  FontMetrics fm = g.getFontMetrics();
  if (down)
    g.drawString(label, ((width - fm.stringWidth(label)) / 2) + 2,
      ((height + fm.getMaxAscent() - fm.getMaxDescent()) / 2) + 1);
  else
    g.drawString(label, (width - fm.stringWidth(label)) / 2,
      (height + fm.getMaxAscent() - fm.getMaxDescent()) / 2);
  // Paint the focus rect
  if (hasFocus) {
    g.setColor(Color.gray);
    g.drawRect(4, 4, width - 8, height - 8);
  }
}
```

The `paint()` method starts off by getting the width and height of the bean, filling the background, and painting a 3D effect around the edges. Notice that the 3D effect is painted differently depending on the value of the `down` member variable. The foreground label text is painted next by selecting the appropriate font and calculating the coordinates so that the text is centered within the bean. Finally, if the `hasFocus` member variable is set to `true`, a focus rectangle is drawn on the bean to indicate that it has the input focus.

The `getPreferredSize()` method is used to return the favored size of the bean to any interested party, including itself. When I say "favored size," I mean the ideal visual size of the bean so that the label text is positioned in the bean with a proper spacing from the edges. The calculation of this size takes into account the selected font and the label text. Following is the code for the `getPreferredSize()` method:

```java
public Dimension getPreferredSize() {
  // Calculate the preferred size based on the label text
```

```
FontMetrics fm = getFontMetrics(getFont());
return new Dimension(fm.stringWidth(label) + TEXT_XPAD,
  fm.getMaxAscent() + fm.getMaxDescent() + TEXT_YPAD);
}
```

Event-Registration Methods

The event-registration methods in the fancy button bean are used to enable the addition and removal of listeners for the bean's action events. The code for these methods follows:

```
public synchronized void addActionListener(ActionListener l) {
  actionListener = AWTEventMulticaster.add(actionListener, l);
}
public synchronized void removeActionListener(ActionListener l) {
  actionListener = AWTEventMulticaster.remove(actionListener, l);
}
```

These methods simply add and remove action listeners from the actionListener vector, which is the ActionListener interface used to keep up with what receives action events. The listeners themselves are managed by the underlying AWTEventMulticaster class, which is a helper class in the Java API designed to keep track of event listeners.

Event-Processing Methods

The fancy button bean provides a variety of event-processing methods, primarily because the bean must listen for a few different types of input events to function properly. The first of these methods, processActionEvent(), isn't related to processing an input event, however; instead, it is used to dispatch action events to all the registered action event listeners. Following is the code for this method:

```
protected void processActionEvent(ActionEvent e) {
  // Deliver the event to all registered action event listeners
  if (actionListener != null)
    actionListener.actionPerformed(e);
}
```

The processActionEvent() method is responsible for firing actionPerformed events to all registered event listeners. It does this by calling the actionPerformed() method on the actionListener member, which represents a chain of event listeners. The actionPerformed() method is the only method defined in the ActionListener interface and is typically called any time an action occurs in an event source such as a bean. In the case of the fancy button bean, an *action* is defined as a button push, but an action can mean other things in other beans.

The fancy button bean uses four other event-processing methods, although they act a little differently than processActionEvent(). Following is the code for the first of these methods, processFocusEvent():

```
protected void processFocusEvent(FocusEvent e) {
  // Get the new focus state and repaint
```

```
      switch(e.getID()) {
        case FocusEvent.FOCUS_GAINED:
          hasFocus = true;
          repaint();
          break;
        case FocusEvent.FOCUS_LOST:
          hasFocus = false;
          repaint();
          break;
      }
      // Let the superclass continue delivery
      super.processFocusEvent(e);
    }
```

This method is called whenever the focus for the bean changes. Its only function is to monitor changes in the bean's focus and to update the appearance of the bean accordingly. The processMouseEvent() method is a little more interesting in that it responds to mouse button presses and releases. Following is the code for this method:

```
protected void processMouseEvent(MouseEvent e) {
    // Track mouse presses/releases
    switch(e.getID()) {
      case MouseEvent.MOUSE_PRESSED:
        down = !down;
        repaint();
        break;
      case MouseEvent.MOUSE_RELEASED:
        if (down && !sticky) {
          fireActionEvent();
          down = false;
          repaint();
        }
        break;
    }
    // Let the superclass continue delivery
    super.processMouseEvent(e);
}
```

The processMouseEvent() method is responsible for trapping mouse button presses and releases and making sure that the bean behaves appropriately. When the mouse button is pressed, the down member variable is toggled and the bean is repainted. However, when the mouse button is released, the down and sticky member variables are first checked to determine the state of the button. If the bean isn't in sticky mode and is down, an action event is fired by the fireActionEvent() method, which you learn about in the "Support Methods" section. The down member variable is then set to false and the bean is repainted.

The processMouseMotionEvent() method is used to respond to events related to the movement of the mouse. Following is the code for this method:

```
protected void processMouseMotionEvent(MouseEvent e) {
    // Track mouse drags
    if (e.getID() == MouseEvent.MOUSE_DRAGGED && !sticky) {
      Point pt = e.getPoint();
      if ((pt.x < 0) || (pt.x > getSize().width) ||
          (pt.y < 0) || (pt.y > getSize().height)) {
```

```
      if (down) {
        down = false;
        repaint();
      }
    }
    else if (!down) {
      down = true;
      repaint();
    }
  }
  // Let the superclass continue delivery
  super.processMouseMotionEvent(e);
}
```

The processMouseMotionEvent() method is responsible for detecting mouse drags and making sure that the bean behaves properly. The only purpose of responding to mouse drags is so that the bean button raises up when the mouse is dragged off it (unless it's in sticky mode; in sticky mode, drags have no meaning because the bean changes state as soon as the mouse button is pressed). If the bean isn't in sticky mode, the coordinates of the mouse are checked by the processMouseMotionEvent() method to see whether they fall within the bean's bounding rectangle. If not, processMouseMotionEvent() restores the bean button to its raised position by setting the down member to **false**. If the mouse is within the bounding rectangle for the bean and the bean is raised, the down member is set to **true**.

The last of the event-processing methods is the processKeyEventMethod(), which is used to respond to key presses. Following is the code for this method:

```
protected void processKeyEvent(KeyEvent e) {
  // Simulate a mouse click for certain keys
  if (e.getKeyCode() == KeyEvent.VK_ENTER ||
      e.getKeyChar() == KeyEvent.VK_SPAOE) {
    if (sticky) {
      down = !down;
      repaint();
    }
    else {
      down = true;
      repaint();
      fireActionEvent();
      down = false;
      repaint();
    }
  }
  // Let the superclass continue delivery
  super.processKeyEvent(e);
}
```

The processKeyEventMethod() is used to provide a keyboard interface for the bean. If the bean has focus and the Enter key or spacebar is pressed, the action is treated just like clicking the mouse on the bean. The mouse click is simulated by setting the down member to **true**, firing an action event by calling fireActionEvent(), and then setting the down member to **false**. This is kind of a tricky way to get extra functionality without doing much work—something I'm always in favor of!

> **NOTE**
>
> You may be a little confused at this point about the processXXXEvent() methods; one of them is used to dispatch events and the others are used to respond to events. The reason for this apparent inconsistency is that the event-processor methods that respond to events are overridden versions of superclass methods. The original superclass versions are responsible for dispatching the events to listeners; your versions are free to just add response code.
>
> Notice that all four of these methods call their respective superclass versions, which is a sure sign that the superclass methods are doing some additional work. In the case of the processActionEvent() method, there is no superclass version, so it must take on the responsibility of dispatching events to registered listeners.

Support Methods

The fancy button bean uses two private support methods you haven't learned about yet: sizeToFit() and fireActionEvent(). These two methods provide functionality that the bean needs only internally, which is why they are declared as private. Nevertheless, they play a vital role in the inner workings of the bean. The code for the sizeToFit() method follows:

```
private void sizeToFit() {
  // Resize to the preferred size
  Dimension d = getPreferredSize();
  setSize(d.width, d.height);
  Component p = getParent();
  if (p != null) {
    p.invalidate();
    p.doLayout();
  }
}
```

The sizeToFit() method is responsible for sizing the bean to fit the label text with just enough space between the text and the border so that the button looks visually appealing. The getPreferredSize() method is used to get the optimal button size, which is then used to resize the bean. Note that calling the setSize() method alone isn't sufficient to resize the bean; you must also notify the bean's parent to lay out the bean again by calling the invalidate() and doLayout() methods on the parent.

The fireActionEvent() method is also important to the internal functioning of the bean. Following is its code:

```
private void fireActionEvent() {
  processActionEvent(new ActionEvent(this, ActionEvent.ACTION_PERFORMED,
    null));
}
```

The `fireActionEvent()` method is simple in that it consists of only a single call to the `processActionEvent()` method. The purpose of providing the `fireActionEvent()` method is to clean up the task of firing an action event by hiding the creation of the `ActionEvent` object passed into `processActionEvent()`. This isn't a big deal, but it does make the code calling `fireActionEvent()` in other methods a little cleaner.

Additional Overhead

You've now covered all the source code for the fancy button bean itself. Although the `FancyButton` class is all you really need to have a fully functioning bean, there is actually one other class worth mentioning: `FancyButtonBeanInfo`. It is possible to provide explicit information about a bean in an associated bean information class. Part of this explicit information is the graphical icons used to display a bean for selection purposes in application builder tools. It is easy to provide selection icons for a bean through a bean information class. Following is the complete source code for the `FancyButtonBeanInfo` class, which is a bean information class that defines selection icons for the fancy button bean:

```
// FancyButtonBeanInfo Class
// FancyButtonBeanInfo.java
package JUL.Source.Chap41.FancyButton;
// Imports
import java.beans.*;
public class FancyButtonBeanInfo extends SimpleBeanInfo {
  // Get the appropriate icon
  public java.awt.Image getIcon(int iconKind) {
    if (iconKind == BeanInfo.ICON_COLOR_16x16) {
      java.awt.Image img = loadImage("FancyButtonIcon16.gif");
      return img;
    }
    if (iconKind == BeanInfo.ICON_COLOR_32x32) {
      java.awt.Image img = loadImage("FancyButtonIcon32.gif");
      return img;
    }
    return null;
  }
}
```

The only method defined in the `FancyButtonBeanInfo` class is `getIcon()`, which is typically called by application builder tools to retrieve an icon representing the bean. Notice that two icons are actually provided by the bean information class using different resolutions. The first icon is 16×16 pixels in size; the second is 32×32 pixels. These two icons give application builder tools some degree of flexibility in representing beans graphically for selection. The BeanBox tool that comes with the BDK uses the 16×16 size icons. Both of the bean icons are provided as GIF 89A images, which is pretty standard for Java. Figure 41.1 shows how the icons look for the fancy button bean.

FIGURE 41.1.

The bean information icons for the fancy button bean.

One final part of the fancy button bean is required before the bean can be used in an application builder tool. I'm referring to the manifest file required by the JAR file in which the bean is placed. As you learned in Chapter 40, "Creating Your Own Beans," beans must be distributed in a JAR file along with an appropriate manifest file describing the contents of the JAR file.

I'm not going to go into the details of manifest files because you really need to know very little about them in most scenarios. In the simple case of packaging up a bean for distribution, all you have to do is provide a few pieces of information. Signing a file for security purposes is a little more involved, but you don't need to worry about that now. Here is the code for the fancy button bean's manifest file, `FancyButton.mf`:

```
Manifest-Version: 1.0
Name: JUL/Source/Chap41/FancyButton/FancyButton.class
Java-Bean: True
```

As you can see, the manifest file is very simple; you basically provide the name of your bean class and specify that it is, in fact, a bean. It is important to note that the package of the bean is specified as the bean's path in the manifest file. This is the only additional overhead you have to place in the JAR file so that application builder tools can extract information about your bean.

Of course, before you build the JAR file, you still have to compile all the bean's Java source code files into classes using the JDK compiler (`javac`). Before doing this, you have to make sure that you have the CLASSPATH environment variable set so that the compiler can find the bean's classes. This is necessary because the fancy button bean is defined as being part of a package (`JUL.Source.Chap41.FancyButton`). You can basically add the root path above the bean package hierarchy to the listing of paths in CLASSPATH. This directory is the parent directory of the JUL directory. If you installed the source code off the CD-ROM into a directory called Stuff, you end up with a directory structure like this:

```
\Stuff\JUL\Source\Chap41\FancyButton
```

In this case, you add the path `\Stuff` to CLASSPATH so that the compiler can locate support classes for the fancy button bean. After setting CLASSPATH, you should be able to compile the fancy button bean by executing the following two commands:

```
javac FancyButton.java
javac FancyButtonBeanInfo.java
```

Beans in a JAR File

With the bean successfully compiled, you are ready to create the JAR file for it. Unfortunately, creating the JAR file for a bean isn't quite as straightforward as you may think. As you know, the fancy button bean is part of a package, which means that the classes and related resource files for the bean are found within a hierarchical directory structure dictated by the package name. This directory structure has implications that affect how the bean is placed in a JAR file because classes are always loaded with respect to a package hierarchy. In other words, classes that reside in a package are always referenced from a directory structure that matches the package name, even when the classes are part of a JAR file. Therefore, the classes and resource files for a bean must preserve their directory structure when they are placed in a JAR file.

The package hierarchy of a bean is enforced in a JAR file by way of the manifest file. As you saw a little earlier in this chapter, the fancy button bean's manifest file includes path information based on the package name of the bean. Although the manifest file handles the problem of enforcing a package hierarchy on a bean in a JAR file, it doesn't address a subtle problem in creating the JAR file in the first place. The problem I'm referring to has to do with the fact that the jar utility specifically looks for a bean class file that matches the package directory structure whenever it is used to create a JAR file for a bean. The problem is made more apparent because the jar utility won't even find a bean class file if the utility is run in the same directory where the file is located. The reason for this is that the jar utility tries to traverse a package directory structure to find the class. The solution is to execute the jar utility from a directory *above* the package directory structure where the bean files are located. In this case, you run the jar utility from the directory just above the JUL directory.

Even though the jar utility expects the bean class to be located within a directory structure, it doesn't automatically know to look for the class files and resources in this structure. This means that you must specify explicit paths when you execute the jar utility from the directory above the package hierarchy. To build a JAR file that contains the fancy button bean and its resources, execute the following command in the directory above the bean package hierarchy:

```
jar cfm JUL\Source\Chap41\FancyButton\FancyButton.jar
  JUL\Source\Chap41\FancyButton\FancyButton.mf
  JUL\Source\Chap41\FancyButton\*.class
  JUL\Source\Chap41\FancyButton\*.gif
```

In this command, notice that the paths to all the files used by the jar utility are explicitly declared. This is necessary because the utility is being executed from the top of the bean package hierarchy. If you're thinking that this seems like a roundabout way of doing things, you're exactly right. However, as of the beta 3 release of the BDK, this was the only way to build JAR files that contain beans that are part of a package. Hopefully, JavaSoft is working out a better approach for the final release of the BDK, which may be available by the time you read this. Check the JavaSoft Web site (www.javasoft.com) for the latest information.

One other small problem must be addressed in regard to the jar command just described. Many operating system shells don't provide a big enough command-line buffer to enter commands that long. Fortunately, there is an easy solution to this problem. I created a simple batch file that can be used to add any bean and its associated resources to a JAR file without concern about the length of the command. Here are the contents of this batch file, which I named beanjar.bat:

```
@echo off
echo Jar'ing %2...
jar cfm %1\%2.jar %1\%2.mf %1\*.class %1\*.gif %1\*.au
echo Rejar'ing finished.
```

This batch file takes two arguments: a path and a bean name. The path argument describes the relative path of the bean's class files and resources; the bean name is the name of the main bean class file without the .class extension.

NOTE

The beanjar.bat batch file is intended to be an all-purpose utility for creating JAR files for beans. For this reason, it attempts to add all the classes, images, and sounds for a bean to the JAR file, even if a bean doesn't necessarily use images or sounds. For beans that don't use images or sounds, an error message appears stating that no files could be found matching the *.gif and *.au wildcards. You can just ignore this error message if your bean doesn't rely on image or sound resources.

Following is an example of creating a JAR file that contains the fancy button bean using the beanjar.bat batch file:

```
beanjar JUL\Source\Chap41\FancyButton FancyButton
```

Keep in mind that this command must still be executed from the top of the package directory hierarchy for the bean. After you execute this command, you should have a JAR file that contains the fancy button bean that is ready to be distributed and used.

NOTE

 Keep in mind that the complete source code and related resources for the fancy button bean are located on the accompanying CD-ROM.

Testing the Fancy Button Bean

The previous section mentioned that most application builder tools, including the BeanBox test container, require beans to be packaged as JAR files. You just created a JAR file that contains the fancy button bean, which you will now test in the BeanBox. To add the bean to the BeanBox, you must first copy the JAR file to the jars directory beneath your BDK installation. If you installed the BDK according to the instructions in the previous chapter, the appropriate directory is \jdk\beans\jars. The reason for copying the JAR file to this directory is that the BeanBox looks in this directory for all the beans to add to its ToolBox.

> **NOTE**
>
> As of this writing, the JavaBeans architects were in the process of working out a better way to integrate new beans into the BeanBox. One of the possible solutions was a new menu command under the Edit menu that would let you add beans using a file-selection dialog box. Check your version of the BeanBox to see whether it supports this functionality.

You launch the BeanBox by executing the run.bat batch file, which you learned about in the previous chapter. The BeanBox should appear with your fancy button bean added to the ToolBox. Figure 41.2 shows what the ToolBox looks like with the bean added.

> **NOTE**
>
> Keep in mind that the run.bat batch file alters the CLASSPATH environment variable so that the BeanBox can run properly. You have to manually set CLASSPATH back to its original value before compiling any additional beans.

FIGURE 41.2.
The BeanBox ToolBox window with the fancy button bean added.

In the figure, notice that the last bean in the ToolBox is the fancy button bean, complete with the 16×16 icon you specified in the bean information class. Add the fancy button bean to the BeanBox by clicking it in the ToolBox and then clicking the main container window. Figure 41.3 shows the newly added fancy button bean.

FIGURE 41.3.

The BeanBox main container window with the fancy button bean added.

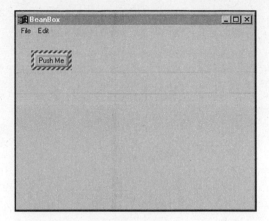

Now that the bean has been added to the container window, the real fun begins. Check out Figure 41.4, which shows the PropertySheet window for the fancy button bean.

FIGURE 41.4.

The BeanBox PropertySheet window for the fancy button bean.

The PropertySheet window shows all the properties for the bean, including the inherited foreground color, background color, font, and name properties, as well as your own sticky and label properties. All these properties are fully editable using the PropertySheet window. Try editing the label and font for the bean because they impact the appearance the most. Figure 41.5 shows the bean with the label and font properties modified.

You should also try out the sticky mode for the bean just to make sure that it works the way you expected it to. Also keep in mind that the bean is designed to fire action events whenever it is clicked, so you can easily wire it to other beans just as you did with the OurButton bean in the previous chapter. Because you already know how to wire buttons to other beans, I'll let you explore that use of the fancy button bean on your own.

FIGURE 41.5.

*The BeanBox main
container with a
modified fancy button
bean.*

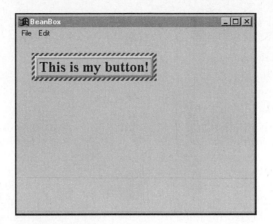

Enhancing the Fancy Button Bean

The last topic of this chapter deals with some areas in which the fancy button bean can be improved. I did all the work for you in developing the guts of the bean, so I want to give you some ideas about some modifications you can make yourself. No matter how good a bean is, there is always room for improvement in one way or another, and this bean is no different. Following are a few suggestions for ways to add more features to the bean:

- Add support for images
- Add button down/up events for the sticky mode

The first suggestion involves adding support for images, which means that the button would display an image along with the label text. As you are no doubt aware, image buttons are popular in most graphical environments. This addition can be as simple as adding a string property that holds the filename for an image drawn in the paint() method.

The second suggestion is related to the sticky mode of the button. In some situations, it may be useful for the button to fire events based on the state changing while it is in the sticky mode. In other words, it might be nice to know when the button is being pushed and raised. Providing this functionality consists of adding a new event interface and providing event types for the button being pushed and raised in the sticky mode.

You may not feel up to the challenge of implementing these suggestions just yet because this was your first bean. However, at least try to think about the conceptual aspects of modifying the bean to support these features. Doing so will help you a great deal in gaining bean design experience.

Summary

This chapter introduced you to the fine art of JavaBeans programming at a practical level; you built your very first bean! Although the theory you learned in the last few chapters was important in its own right, this chapter finally showed you how to do something real with JavaBeans. You started the chapter with an idea for a fancy button bean, carried it through a preliminary design, and completed its implementation. You then took the bean for a spin and finished off by brainstorming some ways to improve it on your own. How empowering!

One of the most important things you learned in this chapter is how little JavaBeans programming differs from traditional Java programming. This chapter should have proved to you that beans are just Java classes with some extra features thrown in. This is no accident, seeing how the folks at JavaSoft wanted to make it easy for Java programmers to shift to JavaBeans programming. You should have been able to follow along in this chapter without too much trouble because the bean you developed is so similar to normal AWT Java classes.

IN THIS PART

Java Databases

Databases and Java

by Shelley Powers

IN THIS CHAPTER

Java is an ideal language for persistent data storage. By using class inheritance and data encapsulation, a Java application developed to work with one type of data storage can be ported or extended to work with another. An example is an application currently working with an RDBMS (Relational Database Management System) that is extended to use RMI (Remote Method Invocation) to store data in a file.

A common misconception with Java is that database access can occur only with the JDBC (Java Database Connection) API. Although the JDBC provides a handy set of lower level classes to manage database connections and transactions, it is not a mandatory component. Several chapters in this book reference the mSQL JDBC driver (included on the CD-ROM that accompanies this book) written by George Reese. George wrote his driver to run with the `MsqlJava` classes created by Darryl Collins. `MsqlJava` uses the `Socket` classes included in the `java.net` package and the data input and output stream classes included in the `java.io` package. If you wanted to, you could as easily connect to an mSQL database using `MsqlJava` instead of the mSQL JDBC driver.

Additional efforts are underway to establish a standard Java class API to interface with object DBMSes (Database Management Systems). Companies are also creating their own optimized data access classes, such as Microsoft's DAO (Data Access Object) classes.

As an alternative to persistent storage of data in database management systems, Java can also be used to store data to files using object serialization.

A History of Java and Data Access

Version 1.0 of the Java Developer's Kit was released in January 1996. This kit contained all the classes necessary to implement database access—although developers had to code their own connections.

The JDK contained core classes grouped together into packages; two of these (`java.net` and `java.io`) provide the classes necessary to connect to a database and send and receive data. However, most of us do not want to create a socket and stream data to and from it to implement a simple transaction.

In February 1996, Sun released the JDBC as a separate package under the name `java.sql`. With the release of JDK 1.1, the JDBC package is *not* included as part of the core Java classes. Chapter 19, "The SQL Package," contains an overview of this package as well as a description of how the JDBC works and a list of the major classes and interfaces.

The JDBC API is based on the SQL CLI (Call Level Interface). This standard explains how to access databases with function calls embedded in applications. The SQL CLI also forms the basis for the ODBC standard from Microsoft. You can read more about this standard at `http://www.jcc.com/sql_stnd.html`.

The JDBC consists of a basic set of interfaces and a `DriverManager` class used as the basis for several drivers. *Drivers* provide the functionality specific to a database or database middleware layer. With the JDBC, Sun also released a basic ODBC driver known as the *JDBC-ODBC bridge* (created by Intersolv for Sun and meant to connect to ODBC-compliant databases).

Certain limitations became immediately apparent when using the JDBC. First, the JDBC-ODBC bridge used native method calls and a DLL (Dynamic Link Library) to connect to a database, prohibiting its use in applets accessible through the Internet. Because of applet security issues, the JDBC limits network connectivity to the same host from which the applet was downloaded. For use with an applet, databases must be installed on the same server as the HTTP server—a potential security risk. A workaround is to have the driver access a middleware layer, which in turn accesses a database located elsewhere; several companies have produced this type of driver.

Java and Object Databases

Information about accessing data using Java can be found at the JavaSoft site `http://www.javasoft.com/jdbc/`. In addition to listing drivers and information about the uses of JDBC, the site also references current efforts to bind the work of the ODMG (Object Database Management Group) with Java to create an API for accessing object-based databases.

The ODMG plans to release a specification that includes this Java-to-ODMG binding some time in 1997. The specification is expected to cover issues of persistence and to include a set of classes created in Java that will map directly to the ODMG objects.

For those who are impatient to try this technology, implementations of object-based persistent data stores using Java do currently exist. As this book goes to press, two companies (POET Software and Object Design, Inc.) have implementations of this technology; you can download them for evaluation from the Internet. Additionally, the JDK 1.1 has a set of object serialization classes included in the `java.io` package that facilitate storage of objects.

Object Serialization

Object serialization is covered in more detail in Chapter 31, "Persistence and Java Serialization," but a brief overview of how this technology works will clarify the next section covering specific products.

Object serialization simply means to store an object in such a way that the object can be retrieved—as an object—from the store. Objects can be manipulated in memory and can reference their members and any associations. With serialization, you can also store these same objects in a persistent format (such as a system file) for later retrieval.

At its simplest, object serialization is not very difficult. Listing 42.1 shows class
ObjectServer with two methods: wrtobj() and rdobj(). The first method creates a
Hashtable object and inserts three values into it. The newly created object is then
serialized to a file named HASH. The second method, rdobj(), opens this new file and uses serialization to read the object back in. After the Hashtable object is read, one of its elements is
accessed and the value of the element is written to standard output. The complete source code
for this application can be found on the CD-ROM that comes with this book.

Listing 42.1. The ObjectServer class.

```
//
// Example using object serialization
//
import java.io.*;
import java.util.*;
// class
public class ObjectServer
{
public static void main(String arg[]) {
    try {
        wrtobj();
        rdobj();
    }
    catch(Exception e) {
        System.out.println(e.getMessage());
    }
}
// create object
// serialize to file
public static void wrtobj()
{
    // create the hashtable object
    Hashtable numbers = new Hashtable();
    numbers.put("one", new Integer(1));
    numbers.put("two", new Integer(2));
    numbers.put("three", new Integer(3));
    // serialize the object to a file
    try {
        FileOutputStream outFile = new FileOutputStream("hash");
        ObjectOutput  outStream  =  new  ObjectOutputStream(outFile);
        outStream.writeObject(numbers);
        outStream.flush();
    }
    catch(IOException e) {
        System.out.println(e.getMessage());
    }

}
// open serialization file
// read in object
// access object member
public static void rdobj()
{
    Hashtable numbers;
```

```
    // open the file and read in the serialized object
    try {
        FileInputStream inFile = new FileInputStream("hash");
        ObjectInputStream inStream = new ObjectInputStream(inFile);
        numbers = (Hashtable)inStream.readObject();
        }
        catch(IOException e) {
            System.out.println(e.getMessage());
        }
        catch(ClassNotFoundException e) {
            System.out.println(e.getMessage());
        }
    // access the hashtable value and print out
    Integer ivalue = (Integer)numbers.get("one");
    if (ivalue != null) {
        System.out.println("one = " + ivalue);
    }
}
}
```

Listing 42.2 shows the result of running this Java application using `java.exe`.

Listing 42.2. The output from the `ObjectServer` application.

```
E:\JDK\java\bin java objser
one = 1
```

One thing you probably noticed in Listing 42.1 is that object serialization involves reading and writing from a file. Because of this file access, applet security implemented with most browsers prohibits this code from being used in an untrusted applet. Later in this chapter, RMI (Remote Method Invocation) is used with the object serialization class to serialize the data to the Web server machine. You can read more about using digital authorization to create trusted applets and other security issues in Chapter 16, "The Security Package," Chapter 34, "Java Security," and Chapter 37, "Code Signing and JAR Security."

ObjectStore PSE for Java and the Java Software Development Kit

Object Design, Inc., manufactures the product ObjectStore PSE (Persistent Storage Engine) for Java; ObjectStore provides single-use persistent storage. The company provides a free downloadable version of this product at their Web site at `http://www.odi.com`. Their fully functional version of this product, ObjectStore PSE Pro for Java, can also be purchased from the Object Design, Inc., site. The company has created an API and a toolset to give you the ability to create persistent Java stores.

To use the product in your Java applet or application, you first initialize ObjectStore:

```
ObjectStore.initialize(null, null);
```

42

DATABASES AND JAVA

Type the following lines to create a database and a transaction:

```
Database db = Database.create (sname, Database.allRead ¦ Database.allWrite);
Transaction tr = Transaction.begin(Transaction.update);
```

The objects are then stored using a `createRoot()` method call, which appends the object to the database. For example, the following example creates the `Rose` object in the `Flower` class with a constructor that takes two strings and an integer:

```
Flower rose = new Flower("rose", "perennial",1);
db.createRoot("Rose", rose);
tr.commit();
```

To read the object, a transaction is created, the object is retrieved from the database, and the object members (including any associated objects) are accessed directly:

```
Transaction tr = Transaction.begin(Transaction.readOnly);
Flower someflower = (Flower)db.getRoot("Rose");
String s = someflower.name;
tr.commit();
```

ObjectStore PSE does require that a *postprocessor* be used on the class file to make the class object capable of persistence.

> **NOTE**
>
> ObjectStore PSE for Java has been licensed by Netscape and will be included with the final released version of Netscape Communicator. Additionally, Microsoft has licensed the product and is bundling it with the Microsoft SDK for Java.

POET Software has created its own Java API to handle persistent storage; that product is called the POET Java Software Development Kit (SDK). The product can be downloaded for evaluation from the POET Web site at `http://www.poet.com`. Information about POET Software's Java SDK product is a bit sketchy at the time this book goes to press because the product is in beta release and most of the documentation is about POET Software's other products.

From the examples, it looks as if the POET product works in a manner similar to ObjectStore PSE except that you can work with remote as well as local persistent data stores. You would have to establish a connection, open a database, create an object, and store it.

Java and Persistent Data Storage on the Host

The previous examples of data storage using some form of object serialization all had one thing in common: The data was stored on the client machine rather than on the server.

In addition to the interim release of the JDBC, Sun has also released a Java API for RMI. This API provides a set of classes that allow methods to be invoked on the client from a Java server based on the Web server. With the concept of trusted applets, the methods are eventually accessible from a Java server located anywhere.

As are the JDBC classes, the RMI classes are part of the core Java class library Sun is releasing with JDK version 1.1. A more detailed description of RMI is given in Chapter 17, "The RMI Package."

To use this technique with object serialization, you must follow several steps. Returning to the earlier example, which serialized a `Hashtable` object, the sample class is extended to include RMI. First, the interface for the remote object is created as shown in Listing 42.3.

Listing 42.3. The `objser` object interface.

```
//
// interface for remote object
//
package my.objser;
public interface objser extends java.rmi.Remote {
    void wrtobj() throws java.rmi.RemoteException;
    int rdobj() throws java.rmi.RemoteException;
}
```

Note the same two methods created in the original class `ObjectServer` shown in Listing 42.1. After the interface is created and installed on the `CLASSPATH`, under its own package folder of `my.objser`, the object serialization server is created as shown in Listing 42.4.

Listing 42.4. The `objimp` object serialization server.

```
//
// Object Serialization Server
//
package my.objser;
import java.rmi.*;
import java.rmi.server.UnicastRemoteObject;
import java.io.*;
import java.util.*;
public class objimp
    extends UnicastRemoteObject
    implements objser
{
    public objimp(String s) throws java.rmi.RemoteException {
    super();
    }

// create object
// serialize to file
public void wrtobj()
{
    System.out.println("creating hashtable");
    Hashtable numbers = new Hashtable();
```

continues

Listing 42.4. continued

```java
        numbers.put("one", new Integer(1));
        numbers.put("two", new Integer(2));
        numbers.put("three", new Integer(3));
        try {
            FileOutputStream outFile = new FileOutputStream("hash");
            ObjectOutput  outStream  =  new  ObjectOutputStream(outFile);
            outStream.writeObject(numbers);
            outStream.flush();
        }
        catch(IOException e) {
            System.out.println(e.getMessage());
        }
    }
    // open serialization file
    // read in object
    // access object member
    public int rdobj()
    {
        Hashtable numbers;
        System.out.println("reading in from file");
        try {
            FileInputStream inFile = new FileInputStream("hash");
            ObjectInputStream inStream = new ObjectInputStream(inFile);
            numbers = (Hashtable)inStream.readObject();
            Integer ivalue = (Integer)numbers.get("one");
            if (ivalue != null) {
                int i = ivalue.intValue();
                return i;
            }
            else
                return 0;
            }
            catch(IOException e) {
                System.out.println(e.getMessage());
            }
            catch(ClassNotFoundException e) {
                System.out.println(e.getMessage());
            }
            return 0;
    }
    public static void main(String args[])
    {
        // Create and install the security manager
        System.setSecurityManager(new RMISecurityManager());
        try {
            objimp obj = new objimp("HelloServer");
            Naming.rebind("HelloServer", obj);
            System.out.println("ObjectImpl created and bound
               in the registry to the name HelloServer");
        }
        catch (Exception e) {
            System.out.println("ObjectImpl.main: an exception occurred:");
            e.printStackTrace();
            }
        }
}
```

The objimp class should be installed in the same package location created for the objser interface. The actual methods used with this class are very similar to those in the original class (shown in Listing 42.1) except that the methods are not defined as static. Interface methods cannot be created with the static modifier because they are overridden in the server. In the main() method for the class, the server is created and bound.

Finally, an applet is created to access the object from the server and to invoke the wrtobj() and rdobj() methods. The results are shown in Listing 42.5.

Listing 42.5. The ObjectApplet class that calls the server object.

```
//
// object serialization applet
//
package my.objser;
import java.awt.*;
import java.rmi.*;
public class ObjectApplet extends java.applet.Applet {
    String message;
    public void init() {
    try {
        objser obj = (objser)
        Naming.lookup("//" + getCodeBase().getHost() + "/HelloServer");
        message = "host is " + getCodeBase().getHost();
        obj.wrtobj();
        int i = obj.rdobj();
        message = message + " value is " + i;
     } catch (Exception e) {
        System.out.println("HelloApplet: an exception occurred:");
        e.printStackTrace();
        }
    }

    public void paint(Graphics g) {
       g.drawString(message, 25, 50);
    }
}
```

Next, an HTML file is created that contains a reference to the new applet, as shown in Listing 42.6.

Listing 42.6. Creating the Object.htm file with reference to the ObjectApplet class.

```
<HTML>
<title>Object Serialization</title>
<center> <h1>Object Serialization - remotely</h1> </center>
<p>
<applet codebase="./classes"
    code="my.objser.ObjectApplet"
    width=500 height=120>
</applet>
</HTML>
```

After the Java classes are created and compiled, stub methods must be created to provide access to the server methods. This is done using the `rmic` tool, provided in the JDK 1.1:

```
rmic -d c:\webshare\wwwroot\classes my.objser.objimp
```

The `-d` flag is used to direct the tool to place the generated classes in the same directory as the server class. This command generates two files for `objimp.class`: `objimp_Skel.class` and `objimp_Stub.class`.

The next step is to start the RMI registration server. Because this example is being created and run in Windows 95, the command to start the RMI server is as follows:

```
start rmiregistry
```

Finally, the server is started. The `-D` option followed by the `java.rmi.server.codebase` specifies the URL for the stub class for the RMI server:

```
java -Djava.rmi.server.codebase=http://localhost/classes/ my.objser.objimp &
```

The location of the RMI server classes must be on the `CLASSPATH` defined for the Web server. At the time this book goes to press, no browser had yet implemented JDK version 1.1, so the JDK-supplied applet viewer program is used to run the new applet:

```
appletviewer http://localhost/Object.htm &
```

This statement opens the HTML file and starts the `ObjectApplet` applet. Figure 42.1 shows the result of this operation, including the system prints from the server in the window directly under the applet.

FIGURE 42.1.

Running the `ObjectApplet` *applet.*

Object serialization and RMI are effective techniques for storing and accessing data on the server without requiring access to a DBMS.

Java and the JDBC

Probably the most common data access technique in use with Java is the JDBC. Within weeks after the release of JDBC 1.0 in 1996, several drivers were available—most downloadable from the Internet for evaluation or direct use.

As explained in Chapter 19, JDBC implements a two-layer architecture: one layer is implemented by the driver developer, and the other layer is implemented by the application or applet developer. As you also learned in Chapter 19, drivers can fall into four categories: JDBC-ODBC drivers, Native API drivers, Java-Net drivers, and native protocol. Because of limitations on access and the necessity of binaries on the client, the first two categories are better suited to intranet use only; the latter two categories can be used for intranet or Internet access.

With the final release of JDK 1.1 and its incorporation into the more popular browsers, database access with Java through applets will not only be simple to implement, but simple to maintain.

Chapter 43, "Getting Started with JDBC," provides several examples of how to use JDBC in Java-based applications. Chapter 44, "Building Database Applets with JDBC," provides examples of database access through an applet embedded in a browser. However, as an example of how to use the JDBC, the following sections create the beginnings of a database utility using the DatabaseMetaData interface. To orient you in this process, the next section reviews the ResultSetMetaData interface.

The ResultSetMetaData Interface

Chapter 19 covered most of the interfaces and classes in the JDBC but left the DatabaseMetaData and ResultSetMetaData interfaces for this chapter. The DatabaseMetaData interface provides *meta data* (information about the database, its procedures, tables, columns, indexes, transactions, and so on) and is covered in the following section. The ResultSetMetaData class provides information about the result set that is returned by a transaction. Its methods are listed next. Note that each method throws a SQLException exception.

■ public abstract string getCatalogName(int *column*)
Gets the catalog name for the table of the specified column index.

■ public abstract int getColumnCount()
The number of columns in the ResultSet.

■ public abstract int getColumnDisplaySize(int *column*)
The display size of the specified column.

■ `public abstract String getColumnLabel(int column)`
The label to be used with the column if it is stored in the database.

■ `public abstract String getColumnName(int column)`
Returns the name of the column, given the column index.

■ `public abstract int getColumnType(int column)`
The data type of the column, given the column index.

■ `public abstract String getColumnTypeName(int column)`
The specific data type name of the data type for the column, given a column index.

■ `public abstract int getPrecision(int column)`
The precision defined for the column, if any, given a column index.

■ `public abstract int getScale(int column)`
The scale defined for the column, if any, given a column index.

■ `public abstract String getSchemaName(int column)`
The schema defined for the column, if supported in the database and if any exists for the column, given a column index.

■ `public abstract String getTableName(int column)`
The table name of the column, given a column index.

■ `public abstract boolean isAutoIncrement(int column)`
Returns `true` if the column value is automatically incremented when a new row is created; otherwise, returns `false`. Used for numeric identifiers.

■ `public abstract boolean isCaseSensitive(int column)`
Returns `true` if the column is case sensitive, whether case is important or not; otherwise, returns `false`.

■ `public abstract boolean isCurrency(int column)`
Returns `true` if the column is formatted for currency values; returns `false` if the column is not formatted or if currency formatting is not applicable.

■ `public abstract boolean isDefinatelyWritable(int column)`
Returns `true` if the column can be updated; otherwise, returns `false`.

■ `public abstract boolean isNullable(int column)`
Returns `true` if the column value can be set to `null`; otherwise, returns `false`.

■ `public abstract boolean isReadOnly (int column)`
Returns `true` if the column is read only; otherwise, returns `false`.

■ `public abstract boolean isSearchable (int column)`
Returns `true` if the column can be used in a search clause; otherwise, returns `false`.

■ `public abstract boolean isSigned (int column)`
Returns `true` if the value of the column is a signed value (such as a signed integer); otherwise, returns `false`.

■ `public abstract boolean isWritable (int column)`
Returns `true` if the value of the column is writeable; otherwise, returns `false`.

A `ResultSetMetaData` object is created as a result of a method call to a `ResultSet` object:

```
ResultSetMetaData rsmd = rs.getMetaData();
```

Once the object is created, you can use it to find information about the result set, such as a column's name:

```
String sname;
String sallnames = "columns are ";
int icount = rsmd.getColumnCount();
for (i = 0; i < icount; i++) {
    sname = rsmd.getColumnName(i);
    sallnames+=sallnames + sname + ",";
}
```

> **TIP**
>
> When would you use `ResultSetMetaData`? If you work with dynamic SQL, you will need this interface. In addition, if you issue generic SQL statements such as `Select * from sometable`, you will find that `ResultSetMetaData` provides useful information.

The DatabaseMetaData Interface

The `DatabaseMetaData` interface provides information about the database itself, rather than the data it contains. JDBC drivers may or may not implement this class; if the class is not implemented, any of the methods for the class throw a `SQLException` error.

As a handy way to explain the usefulness of the `DatabaseMetaData` interface and to provide a good first step for beginning to work with data access in Java, the Java `dbutil` application was created to work with the JDBC-ODBC bridge. This tool takes five parameters: the ODBC database name as defined with the ODBC Administrator, the user name, the password (sorry, the password is not encrypted), the information category, and the information category option. Among the options the existing tool can provide is information about the database, its procedures, tables, columns, and transactions.

`dbutil` is a Java application; the first method of the application to examine is the `main()` procedure:

```
public static void main(String arg[]) {
    try {
        //connect to ODBC database
        Class.forName("sun.jdbc.odbc.JdbcOdbcDriver");
        String url = "jdbc:odbc:" + arg[0];
        // connect
        Connection con = DriverManager.getConnection(url,arg[1],arg[2]);
        // get databasemetadata object
        DatabaseMetaData dmd = con.getMetaData();
        // get option 1 and 2
        String soption = arg[3];
        String soption2 = arg[4];
```

```
            //check argument to see which load to run
            if (soption.compareTo("procedures") == 0) {
                    // output procedure information
                    output_procedure_info(dmd,soption2);
                    }
            else if (soption.compareTo("database") == 0) {
                    // output database information
                    output_database_info(dmd,soption2);
                    }
            else if (soption.compareTo("tables") == 0) {
                    // output table information
                    output_table_info(dmd,soption2);
                    }
            else if (soption.compareTo("columns") == 0) {
                    // output column information
                    output_column_info(dmd,soption2);
                    }
            else {
                    // output transaction information
                    output_transaction_info(dmd,soption2);
            }
            //close connection
            con.close();
            }
        catch(Exception e) {
            System.out.println(e.getMessage());
            }
    }
```

The `main()` method processes the arguments passed on the command line, using the first to connect to the specific database, the second and third arguments as the user name and password, and the last two arguments to see which options to run. After the connection is made, a `DatabaseMetaData` object is created.

The first information method is `output_procedure_info()`:

```
// output_procedure_info
//
// options are:
//
//      are procedures callable
//      do stored procedures support escape sequences
//
public static void output_procedure_info(DatabaseMetaData dmd,
                                            String soption)
{
    boolean b;

    try {
        // are all procedures callable
        if (soption.compareTo("callable") == 0) {
            b = dmd.allProceduresAreCallable();
            if (b)
                System.out.println("You can call procedures");
            else
                System.out.println("You cannot call procedures");
        }
```

```
            // do stored procedures support escape syntax
            else {
                b = dmd.supportsStoredProcedures();
                if (b)
                    System.out.println("Stored Procedures support escape syntax");
                else
                    System.out.println("Stored Procedures do not support escape syntax");
                }
            }
        catch(SQLException e) {
            System.out.println(e.getMessage());
        }
}
```

This method calls the specific method associated with the DatabaseMetaData object to find the information requested by the user. With this method, all the results from the object calls are of type boolean. The next method, output_table_info(), uses a ResultSet object to process the return from a method call:

```
// output_table_info
//
// options are:
//
//    are tables selectable
//
//    for each schema get the tables
//
public static void output_table_info(DatabaseMetaData dmd,
                                     String soption)
{
    boolean b;
    ResultSet rs;
    ResultSet rs2;
    String tempString = "";
    String resultString = "";
    String sschema;
    try {
        // are tables selectable
        if (soption.compareTo("selectable") == 0) {
            b = dmd.allTablesAreSelectable();
            if (b)
                System.out.println("You can select from all tables");
            else
                System.out.println("You cannot select from all tables");
            }
        // for each schema get table names and types
        else if (soption.compareTo("tables") == 0) {
            rs = dmd.getSchemas();
            while(rs.next()) {
                sschema = rs.getString(1);
                System.out.println("Searching Schema " + sschema + "\n");
                rs2 = dmd.getTables(null,sschema, "%",null);
                while(rs2.next()) {
                    tempString = rs2.getString(3) + " ";
                    tempString+= rs2.getString(4);
                    resultString+= tempString + "\n";
                    }
                }
```

```
            System.out.println("Tables are \n" + resultString);
            }
        }
    catch(SQLException e) {
        System.out.println(e.getMessage());
        }
    }
```

 The entire class is presented in Listing 42.7 and can be found on the CD-ROM that accompanies this book.

Listing 42.7. The `dbutil` database utility class.

```
/*
 * Database Utility
 *
 * Author:   Shelley Powers
 *
 */
import java.sql.*;
import sun.jdbc.odbc.*;
import java.io.*;
public class dbutil
{
public static void main(String arg[]) {
    try {
        //connect to ODBC database
        Class.forName("sun.jdbc.odbc.JdbcOdbcDriver");
        String url = "jdbc:odbc:" + arg[0];
        // connect
        Connection con = DriverManager.getConnection(url,arg[1],arg[2]);
        // get databasemetadata object
        DatabaseMetaData dmd = con.getMetaData();
        // get option 1 and 2
        String soption = arg[3];
        String soption2 = arg[4];
        //check argument to see which load to run
        if (soption.compareTo("procedures") == 0) {
            // output procedure information
            output_procedure_info(dmd,soption2);
            }
        else if (soption.compareTo("database") == 0) {
            // output database information
            output_database_info(dmd,soption2);
            }
        else if (soption.compareTo("tables") == 0) {
            // output table information
            output_table_info(dmd,soption2);
            }
        else if (soption.compareTo("columns") == 0) {
            // output column information
            output_column_info(dmd,soption2);
            }
        else {
            // output transaction information
            output_transaction_info(dmd,soption2);
        }
```

```
            //close connection
            con.close();
            }
        catch(Exception e) {
            System.out.println(e.getMessage());
            }
}
// output_procedure_info
//
// options are:
//
//      are procedures callable
//      do stored procedures support escape sequences
//
public static void output_procedure_info(DatabaseMetaData dmd,
                                        String soption)
{
    boolean b;
    try {
        // are all procedures callable
        if (soption.compareTo("callable") == 0) {
            b = dmd.allProceduresAreCallable();
            if (b)
                System.out.println("You can call procedures");
            else
                System.out.println("You cannot call procedures");
            }
        // do stored procedures support escape syntax
        else {
            b = dmd.supportsStoredProcedures();
            if (b)
                System.out.println("Stored Procedures support escape syntax");
            else
                System.out.println("Stored Procedures do not support escape syntax");
            }
        }
    catch(SQLException e) {
        System.out.println(e.getMessage());
        }
}
// output_database_info
//
// options are:
//
//      get database URL
//      get user name
//      get database schemas
//      get database catalogs
//      is database readonly
//
public static void output_database_info(DatabaseMetaData dmd,
                                        String soption)
{
    boolean b;
    ResultSet rs;
    String s;
    String tempString;
```

continues

42

**DATABASES
AND JAVA**

Listing 42.7. continued

```java
    String stringResult = " ";
    try {
        // get url
        if (soption.compareTo("url") == 0) {
            s = dmd.getURL();
            System.out.println("URL of database is " + s);
        }
        // get user name
        else if (soption.compareTo("user") == 0) {
            s = dmd.getUserName();
            System.out.println("User name is " + s);
        }
        // get schemas
        else if (soption.compareTo("schema") == 0) {
            rs = dmd.getSchemas();
            while(rs.next()) {
                tempString = rs.getString(1) + "\n";
                stringResult+=tempString;
            }
            System.out.println("Database Schemas are: \n" + stringResult);
        }
        // is database readonly
        else if (soption.compareTo("readonly") == 0) {
            b = dmd.isReadOnly();
            if (b)
                System.out.println("Database is readonly");
            else
                System.out.println("Database is not readonly");
        }
        // get database catalogs
        else {
            rs = dmd.getCatalogs();
            while (rs.next()) {

                // get catalog
                tempString = rs.getString(1) + "\n";
                stringResult+=tempString;
            }
            System.out.println("Catalogs are: \n" + stringResult);
        }
    }
    catch(SQLException e) {
        System.out.println(e.getMessage());
    }
}
// output_transaction_info
//
// options are:
//
//      does database support dm transactions
//      does a data definition transaction force a commit
//
public static void output_transaction_info(DatabaseMetaData dmd,
                                    String soption)
{
    boolean b;
```

```
    try {
        // does database support dm transactions
        if (soption.compareTo("dm") == 0) {
            b = dmd.supportsDataManipulationTransactionsOnly();
            if (b)
               System.out.println("You can use data manipulation statements");
            else
               System.out.println("You cannot use data manipulation statements");
        }
        // do ddl statements force a commit
        else {
            b = dmd.dataDefinitionCausesTransactionCommit();
            if (b)
               System.out.println("A data definition statement will force a
                                   commit");
            else
               System.out.println("A data definition statement will not force a
                                   commit");
        }
    }
    catch(SQLException e) {
        System.out.println(e.getMessage());
    }
}
// output_table_info
// options are:
//    are tables selectable
//    for each schema, get the tables
public static void output_table_info(DatabaseMetaData dmd,
                                     String soption)
{
    boolean b;
    ResultSet rs;
    ResultSet rs2;
    String tempString = "";
    String resultString = "";
    String sschema;
    try {
        // are tables selectable
        if (soption.compareTo("selectable") == 0) {
            b = dmd.allTablesAreSelectable();
            if (b)
               System.out.println("You can select from all tables");
            else
               System.out.println("You cannot select from all tables");
        }
        // for each schema get table names and types
        else if (soption.compareTo("tables") == 0) {
            rs = dmd.getSchemas();
            while(rs.next()) {
               sschema = rs.getString(1);
               System.out.println("Searching Schema " + sschema + "\n");
               rs2 = dmd.getTables(null,sschema, "%",null);
               while(rs2.next()) {
                   tempString = rs2.getString(3) + " ";
                   tempString+= rs2.getString(4);
                   resultString+= tempString + "\n";
               }
            }
```

continues

Listing 42.7. continued

```java
                    System.out.println("Tables are \n" + resultString);
                    }
            }
        catch(SQLException e) {
            System.out.println(e.getMessage());
            }
        }
}
// output_column_info
//
// The only option at this time for
// columns is a list of columns for each table and
// each schema
public static void output_column_info(DatabaseMetaData dmd,
                                      String soption)
{
    ResultSet rs;
    ResultSet rs2;
    ResultSet rs3;
    String tempString;
    String resultString = "";
    String sschema;
    String stable;
    try {
      if (soption.compareTo("columns") == 0) {
        // for each schema
        rs = dmd.getSchemas();
        while (rs.next()) {
            sschema = rs.getString(1);
            System.out.println("Searching through schema " + sschema + "\n");
            // for each table
            rs2 = dmd.getTables(null,sschema,"%",null);
            while (rs2.next()) {
                stable = rs2.getString(3);
                System.out.println("Searching through table " + stable + "\n");
                // get and print out columns
                rs3 = dmd.getColumns(null, sschema,stable,"%");
                while (rs3.next()) {
                    tempString = rs3.getString(3) + " ";
                    tempString+= rs3.getString(4) + " ";
                    tempString+= rs3.getString(6) + "\n";
                    resultString+= tempString;
                    }
                System.out.println("Columns are : \n" + resultString + "\n");
                }
            }
        }
    }
    catch(SQLException e) {
        System.out.println(e.getMessage());
        }
    }
}
```

Running the dbutil tool is quite simple. I ran the tool against the Northwind database that comes with Access 97:

```
java dbutil nwind admin dba procedures callable
```

Provided that you have the data source (nwind) established and suitably named, this example returns whether the stored procedures in the database are callable. The results are shown here:

```
You can call procedures
```

Then I ran the same query against a Sybase SQL Anywhere database I had:

```
java dbutil Zoo dba sql procedures callable
```

In this case, the result from the tool was as follows:

```
You cannot call procedures
```

I ran the tables category and the tables option to list the tables in the SQL Anywhere database; the first part of the result (the result is fairly long) is shown in Listing 42.8. Note that the output was directed to a file:

```
java dbutil Zoo dba sql tables tables > tables.out
```

Listing 42.8. The tables.out file: The first several lines of the results of running dbutil against a Sybase SQL Anywhere database.

```
Searching Schema DBA

Searching Schema DBO

Searching Schema SYS

Tables are
app_user TABLE
bogus TABLE
company TABLE
counter TABLE
datawindow_table TABLE
department TABLE
dept_position TABLE
employee TABLE
guest_type TABLE
guests TABLE
obj_dw_table TABLE
pbcatcol TABLE
pbcatedt TABLE
pbcatftm TABLE
pbcattbl TABLE
. . .
```

Running this same command against Northwind results in the following output:

```
[Microsoft][ODBC Microsoft Access 97 Driver]Driver not capable
```

Microsoft Access 97 does not allow for this type of call; an exception occurred.

The JDK 1.1 documentation contains a list of the methods and variables for use with the `DatabaseMetaData` interface, which are too numerous to list here. Use the JDK documentation to modify the tool to suit your needs—or to have a little fun with some very simple coding that provides very useful results.

Summary

This chapter provides an overview and some examples of the different techniques you can use with Java for data storage. Among the techniques examined were these:

- Accessing databases using `java.io` and `java.net`
- Using object serialization
- Using object serialization with ODMS
- Using object serialization and RMI
- Using the JDBC

No single technique can solve every problem. If the business is creating a tracking system and wants to store data locally and upload once a day, using object serialization—with or without RMI—is the best solution. If the company wants to provide direct access to a commercial database, such as Oracle or Sybase, the JDBC is the best solution. If the company wants to store information about an object, object serialization—with or without access to an ODMS— is probably the best solution.

The point is, you should examine your requirements, security issues, the length of time you have to maintain the store, DBMS access, and other information before making a decision about which technique to use. You may find that a combination of more than one provides the best overall solution.

Getting Started with JDBC

by Shelley Powers

IN THIS CHAPTER

The Java Database Connectivity (JDBC) API includes classes that can handle most database access needs. From simple select statements to processing the results of a complex stored procedure to accessing more than one database at a time, the JDBC provides the functionality most applications need.

This chapter provides examples that use the main JDBC classes. For general information about the classes, review Chapter 19, "The SQL Package." Additionally, Chapter 42, "Databases and Java," provides information about accessing data using techniques other than the JDBC.

To use the JDBC, you must have one or more JDBC drivers written specifically to connect to the database types you are using. A list of these drivers can be found at the Sun JavaSoft site at `http://www.javasoft.com/jdbc`.

Connecting to a Database and Making Simple Queries

One very attractive aspect of the JDBC is how easy it is to use. To connect to a database, make a query, and process the results takes no more than a few lines of code, as the following sections demonstrate.

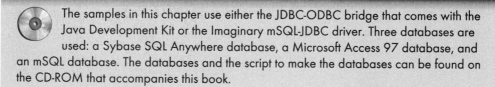

THE SAMPLES IN THIS CHAPTER

The samples in this chapter use either the JDBC-ODBC bridge that comes with the Java Development Kit or the Imaginary mSQL-JDBC driver. Three databases are used: a Sybase SQL Anywhere database, a Microsoft Access 97 database, and an mSQL database. The databases and the script to make the databases can be found on the CD-ROM that accompanies this book.

Database Connections

The database connection string is the only JDBC component that references the particular database being accessed. You must provide a specific driver connection string that uses the protocol defined for the driver. These protocols, currently maintained by JavaSoft, are used by the JDBC `DriverManager` class to determine which driver to load.

Remember to establish the database connection with the ODBC Administrator before using these sample programs. For example, to connect to a Sybase SQL Anywhere database using the JDBC-ODBC bridge, use the following connection string and connection method:

```
//connect to ODBC database
String url = "jdbc:odbc:Zoo";
// connect
Connection con = DriverManager.getConnection(url,"dba", "sql");
```

The second line of the code creates a `String` object that contains the URL for the database. The string also includes the protocol `jdbc`, the subprotocol `odbc`, and the location of the database `Zoo`. The fourth line creates the `Connection` object for the database. Because this example uses the JDBC-ODBC bridge, the database access is through the name defined with the ODBC Administration tool, found in the Control Panel group for Windows NT or 95.

Compare this example with one using the mSQL-JDBC driver and note that the URL string differs in format as well as in content:

```
//connect to database
Class.forName("imaginary.sql.iMsqlDriver");
String url = "jdbc:msql://yasd.com:1112/test";
// connect
Connection con = DriverManager.getConnection(url);
```

With this driver, the subprotocol is `msql`, and the database connection information required by the driver is a double slash followed by the name of the site, the port, and the name of the database. The port number `1112` specifically tells the mSQL-JDBC driver that the database is being run by `root` rather than by some other user name. Specifying a port number of `4333` states that the database is running under another user name, which should also be specified in the connection.

In these two examples, note that the second example loads the driver classes explicitly using the `Class.forName()` method. With this method, the class loader checks for the driver classes in the local path designated by the `CLASSPATH` variable. If the driver classes are not found and the method is called from an applet, the class loader attempts to download them from the network. Chapter 44, "Building Database Applets with JDBC," provides more information about classes and applets.

Another difference between the two examples is that the first connection, for the JDBC-ODBC bridge, uses three parameters: The connection string, the database user name, and the password. The second example, for the mSQL-JDBC driver, passes just the connection string and assumes that the connection is open to all. A third example, which follows (and which also uses the JDBC-ODBC bridge), shows a connection that uses the third `getConnection()` method, which uses a `Properties` class:

```
//connect to ODBC database
      Class.forName("sun.jdbc.odbc.JdbcOdbcDriver");
      String url = "jdbc:odbc:Zoo";
      // connect
      Properties p = new Properties();
      p.put("user", "dba");
      p.put("password","sql");
      Connection con = DriverManager.getConnection(url,p);
```

The benefit of this third technique is that the application can prompt the user for the user name and password so that the password can be entered into an encrypted field and not be hard coded into the application.

Listing 43.1 shows the complete code for connecting to an ODBC database and processing a simple query. Note that, at the end of the application, the `Connection` instance is closed. Unless resources are limited, closing the `Connection` instance is usually not necessary. When the object is no longer in scope (as is the case when the application is no longer running, the applet is unloaded, or the object is contained within a procedure or control structure that ends), normal Java garbage collection frees up the resources.

Listing 43.1. The `sample1` application using JDBC.

```
import java.lang.*;
import java.sql.*;
import sun.jdbc.odbc.*;
public class sample1
{
public static void main(String arg[]) {
int id;
float amount;
Date dt;
String status;
String result;
    try {
        //connect to ODBC database
        Class.forName("sun.jdbc.odbc.JdbcOdbcDriver");
        String url = "jdbc:odbc:Zoo";
        // connect
        Connection con = DriverManager.getConnection(url,"dba", "sql");
        // create Statement object
        Statement stmt = con.createStatement();
        String sqlselect = "Select company_id, order_dt, po_amount, status_cd"
                         + " from dba.purchase_order";
        // run query
        ResultSet rs = stmt.executeQuery(sqlselect);
        // process results
        while(rs.next()) {
                result  = "";
                id      = rs.getInt(1);
                amount  = rs.getFloat(3);
                dt      = rs.getDate(2);
                status  = rs.getString(4);
                result = result.valueOf(id) + " ";
                result+= result.valueOf(amount) + " ";
                result+= dt.toString() + " " + status;
                System.out.println("Values are: " + result);
                }

        //close connection
        con.close();
        }
    catch(Exception e) {
        System.out.println(e.getMessage());
        }
}
}
```

Once a connection is established to the database, it is used to create some kind of statement using the Statement class or one of its extensions.

The Statement Class

A statement for simple querying of a database takes the following form:

```
// create Statement object
Statement stmt = con.createStatement();
```

This type of statement can be used for single-use updates or queries to the database that do not return multiple result sets or update counts.

After the statement is created, it can be used to issue a simple query, as shown here:

```
String sqlselect = "Select company_id, order_dt, po_amount, status_cd"
        + " from dba.purchase_order";
// run query
ResultSet rs = stmt.executeQuery(sqlselect);
```

This example shows how a String object is used to hold the select statement, which is then used in the executeQuery() method call. This method, in turn, generates a ResultSet object containing the results of the query.

The preceding example shows a select statement that accesses all the data in a table. Parameters passed to the Java application can be appended to the SQL statement for a more dynamic query, as shown here:

```
String srch = arg[0];
String sqlselect = "Select company_id, order_dt, po_amount, status_cd"
        + " from dba.purchase_order where company_id = " + srch;
// run query
ResultSet rs = stmt.executeQuery(sqlselect);
```

In addition to searching for specific values, wildcard characters (also referred to as *escape* or *pattern match characters*) can be used in a search. In Java, an underscore character (_) is used to search for a single character, and a percent sign (%) is used to search for zero or more characters, as shown in Listing 43.2.

Listing 43.2. The sample2 application using escape characters.

```
import java.lang.*;
import java.sql.*;
import sun.jdbc.odbc.*;
public class sample2
{
public static void main(String arg[]) {
int id;
float amount;
Date dt;
String status;
String result;
```

continues

43

GETTING STARTED WITH JDBC

Listing 43.2. continued

```java
try {
    //connect to ODBC database
    Class.forName("sun.jdbc.odbc.JdbcOdbcDriver");
    String url = "jdbc:odbc:Zoo";
    // connect
    Connection con = DriverManager.getConnection(url,"dba", "sql");
    // create Statement object
    Statement stmt = con.createStatement();
    String srch = arg[0];
    String sqlselect = "Select company_id, order_dt, po_amount, status_cd"
                + " from dba.purchase_order where company_id = " + srch;
    // run query
    ResultSet rs = stmt.executeQuery(sqlselect);
    // process results
    while(rs.next()) {
            result  = "";
            id      = rs.getInt(1);
            amount  = rs.getFloat(3);
            dt      = rs.getDate(2);
            status  = rs.getString(4);
            result = result.valueOf(id) + " ";
            result+= result.valueOf(amount) + " ";
            result+= dt.toString() + " " + status;
            System.out.println("Values are: " + result);
            }

    //close connection
    con.close();
    }
 catch(Exception e) {
        System.out.println(e.getMessage());
    }
}
}
```

This code in Listing 43.2 looks for any company name that contains the value specified by the variable srch. Notice that the results are pulled from the row using the data type specific to the column. These values are then converted to String values using the valueOf() method. A more efficient method would have been to pull the values in directly as strings using the getString() method, but the example does demonstrate some of the other ResultSet get methods.

> **CAUTION**
>
> If you are using the escape characters, don't forget to include the surrounding quotation marks (") for the pattern-match sequence. Pattern matching is for character-based or like fields; if you forget the quotation marks, you will get an error.

You can also run update statements with the JDBC. Instead of using `executeQuery()`, your application must use `executeUpdate()`.

The update statement can be any valid data modification statement: UPDATE, DELETE, or INSERT. The result is the count of rows impacted by the change. Listing 43.3 shows an example of each of the different types of data manipulation statements.

Listing 43.3. The `sample3` application demonstrating database updates.

```
import java.lang.*;
import java.sql.*;
import sun.jdbc.odbc.*;
public class sample3
{
public static void main(String arg[]) {
    try {
        //connect to ODBC database
        Class.forName("sun.jdbc.odbc.JdbcOdbcDriver");
        String url = "jdbc:odbc:Zoo";
        // connect
        Connection con = DriverManager.getConnection(url,"dba", "sql");
        con.setAutoCommit(false);

        // create Statement object
        Statement stmt = con.createStatement();
        String updatestring = "INSERT INTO RETAIL_ITEM(item_nbr,item_desc,
                qty_per_pkg, "
                + "wholesale_cost, retail_cost, company_id, color, size) "
                + "VALUES(25,'some item', 1, 10.00, 15.00, 1, 'orange', 'M')";
        // run query
        int ct = stmt.executeUpdate(updatestring);
        // process results
        System.out.println("Insert row: " + updatestring.valueOf(ct));
        updatestring = "UPDATE PERSON "
                        + "set zip_cd = '97228' where "
                        + "zip_cd = '97229'";
        // run query
        ct = stmt.executeUpdate(updatestring);
        // process results
        System.out.println("Updated rows: " + updatestring.valueOf(ct));
        //back out modifications
        updatestring = "DELETE FROM RETAIL_ITEM "
                        + "where item_nbr = 25 and company_id = 1";
        // run query
        ct = stmt.executeUpdate(updatestring);
        // process results
        System.out.println("Delete row: " + updatestring.valueOf(ct));
        updatestring = "UPDATE PERSON "
                        + "set zip_cd = '97229' where "
                        + "zip_cd = '97228'";
        // run query
        ct = stmt.executeUpdate(updatestring);
        // process results
        System.out.println("Updated rows: " + updatestring.valueOf(ct));
```

43

GETTING STARTED WITH JDBC

continues

Listing 43.3. continued

```
      //close connection
      con.commit();
      con.close();
      }
    catch(Exception e) {
        System.out.println(e.getMessage());
        }
}
}
```

> **TIP**
>
> In Listing 43.3, note that `autocommit` is turned off for the set of transactions. If you don't turn `autocommit` off, each of the transactions would be committed as soon as it completed, rather than committing after all the transactions have completed. Because we are backing changes out, we want all the transactions to succeed before issuing a commit; otherwise all the transactions will roll back if an exception occurs (the database implements this functionality by default).

The `Statement` object can also be used in a call to a database stored procedure if no dynamic parameters are given. For procedures with `IN`, `OUT`, and `INOUT` parameters, the `CallableStatement` class is used, as explained later in this chapter.

If the statement is a query, it always returns a `ResultSet` object unless an exception occurs. The `ResultSet` object is demonstrated in more detail in the following section.

The ResultSet Class

A query returns a `ResultSet` object. This object contains the results of the query in a form that can be accessed by the application. If the query has no results, the `ResultSet` object contains no rows; otherwise, it contains rows of data matching the query (up to the limit specified for the database). If the database supports doing so, you can set the maximum number of rows using the `Statement` class method `setMaxRows()`. Once the result set is returned, you can use methods to access and process individual columns as shown in Listing 43.4.

Listing 43.4. The `sample4` application with a result set.

```
import java.lang.*;
import java.sql.*;
import sun.jdbc.odbc.*;
public class sample4
{
public static void main(String arg[]) {
int id;
```

```
String name;
String address;
String city;
String state;
String result;
    String srch = arg[0];
    try {
        //connect to ODBC database
        Class.forName("sun.jdbc.odbc.JdbcOdbcDriver");
        String url = "jdbc:odbc:Zoo";
        // connect
        Connection con = DriverManager.getConnection(url,"dba", "sql");
        // create Statement object
        Statement stmt = con.createStatement();
         stmt. setMaxRows(10);
        String sqlselect = "Select company_id, company_name, address_1, city,
                state_cd"
        + " from dba.company where company_name like '%" + srch + "%'";
                // run query
        ResultSet rs = stmt.executeQuery(sqlselect);
        // process results
        while(rs.next()) {
                result  = "";
                id      = rs.getInt(1);
                name    = rs.getString(2);
                address = rs.getString(3);
                city    = rs.getString(4);
                state   = rs.getString(5);
                result = result.valueOf(id) + " ";
                result+= name + " " + address + " ";
                result+= city + " " + state;
                System.out.println("Values are: " + result);
                }
        //close connection
        con.close();
        }
    catch(Exception e) {
        System.out.println(e.getMessage());
        }
}
}
```

Individual data types have matching get*XXX*() methods to retrieve the value in the form the application prefers. You pass to each method the number of the column representing the position it holds in the original select statement, or a text string containing the name of the column. The next() method maintains a cursor that points to the current row being processed. Each call to the method moves the cursor to the next row. When no more rows are found, the next() method returns a value of false.

You can access the columns even if you don't know the order in which the columns will be returned. Using the findColumn() method, you can look for a column with the same name as the one passed to the method; the method returns the column index. You can then use the index used to access the value, as shown in Listing 43.5.

Listing 43.5. The sample5 application using the findColumn() method.

```
// run query
        ResultSet rs = stmt.executeQuery(sqlselect);
        // process results
        while(rs.next()) {
                result  = "";
                id      = rs.getInt(rs.findColumn("company_id"));
                name    = rs.getString(rs.findColumn("company_name"));
                address = rs.getString(rs.findColumn("address_1"));
                city    = rs.getString(rs.findColumn("city"));
                state   = rs.getString(rs.findColumn("state_cd"));
                result = result.valueOf(id) + " ";
                result+= name + " " + address + " ";
                result+= city + " " + state;
                System.out.println("Values are: " + result);
                }
```

This technique is a little convoluted because you can also use the get methods that accept a string representing the column name and return the result. A partial listing of the results of running the sample5 Java application are shown here:

```
java sample5
Values are: 1 Portland T-Shirt Company 18050 Industrial Blvd. Portland, OR
Values are: 2 Tri-State Stuffed Critter 923 Hawthorne Way Vancouver WA
Values are: 3 Tigard Candy Shop 1900 Mountain Rd Tigard OR
Values are: 4 LA T-Shirt Company 13090 SW 108th Ave SW Los Angeles CA
. . .
```

In addition, you can also check to see whether a column value is null by using the wasNull() method after the getXXX() method call:

```
state   = rs.getString("state_cd");
boolean b = rs.wasNull();
if (b) {
. . .
```

The examples in this section introduced and demonstrated the Connection, Statement, and ResultSet classes. The next two sections demonstrate the use of some more complex features of the JDBC and how to access multiple heterogeneous databases.

More Complex Uses of JDBC

Occasionally, a database developer has to program for more complex database access situations. You may want to create a statement and then execute it many times, or call a stored procedure that returns multiple result sets, or issue a dynamic SQL statement. This section covers some techniques for handling these types of statements.

Two of the classes discussed, PreparedStatement and CallableStatement, are extended classes: the former is an extension of Statement and the latter is an extension of PreparedStatement.

In addition to the classes, the following sections also demonstrate and discuss the execute() method of the Statement class.

The PreparedStatement Class

The PreparedStatement class is used to create and compile a statement at the database, and then invoke that statement multiple times. The statement usually has one or more IN parameters that change each time the statement is executed.

Both the executeUpdate() and executeQuery() methods work with the PreparedStatement class. The class is an extension of the standard Statement class; it has the additional flexibility of being stored in a compiled form and run many times.

To create the PreparedStatement class statement, use a SQL string that contains references to one or more unknown parameters:

```
String sqlselect =
            "Select * from retail_item where company_id = ?";
    // create Statement object
    PreparedStatement stmt = con.prepareStatement(sqlselect);
```

Before executing the statement (in this example, it is a query), you must set the IN parameter value:

```
stmt.setInt(1,1);
rs = stmt.executeQuery();
```

After executing the query or update, you can process the results in the same way you process a regular statement:

```
int colcount = rsmd.getColumnCount();
// process results
while(rs.next()) {
        result = "";
        for (int k = 1; k <= colcount; k++) {
                result+= rs.getString(k) + " ";
                }
        System.out.println("Values are: " + result);
        }
```

The only difference between using the PreparedStatement class and the Statement class is that the same statement would then be processed for the former with different parameters.

A full example of using this class is given in Listing 43.6.

Listing 43.6. The sample6 application using the PreparedStatement class.

```
import java.lang.*;
import java.sql.*;
import sun.jdbc.odbc.*;
public class sample6
{
```

continues

Listing 43.6. continued

```java
public static void main(String arg[]) {
String result;
    try {
        //connect to ODBC database
        Class.forName("sun.jdbc.odbc.JdbcOdbcDriver");
        String url = "jdbc:odbc:Zoo";
        // connect
        Connection con = DriverManager.getConnection(url,"dba", "sql");
        con.setAutoCommit(false);
        String sqlselect =
                "Select * from retail_item where company_id = ?";
        // create Statement object
        PreparedStatement stmt = con.prepareStatement(sqlselect);
        ResultSet rs;
        ResultSetMetaData rsmd;
        for (int i = 1; i <= 3; i++) {
                stmt.setInt(1,i);
                rs = stmt.executeQuery();
                rsmd = rs.getMetaData();
                int colcount = rsmd.getColumnCount();
                // process results
                while(rs.next()) {
                    result = "";
                    for (int k = 1; k <= colcount; k++) {
                        result+= rs.getString(k) + " ";
                        }
                    System.out.println("Values are: " + result);
                    }
            }

        //close connection
        con.close();
        }
    catch(Exception e) {
        System.out.println(e.getMessage());
        }
}
}
```

Issuing an update instead of a query is no different except that the IN parameters are used to modify data instead of to select it, and that the executeUpdate() method is used instead of executeQuery():

```java
String sqlselect =
        "Update retail_item set company_id = ? where company_id = ?";
// create Statement object
PreparedStatement stmt = con.prepareStatement(sqlselect);
for (int i = 1; i <= 3; i++) {
        stmt.setInt(1,i);
        stmt.setInt(2, i + 1);
        int count = stmt.executeUpdate();
. . .
```

The purpose of the PreparedStatement class is to compile the query ahead of time, which cuts back on the time necessary to process each query or update. If you are not planning to run the SQL statement multiple times, using the PreparedStatement class is not an effective approach.

PROBLEMS WITH PreparedStatement

The PreparedStatement class may not work if the database does not maintain an open connection between transactions; if the database does not support the use of compiled SQL; or if the JDBC drivers or the database drivers do not support this type of statement. If you use the statement with a JDBC driver that doesn't support it, you get a class exception. If you use the statement with a database or driver that does not support it, you get a SQLException. In my experience, the PreparedStatement class did not work with the ODBC driver for Sybase SQL Anywhere; it also did not work with the driver I had for Microsoft Access at the time this chapter was written. Using the PreparedStatement class resulted in the error Invalid Cursor State, as shown here:

```
java sample6
Values are: 1 Eagle T-Shirt 1 8.50 14.95 1 Black S null
Values are: 4 Wolf T-Shirt 1 8.50 14.95 1 Green S null
Values are: 5 Wolf T-Shirt 1 8.50 14.95 1 Green M null
Values are: 6 Wolf T-Shirt 1 8.50 14.95 1 Green L null
Values are: 19 Snake Shirt 1 13.50 22.00 1 Green S null
Values are: 20 Snake Shirt 1 13.50 22.00 1 Green M null
Values are: 21 Snake Shirt 1 13.50 22.00 1 Green L null
Values are: 22 Cat Shirt 1 8.00 13.00 1 Green XLG null
Values are: 2 Eagle T-Shirt 1 8.50 14.95 1 Black M null
Values are: 3 Eagle T-Shirt 1 8.50 14.95 1 Black L null
Values are: 7 Wolf T-Shirt 1 8.50 14.95 1 Blue L ADSDFS
Values are: 23 Get Wild Tie Dyed T-Shirt 1 10.50 20.95 1 null XL null
Values are: 24 Leopard T-Shirt 1 9.00 14.95 1 Brown L null
Values are: 30 Test 1 12.00 13.00 1 Orange S null
Values are: 40 Cats of the World T-Shirt 1 8.00 14.00 1 Black L null
[Sybase][ODBC Driver]Invalid cursor state
```

The execute() Method

The execute() method is defined for use with the Statement class, which also makes it available for use with the PreparedStatement and CallableStatement classes. This method is used to process an unknown statement, a statement that may return multiple result sets and update counts, or both.

For example, you may have an *ad-hoc* SQL tool that allows the user to enter any valid SQL statement and then process the statement. The user passes in the SQL statement with a program call like this:

```
// create Statement object
Statement stmt = con.createStatement();
String sqlstmt = arg[0];
// run statement
boolean b = stmt.execute(sqlstmt);
```

The result returned from the execute() method is a boolean value: it is false if there are no results or the statement contains an update; it is true if the statement returns at least one result set and no update counts.

If your application cares only about processing result sets from a statement, you can process the results as follows:

```
// if true, result set
        result = "";
        if (b) {
            // process results
            ResultSet rs = stmt.getResultSet();
            ResultSetMetaData rsmd = rs.getMetaData();
            int colcount = rsmd.getColumnCount();
            while(rs.next()) {
                    result = "";
                    for (int i=1; i <= colcount; i++) {
                        result+= rs.getString(i) + " ";
                        }
                    System.out.println("Values are: " + result);
                    }
            }
    . . .
```

Normally, however, your application wants to process all the return results—if only to provide feedback to the user. Listing 43.7 provides a complete example of using the execute() method.

Listing 43.7. The sample7 application using the execute() method.

```
import java.lang.*;
import java.sql.*;
import sun.jdbc.odbc.*;
public class sample7
{
public static void main(String arg[]) {
String result;
    try {
        //connect to ODBC database
        Class.forName("sun.jdbc.odbc.JdbcOdbcDriver");
        String url = "jdbc:odbc:Zoo";
        // connect
        Connection con = DriverManager.getConnection(url,"dba", "sql");
        // create Statement object
        Statement stmt = con.createStatement();
        String sqlstmt = arg[0];
        // run statement
        boolean b = stmt.execute(sqlstmt);
        // if true, result set
        result = "";
        if (b) {
            // process results
            ResultSet rs = stmt.getResultSet();
            ResultSetMetaData rsmd = rs.getMetaData();
            int colcount = rsmd.getColumnCount();
            while(rs.next()) {
                    result = "";
```

```
                    for (int i=1; i <= colcount; i++) {
                        result+= rs.getString(i) + " ";
                        }
                    System.out.println("Values are: " + result);
                    }
                }
            else {
                int ct = stmt.getUpdateCount();
                result = "Update count is " + result.valueOf(ct);
                System.out.println(result);
                }
            //close connection
            con.close();
            }
        catch(Exception e) {
            System.out.println(e.getMessage());
            }
    }
}
```

Running the example and passing in the string `"Select * from retail_item"` returns this result (only the first few lines of the result are shown because the result is fairly lengthy):

```
java sample7 "select * from retail_item"
Values are: 1 Eagle T-Shirt 1 8.50 14.95 1 Black S null
Values are: 2 Chocolate Tigers 5 1.00 1.50 3 null M null
Values are: 3 Stuffed Panda 1 13.50 21.00 2 null L null
Values are: 4 Wolf T-Shirt 1 8.50 14.95 1 Green S null
Values are: 5 Wolf T-Shirt 1 8.50 14.95 1 Green M null
Values are: 6 Wolf T-Shirt 1 8.50 14.95 1 Green L null
Values are: 3 Keychain Zoo Pen 1 .52 1.95 8 null null null
Values are: 8 Taffy Pulls 3 .75 1.25 8 null null null
Values are: 9 Chocolate Pandas 5 1.00 1.50 3 null null null
Values are: 10 Stuffed Giraffe 1 9.95 16.95 2 null null null
```

An application rarely wants to process an unknown statement, but you may want to run a stored procedure that has multiple result sets. This type of procedure is demonstrated in the next section.

PROBLEMS WITH USING CURSORS

The execute() method requires the database to support *cursors*, which enable processing of multiple result sets. The execute() method also requires the database and database driver to support maintaining an open connection after a transaction. If the database does not support these features, the execute() method can result in an error such as invalid cursor state (as happened when I ran the sample7 application with both the Sybase SQL Anywhere ODBC driver and the Microsoft Access ODBC driver). Before spending time coding for something that may not work, test your JDBC and database drivers with the sample7 code in Listing 43.7.

The CallableStatement Class

The `CallableStatement` class is used to accept several parameters for a stored procedure call. The parameters can be defined as input only, output only, or both.

`CallableStatement` is an extension of `PreparedStatement`, which is itself an extension of `Statement`. The `CallableStatement` class adds methods to register and access output parameters.

To create a `CallableStatement` object, issue the procedure call with question marks (?) in place of parameters:

```
String scall = "call new_po(?,?,?,?,?,?,?,?,?,?)";
// create Statement object
CallableStatement stmt = con.prepareCall(scall);
```

You must first set the IN parameters using the appropriate set*XXX*() methods:

```
stmt.setInt(1, 1);
        stmt.setDate(2, dt);
        stmt.setInt(3,1);
        stmt.setDouble(4, 10.00);
        stmt.setString(5,"OP");
        stmt.setInt(6,1);
        stmt.setInt(7,1);
        stmt.setDouble(8, 10.00);
        stmt.setInt(9,61);
```

The last parameter is not set because it is an OUT parameter only. It must be registered using one of the `RegisterOutParameter()` methods:

```
stmt.registerOutParameter(10,java.sql.Types.INTEGER);
```

Because the `new_po()` procedure contains two INSERT commands and multiple result sets, in addition to the one output parameter, the execution method to use for this statement is `execute()`:

```
stmt.registerOutParameter(10,java.sql.Types.INTEGER);
// run statement
stmt.execute();
```

The result sets and update counts are then processed. Listing 43.8 shows all the code that demonstrates the use of `CallableStatement` with two insert commands.

Listing 43.8. The sample8 application using the CallableStatement class.

```
import java.lang.*;
import java.sql.*;
import sun.jdbc.odbc.*;
public class sample8
{
public static void main(String arg[]) {
String result;
Date dt = new Date(97, 12,1);
     try {
         //connect to ODBC database
```

```
        Class.forName("sun.jdbc.odbc.JdbcOdbcDriver");
        String url = "jdbc:odbc:Zoo";
        // connect
        Connection con = DriverManager.getConnection(url,"dba", "sql");
        String scall = "call new_po(?,?,?,?,?,?,?,?,?,?)";
        // create Statement object
        CallableStatement stmt = con.prepareCall(scall);
        stmt.setInt(1, 1);
        stmt.setDate(2, dt);
        stmt.setInt(3,1);
        stmt.setDouble(4, 10.00);
        stmt.setString(5,"OP");
        stmt.setInt(6,1);
        stmt.setInt(7,1);
        stmt.setDouble(8, 10.00);
        stmt.setInt(9,61);
        stmt.registerOutParameter(10,java.sql.Types.INTEGER);
        // run statement
        stmt.execute();
        // get update counts
        boolean cont = true;
        while(cont) {
                int colcount = stmt.getUpdateCount();
                if (colcount > 0) {
                        System.out.println("Updated rows are: " + colcount);
                        stmt.getMoreResults();
                        }
                else {
                        cont = false;
                        }
                }
        cont =true;
        result="";
        while(cont) {
                ResultSet rs = stmt.getResultSet();
                ResultSetMetaData rsms = rs.getMetaData();
                int colcount = rsms.getColumnCount();
                for (int i = 1; i <= colcount; i++) {
                   result+=rs.getString(i) + " ";
                   }
                System.out.println("results are " + result);
                result="";
                cont =   stmt.getMoreResults();
                }
        int po_count = stmt.getInt(10);
        System.out.println("Number of POS is " + po_count);
        //close connection
        con.close();
        }
    catch(Exception e) {
        System.out.println(e.getMessage());
        }
}
}
```

Unfortunately, when I use this code with the JDBC-ODBC bridge to access a Sybase SQL Anywhere database, I get the Function Sequence Error error:

```
java sample8
Updated rows are: 1
[Microsoft] [ODBC Driver Manager] Function sequence error
```

This ODBC DriverManager error occurs because an asynchronously executing function is called when the function is still running from the first call. According to the ODBC documentation, this error occurs when a procedure call or SQL execution statement occurs while a previous call still requires data to be passed in from parameters. After examining the data in the tables, however, I did find that the updates had occurred.

As a workaround to this problem, I modified the code (the modified example is in sample8b.java) to call a stored procedure that contains only the two updates and not the multiple result sets, as shown in Listing 43.9.

Listing 43.9 The sample8b.java application containing the stored procedure call with two updates.

```java
import java.lang.*;
import java.sql.*;
import sun.jdbc.odbc.*;

public class sample8b
{

public static void main(String arg[]) {
String result;

Date dt = new Date(97, 12,1);

    try {

        //connect to ODBC database
        Class.forName("sun.jdbc.odbc.JdbcOdbcDriver");
        String url = "jdbc:odbc:Zoo";

        // connect
        Connection con = DriverManager.getConnection(url,"dba", "sql");

        String scall = "call new_po_copy(?,?,?,?,?,?,?,?,?,?)";

        // create Statement object
        CallableStatement stmt = con.prepareCall(scall);

        stmt.setInt(1, 1);
        stmt.setDate(2, dt);
        stmt.setInt(3,1);
        stmt.setDouble(4, 10.00);
        stmt.setString(5,"OP");
        stmt.setInt(6,1);
        stmt.setInt(7,1);
        stmt.setDouble(8, 10.00);
        stmt.setInt(9,62);
```

```
            stmt.registerOutParameter(10,java.sql.Types.INTEGER);

            // run statement
            stmt.executeUpdate();

            int po_count = stmt.getInt(10);
            System.out.println("Number of POS is " + po_count);

            //close connection
            con.close();
            }
        catch(Exception e) {
            System.out.println(e.getMessage());
            }
    }
}
```

This procedure is then used in an `executeUpdate()` call. The output parameter is printed after the update occurs.

This version of the application worked without error and printed the number of purchase orders in the database, as returned in the `OUT` parameter.

> **TIP**
>
> Chapter 42, "Databases and Java," describes a database utility tool, `dbutil`, that you can modify to get information about what the database, driver, and JDBC driver can process (such as multiple result sets). You should modify this tool to check what your database and drivers can do before you code your application.

Working with Multiple Databases

The last Java application created in this chapter is one that refreshes a table in an mSQL database with the contents of a table in a Microsoft Access database. This example demonstrates the ease with which you can open and maintain multiple database connections at the same time.

The first part of the code loads the mSQL-JDBC driver classes and opens a connection to the mSQL database:

```
//connect to mSQL database
Class.forName("imaginary.sql.iMsqlDriver");
String url = "jdbc:msql://yasd.com:1112/yasd";
// mSQL connection
Connection con = DriverManager.getConnection(url);
// mSQL statement
Statement stmt = con.createStatement();
```

Next, an update is issued to delete the contents from the table being refreshed, in this case, the company table:

```
// clean out existing data
stmt.executeUpdate("DELETE from company");
```

The Access database connection and statement is created next. Note that the mSQL database is remote and that the Access database is local to the application:

```
//connect to Access database
Class.forName("sun.jdbc.odbc.JdbcOdbcDriver");
url = "jdbc:odbc:cityzoo";
// Access Connection
Connection con2 = DriverManager.getConnection(url,"Admin","sql");
// Access Statement
Statement stmt2 = con2.createStatement();
ResultSet rs = stmt2.executeQuery("Select company_id,"
        + "company_name, address_1, address_2, address_3,"
        + "city, state_cd, country_cd, postal_cd, phone_nbr "
        + "from company");
```

The data is pulled from the Access database as strings, which are then concatenated in to an insert string for the mSQL database, as shown in Listing 43.10.

Listing 43.10. The code for `sample9`, which accesses two different databases at the same time.

```
import java.sql.*;
import sun.jdbc.odbc.*;
import java.io.*;
public class sample9
{
public static void main(String arg[]) {
String invalue;
String outvalue;
String id, name, add1, add2, add3,city,state,country,post,phone;
int pos, endpos;
        try {
                System.out.println("Refreshing company...");
                //connect to mSQL database
                Class.forName("imaginary.sql.iMsqlDriver");
                String url = "jdbc:msql://yasd.com:1112/yasd";
                // mSQL connection
                Connection con = DriverManager.getConnection(url);
                // mSQL statement
                Statement stmt = con.createStatement();
                // clean out existing data
                stmt.executeUpdate("DELETE from company");
                //connect to Access database
                Class.forName("sun.jdbc.odbc.JdbcOdbcDriver");
                url = "jdbc:odbc:cityzoo";
                // Access Connection
                Connection con2 = DriverManager.getConnection(url,"Admin","sql");
                // Access Statement
                Statement stmt2 = con2.createStatement();
```

```
ResultSet rs = stmt2.executeQuery("Select company_id,"
    + "company_name, address_1, address_2, address_3,"
    + "city, state_cd, country_cd, postal_cd, phone_nbr "
    + "from company");
// for each line, enter into database
while (rs.next()) {
    // get id
    id = rs.getString(1);
    name = rs.getString(2);
        add1=rs.getString(3);
        add2=rs.getString(4);
        add3=rs.getString(5);
        city=rs.getString(6);
        state=rs.getString(7);
        country=rs.getString(8);
        post=rs.getString(9);
        phone=rs.getString(10);
        // create and execute insert statement
        stmt.executeUpdate("insert into company (company_id,
            company_name,"
            + "address_1,address_2,address_3, "
            + "city,state_cd,country_cd,postal_cd,phone_nbr)
            values("
            + id + ",'" + name + "','" + add1 + "','"
            + add2 + "','"
            + add3 + "','" + city + "','" + state + "','"
            + country + "','" + post +
            "','" + phone + "')");
        }
        stmt.close();
        stmt2.close();
        rs.close();
    }
catch(Exception e) {
    System.out.println(e.getMessage());
        }
}
}
```

43

GETTING STARTED
WITH JDBC

The PreparedStatement class would have been ideal for this type of operation, but the mSQL database does not support cursors, and the drivers for Microsoft Access do not maintain an open connection between transactions. However, the technique that was used works very well— and works fairly quickly, considering that the transactions occurred over a modem.

As a reminder, if you are working with multiple databases at the same time, you must create separate connections and statements for each of the different databases.

Summary

This chapter demonstrates how to use the most common aspects of the JDBC; all the examples use the JDBC-ODBC bridge or the mSQL-JDBC driver. Most SQL statements can be processed with all drivers; however, some statements (such as cursor-based statements) may not work with all drivers or databases. You can usually find a workaround or use a different JDBC-ODBC driver.

Using the JDBC is simple, as this chapter has shown. By using this Java API, you can run simple and complex queries and use all forms of database updates. In addition, the JDBC provides methods and classes that compile statements for later use (the `PreparedStatement` class), execute an unknown SQL statement (the `execute()` method), process multiple results and updates (the `execute()` method), and call procedures with parameters (the `CallableStatement` class).

Refer to Chapter 19, "The SQL Package," for an overview of the JDBC API. You may also want to refer to Chapter 42, "Databases and Java," for an introduction to the JDBC and the beginnings of a handy database utility called `dbutil`. Chapter 44, "Building Database Applets with the JDBC," provides examples of using the JDBC in applets.

Building Database Applets with JDBC

by Shelley Powers

IN THIS CHAPTER

CHAPTER 44

The Java Database Connectivity (JDBC) API was demonstrated in Chapter 43, "Getting Started with JDBC," but none of those examples showed how to use the JDBC to build a database-accessing applet. This chapter explains how to use the JDBC to build applets; this chapter also covers the restrictions on applets and provides examples of some typical uses.

This chapter also demonstrates probably the number one reason for using Java development tools such as Symantec Café or Microsoft Visual J++: it's easy to send information to and from the database using the JDBC but it's not so easy using the AWT (Abstract Window Toolkit) classes. The development tools automate much of the AWT class use and make it much easier to create database forms as shown in the examples.

Database Applets and Security Restrictions

Before the release of the JDK version 1.1, accessing databases from an applet that was downloaded from an HTTP server was restricted in two ways: The applet could not access native methods (that is, it could not access nonJava drivers on the client), and the applet could not access a database that was not located on the same network server as the Web server.

Not being able to access native methods—including database drivers written in C or C++—effectively eliminated the use of the JDBC-ODBC bridge for an applet. The restriction on the database location also seriously hampered most professional uses of this technology. Many companies do not have their database and Web server on the same computer—or even in the same physical location.

USING THE JDBC-ODBC BRIDGE WITH VISUAL J++

So, you created a Java applet or application using Visual J++ and the JDBC-ODBC bridge. When you ran it, however, you got a `java.lang.UnsatisfiedLinkError`. Before you start a long involved process of debugging, note that the first release of the JDBC-ODBC bridge *does not work* with the first release of Visual J++. Visual J++ implements native methods in a different manner than the JDBC-ODBC bridge and the two techniques clash.

How to work around the problem? Compile the application with Visual J++, but run it with the `java.exe` application that comes with JDK 1.1. Alternatively, compile and run the applet or application with the JDK, just make sure that `javac` cannot "see" the Microsoft classes, or you will get a compile time error.

Another limitation for applets (rather than a restriction) is that the original JDBC classes were not included as part of the core Java classes. Therefore, they were not included by the major browsers that allow Java applets. Most browsers prohibit downloading classes from a directory that begins with `java` (to prevent hackers from creating a bad extension of one of the standard Java classes and then overwriting the class in the client when the class is downloaded). Unfortunately, this "security feature" also prevents the downloading of the JDBC classes, turning the original limitation into yet another restriction: the client machine must already have the JDBC classes if any JDBC applet is to work. A workaround that some of the JDBC driver developers created was to copy the JDBC classes to another subdirectory and code their own classes accordingly.

Of course, with the release of the JDK 1.1, several of these restrictions have been either eased or eliminated.

The JDBC classes are now a part of the core Java classes, which means that anyone using a JDK 1.1-compliant browser can have access to the JDBC classes with no additional downloading.

With the new security features in JDK 1.1, an applet can be *digitally signed* as described in Chapter 16, "The Security Package," and Chapter 34, "Java Security." When an applet is digitally signed, it becomes known as a *trusted applet*, which means that it is no longer bound (or as tightly bound) by the traditional applet securities. A trusted applet can, for example, access native methods or access a database located somewhere other than on the Web server.

Loading the Database Applet

If restrictions are not an issue with an applet, what happens when the applet class is downloaded? When an applet that uses the JDBC is downloaded, nothing unusual happens until it tries to connect to a database. The first bit of code to accomplish that feat is the code to load the JDBC driver:

```
Class.forName("imaginary.sql.iMsqlDriver");
```

At this point, the browser or application tries to load the driver classes from the local CLASSPATH. If the driver classes are not found in the designated CLASSPATH, the browser or application attempts to access the driver classes using the ClassLoader(). When ClassLoader() is defined for the implemented object, it accesses the classes it requires from the network as an array of bytes, which are then translated to the necessary classes on the client side.

For example, if an applet is downloaded from a site that uses the mSQL-JDBC driver classes, and the driver is not located on the client, the HTTP log file for the server might look something like this:

```
usr1-dialup22.seattle.mci.net - - [02/Feb/1997:16:56:23 -0500] "GET /book/sample
5.html HTTP/1.0" 200 212
usr1-dialup22.seattle.mci.net - - [02/Feb/1997:16:56:27 -0500] "GET /book/sample
5.class HTTP/1.0" 200 5725
usr1-dialup22.seattle.mci.net - - [02/Feb/1997:16:56:35 -0500] "GET /book/imagin
ary/sql/iMsqlDriver.class HTTP/1.0" 200 2350
ip3.pdx1.pacifier.com - - [02/Feb/1997:16:56:37 -0500] "GET /pbug/member/company
/index.htm HTTP/1.0" 200 2699
usr1-dialup22.seattle.mci.net - - [02/Feb/1997:16:56:38 -0500] "GET /book/imagin
ary/sql/iMsqlConnection.class HTTP/1.0" 200 3661
usr1-dialup22.seattle.mci.net - - [02/Feb/1997:16:56:47 -0500] "GET /book/imagin
ary/sql/msql/MsqlException.class HTTP/1.0" 200 350
```

```
usr1-dialup22.seattle.mci.net - - [02/Feb/1997:16:56:47 -0500] "GET /book/imagin
ary/sql/msql/Msql.class HTTP/1.0" 200 350
usr1-dialup22.seattle.mci.net - - [02/Feb/1997:16:56:47 -0500] "GET /book/imagin
ary/sql/iMsqlResultSet.class HTTP/1.0" 200 350
```

As you can seen, the first access is to the page containing the applet; the second access is to the applet itself; all the accesses that follow are the results of the `ClassLoader()` pulling in the driver classes.

The advantage of this approach is that the person who accesses the applet does not have to take any heroic efforts to run the applet. The disadvantage, of course, is the additional time it takes to download the classes before the applet can run properly. However, once the classes are downloaded, most browsers cache the classes locally, eliminating the need to download the classes again on the next access.

Converting Java Database Applications to Java Applets

As you have learned, using the JDBC classes from an applet is no different than using them from a Java application—as long as restrictions are not an issue. For example, to convert some of the examples from Chapter 43, "Getting Started with JDBC," all you have to do is add the applet code to the top of the file (replacing the `main()` method) and provide an area in which you can access and display information.

The first example in Chapter 43 displayed information from a purchase order table stored in a Sybase SQL Anywhere table. The first step in converting this program is to replace the `main()` method and to redefine the class to extend the `Applet` class. Here is the original code:

```
import java.sql.*;
import sun.jdbc.odbc.*;

public class sample1
{

public static void main(String arg[]) {
```

Here is the code after it has been converted to an applet:

```
import java.applet.*;
import java.awt.*;
import java.awt.event.*;
import java.sql.*;

public class sample1 extends Applet
      implements ActionListener
{
```

Note that the `import` sections in these examples are different: The code for the applet has to include the `Applet` class and the AWT class in addition to the JDBC and driver classes.

The init() method is essential for the applet. This method is where the components necessary for accessing or displaying data are created and laid out (see Listing 44.1; the code is also on the CD-ROM that accompanies this book).

Listing 44.1. The init() method for a database-accessing applet.

```
// set background
    // create layout
    // and place applet components
public void init()
{
        // set background color and font
        setBackground(new Color(255,255,255));
        setFont(new Font("Helvetica", Font.PLAIN, 12));

        // create layout using GridBagLayout
        GridBagLayout gridbag = new GridBagLayout();
        setLayout(gridbag);

        GridBagConstraints Constraints = new GridBagConstraints();

        // define constraints for objects to be added
        Constraints.weightx=1.0;
        Constraints.weighty=0.0;
        Constraints.insets = new Insets(4, 2, 4, 2);

        Constraints.anchor=GridBagConstraints.CENTER;
        Constraints.fill = GridBagConstraints.NONE;
        Constraints.gridwidth = GridBagConstraints.REMAINDER;

        // create search button and add
        searchButton = new Button("Get all POs");

        gridbag.setConstraints(searchButton, Constraints);
        add(searchButton);
        searchButton.addActionListener(this);

        // create results text area
        textResult = new TextArea(7,80);

        // add with constraints to layout
        // change Y constraint to take up remainder of
        // height allocated to applet
        Constraints.weighty=1.0;

        gridbag.setConstraints(textResult,Constraints);
        add(textResult);
}
```

Now you can see why Java tools are becoming so popular. Connecting to the database and accessing the data are fairly trivial compared to creating the display. (And this example is a fairly simple one!)

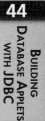

After the display is created, you code an event handler that captures the click of the searchButton button created in the init() method. The handler calls a method that finally connects to the database:

```
// handleEvent
   //
   // Overriding handleEvent allows us to
   // capture the search button push
   //
   // call super.handleEvent to allow other
   // events to be processed correctly

public void actionPerformed(ActionEvent event) {

    if (event.getSource() == searchButton) {
        processRequest();
    }
}
```

The handler must invoke the ancestor code for all events it does not process directly. The processRequest() method shown in the event-handler code connects to the database, accesses the data, and displays it as shown in Listing 44.2 (the code is also located on the CD-ROM that accompanies this book). The output is literally a direct copy of the original code, except that the query output is displayed in a field rather than to system output.

Listing 44.2. The sample1.class code performing a simple query.

```
// processRequest
   //
   // This method will load the database driver,
   // connect to the database, create the retrieval statement,
   // and output the results.
   private synchronized void processRequest()
   {
    String stringResult = "";
    String result;

    try {

        //connect to ODBC database
        Class.forName("sun.jdbc.odbc.JdbcOdbcDriver");
        String url = "jdbc:odbc:Zoo";

        // connect
        Connection con = DriverManager.getConnection(url,"dba", "sql");

        // create Statement object
        Statement stmt = con.createStatement();

        String sqlselect = "Select company_id, order_dt, po_amount, status_cd"
                    + " from dba.purchase_order";

        // run query
        ResultSet rs = stmt.executeQuery(sqlselect);
```

```
        // process results - could have processed in a loop
    while(rs.next()) {
            result = "";
            result = rs.getString(1) + "\t";
            result+= rs.getString(3) + "\t";
            result+= rs.getDate(2) + "\t";
            result+= rs.getString(4) + "\n";
            stringResult+=result;
            }

    textResult.setText(stringResult);

    // close result set and statement
    rs.close();
    stmt.close();
    }
    // catch all exceptions and print out exception message
    catch (Exception e) {
        textResult.setText(e.getMessage());
    }
  }
```

What's the main difference between this method and the same processing approach in the original code in Listing 44.1? Aside from using different result set access methods, the difference is in one line:

```
textResult.setText(stringResult);
```

compared to:

```
System.out.println("Values are: " + result);
```

If you run the applet using the applet viewer utility that comes with the JDK, your results will look similar to those shown in Figure 44.1. Note that to use this utility, you must embed the applet into an HTML file and run that file. The samples in this chapter all come with associated HTML files.

Figure 44.1.

A simple database query applet.

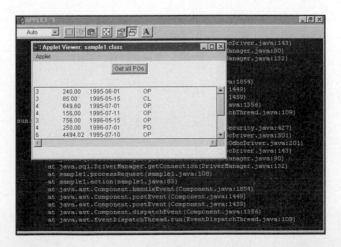

To convert a Java database application to a Java applet, follow these steps:

1. Add in the `import` statements for the `Applet` and AWT classes. Applets require the `Applet` class; most applets use some form of interface component, which the AWT classes provide.

2. Replace the `main()` method with an implementation of the `Applet` class. Note, however, that you can keep the `main()` function. The applet should work correctly.

3. (Optional) Add a constructor, a destructor, an optional `getAppletInfo()` method, `start()`, `stop()`, and `paint()` applet methods, and any other methods you think apply. The default behavior for these `Applet` methods is handled by the `Applet` class if you do not override the methods.

4. Add an `init()` method and create your data access and display components in this method.

5. Make sure that the code accesses data from components rather than from the command line or system input, and that it displays data to components rather than to the system output.

You can find more information about creating applets in Chapter 8, "Introduction to Applet Programming"; you can find more information about using the interface components of the AWT in Chapter 22, "Creating User Interface Components."

A Simple Update Applet

If you want your applet to make a modification to the data in the database, you must provide components for the user to use to input data.

 In this section, you create a sample applet that accesses data from the user and updates the `retail_item` table from the sample Sybase SQL Anywhere database, `Zoo`, included on the CD-ROM that accompanies this book.

The `retail_item` table contains the following fields:

Field	Description
item_nbr	Integer field containing item identifier
item_desc	Text field containing item description
qty_per_pkg	Integer field containing the number of items contained in each package sold
wholesale_cost	Numeric field containing the wholesale cost of the item
retail_cost	Numeric field containing the retail cost of the item
company_id	Integer identifier of the company that makes the item
color	Optional color of the item

Field	Description
size	Optional size of the item
company_item_identifier	Not used in this example

The fields used to reference the `retail_item` columns just mentioned must be available to all methods for the class. These fields are defined as `private` members of the class:

```
private Button        updateButton;
private TextField     itemNbr;
private TextField     itemDesc;
private TextField     itemQty;
private TextField     itemWholesale;
private TextField     itemRetail;
private TextField     itemCompany;
private TextField     itemColor;
private TextField     itemSize;
private TextField     textResult;
```

The fields are defined as `private` only because they are not available to any other class; however, they could just as easily have been defined as `public`.

 Next, the components must be created and laid out. The `init()` method of the sample class looks similar to Listing 44.3 if we limit our AWT layout classes to the `BorderLayout` and `FlowLayout` classes. This code can also be found on the accompanying CD-ROM.

Listing 44.3. The `init()` method of the sample applet.

```
// set background
   // create layout
   // and place applet components
public void init()
{
        // set background color and font
        setBackground(new Color(255,255,255));
        setFont(new Font("Helvetica", Font.PLAIN, 12));

        // create borderlayout
        setLayout(new BorderLayout(5,5));

        // create upperpanel
        Panel upperpanel = new Panel();
        upperpanel.setLayout(new BorderLayout());

        // create top panel of upper panel
        Panel uppertoppanel = new Panel();
        uppertoppanel.setLayout(new FlowLayout(1,5,5));

        uppertoppanel.add(new Label("Item Nbr:"));
        itemNbr = new TextField("",5);
        uppertoppanel.add(itemNbr);
```

continues

44

BUILDING
DATABASE APPLETS
WITH JDBC

Listing 44.3. continued

```
uppertoppanel.add(new Label("Item Desc:"));
itemDesc = new TextField("", 25);
uppertoppanel.add(itemDesc);

upperpanel.add("North", uppertoppanel);

// create bottom panel of upper panel
Panel upperbotpanel = new Panel();
upperbotpanel.setLayout(new FlowLayout(1,5,5));

upperbotpanel.add(new Label("Item Qty:"));
itemQty = new TextField("",3);
upperbotpanel.add(itemQty);

upperbotpanel.add(new Label("Item Wholesale Cost:"));
itemWholesale = new TextField("", 7);
upperbotpanel.add(itemWholesale);

upperpanel.add("South", upperbotpanel);

// add to main borderlayout
add("North", upperpanel);

// create middlepanel
Panel middlepanel = new Panel();
middlepanel.setLayout(new BorderLayout());

// create top panel of middle panel
Panel middletoppanel = new Panel();
middletoppanel.setLayout(new FlowLayout(1,5,5));

middletoppanel.add(new Label("Item Retail:"));
itemRetail = new TextField("",7);
middletoppanel.add(itemRetail);

middletoppanel.add(new Label("Item Company:"));
itemCompany = new TextField("", 3);
middletoppanel.add(itemCompany);

middlepanel.add("North", middletoppanel);

// create bottom panel of middle panel
Panel middlebotpanel = new Panel();
middlebotpanel.setLayout(new FlowLayout(1,5,5));

middlebotpanel.add(new Label("Item Color:"));
itemColor = new TextField("",8);
middlebotpanel.add(itemColor);

middlebotpanel.add(new Label("Item Size:"));
itemSize = new TextField("", 8);
middlebotpanel.add(itemSize);

middlepanel.add("South", middlebotpanel);

add("Center", middlepanel);
```

```
        // add bottom layer
        Panel botpanel = new Panel();
        botpanel.setLayout(new FlowLayout(1,5,5));
        updateButton = new Button("   Update   ");
        updateButton.addActionListener(this);

        botpanel.add(updateButton);

        textResult = new TextField("", 25);
        botpanel.add(textResult);

        add("South", botpanel);
}
```

The `BorderLayout` container class allows you to insert components using the geographical place names "`North`", "`South`", "`East`", "`West`", and "`Center`". Alternatively, the `FlowLayout` container class allows you to add components that are placed one after another in a linear manner. Both layout managers are relatively simple to use. In Listing 44.3, notice the use of the `panel` object. The `panel` object allows you to implement a different layout container, which is then inserted into another layout container, and so on. This capability allows developers to use a variety of layouts to display components.

Once the layout is created, you create the event handler for the update button:

```
// handleEvent
    //
    // Overriding handleEvent allows us to
    // capture the search button push
    //
    // call super.handleEvent to allow other
    // events to be processed correctly

public void actionPerformed(ActionEvent event) {
    if (event.getSource() == updateButton) {
        processRequest();
    }
}
```

 Finally, the code to process the database update is created, as shown in Listing 44.4. This file can also be found on the accompanying CD-ROM.

Listing 44.4. The `sample2.class` code to update a database table.

```
// processRequest
//
// This method will load the database driver,
// connect to the database, create the retrieval statement
// and output the results.
private synchronized void processRequest()
{
    String stringResult = "";
```

continues

Listing 44.4. continued

```java
String result;

String stringNbr,
       stringDeso,
       stringQty,
       stringWholesale,
       stringRetail,
       stringCompany,
       stringColor,
       stringSize;

try {

//connect to ODBC database
Class.forName("sun.jdbc.odbc.JdbcOdbcDriver");
String url = "jdbc:odbc:Zoo";

// connect
Connection con = DriverManager.getConnection(url,"dba", "sql");

textResult.setText("Connected...");

// create Statement object
Statement stmt = con.createStatement();

// get insert values
stringNbr = itemNbr.getText();
stringDesc = itemDesc.getText();
stringQty = itemQty.getText();
stringWholesale = itemWholesale.getText();
stringRetail = itemRetail.getText();
stringCompany = itemCompany.getText();
stringColor = itemColor.getText();
stringSize = itemSize.getText();

String updatestring = "INSERT INTO RETAIL_ITEM(item_nbr,item_desc,
       qty_per_pkg, "
       + "wholesale_cost, retail_cost, company_id, color, size) "
       + "VALUES(" + stringNbr + ",'" + stringDesc +
       "'," + stringQty + "," + stringWholesale + "," +
       stringRetail + "," + stringCompany + ",'" +
       stringColor + "','" + stringSize + "')";

// run query
textResult.setText("Working...");
int ct = stmt.executeUpdate(updatestring);

textResult.setText("completed");

// close statement
stmt.close();
}
// catch all exceptions and print out exception message
catch (Exception e) {
    textResult.setText(e.getMessage());
}

}
```

As you can see from this example, the values are accessed from the AWT components and then used to create an update string. Once the update string is created and executed, the results of the update are output to the results field. Notice that the code also outputs text strings that inform the user of the progress of the update. This notification is essential, especially for longer transactions. If you don't have such a notification scheme, your user will wonder whether an error has occurred.

The example just shown is simpler than you would find in a real-world business application. The example does no checking to make sure that mandatory fields are filled in and does no checking to see whether the user entered appropriate values. Also, a production-quality applet would probably use a drop-down list for the company identifier field and would pull in values from the database and load them to the list when the applet is initialized.

If you run this sample applet using the applet viewer, you should see something similar to Figure 44.2 when the applet loads. In the figure, behind the applet is the DOS window containing the class activity of the applet. If you type some values, the applet looks similar to Figure 44.3.

FIGURE 44.2.

The sample2 applet after being loaded.

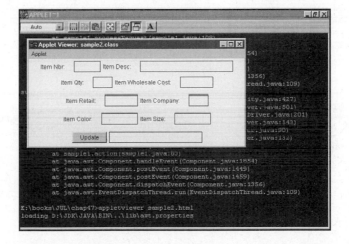

After you enter the values and click the Update button, the applet runs. In Figure 44.4, note that the result field shows the value completed. This notification means that the record was successfully entered into the database.

Now that you have added data to the database, you may find it handy to review the data for accuracy. The next section creates a simple query-based applet to do just that.

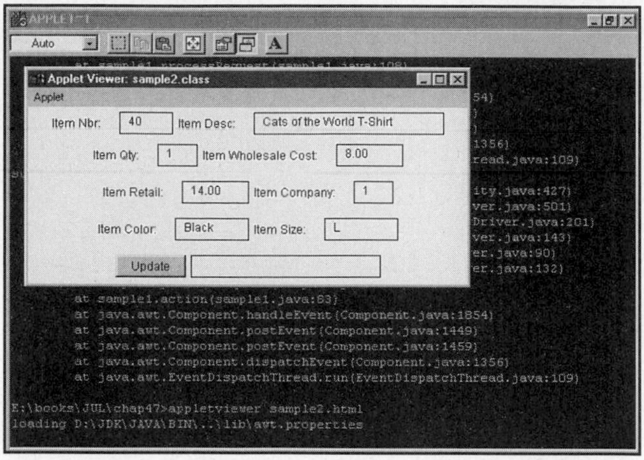

FIGURE 44.3.

The `sample2` *applet after data has been typed into AWT components.*

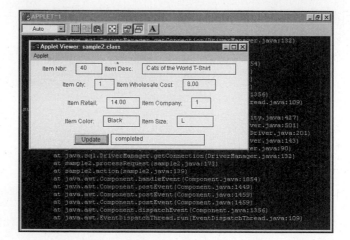

FIGURE 44.4.

The `sample2` *applet after the record insert is completed.*

A Simple Query Applet

Once you have successfully created an applet that enters data into a database, you will want to create an applet that enables one or more people to view the data.

Creating an applet to display data is no different than creating one to update a database. AWT components that must be accessed by both the `init()` method and the database-processing method are usually defined as members of the `Applet` class. In the next example, the `retail_item` table from the preceding example is used as the basis for a query. The user can view all the records of the table or can choose to view retail items of a certain color, size, or both. Based on these criteria, two components must be created to access the two query values of color and size. Additional components are a button that runs the query and a text field that displays the results. Following is the definition of the members for the new applet:

```
Choice      colorChoice;
Choice      sizeChoice;
Button      searchButton;

TextArea    resultsTextArea;
```

 For this applet, I decided to use drop-down list boxes (also called *choice components*) for the two query values. This arrangement assists users by providing a list of valid query values. The init() method uses a combination of BorderLayout, FlowLayout, and GridBagLayout container layout classes (see Listing 44.5 and the accompanying CD-ROM). I used the GridBagLayout class because it allows the developer to define a component that takes up the remainder of the space allocated to the applet (both vertically and horizontally).

Listing 44.5. The init() method for the query applet.

```
// init()
    //
    // method will instantiate the applet
    //
    // the applet objects will be created and placed
    // in this method
    //

public void init()
{
        Panel       layout_area;
        Panel       search_area;
        Panel       result_area;

        // set background to white
        setBackground(new Color(255,255,255));

        // create border layout as default
        setLayout(new BorderLayout());

        layout_area = new Panel();
        layout_area.setLayout(new BorderLayout());

        // add layout_area to top of background panel
        add("North",layout_area);

        // add top label to layout
        setFont(new Font("Helvetica",Font.BOLD,12));
        layout_area.add("North",new Label("Enter value(s) to search on:"));
        setFont(new Font("Helvetica",Font.PLAIN,12));

        // create gridlayout search panel
        // add to background layout
        {
            search_area = new Panel();
            search_area.setLayout(new FlowLayout(1,5,5));
            layout_area.add("Center",search_area);

            // create color Choice object
            // add to layout with label
```

continues

Listing 44.5. continued

```java
                // create Choice object colorChoice
                // add colors to Choice object
                colorChoice = new Choice();
                search_area.add(colorChoice);

                colorChoice.addItem("");
                colorChoice.addItem("Red");
                colorChoice.addItem("Orange");
                colorChoice.addItem("Navy");
                colorChoice.addItem("Green");
                colorChoice.addItem("Yellow");
                colorChoice.addItem("White");
                colorChoice.addItem("Black");
                colorChoice.addItem("Blue");
                colorChoice.addItem("Purple");

                search_area.add(new Label("Color:"));

                // create Choice object sizeChoice
                // add sizes to Choice object
                sizeChoice = new Choice();
                search_area.add(sizeChoice);

                sizeChoice.addItem("");
                sizeChoice.addItem("T");
                sizeChoice.addItem("J");
                sizeChoice.addItem("S");
                sizeChoice.addItem("M");
                sizeChoice.addItem("L");
                search_area.add(new Label("Size:"));

                search_area.add(new Label("      "));
                searchButton = new Button("  Search  ");
                searchButton.addActionListener(this);
                search_area.add(searchButton);
        }

        // create another panel for the result set
        // make the type of layout GridBagLayout
        {
                result_area = new Panel();

                // add results label
                setFont(new Font("Helvetica",Font.BOLD,12));
                add("Center", new Label("Results:"));
                setFont(new Font("Courier",Font.PLAIN,12));

                add("South",result_area);

                GridBagLayout gridbag = new GridBagLayout();
                result_area.setLayout(gridbag);

                GridBagConstraints Constraints = new GridBagConstraints();
                Constraints.weightx=1.0;
                Constraints.weighty=1.0;
                Constraints.anchor = GridBagConstraints.CENTER;
                Constraints.fill = GridBagConstraints.BOTH;
                Constraints.gridwidth = GridBagConstraints.REMAINDER;
```

```
                // create results text area
                resultsTextArea = new TextArea(15,60);

                // add with constraints to layout
                gridbag.setConstraints(resultsTextArea,Constraints);
                result_area.add(resultsTextArea);

                resultsTextArea.setEditable(false);
        }
}
```

After each Choice component is created, data values are added to it using the addItem() method. When the user clicks the down arrow for the component, a list box opens, displaying the values that have been added to it. The user can then click any one of these options to make it the selected item for that component.

USING DIFFERENT FONTS

As you can see in the preceding code samples, you can use different fonts and sizes in the same applet. You may find it effective to use a larger font for buttons and labels and a smaller font for the displayed result.

 Listing 44.6 shows the rest of the query applet, which includes the event handler, the database connection method, and a method that gets the query values and builds a where clause for the query. You can also find this code on the CD-ROM that accompanies this book.

Listing 44.6. sample3: A simple database query applet.

```
// check to see if event was search button being
   // pressed;
   // if so
   //        connect to database
   //        create query
   //        send statement
   //        process results
   //   else
   //        disregard
   //
    public void actionPerformed(ActionEvent event) {
     if (event.getSource() == searchButton) {
         processRequest();
         }
     }

  // process_request
  //
  // connect to database
```

continues

Listing 44.6. continued

```java
// build where clause
// retrieve data
// output results
public void processRequest()
  {
      String whereString = "";
      String stringSelect = "";
      String tempString = "";
      String stringResult = "";

      try {
          resultsTextArea.setText("working...");

          //connect to database
          Class.forName("sun.jdbc.odbc.JdbcOdbcDriver");
          String url = "jdbc:odbc:Zoo";

          // connect
          con = DriverManager.getConnection(url, "dba", "sql");

          // create Statement
          stmt = con.createStatement();

          whereString = buildWhere();

          // execute statement
          stringSelect = "Select retail_item.item_nbr," +
              "retail_item.item_desc,retail_item.qty_per_pkg," +
              "retail_item.color," +
              "retail_item.size,retail_item.retail_cost " +
              "from retail_item" + whereString;

          rs =  stmt.executeQuery(stringSelect);

          resultsTextArea.setText("Processing Results...");

          while (rs.next()) {

              // get item number
              tempString = rs.getString(1) + "\t";
              stringResult+=tempString;

              // get description
              tempString=rs.getString(2) + "\t";
              stringResult+=tempString;

              // get qty
              tempString = rs.getString(3) + "\t";
              stringResult+=tempString;

              // get color
              tempString = rs.getString(4) + "\t";
              if (rs.wasNull()) {
                      tempString = "\t\t";
                      }
              stringResult+=tempString;
```

```
              // get size
              tempString = rs.getString(5) + "\t";
              if (rs.wasNull()) {
                      tempString = "\t\t";
                      }
              stringResult+=tempString;

              // get retail cost
              tempString="$" + rs.getString(6) + "\n";
              stringResult+=tempString;
      }
      if (stringResult == "") {
          stringResult = "No Data Found for Query \n" + stringSelect;
      }
      resultsTextArea.setText(stringResult);

      stmt.close();
      rs.close();
      }

      catch (Exception e) {
          resultsTextArea.setText(e.getMessage());
      }
}

// buildWhere
//
// check Choice components
// if an item is selected and is not
//   the one at position 0, access the selected item
// if choice is category, access the category code
// return generated where clause
public String buildWhere()
{
    String colorString = null;
    String sizeString = null;
    String whereString = null;

    int colorInt = colorChoice.getSelectedIndex();
    if (colorInt > 0) {
        colorString = colorChoice.getSelectedItem();
    }

    int sizeInt = sizeChoice.getSelectedIndex();
    if (sizeInt > 0) {
        sizeString = sizeChoice.getSelectedItem();
    }

    if (colorString != null) {
        whereString = " Where ";
        whereString = whereString + " retail_item.color = '" + colorString +"'";
    }

    if (sizeString != null) {
        if (whereString == null) {
            whereString = " Where ";
        }
```

continues

Listing 44.6. continued

```
            else {
                whereString = whereString + " and ";
            }
            whereString = whereString + " retail_item.size = '" + sizeString +
                "'";
        }
    if (whereString == null) {
        whereString = "";
    }
    return whereString;
}
```

The applet checks to see whether the user selected a color and size value and uses these to modify the query string. The results are parsed with a tab character (/t) appended to add some white space between the fields. The results are then displayed in the TextArea result field.

Also consider the processRequest() method; it uses the JDBC wasNull() method to check the code to see whether a value is returned from some fields. This function is called after the get method to see whether the returned result is null. You should make this check on any field defined as optional (that is, any field for which null values are allowed) in the database. Figure 44.5 shows the newly loaded applet in the applet viewer.

TIP

Use the result field to display the query string if no data is found. In this way, you can determine whether no data was found because there was none to match the query, or because the query did not contain all the components you assumed it would contain.

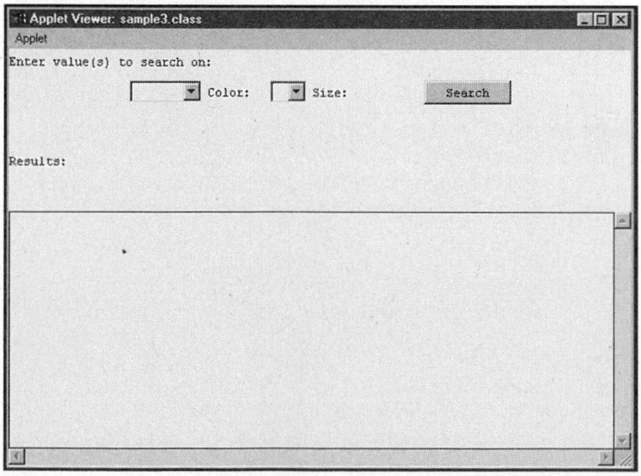

FIGURE 44.5.

The sample3 *applet after loading.*

If you select all the `Black` retail items and run the applet, you see results similar to those shown in Figure 44.6. If you select all the `Black` retail items of size `L` (large), you see a smaller subset of records, as shown in Figure 44.7.

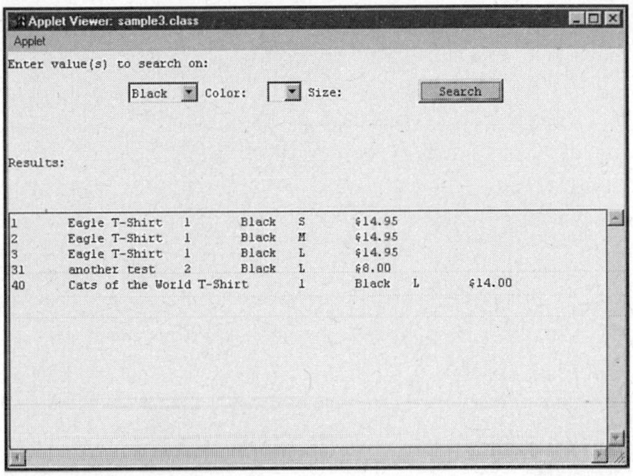

FIGURE 44.6.

The sample3 *applet with all* Black *retail items selected.*

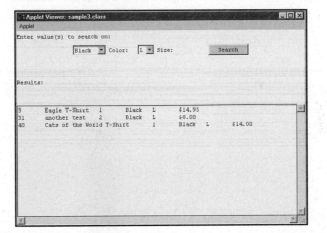

FIGURE 44.7.

The sample3 *applet with all* Black Large *retail items selected.*

Summary

This chapter introduced the techniques of using the JDBC with applets. Not all JDBC technology is accessible by an applet, although these restrictions and limitations have improved with the new security features of the JDK 1.1.

You use the JDBC from an applet no differently than you use the JDBC from an application—except that you must use the AWT component classes to provide a way to access and display data. Although this chapter did not explain the AWT, it did demonstrate how to display query results and access data for a database update.

X PART

IN THIS PART

Integrating Java with Other Technologies

Building VRML 2 Behaviors in Java

by Justin Couch
revised by Bruce Campbell

IN THIS CHAPTER

You've probably had enough of buttons, menus, and creating a hundred and one pictures for animations. Now you're looking for something a little different. If you have been following the computing press, you may have noticed discussions about another hot Web technology called VRML—the Virtual Reality Modeling Language. VRML is designed to produce the 3D equivalent of HTML: a three-dimensional scene defined in a machine-neutral format that can be viewed by anyone with an appropriate viewer. VRML is similar to HTML in that it can be created with a simple ASCII editor such as Notepad and delivered across the Web by the same Web server that delivers HTML documents.

The first version of the standard, VRML 1, produced static scenes that could be visited by anyone with a VRML 1 browser or appropriate VRML 1 plug-in viewer created for use with the Netscape Navigator or Internet Explorer browser. VRML 1 is a derivative of Silicon Graphic's Open Inventor file format. In that first version, a user could visit a 3D scene by walking or flying around, but there was no way to interact with the scene apart from clicking on the 3D equivalent of hypertext links. This was a deliberate decision on the part of the designers. VRML 1 was enough to get the art community interested in creating some beautiful virtual places.

In December 1995, the VRML community decided to drop planned revisions to version 1 and head straight to a fully interactive version, VRML 2. One of the prime requirements for VRML 2 was the ability to support programmable behaviors. Of the seven proposals, the Moving Worlds submission by Sony and SGI came out as the favorite among the 2,000 members of the VRML mailing list. Contained in a draft proposal for VRML 2 was a Java API for creating behaviors for objects in a VRML 2 scene.

Effectively combining VRML and Java requires a good understanding of how both languages work. This chapter introduces the Java implementation of the VRML API and shows you how to get the most from a dynamic virtual world. For specifics about VRML 2, *Teach Yourself VRML 2 in 21 days*, published by Sams.net, is an excellent reference book.

Interestingly enough, Sony has implemented a Java API in its CommunityPlace VRML 2 viewer. This Java API is somewhat different than the Java API implemented by SGI in its CosmoPlayer VRML 2 viewer. Although they use the same basic class structure, you can think of Sony's approach as adding Java scripting to the VRML 2 node structure and SGI's approach as providing VRML 2 3D graphics output capabilities to any Java program. Each of these approaches to integrating Java with VRML has its strengths and weaknesses. Both methods are covered in this chapter with appropriate code examples. SGI has promoted a VRML-specific scripting language called VRMLscript, which you can use instead of Java when you are scripting behaviors; VRMLscript is similar to Sony's interpretation of intranode scripting. Consult a VRML 2 reference for the specifics of VRMLscript. VRMLscript is an appropriate alternative for Java scripting on many occasions, but is more similar to JavaScript than it is to the Java language itself.

Making the World Behave

Within the virtual reality environment, any dynamic change in a virtual world is regarded as a *behavior*. This change can be something as simple as an object changing color when it is touched or something as complex as autonomous, semi-intelligent agents that look and act like humans, such as Neal Stephenson's Librarian from his visionary, sci-fi novel *Snow Crash*.

To understand how to create behaviors for virtual objects, you have to understand how VRML works. Although this section won't delve into a lengthy discussion of VRML, a few basic concepts are reviewed. To start with, VRML is a separate language from the Java programming language used in scripts. The Java VRML classes interact only with a preexisting VRML scene contained in a file with a .wrl extension. The scene is developed using the VRML language to create a collection of VRML nodes; the scene is then associated with a rectangular region within the browser window. The VRML browser then provides a consistent method for moving around in the scene and interacting with it. Although it is possible to create a VRML browser exclusively in Java, both Sony and SGI have compiled machine-dependent browsers for the purposes of rendering speed. Even with a VRML browser written in Java, a scene must be created using VRML, which the Java VRML classes can then dynamically change over time.

Within Sony's CommunityPlace Java API, each virtual object can have its own script attached to it. Creating a highly complex world in this manner requires writing many short scripts. For more interesting behaviors, a longer, heavyweight script can combine the VRML API classes with Java's thread and networking classes.

To minimize the amount of external programming, the VRML specification contains a number of nodes to create common behaviors within the .wrl file itself. These nodes are of two types: sensors and interpolators. *Sensor nodes* initiate events when the user interacts with the sensor. Sensors are associated with virtual objects, timers, and locations in three-dimensional space. A *location* is a 3D volume defined by a cylinder, disk, plane, sphere, or point. Sensors initiate events based on touch (such as a mouse click), time, or proximity (to the user's viewpoint). *Interpolators* change a virtual object over time between specific end-point values defined by the VRML author. Interpolators are available for changing color, scale, position, and orientation over time. By using the specifics of VRML 2, a sensor can turn on a timer that then interpolates the value of a virtual object's characteristic over time. An example is a virtual doorbell that senses a user's mouse click and turns on an orientation interpolator that opens a door slowly over a specific time period. This door example is easily included in a VRML scene without Java.

An Overview of VRML

The VRML world description uses a traditional hierarchical scene-graph approach reminiscent of PEX/PHIGS and other 3D toolkits. A *scene graph* is a document used to express the hierarchical relationships between all the objects in a scene. The word *graph* as used in the term *scene graph* refers to an organization of objects described by certain mathematical characteristics. In a graph, each object in the scene is called a *node*, and each connecting line is called an *edge*. Each node within a scene graph has a parent, and each parent can have multiple children. As an example of a hierarchical VRML scene graph, a body Transform node can include two leg Transform nodes, each of which can contain a foot Transform node, which can contain five toe Transform nodes. The toe Transform node can have children nodes that define its geometry, texture, and color as well as a sensor to make it interactive.

Surprisingly, VRML nodes can be represented in a semiobject-oriented manner that meshes well with Java. Each node has a number of fields. These fields can be accessed by other nodes only if they are explicitly declared to be accessible. You can declare a field as read or write only, or you can define it to require a specific method to access its value. In VRML syntax, the four types of field access are described as follows:

- **field:** Hidden from general access—a private field
- **eventIn:** Sends a value to a node—a write-only field
- **eventOut:** Sends a value from a node—a read-only field
- **exposedField:** Publicly accessible for both read and write

The official VRML 2 node definition specifies the standard accessibility of each field in a node; you must then consider accessibility when you are writing behavior scripts. Most scripts are written to process a value being passed to the script in the form of an eventIn field, which then passes the result back through an eventOut field. Any internal values are kept in fields. The Script can be defined as a node within the scene graph. These Script nodes are not permitted to have exposedFields because of the updating and implementation ramifications within the event system.

Although a node can consist of a number of input and output fields, these fields do not all have to be connected. Usually, the opposite is the case—only a few of the available connections are made. VRML requires explicit connection of nodes using the ROUTE keyword, as shown here:

```
ROUTE fromNode.fieldname1 TO toNode.fieldname2
```

The only restriction when connecting fields is that the two fields be of the same type. No casting of types is permitted.

This route mechanism can be very powerful when combined with scripting. Basically, both a VRML ROUTE statement and a Java script can send an eventIn field or process an eventOut field. The specification allows both fan in and fan out of events. *Fan in* occurs when many nodes send an event to a single eventIn field of a node. *Fan out* is the opposite: one eventOut object is connected to many other eventIn objects. Fan out is handy when you want one script to control a number of different objects at the same time; for example, a light switch eventOut object turning on multiple lights simultaneously.

If two or more events fan in on a particular eventIn object, the results are undefined. You should be careful to avoid such situations unless the ambiguity is intended. An example of this situation is when two separate animation scripts set the position of the same virtual object. To avoid this situation in a complicated animated scene, create an event graph with arrows showing the direction of events firing from one node to another. Then make sure that any two or more events coming in to the same node cannot possibly fire at the same time.

All VRML data types follow the standard programming norms. There are integer, floating-point, string, and boolean standard types as well as specific types for handling 3D graphics such as points, vectors, image, and color. To deal with the extra requirements of the VRML scene, node and time types have been added. The node data type contains an instance pointer to a particular node in the VRML scene graph (such as a virtual toe or foot). Individual fields within a node are not accessible directly. Individual field references in behaviors programming is rarely necessary because communication is on an event-driven model. When field references are needed within the API, a node instance and field string description pair are used.

Except for the boolean and time types, which are always single, values can be either single or multivalued. The distinction is made in the field name. An SF prefix is used for single-valued fields and an MF prefix is used for multivalued fields. For example, type SFInt32 defines a single integer; type MFInt32 defines an array of integers. The Script node definition in the next section contains an MFString and a SFBool. The MFString is used to contain a collection of URLs, each kept in its own separate substring, but the SFBool contains a single boolean flag controlling a condition.

The VRML Script Node

The Script node provides the way to integrate a custom behavior into VRML. Behaviors can be programmed in any language supported by the browser and for which an implementation of the API can be found. In the final specification of VRML 2, sample APIs were provided for Java, C, and also VRML's own scripting language, VRMLscript—a derivative of Netscape's JavaScript. The Script node is defined as shown here:

```
Script {
  exposedField MFString url                []
  field        SFBool   directOutput       FALSE
  field        SFBool   mustEvaluate       FALSE
  # And any number of:
  eventIn      eventTypeName eventName
  field        fieldTypeName fieldName initialValue
  eventOut     eventTypeName eventName
}
```

Unlike standard HTML, VRML enables multiple target files of an open location request to be specified in order of preference. The url field contains any number of strings specifying URLs or URNs to the desired behavior script. For compiled Java scripts, this would be the URL of the .class file, but the url list is not limited to just one script type.

Apart from specifying the behavior file, VRML also enables control over how the Script node performs within the scene graph. The mustEvaluate field tells the browser how often the script should be run. If this field is set to TRUE, the browser must send events to the script as soon as they are generated, forcing an execution of the script. If the field is set to FALSE, in the interests of optimization, the browser may elect to queue events until the outputs of the script are required by the browser. A TRUE setting is most likely to cause browser performance to degrade because of the constant context-swapping needed; a FALSE setting queues events to keep the context-swapping to a minimum. Unless you are performing something the browser is not aware of (such as using a networking or database functionality), you should set the mustEvaluate field to FALSE.

The directOutput field controls whether the script has direct access for sending events to other nodes. Java methods require the node reference of other nodes when setting field values. If, for example, a script is passed an instance of a Transform node, and the directOutput field is set to TRUE, the script can send an event directly to that node. To add a new default box to this group, the script would contain the following code:

```
SFNode     group_node = (SFNode)getField("group_node");
group_node.postEventIn("add_children", (Field)CreateVRMLfromString("Box"));
```

If directOutput is set to FALSE, it requires the Script node to have an eventOut field with the corresponding event type specified (an MFNode in this case), and a ROUTE connecting the script with the target node.

There are advantages to both approaches. When the scene graph is static in nature, the second approach (using known events and ROUTE statements) is much simpler. However, in a scene in which objects are being generated on the fly, static routing and events do not work and the first approach is required.

VRML Data Types in Java

The API is built around two Java interfaces defined in the package vrml. The eventIn and Node interfaces are defined as follows:

```
interface eventIn {
    public String       getName();
    public SFTime        getTimeStamp();
    public ConstField    getValue();
}
interface Node {
    public ConstField getValue(String fieldName)
        throws InvalidFieldException;
```

```
    public void postEventIn(String eventName, Field eventValue)
        throws InvalidEventInException;
}
```

In addition to these two interfaces, each of the VRML field types also has two class definitions that are subclasses of `Field`: a standard version and a restricted, read-only version. The `Const*` definitions are used only in the `eventIn` fields defined in individual scripts. Unless that field class has an exception explicitly defined, these class definitions are guaranteed not to generate exceptions.

For nonconstant fields, each class has at least the `setValue()` and `getValue()` methods that return the Java equivalent of the VRML field type. For example, a `SFRotation` class returns an array of floats mapping to the x, y, z, and orientation, but the `MFRotation` class returns a two-dimensional array of floats. The multivalued field types also have a `set1Value()` method, which enables the caller to set an individual element.

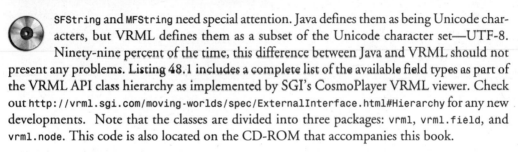 `SFString` and `MFString` need special attention. Java defines them as being Unicode characters, but VRML defines them as a subset of the Unicode character set—UTF-8. Ninety-nine percent of the time, this difference between Java and VRML should not present any problems. Listing 48.1 includes a complete list of the available field types as part of the VRML API class hierarchy as implemented by SGI's CosmoPlayer VRML viewer. Check out `http://vrml.sgi.com/moving-worlds/spec/ExternalInterface.html#Hierarchy` for any new developments. Note that the classes are divided into three packages: `vrml`, `vrml.field`, and `vrml.node`. This code is also located on the CD-ROM that accompanies this book.

Listing 45.1. The VRML API class hierarchy.

```
java.lang.Object
  |
  +- vrml.Event
  +- vrml.Browser
  +- vrml.Field
  |        +- vrml.field.SFBool
  |        +- vrml.field.SFColor
  |        +- vrml.field.SFFloat
  |        +- vrml.field.SFImage
  |        +- vrml.field.SFInt32
  |        +- vrml.field.SFNode
  |        +- vrml.field.SFRotation
  |        +- vrml.field.SFString
  |        +- vrml.field.SFTime
  |        +- vrml.field.SFVec2f
  |        +- vrml.field.SFVec3f
  |        |
  |        +- vrml.MField
  |        |        +- vrml.field.MFColor
  |        |        +- vrml.field.MFFloat
  |        |        +- vrml.field.MFInt32
  |        |        +- vrml.field.MFNode
  |        |        +- vrml.field.MFRotation
```

continues

45

**BUILDING VRML 2
BEHAVIORS IN JAVA**

Listing 45.1. continued

```
   ¦          ¦        +- vrml.field.MFString
   ¦          ¦        +- vrml.field.MFTime
   ¦          ¦        +- vrml.field.MFVec2f
   ¦          ¦        +- vrml.field.MFVec3f
   ¦          ¦
   ¦          +- vrml.ConstField
   ¦                  +- vrml.field.ConstSFBool
   ¦                  +- vrml.field.ConstSFColor
   ¦                  +- vrml.field.ConstSFFloat
   ¦                  +- vrml.field.ConstSFImage
   ¦                  +- vrml.field.ConstSFInt32
   ¦                  +- vrml.field.ConstSFNode
   ¦                  +- vrml.field.ConstSFRotation
   ¦                  +- vrml.field.ConstSFString
   ¦                  +- vrml.field.ConstSFTime
   ¦                  +- vrml.field.ConstSFVec2f
   ¦                  +- vrml.field.ConstSFVec3f
   ¦                  ¦
   ¦                  +- vrml.ConstMField
   ¦                          +- vrml.field.ConstMFColor
   ¦                          +- vrml.field.ConstMFFloat
   ¦                          +- vrml.field.ConstMFInt32
   ¦                          +- vrml.field.ConstMFNode
   ¦                          +- vrml.field.ConstMFRotation
   ¦                          +- vrml.field.ConstMFString
   ¦                          +- vrml.field.ConstMFTime
   ¦                          +- vrml.field.ConstMFVec2f
   ¦                          +- vrml.field.ConstMFVec3f
   ¦
   +- vrml.BaseNode
           +- vrml.node.Node
           +- vrml.node.Script
java.lang.Exception
       java.lang.RuntimeException
               vrml.InvalidRouteException
               vrml.InvalidFieldException
               vrml.InvalidEventInException
               vrml.InvalidEventOutException
               vrml.InvalidExposedFieldException
               vrml.InvalidNavigationTypeException
               vrml.InvalidFieldChangeException
       vrml.InvalidVRMLSyntaxException
```

Integrating Java Scripts with VRML

At some point, each VRML Script node is connected with a list of instructions that brings the VRML objects to life. For simple animations, VRMLscript is an appropriate language to use for coding behaviors. If you need more complexity, the thread and networking features of the Java environment make Java a more capable language for coding behaviors efficiently. Java can be used to create VRML behaviors by extending the Script class or by tying VRML-aware classes together with a VRML scene in an HTML document.

The Script Class Definition

Sony's CommunityPlace VRML viewer includes the `Script` class as part of its Java API. Remember that SGI's CosmoPlayer Java API does not include the `Script` class because you are expected to use VRMLscript for your intranode scripting. The definition of Sony's Java `Script` class follows; as this book goes to press, SGI has not yet included a `Script` class in its API.

```
Class Script implements Node {
    public void processEvents(Events [] events)
        throws Exception;
    public void eventsProcessed()
        throws Exception
    protected Field getEventOut(String eventName)
        throws InvalidEventOutException;
    protected Field getField(String fieldName)
        throws InvalidFieldException
}
```

When you create a script, you are expected to subclass the `Script` class definition to provide the necessary functionality. The class definition deliberately leaves the definition of the codes for the exceptions up to you so that you can create tailored exceptions and handlers.

The `getField()` method returns the value of the field nominated by the given string. This method is how the Java script gets the values from the VRML `Script` node fields. This method is used for all fields and `exposedField` fields. To the Java script, an `eventOut` looks just like another field. There is no need to write an `eventOut` function—the value is set by calling the appropriate field type's `setValue()` method.

Dealing with Event Input

Every `eventIn` field specified in the VRML `Script` node definition requires a matching `public` method in the Java implementation. The method definition takes this form:

```
public void <eventName>(Const<eventTypeName> <variable name>,
            SFTime <variable name>);
```

The method must have the same name as the matching `eventIn` field in the VRML script description. The second field corresponds to the timestamp of when the event was generated. The `SFTime` field is particularly useful when the `mustEvaluate` field is set to `FALSE`, meaning that an event may be queued for some time before finally being processed.

Because `Script` is an implementation of the `Node` interface, it contains the `postEventIn()` method. Earlier in this chapter, you learned that you should not call the `eventIn` methods of other scripts directly. To facilitate direct internode communication, the `postEventIn()` method enables you to send information to other nodes while staying within the VRML event-handling system. The arguments are a `String` specifying the `eventIn` field name and a `Field` containing the value. The value is a VRML data type cast to `Field`. The use of `PostEventIn()`, as available in Sony's CommunityPlace API, is shown in the following example and is also used later in this chapter when a simple dynamic world is constructed.

```
//The node we are getting is a translation
Node translation;
float[3] translation_details;
translation[0] = 0.0f;
translation[1] = 2.3f;
translation[2] = -0.4f;
translation.postEventIn("translation", (Field)translation);
```

SGI's CosmoPlayer API does not use a postEventIn() method. Instead, it uses the following syntax that, in effect, does the same thing:

```
Node translation = browser.getNode("box");
EventInSFVec3f set_translation =
    (EventInSFVec3f)material.getEventIn("translation");
float[] val = new float[3];
val[0] = 0.0f;
val[1] = 2.3f;
val[2] = -0.4f;
set_translation.setValue(val);
```

Remember that SGI's API does not contain the Script class. The event-processing methods, processEvents() and eventsProcessed(), are described later in this chapter.

The First Behavior—A Color-Changing Box

Now you are ready to put this all together to create a color-changer behavior that toggles a box's color between red and blue. Figure 45.1 shows a simple VRML box that has turned blue as a result of a user's mouse click (trust me; although the figure is shown in black and white, the box really is blue!). The following sections show you how to create the example for both the CommunityPlace and CosmoPlayer VRML viewers. The CommunityPlace example requires five components: a Box primitive, a TouchSensor object, a Material node, the Script node, and the Java script. The CosmoPlayer example requires a Box primitive, a TouchSensor object, a Material node, the Java script, and an HTML document to associate the Java script with the VRML scene.

The CommunityPlace Version

For the CommunityPlace viewer, the basic VRML scene consists of a TouchSensor-enabled, red box placed at the scene origin (0,0,0) with an associated Script node and a couple of ROUTE statements. Listing 45.2 shows the complete VRML scene, which was created using a simple text editor. In fact, all the VRML scenes in this chapter were typed by hand into the Notepad text editor that is a part of the Windows operating system. You can find the code in Listing 45.2 on the CD-ROM that accompanies this book.

FIGURE 45.1.

The color-changing box example.

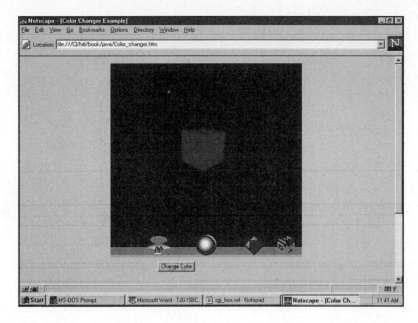

Listing 45.2. The VRML scene graph for CommunityPlace.

```
#VRML V2.0 utf8
#filename: s_box.wrl
Transform {
    bboxSize    1 1 1
    children [
        Shape {
            appearance Appearance {
                material DEF cube_material Material {
                    diffuseColor 1 0 0 #start red.
                }
            }
            geometry Box {size 1 1 1}
        } # end of shape definition
        # Now define a TouchSensor node. This node takes in the
        # geometry of the parent transform. Default behavior OK.
        DEF cube_sensor TouchSensor {}
    ]
}
DEF color_script Script {
    url    "s_color_changer.class"
    # now define our needed fields
    field    SFBool        isRed          TRUE
    eventIn  SFBool        clicked
    eventOut SFColor       color_out
}
ROUTE cube_sensor.isActive TO color_script.clicked
ROUTE color_script.color_out TO cube_material.set_diffuseColor
```

The Script node acts as the color changer. It takes input from the TouchSensor object and outputs the new color to the Material node. The Script node must also keep internal track of the color. This is done by reading in the value from the Material node, but for demonstration purposes, an internal flag is included in the script. No fancy processing or event sending to other nodes is necessary, so both the mustEvaluate and directOutputs fields can be left at the default setting of null.

 Finally, the Java script shown in Listing 45.3 is compiled to produce the color_changer.class file that is referenced in Listing 45.2 in the Script node's behavior field. You can find this code on the CD-ROM that accompanies this book.

Listing 45.3. The sample Java script for CommunityPlace.

```
//filename: s_color_changer.java
import vrml.field.*;
import vrml.node.*;
import vrml.*;
class s_color_changer extends Script {
    // declare the field
    private SFBool    isRed = (SFBool)getField("isRed");
    // declare the eventOut
    private SFColor  color_out = (SFColor)getEventOut("color_out");
    // declare color float array
    float[] color;
    // declare eventIns
    public void clicked(ConstSFBool isClicked, ConstSFTime ts) {
        // called when the user clicks or touches the cube or
        // stops touching/click so first check the status of the
        // isClicked field. We will only respond to a button up.
        if(isClicked.getValue() == false) {
            // now check whether the cube is red or blue
            if(isRed.getValue() == true)
                isRed.setValue(false);
            else
                isRed.setValue(true);
        }
    }
    // finally the event processing call
    public void eventsProcessed() {
        if(isRed.getValue() == true) {
            color = new float[3];
            color[0] = 0.0f;
            color[1] = 0.0f;
            color[2] = 1.0f;
            color_out.setValue(color);
        }
        else {
            color = new float[3];
            color[0] = 1.0f;
            color[1] = 0.0f;
            color[2] = 0.0f;
            color_out.setValue(color);
        }
    }
}
```

The CosmoPlayer Version

 For the CosmoPlayer viewer, the basic VRML scene consists of a TouchSensor-enabled, red box placed at the scene origin (0,0,0) but does *not* include a Script node or the ROUTE statements used with the CommunityPlace example. As you see in Listing 45.4 (which is also located on the CD-ROM that accompanies this book), the routing is done within the Java script itself.

Listing 45.4. The VRML scene graph for CosmoPlayer.

```
#VRML V2.0 utf8
#filename: sgi_box.wrl
Transform {
    bboxSize    1 1 1
    children [
        Shape {
            appearance Appearance {
                material DEF cube_material Material {
                    diffuseColor    1.0 0 0 #start red.
                }
            }
            geometry Box {size 1 1 1}
        } # end of shape definition
        # Now define a TouchSensor node. This node takes in the
        # geometry of the parent transform. Default behavior OK.
        DEF cube_sensor TouchSensor {}
    ]
}
```

 Instead of connecting the Java script to the VRML scene within the VRML file, the connection is made in an HTML document. This approach has one big advantage: You can use the Java AWT to control your VRML scene interaction. The HTML code is provided in the file Color_changer.htm, as shown in Listing 45.5, and can be found on the CD-ROM.

Listing 45.5. The HTML document for the color-changer example in CosmoPlayer.

```
<HTML>
<HEAD>
<TITLE>Color Changer Example</TITLE>
</HEAD>
<BODY>
<CENTER>
<EMBED SRC="sgi_box.wrl" BORDER=0 HEIGHT="400" WIDTH="400">
</CENTER>
<APPLET CODE="sgi_color_changer.class" MAYSCRIPT>
</APPLET>
</BODY>
</HTML>
```

45

BUILDING VRML 2 BEHAVIORS IN JAVA

In the HTML file, you connect the box.wrl VRML file to the Color_changer.class Java class using the <EMBED> and <APPLET> HTML tags. Note that you can set the HEIGHT and WIDTH of the VRML scene to whatever size you want; any Java controls you include in the .class file appear in an area following your VRML scene.

 Finally, the Java sgi_color_changer class source code is shown in Listing 45.6 (this code can also be found on the CD-ROM). This code creates the Java controls and connects them to the VRML scene for visitors to use to interact with the scene. The code in Listing 45.6 allows a user to interact with the VRML scene using Java AWT controls such as buttons and checkboxes, which are made available in a separate control panel. The code in Listing 45.7 allows a user to interact with the VRML scene by clicking on VRML objects in the scene itself.

Listing 45.6. The sample Java script for CosmoPlayer.

```java
//filename: sgi_color_changer.java
import java.awt.*;
import java.applet.*;
import vrml.external.field.EventOut;
import vrml.external.field.EventInSFColor;
import vrml.external.Node;
import vrml.external.Browser;
import vrml.external.exception.*;
import netscape.javascript.JSObject;
public class sgi_color_changer extends Applet {
  TextArea output = null;
  Browser browser = null;
  Node material = null;
  EventInSFColor diffuseColor = null;
  boolean red = true;
  boolean error = false;
  public void init() {
    add(new Button("Change Color"));
    JSObject win = JSObject.getWindow(this);
    JSObject doc = (JSObject) win.getMember("document");
    JSObject embeds = (JSObject) doc.getMember("embeds");
    browser = (Browser) embeds.getSlot(0);
    // Now we've got the handle to the VRML Browser.
    try {
      // Get the material node...
      material = browser.getNode("cube_material");
      // Get the diffuseColor EventIn
      diffuseColor = (EventInSFColor) material.getEventIn("set_diffuseColor");
    }
    catch (InvalidNodeException ne) {
      showStatus("Failed to get node:" + ne);
      error = true;
    }
    catch (InvalidEventInException ee) {
      showStatus("Failed to get EventIn:" + ee);
      error = true;
    }
```

```
    catch (InvalidEventOutException ee) {
      showStatus("Failed to get EventOut:" + ee);
      error = true;
    }
  }

  public boolean action(Event event, Object what) {
    if (error)
      {
        showStatus("Problems! Had an error during initialization");
        return true;  // Uh oh...
      }
    if (event.target instanceof Button)
      {
        Button b = (Button) event.target;
        if (b.getLabel() == "Change Color") {
            if (red) {
                showStatus ("Blue!");
                float[] val = new float[3];
                val[0] = 0.2f;
                val[1] = 0.2f;
                val[2] = 0.8f;
                diffuseColor.setValue(val);
                red = false;
            }
            else {
                showStatus("Red!");
                float[] val = new float[3];
                val[0] = 0.8f;
                val[1] = 0.2f;
                val[2] = 0.2f;
                diffuseColor.setValue(val);
                red = true;
            }
        }
      }
    return true;
  }
}
```

So that you can click the box and change the color from within the VRML scene instead of from a Java AWT button, SGI's browser sets up an event callback in the Java class by implementing EventOutObserver. The EventOutObserver sets up event awareness for the VRML scene. If you want to interact with the cube within the VRML itself instead of from a Java AWT button, just replace sgi_color_changer.class with Color_changer.class, compiled from the source code in Listing 45.7. This code can also be found on the CD-ROM that accompanies this book.

Listing 45.7. An alternative Java script for CosmoPlayer.

```java
//filename: Color_changer.java
import java.awt.*;
import java.applet.*;
import vrml.external.field.EventOut;
import vrml.external.field.EventInSFColor;
import vrml.external.field.EventOutSFColor;
import vrml.external.field.EventOutSFTime;
import vrml.external.field.EventOutObserver;
import vrml.external.Node;
import vrml.external.Browser;
import vrml.external.exception.*;
import netscape.javascript.JSObject;
public class Color_changer extends Applet implements EventOutObserver {
  TextArea output = null;
  Browser browser = null;
  Node material = null;
  EventInSFColor diffuseColor = null;
  EventOutSFColor outputColor = null;
  EventOutSFTime touchTime = null;
  boolean red = true;
  boolean error = false;
  public void init() {
    JSObject win = JSObject.getWindow(this);
    JSObject doc = (JSObject) win.getMember("document");
    JSObject embeds = (JSObject) doc.getMember("embeds");
    browser = (Browser) embeds.getSlot(0);
    // Now we've got the handle to the VRML Browser.
    try {
      // Get the material node...
      material = browser.getNode("cube_material");
      // Get the diffuseColor EventIn
      diffuseColor = (EventInSFColor) material.getEventIn("set_diffuseColor");
      // Get the Touch Sensor
      Node sensor = browser.getNode("cube_sensor");
      // Get its touchTime EventOut
      touchTime = (EventOutSFTime) sensor.getEventOut("touchTime");
      // Set up the callback
      touchTime.advise(this, new Integer(1));
      // Get its diffuseColor EventOut
      outputColor = (EventOutSFColor) material.getEventOut("diffuseColor");
      // Set up its callback
      outputColor.advise(this, new Integer(2));
    }
    catch (InvalidNodeException ne) {
      add(new TextField("Failed to get node:" + ne));
      error = true;
    }
    catch (InvalidEventInException ee) {
      add(new TextField("Failed to get EventIn:" + ee));
      error = true;
    }
    catch (InvalidEventOutException ee) {
      add(new TextField("Failed to get EventOut:" + ee));
      error = true;
    }
  }
```

```
public void callback(EventOut who, double when, Object which) {
  Integer whichNum = (Integer) which;
  if (whichNum.intValue() == 1) {
      if (red) {
              showStatus ("Blue!");
              float[] val = new float[3];
              val[0] = 0.2f;
              val[1] = 0.2f;
              val[2] = 0.8f;
              diffuseColor.setValue(val);
              red = false;
      }
      else {
              showStatus("Red!");
              float[] val = new float[3];          ,
              val[0] = 0.8f;
              val[1] = 0.2f;
              val[2] = 0.2f;
              diffuseColor.setValue(val);
              red = true;
      }
  }
  if (whichNum.intValue() == 2) {
    // Make the new color of the sphere and timestamp
    // show up in the textarea.
    float[] val = outputColor.getValue();
    showStatus("Got color " + val[0] + ", " + val[1] + ", " +
                          val[2] + " at time " + when + "\n");
  }
 }
}
```

Of course, you can combine both the Java controls and the VRML node callback routine in the same Java file.

That's it. Now you have a cube that changes color when you click it. The code looks almost identical for changing a virtual object's translation, rotation, or scale in the VRML scene. All other eventIns can be accessed in similar fashion—including the current scene viewpoint. Creating more complex behaviors is just a variation of this scheme, with more Java code and fields. Although the basic user input usually comes from sensors, in the SGI approach the events can come from any Java program—including a program that embeds all kinds of physics to handle interactions between the objects drawn to the screen in the VRML scene. This approach creates many scientific visualization opportunities.

Even with Sony's approach, scripts are not restricted to input methods based on eventIn fields. One example is a stock market tracker that runs as a separate thread. It can constantly receive updates from the network, process them, and then send the results through a public method to the script, which then puts the appropriate results into the 3D world.

The Browser Class

Behaviors using the methods presented in the color-changer box examples work for many simple systems. Effective virtual reality systems, however, require more than just being able to change the color and shape of objects that already exist in the virtual world. As a thought experiment, consider a virtual taxi: A user should be able to step inside and instruct the cab where to go. Using the techniques from the preceding examples, the cab would move off, leaving the user in the same place. The user does not "exist" as part of the scene graph—the user is known to the browser but not to the VRML scene-rendering engine. Clearly, a greater level of control is needed.

Changing the Current Scene

The VRML 2 specification defines a series of actions the programmer can access to set and retrieve information about the virtual world. Within the Java implementation of the API, world information is provided in the Browser class. The Browser class provides all the functions a programmer needs that are not specific to any particular part of the scene graph.

To define a system-specific behavior, the first functions you must define are these:

```
public static String getName();
public static String getVersion();
```

These strings are defined by the browser writer and identify the browser in some unspecified way. If this information is not available, empty strings are returned.

If you are programming expensive calculations, you may want to know how they affect the rendering speed (frame rate) of the system. The getCurrentFrameRate() method returns the value in frames per second. If this information is not available, the return value is 100.0.

```
public static float getCurrentFrameRate();
```

In systems that use prediction, two more handy pieces of information to know are what mode the user is navigating the scene in, and at what speed the user is traveling. Similar to the getName() method, the string returned to describe the navigation type is browser dependent. VRML defines that, at a minimum, the following four navigation types must be supported: WALK, EXAMINE, FLY, and NONE. However, if you are building applications for an intranet and you know what type of browser is used, this navigation information can be quite handy for varying the behavior, depending on how the user approaches the object of interest. Information about navigation is available from the following methods:

```
public static String getNavigationType();
public static void   setNavigationType(String type)
    throws InvalidNavigationTypeException;
public static float getNavigationSpeed();
public static void  setNavigationSpeed(float speed);
public static float getCurrentSpeed();
```

The difference between *navigation speed* and *current speed* is in the definition. VRML 2 defines a navigationInfo node that contains default information about how to act if given no other external cues. The navigation speed is the default speed in units per second; these units are defined for each browser by the individual browser developers. There is no specification about what this speed represents, only hints. A reasonable estimate of the navigation speed is the movement speed in WALK and FLY mode and the movement speed used in panning and dollying in EXAMINE mode, encountered when a user has not selected any speed controls. The current speed is the actual speed at which the user is traveling at that point in time. This is the speed that the user has set with the browser controls. Speed controls, when they are provided by the browser developer, allow the user to vary from the default navigation speed. For example, a browser with a default speed of 70 pixels/second may slow down to 40 pixels/second when the user selects the slow speed control from an available menu.

Having two different descriptions of speed may seem wasteful, but it comes in quite handy when moving between different worlds. The first world may be a land of giants, where traveling at 100 units per second is considered slow, but in the next world, which models a molecule that is only 0.001 units across, this speed would be ridiculously fast. The navigation speed value can be used to scale speeds to something reasonable for the particular world.

Also contained in the navigationInfo node is a boolean field for a headlight. The *headlight* is a directional light that points in the direction the user is facing. Where the scene creator has used other lighting effects (such as radiosity), the headlight is usually turned off. In the currently available browsers, the headlight field has led to software bugs (for example, turning off the headlight results in the whole scene going black). It is recommended that you do not use the headlight feature within the behaviors because the browser includes logic to determine when best to use the headlight. For example, the headlight is usually disabled when the browser is showing the effects of a single point of light. If you have to access the headlight, the following functions are provided by the Browser class:

```
public static boolean getHeadlight();
public static void setHeadlight(boolean onOff);
```

The methods described in this section enable you to change individual components of the world. The other approach is to completely replace the world with some internally generated one. This approach enables you to use VRML to generate new VRML worlds on the fly—assuming that you already are part of a VRML world (you cannot use this approach in an application to generate a 3D graphics front-end). Use the following statement to replace the current world with an internally generated one:

```
public static void replaceWorld(node nodes[]);
```

This is a nonreturning call that unloads the current scene graph and replaces it with a new one.

45

BUILDING VRML 2 BEHAVIORS IN JAVA

Modifying the Scene

There is only so much you can do with what is already available in a scene. Complex worlds use a mix of static and dynamically generated scenery to achieve their impressive special effects. You can dramatically change a VRML scene while a user is visiting it. The fact that nodes are embedded within other nodes in a scene graph makes VRML very flexible for changing just the specific part of the scene you want to change.

You can query the current world to find out the URL from which it was originally loaded. Your Java code can then contain different paths based on the current world:

```
public static String getWorldURL();
```

GetWorldURL() returns the URL of the root of the scene graph rather than the URL of the currently occupied part of the scene. VRML enables a complex world to be created using a series of small files that are included in the world—a technique called *inlining* in VRML parlance.

You can change your VRML scene dynamically by using the following three browser methods:

```
public static void loadWorld(String[] url);
public static Node createVrmlFromString(String vrmlSyntax);
public static void createVrmlFromURL(String[] url,
                                     Node      node,
                                     String    eventInName);
```

To completely replace the scene graph, you call the loadWorld() method. As with all URL references in VRML, an array of strings are passed. These strings are a list of URLs and URNs to be loaded in order of preference. Should the load of the first URL fail, the browser attempts to load the second, and so on until a scene is loaded or the browser reaches the end of the list. If the load fails, the VRML viewer can notify the user as the developer sees fit. The specification also states that it is up to the browser whether the loadWorld() call blocks or starts a separate thread when loading a new scene.

In addition to replacing the whole scene, you may want to add bits at a time to a scene. You can do this in one of two ways. If you are very familiar with VRML syntax, you can create strings on the fly and pass them to the createVrmlFromString() call. The node that is returned can be added to the scene to produce dynamic results.

Perhaps the most useful of the preceding three functions is the createVrmlFromURL() method. From the definition, you may have noticed that, along with a list of URLs, the method also takes a node instance and a string that refers to an eventIn field name. This call is a nonblocking call that starts a separate thread to retrieve the given file from the URL, converts it into the VRML viewer's internal representation, and then finally sends the newly created list of nodes to the specified node's eventIn field. The eventIn field type must be an MFNode. The Node reference can be any sort of node, not just a part of the script node. This arrangement enables the script writer to add new nodes directly to the scene graph without having to write extra functionality in the script.

With both of the create methods, the returned nodes do not become visible until they have been added to some preexisting node in the scene. Although it is possible to create an entire scene on the fly within a standalone applet, there is no way to make the scene visible unless there is an exiting node instance to which you can add the dynamically generated scene.

Once you have created a set of new nodes, you also want to be able to link them together to get a behavior system similar to the one in the original world. The `Browser` class defines methods for dynamically adding and deleting `ROUTE` statements between nodes:

```
public void addRoute(Node fromNode, String fromEventOut,
                     Node toNode,   String toEventIn)
    throws InvalidRouteException;
public void addRoute(Node fromNode, String fromEventOut,
                     Node toNode,   String toEventIn)
    throws InvalidRouteException;
```

For each of these methods, you must know the node instance for both ends of the `ROUTE`. In VRML, you cannot obtain an instance pointer to an individual field in a node. It is also assumed that if you know you will be adding a `ROUTE`, you also know what fields you are dealing with, so a string is used to describe the field name corresponding to an `eventIn` or `eventOut` field. Exceptions are thrown if either of the nodes or fields does not exist or an attempt to delete a nonexistent `ROUTE` is made.

You now have all the tools required to generate a world on the fly, respond to user input, and modify the scene. The only thing that remains is to acquire the wisdom to create responsive worlds that won't get bogged down in Java code.

The Script Execution Model

When tuning the behaviors in a virtual world, the methods used depend on the execution model. The VRML API gives you a lot of control over exactly how scripts are executed and how events passed to it are distributed.

The arrival of an `eventIn` field at a `Script` node causes the execution of the matching method. There is no other way to invoke a method. A script can start an asynchronous thread, which in turn can call another non-`eventIn` method of the script or can even send events directly to other nodes. The VRML 2 specification makes no mention about scripts containing non-`eventIn` public methods. Although it is possible to call an `eventIn` method directly, it is in no way encouraged. Such programming interferes with the script execution model by preventing browser optimization and can affect the running of other parts of the script. Calling an `eventIn` method directly can also cause performance penalties in other parts of the world, not to mention reentrancy problems within the `eventIn` method itself. If you find it necessary to call an `eventIn` method of the script, use the `postEventIn()` method so that the operation of the browser's execution engine is not affected.

Unless the mustEvaluate field is set, all the events are queued in timestamp order from oldest to newest. For each queued event, the corresponding eventIn method is called. Each eventIn field calls exactly one method. If an eventOut fans out to a number of eventIns, multiple eventIns are generated—one for each node. Once the queue is empty, the eventsProcessed() method for that script is called. The eventsProcessed() method enables any post-event processing to be performed.

A typical use of this post-processing was shown in the example of the color-changing cube, earlier in this chapter. In that example, the eventIn method just took the data and stored it in an internal variable. The eventsProcessed() method took the internal value and generated the eventOut. This approach was overkill for such simple behavior. Normally, such simplistic behavior uses VRMLscript instead of Java. However, the separation of data processing from data collection is very effective in a high-traffic environment, in which event counts are very high and the overhead of data processing is best absorbed into a single, longer run instead of many short runs.

Once the eventsProcessed() method has completed execution, any eventOuts generated as a result are sent as events. If the script generates multiple eventOuts for a single eventOut field, only one event is sent. All eventOuts generated during the execution of the script have the same timestamp.

If your script has spawned a thread, and that script is removed from the scene graph, the browser is required to call the shutdown() method for each active thread to facilitate a graceful exit.

If you want to maintain static data between invocations of the script, it is recommended that your VRML Script node have fields to hold the values. Although it is possible to use static variables within the Java class, VRML makes no guarantees that these variables will be retained, especially if the script is unloaded from memory.

If you are a hardcore programmer, you probably want to keep track of all the event-handling mechanisms yourself. VRML provides the facility to do this with the processEvents() method. This method is called when the browser decides to process the queued eventIns for a script. The method is sent an array of the events waiting to be processed, which you can then do with as you please. Graphics programmers should already be familiar with event-handling techniques from the Microsoft Windows, Xlib, or Java AWT system.

Circular Event Loops

The ROUTE syntax makes it very easy to construct circular event loops. Circular loops can be quite handy. The VRML specification states that if the browser finds event loops, it only processes each event once per timestamp. Events generated as a result of a change are given the same timestamp as the original change because events are considered to happen instantaneously. When event loops are encountered in this situation, the browser enforces a breakage of the loop. The following sample script from the VRML specification uses VRMLscript to explain this process:

```
DEF S Script {
    eventIn   SFInt32   a
    eventIn   SFInt32   b
    eventOut  SFInt32   c
    field     SFInt32   save_a   0
    field     SFInt32   save_b   0
    url       "data:x-lang/x-vrmlscript, TEXT;
        function a(val) { save_a = val; c = save_a+save_b;}
        function b(val) { save_b = val; c = save_a+save_b;}
}
ROUTE S.c to S.b
```

S computes c=a+b with the ROUTE, completing a loop from the output c back to input b. After the initial event with a=1, the script leaves the eventOut c with the value of 1. This causes a cascade effect, in which b is set to 1. Normally, this generates an eventOut on c with the value 2, but the browser has already seen that the eventOut c has been traversed for this timestamp, and therefore enforces a break in the loop. This leaves the values save_a=1, save_b=1, and the eventOut c=1.

Creating Efficient Behaviors

For all animation programming, the ultimate goal is to keep the frame rate as high as possible. In a multithreaded application like a VRML browser, the less time spent in behaviors code, the more time that can be spent rendering. Virtual reality behavior programming in VRML is still very much in its infancy. This section outlines a few common-sense approaches to keeping up reasonable levels of performance—not only for the renderer, but also for the programmer.

The first technique is to use Java only where necessary. This may sound a little strange in a book about Java programming, but consider the resources required to have not only a 3D-rendering engine but a Java VM loaded to run even a simple behavior; also consider that the majority of your viewers may be people using low-end PCs. Because most VRML browsers specify that a minimum of 16M of RAM is required (and 32M is recommended), also loading the Java VM into memory requires lots of swapping to keep the behaviors going. The inevitable result is bad performance. For this reason, the interpolator nodes and VRMLscript were created—built-in nodes for common basic calculations and a small, light language to provide basic calculation abilities. Use of Java should be limited to the times when you require the capabilities of a full programming language, such as for multithreading and network interfaces.

When you do have to use Java, keep the amount of calculation in the script to a minimum. If you are producing behaviors that require either extensive network communication or data processing, these behaviors should be kept out of the Script node and sent off in separate threads. The script should start the thread as either part of its constructor or in response to some event and then return as soon as possible.

In VR systems, frame rate is king. Don't aim to have a one-hundred percent correct behavior if it leads to half the frame rate when a ninety-percent correct behavior will do. It is amazing how users don't notice an incorrect behavior, but as soon as the picture update slows down, they start to complain. Every extra line of code in the script delays the return of the CPU back to the renderer. In military simulations, the goal is to achieve 60fps; even for Pentium-class machines, your goal should be to maintain at least 20fps. Much of this comes down not only to how detailed the world is, but also to how complex the behaviors are. As always, the tradeoff between accuracy and frame rate is up to the individual programmer and the requirements of the application. Your user will typically accept that a door does not open smoothly as long as he or she can move around without watching individual frames redraw.

Don't play with the event-processing loop unless you *really* must. Your behaviors code will be distributed on many different types of machines and browsers. Each browser writer knows best how to optimize the event-handling mechanism to mesh with its internal architecture. With windowing systems, dealing with the event loop is a must if you are to respond to user input, but in virtual reality, you don't have control over the whole system. The `processEvents()` method applies only to the individual script, not as a common method across all scripts. So although you think you are optimizing the event handling, you are doing so only for one script. In a reasonably sized world, another few hundred scripts may also be running, so the optimization of an individual script isn't generally worth the effort.

Changing the Scene

Add to the scene graph only what is necessary. If you can modify existing primitives, do so instead of adding new ones. Every primitive you add to a scene requires the renderer to convert the scene to its internal representation and then reoptimize the scene graph to take the new objects into account. When it modifies existing primitives, the browser is not required to re-sort the scene graph structure, saving computation time. A cloudy sky is better simulated using a multiframed texture map image format (such as MJPEG or PNG) on the background node than using lots of primitives that are constantly modified or dynamically added.

If your scene requires objects to be added and removed on the fly, and many of these objects are the same, don't just delete them from the scene graph. It is better to *remove* them from a node and keep an instance pointer to them so that they can be reinserted at a later time. At the expense of a little extra memory, you save time. If you don't take the time now, you may later have to access the objects from a network or construct them from the ground up from a string representation.

Another trick is to create VRML objects but not add them to the visual scene graph. VRML scripting enables objects to be created but not added to the scene graph. Any object not added isn't drawn. For node types such as sensors, interpolators, and scripts, there is no need for these objects to be added because they are never drawn. Doing so causes extra events to be generated, resulting in a slower system. Normal Java garbage collection rules apply when these nodes are no longer referenced. VRML, however, adds one little extra: Adding a ROUTE to any object is the same as keeping a reference to the object. If a script creates a node, adds one or more ROUTE statements, and then exits, the node stays allocated and it functions properly. You can use this approach to set up a VRML node that does not use events for its visualization.

There are dangers in this approach. Once you lose the node instance pointer, you have no way to delete the node. You need this pointer if you are to delete the ROUTE. Deleting ROUTE statements to the object is the only way to remove these floating nodes. Therefore, you should always keep the node instance pointers for all floating nodes you create so that you can delete the ROUTE statements to them when they're no longer needed. You must be particularly careful when you delete a section of the scene graph that has the only routed eventIn to a floating node that also contains an eventOut to a section of an undeleted section. This situation creates the VRML equivalent of memory leaks. The only way to remove this node is to replace the whole scene or to remove the part of the scene referenced by the eventOut.

Dynamic Worlds—Creating VRML on the Fly

This section develops a framework for creating worlds on the fly. Dynamically changing worlds add tremendous potential to your VRML scenes. You can develop cyberspace protocol-based, seamless worlds in which a visitor can take an object from one world and use or leave it in another world. You can provide a VRML toolkit with which a visitor creates new VRML objects from existing ones and saves them as separate VRML files. But for starters, you may just want to add a few new objects or eliminate objects as a visitor interacts with your scene. The next sections provide an example of a dynamic world for both CommunityPlace and CosmoPlayer. The example primarily familiarizes you with the createVrmlFromString(String *vrmlSyntax*), createVrmlFromURL(String[] *url*, Node *node*, String *event*), and loadURL(String[] *url*, String[] *parameter*) methods of the Browser class. Figure 45.2 shows the sample VRML scene before it dynamically changes.

FIGURE 45.2.

A simple VRML scene based on the VRML logo.

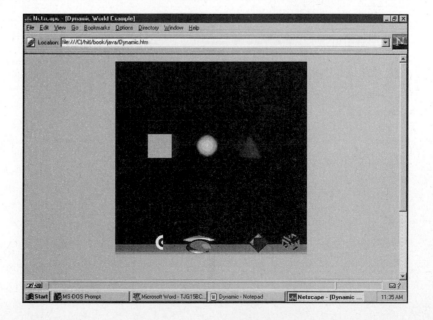

Creating the VRML Source File

If you are to add new objects to a VRML scene, a placeholder node must already exist in the
.wrl file. This placeholder need not be anything more sophisticated than the following empty
Transform node:

```
DEF root_node Transform { }
```

In fact, this statement can be the entire starting world if the world is to be built using Java
AWT controls. More typically, however, other objects are already in the world when it is loaded
and the Transform node becomes just another potential node to which you can add new objects. The Transform node has two eventIn fields—addChildren and removeChildren—that can
be used to add or delete multiple children from within the node.

In the following code example, three objects exist in the VRML scene when the world is first
loaded. Each object enables an event that dynamically changes the world. Using the three primitive shapes that form the VRML logo, the red cube enables the createVrmlFromURL() method,
the green sphere enables the createVrmlFromString() method, and the blue cone takes the user
to another VRML world by using the loadURL() method. The cube, sphere, and cone are each
children of Transform nodes to make sure that they are located in different parts of the world
(all objects are located at the Transform node's origin by default). The code that creates the
cube Transform node follows:

```
DEF cube Transform {
    children [
        DEF cube_sensor TouchSensor{}
        Shape {
            appearance Appearance {
                material Material {
                    diffuseColor 1 0 0
                }
            }
            geometry Box { size  1 1 1}
        }
        # note: script node goes here for CommunityPlace
    ]
    bboxSize     1 1 1
    translation -2 0 0
}
```

Notice that the TouchSensor itself has been defined (with DEF) as has the whole Transform node.
The TouchSensor is the object that triggers events. Without a defined sensor, the cube has no
way to interact with the rest of the scene. Any mouse click (or touch, if the user has a dataglove)
on the cube does nothing. As you soon see, the other two nodes are similar in definition. The
Shape node contains the appearance of the cube (in this case, a bright red color) as well as the
geometry of the cube (which is 1 unit wide, 1 unit tall, and 1 unit deep). The bboxSize field
defines a bounding box that helps the VRML viewer render the cube efficiently. The
translation field places the cube two units to the right from the (0,0,0) origin of the VRML
scene.

Keeping this VRML primer in mind, you are ready to follow the example for both the CommunityPlace and CosmoPlayer VRML viewers.

The CommunityPlace Version of the Dynamic World Example

The following sections break down the process for creating the dynamically changing world for the CommunityPlace browser.

> **NOTE**
>
> For demonstration purposes, the separate scripts are described and grouped with their appropriate objects. It makes no difference if you have lots of small scripts or one large one. If you are a VR scene creator, it is probably better to have one large script to keep track of the scene graph if you want to save a VRML file with the changes. If you are creating a virtual factory of reusable, plug-and-play component VRML objects, you may prefer to use many small scripts, perhaps with some "centralized" script to act as the system controller.

Defining the Script Nodes

Once the basic VRML file is defined, you must add behaviors. The VRML file stands on its own at this point. You can click objects, but nothing happens. Because each object has its own behavior, the requirement for each script is different. Each script requires one eventIn, which is the notification from its TouchSensor().

The example presented does not have any real-time constraints, so the mustEvaluate field for each object is left with the default setting of FALSE. For the cone object, no outputs are sent directly to nodes, so the directOutputs field is left at FALSE. For the sphere object, outputs are sent directly to the Group node, so the directOutputs field is set to TRUE. The directOutputs field for the cube object must also be set to TRUE for reasons explained in the next section.

In addition to eventIn, the box_script example also needs an eventOut to send the new object to the Group node that is acting as the scene root. Good behavior is desirable if the user clicks the cube more than once, so an extra internal variable is added, keeping the position of the last object that was added. Each new object added is translated two units along the z axis from the previous one. A field is also needed to store the URL of the sample file that will be loaded. The box_script definition follows:

```
DEF box_script Script {
    url             "box_script.class"
    directOutputs   TRUE
    eventIn         SFBool    isClicked
    eventIn         MFNode    newNodes
```

```
    eventOut      MFNode     childlist
    field         SFInt32    zposition   0
    field         SFNode     thisScript  USE box_script
    field         MFNode     newUrl      []
}
```

Notice that there is an extra eventIn. Because some processing must be done on the node re-turned from the createVrmlFromURL() method, you must provide an eventIn for the argument. If you do not have to process the returned nodes, use the root_node.add_children() method instead.

The other interesting point to note is that the script declaration includes a field that is a refer-ence to itself. At the time this chapter was written, the draft specifications for VRML 2 did not specify how a script was to refer to itself when calling its own eventIns. To play it safe, the method in the preceding declaration is guaranteed to work. However, it should be possible for the script to specify the this keyword as the node reference when referring to itself. Check the most current version of the specification, available at http://vag.vrml.org/, for more infor-mation.

To show the use of direct outputs, the sphere uses the postEventIn() method to send the new child directly to root_node. To do this, a copy of the name that was defined for the Group is taken; when this copy is resolved in Java, it essentially becomes an instance pointer to the node. Using direct writing to nodes means that you no longer require the eventOut from the cube's script, but you do keep the other fields:

```
DEF sphere_script Script {
    url            "sphere_script.class"
    directOutputs  TRUE
    eventIn        SFBool     isClicked
    field          SFNode     root        USE root_node
    field          SFInt32    zposition   0
}
```

The script for the cone is very simplistic. When the user clicks the cone, all it does is fetch some named URL and set the URL as the new scene graph: a simple cylinder.

```
DEF cone_script Script {
    url         "cone_script.class"
    eventIn     SFBool     isClicked
    field       MFString   target_url ["cylinder.wrl"]
}
```

Completing the VRML Description

Now that you have defined the scripts, you must wire them together. A number of routes are added between the sensors and scripts, as shown in Listing 45.8.

Listing 45.8. The main world VRML description for CommunityPlace.

```
#VRML V2.0 utf8
#filename: s_dynamic.wrl
# first the pseudo root
DEF root_node Transform { bboxSize    1000 1000 1000}
# The cube
Transform {
    children [
        DEF cube_sensor TouchSensor{}
        Shape {
            appearance Appearance {
                material Material {
                    diffuseColor 1 0 0
                }
            }
            geometry Box { size  1 1 1}
        }
        DEF box_script Script {
            url         "box_script.class"
            directOutputs TRUE
            eventIn     SFBool     isClicked
            eventIn     MFNode     newNodes
            eventOut    MFNode     childList
            field       SFInt32    zPosition    0
            field       SFNode     thisScript   USE box_script;
            field       MFString   newUrl ["cylinder.wrl"]
        }
    ]
    bboxSize    1 1 1
    translation  2 0 0
}
ROUTE cube_sensor.isActive TO cube_script.isClicked
ROUTE cube_script.childlist TO root_node.add_children
# The sphere
Transform {
children [
        DEF sphere_sensor TouchSensor {}
        Shape {
            appearance Appearance {
                material Material {
                    diffuseColor 0 1 0
                }
            }
            geometry Sphere { radius    0.5 }
        }
        DEF sphere_script Script {
            url         "sphere_script.class"
            directOutputs TRUE
            eventIn     SFBool     isClicked
            field       SFNode     root       USE root_node
            field       SFInt32    zPosition  0
        }
    ]
```

continues

Listing 45.8. continued

```
    # no translation needed as it is the origin already
    bboxSize    1 1 1
}
ROUTE sphere_sensor.isActive TO sphere_script.isClicked
# The cone
Transform {
    children [
        DEF cone_sensor TouchSensor {}
        Shape {
            appearance Appearance {
                material Material {
                    diffuseColor 0 0 1
                }
            }
            geometry Cone {
                bottomRadius   .5
                height         1
            }
        }
        DEF cone_script Script {
            url        "cone_script.class"
            eventIn    SFBool    isClicked
        }
    ]
    bboxSize       1 1 1
    translation  -2 0 0
}
ROUTE cone_sensor.isActive TO cone_script.isClicked
# end of file
```

The box sensor adds objects to the scene graph from an external file. This external file, shown in Listing 45.9, contains a `Transform` node with a single `Cylinder` as a child. Because the API does not permit you to create node types and you have to place the newly created box at a point other than the origin, you must use a `Transform` node. Although you can just load a box from the external scene and then create a `Transform` node with the `createVrmlFromString()` method, this approach requires more code and slows execution speed. Remember that behavior writing is about getting things done as quickly as possible; the more you can move to external static file descriptions, the better.

Listing 45.9. The external VRML world file.

```
#VRML V2.0 utf8
#filename: cylinder.wrl
Transform {
  children
      Shape {
        appearance Appearance {
            material Material {
                diffuseColor 1 1 .85
            }
        }
    }
```

```
      geometry Cylinder {}
    }
  translation 0 4 0
}
# end of file
```

Organizing the Java Behaviors

Probably the most time-consuming task for someone writing a VRML scene with behaviors is deciding how to organize the various parts in relation to the scene graph structure. In a simple example like the one in Listing 45.8, there are two ways to arrange the scripts. Imagine what can happen in a moderately complex file of two or three thousand objects!

 All the scripts in this example are simple. When the node is received back in newNodes eventIn, the node must be translated to the new position. Ideally, you would like to do this directly by setting the translation field, but you are not able to do so because the translation field is encapsulated within the received node. The only way to translate the node to the new position is to post an event to the node, naming that field as the destination (which is the reason you set directOutputs to TRUE). After this is done, you can then call the add_children() method. Because all the scripts are short, the processEvents() method is not used because the risk to browser execution interruption is minimal. Shorter scripts are less likely to significantly impair the browser's usual processing. Listing 45.10 shows the complete source code for the cube script; this code can also be found on the CD-ROM that accompanies this book.

Listing 45.10. Java source for the cube script.

```
//filename: box_script.java
import vrml.field.*;
import vrml.node.*;
import vrml.*;
class box_script extends Script {
    private SFInt32  zPosition  = (SFInt32)getField("zPosition");
    private SFNode   thisScript = (SFNode)getField("thisScript");
    private MFString newUrl     = (MFString)getField("newUrl");
    // declare the eventOut field
    private MFNode   childList  = (MFNode)getEventOut("childList");
    // now declare the eventIn methods
    public void isClicked(ConstSFBool clicked, SFTime ts)
    {
        // check to see if picking up or letting go
        if(clicked.getValue() == false)
// Note: as of the writing of this book, Sony's CommunityPlace Java API had yet to
// implement the createVrmlFromURL and postEventIn methods
            Browser.createVrmlFromUrl(newUrl.getValue(),
                                  thisScript, "newNodes");
    }
```

continues

Listing 45.10. continued

```java
public void newNodes(ConstMFNode nodelist, SFTime ts)
{
    Node[]  nodes = (Node[])nodelist.getValue();
    float[] translation={0.0f,0.0f,0.0f};
    // Set up the translation
    zPosition.setValue(zPosition.getValue() + 2);
    translation[0] = zPosition.getValue();
    translation[1] = 0;
    translation[2] = 0;
    // There should only be one node with a transform at the
    // top. No error checking.
    nodes[0].postEventIn("translation", (Field)translation);
    // now send the processed node list to the eventOut
    childList.setValue(nodes);
}

}
```

Listing 45.11 (the code can also be found on the CD-ROM) shows the `sphere_script` class, which is similar to the `cube_script` class, except that you have to construct the text-string equivalent of the `cylinder.wrl` file. This is a straightforward string buffer problem. All you have to do is make sure that the `Transform` node of the newly added object has an appropriate value for the `translation` field to avoid a collision with the existing world objects.

Listing 45.11. Java source for the sphere script.

```java
//filename: sphere_script.java
import vrml.field.*;
import vrml.node.*;
import vrml.*;
class sphere_script extends Script {
    private SFInt32  zPosition = (SFInt32)getField("zPosition");
    private SFNode   root      = (SFNode)getField("root");
    // now declare the eventIn methods
    public void isClicked(ConstSFBool clicked, SFTime ts)
    {
        StringBuffer vrml_string = new StringBuffer();
        MFNode       nodes=null;
        // set the new position
        zPosition.setValue(zPosition.getValue() + 2);
        // check to see if picking up or letting go
        if(clicked.getValue() == false)
        {
            vrml_string.append("Transform { bboxSize 1 1 1 ");
            vrml_string.append("translation ");
            vrml_string.append(zPosition.getValue());
            vrml_string.append(" 0 0 ");
            vrml_string.append("children [ ");
            vrml_string.append("sphere { radius 0.5} ] }");
            nodes.setValue(
                    Browser.createVrmlFromUrl(vrml_string));
```

```
// Note: as of the writing of this book, Sony's CommunityPlace Java API had yet to
// implement the createVrmlFromURL and postEventIn methods
            root.postEventIn("add_children", (Field)nodes);
        }
    }
}
```

 The cone_script class is the easiest of the lot. As soon as it receives a confirmation of a touch, it starts to load another world specified by the URL. Listing 45.12 reveals the source code; the code is also located on the CD-ROM that accompanies this book.

Listing 45.12. Java Source for the cone script.

```
//filename: cone_script.java
import vrml.field.*;
import vrml.node.*;
import vrml.*;
class cone_script extends Script {
    SFBool   isClicked = (SFBool)getField("isClicked");
    // The eventIn method
    public void isClicked(ConstSFBool clicked, SFTime ts)
    {
        if(clicked.getValue() == false) {
            String s[] = new String[1] ;
            s[0] = "cylinder.wrl";
            String t[] = new String[1] ;
            t[0] = "target=info_frame";
            getBrowser().loadURL( s,t );
        }
    }
}
```

By compiling the preceding Java code samples and placing these and the two VRML source files in your Web directory, you can serve this basic dynamic world to the rest of the world. The rest of the world will get the same behavior as you do—regardless of what system individual users are running.

The CosmoPlayer Version of the Dynamic World Example

The following sections break down the process for creating the dynamically changing world for the CosmoPlayer browser.

The Complete VRML Description

 As Listing 45.13 shows, the VRML 2 file for CosmoPlayer contains no Script nodes or ROUTE statements. Instead, all scripting is done in the Java class, which is tied to the .wrl file in the HTML document, Dynamic.htm. This code is also located on the CD-ROM that accompanies this book.

Listing 45.13. The main world VRML description for CosmoPlayer.

```
#VRML V2.0 utf8
#filename: sgi_dynamic.wrl
DEF root_node Transform { },
DEF cube Transform {
    children [
        DEF cube_sensor TouchSensor{}
        Shape {
            appearance Appearance {
                material Material {
                    diffuseColor 1 0 0
                }
            }
            geometry Box { size    1 1 1}
        }
    ]
    bboxSize     1 1 1
    translation -2 0 0
},
DEF sphere Transform {
    children [
        DEF sphere_sensor TouchSensor{}
        Shape {
            appearance Appearance {
                material Material {
                    diffuseColor 0 1 0
                }
            }
            geometry Sphere { radius .5 }
        }
    ]
    bboxSize     1 1 1
    translation  0 0 0
},
DEF cone Transform {
    children [
        DEF cone_sensor TouchSensor{}
        Shape {
            appearance Appearance {
                material Material {
                    diffuseColor 0 0 1
                }
            }
            geometry Cone {
                bottomRadius .5
                height       1
            }
        }
    ]
    bboxSize     1 1 1
    translation  2 0 0
}
```

The HTML File

The HTML file in Listing 45.14 is almost identical to the one used in the first behavior example in Listing 45.5, earlier in this chapter. We only have to change the document title to Dynamic World Example, the SRC tag value to Dynamic.wrl, and the CODE tag value to Dynamic.class. With these changes, the HTML document will load the VRML file in a 400×400 pixel area within the browser window. The Java class is associated with the VRML scene and even provides an area for any AWT controls instantiated in the Java source code.

Listing 45.14. The HTML document.

```
<HTML>
<HEAD>
<TITLE>Dynamic World Example</TITLE>
</HEAD>
<BODY>
<CENTER>
<EMBED SRC="sgi_dynamic.wrl" BORDER=0 HEIGHT="400" WIDTH="400">
</CENTER>
<APPLET CODE="sgi_dynamic.class" MAYSCRIPT>
</APPLET>
</BODY>
</HTML>
```

The Java File

The source code in Listing 45.15 compiles without any warnings when you use the JDK 1.1 from Sun and the beta 3 version of CosmoPlayer 1.0. In the listing, I have commented out the lines that have not yet been implemented by SGI so that you can compare them to the VRML Consortium's suggested Java API at http://vrml.vag.org. As of this writing, neither the createVrmlFromURL() nor the loadURL() method had been implemented for the Windows 95/NT 4.0 CosmoPlayer viewer. Note that SGI has implemented a method declared as replaceWorld(Node *node*), which works like the loadURL() method when you use a string parameter that refers to the URL of a .wrl file. As usual, you can find the code presented in Listing 45.15 on the CD-ROM that accompanies this book.

Listing 45.15. The Java source code for CosmoPlayer.

```
//filename: sgi_dynamic.java
import java.awt.*;
import java.applet.*;
import vrml.external.field.*;
import vrml.external.Node;
import vrml.external.Browser;
```

continues

Listing 45.15. continued

```
import vrml.external.exception.*;
import netscape.javascript.JSObject;
public class sgi_dynamic extends Applet  implements EventOutObserver{
  boolean error = false;
  // Browser we're using
  Browser browser;
  // Root of the scene graph (to which we add our nodes)
  Node root=null;
  Node sensor[] = {null,null,null};
  // Shape group hierarchy
  Node[] shape[] = {null,null};
  Node[] scene = null;
  // EventIns of the TouchSensors
  EventOutSFTime touchTime[] = {null,null,null};
  // EventIns of the root node
  EventInMFNode addChildren;
  EventInMFNode removeChildren;
  public void init() {
    JSObject win = JSObject.getWindow(this);
    JSObject doc = (JSObject) win.getMember("document");
    JSObject embeds = (JSObject) doc.getMember("embeds");
    browser = (Browser) embeds.getSlot(0);
    try {
      // Get root node of the scene, and its EventIns
      root = browser.getNode("root_node");
      sensor[0] = browser.getNode("cube_sensor");
      sensor[1] = browser.getNode("sphere_sensor");
      sensor[2] = browser.getNode("cone_sensor");
      for(int x=0;x<3;x++) {
          touchTime[x] = (EventOutSFTime) sensor[x].getEventOut("touchTime");
          touchTime[x].advise(this, new Integer(x));
      }
      addChildren = (EventInMFNode) root.getEventIn("addChildren");
      removeChildren = (EventInMFNode) root.getEventIn("removeChildren");
      // Create shapes to be added on the fly--can reassign new strings at any
      // time
      //NOTE: as of beta 3 of CosmoPlayer 1.0 for Windows95/NT 4.0, the
      //createVRMLFromURL method was not implemented:
      //shape[0] = browser.createVrmlFromURL("cylinder.wrl",root,"addChildren");
      shape[0] = browser.createVrmlFromString("Transform {\n" +
                                        " children\n" +
                                        "  Shape {\n" +
                                        "    appearance Appearance {\n" +
                                        "     material Material {\n" +
                                        "      diffuseColor 0 1 1\n" +
                                        "     }\n" +
                                        "    }\n" +
                                        "    geometry Cylinder {}\n" +
                                        "  }\n" +
                                        " translation 0 -4 0\n" +
                                        "}\n");
      shape[1] = browser.createVrmlFromString("Transform {\n" +
                                        " children\n" +
                                        "  Shape {\n" +
```

```
                                          "    appearance Appearance {\n" +
                                          "      material Material {\n" +
                                          "        diffuseColor 1 1 .85\n" +
                                          "      }\n" +
                                          "    }\n" +
                                          "    geometry Cylinder {}\n" +
                                          "  }\n" +
                                          " translation 0 4 0\n" +
                                          "}\n");
        Node[] scene = browser.createVrmlFromString("Transform {\n" +
                                          " children\n" +
                                          "  Shape {\n" +
                                          "    appearance Appearance {\n" +
                                          "      material Material {\n" +
                                          "        diffuseColor 1 1 .85\n" +
                                          "      }\n" +
                                          "    }\n" +
                                          "    geometry Sphere {radius 2}\n"+
                                          "  }\n" +
                                          " translation 0 0 0\n" +
                                          "}\n");
      }
      catch (InvalidNodeException e) {
        showStatus("PROBLEMS!: " + e + "\n");
        error = true;
      }
      catch (InvalidEventInException e) {
        showStatus("PROBLEMS!: " + e + "\n");
        error = true;
      }
      catch (InvalidVrmlException e) {
        showStatus("PROBLEMS!: " + e + "\n");
        error = true;
      }

      if (error == false)
        showStatus("Ok...\n");
    }
    public void callback(EventOut who, double when, Object which) {
      Integer whichNum = (Integer) which;
      if (whichNum.intValue() == 0) {
        addChildren.setValue(shape[0]);
      }
      else if (whichNum.intValue() == 1) {
        addChildren.setValue(shape[1]);
      }
      else if (whichNum.intValue() == 2) {
        //NOTE: as of beta3 of CosmoPlayer 1.0 for Windows95, the loadURL method
        //was not implemented:
        //loadURL("cylinder.wrl","");
        browser.replaceWorld(scene);
      }
    }
}
```

The Java source code contains a object and event declaration and an initialization section that connects the Java variables to the VRML scene graph nodes and sets up the callback. Then it defines three nodes: `shape[0]` is a cyan cylinder, `shape[1]` is a yellow cylinder, and `scene` is another yellow cylinder centered at the origin. The callback listens for any events generated by the user. When the cube's sensor is activated, `shape[0]` is added to the VRML scene graph with the `addChildren()` method. When the sphere's sensor is activated, `shape[1]` is added to the VRML scene graph with the `addChildren()` method. When the cone's sensor is activated, the current VRML scene graph is replaced with the `scene` node through the `replaceWorld()` method of the browser object. Although not used in this example, the `removeChildren()` method is called in exactly the same way as the `addChildren()` method when you want to remove a single node from the VRML scene graph.

Creating Reusable Behaviors

It would be problematic if you had to rewrite this code every time you wanted to use it in another file. Although you could reuse the Java bytecodes, this means that you would need identical copies of the script declaration every time you wanted to use it. Redundancy is not a particularly nice practice from the software engineering point of view, either. Eventually, you will be caught by the cut-and-paste error of having extra pieces of ROUTE statements (and extra fields) floating around that could accidentally be connected to nodes in the new scene, resulting in difficult-to-trace bugs.

VRML 2 provides a mechanism similar to the C/C++ `#include` directive and `typedef` statements all rolled into one—the `PROTO` and `EXTERNPROTO` statement pair. The `PROTO` statement acts like a `typedef`: you use `PROTO` with a node and its definition and then you can use that name as though it were an ordinary node within the context of that file.

If you want to access that prototyped node outside of that file, you can use the `EXTERNPROTO` statement to include it in the new file and then use it as though it were an ordinary node.

Although this approach is useful for creating libraries of static parts, where it really comes into its own is in creating canned behaviors. A programmer can create a completely self-contained behavior and, in the best object-oriented tradition, provide interfaces to only the behaviors he or she wants. The syntax of the `PROTO` and `EXTERNPROTO` statements follow:

```
PROTO prototypename [ # any collection of
    eventIn        eventTypeName eventName
    eventOut       eventTypeName eventName
    exposedField   fieldTypeName fieldName initialValue
    field          fieldTypeName fieldName initialValue
] {
    # scene graph structure. Any combination of
    # nodes, prototypes, and ROUTEs
}
EXTERNPROTO prototypename [ # any collection of
    eventIn        eventTypeName eventName
    eventOut       eventTypeName eventName
```

```
    exposedField   fieldTypeName fieldName
    field          fieldTypeName fieldName
]
"URL" or [ "URN1" "URL2"]
```

You can then add a behavior to a VRML file by using just the *prototypename* in the file. For example, if you have a behavior that simulates a taxi, you may want to have many taxis in a number of different worlds representing different countries. The cabs are identical except for their color. Note again the ability to specify multiple URLs for the behavior. If the browser cannot retrieve the first URL, it tries the second until it gets a cab.

A taxi can have many attributes (such as speed and direction) that the user of the cab need not really discriminate. To incorporate a virtual taxi into your world, all you really care about is a few things such as being able to signal a cab, get in, tell it where to go, pay the fare, and then get out when it has reached its destination. From the world authors' point of view, how the taxi finds its virtual destination is unimportant. A declaration of the taxi prototype file might look like the following:

```
#VRML V2.0 utf8
# Taxi prototype file taxi.wrl
PROTO taxicab [
    exposedField SFBool      isAvailable   TRUE
    eventIn      SFBool      inCab
    eventIn      SFString    destination
    eventIn      SFFloat     payFare
    eventOut     SFFloat     fareCost
    eventOut     SFInt32     speed
    eventOut     SFVec3f     direction
    field        SFColor     color        1 0 0
    # rest of externally available variables
] {
    DEF root_group Transform {
        # Taxi shape description here
    }
    DEF taxi_script Script {
        url    ["taxi.class"]
        # rest of event and field declarations
    }
    # ROUTE statements to connect it altogether
}
```

To include the taxi in your world, the file would look something like the following:

```
#VRML V2.0 utf8
#
# myworld.wrl
EXTERNPROTO taxi [
    exposedField SFBool      isAvailable
    eventIn      SFBool      inCab
    eventIn      SFString    destination
    eventIn      SFFloat     payFare
    eventOut     SFFloat     fareCost
    eventOut     SFInt32     speed
    eventOut     SFVec3f     direction
    field        SFColor     color
    # rest of externally available variables
]
```

```
[ " http://myworld.com/taxi.wrl", "http://yourworld.com/taxi.wrl"]
# some scene graph
#....
Transform {
    children [
        # other VRML nodes. Then we use the taxi
        DEF my_taxi taxi {
            color  0 1. 0
        }
    ]
}
```

Here is a case in which you are likely to use the postEventIn() method to call a cab. Somewhere in the scene graph, you have a control that your avatar uses to query a nearby cab for its isAvailable field. (An *avatar* is the virtual body used to represent you in the virtual world.) If the isAvailable field is TRUE, the avatar sends the event to flag the cab. Apart from the required mechanics to signal the cab with the various instructions, the world creator does not care how the cab is implemented. By using the EXTERNPROTO call, the world's creator and users can always be sure of getting the latest version of the taxi implementation and that the taxi will exhibit uniform behaviors regardless of which world the users are in.

CommunityPlace's approach to the VRML/Java API is set up to take advantage of using Java within prototyped intranode behaviors. CosmoPlayer, on the other hand, leaves intranode behavior scripting to VRMLscript. You can take advantage of Java class reusability directly within the CosmoPlayer VRML/Java API. For example, you can create a bounce class in Java that many different types of VRML objects could inherit in the Java source code itself. The bounce class would define how to deform an object as it hits an obstacle and changes direction; the class would be written only once, yet take advantage of full reusability.

The Future: VRML, Java, and AI

The information in this chapter has so far relied on static, predefined behaviors available either within the original VRML file or retrievable from somewhere on the Internet.

One exciting goal of VR worlds is to be able to create autonomous agents that have some degree of artificial intelligence. Back in the early days of programming, self-modifying code was common, but it faded away as more resources and higher-level programming languages removed the need. A VR world can take advantage of self-modifying code.

Stephenson's Librarian from *Snow Crash* is just one example of how an independent agent can act in a VR world. His model was very simple—a glorified version of today's 2D HTML-based search engine that, when requested, searched the U.S. Library of Congress for information related to a desired topic (the Librarian also has speech recognition and synthesis capabilities). The next generation of intelligent agents will include learning behavior as well.

The VRML API enables you to go the next step further—a virtual assistant that can modify its own behavior to suit your preferences. This is not just a case of loading in some canned behaviors. By combining VRMLscript and Java behaviors, you can create customized behaviors on the fly by concatenating the behavior strings and script nodes, calling the `createVrmlFromString()` method, and adding it to the scene graph in the appropriate place. Although doing so is probably not feasible with current Pentium-class machines, the next generation of processors will probably make it so.

Summary

With the tools presented in this chapter, you should be able to create whatever you require of cyberspace. There is only so much you can do with a 2D screen in terms of new information-presentation techniques. The third dimension of VRML enables you to create experiences that are far beyond what you expect of today's Web pages. 3D representation of data and VR behaviors programming is still very much in its infancy—so much so that, at the time of this writing, only Sony's CommunityPlace, SGI's CosmoPlayer, and Netscape's Live3D viewers were available for testing, and even then, many parts of these viewers were not implemented. In fact, the Live3D API works only with VRML 1 and is quite different from what is suggested by the VRML 2 standard.

If you are serious about creating behaviors, you *must* learn VRML thoroughly. Many little problems can catch the unwary, particularly the peculiarities of VRML syntax when it comes to ordering objects within the scene graph. An object placed at the wrong level severely restricts its actions. A book on VRML is a must for this work. For a good reference on VRML 2, check out *Teach Yourself VRML 2 in 21 Days*, by Chris Marrin and Bruce Campbell (published by Sams.net Publishing).

Whether you are creating reusable behavior libraries, an intelligent postman that brings the mail to you wherever you are, or simply a functional Java machine for your virtual office, the excitement of behavior programming is catching.

Integrating Java and JavaScript

by Rick Darnell

CHAPTER 46

By itself, Java is a significant development because of its ability to stretch the behavior of your Web pages far beyond what was ever imagined for the World Wide Web. Java can become even more powerful when harnessed with JavaScript.

As you know from other chapters, Java is powerful enough to add animation, sound, and other features to an applet—but it's very cumbersome to directly interact with an HTML page. JavaScript isn't big or powerful enough to match Java's programming power, but it is uniquely suited to work directly with the elements that comprise an HTML document.

By combining the best features of Java and JavaScript, your applet can interact with your Web page, offering a new level of interactivity.

Setting the Stage

For Java and JavaScript to interact on your Web pages, they both must be active and enabled in the user's browser.

To make sure that both features are active in Netscape Navigator when the user views Java applets, include these simple directions on the opening page of your Web site for the user to follow:

1. Choose Options, Network Preferences from the menu bar. The Preferences dialog box appears.
2. Select the Languages tab from the Preferences dialog box (see Figure 46.1).
3. Both Java and JavaScript are enabled by default. If this has changed, make sure that both checkboxes are selected.

Figure 46.1.

The Languages tab in the Network Preferences dialog box controls whether or not Java applets and JavaScript commands are processed for HTML documents.

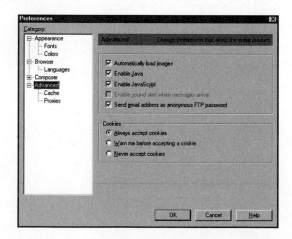

The steps to include to make sure that both languages are active in Microsoft Internet Explorer are similar to the steps for Navigator:

1. Choose View, Options from the menu bar. The Options dialog box appears.
2. Select the Security tab from the Options dialog box (see Figure 46.2).
3. Make sure that the Enable Java Programs checkbox is selected. The scripting languages available in Internet Explorer—JavaScript and VBScript—are automatically enabled; there is no way to disable them.

FIGURE 46.2.

Internet Explorer controls which language features are enabled from the Security tab in the Options dialog box.

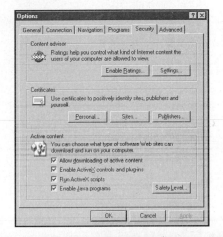

NOTE

Netscape Navigator also includes a Java Console for displaying applet-generated messages (see Figure 46.3). In addition to system messages such as errors and exceptions, the Java Console is where any messages generated by the applet using the `java.lang.System` package (including `System.out.println`) are displayed. To display the Console, select Options, Show Java Console from the Netscape Navigator menu bar.

The Microsoft Internet Explorer can show the results of system messages also, but not in real time as Navigator's Java Console can do. All messages are saved in `javalog.txt` in `C:\Windows\Java`. To make sure that this feature is active, select View, Options from the menu bar, select the Advanced tab in the Options dialog box, and make sure that the Java Logging checkbox is selected.

continues

continued

FIGURE 46.3.

The Java Console displays any system messages generated by the applet.

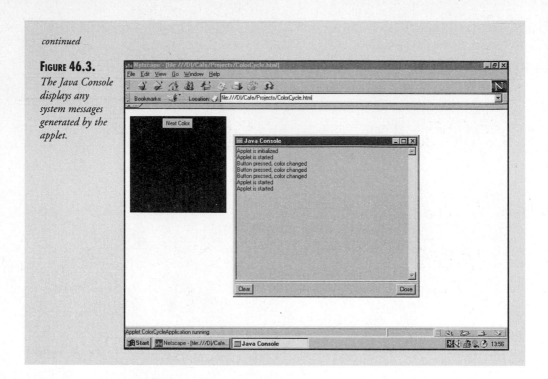

JavaScript Talking to Java

The first and most commonly used communication feature is to modify applet behavior from JavaScript. This is really quite easy to do with the right information, and doing so enables your applet to respond to events on the HTML page—including interacting with forms.

Java syntax is very similar to other JavaScript syntax, so if you're already familiar with either scripting language, adding Java control is an easy step.

Calling Java Methods

With Navigator 3.0 and later, Netscape provides an object called Packages. The Packages object allows JavaScript to invoke native Java methods directly. This object is used in much the same way as the Document or Window object is in regular JavaScript.

> **NOTE**
>
> As you'll recall from earlier discussions, groups of related classes are combined in a construct called a *package*. Classes from a package can be used by outside classes by using the import command.

Just to confuse things, that's not the case with the JavaScript version of `Packages`. In JavaScript, the `Packages` object is the parent object used to invoke native Java methods, such as `Packages.System.out.println("Say Howdy")`.

CAUTION

Invoking native Java methods from JavaScript is possible only within Netscape Navigator 3.0 or later. Microsoft Internet Explorer doesn't include support for the JavaScript-to-Java packages in its 3.01 release, but may include its own version of this capability in later versions.

The source of the problem is that JavaScript is implemented individually for each browser; what Netscape includes for JavaScript isn't the same as what Microsoft includes for JScript. However, Microsoft and Netscape are already working to standardize JavaScript so that it will work the same across both browser platforms.

Internet Explorer still includes support for all the now-standard features of JavaScript, including control and manipulation of windows, documents, and forms, although it still does not include other standard items, such as images.

Here is the syntax to call a Java package from JavaScript directly:

```
[Packages.]packageName.className.methodName
```

The object name is optional for the three default packages—`java`, `sun`, and `netscape`. These three packages can be referenced by their package name alone, as shown here:

```
java.className.methodName
sun.className.methodName
netscape.className.methodName
```

Together with the package name, the object and class names can result in some unwieldy and error-prone typing. This is why you can also create new variables using the `Package` product. The following code assigns a Java package to the variable `System` and then uses the `System` variable to call a method in the package:

```
var JavaSystem = Package.java.lang.System;
JavaSystem.out.println("Hello from Java in JavaScript.");
```

Controlling Java Applets

Controlling an applet with a script is a fairly easy matter, but it does require some knowledge of the applet you're working with. Any public variable, method, or property within the applet is accessible through JavaScript.

> **TIP**
>
> If you're changing the values of variables within an applet, the safest way to do so is to create a new method within the applet for that specific purpose. The method can accept the value from JavaScript, perform any error checking, and then pass the new value along to the rest of the applet. This arrangement helps prevent unexpected behavior or applet crashes.

You have to know which methods, properties, and variables in the applet are public. Only the public items in an applet are accessible to JavaScript.

> **TIP**
>
> Two public methods are common to all applets, and you can always use them—start() and stop(). These methods provide a handy way to control when the applet should be active and running.

There are five basic activities common to all applets (as opposed to one basic activity for applications). An applet has more activities to correspond to the major events in its life cycle on the user's browser. None of the activities have any definitions. You must override the methods with a subclass within your applet. Here are the five activities common to all applets:

- **Initialization:** This activity occurs after the applet is first loaded. This activity can include creating objects, setting state variables, and loading images.
- **Starting:** After being initialized or stopped, an applet is started. The difference between being initialized and starting is that the former happens only once; the latter can occur many times.
- **Painting:** The paint() method is how the applet actually gets information to the screen—from simple lines and text to images and colored backgrounds. Painting can occur a lot of times in the course of an applet's life.
- **Stopping:** Stopping suspends applet execution and stops the applet from using system resources. This activity can be an important addition to your code because an applet continues to run even after a user leaves the page.
- **Destroying:** This activity is the extreme form of stopping. Destroying an applet begins a clean-up process in which running threads are terminated and objects and resources are released.

With this information in hand, getting started begins with the <APPLET> tag. It helps to give a name to your applet to make JavaScript references to it easier to read. The following snippet of code shows the basic constructor for an HTML applet tag that sets the stage for JavaScript control of a Java applet. The tag is identical to the tags you used in previous chapters to add applets, except that a new attribute is included for a name:

```
<APPLET CODE="UnderConstruction.class" NAME="AppletConstruction" WIDTH=60 HEIGHT=60>
</APPLET>
```

Assigning a name to your applet isn't absolutely necessary because JavaScript creates an array of applets when the page is loaded. However, doing so makes for a much more readable page.

CAUTION

Like the JavaScript `Packages` object, the JavaScript `applets` array is currently available only in Netscape Navigator 3.0 or later. This doesn't leave Microsoft Internet Explorer completely out in the cold—JavaScript can still reference an applet in Explorer using the applet's name.

To use a method of the applet from JavaScript, use the following syntax:

```
document.appletName.methodOrProperty
```

TIP

Netscape Navigator 3.0 uses an `applets` array to reference all the applets on a page. The `applets` array is used according to the following syntax:

```
document.applets[index].methodOrProperty
document.applets[appletName].methodOrProperty
```

These two methods also identify the applet you want to control, but the method using the applet's name without the `applets` array is the easiest to read and requires the least amount of typing.

Like other arrays, one of the properties of `applets` is `length`, which returns how many applets are in the document.

This array of applets is not currently available in the Microsoft Internet Explorer 3.0 implementation of JavaScript.

One of the easy methods of controlling applet behavior is starting and stopping its execution. You start and stop an applet using the `start()` and `stop()` methods common to every applet. Use a form and two buttons to add the functions to your Web page (see Figure 46.4). The following code snippet is a basic example of the HTML code needed to add the buttons, with the name of the applet substituted for *appletName*:

```
<FORM>
<INPUT TYPE="button" VALUE="Start" onClick="document.appletName.start()">
<INPUT TYPE="button" VALUE="Stop" onClick="document.appletName.stop()">
</FORM>
```

FIGURE 46.4.

One of the simplest ways to control an applet is to use buttons that start and stop it.

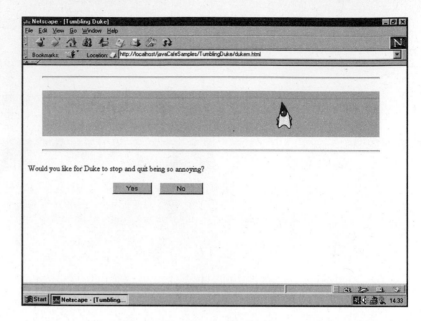

You can also call other methods, depending on their visibility to the world outside the applet. JavaScript can call any Java method or variable by using a `public` declaration.

> **TIP**
>
> Any variable or method within the applet that doesn't include a specific declaration of scope is `protected` by default. If you don't see the `public` declaration, it's not.

The syntax to call applet methods from JavaScript is simple and can be integrated with browser events, such as the button code snippet just shown. The basic syntax for calling an applet method from JavaScript is shown here:

```
document.appletName.methodName(arg1,...,argx)
```

To call the `stop()` method from the `underConstructionApplet` applet within an HTML page, the syntax is as follows (assuming that the applet is the first one listed on the page):

```
document.underConstructionApplet.stop();
```

Here's how you do it with Navigator (again, assuming that the applet is the first one listed on the page):

```
document.applets[0].stop();
```

Integrating the `start()` and `stop()` methods for this applet with the applet tag and button code snippet used earlier results in the following code:

```
<APPLET CODE="UnderConstruction" NAME="underConstructionApplet"
    WIDTH=60 HEIGHT=60></APPLET>
<FORM>
<INPUT TYPE="button" VALUE="Start"
    onClick="document.underConstructionApplet.start()">
<INPUT TYPE="button" VALUE="Stop"
    onClick="document.underConstructionApplet.stop()">
</FORM>
```

Java Talking to JavaScript

The Netscape classes provided with Netscape Navigator 3.0 and later enable Java to take a direct look at your HTML page through JavaScript objects. This new set of classes is called *LiveConnect*. To implement this functionality, you must import the `netscape.javascript.JSObject` class when the applet is created.

> **TIP**
>
> The `netscape.javascript.JSObject` class is included with the other class files in the `Netscape` folder in the `java_30` file for Netscape 3.0, and in the `java_40` file for Netscape 4.0. In Windows, the complete location is `\Program Files\Netscape\Navigator\Program\java\classes`. For version 4.0, the `Navigator` directory name changes to `Communicator`.
>
> To enable the Java compiler to find the packages, you have to move the Netscape class files to your `Java/Lib/` directory and give them a `zip` extension. Then make sure that the new file is added to your `CLASSPATH` attribute. The `netscape.javascript.JSObject` class extends the standard Java `Object` class, so the newly created `JSObject` objects are treated as other Java objects.

To include the `JSObject` class as part of your applet, use the `import` command as you normally do to include any other class package:

```
import netscape.javascript.JSObject;
```

Another important addition is necessary in the applet tag: `MAYSCRIPT`. This security feature gives specific permission for the applet to access JavaScript objects. Here's how to include the tag:

```
<APPLET CODE="colorPreview.class" WIDTH=50 HEIGHT=50 NAME="Preview" MAYSCRIPT>
```

Without the `MAYSCRIPT` parameter, any attempt to access JavaScript from the applet results in an exception. If you want to exclude an applet from accessing the page, simply leave out the `MAYSCRIPT` parameter.

Java and JavaScript Values

The JSObject class gives Java the capability to look at and change objects defined through JavaScript. This requires certain assumptions, especially when passing or receiving values from Java. To ensure compatibility, every JavaScript value is assigned some form from java.lang.Object:

- **Objects.** Any object sent or received from Java remains in its original object wrapper.
- **Java numbers.** Because JavaScript doesn't support the variety of numerical types Java does (byte, char, short, int, long, float, and double), Java numbers lose their specific type and become a basic JavaScript number.
- **JavaScript numbers.** There's no way to tell what kind of number Java may be receiving from JavaScript. So all JavaScript numbers are converted to a Java float.
- **Booleans and strings.** These types are passed essentially unchanged. Java booleans become JavaScript booleans and vice versa. The same is true for strings.

Looking at the JavaScript Window

To get a handle on JavaScript objects—including form items and frames—you must first create an object to hold the current Navigator window. The getWindow() method provides the means to do this.

First, you have to create a new variable of type JSObject. Then, using the JSObject class, assign the window to the variable:

```
JSObject jsWin;
jsWin = JSObject.getWindow(this);
```

TIP

This type of work is typically accomplished within the applet's init() method.

After you have a handle on the window, you can start to break it into its various components with getMember(). This method returns a specific object from the next level of precedence. For example, to get a handle on a form on a Web page with a form called response, you can use the following set of statements:

```
jsWin = JSObject.getWindow(this);
JSObject jsDoc = (JSObject) jsWin.getMember("document");
JSObject responseForm = (JSObject) jsDoc.getMember("response");
```

In JavaScript, this form is referred to as window.document.response. Note that each JavaScript object is assigned to its own variable in Java and is not a property of a parent object. The form in Java is contained in responseForm, not in jsWin.jsDoc.responseForm.

> **NOTE**
>
> All parts of an HTML document exist in JavaScript in set relationships to each other. This arrangement is called *instance hierarchy* because it works with specific items on the page, rather than with general classes of items.
>
> At the top of the pyramid is the `window` object. It is the parent of all other objects. Its children include `document`, `location`, and `history`, which share a precedence level. The `document` object's children include objects specific to the page, such as forms, links, anchors, and applets.
>
> The Java `netscape` package recognizes and uses this hierarchy through its `getWindow()` and `getMethod()` methods. The first gets the `window` object (the highest object); the latter returns individual members of the next level.

So far, you've retrieved only broad objects, such as windows and forms. Getting a specific value from JavaScript follows the same principles, although now you need a Java variable of the proper type to hold the results instead of an instance of `JSObject`.

> **TIP**
>
> Don't forget about passing numbers between JavaScript and Java. All JavaScript numbers are converted to a `float` type. You can cast it to another Java type if necessary once the value is in the applet.

Returning to the form example described earlier in this section, suppose that there is a text field (`name`), a number (`idNum`), and a checkbox (`member`). You can retrieve each of these values from JavaScript using the following commands:

```
jsWin = JSObject.getWindow(this);
JSObject jsDoc = (JSObject) jsWin.getMember("document");
JSObject responseForm = (JSObject) jsDoc.getMember("response");
JSObject nameField = (JSObject) responseForm.getMember("name");
JSOBject idNumField = (JSObject) responseForm.getMember("idNum");
JSOBject memberField = (JSObject) responseForm.getMember("memberField");
String nameValue = (String) nameField.getMember("value");
Float idNumValue = (Float) idNumField.getMember("value");
Boolean memberValue = (Boolean) memberField.getMember("checked");
```

This chunk of code quickly becomes unwieldy, especially when several values are needed from JavaScript. If you have to access more than several elements on a page, it can help to create a new method to handle the process.

The `getElement()` method defined in the next code snippet accepts the name of a form and element on an HTML page as arguments and returns the `JSObject` that contains it:

```
protected JSObject getElement(String formName, String elementName) {
    JSObject jsDoc = (JSObject) JSObject.getWindow().getMember("document");
    JSObject jsForm = (JSObject) jsDoc.getMember(formName);
    JSObject jsElement = (JSObject) jsElement.getMember(elementName);
    return jsElement;
}
```

This simple method creates the intervening `JSObject` objects needed to get to the form element, making the retrieval as easy as knowing the form and element name. If the form or form element is not included on the page, the method throws an exception and halts the applet. And because the instances of `JSObject` are contained within the method, system resources are conserved.

To change a JavaScript value from an applet, use the `JSObject.setMember()` method. The syntax is `setMember(name, value)`, where *name* is the name of the JavaScript object, and *value* is its new value. The following snippet uses the `getElement()` method just defined to get the `name` element from the `response` form, and then uses the `JSObject`'s `setMember()` method to set its value to `Your Name Here`. This is equivalent to the `this.name = newValue` statement in JavaScript.

```
JSObject nameField = getElement("response","name");
nameField.setMember("name","Your Name Here");
```

The `getWindow()` and `getMember()` methods just described are the basic methods used when interfacing with JavaScript. Together, they make receiving values from an HTML page with JavaScript a straightforward task—even if the process is a little cumbersome in the number of statements required.

Getting Values Using Indexes

If your applet is designed to work with a variety of HTML pages that may contain different names for forms and elements, you can use the JavaScript arrays with the `JSObject` slot methods. If the desired form is always the first to appear on the document and the element is the third, then the form name is `forms[0]` and the element is `elements[2]`.

After retrieving the document object using `getWindow()` and `getMember()`, use `getSlot(index)` to return a value within it. For example, in an HTML document containing three forms, the second is retrieved into Java using the following commands:

```
JSOBject jsWin = JSObject.getWindow(this);
JSObject jsDoc = (JSObject) jsWin.getMember("document");
JSObject jsForms = (JSObject) jsDoc.getMember("forms");
JSObject jsForm1 = (JSObject) jsForms.getSlot(1);
```

Using `setSlot()`, the same process is used to load a value into an array. The syntax is shown here:

```
JSObject.setSlot(index,value);
```

In this syntax, the *index* is an integer and the *value* is a `String`, `boolean`, or `float`.

> **TIP**
>
> One rule that must stand firm is the placement of the form and the elements within it. When the applet is used with more than one document, the forms and elements must be in the same relative place every time to avoid exceptions and unpredictable results.

Using JavaScript Methods in Java

The `netscape` class package provides two methods to call JavaScript methods from within an applet: `call()` and `eval()`. The syntax differs slightly for the two methods, but the outcome is the same.

> **TIP**
>
> You need a handle for the JavaScript window before you can use the `call()` and `eval()` methods.

There are two ways to invoke these methods. The first uses a specific window instance; the second uses `getWindow()` to create a JavaScript window just for the expression:

```
jsWin.callOrEval(arguments)
JSOBject.getWindow().callOrEval(arguments)
```

The `call()` method separates the method from its arguments. This is useful for passing Java values to the JavaScript method. The syntax is `call("method", args)`, where *method* is the name of the JavaScript method you want to call and *args* is an array of the arguments you want to pass.

The `eval()` method, on the other hand, uses a string that appears identical to the way a method is called within JavaScript. The syntax is `eval("expression")`, where *expression* is a complete method name along with its arguments, such as `document.writeln('Your name here.'")`. The entire statement is wrapped within a string and passed to JavaScript. Here's what it looks like when you include the string with the `eval()` expression:

```
eval("document.writeln(\'Your name here.\');")
```

TIP

To pass quotation marks as quotation marks to JavaScript within a Java string, use the backslash character before each occurrence.

Summary

Netscape's LiveConnect gives you a whole set of tools to get from JavaScript to Java and back again. The marriage of these two Web technologies can open up a whole new world of how to interact with your users. By using simple statements and definitions—already a part of both languages—you can make a previously static Web page communicate with an applet embedded in it; in return, the Web page can react to the output of the applet.

JavaScript-to-Java communication is a simple extension of JavaScript's functionality. As long as your applets have names, any applet's `public` method is accessible to your HTML page. And using the new Netscape package `netscape.javascript` makes the process a two-way street: Your Java applet can invoke JavaScript functions and look at the structure of your Web page as represented by the JavaScript document object.

This combination is one more set of capabilities in your toolbox that you can use to meet your users' needs.

Integrating Java and ActiveX

by Michael Morrison

IN THIS CHAPTER

CHAPTER 47

With the full force of Microsoft behind it, it's no surprise that ActiveX has received tons of press attention lately. As an Internet developer, you probably have some degree of confusion about how ActiveX fits into the Internet landscape. More specifically, you may be worried about what impact ActiveX will have on Java. This chapter takes a close look at Java and ActiveX and where each fits in the world of Internet development. This chapter also discusses an ActiveX technology that enables the integration of Java and ActiveX.

The goal of this chapter is to give you some perspective on the relationship between Java and ActiveX. In doing so, you learn the details surrounding what each technology offers and why they don't necessarily have to be viewed as direct competitors. You also learn about a specific technology that aims to allow Java and ActiveX to happily coexist.

Technological Goals

In a general sense, Java and ActiveX both try to achieve the same goal: to bring interactivity to the Web. Because this is a very general goal, you probably realize that many different approaches can be taken to reach it. Java and ActiveX definitely take different routes to delivering interactivity to the Web, and for good reason; they're widely divergent technologies that come from two unique companies. Let's take a look at each technology and see what it accomplishes in its pursuit to liven up the Web.

The Java Vision

First and foremost, Java is a programming language. It certainly is other things as well, but the underlying strength of the Java technology is the structure and design of the Java language itself. The architects at Sun wanted to take many of the powerful features in C++ and build a tighter, easier-to-use, and more secure object-oriented language. They succeeded in a big way: Java is indeed a very clean, easy-to-use language with lots of advanced security features. The time spent designing the Java language is paying off well for Sun, because the language's structure is the primary cause of the C++ programmer migration to Java.

However, the Java language without its standard class libraries and Internet support would be nothing more than competition for C++. In fact, the Java language, as cool as it is, would probably fail in a head-to-head match up with C++ strictly from a language perspective. This is because C++ is firmly established in the professional development community, and programmers need a very compelling reason to learn an entirely new language. Sun realized this and was smart enough to present Java as much more than just another programming language.

The basic Java technology consists of the Java language, the Java class libraries, the Java runtime system, and the JavaScript scripting language. It's the combination of all these parts that makes the Java technology so exciting. Java is the first large-scale effort at creating a truly cross-platform programming language with lots of functionality from the start. Couple the slick language and cross-platform aspects of Java with its ability to seamlessly integrate Java programs into the Web environment and you can easily see its appeal.

This integration of the Web into the Java technology is no accident; Sun simply saw the potential to capitalize on a technology they had been developing for a while by fitting it to the rapidly growing needs of the Internet. This pretty much sums up the primary aim of Java: to provide a way to safely integrate cross-platform interactive applications into the Web environment using an object-oriented language. Keep in mind, however, that new innovations such as JavaBeans, JavaOS, and Java microprocessors are rapidly altering and expanding Sun's vision of the Java technology.

The ActiveX Vision

Microsoft has different ideas for the Internet than Sun does. Unlike Sun, Microsoft initially didn't realize the immediate potential of the Internet, or at least didn't see how fast it was all happening. In fact, it wasn't until the excitement surrounding Java had begun to peak that Microsoft finally decided it had to rethink things in regard to the Internet and the Web.

The connection was finally made somewhere in Redmond that the Internet would significantly affect personal computing. The company couldn't just sit idly by and see what happened; it could either take action to capitalize on the Internet or get burnt by not accepting it as a major shift in the way we all use computers. When Microsoft finally came to terms with the fact that the Internet was rapidly changing the face of computing—even personal computing—the company quickly regrouped and decided to figure out a way to get a piece of the Internet action. Keep in mind that Microsoft has never been content with just *a* piece of the action; it wants the *largest* piece of the action!

Unlike Sun, Microsoft already had a wide range of successful commercial software technologies; it just had to figure out which one of them would scale best to the Internet. It turned out that one of the company's most successful technologies was ideally suited for the Internet: OLE (Object Linking and Embedding). Microsoft saw OLE as a powerful, stable technology with lots of potential for the Internet, and it was right; ActiveX is basically OLE revamped for the Internet.

Unlike Java, however, ActiveX isn't just meant to be a way to add interactivity to the Web. Sure, that's part of it, but Microsoft isn't the type of company to just hand out technologies for the good of humanity. OLE is a technology deeply ingrained in most of Microsoft's commercial products, as well as many other commercial Windows applications. By simply migrating OLE to the Internet (through ActiveX), Microsoft effectively assumes a huge market share of Internet products overnight. Suddenly, every piece of code written based on OLE can now be considered ActiveX-enabled with little extra work. Microsoft's new goal of migrating desktop software to the Internet suddenly looks quite attainable.

Although Microsoft is certainly looking to bring interactive applications to the Web with ActiveX, it is also looking to make sure that many of those interactive applications are Microsoft applications. This situation also ensures that Windows remains a strong presence on the Internet because OLE is essentially a Windows-derived technology. Although strategically ideal, the selection of OLE as the technological underpinnings for ActiveX has much more to do with the fact that OLE is a slick technology already tweaked for distributed computing; it's just the icing on the cake that OLE is already firmly established in the PC software community.

Microsoft isn't the only company to benefit from the positioning of ActiveX. Every PC software developer that uses OLE in its applications will benefit from ActiveX just as easily as Microsoft. Because the PC development community is by far the largest in the industry, end users also benefit greatly because many software companies will be building ActiveX applications from existing OLE code that is already stable.

In the discussion of ActiveX thus far, little has been said about programming languages. Unlike Java, ActiveX has nothing to do with a specific programming language; you can write ActiveX code in any language you choose that supports Microsoft's COM specification. Just in case you don't realize it, this is a big deal! Although Java is a very cool language, many programmers don't like being forced to learn a new language just to exploit the capabilities of the Internet. On the other hand, writing ActiveX controls in C++ is a little messier than writing Java applets in Java.

Under the Hood

Okay, so you have an idea about what each technology is trying to accomplish—but what does each actually deliver? It turns out that Java and ActiveX are surprisingly different in their implementations, especially considering how similar their ultimate goals are.

Under Java's Hood

The Java technology can be divided into five major components:

- The Java language
- The Java class libraries
- The Java runtime system
- The JavaScript scripting language
- The JavaBeans component technology

The Java language provides the programmatic underpinnings that make the whole Java system possible. It is the Java language that shines the brightest when you compare Java and ActiveX. The Java class libraries, which go hand in hand with the language, provide a wide array of features guaranteed to work on any platform. This is a huge advantage Java has over almost every other programming language in existence. Never before has a tight, powerful language been delivered that offers a rich set of standard classes in a cross-platform manner.

The Java runtime system is the component of Java that gets the least press attention, but ultimately makes many of Java's features a reality. The Java runtime system includes a *virtual machine*, which stands between Java bytecode programs and the specific processor inside a computer system. It is the responsibility of the virtual machine to translate platform-independent bytecodes to platform-specific native machine code. In doing so, the virtual machine provides the mechanism that makes Java platform-independent. Unfortunately, the virtual machine is also responsible for the performance problems associated with Java. These problems have been, and will continue to be, improved on thanks to just-in-time Java compilers and other related technologies.

The JavaScript scripting language is the Java component that allows you to embed scripted Java programs directly into HTML code. The primary purpose of JavaScript is to allow Web developers who aren't necessarily programmers to add interactivity to their Web pages in a straightforward manner.

The JavaBeans component technology is Java's way of providing a reusable, component-based software API. The JavaBeans technology allows developers to build applications from prebuilt software components that can easily be integrated in visual application builder tools. JavaBeans represents a significant step forward for Java because it helps solidify Java's status as a modern and elegant development language.

Under ActiveX's Hood

The ActiveX technology can be divided into the following major components:

- ActiveX controls
- ActiveX scripting (VBScript)
- ActiveX documents
- ActiveX server-side scripting (ISAPI)

ActiveX controls are self-contained executable software components that can be embedded within a Web page or a standalone application. Acting as an extension to OLE controls, ActiveX controls can be employed to perform a wide range of functions, both with and without specific support for the Internet. ActiveX controls are essentially Microsoft's answer to Java applets, although ActiveX controls are significantly more open-ended than Java applets. In the same sense, JavaBeans is Sun's answer to ActiveX controls. ActiveX controls and JavaBeans components are designed to address the same need: a component software solution extensible enough to be used on the Web.

Where ActiveX controls are Microsoft's answer to Java applets, VBScript is Microsoft's answer to JavaScript. Built on the highly successful Visual Basic programming language, VBScript provides much of the same functionality as JavaScript, but in an environment already familiar to many PC developers.

ActiveX documents are similar to ActiveX controls, except that they are focused on the representation and manipulation of a particular data format, such as a Word document or an Excel spreadsheet. There is no logical equivalent in Java to ActiveX documents; ActiveX documents are a piece of the ActiveX technology that is completely foreign to Java.

The final component of ActiveX is the ISAPI scripting language and server support. ISAPI provides a more powerful answer to CGI scripting, which has long been used to provide pseudo-interactivity for Web pages. ISAPI even goes a step further by providing a way to build filters into Web servers. Java servlets will eventually provide a similar functionality as ISAPI scripting.

A Peaceful Coexistence

Even though Java and ActiveX are perceived as competing technologies in a lot of ways, understand that I don't necessarily see Java and ActiveX as an either/or proposition. The software development community is far too diverse to say that one technology surpasses another in every possible way. In addition, consider that both of these technologies are in a constant state of flux, with new announcements and releases popping up weekly. In my opinion, it's foolish to think that a single software technology will take the Internet by storm and eliminate all others. Java will naturally find its way to where it is best suited, as will ActiveX. Likewise, smart software developers will keep up with both technologies and learn to apply each in cases where the benefits of one outweigh the other.

And in case you're getting nervous about having to learn two completely new types of programming, here's some reassuring news: Microsoft has a technology that allows developers to integrate Java applets with ActiveX controls. What does that mean? Well, because ActiveX is language independent, it means you can write ActiveX controls in Java. Furthermore, it means you can access ActiveX controls from Java applets and vice versa. To me, this is a very exciting prospect: the ability to mix two extremely powerful yet seemingly divergent technologies as you see fit.

The technology I'm talking about is an ActiveX control that acts as a Java virtual machine. What is a Java virtual machine? A *Java virtual machine* is basically a Java interpreter, which means that it is ultimately responsible for how Java programs are executed. By implementing a Java virtual machine in an ActiveX control, Microsoft has effectively integrated Java into the ActiveX environment. This integration goes well beyond just being able to execute Java applets as if they were ActiveX controls; it provides a way for ActiveX controls and Java applets to interact with each other. It also provides a way of using JavaBeans components as if they were ActiveX controls.

Microsoft's willingness to embrace Java as a way to develop ActiveX objects should give you a clue about the uniqueness of each technology. It could well end up that Java emerges as the dominant programming language for the Internet, while ActiveX emerges as the distributed interactive application standard. I know this seems like a confusing situation, but it does capitalize on the strengths of both Java and ActiveX. On the other hand, JavaBeans could emerge as a serious contender on the component front and give ActiveX some competition.

Fortunately, both Microsoft and Sun are showing some degree of interest in supporting each other's technologies. Microsoft has a variety of different Java efforts under way, including a highly optimized Java VM, a native Java compiler, and a Windows-specific Java API, among other things. Similarly, Sun has expressed a great deal of interest in ensuring that JavaBeans components can be successfully integrated with ActiveX.

The main point is that ActiveX and Java are both strong in different ways, which puts them on a collision course of sorts. The software development community is pretty objective; if programmers can have the best of both worlds by integrating ActiveX and Java, then why not do it? No doubt both Sun and Microsoft will have a lot to say about this prospect in the near future. The ActiveX Java virtual machine is a major step in the right direction.

Integrating Java and ActiveX

As you just learned, the ActiveX Java virtual machine (VM) control allows Java programs to run within the context of an ActiveX control. What does this really mean from the perspective of a developer wanting to mix Java and ActiveX? It means you can treat a Java class just like an ActiveX control and interact with it from other ActiveX controls. In other words, the Java VM control gives a Java class the component capabilities of an ActiveX control.

You now understand that Java classes and ActiveX controls can interact with each other through the Java VM control, but you're probably still curious about the specifics. One of the most important issues surrounding Java's integration with ActiveX is the underlying Component Object Model (COM) protocol used by ActiveX. COM is a component software protocol that is the basis for ActiveX. The importance it has in regard to Java is that Java's integration with ActiveX really has more to do with COM rather than the specifics of ActiveX. So, when I refer to Java integrating with ActiveX, understand that the COM protocol is really what is making things happen under the hood.

This brings us to the different scenarios under which Java and ActiveX can coexist. Keep in mind that some of these scenarios require not only the Java VM control at runtime but also support for Java/ActiveX integration at development time. In other words, you may have to use a development tool that supports Java/ActiveX integration, such as Microsoft Visual J++. Following is a list of the different situations possible when integrating Java and ActiveX using the Java VM control:

- Using an ActiveX control as a Java class
- Using JavaBeans or a Java class as an ActiveX control
- Manipulating a Java applet through ActiveX scripting

Using an ActiveX Control as a Java Class

It is possible to use an ActiveX control just as you would a Java class in Java source code. To do this, you must create a Java class that wraps the ActiveX control and then import the class just as you would any other Java class defined in another package. The end result is that an ActiveX control appears just like a Java class at the source code level. Because we are talking about Java source code here, the Java compiler has to play a role in making this arrangement work. This approach requires support for Java/ActiveX integration in the Java compiler. The Visual J++ Java compiler includes this exact support.

Visual J++ includes a tool that automatically generates Java wrapper classes for ActiveX controls. You can then import these wrapper classes into your Java code and use them just like any other Java class. Of course, behind the scenes, the ActiveX control is actually doing all the work, but from a strictly programming perspective, the Java wrapper class is all you have to be concerned with.

Using a Java Class or a JavaBean as an ActiveX Control

Just as you can use an ActiveX control as a Java class, you can also use a Java class as an ActiveX control. Because ActiveX controls are manipulated through interfaces, you have to design Java classes a little differently so that they fit into the ActiveX framework. You must first define an interface or a set of interfaces for the class, using the Object Description Language (ODL) that is part of COM. You then implement these interfaces in a Java class. Finally, you assign the Java class a global class identifier and register it as an ActiveX control using a registration tool such as JavaReg, which ships with Visual J++.

I know this procedure is a little messier than simply compiling a Java class, but consider what you are gaining by taking these extra steps. You are using one set of source code and just one executable to act as both a Java object and an ActiveX control, with relatively little work. Users can then take advantage of all the benefits of component software by using your Java class as an ActiveX control.

Although no ActiveX environments supporting JavaBeans have been released as of this writing, it is expected that JavaBeans components will fit into ActiveX much more smoothly than other Java classes do. We have this expectation because JavaBeans components already have well-defined interfaces, which is a formal requirement of ActiveX. Additionally, Sun is working toward specifically ensuring that JavaBeans is in some way compatible with ActiveX.

Manipulating a Java Applet through ActiveX Scripting

Another less obvious scenario involving Java and ActiveX is the ability to manipulate Java applets through ActiveX scripting code. The ActiveX scripting protocol, which supports both VBScript and JavaScript, allows you access to all public methods and member variables defined in a Java applet or JavaBeans component. The ActiveX protocol is specifically designed to expose the public methods and member variables for `Applet`-derived classes, so any other classes to which you want scripting access must be manipulated indirectly through public methods in the applet. You learn the specifics of using VBScript to control Java applets in Chapter 48, "Using Java with VBScript."

Summary

This chapter took an objective look at Java and ActiveX and where they fit in the quest to make the Web interactive. You learned not only about the philosophy and reasoning behind each technology, but also why the technologies don't necessarily have to be considered competition for each other. You finished up the chapter by learning about Microsoft's plans to integrate Java and ActiveX. This combination of two powerful technologies, although a little confusing at first, is crucial for Web developers because it lessens the need to pick one technology over the other. Possibly the biggest benefit is the peace of mind in knowing that you can continue working with Java without fear that Microsoft and ActiveX will erode your efforts.

This chapter also touched on your ability to use VBScript to control Java applets. The next chapter gives the details about how VBScript works and what benefits it offers.

Using Java with VBScript

by John J. Kottler

IN THIS CHAPTER

CHAPTER 48

The World Wide Web is one of the fastest growing forms of communication today. Not only in the sheer volume of users and computers attached to the Internet, but also in the quality of material found at the countless Web sites. Just over a year ago, typical commercial Web sites featured graphics and text with very little else. Today, however, it is common to find sites that incorporate numerous technologies such as enhanced multimedia, client-side scripting, and Java or ActiveX applications.

But just as creating a useful Web site requires more than pretty pictures, creating an interactive Web site requires much more attention to the coordination of events that a user experiences. Throughout this book, you have learned how to assemble the newest technologies available using traditional HTML as well as script languages like JavaScript and VBScript. In this chapter, you learn how to harness the power of Java applets and share data between those applets and the Web browser using the VBScript language. This chapter does not attempt to teach you the Java language or VBScript; instead, it demonstrates how to integrate the two technologies.

Wake Up and Smell the Java

No other development language has recently caught the attention of the media and computer industry like Sun Microsystems' Java (`www.javasoft.com`). Java grew from an initiative within Sun to create a development environment for small electronic devices such as pagers and cellular phones. Because of this initial requirement, Java appealed to Web site developers who wanted to create usable applications on their pages. For Internet development, it is necessary that applications do not use a large amount of space because the size of the application directly relates to the amount of time required to download it from the Internet. The Java language is based on the C++ computer programming language, with which many developers are already acquainted. These two reasons alone have greatly contributed to the popularity of Java.

Additionally, this robust development language allows developers to create truly unique Windows-style applications that run effortlessly within the confines of an Internet Web browser. Java has become the development language of choice for many Web developers because it offers various advantages for use with the Internet:

- Java is an object-oriented development environment, which allows developers to create modules for applications that can be shared and reused by other applications.
- Java produces highly secure executable programs that cannot be altered or misused.
- Java is a development environment in which a program can be written once, but executed on any type of machine.

In a world as diverse as the Internet, each of these features is indispensable. But as appealing as Java is by itself for use on the Internet, it is a development language that is not intended for the faint of heart. The ease of HTML is replaced with a C++ programming language syntax that is foreign to many users. Therefore, it is common to find many sites reusing common Java applets that can be tweaked appropriately for the site, instead of creating entirely new ones. But how is this "tweaking" accomplished and how can these Java applets communicate with more familiar HTML Web pages?

The VBScript Glue

Java applets alone on a Web page cannot communicate directly with each other or with other elements on the Web page. When creating truly interactive Web pages, this communication is essential. Imagine an orchestra in which all the members played their instruments however they wanted. The result would be far from pleasant! However, if everyone followed a musical "script" that coordinated their efforts and communicated to them when to do what, the result would be a beautiful arrangement.

The same holds true for Web page development. Although not quite as dramatic as independent musicians in an orchestra, multiple Java applets executing aimlessly on a page add little value to the overall use of the page. But when the applets are directed appropriately using predefined commands like those found in a scripting language embedded within the Web browser, the result is significantly more valuable. In a sense, scripting languages such as VBScript and JavaScript are the glue that hold Web pages and objects on those pages together.

In this chapter, you will learn how the VBScript scripting language ties Java applets and Web page material together. With VBScript, you can modify and interrogate the nature of Java applets, which allows you to create pages that extend beyond the traditional capabilities of HTML. You will also learn how it is possible to implement a mechanism with which a Java applet can notify VBScript when a particular event occurs.

> **NOTE**
>
> To establish this communication between Java applets and VBScript, it is essential that you understand the basic concepts of object-oriented technology. You may want to review Chapter 3, "Java Language Fundamentals," to brush up on your object-oriented skills.

The Infamous Marquee

In this section, you learn how to use VBScript to control and be controlled by a Java applet. The examples that follow use a Marquee applet. Developers who are familiar with the extended HTML tags that Microsoft's Internet Explorer provides will recall the <MARQUEE> tag. This tag allows the Web page designer to specify text that scrolls across the Web page. This same effect can be accomplished using the Marquee Java applet, which can then be used on any Java-enabled Web browser. Figure 48.1 shows a sample of this applet in use with a blue textual message that scrolls from right to left on top of a white background. Portions of the Java source code for this applet are given in Listing 48.1. A complete copy of the source code for this application is available on the CD-ROM that accompanies this book.

FIGURE 48.1.

The Marquee Java applet scrolls text horizontally within a defined region of the Web page.

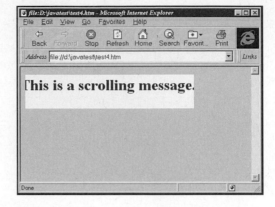

Listing 48.1. The Java source code for the Marquee applet features public variables (properties) and methods for VBScript.

```java
import java.awt.*;

public class Marquee extends java.applet.Applet implements Runnable {
//  These are PUBLIC variables, meaning that they can act as
//  properties which can be modified by JavaScript/VBScript
    public  String  MessageText;
    public  int     MouseClick=0;

//  If a user clicks within the Java applet, this event will
//  be triggered.
    public boolean mouseDown(Event evnt, int x, int y){
        MouseClick=1;
        return true;
    }

//  When the mouse button is released after being clicked,
//  this event will be triggered.
    public boolean mouseUp(Event evnt, int x, int y){
        MouseClick=0;
        return true;
    }

//  This method will be used by JavaScript/VBScript to update
//  text that appears within the Java applet.
    public void setText(String s) {
        MessageText=s;
    }
```

```
        }

    //  NOTE:
    //  The full source for the init, paint, update and thread control
    //  routines can be found on the CD-ROM that accompanies this book.


        }

}
```

Marquee's Properties

The Marquee applet in Listing 48.1 allows the user to specify numerous settings using <PARAM> tags for the applet when embedding the applet on a Web page. However, these tags only specify settings when the applet is first started. You cannot dynamically change settings in the Marquee applet using the <PARAM> tag.

Therefore, the Marquee applet also contains two additional properties declared in the Java application as public variables. The public statement allows other applications or scripting languages such as VBScript to "see" these variables as properties to the Java object. In Listing 48.1, notice that MouseClick and MessageText are two properties that can be interrogated and set by VBScript.

With these two properties available to VBScript, it is possible for a VBScript application to examine what the current message is and change it while the applet is running. The MouseClick property can be set or read as well; however, it is dedicated in this case to handling events, as discussed later in this chapter.

Marquee's Method

Because all the functions in the Marquee Java applet are public functions, they are all technically available for another application such as a Web browser to invoke. However, an additional method specifically for the Marquee applet has been provided to set the scrolling text. The setText() method instructs the Java applet to change the content of the message being scrolled. Notice that the setText() method expects a string as a parameter to the method. This string is the text you pass from VBScript to the Java applet and is the text that should be displayed in the marquee.

Marquee's Event

At the top of Listing 48.1, notice that two events are trapped in the Marquee applet: mouseDown and mouseUp. When a user presses the mouse button down over the Marquee applet, the mouseDown event is triggered in the Java applet. Likewise, when a user releases the mouse button, the mouseUp event is triggered. These events are typical for creating interactive Java applets. In the case of the Marquee applet, we are going to use these events to capture when a user clicks on the applet. If a user clicks on the applet, we want to notify a VBScript application on a Web page to take appropriate action. Later in this chapter, you learn how to simulate event trapping in VBScript.

Embedding Marquee on a Page

Now that you have a Java applet that you want to use on a Web page, you must place it on the page. Both Netscape Navigator 2.x and 3.x as well as Microsoft Internet Explorer 3.x support Java applets and their respective tags: <APPLET> and <PARAM>. You can use these two tags to instruct the browser to insert the Java Marquee applet and set its properties accordingly. Listing 48.2 shows the Marquee applet embedded within a simple HTML page.

Listing 48.2. The <APPLET> and <PARAM> tags are used to embed the Marquee Java applet on a Web page.

```
<HTML>
<TITLE>
Sample Java Applet
</TITLE>

<BODY>
<APPLET NAME=Marquee CODE="Marquee.class" WIDTH=350 HEIGHT=70>
<PARAM NAME=BGCOLOR VALUE ="FFFFFF">
<PARAM NAME=TEXTCOLOR VALUE="FF0000">
<PARAM NAME=SPEED VALUE="5">
<PARAM NAME=TEXT VALUE="Enter your text here.">
</APPLET>
</BODY>
</HTML>
```

NOTE

Each Java applet on a Web page must be uniquely identified by a name (which is specified by the NAME property of the <APPLET> tag) to be used properly within scripts. Names for applets allow scripts to determine which applets should be affected. The names assigned to applets must consist of standard alphanumeric characters and cannot contain spaces.

Controlling Java with VBScript

So you have a Web page with a Java applet that displays scrolling text. Now what? In some cases, this may be just enough. At times, a Web page developer may want to scroll important messages or advertisements using a marquee and little else. However, there may be times when the marquee's message should change dynamically. For example, a marquee that displays Good Morning to a user should display Good Evening at night. You can develop a VBScript routine that first determines the time of day and then sets the marquee's message appropriately.

Invoking Java Methods

Let's make the Marquee applet interactive to the user. People love seeing their name in lights, so we will create a Web page that accepts text input from an HTML input control and sets the marquee's text to what the user enters. Listing 48.3 shows a simple Web page with the Marquee applet, an entry field, and a button that updates the marquee when clicked. Figure 48.2 gives you an idea of what this page looks like.

Listing 48.3. The Marquee applet can be updated using VBScript.

```
<HTML>
<BODY>
<APPLET  NAME=Marquee CODE="Marquee.class" WIDTH=350 HEIGHT=70>
<PARAM   NAME=BGCOLOR VALUE="FFFFFF">
<PARAM   NAME=TEXTCOLOR VALUE="FF0000">
<PARAM   NAME=SPEED VALUE="5">
<PARAM   NAME=TEXT VALUE="Enter your text here.">
</APPLET>

<FORM>
<INPUT   NAME="InputText"
         TYPE=TEXT
         SIZE=35
        VALUE="Enter your text here."
>
<INPUT   TYPE=BUTTON
         WIDTH=200
         VALUE="Change Text"
       onClick="document.Marquee.setText(form.InputText.value)"
>
</FORM>
</BODY>
```

48

FIGURE 48.2.

An entry field can be used to type a message to be displayed in the Marquee applet.

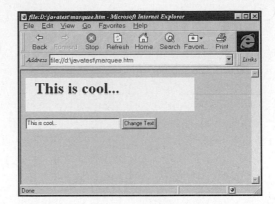

If you are familiar with VBScript or JavaScript, you will quickly realize that calling methods of Java applets is similar to calling VBScript/JavaScript or ActiveX functions. In Listing 48.3, the entry field named InputText holds whatever text the user enters. When a user clicks the Change Text button, a single line of VBScript code is invoked. This single line simply calls the setText() method of the Marquee applet, passing the string from the input field as a parameter for the method.

In general, applet methods can be addressed in VBScript using the following notation:

```
result = document.Applet Name.Applet Method(Method Parameter)
```

In this syntax, *Applet Name* is the name you used in the <APPLET> tag that uniquely identifies the Java applet on the Web page. Likewise, *Applet Method* is the name of the method an applet supports that you want to invoke. In addition, some methods may return a value that can be stored in a variable in VBScript, can be tested, or can be used in conjunction with other VBScript functions. According to the source code in Listing 48.1 for the Marquee applet, the void statement for the setText() method indicates that no value is to be returned. If an applet performed some mathematical computation, that method could return the result to VBScript.

It is common to invoke a method in a Java applet with some form of data passed to the method. For example, if you were going to use a modem to dial a phone number, you would pass the phone number to the dialing function in the modem. Just as a Java applet does not necessarily return a result value, a method can be designed that does not require input parameters.

Reading and Writing Properties

Just as you can use methods provided by a Java applet in VBScript, you can also alter the properties of an object or determine the properties' current values. To the current Marquee example, let's add a second button for a crude guessing game. When a user types a phrase and clicks the Change Text button, the Java applet changes the text in the marquee. When a user then clicks the new Guess Secret Message button, the VBScript code checks the text in the Java applet to see whether it is the secret message. The Guess Secret Message button then posts a message indicating whether or not the user guessed the message correctly. Listing 48.4 presents the new HTML file for this simple game page; Figure 48.3 shows the screen after guessing the correct phrase.

Listing 48.4. The `MessageText` property of the `Marquee` applet can be read by VBScript and tested to create interactive Web pages.

```
<HTML>
<BODY>

<APPLET NAME=Marquee CODE="Marquee.class" WIDTH=350 HEIGHT=70>
<PARAM NAME=BGCOLOR VALUE="FFFFFF">
<PARAM NAME=TEXTCOLOR value="FF0000">
<PARAM NAME=SPEED value="5">
<PARAM NAME=TEXT VALUE="Enter your text here.">
</applet>

<FORM>
<INPUT   NAME="InputText"
         TYPE=text
         SIZE=35
         VALUE="Enter your text here."
>
<INPUT   TYPE=button
         WIDTH=200
         VALUE="Change Text"
      onClick="document.Marquee.setText(form.InputText.value)"
>
<P>
<INPUT   TYPE=button
         VALUE="Guess Secret Message"
      LANGUAGE="VBScript"
      onclick="if document.Marquee.MessageText='VBScript & Java' then
                   alert('You guessed the secret message!')
               else
                   alert('Nope sorry, try again.')
               end if"
>
</FORM>
</BODY>
```

Just like Java methods, properties for applets can be addressed using the following syntax:

To read a property's value:

```
result = document.Applet Name.Applet Property
```

To set a property:

```
document.Applet Name.Applet Property = Value
```

In this syntax, *Applet Name* indicates the name of the Java applet that was used in the `<APPLET>` tag for the Web page; *Applet Property* is the name of the variable you want to view or change in the Java application. Properties can be stored in variables in VBScript, used in conditional testing, or combined with other VBScript applications. You can also set properties by assigning values to them. In a sense, properties can be treated as variables in your VBScript applications.

FIGURE 48.3.

A simple guessing game can be made because VBScript can read the `MessageText` *property in the* `Marquee` *applet.*

In the computer modem example, the auto-answer capability can be turned on or off. A program can examine the auto-answer property and determine whether it is enabled or disabled. If it is disabled, this property can be changed to a desired setting.

> **NOTE**
>
> The names of methods, properties, and respective parameters for various Java applets vary widely. You must consult either the documentation included with the applet or its source code to determine which capabilities are available for the applet.
>
> If you are creating your own Java applets, note that functions and variables declared in a Java applet's source code that are to be treated as methods or properties for VBScript must be `public`. If functions or variables are not public, other applications or languages cannot "see" or use them as methods.

Properties versus Methods

As we examined the Marquee Java applet along with its properties and methods, you may have asked yourself this common question: "When should I use properties and when should I use methods?" In the Marquee example, the results of the setText() method could have just as easily been implemented by adjusting the MessageText property. If you are creating original Java applets, the decision is up to you when to create methods or properties for use by VBScript. You can base this decision on what makes logical sense. When using commercial or prewritten Java applets or applets without source code, however, you may not have a choice. Each developer will undoubtedly create Java methods and properties to be used by VBScript as logically as possible, although the logic may escape you at times.

In general, *properties* are the characteristics of an object and should be used to change the description of an object. Assume that we have a Java applet that plays video content. Some properties for that object are the filename of the video file to play, the current playback position in the video stream, and the option to display or hide VCR-style control buttons.

Methods, on the other hand, are typically used to instruct an object to actually perform an *action*. Properties typically set static values that in themselves do nothing; methods do the actual work. However, some methods perform differently based on the current properties for an object. Using the video player example again, assume that there are methods for playing and stopping content. We can assume that the playback method plays from the current playback position in the video stream. If the stop and playback methods were invoked immediately after each other, playback would continue from wherever it had stopped last. If, on the other hand, a VBScript program stopped playback, changed the playback position property, and then issued a request to play the stream, the playback method would play from the new position indicated by the position property.

Triggering VBScript with Java Events

So far, you have learned how to control Java applets by invoking methods or changing an applet's properties. The third key component to object-oriented technology has not been addressed: events. In the beginning of this chapter, you saw that the Marquee applet traps an event when a user presses the mouse button and traps another when the button is released. The Marquee applet was designed so that when a user clicks on the marquee, a specific action can be taken by the VBScript application for a Web page. For this example, the VBScript application will simply post a message indicating that a user has clicked the marquee.

VBScript (and JavaScript, for that matter) allows developers to control Java applets through methods and properties, but makes no provision for handling events trapped by a Java applet. Other technologies such as ActiveX provide a mechanism by which, if a particular event occurs in the ActiveX control, corresponding VBScript code can be executed in place of the typical ActiveX code.

NOTE

VBScript allows the trapping of events within a VBScript application. Events for ActiveX objects, for example, can be defined and trapped in VBScript by including a subroutine for each event. This subroutine's name must be identified using the ActiveX object name (determined in the <OBJECT> tag for the ActiveX control), followed by an underscore (_), and the name of the event to handle in VBScript.

For example, the ActiveMovie ActiveX control, which is used to display video content and Microsoft NetShow media, contains an Error event. As its name implies, this event is triggered whenever an error is encountered. If a VBScript subroutine is created for this event, all error handling can be customized by VBScript rather than using the default actions provided by ActiveMovie. The following code shows how to implement this error handling for ActiveMovie using VBScript:

```
sub MyActiveMovieControl_Error()
    ' Code to perform when errors occur...
end sub
```

When proper subroutines are established in VBScript for events, actions triggered in an ActiveX control can notify the VBScript application automatically and the results can be handled by custom VBScript code.

More information about Microsoft ActiveX and NetShow can be found at the Microsoft Web site:

www.microsoft.com/netshow

Because there is no inherent way to handle Java events in VBScript, we must simulate the process of notifying VBScript when particular events take place in the applet. To do this, we must use the properties of the object that VBScript can access and use a VBScript function that polls these properties on a regular interval. If properties are polled on a consistent basis, we can determine when they change their state in VBScript. If we set aside properties specifically tied to events triggered in the Java applet, the VBScript application can poll for those event properties to change, indicating that an event occurred.

The Timer Event

Because we want to check a Java applet's property on a timed interval, the first step in executing this scenario is to use an ActiveX timer control in VBScript. A timer control can be found at Microsoft's Web site at this URL:

http://activex.microsoft.com/controls/iexplorer/ietimer.ocx

Listing 48.5 displays the tags necessary to embed an ActiveX timer control into an HTML file.

Listing 48.5. The timer control is an ActiveX control that can be used easily with VBScript.

```
<OBJECT
            ID="TimerControl"
       CLASSID="clsid:59CCB4A0-727D-11CF-AC36-00AA00A47DD2"
       CODEBASE="http://activex.microsoft.com/controls/
                 iexplorer/ietimer.ocx#Version=4,70,0,1161"
          TYPE="application/x-oleobject"
         ALIGN=middle
>
<PARAM NAME="Interval" VALUE="100">
<PARAM NAME="Enabled" VALUE="True">
</OBJECT>
```

This control expects numerous parameters, but the two of importance are `Interval` and `Enabled`. The `Enabled` parameter is equivalent to a switch that turns the timer control on or off. When set to `true`, the timer is turned on.

When the timer is enabled, a `Timer` event is sent to the VBScript for the Web page on a regular interval. This interval is determined by the `Interval` parameter in the `<OBJECT>` tag for the timer control. Time is measured in milliseconds; a value of `1000` is equivalent to a one-second interval. In the sample code shown in Listing 48.5, the interval is set to `100` milliseconds, which is rather quick. The interval is made short because we do not want a user to experience a long delay between clicking the Java applet to trigger an event and seeing the results posted by VBScript. The shorter this delay is, the quicker the response.

> **NOTE**
>
> The `Interval` property of the `Timer` ActiveX control can be adjusted to trigger the `Timer` event after any given amount of time. Longer delays are suitable for other types of applications that may use timers (such as a clock that updates every second or minute). But a shorter duration is required to emulate the *immediate* triggering of VBScript code by a Java applet.

When the parameters are set appropriately for the timer control, the timer triggers an event in VBScript every given number of milliseconds. In this example, the VBScript event `TimerControl_Timer` is executed every 100 milliseconds. The code in the `TimerControl_Timer` function can then read a Java applet's property and determine when it has changed. Listing 48.6 shows a sample of appropriate VBScript code for detecting changes in the `Marquee` applet's `MouseClick` property.

Listing 48.6. Once a timer control is enabled on a Web page, VBScript can check Java properties on a regular basis to determine when they change.

```
<SCRIPT LANGUAGE="VBScript">
sub TimerControl_Timer()
    if document.Marquee.MouseClick=1 then
        document.Marquee.MouseClick=0
        alert("You clicked on the Java applet!")
    end if
End Sub
</SCRIPT>
```

In this case, the mouseDown event in the Marquee applet's source code assigns the public variable MouseClick the value of 1. Likewise, the mouseUp event resets this property to 0. Because these properties are available for interrogation in VBScript and are tied closely to the events in the applet, they can be used to notify VBScript when the event has occurred.

TIP

As shown in Listing 48.6, it is recommended that you reset the properties for an event where appropriate. Although the Java applet should reset the property automatically, there may be occasions when it will not. Resetting the properties when you are finished using them is good practice to avoid these events from triggering more than the number of times expected.

For example, in Listing 48.6, if the mouseClick property was not reset, a new alert box would appear every 100 milliseconds!

NOTE

Although we have discussed how to implement a timer in VBScript using only ActiveX controls, you can also implement this same technique using JavaScript. Instead of using a timer control, JavaScript uses the setTimeOut() function available in the language. This function instructs JavaScript to execute a particular function on a regular interval. By placing the setTimeOut() function within the function to be called regularly, a looping condition can occur, in which the function is called continuously on a given interval. The only exception to note in this implementation is the use of the <BODY> tag, which uses the onLoad event to initiate the entire timer process. The following code shows how to implement a timer in JavaScript:

```
<BODY onLoad="tf=setTimeOut('TimerFunc()',100)">
...
</BODY>
```

```
<SCRIPT LANGUAGE="JavaScript">
function TimerFunc(){

    tf=window.setTimeout("TimerFunc()",100);

    if (document.Marquee.MouseClick==1){
        document.Marquee.MouseClick=0;
        alert("You clicked on the Java applet!");
    }
  }
</SCRIPT>
```

On the Java Side

As you can see, it is possible to trigger VBScript functions when an event occurs in a Java applet on a Web page. However, for this to work correctly, there must be appropriate properties available for VBScript to use.

In the Marquee applet, a special MouseClick property was designed explicitly for this purpose. When a user clicks the mouse button over the Java applet, the applet's mouseDown event is triggered, setting the MouseClick property to 1. The VBScript code for the Web page can then interrogate the MouseClick property to "see" when it changes from 0 to 1 and act accordingly. Likewise, the mouseUp event for the Marquee applet resets the MouseClick property to 0 so that a user can click the applet and trigger the VBScript code again in the future.

The MouseClick property was specifically designed for use with VBScript to indicate when the mouse button is down or up. When designing your own Java applets or modifying applets for which you have the source code, it is easy to add dedicated properties for events to be captured by VBScript. When reusing Java applets that you cannot modify, it becomes increasingly difficult to implement similar event trapping techniques in VBScript—mainly because you cannot add your own custom properties to interrogate with VBScript.

If you use Java applets for which you do not have the source, you may still be able to trap events with VBScript. To do so, however, you must think of other properties that the applet does support that may indicate when particular events occurred. Consider the fictitious video player applet discussed earlier. Assume that we do not have the source code for this applet and want to create a routine in VBScript that performs a specific action when the playback stops. If the applet supports a CurrentPosition property, we can still implement a "stop" event in VBScript. If this CurrentPosition property updates continuously to indicate the position in the video file at which playback is located, it is possible to simply watch this property with a VBScript timer subroutine to determine when the position does not move anymore. This is essentially the same as indicating that the playback of the video stream has stopped.

Summary

In this chapter, you learned how to interface Java applets with VBScript. You saw how to change properties of Java applets and invoke methods that applets support. You also learned how to simulate event trapping in VBScript and JavaScript. With this knowledge, you can implement more complex Web pages that effectively communicate with Java applets to create unique applications. In Chapter 49, "Developing Intranet Applications with Java," you learn how to leverage Java technology to increase the functionality of an organization's intranet.

XI
PART

IN THIS PART

Applied Java

Developing Intranet Applications with Java

by Jerry Ablan

IN THIS CHAPTER

Now that you know all about Java, you probably want to put it to good use. Writing applets that animate text and graphics on your personal Web pages gets stale after a while. Most likely, you want to build something to show your boss at work. So why not develop some intranet applications?

Intranets are the hot new internal webs springing up all over the corporate landscape. Some intranets are broad and diverse while others are skimpy. In addition to providing timely company information such as corporate news and the current price of the company stock, these webs can bring the employees closer. Just like the water cooler of the past, the intranet is the new corporate hangout.

But many companies don't even have intranets. Some companies still don't have e-mail. If your company does not yet have an intranet, perhaps developing an application in Java can help get the project started. You never know....

This chapter covers some basic topics regarding intranet applications and Java. In particular, it covers the following areas:

- The anatomy of an intranet application
- Putting together an application framework for intranet applications
- Using the framework to build intranet applications

This chapter discusses an intranet application framework developed in the book *Developing Intranet Applications with Java* (published by Sams.net). The book takes you step-by-step through the design and implementation of an intranet application framework, and then through eight sample intranet applications.

> **NOTE**
>
> The framework software developed in *Developing Intranet Applications with Java* is called the *Java Intranet Framework*, or JIF. Applications created with JIF are called *jiflets*. For your convenience, the JIF source code is provided on the CD-ROM that comes with this book.

The Anatomy of an Intranet Application

Intranet applications are like a corporate application suite, which includes word processors, project planners, spreadsheets, and many other useful and productive applications. Intranet applications encompass all departments and touch many types of data. But unlike the business productivity application suites available today, your intranet applications should all share a common foundation.

Creating a suite of applications from scratch is tedious and boring. Cutting and pasting code is easy, but that goes against all object-oriented programming practices. What is needed is a basic structure from which you can build your applications. This foundation should be flexible, stable, and extensible. Once developed, it will become your intranet application framework.

The next sections introduce you to four standards that all your applications can share. These standards provide a flexible, stable, and extensible foundation for developing intranet applications. Together, these four standards produce a prototype, or model application, you can use as a base when developing other intranet applications.

A Quick Overview of Intranet Applications

On an intranet, the applications that are built share much of the same functionality. Sure, they all do different things, but they do a lot of the same things. These commonalities should become the foundation for your intranet application framework. They are the base and are truly your application standards.

Your primary design goal should be to provide a set of standard application features. These features create a familiar atmosphere for all your intranet applications. Familiarity provides users with a sense of comfort because they don't have to learn an entirely new program. Apple Computer capitalized on this idea years ago when it introduced the Macintosh computer. If you learned how to use the Mac, then you knew how to run almost every Macintosh application ever written. It was the consistency and adherence to set standards that made this possible. Microsoft Windows has since capitalized on the same concept. The design presented in this chapter is not quite a Macintosh but it does provides something similar: consistency.

The following four standard features are what we suggest you should provide in your intranet application design:

- Standard configuration file processing
- Standard logging to screen or disk
- Standard database connectivity
- Standard look and feel

The following sections examine each feature individually, show an example, and then point you in the right direction to find more information regarding each particular standard.

Configuration File Processing

Using configuration parameters in programming can be a real hassle unless a stable foundation is in place. Generally, you end up coding a new configuration scheme with each application. What you can create is a class that provides a solid method of getting configuration parameters. This method encompasses configuration files on disk and overridden parameters passed in by way of the command line of the application.

The configuration file in Listing 49.1 is an example of the kind of configuration files the applications have.

Listing 49.1. A sample configuration file.

```
# Configuration file for Employee Maintenance
WindowTitle=Employee Maintenance
server=tcp-loopback.world
user=munster
password=
```

At the start of the application, you can read the configuration file into memory. The parameters can then be merged with any configuration parameters passed in by way of the command line. The applications then need a consistent method of retrieving these parameters from the configuration parameter storage area. A good idea is to model the retrieval method after the method used in regular Java applets.

> **NOTE**
>
> In the `jif.util` package, found on the CD-ROM that accompanies this book, is the Java class that implements the design goal of a consistent way to get configuration parameters. It is called `ConfigProperties`.

Logging to Disk or Screen

For tracking problems during the development cycle and for error logging after your application has been deployed, a log file is just the ticket. A common log file is even better for all your applications and users. A common log file is easily searched and filtered for errors. This standard logging mechanism is the first standard feature you should consider developing.

To facilitate such a log file, you must create it on disk. You should append to the log file each time; it should never be overwritten. If you overwrite the file, information from a previous session will be lost. You know how annoying that can be!

But what if the disk log fails to open, or if it can't be written to? You need a backup log. The failed log entries could go to the screen.

This screen logging facility produces the same log information to a window, using the `System.out` facility. When an application fails to create a disk log, all log output can then go to the screen. You can also automatically use this screen log if no disk log is specified or if there is an error creating one.

Common Log Entries

The entries in the log file should follow a standard—a standard that is easy to view and search. This log-file format should be used across all your intranet applications—and possibly your non-intranet applications as well. This log-file format should be simple enough so that other programs may use it.

In the future, you may find that you will use a third-party network management tool that can monitor your intranet applications and their log files. These tools can be a lifesaver in a pinch, so why not think about their needs as well?

Therefore, the following log-file format provides a good idea of what to go with as the design. It includes all the information needed in an easy-to-use format:

`application¦user¦date¦level¦entry`

In this format, the following fields are used:

Field	Description
application	The name of the application
user	The user who is running the application
date	The date of the log entry
level	A single character that indicates the severity of the entry

The severity levels are up to you to define. As a suggestion however, we offer the following:

Suggested Rating	Meaning	Comment
D	Debug	This level is useful for displaying information to the log file during the development stage. When you deploy the application, these messages can easily be filtered from the output.
I	Informational	This level is for information that is not important. Startup and shutdown messages are considered informational.
W	Warning	This level is for semi-important information. When things don't go exactly as planned, but your program can continue, this is a good place for a warning.

continues

49

DEVELOPING
INTRANET
APPLICATIONS

Suggested Rating	Meaning	Comment
E	Error	This level is for important information. When your program encounters any kind of error, this is the level to use.
F	Fatal	This level is for very important information. When your program can no longer run because of some event, this is the level to use.

Listing 49.2 shows some sample log entries.

Listing 49.2. Sample log entries.

```
Employee¦960909¦I¦Application [Employee] started at Sun Sep 09 22:27:33  1996
Employee¦960909¦I¦Server = mars.mcs.net
Employee¦960909¦I¦Title = Employee Maintenance
Employee¦960909¦I¦User = munster
Employee¦960909¦I¦Password = spot
Employee¦960909¦I¦Application [Employee] ended at Sun Sep 09 22:28:38  1996
```

At startup, all your intranet applications should write several things to the log:

- A startup message showing the application and time/date of startup
- Optionally, the contents of the configuration file
- Optionally, any arguments passed in on the command line

At shutdown, your application can write a corresponding entry to its startup message. Refer back to Listing 49.2 for examples of shutdown entries.

NOTE

In the `jif.log` package, found on the CD-ROM that accompanies this book, are the Java classes that implement the design goal of consistent, or common, log-file formatting. They are called `DiskLog` and `ScreenLog`.

Database Connectivity

Connecting to databases with Java is a key point in your intranet application design stage. Various methods are currently available. Some are HTTP server extensions that return data in HTML format. Others are nonportable system-dependent solutions. A more Java-like option is JDBC.

It appears today that JDBC is the strongest supported database standard for Java. For this reason alone, JDBC has been chosen as the database connectivity package for the intranet application in this chapter. Using JDBC allows us to choose from almost any database and provides the flexibility to change databases once coding is complete.

To simplify database connectivity just a bit, we can create a class that encapsulates the more monotonous aspects of connecting and disconnecting from a database server. This new class provides a connection strategy that is simple to use and easily extensible. This class also encapsulates much of the rudimentary JDBC initialization and cleanup. All we have to do is extend this class for each database we need to connect with.

Listing 49.3 shows how easy your JDBC database connection class should be to use.

Listing 49.3. How we want to use our database connector class.

```
//  Make the connection...
if ( myConnector.connect( "username", "password", "dbservername" ) )
{
    //  Connection successful…
}
else
{
    //  Connection failed…
}
```

As you can see, the connect() method is called with the connection parameters necessary to make the connection. The exception handling is handled for you in the class, returning nothing but a simple true or false. This return value indicates the connection state as well.

> **NOTE**
>
> On the CD-ROM that accompanies this book, in the jif.sql package, are the Java classes that implement the design goal of consistent database connectivity. The DBConnector class is the abstract base for many of the database classes. Also provided in the jif.sql package on the CD-ROM are classes that connect to Oracle, Sybase, Microsoft SQL Server, ODBC, and mSQL.

Look and Feel

The final standard your intranet applications should follow is that they should have a consistent look and feel. This is achieved through the use of standard font and a consistent component layout.

Figure 49.1 shows the standard look and feel of the model intranet application. This application is the ever-present and highly overrated `Hello World` example.

FIGURE 49.1.

The standard intranet application look and feel.

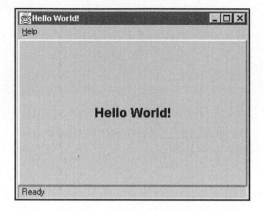

Referring to Figure 49.1, you see the following standard application attributes:

- **A standard Java font.** We choose Dialog, size 12. In Windows 95, the standard font is 8-point MS Sans Serif.
- **A status bar.** The status bar is along the bottom and is used to display messages to the user.

You may notice that there is a menu option shown in Figure 49.1. However, no menu standard is included as part of the standard look and feel for intranet applications. Because the menu varies from application to application, it is not fair to impose a rigid menu structure on applications that may not even need a menu. Therefore, menus are not part of the application design.

> **NOTE**
>
> On the CD-ROM that accompanies this book, in the `jif.awt` package, are the Java classes that implement the design goal of a consistent look and feel. The `StatusBar` class in particular provides a single-line text output area for your applications. There are many other user interface classes in the `jif.awt` package as well. These can all be used to enhance and beautify your intranet applications.

Creating an Intranet Application Framework

Now you have an idea of the types of building blocks you can use in your intranet applications. We've covered four standard features that can create a sense of consistency for you and your users. Now we can take these features and mold them into an *application framework*.

An application framework is, in its simplest form, an application that does nothing. However, a better definition is this: An application framework provides developers with the necessary foundation from which they can build solid applications.

> **NOTE**
>
> Those of you familiar with Borland C++ or Visual C++ are aware of the benefits of a foundation framework. Using the tools provided by Borland C++ or Visual C++, you can generate a complete application shell in minutes. You, the programmer, are left with the job of providing content for the application. The tedious parts like printing and window management are already done for you. Application frameworks are one of the better advances in developer technology in years.

We'll name our framework the *Java Intranet Framework* because it provides a framework for creating intranet applications with Java. Not to mention the cool acronym: JIF!

How to Package the Application Framework

The best way to package the application framework is in groups of functionality. As you recall, we have four functionality groups: utilities, logging, database, and user interface. These fit perfectly into four functionality packages.

Naming our packages is quite simple: We use `jif` as our base package name and then add on the specifics. For example, the utilities package is called `util`, similar to the `java.util` package. Table 49.1 shows the package names we have chosen, along with the class functionality contained within each.

Table 49.1. The Java Intranet Framework packages.

Package Name	Description
`jif.awt`	Standard user interface classes and `java.awt` extensions
`jif.log`	Standard logging classes
`jif.sql`	Standard database connectivity classes and `java.sql` extensions
`jif.util`	Standard utility classes and `java.util` extensions

The jif.sql package name does not really contain SQL functionality. However, the name is chosen to be consistent with the JDBC class hierarchy that lives in the java.sql package.

> ### TIP
>
> Placing Java classes into packages is simple. In each file, add a line of code that defines the package to which the class belongs. These statements are package statements as discussed in Chapter 5, "Classes, Packages, and Interfaces."
>
> In addition to adding the package statements to your source code, you must also move all the classes into a directory hierarchy that represents the package hierarchy.

Constructing the Foundation

Now that we're headed toward building a framework, we need to use our classes to construct our foundation so that we can build intranet applications. What we really need is something to model our framework on.

An excellent implementation of application direction and structure is Java's own Applet class. This class is a self-contained mini-application that runs in a special applet viewer program or from an HTML World Wide Web page.

Making the Framework Easy to Use

To make our jiflets easy to work with, we've modeled them after Java's own Applet class. The jiflet is a Java application that provides the standard features of our intranet application in an easy-to-use wrapper. These features include all four outlined earlier, plus many of the features in a standard Java applet.

One such feature is an init() method that is called automatically by the framework. The init() method is a centralized location in which you can place all your initialization code.

Another feature our jiflet should contain is a standard way to get configuration parameters. We can retrieve parameters from the configuration file with a method like the java.Applet.getParameter() method.

In fact, the following methods are available both in applets and jiflets:

- `public void init()`
- `public boolean isActive()`
- `public void destroy()`
- `public String getParameter( String name )`
- `public void resize(Dimension d)`
- `public void resize(int width, int height)`
- `public void showStatus(String msg)`

The only features really missing from jiflets that appear in applets are the multimedia methods. These multimedia methods provide a clean way for applets to load images and sound files off of a network. Because jiflets represent intranet applications, these features are not usually necessary.

With the design goals laid out, let's look into the implementation of the classes.

The Jiflet Class

The `Jiflet` class is the intranet application version of Java's own `Applet` class. It provides you with a framework to develop intranet applications quickly and easily. It brings together all the usefulness of the other JIF packages into a single, easy-to-use component.

Let's take a look at the `Jiflet` class in detail. We start with the instance variables, move to the constructors, and then on to each of the methods. After finishing this chapter, you should have a good understanding of the `Jiflet` class: how to use it and how to use it to develop intranet applications with Java.

Instance Variables

The `Jiflet` class contains the following instance variables:

```
protected boolean          activeFlag = false;
protected DiskLog          appLogFile;
protected String           appName;
protected boolean          appVerbosity = false;
protected ConfigProperties configProperties;
protected ScreenLog        defaultLog;
private   DBConnector      myConnector = null;
protected StatusBar        myStatusBar = null;
private   int              oldCursor = -1;
```

Let's look at each one and how it is used.

activeFlag

```
protected boolean              activeFlag = false;
```

The activeFlag variable is used to denote the activeness of a jiflet. Its state can be queried with the Jiflet.isActive() method. The activeFlag variable is set to true right before the run() method is called and set to false after the destroy() method is called.

appLogFile

```
protected DiskLog              appLogFile;
```

The appLogFile variable is the log file object for the jiflet. During construction, this object is created like so:

```
appLogFile = new DiskLog( logPath, DiskLog.createLogFileName(), appName );
```

In this syntax, logPath is a configurable location in which all log files are placed. The DiskLog.createLogFileName() method creates a standard log filename. Finally, appName is used on the standard log entry to identify the application that generates it.

appName

```
protected String               appName;
```

The appName string holds the name of the application that is running. This string is usually passed in at construction.

appVerbosity

```
protected boolean              appVerbosity = false;
```

If you choose, your jiflet can be configured to report more information about certain things. This *verbosity* level is turned on or off with the appVerbosity boolean instance variable. It defaults to false and can be set with the Jiflet.setVerboseMode() method.

configProperties

```
protected ConfigProperties     configProperties;
```

The configProperties object holds the combined program arguments and the configuration parameters read from the application's configuration file. Access to this variable is through the Jiflet.getParameter() methods.

defaultLog

```
protected ScreenLog          defaultLog;
```

The `defaultLog` variable is a default log in case the real application log cannot be created. This log writes its entries to the standard output device of the operating system.

myConnector

```
private DBConnector          myConnector = null;
```

The `myConnector` variable holds the `DBConnector` object associated with this jiflet. This variable can be set and retrieved with the `Jiflet.setConnector()` and `Jiflet.getConnector()` methods.

myStatusBar

```
protected StatusBar          myStatusBar = null;
```

The `myStatusBar` variable holds the instance of the `StatusBar` object created for the jiflet. The status can be set and cleared with the `Jiflet.showStatus()` and `Jiflet.clearStatus()` methods.

oldCursor

```
private int                  oldCursor = -1;
```

The `oldCursor` private variable is used to store the value of the cursor while a "wait" cursor is displayed. This variable is used by the `Jiflet.startWait()` and `Jiflet.endWait()` methods.

Constructors

There are four ways to construct a jiflet. These are defined by four separate constructors. Each of these four constructors is useful for different purposes. For the most part, most of your jiflets use the fourth incarnation. Let's take a look at each constructor.

Three of the constructors call the fourth constructor. This master constructor is where all the jiflet initialization takes place. Listing 49.4 shows the complete source code for this constructor.

49

Listing 49.4. The jiflet's master constructor.

```
/**
 * Creates a Jiflet with a title, a name, arguments, and optionally
 * verbose.
 *
 * @param title The window title
 * @param name The name of the application
 * @param args The arguments passed in to the program
```

continues

Listing 49.4. continued

```
 * @param verbosity On/Off setting indicating verbosity of log entries
 * @see #setVerboseMode
 */
public
Jiflet( String title, String name, String args[], boolean verbosity )
{
    //    Call the superclass...
    super( title );

    //    Copy title to name...
    if ( name.equals( "" ) )
        name = title;

    //    Set the color...
    setBackground( Color.lightGray );

    //    Center and show our window!
    center();

    //    Add a status bar...
    enableStatusBar();

    //    Save my application name...
    appName = name;

    //    Create a default log...
    defaultLog = new ScreenLog( appName );

    //    Parse any passed in arguments...
    //    Parse the configuration file if available...
    configProperties = new ConfigProperties( args, appName + ".cfg" );

    //    Reset the title...
    setTitle( getParameter( "Title", title ) );

    //    Construct a log file name...
    String logPath = getParameter( "LogPath", "" );

    //    Open the log file...
    try
    {
        if ( logPath.equals( "" ) )
        {
            appLogFile = new DiskLog( appName );
        }
        else
        {
            appLogFile = new DiskLog( logPath,
                DiskLog.createLogFileName(),
                appName );
        }
    }
```

```
catch ( IOException e )
{
    //    Write errors to the screen...
    errorLog( "Error opening log file for [" +
        appName + "] (" + e.toString() + ")" );

    appLogFile = null;
}

//    Turn on verbose mode...
setVerboseMode( verbosity );

//    Denote construction...
log( "Application [" + appName + "] started at " +
    ( new Date() ).toString() );

//    Call my init!
init();

//    We are now active!
activeFlag = true;

//    Call my run...
run();
}
```

Because the `Jiflet` class descends from Java's `Frame` class, we first need to call the superclass's constructor with a title. Then the following is done:

- The background color is set to light gray.
- The jiflet is centered on the screen.
- The status bar is created and enabled.
- The default log is opened.
- The configuration file is read into memory and combined with the program arguments.
- The `LogPath` configuration option is retrieved from the configuration.
- The actual disk log file is created.
- Verbose mode is turned on or off depending on the value passed in.
- A message is written to the log, stating that the jiflet has started.
- The user's implemented `init()` method is called.
- The `run()` method is called. By default, the `show()` method of the `Frame` is called to display the jiflet on the screen.

49

DEVELOPING INTRANET APPLICATIONS

Listing 49.5 shows the other three constructors available for creating `Jiflet` objects.

Listing 49.5. Three more constructors for creating `Jiflet` objects.

```
public
Jiflet()
{
    this( "Generic Jiflet", "Jiflet", null, false );
}

public
Jiflet( String title )
{
    this( title, "", null, false );
}

public
Jiflet( String title, String name, String args[] )
{
    this( title, name, args, false );
}
```

As you see, all three of these constructors call the main constructor, setting some values to `null` or blanks.

Methods

Many methods are available in the `Jiflet` class. The following sections document their arguments and what purpose they serve.

setVerboseMode()

```
public void
setVerboseMode( boolean whichWay )
```

The `setVerboseMode()` method turns on or off verbose mode. If verbose mode is turned on, all log entries created with the `Jiflet.verboseLog()` method are actually passed to the log object. If verbose mode is turned off, all log entries created this way are ignored.

> **TIP**
>
> The `setVerboseMode()` method, in conjunction with `Jiflet.verboseLog()`, offers an excellent debugging tool. Simply enable verbose mode when you need more detail; in your code, provide that detail with the `Jiflet.verboseLog()` method.

verboseLog()

```
//****************************************************************************
//* verboseLog                                                               *
//****************************************************************************

    public void
    verboseLog( char logLevel, String logEntry )

    public void
    verboseLog( String logEntry )
```

The verboseLog() method creates a log entry that is written to the log file only if the verbose mode flag is set to true.

The second constructor defaults to a log level of I (for informational).

errorLog()

```
//****************************************************************************
//* errorLog                                                                 *
//****************************************************************************

    public void
    errorLog( String logEntry )
```

The errorLog() method allows you to create error log entries without specifying an error logging level each time. It is simply a convenience method.

log()

```
//****************************************************************************
//* log                                                                      *
//****************************************************************************

    public void
    log( char logLevel, String logEntry )

    public void
    log( String logEntry )
```

The log() method creates a log entry that is written to the log file. If there is an error, or the log file is not open, the output goes to the screen.

The second constructor defaults to a log level of I (for informational).

handleEvent()

```
//****************************************************************************
//* handleEvent                                                              *
//****************************************************************************

    public boolean
    handleEvent( Event anEvent )
```

The handleEvent() method overrides the default Frame.handleEvent() method. It listens for destruction events so that the jiflet can close itself down cleanly.

action()

```
//*****************************************************************************
//* action                                                                    *
//*****************************************************************************

    public boolean
    action( Event event, Object arg )
```

The action() method receives ACTION_EVENT events from the event system. It listens for menu events and passes them to Jiflet.handleMenuEvent().

handleMenuEvent()

```
//*****************************************************************************
//* handleMenuEvent                                                           *
//*****************************************************************************

    protected boolean
    handleMenuEvent( Event event, Object arg )
```

The handleMenuEvent() method is a placeholder for menu events. This method does nothing in the Jiflet class. It must be overridden by derived classes to include any functionality.

shutDown()

```
//*****************************************************************************
//* shutDown                                                                  *
//*****************************************************************************

    public boolean
    shutDown( int level )
```

The shutDown() method is the central point of exit for the jiflet. With the exception of a program crash, the jiflet always exits through this method. The method is responsible for writing a log entry for the application ending, and it calls the Jiflet.destroy() method. The level argument is passed to the operating system as a return value for the calling program.

suicide()

```
//*****************************************************************************
//* suicide                                                                   *
//*****************************************************************************

    public void
    suicide( Exception e, String logLine, int level )

    public void
    suicide( String logLine )

    public void
    suicide( String logLine, int level )

    public void
    suicide( Exception e )
```

```
    public void
    suicide( Exception e, String logLine )
```

The suicide() method allows a jiflet to gracefully kill itself. Depending on the circumstances, you may or may not want a log entry written, and you may or may not have an exception that caused your program's death.

center()

```
//******************************************************************************
//* center                                                                     *
//******************************************************************************

    public void
    center()
```

The center() method centers the jiflet window on the screen.

enableStatusBar()

```
//******************************************************************************
//* enableStatusBar                                                            *
//******************************************************************************

    public void
    enableStatusBar( String text )

    public void
    enableStatusBar()
```

The enableStatusBar() method creates a status bar with or without text and adds it to the jiflet's layout.

clearStatus()

```
//******************************************************************************
//* clearStatus                                                                *
//******************************************************************************

    public void
    clearStatus()
```

The clearStatus() method clears the text in the status bar.

showStatus()

```
//******************************************************************************
//* showStatus                                                                 *
//******************************************************************************

    public void
    showStatus( String text )
```

The showStatus() method sets the text in the status bar.

49

DEVELOPING
INTRANET
APPLICATIONS

setConnector()

```
//****************************************************************************
//* setConnector                                                             *
//****************************************************************************

    protected void
    setConnector( DBConnector aConnector )
```

The setConnector() method sets the DBConnector object associated with this jiflet.

getConnector()

```
//****************************************************************************
//* getConnector                                                             *
//****************************************************************************

    public DBConnector
    getConnector()
```

The getConnector() method returns the previously associated DBConnector object to the caller.

startWait()

```
//****************************************************************************
//* startWait                                                                *
//****************************************************************************

    public void
    startWait()
```

The startWait() method is a luxury method. It changes the cursor to the system default "wait" cursor. Usually an hourglass, this cursor indicates that a lengthy process is occurring.

endWait()

```
//****************************************************************************
//* endWait                                                                  *
//****************************************************************************

    public void
    endWait()
```

The endWait() method returns the cursor to its previous state if called after a Jiflet.startWait() call. Otherwise, this method does nothing.

getParameter()

```
//***************************************************************************
//* getParameter                                                            *
//***************************************************************************

    public String
    getParameter( String key )

    public String
    getParameter( String key, String defaultValue )
```

The `getParameter()` method is identical to Java's `Applet.getParameter()` method. It returns the value associated with the *key* passed. You can also pass in a default value in case the key is not found. These parameters are looked for in the `configProperties` instance variable.

canClose()

```
//***************************************************************************
//* canClose                                                                *
//***************************************************************************

    public boolean
    canClose()
```

The `canClose()` method is called before the jiflet is allowed to close. It provides you with a place to catch an unwanted departure. The default implementation returns `true`. Override this method to add your own functionality. An example of its use is to catch users before they exit to see whether they have saved their work.

Within your overridden copy, you can ask users whether they want to save their work. If they say no, return `true`, closing the jiflet. If they say yes, save their work and then return `true`, closing the jiflet. You can also offer them a cancel option, which returns `false`.

isActive()

```
//***************************************************************************
//* isActive                                                                *
//***************************************************************************

    public boolean
    isActive()
```

The `isActive()` method returns `true` if the jiflet is currently active; otherwise it returns `false`. The `isActive()` method is similar to the `Applet.isActive()` method. A jiflet is considered active right before its `run()` method is called.

Wrapping Up Jiflets

Now that we have this new `Jiflet` class, we need to place it somewhere. Again we borrow from the example set by Sun and place it in a package called `jif.jiflet`. This package contains the `Jiflet` class.

Programming with Jiflets

Now that we've created a class that implements the design goals, let's take it for a test drive. Remember that because we've modeled our jiflet on Java's `Applet` class, creating a jiflet should be quite simple.

The Smallest Jiflet

The smallest possible jiflet simply prints a string on the screen and does nothing else. Listing 49.6 shows the source code for our smallest jiflet.

Listing 49.6. The smallest jiflet.

```
//****************************************************************************
//* Imports                                                                  *
//****************************************************************************

import                     jif.jiflet.Jiflet;
import                     java.awt.Label;

//****************************************************************************
//* SmallJiflet                                                              *
//****************************************************************************

public class
SmallJiflet
extends Jiflet
{

//****************************************************************************
//* main                                                                     *
//****************************************************************************

    public static void
    main( String[] args )
    {
        new SmallJiflet();
    }

//****************************************************************************
//* init                                                                     *
//****************************************************************************

    public void
    init()
    {
```

```
        add( "Center", new Label( "I'm a small jiflet" ) );
        pack();
    }

//*********************************************************************
//* run                                                               *
//*********************************************************************

    public void
    run()
    {
        show();
    }

}
```

The main() method is called by the Java interpreter to run your program. It is required to create the class that is your program. It is in the main() method that we create an instance of SmallJiflet.

The pack() method readjusts the size of the jiflet to accommodate all the user interface objects contained within it. The pack() method is necessary because, unlike an applet, we have no predefined width or height.

The output of our small jiflet is shown in Figure 49.2.

FIGURE 49.2.
The output of
SmallJiflet.

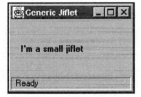

Extending Jiflets for Real-World Use

Now that you have a basic understanding of the Java Intranet Framework (JIF), the rest of this chapter extends the jiflet concept into a form that can be easily used for building database-aware intranet applications.

A jiflet, as you know, is the smallest application that can be built with JIF. However, it does absolutely nothing but look pretty. After building several applications using JIF, it becomes apparent that they all share much of the same code. Each application goes through the following life cycle:

1. Construct the jiflet.
2. Construct the user interface.
3. Handle events until the program ends.

Pretty boring, but such is life when you are only binary information. The pattern that becomes evident to you is that each application has a monotonous bunch of initialization code and a user interface that must be copied from application to application. But this base initialization is not in the Jiflet class. Jiflets have to remain pure.

The result is three new abstract classes: SimpleDBJiflet, SimpleDBUI, and DBRecord.

The philosophy is that a SimpleDBJiflet has a user interface defined by a SimpleDBUI. The two work together to present a pleasant atmosphere for the user. Together, they allow the user to manipulate a single set of database data. This database information is represented by the DBRecord class.

By extending these three abstract classes (and filling in the blanks as it were), you can create powerful database applications in a matter of hours!

The DBRecord Class

The DBRecord class is the smallest of the three new classes. This class represents a single set of database data. The data represented by this class is defined in its subclasses, therefore DBRecord is an abstract class. The source code for this class is shown in Listing 49.7.

Listing 49.7. The DBRecord class.

```
//*****************************************************************************
//* Package                                                                   *
//*****************************************************************************

package                         jif.sql;

//*****************************************************************************
//* Imports                                                                   *
//*****************************************************************************

//    JIF imports
import                          jif.sql.*;
import                          jif.awt.*;

//    Java imports
import                          java.sql.*;

//*****************************************************************************
//* DBRecord                                                                  *
//*****************************************************************************

public abstract class
DBRecord
{
```

```
//*****************************************************************************
//* Members                                                                  *
//*****************************************************************************
    //    An indicator for data changes...
    protected boolean           dataChange = false;
    protected boolean           isNewRecord = false;


//*****************************************************************************
//* Constructor                                                              *
//*****************************************************************************
    public
    DBRecord()
    {
        clear();
    }

    public
    DBRecord( ResultSet rs )
    {
        parseResultSet( rs );
    }


//*****************************************************************************
//* parseResultSet                                                           *
//*****************************************************************************
    /**
    * Parses a "SELECT * ..." result set into itself
    */
    public boolean
    parseResultSet( ResultSet rs )
    {
        isNewRecord = false;
        return( isNewRecord );
    }


//*****************************************************************************
//* update                                                                   *
//*****************************************************************************
    /**
    * Requests update SQL from the JifPanel and sends it to the database
    * via the DBConnector object passed in.
    */
    public abstract boolean
    update( DBConnector theConnector, JifPanel ap );


//*****************************************************************************
//* deleteRow                                                                *
//*****************************************************************************
    /**
    * Constructs delete SQL for the current row
    */
    public abstract boolean
    deleteRow( DBConnector theConnector );
```

49

DEVELOPING
INTRANET
APPLICATIONS

continues

Listing 49.7. continued

```
//******************************************************************************
//* setDataChange                                                              *
//******************************************************************************

    /**
     * Sets a flag indicating that data has changed...
     */
    public boolean
    setDataChange( boolean onOff )
    {
        dataChange = onOff;
        return( dataChange );
    }


//******************************************************************************
//* clear                                                                      *
//******************************************************************************

    /**
     * Clears all the variables...
     */
    public void
    clear()
    {
        isNewRecord = true;
        setDataChange( false );
    }



//******************************************************************************
//* canSave                                                                    *
//******************************************************************************

    /**
     * Checks to see if all required fields are filled in
     */
    public boolean
    canSave()
    {
        //    Everything is filled in!
        return( true );
    }


//******************************************************************************
//* didDataChange                                                              *
//******************************************************************************

    public boolean
    didDataChange()
    {
        return( dataChange );
    }
```

```
//*****************************************************************************
//* setNewStatus                                                              *
//*****************************************************************************

    public void
    setNewStatus( boolean how )
    {
        isNewRecord = how;
    }

//*****************************************************************************
//* getNewStatus                                                              *
//*****************************************************************************

    public boolean
    getNewStatus()
    {
        return( isNewRecord );
    }

}
```

The DBRecord class can be constructed with or without data. The data required to construct this class is a JDBC ResultSet object. This object is passed to the parseResultSet() method. In your derived class, you must override this method to read in the data from the ResultSet into instance variables.

To complete the class, you must provide two additional methods in your derived class: update() and deleteRow(). update() is called when someone wants you to save the information that your class contains. deleteRow() is called when someone wants you to delete the information your class contains.

The class provides a clear() method, which you override to clear out your instance variables. The clear() method is called, for example, when the user presses the New or Clear button.

The DBRecord class has two indicators: dataChange and isNewRecord. The boolean value dataChange indicates that the data has changed in the record; the boolean value isNewRecord indicates whether the record exists in the database.

The dataChange value must be manually set and reset. This is done to some degree by the SimpleDBJiflet class. For example, when a record is saved to the database, the dataChange value is set to false. This setting is made by way of the setDataChange() method.

Access methods are provided for you to get at these indicators. getNewStatus() and setNewStatus() allow access to the isNewRecord indicator. setDataChange() and didDataChange() provide access to the dataChange indicator.

Finally, the class provides a method called canSave(). This method returns a boolean value indicating whether the record is eligible to be saved to the database. Eligibility depends completely on the table the record represents. The canSave() method allows you to validate the data that the user has entered and give it the thumbs up or down.

49

DEVELOPING INTRANET APPLICATIONS

NOTE

The DBRecord class is part of the `jif.sql` package, included on the CD-ROM that accompanies this book.

A complete example is in order. Listing 49.8 is a complete DBRecord derivation for a table that represents Conference Rooms.

Listing 49.8. A DBRecord subclass.

```
//*****************************************************************************
//* Package                                                                   *
//*****************************************************************************

package                        jif.common;

//*****************************************************************************
//* Imports                                                                   *
//*****************************************************************************

//    JIF imports
import                         jif.sql.*;
import                         jif.awt.*;

//    Java imports
import                         java.sql.*;

//*****************************************************************************
//* ConfRoomRecord                                                            *
//*****************************************************************************

/**
 * A class that encapsulates a row in the conference room table...
 */
public class
ConfRoomRecord
extends DBRecord
{

//*****************************************************************************
//* Constants                                                                 *
//*****************************************************************************

    public final static String     TABLE_NAME = "conf_room";

//*****************************************************************************
//* Members                                                                   *
//*****************************************************************************

    //    A variable for each table column...
    public int                     room_nbr = -1;
    public int                     floor_nbr = -1;
    public String                  desc_text = "";
```

```
//*****************************************************************************
//* Constructor                                                               *
//*****************************************************************************

    public
    ConfRoomRecord()
    {
        clear();
    }

    public
    ConfRoomRecord( ResultSet rs )
    {
        parseResultSet( rs );
    }

//*****************************************************************************
//* parseResultSet                                                            *
//*****************************************************************************

    public boolean
    parseResultSet( ResultSet rs )
    {
        clear();

        try
        {
            //    Suck out the data...
            room_nbr = rs.getInt( "room_nbr" );
            floor_nbr = rs.getInt( "floor_nbr" );
            desc_text = rs.getString( "desc_text" );
            return( super.parseResultSet( rs ) );
        }
        catch ( SQLException e )
        {
            //    Signal an error...
            clear();
            return( false );
        }
    }

//*****************************************************************************
//* update                                                                    *
//*****************************************************************************

    /**
     * Requests update SQL from the JifPanel and sends it to the database
     * via the DBConnector object passed in.
     */
    public boolean
    update( DBConnector theConnector, JifPanel ap )
    {
        boolean         success = true;
```

continues

Listing 49.8. continued

```java
        try
        {
            //    No update if nothing to do...
            if ( dataChange )
            {
                String    sql;

                //    Generate some SQL!
                if ( getNewStatus() )
                    sql = ap.generateInsertSQL( TABLE_NAME );
                else
                    sql = ap.generateUpdateSQL( TABLE_NAME );

                if ( !sql.equals( "" ) )
                    theConnector.getStatement().executeUpdate( sql );
            }
        }
        catch ( SQLException e )
        {
            theConnector.errorLog( e.toString() );
            success = false;
        }

        return( success );
    }


//*****************************************************************************
//* deleteRow                                                               *
//*****************************************************************************

    /**
    * Removes this record from the database...
    */
    public boolean
    deleteRow( DBConnector theConnector )
    {
        boolean        success = true;

        //    Nothing to do...
        if ( getNewStatus() )
            return( false );

        String sql = "delete from " + TABLE_NAME + " where room_nbr " +
            "= " + Integer.toString( room_nbr ) + " and floor_nbr " +
            "= " + Integer.toString( floor_nbr );
        try
        {
            theConnector.getStatement().executeUpdate( sql );
        }
        catch ( SQLException e )
        {
            theConnector.errorLog( e.toString() );
            success = false;
        }
        return( success );
    }
```

```
//****************************************************************************
//* clear                                                                    *
//****************************************************************************

    /**
     * Clears all the variables...
     */
    public void
    clear()
    {
        super.clear();

        room_nbr = -1;
        floor_nbr = -1;
        desc_text = "";
    }

}
```

The SimpleDBUI Class

The `SimpleDBUI` class encapsulates the nonvisual side of the user interface that is necessary for proper application functionality. The class extends the `JifPanel` class by providing some default buttons and methods for moving data to and from the user interface components. The source code for this class is shown in Listing 49.9.

Listing 49.9. The SimpleDBUI class.

```
//****************************************************************************
//* Package                                                                  *
//****************************************************************************

package                         jif.awt;

//****************************************************************************
//* imports                                                                  *
//****************************************************************************

import                          java.awt.*;
import                          jif.sql.*;
import                          jif.jiflet.*;
import                          jif.common.*;

//****************************************************************************
//* SimpleDBUI                                                               *
//****************************************************************************

public abstract class
SimpleDBUI
extends JifPanel
{
```

continues

Listing 49.9. continued

```java
//******************************************************************************
//* Members                                                                    *
//******************************************************************************

    SimpleDBJiflet                  myJiflet;

    //    Some standard buttons...
    public Button                   saveButton = new Button( "Save" );
    public Button                   clearButton = new Button( "Clear" );
    public Button                   newButton = new Button( "New" );
    public Button                   deleteButton = new Button( "Delete" );
    public Button                   chooseButton = new Button( "Choose" );
    public Button                   closeButton = new Button( "Close" );

//******************************************************************************
//* Constructor                                                                *
//******************************************************************************

    public
    SimpleDBUI( SimpleDBJiflet jiflet )
    {
        setJiflet( jiflet );
        setFont( new Font( "Dialog", Font.PLAIN, 12 ) );
    }

//******************************************************************************
//* getJiflet                                                                  *
//******************************************************************************

    public SimpleDBJiflet
    getJiflet()
    {
        return( myJiflet );
    }

//******************************************************************************
//* setJiflet                                                                  *
//******************************************************************************

    public void
    setJiflet( SimpleDBJiflet jiflet )
    {
        myJiflet = jiflet;
    }

//******************************************************************************
//* moveToScreen                                                               *
//******************************************************************************

    /**
     * Moves data from a DBRecord object to the fields on the screen
     * for editing.
     */
    public abstract void
    moveToScreen();
```

```
//****************************************************************************
//* clearScreen                                                              *
//****************************************************************************

    /**
     * Clears the screen fields
     */
    public abstract void
    clearScreen();

//****************************************************************************
//* moveFromScreen                                                           *
//****************************************************************************

    /**
     * Moves data from the fields on the screen to a DBRecord object.
     */
    public abstract void
    moveFromScreen();

//****************************************************************************
//* action                                                                   *
//****************************************************************************

    public boolean
    action( Event event, Object arg )
    {
        //    Smart JIF components generate ACTION_EVENTs when changed...
        if ( event.target instanceof SQLFactoru )
        {
            //    Notify dad...
            sendJifMessage( event, DATA_CHANGE );
            return( true );
        }

        //    User pressed Save...
        if ( event.target == saveButton )
        {
            //    Notify dad...
            sendJifMessage( event, SAVE );
            return( true );
        }

        //    User pressed New...
        if ( event.target == newButton )
        {
            //    Notify dad...
            sendJifMessage( event, NEW );
            return( true );
        }

        //    User pressed Choose
        if ( event.target == chooseButton )
        {
```

continues

Listing 49.9. continued

```
            //    Notify dad...
        sendJifMessage( event, CHOOSE );
        return( true );
    }

    //    User pressed Close
    if ( event.target == closeButton )
    {
        //    Notify dad...
        sendJifMessage( event, CLOSE );
        return( true );
    }

    //    User pressed Delete
    if ( event.target == deleteButton )
    {
        //    Notify dad...
        sendJifMessage( event, DELETE );
        return( true );
    }

    //    User pressed Clear
    if ( event.target == clearButton )
    {
        //    Notify dad...
        sendJifMessage( event, CLEAR );
        return( true );
    }

    //    Not handled...
    return( false );
    }

}
```

Being abstract, the `SimpleDBUI` class is not very complex. The first thing you notice about the class is that we create a slew of buttons:

```
public Button              saveButton = new Button( "Save" );
public Button              clearButton = new Button( "Clear" );
public Button              newButton = new Button( "New" );
public Button              deleteButton = new Button( "Delete" );
public Button              chooseButton = new Button( "Choose" );
public Button              closeButton = new Button( "Close" );
```

These are the standard buttons that the `SimpleDBUI` knows about. They are defined as `public` so that you can access them outside the user interface. Unless they are placed on a panel or shown in some manner on the screen, they are really never used; therefore they do not generate messages.

When these buttons are shown on the screen and subsequently clicked by the user, an ACTION_EVENT event is generated. This event is translated into a JifMessage by the action() event handler method. The message is then sent on to the parent, presumably a SimpleDBJiflet, and processed there.

The SimpleDBUI class is expected to move data in and out of a DBRecord class. It does this using three methods: moveToScreen(), moveFromScreen(), and clearScreen(). This class has access to the current DBRecord by way of the jiflet. By calling the SimpleDBJiflet's getDBRecord() method, a reference to the current DBRecord is provided.

The moveToScreen() method moves data from the DBRecord to the screen components. The moveFromScreen() method moves data from the screen components to the DBRecord. And clearScreen() clears out the screen components. This last method does not touch the DBRecord really, but a clearScreen() followed by a moveFromScreen() clears out the DBRecord.

> **NOTE**
>
> The SimpleDBUI class is part of the jif.awt package, included on the CD-ROM that accompanies this book.

 A simple SimpleDBUI derivation is shown in Listing 49.10. This is from the Online In/Out Board application. This application is provided for you on the CD-ROM that accompanies this book.

Listing 49.10. A SimpleDBUI subclass.

```
//*****************************************************************************
//* imports                                                                  *
//*****************************************************************************

import                         java.awt.*;

import                         jif.awt.*;
import                         jif.sql.*;
import                         jif.jiflet.*;
import                         jif.common.*;


//*****************************************************************************
//* InOutBoardUI                                                             *
//*****************************************************************************

public class
InOutBoardUI
extends SimpleDBUI
{
```

continues

Listing 49.10. continued

```java
//*****************************************************************************
//* Members                                                                   *
//*****************************************************************************
    List                    empList;

//*****************************************************************************
//* Constructor                                                               *
//*****************************************************************************

    public
    InOutBoardUI( SimpleDBJiflet jiflet )
    {
        super( jiflet );
        setLayout( new BorderLayout() );

        empList = new List();
        empList.setFont( new Font( "Helvetica", Font.BOLD, 14 ) );
        add( "Center", empList );
        empList.enable();

        JifPanel p = new JifPanel();
        p.setLayout( new FlowLayout( FlowLayout.CENTER, 5, 5 ) );
        saveButton.setLabel( "Toggle" );
        saveButton.disable();
        p.add( saveButton );
        add( "South", p );

        //    Set the focus to the first field...
        setFocus( empList );
    }

//*****************************************************************************
//* moveToScreen                                                              *
//*****************************************************************************

    /**
     * Moves data from an InOutBoardRecord object to the fields on the screen
     * for editing.
     */
    public void
    moveToScreen()
    {
        if ( getJiflet().getDBRecord() == null )
            return;

        //    Cast one off...
        EmployeeRecord er = ( EmployeeRecord )getJiflet().getDBRecord();
        String s = er.first_name + " " + er.last_name + " is ";

        if ( er.in_out_ind.equalsIgnoreCase( "Y" ) )
            s += "in";
        else
            s += "out";

        empList.addItem( s );
    }
```

```
//******************************************************************************
//* clearScreen                                                                *
//******************************************************************************

    /**
     * Clears the record out...
     */
    public void
    clearScreen()
    {
        empList.clear();
    }

//******************************************************************************
//* moveFromScreen                                                             *
//******************************************************************************

    /**
     * Moves data from the fields on the screen to an EmployeeRecord object.
     */
    public void
    moveFromScreen()
    {
        //     Does nothing…
        return;
    }

}
```

The SimpleDBJiflet Class

The SimpleDBJiflet class pulls together the DBRecord and SimpleDBUI classes into a cool little hunk of code. This class encapsulates much of the necessary menu and database initialization that must be done for each application.

The SimpleDBJiflet class extends the Jiflet class and adds the following functionality:

■ A File menu with standard database connectivity

■ A Help menu with a working About dialog box

■ A standard method of communicating with the user interface

■ Record saving and deleting

■ Data modification notification

Although they are not functional on their own, these features keep you from doing the legwork of cutting and pasting from app to app. The beauty of object-oriented programming and Java is that you can stuff all this functionality into an abstract base class and fill in the blanks. That is all that has been done here.

The File and Help Menus

The `SimpleDBJiflet` class creates two menus: a File menu and a Help menu. The File menu contains two items: Connect and Exit.

The first option, Connect, connects and disconnects the application to and from the database. This functionality is provided completely as long as the jiflet has a valid `DBConnector` set for itself.

After a database connection is established, the Connect menu option changes to Disconnect automatically. When the Disconnect option is selected, it disconnects the application from the database and the option changes back to Connect.

The second menu option, Exit, disconnects any connected `DBConnector` and closes the application. The Exit option can include writing information to a log file or to the screen. It depends on the configuration of the jiflet.

The Help menu has a single menu item that brings up an About dialog box. If you are not familiar with these critters, they are simply brag boxes for the authors of programs. Some of these dialog boxes actually show useful information, but most just show the program name and a fancy icon along with some copyright information.

Should your jiflet be any different? You're just as proud of your creation as other authors are! Well, set a copyright message with the method `setCopyright()`, and an About dialog box displays automagically! Figure 49.3 shows the About dialog box for the employee maintenance program. Nothing too fancy, just the text and a little icon.

FIGURE 49.3.

The employee maintenance About dialog box.

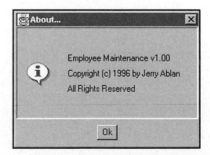

> **TIP**
>
> A nice extension to the `Jiflet` class allows custom icons to be associated with the application. Then in their About dialog boxes, the custom icon displays instead of the stock information icon.

The only code required to get that nice About box in the derived `Employee` program is the following:

```
setCopyright( "Employee Maintenance v1.00\n" +
    "Copyright (c) 1996 by Jerry Ablan\n" +
    "All Rights Reserved" );
```

Not a lot of code for such a nice feature! By the way, the About menu item is disabled until you call the `setCopyright()` method.

Standard Communications: `JifMessage`

In object-oriented programming, objects communicate with each other by way of messages. But at what point should objects know about the inside workings of other objects? Some purists argue *never*! Some argue *sometimes*. It is usually, however, a matter of convenience.

While designing many of the applications for this book, I felt that the user interface should be able to manage itself, because it doesn't know about the application driving it. However, I felt that the application needed to know a little about the user interface. Otherwise, you really can't provide any nice bells and whistles. One such feature is to enable and disable the Save button when a data item is modified. This is an excellent visual clue to the user that a change has been made, intentionally or not.

To feel politically correct—OOP-wise—and to not let my user interface design creep into my application design, I created the `JifMessage` interface. Listing 49.11 is the source code for the `JifMessage` interface.

Listing 49.11. The `JifMessage` interface.

```
//****************************************************************************
//* Package                                                                  *
//****************************************************************************

package                         jif.jiflet;

//****************************************************************************
//* Imports                                                                  *
//****************************************************************************

import                          java.awt.Event;
```

continues

Listing 49.11. continued

```
//*************************************************************************
//* JifMessage                                                           *
//*************************************************************************

public interface
JifMessage
{

//*************************************************************************
//* Members                                                              *
//*************************************************************************

    public static final int      NEW = 0;
    public static final int      CLEAR = 1;
    public static final int      SAVE = 2;
    public static final int      DELETE = 3;
    public static final int      CUT = 4;
    public static final int      COPY = 5;
    public static final int      PASTE = 6;
    public static final int      HELP_WINDOW = 7;
    public static final int      HELP_CONTEXT = 8;
    public static final int      HELP_ABOUT = 9;
    public static final int      HELP_HELP = 10;
    public static final int      DATA_CHANGE = 11;
    public static final int      CHOOSE = 12;
    public static final int      CLOSE = 13;

//*************************************************************************
//* sendJifMessage                                                       *
//*************************************************************************

    public void
    sendJifMessage( Event event, int msg );

}
```

Again, the `JifMessage` interface is nothing fancy—simply a list of constants and a consistent method of sending them, which is up to the implementor of this interface. As you can see, many standard actions are represented by the constants in this class: New, Save, Delete, Close, and so on.

After creating this interface, we have to implement it somewhere. I felt that the `JifPanel` class is an excellent spot. Because most user interfaces are created with `JifPanels`, placing the interface there provides a consistent and standard method of communication with its parent. Listing 49.12 is the code added to the `JifPanel` class to implement this interface.

Listing 49.12. Sending a `JifMessage`.

```
//*************************************************************************
//* sendJifMessage                                                       *
//*************************************************************************

    public void
    sendJifMessage( Event event, int msg )
    {
        event.target = this;
        event.arg = new Integer( msg );
        getParent().postEvent( event );
    }
```

Nothing too tricky here, either. The `sendJifMessage()` method takes as arguments an event and the message to send. It changes the target of the event to itself (the `JifPanel` instance) and sets the argument of the event to the message. It then sends the message along to the parent.

Here's a quick example of how it is used. In the `SimpleDBUI` class, there is a built-in Save button. When the user clicks this button, the class automatically sends a `JifMessage.SAVE` event to its parent. The parent needs only to listen for these `JifMessage` events to know what the child wants it to do.

The code for sending from the child looks exactly like this:

```
//    User pressed Save...
if ( event.target == saveButton )
{
    //    Notify dad...
    sendJifMessage( event, JifMessage.SAVE );
    return( true );
}
```

The code for receiving in the parent looks like this:

```
public boolean
action( Event event, Object arg )
{
    switch ( ( ( Integer )arg ).intValue() )
    {
        case JifMessage.DELETE:
            delDlg = new ResponseDialog( this,
                "Delete Confirmation",
                "Are you sure you want to delete this record?",
                "Yes,No" );

            delDlg.show();
            break;
    }
}
```

49

DEVELOPING
INTRANET
APPLICATIONS

Now that there is a standard way of communicating, we can add some standard features like saving and deleting.

Record Saving and Deleting

A nice feature for a program to have is a standard method of saving and deleting. Now that we know when the user wants us to save or delete (by way of a JifMessage), we need some standard methods for doing this.

Enter the saveRecord() and deleteRecord() methods. These two methods provide a way to save and delete the information stored in the DBRecord of the jiflet. When the SimpleDBUI sends the SAVE or DELETE JifMessage to the jiflet, one of these methods is called.

The methods are declared as shown in Listing 49.13.

Listing 49.13. Declaring the saveRecord() and deleteRecord() methods.

```
//******************************************************************************
//* saveRecord                                                                 *
//******************************************************************************

    public boolean
    saveRecord()
    {
        //    If we are not connected, do nothing...
        if ( !getConnector().connected() )
        {
            MessageBox mb = new MessageBox( this, "Hold on there!",
                "You must connect with the database\n" +
                "before you can save any data.\n\n" +
                "Connect first, then try this again!",
                MessageBox.EXCLAMATION );

            mb.show();
            return( false );
        }

        //    Move the data back to the DBRecord...
        getUIPanel().moveFromScreen();

        //    Check to see if all fields are filled in...
        if ( getDBRecord().canSave() )
        {
            //    Save it...
            if ( getDBRecord().update( getConnector(), getUIPanel() ) )
            {
                //    Indicate that it was saved...
                getDBRecord().setDataChange( false );
                setStatus( "Record saved..." );
            }
            else
                setStatus( "Record not saved..." );

            return( true );
        }
```

```
        else
        {
            MessageBox mb = new MessageBox( this, "Cannot Save!",
                "All required fields must be entered!",
                MessageBox.EXCLAMATION );

            mb.show();
        }

        return( false );
    }

//******************************************************************************
//* deleteRecord                                                               *
//******************************************************************************

    public boolean
    deleteRecord()
    {
        //    If we are not connected, do nothing...
        if ( !getConnector().connected() )
        {
            MessageBox mb = new MessageBox( this, "Hold on there!",
                "You must connect with the database\n" +
                "before you can delete any data.\n\n" +
                "Connect first, then try this again!",
                MessageBox.EXCLAMATION );

            mb.show();
            return( false );
        }

        //    Move the data back to the DBRecord...
        getUIPanel().moveFromScreen();

        //    Kill it!
        if ( getDBRecord().deleteRow( getConnector() ) )
        {
            //    Indicate that it was saved...
            getDBRecord().clear();
            getUIPanel().moveToScreen();
            setStatus( "Record deleted..." );
            return( true );
        }
        else
            setStatus( "Record not deleted..." );

        return( false );
    }
```

Having these methods in the base class allows you to override them in your derived classes, thus enhancing the functionality. One functionality is to modify two tables instead of one. Or perhaps your jiflet does not save any data but you use the Save button and mechanism for some other sort of notification. It is up to you. Be creative!

49

DEVELOPING
INTRANET
APPLICATIONS

Data Change Notification

The last function that the SimpleDBJiflet class provides is data change notification.

When the SimpleDBUI class contains one of the JIF Component extensions (such as JifTextField), it is notified when the user changes the data. This notification is passed along to the SimpleDBJiflet class. The SimpleDBJiflet class then manages the enabling and disabling of the Save, New, and Delete buttons.

The status of the record depends on the state of the DBRecord at the time. If the record is new, it can't be deleted but it can be saved or cleared (New). If the record has not been changed and is not new, it can be saved, deleted, or cleared. This is not a very complex set of rules, but it is a hassle to code for each application. You'll find it refreshing when your Save button lights up after you type your first character.

Summary

This chapter thoroughly covered an intranet application framework. You had an intimate encounter with the Jiflet class, which is part of the Java Intranet Framework. This base, or framework, is provided for you on the CD-ROM that accompanies this book. You can use it to create your own intranet applications with Java.

Java Game Programming

by Tim Macinta

IN THIS CHAPTER

Creating games with Java is a lot like creating games with other languages. You have to deal with the design of movable objects (often referred to as *sprites*), the design of a graphics engine to keep track of the movable objects, and double buffering to make movement look smooth. There is a good chance that future versions of Java will provide built-in support for sprites and double buffering, but for now, we have to add the support ourselves. This chapter covers methods for creating these standard building blocks of games using Java.

Thankfully, Java takes care of a lot of the dirty work you would have to do if you were writing a game in another language. For example, Java provides built-in support for transparent pixels, making it easier to write a graphics engine that can draw nonrectangular objects. Java also has built-in support for allowing several different programs to run at once—perfect for creating a world with a lot of creatures, each with its own special methods for acting. However, the added bonuses of Java can turn into handicaps if you do not use them properly. This chapter explains how to use the advantages of Java to write games and how to avoid the pitfalls that accompany the power.

Selecting an Appropriate Version of Java

Before you set out to write a game in Java, you must first decide which version of Java you are going to use. Should you use the most recent version of Java (currently 1.1) or should you use an older version so that more people can use your game? This decision depends largely on how you plan to distribute your game. If you plan to distribute your game as an application, the decision is pretty simple: use the latest version of Java because you can take advantages of the latest improvements; if the user doesn't have the latest version of Java, you can just ship it with your application.

However, if you plan to distribute your game as an applet, the choice is a little more complicated. Should you use the latest version of Java so that you have a much richer set of class libraries to work with, or should you use the 1.0 version of Java so that you can reach the largest audience? For now, the solution is to use the 1.0 version of Java. Currently, Netscape Navigator 4.0 and HotJava are the only Web browsers that support the Java 1.1 API—and most users are not yet using these browsers. In the future, the Java 1.1 API will be widespread enough that it will be reasonable to write a game using the 1.1 API. For now, however, it's best to play it safe and use the Java 1.0 API so that everybody who has a Java-enabled browser can use the game.

This chapter covers what you need to know to write games in both the Java 1.0 and the 1.1 API. Most of what you need to know to write games in Java does not depend on whether or not you are using the Java 1.0 or the 1.1 API. The main issue between the different APIs is the issue of handling user input. This difference is really only of secondary importance because the bulk of the code in this chapter is the same regardless of what API you use it for.

Consequently, all the examples in this chapter are first shown with code that conforms to the Java 1.0 API. If there is a different way of doing things with the Java 1.1 API, an alternative that conforms to the Java 1.1 API is also provided. Don't forget that the Java 1.1 API is backward compatible with the Java 1.0 API, so the 1.0 examples work regardless of which version of Java you use (the Java 1.1 API example just shows a better way of doing things in the newer version of Java). The Java 1.1 versions of the examples are in the Chap50/jdk1_1 directory on the CD-ROM that accompanies this book; the Java 1.0 versions of the examples are in the Chap50 directory.

Graphics: Creating a Graphics Engine

A graphics engine is essential to a well-designed game in Java. A *graphics engine* is an object that is given the duty of painting the screen. The graphics engine keeps track of all objects on the screen at one time, the order in which to draw the objects, and the background to be drawn. By far, the most important function of the graphics engine is the maintenance of movable object blocks.

Movable Object Blocks in Java

So what's the big fuss about movable object blocks (MOBs)? Well, they make your life infinitely easier if you're interested in creating a game that combines graphics and user interaction—as most games do. The basic concept of a movable object is that the object contains both a picture that will be drawn on the screen and information that tells you where the picture is to be drawn on the screen. To make the object move, you simply tell the movable object (more precisely, the graphics engine that contains the movable object) which way to move and you're done—redrawing is automatically taken care of.

The bare-bones method for making a movable object block in Java is shown in Listing 50.1. As you can see, the movable object consists merely of an image and a set of coordinates. You may be thinking, "Movable objects are supposed to take care of all the redrawing that needs to be done when they are moved. How is that possible with just the code in Listing 50.1?" Redrawing is the graphics engine's job. Don't worry about it for now; it's covered a little later.

NOTE

 If you don't feel like typing all the code from Listings 50.1 through 50.4, you can find finished versions of all the code in the CHAP50 directory on the CD-ROM that accompanies this book. The files that correspond to Listings 50.1 through 50.4 are called MOB.java, GraphicsEngine.java, Game.java, and example.html. You can see the final version of the GraphicsEngine test by viewing the page titled example.html with a Java-enabled browser.

Listing 50.1. MOB.java: The code to create a bare-bones movable object block (MOB).

```java
import java.awt.*;

public class MOB {
    public int x = 0;
    public int y = 0;
    public Image picture;

        public MOB(Image pic) {
            picture=pic;
        }
}
```

As you can see in Listing 50.1, the constructor for our movable object block (MOB) takes an Image and stores it away to be drawn when needed. After we instantiate a MOB (that is, after we call the constructor), we have a movable object that we can move around the screen just by changing its x and y values. The engine will take care of redrawing the movable object in the new position, so what else is there to worry about?

One thing to consider is the nature of the picture that is going to be drawn every time the movable object is drawn. Consider the place in which the image probably will originate. In all likelihood, the picture will either come from a GIF or JPEG file, which has one very important consequence—it will be rectangular. So what? Think about what your video game will look like if all your movable objects are rectangles. Your characters will be drawn, but so will their backgrounds. Chances are, you'll want to have a background for the entire game and it would be unacceptable if the unfilled space on character images covered up your background just because the images were rectangular and the characters were of another shape.

When programming games in other languages, this problem is often resolved by examining each pixel in a character's image before drawing it to see whether it's part of the background. If the pixel is not part of the background, it's drawn as normal. If the pixel is part of the background, it's skipped and the rest of the pixels are tested. Pixels that aren't drawn usually are referred to as *transparent pixels*. If you think this seems like a laborious process, it is. Fortunately, Java has built-in support for transparent colors in images, which simplifies your task immensely. You don't have to check each pixel for transparency before it's drawn because Java can do that automatically. Java even has built-in support for different levels of transparency. For example, you can create pixels that are 20 percent transparent to give your images a ghost-like appearance. For now, however, we'll deal only with fully transparent pixels.

NOTE

Whether or not you know it, you are probably already familiar with transparent GIFs. If you have ever stumbled across a Web page with an image that wasn't perfectly rectangular, you were probably looking at a transparent GIF.

Java's capability to draw transparent pixels makes the task of painting movable objects on the screen much easier. But how do you tell Java which pixels are transparent and which pixels aren't? You could load the image and run it through a filter that changes the ColorModel, but that would be doing it the hard way. Fortunately, Java supports transparent GIF files. Whenever a transparent GIF file is loaded, all the transparency is preserved by Java. That means your job just got a lot easier.

> **NOTE**
>
> A new Adobe PhotoShop plug-in allows you to save your images as transparent (and interlaced) GIFs. You can download it from http://www.adobe.com.

Now the problem becomes how to make transparent GIFs. This part is easier than you think. Simply use your favorite graphics package to create a GIF file (or a picture in some other format that you can eventually convert to a GIF file). Select a color that doesn't appear anywhere in the picture and fill all areas that you want to be transparent with the selected color. Make a note of the RGB value of the color that you use to fill in the transparent places. Now you can use a program to convert your GIF file into a transparent GIF file. I use Giftool, distributed by Home Pages, Inc., to make transparent GIF files. You simply pass to Giftool the RGB value of the color you selected for transparency, and Giftool makes that color transparent inside the GIF file. Giftool is also useful for making your GIF files interlaced. *Interlaced GIF files* are the pictures that initially appear with block-like edges and keep getting more defined as they continue to load.

Construction of a Graphics Engine

Now you have movable objects that know where they're supposed to be and don't eat up the background as they go there. The next step is to design something that will keep track of your movable objects and draw them in the proper places when necessary. This is the job of the GraphicsEngine class. Listing 50.2 shows the bare bones of a graphics engine—the minimum you need to handle multiple movable objects. Even this engine leaves out several things nearly all games need, but we'll get to those things later. For now, let's concentrate on how this bare-bones system works to give you a solid grasp of the basic concepts.

Listing 50.2. GraphicsEngine.java: A bare-bone graphics engine that tracks your movable objects.

```
import java.awt.*;
import java.awt.image.*;

public class GraphicsEngine {
  Chain mobs = null;
```

continues

Listing 50.2. continued

```java
public GraphicsEngine() {}

public void AddMOB (MOB new_mob) {
  mobs = new Chain(new_mob, mobs);
}

public void paint(Graphics g, ImageObserver imob) {
  Chain temp_mobs = mobs;
  MOB mob;
  while (temp_mobs != null) {
    mob = temp_mobs.mob;
    g.drawImage(mob.picture, mob.x, mob.y, imob);
    temp_mobs = temp_mobs.rest;
  }
}
}

class Chain {
  public MOB mob;
  public Chain rest;

  public Chain(MOB mob, Chain rest) {
    this.mob = mob;
    this.rest = rest;
  }

}
```

Introducing Linked Lists

Before we detail how the GraphicsEngine class works, let's touch on the Chain class. The Chain class looks rather simple—and it can be—but don't let that fool you. Entire languages such as LISP and Scheme have been built around data structures that have the same function as the Chain class. The Chain class is simply a data structure that holds two objects. Here, we're calling those two objects item and rest because we are going to use Chain to create a linked list. The power of the Chain structure—and structures like it—is that it can be used as a building block to create a multitude of more complicated structures. These structures include circular buffers, binary trees, weighted di-graphs, and linked lists, to name a few. Using the Chain class to create a linked list is suitable for our purposes.

Our goal is to keep a list of the moveable objects that have to be drawn. A linked list suites our purposes well because a linked list is a structure used to store a list of objects. It is referred to as a "linked" list because each point in the list contains an object and a link to a list with the remaining objects.

> **NOTE**
>
> The concept of a linked list—the Chain class in this case—may be a little hard to grasp at first because it is defined recursively. If you don't understand it right away, don't worry. Try to understand how the Chain class is used in the code first and study Figure 50.1; then the technical explanation should make more sense.

To understand what a linked list is, think of a train as an example: Consider the train to be the first car followed by the rest of the train. The "rest of the train" can be described as the second car followed by the remaining cars. This description can continue until you reach the last car, which can described as the caboose followed by nothing. A Chain class is analogous to a train. A Chain can be described as a movable object followed by the rest of the Chain, just as a train can be described as a car followed by the rest of the train. And just as the rest of the train can be considered a train by itself, the rest of the Chain can be considered a Chain by itself, and that's why the rest is of type Chain.

From the looks of the constructor for Chain, it appears that you need an existing Chain to make another Chain. This makes sense when you already have a Chain and want to add to it, but how do you start a new Chain? To do this, create a Chain that is an item linked to nothing. How do you link an item to nothing? Use the Java symbol for nothing—null—to represent the rest Chain. If you look at the code in Listing 50.2, that's exactly what we did. Our instance variable mobs is of type Chain and it is used to hold a linked list of movable objects. Look at the method AddMOB() in Listing 50.2. Whenever we want to add another movable object to the list of movable objects we're controlling, we simply make a new list of movable objects that has the new movable object as the first item and the old Chain as the rest of the list. Notice that the initial value of mobs is null, which is used to represent nothing.

> **NOTE**
>
> You may wonder why we even bothered making a method called AddMOB() when it only ended up being one line long. The point in making short methods like AddMOB() is that if GraphicsEngine were subclassed in the future, it would be a lot easier to add functionality if all you have to do is override one method as opposed to changing every line of code that calls AddMOB(). For example, if you wanted to sort all your moveable objects by size, you can just override AddMOB() so that it stores all the objects in a sorted order to begin with.

Painting Images from a List

Now that we have a method for keeping a list of all the objects that have to be painted, let's review how to use the list. The first thing you should be concerned about is how to add new objects to the list of objects that have to be painted. You add a new object to the list by using the AddMOB() method shown in Listing 50.2. As you can see from the listing, all the AddMOB() method does is to replace the old list of objects stored in mobs with a new list that contains the new object and a link to the old list of objects.

How do we use the list of movable objects once AddMOB() has been called for all the movable objects we want to handle? Take a look at the paint() method. The first thing to do is copy the pointer to mobs into a temporary Chain called temp_mobs. Note that the *pointer* is copied, not the actual contents. If the contents were copied instead of the pointer, this approach would take much longer and would be much more difficult to implement. "But I thought Java doesn't have pointers," you may be thinking at this point. That's not exactly true; Java doesn't have pointer arithmetic, but pointers are still used to pass arguments, although the programmer never has direct access to these pointers.

temp_mobs now contains a pointer to the list of all the movable objects to be drawn. The task at hand is to go through the list and draw each movable object. The variable mob is used to keep track of each movable object as we get to it. The variable temp_mobs represents the list of movable objects we have left to draw (that's why we started it off pointing to the whole list). We'll know all our movable objects have been drawn when temp_mobs is null, because that will be just like saying the list of movable objects left to draw is empty. That's why the main part of the code is encapsulated in a while loop that terminates when temp_mobs is null.

Look at the code inside the while loop of the paint() method. The first thing that is done is to assign mob to the movable object at the beginning of the temp_mobs Chain so that there is an actual movable object to deal with. Now it's time to draw the movable object. The g.drawImage command draws the movable object in the proper place. The variable mob.picture is the picture stored earlier when the movable object was created. The variables mob.x and mob.y are the screen coordinates at which the movable object should be drawn; notice that paint() looks at these two variables every time the movable object is drawn, so changing one of these coordinates while the program is running has the same effect as moving it on the screen. The final argument passed to g.drawImage, imob, is an ImageObserver responsible for redrawing an image when it changes or moves. Don't worry about where you get an ImageObserver from; chances are, you'll be using the GraphicsEngine class to draw inside a Component (or a subclass of Component such as Applet), and a Component implements the ImageObserver interface so that you can just pass the Component to GraphicsEngine whenever you want to repaint.

The final line inside the while loop shortens the list of movable objects that have to be drawn. It points temp_mobs away from the Chain that it just drew a movable object off the top of and points it to the Chain that contains the remainder of the MOBs. As we continue to cut down the list of MOBs by pointing to the remainder, temp_mobs eventually winds up as null, which ends the `while` loop with all our movable objects drawn. Figure 50.1 provides a graphical explanation of this process.

FIGURE 50.1.

A graphical representation of a Chain.

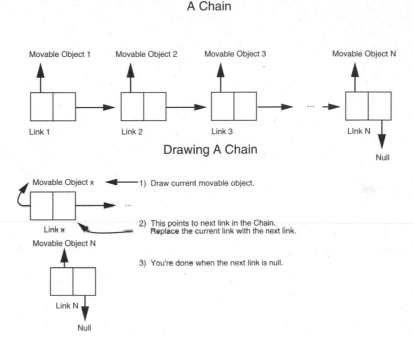

Installing the Graphics Engine

The graphics engine in Listing 50.2 certainly had some important things left out, but it does work. Let's go over how to install the `GraphicsEngine` inside a `Component` first, and then go back and improve on the design of the graphics engine and the MOB.

Listing 50.3 shows an example of how to install the `GraphicsEngine` inside a `Component`. It just so happens that the `Component` we're installing it in is an `Applet` (remember that `Applet` is a subclass of `Component`), so we can view the results with a Web browser. Keep in mind that the same method called to use the `GraphicsEngine` inside an `Applet` can also be used to install the `GraphicsEngine` inside other `Components`.

> **NOTE**
>
>
> Remember that you can find all the code presented in the listings in this chapter on the CD-ROM that accompanies this book.

Before trying to understand the code in Listing 50.3, it would be a good idea to type and compile Listings 50.1 through 50.3 so that you can get an idea of what the code does. Save each listing with the filename specified in each listing's heading and compile the code by using the javac command on each of those files.

In addition to compiling the code in Listings 50.1 through 50.3, you must also create the HTML file shown in Listing 50.4. (Use a Java-enabled browser or the JDK applet viewer to view this file once you have compiled everything.) As the final step, you must place a small image file to be used as the movable object in the same directory as the code and either rename it to one.gif or change the line inside the init() method in Listing 50.3 that specifies the name of the picture being loaded.

If you want to use the JDK 1.1 alternative version of this applet, simply save the code in Listing 50.5 to a file named Game.java instead of using the code in Listing 50.3. Of course, if you do use the JDK 1.1 alternative, you must make sure that your browser or applet viewer is Java 1.1 compliant.

Listing 50.3. Game.java: This sample applet illustrates the GraphicsEngine class in Java 1.0.

```java
import java.awt.*;
import java.applet.Applet;
import java.net.URL;

public class Game extends Applet {
  GraphicsEngine engine;
  MOB picture1;

  public void init() {
    try {
      engine = new GraphicsEngine();
      Image image1 = getImage(new URL(getDocumentBase(), "one.gif"));
      picture1 = new MOB(image1);
      engine.AddMOB(picture1);
    }
    catch (java.net.MalformedURLException e) {
      System.out.println("Error while loading pictures...");
      e.printStackTrace();
    }
  }

  public void update(Graphics g) {
    paint(g);
  }

  public void paint(Graphics g) {
    engine.paint(g, this);
  }

  public boolean mouseMove (Event evt, int mx, int my) {
    picture1.x = mx;
    picture1.y = my;
```

```
      repaint();
      return true;
   }
}
```

Listing 50.4. This code must be in an HTML file if you are to view the applet.

```
<html>
<head>
<title>GraphicsEngine Example</title>
</head>

<body>
<h1>GraphicsEngine Example</h1>

<applet code="Game.class" width=200 height=200>
</applet>
</body>
</html>
```

Listing 50.5. Game.java: This sample applet illustrates the GraphicsEngine class in Java 1.1.

```
import java.awt.event.*;
import java.awt.*;
import java.applet.Applet;
import java.net.URL;

public class Game extends Applet implements MouseMotionListener {
  GraphicsEngine engine;
  MOB picture1;

  public void init() {
    addMouseMotionListener(this);
    try {
      engine = new GraphicsEngine(this);
      Image image1 = getImage(new URL(getDocumentBase(), "one.gif"));
      picture1 = new MOB(image1);
      engine.AddMOB(picture1);
    }
    catch (java.net.MalformedURLException e) {
      System.out.println("Error while loading pictures...");
      e.printStackTrace();
    }
  }

  public void update(Graphics g) {
    paint(g);
  }
```

continues

Listing 50.5. continued

```java
public void paint(Graphics g) {
  engine.paint(g, this);
}

public void mouseDragged (MouseEvent evt) {
}

public void mouseMoved (MouseEvent evt) {
  picture1.x = evt.getX();
  picture1.y = evt.getY();
  repaint();
}
}
```

Once you have the example up and running, the image you selected should appear in the upper-left corner of the applet's window. Pass your mouse over the applet's window. The image you have chosen should follow your pointer around the window. If you use the images off the CD-ROM that accompanies this book, you should see something similar to Figure 50.2.

FIGURE 50.2.

This is what the example of the bare-bones GraphicsEngine *should look like.*

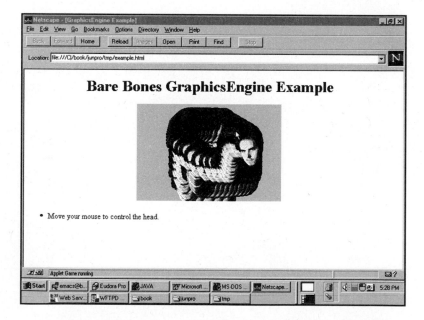

Let's go over how the code that links the GraphicsEngine to the applet called Game works. Our instance variables are engine, which controls all the movable objects we can deliver, and picture1, a movable object that draws the chosen image.

Take a look at the fairly straightforward init() method. You initialize engine by setting it equal to a new GraphicsEngine. Next, the image you chose is loaded with a call to getImage(). This line creates the need for the try and catch statements that surround the rest of the code to catch any invalid URLs. After the image is loaded, it is used to create a new MOB, and picture1 is initialized to this new MOB. The work is completed by adding the movable object to engine so that engine will draw it in the future. The remaining lines (the lines inside the catch statement) are there to provide information about any errors that occur.

The update() method is used to avoid flickering. By default, applets use the update() method to clear the window they live in before they repaint themselves with a call to their paint() method. This can be a useful feature if you're changing the display only once in a while, but with graphics-intensive programs, this can create a lot of flicker because the screen refreshes itself frequently. Because the screen refreshes itself so often, once in a while, it catches the applet at a point at which it has just cleared its window and hasn't yet had a chance to redraw itself. This situation is what causes flicker.

The flicker was eliminated here simply by leaving out the code that clears the window and going straight to the paint() method. If you already ran this example applet, you have probably already noticed that, although not clearing the screen solves the problem of flickering, it creates another problem: The movable object is leaving streaks! (If you haven't run the applet yet, you can see the streaks in Figure 50.2.) Don't worry; the streaks will be eliminated a little later when we introduce double buffering into our graphics engine.

As you can see, the Game.paint() method consists of one line: a call to the paint() method in engine. It might seem like a waste of time going from update() to paint() to engine.paint() just to draw one image. Once you have a dozen or more movable objects on the screen at once, however, you'll appreciate the simplicity of being able to add the object in the init() method and then forget about it the rest of the time, letting the engine.paint() method take care of everything.

Finally, we have the mouseMove() method (or the mouseMoved() method if you used the Java 1.1-compliant example in Listing 50.5). This is what provides the tracking motion so that the movable object follows your pointer around the window. There are, of course, other options for user input; these are discussed later in this chapter. The tracking is accomplished simply by setting the coordinates of the movable object to the position of the mouse. The call to repaint() just tells the painting thread that something has changed; the painting thread calls paint() when it gets around to it, so you don't have to worry about redrawing any more. To finish up, true is returned to inform the caller that the mouseMove() event was taken care of (if you're using the Java 1.1 example, nothing is returned because nothing has to be returned).

> **NOTE**
>
> The AWT event model underwent a major overhaul in Java 1.1; one of the things that changed was that methods that handle events don't return anything anymore. The AWT no longer has to know whether or not the mouseMove() method was taken care of because it is now implicitly taken care of when you register an observer with a component.

Improving the Bare-Bones Engine

Now that the framework has been laid for a functional graphics engine, it's time to make improvements. Let's start with movable objects. What should you consider when thinking about the uses movable objects have in games? Sooner or later, chances are that you'll want to write a game with a lot of movable objects. It would be much easier to come up with some useful properties that you want all your movable objects to have now so that you don't have to deal with each movable object individually later.

One area that merits improvement is the order in which movable objects are painted. What if you had a ball (represented by a movable object) that was bouncing along the screen, and you wanted it to travel in front of a person (also represented by a movable object)? How could you make sure that the ball was drawn *after* the person every time, to make it look like the ball was is in front of the person? You could make sure that the ball is the first movable object added to the engine, ensuring that it's always the last movable object painted. However, that approach can get hairy if you have 10 or 20 movable objects that all have to be in a specific order. Also, what if you wanted the same ball to bounce back across the screen later on, but this time behind the person? The method of adding movable objects in the order you want them drawn obviously wouldn't work, because you would be switching the drawing order in the middle of the program.

What you need is some sort of prioritization scheme. The improved version of the graphics engine will implement a scheme in which each movable object has an integer that represents its priority. The movable objects with the highest priority number are drawn last and thus appear in front.

Listing 50.6 shows the changes that have to be made to the MOB class to implement prioritization. Listing 50.7 shows the changes that have to be made to the GraphicsEngine class, and Listing 50.8 shows the changes that have to be made to the Game applet. Several other additional features have also been added in these listings, and we'll touch on those later.

Once again, a version of this applet that conforms to the JDK 1.1 API is provided. If you prefer to use a Java 1.1 example, simply use the code in Listing 50.9 for the changes that have to be made to Game instead of using the code in Listing 50.8.

> **NOTE**
>
> Our prioritization scheme does not impose any restrictions on the priority of each object. There is no need to give objects sequential priorities (that is, you can give objects priorities like 1, 5, and 20 instead of using priorities 1, 2, and 3). You can also assign the same priority to more than one object if you don't care which object is drawn on top (that is, you can leave all your objects with the default priority of 0).

The heart of the prioritization scheme lies in the new version of `GraphicsEngine.paint()`. The basic idea is that before any movable objects are drawn, the complete list of movable objects is sorted by priority. The highest priority objects are put at the end of the list so that they are drawn last and appear in front; the lowest priority objects are put at the beginning of the list so that they are drawn first and appear in back. A bubble-sort algorithm is used to sort the objects. Bubble-sort algorithms are usually slower than other algorithms, but they tend to be easier to implement. In this case, the extra time taken by the bubble-sort algorithm is relatively negligible because the majority of time within the graphics engine is eaten up displaying the images.

 Update your code in the files `MOB.java`, `GraphicsEngine.java`, and `Game.java` with the updated code shown in Listings 50.6, 50.7, and 50.8 (or 50.9 for the Java 1.1 version). Compile the updated versions of all three files and add an image called `background.jpg` to your directory (this image is the background image for the applet). You should see something that looks like Figure 50.3 (especially if you're using the files from the CD-ROM that accompanies this book). After getting the example up and running, look at the `init()` method in the `Game` class and pay particular attention to the priorities assigned to each movable object. From looking at the `mouseMove()` method, you should be able to see that the first five movable objects line up in a diagonal line of sorts (as long as you move the mouse slowly). If you move the mouse slowly, you should see that three of the first five movable objects are noticeably in front of the other two. This should make sense if you examine the priorities they were assigned inside the `Game.init()` method.

Also notice that the bouncing object is always in front of the object you control with your mouse. This is because the bouncing object was assigned a higher priority than all the other objects. Now press the S key. The first object your mouse controls should now be displayed in front of the bouncing object. Take a look at the `Game.keyDown()` method to see why this occurs (look at the `Game.keyTyped()` example if you are using the Java 1.1 example). You will see that pressing the S key toggles the priority of `picture1` between a priority that is lower than the bouncing object and a priority that is higher than the bouncing object.

FIGURE 50.3.

What the final version of the GraphicsEngine *example should look like.*

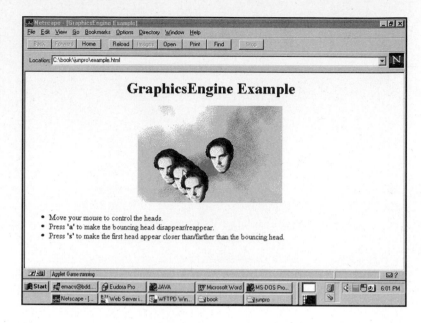

Listing 50.6. MOB.java: The enhanced version of the MOB class.

```java
import java.awt.*;

public class MOB {
  public int x = 0;
  public int y = 0;
  public Image picture;
  public int priority = 0;
  public boolean visible = true;

  public MOB(Image pic) {
    picture=pic;
  }
}
```

Listing 50.7. GraphicsEngine.java: The enhanced version of the GraphicsEngine class.

```java
import java.awt.*;
import java.awt.image.*;

public class GraphicsEngine {
  Chain mobs = null;
  public Image background;
  public Image buffer;
  Graphics pad;

  public GraphicsEngine(Component c) {
    buffer = c.createImage(c.size().width, c.size().height);
    pad = buffer.getGraphics();
  }
```

```java
public void AddMOB (MOB new_mob) {
  mobs = new Chain(new_mob, mobs);
}

public void paint(Graphics g, ImageObserver imob) {

  /* Draw background on top of buffer for double buffering. */

  if (background != null) {
    pad.drawImage(background, 0, 0, imob);
  }

  /* Sort MOBs by priority */

  Chain temp_mobs = new Chain(mobs.mob, null);
  Chain ordered = temp_mobs;
  Chain unordered = mobs.rest;
  MOB mob;
  while (unordered != null) {
    mob = unordered.mob;
    unordered = unordered.rest;
    ordered = temp_mobs;
    while (ordered != null) {
    if (mob.priority < ordered.mob.priority) {
      ordered.rest = new Chain(ordered.mob, ordered.rest);
      ordered.mob = mob;
      ordered = null;
    }
    else if (ordered.rest == null) {
      ordered.rest = new Chain(mob, null);
      ordered = null;
    }
    else {
      ordered = ordered.rest;
    }
    }
  }

  /* Draw sorted MOBs */

  while (temp_mobs != null) {
    mob = temp_mobs.mob;
    if (mob.visible) {
    pad.drawImage(mob.picture, mob.x, mob.y, imob);
    }
    temp_mobs = temp_mobs.rest;
  }

  /* Draw completed buffer to g */

  g.drawImage(buffer, 0, 0, imob);

  }
}
```

continues

Listing 50.7. continued

```
class Chain {
  public MOB mob;
  public Chain rest;

  public Chain(MOB mob, Chain rest) {
    this.mob = mob;
    this.rest = rest;
  }
}
```

Listing 50.8. Game.java: An extended example showing the properties of the GraphicsEngine class in Java 1.0.

```
import java.awt.*;
import java.applet.Applet;
import java.net.URL;

public class Game extends Applet implements Runnable {
  Thread kicker;
  GraphicsEngine engine;
  MOB picture1, picture2, picture3, picture4, picture5, picture6;

  public void init() {
    try {
      engine = new GraphicsEngine(this);
      engine.background = getImage(new URL(getDocumentBase(), "background.jpg"));
      Image image1 = getImage(new URL(getDocumentBase(), "one.gif"));
      picture1 = new MOB(image1);
      picture2 = new MOB(image1);
      picture3 = new MOB(image1);
      picture4 = new MOB(image1);
      picture5 = new MOB(image1);
      picture6 = new MOB(image1);
      picture1.priority = 5;
      picture2.priority = 1;
      picture3.priority = 4;
      picture4.priority = 2;
      picture5.priority = 3;
      picture6.priority = 6;
      engine.AddMOB(picture1);
      engine.AddMOB(picture2);
      engine.AddMOB(picture3);
      engine.AddMOB(picture4);
      engine.AddMOB(picture5);
      engine.AddMOB(picture6);
    }
    catch (java.net.MalformedURLException e) {
      System.out.println("Error while loading pictures...");
      e.printStackTrace();
    }
  }
```

```java
public void start() {
  if (kicker == null) {
    kicker = new Thread(this);
  }
  kicker.start();
}

public void run() {
  requestFocus();
  while (true) {
    picture6.x = (picture6.x+3)%size().width;
    int tmp_y = (picture6.x % 40 - 20)/3;
    picture6.y = size().height/2 - tmp_y*tmp_y;
    repaint();
    try {
   kicker.sleep(50);
    }
    catch (InterruptedException e) {
    }
  }
}

public void stop() {
  if (kicker != null && kicker.isAlive()) {
    kicker.stop();
  }
}

public void update(Graphics g) {
  paint(g);
}

public void paint(Graphics g) {
  engine.paint(g, this);
}

public boolean mouseMove (Event evt, int mx, int my) {
  picture5.x = picture4.x-10;
  picture5.y = picture4.y-10;
  picture4.x = picture3.x-10;
  picture4.y = picture3.y-10;
  picture3.x = picture2.x-10;
  picture3.y = picture2.y-10;
  picture2.x = picture1.x-10;
  picture2.y = picture1.y-10;
  picture1.x = mx;
  picture1.y = my;
  return true;
}

public boolean keyDown (Event evt, int key) {
  switch (key) {
  case 'a':
    picture6.visible = !picture6.visible;
    break;
```

continues

Listing 50.8. continued

```
    case 's':
      if (picture1.priority==5) {
    picture1.priority=7;
      }
      else {
    picture1.priority=5;
      }
      break;
    }
    return true;
  }
}
```

Listing 50.9. Game.java: An extended example showing the properties of the GraphicsEngine class in Java 1.1.

```
import java.awt.event.*;
import java.awt.*;
import java.applet.Applet;
import java.net.URL;

public class Game extends Applet implements Runnable, MouseMotionListener,
        KeyListener {
  Thread kicker;
  GraphicsEngine engine;
  MOB picture1, picture2, picture3, picture4, picture5, picture6;

  public void init() {
    addMouseMotionListener(this);
    addKeyListener(this);
    try {
      engine = new GraphicsEngine(this);
      engine.background = getImage(new URL(getDocumentBase(), "background.jpg"));
      Image image1 = getImage(new URL(getDocumentBase(), "one.gif"));
      picture1 = new MOB(image1);
      picture2 = new MOB(image1);
      picture3 = new MOB(image1);
      picture4 = new MOB(image1);
      picture5 = new MOB(image1);
      picture6 = new MOB(image1);
      picture1.priority = 5;
      picture2.priority = 1;
      picture3.priority = 4;
      picture4.priority = 2;
      picture5.priority = 3;
      picture6.priority = 6;
      engine.AddMOB(picture1);
      engine.AddMOB(picture2);
      engine.AddMOB(picture3);
      engine.AddMOB(picture4);
      engine.AddMOB(picture5);
      engine.AddMOB(picture6);
    }
```

```java
      catch (java.net.MalformedURLException e) {
        System.out.println("Error while loading pictures...");
        e.printStackTrace();
      }
    }

    public void start() {
      if (kicker == null) {
        kicker = new Thread(this);
      }
      kicker.start();
    }

    public void run() {
      requestFocus();
      while (true) {
        picture6.x = (picture6.x+3)%size().width;
        int tmp_y = (picture6.x % 40 - 20)/3;
        picture6.y = size().height/3 + tmp_y*tmp_y;
        repaint();
        try {
          kicker.sleep(50);
        }
        catch (InterruptedException e) {
        }
      }
    }

    public void stop() {
      if (kicker != null && kicker.isAlive()) {
        kicker.stop();
      }
    }

    public void update(Graphics g) {
      paint(g);
    }

    public void paint(Graphics g) {
      engine.paint(g, this);
    }

    public void mouseDragged (MouseEvent evt) {
    }

    public void mouseMoved (MouseEvent evt) {
      int mx = evt.getX();
      int my = evt.getY();
      picture5.x = picture4.x-10;
      picture5.y = picture4.y-10;
      picture4.x = picture3.x-10;
      picture4.y = picture3.y-10;
      picture3.x = picture2.x-10;
      picture3.y = picture2.y-10;
      picture2.x = picture1.x-10;
      picture2.y = picture1.y-10;
```

continues

Listing 50.9. continued

```
      picture1.x = mx;
      picture1.y = my;
   }

   public void keyPressed (KeyEvent evt) {
   }

   public void keyReleased (KeyEvent evt) {
   }

   public void keyTyped (KeyEvent evt) {
      switch (evt.getKeyChar()) {
      case 'a':
         picture6.visible = !picture6.visible;
         break;
      case 's':
         if (picture1.priority==5) {
            picture1.priority=7;
          }
         else {
            picture1.priority=5;
         }
         break;
      }
   }
}
```

Double Buffering

Two big features also implemented in the improved code are double buffering and the addition of a background image. This is accomplished entirely in GraphicsEngine (as shown in Listing 50.7). Notice the changes in the constructor for GraphicsEngine. The graphics engine now creates an image so that it can do off-screen processing before it's ready to display the final image. The off-screen image is named buffer, and the Graphics context that draws into that image is named pad.

Now take a look at the changes to the paint() method in GraphicsEngine. Notice that, until the end, all the drawing is done into the Graphics context pad instead of the Graphics context g. The background is drawn into pad at the beginning of the paint() method and then the movable objects are drawn into pad after they have been sorted. Once everything is drawn into pad, the image buffer contains exactly what we want the screen to look like; so we draw buffer to g, which causes it to be displayed on the screen.

Invisibility and Other Possible Extensions

Another feature that was added to the extended version of the movable objects was the capability to make your movable objects disappear when they aren't wanted. This was accomplished by giving MOB a flag called visible. Take a look at the end of GraphicsEngine.paint() method in Listing 50.7 to see how this works. This feature comes in handy when you have an object you want to show only part of the time. For example, you can make a bullet a movable object. Before the bullet is fired, it is in a gun and should not be visible, so you set visible to false and the bullet isn't shown. Once the gun is fired, the bullet can be seen, so you set visible to true and the bullet is shown. Run the Game applet and press the A key a few times. As you can see from the keyDown() method (or the keyTyped() method if you are using the Java 1.1 example), pressing the A key toggles the visible flag of the bouncing object between true and false.

By no means do the features shown in Listings 50.6, 50.7, and 50.8 exhaust the possibilities of what can be done with the structure of movable objects. Several additional features can easily be added, such as a centering feature for movable objects so that they are placed on the screen based on their center rather than their edge, an animation feature so that a movable object can step through several images instead of just displaying one, the addition of velocity and acceleration parameters, or even a collision-detection method that allows you to tell when two movable objects have hit each other. Feel free to extend the code to accommodate your needs.

Using the Graphics Engine to Develop Games

We haven't actually written a game yet, but we have laid the foundation for writing games. You now have objects you can move around the screen simply by changing their coordinates. These tools have been the building blocks for games since the beginning of graphics-based computer games. Use your imagination and experiment. If you need more help extending the concepts described here concerning the creation of games with movable objects and their associated graphics engines, pick up a book devoted strictly to game programming. *Tricks of the Game-Programming Gurus* (published by Sams.net Publishing) and *Teach Yourself Internet Game Programming with Java* (also published by Sams.net Publishing) are good titles.

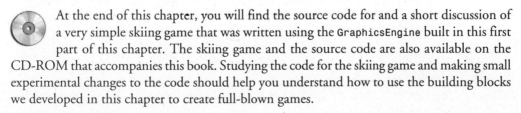 At the end of this chapter, you will find the source code for and a short discussion of a very simple skiing game that was written using the GraphicsEngine built in this first part of this chapter. The skiing game and the source code are also available on the CD-ROM that accompanies this book. Studying the code for the skiing game and making small experimental changes to the code should help you understand how to use the building blocks we developed in this chapter to create full-blown games.

50

JAVA GAME
PROGRAMMING

Sounds

We've spent all this time learning how to do the graphics for a game in Java, but what about sounds? Sound support in Java is very sparse. The Java development team worked hard on the version 1.x releases of Java but unfortunately didn't have time to incorporate a lot of sound support.

> **NOTE**
>
> Although it's possible to develop much better sound control using the undocumented `sun.audio.*` classes, doing so is generally a bad idea for several reasons. First of all, the `sun.audio.*` classes are not part of the core Java API, so there is no guarantee that they will always be there in every implementation of the virtual machine. Second, JavaSoft is currently working on adding better audio support to the Java core classes, so you won't have to worry about the lack of functionality in the future.

Check out `java.applet.AudioClip` in Java 1.0 or Java 1.1 to discover the full extent of sound use. There are only three methods: `loop()`, `play()`, and `stop()`. This simple interface makes life somewhat easier. Use `Applet.getAudioClip` to load an `AudioClip` in the AU format and you have two choices: Use the `play()` method to play it at specific times or use the `loop()` method to play it continuously. The applications for each are obvious. Use the `play()` method for something that's going to happen once in a while, such as the firing of a gun; use the `loop()` method for something that should be heard all the time, such as background music or the hum of a car engine.

Java-Specific Game Design Issues

When thinking about the design of your game, there are some Java-specific design issues you must consider. One of Java's most appealing characteristics is that it can be downloaded through the Web and run inside a browser. This networking aspect brings several new considerations into play. Java is also meant to be a cross-platform language, which has important ramifications in the design of the user interface and for games that rely heavily on timing.

Picking a User Interface

When picking a user interface, you should keep several things in mind. Above all, remember that your applet should be able to work on all platforms because Java is a cross-platform language. If you choose to use the mouse as your input device, keep in mind that regardless of how many buttons your mouse has, a Java mouse has only one button. Although Java can read from any button on a mouse, it considers all buttons to be the same button. The Java development team made the design choice to have only one button so that Macintosh users wouldn't get the short end of the stick.

If you use the keyboard as your input device, it is even more critical for you to remember that although the underlying platforms might be vastly different, Java is platform independent. This becomes a problem because the different machines that Java can run on may interpret keystrokes differently when more than one key is held down at once. For example, you may think it worthwhile to throw a supermove() method in your game that knocks an opponent off the screen, activated by holding down four secret keys at the same time. However, doing this might destroy the platform independence of your program because some platforms may not be able to handle four keystrokes at once. The best approach is to design a user interface that doesn't call into question whether it is truly cross-platform. Try to get by with only one key at a time, and stay away from control and function keys in general because they can be interpreted as browser commands by the different browsers in which your applet runs.

Limiting Factors

As with any programming language, Java has its advantages and its disadvantages. It's good to know both so that you can exploit the advantages and steer clear of the disadvantages. Several performance issues arise when you are dealing with game design in Java—some of which are a product of the inherent design of Java and some of which are a product of the environment in which Java programs normally run.

Downloading

One of the main features of Java is that it can be downloaded and run across the Net. Because automatically downloading the Java program you want to run is so central to the Java software model, the limitations imposed by using the Net to get your Java bear some investigation. First, keep in mind that most people with a network connection aren't on the fastest lines in the world. Although you may be ready to develop the coolest animation ever for a Java game, remember that nobody will want to see it if it takes forever to download. It is a good idea to avoid extra frills when they are going to be costly in terms of download time.

One trick you can use to get around a lengthy download time is to download everything you can in the background. For example, you can send level one of your game for downloading, start the game, and while the user plays level one, download levels two and up in a background thread. This task is simplified considerably with the java.awt.MediaTracker. To use the MediaTracker class, simply add all your images to MediaTracker with the addImage() method and then call checkAll() with true as an argument.

NOTE

Java 1.1 includes the ability to store all your images, classes, and other files in a JAR file. A JAR file is a new type of Java Archive file, created (among other reasons) to speed up

continues

50

JAVA GAME PROGRAMMING

continued

network transfers by reducing the number of connections. Another option for packaging everything together is supplied by some browsers, such as Netscape 3.0; these browsers allow you to store all your classes in one ZIP file.

Opening a network connection can take a significant amount of time. If you have 30 or 40 pictures to send for downloading, the time this takes can quickly add up. One trick that can help decrease the number of network connections you have to open is to combine several smaller pictures into one big picture. You can use a paint program or an image-editing program to create a large image that is made up of your smaller images placed side by side. You then send for downloading only the large image. This approach decreases the number of network connections you have to open and can also decrease the total number of bytes contained in the image data. Depending on the type of compression used, if the smaller images that make up your larger image are similar, you will probably achieve better compression by combining them into one picture. Once the larger picture has been loaded from across the network, the smaller pictures can be extracted using the `java.awt.image.CropImageFilter` class to crop the image for each of the original smaller images.

Execution Speed

Another thing you should keep in mind with applets is timing. Java is remarkably fast for an interpreted language, but graphics handling usually leaves something to be desired when it comes to rendering speed. Your applet probably will be rendered inside a browser, which slows it down even more. If you are developing your applets on a state-of-the-art workstation, keep in mind that a large number of people will be running Java inside a Web browser on much slower PCs. When your applets are graphics intensive, it's always a good idea to test them on slower machines to make sure that the performance is acceptable. If you find that an unacceptable drop in performance occurs when you switch to a slower platform, try shrinking the `Component` that your graphics engine draws into. You may also want to try shrinking the images used inside your movable objects because the difference in rendering time is most likely the cause of the drop in performance.

Another thing to watch out for is poor threading. A top-of-the-line workstation may allow you to push your threads to the limit, but on a slow PC, computation time is often far too precious. Improperly handled threading can lead to some bewildering results. In the `run()` method in Listing 50.8, notice that we tell the applet's thread to sleep for 50 milliseconds. Try taking this line out and seeing what happens. If you're using the applet viewer or a browser, it will probably lock up or at least appear to respond very slowly to mouse clicks and keystrokes. This happens because the applet's thread, `kicker`, eats up all the computation time and there's not much time left over for the painting thread or the user input thread. Threads can be extremely useful, but you have to make sure that they are put to sleep once in a while to give other threads a chance to run.

Fortunately, there is hope on the horizon concerning the relatively slow execution speed of Java. Just-in-time compilers, which greatly enhance the performance of Java, are starting to appear. Just-in-time compilers compile Java bytecode into native machine code on the fly so that Java programs can be run almost as fast as compiled languages such as C and C++.

A Simple Example: The Skiing Game

 The code in Listing 50.10 shows a simple example of a game that has been built using the GraphicsEngine developed in the first part of this chapter. The game is also provided in the file Ski.java on the CD-ROM that accompanies this book, so that you don't have to bother typing it in.

As usual, Listing 50.11 provides an alternative version of this game that uses the features in the JDK 1.1. Use Listing 50.11 instead of Listing 50.10 if you want to use the Java 1.1-specific version.

Listing 50.10. Ski.java: A very simple game that shows how to use the GraphicsEngine to create games in Java 1.0.

```
import java.awt.*;
import java.applet.Applet;
import java.net.URL;

public class Ski extends Applet implements Runnable {
  Thread kicker;
  GraphicsEngine engine;
  MOB tree1, tree2, tree3, player;
  int screen_height = 1, screen_width = 1, tree_height = 1, tree_width = 1;
  int player_width = 1, player_height = 1;
  int step_amount = 10;

  public void init() {
    try {
      engine = new GraphicsEngine(this);
      Image snow = getImage(new URL(getDocumentBase(), "snow.jpg"));
      engine.background = snow;
      Image tree = getImage(new URL(getDocumentBase(), "tree.gif"));
      MediaTracker tracker = new MediaTracker(this);
      tracker.addImage(tree, 0);
      tracker.addImage(snow, 0);
      tree1 = new MOB(tree);
      tree2 = new MOB(tree);
      tree3 = new MOB(tree);
      Image person = getImage(new URL(getDocumentBase(), "player.gif"));
      tracker.addImage(person, 0);
      tracker.waitForID(0);
      tree_height = tree.getHeight(this);
      tree_width = tree.getWidth(this);
```

continues

Listing 50.10. continued

```java
    player_width =   person.getWidth(this);
    player_height =   person.getHeight(this);
    player = new MOB(person);

    screen_height = size().height;
    screen_width = size().width;

    player.y = screen_height/2;
    player.x = screen_width/2;

    tree1.x = randomX();
    tree1.y = 0;

    tree2.x = randomX();
    tree2.y = screen_height/3;

    tree3.x = randomX();
    tree3.y = (screen_height*2)/3;

    player.priority = player.y-(tree_height-player_height);
    tree1.priority = tree1.y;
    tree2.priority = tree2.y;
    tree3.priority = tree3.y;

    engine.AddMOB(player);
    engine.AddMOB(tree1);
    engine.AddMOB(tree2);
    engine.AddMOB(tree3);
  }
  catch (Exception e) {
    System.out.println("Error while loading pictures...");
    e.printStackTrace();
  }
}

public void start() {
  if (kicker == null) {
    kicker = new Thread(this);
  }
  kicker.start();
}

public void run() {

  while (true) {
    increment(tree1);
    increment(tree2);
    increment(tree3);
    if (hit(tree1) || hit(tree2) || hit(tree3)) {
      step_amount = 0;
    }
```

```
      else step_amount++;
      repaint();
      try {
        kicker.sleep(100);
      }
      catch (InterruptedException e) {
      }
    }
  }

  public void increment(MOB m) {
    m.y -= step_amount;
    if (m.y < -tree_height) {
      m.y = m.y+screen_height+2*tree_height;
      m.x = randomX();
    }
    m.priority = m.y;
  }

  public boolean hit(MOB m) {
    return (m.y < player.priority+tree_height/2 && m.y >= player.priority && m.x >
            player.x-tree_width && m.x < player.x+player_width);
  }

  public int randomX() {
    return (int) (Math.random()*screen_width);
  }

  public void stop() {
    if (kicker != null && kicker.isAlive()) {
      kicker.stop();
      kicker = null;
    }
  }


  public void update(Graphics g) {
    paint(g);
  }

  public void paint(Graphics g) {
    engine.paint(g, this);
  }

  public boolean mouseMove (Event evt, int mx, int my) {
    player.x = mx - player_width/2;
    return true;
  }
}
```

Listing 50.11. Ski.java: A very simple game that shows how to use the GraphicsEngine to create games in Java 1.1.

```java
import java.awt.event.*;
import java.awt.*;
import java.applet.Applet;
import java.net.URL;

public class Ski extends Applet implements Runnable, MouseMotionListener {
  Thread kicker;
  GraphicsEngine engine;
  MOB tree1, tree2, tree3, player;
  int screen_height = 1, screen_width = 1, tree_height = 1, tree_width = 1;
  int player_width = 1, player_height = 1;
  int step_amount = 10;

  public void init() {
    addMouseMotionListener(this);
    try {
      engine = new GraphicsEngine(this);
      Image snow = getImage(new URL(getDocumentBase(), "snow.jpg"));
      engine.background = snow;
      Image tree = getImage(new URL(getDocumentBase(), "tree.gif"));
      MediaTracker tracker = new MediaTracker(this);
      tracker.addImage(tree, 0);
      tracker.addImage(snow, 0);
      tree1 = new MOB(tree);
      tree2 = new MOB(tree);
      tree3 = new MOB(tree);
      Image person = getImage(new URL(getDocumentBase(), "player.gif"));
      tracker.addImage(person, 0);
      tracker.waitForID(0);
      tree_height = tree.getHeight(this);
      tree_width = tree.getWidth(this);
      player_width =  person.getWidth(this);
      player_height =  person.getHeight(this);
      player = new MOB(person);

      screen_height = size().height;
      screen_width = size().width;

      player.y = screen_height/2;
      player.x = screen_width/2;

      tree1.x = randomX();
      tree1.y = 0;

      tree2.x = randomX();
      tree2.y = screen_height/3;

      tree3.x = randomX();
      tree3.y = (screen_height*2)/3;

      player.priority = player.y-(tree_height-player_height);
      tree1.priority = tree1.y;
      tree2.priority = tree2.y;
      tree3.priority = tree3.y;
```

```java
      engine.AddMOB(player);
      engine.AddMOB(tree1);
      engine.AddMOB(tree2);
      engine.AddMOB(tree3);
    }
    catch (Exception e) {
      System.out.println("Error while loading pictures...");
      e.printStackTrace();
    }
  }

  public void start() {
    if (kicker == null) {
      kicker = new Thread(this);
    }
    kicker.start();
  }

  public void run() {

    while (true) {
      increment(tree1);
      increment(tree2);
      increment(tree3);
      if (hit(tree1) || hit(tree2) || hit(tree3)) {
        step_amount = 0;
      }
      else step_amount++;
      repaint();
      try {
        kicker.sleep(100);
      }
      catch (InterruptedException e) {
      }
    }
  }

  public void increment(MOB m) {
    m.y -= step_amount;
    if (m.y < -tree_height) {
      m.y = m.y+screen_height+2*tree_height;
      m.x = randomX();
    }
    m.priority = m.y;
  }

  public boolean hit(MOB m) {
    return (m.y < player.priority+tree_height/2 && m.y >= player.priority && m.x >
            player.x-tree_width && m.x < player.x+player_width);
  }

  public int randomX() {
    return (int) (Math.random()*screen_width);
  }
```

continues

Listing 50.11. continued

```
public void stop() {
  if (kicker != null && kicker.isAlive()) {
    kicker.stop();
    kicker = null;
  }
}

public void update(Graphics g) {
  paint(g);
}

public void paint(Graphics g) {
  engine.paint(g, this);
}

public void mouseDragged (MouseEvent evt) {
}

public void mouseMoved (MouseEvent evt) {
  player.x = evt.getX() - player_width/2;
}
}
```

Playing the Game

To play the game, simply use a Java-enabled browser or the JDK applet viewer to view the file called `ski.html`. You should see something like Figure 50.4. Once the game is properly running, you see a skier and three trees on the screen.

Use the mouse to control the skier. Moving your mouse left and right without holding the mouse button down causes the skier to move left and right. You cannot move the player up and down.

The object of the game is to avoid hitting the trees. Notice that as long as you avoid hitting the trees, you continue to accelerate. Hence, the longer you avoid hitting the trees, the faster you go. Hitting a tree brings the skier to a halt, and you have to start accelerating from a standstill again.

Understanding the Code

The skiing game basically grew out of the `GraphicsEngine` example developed earlier in this chapter. Support for things that weren't needed (like a bouncing head) was removed, and support for new things (like moving trees) was added. Tweaking code like this is an excellent way to learn a language and to learn new programming methods. Don't be afraid to tweak the code yourself—experimenting with existing code is a great way to build up some experience before attempting to write something from scratch.

Figure 50.4.

A simple skiing game applet that uses the GraphicsEngine.

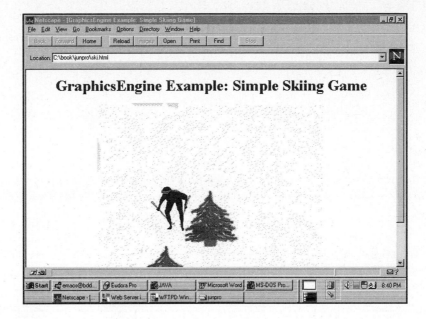

Initializing Everything

As its name implies, the init() method is in charge of initializing the applet. It is called once and only once at the beginning of the applet's life cycle. In the case of the skiing game, the init() method takes care of creating the graphics engine to handle all the objects (loading the images for the background, the trees, and the skier; creating new MOBs from these images; adding these MOBs to the graphics engine; and gathering information about the size of the images).

The start() method is also part of the initialization process, but unlike the init() method, it can be called more than once. The idea behind the start() method is that it is called every time the Web page it's in is viewed; the start() method can be called several times if the user goes back to the same Web page several times in the same session.

The start() method is used just to start a thread. The thread is used to move the trees. The thread is stopped when the user leaves the Web page because the stop() method (which is called every time the Web page is left) contains code that stops the thread.

Creating Movement

The movement of the trees is accomplished inside the run() method. Inside the run() method, the increment() method is called for each of the trees, causing them to move up the screen.

Whenever a tree has gone so far up the screen that it is no longer visible, it is placed at the bottom of the screen at a random position, creating the illusion that there are an infinite number of trees when in fact there are only three.

The run() method also checks to see whether or not the skier has hit a tree. If the skier has hit a tree, the variable step_amount is set to zero. If the skier has not hit a tree, the variable step_amount is increased by 1. The variable step_amount is used to decide how far to move the tree up the screen each time. If the skier has hit a tree, the trees don't move at all that particular time (because the skier has stopped). If the skier hasn't hit a tree, the trees move up by step_amount number of pixels. step_amount is increased by 1 each time the skier passes (that is, does not hit) a tree. Because step_amount increases, this makes the trees move up the screen faster, creating the illusion that the skier is accelerating.

Finally, the movement of the skier is controlled completely by the mouse. Because the mouseMove() method is called every time the mouse is moved, all we have to do is override the mouseMove() method so that whenever the mouse moves, we move the player. If you want to use the JDK 1.1 version, all you have to do is override the mouseMoved() method.

Summary

In this chapter, we developed a basic Java graphics engine that can be used for game creation. This graphics engine incorporated movable objects with prioritization and visibility settings, double buffering, and a background image. We also went over a very simple example of a game that was built using the tools presented in the chapter. However, the focus was on the construction of the tools rather than the construction of the example game because the tools can be expanded to produce a multitude of games.

This chapter also touched on issues you should keep in mind when developing games with Java. It is important to remember that Java is a cross-platform language. When you develop your games, you should be aware that people will want to run them on machines that may not have the same capabilities as your development machine.

Advanced Image Processing

by K.C. Hopson and Stephen Ingram

IN THIS CHAPTER

CHAPTER 51

This chapter teaches you the more advanced concepts involved in Java images. It leads off by introducing Java's fundamental image model. Image filters are explored, and two advanced filters are explained, including a special-effects filter. This chapter ends by using a custom filter to present Mandelbrot sets (visually striking images from chaos theory).

To really appreciate the power behind Java images, you have to understand the consumer/producer model in detail. Powerful graphics applications use the advantages of this model to perform their visual wizardry. In particular, you can write effective image filters only if you understand the underlying model.

The Image Model

True to Java's object-oriented design, images are not presented by a single class. Rather, a richer and more specialized class system is used. The designers of Java wanted an extensible image system that would allow image manipulation as well as support for a wide variety of image formats. The best way to meet these requirements was to devolve image presentation into its requisite parts. An image producer understands a particular image format but is unaware of the details behind image display. Instead, the producer renders its contents through an image consumer interface. By separating production from consumption, Java allows multiple image filters to be inserted between the base image and its eventual display.

Image Producers

The `ImageProducer` interface has the following methods:

- `public void addConsumer(ImageConsumer ic);`

- `public boolean isConsumer(ImageConsumer ic);`

- `public void removeConsumer(ImageConsumer ic);`

- `public void startProduction(ImageConsumer ic);`

- `public void requestTopDownLeftRightResend(ImageConsumer ic);`

All the methods require an `ImageConsumer` object. There are no back doors; an `ImageProducer` can output only through an associated `ImageConsumer`. A given producer can have multiple objects as client consumers, although this is not usually the case. Typically, as soon as a consumer registers itself with a producer using `addConsumer()`, the image data is immediately delivered through the consumer's interface.

Image Consumers

The `ImageProducer` interface is clean and straightforward, but the `ImageConsumer` is quite a bit more complex. It has the following methods:

- ■ public void setDimensions(int *width*, int *height*);

- ■ public void setProperties(Hashtable *props*);

- ■ public void setColorModel(ColorModel *model*);

- ■ public void setHints(int *hintflags*);

- ■ public void setPixels(int *x*, int *y*, int *w*, int *h*, ColorModel *model*,
  byte *pixels*[], int *off*, int *scansize*);

- ■ public void setPixels(int *x*, int *y*, int *w*, int *h*, ColorModel *model*,
  int *pixels*[], int *off*, int *scansize*);

- ■ public void imageComplete(int *status*);

Figure 51.1 shows the normal progression of calls to the ImageConsumer interface. Several methods are optional: setProperties(), setHints(), and setColorModel(). The core method is setDimensions(), followed by one or more calls to setPixels(). Finally, when there are no more setPixels() calls, imageComplete() is invoked.

FIGURE 51.1.

Normal flow of calls to an ImageConsumer *interface.*

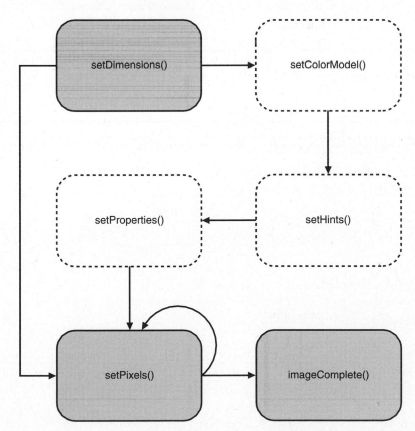

Each image has fixed rectangular dimensions, which are passed in setDimensions(). The consumer saves this data for future reference. The setProperties() method has no discernible use right now, and most consumers don't do anything with it. The hint flags, however, are a different story. *Hints* are supposed to give clues about the format of the producer's data. Table 51.1 lists the values for hint flags.

Table 51.1. The values for the hintflags parameter for setHints().

Name	*Meaning*
RANDOMPIXELORDER=1	Make no assumptions about the delivery of pixels.
TOPDOWNLEFTRIGHT=2	Pixel delivery will paint in top to bottom, left to right.
COMPLETESCANLINES=4	Pixels will be delivered in multiples of complete rows.
SINGLEPASS=8	Pixels will be delivered in a single pass. No pixel will appear in more than one setPixel() call.
SINGLEFRAME=16	The image consists of a single static frame.

When all the pixel information has been transmitted, the producer calls imageComplete(status). The status parameter has one of three values: IMAGEERROR=1, SINGLEFRAMEDONE=2, or STATICFRAMEDONE=3.

SINGLEFRAMEDONE indicates that additional frames will follow; for example, a video camera would use this technique. Special-effects filters can also use SINGLEFRAMEDONE. STATICFRAMEDONE is used to indicate that no more pixels will be transmitted for the image. The consumer should remove itself from the producer after receiving STATICFRAMEDONE.

Two setPixels() calls provide the image data. Keep in mind that the image size was set in advance by setDimensions(). The array within setPixels() calls does not necessarily contain all the pixels within an image. In fact, the calls usually contain only a rectangular subset of the total image. Figure 51.2 shows a rectangle of setPixels() within an entire image.

The row size of the array is the scansize. The width and height (*w* and *h*) parameters indicate the usable pixels within the array, and the offset (*off*) contains the starting index. It is up to the consumer to map the passed array onto the entire image. The subimage's location within the total image is contained in the *x* and *y* parameters.

The ColorModel contains all the necessary color information for the image. The call to setColorModel() is purely informational because each setPixels() call passes a specific ColorModel parameter. No assumptions should be made about the ColorModel from the setColorModel() calls.

FIGURE 51.2.

The relationship of `setPixels()` *calls to an entire image.*

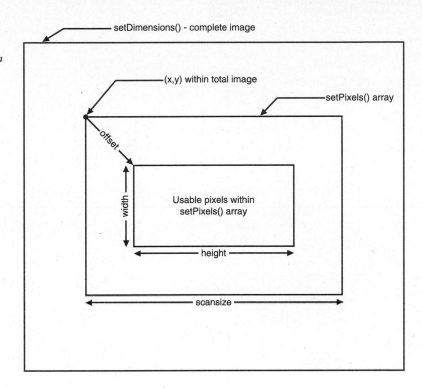

Filtering an Image

Image filters sit between an `ImageProducer` and an `ImageConsumer` and must implement both these interfaces. Java supplies two separate classes for using filters: `FilteredImageSource` and `ImageFilter`.

The `FilteredImageSource` Class

The `FilteredImageSource` class implements the `ImageProducer` interface, which allows the class to masquerade as a real producer. When a consumer attaches to the `FilteredImageSource`, it's stored in an instance of the current filter. The filter class object is then given to the actual `ImageProducer`. When the image is rendered through the filter's interface, the data is altered before being forwarded to the actual `ImageConsumer`. Figure 51.3 shows the filtering operation.

The following is the constructor for `FilteredImageSource`:

```
FilteredImageSource(ImageProducer orig, ImageFilter imgf);
```

FIGURE 51.3
Image filtering classes.

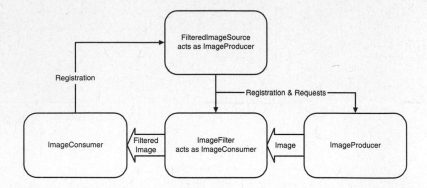

Producer and filter are stored until a consumer attaches itself to the `FilteredImageSource`. The following lines show how an application sets up a filter chain:

```
// Create the filter
ImageFilter filter = new SomeFilter();
// Use the filter to get a producer
ImageProducer p = new FilteredImageSource(myImage.getSource(), filter);
// Use the producer to create the image
Image img = createImage(p);
```

Writing a Filter

Filters always extend the `ImageFilter` class, which implements all the methods for an `ImageConsumer`. In fact, the `ImageFilter` class is itself a pass-through filter. It passes the data without alteration but otherwise acts as a normal image filter. The `FilteredImageSource` class works only with `ImageFilter` and its subclasses. Using `ImageFilter` as a base frees you from having to implement a method you have no use for, such as `setProperties()`. `ImageFilter` also implements one additional method:

```
public void resendTopDownLeftRight(ImageProducer ip);
```

When a `FilteredImageSource` gets a request to resend through its `ImageProducer` interface, it calls the `ImageFilter` instead of the actual producer. `ImageFilter`'s default resend function calls the producer and requests a repaint. There are times when the filter does not want to have the image regenerated, so it can override this call and simply do nothing. One example of this type of filter is described in the section "Dynamic Image Filter: `FXFilter`," later in this chapter. A special-effects filter can simply remove or obscure certain parts of an underlying image. To perform the effect, the filter merely has to know the image dimensions, not the specific pixels it will be overwriting. `setPixel()` calls are safely ignored, but the producer must be prevented from repainting. If your filter does not implement `setPixels()` calls, a subsequent resend request destroys the filter's changes by writing directly to the consumer.

> **NOTE**
>
> If setPixels() is not overridden in your filter, you will probably want to override resendTopDownLeftRight() to prevent the image from being regenerated after your filter has altered the image.

Static Image Filter: Rotation

Rotation is a common image manipulation. Unfortunately, no standard Java filter performs this operation. This apparent oversight provides us with an excellent opportunity to develop your first filter.

Static filters perform their manipulations and then issue a STATICFRAMEDONE. Because all the alterations are applied at one time, the filter is said to be *static*. If a filter applies its changes in stages, it is considered to be a *dynamic* filter.

Pixel Rotation

To perform image rotation, you have to use some math. You can perform the rotation of points with the following formulas:

```
new_x = x * cos(angle) - y * sin(angle)
new_y = y * cos(angle) + x * sin(angle)
```

Rotation is around the z axis. Positive angles cause counterclockwise rotation; negative angles cause clockwise rotation. These formulas are defined for Cartesian coordinates. The Java screen is actually inverted, so the positive y-axis runs down the screen, not up. To compensate for this, invert the sign of the sine coefficients:

```
new_x = x * cos(angle) + y * sin(angle)
new_y = y * cos(angle) - x * sin(angle)
```

In addition, the sine and cosine functions compute the angle in radians. The following formula converts degrees to radians:

```
radians = degrees * PI/180;
```

This works because there are 2*PI radians in a circle. That's all the math you need; now you can set up the ImageConsumer routines.

Handling setDimensions()

The setDimensions() call tells you the total size of the image. Record the size and allocate an array to hold all the pixels. Because this filter rotates the image, the size may change. In an extreme case, the size can grow much larger than the original image because images are rectangular. If you rotate a rectangle 45 degrees, a new rectangle must be computed that contains all the pixels from the rotated image, as shown in Figure 51.4.

FIGURE 51.4.

*The new bounding
rectangle after rotation.*

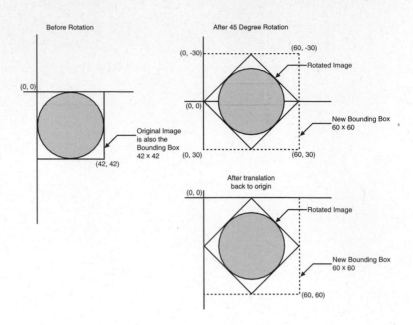

To calculate the new bounding rectangle, each vertex of the original image must be rotated. After rotation, the new coordinate is checked for minimum and maximum x and y values. After all four points are rotated, you'll know what the new bounding rectangle is. Record this information as rotation space and inform the consumer of the size after rotation.

Handling `setPixels()`

The `setPixels()` calls are very straightforward. Simply translate the pixel color into an RGB value and store it in the original image array allocated in `setDimensions()`.

Handling `imageComplete()`

The `imageComplete()` method performs all the work. After the image is final, populate a new rotation space array and return it to the consumer through the consumer's `setPixels()` routine. Finally, invoke the consumer's `imageComplete()` method. Listing 51.1 contains the entire filter; the code is also located on the CD-ROM that accompanies this book.

Listing 51.1. The `SpinFilter` class.

```
import java.awt.*;
import java.awt.image.*;
public class SpinFilter extends ImageFilter
{
    private double angle;
    private double cos, sin;
    private Rectangle rotatedSpace;
```

```
private Rectangle originalSpace;
private ColorModel defaultRGBModel;
private int inPixels[], outPixels[];
SpinFilter(double angle)
{
    this.angle = angle * (Math.PI / 180);
    cos = Math.cos(this.angle);
    sin = Math.sin(this.angle);
    defaultRGBModel = ColorModel.getRGBdefault();
}
private void transform(int x, int y, double out[])
{
    out[0] = (x * cos) + (y * sin);
    out[1] = (y * cos) - (x * sin);
}
private void transformBack(int x, int y, double out[])
{
    out[0] = (x * cos) - (y * sin);
    out[1] = (y * cos) + (x * sin);
}
public void transformSpace(Rectangle rect)
{
    double out[] = new double[2];
    double minx = Double.MAX_VALUE;
    double miny = Double.MAX_VALUE;
    double maxx = Double.MIN_VALUE;
    double maxy = Double.MIN_VALUE;
    int w = rect.width;
    int h = rect.height;
    int x = rect.x;
    int y = rect.y;
    for ( int i = 0; i < 4; i++ )
    {
        switch (i)
        {
        case 0: transform(x + 0, y + 0, out); break;
        case 1: transform(x + w, y + 0, out); break;
        case 2: transform(x + 0, y + h, out); break;
        case 3: transform(x + w, y + h, out); break;
        }
        minx = Math.min(minx, out[0]);
        miny = Math.min(miny, out[1]);
        maxx = Math.max(maxx, out[0]);
        maxy = Math.max(maxy, out[1]);
    }
    rect.x = (int) Math.floor(minx);
    rect.y = (int) Math.floor(miny);
    rect.width = (int) Math.ceil(maxx) - rect.x;
    rect.height = (int) Math.ceil(maxy) - rect.y;
}
/**
 * Tell the consumer the new dimensions based on our
 * rotation of coordinate space.
 * @see ImageConsumer#setDimensions
 */
public void setDimensions(int width, int height)
{
```

Listing 51.1. continued

```java
        originalSpace = new Rectangle(0, 0, width, height);
        rotatedSpace = new Rectangle(0, 0, width, height);
        transformSpace(rotatedSpace);
        inPixels = new int[originalSpace.width * originalSpace.height];
        consumer.setDimensions(rotatedSpace.width, rotatedSpace.height);
    }
    /**
     * Tell the consumer that we use the defaultRGBModel color model
     * NOTE: This overrides whatever color model is used underneath us.
     * @param model contains the color model of the image or filter
     *              beneath us (preceding us)
     * @see ImageConsumer#setColorModel
     */
    public void setColorModel(ColorModel model)
    {
        consumer.setColorModel(defaultRGBModel);
    }
    /**
     * Set the pixels in our image array from the passed
     * array of bytes.  Xlate the pixels into our default
     * color model (RGB).
     * @see ImageConsumer#setPixels
     */
    public void setPixels(int x, int y, int w, int h,
                ColorModel model, byte pixels[],
                int off, int scansize)
    {
        int index = y * originalSpace.width + x;
        int srcindex = off;
        int srcinc = scansize - w;
        int indexinc = originalSpace.width - w;
        for ( int dy = 0; dy < h; dy++ )
        {
            for ( int dx = 0; dx < w; dx++ )
            {
                inPixels[index++] = model.getRGB(pixels[srcindex++] & 0xff);
            }
            srcindex += srcinc;
            index += indexinc;
        }
    }
    /**
     * Set the pixels in our image array from the passed
     * array of integers.  Xlate the pixels into our default
     * color model (RGB).
     * @see ImageConsumer#setPixels
     */
    public void setPixels(int x, int y, int w, int h,
                ColorModel model, int pixels[],
                int off, int scansize)
    {
        int index = y * originalSpace.width + x;
        int srcindex = off;
        int srcinc = scansize - w;
        int indexinc = originalSpace.width - w;
        for ( int dy = 0; dy < h; dy++ )
        {
            for ( int dx = 0; dx < w; dx++ )
```

```
                {
                    inPixels[index++] = model.getRGB(pixels[srcindex++]);
                }
                srcindex += srcinc;
                index += indexinc;
            }
        }
        /**
         * Notification that the image is complete and there will
         * be no further setPixel calls.
         * @see ImageConsumer#imageComplete
         */
        public void imageComplete(int status)
        {
            if (status == IMAGEERROR || status == IMAGEABORTED)
            {
                consumer.imageComplete(status);
                return;
            }
            double point[] = new double[2];
            int srcwidth = originalSpace.width;
            int srcheight = originalSpace.height;
            int outwidth = rotatedSpace.width;
            int outheight = rotatedSpace.height;
            int outx, outy, srcx, srcy;
            outPixels = new int[outwidth * outheight];
            outx = rotatedSpace.x;
            outy = rotatedSpace.y;
            double end[] = new double[2];
            int index = 0;
            for ( int y = 0; y < outheight; y++ )
            {
                for ( int x = 0; x < outwidth; x++)
                {
                    // find the originalSpace point
                    transformBack(outx + x, outy + y, point);
                    srcx = (int)Math.round(point[0]);
                    srcy = (int)Math.round(point[1]);
                    // if this point is within the original image
                    // retreive its pixel value and store in output
                    // else write a zero into the space. (0 alpha = transparent)
                    if ( srcx < 0 || srcx >= srcwidth ||
                        srcy < 0 || srcy >= srcheight )
                    {
                        outPixels[index++] = 0;
                    }
                    else
                    {
                        outPixels[index++] = inPixels[(srcy * srcwidth) + srcx];
                    }
                }
            }
            // write the entire new image to the consumer
            consumer.setPixels(0, 0, outwidth, outheight, defaultRGBModel,
                            outPixels, 0, outwidth);
            // tell consumer we are done
            consumer.imageComplete(status);
        }
    }
}
```

The rotation is complex. First, as Figure 51.4 shows, the rotated object is not completely within the screen's boundary. All the rotated pixels must be translated back in relation to the origin. You can do this easily by assuming that the coordinates of rotated space are really 0,0—the trick is how the array is populated. An iteration is made along each row in rotated space. For each pixel in the row, the rotation is inverted. This yields the position of this pixel within the original space. If the pixel lies within the original image, grab its color and store it in rotated space; if it doesn't, store a transparent color.

A Dynamic Image Filter: `FXFilter`

The `SpinFilter` is static; the `FXFilter` is dynamic. A *static filter* alters an image and sends `STATICIMAGEDONE` when the alteration is done; a *dynamic filter* makes the effect take place over multiple frames, much like an animation. The `FXFilter` has three effects: wipe left, wipe right, and wipe from center out. Each effect operates by erasing the image in stages. The filter calls `imageComplete()` many times, but instead of passing `STATICIMAGEDONE`, it specifies `SINGLEFRAMEDONE`.

Each of the wipes operates by moving a column of erased pixels over the length of the image. The width of the column is calculated to yield the number of configured iterations.

In `setHints()`, the consumer is told that the filter will send random pixels. This causes the consumer to call `resendTopDownLeftRight()` when the image is complete. The filter must intercept the call to avoid having the just-erased image repainted by the producer in pristine form.

 The filter has two constructors. If you don't specify a color, the image dissolves into transparency, allowing you to phase one image into a second image. You can also specify an optional color, which causes the image to gradually change into the passed color. You can dissolve an image into the background by passing the background color in the filter constructor. The number of iterations is completely configurable. There is no hard-and-fast formula for performing these effects, so feel free to alter the values to get the result you want. Listing 51.2 contains the source code for the filter; the code is also located on the CD-ROM that accompanies this book.

Listing 51.2. The special-effects filter.

```
public class FXFilter extends ImageFilter
{
    private int outwidth, outheight;
    private ColorModel defaultRGBModel;
    private int dissolveColor;
    private int iterations = 10;
    private Thread runThread;
    private int inPixels[];
    public static final int WIPE_LR =  1;
    public static final int WIPE_RL =  2;
    public static final int WIPE_C =   3;
    private int type = WIPE_C;
```

```java
/**
 * Dissolve to transparent constructor
 */
FXFilter()
{
    defaultRGBModel = ColorModel.getRGBdefault();
    dissolveColor = 0;
}
/**
 * Dissolve to the passed color constructor
 * @param dcolor contains the color to dissolve to
 */
FXFilter(Color dcolor)
{
    this();
    dissolveColor = dcolor.getRGB();
}
/**
 * Set the type of effect to perform.
 */
public void setType(int t)
{
    switch (t)
    {
    case WIPE_LR:  type = t; break;
    case WIPE_RL:  type = t; break;
    case WIPE_C:   type = t; break;
    }
}
/**
 * Set the dissolve iterations. (Optional, will default to 10)
 * @param num contains the number of times to loop.
 */
public void setIterations(int num)
{
    iterations = num;
}
/**
 * @see ImageConsumer#setDimensions
 */
public void setDimensions(int width, int height)
{
    outwidth = width;
    outheight = height;
    inPixels = new int[width * height];
    consumer.setDimensions(width, height);
}
public void setPixels(int x, int y, int w, int h,
              ColorModel model, byte pixels[],
              int off, int scansize)
{
    int index = y * outwidth + x;
    int srcindex = off;
    int srcinc = scansize - w;
    int indexinc = outwidth - w;
```

continues

Listing 51.2. continued

```java
        for ( int dy = 0; dy < h; dy++ )
        {
            for ( int dx = 0; dx < w; dx++ )
            {
                inPixels[index++] = model.getRGB(pixels[srcindex++] & 0xff);
            }
            srcindex += srcinc;
            index += indexinc;
        }
    }
    public void setPixels(int x, int y, int w, int h,
                ColorModel model, int pixels[],
                int off, int scansize)
    {
        int index = y * outwidth + x;
        int srcindex = off;
        int srcinc = scansize - w;
        int indexinc = outwidth - w;
        for ( int dy = 0; dy < h; dy++ )
        {
            for ( int dx = 0; dx < w; dx++ )
            {
                inPixels[index++] = model.getRGB(pixels[srcindex++]);
            }
            srcindex += srcinc;
            index += indexinc;
        }
    }
    /**
     * Override this method to keep the producer
     * from refreshing our dissolved image
     */
    public void resendTopDownLeftRight(ImageProducer ip)
    {
    }
    /**
     * Notification that the image is complete and there will
     * be no further setPixel calls.
     * @see ImageConsumer#imageComplete
     */
    public void imageComplete(int status)
    {
        if (status == IMAGEERROR || status == IMAGEABORTED)
        {
            consumer.imageComplete(status);
            return;
        }
        if ( status == SINGLEFRAMEDONE )
        {
            runThread = new RunFilter(this);
            runThread.start();
        }
        else
            filter();
    }
```

Advanced Image Processing

ADVANCED IMAGE
PROCESSING

```java
public void filter()
{
    switch ( type )
    {
    case WIPE_LR:   wipeLR();        break;
    case WIPE_RL:   wipeRL();        break;
    case WIPE_C:    wipeC();         break;
    default:        wipeC();     break;
    }
    consumer.imageComplete(STATICIMAGEDONE);
}
/**
 * Wipe the image from left to right
 */
public void wipeLR()
{
    int xw = outwidth / iterations;
    if ( xw <= 0 ) xw = 1;
    int total = xw * outheight;
    int dissolvePixels[] = new int[total];
    for ( int x = 0; x < total; x++ )
        dissolvePixels[x] = dissolveColor;
    for ( int t = 0; t < (outwidth - xw); t += xw )
    {
        setPixels(t, 0, xw, outheight,
                        defaultRGBModel, dissolvePixels,
                        0, xw);
        // tell consumer we are done with this frame
        consumer.setPixels(0, 0, outwidth, outheight,
            defaultRGBModel, inPixels, 0, outwidth);
        consumer.imageComplete(ImageConsumer.SINGLEFRAMEDONE);
        Thread.yield();
    }
}
/**
 * Wipe the image from right to left
 */
public void wipeRL()
{
    int xw = outwidth / iterations;
    if ( xw <= 0 ) xw = 1;
    int total = xw * outheight;
    int dissolvePixels[] = new int[total];
    for ( int x = 0; x < total; x++ )
        dissolvePixels[x] = dissolveColor;
    for ( int t = outwidth - xw - 1; t >= 0; t -= xw )
    {
        setPixels(t, 0, xw, outheight,
                        defaultRGBModel, dissolvePixels,
                        0, xw);
        // tell consumer we are done with this frame
        consumer.setPixels(0, 0, outwidth, outheight,
                defaultRGBModel, inPixels, 0, outwidth);
        consumer.imageComplete(ImageConsumer.SINGLEFRAMEDONE);
        Thread.yield();
    }
}
```

Listing 51.2. continued

```
/**
 * Wipe the image from the center out
 */
public void wipeC()
{
    int times = outwidth / 2;
    int xw = times / iterations;
    if ( xw <= 0 ) xw = 1;
    int total = xw * outheight;
    int dissolvePixels[] = new int[total];
    for ( int x = 0; x < total; x++ )
        dissolvePixels[x] = dissolveColor;
    int x1 = outwidth /2;
    int x2 = outwidth /2;
    while ( x2 < (outwidth - xw) )
    {
        setPixels(x1, 0, xw, outheight,
                        defaultRGBModel, dissolvePixels,
                        0, xw);
        setPixels(x2, 0, xw, outheight,
                        defaultRGBModel, dissolvePixels,
                        0, xw);
        // tell consumer we are done with this frame
        consumer.setPixels(0, 0, outwidth, outheight,
                defaultRGBModel, inPixels, 0, outwidth);
        consumer.imageComplete(ImageConsumer.SINGLEFRAMEDONE);
        Thread.yield();
        x1 -= xw;
        x2 += xw;
    }
}
}
class RunFilter extends Thread
{
    FXFilter fx = null;
    RunFilter(FXFilter f)
    {
        fx = f;
    }
    public void run()
    {
        fx.filter();
    }
}
```

You need `RunFilter` for image producers created from a memory image source. GIF and JPEG images both spawn a thread for their producers. Because the filter has to loop within the `imageComplete()` method, a separate thread is necessary for production. Memory images do not spawn a separate thread for their producers, so the filter has to spawn its own.

The only way to differentiate the producers is to key on their status. GIF and JPEG image producers send `STATICIMAGEDONE`; memory images send `SINGLEFRAMEDONE`.

NOTE

If you spawn an additional thread for GIF and JPEG images, you won't be able to display the image at all. Producers that are already a separate thread must operate within their existing threads.

The Mandelbrot Set Project

A new project, one that views the Mandelbrot set, gives you examples of some of the more advanced concepts to which you have been introduced. The Mandelbrot set is the most spectacular example of *fractals*, one of the hot scientific topics of recent years. With the applets in this chapter, you can view or generate an original Mandelbrot image.

Because the Mandelbrot set can take a while to generate (it requires millions of calculations), you have a chance to combine threads and image filters so that you can view the set as it's being generated. You may also want to save the Mandelbrot images. The BmpClass file, found on the CD-ROM that accompanies this book, converts a BMP-formatted file into a Java image.

The applet in the Mandelbrot example, MandelApp, generates the full Mandelbrot set. Depending your computer, this process can take a little while; for example, on a 486DX2-50 PC, the process takes a few minutes. When the image is complete (as indicated by a message on the browser's status bar), you can save the image to a BMP-formatted file by clicking anywhere on the applet's display area. The file is called mandel.bmp. Remember to run this applet from a program, such as the applet viewer, that lets applets write to disk.

How It Works

Because it can take quite a while to generate the Mandelbrot set, the program was designed by combining a calculation thread with an image filter so that you can see the results as they are generated. However, understanding how the classes interrelate is a little tricky. Figure 51.5 shows the workflow involved in producing a Mandelbrot image. Understanding this flow is the key to understanding this project.

The process begins when an applet displaying Mandelbrot sets constructs a Mandelbrot object. The Mandelbrot object, in turn, creates an instance of the CalculatorImage class. The Mandelbrot set passes itself as a part of the CalculatorImage constructor. It is referenced as a CalculatorProducer object, an interface that the Mandelbrot class implements. This interface implementation is used to communicate with the image filter.

Figure 51.5.

*The workflow involved
in producing a
Mandelbrot image.*

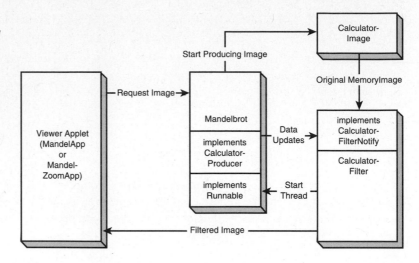

In the next step, the applet requests a `Mandelbrot` image. This request is initiated by calling the `getImage()` method of the `Mandelbrot` object, which in turn leads to a call to a like-named method of the `CalculatorImage` object. At this point, the `CalculatorImage` object creates a color palette by using an instance of the `ImageColorModel` class and then creates a `MemoryImageSource` object. This object, which implements `ImageProducer`, produces an image initialized to all zeros (black); it's combined with an instance of the `CalculatorFilter` class to produce a `FilteredImageSource`.

When the `MemoryImageSource` object produces its empty image, it is passed to the `CalculatorFilter`, which takes the opportunity to produce the calculated image. It does this by kicking off the thread of the image to be calculated. The `CalculatorFilter` doesn't know that it is the Mandelbrot set that's being calculated; it just knows that some calculation must occur in the `CalculatorProducer` object in which it has a reference.

Once the `Mandelbrot` thread is started, it begins the long calculations required to produce a Mandelbrot set. Whenever the thread finishes a section of the set, it notifies the filter with new data through the `CalculateFilterNotify` interface. The filter, in turn, lets the viewing applet know that it has new data to display by updating the corresponding `ImageConsumer`, which causes the applet's `imageUpdate()` method to be called. This call causes a repaint, and the new image data is displayed. This process repeats until the full image is created.

As you have probably observed, this is a complicated process. The `Calculator` classes are meant to provide a generic approach toward manipulating images that require long calculations. You can replace the `Mandelbrot` class with some other calculation thread that implements `CalculatorProducer`, and everything should work. A good exercise is to replace `Mandelbrot` with another fractal calculation or some other scientific imaging calculation. (I found that replacing `Mandelbrot` with a `Julia` fractal class calculation was very easy.)

Some of the classes in this project are now presented with their full source code to explain the advanced image processing. The other classes can be found on the CD-ROM that accompanies this book.

The Mandelbrot Class

 The Mandelbrot class, shown in Listing 51.3, calculates the Mandelbrot set. It implements the Runnable interface (so that it can run as a thread) and also implements the CalculatorProducer interface (so that it can update an image filter with the progress made in its calculations). This code is also located on the CD-ROM that accompanies this book.

Listing 51.3. The Mandelbrot class.

```java
import java.awt.image.*;
import java.awt.Image;
import java.lang.*;
// Class for producing a Mandelbrot set image...
public class Mandelbrot implements Runnable, CalculatorProducer {
    int width;  // The dimensions of the image...
    int height;
    CalculateFilterNotify filter; // Keeps track of image production...
    int pix[]; // Pixels used to construct image...
    CalculatorImage img;
    // General Mandelbrot parameters...
    int numColors = 256;
    int maxIterations = 512;
    int maxSize = 4;
    double RealMax,ImagineMax,RealMin,ImagineMin;  // Define sizes to build...
    private Boolean stopCalc = new Boolean(false);  // Stop calculations...
    // Create standard Mandelbrot set
    public Mandelbrot(int width,int height) {
        this.width = width;
        this.height = height;
        RealMax = 1.20;  // Default starting sizes...
        RealMin = -2.0;
        ImagineMax = 1.20;
        ImagineMin = -1.20;
    }
    // Create zoom of Mandelbrot set
    public Mandelbrot(int width,int height,double RealMax,double RealMin,
     double ImagineMax,double ImagineMin) {
        this.width = width;
        this.height = height;
        this.RealMax = RealMax;  // Default starting sizes...
        this.RealMin = RealMin;
        this.ImagineMax = ImagineMax;
        this.ImagineMin = ImagineMin;
    }
    // Start producing the Mandelbrot set...
    public Image getImage() {
        img = new CalculatorImage(width,height,this);
        return img.getImage();
    }
```

continues

Listing 51.3. continued

```java
// Start thread to produce data...
public void start(int pix[],CalculateFilterNotify filter) {
    this.pix = pix;
    this.filter = filter;
    new Thread(this).start();
}
// See if user wants to stop before completion...
public void stop() {
    synchronized (stopCalc) {
        stopCalc = Boolean.TRUE;
    }
    System.out.println("GOT STOP!");
}
// Create data here...
public void run() {
    // Establish Mandelbrot parameters...
    double Q[] = new double[height];
    // Pixdata is for image filter updates...
    int pixdata[] = new int[height];
    double P,diffP,diffQ, x, y, x2, y2;
    int color, row, column,index;
    System.out.println("RealMax = " + RealMax + " RealMin = " + RealMin +
        " ImagineMax = " + ImagineMax + " ImagineMin = " + ImagineMin);
    // Setup calculation parameters...
    diffP = (RealMax - RealMin)/(width);
    diffQ = (ImagineMax - ImagineMin)/(height);
    Q[0] = ImagineMax;
    color = 0;
    // Setup delta parameters...
    for (row = 1; row < height; row++)
        Q[row] = Q[row-1] - diffQ;
    P = RealMin;
    // Start calculating!
    for (column = 0; column < width; column++) {
        for (row = 0; row < height; row++) {
            x = y = x2 = y2 = 0.0;
            color = 1;
            while ((color < maxIterations) &&
                ((x2 + y2) < maxSize)) {
                    x2 = x * x;
                    y2 = y * y;
                    y = (2*x*y) + Q[row];
                    x = x2 - y2 + P;
                    ++color;
            }
            // plot...
            index = (row * width) + column;
            pix[index] = (int)(color % numColors);
            pixdata[row] = pix[index];
        } // end row
        // Update column after each iteration...
        filter.dataUpdateColumn(column,pixdata);
        P += diffP;
```

```
            // See if we were told to stop...
            synchronized (stopCalc) {
                if (stopCalc == Boolean.TRUE) {
                    column = width;
                    System.out.println("RUN: Got stop calc!");
                }
            }  // end sync
        } // end col
        // Tell filter that we're done producing data...
        System.out.println("FILTER: Data Complete!");
        filter.setComplete();
    }
    // Save the Mandelbrot set as a BMP file...
    public void saveBMP(String filename) {
        img.saveBMP(filename,pix);
    }
}
```

There are two constructors for the Mandelbrot class. The default constructor produces the full Mandelbrot set and takes the dimensions of the image to calculate. The Real and Imagine variables in the constructors and the run() method are used to map the x,y axis to the real and imaginary portions of c in the following formula:

$$z_{n+1} = z_n^2 + c$$

A few other variables are worth noting. The variable maxIterations represents when to stop calculating a number. If this number (set to 512 in the code) is reached, the starting value of c takes a long time to head toward infinity. The variable maxSize is a simpler indicator of how quickly the current value grows. How the current calculation is related to these variables is mapped to a specific color; the higher the number, the slower the growth. If you have a fast computer, you can adjust these variables to get a richer or duller expression of the Mandelbrot set.

Once the thread is started (by the CalculatorFilter object through the start() method), the run() method calculates the Mandelbrot values and stores a color corresponding to the growth rate of the current complex number into a pixel array. When a column is complete, run() uses the CalculateFilterNotify interface to let the related filter know that new data has been produced. The method also checks to see whether you want to abort the calculation. Note how it synchronizes the stopCalc boolean object in the run() and stop() methods.

The calculation can take a while to complete (it takes a couple minutes on a 486-based PC). Nevertheless, this performance is quite a testament to Java! With other interpreted, portable languages, you may be tempted to use your computer's reset button because the calculations take so long. With Java, you get fast visual feedback on how the set unfolds.

A good exercise is to save any partially developed Mandelbrot set; you can use the saveBMP() method to accomplish that task. You also need some kind of data file to indicate where the calculation was stopped.

The code for the following interfaces and classes (the `CalculateFilterNotify` interface, the `CalculatorProducer` interface, the `CalculatorFilter` class, and the `CalculatorImage` class) is located on the CD-ROM that accompanies this book.

The `CalculateFilterNotify` Interface

The `CalculateFilterNotify` interface defines the methods necessary to update an image filter that works with a calculation thread. As shown in Listing 51.4, the data methods are used to convey a new batch of data to the filter. The `setComplete()` method indicates that the calculations are complete.

Listing 51.4. The `CalculateFilterNotify` interface.

```
/* Interface for defining methods for updating a
   Calulator Filter... */
public interface CalculateFilterNotify {
    public void dataUpdate();    // Update everything...
    public void dataUpdateRow(int row); // Update one row...
    public void dataUpdateColumn(int col,int pixdata[]);  // Update one column...
    public void setComplete();
}
```

The `CalculatorProducer` Interface

The `CalculatorProducer` interface, shown in Listing 51.5, defines the method called when a calculation filter is ready to kick off a thread that produces the data used to generate an image. The `CalculateFilterNotify` object passed to the `start()` method is called by the producer whenever new data is yielded.

Listing 51.5. The `CalculatorProducer` interface.

```
// Interface for a large calculation to produce image...
interface CalculatorProducer {
    public void start(int pix[],CalculateFilterNotify cf);
}
```

The `CalculatorFilter` Class

The `CalculatorFilter` class, shown in Listing 51.6, is a subclass of `ImageFilter`. Its purpose is to receive image data produced by some long calculation (such as the one used on the Mandelbrot set) and to update any consumer with the new data's image. The `CalculatorProducer`, indicated by the variable cp, is what produces the data.

Listing 51.6. The CalculatorFilter class.

```java
import java.awt.image.*;
import java.awt.Image;
import java.awt.Toolkit;
import java.lang.*;
public class CalculatorFilter extends ImageFilter
 implements CalculateFilterNotify {
   private ColorModel defaultRGBModel;
   private int width, height;
   private int pix[];
   private boolean complete = false;
   private CalculatorProducer cp;
   private boolean cpStart = false;
   public CalculatorFilter(ColorModel cm,CalculatorProducer cp) {
      defaultRGBModel = cm;
      this.cp = cp;
   }
   public void setDimensions(int width, int height) {
      this.width = width;
      this.height = height;
      pix = new int[width * height];
      oonsumer.setDimensions(width,height);
   }
   public void setColorModel(ColorModel model) {
      consumer.setColorModel(defaultRGBModel);
   }
   public void setHints(int hints) {
      consumer.setHints(ImageConsumer.RANDOMPIXELORDER);
   }
   public void resendTopDownLeftRight(ImageProducer p) {
    }
   public void setPixels(int x, int y, int w, int h,
      ColorModel model, int pixels[],int off,int scansize) {
   }
   public void imageComplete(int status) {
     if (!cpStart) {
        cpStart = true;
        dataUpdate();  // Show empty pixels...
        cp.start(pix,this);
     } // end if
     if (complete)
        consumer.imageComplete(ImageConsumer.STATICIMAGEDONE);
   }
   // Called externally to notify that more data has been created
   // Notify consumer so they can repaint...
   public void dataUpdate() {
     consumer.setPixels(0,0,width,height,
             defaultRGBModel,pix,0,width);
     consumer.imageComplete(ImageConsumer.SINGLEFRAMEDONE);
   }
   // External call to update a specific pixel row...
   public void dataUpdateRow(int row) {
     // The key thing here is the second to last parameter (offset)
     // which states where to start getting data from the pix array...
     consumer.setPixels(0,row,width,1,
             defaultRGBModel,pix,(width * row),width);
```

continues

Listing 51.6. continued

```
        consumer.imageComplete(ImageConsumer.SINGLEFRAMEDONE);
    }
    // External call to update a specific pixel column...
    public void dataUpdateColumn(int col,int pixdata[]) {
        // The key thing here is the second to last parameter (offset)
        // which states where to start getting data from the pix array...
        consumer.setPixels(col,0,1,height,
                defaultRGBModel,pixdata,0,1);
        consumer.imageComplete(ImageConsumer.SINGLEFRAMEDONE);
    }
    // Called from external calculating program when data has
    // finished being calculated...
    public void setComplete() {
        complete = true;
        consumer.setPixels(0,0,width,height,
            defaultRGBModel,pix,0,width);
        consumer.imageComplete(ImageConsumer.STATICIMAGEDONE);
    }
}
```

Because the ImageFilter class was explained earlier in this chapter, issues related to this class are not repeated here. However, a couple of things should be pointed out. When the image is first requested, the filter gets the dimensions the consumer wants by calling the setDimensions() method. At this point, the CalculatorFilter allocates a large array holding the color values for each pixel.

When the original ImageProducer is finished creating the original image, the filter's imageComplete() method is called, but the filter must override this method. In this case, the CalculatorFilter starts the CalculatorProducer thread, passing it the pixel array to put in its updates. Whenever the CalculatorProducer has new data, it calls one of the four methods specified by the CalculateFilterNotify interface: dataUpdate(), dataUpdateRow(), dataUpdateColumn(), or setComplete(). The dataUpdateColumn() method is called by the Mandelbrot calculation because it operates on a column basis. In each of these cases, the filter updates the appropriate consumer pixels by using the setPixels() method, then calls the consumer's imageComplete() method to indicate the nature of the change. For the three data methods, the updates are only partial, so a SINGLEFRAMEDONE flag is sent. The setComplete() method, on the other hand, indicates that everything is complete, so it sets a STATICIMAGEDONE flag.

The CalculatorImage Class

The CalculatorImage class, shown in Listing 51.7, is the glue between the CalculatorProducer class that produces the image data and the CalculatorFilter that manages it.

Listing 51.7. The CalculatorImage class.

```
// This class takes a CalculatorProducer and sets up the
// environment for creating a calculated image.  Ties the
// producer to the CalculatorFilter so incremental updates can
// be made...
public class CalculatorImage {
    int width;  // The dimensions of the image...
    int height;
    CalculatorProducer cp;  // What produces the image data...
    IndexColorModel palette;  // The colors of the image...
    // Create Palette only once per session...
    static IndexColorModel prvPalette = null;
    int numColors = 256;  // Number of colors in palette...
    // Use defines how big of an image they want...
    public CalculatorImage(int width,int height,CalculatorProducer cp) {
        this.width = width;
        this.height = height;
        this.cp = cp;
    }
    // Start producing the Calculator image...
    public synchronized Image getImage() {
        // Hook into the filter...
        createPalette();
        ImageProducer p = new FilteredImageSource(
         new MemoryImageSource(width,height,palette,
             (new int[width * height]),0,width),
              new CalculatorFilter(palette,cp));
        // Return the image...
        return Toolkit.getDefaultToolkit().createImage(p);
    }
    // Create a 256 color palette...
    // Use Default color model...
    void createPalette() {
        // Create palette only once per session...
        if (prvPalette != null) {
            palette = prvPalette;
            return;
        }
        // Create a palette out of random RGB combinations...
        byte blues[], reds[], greens[];
        reds = new byte[numColors];
        blues = new byte[numColors];
        greens = new byte[numColors];
        // First and last entries are black and white...
        blues[0] = reds[0] = greens[0] = (byte)0;
        blues[255] = reds[255] = greens[255] = (byte)255;
        // Fill in other entries...
        for ( int x = 1; x < 254; x++ ){
         reds[x] = (byte)(255 * Math.random());
         blues[x] = (byte)(255 * Math.random());
         greens[x] = (byte)(255 * Math.random());
        }
        // Create Index Color Model...
        palette = new IndexColorModel(8,256,reds,greens,blues);
        prvPalette = palette;
    }
```

continues

Listing 51.7. continued

```
// Save the image set as a BMP file...
public void saveBMP(String filename,int pix[]) {
    try {
        BmpImage.saveBitmap(filename,palette,
            pix,width,height);
    }
    catch (IOException ioe) {System.out.println("Error saving file!"); }
  }
}
```

When an image is requested with the `getImage()` method, the `CalculatorImage` class creates a color palette through an instance of the `ImageColorModel` class and then creates a `MemoryImageSource` object. This `ImageProducer` object produces an image initialized to all zeros (black). It is combined with an instance of the `CalculatorFilter` class to produce a `FilteredImageSource`. When the `createImage()` method of the Abstract Windowing Toolkit (AWT) class is called, production of the calculated image begins.

The color palette is a randomly generated series of pixel values. Depending on your luck, these color combinations can be attractive or uninspiring. The `createPalette()` method is a good place to create a custom set of colors for this applet—if you want to have some control over its appearance. You should replace the random colors with hard-coded RGB values; you may also want to download a URL file that specifies a special color map.

The Mandelbrot Applet

Listing 51.8 shows the complete code for the Mandelbrot applet, `MandelApp`; the code is also located on the CD-ROM that accompanies this book. The applet does only a few things. When the applet starts, it gets the Mandelbrot image, forcing it to begin being created. The `imageUpdate()` method is called to repaint the applet whenever there is some new data to be displayed. The only other thing the applet does is to wait for a mouse click to indicate that you want to save the image. The mouse click is handled by a listener class, `MandelMouseListener`. Recall that this is an example of the Java 1.1 delegation model for events.

Listing 51.8. The `MandelApp` class.

```
// Listener for mouse clicks...
class MandelMouseListener implements MouseListener
{
    MandelApp app;
    public MandelMouseListener(MandelApp app) {
        this.app = app;
    }
    public void mouseClicked(MouseEvent e)
    {
        app.saveImage();
    }
    public void mousePressed(MouseEvent e)
```

```java
        {
        }
        public void mouseReleased(MouseEvent e)
        {
        }
        public void mouseEntered(MouseEvent e)
        {
        }
        public void mouseExited(MouseEvent e)
        {
        }
}
// This applet displays the Mandlebrot set through
// use of the Mandelbrot class...
public class MandelApp extends Applet  {
    Image im;    // Image that displays Mandelbrot set...
    Mandelbrot m; // Creates the Mandelbrot image...
    int NUMCOLS = 640;   // Dimensions image display...
    int NUMROWS = 350;
    boolean complete = false;
    // Set up the Mandelbrot set...
    public void init() {
        m = new Mandelbrot(NUMCOLS,NUMROWS);
        im = m.getImage();
        // Hook the listener to the app...
        addMouseListener(new MandelMouseListener(this));
    }
    // Will get updates as set is being created.
    // Repaint when they occur...
    public boolean imageUpdate(Image im,int flags,
        int x, int y, int w, int h) {
        if ((flags & FRAMEBITS) != 0) {
            showStatus("Calculating...");
            repaint();
            return true;
        }
        if ((flags & ALLBITS) != 0) {
            showStatus("Image Complete!");
            repaint();
            complete = true;
            return false;
        }
        return true;
    }
    // Paint on update...
    public void update(Graphics g) {
        paint(g);
    }
    public synchronized void paint(Graphics g) {
        g.drawImage(im,0,0,this);
    }
    // Save Bitmap when image complete...
    public void saveImage() {
      if (complete) {
          showStatus("Save Bitmap...");
          m.saveBMP("mandel.bmp");
          showStatus("Bitmap saved!");
      } // end if
    }
}
```

Summary

This chapter covered advanced image concepts and demonstrated the writing and use of image filters, rotation concepts, and special effects. Finally, a Mandelbrot applet was developed to explain the principles presented in this chapter.

Images give Java tremendous flexibility. Once you master image concepts, the endless possibilities of the Java graphics system are yours to explore.

Java Internationalization

by Glenn Vanderburg

IN THIS CHAPTER

CHAPTER 52

As the world grows smaller—because of the continued success of the Internet as well as other developments—it is becoming more important to write software for the world rather than for one just language or culture. Writing internationalized applications has been an extremely challenging task, partly because the problems were not well understood, and partly because good tools and facilities to help with the task have been hard to come by.

Java is intended to be the programming language for the Internet; for it to succeed in that role, it has to provide some of those tools for programmers. It should be easy to write internationalized programs in Java.

Java 1.1 is a big step ahead of other programming languages. Java now has unprecedented support for internationalization: a full array of APIs and facilities to assist programmers in developing for a global market. In this chapter, you learn about the problems of internationalization and how to use Java's internationalization features to solve those problems in your programs.

About Internationalization

Internationalization is a large topic—and a complex one. There are facets to internationalization that have never occurred to most programmers. In fact, the size of the topic is one of the reasons that good internationalization facilities are so rare: Very few programmers or groups of programmers have the understanding necessary to design and build tools and libraries to support the task.

Internationalization is the process of writing a program (or modifying an existing program) so that it is ready to support other languages and cultures. Note that internationalization does not include actually translating messages and other tasks specific to supporting a particular language; that job is called *localization*. A more concise definition of internationalization is this: preparing a program to be localized.

"But," you ask, "if that's all internationalization is, what's the big deal? It seems that localization is the hard part." Localization certainly is difficult, but internationalization has its own challenges. The typical program, before being internationalized, has messages, prompts, and textual labels scattered throughout the code. That's bad enough, but nonlocalized data isn't the worst problem. Most programs contain hidden assumptions about the meaning and proper format of various constructs, such as numbers, currency values, times, dates, sort order, and capitalization rules.

Programs like that are hard to localize because finding all the locale-dependent data is difficult—and finding the hidden assumptions about language and culture is even more difficult. Furthermore, because all the locale dependencies are intertwined with the application code, localizing such programs frequently involves creating entirely new versions for each new locale. Those versions must be supported and maintained in parallel, which is—to say the least— a support nightmare.

It is far better to internationalize programs first, before localizing them. Internationalized programs can usually be switched easily between any of the supported locales, whether at run time or when the program is shipped to customers. An internationalized program has locale-sensitive data grouped together in just a few parts of the program or in external data files. Additionally, code that depends on locale-specific assumptions is replaced with calls to a few special routines that encapsulate those assumptions.

Thus, internationalization depends on two types of techniques: program structuring techniques and disciplined use of library facilities. In addition, an internationalized program uses three kinds of data:

- **Internal data.** Messages, labels, icons, and other "resources" that can be considered part of the program itself.
- **System data.** Information obtained from the runtime platform, such as date and time information or system properties. (System data is usually a tiny portion of the information manipulated by a program, but it is no less important for purposes of internationalization.)
- **User data.** Text, images, or other information supplied at run time at the direction of the user of the program (this kind of data is also called "documents").

Internationalization isn't an absolute quality. Some programs are more thoroughly internationalized than others. Many programs can support multiple European languages, but are prohibitively difficult to localize for a right-to-left or vertical writing system. Some internationalized programs can be switched between locales when they are run; others require recompilation. Finally, some programs require a particularly strong form of internationalization so that they can actually support multiple languages and locales simultaneously. As an example of such a program, consider a word processor to be used by a linguist. That program would have to allow the use of multiple languages and alphabets in a single document. Such programs are called *multilingual* (or, in some cases, *multilocale*) programs. Although this extreme variety of internationalization has its own name, it is still a form of internationalization.

An Overview of Java's Internationalization Features

Most of Java's internationalization facilities fall into the category of library routines that encapsulate rules and assumptions about dealing with different types of locale-sensitive data. There are classes for representing and comparing times, dates, numbers, and currency values. Other classes assist with sorting and classifying text and characters. Additionally, Java provides facilities for formatting and parsing those objects for display, either alone or embedded in other localized text (such as GUI labels or error messages).

Java also provides some help with the program structure issues that are an important part of internationalization. The mechanism for managing internal data related to localization is the `ResourceBundle` class. This class is versatile enough to support many different ways of storing and representing the data, and the Java 1.1 library contains two simple but useful implementations that are very useful for internationalization.

Underneath nearly every part of Java's internationalization support is the Unicode character set. With the release of Java 1.1, Unicode support in the Java language and its libraries is extremely thorough. Having Unicode as the native character set for strings and characters in the language simplifies the rest of the internationalization task immensely.

All these Java facilities are designed to support dynamic localization, even to the point of supporting multilingual programs. There is no global state that affects the entire program, no "system locale" that must be changed. Instances of the `Locale` class represent particular locales. All the locale-sensitive methods in the Java libraries can take a `Locale` object as an argument so that locales can be easily changed from one operation to the next. There are "default locales" that make certain operations easier in programs that use only one locale at a time, but they are implemented so that they do not impact full multilingual support when it is needed.

In describing the goals for the Java internationalization facilities, JavaSoft's design specification document contains this statement:

> *Java programs should be internationalized by default. This implies that it should be easier than not to write internationalized Java code.*

That goal was perhaps a little unrealistic, and it certainly wasn't realized in every respect. It still takes discipline and a little extra work to make proper use of the library facilities and to structure things properly. But it's notable that little or none of the extra work is particularly cumbersome; in some respects, it actually *is* easier to do it the right way. Certainly, internationalization is easier in Java 1.1 than it has ever been before.

Locales

`Locale` objects are tokens that represent locales. In Java, *locales* are defined as geographic, political, or cultural regions. For practical purposes, a locale is usually the combination of a language and a set of cultural rules and assumptions (regardless of the geographical designation). In most respects, although they are represented as objects rather than strings, `Locale` objects function simply as names: they don't really have any behavior or semantics apart from identifying locales. In fact, there is a standard form for representing a locale name as a string. It is relatively easy to convert between the string representation and a `Locale` object and back again.

To construct a `Locale`, you must supply a language name because language is the single-most important characteristic of a locale. You can also specify a country name, which helps to distinguish between different cultural conventions used by speakers of the same language. For example, English speakers in the United States do many things differently than those in the United Kingdom; Brazilians have some customs that would be unfamiliar to people in Portugal, even though Portuguese is the dominant language in both countries. Here are some examples of how to construct `Locale` objects for various situations:

```
new Locale("en", "")       // Default English/American locale
new Locale("en", "GB")     // English locale for Great Britain
new Locale("fr", "CH")     // French locale for Switzerland
```

The names used for the languages and countries are the two-letter international standard language and country codes. The API documentation for the `Locale` class contains pointers to Web pages with complete lists. Confusingly, language codes are always two lowercase letters, but country codes are two uppercase letters. The `Locale` constructors aren't picky about case, but they do convert their parameters to the appropriate case when they are called. When you call the `toString()` method, the result is the two codes concatenated with an intervening underscore, or just the language code if no country is specified.

There is also a constructor that takes three parameters—all strings—to provide a way to specify additional variant locales, including cultural or linguistic enclaves within a single country and language group. For example, among the locales supported by Java 1.1 are two locales for the country of Norway. Norwegian is the language for both locales, but there is a minor difference: they use different names for some of the days of the week. The default Norwegian locale, Bokmål, has a string representation no_NO_B, but because it is the default, it is the locale you get if you omit the variant token or specify only the language token. The other Norwegian locale, Nynorsk, must be specified explicitly; its string representation is no_NO_NY. Here are some examples:

```
new Looale("no", "")        // Bokmål, no_NO_B
new Locale("no", "NO")      // Bokmål, no_NO_B
new Locale("no", "NO", "B") // Bokmål, no_NO_B
new Locale("no", "NO", "NY")// Nynorsk, no_NO_NY
```

Although a `Locale` is just a form of name, if it is to actually be useful, it must refer to something that really exists. Many internationalization support classes use the locale name to find resources or rules of various kinds for a particular locale. Java 1.1 includes support for the locales listed in Table 52.1.

Table 52.1. Locales supported in Java 1.1.

Minimal Name	Full Name	Language	Country
ar	ar_EG	Arabic	Egypt
be	be_BY	Belorussian	Belarus
bg	bg_BG	Bulgarian	Bulgaria
ca	ca_ES	Catalan	Spain

continues

Table 52.1. continued

Minimal Name	Full Name	Language	Country
cs	cs_CZ	Czech	Czech Republic
da	da_DK	Danish	Denmark
de	de_DE	German	Germany
de_AT	de_AT	German	Austria
de_CH	de_CH	German	Switzerland
el	el_GR	Greek	Greece
en_CA	en_CA	English	Canada
en_GB	en_GB	English	United Kingdom
en_IE	en_IE	English	Ireland
(none)	en_US	English	United States
es	es_ES	Spanish	Spain
et	et_EE	Estonian	Estonia
fi	fi_FI	Finnish	Finland
fr	fr_FR	French	France
fr_BE	fr_BE	French	Belgium
fr_CA	fr_CA	French	Canada
fr_CH	fr_CH	French	Switzerland
hr	hr_HR	Croatian	Croatia
hu	hu_HU	Hungarian	Hungary
is	is_IS	Icelandic	Iceland
it	it_IT	Italian	Italy
it_CH	it_CH	Italian	Switzerland
iw	iw_IL	Hebrew	Israel
ja	ja_JP	Japanese	Japan
ko	ko_KR	Korean	Korea
lt	lt_LT	Lithuanian	Lithuania
lv	lv_LV	Latvian	Latvia
mk	mk_MK	Macedonian	Macedonia
nl	nl_NL	Dutch	Netherlands
nl_BE	nl_BE	Dutch	Belgium
no	no_NO_B	Norwegian (Bokmål)	Norway
no_NO_NY	no_NO_NY	Norwegian (Nynorsk)	Norway

Minimal Name	Full Name	Language	Country
pl	pl_PL	Polish	Poland
pt	pt_PT	Portuguese	Portugal
ro	ro_RO	Romanian	Romania
ru	ru_RU	Russian	Russia
sh	sh_SP	Serbian (Latin)	Serbia
sk	sk_SK	Slovak	Slovakia
sl	sl_SI	Slovene	Slovenia
sq	sq_AL	Albanian	Albania
sr	sr_SP	Serbian (Cyrillic)	Serbia
sv	sv_SE	Swedish	Sweden
tr	tr_TR	Turkish	Turkey
uk	uk_UA	Ukrainian	Ukraine
zh	zh_CN	Chinese	China
zh_TW	zh_TW	Chinese	Taiwan

The `Locale` class is found in the `java.util` package.

Resource Bundles

Resource bundles can be used to solve the structuring problem associated with internationalizing internal data. Using resource bundles, locale-sensitive data can be grouped together in one place—or just a few places—so that it can be localized easily.

Resource bundles implement special support for locales. In particular, the `java.util.ResourceBundle` class provides methods that search for bundles associated with a particular locale. The search process tries several variations, starting with the specified locale, falling back to the default locale, and finally settling for a nonlocalized bundle. The search does not fail unless there simply isn't a resource bundle by the requested name at all. That's convenient, and it is usually what you want: If the program hasn't been localized for a particular locale, it is probably better to continue running without localization than simply to fail.

As an example of how the search process works, assume that your program makes use of a resource bundle called `MessageBundle`. Also assume that the default locale is `fr_CA`, and the bundle is requested for the `no_NO_NY` (a situation that might occur if the user is a Norwegian living in Quebec). Now suppose that the application makes the following call:

```
ResourceBundle.getBundle("MessageBundle", new Locale("no", "NO", "NY"))
```

In response, the search tests for the existence of these bundles, in the following order:

1. `MessageBundle_no_NO_NY`
2. `MessageBundle_no_NO`
3. `MessageBundle_no`
4. `MessageBundle_fr_CA`
5. `MessageBundle_fr`
6. `MessageBundle`

In other words, the search starts with the specified locale and looks for progressively less-specific alternatives; if none are found, the search starts over again with the default locale; finally, if none of the bundles associated with the default locale is found, the default bundle is tried. If no bundle is found with any of those names, the `MissingResourceException` exception is thrown.

Resource bundles can be used for any type of data, and the `ResourceBundle` class can be extended to support any kind of storage mechanism. That's a useful flexibility for internationalization because any kind of data used by a program may have to be localized, including messages, prompts, labels, icons, sound files, and images.

Manipulating Data

Programmers have developed many tricks for quickly dealing with various kinds of data. But it's surprising how often those tricks incorporate cultural or language assumptions. For example, how does one sort a list of words in a language that uses accents and diacritical marks? The problem usually comes as a surprise to English-speaking programmers who are unaccustomed to using accented letters. An even bigger surprise is the revelation that there is no one answer to the question! Different languages and cultures have different rules about how to alphabetize a, á, and â, for example. There are many such issues to be considered for text, dates and times, currency values, and other kinds of data.

Fortunately, the Java libraries provide assistance for handling dates, times, and textual information in a locale-independent way. The next two sections explain the relevant facilities.

Dates and Times

The world doesn't have as many calendar systems as it does languages, but it has enough to be troublesome for the programmer writing international applications. In addition to the standard Gregorian calendar used by most of the world, Chinese, Hebrew, and Islamic calendars are in wide use.

In Java 1.1, dates are represented by instances of the `java.util.Date` class. Times are represented that way, too; after all, a time is nothing more than a very precise date.

To represent any date, *some* calendar system must be chosen. The `Date` class implements one particular calendar system, in which times are represented as the number of milliseconds since the first instant of January 1, 1970, GMT (Greenwich mean time). The number can be negative, to indicate times before that demarcation point. That may not seem like a particularly useful calendar to you; in fact, it is not meant for human consumption. The purpose of this calendar system is to be a simple, uniform calendar for representing times within the Java library.

As such, `Date` objects are really useful only for comparing with other `Date` objects. The class provides comparison methods so that it is easy to tell how one `Date` relates to another. More complicated operations, such as learning about months, years, and days of the week, are the job of the `Calendar` classes.

`Calendar` provides a generalized view of different calendar systems; particular calendar systems are supported by subclasses of `Calendar`. The primary purpose of `Calendar` objects is to convert between `Date` objects and integer values for year, month, day of month, day of week, hour, minute, second, and so on. (The documentation for the various calendar classes calls these values *fields*.) You can change the time a `Calendar` object represents by providing a new `Date` object, or by changing the integer values that represent the portions of the calendrical date specification. For example, given a `Date` object `d1`, you can calculate another date one week later by doing the following:

```
Calendar cal = Calendar.getInstance();    // acquire a localized Calendar object
cal.setTime(d1);                          // set the Calendar's time value

cal.set(Calendar.WEEK_OF_MONTH,           // set the "week-of-month" field to
   cal.get(Calendar.WEEK_OF_MONTH) + 1);  //   the current value plus one

Date d2 = cal.getTime();                  // now retrieve a new Date object
```

There are some interesting details in this code fragment, so I'll discuss the code step by step. First, note that I didn't just create a new instance of `Calendar` with a constructor. Instead, I used the "factory method" `getInstance()` to get a new `Calendar` object. The `getInstance()` method creates an object appropriate for the default locale. There is also a version of the method that takes a `Locale` object as a parameter and creates an object appropriate for the specified locale. This is a pattern common to most of the internationalization classes discussed in the rest of this chapter.

After creating the `Calendar` object, I had to set the time it represented, using my `d1` object. That's a bit cumbersome; hopefully, some future version of `Calendar` will allow a `Date` object to be specified as a parameter to the `getInstance()` method for automatic initialization.

Next, I advanced the week by 1. First I queried the current week of the month, added 1, and reset the same field. The `Calendar` class can represent dates in terms of the following different fields, denoted by named constants:

Field Name	Description
AM_PM	Before or after noon
DATE	The day of the month
DAY_OF_MONTH	The day of the month (synonym for DATE)
DAY_OF_WEEK	The day of the week
DAY_OF_WEEK_IN_MONTH	Occurrence of this day of the week in this month (for example, Tuesday the 10th is the second Tuesday of the month)
DAY_OF_YEAR	The day of the year
DST_OFFSET	Offset from UTC for daylight saving time in this time zone
ERA	The era in which this date occurs (for example, A.D. or B.C.)
HOUR	Hour in 12-hour clock
HOUR_OF_DAY	Hour in 24-hour clock
MILLISECOND	Milliseconds within the second
MINUTE	The minute of the hour
MONTH	The month of the year
SECOND	The second within the minute
WEEK_OF_MONTH	The week of the month
WEEK_OF_YEAR	The week of the year
YEAR	The year within the era
ZONE_OFFSET	Offset from UTC in this time zone

Any of these fields can be retrieved from a `Calendar` object with the `get()` method or be set with the `set()` method. All the fields are stored as integers; to translate to textual representations, use the `DateFormat` class described in "Formatted Output and Input," later in this chapter.

After changing the week of the month, I was able to retrieve the new `Date` object, which represents the moment exactly one week after the original `Date`. Notice that there are a couple of funny things going on in this step.

The first question you might ask is this: What if the WEEK_OF_MONTH field was already set to 5? By incrementing it, we set the new date to be in the sixth week of the month. But that doesn't make any sense because months don't have six weeks.

The answer is that `Calendar` objects, by default, are very permissive about the way dates are specified. If you specify a date as being in the seventh week of the twelfth month, the calendar assumes that you mean the second week of the first month of the following year. If you specify a time as `25:00`, the resulting time is `1:00` A.M. of the following day. This behavior can be turned off by calling `setLenient(false)`.

Another question may have occurred to you: How does the calendar make sense of the fields after the `WEEK_OF_MONTH` field is incremented? After all, the calendar also knows about fields representing the day of the year and the day of the month. It seems as though changing just one of the fields would cause a conflict with some of the other fields.

The answer is that `Calendar` keeps track of which fields are explicitly set and gives them precedence over fields that have been inferred from the time value. Because we set only the `WEEK_OF_MONTH` field, that value has precedence over other fields that contain contradictory information. In fact, `Calendar` has rules for choosing between contradictory fields even if they have all been explicitly set, but in our example, those rules aren't required.

Java 1.1 includes one specialized calendar implementation, `GregorianCalendar`, which implements the standard calendar system used by most western countries.

Time Zones

`Calendar` can localize its operations based on locales, and it can also understand time zones. Instances of `java.util.TimeZone` represent time zones and incorporate knowledge about time zones around the world, including offsets from GMT and rules about daylight saving time. Other classes in the Java library in addition to the `Calendar` class make use of `TimeZone`, including `DateFormat` (discussed in "Formatted Output and Input," later in this chapter).

There are several ways to create `TimeZone` objects. To get the current time zone where the computer is running, use the `getDefault()` method. If you want an object for a particular zone, call `getTimeZone()` with a string containing that zone's ID (for example, United States Central Standard Time uses an ID of `CST`). You can also create a `TimeZone` using the constructor and set an explicit offset from GMT using the `setRawOffset()` method.

Most of the time, you don't have to query or manipulate `TimeZone` objects directly; you can just create the appropriate instances and pass them, as needed, to other objects (such as `Calendar`) which use the time zone information appropriately. Therefore, you can think of `TimeZone` objects as similar to `Locale` objects: they primarily serve as names or tokens.

Text Processing

Textual data presents an entirely different class of problems. As I write this chapter, I am (not surprisingly) using a word processing program. It is instructive to consider the various ways in which such an application uses and manipulates text, and what kinds of problems might be involved where internationalization is concerned.

For one thing, the interface for most word processors makes copious use of lists of names: styles, fonts, cross-reference tags, and so on. Such lists are ordered alphabetically. Sorting localized text is an internationalization problem, not merely because of different alphabets, but also because of different rules used across cultures.

When I use the arrow keys to move around in my document, the cursor moves one letter or line at a time. But by holding down various combinations of modifier keys, I can move (or, for that matter, delete or select text) by other units: words, sentences, or paragraphs. Furthermore, my word processor adjusts line breaks as I type. But Unicode complicates the task of recognizing boundaries between textual units, including acceptable places for line breaking. In addition, Unicode incorporates the concept of *combining characters*: two 16-bit Unicode characters (usually a base character and an accent mark) that combine to produce the appearance of one character. So even moving letter by letter is related to internationalization!

When I search for text in my document, I can choose whether the search should be sensitive to the difference between uppercase and lowercase letters. The program can also change the capitalization of text automatically, whether at my direction or in the process of formatting headings or entries in the table of contents. The difference between uppercase and lowercase is easy to deal with in ASCII, but the issue is much more complicated in an international character set like Unicode.

Java 1.1 provides features for dealing with all these issues. They are divided into three categories: collation, text boundaries, and character classification.

Collation

The term *collation* refers to the act of comparison. It can also refer to sorting, but the Java library uses it in the first sense. Java 1.1 does not provide sorting routines, but it does provide the collation facilities—the comparison facilities—required to implement sort routines on text objects.

The primary collation class is called `java.text.Collator`. As with many of the Java internationalization classes, `Collator` objects are not created directly using the constructor; instead, they are created using the static `Collator.getInstance()` and `Collator.getInstance(Locale)` methods, which create localized versions of `Collator`.

The basic collation functionality of `Collator` lies in the `compare(String, String)` method. Just as similar facilities in other languages such as C, this method returns an integer value: zero if the strings are equal, less than or greater than zero if the first string is, respectively, less than or greater than the second. If you are interested only in whether the strings are equal, the convenience method `equals(String, String)` returns a boolean value indicating equality.

For one-time comparisons, calls to `compare()` and `equals()` are sufficient. If certain strings are to be compared multiple times (as might happen when sorting a list of strings), it is better to use `CollationKey` objects. The `getCollationKey(String)` method returns an instance of

CollationKey that represents the given string for purposes of comparison within the Collator object's locale. In general, CollationKey objects can be compared more efficiently than String objects can be. Given two CollationKey objects called k1 and k2, you compare them in this way:

```
k1.compareTo(k2)
```

You can also retrieve the original source string from a CollationKey, using the getSourceString() method, so that you don't have to keep track of which keys represent which strings.

The way Collator objects decide on the relationship between two strings can be tuned to follow desired conventions. The *strength* of a comparison refers to how literal it is. For example, an extremely strong comparison considers a and A to be different characters; a weaker comparison might consider a, A, ä, and Å to be all the same. Four strength levels are provided. The precise meaning of the strength values depends on the locale, but here are some common definitions:

- PRIMARY: Two characters are considered to be the same if their base letters are the same, regardless of accents, other diacritical marks, or case distinctions. This is the weakest kind of collation.

- SECONDARY: Two characters are considered to be the same if the base letter and any diacritical marks are the same, regardless of case distinctions.

- TERTIARY: Two characters are considered to be the same only if they have the same base letter, the same diacritical marks, and the same case.

- IDENTICAL: Two characters are considered to be the same only if they have the same bit pattern. This is the strongest form of collation.

It may seem that there is no difference between TERTIARY and IDENTICAL, but there is a difference. Unicode may provide more than one way to specify the same letter—for example, the character ë can be specified either as a single 16-bit character or as a combination of e and a combining ¨ mark. The two versions are considered equal under a TERTIARY comparison but are different under the rules for IDENTICAL comparisons.

The strength a Collator object uses for comparisons can be set with the setStrength() method; the strength can be queried using getStrength().

Text Divisions and Boundaries

The BreakIterator class provides a locale-independent way to find the boundaries between certain kinds of textual elements, such as words and sentences. BreakIterator is even helpful for finding boundaries between printable characters; again, this is because two 16-bit Unicode characters can combine to produce one printed glyph. (It wouldn't be a good idea to try to put the insertion cursor between a letter and its accent!)

Once again, you don't create instances of `BreakIterator` with a constructor. There are actually several different static factory methods for creating `BreakIterator` objects, depending on what kind of textual element you want to learn about:

- `getCharacterInstance()` returns a `BreakIterator` that can find boundaries between characters
- `getLineInstance()` returns a `BreakIterator` that can find valid places for line breaks
- `getSentenceInstance()` returns a `BreakIterator` that can find sentence boundaries
- `getWordInstance()` returns a `BreakIterator` that can find word boundaries

Each of these methods comes in two varieties: one with a `Locale` parameter, and one with no parameter (this form uses the default locale).

Once you have a `BreakIterator` object, how do you use it? First, you must inform the object about the text you want to examine, using the `setText(String)` method. Then you can move through the text looking at boundaries using the `first()`, `last()`, `next()`, and `previous()` methods. Each of these methods moves the current position of the `BreakIterator` to the requested boundary and returns the integer position of that boundary within the text. The `next()` and `previous()` methods return a special value, `BreakIterator.DONE`, if there are no more boundaries in the requested direction. Additionally, the `next()` method has a variant that takes an integer parameter for moving ahead by multiple boundaries in one step.

Iterating through text with a `BreakIterator` is a little more complicated than traversing a data structure using an `Enumeration` object. The reason is that the information you get back from a `BreakIterator` is usually not the complete element you are interested in; instead, it is the start or end point of that element within the text. You must save that value and then find the other boundary before you can do useful things. This is a case in which it makes sense to declare and use two loop variables in a `for` statement. For example, here is a code fragment that loops through all the words in a `String` called `textBuffer`, printing them as it goes:

```
BreakIterator words = BreakIterator.getWordInstance();
words.setText(textBuffer);

for (    int start = words.first(), end = words.next();
         end != BreakIterator.DONE;
         start = end, end = words.next()) {
    System.out.println(textBuffer.substring(start,end));
}
```

Another method, `current()`, returns the index of the current boundary without changing or moving the current point. The `following(int)` method returns the first boundary after the specified position in the text.

What do you do if you need some of the `BreakIterator` facilities but can't afford to store your application's text in a `String` object? If efficiency or ease of access dictate that you use a text data structure (such as a *trie*—a specialized text data structure) instead of a string, you should define a `CharacterIterator` class for that data structure. `CharacterIterator` is an interface, similar in some ways to the java.util.Enumeration interface. It provides an abstract interface for iterating over the elements in a data structure. Classes that implement CharacterIterator don't have to contain all the data; they just have to know how to read it sequentially from the data structure and how to keep track of the current position. CharacterIterator differs from Enumeration in that it is specialized for character data and allows bidirectional scanning.

BreakIterator actually has two setText() methods: One takes a String parameter, and the other takes a CharacterIterator parameter. Once you build a CharacterIterator for your data structure, you can use the BreakIterator facilities to analyze the text stored there.

Character Classification

Even with all the useful text-handling facilities already described, occasionally a program has to work at the level of individual characters. Operations that were trivial using the ASCII character set (such as converting between uppercase and lowercase) are much more complicated with Unicode.

The java.lang.Character class contains several methods for making various tests on character values and for converting them in some way. You can test for the case of a character, or learn whether it is a whitespace character, for example, and you can convert between uppercase and lowercase and back again.

Input and Output

Manipulating data is all very well and good, but at some point, it comes down to reading that data from somewhere and writing (or displaying) it. Java provides facilities to help with several aspects of internationalized I/O, including Unicode streams and formatting and parsing classes.

Unicode Streams

In Java 1.1, the java.io package contains several I/O stream classes that read and write Unicode data. These classes are called *readers* and *writers*, and extend the Reader and Writer classes.

Because the String and char data types in Java represent Unicode data, Unicode I/O streams are the natural and preferred mechanism for text input and output. And it doesn't take any extra work to use them instead of the byte-oriented streams. I won't go into much detail about Unicode streams in this chapter; if you want more details about Unicode I/O streams, see Chapter 12, "The I/O Package."

Formatted Output and Input

The hard part about internationalized input and output is formatting and parsing. Data that is intrinsically textual can be read, manipulated, and written again rather easily, but what about data that is represented as text but must be manipulated in some other form? How do you convert back and forth between the values and their textual representations in a locale-independent way?

That's the job of the `Format` classes. The `java.text` package contains the abstract `Format` class, which describes a generic facility for formatting and parsing textual data representations. Several subclasses of `Format` perform internationalized handling of data types such as `Date` and numeric values, plus messages for users.

The interface defined by the `Format` class consists of four methods: two for formatted output, and two for parsing formatted input. The intent is that strings generated by `Format` and its subclasses can also be reparsed by those same classes to generate an equivalent object or set of objects.

The primary formatting method is `format(Object)`, which returns a formatted string. The other formatting method is more complicated: `format(Object, StringBuffer, FieldPosition)` returns the `StringBuffer` object that is passed as the second parameter, after appending the formatted value to it. Subclasses of `Format` use the `FieldPosition` object to communicate information about the formatting process. When the method is called, the `FieldPosition` parameter contains an integer, the *field identifier*, which the caller uses to express interest in a particular portion of the formatted string. When the method returns, the `FieldPosition` object has been updated to contain the beginning and ending positions of that field within the `StringBuffer`. Such information might be useful for choosing appropriate sizes for GUI elements, and this variation of the `format()` method is useful for building a formatted string in pieces.

The two parsing methods parallel the formatting methods. `ParseObject(String)` returns an `Object` created from the information in the string. `ParseObject(String, ParsePosition)` also returns an `Object` representing the parsed value, but the `ParsePosition` parameter is used to control the current position when parsing a string piece by piece. Instances of `ParsePosition` contain an integer representing a position within a string. When the method is called, the `ParsePosition` parameter indicates where in the string the method should begin parsing; when the method returns, the parameter has been updated to point to the first character following the parsed value. Thus, it is ready to pass to the next `ParseObject` method to parse the next piece of the string.

Once again, `Format` is an abstract class and doesn't provide implementations of all these methods. It does provide default implementations of the simple, single-parameter versions, which work by calling the more general methods so that you can build a working `Format` object simply by supplying implementations for only two methods.

Formatting and Parsing Individual Objects

The Java 1.1 library provides specialized subclasses of `Format` for handling two kinds of locale-sensitive data: dates and numbers. `DateFormat` and `NumberFormat` each provide the following facilities:

■ Static `getInstance()` methods that create instances specialized for a particular locale or for the default locale

■ Specialized `getInstance()` methods, such as `NumberFormat.getCurrencyInstance()`, for creating instances specialized for certain *interpretations* of the data

■ Static constants that identify various parts of a formatted value, for use as the field identifiers in `FieldPosition` objects (for example, `DateFormat.MONTH_FIELD`)

■ Methods for setting various style properties for the formatted values (for example, `NumberFormat.setMaximumFractionDigits()`)

■ Various specialized versions of `format()` that take parameters of the appropriate type instead of `Object`

■ Specialized `parse()` methods that return the appropriate type instead of `Object` (these methods can't be versions of `parseObject()` because methods can't be overloaded on the return type)

`DateFormat` can format and parse `Date` objects as dates, or times, or both. `NumberFormat` can interpret *numbers*—that is, values of any of the Java numeric types—as ordinary numbers, currency values, or percentages. When parsing numbers using the `parse()` method, numbers are returned as instances of `java.lang.Number`.

You may be surprised to learn that, even though `DateFormat` and `NumberFormat` provide all those extra facilities on top of the interface defined by `Format`, they don't actually implement the parsing and formatting functions! `DateFormat` and `NumberFormat` are themselves abstract classes. You must create instances using `getInstance()` or one of its variants.

When you call `getInstance()` on one of these classes, you get a preconfigured instance of `DecimalFormat` (for numbers) or `SimpleDateFormat` (for dates). These classes can be configured with rules and patterns to format and parse values according to the conventions of a wide variety of locales. The configuration rules are documented in the API documentation, and it's possible to use these classes directly to handle specialized formatting and parsing needs. Unless you really need something special, though, it's best to just call one of the `getInstance()` methods on `DateFormat` or `NumberFormat` and use the object that is returned.

Why? If `DecimalFormat` and `SimpleDateFormat` are so configurable, why aren't they the standard objects? Why the extra level of inheritance, with abstract classes that don't actually provide an implementation of the core functionality? The answer is that, as configurable as they are, `DecimalFormat` and `SimpleDateFormat` may not be flexible enough to handle all the locales in the world. Some locales may require entirely new formatting classes to be written if they are to be supported correctly. If you asked for a format object for such a locale, you would actually get an instance of one of the new classes. Keeping the basic interface definition and factory methods in a separate class, independent of the actual functionality, makes it easier to support such atypical locales without having to modify any of the classes in the core library.

Formatting and Parsing Textual Messages

Being able to format and parse dates, times, and numbers is nice, but such items rarely occur in isolation; usually they are embedded in other text. The `MessageFormat` class is designed for formatting and parsing textual strings that may incorporate other data items. Error messages are a prime example of what `MessageFormat` is good for, but the facility can be used to prepare any text meant for human conceptions, including GUI elements and printed reports.

In many respects, `MessageFormat` is similar to C's `printf()` function. In fact, there is a static method, `MessageFormat.format(String, Object[])`, which is very similar indeed. One parameter is a format string that functions as a pattern, with embedded format specifiers indicating how the other parameters should be processed and substituted into the pattern string. Unlike `printf()`, however, the `format()` method doesn't actually print the formatted message; it just returns it as a `String`. Because Java doesn't permit methods to take a variable number of parameters, the additional items are passed as an `Object` array. Also, the syntax for format specifiers is different; among other things, they incorporate the number of the data item to which they refer. This is because localization of text often involves changing not only the words, but the structure of sentences. Thus, the item that occurs first in the English version of a sentence may have to come last in the German version. (Format patterns are usually taken from a localized resource bundle rather than being included directly in the code.)

Format specifiers within patterns are surrounded by curly braces. Here is a simple example:

```
MessageFormat.format("No entry for {0} in the database", new Object[] {name});
```

The format specifier `{0}` indicates that the first element of the array (with index `0`) should be substituted into the string at that point. The element should be a `String`.

What if one of your data items is not a `String`? One solution is to format it separately (for example, with `NumberFormat` or `DateFormat`) and use the resulting `String`. There's no need to do that, however, because you can include the fact that the element is a number or date in the format specifier. This example includes a number, a string, and a date:

```
// numAppt is an int, pName is a String, and apptDate is a Date

MessageFormat.format("{0,number} appointments for {1} on {2,date,medium}",
                new Object[] {new Integer(numAppt), pName, apptDate});
```

There are four possibilities for the type selector after the comma: date, time, number, and choice. The date selector results in a call to DateFormat.getDateInstance() to do the formatting; the time selector results in a call to DateFormat.getTimeInstance(). The number selector by itself uses NumberFormat.getInstance(), but style options can be specified to modify that behavior. The choice selector is explained in the next section.

If the type selector is followed by another comma, then whatever follows (up to the curly brace that ends the format specifier) is a *style option*. The format specifier for the date in the preceding example includes the style option medium, which is one of the styles for dates and times. The others are short, long, and full, and they correspond to the SHORT, MEDIUM, LONG, and FULL constants that DateFormat provides for selecting styles with the getInstance() methods. Additionally, the style for a date or time format can be a valid configuration pattern understood by the SimpleDateFormat class.

The valid styles for number formats are currency, percent, and integer; these styles modify the way the number is interpreted appropriately. The style can also be a configuration pattern accepted by the DecimalFormat class.

So far, I've discussed only the static format(String, Object[]) method. But instances of MessageFormat are useful, too. In fact, the static method is implemented in terms of a throwaway instance:

```
public static String format(String pattern, Object[] arguments) {
    MessageFormat temp = new MessageFormat(pattern);
    return temp.format(arguments);
}
```

Why might you want to create an instance of MessageFormat? There are several possible reasons. For one thing, it would be a good thing to do if you had to print the same message multiple times with different data values. Because parsing and processing the format pattern is reasonably expensive, it would be a good idea to do so only once if the pattern is going to be reused many times. Another reason is that the static version of the method uses the default locale, whereas instances can be created for specific locales. Therefore, you should never use the static method in a *multilingual* program. You would also create an instance of MessageFormat if you were using it to parse text rather than to format it (more about that topic later).

The final reason why MessageFormat instances are useful is that they give us more flexibility. With an instance, you can build a pattern programmatically. For example, the preceding example used three different objects; but you could have written it this way:

```
MessageFormat msg = new MessageFormat("{0} appointments for {1} on {2}");
msg.setFormat(0, NumberFormat.getInstance());
// format 1, for the string, is already set.
msg.setFormat(2, DateFormat.getDateInstance(Date.MEDIUM));

msg.format(new Object[] {new Integer(numAppt), pName, apptDate});
```

That seems like an awful lot of trouble to go through when you could just encode the information in the format string. But it can be useful in some complicated situations—and it is particularly useful if you have to include some data that is not a number, date, time, or string. You can extend the `Format` class to handle locale-independent formatting of any data type you want, but you can't extend the `MessageFormat` format specifier syntax to support your new `Format` classes. You can, however, make use of the new classes by explicitly including them with the `setFormat()` method, as just shown.

I mentioned earlier that the format specifiers include the ordinal number of the array element to which they refer, so that they can be reordered if necessary during the localization process. It's important to note that the numbers used to identify the specifiers in the `setFormat()` call are different from the numbers actually included in the format specifiers. The numbers used by the `setFormat()` method always refer to the specifiers in the order they occur in the pattern string, starting with zero. That's a problem for internationalization, because when the order of the specifiers changes during localization, the numbers used to set the format objects for the message have to change, too. I hope this problem is resolved in a future Java release.

As you can with the other subclasses of `Format`, you can use `MessageFormat` for parsing as well as formatting. The `parse()` methods return arrays of `Object`, and the patterns are the same as for formatting. The intent is that a message formatted with a pattern can be parsed with the same pattern. Although this logic may fail in some situations (including some uses of `ChoiceFormat`, described in the next section), it works in general.

There are two other things to know about `MessageFormat`. There is currently an arbitrary limit of 10 format specifiers for a single pattern. There's no need for a limit at all, and a comment in the source code indicates that this limit may someday be removed. (On the other hand, if you are using format patterns with 83 specifiers, you should probably consider a different strategy.)

> **TIP**
>
> If you have to include a { or } character in a format pattern, you must enclose it within the string in single quotation marks. If you have to include a single quote character, double it. This quoting mechanism is, in my opinion, a little strange and inconsistent with the backslash-quoting mechanism used for the first level of quoting in Java strings. However, there are problems with using that mechanism in this case as well, so it is difficult to say whether another option may have been better. Just remember to be on the lookout for occasions when any of those three characters must appear in a string formatted by `MessageFormat`.

The ChoiceFormat Class

Occasionally, some part of the text surrounding a value has to change depending on the value itself. There are many examples of this, but the classic example involves singular and plural forms of words. There was a time when computer users accepted messages like There were 1 match(es) found, but today, people expect better.

Java 1.1 provides the ChoiceFormat class for solving this problem. Assuming that the variable numMatches contains the number of matches found, here's one simple way to format the preceding message:

```
MessageFormat msg = new MessageFormat("There {0} found.");

double[] limits = {0, 1, 2};
String[] choices = {"were no matches",
                    "was 1 match",
                    "were {0,number} matches"};
ChoiceFormat = new ChoiceFormat(limits, choices);
msg.setFormat(0, choice);

msg.format(new Object[] {numMatches})
```

The ChoiceFormat object is created with two arrays: an array of limits and an array of choices. The two arrays should be the same size. The limits array consists of double values, sorted in ascending order. The choices array consists of String values. ChoiceFormat is invoked to format a number. It compares that number to the numbers in the limits array, and formats the number using the element of the choices array that corresponds to the chosen limit. If there are N entries in each array, and we call the number to be formatted x, the matching element is chosen this way:

1	if $x <$ limit[1]
i	if limit[i] $<= x <$ limit[i+1]
N	if limit[N] $<= x$

The selected choice is substituted into the pattern and processed recursively. Note that the third choice in the preceding example—used when numMatches is 2 or greater—has a format specifier embedded within it. That specifier is used to format the number into the message if the third choice is selected.

That's a bit cumbersome, but fortunately there's an easier way. The ChoiceFormat class understands patterns of its own, and you can embed those patterns in the format specifiers for MessageFormat. For example, the previous message can also be specified like this:

```
MessageFormat.format("There {0,choice,0#were no matches¦1#was 1 match¦"
                + "2#were {0,number} matches} found.");
```

ChoiceFormat can also be used to parse strings like this one.

Internationalizing Graphical Interfaces

Java 1.1 provides a new feature for the AWT package that is designed to help with internationalizing graphical interfaces. In Java 1.0, buttons and several other kinds of components displayed their names as a user-visible label. In some cases, the name was useful for determining which button was clicked and was hard-coded into the application, making the label text difficult to localize. Java 1.1 components have an explicit `label`, distinct from the name, that is used for the user-visible display if it has been set. This separation of values allows the label to be localized while enabling you to use the same component name in all locales.

Summary

In this chapter, you learned about internationalization and all the Java 1.1 features that support this task. Internationalization is primarily a problem of managing program structure so that locale-sensitive data and operations are easy to find, and of using appropriate facilities to manipulate certain kinds of data.

Java's resource bundles help with the structuring issues, and a wide variety of other facilities are included for manipulating, formatting, and parsing locale-sensitive data, including dates, times, numbers, and text, in an internationalized manner.

Related Java Technologies

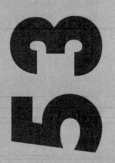

Just-in-Time Compilers

by Michael Morrison

IN THIS CHAPTER

Java programs have been criticized from early on because of their relatively slow execution speeds. Admittedly, compared to natively compiled programs written in languages like C/C++ or Pascal, Java programs are pretty sluggish. However, this complaint has to be weighed heavily against the inherently cross-platform nature of Java, which simply isn't possible with native programs such as those generated by C/C++ and Pascal compilers. In an attempt to alleviate the inherent performance problems associated with processor-independent Java executables, various companies are offering just-in-time (JIT) Java compilers, which compile Java bytecode executables into native programs just before execution.

This chapter explores JIT compilers and how they impact the overall landscape of Java. You learn all about the Java virtual machine and how JIT compilers fit into its organization. Furthermore, you learn about specific types of Java programs that benefit the most from JIT compilation. By the end of this chapter, you'll have a lot better understanding of this exciting technology and how it can improve the performance of your own Java programs.

Understanding the Java VM

To fully understand what a just-in-time (JIT) compiler is and how it fits into the Java runtime system, you must have a solid understanding of the Java virtual machine (VM). The Java VM is a software abstraction for a generic hardware platform and is the primary component of the Java system responsible for portability. The purpose of the VM is to allow Java programs to compile to a uniform executable format, as defined by the VM, that can be run on any platform. Java programs execute within the VM itself, and the VM is responsible for managing all the details of actually carrying out platform-specific functions.

When you compile a Java program, it is compiled to be executed under the VM. Contrast this to C/C++ programs, which are compiled to be run on a real (non-virtual) hardware platform, such as a Pentium processor running Windows 95. The VM itself has characteristics very much like a physical microprocessor, but it is entirely a software construct. You can think of the VM as an intermediary between Java programs and the underlying hardware platform on which all programs must eventually execute.

Even with the VM, at some point, all Java programs must be resolved to a particular underlying hardware platform. In Java, this resolution occurs within each particular VM implementation. The way this works is that Java programs make calls to the VM, which in turn routes them to appropriate native calls on the underlying platform. Knowing this, it's fairly obvious that the VM itself is highly platform dependent. In other words, each different hardware platform or operating system must have a unique VM implementation that routes the generic VM calls to appropriate underlying native services.

Because a VM must be developed for each different platform, it is imperative that it be as lean as possible. Another benefit of having a compact VM is the ability to execute Java programs on systems with fewer resources than desktop computer systems. For example, JavaSoft has plans to use Java in consumer electronics devices such as televisions and cellular phones. A compact, efficient VM is an essential requirement in making Java programs run in highly constrained environments such as these.

Just as all microprocessors have instruction sets that define the operations they can perform, so does the Java VM. VM instructions compile into a format known as *bytecode*, which is the executable format for Java programs that can be run under the VM. You can think of bytecodes as the machine language for the VM. It makes sense, then, that the JDK compiler generates bytecode executables from Java source files. These bytecode executables are always stored as .class files. Figure 53.1 shows the role of the VM in the context of the Java environment.

FIGURE 53.1.

The role of the VM in the Java environment.

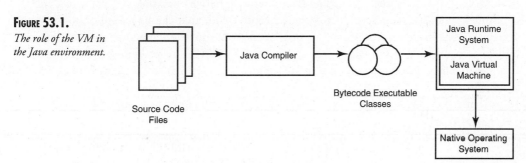

In Figure 53.1, notice how the VM is nestled within the Java runtime system. It is through the VM that executable bytecode Java classes are executed and ultimately routed to appropriate native system calls. A Java program executing within the VM is executed a bytecode at a time. With each bytecode instruction, one or more underlying native system calls may be made by the VM to achieve the desired result. In this way, the VM is completely responsible for handling the routing of generic Java bytecodes to platform-specific code that actually carries out a particular function. The VM has an enormous responsibility and is really the backbone of the entire Java runtime environment. For more gory details about the inner workings of the VM, refer to Chapter 33, "Java Under the Hood: Inside the Virtual Machine."

JIT Compilers and the VM

JIT compilers alter the role of the VM a little by directly compiling Java bytecode into native platform code, thereby relieving the VM of its need to manually call underlying native system services. The purpose of JIT compilers, however, isn't to allow the VM to relax. By compiling bytecodes into native code, execution speed can be greatly improved because the native code can be executed directly on the underlying platform. This stands in sharp contrast to the VM's approach of interpreting bytecodes and manually making calls to the underlying platform. Figure 53.2 shows how a JIT compiler alters the role of the VM in the Java environment.

FIGURE 53.2.

The role of the VM and JIT compiler in the Java environment.

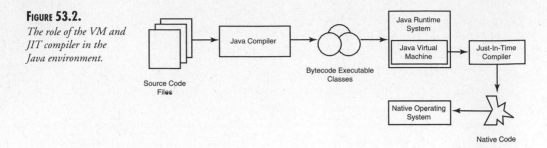

Notice that instead of the VM calling the underlying native operating system, it calls the JIT compiler. The JIT compiler in turn generates native code that can be passed on to the native operating system for execution. The primary benefit of this arrangement is that the JIT compiler is completely transparent to everything except the VM. The really neat thing is that a JIT compiler can be integrated into a system without any other part of the Java runtime system being affected. Furthermore, users don't have to fool with any configuration options; their only clue that a JIT compiler is even installed may simply be the improved execution speed of Java programs.

The integration of JIT compilers at the VM level makes JIT compilers a legitimate example of component software; you can simply plug in a JIT compiler and reap the benefits with no other work or side effects.

Inside a JIT Compiler

Even though JIT compiler integration with the Java runtime system may be transparent to everything outside the VM, you're probably thinking that there are some tricky things going on inside the VM. In fact, the approach used to connect JIT compilers to the VM internally is surprisingly straightforward. In this section, I describe the inner workings of Borland's AppAccelerator JIT compiler, which is the JIT compiler used in Netscape Navigator 3.0. Although other JIT compilers, such as Microsoft's JIT compiler in Internet Explorer, may differ in some ways, they ultimately must tackle the same problems. By understanding Borland's approach with AppAccelerator, you gain insight into the implementation of JIT compilers in general.

The best place to start describing the inner workings of the AppAccelerator JIT compiler is to quickly look at how Java programs are executed *without* a JIT compiler. A Java class that has been loaded into memory by the VM contains a V-table (virtual table), which is a list of the addresses for all the methods in the class. The VM uses the V-table whenever it has to make a call to a particular method. Each address in the V-table points to the executable bytecode for the particular method. Figure 53.3 shows the physical V-table layout for a Java class.

NOTE

The term *V-table* is borrowed from C++, where it stands for *virtual table*. In C++, V-tables are attached to classes that have *virtual methods*, which are methods that can be over-ridden in derived classes. In Java, all methods are virtual, so all classes have V-tables.

FIGURE 53.3.

The physical V-table layout for a Java class.

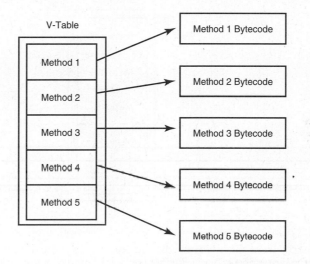

When a JIT compiler is first loaded, the VM pulls a little trick with the V-table to make sure that methods are compiled into native code rather than executed. What happens is that each bytecode address in the V-table is replaced with the address of the JIT compiler itself. Figure 53.4 shows how the bytecode addresses are replaced with the JIT compiler address in the V-table.

FIGURE 53.4.

The physical V-table layout for a Java class with a JIT compiler present.

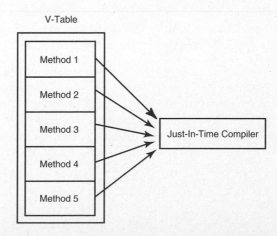

When the VM calls a method through the address in the V-table, the JIT compiler is executed instead. The JIT compiler steps in and compiles the Java bytecode into native code and then patches the native code address back to the V-table. From now on, each call to the method results in a call to the native version. Figure 53.5 shows the V-table with the last method JIT compiled.

FIGURE 53.5.

The physical V-table layout for a Java class with one JIT-compiled method.

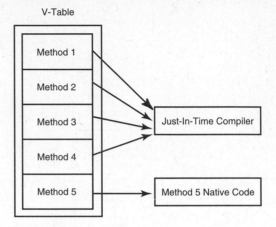

One interesting aspect of this approach to JIT compilation is that it is performed on a method-by-method basis. In other words, the compilation is performed on individual methods, as opposed to entire classes. This is very different from what most of us think of in terms of traditional compilation. Just remember that JIT compilation is anything but traditional!

Another added benefit of the method-by-method approach to compilation is that methods are compiled only when they are called. The first time a method is called, it is compiled; subsequent calls result in the native code being executed. This approach results in only methods being compiled that are actually used, which can yield huge performance benefits. Consider the case of a class in which only four out of ten methods are called. The JIT compiler compiles only those four methods, resulting in a 60-percent savings in compile time (assuming that the compile time for each of the methods is roughly the same).

Just in case you're worried about the original bytecode once a method has been JIT compiled, don't worry, it's not lost. To be honest, I didn't completely tell the truth about how the V-table stores method address information. What really happens is that each method has two V-table entries: one for the bytecode and one for the native code. The native code address is the one that is actually set to the JIT compiler's address. This V-table arrangement is shown in Figure 53.6.

FIGURE 53.6.

The physical V-table layout for a Java class with both bytecode and native code entries.

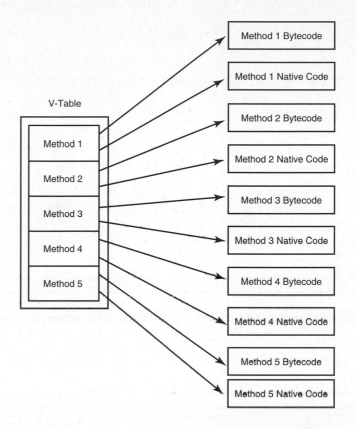

The purpose of having both bytecode and native code entries in the V-table is to allow you to switch between which one is executed. In this way, you can simultaneously execute some methods as bytecode and some using JIT-compiled native code. It isn't immediately apparent what benefits this arrangement will have, but the option of conditionally using the JIT compiler at the method level is something that may come in handy.

Okay, so the JIT compiler is integrated with the VM primarily through the V-table for each class loaded into memory. That's fine, but how is the JIT compiler installed and recognized by the VM in the first place? When the VM is first loaded, it looks for the JIT compiler and loads it if it is found. After loading, the JIT compiler installs itself by hooking into the VM and modifying the class-loading mechanism to reference the compiler. From this point on, the VM doesn't know or care about the compiler. When a class is loaded, the compiler is notified through its hook to the VM and the V-table trickery is carried out.

53

JUST-IN-TIME
COMPILERS

Security and JIT Compilers

You may have some concerns about how JIT compilers impact the security of Java programs—because they seem to have a lot of say over what gets executed and how. You'll be glad to know that JIT compilers alter the security landscape of Java very little. The reason is that JIT compilation is performed as the last stage of execution, after the bytecode has been fully checked by the runtime system. This is very important because native code can't be checked for security breaches like Java bytecode can be. So it is imperative that JIT compilation occur on bytecode that has already been security checked by the runtime system.

It is equally important that native code (code that has been JIT compiled) is executed directly from memory and isn't cached on a local file system to be executed later. Again, doing so would violate the whole idea of checking every Java program immediately before execution. Actually, this approach wouldn't qualify as JIT compilation anyway, because the code wouldn't really be compiled just in time.

In terms of security, the cleanest and safest approach to JIT compilation is to compile bytecode directly to memory and throw it away when it is no longer needed. Because native code is disposable in this scenario, it is important that it can be quickly recompiled from the original bytecode. This is where the approach of compiling only methods as they are called really shines.

JIT Compiler Performance

None of the details surrounding JIT compilers would really matter if they didn't perform their job and speed up the execution speed of Java programs. The whole point of JIT compilation is to realize a performance gain by compiling VM bytecode to native code at run time. Knowing this, let's take a look at just how much of a performance improvement JIT compilers provide.

In assessing JIT compiler performance, it's important to understand exactly where performance gains are made. One common misconception surrounding JIT compilation is the amount of code affected. For example, if a particular JIT compiler improves the execution speed of bytecode by an order of ten (on average), it seems only logical that a Java program executing under this JIT compiler would run ten times faster. However, this isn't the case. The reason is that many programs, especially applets, rely heavily on the Java AWT, which on the Windows platform is written entirely in native C. Because the AWT is already written in native code, programs that rely heavily on the AWT don't reap the same performance gains as programs that depend on pure Java bytecode. A heavily graphical program that makes great use of the AWT may see performance gains by an order of only two or three.

On the other hand, a heavily processing-intensive Java program that uses lots of floating-point math may see performance gains closer to an order of fifteen. This happens because native Pentium code on a Windows machine is very efficient with floating-point math. Of course, other platforms may differ in this regard. Nevertheless, this will probably remain a common theme across all platforms: Nongraphical programs are less affected by JIT compilation than computationally intensive programs.

Now that I've tempered your enthusiasm a little for how greatly JIT compilation impacts performance, let's look at some hard numbers that show the differences between interpreted and JIT-compiled code across different JIT compiler implementations. Figure 53.7 shows a graph of Netscape Navigator 3.0's performance benchmarks for various JIT-compiled Java operations as measured using Pendragon Software's CaffeineMark 2.01 benchmark suite.

FIGURE 53.7.

Performance benchmarks for various JIT-compiled Java operations in Netscape Navigator 3.0.

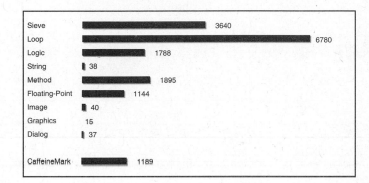

In looking at Figure 53.7, you may be wondering exactly what the numbers mean. The numbers show the relative performance of Netscape Navigator as compared to the Symantec Café applet viewer running in debug mode. The Café applet viewer produces scores of exactly 100 on all benchmark tests, so scores above 100 represent a higher browser execution speed than the Café applet viewer. Likewise, scores lower than 100 represent slower browser execution. You can see that, in some areas, Navigator blows away the Café applet viewer with scores in the thousands. In other areas, however, the JIT-compiled Navigator code slips a little and is actually slower than the interpreted code. Most of these areas are related to graphics operations, which highlights the fact that Café has more efficient graphics support than Navigator.

Figure 53.8 shows the results of running the same benchmark tests on the JIT compiler in Microsoft Internet Explorer 3.0.

FIGURE 53.8.

Performance benchmarks for various JIT-compiled Java operations in Microsoft Internet Explorer 3.0.

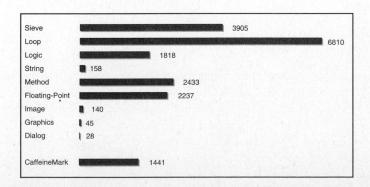

It's interesting to note that Internet Explorer outperformed Navigator on all tests except one. This is expected because Microsoft claims to have the fastest Java implementation around. Even so, this is still the first round of support for JIT compilers, so expect to see plenty of competition in the future between the JIT compiler implementations in different browsers. Marketing hype aside, you can see from these figures that JIT compilation improves performance significantly in many areas, regardless of your browser of choice. Navigator and Internet Explorer both show an overall performance improvement that is over eleven times faster than Café's interpreted approach. Just remember that this improvement depends largely on the type of applet you are running and whether it is processing or graphics intensive.

Alternatives to JIT Compilers

At this point, I hope I have made a pretty decent case in support of JIT compilers as a way of improving the overall performance of Java. Before we settle down with JIT compilers as the only answer to Java's performance woes, it's important to investigate whether there may be other alternatives. I could make some guesses about how Java performance can be improved with other means, but I don't really have to because a couple of other avenues are already being investigated. The rest of this chapter focuses on these other approaches and what they have to offer.

The first alternative to JIT compilers involves *rewriting the Java interpreter* to be more efficient. Faster, more efficient Java interpreters have already been developed by companies such as Microsoft and have improved the performance of Java code by a factor of two or three over the speed of the standard JDK interpreter. Even so, there are practical limitations surrounding interpreted code as a whole. In other words, faster interpreters are great, but they can never single-handedly boost the performance of Java to any large extent. A more aggressive approach is necessary to reap significant gains.

Another approach involves the use of *flash compilers*, which are definitely more aggressive than optimized Java interpreters. Unlike JIT compilers, in which the interpreter selectively compiles functions, flash compilers compile all class files as they are downloaded from a server. This approach completely bypasses the Java interpreter, alleviating the associated overhead. Flash compilers fully compile applets and applications to machine code, resulting in execution speeds on the order of compiled languages such as C++. Furthermore, the compiled machine code can be cached for later execution. The ability to cache code is particularly beneficial on corporate intranets, where users regularly execute the same applets and applications.

Asymetrix has developed a fully functioning flash compiler as part of its SuperCede integrated development environment. The SuperCede flash compiler is also available as a separate Web browser plug-in. The SuperCede flash compiler can generate code with minimal optimizations (for users who want to optimize for download time) or with maximum optimizations (for users who want to optimize for execution speed). The SuperCede flash compiler is implemented in the SuperCede virtual machine, which is the only Java virtual machine to support interoperability between Java and ActiveX.

It is difficult to predict if or how JIT compilers, flash compilers, and improved interpreters will coexist as Java matures. For the time being, it looks as if JIT compilers are the strongest candidates for widespread performance gains, as is evidenced by their inclusion in the two most popular Web browsers (Netscape Navigator and Microsoft Internet Explorer). However, the future is still wide open and Java has plenty of room to improve in terms of performance.

Summary

In this chapter, you learned about just-in-time (JIT) compilers and how they impact the Java runtime system. You began the chapter by peering into the runtime system to see exactly where JIT compilers fit in. In doing so, you learned a great deal about the Java virtual machine (VM), which is largely responsible for the integration of JIT compilers into the runtime system. Once you gained an understanding of how JIT compilers relate to the VM, you moved on to learning about the details of a particular JIT compiler implementation. This look into the inner workings of a real JIT compiler helped give you insight into what exactly a JIT compiler does.

Even though the technical details of JIT compilers are important to understand, little of it would be meaningful if JIT compilers didn't deliver on their promise to improve Java execution speed. For this reason, you spent some time learning about the specific areas where JIT compilers improve Java performance. You also saw benchmark tests comparing JIT compiler performance in the two most popular Web browsers available. Through these benchmark tests, you were able to get an idea of how dramatically JIT compilation can improve performance. You finished up the chapter by looking at a couple of other approaches to improving the performance of Java code and how these other options relate to JIT compilers.

Remote Objects and the Java IDL System

by Mike Fletcher

IN THIS CHAPTER

CHAPTER 54

One of Java's most useful new features is its ability to invoke methods on objects running on a remote virtual machine. This Remote Method Invocation (RMI) facility, along with the CORBA (Common Object Request Broker Architecture) IDL (Interface Definition Language) compiler libraries, make Java a very attractive platform for client/server applications.

This chapter covers both the Java native remote method system and the CORBA interface. An overview of the two different systems is given first, followed by examples using both.

Using Objects in a Networked Environment

From the start, Java has had network capabilities in the form of the classes in the java.net package. The functionality provided by these classes is very low level (raw network streams, or packets). The introduction of the Remote Method Invocation classes and the CORBA interface has raised the level of abstraction. These two packages provide a way of accessing data and methods in the form of objects over a network.

The development and widespread deployment of networks has changed how computers are used. The trend in network computing over the past few years has been towards *client/server* systems. In client/server systems, a local application (the client) provides the interface to a remote database or application (the server). The Web itself is an example of a client/server system: the Web browsers are the clients and the Web sites are the servers.

Client/server systems rely on network services to communicate information between themselves, but for the most part, that is all they send: information. Distributed object systems combine client/server systems with another trend in computing: object-oriented programming. Rather than sending just information, distributed object systems transmit both data and code to manipulate that data. Another benefit of distributed objects is the ability for an object on one host to invoke a method on an object located on a remote host across the network.

Imagine that you were writing a tic-tac-toe game to be played over the network. In a conventional client/server approach, you would need to worry about things such as creating network connections between players and developing a protocol for sending moves back and forth. This is not to say that the game could not be developed, simply that there is a lot more work to be done to do so.

With a distributed object system, many of these lower level details are hidden from the programmer. For example, the server object would have a method that registers a player's move. A player's client would simply obtain a reference to the server object and call the appropriate method on this object (just as if the server object resided on the same machine).

A system for distributed objects has to take many things into consideration: How are remote objects referenced? What representation is used for transmitting an object or parameters for a method call (a process known as *marshaling* in distributed object circles)? What character set is used for strings? Are integers represented as little-endian (the low order byte of a word comes first, as with Motorola processors) or big-endian (the high order byte of a word comes first, as with Intel processors)? What happens if there is a network problem during a method call?

Sun Microsystems is no stranger to solving such problems. Its Remote Procedure Call (RPC) and External Data Representation (XDR) protocols have been in wide use on UNIX platforms for many years. The Network File System (NFS), used to share file systems between machines, and the Network Information System (NIS, formerly known as YP), used to provide a distributed database of configuration information (such as user accounts or host name to IP address databases), are both implemented using RPC.

Why Two Different Solutions?

You may be asking yourself why Sun is providing two different solutions to solve the same problem. The answer is that each of the remote object systems has its own particular advantages.

The RMI system provides Java-native access to remote objects. Because it is written specifically for Java in Java, the RMI system allows transparent access to remote objects. Once a reference is obtained for a remote object, it is treated just like any other Java object. The code accessing the remote object may not even be aware that the object does not reside on the same host. The downside to this approach is that the RMI system may only be used to interface to servers written in Java.

The IDL interface provides access to clients and servers using the industry standard CORBA protocol specifications. An application that uses the IDL compiler can connect to any object server that complies with the CORBA standards and uses a compatible transport mechanism. Unlike the RMI system, CORBA is intended to be a language-neutral system. Objects must be specified using the OMG Interface Definition Language, and access must be through library routines that translate the calls into the appropriate CORBA messages.

Remote Method Invocation System

The RMI system uses Java interfaces and a special "stub" compiler to provide transparent access to remote objects. An interface is defined by specifying the methods provided by the remote object. Next, a server class is defined to implement the interface. The stub compiler is invoked to generate classes that act as the glue between the local representation of an object and the remote object residing on the server.

The RMI system also provides a naming service that allows servers to bind object references to URLs such as `rmi://foohost.com/ObjectName`. A client passes a URL to the `Naming` class's `lookup()` method, which returns a reference to an object implementing the appropriate interface.

Interface Definition Language and CORBA

CORBA is a part of the Object Management Group's (OMG) Object Management Architecture. The OMG is an industry consortium formed in 1989 to help provide standards for object-oriented technology. The architecture consists of four standards:

- **Common Object Request Broker Architecture (CORBA).** This standard specifies the interactions between a client object and an Object Request Broker (ORB). The ORB receives an invocation request, determines which object can handle the request, and passes the request and parameters to the servicing object.
- **Common Object Services Specification (COSS).** COSS provides a standard interface for operations such as creating and relocating objects.
- **Common Facilities.** This standard specifies common application functionalities such as printing, e-mail, and document management.
- **Applications Objects.** These standard objects provide for common business functions.

NOTE

For a more complete introduction to CORBA and related standards, check out the OMG's home page at http://www.omg.org/. Another useful URL is http://www.omg.org/ed.htm, which has a pointer to a list of books on distributed objects (and CORBA in particular).

The Java IDL system provides a mapping from the CORBA object model into Java classes. The IDL compiler provides stub classes. These stubs call an ORB core that handles details such as determining the transport mechanism to use (such as Sun's NEO or the OMG's Internet Inter-ORB Protocol (IIOP)) and marshaling parameters.

Using the `java.rmi` Package

Let's take a look at the Java-native remote method system. The following sections provide a more detailed explanation of how the RMI system works and what you need to do to use it. A sample service is developed that provides `java.io.InputStream` and `java.io.OutputStream` compatible access to a file located on a remote machine.

An Overview of `java.rmi`

The RMI system consists of several different classes and interfaces. The following sections give brief explanations of what the important ones do and how they are used.

The java.rmi.Remote Interface

The RMI system is based on remote interfaces through which a client accesses the methods of a remote object. These interfaces must be declared to extend java.rmi.Remote, and each method of an interface must indicate that it throws java.rmi.RemoteException in addition to any other exceptions.

The java.rmi.server.RemoteServer Class

The RemoteServer provides a superclass for servers that provide remote access to objects. The second step in developing an RMI server is to create a server class that implements your remote interface. This server class should extend one of the subclasses of RemoteServer (the UnicastRemoteObject is the only RemoteServer subclass provided by the RMI system at this time) and must contain the actual code for the methods declared in the remote interface.

After the server class has been created, the RMI stub compiler (rmic) is given the interface for the class and the server that provides the implementation used to create several "glue" classes. These glue classes work behind the scenes to handle all the nasty details such as contacting the remote virtual machine, passing arguments, and retrieving a return value (if any).

The java.rmi.Naming Class

The Naming class provides a way for server classes to make remote objects visible to clients. All the Naming class's methods are static and do not require an instance to use. A server that wants to make an object available calls the bind() or rebind() method with the name of the object (passed as a String) and a reference to an object implementing an interface extending Remote. Clients can call the lookup() method with a String representation of the URL for the object they want to access. RMI URLs are of the form rmi://host[:port]/name, where *host* is the name of the host on which the object's server resides (with an optional *port* number) and *name* is the name of the object.

Exceptions

The RMI package provides several exceptions used to indicate errors during remote method calls. The most common exception is the generic RemoteException used to indicate that some sort of problem occurred during a call. All methods of an interface extending the Remote interface must note that they can throw this exception. Several other more specific exceptions such as StubNotFoundException (thrown when the RMI system cannot find the glue classes generated by rmic) and RemoteRuntimeException (thrown when a RuntimeException occurs on the server during a method call) are subclasses of RemoteException.

The Naming class has two exceptions—NotBoundException and AlreadyBound—that are thrown to indicate that a given name either hasn't been bound to an object or has already been bound. All the naming methods can also throw a java.net.UnknownHostException if the host specified in the URL is invalid; they can throw a `java.net.MalformedURLException` if the given URL is not syntactically correct.

RMI Example Architecture

To demonstrate the `java.rmi` package, we will create a (very simple) file server. This server accepts requests from a remote caller and returns a `RemoteObject` that is used by wrapper classes to provide `java.io.InputStream` and `java.io.OutputStream` objects that read or write from the remote file.

The `RemoteInputHandle` Interface

First off, we define the interface with which our input wrapper class interacts with the remote file (see Listing 54.1). The `RemoteInputHandle` class provides methods that correspond to those required by the `java.io.InputStream` abstract class. The interface simply defines the methods required for an `InputStream` object. Each method can throw a `RemoteException` as noted in the `throws` clause.

Listing 54.1. The `RemoteInputHandle` interface.

```
import java.rmi.*;
import java.io.IOException;
public interface RemoteInputHandle
    extends Remote
{
  public int available( )
    throws IOException, RemoteException;

  public void close( )
    throws IOException, RemoteException;

  public void mark( int readlimit )
    throws RemoteException;

  public boolean markSupported( )
    throws RemoteException;

  public int read( )
    throws IOException, RemoteException;

  public int read( byte b[] )
    throws IOException, RemoteException;

  public int read( byte b[], int off, int len )
    throws IOException, RemoteException;

  public void reset( )
    throws IOException, RemoteException;

  public long skip( long n )
    throws IOException, RemoteException;
}
```

The `RemoteInputHandleImpl` Class

Next up is the `RemoteInputHandleImpl` class, which provides the implementation for the `RemoteInputHandle` interface just defined (see Listing 54.2). The `RemoteFileServerImpl` class creates a new input handle implementation when a `RemoteInputHandle` is requested. The constructor for the implementation class takes one argument: the `InputStream` for which we are providing remote access. This makes the handle more useful because we can provide remote access to any local object that extends `InputStream`. This stream is saved in an instance variable (`inStream`) after the `UnicastRemoteServer` superclass's constructor is called. The superclass constructor is called because it has to set things up to listen for requests from remote clients.

Listing 54.2. The `RemoteInputHandleImpl` class.

```
import java.rmi.*;
import java.rmi.server.UnicastRemoteObject;
import java.rmi.RMISecurityManager;

public class RemoteInputHandleImpl
    extends UnicastRemoteObject
    implements RemoteInputHandle
{
  private InputStream inStream;
  public RemoteInputHandleImpl( InputStream in )
    throws RemoteException
  {
    super( );

    inStream = in;
  }
```

Next comes the actual code implementing the methods of the `RemoteInputHandle` interface (see Listing 54.3). Each method simply calls the corresponding method on `inStream` and returns the return value from that call (as appropriate). The RMI system takes care of returning the result—as well as any exceptions that occur—to the calling object on the remote machine.

Listing 54.3. The methods of the `RemoteInputHandleImpl` class.

```
public int available( )
  throws IOException, RemoteException
{
  return inStream.available();
}

public void close( )
  throws IOException, RemoteException
{
  inStream.close( );
}
```

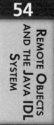

54

REMOTE OBJECTS
AND THE JAVA IDL
SYSTEM

continues

Listing 54.3. continued

```
public synchronized void mark( int readlimit )
  throws RemoteException
{
  inStream.mark( readlimit );
}

public boolean markSupported( )
  throws RemoteException
{
  return inStream.markSupported( );
}

public int read( )
  throws IOException, RemoteException
{
  return inStream.read( );
}

public int read( byte b[] )
  throws IOException, RemoteException
{
  return inStream.read( b );
}

public int read( byte b[], int off, int len )
  throws IOException, RemoteException
{
  return inStream.read( b, off, len );
}

public synchronized void reset( )
  throws IOException, RemoteException
{
  inStream.reset( );
}

public long skip( long n )
  throws IOException, RemoteException
{
  return inStream.skip( n );
}
}
```

The `RemoteInputStream` Class

The `RemoteInputStream` class extends the abstract `InputStream` class and uses the `RemoteInputHandle` interface. The constructor first contacts a `RemoteFileServer` to obtain a `RemoteInputHandle` reference for the path given and then stores this handle in an instance variable. The `InputStream` methods are mapped into the corresponding calls on the `RemoteInputHandle` (that is, the `RemoteInputStream` read() method calls the read() method on the `RemoteInputHandle` reference obtained by the constructor).

> **NOTE**
>
> You may wonder why we are using a wrapper class when all it does is turn around and call the same method on the interface. The reason is that we want to provide a class that can be used any place an `InputStream` or `OutputStream` can be used. Although this approach increases the overhead because we have to make an extra method call, the ability to use our remote streams as drop-in replacements outweighs the cost of that extra call.
>
> For example, you can create a `PrintStream` using a `RemoteOutputStream` for a log file for an application. Anything you print to this `PrintStream` is written to the log file on the remote machine. Without the wrapper class, you would have to individually extend each class to use the `RemoteInputHandle` or `RemoteOutputHandle` as needed.

We'll start out with the necessary imports and the class definition (see Listing 54.4). We need access to the `java.io` classes because the `RemoteInputStream` extends `InputStream`. We also need access to the RMI `Naming` class so that we can use the `lookup()` method to get a `RemoteInputHandle` from the server. There are two constructors for the class: One takes a path name as the argument and contacts the file server residing on the same host, and the other takes a remote host name to contact as well.

Listing 54.4. The RemoteInputStream class.

```
import java.io.*;
import java.rmi.RemoteException;
import java.rmi.Naming;
import java.rmi.NotBoundException;

public class RemoteInputStream
    extends InputStream
{
  private RemoteInputHandle in;

  public RemoteInputStream( String path )
    throws IOException, RemoteException, NotBoundException
  {
    String url = "rmi://localhost/RFSI";
    RemoteFileServer rfs = (RemoteFileServer) Naming.lookup( url );
    in = rfs.getInStream( path );
  }

  public RemoteInputStream( String path, String host )
    throws IOException, RemoteException, NotBoundException
  {
    String url = "rmi://" + host + "/RFSI";
    RemoteFileServer rfs = (RemoteFileServer) Naming.lookup( url );
    in = rfs.getInStream( path );
  }
```

54

REMOTE OBJECTS
AND THE JAVA IDL
SYSTEM

Next, each of the `InputStream` methods is defined (see Listing 54.5). The code for each method tries to call the corresponding method on the handle object. If a `RemoteException` occurs, an `IOException` is thrown with the message from the `RemoteException` as its message.

Listing 54.5. The `InputStream` methods of the `RemoteInputStream` class.

```
public int available( )
  throws IOException
{
  try {
    return in.available( );
  } catch( RemoteException e ) {
    throw new IOException( "Remote error: " + e );
  }
}

public void close( )
  throws IOException
{
  try {
    in.close( );
  } catch( RemoteException e ) {
    throw new IOException( "Remote error: " + e );
  }
}

public synchronized void mark( int readlimit )
{
  try {
    in.mark( readlimit );
  } catch( Exception e ) {
    System.err.println(
        "RemoteInputStream::mark: Remote error: " + e );
  }
}

public boolean markSupported( ) {
  try {
    return in.markSupported( );
  } catch( RemoteException e ) {
    return false;          // Assume mark not supported
  }
}

public int read( )
  throws IOException
{
  try {
    return in.read( );
  } catch( RemoteException e ) {
    throw new IOException( "Remote error: " + e );
  }
}

public int read( byte b[] )
  throws IOException
{
```

```
    try {
      return in.read( b );
    } catch( RemoteException e ) {
      throw new IOException( "Remote error: " + e );
    }
  }

  public int read( byte b[], int off, int len )
    throws IOException
  {
    try {
      return in.read( b, off, len );
    } catch( RemoteException e ) {
      throw new IOException( "Remote error: " + e );
    }
  }

  public synchronized void reset( )
    throws IOException
  {
    try {
      in.reset( );
    } catch( RemotcExccption e ) {
      throw new IOException( "Remote error: " + e );
    }
  }

  public long skip( long n )
    throws IOExoeption
  {
    try {
      return in.skip( n );
    } catch( RemoteException e ) {
      throw new IOException( "Remote error: " + e );
    }
  }
}
```

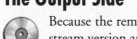

The Output Side

Because the remote interface, implementation, and the wrapper class for the output stream version are, for the most part, identical to those for input stream, they are not given here. The methods in the interface correspond to those for `java.io.OutputStream` instead of `InputStream`, and the `RemoteOutputStream` object extends `OutputStream`. The complete code for all the output classes is contained on the CD-ROM that accompanies this book.

The RemoteFileServer Interface and the RemoteFileServerImpl Class

The `RemoteFileServer` interface provides two methods that the remote input and output stream classes use to obtain handles (see Listing 54.6).

Listing 54.6. The `RemoteFileServer` interface.

```
public interface RemoteFileServer
    extends java.rmi.Remote
{

  public RemoteOutputHandle getOutStream( String path )
    throws java.rmi.RemoteException;

  public RemoteInputHandle getInStream( String path )
    throws java.rmi.RemoteException;
}
```

The server itself is very simple. It consists of a constructor that calls the `UnicastRemoteServer` superclass, a method that does some sanity checking on the path names requested, implementations of the interface methods, and a `main()` method that allows the server to be started (see Listing 54.7). We start off as usual with the `import` statements, class declaration, and the constructor. Note that there is a `static` class variable `PATH_SEPARATOR`, which should be changed to whatever character separates directory components on your operating system.

Listing 54.7. The `RemoteFileServerImpl` class.

```
import java.io.*;
import java.rmi.*;
import java.rmi.server.UnicastRemoteServer;
import java.rmi.server.StubSecurityManager;

public class RemoteFileServerImpl
    extends UnicastRemoteServer
    implements RemoteFileServer
{
  // Path component separator.  Change as appropriate to your OS.
  public static char PATH_SEPARATOR = '/';

  public RemoteFileServerImpl( )
    throws RemoteException
  {
    super( );      // Call superclass' constructor
    // No class specific initialization needed.
  }
```

The `checkPathName()` method shown in Listing 54.8 does some rudimentary checking to ensure that the path name does not point outside the current directory or one of its subdirectories. The code that checks for an *absolute path* (that is, a path that starts at the root directory or with a specific drive) should be edited as appropriate for your platform.

Listing 54.8. The `RemoteFileServerImpl.checkPathName()` method.

```
public boolean checkPathName( String path )
{
  // No absolute path names (i.e. ones beginning with a slash or drive)
  // UNIX Version
  if( path.charAt( 0 ) == PATH_SEPARATOR ) {
    return false;
  }
  // Wintel Version
  /*
    if( path.charAt( 1 ) == ':' && path.charAt( 2 ) == PATH_SEPARATOR ) {
      return false;
    }
  */

// No references to parent directory with ".."
  for( int i = 0; i < path.length() - 1; i++ ) {
    if( path.charAt( i ) == '.'
        && path.charAt( i + 1 ) == '.' ) {
      return false;
    }
  }
  return true;      // Path's OK
}
```

Next comes the code implementing the methods of our remote interface (see Listing 54.9). Each calls `checkPathName()` on the path and then tries to open either a `FileInputStream` or `FileOutputStream` as appropriate. Any exception that occurs while obtaining a stream is rethrown as a `RemoteException` (although there is no reason the interface cannot throw the appropriate exceptions). Once the stream has been opened, a `RemoteInputHandleImpl` or `RemoteOutputHandleImpl` object is created as appropriate with the just-opened stream. The handle is then returned to the caller.

Listing 54.9. The methods of the `RemoteFileServerImpl` class.

```
public RemoteInputHandle getInStream( String path )
  throws java.rmi.RemoteException
{
  FileInputStream file = null; // Used to hold file for input

  // Log that we're opening a stream
  System.err.println( "RFSI::getInStream( \"" + path + "\" )" );

  // Check that the path name is legal or gripe
  if( !checkPathName( path ) ) {
    RemoteException e =
      new RemoteException( "Invalid pathname '" + path + "'." );
    throw e;
  }
```

54

REMOTE OBJECTS
AND THE JAVA IDL
SYSTEM

continues

Listing 54.9. continued

```
    // Try and open a FileInputStream for the path
    try {
      file = new FileInputStream( path );
    } catch( FileNotFoundException e ) {
      // File doesn't exist, so throw remote exception with that message
      RemoteException r =
        new RemoteException( "File does not exist: "
                              + e.getMessage() );
      throw r;
    } catch( IOException e ) {
      // Problem opening file, so throw exception saying that
      RemoteException r =
        new RemoteException( "Error opening file: "
                              + e.getMessage() );
      throw r;
    }

    // Return value is a RemoteInputHandle for an RIH implementation
    // object created with the file we just opened as its input stream.
    RemoteInputHandle retval =
      new RemoteInputHandleImpl( file );
    return retval;        // Return handle to caller
  }

  public RemoteOutputHandle getOutStream( String path )
    throws java.rmi.RemoteException
  {
    FileOutputStream file = null; // Used to hold file for output
    // Log that we're opening a stream
    System.err.println( "RFSI::getOutStream( \"" + path + "\" )" );
    // Check that the path name is legal or gripe
    if( !checkPathName( path ) ) {
      RemoteException e =
        new RemoteException( "Invalid pathname '" + path + "'." );
      throw e;
    }

    // Try and open FileOutputStream for the path
    try {
      file = new FileOutputStream( path );
    } catch( IOException e ) {
      // Problem opening file for output, so throw exception saying so
      RemoteException r =
        new RemoteException( "Error opening file: "
                              + e.getMessage() );
      throw r;
    }

    // Return value is a RemoteOutputHandle for an ROH implementation
    // object created with the file just opened as its output stream
    RemoteOutputHandle retval = new RemoteOutputHandleImpl( file );
    return retval;      // Return the handle
  }
```

Finally, we come to the `main()` method, which can be used to start a standalone server from the command line (see Listing 54.10). The first thing this method does is to create a `StubSecurityManager`—a `SecurityManager` context appropriate for a standalone remote object server. Next, `main()` creates a `RemoteFileServerImpl` object and binds it to the name `RFSI`. If an exception occurs during object creation or binding, the name of the exception is noted and the server exits.

Listing 54.10. The `RemoteFileServerImpl.main()` method.

```
public static void main( String args[] )
{
  // Create and install stub security manager
  System.setSecurityManager( new StubSecurityManager( ) );

  try {
    System.err.println( "RFSI::main: creating RFSI." );

    // Create a new server implementation object
    RemoteFileServerImpl i = new RemoteFileServerImpl( );

    // Bind our server object to a name so clients may contact us.
    /* The URL will be "rmi://host/RFSI", with host replaced with */
    // the name of the host we're running on.
    String name = "RFSI";
    System.err.println( "RFSI::main: binding to name: " + name );
    Naming.rebind( name, i );
  } catch( Exception e ) {
    // Problem creating server.  Log exception and die.
    System.err.println( "Exception creating server: "
                        + e + "\n" );
    e.printStackTrace( System.err );
    System.exit( 1 );
  }
}
```

The `rfsClient` Class

To demonstrate how to use our remote files, we now develop a very simple client that opens a remote output file and writes a message to it (see Listing 54.11). An input stream is obtained and the stream's contents are read back. The output filename is defined as `outputfile` and the input filename defaults to `inputfile` (however, if an argument is given on the command line, that name is used instead). The host contacted is defined as the local host, but you can change the URL used to point to a remote machine if you have access to more than one host.

Listing 54.11. The rfsClient class.

```java
import java.io.*;
import java.rmi.*;

public class rfsClient
{
  public static void main( String args[] ) {
    System.setSecurityManager( new java.rmi.RMISecurityManager() );

    // Contact remote file server running on same machine
    String url = "rmi://localhost/";

    // Default name of file to read
    String infile = "inputfile";

    // Try and open an output stream to a file called "outputfile"
    try {
      OutputStream out = new RemoteOutputStream( "outputfile");
      PrintWriter ps = new PrintWriter( out );
      ps.println( "Testing println on remote file." );
      ps.println( new java.util.Date() );
      ps.flush();
      ps.close();
      ps = null;
      out = null;
    } catch( Exception e ) {
      System.err.println( "Error on getOutStream: " + e );
      e.printStackTrace();
      System.exit( 1 );
    }

    // If we were given a command line argument, use that as the
    // input file name
    if( args.length != 0 ) {
      infile = args[ 0 ];
    }

    // Try and open an output stream on a file
    try {
      InputStream in = new RemoteInputStream( infile );
      DataInputStream ds = new DataInputStream( in );
      // Read each line of the file and print it out
      try {
        String line = ds.readLine( );
        while( line != null ) {
          System.err.println( "Read: " + line );
          line = ds.readLine( );
        }
      } catch( EOFException e ) {
        System.err.println( "EOF" );
      }
    } catch( Exception e ) {
      System.err.println( "Error on getInStream: " + e );
      e.printStackTrace( );
      System.exit( 1 );
    }
    System.exit( 0 );      // Exit gracefully
  }
}
```

Using the IDL Compiler

The following sections cover the CORBA-based IDL compiler and support classes. First, we'll explain exactly what the IDL compiler does and how it maps objects from the IDL definitions to Java equivalents. A simple example using the IDL system is also given.

The IDL-to-Java Compiler

The IDL compiler takes an object definition in the CORBA IDL format and generates a Java version. Table 54.1 shows several of these mappings.

Table 54.1. Sample IDL-to-Java mappings.

IDL Feature	Java Mapping
module	package
boolean	boolean
char	char
octet	byte
string	java.lang.String
short	short
long	int
long long	long
float	float
enum	A Java class with a static final int member for each enum member
struct	A Java class; all methods and instance variables are public
interface	A Java interface; the compiler also generates a stub that implements the interface if you choose
exception	A Java class that extends the omg.corba.UserException class

As Table 54.1 shows, most of the mappings are straightforward. Some IDL constructs do not have a direct Java equivalent. One example of this is a union (a structure that can hold one of several different types of components); in this case, the union is a class with a discriminator (which indicates the type of information the union currently holds) and access methods for each possible content type.

Another difference between Java and the IDL model is in the way parameters are passed to method calls. Java passes all parameters by value; the IDL model defines three ways parameters can be passed: in (which is a pass-by value, just as it is with Java); out (which is a pass-by reference—meaning that the parameter is passed so that it can be modified); and inout (which is a cross between a pass-by value and a pass-by reference—the value remains the same until the method returns).

IDL Support Classes

With the java.rmi system, the remote objects are themselves servers. The CORBA model depends on a separate request broker to receive requests and actually call methods. The IDL system provides a class to represent the ORB. The generic ORB object provides a very important method: resolve(). This method takes a URL and a remote object reference created from a stub class of the appropriate type and binds the reference to the server. The format for IDL URLs is idl:*orb package*://*hostname[:port]*/*object*, where *orb package* is the Java package that provides access to a given type of ORB (sunw.door is the simple ORB that comes with the IDL package, sunw.neo is Sun's NEO ORB, and so on); *hostname* and the optional *port* are used to determine where to contact the ORB; and *object* is the name of the object requested from the ORB.

The CORBA runtime system also defines mappings from the standard CORBA exceptions to Java exceptions. All IDL-defined exceptions are subclasses of one of two classes: sunw.corba.SystemException (for all exceptions raised by the CORBA system itself) and sunw.corba.UserException (used as the superclass for all user-defined exceptions in IDL objects).

IDL System Example

To demonstrate the use of the IDL compiler and the CORBA interface, we will develop a simple example. Our object will represent a conference room. The goal is to allow clients to query the state of the room (whether it is available or in use).

Room IDL Definition

The first step in creating our example is to write the IDL definition for the object. The interface defines an enumerated type, roomStatus, which notes whether the room is in use or available. A room has (for our purposes) two attributes: a name and a status. The interface also provides a method to set the status of the room.

The IDL-to-Java compile (idlgen) takes this definition and creates several interfaces and classes. These classes are placed in a package called unleashed. The classes implementing the roomStatus enumeration are placed in the unleashed.Room package as shown in Listing 54.12.

Listing 54.12. The IDL for a room (room.idl).

```
module unleashed {
  interface Room {
    // Status of a room
    enum roomStatus { available, inUse };
```

```
  // Room name
  readonly attribute string Name;

  // Current room status
  readonly attribute roomStatus Status;

  // Method to set the status of the Room
  void setStatus( in roomStatus newStatus );
  };
};
```

The RoomImpl Class

The first class that must be defined is the implementation object for the room object (see Listing 54.13). This is analogous to creating a subclass of RemoteServer when using the RMI classes. Unlike the RMI system, however, the server is a separate ORB object.

The implementation must implement the unleashed.RoomServant interface (which was generated by idlgen). The RoomImpl class has two instance variables to hold the name of the room and its status. The constructor takes two arguments, which are copied into these instance variables. Normally, each attribute of an interface has a get() and set() method defined for it (get*Attribute*() and set*Attribute*()). Because both of the attributes on the room interface are read-only, only the getName() and getStatus() methods are defined by the compiler. Our implementation simply returns the contents of the instance variables. The setStatus() method likewise performs a bounds check (using the enumeration class created by the compiler) to set the status member.

Listing 54.13. The unleashed.RoomImpl class.

```
package unleashed;

public class RoomImpl implements unleashed.RoomServant
{
  private String name;
  private int status;
  public RoomImpl( String n, int s )
    throws sunw.corba.EnumerationRangeException
  {
    name = n;
    status = unleashed.Room.roomStatus.narrow( s );
  }
  public String getName( ) {
    return name;
  }
  public int getStatus( ) {
    return status;
  }
  public void setStatus( int newStatus ) {
    status = unleashed.Room.roomStatus.narrow( newStatus );
  }
}
```

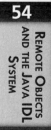

54

REMOTE OBJECTS
AND THE JAVA IDL
SYSTEM

The RoomServer Class

Now that we have the implementation for the room object, we have to create a server class (see Listing 54.14). The server uses the simple `sunw.door` ORB that comes with the IDL system. It first calls `sunw.door.Orb.initialize()` to start the ORB listening for requests from clients. An implementation object is created and passed to the `RoomSkeleton.createRef()` method. This method, created by the IDL compiler, returns a `RoomRef` suitable for passing to the ORB's `publish()` method. This accomplishes the same thing as using the `java.rmi.Naming.bind()` method—that is, binding the object reference to a name accessible by a URL.

Listing 54.14. The RoomServer class.

```
package unleashed;

public class RoomServer
{
  static String pathName = "room.server";
  public static void main( String arg[] ) {
    sunw.door.Orb.initialize( );
    try {
      RoomRef r =
        RoomSkeleton.createRef(
          new RoomImpl( "Room 203", unleashed.Room.roomStatus.available ) );
      sunw.door.Orb.publish( pathName, r );
    } catch( sunw.door.naming.Failure e ) {
      System.err.println( "Couldn't bind object in naming context: " + e );
      System.exit( 1 );
    }
    System.err.println( "Room server setup and bound on port "
                        + sunw.door.Orb.getDefaultPort() );
  }
}
```

The Client Applet

The last step is to create a client to access the remote object. `RoomClient` is an applet that connects to a room object and provides a way of querying the current status and changing the status. An instance variable of type `unleashed.RoomRef` is used to hold the currently active remote object reference. The `init()` method creates the user interface. A `TextField` is created to allow the user to enter the host name to connect to. Fields are also created to show the name and status of the room once a server has been contacted. Finally, three buttons are created: one to cause the applet to connect to the room object, one to request that the room be reserved (marked as "in use"), and one to request that the room be released (marked as "available").

The `connect()` method uses the host name entered by the user to construct a URL for the room server residing on that machine. The URL assumes that the server is running on the default `sunw.door` ORB port. The `connect()` method creates a reference to a `RoomStub` and uses the sunw.corba.Orb.resolve() method to resolve the URL to an object reference. If an exception occurs, the error message is displayed in the applet's status area and printed to System.err.

The updateStatus() method uses the room reference obtained by connect() to determine the name and status of the room. The information is printed to the corresponding field of the interface. Any exceptions are noted in the status line and logged to System.err. Both reserve() and release() call the setStatus() method on the RoomRef object. The only difference between the two methods is the constant from the unleashed.Room.roomStatus class they use.

Finally, the action() method is called whenever the user clicks one of the buttons. This method determines which button was clicked and calls the corresponding method. Listing 54.15 shows the complete RoomClient class; Figure 54.1 shows the RoomClient applet in use.

Listing 54.15. The RoomClient class.

```
import java.net.URL;
import java.awt.*;
import java.applet.Applet;
public class RoomClient extends Applet
{
  unleashed.RoomRef r;
  String serverUrl;
  TextField nameField;
  TextField statusField;
  TextField hostField;
  Button connectButton;
  Button reserveButton;
  Button releaseButton;

  public void init( ) {
    Panel p;
    setLayout( new BorderLayout() );
    p = new Panel();
    p.setLayout( new FlowLayout() );
    p.add( new Label( "Host: " ) );
    p.add( hostField = new TextField( 30 ) );

    add( "North", p );

    Panel stats = new Panel();
    stats.setLayout( new GridLayout( 2, 1 ) );
    p = new Panel( );
    p.setLayout( new GridLayout( 1, 2 ) );
    p.add( new Label( "Room Name: " ) );
    p.add( nameField = new TextField( 30 ) );
    stats.add( p );
    p = new Panel( );
    p.setLayout( new GridLayout( 1, 2 ) );
    p.add( new Label( "Room status: " ) );
    p.add( statusField = new TextField( 10 ) );
    stats.add( p );
```

continues

Listing 54.15. continued

```
    add( "Center", stats );

    p = new Panel( );
    p.setLayout( new GridLayout( 1, 3 ) );
    p.add( connectButton = new Button( "Connect" ) );
    p.add( reserveButton = new Button( "Reserve" ) );
    p.add( releaseButton = new Button( "Release" ) );

    add( "South", p );

    // Name and status fields not editable
    nameField.setEditable( false );
    statusField.setEditable( false );
    updateStatus();
  }

  public void connect( ) {
    String host = hostField.getText();
    if( host == null || host.length() == 0 ) {
      showStatus( "Enter a hostname first." );
      return;
    }

    serverUrl =
      "idl:sunw.door://"
        + host + ":" + sunw.door.Orb.getDefaultPort()
          + "/room.server";
    showStatus( "Connecting to room server on " + host );

    try {
      r = unleashed.RoomStub.createRef();
      sunw.corba.Orb.resolve( serverUrl, r );
    } catch( Exception e ) {
      System.err.println( "Couldn't resolve: " + e );
      showStatus( "Couldn't resolve room server: " + e );
      return;
    }
    updateStatus( );
  }

  public void updateStatus( ) {
    if( r == null ) {
      nameField.setText( "" );
      statusField.setText( "" );
      showStatus( "Not Connected" );
      return;
    }

    // Get room name and stick it in text field
    try {
      String name = r.getName();
      nameField.setText( name );
    } catch( sunw.corba.SystemException e ) {
      System.err.println( "Error getting room name: " + e );
      showStatus( "Error getting room name: " + e );
    }
```

```java
    try {
      switch( r.getStatus( ) ) {
      case unleashed.Room.roomStatus.available:
        statusField.setText( "available" );
        break;
      case unleashed.Room.roomStatus.inUse:
        statusField.setText( "in use" );
        break;
      }
    } catch( sunw.corba.SystemException e ) {
      System.err.println( "Error getting room status: " + e );
      showStatus( "Error getting room status: " + e );
    }
  }

  public void reserve( ) {
    if( r == null ) {
      showStatus( "You must connect to a server first." );
      return;
    }

    try {
      r.setStatus( unleashed.Room.roomStatus.inUse );
    } catch( sunw.corba.SystemException e ) {
      System.err.println( "Error setting room status: " + e );
      showStatus( "Error reserving room: " + e );
    }
    updateStatus( );
  }

  public void release( ) {
    if( r == null ) {
      showStatus( "You must connect to a server first." );
      return;
    }

    try {
      r.setStatus( unleashed.Room.roomStatus.available );
    } catch( sunw.corba.SystemException e ) {
      System.err.println( "Error setting room status: " + e );
      showStatus( "Error reserving room: " + e );
    }
    updateStatus( );
  }

  public boolean action( Event e, Object o )
  {
    if( "Connect".equals( o ) ) {
      connect();
      return true;
    }
    if( "Reserve".equals( o ) ) {
      reserve( );
      return true;
    }
```

54

REMOTE OBJECTS
AND THE JAVA IDL
SYSTEM

continues

Listing 54.15. continued

```
    if( "Release".equals( o ) ) {
      release( );
      return true;
    }
    return false;
  }
}
```

Figure 54.1.

The RoomClient
applet in action.

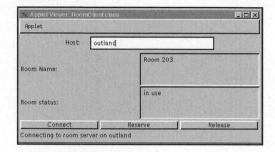

Summary

You should now have an idea how both of the distributed object systems for Java work. Both systems have their advantages and disadvantages. Hopefully, you now know enough to choose the one that best fits your application.

Serving the Net with Jeeves

by Mike Fletcher

IN THIS CHAPTER

This chapter discusses Jeeves, Sun's Java-based Web server. The chapter starts with an introduction to Web servers for those not familiar with them and continues with a discussion of how Jeeves differs from other servers. An overview of some of Jeeves's features follows, including a sample "servlet" (a Java class that runs in the server to dynamically create content) and an introduction to the servlet API.

How the Other Half Lives: Web Servers

Web servers are the compliment to Web browsers. When you type a URL or click a link, your browser contacts the HTTP server residing on the host from which you want to retrieve content. Using the HTTP protocol, the browser indicates what resource it wants to obtain, and the server sends back the requested data (or an error if the request fails).

You may sometimes hear an HTTP server referred to as an HTTP *daemon*. No, it doesn't mean you need to have your PC exorcised. This usage comes from UNIX terminology for a process that provides system services. (In mythology, a daemon is a *helpful* spirit.) A typical UNIX system has several daemon processes that provide services such as FTP, Telnet, and e-mail. Daemons can start running at system boot time, or they can be started by a process called `inetd`. The `inetd` daemon determines what service is requested by the port on which the request comes in. For performance reasons, an HTTP daemon is usually started at boot time rather than from `inetd` to avoid the overhead of starting up a new process every time a Web page is requested.

Originally, Web servers were limited to returning HTML content from files located on the server's file systems. Originally, the only interaction between a client and a server was a simple search facility. A page would be marked as `ISINDEX`, which indicated to the client that an argument could be appended to the URL for the page.

To provide interaction between a client browsing the Web and a server returning content, *forms* were added to the HTML standard. With the added capabilities provided by forms, the Web started moving towards its much more interactive form. Web servers also changed to support the new interaction. The Common Gateway Interface (CGI) is a standard interface that allows an HTTP server to interact with an external application. The CGI specification defines things such as how an external application is given command-line options and what environment variables contain information.

What Makes Jeeves Different from Other HTTP Servers?

Although it provides necessary functionality in today's interactive Web, CGI has some problems. One of the worst is that of security. When users access a URL provided by a CGI program, they run a program on your Web server. If a CGI program is not carefully written, it could allow a malicious user to gain access to your server or destroy data. This problem can be avoided, but it is something to be aware of.

Another problem with CGI programs is that a separate external program must be started up each time someone requests a URL provided by a CGI program. This extra overhead may not be noticed on an average Web server, but it can make a difference. Several alternatives to CGI exist to address this problem, such as the FastCGI specification from Open Market (which uses persistent external processes to handle requests) or Netscape's server API (which is a C interface that allows code that handles requests to be dynamically linked into the Web servers).

Jeeves addresses both these concerns. In addition to providing the usual CGI interface, Jeeves supports servlets. A *servlet* is a Java object run by Jeeves to handle a request from a client. Servlets can be loaded from the local machine on which the Web server is running, or they can be loaded over the network. Untrusted code loaded over the network is treated similarly to classes loaded by a Web browser and is limited in what it can access.

Jeeves also takes advantage of Java's threading capabilities. In addition to using multiple threads to dispatch incoming requests, servlets can be run in their own threads. This capability reduces the overhead necessary to dispatch requests for dynamic documents, especially on multi-processor machines.

HTTP Server Administration Made Easy

Most HTTP servers, especially the freely available UNIX versions, must be configured by editing a set of configuration files with an editor. Unless you are intimately familiar with your server, it is easy to make mistakes. Jeeves' configuration is handled by means of an interactive applet accessed through your browser (see Figure 55.1). Although the information is stored in files that can be edited, Jeeves's fill-in-the-blank configuration is much easier to use than searching through manual pages for the exact syntax to turn off this or that feature.

To access the server configuration screens from the `Configuration` applet, you must authenticate yourself to the server with a user name and password. The list box on the left side of the screen shows the different groups of settings you can configure. To the right are the various fields, buttons, and what-not that let you do the actual configuring of the server. Table 55.1 explains what the different sections control.

Table 55.1. Jeeves configuration groups.

Section	Explanation
HTTP Configuration	Sets HTTP protocol parameters.
Log Configuration	Defines names used for log files that track server accesses and errors.

continues

Table 55.1. continued

Section	Explanation
File Aliasing	Controls the mapping of URLs to files and directories.
Servlet Aliasing	Controls the mapping of URLs to servlets.
Servlet Loading	Defines where the code for servlets is loaded from and any parameters passed to the servlet.
MIME Section	Sets up mappings from file extensions to the MIME type returned.
Users, Groups, and ACLs	These three sections control the creation, deletion, and modification of access control-related settings.
Resource Protection	Allows you to grant privileges using the information entered with the preceding sections. More information on this is provided in "Access Control," later in this chapter.
Reauthenticate	Lets you enter (authenticate) yourself to the server with your user name and password. It allows you to log in as a different user, or to reconnect to the server if you have restarted the server while leaving your browser to run the admin applet.

FIGURE 55.1.

The Jeeves Configuration *applet.*

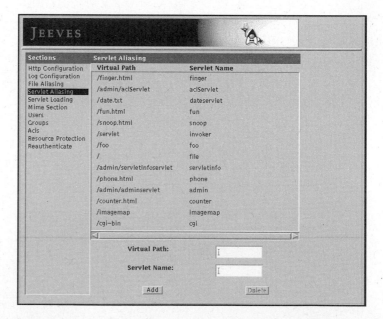

HTTP Configuration

The HTTP Configuration section of the Jeeves Configuration applet enables control of the settings related to the HTTP protocol. In this section, you set the port on which the server listens. You can also define the maximum number of connections the server will accept. Related to this are the minimum and maximum numbers of threads that can start to handle requests.

Jeeves provides support for the HTTP "keep-alive" directive. This extension to the HTTP protocol allows a client to ask that a connection be kept open and used to retrieve multiple URLs. The HTTP Configuration section has fields for setting the maximum number of requests for each keep-alive session and a timeout value (to prevent a client from monopolizing a connection).

Log Configuration

The Log Configuration section of the Jeeves Configuration applet lets you define the names of the log files to which Jeeves will write information. The level of information written to each log can be customized depending on the log. For example, the access_log (logs which pages are being retrieved) and the referer_log (logs which page the browser came from before your page) can be either on or off. The error_log (records any errors the server encounters, such as trying to retrieve a nonexistent page) can be turned off, set to log only major problems, set to log major and minor problems, or set to record all errors.

In addition to the access log (which tracks the resources being accessed by clients) and the error log (which notes errors such as when nonexistent files are requested), Jeeves provides an event log for servlets. Servlets can use the log() method of the java.servlet.Servlet class to write a String to the event log.

File Aliasing

Although the primary purpose of an HTTP server is to return files in response to client requests, you don't want to give out access to your complete file system to just anyone. The File Aliasing section of the Jeeves Configuration applet allows you to map URLs to particular directories or files. This facility also lets you give an easy-to-remember URL to a particular resource. For example, if you have a page with a feature that changes monthly, you can set the URL http://myhost.com/features/current to point to the current month's page.

Servlet Aliasing and Servlet Loading

The Servlet Aliasing and Servlet Loading sections of the Jeeves Configuration applet provide control over a server's Java servlets. Servlet Aliasing is the servlet equivalent of the File Aliasing section (just described). The Servlet Aliasing section allows mappings between URLs and servlet names. The Servlet Loading section sets mappings from servlet names to the Java class for the servlet. The location from which the servlet code is loaded (that is, from the local disk or from the network) and any parameters to be passed to the servlet can be defined here as well.

MIME Section

The MIME Section of the Jeeves `Configuration` applet controls the mappings between file extensions and MIME content types. These mappings let a browser know what type of resource it is retrieving so that it can handle it properly. For example, if you have several Microsoft Word documents, you can use this configuration to tell Jeeves to return a content type of `application/msword` for all files that have the file extension `.doc`. Assuming that the client's browser is properly configured, it automatically launches the application to view the file.

Users, Groups, ACLs, and Resource Protection

The Users, Groups, ACLs, and Resource Protection sections of the Jeeves `Configuration` applet allow you to control who can access resources on your server. Refer to the following section, "Access Control," for a detailed description of how Jeeves provides resource controls.

Access Control

Jeeves provides a very flexible system for controlling access to Web pages and servlets. Privileges can be granted to users (referred to as *principals* in this context), groups of users, or network hosts.

Each user has an account name (which must be unique) and a password. The User Section of the Configuration applet allows you to create and delete user accounts as well as modify a user's password. Likewise, the Groups section allows the creation and deletion of groups of users. Individual user accounts can be assigned or removed from groups.

Access Control Lists (ACLs) are the basis for resource controls with Jeeves. An ACL can be made up of any combination of users, groups, and network hosts. Membership in an ACL can be either positive (the entity is in the list) or negative (the entity is not in the list). In addition to keeping track of which entities are in the ACL, the ACL defines which HTTP request (that is, `GET` or `POST`) can be sent. Once you have created an ACL, the Resource Protection section of the `Configuration` applet enables you to assign lists to a particular URL. Figure 55.2 shows what the ACL Configuration screen looks like.

The practical upshot of this arrangement is that Jeeves gives you very flexible control over deciding who can get what from your server. For example, you can create an ACL that contains the host names for each department's machines. Engineering documents can be specified as available to the developer ACL and the quality assurance ACL. This information is available only to those two departments—the marketing department's machines are not allowed to retrieve it. If the marketing people want to track who is accessing a particular resource, individual user accounts (or a group account) can be placed in an ACL and that ACL can be assigned to the URL in question.

FIGURE 55.2.

*The Access Control List
Configuration section.*

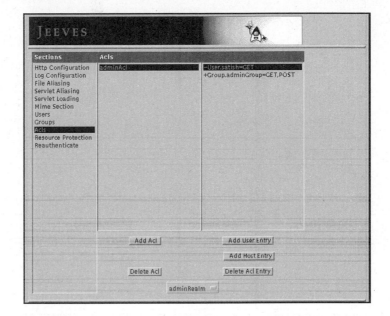

The Servlet API

The API for servlets is similar to that for applets. Servlets must subclass the `java.servlet.GenericServlet` class and override the `service(ServletRequest, ServletResponse)` method. Servlets should extend one of the base servlet classes that implement the `Servlet` interface (such as `GenericServlet` or `HttpServlet`). Like the `java.applet.Applet` class, the `GenericServlet` class provides a method to retrieve parameters: `getInitParameter()`. The `getServletContext()` method obtains a `ServletContext` object, which provides references to other servlets; the method also provides a way to find out what server the servlet is running on.

If a servlet needs special initialization, an `init()` method can be provided. This method is called when the servlet class is loaded. A servlet can contain a `getServletInfo()` method to return information about what the servlet does and its author. Jeeves displays this information in the `Configuration` applet.

The most important method for a servlet is the `service()` method. This method is invoked by the server whenever a request is received. Each time a client requests a URL corresponding to a servlet, Jeeves calls the `service()` method with two parameters: an object implementing the `ServletRequest` interface and an object implementing the `ServletResponse` interface.

The ServletRequest interface provides information similar to that passed to a CGI program in other servers. The interface defines methods to retrieve information such as the URL for the request, the remote host and port the request was received from, and any user authentication information.

The ServletResponse interface contains methods that enable a servlet to communicate the results of a request back to the client that asked for it. A getOutputStream() method provides an OutputStream object that writes to the client. Several methods are provided to set HTTP information such as the response code, the MIME Content-Type of the reply, and the status message returned.

The GenericServlet is intended to be used as a base class for servicing any generic request; the java.servlet.http.HttpServlet, on the other hand, is specifically intended for servicing requests received from the HTTP protocol. The service() method for an HttpServlet receives an HttpServletRequest and an HttpServletResponse as parameters. The HTTP-specific versions extend the ServletRequest and ServletResponse interfaces to provide information specific to an HTTP request, such as the URL requested and any HTTP headers.

Sample Servlet: A Simple Phone Database

We finish off this chapter with a sample servlet. This servlet reads a text file containing people's names, titles, and phone numbers and stores this information in a java.util.Hashtable. When a client requests the URL corresponding to the servlet, the servlet returns a form with a text field. The user can enter a name in the field and click the Submit button. The servlet searches its hash table and returns the corresponding phone number if it exists.

First off are the import statements and class definition. Listing 55.1 defines the Hashtable phoneList and initializes it to null.

NOTE

 All the code in addition to a sample phone list for the servlet example in this chapter can be found on the CD that accompanies this book.

Listing 55.1. The phoneSearch servlet.

```
import java.io.*;
import java.util.*;
import java.servlet.*;
import java.servlet.http.*;
public
class phoneSearch extends HttpServlet {
  // Hashtable to hold phone list information.  Loaded by init()
  Hashtable phoneList = null;
```

Next we define the init() method. As with an applet, this method is called automatically after the class is loaded. The init() code takes care of opening the phone database file and then calls the readDatabase() method to load the information into the hash table. It uses the Servlet.log() method to provide status updates that are written into the server's event log (see Listing 55.2).

Listing 55.2. The phoneSearch.init() method.

```
// Initialize servlet.  Reads in phone database from file.
public void init( ) throws ServletException
{
  FileInputStream infile = null; // For reading data file
  String phoneFile = null;       // Filename of database
  // Log when we start up.
  log( "phoneSearch Servlet Started." );
  // If a filename is given in our parameters, use it
  if( (phoneFile = getInitParameter( "file" )) == null ) {
    phoneFile = "phone.txt";   // otherwise default to phone.txt
  }

  // Log what phone database file we're using
  log( "Using phone database file '" + phoneFile + "'." );
  // Try and open the phone database file
  try {
    infile = new FileInputStream( phoneFile );
  } catch( FileNotFoundException e ) {
    log( "Database file '" + phoneFile + "' does not exist." );
    log( "Error was: " + e.getMessage() );
    throw new ServletException( e.getMessage() );    // Rethrow exception
  } catch( IOException e ) {
    log( "I/O Error opening database file '" + phoneFile + "'." );
    log( "Error was: " + e.getMessage() );
    throw new ServletException( e.getMessage() );    // Rethrow exception
  }
  // Read the database into our hashtable
  try {
    readDatabase( new DataInputStream( infile ) );
  } catch( java.io.IOException e ) {
    throw new ServletException( "Error opening database file:"
                                + e.getMessage() );
  }
  // Log that we're ready for business.
  log( "Read database.  phoneSearch ready." );
}
```

The readDatabase() method takes a DataInputStream from which it reads the phone information (see Listing 55.3). Lines starting with a # character are ignored. Each line should have three fields: the person's name, title, and phone number. The format of each line is the three fields separated by pipe (¦) characters. If the line does not contain a ¦ character, we note the line number to the event log and go on to the next line of the file. Correctly formatted lines are split into two parts: the name field, and the title and phone fields. The title and phone string is inserted into the hash table with the name (converted to all lowercase) as the key.

55

SERVING THE NET WITH JEEVES

Listing 55.3. The phoneSearch.readDatabase() method.

```java
public void readDatabase( DataInputStream in )
  throws IOException
{
  int pos, oldpos, lineNumber;
  String name, info;
  // Get an empty hashtable
  phoneList = new Hashtable( );
  lineNumber = 0;     // Initialize line numbers
  try {
    try {
      // Read in first line
      String line = in.readLine( );
      // While there are lines to read . . .
      while( line != null ) {
        lineNumber++;     // Increment line count
        // Allow comment lines starting with an octothorpe
        if( line.charAt( 0 ) == '#' ) {
          line = in.readLine( ); // Read next line && loop
          continue;
        }
        // If line doesn't have a ¦ character, log it and go on
        if( (pos = line.indexOf( '¦' )) < 0 ) {
          log( "Malformed phone database line at line " + lineNumber );
          line = in.readLine( ); // Read next line && loop
          continue;
        }
        // Copy name from line
        name = line.substring( 0, pos ).toLowerCase();
        // Leave title and # with ¦ separator as one item
        info = line.substring( pos + 1, line.length() );
        // Place info into hashtable with name as key
        phoneList.put( name, info );
        line = in.readLine( ); // Read next line
      }
    } catch( EOFException e ) {
      ;
    }
  } catch( IOException e ) {
    log( "Error while reading database: " + e.getMessage( ) );
    throw e;
  }
  log( "phoneSearch read " + lineNumber + " lines." );
  log( "phoneSearch hashtable has " + phoneList.size() + " items." );
  return;     // Done reading database
}
```

The service() method is the heart of any servlet. Whenever Jeeves receives a request for a URL that maps to a servlet, it calls that servlet's service() method. Two parameters are passed with this call: one representing the request (an object implementing the ServletRequest interface) and one representing the servlet's reply (an object implementing the ServletResponse interface). Because we are extending the HttpServlet class, the parameters are an HttpServletRequest and an HttpServletResponse. The servlet can use information from the HttpServletRequest to determine how it was called and who called it. The `HttpServletResponse` allows the servlet to set the HTTP headers for its reply, as well as provide an `OutputStream` on which to write the reply.

Listing 55.4. The `phoneSearch.service()` method.

```
public void service( HttpServletRequest req, HttpServletResponse res )
  throws ServletException, IOException
{
  PrintWriter out = new PrintWriter( res.getOutputStream() );
  // Set our content type, that the output shouldn't be cached
  res.setContentType( "text/html" );
  res.setHeader( "Pragma", "no-cache" );
  // Write out HTML for our search form
  out.println( "<html>" );
  out.println( "<head><title>Phone List Example Servlet</title></head>" );
  out.println( "<body bgcolor=\"#ffffff\">" );
  // Start of form
  out.println( "<form method=\"GET\">" );
  out.println( "<h1>Phone List Servlet</h1><hr>" );
  // Print some instructions for our user
  out.println( "Enter the name of the person you want to search for." );
  out.println( "Names are recorded as all lowercase.  Search terms" );
  out.println( "are converted to all lowercase." );
  // Create a text field for search term
  out.print( "<p><input TYPE=\"text\" NAME=\"search\" VALUE=\"" );
  // See if we were given a query parameter (i.e. someone's called
  // us already).
  String search = req.getParameter( "search" );
  // If we have search will be non-null and we will use that
  // as the default value in our input box
  if( search != null )
    out.print( search );
  out.println( "\">" );     // Finish tag for search INPUT
  // Create a submit button
  out.println( "<input TYPE=\"submit\" NAME=\".submit\"><p><hr>" );
  // If we were given a search parameter and its length is non-zero
  if( search != null && search.length() != 0 ) {
    // Make the search item all lowercase
    search = search.toLowerCase();
    // See if search term is a key in hashtable
    String info = (String) phoneList.get( search );
    if( info != null ) {
      // Find separator in info
      int pos;
      pos = info.indexOf( '¦' );
      // Format the data in a spiffy table
      out.println( "<table width=\"75%\" border=\"2\">" );
      out.println( "<tr><th>Name</th><th>Title</th><th>Phone</th></tr>" );
      // Print out a row with the data from the query and hashtable
      out.println( "<tr><td>" + search + "</td>" );
      out.println( "<td>" + info.substring( 0, pos ) + "</td>" );
      out.println( "<td>" + info.substring( pos + 1, info.length() ) + "</td>" );
      out.println( "</table>" ); // Mark the end of our table
```

continues

Listing 55.4. continued

```
    } else {
      // Search term wasn't in hashtable, so let them know that
      out.println( "No one by the name '" + search + "' was found." );
    }
  }
  // Close out form, body, and html tags
  out.println( "<p></form>" );
  out.println( "</body></html>" );
  out.flush();
  out.close();
  return;    // We're done
}
```

Last are the getServletInfo() and destroy() methods (see Listing 55.5). The getServletInfo() method should return a String with information such as what the servlet does, who the author is, and information about the version. The destroy() method for this servlet just logs to the event log the fact that it was called. If you have a servlet that has, for example, connections to a database or information that has to be written out to disk, the destroy() method can handle those tasks.

Listing 55.5. The phoneSearch.getServletInfo() and phoneServlet.destroy() methods.

```
// Provide a little information about what servlet does
public String getServletInfo( )
{
  return "Simple Phone Database";
}
public void destroy( )
{
  // Log when we're destroyed
  log( "phoneSearch Servlet destroy() called." );
}
}
```

Using the phoneSearch Servlet

 The simplest way to use the servlet created in this chapter is to compile the code (phoneSearch.java, located on the CD-ROM that accompanies this book) and place the class file into the servlet directory under the main Jeeves directory. The phone database file should be placed in the Jeeves root directory and be named phone.txt. If you name the file differently or place it in another directory (in the servlet directory, for example), you must specify the location with the file parameter in the Servlet Loading section of the Configuration applet. Figure 55.3 shows the phoneSearch servlet in action.

FIGURE 55.3.

The phoneSearch *servlet in action.*

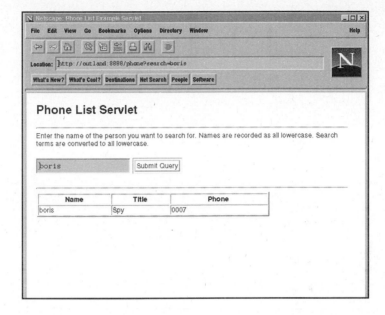

Summary

After reading this chapter, you should have an understanding of Jeeves's capabilities and what sets it apart from other HTTP servers. You should have an idea how to configure Jeeves to map URLs to different files or servlets, as well as how to write your own servlets to provide dynamic content.

Netscape's Internet Foundation Classes

by William R. Stanek

IN THIS CHAPTER

As Java evolves, it becomes increasingly apparent that there are many ways it can be improved—especially when it comes to the graphical user interface contained in the Abstract Windowing Toolkit (AWT). Because Java is an object-oriented programming language, the user interface can be easily extended with a set of advanced and fully customizable components. This is where the Netscape Internet Foundation Classes (IFC) come into the picture.

Netscape's IFC features enhancements to Java's user interface that you simply cannot find in Java 1.1. But best of all, if you use the IFC, you can finally unleash the multimedia capabilities of your system. The IFC features extensive support for images, sounds, and animation. The IFC packages are included with Netscape Navigator 4.0 and later. If you don't use Netscape Navigator, you can still use Netscape IFC, but you will have to download the developer kit.

The Next Generation of AWT: The IFC

With the Internet Foundation Classes, Netscape establishes itself as a leader in Java development. Keep in mind that the Internet Foundation Classes are designed to compliment Java's Abstract Windowing Toolkit (AWT). As such, the IFC does not replace the AWT; it enhances the AWT.

Because the IFC APIs and packages are layered on top of Java's AWT, the IFC is fully compatible with existing versions of the Java programming language (see Figure 56.1). Before Netscape finalized IFC version 1, the company made several important changes to the interface to ensure that the IFC is compatible with future versions of Java.

> **NOTE**
>
> The IFC APIs and packages are bundled with Netscape Communicator and Navigator version 4.0 and later. This means that the IFC APIs are available to applets you want to run in your Netscape browsers. Because Netscape IFC is 100-percent Java based, the classes can be used with just about any Java-capable browser. If you want to use IFC classes with standalone applications, you can bundle the classes with the application, but you are subject to the terms of the Netscape ONE license. Specifically, you must sign the Netscape ONE license before you distribute IFC Java source code. You can find more information at this URL: `developer.netscape.com`.

The IFC is designed to help developers create advanced applications in less time and with greater efficiency. The most important area in which the IFC comes to the developer's aid is the enhanced user interface. If you use this interface, your programs can perform many advanced tasks simply by calling methods of the interface objects. This means that you get the level of functionality you need with a limited amount of fuss and programming.

Behind the many predefined actions and operations of the interface are the interface components themselves. To be truly useful, components such as selection lists, popup windows, and dialog boxes should be fully customizable. It is no surprise, then, that all the components of the IFC are completely customizable. The modular design of the components also makes it easy to override their default look and feel, giving you advanced control with minimal coding.

FIGURE 56.1.

Netscape's IFC is layered on top of Java's AWT.

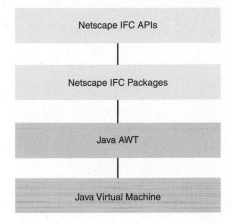

| Netscape IFC APIs |
| Netscape IFC Packages |
| Java AWT |
| Java Virtual Machine |

With IFC, even a simple button becomes an avenue to a multimedia feast without extensive coding. Stitch a few simple lines of code together and your IFC-enhanced buttons can have images, sounds, and animation associated with them.

What's in the IFC?

Netscape IFC is divided into two package libraries:

- `netscape.application`
- `netscape.util`

Overview of the `netscape.application` Package

The `netscape.application` package supplies you with top-level classes for creating user interfaces of applications; it also provides services such as event handling and drawing. The complete list of classes, interfaces, and exceptions supported by `netscape.application` is shown in Table 56.1.

Table 56.1. The `netscape.application` package summary.

Classes	Interfaces	Exception
AWTCompatibility	ApplicationObserver	HTMLParsingException
AWTComponentView	DragDestination	
Alert	DragSource	
Application	DrawingSequenceOwner	
BezelBorder	EventFilter	
Bitmap	EventProcessor	
Border	ExtendedTarget	
Button	LayoutManager	
Color	ScrollBarOwner	
ColorChooser	Scrollable	
ColorWell	Target	
CommandEvent	TextFieldOwner	
ContainerView	TextFilter	
DebugGraphics	TextViewOwner	
DragSession	Window	
DragWell	WindowOwner	
DrawingSequence		
EmptyBorder		
Event		
EventLoop		
ExternalWindow		
FileChooser		
Font		
FontChooser		
FontMetrics		
FoundationApplet		
FoundationPanel		
Graphics		
GridLayout		
Image		
ImageAttachment		
ImageSequence		

Netscape's Internet Foundation Classes

CHAPTER 56

1271

56

NETSCAPE'S
INTERNET FOUNDA-
TION CLASSES

Classes	*Interfaces*	*Exception*
InternalWindow		
InternalWindowBorder		
KeyEvent		
LineBorder		
ListItem		
ListView		
Menu		
MenuItem		
MouseEvent		
PackConstraints		
PackLayout		
Point		
Polygon		
Popup		
PopupItem		
Range		
Rect		
RootView		
ScrollBar		
ScrollGroup		
ScrollView		
Size		
Slider		
Sound		
TargetChain		
TextAttachment		
TextField		
TextParagraphFormat		
TextView		
Timer		
View		
WindowContentView		

Overview of the `netscape.util` Package

The `netscape.util` package provides the necessary utility classes for the IFC, such as timers and archives. The complete list of classes, interfaces, and exceptions supported by `netscape.util` is shown in Table 56.2.

Table 56.2. The `netscape.util` package summary.

Classes	Interfaces	Exceptions
Archive	Codable	CodingExceptionInconsistencyException
Archiver	Comparable	DeserializationException
ClassInfo	Decoder	NoSuchElementException
ClassTable	Encoder	InconsistencyException
Deserializer	Enumeration	
FormattingSerializer		
Hashtable		
Serializer		
Sort		
Unarchiver		
Vector		

Overview of the IFC Object Framework

Together, the `netscape.application` and `netscape.util` packages form a library with an extensive object framework. As Table 56.3 shows, you can find objects for interface components, windowing, animation, and much more.

Table 56.3. Object framework in the IFC.

Framework	Description
Animation	Enables advanced animation with line art and images; includes methods for buffering, flicker control, and transparency.
Application Components	Provides key application components such as buttons, checkboxes, radio buttons, and text fields.
Composite Components	Creates complex interface components such as file choosers, font choosers, and color choosers.

Netscape's Internet Foundation Classes

CHAPTER 56

1273

56

NETSCAPE'S
INTERNET FOUNDA-
TION CLASSES

Framework	Description
Drag-and-Drop	Enables drag-and-drop features among components of an application.
Event Drawing	Provides essential event-handling methods and allows objects called by an event to draw themselves.
Multifont Text/Image Object	Allows for the display of multiple fonts in text elements; also allows for the display of embedded images.
Object Persistence	Allows objects to maintain their state so that they can be reused later to initialize an application with user preferences.
Timers	Enables multitasking without having to use multithreading.
Windowing	Allows you to use internal and external windows.

Installing the IFC

To compile and run Java programs that use IFC classes, you need a *developer environment*. The developer environment is found in the IFC SDK, which includes documentation, reference resources, and examples. You should install a developer environment on the system you plan to use for the development of IFC-enhanced Java programs.

If you just want to run Java programs that use IFC classes, you need a *user environment*. The IFC user environment is included with Netscape Communicator version 4.0 and later. However, you can install the IFC on any system to which Java has been ported. All you need is Java, a Java-compatible browser, and the IFC user download.

To obtain the IFC SDK or IFC user download, visit the Web page shown in Figure 56.2. The URL for the IFC Developer Central is `http://developer.netscape.com/library/ifc/index.html`. Netscape archived the IFC files using several different compression formats (such as `zip`, `gzip`, and `tar`). Because the IFC is written completely in Java, you do not have to download different archive files for different systems.

The sections that follow look at the installation process by platform. There are separate installation sections for UNIX, Windows 95, Windows NT, and Macintosh systems. After you read the setup procedures for your system, jump ahead to the section called "Creating IFC-Enhanced Applets and Applications."

Keep in mind that the installation process is similar regardless of whether you plan to install a user environment or a developer environment. The key difference is that you use different filenames to retrieve and install the IFC archive file.

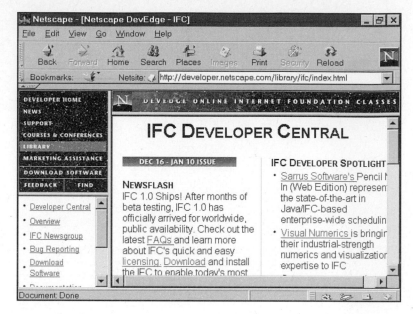

Quick Setup for UNIX

The IFC archive file you probably want to use for UNIX systems is the one compressed using `gzip` and `tar`. After you obtain the IFC archive, check to make sure that the size of the file you downloaded matches the file size listed on the Web site. If the file sizes are not identical, your file may have been corrupted during download. In that case, delete the file from your system and download the IFC archive again.

After you move the archive file to the base directory you want to use for installation (for example, `/home/users`), you can unzip and unpack the archive using the following command:

```
gunzip ifc60.tar.gz ¦ tar xf -
```

> **NOTE**
>
> The `gunzip` command lists the contents of the compressed files and directories. The output of this command is sent to the UNIX tape-archive command `tar`, which extracts the files and directories but does not list the extraction to the screen.

Next, you have to let your system know where you installed the IFC class files. To do this, you use the `CLASSPATH` environment variable. `CLASSPATH` tells the Java interpreter and compiler where to look for your class files. When you installed Java, you probably assigned a value to the `CLASSPATH` variable. Do not remove this value; simply add another file path for the IFC classes.

Netscape's Internet Foundation Classes

CHAPTER 56

1275

56

NETSCAPE'S
INTERNET FOUNDA-
TION CLASSES

C shell users will want to edit the .cshrc file in their home directory and update the statement that sets the CLASSPATH variable. If you installed the IFC class files in $HOME/ifc11/classes, you can update the CLASSPATH variable as follows:

```
setenv CLASSPATH java/classes:java/lib/classes.zip:$HOME/ifc11/classes
```

If the CLASSPATH variable is not set in your .cshrc file, enter only the path to the IFC files, as shown here:

```
setenv CLASSPATH $HOME/ifc11/classes
```

For these changes to take effect in the current command-tool or shell environment, you must source your .cshrc file or enter the setenv command at the shell prompt. This action updates the current environment settings.

If you are using the Bourne shell as your main UNIX shell, you can set the CLASSPATH in your .profile file. Do this by editing the .profile file in your home directory and updating the statements that set and export the CLASSPATH variable's path, as shown here:

```
CLASSPATH=java/classes;java/lib/classes.zip;$HOME/ifc11/classes
export CLASSPATH
```

For these changes to take effect in the current command-tool or shell environment, you must set the CLASSPATH variable and export it from the command line, like this:

```
CLASSPATH=$HOME/ifc11/classes;export CLASSPATH
```

> **NOTE**
>
> If you use the command-line Java tools in the current command tool, sourcing .cshrc or exporting CLASSPATH will work. However, if you want to run IFC applets outside the context of the current command tool, you should log out and then log back in.

Quick Setup for Windows 95

The IFC archive file you probably want to use for Windows 95 systems is the one that is zipped. After you obtain the IFC archive, check to make sure that the size of the file you downloaded matches the file size listed on the Web site. If the file sizes are not identical, your file may have been corrupted during download. In that case, delete the file from your system and download the IFC archive again.

To install the IFC from the MS-DOS prompt, follow these steps:

1. Open a DOS window.
2. Change to the directory that contains the IFC archive file.

3. Move the archive file to the location you want to install it. To install the IFC 1.1 in `c:\ifc11`, for example, use the following command:

   `move ifc60.zip c:\`

4. Unzip the archive file with an unzip utility that supports long filenames. Be sure to extract the directory structure.

After installing the IFC, update your `AUTOEXEC.BAT` file so that your computer can find the IFC class files. To do this, type the following at the DOS prompt:

`EDIT C:\AUTOEXEC.BAT`

Now you have to let your system know where you installed the IFC class files. To do this, use the `CLASSPATH` environment variable. `CLASSPATH` tells the Java interpreter and compiler where to look for your class files. When you installed Java, you probably assigned a value to the `CLASSPATH` variable. Do not remove this value; simply add another file path for the IFC classes.

If you installed the IFC under the `C:\` directory, update the line that sets the `CLASSPATH` variable as follows:

`SET CLASSPATH=C:\JAVA\LIB\CLASSES.ZIP;C:\ifc11\classes;`

When you are finished, save and close your `AUTOEXEC.BAT` file. If you reboot your computer, you ensure that the working environment is set for all future sessions.

Quick Setup for Windows NT

The IFC archive file you probably want to use for Windows NT systems is the one compressed using `zip`. After you obtain the IFC archive, check to make sure that the size of the file you downloaded matches the file size listed on the Web site. If the file sizes are not identical, your file may have been corrupted during download. In that case, delete the file from your system and download the IFC archive again.

To install the IFC from the MS-DOS prompt, follow these steps:

1. Open a DOS window.

2. Change to the directory that contains the IFC archive file.

3. Move the archive file to the location you want to install it. To install the IFC 1.1 in `c:\ifc11`, for example, use the following command:

   `move ifc60.zip c:\`

4. Unzip the archive file with an unzip utility that supports long filenames. Be sure to extract the directory structure.

After installing the IFC, create a user environment variable called `CLASSPATH`. `CLASSPATH` tells the Java interpreter and compiler where to look for your class files. When you installed Java, you probably assigned a value to the `CLASSPATH` variable. Do not remove this value; simply add another file path for the IFC classes.

If the `CLASSPATH` variable already exists on your system, double-click the System icon in the Control Panel, select the user environment variable, and then update it as follows:

```
C:\JAVA\LIB\CLASSES.ZIP;C:\ifc11\classes;
```

If the `CLASSPATH` variable does not exist on your system, double-click the System icon in the Control Panel and create the user environment variable with the following value:

```
C:\JAVA\LIB\CLASSES.ZIP;C:\ifc11\classes;
```

NOTE

If you did not install the IFC to the recommended location, you must enter the proper file path.

Quick Setup for Macintosh

The IFC archive file you probably want to use for Macintosh systems is the one that is zipped. After you obtain the IFC archive, check that the size of the file you downloaded matches the file size listed on the Web site. If the file sizes are not identical, your file may have been corrupted during download. In that case, delete the file from your system and download the IFC archive again.

NOTE

Hopefully, Netscape has woken up by the time you read this and has realized that Mac users prefer Mac compression formats. If so, you should use StuffIt to decompress the Macintosh binary file and `DeHQX` or `BinHex4` to decompress the hqx file. If you used `Fetch` or `Anarchie` to download the files, the archive file was automatically decompressed when the download finished. If not, you can use StuffIt Expander or DropStuff with Expander Enhancer to decompress the `tar` or `zip` file.

Before you can install the IFC, you must decompress the IFC archive file with an unzip utility. For IFC 1.1, this action creates a folder called `ifc11` under the installation folder.

Next, create the following folder in the System folder: Preferences | Netscape | Java | `netscape-classes`. Then copy the contents of the `ifc11/classes` folder into the `netscape-classes` folder. If the copy is successful, the `netscape-classes` folders should have folders called `netscape ¦ application` and `netscape ¦ util`.

> **NOTE**
>
> If you installed Netscape Communicator version 4.0 or later, these folders should already exist. In this case, all you have to do is check for the existence of the folders.

Creating IFC-Enhanced Applets and Applications

In Java 1.1, there is no way for system classes to look up an applet's class by name. This presents a slight problem for IFC developers and requires a workaround. The way you implement the workaround depends on whether you are developing a standalone application or an applet.

> **NOTE**
>
> To compile IFC-enhanced programs, you must install the Java Development Kit *and* the IFC. If you have not already done so, do it now. To run IFC-enhanced programs, you must have the IFC and a Java-compatible browser.

Working with Applications

Applications are standalone programs that do not run within a browser. When you develop an application that uses the IFC, start by creating a separate folder for the application. In this folder, create a file called `NetscapeApplet.java` with the contents shown in Listing 56.1. You can also find this code on the CD-ROM that accompanies this book.

Listing 56.1. `NetscapeApplet.java` source code.

```
import netscape.application.*;
import netscape.util.*;
public class NetscapeApplet extends FoundationApplet {
    public Class classForName(String className)
        throws ClassNotFoundException {
        return Class.forName(className);
    }
}
```

Then create the `.java` source files for your application in the same directory. Be sure that the main class is a subclass of the `Application` class and that you import `netscape.application` and `netscape.util`. Here are the statements that accomplish these goals:

```
import netscape.application.*;
import netscape.util.*;
```

```
public class myApplication extends Application {
    //main class definitions here
}
```

When you compile the application, compile all the .java files at the same time using the following command:

```
javac *.java
```

You can now run your application using the Java interpreter.

> **TIP**
>
> If the program does not compile, double-check the file paths set in the CLASSPATH variable.

Working with Applets

Applets are programs run within a browser. When you develop an applet that uses the IFC, start by following the steps outlined in the preceding section. If the applet compiles successfully, you can then create an HTML page to run the applet.

Unlike traditional applets, IFC-enhanced applets are not executed by their class name. Instead, you execute the applet by invoking the NetscapeApplet class with a parameter called ApplicationClass. The ApplicationClass parameter tells the IFC the name of the main class file for your application:

```
<APPLET CODE="NetscapeApplet">
<PARAM NAME="ApplicationClass" VALUE="AppName">
</APPLET>
```

In this syntax, *AppName* is the actual name of the main class file for the applet.

Testing the Installation

Listing 56.2 shows the code for a Web page with a script you can use to test the installation of the Netscape Internet Foundation Classes. This script uses the releaseName() function of netscape.application.Application to test for the presence of the IFC.

 Load this page in a browser on your development or user platform to test the installation of the IFC. If a problem occurs, you will see an error similar to the one shown in Figure 56.3. You can also find this code on the CD-ROM that accompanies this book.

> **TIP**
>
> In the IFC check script, be sure to match the IFC version reference with the actual version you installed on your system. The script currently checks for IFC version 1.0. Keep in mind that the Netscape IFC is integrated into Netscape Navigator 4.0. This script is designed to be used with browsers other than Netscape Navigator 4.0.

Listing 56.2. Check your installation with this script.

```
<HTML>
<HEAD>
<TITLE>Check IFC Installation</TITLE>
<SCRIPT LANGUAGE="JavaScript">
<!--
browserName = navigator.appName
window.onerror = errorMessage
function errorMessage() {
    if (confirm("It appears you do not have the current version
                of Netscape IFC installed. \n\nWould you like to download the
                current release of IFC now?")) {
        window.open('http://developer.netscape.com/library/ifc/index.html', '')
    }
    return true
}function CheckIFC() {
    if (browserName.lastIndexOf('Netscape') != -1) {
        var app = netscape.application.Application
        var release = app.releaseName()
        if (release != "IFC 1.0") {
            errorMessage()
            return
        }
    window.confirm("Version: " + release + "\n\n
        of the IFC is properly installed on your system.");
    } else if (browserName.lastIndexOf('Microsoft Internet Explorer') != -1) {
        window.confirm("Verification does not work for Internet Explorer 3.0")
    } else {
        window.alert("Unable to determine if IFC has been installed properly.")    }
}// -->
</SCRIPT>
</HEAD>
<BODY BGCOLOR="#FFFFFF">
<DIV ALIGN="CENTER">
<H1>Check Netscape IFC Installation</H1>
<P ALIGN=LEFT>You can check the IFC installation by clicking on the
 button below. If the IFC <EM>is</EM> installed properly, you will
 see a message telling you what version you currently have installed
 on your system. If the IFC <EM>is not</EM> installed properly, you
 will see an error message and have the opportunity to download the
 IFC from the IFC Developer Central.</P>
<FORM>
<INPUT TYPE="button" VALUE="Check IFC Installation" onClick="CheckIFC()">
</FORM>
</DIV>
</BODY>
</HTML>
```

Netscape's Internet Foundation Classes

CHAPTER 56

1281

56

NETSCAPE'S
INTERNET FOUNDA-
TION CLASSES

FIGURE 56.3.
*The IFC is not installed
properly on this system.*

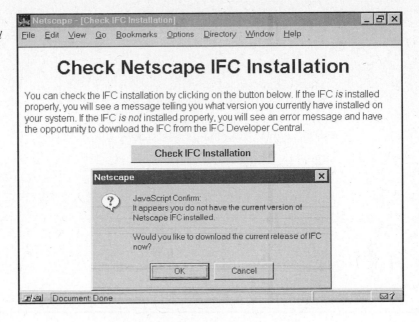

Summary

The programmers at Netscape saw a window of opportunity to develop Java's user interface to its full potential—and they carried it 49 yards for a touchdown. As you have seen, the Netscape Internet Foundation Classes are not a replacement for Java classes; rather, the IFC is layered on top of Java's Abstract Windowing Toolkit and is designed to compliment it. To learn more about Netscape IFC, you may want to look for the *Netscape ONE Developer's Guide* (published by Sams Publishing). In this guide, you will find a detailed walk-through of all the frameworks in the IFC as well as applets and applications that use Netscape IFC components.

Java into the Future

by Michael Morrison

CHAPTER 57

This chapter wraps up your journey through Java by peering into the crystal ball and taking a look at what lies ahead for Java. More specifically, this chapter discusses new API extensions for Java development, the JavaOS operating system, and Java microprocessors.

Most of the new API extensions are available in white-paper form, with early implementations becoming available in the near future. If you aren't familiar with *white papers*, they are technical documents describing the goals of a new technology. The JavaOS is a new compact operating system based on and fully supporting the Java platform. Java microprocessors are full-blown microprocessors geared toward supporting the Java virtual machine.

The emerging Java technologies you learn about in this chapter are still in their early stages as of this writing, which means that I can give you only a preliminary look at what they have to offer. Nevertheless, you should be able to take from this chapter a better understanding of where Java is headed and what it might mean to your own development efforts. You should check out JavaSoft's Web site (www.javasoft.com) to get the latest scoop on the status of these technologies; this site will always contain the most up-to-date information regarding these technologies.

Java API Overview

Java version 1.1, the latest Java release as of this writing, is now being referred to by JavaSoft as the *core Java API*. The core Java API defines the minimal set of functionality a Java implementation must support to be considered Java compliant. For example, when someone undertakes the job of supporting Java on a particular platform, that person must fully implement the core Java API. This guaranteed support for the core API is what allows Java developers the luxury of being able to write Java programs once and having them run on any Java-compliant platform.

In the near future, JavaSoft plans to expand on the core API by introducing new APIs that address more applied development needs. The new APIs cover a wide range of areas and will ultimately save developers a great deal of time by establishing a consistent approach to certain development issues, reducing the need for custom coding. Some of these new APIs may merge with the core API in a future release of Java; other APIs will remain extensions. Regardless of their ultimate relationship to the core API, the new extension APIs are referred to as the *standard extension APIs* because they extend the current core API as we know it.

The standard extension APIs are divided into a set of individual APIs that target different development needs. Following are the major components of the standard extension APIs:

- Commerce API
- Management API
- Server API

- Media API
- Embedded API

The following sections explain each of these APIs and how they impact the Java software platform.

The Commerce API

As the role of the Internet continues to evolve from being an information source to being a retail marketplace, the need for a secure commercial transaction protocol is also growing. Both Internet vendors and shoppers alike are eagerly awaiting the inevitable migration of shopping to the Web. Beyond shopping, there are also other important areas of financial transactions (such as investment trading) that can benefit greatly from a secure standard. JavaSoft has provided an answer to the problem of secure purchasing with the Commerce API, a Java API extension that provides the overhead for Java programs to support secure purchasing and financial management.

The Java Commerce API aims to provide developers with an elegant solution to the problem of commercial transactions on the Web. The goal is to make purchasing goods a seamless yet secure part of the Web experience. To this end, the Commerce API is being pushed by JavaSoft as an open, extensible environment for financial management on the Web. The long-term plan for the Commerce API is for integration into the Java software platform—partially with the core API and partially as a standard extension. It isn't clear yet which components will make it into the core API and which will remain separate.

The Commerce API consists of the following primary components:

- **Infrastructure.** The infrastructure of the Commerce API is the architectural framework that defines the interactions between the other components of the API. This infrastructure is also what gives the API its extensibility to support future commerce extensions.

- **Information database.** The database component serves as a repository for user information such as payment methods and the user's shipping address. The database component contains encryption features so that user information can be kept completely private. Alternatively, commerce service providers have the option of sharing user information with one another.

- **Payment cassettes.** The Commerce API makes use of *cassettes*, which are software modules that implement specific financial protocols. A payment cassette defines the protocol for making electronic payments. Examples of payment cassettes include credit cards, debit cards, and (eventually) digital cash. A user can have multiple payment cassettes that represent different payment instruments, much like we carry different payment instruments in our wallets or purses. In fact, one of the classes in the Commerce API specifically models an electronic wallet.

■ **Service cassettes.** Service cassettes are the second kind of software module used by the Commerce API to implement specific financial protocols. Service cassettes serve to model any type of value-added financial service such as financial analysis or tax preparation modules. For example, you can feasibly purchase a service cassette to help you balance your electronic checkbook or assess the value of your stock portfolio.

■ **Administrative interfaces.** This component of the Commerce API includes dialog boxes and other graphical interfaces used to retrieve information from the user and to configure commerce options.

For more information on the Commerce API, check out JavaSoft's Commerce API Web site, located at this URL:

```
http://www.javasoft.com/products/commerce/
```

The Management API

The Management API is designed to answer the needs of integrated network management systems. It includes a wide range of interfaces, classes, and applets to facilitate the development of integrated management solutions. The primary goal of the Management API is to provide a unified approach to handling the complexities involved in developing and maintaining resources and services on a heterogeneous network. Using the Management API, Java developers can rapidly develop network management applications supporting a wide range of systems on large and often complex networks. JavaSoft plans to keep the Management API as a separate extension from the core API.

The Management API includes the following core components:

■ **Admin View Module (AVM).** The AVM is an extension of the Java Abstract Windowing Toolkit (AWT), enhanced to provide specific support for creating integrated management applications. The classes implemented in the AVM serve as a basis for developing sophisticated graphical user interfaces. For example, the AVM includes support for graphical tables, charts, graphs, and visual gauges.

■ **Base object interfaces.** The base object interfaces define the core object types used for distributed resources and services in a management system. Using the base object interfaces, developers can define abstractions for a variety of attributes associated with a managed enterprise environment.

■ **Managed container interfaces.** The managed container interfaces define a way to group together managed objects for better organization. This organization facilitates a more group-oriented approach to keeping up with managed resources, which can be a great benefit in complex systems.

■ **Managed notification interfaces.** The managed notification interfaces define a core foundation of managed event-notification services. Developers are free to develop more advanced application-specific notification services by extending these services.

- **Managed data interfaces.** The managed data interfaces provide a way to link managed object attributes to relational databases using JDBC. In doing so, the managed data interfaces establish a transparent link between management resources and external databases.

- **Managed protocol interfaces.** The managed protocol interfaces use the Java Security APIs and Java RMI to add secure distributed object support to the core functionality provided by the base object interfaces.

- **Simple Network Management Protocol (SNMP) interfaces.** The SNMP interfaces extend the managed protocol interfaces to provide support for SNMP agents. SNMP is a relatively simple protocol originally developed to solve communication problems between different types of networks and gather network statistics. Because SNMP is the most popular management protocol in use, its support through the SNMP interfaces is an important part of the Management API.

- **Applet integration interfaces.** The applet integration interfaces component of the Management API specifies how Java applets can be integrated with the Management API to provide management solutions. Applet developers use the applet integration interfaces to build management support into their applets.

For more information on the Management API, refer to JavaSoft's Management API Web site, located at this URL:

```
http://www.javasoft.com/products/JavaManagement/
```

The Server API

After the success of Java and its immediate use for developing client-side applets, JavaSoft decided to take steps to make Java a more viable alternative for server-side applications. The Server API is JavaSoft's answer to the need for more complete server-oriented support in Java. The Server API provides a wide range of server functionality including support for administration, accessibility control, and dynamic resource handling. Also included in the Server API is the Servlet API, which provides a framework for extending servers with servlets. A *servlet* is a Java object that extends the functionality of an information server, such as an HTTP server. You can think of servlets as the server equivalents of client-side Java applets.

The Servlet API provides the overhead necessary for creating servlets and interfacing them with information servers. The Servlet API is equipped to handle the entire servlet/server relationship, with an emphasis on keeping things stable and simple. All that is required to run servlets is a server that supports the Servlet API.

JavaSoft has grouped the Server and Servlet APIs under its new Internet server framework known as *Jeeves*. To get more information about the APIs, check out Chapter 55, "Serving the Net with Jeeves." You may also want to visit JavaSoft's Jeeves Web site, located at this URL:

```
http://jeeves.javasoft.com/products/java-server/webserver/index.shtml
```

The Media API

Possibly the weakest area of the core Java API as we know it is its support for media. Currently, the Java API supports only static GIF and JPEG images and wave sounds in the AU sound format. Clearly, this limited media support won't cut it in the long run. Sure, developers can hack their own media implementations to some extent, but they can already do that in a variety of other languages and platforms. Java was supposed to make things easier, right?

JavaSoft realized this weakness and is remedying things with the Media API, which is slated to include support for a dizzying array of media types that will no doubt put Java on the map as a serious multimedia platform. The Media API includes classes that model media types such as full-motion video, audio, 2D and 3D graphics, telephony, and more. Furthermore, the structure of the API is such that many of these media types will rely on the same underlying facilities. For example, all time-based media (such as video and audio) will use the same underlying timing mechanism, meaning that synchronization won't be a problem.

The Media API is designed to be very open and extensible—which is important considering that the world of multimedia is always changing. JavaSoft plans to integrate the Media API into the Java platform both as core API additions and as standard extension APIs.

The following API subsets comprise the Media API:

- **Media Framework API.** The Media Framework API handles the low-level timing functionality required by many of the other media APIs. This API includes support for timing and synchronization, both of which are critical to media types that must function together in harmony. *Synchronization* refers to how different time-based media elements agree with each other in time. For example, it is important for the sound track of a movie to remain synchronized with the picture.

  Also included in the Media Framework API is support for streaming, compression, and live data sources. *Streaming* is the process of interacting with data while it is still being transferred. For example, a streaming audio player begins playing audio as soon as a certain minimal amount of data has been transferred.

- **2D Graphics API.** The 2D Graphics API extends the functionality of the AWT classes to provide wider support for 2D graphics primitives and a variety of different graphical output devices, such as printers. Another important addition to the 2D Graphics API is the definition of a uniform graphical model that brings many graphics functions into one structure.

- **Animation API.** The Animation API uses the 2D Graphics API as a basis for its implementation of animated 2D graphics objects, or *sprites*. The Animation API also relies on the Media Framework API for maintaining timing and synchronization.

- **3D Graphics API.** The 3D Graphics API provides the overhead necessary to generate high-performance 3D graphics. This API implements 3D graphics by supporting a model of 3D graphical objects that can be rendered at high speeds. The 3D Graphics

API also includes support for VRML, which is a very popular 3D modeling language. To pull off all this functionality, the 3D Graphics API relies heavily on the functions provided by many of the other media APIs.

■ **Video API.** The Video API brings full-motion video to Java. The API provides the framework for managing and processing video in either a streaming or stored scenario.

■ **Audio API.** Similar to the Video API in some ways, the Audio API also provides support for both streaming and stored media. However, the media supported by the Audio API consists of either sampled or synthesized audio. The Audio API even contains classes for implementing 3D spatial audio.

■ **Musical Instrument Digital Interface (MIDI) API.** The MIDI API brings timed musical events to Java by way of the popular MIDI standard. MIDI defines a protocol for communicating and storing time-based events, such as those generated by a musical instrument. MIDI is an efficient way to represent both musical pieces as well as more general timing resources. Expect to hear the Web much differently once this API catches on!

■ **Share API.** The Share API is probably the most interesting of the media APIs, simply because it's the least obvious. It defines a means by which live, multiparty communication can take place over a network. The Share API provides support for both synchronization and session management. I wouldn't be surprised to see multiplayer games and "chat" applets take on a new feel once this API is out.

■ **Telephony API.** The Telephony API gives Java the capability to interact with telephones. Most important telephone functions are supported in this API, including teleconferencing and caller ID, among others.

The Embedded API

The last of the standard extension APIs is the Embedded API, which defines a minimal set of Java functionality specifically targeted for embedded systems applications, such as consumer electronics devices. An *embedded system* is a scaled-down computer system programmed to perform a particular function within an electronic device. The Embedded API is the only API that doesn't really add anything to the Java core API. In fact, the Embedded API will more than likely be a subset of the core API, because only a part of the core functionality is needed in embedded applications. For example, because most embedded systems have no graphical output to speak of, the entire AWT is really unnecessary. Likewise, a network connection is unlikely in an embedded system, so there is no need to include the Java networking package.

More than likely, the Embedded API will consist of the following packages from the core API: language, utilities, and I/O. Beyond those, it's possible that Embedded API extensions could be developed to support specialized networking and output requirements. Because the Embedded API is itself a subset of the core API, it will more than likely be treated as an extension API.

57

JAVA INTO THE
FUTURE

JavaOS

Even though Java has been touted largely as a neat new programming language, it is, in fact, much more than that. Java is also a very powerful and compact runtime system that, in many ways, mimics the facilities provided by a full-blown operating system. Knowing this, it wasn't a complete surprise to some that JavaSoft decided to build a complete operating system around the Java technology. This new operating system is called JavaOS and is described by JavaSoft as "a highly compact operating system designed to run Java applications directly on micro-processors in anything from net computers to pagers."

JavaOS is no doubt intended to ride the wave created by Java and its insanely rapid success. However, don't let that statement mislead you into thinking that JavaOS is any less legitimate than the technology it is built on. The idea of building a complete operating system on top of the existing Java technology makes perfect sense. The applications of a compact, efficient operating system that can natively run Java programs are far and wide. In fact, JavaSoft has already made mention of a variety of devices to which the JavaOS technology could be easily applied. These devices include everything from networked computers to cellular telephones; basically any device that can benefit from a compact operating system and support for a powerful programming language like Java.

Overhead

JavaOS has been described by JavaSoft as just enough of an operating system to run the Java virtual machine. With this minimal design goal, it stands to reason that JavaSoft is targeting consumer electronic devices with the JavaOS technology. As part of this approach, JavaOS is specifically designed to be fully ROMable, meaning that it will work well in the embedded systems common to electronic devices. A *ROMable* software technology is one that can be implemented in read-only memory (ROM). ROM is commonly used in electronic devices to store executable system code because there is typically no other storage means beyond random access memory (RAM), which is temporary.

JavaOS has been touted as being able to run with as little as 512K of ROM and 256K of RAM in an embedded environment. Likewise, an entire JavaOS system running on a networked computer requires only 4M of ROM and 4M of RAM. These last figures include space for JavaOS, the HotJava Web browser, and a cache for downloading Web content and applets. JavaOS's minimal requirements set the stage for some unique products such as compact personal digital assistants (PDAs) with complete Internet support.

Industry Support

Because of the success of Java, JavaOS is able to enjoy industry support before its availability in even a preliminary form. An impressive group of technology companies have already announced plans to license JavaOS. Likewise, an equally important group of software tools companies have announced plans to provide development tools for JavaOS. These two areas of support provide the one-two punch necessary for JavaOS to be a success.

JavaSoft is already working with the software tools companies to define a set of APIs for developing applications for JavaOS. Major players on the Java development scene have already announced intentions to enhance their development environments to support JavaOS embedded systems development. This is a pretty major step in the embedded programming world, where many development tools are still fairly primitive compared to the visual tools used by computer applications developers.

> **NOTE**
>
> On a similar front, both the Solaris and Windows platforms are slated to include full support for Java at the operating system level. However, this support will be aimed more at supporting the Java runtime system than serving as an implementation of JavaOS.

Java Microprocessors

As if Sun weren't branching out enough with JavaOS, the company surprised the microprocessor world last year by announcing the development of a line of microprocessors optimized for Java. Microprocessors aren't new to Sun, whose Sun Microelectronics division is responsible for the popular SPARC line of microprocessors. However, the idea of Sun Microelectronics developing microprocessors specifically to support Java no doubt caught a lot of people off guard, including other microprocessor companies!

> **NOTE**
>
> Just so you don't get confused, both JavaSoft and Sun Microelectronics are divisions of Sun Microsystems. Whenever I refer to Sun, I'm referring to the company at large.

Java microprocessors are quite obviously yet another move on Sun's part to capitalize on the success of Java. However, as it does with JavaOS, Sun legitimately has an interesting and potentially lucrative angle in developing Java microprocessors. As it is for JavaOS, the primary target application for Java microprocessors is in embedded systems. Speed is a very critical factor in embedded systems, primarily because of the limited horsepower available in these small systems. Java microprocessors have the potential to significantly increase performance because they are being designed around the highly efficient Java technology. Contrast this with other embedded microprocessors that typically have a more generic design.

Sun is pushing Java microprocessors based on a new microprocessor product paradigm: *simple, secure, and small*. Add to this Sun's promise to deliver Java microprocessors at a fraction of the cost of traditional microprocessors. Sun is clearly appealing to the consumer electronics market, where a compact, low-cost microprocessor would probably rock a lot of boats. Sun has also announced the development of a full range of component-level and board-level products to support the microprocessors.

Although the prospect of a Java microprocessor may seem strange at first, it's not hard to see Sun's motivation. By 1999, the average American home is expected to contain between 50 and 100 microcontrollers. Worldwide, there are also expected to be more than 145 million cellular phone users, with each phone containing at least one microcontroller. And each microcontroller contains at least one microprocessor. Are you starting to get the picture?

> **NOTE**
>
> A *microcontroller* is a miniature computer system, usually implemented on a single circuit board, scaled down to support a limited function such as those required by consumer electronic devices.

The Java processor family consists of three lines of microprocessors:

- picoJAVA
- microJAVA
- UltraJAVA

The next few sections describe these different processor lines and the application for which each is targeted.

picoJAVA

The specification for a minimal Java microprocessor is called picoJAVA and serves as the basic design for all Sun's microprocessors. picoJAVA isn't a physical processor that Sun intends to manufacture and sell; rather, it is the core specification on which all Java microprocessors will be designed and built. The picoJAVA specification will be made readily available for licensing to other chip manufacturers who want to develop their own Java microprocessors. The picoJAVA specification is geared toward a microprocessor with the best price/performance that fully supports the Java virtual machine.

microJAVA

The first physical microprocessor in the works at Sun is microJAVA, which builds application-specific I/O, memory, communications, and control functions onto the picoJAVA core. microJAVA processors are expected to cost anywhere from $25 to $100, which makes them good candidates for a wide range of electronic devices such as telecommunications equipment and other nonnetwork applications such as printers and video games.

UltraJAVA

Sun's high-end Java microprocessor offering is called UltraJAVA. It is designed to encompass the very fastest Java processors available. The UltraJAVA processor line includes support for advanced graphics by virtue of Sun's Visual Instruction Set (VIS), which defines high-performance hardware graphics extensions. Not surprisingly, the UltraJAVA line of processors is primarily targeting high-end 3D graphics and multimedia applications. Even with an expected cost starting at $100, the UltraJAVA processor line may still be a bargain.

Summary

In this chapter, you broke away from the programming aspects of Java and learned about some new technologies based on the Java framework. The first of these is the standard extension APIs, which are planned to expand Java in a variety of directions. These APIs will no doubt boost the appeal of Java to new levels because developers will have much more reusable code to leverage when building custom applications and applets. Although these new APIs ultimately mean more learning curves for developers, they also result in less time spent writing code when that code is best suited to a standard extension. Knowing this, many developers will be forced to rethink their current plans based on the availability of the standard extension APIs because there's no need to reinvent the wheel if it's already in the works.

You also learned about JavaOS, a new operating system based entirely on the Java virtual machine. You then took a look at the new Java microprocessors, which aim to be the first physical Java implementation on silicon. Although JavaOS and Java microprocessors may not directly impact your Java development efforts in the immediate future, they will no doubt play a significant role in Java reaching its maturity as a technology with widespread application. That's reason enough for me to stay informed about the status of these technologies!

Appendixes

Java Language Summary

by Laura Lemay
revised by Billy Barron

This appendix contains a summary or quick reference for the Java language, as described in this book.

> **NOTE**
>
> This is not a grammar overview, nor is it a technical overview of the language itself. It's a quick reference to be used after you already know the basics of how the language works. If you need a technical description of the language, your best bet is to visit the Java Web site (`http://java.sun.com`) and download the actual specification, which includes a full BNF grammar.

Language keywords and symbols are shown in a `monospace font`. Arguments and other parts to be substituted are in `italic monospace`.

Optional parts are indicated by brackets (except in the array syntax section). If there are several options that are mutually exclusive, they are shown separated by pipes (¦) like this:

`[ public ¦ private ¦ protected ] type varname`

Reserved Words

The following words are reserved for use by the Java language itself (some of them are reserved but not currently used). You cannot use these terms to refer to classes, methods, or variable names:

abstract	do	import	public	try
boolean	double	instanceof	return	void
break	else	int	short	volatile
byte	extends	interface	static	while
case	final	long	super	
catch	finally	native	switch	
char	float	new	synchronized	
class	for	null	this	
const	goto	package	throw	
continue	if	private	throws	
default	implements	protected	transient	

Comments

```
/* this is the format of a multiline comment */
// this is a single-line comment
/** Javadoc comment */
```

Literals

number	Type int
number[l ¦ L]	Type long
0xhex	Hex integer
0Xhex	Hex integer
0octal	Octal integer
[*number*].*number*	Type double
number[f ¦ f]	Type float
number[d ¦ D]	Type double
[+ ¦ -] *number*	Signed
numberenumber	Exponent
numberEnumber	Exponent
'*character*'	Single character
"*characters*"	String
""	Empty string
\b	Backspace
\t	Tab
\n	Line feed
\f	Form feed
\r	Carriage return
\"	Double quote
\'	Single quote
\\	Backslash
\uNNNN	Unicode escape (NNNN is hex)
true	Boolean
false	Boolean

Variable Declarations

`[ byte ¦ short ¦ int ¦ long ] varname`	Integer (pick one type)
`[ float ¦ double ] varname`	Floats (pick one type)
`char varname`	Characters
`boolean varname`	Boolean
`classname varname`	Class types
`type varname, varname, varname`	Multiple variables

The following options are available only for class and instance variables. Any of these options can be used with a variable declaration:

`[ static ] variableDeclaration`	Class variable
`[ final ] variableDeclaration`	Constants
`[ public ¦ private ¦ protected ] variableDeclaration`	Access control

Variable Assignments

`variable = value`	Assignment
`variable++`	Postfix Increment
`++variable`	Prefix Increment
`variable--`	Postfix Decrement
`--variable`	Prefix Decrement
`variable += value`	Add and assign
`variable -= value`	Subtract and assign
`variable *= value`	Multiply and assign
`variable /= value`	Divide and assign
`variable %= value`	Modulus and assign
`variable &= value`	AND and assign
`variable ¦ = value`	OR and assign
`variable ^= value`	XOR and assign
`variable <<= value`	Left-shift and assign
`variable >>= value`	Right-shift and assign
`variable >>>= value`	Zero-fill, right-shift, and assign

Operators

`arg + arg`	Addition
`arg - arg`	Subtraction
`arg * arg`	Multiplication
`arg / arg`	Division
`arg % arg`	Modulus
`arg < arg`	Less than
`arg > arg`	Greater than
`arg <= arg`	Less than or equal to
`arg >= arg`	Greater than or equal to
`arg == arg`	Equal
`arg != arg`	Not equal
`arg && arg`	Logical AND
`arg ¦¦ arg`	Logical OR
`! arg`	Logical NOT
`arg & arg`	AND
`arg ¦ arg`	OR
`arg ^ arg`	XOR
`arg << arg`	Left-shift
`arg >> arg`	Right-shift
`arg >>> arg`	Zero-fill right-shift
`~ arg`	Complement
`(type)thing`	Casting
`arg instanceof class`	Instance of
`test ? trueOp : falseOp`	Ternary (if) operator

Objects

`new class();`	Create new instance
`new class(arg,arg,arg...)`	New instance with parameters
`new type(arg,arg,arg...)`	Create new instance of an anonymous class
`Primary.new type(arg,arg,arg...)`	Create new instance of an anonymous class

`object.variable`	Instance variable
`object.classvar`	Class variable
`Class.classvar`	Class variable
`object.method()`	Instance method (no arguments)
`object.method(arg,arg,arg...)`	Instance method
`object.classmethod()`	Class method (no arguments)
`object.classmethod(arg,arg,arg...)`	Class method
`Class.classmethod()`	Class method (no arguments)
`Class.classmethod(arg,arg,arg...)`	Class method

Arrays

> **NOTE**
>
> The brackets in this section are parts of the array creation or access statements. They do not denote optional parts as they do in other parts of this appendix.

`type varname[]`	Array variable
`type[] varname`	Array variable
`new type[numElements]`	New array object
`new type[] {initializer}`	New anonymous array object
`array[index]`	Element access
`array.length`	Length of array

Loops and Conditionals

`if ( test) block`	Conditional
`if ( test ) block` `else block`	Conditional with `else`

```
switch (test) {                           switch (only with int
 case value : statements                  or char types)
  case value : statements
  ...
 default : statement
}


for (initializer; test; change ) block    for loop


while ( test ) block                       while loop


do block                                   do loop
while (test)


break [ label ]                            Break from loop or switch


continue [ label ]                         continue loop


label:                                     Labeled loop
```

Class Definitions

```
class classname block                      Simple class definition
```

Any of the following optional modifiers can be added to the class definition:

```
[ final ] class classname block            No subclasses
[ abstract ] class classname block         Cannot be instantiated
[ public ] class classname block           Accessible outside
                                           package
class classname [ extends Superclass ] block   Define superclass
class classname [ implements interfaces ] block Implement one or more
                                           interfaces
```

Method and Constructor Definitions

The basic method looks like this, where *returnType* is a type name, a class name, or void:

`returnType methodName() block`	Basic method
`returnType methodName(parameter, parameter, ...) block`	Method with parameters

Method parameters look like this:

`type parameterName`

Method variations can include any of the following optional keywords:

`[ abstract ] returnType methodName() block`	Abstract method
`[ static ] returnType methodName() block`	Class method
`[ native ] returnType methodName() block`	Native method
`[ final ] returnType methodName() block`	Final method
`[ synchronized ] returnType methodName() block`	Thread lock before executing
`[ public ¦ private ¦ protected ] returnType methodName()`	Access control

Constructors look like this:

`classname() block`	Basic constructor
`classname(parameter, parameter, parameter...) block`	Constructor with parameters
`[ public ¦ private ¦ protected] classname() block`	Access control

In the method/constructor body, you can use these references and methods:

`this`	Refers to current object
`classname.this`	Refers to a particular inner class object
`super`	Refers to superclass
`super.methodName()`	Calls a superclass's method
`this(...)`	Calls class's constructor
`super(...)`	Calls superclass's constructor
`type.class`	Returns the class object for the type
`return [ value ]`	Returns a value

Importing

```
import package.className          Imports specific class name
import package.*                  Imports all classes in package
package packagename               Classes in this file belong to this package
interface interfaceName [ extends anotherInterface ] block
[ public ] interface interfaceName block
[ abstract ] interface interfaceName block
```

Guarding

```
synchronized ( object ) block    Waits for lock on object


try block                        Guarded statements
catch ( exception ) block        Executed if exception is thrown
[ finally block ]                Always executed


try block                        Same as previous example (can
[ catch ( exception ) block ]    use optional catch or finally
finally block                    but not both)
```

Class Hierarchy Diagrams

by Charles Perkins

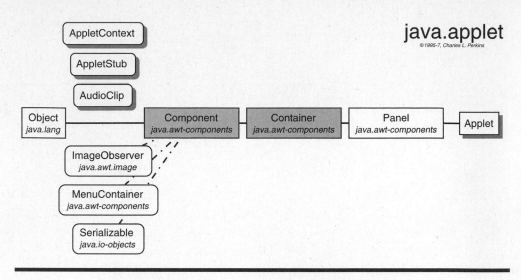

java.applet
©1995-7, Charles L. Perkins

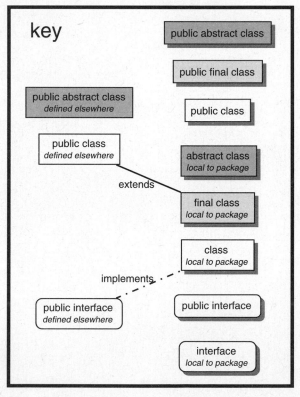

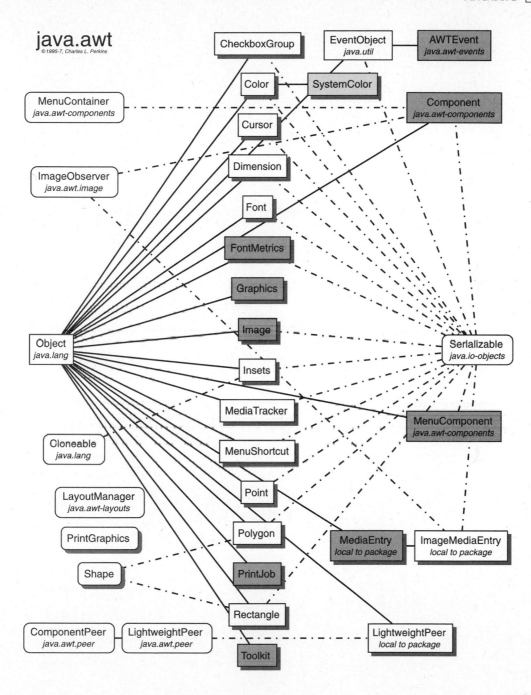

java.awt

©1995-7, Charles L. Perkins

java.awt-components

© 1995-7, Charles L. Perkins

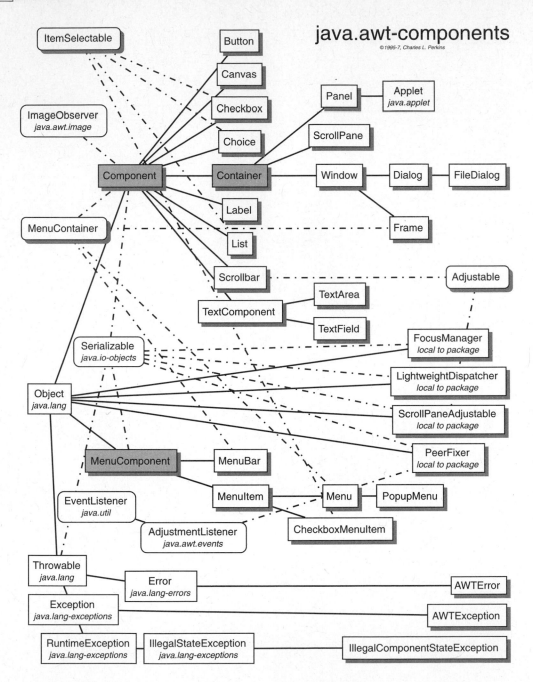

java.awt-layouts

© 1995-7, Charles L. Perkins

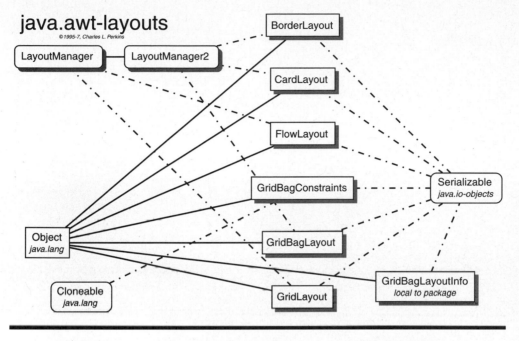

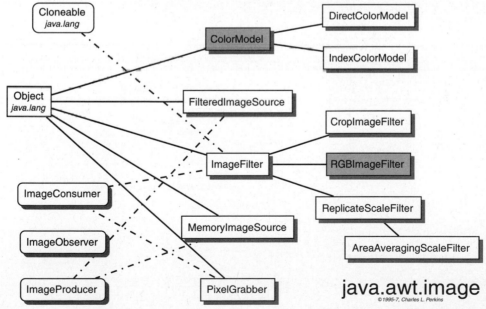

java.awt.image

© 1995-7, Charles L. Perkins

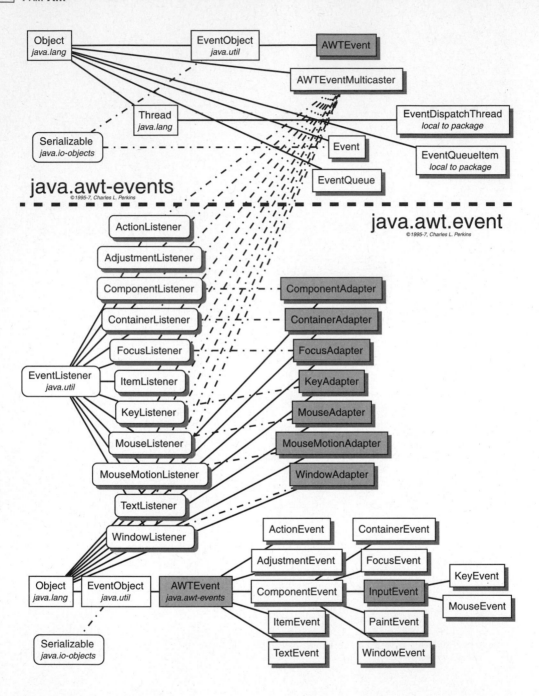

java.awt-events
© 1995-7, Charles L. Perkins

java.awt.event
© 1995-7, Charles L. Perkins

\<unnamed\> (java/awt/test)

© 1995-7, Charles L. Perkins

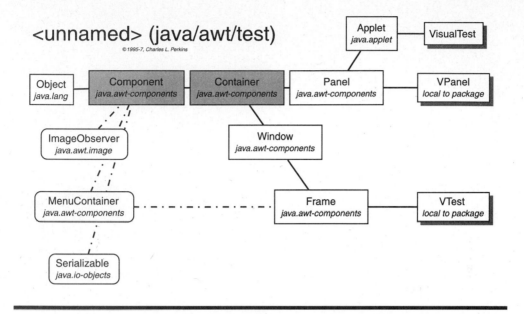

java.awt.datatransfer

® 1995-7, Charles L. Perkins

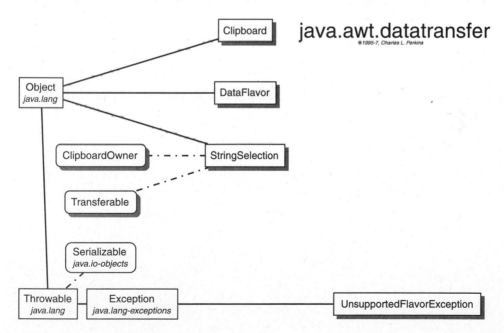

java.awt.peer

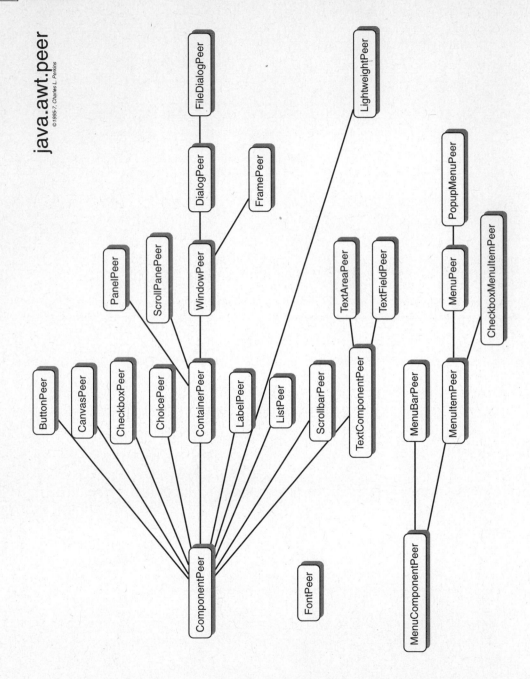

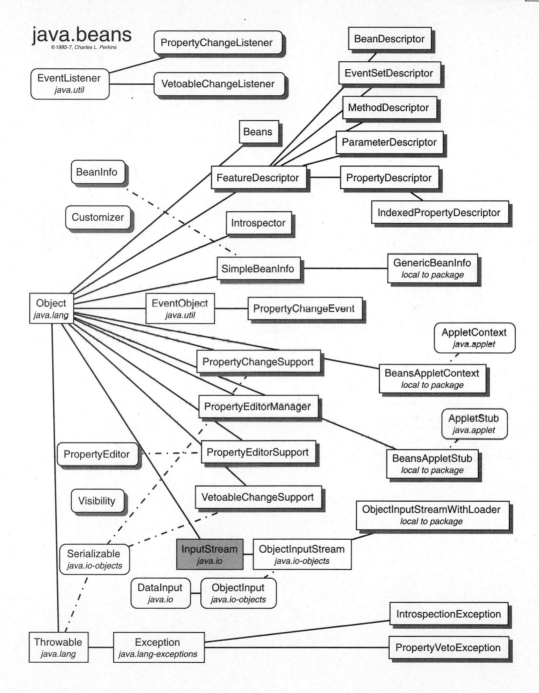

java.beans

PropertyChangeListener

EventListener
java.util

VetoableChangeListener

BeanDescriptor

EventSetDescriptor

MethodDescriptor

Beans

ParameterDescriptor

FeatureDescriptor

PropertyDescriptor

BeanInfo

IndexedPropertyDescriptor

Customizer

Introspector

SimpleBeanInfo

GenericBeanInfo
local to package

Object
java.lang

EventObject
java.util

PropertyChangeEvent

AppletContext
java.applet

PropertyChangeSupport

BeansAppletContext
local to package

PropertyEditorManager

AppletStub
java.applet

PropertyEditor

PropertyEditorSupport

BeansAppletStub
local to package

Visibility

VetoableChangeSupport

ObjectInputStreamWithLoader
local to package

Serializable
java.io-objects

InputStream
java.io

ObjectInputStream
java.io-objects

DataInput
java.io

ObjectInput
java.io-objects

IntrospectionException

Throwable
java.lang

Exception
java.lang-exceptions

PropertyVetoException

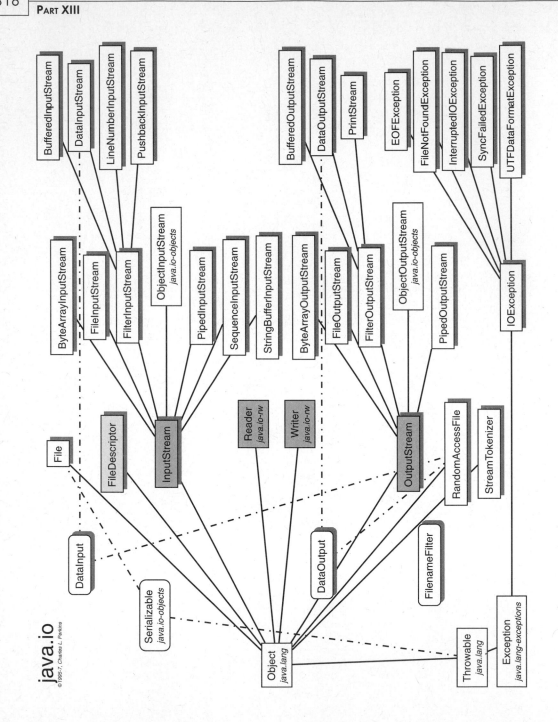

java.io
© 1995-7, Charles L. Perkins

java.io-rw
©1995-7, Charles L. Perkins

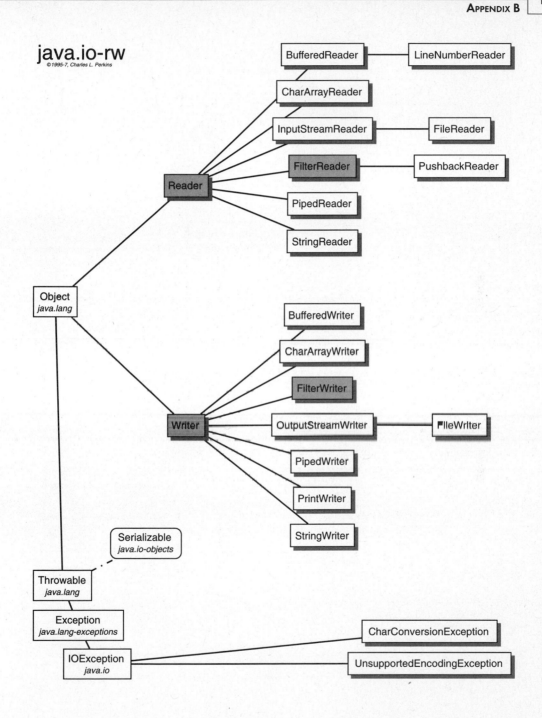

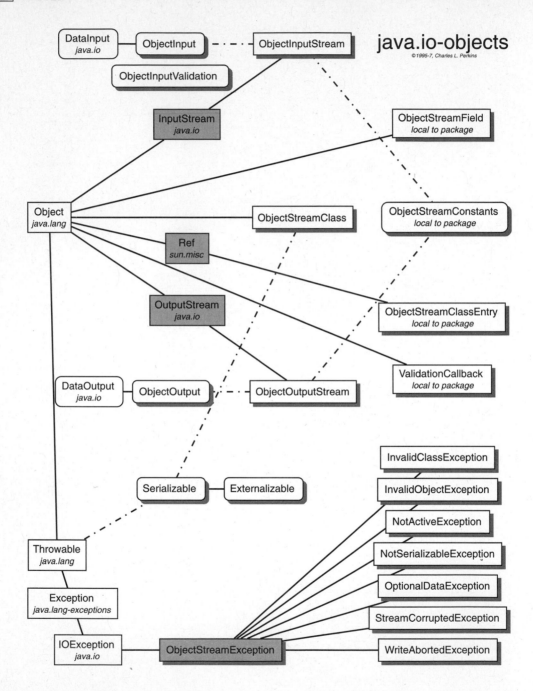

java.io-objects
©1995-7, Charles L. Perkins

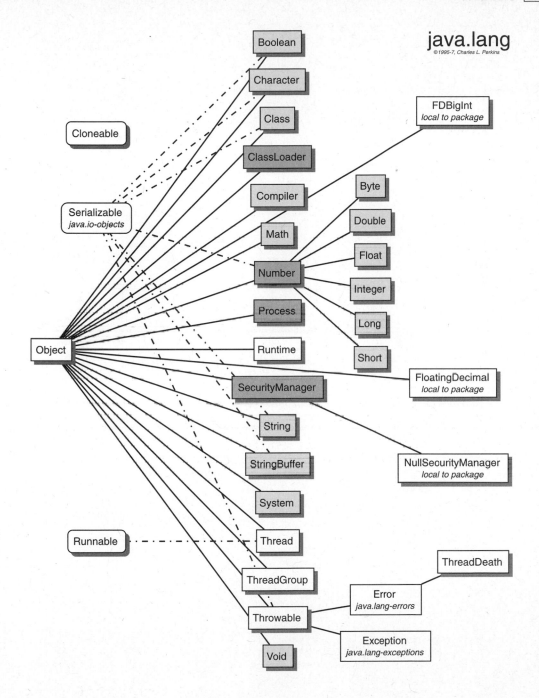

java.lang
©1995-7, Charles L. Perkins

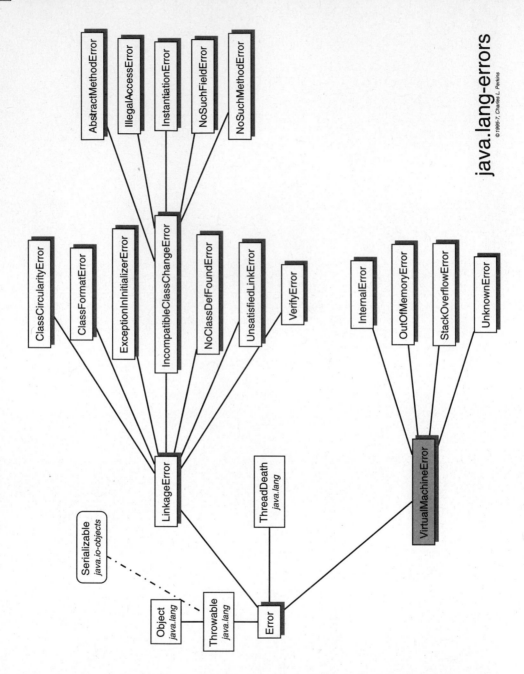

java.lang-errors

©1995-7, Charles L. Perkins

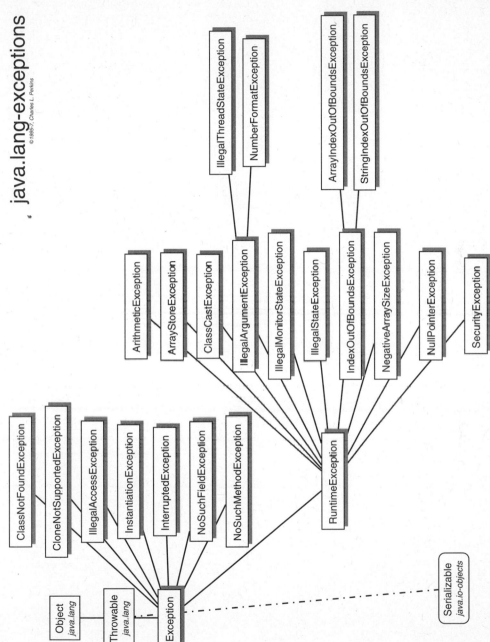

java.lang-exceptions

© 1995-7, Charles L. Perkins

java.lang.reflect

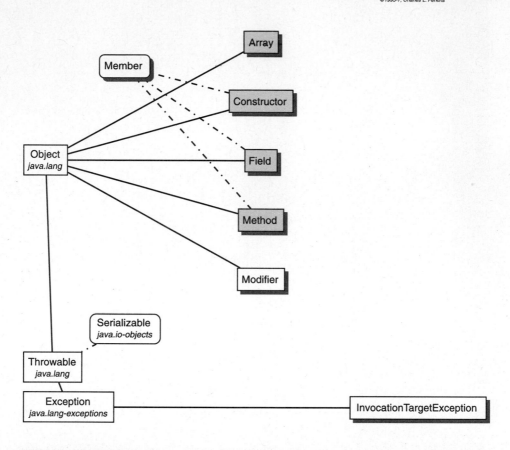

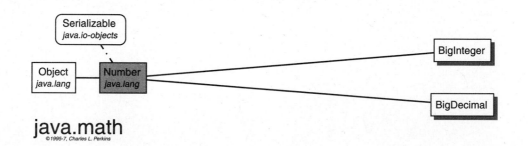

java.math

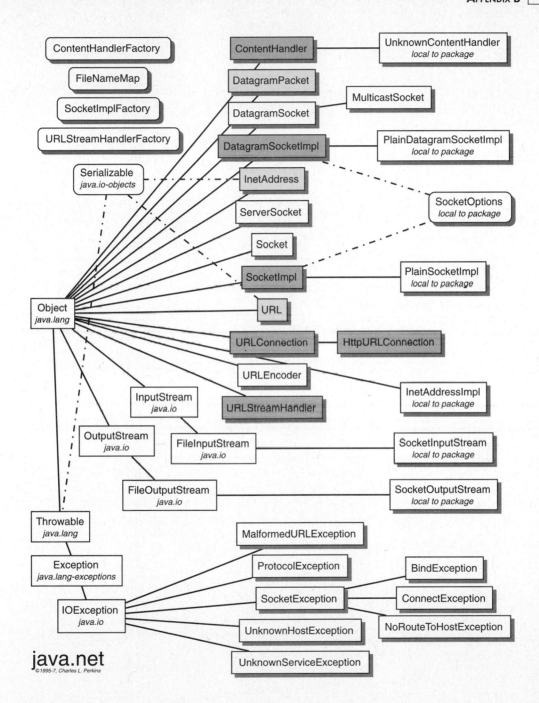

ContentHandlerFactory

FileNameMap

SocketImplFactory

URLStreamHandlerFactory

Serializable
java.io-objects

Object
java.lang

ContentHandler → UnknownContentHandler *local to package*

DatagramPacket

DatagramSocket — MulticastSocket

DatagramSocketImpl — PlainDatagramSocketImpl *local to package*

InetAddress

ServerSocket

Socket

SocketImpl — PlainSocketImpl *local to package*

SocketOptions *local to package*

URL

URLConnection — HttpURLConnection

URLEncoder

URLStreamHandler

InetAddressImpl *local to package*

InputStream
java.io

OutputStream
java.io

FileInputStream
java.io — SocketInputStream *local to package*

FileOutputStream
java.io — SocketOutputStream *local to package*

Throwable
java.lang

Exception
java.lang-exceptions

IOException
java.io

MalformedURLException

ProtocolException

SocketException — BindException

ConnectException

NoRouteToHostException

UnknownHostException

UnknownServiceException

java.net
©1995-7, Charles L. Perkins

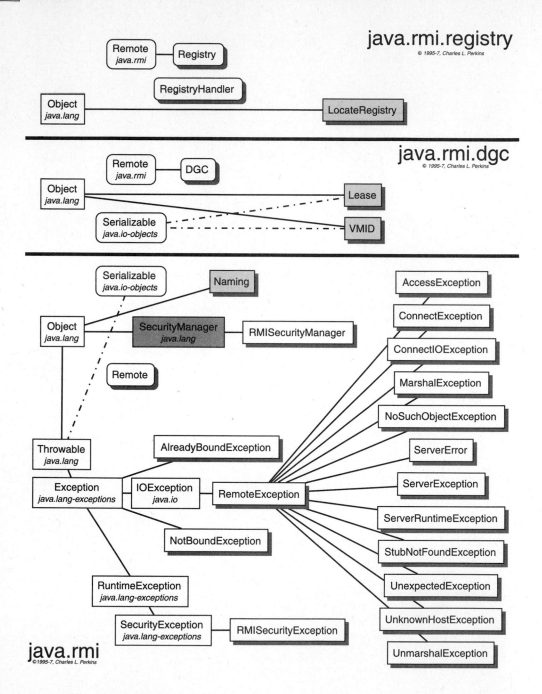

java.rmi.registry
© 1995-7, Charles L. Perkins

java.rmi.dgc
© 1995-7, Charles L. Perkins

java.rmi
©1995-7, Charles L. Perkins

java.rmi.server
©1995-7, Charles L. Perkins

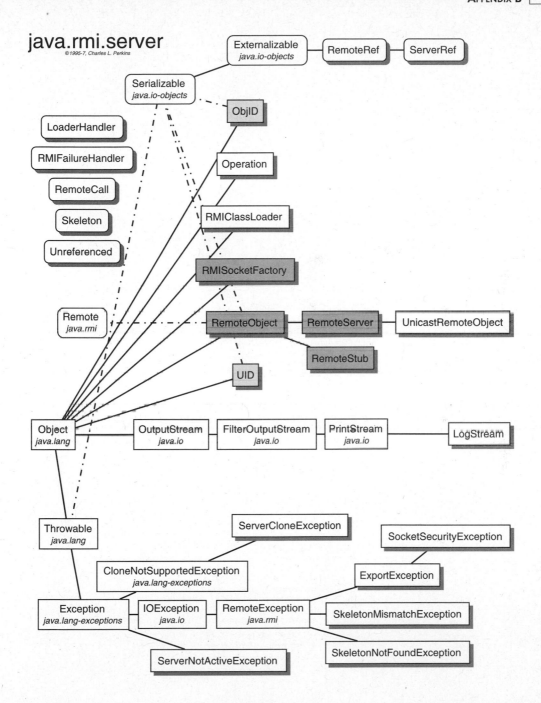

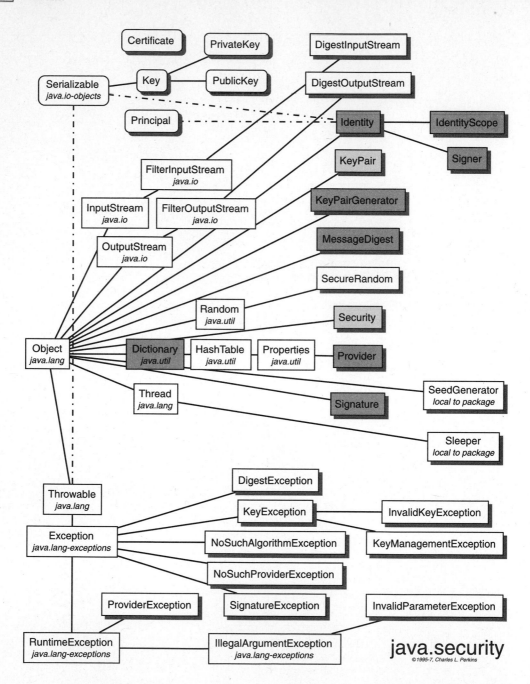

java.security
©1995-7, Charles L. Perkins

java.security.interfaces

© 1995-7, Charles L. Perkins

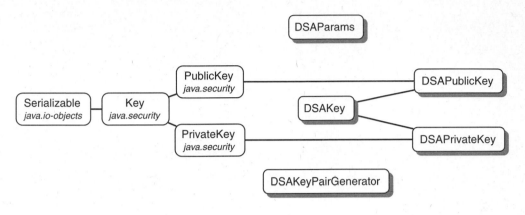

java.security.acl

© 1995-7, Charles L. Perkins

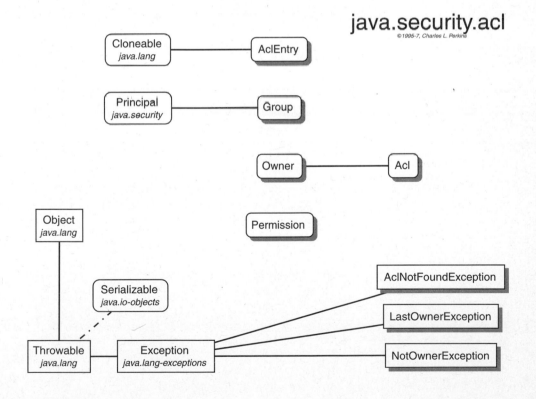

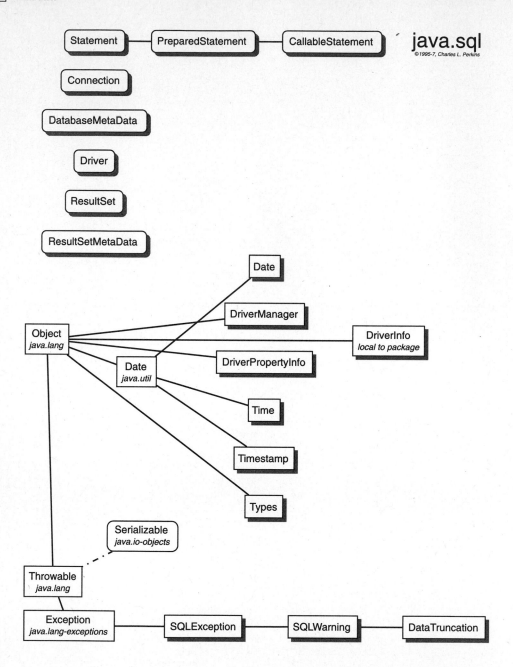

Statement — PreparedStatement — CallableStatement

java.sql
©1995-7, Charles L. Perkins

Connection

DatabaseMetaData

Driver

ResultSet

ResultSetMetaData

Date

DriverManager

Object
java.lang

DriverInfo
local to package

Date
java.util

DriverPropertyInfo

Time

Timestamp

Types

Serializable
java.io-objects

Throwable
java.lang

Exception
java.lang-exceptions

SQLException — SQLWarning — DataTruncation

java.text

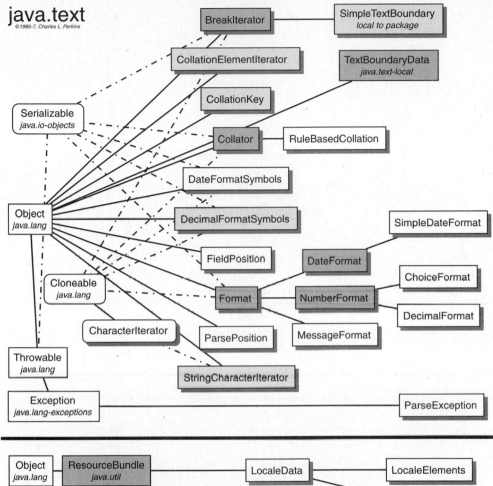

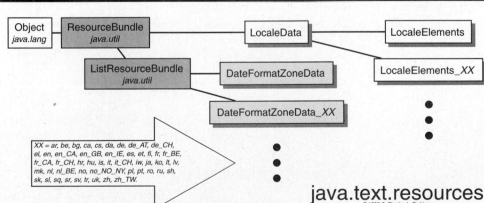

XX = ar, be, bg, ca, cs, da, de, de_AT, de_CH, el, en, en_CA, en_GB, en_IE, es, et, fi, fr, fr_BE, fr_CA, fr_CH, hr, hu, is, it, it_CH, iw, ja, ko, lt, lv, mk, nl, nl_BE, no, no_NO_NY, pl, pt, ro, ru, sh, sk, sl, sq, sr, sv, tr, uk, zh, zh_TW.

java.text.resources

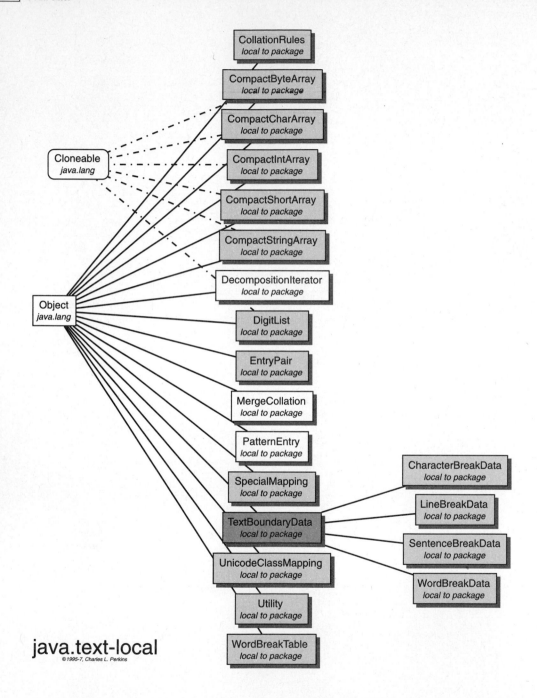

CollationRules
local to package

CompactByteArray
local to package

CompactCharArray
local to package

Cloneable
java.lang

CompactIntArray
local to package

CompactShortArray
local to package

CompactStringArray
local to package

DecompositionIterator
local to package

Object
java.lang

DigitList
local to package

EntryPair
local to package

MergeCollation
local to package

PatternEntry
local to package

SpecialMapping
local to package

CharacterBreakData
local to package

LineBreakData
local to package

TextBoundaryData
local to package

SentenceBreakData
local to package

UnicodeClassMapping
local to package

WordBreakData
local to package

Utility
local to package

java.text-local
©1995-7, Charles L. Perkins

WordBreakTable
local to package

java.util
©1995-7, Charles L. Perkins

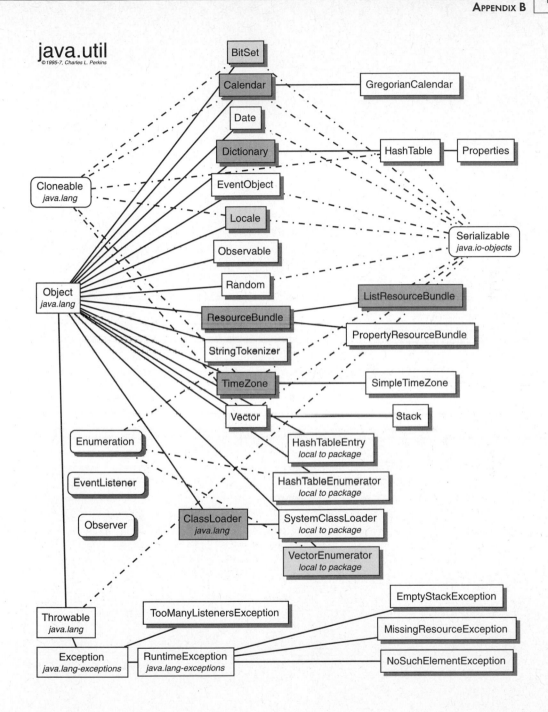

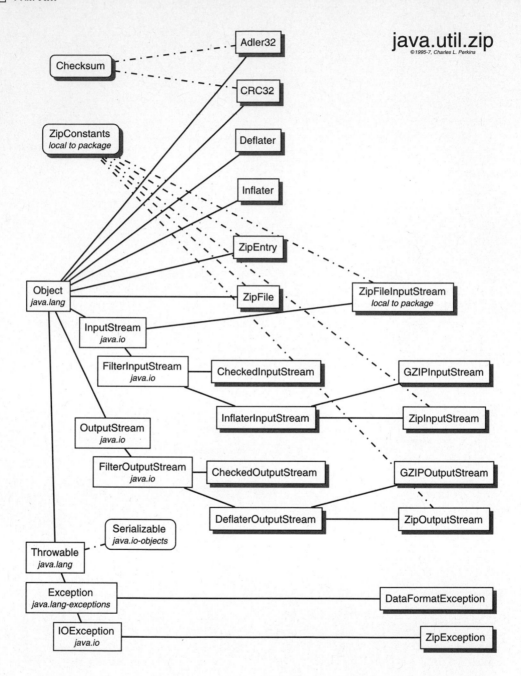

java.util.zip

©1995-7, Charles L. Perkins

Java Class Library

by Laura Lemay
revised by Billy Barron and Jeff Shockley

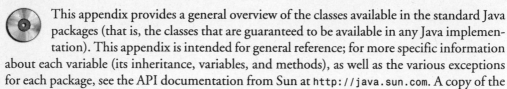

This appendix provides a general overview of the classes available in the standard Java packages (that is, the classes that are guaranteed to be available in any Java implementation). This appendix is intended for general reference; for more specific information about each variable (its inheritance, variables, and methods), as well as the various exceptions for each package, see the API documentation from Sun at http://java.sun.com. A copy of the 1.1 API documentation is on the CD-ROM included with this book.

java.lang

The java.lang package contains the classes and interfaces that are the core of the Java language.

Interfaces

Cloneable	Interface indicating that an object may be copied or cloned
Runnable	Methods for classes that want to run as threads
Serializable	Interface for tagging an object that can be serialized (Java 1.1)

Classes

Boolean	Object wrapper for boolean values
Byte	Object wrapper for byte values (Java 1.1)
Character	Object wrapper for char values
Class	Runtime representations of classes
ClassLoader	Abstract behavior for handling loading of classes
Compiler	System class that gives access to the Java compiler
Double	Object wrapper for double values
Float	Object wrapper for float values
Integer	Object wrapper for int values
Long	Object wrapper for long values
Math	Utility class for math operations
Number	Abstract superclass of all number classes (Integer, Float, and so on)
Object	Generic Object class, at top of inheritance hierarchy
Process	Abstract behavior for processes such as those spawned using methods in the System class
Runtime	Access to the Java runtime system
SecurityManager	Abstract behavior for implementing security policies
Short	Object wrapper for short values (Java 1.1)

String	Character strings
StringBuffer	Mutable strings
System	Access to Java's system-level behavior, provided in a platform-independent way.
Thread	Methods for managing threads and classes that run in threads
ThreadDeath	Class of object thrown when a thread is asynchronously terminated
ThreadGroup	A group of threads
Throwable	Generic exception class; all objects thrown must be a Throwable
Void	Object wrapper for void types (Java 1.1)

java.lang.reflect (Java 1.1)

The java.lang.reflect package is used to find out information about loaded classes such as what methods and fields they have.

Interfaces

Member	Methods to find out information about a member

Classes

Array	Methods to dynamically create and access arrays
Constructor	Methods to find out about and access constructors
Field	Methods to find out about and access variables
Method	Methods to find out about and access methods
Modifier	Decoder for static class and member access modifiers

java.math (Java 1.1)

The java.math package contains two classes that can hold numbers of arbitrary size.

Classes

BigDecimal	A very big floating-point number
BigInteger	A very big integer number

C

JAVA CLASS LIBRARY

`java.util`

The `java.util` package contains various utility classes and interfaces, including random numbers, system properties, and other useful classes.

Interfaces

Enumeration	Methods for enumerating sets of values
EventListener	Methods for listening to events (Java 1.1)
Observer	Methods for enabling classes to be `Observable` objects

Classes

BitSet	A set of bits
Calendar	A generic calendar (Java 1.1)
Date	The current system date as well as methods for generating and parsing dates
Dictionary	An abstract class that maps between keys and values (superclass of `HashTable`)
EventObject	A event object associated with another object (Java 1.1)
GregorianCalendar	A Gregorian calendar, which is the type you probably use (Java 1.1)
Hashtable	A hash table
ListResourceBundle	A resource supplier for a `Locale` (Java 1.1)
Locale	A description of a geographic location (Java 1.1)
Observable	An abstract class for observable objects
Properties	A hash table that contains behavior for setting and retrieving persistent properties of the system or a class
PropertyResourceBundle	A resource supplier which uses properties from a file (Java 1.1)
Random	Utilities for generating random numbers
ResourceBundle	A set of objects related to a `Locale` (Java 1.1)
SimpleTimeZone	A simplified time zone (Java 1.1)
Stack	A stack (a last-in-first-out queue)
StringTokenizer	Utilities for splitting strings into individual "tokens"
TimeZone	A generic time zone (Java 1.1)
Vector	A growable array of `Objects`

`java.util.zip` (Java 1.1)

The `java.util.zip` package provides classes for dealing with ZIP and GZIP files.

Interfaces

Checksum	Methods for calculating a checksum

Classes

Adler32	Calculates an Adler 32 checksum
CRC32	Calculates a CRC 32 checksum
CheckedInputStream	Input stream with an associated checksum
CheckedOutputStream	Output stream with an associated checksum
Deflator	Compressor for uncompressed files
DeflatorOutputStream	Output stream that compresses files
GZIPInputSteam	Input stream from a GZIP file
GZIPOutputStream	Output stream to a GZIP file
Inflater	Decompressor for compressed files
InflaterInputStream	Input stream that decompresses files
ZipEntry	A file entry inside a ZIP file
ZipFile	A whole ZIP file
ZipInputStream	Input stream from a ZIP file
ZipOutputStream	Output stream to a ZIP file

`java.io`

The `java.io` package provides input and output classes and interfaces for streams and files.

Interfaces

DataInput	Methods for reading machine-independent typed input streams
DataOutput	Methods for writing machine-independent typed output streams
Externalizable	Methods to write/read an object's contents with a stream (Java 1.1)
FilenameFilter	Methods for filtering filenames

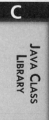

`ObjectInput`	Methods for reading objects (Java 1.1)
`ObjectInputValidation`	Methods to validate an object (Java 1.1)
`ObjectOutput`	Methods for writing objects (Java 1.1)
`Serializable`	Tag to say that this class can be serialized (Java 1.1)

Classes

`BufferedInputStream`	A buffered input stream
`BufferedOutputStream`	A buffered output stream
`BufferedReader`	A buffered reader (Java 1.1)
`BufferedWriter`	A buffered writer (Java 1.1)
`ByteArrayInputStream`	An input stream from a byte array
`ByteArrayOutputStream`	An output stream to a byte array
`CharArrayReader`	A reader from an array of characters (Java 1.1)
`CharArrayWriter`	A writer to an array of characters (Java 1.1)
`DataInputStream`	Enables you to read primitive Java types (`ints`, `chars`, `booleans`, and so on) from a stream in a machine-independent way
`DataOutputStream`	Enables you to write primitive Java data types (`ints`, `chars`, `booleans`, and so on) to a stream in a machine-independent way
`File`	Represents a file on the host's file system
`FileDescriptor`	Holds onto the UNIX-like file descriptor of a file or socket
`FileInputStream`	An input stream from a file, constructed using a filename or descriptor
`FileOutputStream`	An output stream to a file, constructed using a filename or descriptor
`FileReader`	A reader from a file, constructed using a filename or descriptor (Java 1.1)
`FileWriter`	A writer to a file, constructed using a filename or descriptor (Java 1.1)
`FilterInputStream`	Abstract class that provides a filter for input streams (and for adding stream functionality such as buffering)
`FilterOutputStream`	Abstract class that provides a filter for output streams (and for adding stream functionality such as buffering)

FilterReader	A class that provides a filter for readers (and for adding functionality such as buffering) (Java 1.1)
FilterWriter	A class that provides a filter for writers (and for adding functionality such as buffering) (Java 1.1)
InputStream	An abstract class representing an input stream of bytes; the parent of all input streams in this package
LineNumberInputStream	An input stream that keeps track of line numbers
ObjectInputStream	A class that deserializes data and objects (Java 1.1)
ObjectOutputStream	A class that serializes data and objects (Java 1.1)
ObjectStreamClass	A descriptor for classes that can be serialized (Java 1.1)
OutputStream	An abstract class representing an output stream of bytes; the parent of all output streams in this package
OutputStreamWriter	A bridge between byte and character streams (Java 1.1)
PipedInputStream	A piped input stream, which should be connected to a PipedOutputStream to be useful
PipedOutputStream	A piped output stream, which should be connected to a PipedInputStream to be useful (together they provide safe communication between threads)
PipedReader	A piped reader, which should be connected to a PipedWriter to be useful (Java 1.1)
PipedWriter	A piped writer, which should be connected to a PipedReader to be useful (Java 1.1)
PrintStream	An output stream for printing (used by System.out.println(...))
PrintWriter	A writer for printing (Java 1.1)
PushbackInputStream	An input stream with a pushback buffer
PushbackReader	A reader with a pushback buffer (Java 1.1)
RandomAccessFile	Provides random access to a file, constructed from filenames, descriptors, or objects
Reader	An abstract class representing an input character stream; the parent of all readers in this package (Java 1.1)
SequenceInputStream	Converts a sequence of input streams into a single input stream
StreamTokenizer	Converts an input stream into a series of individual tokens

StringBufferInputStream	An input stream from a `String` object
StringReader	A reader from a `String` object (Java 1.1)
StringWriter	A writer to a `String` object (Java 1.1)
Writer	An abstract class representing an output character stream; the parent of all writers in this package (Java 1.1)

java.net

The `java.net` package contains classes and interfaces for performing network operations, such as sockets and URLs.

Interfaces

ContentHandlerFactory	Methods for creating `ContentHandler` objects
FileNameMap	Methods for mapping between filenames and MIME types (Java 1.1)
SocketImplFactory	Methods for creating socket implementations (instance of the `SocketImpl` class)
URLStreamHandlerFactory	Methods for creating `URLStreamHandler` objects

Classes

ContentHandler	Abstract behavior for reading data from a URL connection and constructing the appropriate local object, based on MIME types
DatagramPacket	A datagram packet (UDP)
DatagramSocket	A datagram socket
DatagramSocketImpl	Abstract base class for datagram and multicast sockets (Java 1.1)
HttpURLConnection	A connection can handle the HTTP protocol (Java 1.1)
InetAddress	An object representation of an Internet host (host name, IP address)
MulticastSocket	A server-side socket with support for transmitting data to multiple client sockets (Java 1.1)
ServerSocket	A server-side socket
Socket	A socket
SocketImpl	An abstract class for specific socket implementations
URL	An object representation of a URL

URLConnection	Abstract behavior for a socket that can handle various Web-based protocols (http, ftp, and so on)
URLEncoder	Turns strings into x-www-form-urlencoded format
URLStreamHandler	Abstract class for managing streams to objects referenced by URLs

java.awt

The java.awt package contains the classes and interfaces that make up the Abstract Windowing Toolkit.

Interfaces

Adjustable	Methods for objects with adjustable numeric values (Java 1.1)
EventSource	Methods for objects that generate events (Java 1.1)
ItemSelectable	Methods for objects that contain a set of selectable items (Java 1.1)
LayoutManager	Methods for laying out containers
LayoutManager2	Methods for laying out containers based on a constraints object (Java 1.1)
MenuContainer	Methods for menu-related containers
PrintGraphics	Methods for providing a print graphics context (Java 1.1)
Shape	Methods for geometric shapes (Java 1.1)

Classes

AWTEvent	The parent of all AWT events (Java 1.1)
AWTEventMulticaster	A multicast event dispatcher (Java 1.1)
BorderLayout	A layout manager for arranging items in border formation
Button	A UI pushbutton
Canvas	A canvas for drawing and performing other graphics operations
CardLayout	A layout manager for HyperCard-like metaphors
Checkbox	A checkbox
CheckboxGroup	A group of exclusive checkboxes (radio buttons)
CheckboxMenuItem	A toggle menu item

Choice	A popup menu of choices
Color	An abstract representation of a color
Component	The abstract generic class for all UI components
Container	Abstract behavior for a component that can hold other components or containers
Cursor	A screen cursor (Java 1.1)
Dialog	A window for brief interactions with users
Dimension	An object representing width and height
Event	An object representing events caused by the system or based on user input
EventQueue	A queue of events waiting to be processed (Java 1.1)
FileDialog	A dialog box for getting filenames from the local file system
FlowLayout	A layout manager that lays out objects from left to right in rows
Font	An abstract representation of a font
FontMetrics	Abstract class for holding information about a specific font's character shapes and height and width information
Frame	A top-level window with a title
Graphics	Abstract behavior for representing a graphics context and for drawing and painting shapes and objects
GridBagConstraints	Constraints for components laid out using GridBagLayout
GridBagLayout	A layout manager that aligns components horizontally and vertically based on their values from GridBagConstraints
GridLayout	A layout manager with rows and columns; elements are added to each cell in the grid
Image	An abstract representation of a bitmap image
Insets	Distances from the outer border of the window; used to lay out components
Label	A text label for UI components
List	A scrolling list
MediaTracker	A way to keep track of the status of media objects being loaded over the Net
Menu	A menu that can contain menu items and is a container on a menu bar

MenuBar	A menu bar (container for menus)
MenuComponent	The abstract superclass of all menu elements
MenuItem	An individual menu item
MenuShortcut	A keyboard shortcut for a menu item (Java 1.1)
Panel	A container that is displayed
Point	An object representing a point (x and y coordinates)
Polygon	An object representing a set of points
PopupMenu	A menu that pops up (Java 1.1)
PrintJob	A job to be printed (Java 1.1)
Rectangle	An object representing a rectangle (x and y coordinates for the top-left corner, plus width and height)
ScrollPane	A container with automatic scrolling (Java 1.1)
Scrollbar	A UI scrollbar object
SystemColor	A class containing the GUI colors for a system (Java 1.1)
TextArea	A multiline, scrollable, editable text field
TextComponent	The superclass of all editable text components
TextField	A fixed-size editable text field
Toolkit	Abstract behavior for binding the abstract AWT classes to a platform-specific toolkit implementation
Window	A top-level window, and the superclass of the Frame and Dialog classes

java.awt.datatransfer (Java 1.1)

The java.awt.datatransfer package is a subpackage of the AWT that provides interfaces and methods for talking to the clipboard.

Interfaces

ClipboardOwner	Methods for classes providing data to a clipboard
Transferable	Methods for classes providing data to a transfer operation

Classes

Clipboard	The clipboard itself
DataFlavor	The opaque concept of a data format
StringSelection	A transfer agent for a string

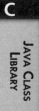

java.awt.event (Java 1.1)

The java.awt.event package is a subpackage of the AWT that implements the new event model for Java 1.1.

Interfaces

ActionListener	Methods for listening to an action event
AdjustmentListener	Methods for listening to an adjustment event
ComponentListener	Methods for listening to a component event
FocusListener	Methods for listening to a focus event
ItemListener	Methods for listening to an item event
KeyListener	Methods for listening to a keyboard event
MouseListener	Methods for listening to a mouse event
MouseMotionListener	Methods for listening to a mouse motion event
TextListener	Methods for listening to a text event
WindowListener	Methods for listening to a window event

Classes

ActionEvent	An action event
AdjustmentEvent	An adjustment event generated from an adjustable object
ComponentAdapter	An adapter that listens to component events
ComponentEvent	A component event
ContainerAdapter	An adapter that listens to container events
ContainerEvent	A container event
FocusAdapter	An adapter that listens to focus events
FocusEvent	A focus event
InputEvent	An input event
ItemEvent	An item event generated from an ItemSelectable object
KeyAdapter	An adapter that listens to keyboard events
KeyEvent	A keyboard event
MouseAdapter	An adapter that listens to mouse events
MouseEvent	A mouse event
MouseMotionAdapter	An adapter that listens to mouse motion events, such as drag

PaintEvent	A component-level paint event
TextEvent	A text event generated by a TextComponent
WindowAdapter	An adapter that listens to window events
WindowEvent	A windowing event

java.awt.image

The java.awt.image package is a subpackage of the AWT that provides interfaces and classes for managing bitmap images.

Interfaces

ImageConsumer	Methods for receiving image data created by an ImageProducer
ImageObserver	Methods to track the loading and construction of an image
ImageProducer	Methods for producing image data received by an ImageConsumer

Classes

AverageScaleFilter	A filter that scales an image based on an average algorithm (Java 1.1)
ColorModel	An abstract class for managing color information for images
CropImageFilter	A filter for cropping images to a particular size
DirectColorModel	A specific color model for managing and translating pixel color values
FilteredImageSource	An ImageProducer that takes an image and an ImageFilter object and produces an image for an ImageConsumer
ImageFilter	A filter that takes image data from an ImageProducer, modifies it in some way, and hands it off to an ImageConsumer
IndexColorModel	A specific color model for managing and translating color values in a fixed-color map
MemoryImageSource	An image producer that gets its image from memory; used after constructing an image by hand
PixelGrabber	An ImageConsumer that retrieves a subset of the pixels in an image

| ReplicateScaleFilter | A filter that scales an image (Java 1.1) |
| RGBImageFilter | Abstract behavior for a filter that modifies the RGB values of pixels in RGB images |

java.awt.peer

The java.awt.peer package is a subpackage of AWT that provides the (hidden) platform-specific AWT classes (for example, Motif, Macintosh, and Windows 95) with platform-independent interfaces to implement. Thus, callers using these interfaces need not know which platform's window system these hidden AWT classes are currently implementing.

Each class in the AWT that inherits from either Component or MenuComponent has a corresponding peer class. Each of those classes is the name of the Component with -Peer added (for example, ButtonPeer, DialogPeer, and WindowPeer). Because each one provides similar behavior, they are not enumerated here.

java.applet

The java.applet package provides applet-specific behavior.

Interfaces

AppletContext	Methods to refer to the applet's context
AppletStub	Methods for implementing applet viewers
AudioClip	Methods for playing audio files

Classes

| Applet | The base applet class |

java.beans

The java.beans package contains the classes and interfaces that make the JavaBeans technology possible.

Interfaces

| BeanInfo | Methods that can be used to find out information explicitly provided by a bean |
| Customizer | Methods that define the overhead to provide a complete visual editor for a bean |

PropertyChangeListener	Method that is called when a bound property is changed
PropertyEditor	Methods that provide support for GUIs that allow users to edit a property value of a given type
VetoableChangeListener	Methods that are called when a constrained property is changed
Visibility	Methods used to determine whether a bean requires a graphical user interface and whether a graphical user interface is available for the bean to use

Classes

BeanDescriptor	Provides global information about a bean
Beans	Provides some general-purpose beans control methods
EventSetDescriptor	Represents a set of events that a bean is capable of generating
FeatureDescriptor	Serves as a common base class for the EventSetDescriptor, MethodDescriptor, and PropertyDescriptor classes
IndexedPropertyDescriptor	Provides methods for accessing the type of an indexed property along with its accessor methods
Introspector	Provides the overhead necessary to analyze a bean and determine its public properties, methods, and events
MethodDescriptor	Provides methods for accessing information such as a method's parameters
ParameterDescriptor	Allows bean implementors to provide additional information for each of their parameters
PropertyChangeEvent	Stores information relating to a change in a bound or constrained property
PropertyChangeSupport	A helper class for managing listeners of bound and constrained properties
PropertyDescriptor	Provides methods for accessing the type of a property along with its accessor methods and describes whether it is bound or constrained
PropertyEditorManager	Provides a way of registering property types so that their editors can be easily found

PropertyEditorSupport	A helper class implementing the PropertyEditor interfaces that is used to make the construction of custom property editors a little easier
SimpleBeanInfo	A support class designed to make it easier for bean developers to provide explicit information about a bean
VetoableChangeSupport	A helper class for managing listeners of bound and constrained properties

java.rmi

The java.rmi package contains the classes and interfaces that enable the programmer to create distributed Java-to-Java applications, in which the methods of remote Java objects can be invoked from other Java virtual machines, possibly on different hosts.

Interfaces

| Remote | Methods for identifying all remote objects |

Classes

| Naming | Methods for obtaining references to remote objects based on Uniform Resource Locator (URL) syntax |
| RMISecurityManager | Methods defining the RMI stub security policy for applications (not applets) |

java.rmi.dgc

Interfaces

| DGC | Methods for cleaning connections for unused clients |

Classes

| Lease | Contains a unique VM identifier and a lease duration |
| VMID | Methods for maintaining unique VMID across all Java virtual machines |

java.rmi.registry

Interfaces

Registry	A class used to obtain the registry for different hosts
RegistryManager	Methods used to interface to the private implementation

Classes

LocateRegistry	Used to obtain the bootstrap for the registry on a particular host

java.rmi.server

Interfaces

LoaderHandler	
RMIFailureHandler	Methods for handling when the RMI runtime system is unable to create a Socket or ServerSocket
RemoteCall	Methods for implementing calls to a remote object
RemoteRef	Represents a handle for a remote object
ServerRef	Represents the server-side handle for a remote object implementation
Skeleton	Represents the server-side entity that dispatches calls to the actual remote object implementation
Unreferenced	Methods to receive notification when there are no more remote references to it

Classes

LogStream	Provides a mechanism for logging errors that are of possible interest to those monitoring the system
ObjID	Used to identify remote objects uniquely in a VM
Operation	Holds a description of a Java method
RMIClassLoader	Provides static methods for loading classes over the network
RMISocketFactory	Used by the RMI runtime system to obtain client and server sockets for RMI calls
RemoteObject	Provides the remote semantics of Object by implementing methods for hashCode, equals, and toString

C

JAVA CLASS
LIBRARY

RemoteServer	A superclass to all server implementations that provides the framework to support a wide range of remote reference semantics
RemoteStub	Stub objects are surrogates that support exactly the same set of remote interfaces defined by the actual implementation of the remote object
UID	Abstraction for creating identifiers that are unique with respect to the the host on which it is generated
UnicastRemoteObject	Defines a nonreplicated remote object whose references are valid only while the server process is alive

java.security

The java.security package contains the classes and interfaces that enable the programmer to implement certificates and digital signatures in Java components.

Interfaces

Certificate	Methods for managing a certificate, including encoding and decoding
KeyParams	An interface to alogrithm-specific key parameter interfaces such as DSAParams
Principal	Represents the principal component of a certificate

Classes

DigestInputStream	Represents an input stream that has a message digest associated with it
DigestOutputStream	Represents an output stream that has a message digest associated with it·
Identity	Methods for managing identities, which can be objects such as people, companies, or organizations that can be authenticated using a public key
IdentityScope	Methods for defining the scope of an identity including the name of the identity, its key, and associated certificates
Key	An abstract class representing a cryptographic key
KeyPair	A simple holder for a key pair (a public key and a private key)

MessageDigest	Methods that provide the functionality of a message digest algorithm
PrivateKey	A subclass of Key representing a private key
Provider	Represents a Security Package Provider (SPP) for the Java Security API
PublicKey	A subclass of Key representing a public key
SecureRandom	Generates a random number
Security	Methods for managing Security Package Providers (SPPs)
Signature	Provides the algorithm for digital signatures
Signer	Represents an identity that can also sign

java.security.acl

The java.security.acl package provides the interface to a data structure that guards access to resources.

Interfaces

Acl	An interface representing an Access Control List (ACL), which is a data structure used to guard access to resources
AclEntry	Methods that allow programmers to add, remove, or set permissions for the Principals of each ACLEntry in the ACL
Group	Methods that allow programmers to add or remove a member from the group of Principals
Owner	Represents the owner of an ACL
Permission	Represents the type of access granted to a resource such as a Principal in the ACL

java.security.interfaces

Interfaces

DSAKey	Methods used to authenticate components including Java applets and ActiveX controls distributed on the Web
DSAParams	Methods allowing programmers to get the base, prime, and subprime
DSAPublicKey	An interface to a DSA public key

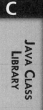

java.sql

The java.sql package includes classes, interfaces, and methods you can use to connect your Java applications to back-end databases.

Interfaces

CallableStatement	Methods used to execute stored procedures and handle multiple result sets
Connection	Represents a session with the database
DatabaseMetaData	An interface allowing programmers to get high-level information about the database
Driver	Methods used to connect to a database
PreparedStatement	Methods for running precompiled SQL statements
ResultSet	Methods for retrieving values from an executed SQL statement
ResultSetMetaData	Methods that provide information about the types and properties of the columns in a ResultSet
Statement	Used for static SQL statements

Classes

Date	Provides methods for formatting and referencing date values
DriverManager	Allows for the managing of a set of JDBC drivers
DriverPropertyInfo	Provides methods for obtaining different properties of a driver
Time	Provides methods for formatting and referencing time values
Timestamp	A wrapper that holds the SQL TIMESTAMP value
Types	Defines constants that are used to identify SQL types

java.text

The java.text package includes classes and methods used to format objects such as numbers, dates, times, and so on to a string, or to parse a given string to an object such as number, date, time, and so on.

Interfaces

CharacterIterator — Methods to traverse a string and return various information about it

Classes

ChoiceFormat — Methods that allow the attaching of formats to numbers

CollatedString — Provides a way to use international strings in a hash table or sorted collection

Collation — Allows the comparing of Unicode text

CollationElementIterator — Provides a way to iterate over an international string

DateFormat — An abstract class that includes several date-time formatting subclasses

DateFormatData — Methods to set the date-time formatting data

DecimalFormat — Methods to format numbers

Format — A base class for all formats

FormatStatus — Used to align formatted objects

MessageFormat — Methods to create concatenated messages

NumberFormat — An abstract class for all number formats including subclasses; you can use their methods to format and parse numbers

NumberFormatData — Encapsulates localizable number format data

ParseStatus — Gets the status of parsing when you parse through a string with different formats

SimpleDateFormat — Methods to format a date or time into a string

SortKey — Methods to do bitwise comparison of strings

StringCharacterIterator — Methods for bidirectional iteration over a string

TableCollation — Implements Collation using data-driven tables

TextBoundary — Used to locate boundaries in given text

Online Java Resources

by Rick Darnell

This appendix lists online resources for the Java programming language, Java-enabled browsers, and other related technologies and projects.

> **CAUTION**
>
> Remember that any URL listed here is subject to change. Java resources are likely to appear or disappear from the World Wide Web just like any other Web page.

Java's Home: JavaSoft

Java's popularity encouraged Sun to create a site devoted specifically to Java and related products and topics at `http://www.javasoft.com/` (see Figure D.1). In addition to news on the development of Java and access to the Java Development Kit, it also includes links to the HotJava browser, JavaBeans, JavaOS, and third-party vendors for JDBC development.

FIGURE D.1.

The official Java Website is a good place to start when looking for information about the latest developments and revisions to Java.

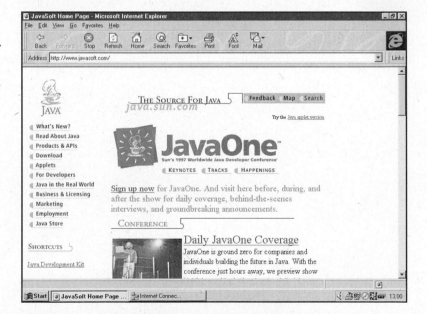

Java Clearing Houses and Information Repositories

A host of sites devoted to Java have sprouted up all over the Web; several others include Java as a major topic or subtopic. Although these sites are not affiliated with Sun Microsystems, they are still very valuable sources of information.

■ **Gamelan**: One of the first and still one of the best, the Gamelan site includes well-ordered links to applets and applications, plus a storehouse of information on Java's development (see Figure D.2). It also includes information and links to JavaScript sites.

`http://www.gamelan.com/`

FIGURE D.2.

Gamelan is probably the most comprehensive collection of links to Java information, applets, and applications on the World Wide Web.

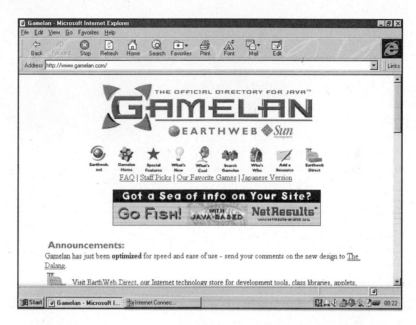

■ **Java Applet Rating Service**: Better known as JARS, this site offers independent reviews and ratings of both commercial and shareware Java applets. It rates its picks by the applets' percentage standings against other applets (top 1 percent, top 5 percent, and so on). It includes indexes by category of applets, with links to sample pages.

`http://www.jars.com/`

■ **Java Developer**: The Java Developer is a public service FAQ site devoted to Java programming and related issues (see Figure D.3). It offers online resources, employment postings, and a large tutorial section called *How do I...?*.

`http://www.digitalfocus.com/faq/`

■ **WWW Virtual Library**: Links to events, reference information, programming resources, and a variety of applets and applications are found on this site.

`http://www.acm.org/~ops/java.html`

■ **The Java User Resource Network**: Also known as Java URN, this site has listings of programming and system consultants and developers (see Figure D.4). It also includes links to other Java sites and applets.

`http://www.nebulex.com/URN`

FIGURE D.3.
Digital Focus provides answers to many Java programming questions.

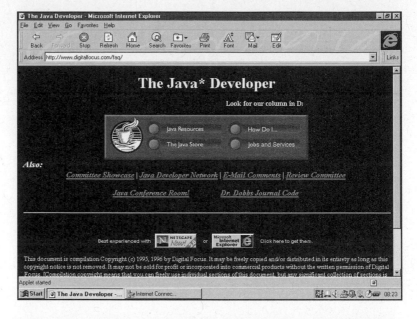

FIGURE D.4.
The Java URN has links to programmers and system consultants when you don't feel like doing it yourself or when you need professional assistance.

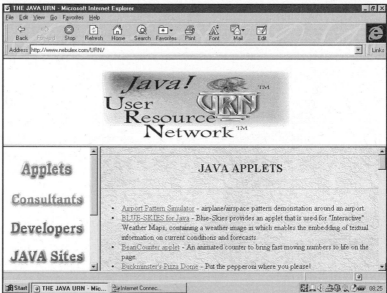

■ **Tucows**: Although it is not limited to Java, the Tucows site includes links to a variety of Java authoring tools, including offerings from big players such as Symantec and Sun. It also includes shareware Java development tools such as JavaPad and Jamba.

```
http://www.tucows.com/
```

■ **JavaWorld**: This online magazine has been at the front of the pack with news about many of the important developments for Java. In addition to news and views, each issue includes hands-on features and tutorials. Back issues are available for browsing.

`http://www.javaworld.com/`

JavaScript Information

JavaScript is one of the harder Web technologies to keep track of. It was originally developed by Netscape for Navigator, although a similar implementation is now in place for Microsoft's Internet Explorer. Official sites are virtually nonexistent, other than a handful of white papers and the JavaScript online manual at Netscape (`http://home.netscape.com/`). The lack of official information has encouraged several hardy souls to develop sites devoted to JavaScript and its use.

■ **JavaScript Index**: The JavaScript Index is a reliable and well-established collection of JavaScript experiments and demonstrations, plus links to an ever-growing list of home pages that showcase a variety of scripting tricks. The site also includes a JavaScript Library, which includes collections of source code from the Web.

`http://www.c2.org/~andreww/javascript/`

■ **Voodoo JavaScript Tutorial**: This is one of the first tutorials published for JavaScript, and it is still a good place for beginners to start. The tutorial is presented in a set of easy steps covering the basics of JavaScript and manipulating frames. It includes examples built into the tutorial pages, along with descriptive text and code samples.

`http://rummelplatz.uni-manneheim.de/~skoch/js/script.htm`

■ `comp.lang.javascript`: A great deal of information passes through the JavaScript newsgroup. Even if you don't post questions, you can still learn a great deal by following the traffic. Several of the established JavaScript gurus also monitor and post to this group.

■ `news://secnews.netscape.com/netscape.navigator`: Although the server is marked as secure, this newsgroup is still open to the general public. Its traffic is monitored by Netscape engineers and representatives, although they're not always quick to respond. JavaScript topics are found here, although they tend to be in the minority.

Java Tools

The entries in this section include software vendors and links to other developers who have worked to make developing Java applets and applications much easier than it was in the days of working with a text editor and the Java class compiler. Sun also has its own offerings. See the reference for `www.javasoft.com`, earlier in this appendix.

- **Symantec**: Symantec has worked hard at staying in the lead with the development of Java authoring tools and add-ons to extend Java's capabilities. Current offerings include Java Café, Visual Café, Café Pro, dbAnywhere, and a just-in-time compiler.

  `http://www.symantec.com/product/index_devtools.html`

- **Microsoft**: Microsoft leaves no stone unturned when it comes to making sure that they have a competitive product in every major market; the world of Java is not immune. Microsoft's offerings include the company's own version of a free Java Software Development Kit, Visual J++ for developing Java applications, the Java virtual machine, and a just-in-time compiler for Internet Explorer.

  `http://www.microsoft.com/workshop/java`

- **WebWare Online**: WebWare is a software wholesale club for purchasing Java products—including software development tools and class libraries.

  `http://www.webwareonline.com/`

Many other applications are designed to speed development of applets and applications, including IBM's AppletAuthor, Aimtech's Jamba, and Natural Intelligence's Roaster.

Java in the Newsgroups

- **`comp.lang.java` (`comp.lang.java.misc`)**: The Java newsgroups found under computer languages (`comp.lang`) host a variety of topics, including Java programming in general, and more specific aspects such as `comp.lang.java.api` for the application programming interface.

- **Digital Espresso**: If you don't feel like browsing through the volumes of postings in the newsgroups, check out this Web site for a summary of the traffic in the Java newsgroups and mailing lists. It was formerly known as—and is sometimes still referred to as—J*** Notes.

  `http://www.io.org/~mentor/DigitalEspresso.html`

Other Related Programming Information

- **Sams Publishing Books Online**: Sams Publishing makes a variety of their titles available online in an HTML format—including several in their Java series: *Peter Norton's Guide to Java Programming*, *Teach Yourself Java in 21 Days*, *The Java Developer's Guide*, and *Developing Professional Java Applets*. All links to online books are on the same page, so look for the Java subheading.

  `http://www.mcp.com/sams/books_online.html`

- **Programming Active Objects in Java**: This discussion by Doug Lea covers object-oriented design issues as they relate to Java and Java applications.

  `http://g.oswego.edu/dl/pats/aopintro.html`

■ **Object-Oriented Information Sources Index**: A searchable index to a variety of object-oriented information sources, including research groups, archives, companies, books, and bibliographies.

```
http://cuiwww.unige.ch/OSG/OOinfo/
```

■ **Object-Oriented Design Online Reference Guide**: A guide to online information sources about object-oriented design created by the lead database engineer for infrastructure at CompuServe.

```
http://www.clark.net/pub/howie/OO/oo_home.html
```

■ **Java Online Bibliography**: Although not all-inclusive, this online index includes key articles and press releases about Java and related technology issues.

```
http://www.december.com/works/java/bib.html
```

■ **Yahoo!**: The folks at Yahoo! have devoted several sections to Java, including a specific area for the HotJava browser.

```
http://www.yahoo.com/Computers_and_Internet/Languages/Java/
http://www.yahoo.com/Business_and_Economy/Companies/Computers/Software/Java/
http://www.yahoo.com/Computers_and_Internet/Internet/World_Wide_Web/Browsers/
     HotJava/
```

What's on the CD-ROM

On the *Java 1.1 Unleashed,* Third Edition, CD-ROM that accompanies this book, you will find all the sample files presented in this book along with a wealth of other applications and utilities.

> **NOTE**
>
> Refer to the readme.wri file on the CD-ROM (Windows) or the Guide to the CD-ROM file (Macintosh) for the latest listing of software.

Windows Software

Here is a list of the **Java products** you can find on the CD-ROM:

- Sun's Java Development Kit for Windows 95/NT, version 1.1.1 (Solaris versions included)
- Sun's JavaBeans Development Kit for Windows 95/NT (Solaris versions included)
- Trial version of Jamba for Windows 95/NT
- JPad
- JPad Pro demo
- Kawa demo
- Studio J++ demo
- Javelin demo
- JDesigner Pro database wizard for Java

Here is a list of the **HTML tools** you can find on the CD-ROM:

- Hot Dog 32-bit HTML editor
- HoTMetaL HTML editor
- HTMLed HTML editor
- WebEdit Pro HTML editor
- Spider 1.2 demo
- Web Analyzer demo

Here are the **graphics, video, and sound applications** you can find on the CD-ROM:

- Goldwave sound editor, player, and recorder
- MapThis imagemap utility
- Paint Shop Pro
- SnagIt screen-capture utility

- ThumbsPlus image viewer and browser
- Image Library from The Rocket Shop

Here's a list of the **utilities** you can find on the CD-ROM:

- Adobe Acrobat viewer
- WinZip for Windows NT/95
- WinZip Self-Extractor

Macintosh Software

Here's a list of the **Java products** you can find on the CD-ROM:

- Sun's Java Developer's Kit for Macintosh v1.0.2
- Sample applets
- Sample JavaScripts

Here's a list of the **HTML tools** you will find on the CD-ROM:

- BBEdit 3.5.1 freeware
- BBEdit 4.0 demo
- WebMap

Here's a list of the **graphics applications** you can find on the CD-ROM:

- Graphic converter
- GIFConverter
- Image Library from The Rocket Shop

Here's a list of the **utilities** you can find on the CD-ROM:

- Adobe Acrobat reader
- SnagIt Pro screen-capture utility
- SoundApp
- Sparkle
- ZipIt 1.3.5 for Macintosh

ABOUT THE SOFTWARE

Please read all the documentation associated with a third-party product (usually contained in files named readme.txt or license.txt) and follow all guidelines.

Glossary

accessor method   A public method defined in a bean that reads or writes the value of a property.

ActiveX   A family of technologies developed by Microsoft to combine computing ability with Internet connectivity.

ActiveX control   A software module with OLE capabilities that can easily be embedded in Web pages or programs.

anchor   A part of a hypertext document that is either the source or destination of a hypertext link. A *link* can extend from an anchor to another document, or from another document to an anchor. When anchors are the starting points of these links, they are typically highlighted or otherwise identified in the hypertext browser as *hotspots*.

API (Application Programming Interface)   The set of Java packages and classes—included in the Java Development Kit (JDK)—that programmers use to create applets.

applet   A Java program that can be included in an HTML page with the APPLET element and observed in a Java-enabled browser.

application (Java)   A computer program, written in Java, that executes independently of a Java-enabled browser through the Java interpreter included in the Java Development Kit.

ASCII (American Standard Code for Information Interchange)   A 7-bit character code that can represent 128 characters, some of which are control characters used for communications control and cannot be printed.

attribute   A property of an HTML element, specified in the start tag of the element. The attribute list of the APPLET element is used to identify the location of applet source code (with the Codebase attribute) and the name of the Java class (with the Code attribute).

bean   A compact, portable, reusable, serializable, Java software component that includes support for automatic integration with visual application builder tools.

block (Java)   The code between matching curly braces { and }.

boolean   A data type that has a value of true or false.

bound property   A JavaBeans property that provides notifications to an interested party based on changes in its value.

browser   A software program used to observe the Web. Also a synonym for a Web client.

bytecode   The machine-readable code created as the result of compiling a Java language source file. This is the code distributed across the network to run an applet. Bytecodes are architecture neutral; the Java-capable browser ported to a particular platform interprets them.

cast (verb)   To change an expression from one data type to another.

CERN (Centre European pour la Recherche Nucleaire)   The European laboratory for particle physics, where the World Wide Web originated in 1989. (See `http://www.cern.ch/`.)

CGI (Common Gateway Interface)   A standard for programs to interface with Web servers.

child class   A subclass of a class (its parent class). It inherits `public` and `protected` data and methods from the parent class.

class   A template for creating objects. A class defines data and methods and is a unit of organization in a Java program. It can pass its `public` data and methods to its subclasses.

client   A software program that requests information or services from another software application (*server*) and displays this information in a form required by its hardware platform.

COM (Component Object Model)   A binary standard developed by Microsoft for representing software components in a distributed environment.

compiler   A software program that translates human-readable source code into machine-readable code.

constrained property   A JavaBeans property that allows an interested party to perform a validation on a new property value before accepting the modification.

constructor   A method named after its class. A constructor method is invoked when an object of that class is made.

container   A context in which components can be grouped together and interacted with.

content handler   A program loaded into the user's HotJava browser that interprets files of a type defined by the Java programmer. The Java programmer provides the necessary code for the user's HotJava browser to display and interpret this special format.

CORBA (Common Object Request Broker Architecture)   The industry standard for representing distributed objects.

CPU   Central Processing Unit.

cross-platform   A term used to indicate that a piece of software can run on any operating system platform.

customizer   A user interface that provides a specialized way of visually editing bean properties.

design patterns   Rules used to determine information about a bean from its reflected method names and signatures.

digital signature   A security technique that involves the attachment of a code to a software component that identifies the vendor of the component.

domain name   The alphanumeric name for a computer host; this name is mapped to the computer's numeric Internet Protocol (IP) address.

DTD (Document Type Definition)   A specification for a markup language such as HTML.

element   A unit of structure in an HTML document. Many elements have start and stop tags; some have just a single tag, and some can contain other elements.

event   Something that happens within a component that an application or other component may want to know about and possibly react to.

event adapter   An intermediary placed between an event source and a listener that provides additional event delivery behavior.

event listener   An applet, application, or JavaBeans component capable of responding to events.

event source   A component capable of generating events.

event state object   An object used to store information associated with a particular event.

externalization mechanism   A way to store and retrieve an object through some type of customized, externally defined format.

FTP (File Transfer Protocol)   A way to exchange files across a network.

garbage collection   The process by which memory allocated for objects in a program is reclaimed. Java automatically performs this process.

getter method   An accessor method that reads, or gets, the value of a property.

Gopher   A protocol for disseminating information on the Internet using a system of menus.

home page   An entry page for access to a local web. Also, a page that a person or company defines as a principal page, often containing links to other pages containing personal or professional information.

HotJava   A Web browser designed to execute applets written in the Java programming language.

hotspot   An area on a hypertext document that a user can click to retrieve another resource or document.

HTML (HyperText Markup Language)   The mechanism used to create Web pages. Web browsers display these pages according to a browser-defined rendering scheme.

HTTP (HyperText Transfer Protocol)   The native protocol of the Web, used to transfer hypertext documents.

hypermedia   Hypertext that includes multimedia: text, graphics, images, sound, and video.

hypertext   Text that is not constrained to a single sequence for observation; Web-based hypertext is not constrained to a single server for creating meaning.

imagemap   A graphic inline image on an HTML page that potentially connects each pixel or region of an image to a Web resource. The user retrieves the resources by clicking the image.

indexed properties   A property that represents an array of values.

inner class   A Java class defined as a member of another class, locally within a block of statements or anonymously within an expression.

instance   An object.

interface   A set of methods that Java classes can implement.

Internet   The cooperatively run, globally distributed collection of computer networks that exchange information using the TCP/IP protocol suite.

introspection   The mechanism that exposes the functionality of a component to the outside world.

Java   An object-oriented programming language for creating secure, distributed, platform-independent applications.

Java-enabled browser   A World Wide Web browser that can display Java applets.

language-independent   A term used to indicate that a piece of software can be developed in any programming language.

link   A connection between one hypertext document and another.

LiveConnect   A technology included with Netscape Navigator that provides a way of interconnecting different types of executable content.

low-level events   Events that correspond to a low-level input or visual interface interaction.

Matrix   The set of all networks that can exchange electronic mail either directly or through gateways—including the Internet, BITNET, FidoNet, UUCP, and commercial services such as America Online, CompuServe, Delphi, and Prodigy. This term was coined by John S. Quarterman in his book *The Matrix* (Digital Press, 1990).

method   A function that can perform operations on data.

MIME (Multipurpose Internet Mail Extensions)   A specification for multimedia document formats.

Mosaic   A graphical Web browser originally developed by the National Center for Supercomputing Applications (NCSA). It now includes a number of commercially licensed products.

multicast event source   An event source capable of generating events for retrieval by any number of listeners.

native methods   Class methods declared in a Java class but implemented in C.

navigating   The act of observing the content of the Web for some purpose.

NCSA (National Center for Supercomputing Applications)   Developers and distributors of NCSA Mosaic at the University of Illinois at Champaign-Urbana.

Net   An informal term for the Internet or a subset (or a superset) of the Matrix in context. For example, a computerized conference using e-mail may take place on a BITNET host that has an Internet gateway, thus making the conference available to anyone on either of these networks. In this case, the developer might say, "Our conference will be available on the Net." Although you may even consider discussion forums on commercial online services to be "on the Net," these forums are not accessible from the Internet.

newsgroup   Internet message bases that provide forums for exchanging ideas, information, and opinions.

object   A variable defined as being a particular class type. An object has the data and methods as specified in the class definition.

object-oriented   A term specifying that a piece of software is composed of objects, which are self-contained modules that contain both data and procedures that act on the data.

OLE (Object Linking and Embedding)   A COM-based technology developed by Microsoft that provides a wide range of services, including application automation, reusable controls, version management, standardized drag-and-drop, documents, object linking and embedding, and visual editing.

OpenDoc   An open, multiplatform, component software architecture heavily backed by Apple and IBM.

overload (verb)   To use the same name for several items in the same scope; Java methods can be overloaded.

package (Java)   A set of classes with a common high-level function declared with the `package` keyword.

packet   A set of data handled as a unit in data transmission.

page   A single file of HyperText Markup Language.

parameter (HTML)   A name and value pair identified by the `Name` and `Value` attributes of the `PARAM` element used inside an `APPLET` element.

parameter list (Java)   The set of values passed to a method. The definition of the method describes how these values are manipulated.

parent class   The originating class of a given subclass.

persistence   The means by which a component is stored to and retrieved from a nonvolatile location such as a hard disk.

platform   A term referring to a particular operating system and runtime environment, such as Windows 95 or Solaris.

property   A discrete, named attribute of a JavaBeans component that determines its appearance and behavior.

property editor   A user interface that enables the visual editing of a particular property type.

property sheet   A user interface containing property editors for all the exported properties of a JavaBeans component.

protocol handler   A program loaded into the user's HotJava browser that interprets a protocol. These protocols include standards such as HTTP, as well as programmer-defined protocols.

reflection   The process of studying a bean to determine information about its functionality and public facilities.

RMI (Remote Method Invocation)   The execution of methods on remote Java objects located on other Java virtual machines—and sometimes on different hosts.

robot   A term for software programs that automatically explore the Web for a variety of purposes. Robots that collect resources for later database queries by users are sometimes called *spiders*.

scope   The program segment in which a reference to a variable is valid.

semantic events   Events that correspond to high-level visual interface actions based on the semantics of a bean.

serialization   The process of storing or retrieving information through a standard protocol.

server   A software application that provides information or services based on requests from client programs.

setter method   An accessor method that writes, or sets, the value of a property.

SGML (Standard Generalized Markup Language)   A standard for defining markup languages; HTML is an instance of SGML. (See `http://www.sgmlopen.org/`.)

site   The file section of a computer on which Web documents (or other documents served in another protocol) reside—for example, a Web site, a Gopher site, or an FTP site.

software component   A piece of software isolated into a discrete, easily reusable structure.

Solaris   Sun Microsystem's software platform for networked applications. Solaris includes the operating system, SunOS.

Sparc (Scalable Processor ARChitecture)   A microprocessor architecture based on very efficient handling of a small set of instructions. (See `http://www.sparc.com/`.)

spider   A software program that traverses the Web to collect information about resources for later queries by users who want to find resources. Major species of active spiders include Lycos and WebCrawler.

surfing   The act of navigating the Web, typically using techniques for rapidly traversing content, to find subjectively valuable resources.

tag   The code used to make up part of an HTML element. For example, the TITLE element has a start tag, `<TITLE>`, and an end tag, `</TITLE>`.

TCP/IP (Transmission Control Protocol/Internet Protocol)   The set of protocols used for network communication on the Internet.

unicast event source   An event source capable of generating events for retrieval by only one listener.

Unicode   A 16-bit character set that supports many world languages.

URL (Uniform Resource Locator)   The scheme for addressing on the Web. A URL identifies a resource on the Web.

Usenet   A system for disseminating asynchronous text discussion among cooperating computer hosts. The Usenet discussion space is divided into *newsgroups*, each concerned with a particular topic or subtopic.

versioning   The inevitable tendency for an object to evolve over time and gain new functionality.

virtual machine   The hypothetical microprocessor on which Java bytecodes execute.

visual component   A type of software component that has a visual representation requiring physical space on the display surface of a parent application.

VRML (Virtual Reality Modeling Language)   A specification for three-dimensional rendering used in conjunction with Web browsers.

web   A set of hypertext pages that are considered a single work. Typically, a single web is created by one author or cooperating authors and is deployed on a single server with links to other servers—that is, it is a subset of the Web.

Web (World Wide Web)   A hypertext information and communication system popularly used on the Internet computer network with data communications operating according to a client/server model. Web clients (browsers) can access multiprotocol and hypermedia information using an addressing scheme.

Web server   Software that provides services to Web clients.

white paper   A technical document outlining the goals of a new technology.

wizard   A user interface that uses multiple-step questionnaires to gather information from the user.

WWW   The World Wide Web.

X   X Window System. A windowing system that supports graphical user interfaces to applications.

See also:

Sun's Java Glossary

`http://www.javasoft.com/javacontest/java-P1/project_files/faq/glossary.html`

I

INDEX

Symbols

A

Teach Yourself Java in 21 Days, Professional Reference Edition

Laura Lemay and Michael Morrison

Introducing the first, best, and most detailed guide to developing applications with the hot new Java language from Sun Microsystems. Provides detailed coverage of the hottest new technology on the World Wide Web. Shows readers how to develop applications using the Java language. Includes coverage of browsing Java applications with Netscape and other popular Web browsers. CD-ROM includes the Java Development Kit.

Price: $59.99 USA/$84.95 CDN   *Casual—Accomplished—Expert*
1-57521-183-1   900 pp.   *Internet—Programming*

Java Developer's Reference

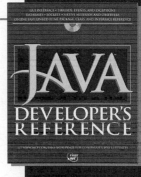

Mike Cohn, et al.

This is the information- and resource-packed development package for professional developers. It explains the components of the Java Development Kit (JDK) and the Java programming language. Everything needed to program Java is included within this comprehensive reference, making it the tool developers will turn to over and over again for timely, accurate information on Java and the JDK. CD-ROM contains source code from the book and powerful utilities. Includes tips and tricks for getting the most from Java and your Java programs. Contains complete descriptions of all the package classes and their individual methods.

Price: $59.99 USA/$84.95 CDN   *Accomplished—Expert*
1-57521-129-7   1,296 pp.   *Internet—Programming*

Developing Intranet Applications with Java

Jerry Ablan

This book shows developers the intricacies of Java intranet development. It teaches how to create interactive databases, multimedia, animations, and sound for use on an intranet. Teaches how to add interactivity to Web databases. Discusses the various ways Java is used and can be used for intranet development. CD-ROM includes source code from the book and powerful Java utilities.

Price: $49.99 USA/$70.95 CDN   *Accomplished—Expert*
1-57521-166-1   528 pp.   *Internet—Intranet*

Peter Norton's Guide to Java Programming

William Stanek & Sams DeWolfe

Peter Norton's Guide to Java Programming is a programmer's guide for Web developers. The highly qualified authors dispense their knowledge of Web programming with Java in an easy-to-understand format that will have you programming Java applets in no time. Teaches about threads and exceptions, Java tools, the Java API, applet reuse and more. Provides the most extensive coverage available on how to enhance Java.

Price: $39.99 USA/$56.95 CDN   *Casual—Accomplished*
1-57521-088-6   800 pp.   *Internet—Programming*

Web Programming with Java

Michael Girdley and Kathryn A. Jones, et al.

This book gets readers on the road to developing robust, real-world Java applications. Various cutting-edge applications are presented, allowing the reader to quickly learn all aspects of programming Java for the Internet. CD-ROM contains source code and powerful utilities. Readers will be able to create live, interactive Web pages.

Price: $39.99 USA/$56.95 CDN   *Accomplished—Expert*
1-57521-113-0   500 pp.   *Internet—Programming*

Web Programming Unleashed

Bob Breedlove, et al.

This comprehensive tome explores all aspects of the latest technology craze—Internet programming. Programmers will turn to the proven expertise of the *Unleashed* series for accurate, day-and-date information on this hot new programming subject. Gives timely, expert advice on ways to exploit the full potential of the Internet. CD-ROM includes complete source code for all applications in the book, additional programs with accompanying source code, and several Internet application resource tools. Covers Internet programming.

Price: $49.99 USA/$70.95 CDN   *Accomplished—Expert*
1-57521-117-3   1,056 pp.   *Internet—Programming*

Web Publishing Unleashed, Professional Reference Edition

William Stanek

Web Publishing Unleashed, Professional Reference Edition, is a completely new version of the first book, combining coverage of all Web development technologies in one volume. It now includes entire sections on JavaScript, Java, VBScript, and ActiveX, plus expanded coverage of multimedia Web development, adding animation, developing intranet sites, Web design, and much more. Includes a 200-page reference section. CD-ROM includes a selection of HTML, Java, CGI, and scripting tools for Windows/MAC—plus the Sams.net Web Publishing Library and electronic versions of top Web publishing books. Covers HTML, CGI, JavaScript, VBScript, and ActiveX.

Price: $69.99 USA/$98.95 CAN   *Intermediate—Advanced*
1-57521-198-X 1,200 pp.   *Internet—Web Publishing*

The World Wide Web Unleashed 1997

John December

This book unleashes the latest Web topics previously known only to the field experts. It is designed to be the only book readers need from their initial logon to the Web to creating their own Web pages. Takes the reader on an updated tour of the Web—highlights sites and outlines browsing techniques. Includes the Sams.net Web 1,000 Directory—the "yellow pages" of the Internet. CD-ROM contains everything from starter software to advanced Web site development tools. Covers the World Wide Web.

Price: $49.99 USA/$70.95 CDN   *All User Levels*
1-57521-184-X 1,300 pp.   *Internet—General/WWW Applications*

Add to Your Sams.net Library Today
with the Best Books for Internet Technologies

ISBN	Quantity	Description of Item	Unit Cost	Total Cost
1-57521-183-1		Teach Yourself Java in 21 Days, Professional Reference Edition (Book/CD-ROM)	$59.99	
1-57521-129-7		Java Developer's Reference (Book/CD-ROM)	$59.99	
1-57521-166-1		Developing Intranet Applications with Java	$49.99	
1-57521-088-6		Peter Norton's Guide to Java Programming (Book/CD-ROM)	$39.99	
1-57521-113-0		Web Programming with Java (Book/CD-ROM)	$39.99	
1-57521-117-3		Web Programming Unleashed (Book/CD-ROM)	$49.99	
1-57521-198-X		Web Publishing Unleashed, Professional Reference Edition (Book/CD-ROM)	$69.99	
1-57521-184-X		The World Wide Web Unleashed 1997 (Book/CD-ROM)	$49.99	
		Shipping and Handling: See information below.		
		TOTAL		

Shipping and Handling: $4.00 for the first book and $1.75 for each additional book. If you need to have it NOW, we can ship product to you in 24 hours for an additional charge of approximately $18.00, and you will receive your item overnight or in two days. Overseas shipping and handling adds $2.00. Prices subject to change. Call between 9:00 a.m. and 5:00 p.m. EST for availability and pricing information on latest editions.

201 W. 103rd Street, Indianapolis, Indiana 46290

1-800-428-5331 — Orders   1-800-835-3202 — FAX   1-800-858-7674 — Customer Service

Book ISBN 1-57521-298-6

MACMILLAN COMPUTER PUBLISHING USA

A VIACOM COMPANY

Technical ---- Support:

If you need assistance with the information in this book or with the CD-ROM accompanying the book, please access the Knowledge Base on our Web site at **http://www.superlibrary.com/general/support**. Our most Frequently Asked Questions are answered there. If you do not find the answer to your questions on our Web site, you may contact Macmillan Technical Support at **(317) 581-3833** or e-mail us at **support@mcp.com**.

Installing the CD-ROM

The CD-ROM that accompanies this book contains all the source code and project files developed by the authors, plus an assortment of evaluation versions of third-party products. To install the disc, follow the steps for your appropriate system.

Windows 95/NT 4 Installation Instructions

1. Insert the CD-ROM into your CD-ROM drive.
2. From the Windows 95 desktop, double-click the My Computer icon.
3. Double-click the icon representing your CD-ROM drive.
4. Double-click the icon titled setup.exe to run the CD-ROM installation program..
5. Follow the on-screen instructions.

Windows NT 3.51 Installation Instructions

1. Insert the CD-ROM into your CD-ROM drive.
2. From File Manager or Program Manager, choose Run from the File menu.

3. Type **<drive>\setup** and press Enter, where <drive> corresponds to the drive letter of your CD-ROM. For example, if your CD-ROM is drive D, type **D:\SETUP** and press Enter.

4. Follow the on-screen instructions.

NOTE

Windows NT 3.51 users will be unable to access the \WIN95NT4 directory because it was left in its original long filename state with a combination of uppercase and lowercase letters. This was done to allow Windows 95 and Windows NT 4 users direct access to those files on the CD-ROM. All other directories were translated in compliance with the Windows NT 3.51 operating system and can be accessed without trouble. Attempting to access the \WIN95NT4 directory causes no harm; you simply cannot read the contents of the directory.

Macintosh Installation Instructions

1. Insert the CD-ROM into your CD-ROM drive.

2. When an icon for the CD appears on your desktop, open the disc by double-clicking that icon.

3. Double-click the icon titled Guide to the CD-ROM.

4. Follow the on-screen instructions.

10. **Governing Law.** Any action related to this License will be governed by California law and controlling U.S. federal law. No choice of law rules of any jurisdiction will apply.

11. **Severability.** If any of the above provisions are held to be in violation of applicable law, void, or unenforceable in any jurisdiction, then such provisions are herewith waived to the extent necessary for the License to be otherwise enforceable in such jurisdiction. However, if, in Sun's opinion, deletion of any provisions of the License by operation of this paragraph unreasonably compromises the rights or increases the liabilities of Sun or its licensors, Sun reserves the right to terminate the License and refund the fee paid by Licensee, if any, as Licensee's sole and exclusive remedy.

4. **Trademarks and Logos.** This License does not authorize Licensee to use any Sun name, trademark, or logo. Licensee acknowledges that Sun owns the Java trademark and all Java-related trademarks, logos, and icons including the Coffee Cup and Duke ("Java Marks") and agrees: (i) to comply with the Java Trademark Guidelines at http://java.sun.com/trademarks.html; (ii) to not do anything harmful to or inconsistent with Sun's rights in the Java Marks; and (iii) to assist Sun in protecting those rights, including assigning to Sun any rights acquired by Licensee in any Java Mark.

5. **Disclaimer of Warranty.** Software is provided "AS IS," without a warranty of any kind. ALL EXPRESS OR IMPLIED REPRESENTATIONS AND WARRANTIES, INCLUDING ANY IMPLIED WARRANTY OF MERCHANTABILITY, FITNESS FOR A PARTICULAR PURPOSE OR NON-INFRINGEMENT, ARE HEREBY EXCLUDED.

6. **Limitation of Liability.** SUN AND ITS LICENSORS SHALL NOT BE LIABLE FOR ANY DAMAGES SUFFERED BY LICENSEE OR ANY THIRD PARTY AS A RESULT OF USING OR DISTRIBUTING SOFTWARE. IN NO EVENT WILL SUN OR ITS LICENSORS BE LIABLE FOR ANY LOST REVENUE, PROFIT, OR DATA, OR FOR DIRECT, INDIRECT, SPECIAL, CONSEQUENTIAL, INCIDENTAL, OR PUNITIVE DAMAGES, HOWEVER CAUSED AND REGARDLESS OF THE THEORY OF LIABILITY, ARISING OUT OF THE USE OF OR INABILITY TO USE SOFTWARE, EVEN IF SUN HAS BEEN ADVISED OF THE POSSIBILITY OF SUCH DAMAGES.

7. **Termination.** Licensee may terminate this License at any time by destroying all copies of Software. This License will terminate immediately without notice from Sun if Licensee fails to comply with any provision of this License. Upon such termination, Licensee must destroy all copies of Software.

8. **Export Regulations.** Software, including technical data, is subject to U.S. export control laws, including the U.S. Export Administration Act and its associated regulations, and may be subject to export or import regulations in other countries. Licensee agrees to comply strictly with all such regulations and acknowledges that it has the responsibility to obtain licenses to export, re-export, or import Software. Software may not be downloaded, or otherwise exported or re-exported (i) into, or to a national or resident of Cuba, Iraq, Iran, North Korea, Libya, Sudan, Syria, or any country to which the U.S. has embargoed goods; or (ii) to anyone on the U.S. Treasury Department's list of Specially Designated Nations or the U.S. Commerce Department's Table of Denial Orders.

9. **Restricted Rights.** Use, duplication, or disclosure by the United States government is subject to the restrictions as set forth in the Rights in Technical Data and Computer Software Clauses in DFARS 252.227-7013(c) (1) (ii) and FAR 52.227-19(c) (2) as applicable.

Java™ Development Kit Version 1.1 Binary Code License

This binary code license ("License") contains rights and restrictions associated with use of the accompanying software and documentation ("Software"). Read the License carefully before installing the Software. By installing the Software, you agree to the terms and conditions of this License.

1. **Limited License Grant.** Sun grants to you ("Licensee") a non-exclusive, non-transferable limited license to use the Software without fee for evaluation of the Software and for development of Java™-compatible applets and applications. Licensee may make one archival copy of the Software and may redistribute complete, unmodified copies of the Software to software developers within Licensee's organization to avoid unnecessary download time, provided that this License conspicuously appears with all copies of the Software. Except for the foregoing, Licensee may not redistribute the Software in whole or in part, either separately or included with a product. Refer to the Java Runtime Environment Version 1.1 binary code license (http://java.sun.com/products/JDK/1.1/index.html) for the availability of runtime code which may be distributed with Java-compatible applets and applications.

2. **Java Platform Interface.** Licensee may not modify the Java Platform Interface ("JPI", identified as classes contained within the java package or any subpackages of the java package), by creating additional classes within the JPI or otherwise causing the addition to or modification of the classes in the JPI. In the event that Licensee creates any Java-related API and distributes such API to others for applet or application development, Licensee must promptly publish an accurate specification for such API for free use by all developers of Java-based software.

3. **Restrictions.** Software is confidential copyrighted information of Sun, and title to all copies is retained by Sun and/or its licensors. Licensee shall not modify, decompile, disassemble, decrypt, extract, or otherwise reverse engineer Software. Software may not be leased, assigned, or sublicensed, in whole or in part. Software is not designed or intended for use in online control of aircraft, air traffic, aircraft navigation, or aircraft communications; or in the design, construction, operation or maintenance of any nuclear facility. Licensee warrants that it will not use or redistribute the Software for such purposes.